I0799702

NZC

2021 NEW ZEALAND CRICKET ALMANACK

EDITED BY
FRANCIS PAYNE
IAN SMITH

mower

The editors welcome contributions from readers for inclusion in the *2022 Almanack*

Please correspond directly with the editors:

Francis Payne,
97 Bond Crescent,
Forrest Hill,
AUCKLAND.
Phone: (09) 410-5259
Email: francisp@xtra.co.nz

Ian Smith,
98C Taita Drive,
Lower Hutt,
WELLINGTON.
Phone: (04) 976-6477
Email: ianelizabeth2@outlook.com

Front cover: The jubilant New Zealand squad after the test championship final

Photosport

ISBN 978-1-990003-23-3

A Mower Book

Published in 2021 by Upstart Press Ltd
Level 6, BDO Tower, 19-21 Como Street, Takapuna, Auckland, New Zealand
Printed by 1010 Printing Co. Ltd, China

CONTENTS

NZC

Office Bearers

2020/21

Patron

Her Excellency The Right Honourable Dame Patsy Reddy GNZM, QSO
Governor-General of New Zealand

President

D.A. Hockley CNZM, MNZM

Board

G.J. Barclay *(chairman, retired December 2020)*
M.C. Snedden CNZM *(chairman, elected December 2020)*
G.I. Allott, A.W. Campbell, J.M. Lloyd, K.M. Malloy,
D.M. Puketapu, R.J. Rolls, R.G. Twose *(co-opted January 2021)*

Chief Executive Officer

D.J. White

Auditors

PWC

Bankers

ANZ Bank

Life Members

S.L. Boock ONZM, J.G. Bracewell, M.J. Brito, J.V. Coney MBE
J.J. Crowe, D.S. Currie QSO, E.C. Drumm MNZM, S.P. Fleming ONZM,
I.W. Gallaway QSO, MBE *(deceased)* Sir Richard Hadlee MBE, D.A. Hockley CNZM, MNZM
G.P. Howarth OBE, A.R. Isaac CNZM, B.B. McCullum ONZM, J.D. McCarthy
P.F. McKelvey CNZM, MBE, L.J. Murdoch ONZM, MBE, D.O. Neely MNZM, MBE
Hon. Justice B.J. Paterson CNZM, OBE, QC, J.R. Reid CNZM, OBE *(deceased)*
I.D.S. Smith MBE, Y.G. Taylor, G.M. Turner, D.L. Vettori ONZM
Sir Allan Wright KBE, J.G. Wright MBE

Honorary Cricket Members

J.C. Alabaster, S.E. Bond, B.F. Bowden, B.A. Brentnall, B.L. Cairns
F.J. Cameron MBE, E.J. Chatfield MBE, R.O. Collinge, A.E. Dick
G.T. Dowling OBE, J.W. Guy, D.R. Hadlee, B.F. Hastings, A. McKenna
V. Pollard, J.F. Reid *(deceased)*, B.W. Sinclair MNZM, J.T. Sparling

National Code of Conduct Commissioner

M. Heron QC

Statistician

F. Payne

FROM THE EDITORS

The 74th edition of the *New Zealand Cricket Almanack* finds the Black Caps on top of the world after a year in cricket like no other. The number one ranked test side and winners of the inaugural World Test Championship.

The Year in Cricket

This edition starts with the White Ferns in Australia in September and ends with New Zealand in England in June. Despite the pandemic, New Zealand Cricket delivered a full season of international and domestic cricket.

The Black Caps hosted West Indies, Pakistan, Australia and Bangladesh before heading to England where they defeated the home side in a two-match test series and were victorious in the historic test championship final against India. West Indies and Pakistan brought extended squads to New Zealand which took part in a series of A team games.

The White Ferns toured Australia and then had home series against England and Australia. There were the usual domestic programmes and most age-group cricket continued. Domestic cricket once more started in October and this season finished in April. The domestic Twenty20 competition again featured men's and women's double-headers.

The Black Caps

It was a year to savour for the Black Caps. As well as winning the test championship and being the number one ranked test side, they were also the top rated one-day side and were third in the Twenty20 rankings. Kane Williamson was the number one test batsman and New Zealand players were prominent in all player ranking categories.

New Zealand won six of the seven test matches they played, won all three one-day internationals and ten of the thirteen Twenty20 games which produced a result. Their only losses during the year were in three Twenty20 games but all those series were won. The Black Caps played eight series across all formats (excluding the one-off test championship final) and won every one of them.

The Black Caps' season started with two test wins against West Indies and two Twenty20 victories and an abandoned game. New Zealand also won both tests against Pakistan and won the Twenty20 series 2-1. Pakistan were the stronger of the two visiting sides but both teams suffered from catching lapses in the test matches which often proved very expensive indeed.

Australia came to New Zealand for a five-game Twenty20 series. New Zealand won the first two matches, Australia the next two before New Zealand clinched the series with a seven wicket win at Wellington in the final game.

Bangladesh rounded out the home season with three one-day internationals and three Twenty20s. Apart from the second one-day match, Bangladesh were outclassed and continued their unenviable record against New Zealand in New Zealand which reads played 32, lost 32 across all formats.

New Zealand played two tests against England prior to the test championship final (although they are not part of the next championship cycle). The first match at Lord's was drawn but was notable for Devon Conway making 200 on his test debut. New Zealand then gained a convincing four-day win in the second test at Edgbaston.

The test championship final went to a sixth day after considerable rain interruptions. In a tense affair, New Zealand finally gained the ascendency on the last day and eventually won by eight wickets. It was absolutely fitting that New Zealand's champion pair of batsmen, Kane Williamson and Ross Taylor, were together in the middle when the historic win was achieved.

Williamson was the dominant batsman over the year while the New Zealand bowlers were relentless. The four-pronged pace attack of Tim Southee, Trent Boult, Neil Wagner and Kyle Jamieson was outstanding.

Such were New Zealand's riches, they were able to leave out players in successive games in England who had achieved the following in their previous test: Daryl Mitchell (century against Pakistan); Tim Southee (6-43 at Lord's); Matt Henry (player of the match at Edgbaston) and Will Young (82 in the same game).

Williamson (754 runs in just five tests) and Jamieson (37 wickets at 13 in six tests) are our Players of the Year. Conway (who averaged over fifty in all three formats) and Southee (30 wickets at 20 in six tests) would normally have been frontrunners for inclusion but this was no ordinary year.

The White Ferns

The White Ferns had an extensive programme of 18 matches (nine one-day games and nine Twenty20s) spread across home and away series against Australia and a visit from England. Women's international cricket was played in New Zealand as late as April for the first time.

Three wins (two of which came with a series already decided) was an extremely disappointing return for the White Ferns. Their chance of a Twenty20 series win against Australia was thwarted when the deciding game at Auckland was washed out.

Amy Satterthwaite returned to the side after maternity leave and showed her class with an outstanding unbeaten century against England at Dunedin in the White Ferns' only one-day success. Sophie Devine was unable to bring her domestic form to the international stage, reaching thirty just once in 13 innings. She again captained the side but withdrew during the Australian series with Satterthwaite taking over.

Suzie Bates was injured in Australia and missed the rest of the season but Brooke Halliday showed promise with fifties in each of her first two one-day international innings. Fran Jonas, a sixteen-year-old left-arm spinner, also made her White Ferns debut during the season.

Amelia Kerr was New Zealand's leading wicket taker across all games with 17 victims while Leigh Kasperek took nine wickets in the only two one-day matches in which she appeared. This included an outstanding 6-46 at Mount Maunganui, the best figures by any player against Australia in one-day internationals.

The Domestic Scene

Domestic cricket started in October and ran through until April with Canterbury completely dominant. They won an unprecedented four competitions and were beaten finalists in the fifth.

The men's side won the Plunket Shield (with two full rounds remaining) and the Ford Trophy but went down to Wellington in a last-over finish in the Super Smash Twenty20 final.

The Canterbury women's team also won their Super Smash final in the last over, recovering from 60-6 to successfully chase Wellington's 125 without further loss. They also won the Hallyburton Johnstone Shield final against Auckland. The Super Smash finals were played as a Wellington-Canterbury double-header at the Basin Reserve.

The Hawke Cup again moved around the provinces. Nelson took the trophy from Canterbury Country in the season's first challenge but then immediately lost to North Otago, who had not held the Hawke Cup for five years. North Otago then lost their first defence to Hawke's Bay who successfully held off Hamilton's challenge in the last game of the season.

Changes

During the year former New Zealand players John F. Reid, John R. Reid, Bruce Taylor and John Ward passed away. Dean Brownlie, James Baker, Anton Devcich and BJ Watling, New Zealand's most successful wicketkeeper-batsman, announced their retirements. Otago coach Rob Walter was named to take over at Central Districts while his replacement at Otago is former Zimbabwe international Dion Ebrahim.

Coming Up

Despite the difficulties presented by the pandemic, the cricket continues. The White Ferns have three Twenty20s and five one-day internationals scheduled for September in England. The Black Caps are due to visit Bangladesh, Pakistan, United Arab Emirates (for the Twenty20 World Cup) and India. Bangladesh, the Netherlands and South Africa are set down to tour New Zealand and the women's fifty-over World Cup will begin in New Zealand in March 2022.

Acknowledgments

We again wish to thank the associations, scorers and officials throughout the country who supplied information to us. In particular, we would like to acknowledge the help of Catherine Campbell and the rest of the staff at New Zealand Cricket.

We are also grateful to Evan Watkin, Lindsay Knight, Euan West and Brian Adams for their help with obituaries and other information.

Francis Payne & Ian Smith
July 2021

DIARY OF THE SEASON

July

3 Graeme Aldridge and Joanne Broadbent are named as Northern Districts' men's and women's coaches for the 2020/21 season. Aldridge had been part of Northern's coaching contingent for several seasons while Broadbent was assistant coach in 2019/20.

30 New Zealand Cricket's umpire panels remain unchanged for 2020/21. They are International: Chris Brown, Shaun Haig, Wayne Knights. National: Brent Bowden, John Bromley, John Dempsey, Ash Mehrotra, Tim Parlane, Derek Walker. (Brown, Haig and Knights will also serve on the national panel when available). Reserve: Cory Black, Kim Cotton, Tyron Davies, Lui Els, Kannan Jagannathan, Damian Morrow, Pete Pasco, Eugene Sanders, Tim Shirriffs, Allen Stanley, Garth Stirrat, Glen Walklin.

August

4 Hamish Rutherford re-signs with Worcestershire for the Twenty20 Blast, which was delayed due to the coronavirus outbreak. Rutherford also played for the county in 2019.

8 The Women's Cricket World Cup due to be played in February in New Zealand is postponed for a year due to the disruption caused by Covid-19.

18 Eight of New Zealand's most promising women's players sign development contracts for 2020/21. They are: Bella Armstrong, Skye Bowden, Rebecca Burns, Eden Carson, Katie Gurrey, Fran Jonas, Jacinta Savage and Jess Watkin.

19 Craig Cumming is named as coach of the Otago women's team. Cumming is a level three qualified coach and has been involved in coaching throughout the Otago Cricket Pathway's Programme in both the men's and women's game for five years.

25 Rhys Morgan is appointed as Canterbury women's coach for 2020/21. A former Wellington first-class cricketer, Morgan had previously coached the Wellington under 19 men and women and the Wellington A women's side. He also held several national coaching roles in Fiji as well as being a batting consultant for the Bangladesh test team.

26 Craig McMillan is confirmed as Bangladesh batting consultant for their tour to Sri Lanka in October.

Central Districts women's coach Jamie Watkins is named in a newly created role to oversee the development of women's cricket throughout the association. He will move to a full-time position with CDCA for the first time and continue in his coaching role.

September

2 Gary Stead is reappointed as New Zealand coach for a further three-year term. He will continue as coach in all three formats of the game up until the conclusion of the ICC Cricket World Cup 2023.

17 Shane Jurgensen signs a two-year contract extension as New Zealand bowling coach. This will take him through to the end of 2022 and span two Twenty20 World Cups: in India in 2021 and Australia the following year.

19 Craig McMillan withdraws from his role as batting consultant for Bangladesh's tour of Sri Lanka following the death of his father.

October

31 Adam Milne is released from his 2020/21 Central Districts contract after agreeing to play for Sydney Thunder in the Big Bash League. Joey Field is subsequently named as his replacement on Central's contract list.

November

4 Otago coach Rob Walter has his contract extended until April 2023, following an improved performance by the team in 2019/20. Otago were the only team to finish in the top three of each of the domestic competitions, contesting the Ford Trophy final for the second straight year, and losing a home Super Smash elimination final. Former New Zealand under 19 assistant coach Adam Miles will work alongside Walter.

11 Anna Campbell and Rebecca Rolls are elected to the New Zealand Cricket board following its annual general meeting. They replace outgoing members Liz Dawson and Don Mackinnon on the eight-strong board, with Diana Puketapu re-elected for a further term. Campbell has been heavily involved in community cricket and was formerly on the board of the Otago Cricket Association. She is a geneticist and the managing director of AbacusBio. Rolls, a former cricket and football international, has had a long career in the public service, holding a number of senior leadership roles.

The meeting heard that NZC's budgeted loss for the year of $2.4m had been turned into a surplus of $1.5m, partly due to a significant reduction in activity because of the onset of COVID-19, along with widespread operational savings across the organisation. Greg Barclay was returned as chairman at the new board's first meeting immediately following the AGM formalities.

12 Heath Mills is named chairman of the Federation of International Cricketers' Associations board following the expiration of Tony Irish's term. Mills had been the chief executive of the New Zealand Players' Association and FICA Board Member since 2002.

13 Colin Munro signs with the Perth Scorchers for the Big Bash League and is released from his 2020/21 Auckland contract. He is subsequently replaced by Ryan Harrison.

19 Jackson Latham is given a Canterbury contract after Andrew Hazeldine is ruled out of the season due to illness.

25 Greg Barclay is elected as the International Cricket Council chairman. He fills the role vacated by Shashank Manohar who stepped down in July. Imran Khwaja had been interim chairman in the meantime.

December

2 Martin Snedden is elected chairman of the New Zealand Cricket board, replacing Greg Barclay, who was required to stand down from the position after being elected chairman of the ICC. Snedden is a former NZC chief executive and member of the board from 1990-1992, 1999-2001 and from 2013 until present. He will also become NZC's representative on the ICC board, a role he was previously seconded to in 2013 and 2014. He was also a member of the ICC chief executives' committee from 2001 to 2007.

15 Mitchell McClenaghan signs for Otago for the 2020/21 Super Smash season. He had recently completed a sixth year with 2020 IPL champions Mumbai Indians.

January

1 The New Year's Honours list sees Debbie Hockley named a Companion of the New Zealand Order of Merit (CNZM) for services to cricket while Kendra Cocksedge is made a Member of the New Zealand Order of Merit (MNZM) for services to rugby. Cocksedge played 43 games for Central Districts women's cricket team from 2004/05 to 2007/08.

26 New Zealand Cricket announce that Dream11 has extended its naming rights partnership with the men's and women's Super Smash competitions for a further six years.

February

15 New Zealand Cricket announce they have co-opted Roger Twose as a director to replace Greg Barclay (who was required to step down upon his election to the ICC chair) and has appointed Steve Tew to the position of board observer. Former international Twose has served on NZC's High Performance Advisory Group for the last 10 months and is an investment committee member for two Willis Bond Capital Partners' private equity funds totalling $232 million. Tew was CEO of New Zealand Rugby from 2008 to 2019.

18 New Zealand's Mark Coles is named coach of the Scotland women's team. Coles, who has over 20 years' experience as a professional cricket coach, becomes the first full-time coach of the women's national team. During Coles' two-year tenure as coach of the Pakistan women's side they moved up to fifth in the ICC women's championship table.

22 Former umpire Mike Spring dies in Tauranga aged 78. He stood in eight first-class and seven one-day matches in the 1980s and in one game of the 1981/82 women's world cup.

27 Wellington announce the extension of coach Glenn Pocknall's contract until May 2024.

March

2 Jeetan Patel is appointed as England's full-time spin bowling coach, having previously done short-term stints in the job as a consultant.

4 Lockie Ferguson signs with Yorkshire for the Twenty20 Blast competition. Yorkshire confirmed Ferguson's acquisition for all the group matches in June and July, subject to any international involvement.

11 A new $4.5 million cricket training facility for Hagley Park has received Christchurch City Council approval. It will also be able to accommodate basketball, netball, hockey and futsal. It is hoped to build the facility in time for the Women's Cricket World Cup in March 2022. The centre will be called The Sir Richard Hadlee Sports Centre, after the sporting trust in his name donated $800,000 towards its construction.

April

7 Joanne Broadbent extends her contract as Northern Districts' women's coach for a further two seasons.

13 The New Zealand Cricket awards are held online.

New Zealand umpire of the year: Chris Brown
Men's domestic player of the year: Daryl Mitchell
Women's domestic player of the year: Frances Mackay
Ruth Martin Cup *(women's domestic batting)*: Kate Ebrahim
Phyl Blackler Cup *(women's domestic bowling)*: Sarah Asmussen
Dream11 Super Smash men's player of the year: Finn Allen
Dream11 Super Smash women's player of the year: Amelia Kerr
Redpath Cup *(first-class batting)*: Kane Williamson
Winsor Cup *(first-class bowling)*: Kyle Jamieson
ANZ women's one-day international player of the year: Amy Satterthwaite
ANZ women's Twenty20 international player of the year: Amelia Kerr
ANZ test player of the year: Kane Williamson
ANZ men's one-day international player of the year: Devon Conway
ANZ men's Twenty20 international player of the year: Devon Conway
Sir Richard Hadlee medal for player of the year: Kane Williamson
Bert Sutcliffe medal for outstanding service: Jeff Crowe

19 Finn Allen is signed by Lancashire for the 2021 Vitality Blast campaign.

Rob Walter steps down from his role as Otago coach after accepting a three-year contract with Central Districts. Current Central coach Aldin Smith moves into a performance and pathway coaching role.

19 Matt McEwan announces his retirement. He took 158 wickets at 26.79 in 47 first-class games for Canterbury, Wellington and Auckland.

Dean Brownlie also announces his retirement. He played 14 tests, 16 one-day internationals and five Twenty20 internationals and scored 6208 runs at 40.05 in 94 first-class games.

21 Gloucestershire sign Glenn Phillips for their 2021 Twenty20 campaign.

22 Lance Dry is named as Wellington's women's coach while Luke Woodcock is appointed as specialist batting coach for the women's side and Cricket Wellington pathway players.

27 James Neesham signs for Essex in the T20 Blast competition.

28 Nathan Smith announces he will move from Otago to Wellington for the 2021/22 season.

May

3 James Baker announces his retirement. He played 76 first-class games, all for Northern Districts, taking 201 wickets at 29.65.

5 Colin de Grandhomme *(Hampshire)* and Devon Conway *(Somerset)* sign up for the second half of the T20 Blast competition.

6 After 12 years with Northern Districts, Felicity Leydon-Davis moves to Otago for the 2021/22 domestic season.

12 BJ Watling announces his decision to retire from all cricket after the tour of England. In 75 tests he scored 3790 runs and made 265 wicketkeeping dismissals. In 178 first-class games he made 10,034 runs and had 417 dismissals. He also played 28 one-day internationals and five Twenty20 internationals.

14 The 20 players offered New Zealand Cricket men's contracts for 2021/22 are Tom Blundell, Trent Boult, Devon Conway, Colin de Grandhomme, Lockie Ferguson, Martin Guptill, Matt Henry, Kyle Jamieson, Tom Latham, Daryl Mitchell, Henry Nicholls, James Neesham, Glenn Phillips, Mitchell Santner, Ish Sodhi, Tim Southee, Ross Taylor, Neil Wagner, Kane Williamson and Will Young. Mitchell and Phillips appear on the list for the first time while Ajaz Patel and BJ Watling drop out.

22 Daryl Mitchell signs with Middlesex for the last nine group matches of the Vitality Blast.

26 The 17 players offered New Zealand Cricket women's contracts for 2021/22 are Suzie Bates, Sophie Devine, Lauren Down, Maddy Green, Brooke Halliday, Hayley Jensen, Leigh Kasperek, Amelia Kerr, Jess Kerr, Frances Mackay, Jess McFadyen, Rosemary Mair, Katey Martin, Thamsyn Newton, Hannah Rowe, Amy Satterthwaite, Lea Tahuhu. Halliday, Mackay and McFadyen are offered contracts for the first time while Natalie Dodd, Holly Huddleston, Katie Perkins and Anna Peterson drop off the list.

June

1 Garth Stirrat, who was a member of New Zealand Cricket's reserve umpires panel, announces his retirement. He stood in nine first-class games, 17 one-day fixtures, 12 Twenty20 matches and four women's internationals.

Derbyshire re-sign Logan van Beek for the Twenty20 Blast competition for 2021. He played for the county in all formats in 2019 and replaces Billy Stanlake who suffered a stress fracture in his back.

2 Dion Ebrahim is named as the new Otago coach. The former Zimbabwe international joins Otago from Central Districts, where he filled the assistant coach role during the 2020/21 season and was previously assistant coach and performance coach at Canterbury over a five year period.

7 Former White Fern Janice Stead is appointed a Member of the New Zealand Order of Merit for services to sport and the community in the 2021 Queen's Birthday Honours list.

10 Kyle Jamieson signs for Surrey and will be available for selection in the Twenty20 Blast and the final two games in the group stage of the county championship.

Wes Armstrong, head groundsman at the Basin Reserve from 1971 to 1994, passes away in Wellington aged 88.

July

5 Denise Craig, who chaired the New Zealand Women's Cricket Council in the early 1990s, passes away in Wellington aged 79. She represented Wellington as a wicketkeeper, was a national selector and managed the White Ferns at home and in Australia. She was also the first coach and selector of the Central Districts women's side in 1979.

14 The six Major Associations announce their 16 contracted players for 2021/22. Notable changes are George Worker *(Central Districts)* to Auckland, Nathan Smith *(Otago)* to Wellington and Jake Gibson *(Northern Districts)* to Otago. Adithya Ashok and Matthew Gibson *(Auckland)*, Will O'Rourke *(Canterbury)*, Kristian Clarke *(Northern Districts)* and Callum McLachlan *(Wellington)* have not previously appeared at provincial level.

16 Kate Ebrahim announces her availability for Otago for the 2021/22 season following her husband Dion's appointment as Otago men's coach.

19 Anton Devcich announces his retirement. He played in 12 one-day internationals and four Twenty20 internationals and scored 2826 runs and took 51 wickets in 56 first-class matches.

PLAYERS OF THE YEAR

Kyle Jamieson had a stellar season in first-class cricket. In the period under review he took 37 wickets in six test matches (at an average of just 13) and 20 wickets at 10 apiece in three games for Auckland.

Jamieson started the season with five wicket hauls in each of his three Plunket Shield games with a best of 5-39 against Otago. In the game against Wellington he reached 100 first-class wickets and when the test matches came he continued his great form.

He started with 2-25 and 2-42 in the first test against West Indies and in the second test had career best figures of 5-34. He took five wickets in the first test against Pakistan and in the second had a five wicket haul in each innings for match figures of 11-117.

In the test against England at Lord's he took 3-85 and 0-28 (the only first-class innings where he failed to take a wicket) before getting 5-31 and 2-30 in the test championship final. He bowled 46 overs in the match, conceding just 61 runs.

Jamieson took five wickets in the Super Smash for Auckland and got four wickets in international Twenty20 games. He was awarded one of the biggest contracts in the Indian Premier League and after the test matches in England was contracted to Surrey. He has quickly risen to the top level of bowlers with his outstanding record of 46 wickets in just eight tests.

Kane Williamson's only first-class games during the season were five test matches but in those five games he amassed 754 runs at an average of 107. This included scores of 251 against West Indies and 129 and 238 against Pakistan.

In the final of the World Test Championship, in a low scoring game where batting conditions were often difficult, he made scores of 49 and 52 not out, steering New Zealand to its historic win on the sixth day of the match.

Williamson's 49 in almost five hours on the fifth day was a crucial innings which enabled New Zealand to gain a slight advantage which they never relinquished. He was fittingly in the middle with Ross Taylor when the winning runs came.

Williamson played seven Twenty20 internationals, scoring 140 runs, and also played two Twenty20 games for Northern Districts, making 34 and 79, both times unbeaten.

He again had a contract in the Indian Premier League and was also due to play in England but a troublesome elbow injury, which forced him to miss some international games during the year, saw him withdraw. Williamson finished the season with 7230 runs in test cricket at 53.95, just 334 runs behind Taylor's New Zealand record.

PROMISING PLAYERS

Finn Allen transferred from Auckland to Wellington for the 2020/21 season and couldn't have had a worse start getting a pair in his first Plunket Shield game. He then scored just 40 runs in the next two games.

He missed the first three Ford Trophy matches due to concussion but scored 30 against Auckland in his first appearance. When the Dream11 Super Smash began Allen literally started with a bang getting a 20-ball fifty in the first match. He proceeded to score another 20-ball half-century against Otago before getting a fifty from just 16 balls against Central Districts. He was the top scorer in the tournament with 512 runs at 56.88 with a very impressive strike rate of 193.

He then resumed in the Ford Trophy and scored his maiden hundred against Otago. This came off only 50 balls and equalled Peter Fulton's New Zealand record for the fastest one-day domestic century. Allen was then called up to the New Zealand Twenty20 side against Bangladesh. He was dismissed first ball on debut but made 71 off 29 balls in the third game.

After some withdrawls from the Indian Premier League he was awarded a contract with the Rajasthan Royals but didn't play a game before that tournament was halted. He was also signed by Lancashire to play in the Twenty20 tournament during the English summer.

Will O'Donnell's appearances in his first two seasons for Auckland had been mainly confined to Ford Trophy games. He started his third season in the one-day competition and after the first game never looked back. He had five successive innings over fifty with the last of them (106 against Wellington) being his maiden century.

He then scored 212 runs in the Super Smash at 35.33 and a strike rate of 124. Resuming in the Ford Trophy he scored a further two fifties in four innings to end up as the leading scorer in the competition with with 537 runs at 53.70.

O'Donnell then joined his brother in the Plunket Shield side and had two fifties prior to the final game against Wellington where he scored his maiden first-class century and another hundred in the second innings. He became the ninth Auckland player to score a century in each innings of a game and finished with 375 runs at 75 in the Plunket Shield. He has certainly shown he has the temperament for all formats of cricket

Michael Rae started the Plunket Shield season getting 11 wickets in the first four games. He was then selected to play in the first-class game for New Zealand A against the touring West Indies side at Queenstown.

In his first game in the Ford Trophy he achieved the third-best figures in New Zealand one day cricket when he took 7-35 against Auckland. This was the best for Otago in the domestic competition. He then played for New Zealand A against Pakistan A at Whangarei.

In five Super Smash games he took three wickets before returning for the remainder of the Ford Trophy competition, taking 4-39 against Canterbury.

When the Plunket Shield resumed he took 4-89 against Auckland, 5-62 (plus a hat-trick and eight wickets in the match) against Central Districts and 4-55 against Northern Districts.

He ended the season with 29 wickets at 34 in the Plunket Shield, which included his 100th first-class victim. He played in every first-class game during the season and held the attack together when Otago suffered injuries which depleted their fast bowling stocks.

HAPPENINGS

As far as can be ascertained there are fourteen surviving New Zealand first-class cricketers who were born in 1930 or earlier. Any additions or amendments to the following list are very welcome:

		Born
A.P. Arnold	*Canterbury*	16.10.1926
W.C. Crump	*Auckland*	3. 2.1928
D.J. Reid	*Canterbury*	17.10.1928
J.D. Alderson	*Canterbury*	3. 2.1929
H.N. Dellow	*Canterbury*	14. 2.1929
G.E. Royfee	*Canterbury*	20. 2.1929
J.W.F. Kiddey	*Canterbury*	5. 7.1929
T.G. McMahon	*Wellington*	8.11.1929
D.V. Spence	*Central Districts*	8. 1.1930
P.M. McCaw	*Wellington*	10. 2.1930
I.B. Leggat	*Central Districts*	7. 6.1930
J.C. Alabaster	*Otago*	11. 7.1930
J.A. Harliwich	*Canterbury*	14. 7.1930
I.N. Brennan	*Wellington*	17. 7.1930

Missing from the previous year's list of oldest players are Alan Burgess, Iain Gallaway and Jack Tynan (who were the three oldest), Doug Bowden, John Reid and Trevor Malloch.

Obituaries for Burgess, Gallaway and Reid appear in this edition. Bruce Pairaudeau, born 14 April 1931, is the oldest Northern Districts player and Trevor McMahon is New Zealand's oldest living test cricketer.

• • •

Jack Tynan, who died at Christchurch on 23 August 2020, was Wellington's oldest surviving player. He played four times for Wellington in the 1950s. He was also a former New Zealand hockey captain and led the team at the Melbourne 1956 Olympic Games where they finished in sixth place.

Doug Bowden, who was Central Districts' oldest surviving player, died at Taupo on 20 January 2021. He was a member of Central's first Plunket Shield team which met Wellington at the Basin Reserve on 1 December 1950. He played 16 matches for Central Districts.

Trevor Malloch, who died at Feilding on 2 November 2020, played twice for Wellington in 1953/54. He was awarded a Queen's Service Medal in the 2004 Queen's Birthday Honours for Public Service. He had been Wellington's oldest surviving first-class player.

• • •

Auckland's oldest player, Bill Crump, became a first-class cricketer in unusual circumstances. Forty years after the games had taken place, the ICC ruled that Fiji's matches against the major associations in New Zealand in 1947/48 were first-class despite the New Zealand Cricket Council's original and subsequent rulings that they should not be considered as such. Fiji played twice against Auckland, Crump keeping wicket in the second game.

• • •

Australian-born off-spinner Des Ferrow, who died at Tauranga on 5 December 2020 aged 87, played in Northern Districts' first Plunket Shield game, against Auckland at Seddon Park, which began on Christmas Day 1956. Ferrow had the distinction of capturing the first wicket for Northern in first-class cricket, having Auckland opener Dave Perry caught by Peter Smith. Ferrow finished with 4-50 from 27 overs.

Ferrow played three further games for Northern and continued to play for Bay of Plenty into the 1960s. Dave Hoskin, who bowled the first over for Northern Districts, and Auckland batsman Roger Harris are the only survivors from that historic game.

Keith Butler, who died at Auckland on 29 September 2020 aged 86, played just one first-class game, for Auckland against Fiji in 1953/54, but it was a remarkable one.

After no play on the first two days, the scores on the final day were: Auckland 96-7 in 43 overs, Fiji 121-6 in 28.2 overs, Auckland 106-7 in 33 overs and Fiji 83-3 in 13.3 overs to win by seven wickets. This is the last occasion that a first-class game in New Zealand has been completed in one day. The other six instances were all prior to 1900.

Butler bowled just six overs in the game without success but top scored with 24 in Auckland's second innings.

• • •

While not a first-class cricketer, Derek Geoffrey Hamilton (born 30 June 1923) is probably the oldest surviving player to have appeared for a New Zealand representative team. He played for Royal New Zealand Air Force and New Zealand Services sides in England in 1944 and 1945.

Hamilton was a left-arm spinner from Christchurch and took nine wickets in one match for Services against a strong Australian Air Force side. In their review of services cricket in the 1945 edition, *Wisden* said "Hamilton showed natural ability...his accuracy was almost uncanny. Against the Australians he opened with eight maiden overs and altogether conceded only 40 runs in 25 overs while taking six wickets."

• • •

A Royal New Zealand Air Force team picture has been reproduced in the illustrations section. It was taken before a game against Cross Arrows at Lord's on 8 September 1944. The photograph was taken outside the Harris Garden in front of the memorial plaque to Lord Harris and contains some notable names.

New Zealand test wicketkeeper Ken James, the captain of the team, is seated between Bill Jordan and Sir Pelham Warner. Jordan was New Zealand's longest-serving high commissioner to the United Kingdom from 1936 to 1951. He presented the William Jordan Trophy which was to be contested for in tests between New Zealand and England.

Warner was a former England captain and long-serving administrator who was knighted for his services to cricket in 1937. The Warner Stand at Lord's is named after him.

• • •

Robbie O'Donnell (27 games for Auckland) led his team in every match in the three domestic competitions in 2020/21 while Cole McConchie captained Canterbury in 27 out of 31 games. Central Districts, Northern Districts and Otago appointed different captains for the first-class and limited-overs formats.

	Official captain	***Replacement/Alternate***
Auckland	Robbie O'Donnell	–
Canterbury	Cole McConchie	Leo Carter
Central Districts	Greg Hay	Tom Bruce, George Worker
Northern Districts	Joe Carter	Anton Devcich
Otago	Hamish Rutherford	Nick Kelly, Jacob Duffy
Wellington	Michael Bracewell	Fraser Colson, Troy Johnson

• • •

BJ Watling reached a major milestone when he caught Abid Ali off Trent Boult's bowling in Pakistan's second innings of the test at Bay Oval on 29 December. It was Watling's 400th wicketkeeping dismissal in first-class cricket and he was just the fifth New Zealand player to reach the mark.

Most first-class wicketkeeping dismissals by New Zealand players are Gareth Hopkins 455, Kruger van Wyk 435, Ian Smith 426, Ken James 422, BJ Watling 417.

New Zealand played seven test matches during the past twelve months, winning six and drawing one. Kane Williamson (754) was the leading run scorer while Kyle Jamieson took the most wickets (37).

Williamson (three), Henry Nicholls (two) and Devon Conway and Daryl Mitchell scored centuries. Jamieson (four times) and Tim Southee (twice) took five wickets in an innings and Jamieson took ten in a match. Nicholls, Tom Latham and Ross Taylor were the only players to appear in every game.

• • •

New Zealand took part in just three one-day internationals in the same period, winning them all. Devon Conway was the leading scorer with 225 runs. Conway, Tom Latham and Daryl Mitchell each scored centuries. James Neesham took the most wickets (seven) while Matt Henry (3.48 runs per over) was the most economical bowler.

• • •

New Zealand played 14 Twenty20 internationals over the year, winning ten, losing three with one no result. Devon Conway was again the leading scorer with 473 runs while Tim Southee (21) was the leading wicket taker.

Glenn Phillips scored the only century while Conway (4), Martin Guptill, Tim Seifert and Kane Williamson (2) and Phillips, Finn Allen and Will Young made fifties. Lockie Ferguson, who played in five games, had the best economy rate of 6.26 runs per over. Conway, Guptill and Phillips appeared in every game.

• • •

The highest run scorer in New Zealand first-class cricket over the past twelve months was Devon Conway who totalled 835, followed by Kane Williamson (754). The most first-class wickets were taken by Kyle Jamieson (57) while Tim Southee took 44.

• • •

A number of New Zealand players have a high ratio of catches per match over their first-class careers. Ross Taylor has 246 in 188 games while Jeet Raval (134 in 126), Martin Guptill (130 in 115), Daryl Mitchell (85 in 78), Tom Bruce (78 in 51), Robbie O'Donnell (67 in 55) and James Neesham (66 in 65) also average at least one catch per game. Included in Taylor's record are 159 catches in 108 test matches.

• • •

By the end of the tour to England, Ross Taylor had taken 344 catches as a fielder for New Zealand in international cricket – 159 in tests, 139 in one-day internationals and 46 in Twenty20 internationals. Stephen Fleming (305), Martin Guptill (201), Kane Williamson (164), Nathan Astle (156) and Daniel Vettori (153) are the only other fielders to have taken 150 catches or more for New Zealand in international cricket.

• • •

Taylor was also the longest-serving player to appear in New Zealand first-class cricket in 2020/21. He made his debut for Central Districts against Canterbury at Timaru on 9 January 2003, batting at number seven and scoring 12 in his only innings (bowled by Craig McMillan, who opened the bowling with Chris Martin).

He was followed by BJ Watling and Will Somerville who both made their debuts in the 2004/05 season. Neil Broom also made his first-class debut in 2002/03 but appeared only in Ford Trophy and Super Smash games in 2020/21.

Broom thus remained on 101 first-class appearances for Otago, meaning Warren Lees' long-standing Otago record of 108 games remained intact. BJ Watling (91 games) was the closest to James Marshall's Northern Districts record of 127 but subsequently announced his retirement, as did James Baker (76 games). Scott Kuggeleijn (59 games) is now next in line.

Luke Woodcock's Wellington record of 143 games (also the record for any New Zealand province) will not be challenged for some time. Tom Blundell (57 matches) has the most first-class games for Wellington amongst current players.

Peter Fulton's Canterbury record of 121 is also safe for the time being with Cameron Fletcher (57 games) being his nearest challenger. The nearest to Tim McIntosh's Auckland record of 102 games is Robbie O'Donnell with 55 appearances while Greg Hay (85 matches) is the nearest challenger to Mathew Sinclair's Central Districts record of 119 games.

• • •

The thirty-first national limited-overs competition for secondary school boys, the Gillette Cup, was played at Lincoln from 10-14 December 2020. A total of 93 teams entered the competition which is organised by each major association, with one winner from each progressing to the final. Christchurch Boys' High School won the tournament for the third time in five years. Angus Sidey *(Christchurch Boys' High School)* was named player of the tournament.

Round 1
New Plymouth Boys' High School 102 lost to **Christchurch Boys' High School** 103-3 by 7 wickets
Wellington College 302-8 defeated **Hamilton Boys' High School** 201 by 101 runs
Otago Boys' High School 228 lost to **Westlake Boys' High School** 229-5 by 5 wickets

Round 2
Westlake Boys' High School 208-9 lost to **Christchurch Boys' High School** 210-6 by 4 wickets
Hamilton Boys' High School 349-5 defeated **Otago Boys' High School** 249-9 by 100 runs
Wellington College 262-9 defeated **New Plymouth Boys' High School** 137 by 125 runs

Round 3
Hamilton Boys' High School 268-4 lost to **Christchurch Boys' High School** 271-5 by 5 wickets
New Plymouth Boys' High School 218 defeated **Westlake Boys' High School** 160 by 58 runs
Wellington College 339-9 defeated **Otago Boys' High School** 328-8 by 11 runs

Round 4
Christchurch Boys' High School 343-6 defeated **Wellington College** 204 by 139 runs
Hamilton Boys' High School 256 defeated **Westlake Boys' High School** 119 by 137 runs
New Plymouth Boys' High School 231 defeated **Otago Boys' High School** 186 by 45 runs

Round 5
Otago Boys' High School 105 lost to **Christchurch Boys' High School** 106-2 by 8 wickets
Hamilton Boys' High School 138 lost to **New Plymouth Boys' High School** 139-6 by 4 wickets
Wellington College 303-7 defeated **Westlake Boys' High School** 302-9 by 1 run

Final placings: Christchurch Boys' High School 1st, Wellington College 2nd, New Plymouth Boys' High School 3rd, Hamilton Boys' High School 4th, Westlake Boys' High School 5th, Otago Boys' High School 6th.

The twenty-seventh national secondary schools girls competition, the Gillette Venus Cup, was played at Palmerston North from 11-13 December 2020.

A total of 65 teams entered the competition which is organised by each major association, with one winner from each progressing to the final. Christchurch Girls' High School won the tournament. Player of the tournament was Nensi Patel *(Tauranga Girls' College)*.

Round 1
Christchurch Girls' High School 140-5 defeated **St Hilda's Collegiate** 49 by 91 runs
Takapuna Grammar School 132-4 defeated **Hutt Valley High School** 90-4 by 42 runs
Tauranga Girls' College 90-3 lost to **St Matthew's Collegiate** 91-4 by 6 wickets

Round 2
St Matthew's Collegiate 84-7 lost to **Christchurch Girls' High School** 87-3 by 7 wickets
Hutt Valley High School 88-9 defeated **St Hilda's Collegiate** 87 by 1 run
Tauranga Girls' College 133-3 defeated **Takapuna Grammar School** 116-6 by 17 runs

Round 3
Hutt Valley High School 106-2 lost to **Christchurch Girls' High School** 107-3 by 7 wickets
Tauranga Girls' College 124-3 defeated **St Hilda's Collegiate** 111 by 13 runs
Takapuna Grammar School 84-9 lost to **St Matthew's Collegiate** 86-4 by 6 wickets

Round 4
Christchurch Girls' High School 124-5 defeated **Tauranga Girls' College** 62 by 62 runs
Hutt Valley High School 108-6 lost to **St Matthew's Collegiate** 110-2 by 8 wickets
Takapuna Grammar School 122-5 lost to **St Hilda's Collegiate** 123-2 by 8 wickets

Round 5
Christchurch Girls' High School 133-5 defeated **Takapuna Grammar School** 108 by 25 runs
Tauranga Girls' College 58-9 lost to **Hutt Valley High School** 59-6 by 4 wickets
St Matthew's Collegiate 122-4 defeated **St Hilda's Collegiate** 83-8 by 39 runs

Playoffs
St Matthew's Collegiate 66 lost to **Christchurch Girls' High School** 68-1 by 9 wickets
Hutt Valley High School 130-5 defeated **Tauranga Girls' College** 72 by 58 runs
St Hilda's Collegiate 82 lost to **Takapuna Grammar School** 85-3 by 7 wickets

Final placings: Christchurch Girls' High School 1st, St Matthew's Collegiate 2nd, Hutt Valley High School 3rd, Tauranga Girls' College 4th, Takapuna Grammar School 5th, St Hilda's Collegiate 6th.

• • •

The Cornwall Cricket Club in Auckland again organised the national club competition which was played from 8-11 April 2021. The format changed from fifty-over to Twenty20. Teams involved were Karaka *(Northern Districts)*, Taieri *(Otago)*, Lancaster Park *(Canterbury)*, Napier Technical Old Boys *(Central Districts)*, Karori *(Wellington)* and Takapuna *(Auckland)*.

Players with first-class experience involved were Robbie and Will O'Donnell, Ross ter Braak and Danru Ferns *(Takapuna)*, Ben McCord and Michael Davidson *(Lancaster Park)*, Ben Lockrose *(Taieri)*, Christian Leopard and Jayden Lennox *(Napier Technical Old Boys)* and Michael Pollard, Andrew Fletcher, Peter Younghusband, Michael Snedden, Jakob Bhula and Tom Blundell *(Karori)*.

In the final **Takapuna** 107-8 (Q.L.M. Sunde 38) defeated **Karori** 69 (W.T. O'Donnell 4-14) by 38 runs.

Tournament awards were: Batting – Jakob Bhula *(Karori)*, Bowling – Ross ter Braak *(Takapuna)*, All-rounder – Todd Watson *(Napier Technical Old Boys)*, Player of the Tournament – Will O'Donnell *(Takapuna)*.

Canterbury won the Plunket Shield for the 2020/21 season, the first time they had won the competition since 2016/17. The overall list of winners of the New Zealand first-class competition (Plunket Shield, Shell Trophy, State Championship) is Auckland 23, Wellington 21, Canterbury 20, Otago 13, Central Districts 11, Northern Districts 8.

This does not include matches from the seasons 1907/08 to 1920/21 when the Plunket Shield was first played on a challenge basis. Otago, whose last success was in 1987/88 (Shell Trophy) have gone by far the longest without winning the title.

Otago also won the one-day competition (Shell Cup) that season when they fielded the same eleven in all five games. Five of those players, Bruce Blair, Stephen Boock, Kevin Burns, Richard Hoskin and Derek Walker also played in all eight Shell Trophy fixtures.

• • •

Canterbury also won the New Zealand domestic one-day competition which was introduced in the 1971/72 season and was played as a knockout format until a round-robin programme was introduced in 1980/81. They had last won the title in 2016/17.

The winners have been: Canterbury (15), Auckland (12), Wellington (8), Northern Districts (7), Central Districts (6), Otago (2).

Canterbury (in 1975/76-1977/78 and 1991/92-1993/94) are the only side to win the competition three times in a row (winning seven times in nine seasons during the 1990s).

• • •

Wellington won the domestic Twenty20 title for the second year in a row, defeating Canterbury in the final. It was Wellington's fourth success in five final appearances.

A summary of winners is: **Auckland** — eight finals, four wins, **Canterbury** — four finals, one win, **Central Districts** — six finals, three wins, **Northern Districts** — four finals, two wins, **Otago** — five finals, two wins, **Wellington** — five finals, four wins.

Nine finals have been won by the team batting first, six by the team batting second while one was abandoned with the higher placed team (Otago) being declared winners.

• • •

In the sixteen years that three titles have been available, no team has won all three in the same season. Canterbury (2005/06) and Auckland (2006/07 and 2010/11) won the one-day and Twenty20 competitions in the same season while Northern Districts won the Plunket Shield and one-day titles in 2009/10 as did Canterbury this past season.

Auckland (in 2015/16), Central Districts (2018/19) and Wellington (2019/20) are the only teams to win the first-class and Twenty20 titles in the same season. Over the 2012/13 and 2013/14 seasons all six teams won a trophy each.

• • •

Canterbury also won both women's competitions, the first time any province had won as many as four competitions in the same season. Canterbury had previously won both women's titles in 2007/08 and 2010/11 with the Canterbury men's team also winning the first-class competition on both occasions (known as the State Championship in 2007/08).

Central Districts (2009/10) are the only other team to win both women's competitions in the same season.

• • •

The third Twenty20 between New Zealand and Bangladesh at Auckland was reduced to a ten-over game. New Zealand scored 141-4 and Bangladesh were bowled out for 76 in 9.3 overs. The only shorter all out innings in Twenty20 internationals are 8.3 overs by Turkey (21) against Czech Republic and 8.5 overs by Turkey (32) against Austria on successive days at Ilfov County, Romania in the Continental Cup in 2019.

With home umpires officiating in international games due to the Covid situation, New Zealand umpire Chris Gaffaney, who was on the ICC's elite panel, stood in all four tests played in New Zealand during the season. Wayne Knights and Chris Brown made their test umpiring debuts, standing in two games each.

Gaffaney also stood in all three one-day internationals and six of the Twenty20s played in New Zealand. Brown officiated in one one-day game and eight Twenty20s, Knights stood in two one-day internationals and eight Twenty20s while Shaun Haig umpired six Twenty20s.

Kim Cotton stood in nine of the twelve women's internationals played in New Zealand during the season. Brown, Ashley Mehrotra, Brent Bowden, John Dempsey and Eugene Sanders were also involved.

Former New Zealand captain Jeff Crowe was the ICC Match Referee throughout the season for the Black Caps' games. The first test against West Indies at Hamilton was his 100th test in that role. In the same game Wayne Knights and his sister Erica made their test debuts as umpire and scorer.

• • •

BJ Watling took 26 catches in five test matches during the 2020/21 season with 16 of these coming off the bowling of Tim Southee, Neil Wagner and Trent Boult. The top three most frequent dismissal combinations for New Zealand in test cricket all feature Watling:

75 c Watling b Southee
57 c Watling b Boult
55 c Watling b Wagner
43 c Smith b Hadlee
42 c McCullum b Martin
37 c Parore b Cairns
35 c Smith b Chatfield

Watling took two of his catches off Southee and one off Wagner as a fielder. Ross Taylor (26) has taken the most catches off Southee in the outfield and also the most off Boult's bowling (19). Southee (16) has taken the most catches by a fielder off Wagner.

The most frequent fielder and bowler combination for New Zealand is 27 by Jeremy Coney and Richard Hadlee followed by Taylor with 26 catches off Southee.

• • •

Tim Southee became the second New Zealand bowler to take 600 wickets in international cricket during the world test championship final against India. Trent Boult had earlier reached 500 wickets in the second test against England. The most wickets for New Zealand bowlers in internationals is: 696 Daniel Vettori, 603 Tim Southee, 589 Richard Hadlee, 507 Trent Boult, 419 Chris Cairns.

• • •

Sean Davey produced the best bowling figures by a player on debut in New Zealand domestic one-day cricket when he took 6-30 for Canterbury against Wellington at Christchurch in November.

Three players had previously taken five wickets in an innings on debut: Leighton Burtt, 5-26 for Canterbury against Auckland in 2005/06, Bevan Small, 5-45 for Central Districts against Auckland in 2011/12 and Jake Gibson, 5-31 for Northern Districts against Auckland in 2019/20. In other List A cricket, Hedley Howarth took 5-22 for New Zealand against New South Wales in 1969/70 on debut.

The best figures on debut overall are by Denys Hobson who had figures of 11.5-3-27-7 for Western Province against Northern Transvaal in 1974/75.

Davey finished with 15 wickets at 20 in the Ford Trophy and was also successful in the longer format with 15 wickets at 18 in the Plunket Shield. He took 5-19 against Central Districts in his third match.

An $8000 portable shade sail appears to have finally solved McLean Park's sunstrike problem for top-level cricket. The rays from the setting sun coming through a narrow gap between two stands had halted play on numerous occasions in the past, including India's one-day international in January 2019 and the Pakistan Twenty20 international on 22 December.

The 12x12 metre shade was successfully trialled in the Twenty20 Super Smash match between Central Districts and Canterbury on 5 February. It was hoisted by a crane, which can go as high as 47 metres, propped up by two beams, weighed down by water drums and tied down with an elaborate system to stop the wind disturbing it. It was placed in the exact position just before the match, with help from a smartphone app which predicts the sun's path on any given day.

The sail cost $8000 to build and, based on its single use, will cost Napier City Council approximately $2000 each time it is used. The council had previously spent $5 million on new drainage and a re-turf at McLean Park after a one-day international against Australia in 2016 was abandoned due to a waterlogged outfield.

• • •

Will O'Donnell and Michael Bracewell both scored a century in each innings of the Plunket Shield match between Auckland and Wellington at Eden Park's outer oval in April. It was the second season in a row that two batsman had each scored two centuries in the same match, something that had happened just twice previously in New Zealand's entire first-class history as this list shows.

Ian Chappell & Greg Chappell	Australia v New Zealand	Wellington	1973/74
Andrew Jones & Asanka Gurusinha	New Zealand v Sri Lanka	Hamilton	1990/91
Joe Carter & Mark Chapman	Auckland v Northern Districts	Auckland	2019/20
Michael Bracewell & Will O'Donnell	Auckland v Wellington	Auckland	2020/21

The last player to score a hundred in each innings for Wellington was Luke Ronchi against Northern Districts in 2012/13 while Jesse Ryder had done so earlier in the same season against Central Districts.

• • •

O'Donnell's hundred in the first innings of the game against Wellington was his first in first-class cricket. He then joined four other players who followed up their first hundred with another one in the second innings. This list is:

Paul Whitelaw (115 & 155)	Auckland v Wellington	1934/35
Graham Gedye (104 & 101)	Auckland v Central Districts	1963/64
Keith Thomson (102 & 102*)	Canterbury v Otago	1966/67
Hamish Rutherford (107 & 118)	Otago v Northern Districts	2011/12
Will O'Donnell (117 & 137*)	Auckland v Wellington	2020/21

• • •

The second and third one-day internationals between the White Ferns and England were played at University Oval in Dunedin. This was the first time the White Ferns had played at the venue, after their Twenty20 international against South Africa had been abandoned due to persistent rain the season before.

It was also the first time the White Ferns had played in Dunedin since 13 February 1999 when they met South Africa at Carisbrook.

Katey Martin, with almost 200 matches for New Zealand, thus played in an international in her home city for the first time. Her Otago team mate Suzie Bates, with well over 200 appearances for New Zealand, was not so lucky though, having missed most of the summer after being injured in Australia early in the season.

Birkenhead's Jasmeet Singh and Parvesh Sethi recorded the highest known opening partnership in all cricket in New Zealand when they amassed a first wicket stand of 455 in a fourth grade game against Grafton at Walker Park in Auckland in December.

The stand was broken in the 40th over when Jasmeet was dismissed for 314 from 149 balls, with 28 fours and 25 sixes. Sethi made 125 off 109 balls. Birkenhead made 503-4 in their 45 overs and dismissed Grafton (who had won the toss) for 95, winning by 408 runs.

The previous highest recorded first wicket partnership in New Zealand was 441 by Jack Mills and Hec Gillespie for Eden against University at Auckland in 1924/25.

• • •

Benji Culhane scored a remarkable century playing for Otago against Auckland at the New Zealand Under 19 cricket tournament at Lincoln in December. He came to the crease with his team at 127-6 and it soon became 138-9.

That's when Culhane took charge, the wicketkeeper-batsman striking 12 fours and eight sixes as he posted 123 from just 94 balls. He found support from Otago's number eleven Ben Seavill who contributed 29 off 43 balls as he and Culhane put on 153 for the last wicket. Culhane was run out off the last ball of the innings with Otago posting 291 batting first.

Despite Culhane's heroics, however, Otago was not able to post a win as Auckland overhauled the target with three overs and four wickets to spare.

Culhane is the son of former All Black first five-eighth Simon Culhane who scored 45 points against Japan at the 1995 World Cup. Culhane senior was a useful cricketer himself, playing at Hawke Cup level for Southland.

• • •

Adam and Liam Beck completed a rare batting double of twins each scoring centuries in the same innings. Playing for Pleasant Point seniors against Celtic in the South Canterbury competition in February, they spearheaded a successful chase in reply to Celtic's 288-6 off their 50 overs.

The twins came together at the end of the 12th over, sharing a century partnership. Adam made 103 from 126 balls, with eight fours and six sixes, while Liam ended unbeaten on 113, hitting 11 fours, as Point completed a seven wicket win with two overs to spare to stay top of the Tweedy Cup points table. Both players have previously appeared for the South Canterbury representative team.

• • •

Roneel Hira produced a remarkable all-round performance in a club game in February. The 34-year-old Hira, who played 15 Twenty20 internationals for New Zealand, reached fifty off just 12 balls, for North Shore against Takapuna at Devonport Domain. He later recalled how he had let two balls go, "one down leg-side and one down the off."

He finished with 73 off 22 balls, including seven sixes and seven fours, in the Hedley Howarth Championship two-day game. Hira also excelled with the ball with match figures of 14-78 from 43 overs. This included eight wickets in the second innings, the first time he had reached that mark.

• • •

Mike Dormer, who played four games for Auckland as wicketkeeper in 1961/62, died at Christchurch on 19 April 2021 aged 83. His major cricketing legacy was as founder of the Willows Cricket Club in Loburn, North Canterbury.

Dormer founded the Willows in 1994 and during his time sent eight youth teams to Sri Lanka and India. Nine players in the current Canterbury team which won the Plunket Shield this past season had been on a Willows tour. With foresight and vision he turned a piece of farmland in North Canterbury into the Willows Cricket Club, which fosters the game among secondary schools to the current day.

The O'Donnell brothers, Robbie and Will, both scored centuries in the same innings for Auckland against Wellington at Eden Park's outer oval in April. The list of centuries by brothers in the same innings in New Zealand first-class cricket is:

Nessie Snedden (139) & Cyril Snedden (119)	Auckland v Hawke's Bay	1920/21
Ian Chappell (145 & 121) & Greg Chappell (247* & 131)	Australia v NZ	1973/74
Martin Crowe (143) & Jeff Crowe (109*)	NZ v South Australia	1989/90
Hamish Marshall (170) & James Marshall (178*)	ND v Canterbury	2009/10
Neil Broom (203*) & Darren Broom (112)	Otago v ND	2010/11
Will O'Donnell (117) & Robbie O'Donnell (142)	Auckland v Wellington	2020/21

The Snedden brothers both recorded their maiden first-class hundreds in the above game (Cyril was making his first-class debut). Nessie took 5-13 in Hawke's Bay's first innings while Cyril took 4-1 in the second. Auckland made 537 and dismissed their opponents for 130 and 53. It was Hawke's Bay's final season as a first-class association.

• • •

Greg Hay equalled the New Zealand provincial record of six successive fifties when he made 93 for Central Districts against Northern Districts at Hamilton in the opening round of the Plunket Shield competition.

Hay had waited 223 days since his previous innings because of two cancelled games at the end of 2019/20 and also had to wait till the fourth day of the first game of the new season to finally get another bat. Northern Districts' first innings did not end until the last day because of weather interruptions.

Hay joined Bert Sutcliffe *(Auckland)*, Bruce Pairaudeau *(Northern Districts)*, Mathew Sinclair *(Central Districts)* and Matthew Bell and James Franklin *(Wellington)* in achieving the feat. His sequence ended when he was dismissed for 5 in his next game.

• • •

During the season, five players reached fifty first-class appearances for their province. Tom Blundell *(Wellington)*, Cameron Fletcher *(Canterbury)* and Ish Sodhi *(Northern Districts)* all achieved this in the opening round of the Plunket Shield followed by Robbie O'Donnell *(Auckland)* and Dane Cleaver *(Central Districts)*.

Sodhi achieved the landmark without even taking the field. For the first three days of the weather-interrupted game against Central Districts he waited while Northern batted and then was replaced by Joe Walker on the fourth day under the Covid replacement rule.

• • •

Mitchell Santner became the 70th New Zealand men's cricket captain when he led the side in the third Twenty20 international against West Indies at Mount Maunganui on 30 November. Santner also opened the bowling but rain came after 2.2 overs and the match was eventually abandoned.

Santner had an opportunity for a more extended period as captain when he again led the side in the first Twenty20 against Pakistan at Auckland in December. He once more opened the bowling and struck the winning runs with a six off Wahab Riaz.

From records available, this appears to be Santner's only games as captain at any representative level including age-group tournaments, Fergus Hickey, Hawke Cup and Provincial A.

New Zealand captains who have opened the bowling in an official international are Harry Cave, Jeremy Coney, Dion Nash, Daniel Vettori, Kyle Mills, Tim Southee and Santner. Southee, with 25 wickets in 19 games, has been used most often in this role.

By the end of the sesason, Robbie O'Donnell had played 55 first-class games, all of which are for Auckland. Shanan Stewart (96 games for Canterbury) holds the overall New Zealand record for most first-class games in a career all for one team. The most first-class games for each New Zealand province without playing for any other first-class side is:

Auckland	68 – Michael Bates
Canterbury	96 – Shanan Stewart
Central Districts	62 – John Smith and Ben Smith
Northern Districts	90 – Cliff Dickeson
Otago	75 – Stu McCullum
Wellington	52 – Brian Cederwall

• • •

A total of 202 New Zealand players have appeared for their province on at least fifty occasions in first-class cricket. The first to do so was wicketkeeper Charlie Boxshall, who played for Canterbury from 1897/98 to 1914/15.

Boxshall, who was born in Victoria and came to New Zealand in the late 1890s, made his first-class debut at 35 and played his last game at the age of 52. He was the New Zealand wicketkeeper from 1898 to 1914 and was aged 51 when he made his last appearance for the national side on their tour of Australia. He remains New Zealand's oldest first-class player and the oldest New Zealand representative.

• • •

History repeated itself when Finn Allen *(Wellington)* dismissed Hamish Rutherford *(Otago)* with his first ball in first-class cricket in the Plunket Shield game at the Basin Reserve in November. In 1988/89 Stephen Hotter, also playing for Wellington, dismissed Hamish's father, Ken, also playing for Otago, with his first-ball. New Zealand players to take a wicket with their first ball in first-class cricket are:

Bowler	***Batsman***			
R.B. Strange	T.H. Dent	Canterbury v Hawke's Bay	Christchurch	1901/02
S.J. Hotter	K.R. Rutherford	Wellington v Otago	Dunedin	1988/89
A.C. Barnes	M.E.L. Lane	Auckland v CD	Palmerston North	1993/94
R.A. Jones	G.E. Bradburn	Wellington v ND	Wellington	2000/01
L.J. Woodcock	C.D. Cumming	Wellington v Otago	Wellington	2001/02
B. Cachopa	Craig Cachopa	Auckland v Wellington	Auckland	2011/12
O.R. Newton	M.L. Guptill-Bunce	Wellington v Auckland	Wellington	2017/18
F.H. Allen	H.D. Rutherford	Wellington v Otago	Wellington	2020/21

• • •

In the same game, Tom Blundell was given out for obstructing the field, shortly after reaching his hundred in the second innings. Blundell had used his hand to try and stop the ball hitting his stumps and would previously have been given out "handled the ball".

However, a change to the laws in 2017 saw handling the ball classed as obstruction. The only players ever given out "handled the ball" in New Zealand first-class cricket are:

Edward Benson	MCC v Auckland	1929/30
Alan Gilbertson	Otago v Auckland	1952/53
Justin Vaughan	Emerging Players v England XI	1991/92
Will Williams	Canterbury v Otago	2012/13

The only other player given out "obstructing the field" is Johnny Hayes for Canterbury against Central Districts at Christchurch in 1954/55. Hayes was dismissed without scoring after the bowler, Fen Cresswell, successfully appealed when Hayes collided with a fieldsman.

An extremely unusual situation occurred during West Indies' tour of New Zealand when the visitors twice played two matches at the same time at opposite ends of the country.

The test match squad was involved in a four-day first-class match at Queenstown from 26 to 29 November while Twenty20 internationals took place at Auckland (27 November) and Mount Maunganui (29 November).

As the game at Auckland was a night game the two teams were not in action simultaneously but the Mount Maunganui game was a day game which saw both West Indies teams in the field at the same time.

• • •

The 2020/21 summer was the fiftieth season of New Zealand domestic one-day cricket. The competition, which began as the New Zealand Motor Corporation Knock-Out in the 1971/72 season, has gone under the names of Gillette Cup (from 1977/78), National Knock-Out (1979/80), Shell Cup (from 1980/81) when it was first contested on a league basis, State Shield (from 2001/02), One-Day Competition (from 2009/10) and the Ford Trophy (from 2011/12).

While 1971/72 saw the beginning of domestic one-day cricket in New Zealand, it was also the last season that New Zealand did not host an international side. The domestic season ended on 23 January and New Zealand began their historic first tour to West Indies eleven days later. The five-match series was drawn 0-0, one of New Zealand's most notable achievements to that time. It was also the last time that New Zealand played a five-match test series.

• • •

When Kane Williamson made 251 against Pakistan in the first test against Pakistan at Hamilton in December, it was just the second time that score had been recorded in test cricket. Walter Hammond also made 251 for England against Australia at Sydney in 1928/29.

The two innings reflect how over rates have changed over the years. Hammond's innings took 461 minutes and he faced 605 balls. Williamson batted for 624 minutes but faced just 412 deliveries. The only other score of 251 in New Zealand first-class cricket is by Chris Harris, who batted for 647 minutes, facing 531 balls for Canterbury against Central Districts at Rangiora in 1996/97.

The test where Hammond played his innings was the one where Don Bradman had been dropped after an unsuccessful debut. Bradman returned for the next test and averaged 102 from then until his retirement in 1948.

• • •

Williamson and Hammond share another record in scoring two double centuries in one season in New Zealand first-class cricket. The list of those who have done so is: Syd Hiddleston 1925/26, Walter Hammond 1932/33, Chris Harris 1996/97, Tom Latham 2013/14, Brendon McCullum 2013/14 and Kane Williamson 2020/21.

The list of players scoring 200 or more in New Zealand first-class cricket most often is: (8) Bert Sutcliffe (including two triple centuries), (5) Mathew Sinclair, Kane Williamson, (4) John R. Reid, Glenn Turner, Brendon McCullum (including one triple century), Tom Latham and Ross Taylor. Turner also had five double centuries and one triple century for Worcestershire.

• • •

When Mitchell Santner dismissed Pakistan's Mohammad Abbas in the test at Bay Oval, it was the first wicket taken by a New Zealand spin bowler in a home test since Santner had dismissed Joe Root at Hamilton the previous season. In between, the New Zealand pace bowlers had taken all 96 wickets to fall in tests which also involved India and West Indies.

One wicket by Santher soon brought two as he also caught and bowled Naseem Shah to end the match and give New Zealand a win by 101 runs. The New Zealand pace attack then accounted for the first eighteen Pakistan wickets in the next test before Kane Williamson dismissed Shaheen Afridi to break the sequence.

Pakistan conceded 64 extras in New Zealand's innings of 659-6 in the second test at Hagley Oval. This was made up of 27 byes, 8 leg byes, 12 no-balls and 17 wides. It fell just short of the most extras conceded in any first-class match in New Zealand which is 66, conceded by Pakistan A against New Zealand Academy at Lincoln in 1998/99.

In that game, however, the no-ball penalty was two runs each and the overall total would be just 39 under current playing conditions.

The record for most extras in a test innings was set by India who conceded 76 in Pakistan's 537 at Bangalore in 2007/08. The most conceded by New Zealand is 62 in England's 526 at Leeds in 2004.

• • •

In the first test against England at Lord's, Devon Conway became the second New Zealand batsman after Mathew Sinclair, and the seventh overall, to score a double century on test debut. Reginald "Tip" Foster (whose 287 against Australia at Sydney in 1903/04 is the highest innings on debut), Lawrence Rowe, Brendon Kuruppu, Jacques Rudolph and Kyle Mayers (second innings) are the others.

Conway's 200 was the highest score by any player making their test debut in England and put him in famous company, eclipsing K.S. Ranjitsinhji, who made 154 not out for England against Australia at Old Trafford in 1896, and W.G. Grace, who scored 152 for England against Australia at the Oval in 1880 (the first test ever played in England). Both Conway and Sinclair were dismissed without scoring in their first innings in first-class cricket.

• • •

Conway's innings was also the highest score against England by a player on test debut. This list reads:

200	Devon Conway (New Zealand)	Lord's	2021
176	George Headley (West Indies)	Bridgetown	1929/30 *(second innings)*
171	Hamish Rutherford (New Zealand)	Dunedin	2012/13
165*	Charles Bannerman (Australia)	Melbourne	1876/77 *(the first ever test match)*

• • •

Two New Zealanders also feature near the top of the list of longest innings played on test debut as follows:

mins				
777	Brendon Kuruppu (201*)	Sri Lanka v New Zealand	Colombo	1986/87
578	Devon Conway (200)	New Zealand v England	Lord's	2021
535	Aminul Islam (145)	Bangladesh v India	Dhaka	2000/01
534	Mathew Sinclair (214)	New Zealand v West Indies	Wellington	1999/00

• • •

Conway opened the batting for New Zealand on test debut at the age of 29. The oldest New Zealand openers on test debut are:

Age			
36	Ray Emery v West Indies	Christchurch	1951/52
34	Graham Gedye v South Africa	Wellington	1963/64
29	Devon Conway v England	Lord's	2021
29	Craig Cumming v Australia	Christchurch	2004/05
29	David White v Pakistan	Karachi	1990/91
29	Mark Richardson v Zimbabwe	Bulawayo	2000/01

Emery was one of the major figures behind the creation of Auckland's international airport. Ray Emery Drive at the airport is named after him.

John Ward, who passed away on 12 January 2021, was one of the last specialist wicketkeepers in test cricket. He played in eight tests for New Zealand from 1963/64 to 1967/68, mostly batting from numbers nine to eleven.

Roy Harford, who was 85 on 30 May, played in three tests in 1967/68 and Barry Milburn played three tests the following season. Harford and Milburn batted at number eleven every time. All three were outstanding wicketkeepers. They are the last of their kind in test cricket.

Milburn was selected for the tour of England, India and Pakistan in 1969 but Ken Wadsworth was preferred as keeper, playing the next 33 tests in succession. Milburn's daughter, Rowan, kept wicket for the Netherlands and New Zealand.

• • •

Gloucestershire wicketkeeper James Bracey made his test debut against New Zealand at Lord's but was bowled by Tim Southee without scoring in his first innings. He was the first England wicketkeeper to be bowled for a duck in his test debut innings in England since Dick Lilley (also at Lord's) in 1896. Gregor MacGregor in 1890 (also at Lord's) is the only other to suffer the same fate.

Bracey was also the first England wicketkeeper to make a duck on debut (first innings) since James Foster at Mohali in 2001/02. He was the first at home since Alan Knott against Pakistan in 1967 (caught Hanif Mohammad bowled Mushtaq Mohammad).

• • •

Devon Conway didn't manage to carry his bat in his test debut (he was last man out) but he did become the first player in test history to be run out for exactly 200. Brian Lara (277 at Sydney in 1992/93) has the highest score by a batsman who was run out while Lou Vincent (224 against Sri Lanka at Wellington in 2004/05) has the New Zealand record.

Other players to be dismissed for exactly 200 in a test are Walter Hammond, Mohsin Khan, David Boon, Steve Waugh, Graeme Smith, Mushfiqur Rahim, Virat Kohli and Ross Taylor.

• • •

Conway was making his test debut at the age of 29. The only older player to reach 150 in his first test innings was W.G. Grace who was 32 when made his debut for England against Australia at The Oval in 1880. This was the very first test played in England.

The next oldest after Conway is Khalid "Billy" Ibadulla who was 28 when he made his debut for Pakistan against Australia at Karachi in 1964/65. Ibadulla had a long career for Warwickshire in county cricket before making his test debut in October 1964. He scored 166 and shared a first wicket stand of 249 with wicketkeeper Abdul Kadir (95) who was also playing in his first test.

Ibadulla then came to New Zealand where he played as the overseas professional for Otago in 1964/65. As it happened, Pakistan made their first tour to New Zealand that season and Ibadulla played for Otago against the touring side, scoring an unbeaten century. He was then drafted into the Pakistan team for the third test, scoring 28 and 9.

He later appeared in two tests on Pakistan's 1967 tour to England. He was appointed as a Member of the New Zealand Order of Merit in the 2004 Queen's Birthday Honours list for services to cricket.

• • •

Ross Taylor set a record for international appearances for New Zealand in the first test against Pakistan at Mount Maunganui. It was his 438th game for New Zealand across all formats, surpassing Daniel Vettori's record. During the season Kane Willliamson and Tim Southee played their 300th games for New Zealand.

Players with the most appearances for New Zealand are: Ross Taylor 443, Daniel Vettori 437, Brendon McCullum 432, Stephen Fleming 395, Martin Guptill 335, Nathan Astle 308, Tim Southee 305, Kane Williamson 303.

Mount Maunganui's Bay Oval missed out on its first sold-out occasion after a coronavirus outbreak in late February forced a last-minute change of plans. Recent upgrades to the ground would have led to it being the venue's biggest crowd.

New Zealand Cricket's original schedule had Black Caps v Australia and White Ferns v England double-headers set down for Wellington, Auckland and Mount Maunganui on 3, 5 and 7 March.

Logistical complications meant that all matches were eventually played at Sky Stadium in Wellington. With the country on alert level two, the first two days were played behind closed doors but spectators were allowed for the final day after the alert level was relaxed.

The other major change to New Zealand's international schedules during the season was the cancellation of the Black Caps' proposed visit to Australia. One-day internationals were meant to be played on 26, 29 and 31 January at Adelaide, Canberra and Hobart as well as one Twenty20 game at Sydney on 1 February.

• • •

Daryl Mitchell did not bat or bowl or take a catch when he made his one-day international debut against Bangladesh at Dunedin on 20 March. This was the first such instance for New Zealand since Mark Bailey against Zimbabwe at Dhaka in the Wills International Cup in October 1998.

This turned out to be Bailey's only official appearance for New Zealand but Mitchell got another chance and hit his maiden century in the third match of the series, bringing up three figures with two off the last ball of the innings.

Bailey did feature for New Zealand on other occasions. He went to West Indies in 1996 as a replacement late in the tour and played three games in Bermuda, including 100 against a Bermuda Board President's XI in his first game.

Bailey also appeared in all three Cricket Max internationals against an England side in 1997/98 and was a member of the New Zealand team when cricket was played for the one and only time at the Commonwealth Games, in Kuala Lumpur in 1998. He played in the third and fourth play-off game when New Zealand defeated Sri Lanka to take the bronze medal.

• • •

Sophie Devine hit the fastest Twenty20 century in women's cricket in the Dream11 Super Smash game between Wellington and Otago at Dunedin on 14 January, reaching three figures from just 36 balls.

Otago batted first and made 128-7 and Wellington replied with 131-0 off 8.4 overs (Devine 108 off 38 balls and Maddy Green 20 off 15). Devine's ball-by-ball sequence was 1 2 3 4 . 4 . . 1 4 4 6 6 1 2 1 1 . 1 4 6 6 4 . 4 1 6 6 1 6 . 6 . 2 1 6 4 4.

The record for the fastest Twenty20 century previously belonged to Deandra Dottin, who made a hundred off 38 balls for West Indies against South Africa at St Kitts in 2010.

• • •

Devon Conway became the first New Zealand batsman to score a double century in his first first-class game in any overseas country when he made 200 against England at Lord's. The previous highest by a New Zealander in England was Matt Horne's 133 against British Universities in 1999 and the record for the previous highest anywhere was also held by Horne who made 181 in Zimbabwe in 1997/98.

The highest scores by a New Zealand batsman in their first first-class game in any overseas country are:

200	Devon Conway	New Zealand v England	Lord's	2021
181	Matt Horne	New Zealand v Mashonaland	Harare	1997/98
173*	Mark Richardson	New Zealand v Boland	Paarl	2000/01
170	Jamie How	New Zealand v New South Wales	Sydney	2008/09
162	Daniel Flynn	New Zealand A v Zimbabwe A	Harare	2010/11
153*	Trevor Franklin	Young New Zealand v Zimbabwe	Harare	1984/85

Tom Latham became the second New Zealand opening batsman to reach 4000 runs in test cricket during the world test championship final. The most runs scored by a New Zealand opening batsman in tests is:

	Mts	*Runs*	*Ave*	*100*
John Wright	80	5260	38.11	12
Tom Latham	58	4027	41.94	11
Glenn Turner	38	2828	45.61	7
Mark Richardson	38	2770	44.67	4
Graham Dowling	36	2177	31.55	3
Martin Guptill	40	2062	27.49	2
Bryan Young	35	2024	32.12	2

• • •

Tim Southee, Trent Boult and Neil Wagner have appeared in 37 test matches together. In those games Southee has taken 171 wickets at 25, Boult 169 at 25 and Wagner 163 at 25. All other bowlers used have taken 154 wickets between them. Kyle Jamieson (28 wickets at 12) is next on the list.

Trent Boult (252 wickets at 25) and Tim Southee (248 wickets at 25) have played in 60 tests together and have taken a combined total of 500 wickets.

At the end of the 49th over of India's first innings in the world test championship final, Boult and Southee had each sent down 2853.2 overs in 139 internationals together and each had conceded 10,051 runs.

• • •

Boult and Southee also have the most wickets for New Zealand in test match victories. Boult tops the list with 177 wickets at 22 in 37 games while Southee has 175 at 21 in 36 wins. Richard Hadlee (173 wickets at 13 in 22 games) is next.

Kane Williamson (4094 runs at 75) has scored the most runs for New Zealand in test match wins. Ross Taylor is next with 3244 runs at 55. Taylor has been on the winning side on 43 occasions, a New Zealand record.

• • •

New Zealand's victory at Birmingham meant that they had won three test series in a row against England for the first time. Tom Latham, Henry Nicholls, Ross Taylor and Neil Wagner played in all six games while BJ Watling (405 runs at 68 in five games) scored the most runs and Tim Southee (26 wickets at 21 in five games) was the most successful bowler. Southee, Wagner and Trent Boult took 73 of the 101 wickets that fell to bowlers.

• • •

Former Otago wicketkeeper Tom Flaws died in Dunedin on 24 June 2021 aged 89. When Otago batsman (and very occasional wicketkeeper) Artie Dick was selected as backup keeper to John Ward for New Zealand in South Africa 1961/62, Dick was somewhat bemused as he didn't keep wicket for province or club, as Flaws was the keeper for both.

Ward subsequently suffered an injury and Dick ended up playing in all five tests in South Africa and equalled the previous world record of 23 dismissals in a series (although South Africa's John Waite took 26). He also scored vital runs.

South Africa had recently left the Commonwealth and were therefore ineligible to be members of the Imperial Cricket Conference (ICC) so the tests should have been regarded as "unofficial", something the New Zealand players were aware of before the tour. However, *Wisden* continued to regard them as official (as they did for South Africa's other tests in the 1960s) and that status still stands today.

Flaws played 27 first-class games for Otago from 1952/53 to 1962/63 taking 44 catches and making as many as 29 stumpings.

OBITUARIES

Alan Thomas BURGESS

Born: *Christchurch, 1 May, 1920*

Died: *Rangiora, 6 January, 2021*

Right-hand batsman, slow left-arm bowler

Alan Burgess had been the world's oldest living first-class cricketer when he passed away at the age of 100.

Burgess grew up in Linwood in Christchurch, attending Phillipstown School alongside future All Black great Fred Allen. Burgess was an apprentice upholsterer after leaving school but sports were his passion.

His father, Tom, umpired the test between New Zealand and England at Lancaster Park in 1932/33. Tom Burgess was born in Blackburn in 1888 and came with his family to New Zealand in 1892. His brother, Walter was the father of Gordon Burgess, father of test batsman Mark. Gordon Burgess played seven matches for Auckland in the 1940s and 1950s and had a long career in cricket administration.

Alan Burgess appeared in 13 first-class matches for Canterbury from 1940/41 to 1951/52 and also for New Zealand Services in England in 1945. He took 6-52 on debut against Otago at Lancaster Park in a match which began on Christmas Day 1940. Tom Burgess was one of the umpires in this game, having been appointed prior to his son being selected.

After being shipped overseas from New Zealand in 1941 Burgess spent almost a year training in the desert with the 20th Canterbury-Otago Battalion in Egypt and was then sent to Italy. Burgess was involved in the Battle of Monte Cassino in 1944 and served as a Sherman tank driver. He fought his way up to Trieste, where he got a call to go to England.

"Getting selected to play for the New Zealand Forces team and playing at Lord's was the highlight." Burgess said. The Services team included famous names such as Stewie Dempster, Ken James, who was the captain, and Martin Donnelly.

In 14 first-class games Burgess made 466 runs at 22.19 and took 16 wickets at 30.68.

Ross Alexander DYKES

Born: *Auckland, 26 February, 1945*

Died: *Auckland, 30 November, 2020*

Left-hand batsman, wicketkeeper

Ross Dykes was one of the great servants of cricket in New Zealand. A dependable wicketkeeper for Auckland in the 1960s and 1970s, Dykes played 31 first-class games, effecting 81 dismissals (57 caught and 24 stumped) and made 723 runs at an average of 20.08. His highest score was 82 against Wellington at Eden Park in January 1972 in a match which Auckland won by just 20 runs.

No sooner had his playing career ended than he began his long service as a selector, first a 12-year stint with Auckland and then a stretch on the New Zealand panel between 1990 and 2005 – broken only by a year off in 1993.

Dykes was convener of selectors between 1996 and 2000; his most notable decision coming in early 1997 when his panel oversaw the selection of an 18-year-old Daniel Vettori, New Zealand's youngest test player.

In this period he was also the manager of several New Zealand teams, taking sides to Bangladesh, India, Pakistan, South Africa, England and Australia.

Dykes moved to Dunedin in 2005 to take over the role as the chief executive of the Otago Cricket Association, admitting at the time he'd never lived more than a kilometre from One Tree Hill in Auckland.

He served that role successfully for a decade, the most significant development during his tenure being the establishment of the University of Otago Oval as New Zealand's seventh test venue. Dykes also acted as an New Zealand Cricket match referee, overseeing first-class games, List A matches and women's internationals.

Iain Watson GALLAWAY

Born: *Dunedin, 26 December, 1922*

Died: *Dunedin, 18 April, 2021*

Right-hand batsman, wicketkeeper

Iain Gallaway, who died in Dunedin aged 98, played three first-class matches as Otago wicketkeeper in the 1940s but is far better remembered for his long career as a cricket and rugby commentator. He was also New Zealand's oldest surviving first-class cricketer.

Gallaway was born in Dunedin and attended Christ's College in Christchurch for five years. He served in the New Zealand-based artillery at the start of the second world war and then joined the navy when he was 20. He was part of the contingent which patrolled the North Sea until peace was declared in 1945.

A past president, and life member of New Zealand Cricket, he was a lawyer by profession, having initially had his heart set on becoming a journalist before the war. On his return, however, following an offer from the *Otago Daily Times*, he changed his mind.

Gallaway was a keen and capable cricketer, keeping wicket for the Carisbrook club in Dunedin and for a variety of services teams in the war. He made his first-class debut against Wellington at Carisbrook in February 1947, scoring 22 in 103 minutes at number ten, sharing a partnership of 79 for the ninth wicket with Lankford Smith.

Gallaway's next game was the famous match against Walter Hammond's MCC side. Bert Sutcliffe, who had played for Auckland in the Plunket Shield (339 runs at 84 that season) had transferred to Dunedin and made his Otago debut in this game.

Sutcliffe, who was a few days away from making his test debut, marked his first game for Otago by scoring 197 and 128 in memorable fashion. In later years, Gallaway would often joke about his own contribution in this match, recalling how, after the eventual dismissal of Sutcliffe in the first innings, and the subsequent raucous ovation from the Carisbrook crowd, he was dismissed first ball and walked off to the continuing applause for the previous batsman.

Gallaway played once more for Otago the following season but was taken ill during the game. In his three matches he scored 26 runs, took seven catches and made one stumping.

He was a pioneer of cricket and rugby radio commentary, developing into New Zealand's pre-eminent sports broadcaster over the ensuing four decades, his gravelly tones, knowledgeable analysis and dry sense of humour making his voice a household favourite.

His most exotic, not to mention challenging assignment, came in 1955 when he was tasked with accompanying the New Zealand team on its maiden tour to Pakistan and India.

With little infrastructure, technology, or resourcing and not a commentary box in sight, Gallaway recalled that he sometimes found himself calling a game from a bough of a tree, or taking up other unorthodox observation points, in order to gain a decent view of proceedings.

He later became a part of Radio New Zealand's Sports Roundup service, bringing cricket commentaries to radio listeners throughout the country on AM frequencies otherwise used by the Concert Programme. Along with the likes of Alan Richards, Colin Snedden, Trevor Rigby and Peter Sharp his voice became synonymous with summer and the game of cricket.

Gallaway eventually became known as "The Voice of Carisbrook" although arguably his favourite cricket ground was Molyneux Park in Alexandra, where Otago hosted many of its fixtures over the Christmas and New Year holiday period. His signature line, *"Not a Cloud in the Sky"*, was the title of his autobiography, published in 1997.

As well as being the Patron of the Otago Cricket Association, he served in a variety of capacities within the OCA and the Dunedin Cricket Association. He was appointed as a Member of the Order of the British Empire in the 1978 Queen's Birthday Honours list for services to rugby and cricket. In the 1986 Queen's Birthday Honours list he was made a Companion of the Queen's Service Order for community service.

He was also a former chairman of the Broadcasting Standards Authority, and a former, and long-serving Chancellor of the Anglican Diocese of Dunedin.

Gallaway was also an international rugby referee, taking charge of the British Lions match against West Coast in 1950 and Australia versus Southland in 1949.

Graham Anthony NEWDICK

Born: *Lower Hutt, 11 January, 1949*

Died: *Bromsgrove, England, 25 August, 2020*

Right-hand batsman, right-arm off-spin bowler

Graham Newdick, who was a dependable opening batsman for Wellington in the 1970s, was a member of the New Zealand side which took part in the Australian domestic one-day competition in 1972.

Newdick represented Hutt Valley while still a teenager and played for Wellington in the Brabin (under 20) and Rothmans Under 23 tournaments.

In 1970, Newdick was a member of the New Zealand Ambassadors side which played 37 games in Chile, Argentina, Brazil, Peru, Grenada, St Vincent, St Lucia, Dominica, Antigua, Portugal, Gibraltar, England, Bermuda, Washington DC, St Louis, California (including Hollywood) and Hawaii.

Other members of the team who appeared in first-class cricket were Bruce Hamilton, John Morrison, Cran Bull, Rod Fulton, John Flaherty, Barry Hadlee and Andy Roberts.

Newdick made his first-class debut the following summer, enjoying a successful first season scoring 460 runs at 46, including 143 in 309 minutes against Auckland on his 22nd birthday. This remained the highest of his four first-class hundreds.

At the end of the 1971/72 season he was selected in a New Zealand team which took part in the Australian Coca-Cola Knockout Cup while the main New Zealand side was in West Indies. Newdick scored 5 in a warm-up game against Victoria Universities and 3 against Victoria in the semi-final, which New Zealand lost. The New Zealand side saw Richard Hadlee in national colours for the first time.

One of Newdick's best seasons came in 1978/79 when he scored 541 runs, including a very patient 119 in 388 minutes against Central Districts at McLean Park. It was his fourth and last century for Wellington.

After bowing out of first-class cricket at the end of 1980/81, Newdick continued to play for Hutt Valley until 1983/84. He also provided yeoman service for the Hutt club and later coached the Wellington College and St Pat's Silverstream first elevens.

Outside cricket, Newdick worked as a carpenter and later worked for the Building and Construction Industry Training Organisation as a mentor to up and coming apprentices.

A handy outside back, who played rugby for the Eastbourne club before playing senior football for Hutt Old Boys, Newdick had moved to England with his wife, Debbie, to be closer to his two sons.

In 61 first-class games Newdick scored 3292 runs at 30.48 and took five wickets at 26.80. He also scored 403 runs at 20.15 in 20 one-day games.

NZC

NEW ZEALAND v PAKISTAN ***(Second Test)*** **— 2020/21**

Back row: T.A. Blundell, T.G. Southee, T.A. Boult, K.A. Jamieson, L.R.P.L. Taylor, D.J. Mitchell, M.J. Henry, H.M. Nicholls.
Front row: M.J. Santner, K.S. Williamson *(captain)*, B-J. Watling, T.W.M. Latham, W.A. Young.

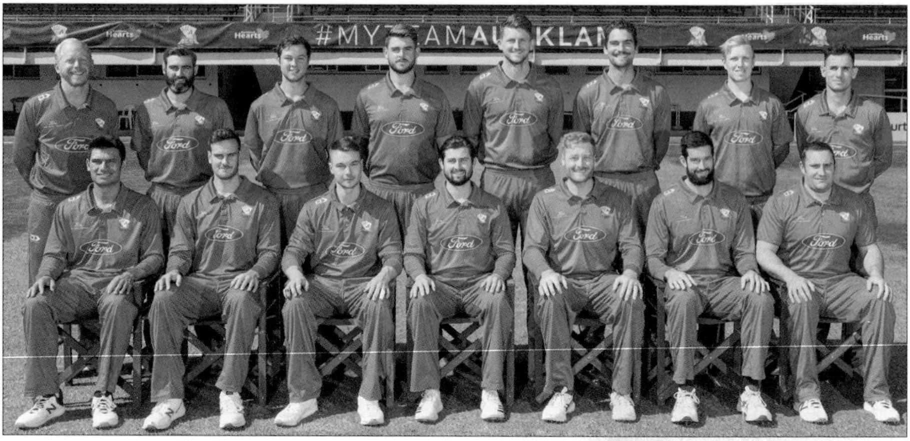

AC

AUCKLAND — 2020/21

Back row: L.J. Delport, B.P. Rodden, R.D. Harrison, W.T. O'Donnell, O.M.R. Pringle, D.K. Ferns, R.M. ter Braak, G.K. Beghin.

Front row: S.M. Solia, B.G. Lister, B.J. Horne, R.R. O'Donnell *(captain)*, M.J. Guptill, W.E.R. Somerville, M.B. McEwan.

AC

AUCKLAND WOMEN — 2020/21

Back row: M.M. Penfold, J.E.I. Prasad, B.G. Armstrong, F.C. Jonas, K.T. Perkins, R.H. McNeill, T.I. Lamb, A.N. Kelly.

Front row: R.S.M. Lili'i, H.R. Huddleston, A.M. Peterson, L.R. Down *(captain)*, S. Shahri.

Photosport

CANTERBURY — 2020/21

Back row: F.W. Sheat, D.J. Mitchell, E.J. Nuttall, W.S.A. Williams, T.D. Astle, K.J. McClure, C.J. Bowes, H.B. Shipley, H.M. Nicholls, J.C.A. Latham, M.J. Henry, M.J. Hay, J.C.T. Boyle.
Front row: T.M. Lortan, M.W. Hay, T.F. van Woerkom, S.B. Davey, C.E. McConchie *(captain)*, L.J. Carter, C.D. Fletcher, T.W.M. Latham.

Photosport

CANTERBURY WOMEN — 2020/21

Back row: L.E.V. Hughes, K.E. Ebrahim, M.J. Banks, E.K. Kench, G.E.S. Sullivan, S.R. Asmussen, L.M.M. Tahuhu.
Second row: K.J. Havill, F.L. Mackay *(captain)*, J.L. Savage. N.B. Cox, K.F.G. Nation
Front row: J.A. Simmons, A.E. Satterthwaite, J. Dean.

Bruce Lim Photography

NORTHERN DISTRICTS — 2020/21

Back row: B. Popli, J.A. Raval, I.S. Sodhi, B.R. Hampton, J.M. Gibson, A. Verma.
Second row: N. Smith *(strength & conditioning)*, S. Krishnamurthy *(assistant coach)*, C. Miles *(strength & conditioning)*, Z.N. Gibson, J.D. Baker, M.J. Fisher, G.W. Aldridge *(coach)*, P. Head *(physiotherapist)*.
Front row: H.R. Cooper, K.D. Clarke, B-J. Watling, A.P. Devcich *(captain)*, J.F. Carter *(captain)*, D.G. Brownlie, J.G. Walker, P.D. Bocock.

Bruce Lim Photography

NORTHERN DISTRICTS WOMEN — 2020/21

Back row: C.R. Sarsfield, E.A.J. Richardson, L.H. Heaps, L.F. Boucher, C.A. Gurrey, S.R. Naidu.
Front row: M.B. Templeton, G.A. Harris, B.M. Halliday *(captain)*, K.G. Anderson, A.M. Ewart, N.H. Patel.

Photosport

OTAGO — 2020/21

Back row: R. Walter *(coach)*, D.N. Phillips, N.G. Smith, T. Muller, J.D. McKay, M.B. Bacon, A.W. McKenzie, M.W. Chu, B. Harrop *(physiotherapist)*, B. Clancy *(strength & conditioning)*.
Front row: C.T. Hawkins, M.D. Rae, J.A. Duffy *(captain)*, H.D. Rutherford *(captain)*, N.F. Kelly, A.K. Kitchen, M.J.G. Rippon, M. Renwick.

Photosport

OTAGO WOMEN — 2020/21

Back row: S.R. Wilson, I.R. James *(captain)*, O.N. Gain, M.B.A. Lamplough, S.A. Oldershaw, G.R. Adams, M.E. Loe, E.J. Carson.
Front row: E.J. Black, M.R. Cowan, K.J. Martin *(captain)*, H.N.K. Jensen, P.M. Inglis, C.G. Blakely.

Derek Hamilton/Rob Franks

Royal New Zealand Air Force v Cross Arrows at Lord's — 1944

Back row: Umpire, J.W. Peake, T.F.C. Geary, R. Gear, C.M. Enting, R.W.H. Carter, D.G. Hamilton, B. Gascoigne, L. Todd, R.W. Metcalf.
Front row: Unknown, P.W. Burton, W.J. Jordan *(New Zealand High Commissioner)*, K.C. James *(captain)*, Sir Pelham Warner.

Photosport

WELLINGTON — 2020/21

Back row: N. Shah *(physiotherapist)*, A. Smith *(strength & conditioning)*, O.R. Newton, B.V. Sears, L.J. Woodcock *(batting coach)*, F.J. Colson, J.D. Gibson, J.D.S. Neesham, T.A. Blundell, L.V. van Beek, F.H. Allen, P.F. Younghusband.

Front row: N. Hogg *(sports psychologist)*, G.D. Pocknall *(coach)*, R. Ravindra, T.M. Johnson, M.G. Bracewell *(captain)*, H.K. Bennett, D.P. Conway, L.R. Dry *(assistant coach)*, G.J. Butler *(video analyst)*.

Dave Lintott Photography

WELLINGTON WOMEN — 2020/21

Back row: K.M. Chandler, X.A.R. Jetly, M.P. Singh, B.C. Molony, D.M. Doughty, N.E. Codyre.

Second row: M. Rao *(assistant coach)*, R. Pettit *(manager)*, O.A. Boivin, R.M. Burns, G.E. Plimmer, C.R. King, I. Tissera *(coach)*.

Front row: L.M. Kasperek, S.F.M. Devine, T.M.M. Newton *(captain)*, M.L. Green *(captain)*, A.C. Kerr, J.M. Kerr, J.T. McFadyen.

Carey Clements

John R. Reid and John F. Reid at the Basin Reserve, Wellington in 2018.

HBCA

HAWKE'S BAY — 2020/21

Back row: D.C. Smidt *(manager)*, I.D. Lange, J.D. Whitley, W.J. Clark, B.P. Stoyanoff, M.J. Edmondson, L.R. Dudding, D.J. Castle *(coach)*.

Front row: B.D. Schmulian, T.J. Watson, C.K. Leopard, A.R. Schaw *(captain)*, J.R. Lennox, G.D. Tryon, B.L. Wiggins, D.R. Thompson.

John Fulton REID

Born: *Auckland, 3 March, 1956*

Died: *Christchurch, 28 December, 2020*

Left-hand batsman, right-arm leg-break bowler, wicketkeeper

John Reid was an accomplished left-handed batsman and later a cricket administrator. He was remembered by his peers as a dependable team-mate who was a great player of spin bowling.

Reid made his first-class debut as a 19-year-old wicketkeeper for Auckland in December 1975 and made his test debut against Pakistan on the same ground in 1978/79, scoring 0 and 19. His next appearance for New Zealand came two seasons later in the home series with India and Reid had scores of 46 in the first test, 123 not out in the rain-ruined second game and 74 in the third.

It was another three years, however, before Reid next gained national selection with the likes of John Wright, Bruce Edgar, Geoff Howarth, Jeff and Martin Crowe and Jeremy Coney being preferred ahead of him.

Reid finally got his chance when Howarth moved up to open on the tour to Sri Lanka in 1984, replacing Edgar, and Reid took over at number three. In the third test at Colombo, Reid scored 180 in 685 minutes.

New Zealand's next assignment was home and away tours to Pakistan in 1984/85 where Reid had a sequence of scores of 106, 21, 97, 148, 3 and 158 not out. He made himself unavailable for the tour to West Indies which followed, to spend time in his day job as a high school geography teacher.

Reid was back in the national side later in the year when New Zealand toured Australia and was part of New Zealand's first test win in Australia (and subsequently their first series win against Australia home or away). The first test at Brisbane will always be remembered for Richard Hadlee's 15-wicket haul but Reid (108) played his part, sharing a third wicket stand of 224 with Martin Crowe (188) as New Zealand went on to win by an innings.

Reid played in all three tests in Australia and the three that followed at home but did little else of note. That appeared to be the end of Reid's career at test and first-class level but two years later he reappeared for one game for Auckland, scoring 112 in 520 minutes in what was his last innings in first-class cricket.

Reid reached 1000 runs in test cricket in just 20 innings, a New Zealand record (since equalled by Mark Richardson).

Teammate John Wright remembered the tours to the sub-continent well, particularly to Sri Lanka. He said while others in the team struggled with the heat, Reid was cool, calm and collected. "John was very calm, unruffled and sensible. He was a good technician cricket-wise," he said.

Following his playing days, Reid moved into administration. He was the first chief executive of Auckland Cricket before roles with New Zealand Cricket in the mid 1990s and then Sparc (now Sport New Zealand) in 2005.

New Zealand Cricket colleague Tim Murdoch said Reid was a "pleasant, courteous, gentleman-like figure" who played an important role establishing the National High Performance Cricket Academy at Lincoln University, alongside Chris Doig.

"That was his passion really. It was initially coaching, then the holistic development of players through the creation of the academy," he said.

Reid also had coaching spells with both the New Zealand men's and women's national sides. He took over as coach of the men's team for the 1994/95 centenary season in New Zealand and was part of the coaching lineup for the 2000 World Cup-winning White Ferns. Catherine Campbell said Reid was a "key member" of the side, providing structure around preparation.

Campbell described Reid as a "visionary", with that vision spanning across all levels of the game. "He had a great love for the community game as well. Of community cricket, of all parts of the game. He didn't have an ego. He wasn't always wanting to be involved at the top of the game which I think was a real trademark of John's," she said. "There would be very few people involved with cricket who didn't have some involvement with John Reid. At club level, at rep level, at New Zealand level, he touched the whole of cricket."

"Cricket was his passion, and he had a great way of looking at cricket. Probably a lot of achievement for New Zealand Cricket that may not necessarily be top of the mind for people, a lot of background work that was very much appreciated by those in that area."

In later years, Reid was active in local government with Selwyn District Council as their major projects property manager since 2015. He oversaw the development of Foster Park and the Selwyn Sports Centre and the sports hall at the centre was named after him.

Reid played in 19 tests for New Zealand, scoring 1296 runs at an average of 46.28, including six centuries and two fifties. In first-class cricket he scored 5650 runs at 38.17 in 101 games. He took six wickets with his leg-spin bowling and took 116 catches and made nine stumpings. He played 25 one-day internationals, scoring 633 runs at 27.52. He had an outstanding one-day record for Auckland, scoring 1517 runs at 54.17.

John Richard REID

Born: *Auckland, 3 June, 1928*

Died: *Auckland, 14 October, 2020*

Right-hand batsman, right-arm fast-medium/off-spin bowler

The term "colossus" is often used but never more aptly than to describe John Reid's standing in New Zealand cricket. When he retired he held the New Zealand test records for most matches, most matches as captain, most runs, most wickets and most catches (and also stood in as wicketkeeper). His 58 tests in succession was a world record at the time. Reid never missed a test over his 16 year career.

Reid was an aggressive, hard-hitting middle-order batsman who had a good eye and was unafraid to hit the ball in the air. Muscular and well-built, he was also a brilliant fielder at gully or cover and a pacy seam bowler.

Reid was born in Auckland but grew up in Wellington. He excelled at sport at Hutt Valley High School, going straight into the First XI and First XV when he entered the third form in 1943. He was part of a remarkable school athletic team. It also included 1950 Empire Games 220 yard gold medallist Don Jowett, legendary All Black wing Ron Jarden and another 1950 Games athlete, hurdler Robert Smith.

Reid was widely tipped to reach higher honours in both rugby and cricket, but his rugby-playing days ended following two bouts of rheumatic fever and a resulting heart murmur.

He made his first-class debut for Wellington against Canterbury at Lancaster Park on 31 December 1947, scoring 79 in his first innings and sharing a partnership of 155 with Eric Tindill. He also gained selection for North Island against the South, scoring 66 but was not seen at the bowling crease in first-class games that season.

The following summer he tallied 355 runs at 50, including his maiden century, opening the batting for the New Zealand XI against the Rest. Selection for the 1949 tour of England duly followed, where Reid made 1488 runs at 41 and took 13 wickets in 25 first-class games.

He made his test debut at Old Trafford in the third match of the series, scoring 50 and 25, sharing a partnership of 116 with Martin Donnelly in the first innings. When Frank Mooney was injured, Reid was asked to keep wickets in the fourth test, scoring 93 in the second innings.

Reid registered the first of four first-class double centuries in 1951/52, making 283 in his second innings against Otago at the Basin Reserve. It was a remarkable innings given the low scoring which had preceded it during the match. Wellington made 159 (Reid out without scoring) and Otago replied with 158 (Reid 5-35, opening the bowling). Wellington then ran up 575-7 before declaring with Reid hitting 41 fours and a six in his 385 minutes at the crease. Otago made 333-8 as the match was drawn.

In 1952 Reid spent the first of three consecutive English summers as a professional with Heywood in the Central Lancashire League, where he developed his fast-medium bowling.

Reid hit his first test century at Cape Town in the third test of the 1953/54 tour to South Africa. He was 19 not out at lunch on the second day and raced through to 135 at tea. The century was a very welcome one because Reid's run of form in tests prior to this had been 11, 11, 0, 3, 6, 1, 9, 7, 6, 0, 3 and 1. Reid scored 1012 runs in first-class matches on tour and took 51 wickets.

New Zealand toured Pakistan and India for the first time in 1955/56. Reid took no time at all to acclimatise to the unfamiliar conditions, taking 7-28 against the Chief Commissioner's XI in the opening tour game and then scoring an unbeaten 150 when New Zealand batted.

Illness took a heavy toll on the New Zealand players on that tour but Reid managed two centuries in the series against India. He made 119 not out at Delhi, sharing an unbeaten stand of 222 with Bert Sutcliffe (230 not out) and 120 in the next test at Calcutta.

New Zealand faced West Indies in a four-test series on their return home. Harry Cave continued as captain for the first test but Reid took over from the second. The fourth test at Eden Park will forever be fondly remembered for New Zealand gaining their first victory in test cricket. Inevitably Reid played his part, top scoring with 84 in the first innings.

Reid transferred to Otago for two seasons the following summer and recorded his best bowling figures in first-class cricket. He took 7-20 as Central Districts were routed for 81 at Carisbrook in 1956/57 and next season scored 201 against Canterbury.

New Zealand endured a difficult time in England in 1958, losing the test series 4-0 and five times being dismissed for under 100. Reid scored 1429 in first-class games at 39 and was named a Wisden cricketer of the year in 1959.

The tour to South Africa in 1961/62 was the pinnacle of Reid's career and a major success for New Zealand, who up till then, had won just one test match and none overseas. New Zealand drew the series 2-2 in dramatic fashion with Reid contributing 546 runs at 60 and proving a match-winner with the ball. In all first-class games he made an astonishing 1915 runs at 68.

In an interview for *Wisden Cricket Monthly* in June 1993, Reid said "I just felt, I don't care what you're bowling, you'll never get me out. I may get myself out but nobody's going to get me out, and that's a hell of a feeling to have."

South Africa won the first test by just 30 runs, Reid (13 and 16) recording a rare failure. The second test was drawn, with Reid unbeaten on 75 at the end.

The third test at Cape Town saw New Zealand gain their first test win overseas. New Zealand made 385 (Reid 92) then bowled South Africa out for 190. New Zealand declared at 212-9 and South Africa were dismissed for 335, New Zealand winning by 73 runs. Reid (2-21 off 14.2 overs) captured the final wicket.

South Africa won the fourth test by an innings, with Reid getting little support as he made 60 (out of 164) and 142 (out of 249).

The fifth test, at Port Elizabeth, saw New Zealand make 275 and South Africa reply with 190 (Reid 2-26 off 14 overs). New Zealand then made 228 (Reid 69) which left South Africa with a target of 314 in more than a day to win the match while a draw would still have given them the series.

New Zealand managed to capture wickets at regular intervals but the South African batting was determined. The eighth wicket fell at 199 but then fast bowlers Peter Pollock and Neil Adcock took control and added 60 in less than an hour. Dick Motz finally bowled Adcock but then number eleven Harry Bromfield proved a stubborn ally for Pollock as the pair inched towards their target.

Frank Cameron finally accounted for Bromfield, who had defended for 36 minutes without scoring, and New Zealand had won by 40 runs and shared the series. An historic moment in New Zealand cricket.

Reid had again been to the fore. His figures were 45-27-44-4 (his victims being all top-order batsmen). Far from fully fit, he had bowled his off-cutters but on others days he was a fast-medium bowler with a feared bouncer.

Another example of what John Reid meant to the New Zealand team came at Christchurch in March 1963. In a seven wicket loss to England he made 100 out of 159 all out, the lowest test total to include a century. Just two other New Zealand batsmen made double figures. He had also top-scored with 74 in the first innings.

That season was also notable for one of Reid's most famous innings when he made 296 against Northern Districts at the Basin Reserve. Reid's innings occupied just 220 minutes and included 35 fours as well as a world record (at the time) 15 sixes. In his previous match, Reid had returned the extraordinary figures of 30-14-29-7 against Auckland.

Reid's fine form with the ball continued next season when he captured 40 wickets in first-class cricket. This included his best test figures of 6-60 (off 35 overs) against South Africa at Carisbrook in Dunedin.

At the end of the 1964/65 season, New Zealand embarked on an extremely arduous tour to India, Pakistan and England. The first seven games were all test matches against India and Pakistan and several of the New Zealand squad had little experience at first-class level.

Reid marked his 50th successive test with four sixes in his first ten balls in a memorable 82 against India at Calcutta. He also scored 88 against Pakistan at Lahore and his final test century came in the next game at Karachi when he made 128 and 76. Reid's last test was against England at Leeds when he made 54 in the first innings.

At the end of the tour, Reid captained a World XI against an England XI at Scarborough in what was to be his last first-class match. This was a notable honour for Reid with the World side including such names as Conrad Hunte, Hanif Mohammad, Garry Sobers, Colin Bland and Rohan Kanhai. By now troubled with knee damage, Reid decided it was a good note on which to end his first-class career.

The only other New Zealand player of uncontested world standing during Reid's era was Bert Sutcliffe, and in 58 tests, 34 of which he was captain, Reid often felt as if he was propping up the side. "It was hard work, you had a lot of responsibility," he said. "You knew jolly well that if you didn't get runs then nobody else would."

Reid was appointed as an Officer of the Order of the British Empire in the 1962 Queen's Birthday Honours list for services to sport, especially cricket. In the 2014 New Year Honours list he became a Companion of the New Zealand Order of Merit for services to cricket. He won New Zealand's highest batting award, the Redpath Cup, on five occasions and the Winsor Cup, for bowling, once.

He was a New Zealand selector between 1958 and 1965 and again between 1975 and 1978. From 1993 to 2002 he was an international match referee, officiating in 50 tests and 98 one-day internationals. On retirement he was made president of New Zealand Cricket in 2003.

He was also involved in the building and running of the John Reid Squash Centre in Wellington, which helped to make squash a popular sport in New Zealand, and which was sold to the New Zealand Squash Rackets Association in the late 1970s.

In 1981 Reid and his wife Norli moved to South Africa, where he coached Northern Transvaal for seven years, and Transvaal for a shorter time. They returned to New Zealand to live in 1992.

Reid had been New Zealand's oldest living test player and also Wellington's oldest surviving first-class cricketer. Reid's son, Richard, played nine one-day internationals for New Zealand.

Reid played 246 first-class matches, amassing 16,128 runs at 41.35 (with 39 centuries) and capturing 466 wickets at 22.60. He scored 3428 runs in 58 tests at 33.28 with six centuries and took 85 wickets at 33.35.

Bruce Richard TAYLOR

Born: *Timaru, 12 July, 1943*

Died: *Lower Hutt, 6 February, 2021*

Left-hand batsman, right-arm fast-medium bowler

Bruce Taylor was one of New Zealand's greatest all-rounders and, on his day, as good as any. His rise to fame was rapid and somewhat accidental.

He made his first-class debut for the New Zealand Under 23 XI in 1963/64 and played two Plunket Shield games for Canterbury the following summer, being called up when Dick Motz was injured. Taylor scored 49 and took 3-57 against Auckland and 5-49 against Northern Districts.

At the end of the season the New Zealand selectors picked their team for a very arduous tour to India, Pakistan and England. The first seven games of the tour were test matches in India and Pakistan.

The 21-year-old Taylor was named in the squad after Gary Bartlett, who was believed to be the selectors' first choice, was ruled out due to fitness concerns.

Taylor did not play the first test in India and was not selected for the second at Calcutta. However, Barry Sinclair fell ill before the game and Taylor was brought in to replace him.

New Zealand batted on the first day and were 233-6 when Taylor, in his first test, came out to join 41-year legend Bert Sutcliffe, who was making a comeback to international cricket after five years. The pair went to stumps at 259-6, Sutcliffe 74, Taylor 13.

The next day they were not separated until the score had reached 396. Taylor was dismissed for 105 made in 158 minutes with fourteen fours and three sixes. Sutcliffe remained unbeaten on 151 when New Zealand declared at 462-9.

Just before stumps Taylor struck for the first time dismissing Farokh Engineer and then immediately had the wicket of nightwatchman Bapu Nadkarni. India ended the day at 101-4 and next day took their score through to 380. Taylor dismissed Chandu Borde, the Nawab of Pataudi and Srinivas Venkataraghavan to finish with figures of 5-86.

There was little time for a result in the four-day game and the match was drawn. Taylor remains the only player to score a century and take five wickets in an innings on his test debut.

In the next test at Bombay, New Zealand made 297 and then dismissed India for just 88, with Taylor having the spectacular figures of 5-26 off 7.3 overs. India followed on and amassed 463-5 (Taylor 3-76) and New Zealand were fortunate to escape with a draw, being 80-8 at the close. Taylor, who came in at 45-6, top scored with 21.

Taylor top scored again in the first test against Pakistan, played on a difficult pitch at Rawalpindi. New Zealand were sent in and found themselves 39-5 before Taylor arrived and hit 76 in 88 minutes to help New Zealand reach 175.

Taylor had the unusual distinction of scoring his first two first-class hundreds in test matches. New Zealand were struggling at 152-6 against West Indies at Eden Park in February 1969 when Taylor arrived at the crease. He took just 30 minutes to reach fifty and his century arrived after 86 minutes. His hundred came off 83 balls, which remained the New Zealand record until beaten by Daniel Vettori 37 years later. Taylor's final tally of 124 came in just 111 minutes and included fourteen fours and five sixes (one of which took Taylor to his century).

Taylor was in the New Zealand party which made the historic first visit to West Indies early in 1972. The five-match series was drawn 0-0, a notable achievement by New Zealand.

In unfamiliar conditions, with Lawrence Rowe seemingly able to score double-centuries at will, New Zealand lost their captain Graham Dowling through injury, Richard Collinge had to leave the tour early and the odds were overwhelmingly in the home side's favour.

However, New Zealand had Glenn Turner's heroics (four double centuries on tour) and Bevan Congdon took over as captain and overnight transformed himself from modest test batsman and occasional bowler to the world's leading test all-rounder over the next few years. Hedley Howarth bowled himself to a standstill (74 overs in one innings alone) and Graham Vivian provided perhaps the best example ever of a player being worth his place in the team for his fielding alone. He and Mark Burgess set fielding standards rarely seen.

Taylor well and truly played his part. He was not selected for the first test in Jamaica where New Zealand, who looked headed for defeat at one stage, came out of the game with an honourable draw. A double century from Turner and a hundred on the last day from Mark Burgess were notable efforts.

Taylor was brought in for the second test at Trinidad, taking seven wickets in the match. In the next, at Barbados, West Indies decided to bat first and their powerful batting lineup was routed for just 133. Taylor finished with 7-74, the first time a New Zealand bowler had taken more than six wickets in a test innings.

New Zealand could, and perhaps should have won this test and thus probably the series. New Zealand were brilliant in the field but ironically it was two catching lapses which allowed Charlie Davis and Garry Sobers (who otherwise had a modest record against New Zealand) to take West Indies to safety in the second innings. This could so easily have been remembered as a most historic win for New Zealand.

Taylor was known as a swashbuckling batsman but one of his very best innings was a rearguard one. The fifth test was played over six days because the series was level. On the last day, New Zealand were 188-7 with no hope of winning and with almost two hours to go. Taylor (42 not out in 106 minutes) and Wadsworth (another attacking batsman, 40 not out in 143 minutes) saved the day and the series.

Taylor had earlier taken 3-74 and 5-41 in the match to give him 27 wickets for the series (four matches) at 17.70. This was a New Zealand record and only bettered since by Richard Hadlee's 33 wickets in three tests in Australia in 1985/86. With his high arm action, Bruce Taylor was a dangerous bowler generating seam movement and bounce.

Taylor's batting was also crucial when Canterbury defeated Les Favell's Australian team at Lancaster Park in February 1967. Canterbury became the first team to defeat an Australian side in a first-class game in New Zealand.

The Australians made 279 (Taylor 3-56) and Canterbury replied with 256. Taylor, batting at number nine, top scored with 69. The visitors were bowled out for 156 in their second innings (Motz 7-56), leaving Canterbury 180 for victory. The home side were struggling before Taylor's unbeaten 37 saw them home.

Taylor's highest score was a monumental 173 against Otago at Carisbrook in January 1973. He joined Jeremy Coney at 42-4 but soon required a runner. John Morrison, who had just been dismissed without scoring, went back out in to the middle and remained there for a partnership which was finally worth 255 runs.

The tour to England in 1973, was Taylor's last outing for New Zealand. He played in all three tests and in his only two one-day internationals. Taylor had played for Wellington from 1970/71, captaining them in 1972/73 and 1973/74 before stepping away from the first-class game. However, he returned for two more seasons in 1978/79, taking a further 38 wickets.

His final game was against West Indies at the Hutt Recreation Ground (when the Basin Reserve was being redeveloped). Wellington gained a famous victory with Ewen Chatfield and Stu Cater capturing all twenty wickets.

Taylor opened the bowling in both innings and failed to take a wicket but recalled "It's quite ironic that game. Chats (Ewen Chatfield) got 13 wickets, Stu Cater got seven and I didn't get one and I felt it was one of the best spells I ever bowled. I kept beating the bat of Haynes and Greenidge all day." Taylor played one final Shell Cup one-day game in 1980/81.

Taylor was later a national selector, helping pick the 1992 World Cup side. He served a year in jail in 1993 after pleading guilty to 22 fraud charges stemming from taking more than $368,000 from Dunedin's John McGlashan College, where he worked.

However, cricket never turned its back on him. He was soon back coaching and joined Wellington's selection panel in the early 2000s.

Later in life, Taylor struggled with health issues, suffering several heart attacks and having a leg amputated in 2016 to fight gangrene.

Taylor made 4579 runs at 24.75 in 141 first-class matches and took 422 wickets at 25.13. In 30 tests he scored 898 runs at 20.40 and took 111 wickets at 26.60.

John Thomas WARD

Born: *Timaru, 11 March, 1937*

Died: *Timaru, 12 January, 2021*

Right-hand batsman, wicketkeeper

John Ward was an outstanding wicketkeeper who played eight test matches in the 1960s. He started out his cricketing career as a leg-spinner and it was only because his Timaru club side Old Boys decided to have a second senior side that Ward picked up the gloves. He recounted that "No one wanted to be the wicketkeeper, so I thought okay I will have a go."

Ward was selected for the 1958 tour to England, as Eric Petrie's understudy, before he had played for his province (Canterbury). Ward's first-class debut was a trial match for the tour between North Island and the South. Ward took five catches and was named in the touring party ahead of Sam Guillen who was not only the Canterbury wicketkeeper at the time but the incumbent New Zealand keeper as well.

Petrie was in outstanding form on the tour and played in all five tests. Ward played in 13 first-class games, making 28 dismissals.

Guillen was still favoured by the Canterbury selectors the following season meaning that Ward did not make his Canterbury debut until 1959/60, with Guillen playing as a batsman.

Ward played in one unofficial test against Ian Craig's Australian team in 1959/60 and also for New Zealand against Dennis Silk's MCC side in 1960/61. He was duly selected as the number one keeper for New Zealand's visit to South Africa in 1961/62 but was injured early in the tour.

Reserve keeper Artie Dick was thus pressed into action for the first test and never looked back, making 23 dismissals and scoring valuable runs. Dick's selection as reserve keeper was a curious one as he did not keep for Otago and was not even the wicketkeeper for his club side.

Dick retained the gloves for the England series in 1962/63 but Ward finally gained his test cap against South Africa the following season. However, Dick, who was the superior batsman, returned for the next two tests and the first two against Pakistan in 1964/65. Ward was recalled for the final test and then chosen as the only specialist keeper for the very arduous tour to India, Pakistan and England in 1965. The first seven games were tests in the subcontinent.

Ward played the first four games (all tests in India) but again suffered injury and Dick was flown out as replacement. Dick played the three tests against Pakistan and the first two in England before Ward was recalled for the last at Leeds, where John Edrich made 310 not out.

Eric Petrie, aged 38, was recalled as the New Zealand wicketkeeper for the 1965/66 series against England and Roy Harford was preferred as keeper when Les Favell's Australian team visited the following season. Harford retained his place for the first three tests against India in 1967/68 but made several mistakes in the third game (despite setting a New Zealand record of five catches in an innings) and was replaced by Ward for the fourth.

This turned out to be Ward's final appearance for New Zealand but he continued to play for Canterbury until 1970/71. Ward's son, Barry, kept wicket for Canterbury in 1986/87.

Ward's favourite Canterbury memory was taking a stumping off quick bowler Dick Motz in a pre-planned move (Northern Districts' Gary Giles was the victim). "Usually things like that never quite work out so we were both happy" Ward said.

Ward had a long association with South Canterbury cricket. As well as captaining the South Canterbury side from 1959 to 1969 he also had two spells as selector from 1970 to 1975 and again from 1982 to 1986. In 1982 he was recognised with Life Membership of the South Canterbury Cricket Association and since 2014 had also been the Patron, fulfilling any duties with a still-keen interest and obvious love of the game that he continued to pass on.

Ward scored 1117 runs at 12.41 in 95 first-class games and took 227 catches and made 27 stumpings. In eight tests he made 75 runs at 12.50 and had 16 catches and one stumping.

WEST INDIES IN NEW ZEALAND

West Indies toured New Zealand playing two tests, three Twenty20 internationals, a four-day first-class game and a three-day warm-up match. The visitors were unable to win a game losing both test matches and the Twenty20 series 2-0 with a game abandoned. The first class match finished in a draw.

Brathwaite was the leading run scorer in the first-class games with 301, including a career best 246 against New Zealand A. Blackwood was the only other player to score a century, reaching three figures in the first test. They were the only players to score 200 runs. Gabriel and Chamar Holder were the leading wicket-takers with six and five.

In the Twenty20s Pollard was the only player to score 100 runs, including a career best 75 not out, while no bowler took more than three wickets.

The squads were: First Class: J.O. Holder *(captain)*, R.L. Chase *(vice-captain)*, J. Blackwood, N.E. Bonner, K.C. Brathwaite, D.M. Bravo, S.S.J. Brooks, J.D. Campbell, R.R.S. Cornwall, J. Da Silva, S.O.Dowrich, S.T. Gabriel, S.O. Hetmyer, C.K. Holder, A.S. Joseph, S.A.R. Moseley, K.M.A. Paul, R.A. Reifer, K.A.J. Roach.

Twenty20: K.A. Pollard *(captain)*, N. Pooran *(vice-captain)*, F.A. Allen, S.S. Cotterell, A.D.S. Fletcher, S.O. Hetmyer, B.A. King, K.R. Mayers, K.M.A. Paul, R. Powell, R. Shepherd, O.R. Thomas, H.R. Walsh, K.O.K. Williams.

Coach, P.V. Simmons; Manager, R.N. Lewis.

West Indies First-class Averages

BATTING	*M*	*I*	*NO*	*HS*	*Agg*	*Ave*	*100s*	*50s*	*Ct*	*St*
K.C. Brathwaite	3	5	0	246	301	60.20	1	-	1	-
J. Blackwood	3	5	0	104	269	53.80	1	2	-	-
R.A. Reifer	1	1	0	46	46	46.00	-	-	-	-
J.O. Holder	3	5	1	61	127	31.75	-	1	4	-
J.D. Campbell	3	5	0	68	155	31.00	-	1	-	-
J. Da Silva	1	2	0	57	60	30.00	-	1	2	-
A.S. Joseph	3	5	0	86	132	26.40	-	1	-	-
D.M. Bravo	3	5	0	93	125	25.00	-	1	-	-
S.O. Dowrich	2	1	0	23	23	23.00	-	-	1	-
S.S.J. Brooks	3	5	0	36	58	11.60	-	-	2	-
R.L. Chase	2	4	0	11	17	4.25	-	-	1	-
K.A.J. Roach	1	2	1	2	2	2.00	-	-	-	-
S.T. Gabriel	2	4	0	2	3	0.75	-	-	-	-
R.R.S. Cornwall	1	1	0	0	0	0.00	-	-	-	-
C.K. Holder	2	3	3	13*	21	-	-	-	-	-

BOWLING	*O*	*M*	*R*	*W*	*Ave*	*Best*	*5w*	*10w*
J.D. Campbell	6	2	30	1	30.00	1-30	-	-
S.T. Gabriel	51	13	182	6	30.33	3-89	-	-
R.R.S. Cornwall	15	3	34	1	34.00	1-34	-	-
K.A.J. Roach	30	7	114	3	38.00	3-114	-	-
K.C. Brathwaite	31	3	80	2	40.00	2-66	-	-
C.K. Holder	54	5	210	5	42.00	3-100	-	-
A.S. Joseph	71	16	246	4	61.50	3-109	-	-
R.L. Chase	38	1	163	2	81.50	2-54	-	-
J.O. Holder	77	22	190	1	190.00	1-45	-	-
D.M. Bravo	5	0	19	0	-	-	-	-
J. Blackwood	12	0	39	0	-	-	-	-
R.A. Reifer	18	2	56	0	-	-	-	-

New Zealand Test Averages

BATTING	M	I	NO	HS	Agg	Ave	100s	50s	Ct	St
K.S. Williamson	1	1	0	251	251	251.00	1	-	1	-
H.M. Nicholls	2	2	0	174	181	90.50	1	-	1	-
K.A. Jamieson	2	2	1	51*	71	71.00	-	1	-	-
T.W.M. Latham	2	2	0	86	113	56.50	-	1	5	-
B-J. Watling	1	1	0	30	30	30.00	-	-	4	-
D.J. Mitchell	2	2	0	42	51	25.50	-	-	1	-
W.A. Young	2	2	0	43	48	24.00	-	-	1	-
L.R.P.L. Taylor	2	2	0	38	47	23.50	-	-	2	-
T.G. Southee	2	2	1	11*	22	22.00	-	-	3	-
T.A. Blundell	2	2	0	14	28	14.00	-	-	2	-
T.A. Boult	2	1	0	6	6	6.00	-	-	1	-
N. Wagner	2	1	1	66*	66	-	-	1	-	-

BOWLING	O	M	R	W	Ave	Best	5w	10w
K.A. Jamieson	53	13	144	11	13.09	5-34	1	-
T.G. Southee	73.4	19	225	12	18.75	5-32	1	-
N. Wagner	58	12	181	9	20.11	4-66	-	-
D.J. Mitchell	7	0	27	1	27.00	1-7	-	-
T.A. Boult	67	14	223	5	44.60	3-96	-	-

West Indies Test Averages

BATTING	M	I	NO	HS	Agg	Ave	100s	50s	Ct	St
J. Blackwood	2	4	0	104	216	54.00	1	1	-	-
J.O. Holder	2	4	1	61	103	34.33	-	1	4	-
J. Da Silva	1	2	0	57	60	30.00	-	1	2	-
J.D. Campbell	2	4	0	68	110	27.50	-	1	-	-
A.S. Joseph	2	4	0	86	110	27.50	-	1	-	-
K.C. Brathwaite	2	4	0	24	55	13.75	-	-	1	-
S.S.J. Brooks	2	4	0	36	53	13.25	-	-	2	-
D.M. Bravo	2	4	0	12	32	8.00	-	-	-	-
R.L. Chase	2	4	0	11	17	4.25	-	-	1	-
K.A.J. Roach	1	2	1	2	2	2.00	-	-	-	-
S.T. Gabriel	2	4	0	2	3	0.75	-	-	-	-
C.K. Holder	1	2	2	13*	21	-	-	-	-	-
S.O. Dowrich	1	-	-	-	-	-	-	-	-	-

BOWLING	O	M	R	W	Ave	Best	5w	10w
S.T. Gabriel	51	13	182	6	30.33	3-89	-	-
K.A.J. Roach	30	7	114	3	38.00	3-114	-	-
A.S. Joseph	53	10	208	4	52.00	3-109	-	-
C.K. Holder	26	1	110	2	55.00	2-110	-	-
R.L. Chase	38	1	163	2	81.50	2-54	-	-
K.C. Brathwaite	3	0	14	0	-	-	-	-
J.O. Holder	58	18	145	0	-	-	-	-

NEW ZEALAND A v WEST INDIES
At John Davies Oval, Queenstown 20, 21, 22 November, 2020

New Zealand A 308-3d (R. Ravindra 112, H.M. Nicholls 76, D.P. Conway 46*, J.F. Carter 41*) and 124-1d (W.A. Young 64*, D.P. Conway 41*) **drew with West Indies A** 366 (D.M. Bravo 135, S.S.J. Brooks 80, K.C. Brathwaite 47, R.L Chase 42, J.A. Duffy 3-49)

NEW ZEALAND A v WEST INDIES — First-class

at John Davies Oval, Queenstown on 26, 27, 28, 29 November, 2020
Toss : West Indies. Umpires : B.F. Bowden & D.J. Walker
Close of play: 1st day: West Indies 353-3, Brathwaite 183, Blackwood 19; 2nd day: NZ A 45-0, Cooper 19, Ravindra 22
3rd day: NZ A 249-4, Young 80, McConchie 25
Match drawn

West Indies won the toss and decided to bat first. Campbell assisted Brathwaite in an opening stand of 111 and Bravo helped added 189 for the second wicket. Brathwaite got his century off 139 balls and then went to his double century after a further 141 deliveries. Bravo and Blackwood both got fifties. Brathwaite's 246 was his highest first-class score and the second highest by a West Indian in New Zealand. McConchie was the most successful bowler with 3-130.

New Zealand A then had an opening stand of 100 with both Cooper and Ravindra getting fifties from 139 and 92 balls respectively. Young and McConchie added 170 for the fifth wicket. Young scored his tenth century from 209 balls and had reached 5000 first class runs when on 56. McConchie reached his fifth hundred off 217 balls. New Zealand A declared at 440-8 and the game was called off.

WEST INDIES

FIRST INNINGS	*Runs*	*Mins*	*Balls*	*6s*	*4s*
K.C.Brathwaite c Young b Rae	246	552	400	1	17
J.D.Campbell b Tickner	45	106	62	-	8
D.M.Bravo* c Tickner b Ravindra	93	221	167	-	11
S.S.J.Brooks c Sears b Rae	5	30	30	-	-
J.Blackwood b Ravindra	53	115	82	-	4
S.O.Dowrich† b Sears	23	53	36	-	2
J.O.Holder c McClure b McConchie	24	80	48	-	1
R.A.Reifer c Rae b McConchie	46	121	107	-	4
R.R.S.Cornwall b McConchie	0	3	5	-	-
A.S.Joseph run out	22	47	32	-	2
C.K.Holder not out	0	14	8	-	-
Extras (lb 7, w 3, nb 4)	14				
TOTAL (162.1 overs)	**571**	673			

NEW ZEALAND A

	Runs	*Mins*	*Balls*	*6s*	*4s*
H.R.Cooper lbw b Holder C.K.	54	193	149	-	5
R.Ravindra lbw b Cornwall	52	149	99	-	5
W.A.Young b Brathwaite	133	371	270	-	11
J.F.Carter c Dowrich b Holder C.K.	1	12	8	-	-
K.J.McClure lbw b Holder J.O.	20	89	53	-	1
C.E.McConchie* not out	124	336	233	1	7
D.Cleaver† b Holder C.K.	10	20	18	-	1
S.M.Solia c sub (J.De Silva) b Brathwaite	0	9	8	-	-
B.V.Sears lbw b Campbell	5	49	41	-	1
B.M.Tickner not out	13	31	29	1	-
M.D.Rae					
Extras (b 3, lb 10, w 1, nb 14)	28				
TOTAL (149 overs) (8 wkts dec)	**440**	630			

Bowling	*O*	*M*	*R*	*W*
NEW ZEALAND A				
Tickner	28	3	113	1
Rae	28	2	100	2
Sears	21	0	76	1
Solia	14	0	43	0
McConchie	36.1	3	130	3
Ravindra	35	7	102	2
WEST INDIES				
Joseph	18	6	38	0
Holder C.K.	28	4	100	3
Holder J.O.	19	4	45	1
Cornwall	15	3	34	1
Brathwaite	28	3	66	2
Reifer	18	2	56	0
Blackwood	12	0	39	0
Bravo	5	0	19	0
Campbell	6	2	30	1

Fall of Wickets

	WI	***NZA***
	1st	*1st*
1st	111	100
2nd	300	130
3rd	322	137
4th	429	186
5th	472	356
6th	483	373
7th	512	377
8th	512	400
9th	565	-
10th	571	-

NEW ZEALAND v WEST INDIES First Twenty20 International

at Eden Park, Auckland on 27 November, 2020 (d/n)
Toss : New Zealand. Umpires : C.M. Brown & W.R. Knights
New Zealand won by 5 wickets (D/L)

New Zealand won the toss and decided to field. Conway and Jamieson made their Twenty20 international debuts.There were three rain interruptions after four balls, two overs and ten overs with the game reduced to 16 overs.

The West Indies innings was full of drama. They had reached 58-0 after 3.1 overs but two overs later were 59-5. Then there was an 84 run stand in 8.1 overs with Pollard getting his highest score in Twenty20 internationals. His fifty came from 30 balls but two wickets then fell quickly before West Indies reached 180-7. Ferguson had career best figures of 5-21, the second best by a New Zealand bowler.

New Zealand had a target of 179 and were soon 63-4 but forties to Conway and Neesham saw them home with four balls to spare. Neesham made his highest score.

WEST INDIES

	Runs	Mins	Balls	6s	4s
A.D.S.Fletcher b Ferguson	34	22	14	3	3
B.A.King c Neesham b Southee	13	28	10	-	2
S.O.Hetmyer c Seifert b Ferguson	0	3	4	-	-
N.Pooran† lbw b Ferguson	1	10	2	-	-
R.Powell c Ferguson b Southee	0	3	3	-	-
K.A.Pollard* not out	75	63	37	8	4
F.A.Allen c Seifert b Ferguson	30	40	26	1	4
K.M.A.Paul c Seifert b Ferguson	0	2	2	-	-
S.S.Cottrell not out	1	15	2	-	-
K.O.K.Williams					
O.R.Thomas					
Extras (lb 6, w 16, nb 4)	26				
TOTAL (16 overs) (7 wkts)	**180**	94			

NEW ZEALAND

	Runs	Mins	Balls	6s	4s
M.J.Guptill c Pooran b Cottrell	5	3	3	-	-
T.L.Seifert† c Powell b Thomas	17	20	13	1	2
D.P.Conway c Thomas b Pollard	41	67	29	1	5
G.D.Phillips b Thomas	22	12	7	3	1
L.R.P.L.Taylor run out	0	6	4	-	-
J.D.S.Neesham not out	48	48	24	3	5
M.J.Santner not out	31	17	18	3	-
K.A.Jamieson					
L.H.Ferguson					
T.G.Southee*					
H.K.Bennett					
Extras (b 4, lb 2, w 3, nb 6)	15				
TOTAL (15.2 overs) (5 wkts)	**179**	88			

Bowling	*O*	*M*	*R*	*W*
NEW ZEALAND				
Southee	3	0	22	2
Jamieson	3	0	26	0
Bennett	2.3	0	50	0
Ferguson	4	0	21	5
Santner	2	0	23	0
Neesham	1.3	0	32	0
WEST INDIES				
Cottrell	4	0	30	1
Allen	2	0	32	0
Thomas	3	0	23	2
Williams	2	0	33	0
Paul	3	0	39	0
Pollard	1.2	0	16	1

Fall of Wickets

	WI	*NZ*
1st	58	7
2nd	58	34
3rd	58	62
4th	58	63
5th	59	140
6th	143	-
7th	146	-
8th	-	-
9th	-	-
10th	-	-

NEW ZEALAND v WEST INDIES Second Twenty20 International

at Bay Oval, Mt Maunganui on 29 November, 2020
Toss : West Indies. Umpires : C.M. Brown & S.B. Haig
New Zealand won by 72 runs

Sodhi replaced Bennett for New Zealand while Mayers replaced Williams for West Indies. The visitors won the toss and decided to bowl first. New Zealand made 238-3 with a record third wicket stand of 184 between Conway and Phillips from 13.3 overs. Phillips scored a maiden century from 46 balls, the fastest by a New Zealand batsman. Conway scored a maiden fifty from 31 balls.

West Indies lost King in the second over and never recovered making 166-9. Pollard again top scored with 28. Jamieson and Santner both took two wickets. This gave New Zealand a series win.

NEW ZEALAND

	Runs	Mins	Balls	6s	4s
M.J.Guptill c Pooran b Allen	34	31	23	2	5
T.L.Seifert† b Thomas	18	25	13	-	3
D.P.Conway not out	65	80	37	4	4
G.D.Phillips c sub (H.R.Walsh) b Pollard	108	72	51	8	10
L.R.P.L.Taylor not out	0	2	0	-	-
J.D.S.Neesham					
M.J.Santner					
I.S.Sodhi					
K.A.Jamieson					
T.G.Southee*					
L.H.Ferguson					
Extras (lb 4, w 5, nb 4)	13				
TOTAL (20 overs) (3 wkts)	**238**	106			

WEST INDIES

	Runs	Mins	Balls	6s	4s
A.D.S.Fletcher run out	20	18	14	2	-
B.A.King b Jamieson	0	5	1	-	-
S.O.Hetmyer c Santner b Sodhi	25	66	32	-	2
K.R.Mayers c Phillips b Neesham	20	24	14	2	-
N.Pooran† c & b Santner	7	6	4	1	-
K.A.Pollard* c Southee b Santner	28	16	15	4	-
R.Powell b Ferguson	9	15	7	-	1
F.A.Allen c Phillips b Southee	15	14	11	2	-
K.M.A.Paul not out	26	20	18	3	-
S.S.Cottrell c Seifert b Jamieson	1	7	4	-	-
O.R.Thomas not out	0	7	0	-	-
Extras (lb 1, w 14)	15				
TOTAL (20 overs) (9 wkts)	**166**	101			

Bowling	*O*	*M*	*R*	*W*
WEST INDIES				
Cottrell	4	0	39	0
Mayers	1	0	10	0
Thomas	4	0	44	1
Paul	4	0	64	0
Allen	3	0	35	1
Pollard	3	0	33	1
Powell	1	0	9	0
NEW ZEALAND				
Southee	4	0	49	1
Jamieson	4	0	15	2
Ferguson	4	0	22	1
Santner	3	0	41	2
Sodhi	4	0	26	1
Neesham	1	0	12	1

Fall of Wickets	***NZ***	***WI***
1st	49	10
2nd	53	28
3rd	237	60
4th	-	72
5th	-	107
6th	-	113
7th	-	132
8th	-	140
9th	-	144
10th	-	

NEW ZEALAND v WEST INDIES Third Twenty20 International

at Bay Oval, Mt Maunganui on 30 November, 2020 (d/n)
Toss : New Zealand. Umpires : S.B. Haig & W.R. Knights
No result

Both sides made changes. Southee, Ferguson and Jamieson joined the New Zealand test squad and were replaced by Bennett, Mitchell and Kuggeleijn. Walsh and Shepherd (debut) replaced Heymyer and Paul.

Santner became New Zealand's eighth Twenty20 international captain and on winning the toss decided to bowl. However heavy rain came after 2.2 overs with the score at 25-1 and no further play was possible.

WEST INDIES

	Runs	Mins	Balls	6s	4s
A.D.S.Fletcher not out	4	12	3	-	1
B.A.King c Neesham b Ferguson	11	6	7	1	1
K.R.Mayers not out	5	5	4	-	1
N.Pooran†					
R.Powell					
K.A.Pollard*					
F.A.Allen					
H.R.Walsh					
R.Shepherd					
S.S.Cottrell					
O.R.Thomas					
Extras (w 5)	5				
TOTAL (2.2 overs) (1 wkt)	**25**	12			

NEW ZEALAND

M.J.Guptill
T.L.Seifert†
D.P.Conway
G.D.Phillips
D.J.Mitchell
J.D.S.Neesham
M.J.Santner*
I.S.Sodhi
S.C.Kuggeleijn
L.H.Ferguson
H.K.Bennett

Bowling	*O*	*M*	*R*	*W*
NEW ZEALAND				
Santner	1	0	12	0
Ferguson	1	0	13	1
Bennett	0.2	0	0	0

Fall of Wickets	***WI***
1st	16
2nd	-
3rd	-
4th	-
5th	-
6th	-
7th	-
8th	-
9th	-
10th	-

NEW ZEALAND v WEST INDIES — First Test

at Seddon Park, Hamilton on 3, 4, 5, 6 December, 2020
Toss : West Indies. Umpires : C.B. Gaffaney & W.R. Knights
Close of play: 1st day: NZ 243-2, Williamson 97, Taylor 31; 2nd day: West Indies 49-0, Brathwaite 20, Campbell 22
3rd day: West Indies 196-6, Blackwood 80, Joseph 59
New Zealand won by an innings and 134 runs

Young made his test debut for New Zealand. West Indies won the toss and decided to bowl first. They had an early success before Latham and Williamson added 154 for the second wicket. Latham got fifty from 126 balls while Williamson went to his 22nd test hundred from 224 deliveries and proceeded to his third double century after 369 balls. He also registered his highest test score. Jamieson scored a maiden fifty before a declaration was made at 519-7. Roach and Gabriel both took three wickets.

West Indies reached 49-0 at the close of the second day but collapsed to be dismissed for 138. Southee took four wickets. No batsman was able to reach 30. Following on 381 behind the visitors were faring no better at 89-6 before Blackwood and Joseph broke the West Indies seventh wicket record against New Zealand by adding 155. Blackwood reached his second century after 135 balls while Joseph scored his maiden fifty off 69 balls. Wagner took four wickets as West Indies were dismissed for 247 giving New Zealand a win by an innings and 134 runs.

NEW ZEALAND

FIRST INNINGS	*Runs*	*Mins*	*Balls*	*6s*	*4s*	*SECOND INNINGS*	*Runs*	*Mins*	*Balls*	*6s*	*4s*
T.W.M.Latham b Roach	86	268	184	1	12						
W.A.Young lbw b Gabriel	5	21	11	-	1						
K.S.Williamson* c Chase b Joseph	251	624	412	2	34						
L.R.P.L.Taylor c Brooks b Gabriel	38	111	68	-	6						
H.M.Nicholls c Holder b Roach	7	49	33	-	1						
T.A.Blundell† lbw b Gabriel	14	91	63	-	2						
D.J.Mitchell c Holder b Roach	9	61	37	-	1						
K.A.Jamieson not out	51	76	64	2	5						
T.G.Southee not out	11	12	10	1	-						
N.Wagner											
T.A.Boult											
Extras (b 11, lb 23, w 1, nb 12)	47										
TOTAL (145 overs) (7 wkts dec)	**519**	658									

WEST INDIES

FIRST INNINGS	*Runs*	*Mins*	*Balls*	*6s*	*4s*	*SECOND INNINGS*	*Runs*	*Mins*	*Balls*	*6s*	*4s*
K.C.Brathwaite c Blundell b Boult	21	131	92	-	1	c Blundell b Southee	10	40	23	-	1
J.D.Campbell c Williamson b Southee	26	117	73	1	2	c Latham b Boult	2	9	3	-	-
S.S.J.Brooks c Taylor b Southee	1	8	7	-	-	(4) c sub (D.P.Conway) b Wagner	2	4	4	-	-
D.M.Bravo b Jamieson	9	50	35	-	-	(3) c Southee b Wagner	12	25	19	-	3
R.L.Chase lbw b Wagner	11	50	29	-	2	lbw b Jamieson	6	35	19	-	1
J.Blackwood c Latham b Southee	23	73	48	-	3	c Southee b Wagner	104	239	141	2	11
J.O.Holder* not out	25	113	73	-	3	lbw b Mitchell	8	32	15	-	1
A.S.Joseph c Mitchell b Southee	0	2	3	-	-	c sub (M.J.Santner) b Jamieson	86	167	125	3	9
K.A.J.Roach b Jamieson	2	30	18	-	-	not out	0	9	2	-	-
S.T.Gabriel lbw b Wagner	1	11	9	-	-	b Wagner	0	3	4	-	-
S.O.Dowrich† absent hurt						absent hurt					
Extras (b 8, lb 7, w 1, nb 3)	19					(lb 7, w 8, nb 2)	17				
TOTAL (64 overs)	**138**	295				(58.5 overs)	**247**	283			

Bowling	*O*	*M*	*R*	*W*	*O*	*M*	*R*	*W*
WEST INDIES								
Roach	30	7	114	3				
Gabriel	25	6	89	3				
Holder	31	12	60	0				
Joseph	31	8	99	1				
Chase	25	0	109	0				
Brathwaite	3	0	14	0				
NEW ZEALAND								
Southee	19	7	35	4	15	2	62	1
Boult	17	5	30	1	15	1	63	1
Jamieson	13	3	25	2	12	2	42	2
Wagner	15	3	33	2	13.5	0	66	4
Mitchell					3	0	7	1

Fall of Wickets	***NZ***	***WI***	***WI***
	1st	*1st*	*2nd*
1st	14	53	4
2nd	168	55	25
3rd	251	55	27
4th	281	79	27
5th	353	79	53
6th	409	119	89
7th	503	119	244
8th	-	135	247
9th	-	138	247
10th	-	-	-

NEW ZEALAND v WEST INDIES — Second Test

at Basin Reserve, Wellington on 11, 12, 13, 14 December, 2020
Toss : West Indies. Umpires : C.M. Brown & C.B. Gaffaney
Close of play: 1st day: NZ 294-6, Nicholls 117, Jamieson 1; 2nd day: West Indies 124-8, Da Silva 2, C.K.Holder 5
3rd day: West Indies 244-6, J.O.Holder 60, Da Silva 25
New Zealand won by an innings and 12 runs

Watling, who had missed the first test through injury, replaced Williamson who was absent on paternity leave, while Chamar Holder and Da Silva replaced Roach and Dowrich who had both returned home. Wagner and Gabriel were both playing their 50th test match.

West Indies again won the toss and decided to bowl. Nine of the first ten New Zealand batsmen reached double figures but Nicholls rode his luck, after being dropped on four occasions, to reach his sixth test hundred after 179 balls. It was the 100th test century at the Basin Reserve. Wagner scored his maiden fifty (36 balls) to get New Zealand to 460. Gabriel and Joseph both took three wickets.

West Indies lost Brathwaite without a run on the board and never recovered, being bowled out for 131. Blackwood was the only player to pass 14 runs as he got fifty from 70 balls. Southee and Jamieson both took five wickets. Southee for the 11th time in a test and for Jamieson the second time.

New Zealand decided to enforce the follow on and Campbell reached his highest test score in reply. However, West Indies then went from 130-2 to 170-6 before Jason Holder and Da Silva added 82. Holder got fifty from 73 balls, four fewer than Da Silva. Boult and Wagner both took three wickets as the visitors made 317. New Zealand won by an innings and 12 runs to give them a 2-0 series win.

NEW ZEALAND

FIRST INNINGS	Runs	Mins	Balls	6s	4s
T.W.M.Latham* c Da Silva b Holder C.K.	27	87	53	-	4
T.A.Blundell b Gabriel	14	35	19	-	2
W.A.Young c Holder J.O. b Gabriel	43	174	87	-	4
L.R.P.L.Taylor c Da Silva b Gabriel	9	19	12	-	1
H.M.Nicholls c Brathwaite b Chase	174	425	280	1	21
B-J.Watling† b Joseph	30	68	51	-	6
D.J.Mitchell lbw b Holder C.K.	42	101	68	-	5
K.A.Jamieson c Holder J.O. b Joseph	20	79	57	-	3
T.G.Southee b Joseph	11	17	12	-	2
N.Wagner not out	66	58	42	4	8
T.A.Boult c Brooks b Chase	6	2	3	1	-
Extras (b 2, lb 7, w 9)	18				
TOTAL (114 overs)	**460**	535			

SECOND INNINGS — Runs Mins Balls 6s 4s

WEST INDIES

FIRST INNINGS	Runs	Mins	Balls	6s	4s	SECOND INNINGS	Runs	Mins	Balls	6s	4s
K.C.Brathwaite c Taylor b Southee	0	9	8	-	-	c Young b Boult	24	48	42	-	3
J.D.Campbell c Latham b Jamieson	14	69	37	-	2	b Jamieson	68	185	109	-	8
D.M.Bravo c & b Southee	7	42	30	-	1	c Nicholls b Boult	4	3	3	-	1
S.S.J.Brooks b Jamieson	14	140	92	-	1	c Watling b Wagner	36	108	72	1	4
R.L.Chase b Jamieson	0	2	1	-	-	c Latham b Jamieson	0	13	7	-	-
J.Blackwood c Latham b Southee	69	145	92	-	11	b Boult	20	48	33	-	1
J.O.Holder* c Boult b Jamieson	9	35	25	-	1	b Southee	61	126	93	2	8
J.Da Silva† c Watling b Southee	3	38	25	-	-	lbw b Wagner	57	135	84	-	6
A.S.Joseph c Watling b Jamieson	0	3	3	-	-	c Watling b Southee	24	18	12	2	3
C.K.Holder not out	8	32	22	-	-	not out	13	37	15	-	3
S.T.Gabriel b Southee	2	8	6	-	-	b Wagner	0	9	6	-	-
Extras (lb 3, w 1, nb 1)	5					(b 1, lb 7, w 1, nb 1)	10				
TOTAL (56.4 overs)	**131**	265				(79.1 overs)	**317**	366			

Bowling	O	M	R	W	O	M	R	W
WEST INDIES								
Gabriel	26	7	93	3				
Holder J.O.	27	6	85	0				
Joseph	22	2	109	3				
Holder C.K.	26	1	110	2				
Chase	13	1	54	2				
NEW ZEALAND								
Southee	17.4	6	32	5	22	4	96	2
Boult	14	5	34	0	21	3	96	3
Wagner	12	5	28	0	17.1	4	54	3
Jamieson	13	4	34	5	15	4	43	2
Mitchell					4	0	20	0

Fall of Wickets	**NZ** *1st*	**WI** *1st*	**WI** *2nd*
1st	31	0	37
2nd	63	22	41
3rd	78	29	130
4th	148	29	131
5th	203	97	134
6th	286	111	170
7th	336	117	252
8th	359	117	282
9th	454	127	307
10th	460	131	317

WEST INDIES A IN NEW ZEALAND

West Indies A played two first-class games in New Zealand against their New Zealand counterpart while the main side was playing New Zealand in Twenty20 and test matches.

Shepherd and Moseley both scored centuries, scoring 232 and 171 runs respectively. Pooran scored 176 runs. Cornwall and Walsh were the leading wicket takers with six wickets each. No bowler took more than three wickets in an innings. Powell captained the side in the first game and Pooran in the second.

The squad was: F.A. Allen, N.E. Bonner, R.R.S. Cornwall, J. Da Silva, B.A. King, P.A.S. McSween, K.R. Mayers, S.A.R. Moseley, K.M.A. Paul, N. Pooran, R. Powell, R.A. Reifer, J.N.T. Seales, R. Shepherd, O.R. Thomas, H.R. Walsh. Coach, A. Coley.

West Indies A First-class Averages

BATTING	*M*	*I*	*NO*	*HS*	*Agg*	*Ave*	*100s*	*50s*	*Ct*	*St*
R. Shepherd	2	4	1	133	232	77.33	1	1	4	-
R.A. Reifer	1	2	1	65	65	65.00	-	1	-	-
N. Pooran	2	4	0	69	176	44.00	-	1	-	-
S.A.R. Moseley	2	4	0	110	171	42.75	1	1	1	-
K.M.A. Paul	1	2	0	43	47	23.50	-	-	1	-
F.A. Allen	2	4	0	35	80	20.00	-	-	1	-
J. Da Silva	1	2	1	15*	17	17.00	-	-	-	-
B.A. King	2	4	0	32	57	14.25	-	-	2	-
R. Powell	2	4	0	27	45	11.25	-	-	1	-
K.R. Mayers	2	4	0	19	30	7.50	-	-	2	-
H.R. Walsh	2	4	1	8	14	4.66	-	-	3	-
J.N.T. Seales	1	2	0	6	7	3.50	-	-	-	-
R.R.S. Cornwall	1	2	0	2	2	1.00	-	-	1	-
O.R. Thomas	1	1	1	0*	0	-	-	-	-	-

BOWLING	*O*	*M*	*R*	*W*	*Ave*	*Best*	*5w*	*10w*
N. Pooran	1	0	3	1	3.00	1-3	-	-
R.R.S. Cornwall	47.5	13	128	6	21.33	3-37	-	-
K.M.A. Paul	5	1	24	1	24.00	1-24	-	-
F.A. Allen	69.3	6	243	5	48.60	3-146	-	-
R.A. Reifer	19	3	49	1	49.00	1-49	-	-
H.R. Walsh	53.5	0	314	6	52.33	3-71	-	-
R. Shepherd	37	10	114	2	57.00	1-12	-	-
K.R. Mayers	23	2	60	1	60.00	1-44	-	-
J.N.T. Seales	21	4	76	1	76.00	1-53	-	-
B.A. King	7	0	28	0	-	-	-	-
R. Powell	6	1	46	0	-	-	-	-
O.R. Thomas	25	4	104	0	-	-	-	-

NEW ZEALAND A v WEST INDIES A — First-class

at Bay Oval, Mt Maunganui on 3, 4, 5, 6 December, 2020
Toss : New Zealand A. Umpires : J.M. Dempsey & T.J. Parlane
Close of play: 1st day: NZ A 10-0, Phillips 8, Seifert 2; 2nd day: NZ A 321-3, Carter 8, McConchie 7
3rd day: West Indies A 57-3, Pooran 25, Mayers 3
New Zealand A won by an innings and 143 runs

New Zealand A decided to bowl first after winning the toss and had the tourists in trouble at 113-7 before Reifer and Shepherd added 199 for the eighth wicket. Reifer got fifty from 132 balls while Shepherd got fifty from 76 balls and a maiden first-class hundred off a further 59. He reached his century with a six and then hit his next three balls for sixes as well. West Indies A were dismissed for 322. Duffy took four wickets and Smith three.

New Zealand A had a 226 run opening stand with both Phillips and Seifert reaching their sixth centuries. Phillips took 138 balls while Seifert needed 231. Cleaver and Smith both got fifties in a seventh wicket stand of 106. New Zealand A made 574.

West Indies A faced a deficit of 252 and lost Moseley in the second over and went from 53-1 to 109-8 with Reifer retired hurt and Thomas absent injured. Kuggeleijn got three wickets as New Zealand A won by an innings and 143 runs.

WEST INDIES A

FIRST INNINGS	*Runs*	*Mins*	*Balls*	*6s*	*4s*	*SECOND INNINGS*	*Runs*	*Mins*	*Balls*	*6s*	*4s*
B.A.King c Phillips b Bracewell	3	5	7	-	-	(2) c Seifert b Kuggeleijn	22	56	36	-	4
S.A.R.Moseley c Seifert b Duffy	2	18	8	-	-	(1) c Cleaver b Duffy	5	6	7	-	1
N.Pooran c Carter b Smith	46	105	74	-	7	c McConchie b Smith	35	120	61	-	4
R.Powell* c Cleaver b Smith	27	66	32	2	2	c Cleaver b Kuggeleijn	0	4	3	-	-
K.R.Mayers c Sodhi b Smith	0	3	3	-	-	c Duffy b Kuggeleijn	11	31	25	-	1
J.Da Silva† c Cleaver b Kuggeleijn	2	28	17	-	-	not out	15	84	51	-	1
R.A.Reifer c Cleaver b Duffy	65	245	162	-	6	retired hurt	0	8	6	-	-
F.A.Allen c Cleaver b Duffy	19	38	31	-	4	c Bracewell b Smith	5	20	14	-	-
R.Shepherd c McConchie b Duffy	133	214	154	7	14	c Chapman b Duffy	11	16	13	1	1
H.R.Walsh lbw b Bracewell	8	10	8	-	2	c & b Sodhi	1	5	4	-	-
O.R.Thomas not out	0	3	1	-	-	absent hurt					
Extras (b 5, lb 7, w 1, nb 4)	17					(nb 4)	4				
TOTAL (82.1 overs)	**322**	370				(36 overs)	**109**	177			

NEW ZEALAND A

	Runs	Mins	Balls	6s	4s
G.D.Phillips c & b Walsh	136	240	184	5	15
T.L.Seifert lbw b Reifer	111	351	241	-	8
M.S.Chapman c Shepherd b Pooran	45	117	84	-	7
J.F.Carter c King b Mayers	35	118	81	-	3
C.E.McConchie b Shepherd	8	48	26	-	-
D.Cleaver† c & b Walsh	85	192	152	-	5
D.A.J.Bracewell c Shepherd b Allen	29	49	38	1	3
N.G.Smith c Walsh b Allen	76	108	84	1	5
S.C.Kuggeleijn c Mayers b Walsh	13	22	19	1	-
I.S.Sodhi b Allen	6	9	9	1	-
J.A.Duffy* not out	0	2	0	-	-
Extras (b 15, lb 10, w 4, nb 1)	30				
TOTAL (152.5 overs)	**574**	629			

Bowling	*O*	*M*	*R*	*W*	*O*	*M*	*R*	*W*
NEW ZEALAND A								
Duffy	18.1	4	47	4	10	3	27	2
Bracewell	17	2	62	2	9	0	37	0
Kuggeleijn	19	4	58	1	8	1	18	3
Smith	10	1	37	3	6	2	17	2
McConchie	8	0	58	0				
Sodhi	10	0	48	0	3	0	10	1
WEST INDIES A								
Thomas	25	4	104	0				
Reifer	19	3	49	1				
Shepherd	20	6	58	1				
Powell	3	0	37	0				
Mayers	16	0	44	1				
Allen	44.5	3	146	3				
Walsh	24	0	108	3				
Pooran	1	0	3	1				

Fall of Wickets

	WIA	*NZA*	*WIA*
	1st	*1st*	*2nd*
1st	3	226	6
2nd	13	306	53
3rd	79	308	53
4th	79	341	68
5th	88	377	85
6th	88	422	93
7th	113	528	106
8th	312	558	109
9th	322	574	-
10th	322	574	-

Reifer retired hurt at 85-5

NEW ZEALAND A v WEST INDIES A — First-class

at Saxton Oval, Nelson on 11, 12, 13, 14 December, 2020
Toss : New Zealand A. Umpires : J.M. Dempsey & G.A. Stirrat
Close of play: 1st day: NZ A 264-4, M.G.Bracewell 93, Ravindra 30; 2nd day: West Indies A 142-5, Moseley 56, Paul 35
3rd day: West Indies A 26-0, King 8, Mayers 15
New Zealand A won by 101 runs

New Zealand A decided to bat after winning the toss and made an imposing 481-7. Michael Bracewell made his ninth century after 200 balls as he and Ravindra added 161. Ravindra got his second hundred and highest score. His hundred came from 155 balls. Cornwall took three wickets.

West Indies made 298 thanks mainly to Moseley getting his fourth hundred off 240 balls. Doug Bracewell took 6-42, his tenth five wicket bag. New Zealand A changed their batting order in their second innings and declared at 174-7. Cornwall got another three wickets as did Walsh.

West Indies were set 358 to win but never really threatened. Moseley got fifty from 115 balls and Pooran had his highest score. Ravindra was the star getting his first five wicket bag and joining the select group of players to have scored a century and taken six wickets in an innings in the same match. West Indies were dismissed for 256 to give New Zealand A a 101 run win.

NEW ZEALAND A

FIRST INNINGS	*Runs*	*Mins*	*Balls*	*6s*	*4s*	*SECOND INNINGS*	*Runs*	*Mins*	*Balls*	*6s*	*4s*
G.D.Phillips c Mayers b Seales	13	45	34	-	1	c Allen b Cornwall	9	14	13	-	1
T.L.Seifert c Moseley b Allen	60	218	162	-	3	lbw b Cornwall	13	25	16	-	2
M.S.Chapman b Paul	45	103	77	1	8	b Cornwall	40	61	45	-	4
M.G.Bracewell c Shepherd b Cornwall	135	298	235	-	14	(7) b Walsh	0	2	1	-	-
J.D.S.Neesham c Paul b Allen	10	58	50	-	-	(4) c Powell b Walsh	38	48	37	-	4
R.Ravindra not out	144	270	174	3	9	(8) c Cornwall b Shepherd	22	29	20	1	1
C.D.Fletcher† lbw b Cornwall	48	84	74	-	5	(9) not out	1	7	1	-	-
D.A.J.Bracewell* c Shepherd b Cornwall	5	16	7	-	-	(6) c King b Walsh	12	13	10	-	1
S.C.Kuggeleijn						(5) not out	34	55	25	2	1
I.S.Sodhi											
B.M.Tickner											
Extras (b 5, lb 6, w 4, nb 6)	21					(lb 4, nb 1)	5				
TOTAL (134.3 overs) (7 wkts dec)	**481**	547				(27.5 overs) (7 wkts dec)	**174**	129			

WEST INDIES A

	Runs	*Mins*	*Balls*	*6s*	*4s*		*Runs*	*Mins*	*Balls*	*6s*	*4s*
S.A.R.Moseley c Fletcher b Bracewell D.A.J.	110	365	267	-	11	(3) c Kuggeleijn b Bracewell M.G.	54	159	126	2	2
B.A.King b Bracewell D.A.J.	0	2	3	-	-	(1) b Ravindra	32	113	74	-	3
K.R.Mayers c Phillips b Bracewell D.A.J.	0	10	5	-	-	(2) c Fletcher b Bracewell D.A.J.	19	49	39	-	3
R.Powell b Kuggeleijn	0	14	9	-	-	c Bracewell M.G. b Ravindra	18	51	42		2
N.Pooran*† c Kuggeleijn b Tickner	26	48	31	-	6	c Fletcher b Ravindra	69	95	63	4	6
F.A.Allen c Bracewell D.A.J. b Sodhi	21	45	29	1	2	c Fletcher b Tickner	35	54	32	2	5
K.M.A.Paul lbw b Bracewell D.A.J.	43	97	56	3	2	c Fletcher b Ravindra	4	12	3	-	1
R.Shepherd not out	77	182	101	4	6	lbw b Tickner	11	19	17	1	-
R.R.S.Cornwall lbw b Bracewell D.A.J.	0	10	6	-	-	b Ravindra	2	15	4	-	-
H.R.Walsh b Bracewell D.A.J.	4	4	4	-	1	not out	1	16	7	-	-
J.N.T.Seales c Fletcher b Tickner	6	30	25	-	1	b Ravindra	1	10	11	-	-
Extras (lb 5, w 1, nb 5)	11					(b 5, lb 2, nb 3)	10				
TOTAL (88.3 overs)	**298**	536				(69.3 overs)	**256**	297			

Bowling	*O*	*M*	*R*	*W*	*O*	*M*	*R*	*W*
WEST INDIES A								
Mayers	7	2	16	0				
Seales	18	4	53	1	3	0	23	0
Shepherd	15	4	44	0	2	0	12	1
Paul	5	1	24	1				
Cornwall	37.5	10	91	3	10	3	37	3
Powell	3	1	9	0				
Allen	22.4	3	82	2	2	0	15	0
King	4	0	16	0	3	0	12	0
Walsh	22	0	135	0	7.5	0	71	3
NEW ZEALAND A								
Bracewell D.A.J.	15	5	42	6	10	1	35	1
Kuggeleijn	16	2	56	1	6	5	4	0
Neesham	7	3	16	0	4	1	19	0
Tickner	12.3	2	34	2	14	5	28	2
Sodhi	17	3	56	1	6	1	15	0
Ravindra	13	0	56	0	19.3	1	89	6
Bracewell M.G.	3	0	17	0	7	1	37	1
Phillips	5	0	16	0	3	0	22	0

Fall of Wickets

	NZA 1st	***WIA 1st***	***NZA 2nd***	***WIA 2nd***
1st	31	1	17	31
2nd	101	5	27	74
3rd	152	7	103	106
4th	187	47	105	159
5th	348	83	124	236
6th	455	162	125	236
7th	481	277	156	248
8th	-	277	-	254
9th	-	282	-	254
10th	-	298	-	256

PAKISTAN A
IN NEW ZEALAND

Pakistan A made a six match tour which included a first-class game against New Zealand A and five unofficial Twenty20 matches against Northern Districts, Wellington, Canterbury and a New Zealand XI. These games took place at the same time as the national side was playing New Zealand in Twenty20 internationals or test matches. Two other games were cancelled.

In the first-class match Fawad Alam and Rohail Nazir both scored centuries while Amad Butt, Mohammad Abbas and Yasir Shah all took five wickets or more.

The squad was: Rohail Nazar *(captain)*, Abdullah Shafiq, Abid Ali, Amad Butt, Azhar Ali, Danish Aziz, Fawad Alam, Haider Ali, Haris Rauf, Hussain Talat, Iftikhar Ahmed, Imran Butt, Khushdil Shah, Mohammad Abbas, Mohammad Hasnain, Musa Khan, Naseem Shah, Shan Masood, Sohail Khan, Usman Qadir, Wahab Riaz, Yasir Shah, Zeeshan Malik. Coach and manager, Ijaz Ahmed.

NEW ZEALAND A v PAKISTAN A

At McLean Park, Napier 10, 11, 12, 13 December, 2020 (First-class)

Match cancelled due to Covid concerns delaying the beginning of training sessions for the Pakistan players

NEW ZEALAND A v PAKISTAN A — First-class

at Cobham Oval, Whangarei on 17, 18, 19, 20 December, 2020
Toss : New Zealand A. Umpires : J.M. Dempsey & D.J. Walker
Close of play: 1st day: NZA 23-1, Ravindra 11, McClure 11; 2nd day: Pakistan A 15-1, Shan Masood 10, Azhar Ali 2
3rd day: Pakistan A 318-9, Mohammad Abbas 0, Naseem Shah 1
Pakistan A won by 89 runs

New Zealand A decided to bowl and after losing two early wickets Pakistan A never really recovered, reaching 194. Azhar made a patient fifty. Nuttall took five wickets and Smith three.

The home side made 224 with Ravindra getting 70. Fletcher and Nuttall added 76 for the ninth wicket. Abbas took four wickets while Amad and Yasir took three each.

Pakistan A were 64-4 before Fawad and Rohail added 215 for the fifth wicket. Both made centuries from 181 and 163 balls respectively. Henry took 6-53 and Rae had three wickets as Pakistan A made 329.

New Zealand A needed 298 to win but never threatened as batsmen got starts but no one made a fifty. Naseem and Amad both took three wickets as the visitors dismissed the home side for 208, giving them an 89 run win.

PAKISTAN A

FIRST INNINGS	*Runs*	*Mins*	*Balls*	*6s*	*4s*	*SECOND INNINGS*	*Runs*	*Mins*	*Balls*	*6s*	*4s*
Shan Masood lbw b Nuttall	8	14	16	-	1	c Bracewell b Henry	14	50	33	-	1
Abid Ali c Fletcher b Nuttall	7	33	25	-	-	b Nuttall	1	6	5	-	-
Azhar Ali c Bracewell b Nuttall	58	297	172	-	3	lbw b Rae	29	102	65	-	3
Imran Butt c Fletcher b Smith	27	100	77	-	4	c Ravindra b Rae	10	43	22	-	-
Fawad Alam c Smith b Nuttall	3	23	10	-	-	c Fletcher b Henry	139	320	233	-	11
Rohail Nazir*† c Carter b Henry	21	55	37	-	4	c Cooper b Henry	100	246	164	2	11
Amad Butt lbw b Nuttall	13	21	21	-	2	c Carter b Henry	0	10	9	-	-
Yasir Shah c Carter b Smith	18	42	33	-	3	c Cooper b Henry	8	20	16	-	1
Sohail Khan c McClure b Smith	0	1	1	-	-	c sub (S.M.Solia) b Rae	3	23	7	-	-
Mohammad Abbas not out	18	40	40	-	2	not out	2	23	10	-	-
Naseem Shah st Fletcher b Rippon	3	14	10	-	-	b Henry	10	18	17	-	2
Extras (b 8, lb 3, w 3, nb 4)	18					(lb 11, nb 2)	13				
TOTAL (73 overs)	**194**	339				(96.3 overs)	**329**	433			

NEW ZEALAND A

	Runs	*Mins*	*Balls*	*6s*	*4s*		*Runs*	*Mins*	*Balls*	*6s*	*4s*
H.R.Cooper c Imran b Abbas	0	10	11	-	-	c Yasir b Sohail	1	6	4	-	-
R.Ravindra lbw b Abbas	70	255	158	1	8	b Amad	17	83	50	-	1
K.J.McClure c Rohail b Amad	24	90	60	-	4	c Rohail b Naseem	22	81	43	1	1
J.F.Carter c Abbas b Amad	1	21	8	-	-	lbw b Naseem	30	74	39	-	5
M.G.Bracewell*c Imran b Amad	0	3	2	-	-	b Naseem	30	79	55	-	5
N.G.Smith lbw b Yasir	40	41	86	-	5	c Rohail b Amad	45	142	108	1	4
C.D.Fletcher† b Abbas	57	139	108	1	6	b Yasir	7	22	19	-	-
M.J.G.Rippon b Yasir	0	3	4	-	-	lbw b Abbas	7	35	16	-	1
M.J.Henry st Rohail b Yasir	9	9	9	-	2	c Amad b Yasir	6	11	6	-	1
E.J.Nuttall not out	14	118	55	-	2	not out	24	73	41	-	5
M.D.Rae lbw b Abbas	0	2	1	-	-	c Fawad b Amad	4	10	9	-	1
Extras (lb 4, w 2, nb 5)	11					(lb 8, w 1, nb 6)	15				
TOTAL (82.5 overs)	**226**	397				(64 overs)	**208**	311			

Bowling	*O*	*M*	*R*	*W*	*O*	*M*	*R*	*W*
NEW ZEALAND A								
Henry	19	3	54	1	25.3	6	53	6
Nuttall	17	1	54	5	5	1	17	1
Rae	15	4	36	0	18	3	85	3
Smith	18	5	29	3	13	4	28	0
Ravindra	1	0	2	0	12	1	48	0
Rippon	3	0	8	1	15	4	44	0
Bracewell					8	1	43	0
PAKISTAN A								
Sohail	18	5	51	0	8	2	27	1
Abbas	21.5	9	40	4	15	5	34	1
Naseem	16	3	55	0	12	1	44	3
Amad	10	3	22	3	11	3	38	3
Yasir	17	2	54	3	17	3	55	2
Fawad					1	0	2	0

Fall of Wickets

	PA *1st*	***NZA*** *1st*	***PA*** *2nd*	***NZA*** *2nd*
1st	16	3	2	2
2nd	17	61	26	42
3rd	66	67	49	42
4th	76	67	64	108
5th	114	134	279	113
6th	131	140	281	128
7th	161	140	295	148
8th	161	150	312	158
9th	178	226	317	200
10th	194	226	329	208

NEW ZEALAND XI v PAKISTAN A

At Cobham Oval, Whangarei 23 December, 2020 (Twenty20)

Match cancelled

NORTHERN DISTRICTS v PAKISTAN A
At Seddon Park, Hamilton   27 December, 2020

Northern Districts 203-2 (T.L. Seifert 99*, K.D. Clarke 40, A.P. Devcich 38*) **defeated Pakistan A** 182-9 (Zeeshan Malik 52, Haider Ali 51, J.H. Brown 3-42) by 21 runs

WELLINGTON v PAKISTAN A
At Basin Reserve, Wellington   29 December, 2020

Pakistan A 91 (J.D. Gibson 3-30) **lost to Wellington** 97-1 (D.P. Conway 48*, R. Ravindra 35*) by 9 wickets

CANTERBURY v PAKISTAN A
At Bert Sutcliffe Oval, Lincoln   1 January, 2021

Canterbury 169-5 (H.J. Chamberlain 66*, T.M. Lortan 51) **lost to Pakistan A** 170-3 (Rohail Nazir 69*, Hussain Talat 53*) by 7 wickets

NEW ZEALAND XI v PAKISTAN A
At Bert Sutcliffe Oval, Lincoln   3 January, 2021

Pakistan A 231-5 (Haider Ali 64, Zeeshan Malik 54, Hussain Talat 44*, Abdullah Shafiq 35) **defeated New Zealand XI** 130 (R.A. Mariu 48, Usman Qadir 3-18) by 101 runs

NEW ZEALAND XI v PAKISTAN A
At Bert Sutcliffe Oval, Lincoln   5 January, 2021

New Zealand XI 181-5 (J.F. Carter 81*) **defeated Pakistan A** 161 (Khushdil Shah 70, Hussain Talat 44, J.J.N.P. Bhula 3-9, A. Ashok 3-24) by 20 runs

(all games were unofficial Twenty20 games)

PAKISTAN IN NEW ZEALAND

Pakistan played three Twenty20 internationals and two test matches against New Zealand. They lost the Twenty20 series 2-1 and the test series 2-0. The team was affected by injuries to captain Babar Azam who never played after fracturing a finger and also to Imam-ul-Haq. The stand-in captain for the Twenty20s, Shadab Khan, was also injured.

Pakistan struggled at times with their batting and were inconsistent and prone to collapses. They also had many lapses in the field which proved very costly. The bowling attack was centred around Shaheen Shah Afridi.

Hafeez scored an unbeaten 99 and Rizwan got 89 in the Twenty20s but these were the only fifties. Rauf took five wickets followed by Faheem and Afridi with four.

In the test matches the only century was scored by Fawad Alam but the leading runs scorers were Rizwan, Faheem and Azhar. These were the only players to get fifties. Afridi took six wickets with Abbas and Naseem taking four each.

The touring party was: Twenty 20: Babar Azam *(captain)*, Abdullah Shafiq, Faheem Ashraf, Haider Ali, Haris Rauf, Hussain Talat, Iftikhar Ahmed, Imad Wasim, Khushdil Shah, Mohammad Hafeez, Mohammad Hasnain, Mohammad Rizwan, Musa Khan, Sarfraz Ahmed, Shadab Khan, Shaheen Shah Afridi, Usman Qadir, Wahab Riaz.

Test: Babar Azam *(captain)*, Abid Ali, Azhar Ali, Faheem Ashraf, Fawad Alam, Haris Sohail, Imam-ul-Haq, Imran Butt, Mohammad Abbas, Mohammad Rizwan, Naseem Shah, Sarfraz Ahmed, Shadab Khan, Shaheen Shah Afridi, Shan Masood, Sohail Khan, Yasir Shah, Zafar Gohar. Coach, Misbah-ul-Haq; Manager, Mansoor Rana.

New Zealand Test Averages

BATTING	*M*	*I*	*NO*	*HS*	*Agg*	*Ave*	*100s*	*50s*	*Ct*	*St*
K.S. Williamson	2	3	0	238	388	129.33	2	-	-	-
H.M. Nicholls	2	3	0	157	224	74.66	1	1	3	-
K.A. Jamieson	2	2	1	32	62	62.00	-	-	1	-
L.R.P.L. Taylor	2	3	1	70	94	47.00	-	1	6	-
T.W.M. Latham	2	3	0	53	90	30.00	-	1	2	-
B-J. Watling	2	3	0	73	85	28.33	-	1	14	-
T.A. Blundell	2	3	0	64	85	28.33	-	1	-	-
M.J. Santner	1	2	1	19	25	25.00	-	-	2	-
N. Wagner	1	1	0	19	19	19.00	-	-	-	-
T.G. Southee	2	1	0	0	0	0.00	-	-	3	-
D.J. Mitchell	1	1	1	102*	102	-	1	-	-	-
T.A. Boult	2	1	1	8*	8	-	-	-	-	-
M.J. Henry	1	-	-	-	-	-	-	-	1	-

BOWLING	*O*	*M*	*R*	*W*	*Ave*	*Best*	*5w*	*10w*
K.A. Jamieson	90.2	40	187	16	11.68	6-48	2	1
K.S. Williamson	5	1	17	1	17.00	1-16	-	-
N. Wagner	49	14	105	4	26.25	2-50	-	-
M.J. Santner	25.3	5	59	2	29.50	2-52	-	-
T.A. Boult	90.3	22	268	9	29.77	3-43	-	-
T.G. Southee	92	30	208	6	34.66	2-33	-	-
M.J. Henry	32	7	93	1	93.00	1-68	-	-
D.J. Mitchell	7	2	14	0	-	-	-	-

Pakistan Test Averages

BATTING	*M*	*I*	*NO*	*HS*	*Agg*	*Ave*	*100s*	*50s*	*Ct*	*St*
Mohammad Rizwan	2	4	0	71	202	50.50	-	3	4	-
Faheem Ashraf	2	4	0	91	186	46.50	-	1	-	-
Azhar Ali	2	4	0	93	173	43.25	-	1	1	-
Zafar Gohar	1	2	0	37	71	35.50	-	-	-	-
Fawad Alam	2	4	0	102	129	32.25	1	-	-	-
Abid Ali	2	4	0	26	76	19.00	-	-	1	-
Shaheen Afridi	2	4	1	8*	25	8.33	-	-	-	-
Haris Sohail	2	4	0	15	28	7.00	-	-	3	-
Naseem Shah	2	4	2	12	13	6.50	-	-	1	-
Mohammad Abbas	2	4	1	5	9	3.00	-	-	1	-
Shan Masood	2	4	0	10	10	2.50	-	-	4	-
Yasir Shah	1	2	0	4	4	2.00	-	-	2	-

BOWLING	*O*	*M*	*R*	*W*	*Ave*	*Best*	*5w*	*10w*
Shaheen Afridi	82.5	15	257	6	42.83	4-109	-	-
Yasir Shah	43	4	134	3	44.66	3-113	-	-
Mohammad Abbas	76	27	180	4	45.00	2-98	-	-
Faheem Ashraf	51	13	164	3	54.66	2-106	-	-
Naseem Shah	63.3	6	292	4	73.00	3-55	-	-
Haris Sohail	6	0	19	0	-	-	-	-
Shan Masood	5	1	23	0	-	-	-	-
Zafar Gohar	32	0	159	0	-	-	-	-

NEW ZEALAND v PAKISTAN First Twenty20 International

at Eden Park, Auckland on 18 December, 2020 (d/n)
Toss : Pakistan. Umpires : S.B. Haig & W.R. Knights
New Zealand won by 5 wickets

Duffy made his debut as New Zealand were without four players from the test squad. Pakistan decided to bat first but Duffy got a wicket in his first over and finished with 4-33. At one stage Pakistan were 39-5 but Shadab and Faheem, who both made their highest scores, saw them through to 153-9. Kuggeleijn had his best bowling figures.

New Zealand were 21-2 before Seifert hit a 35-ball fifty and New Zealand reached 156-5 from 18.5 overs. Rauf got three wickets.

PAKISTAN

	Runs	Mins	Balls	6s	4s
Mohammad Rizwan† c Phillips b Duffy	17	16	17	-	3
Abdullah Shafiq c Chapman b Duffy	0	5	2	-	-
Haider Ali c & b Kuggeleijn	3	14	5	-	-
Mohammad Hafeez c Chapman b Duffy	0	1	1	-	-
Shadab Khan* c Sodhi b Duffy	42	61	32	3	2
Khushdil Shah c Guptill b Sodhi	16	17	20	-	2
Imad Wasim c Tickner b Kuggeleijn	19	22	14	-	2
Faheem Ashraf c Guptill b Tickner	31	30	18	3	2
Wahab Riaz c Santner b Kuggeleijn	9	5	5	1	-
Shaheen Afridi not out	10	8	5	1	-
Haris Rauf not out	0	2	1		
Extras (b 2, lb 1, w 3)	6				
TOTAL (20 overs) (9 wkts)	**153**	95			

NEW ZEALAND

	Runs	Mins	Balls	6s	4s
M.J.Guptill c Shadab b Afridi	6	8	10	-	1
T.L.Seifert† c Faheem b Afridi	57	67	43	1	6
D.P.Conway c & b Rauf	5	9	4	-	1
G.D.Phillips c Khushdil b Rauf	23	24	18	1	2
M.S.Chapman lbw b Rauf	34	33	20	1	4
J.D.S.Neesham not out	15	26	10	2	-
M.J.Santner* not out	12	16	8	1	-
S.C.Kuggeleijn					
I.S.Sodhi					
J.A.Duffy					
B.M.Tickner					
Extras (lb 1, w 3)	4				
TOTAL (18.5 overs) (5 wkts)	**156**	94			

Bowling	*O*	*M*	*R*	*W*
NEW ZEALAND				
Santner	4	0	18	0
Duffy	4	0	33	4
Kuggeleijn	4	0	27	3
Sodhi	4	0	37	1
Tickner	4	0	35	1
PAKISTAN				
Afridi	4	0	27	2
Imad	2	0	14	0
Rauf	4	0	29	3
Faheem	3	0	18	0
Wahab	3.5	0	45	0
Shadab	2	0	22	0

Fall of Wickets	*P*	*NZ*
1st	8	8
2nd	20	21
3rd	20	65
4th	20	110
5th	39	129
6th	79	-
7th	114	-
8th	136	-
9th	149	-
10th	-	-

NEW ZEALAND v PAKISTAN Second Twenty20 International

at Seddon Park, Hamilton on 20 December, 2020 (d/n)
Toss : Pakistan. Umpires : C.M. Brown & S.B. Haig
New Zealand won by 9 wickets

New Zealand made four changes with Williamson, Southee, Jamieson and Boult replacing Chapman, Tickner, Santner and Duffy.

Pakistan again decided to bat and were soon 33-3 with Southee getting all three wickets. Hafeez dominated the innings and made his highest score. He scored 16 from the last three balls to be unbeaten on 99 as Pakistan made 163-6. Southee finished with 4-21.

Guptill made a quick 21 before Seifert and Williamson broke the New Zealand second wicket stand with an unbeaten 129 from 95 balls. Seifert needed 32 balls for his fifty, five fewer than Williamson. He made his highest score as New Zealand won by nine wickets and four balls to spare.

PAKISTAN

	Runs	Mins	Balls	6s	4s
Mohammad Rizwan† c Seifert b Southee	22	26	20	-	4
Haider Ali c Williamson b Southee	8	6	4	1	-
Abdullah Shafiq c & b Southee	0	1	2	-	-
Mohammad Hafeez not out	99	86	57	5	10
Shadab Khan* c Southee b Neesham	4	14	7	-	1
Khushdil Shah c Guptill b Sodhi	14	31	20	-	1
Faheem Ashraf c Williamson b Southee	4	9	5	-	-
Imad Wasim not out	10	11	5	-	2
Wahab Riaz					
Shaheen Afridi					
Haris Rauf					
Extras (lb 2)	2				
TOTAL (20 overs) (6 wkts)	**163**	95			

NEW ZEALAND

	Runs	Mins	Balls	6s	4s
M.J.Guptill c Rauf b Faheem	21	16	11	2	1
T.L.Seifert† not out	84	80	63	3	8
K.S.Williamson* not out	57	64	42	1	8
D.P.Conway					
G.D.Phillips					
J.D.S.Neesham					
K.A.Jamieson					
S.C.Kuggeleijn					
T.G.Southee					
I.S.Sodhi					
T.A.Boult					
Extras (w 2)	2				
TOTAL (19.2 overs) (1 wkt)	**164**	80			

Bowling	*O*	*M*	*R*	*W*
NEW ZEALAND				
Boult	4	0	33	0
Southee	4	0	21	4
Jamieson	4	0	43	0
Kuggeleijn	3	0	33	0
Neesham	2	0	10	1
Sodhi	3	0	21	1
PAKISTAN				
Afridi	4	0	38	0
Rauf	4	0	39	0
Faheem	3.2	0	19	1
Wahab	1	0	19	0
Shadab	4	0	24	0
Imad	3	0	25	0

Fall of Wickets	*P*	*NZ*
1st	16	35
2nd	16	-
3rd	33	-
4th	56	-
5th	119	-
6th	133	-
7th	-	-
8th	-	-
9th	-	-
10th	-	-

NEW ZEALAND v PAKISTAN — Third Twenty20 International

at McLean Park, Napier on 22 December, 2020 (d/n)
Toss : Pakistan. Umpires : C.M. Brown & W.R. Knights
Pakistan won by 4 wickets

New Zealand were unchanged while Pakistan made three changes. Iftikhar, Talat and Hasnain replaced Shafiq, Wasim and Riaz.

Pakistan again won the toss but decided to bowl first. New Zealand had a good start with a 40 run opening stand but then lost three quick wickets. Conway and Phillips then added 51 for the fourth wicket. Conway reached fifty from 39 balls as New Zealand made 173-7. Faheem got three wickets while Afridi and Rauf took two each.

Rizwan and Hafeez added 72 from 49 balls for Pakistan's second wicket. Rizwan reached his maiden fifty off 40 balls to steer the tourists to a four wicket win with two balls remaining. Southee and Kuggeleijn both took two wickets.

NEW ZEALAND

	Runs	Mins	Balls	6s	4s
M.J.Guptill c Shadab b Rauf	19	21	16	1	2
T.L.Seifert† b Faheem	35	36	20	3	2
K.S.Williamson* b Faheem	1	6	4	-	-
D.P.Conway c Shadab b Rauf	63	75	45	1	7
G.D.Phillips c Rauf b Afridi	31	35	20	-	4
J.D.S.Neesham c Shadab b Faheem	2	12	4	-	-
S.C.Kuggeleijn c Iftikhar b Afridi	14	11	6	1	1
T.G.Southee not out	6	7	6	-	-
K.A.Jamieson not out	0	2	0	-	-
I.S.Sodhi					
T.A.Boult					
Extras (lb 1, nb 1)	2				
TOTAL (20 overs) (7 wkts)	**173**	104			

PAKISTAN

	Runs	Mins	Balls	6s	4s
Mohammad Rizwan† c Conway b Jamieson	89	103	59	3	10
Haider Ali c sub (D.J.Mitchell) b Kuggeleijn	11	25	9	-	1
Mohammad Hafeez c sub (D.J.Mitchell) b Kuggeleijn	41	41	29	3	2
Khushdil Shah c sub (D.J.Mitchell) b Neesham	13	16	10	-	2
Faheem Ashraf c Seifert b Southee	2	11	3	-	-
Shadab Khan* c Seifert b Southee	0	1	1	-	-
Iftikhar Ahmed not out	14	8	7	1	1
Hussain Talat not out	0	2	0	-	-
Mohammad Hasnain					
Haris Rauf					
Shaheen Afridi					
Extras (lb 4, w 3)	7				
TOTAL (19.4 overs) (6 wkts)	**177**	105			

Bowling	*O*	*M*	*R*	*W*
PAKISTAN				
Afridi	4	0	43	2
Hasnain	4	0	29	0
Rauf	4	0	44	2
Faheem	4	0	20	3
Shadab	4	0	36	0
NEW ZEALAND				
Boult	4	0	43	0
Southee	4	0	25	2
Jamieson	2.4	0	22	1
Kuggeleijn	4	0	40	2
Sodhi	1	0	6	0
Neesham	4	0	37	1

Fall of Wickets	***NZ***	***P***
1st	40	40
2nd	45	112
3rd	58	141
4th	109	163
5th	128	163
6th	159	171
7th	169	-
8th	-	-
9th	-	-
10th	-	-

NEW ZEALAND v PAKISTAN — First Test

at Bay Oval, Mt Maunganui on 26, 27, 28, 29, 30 December, 2020
Toss : Pakistan. Umpires : C.B. Gaffaney & W.R. Knights
Close of play: 1st day: NZ 222-3, Williamson 94, Nicholls 42; 2nd day: Pakistan 30-1, Abid Ali 19, Mohammad Abbas 0
3rd day: Pakistan 239 all out; 4th day: Pakistan 71-3, Azhar Ali 34, Fawad Alam 21
New Zealand won by 101 runs

New Zealand made one change from its previous test side with Santner replacing Mitchell. Rizwan captained Pakistan for the first time.

Pakistan decided to field first and had early success with both New Zealand openers out for 13. Williamson was then associated in century stands with Taylor and Nicholls. 120 runs were added for the third wicket and 133 for the fourth. Williamson scored fifty from 154 balls and went to his 23rd century off 261 deliveries. Taylor scored fifty from 127 balls and Nicholls took 108 for his half-century. Watling later scored fifty from 111 balls as New Zealand made 431. Afridi took four wickets and Yasir three.

Pakistan made a poor start losing six wickets for 80 before Rizwan and Faheem added 107 for the seventh wicket. Rizwan got fifty from 106 balls, 19 more than Faheem who made his highest score. Pakistan were dismissed for 239.

With a 192 run lead New Zealand had an opening stand of 111. Blundell got fifty from 87 balls, 20 faster than Latham. New Zealand declared at 180-5 with a lead of 372.

Pakistan then lost both openers within three overs and were soon 75-4. Haris became Southee's 300th test wicket. Fawad and Rizwan then added 165 for the fifth wicket from 63.2 overs. Fawad reached his second century off 236 balls and Rizwan got his second fifty of the match from 156 deliveries. Fawad became Watling's 250th victim as a wicket-keeper.

Only three players passed 20 as Pakistan collapsed, losing six wickets for 31 runs and being bowled out for 271. All five major bowlers took two wickets each. Wagner had bowled throughout the innings with two broken toes suffered while batting. New Zealand won by 101 runs.

NEW ZEALAND

FIRST INNINGS	*Runs*	*Mins*	*Balls*	*6s*	*4s*	*SECOND INNINGS*	*Runs*	*Mins*	*Balls*	*6s*	*4s*
T.W.M.Latham c Azhar b Afridi	4	2	3	-	1	c Abid b Naseem	53	185	112	-	3
T.A.Blundell c Yasir b Afridi	5	47	29	-	-	b Abbas	64	149	107	-	7
K.S.Williamson* c Sohail b Yasir	129	476	297	1	12	c Rizwan b Naseem	21	48	33	-	2
L.R.P.L.Taylor c Rizwan b Afridi	70	205	151	1	10	not out	12	39	13	-	1
H.M.Nicholls c Masood b Naseem	56	203	137	-	5	c Abbas b Naseem	11	12	5	-	2
B-J.Watling† c Yasir b Afridi	73	216	145	-	8	run out	5	5	3	-	1
M.J.Santner c Rizwan b Faheem	19	56	43	1	2	not out	6	9	5	-	1
K.A.Jamieson c Rizwan b Abbas	32	87	69	1	1						
T.G.Southee b Yasir	0	11	9	-	-						
N.Wagner c Masood b Yasir	19	54	36	-	2						
T.A.Boult not out	8	15	17	-	-						
Extras (lb 5, w 5, nb 6)	16					(lb 2, w 1, nb 5)	8				
TOTAL (155 overs)	**431**	688				(45.3 overs) (5 wkts dec)	**180**	224			

PAKISTAN

	Runs	*Mins*	*Balls*	*6s*	*4s*		*Runs*	*Mins*	*Balls*	*6s*	*4s*
Shan Masood c Watling b Jamieson	10	66	42	-	-	c Taylor b Southee	0	11	8	-	-
Abid Ali b Jamieson	25	137	104	-	3	c Watling b Boult	0	5	2	-	-
Mohammad Abbas c Taylor b Boult	5	79	55	-	1	(9) lbw b Santner	1	42	26	-	-
Azhar Ali c Watling b Southee	5	48	34	-	-	(3) c Watling b Boult	38	170	120	-	5
Haris Sohail c Nicholls b Southee	3	45	22	-	-	(4) c Santner b Southee	9	69	46	-	-
Fawad Alam c Watling b Wagner	9	80	42	-	-	(5) c Watling b Wagner	102	396	269	-	14
Mohammad Rizwan*† run out	71	205	142	-	8	(6) lbw b Jamieson	60	285	191	-	6
Faheem Ashraf c Watling b Jamieson	91	193	134	1	15	(7) c Watling b Wagner	19	42	28	-	4
Yasir Shah b Boult	4	9	7	-	1	(8) c Southee b Jamieson	0	12	5	-	-
Shaheen Afridi c Latham b Wagner	6	48	30	-	1	not out	8	62	30	-	2
Naseem Shah not out	0	4	3	-	-	c & b Santner	1	34	24	-	-
Extras (b 3, lb 4, w 2, nb 1)	10					(b 16, lb 7, w 2, nb 8)	33				
TOTAL (102.2 overs)	**239**	458				(123.3 overs)	**271**	566			

Bowling	*O*	*M*	*R*	*W*	*O*	*M*	*R*	*W*
PAKISTAN								
Afridi	36	7	109	4	11	0	47	0
Abbas	31	14	49	1	11	2	33	1
Faheem	19	8	40	1	4	1	18	0
Naseem	25	3	96	1	12.3	1	55	3
Yasir	37	4	113	3	6	0	21	0
Masood	2	1	2	0	1	0	4	0
Sohail	5	0	17	0				
NEW ZEALAND								
Southee	26	7	69	2	23	8	33	2
Boult	26	4	71	2	25	9	72	2
Jamieson	23.2	13	35	3	26	13	35	2
Wagner	21	5	50	2	28	9	55	2
Santner	6	2	7	0	19.3	3	52	2
Williamson					2	1	1	0

Fall of Wickets

	NZ 1st	*P 1st*	*NZ 2nd*	*P 2nd*
1st	4	28	111	0
2nd	13	39	139	0
3rd	133	43	147	37
4th	266	51	165	75
5th	281	52	170	240
6th	317	80	-	242
7th	383	187	-	251
8th	388	196	-	259
9th	421	235	-	261
10th	431	239	-	271

NEW ZEALAND v PAKISTAN — Second Test

at Hagley Oval, Christchurch on 3, 4, 5, 6 January, 2021
Toss : New Zealand. Umpires : C.M. Brown & C.B. Gaffaney
Close of play: 1st day: Pakistan 297 all out; 2nd day: NZ 286-3, Williamson 112, Nicholls 89
3rd day: Pakistan 8-1, Abid Ali 7, Mohammad Abbas 1
New Zealand won by an innings and 176 runs

Both sides made changes from the first test. Mitchell and Henry replaced Santner and the injured Wagner for New Zealand while Zafar made his test debut for Yasir. Williamson won the toss and bowled.

Pakistan made 297 with Azhar and Rizwan getting fifties. Rizwan reached 5000 first-class runs during his innings. Jamieson had his third five wicket haul with 5-69.

New Zealand then proceeded to amass 659-6. This was the highest team score at Hagley Oval. Williamson and Nicholls added 369 for the fourth wicket, a record for New Zealand against all comers and the highest stand in New Zealand and Pakistan tests. Nicholls had been caught off a no-ball with the score at 80-3.

Nicholls reached 2000 test runs and Williamson became the third New Zealand player to score 7000 test runs. He reached his 24th test hundred from 140 balls and his two hundred from 327 deliveries. Nicholls got his seventh test century from 212 balls and Mitchell scored a maiden test century from 112 balls. Taylor had earlier reached 12,000 first-class runs.

Pakistan had a deficit of 362 and were dismissed for 186. No one was able to reach 40 while Jamieson had career best figures of 6-48, his fourth five wicket bag. This gave him 11-117 for the game, the best match figures by a New Zealand bowler against Pakistan. The innings and 176 run win pushed New Zealand to number one in the ICC test rankings.

PAKISTAN

FIRST INNINGS	*Runs*	*Mins*	*Balls*	*6s*	*4s*	*SECOND INNINGS*	*Runs*	*Mins*	*Balls*	*6s*	*4s*
Shan Masood lbw b Southee	0	13	8	-	-	c Southee b Jamieson	0	26	25	-	-
Abid Ali c Southee b Jamieson	25	93	53	-	3	c sub (W.A.Young) b Jamieson	26	126	77	-	3
Azhar Ali c Taylor b Henry	93	271	172	-	12	(4) c Watling b Jamieson	37	142	98	-	6
Haris Sohail c Nicholls b Jamieson	1	6	4	-	-	(5) c Watling b Jamieson	15	63	45	-	2
Fawad Alam c Watling b Jamieson	2	13	8	-	-	(6) c Taylor b Boult	16	88	44	-	2
Mohammad Rizwan*† c Watling b Jamieson	61	103	71	-	11	(7) b Jamieson	10	21	18	-	2
Faheem Ashraf c Taylor b Jamieson	48	111	88	-	8	(8) c Watling b Jamieson	28	82	65	-	3
Zafar Gohar c Jamieson b Southee	34	85	62	-	6	(9) c Henry b Boult	37	78	64	-	7
Shaheen Afridi c Nicholls b Boult	4	46	21	-	-	(10) c Taylor b Williamson	7	33	26	-	1
Mohammad Abbas not out	0	14	7	-	-	(3) c Watling b Boult	3	40	29	-	-
Naseem Shah c Latham b Boult	12	10	9	-	3	not out	0	9	1	-	-
Extras (b 2, lb 9, w 6)	17					(b 1, w 4, nb 2)	7				
TOTAL (83.5 overs)	**297**	385				(81.4 overs)	**186**	356			

NEW ZEALAND

	Runs	Mins	Balls	6s	4s
T.W.M.Latham c Sohail b Afridi	33	100	71	-	4
T.A.Blundell lbw b Faheem	16	94	54	-	3
K.S.Williamson* c Masood b Faheem	238	573	364	-	28
L.R.P.L.Taylor c Masood b Abbas	12	42	33	-	1
H.M.Nicholls c Naseem b Abbas	157	398	291	1	18
B-J.Watling† c Sohail b Afridi	7	16	18	-	1
D.J.Mitchell not out	102	146	112	2	8
K.A.Jamieson not out	30	35	22	2	2
M.J.Henry					
T.G.Southee					
T.A.Boult					
Extras (b 27, lb 8, w 17, nb 12)	64				
TOTAL (158.5 overs) (6 wkts dec)	**659**	703			

Bowling	*O*	*M*	*R*	*W*	*O*	*M*	*R*	*W*
NEW ZEALAND								
Southee	23	7	61	2	20	8	45	0
Boult	20.5	3	82	2	18.4	6	43	3
Jamieson	21	8	69	5	20	6	48	6
Henry	17	2	68	1	15	5	25	0
Mitchell	2	1	6	0	5	1	8	0
Williamson					3	0	16	1
PAKISTAN								
Afridi	35.5	8	101	2				
Abbas	34	11	98	2				
Naseem	26	2	141	0				
Faheem	28	4	106	2				
Masood	2	0	17	0				
Gohar	32	0	159	0				
Sohail	1	0	2	0				

Fall of Wickets	**P** *1st*	**NZ** *1st*	**P** *2nd*
1st	4	52	3
2nd	66	52	17
3rd	70	71	46
4th	83	440	79
5th	171	452	88
6th	227	585	98
7th	260	-	126
8th	282	-	145
9th	285	-	171
10th	297	-	186

AUSTRALIA IN NEW ZEALAND

Australia made a five match Twenty20 tour of New Zealand in February/March. The team was selected on the basis that the Australian test side would be touring South Africa at the same time. When that tour was called off Australia decided to use the originally selected players.

Due to Covid restrictions the second, third and fourth games were played with no crowds and the last three games were all played in Wellington. The original schedule had Black Caps v Australia and White Ferns v England double-headers set down for Wellington, Auckland and Mount Maunganui on 3, 5 and 7 March.

After losing the first two games Australia fought back well to level the series but were soundly beaten in the final game. Aaron Finch (197) Marcus Stoinis (140) and Josh Phillippe (105) were the only players to score over 100 runs. Finch scored two fifties during the series. Ashton Agar was the leading wicket-taker with eight wickets. This included a career best of 6-30 which were the best figures by an Australian bowler in Twenty20 internationals.

The touring party was: A.J. Finch *(captain)*, M.S. Wade *(vice-captain)*, A.C. Agar, J.P. Behrendorff, B.R. McDermott, M.R. Marsh, G.J. Maxwell, R.P. Meredith, J.R. Phillippe, J.A. Richardson, K.W. Richardson, D.R. Sams, T. Sangha, D.J.M. Short, M.P. Stoinis, A.J. Turner, A.J. Tye, A. Zampa. Coach, A.B. McDonald; Manager, P. Berthold.

NEW ZEALAND v AUSTRALIA First Twenty20 International

at Hagley Oval, Christchurch on 22 February, 2021 (d/n)
Toss : Australia. Umpires : C.M. Brown & C.B. Gaffaney
New Zealand won by 53 runs

Philippe made his debut for Australia who won the toss and bowled first. They had early success having New Zealand 19-3 before Conway and Phillips added 74 from 50 balls for the fourth wicket. Conway got fifty from 36 balls and went on to his highest score, finishing unbeaten on 99 after only being able to get a single off the last ball. Sams and Jhye Richardson had career best figures as New Zealand made 184-5.

Australia lost four wickets for 19 to the new ball bowlers and never recovered. Marsh top scored with 45 and made his highest score. Sodhi had career best figures of 4-28 as Australia made 131 from 17.3 overs to give New Zealand a 53 run win.

NEW ZEALAND

	Runs	Mins	Balls	6s	4s
M.J.Guptill c Agar b Sams	0	2	3	-	-
T.L.Seifert† b Richardson J.A.	1	11	5	-	-
K.S.Williamson* c Wade b Sams	12	16	13	-	2
D.P.Conway not out	99	79	59	3	10
G.D.Phillips c Marsh b Stoinis	30	34	30	3	-
J.D.S.Neesham c Wade b Richardson J.A.	26	22	15	-	3
M.J.Santner not out	7	15	5	-	1
K.A.Jamieson					
T.G.Southee					
I.S.Sodhi					
T.A.Boult					
Extras (b 2, lb 3, w 4)	9				
TOTAL (20 overs) (5 wkts)	**184**	91			

AUSTRALIA

	Runs	Mins	Balls	6s	4s
M.S.Wade† c Williamson b Boult	12	18	12	1	-
A.J.Finch* c Conway b Southee	1	4	2	-	-
J.R.Philippe c Conway b Boult	2	5	3	-	-
M.R.Marsh c Santner b Jamieson	45	57	33	2	5
G.J.Maxwell c Neesham b Southee	1	5	5	-	-
M.P.Stoinis c & b Sodhi	8	25	11	-	1
A.C.Agar c Jamieson b Sodhi	23	22	13	1	2
D.R.Sams c Jamieson b Sodhi	1	2	3	-	-
J.A.Richardson st Seifert b Santner	11	17	11	1	-
K.W.Richardson c Neesham b Sodhi	5	6	5	-	-
A.Zampa not out	13	8	8	-	2
Extras (lb 1, w 7, nb 1)	9				
TOTAL (17.3 overs)	**131**	87			

Bowling	*O*	*M*	*R*	*W*
AUSTRALIA				
Sams	4	0	40	2
Zampa	3	0	20	0
Richardson J.A.	4	0	31	2
Richardson K.W.	4	0	42	0
Agar	2	0	20	0
Stoinis	2	0	17	1
Maxwell	1	0	9	0
NEW ZEALAND				
Southee	3	0	10	2
Boult	3	0	22	2
Jamieson	3	0	32	1
Neesham	1	0	9	0
Sodhi	4	0	28	4
Santner	3.3	0	29	1

Fall of Wickets	***NZ***	***A***
1st	0	3
2nd	11	8
3rd	19	16
4th	93	19
5th	140	56
6th	-	98
7th	-	99
8th	-	99
9th	-	108
10th	-	131

NEW ZEALAND v AUSTRALIA Second Twenty20 International

at University of Otago Oval, Dunedin on 25 February, 2021
Toss : Australia. Umpires : C.B. Gaffaney & S.B. Haig
New Zealand won by 4 runs

Australia won the toss and decided to field first. Seifert fell in the third over before Guptill and Williamson added 131 for the second wicket from 69 balls. Guptill got fifty from 27 balls, five faster than Williamson. Neesham hit an unbeaten 45 from just 16 balls to get New Zealand to 219-7. Kane Richardson took 3-43.

Australia were 112-3 before Santner took three wickets in an over but Stoinis and Sams added 92 for the seventh wicket from just 36 balls. Stoinis scored 78 from 37 balls and Sams 41 from 15. The match was decided on the last ball with Australia making 215-8 to give New Zealand a 4 run win. Santner was the most successful bowler, taking 4-31.

NEW ZEALAND

	Runs	Mins	Balls	6s	4s
M.J.Guptill c Stoinis b Sams	97	62	50	8	6
T.L.Seifert† c Finch b Richardson K.W.	3	13	6	-	-
K.S.Williamson* b Zampa	53	55	35	3	2
J.D.S.Neesham not out	45	33	16	6	1
G.D.Phillips b Richardson J.A.	8	10	6	1	-
D.P.Conway c Zampa b Richardson K.W.	2	3	1	-	-
M.J.Santner c Maxwell b Richardson K.W.	0	2	1	-	-
T.G.Southee run out	6	5	3	-	1
K.A.Jamieson not out	0	1	0	-	-
I.S.Sodhi					
T.A.Boult					
Extras (lb 1, w 4)	5				
TOTAL (20 overs) (7 wkts)	**219**	95			

AUSTRALIA

	Runs	Mins	Balls	6s	4s
M.S.Wade† c Williamson b Southee	24	19	15	1	3
A.J.Finch* c Phillips b Sodhi	12	40	14	-	1
J.R.Philippe c Conway b Santner	45	39	32	3	2
G.J.Maxwell c Sodhi b Santner	3	9	5	-	-
M.P.Stoinis c Southee b Neesham	78	47	37	5	7
A.C.Agar c Conway b Santner	0	1	1	-	-
M.R.Marsh c Seifert b Santner	0	1	1	-	-
D.R.Sams c Phillips b Neesham	41	30	15	4	2
J.A.Richardson not out	4	4	1	-	1
K.W.Richardson not out	0	1	0	-	-
A.Zampa					
Extras (w 7, nb 1)	8				
TOTAL (20 overs) (8 wkts)	**215**	97			

Bowling	*O*	*M*	*R*	*W*
AUSTRALIA				
Sams	4	0	46	1
Agar	3	0	30	0
Richardson J.A.	4	0	39	1
Richardson K.W.	4	0	43	3
Zampa	4	0	43	1
Stoinis	1	0	17	0
NEW ZEALAND				
Southee	4	0	47	1
Boult	4	0	30	0
Jamieson	4	0	56	0
Santner	4	0	31	4
Sodhi	3	0	41	1
Neesham	1	0	10	2

Fall of Wickets

	NZ	*A*
1st	20	34
2nd	151	70
3rd	173	87
4th	190	112
5th	198	113
6th	199	113
7th	213	205
8th	-	211
9th	-	-
10th	-	-

NEW ZEALAND v AUSTRALIA — Third Twenty20 International

at Sky Stadium, Wellington on 3 March, 2021 (d/n)
Toss : New Zealand. Umpires : C.B. Gaffaney & W.R. Knights
Australia won by 64 runs

Chapman replaced Santner due to illness for New Zealand while Meredith made his debut for Australia. New Zealand decided to bowl first and Australia made 208-4. Finch made 69 and Maxwell scored 70 from 31 balls. This included 26 from one over from Neesham. His 0-60 was the second most expensive bowling figures by a New Zealand bowler in Twenty20 internationals.

New Zealand again lost an early wicket but went from 109-3 to 116-7 in 13 balls, with Agar taking three wickets in an over. He eventually finished with 6-30, the best figures for an Australian bowler in Twenty20 Internationals. It was his second five wicket bag. New Zealand were eventually dismissed for 144 from 17.1 overs giving Australia a 64 run win.

AUSTRALIA

	Runs	Mins	Balls	6s	4s
M.S.Wade† c Guptill b Boult	5	9	6	-	1
A.J.Finch* c Jamieson b Sodhi	69	71	44	2	8
J.R.Philippe c Guptill b Sodhi	43	36	27	1	3
G.J.Maxwell c Seifert b Southee	70	37	31	5	8
M.P.Stoinis not out	9	19	8	-	1
M.R.Marsh not out	6	8	6	-	-
A.C.Agar					
J.A.Richardson					
K.W.Richardson					
A.Zampa					
R.P.Meredith					
Extras (b 1, lb 1, w 2, nb 2)	6				
TOTAL (20 overs) (4 wkts)	**208**	90			

NEW ZEALAND

	Runs	Mins	Balls	6s	4s
M.J.Guptill c Agar b Zampa	43	40	28	3	2
T.L.Seifert† c Stoinis b Meredith	4	9	4	-	1
K.S.Williamson* lbw b Meredith	9	11	6	1	-
D.P.Conway c Stoinis b Agar	38	38	27	1	5
G.D.Phillips c Richardson K.W. b Agar	13	17	10	1	-
J.D.S.Neesham c Wade b Agar	0	4	1	-	-
M.S.Chapman c Zampa b Agar	18	17	10	1	1
T.G.Southee c Maxwell b Agar	5	6	6	-	-
K.A.Jamieson lbw b Agar	11	12	9	-	2
I.S.Sodhi c & b Richardson K.W.	1	4	2	-	-
T.A.Boult not out	0	1	0	-	-
Extras (lb 1, w 1)	2				
TOTAL (17.1 overs)	**144**	89			

Bowling	*O*	*M*	*R*	*W*
AUSTRALIA				
Southee	4	0	37	1
Boult	4	0	39	1
Neesham	4	0	60	0
Jamieson	4	0	38	0
Sodhi	4	0	32	2
AUSTRALIA				
Richardson J.A.	3	0	34	0
Meredith	4	0	24	2
Zampa	2	0	17	1
Richardson K.W.	2.1	0	17	1
Agar	4	0	30	6
Stoinis	1	0	6	0
Maxwell	1	0	15	0

Fall of Wickets	*A*	*NZ*
1st	6	20
2nd	89	48
3rd	153	80
4th	194	109
5th	-	109
6th	-	110
7th	-	116
8th	-	138
9th	-	144
10th	-	144

NEW ZEALAND v AUSTRALIA Fourth Twenty20 International

at Sky Stadium, Wellington on 5 March, 2021 (d/n)
Toss : Australia. Umpires : C.M. Brown & W.R. Knights
Australia won by 50 runs

Santner returned to the New Zealand side in place of Chapman. Australia decided to bat first after winning the toss. Their innings was centred around Finch who made an unbeaten 79 with no other batsman able to score 20. Sodhi took 3-32 as Australia made 156-6. During his innings, Finch became Australia's leading run scorer in Twenty20 internationals.

The New Zealand batsmen struggled with only three reaching double figures and the highest partnership of the innings was the tenth with 24. Kane Richardson took three wickets while Agar, Zampa and Maxwell all took two. New Zealand were bowled out for 106 off 18.5 overs to leave the series level at two games each.

AUSTRALIA

	Runs	Mins	Balls	6s	4s
M.S.Wade† c Sodhi b Santner	14	11	10	1	1
A.J.Finch* not out	79	86	55	4	5
J.R.Philippe c Southee b Sodhi	13	18	17	-	1
G.J.Maxwell c Guptill b Boult	18	12	9	1	2
M.P.Stoinis c Williamson b Sodhi	19	14	13	1	2
A.C.Agar b Boult	0	5	3	-	-
M.R.Marsh c Southee b Sodhi	6	10	6	-	1
J.A.Richardson not out	4	14	7	-	-
A.Zampa					
R.P.Meredith					
K.W.Richardson					
Extras (w 3)	3				
TOTAL (20 overs) (6 wkts)	**156**	86			

NEW ZEALAND

	Runs	Mins	Balls	6s	4s
M.J.Guptill c Maxwell b Agar	7	17	10	-	1
T.L.Seifert† b Richardson K.W.	19	32	28	-	3
K.S.Williamson* c Marsh b Maxwell	8	19	12	-	-
D.P.Conway c Stoinis b Agar	17	39	20	-	1
G.D.Phillips run out	1	6	3	-	-
J.D.S.Neesham c Finch b Zampa	3	7	5	-	-
M.J.Santner b Maxwell	3	6	5	-	-
T.G.Southee c Wade b Richardson K.W.	6	4	4	1	-
K.A.Jamieson c Maxwell b Richardson K.W.	30	25	18	-	5
I.S.Sodhi c Finch b Zampa	0	3	2	-	-
T.A.Boult not out	6	12	6	-	1
Extras (b 1, lb 1, w 4)	6				
TOTAL (18.5 overs)	**106**	87			

Bowling	*O*	*M*	*R*	*W*
NEW ZEALAND				
Southee	4	0	32	0
Boult	4	0	27	2
Santner	4	0	16	1
Jamieson	4	0	49	0
Sodhi	4	0	32	3
AUSTRALIA				
Agar	4	0	11	2
Meredith	3	0	20	0
Richardson J.A.	2	0	16	0
Zampa	4	0	24	2
Richardson K.W.	2.5	0	19	3
Maxwell	3	0	14	2

Fall of Wickets	**A**	**NZ**
1st	18	21
2nd	42	34
3rd	68	36
4th	93	41
5th	97	48
6th	114	57
7th	-	64
8th	-	80
9th	-	82
10th	-	106

NEW ZEALAND v AUSTRALIA — FifthTwenty20 International

at Sky Stadium, Wellington on 7 March, 2021
Toss : Australia. Umpires : C.B. Gaffaney & W.R. Knights
New Zealand won by 7 wickets

Chapman replaced Jamieson for New Zealand and Australia again decided to bat first. Finch and Wade had a second wicket partnership of 66 from 46 balls. Wade top scored with 44 and Sodhi took 3-24 as Australia made 142-8.

Conway opened the innings with Guptill and they had a 106 run opening stand from 71 balls. Guptill got fifty from 31 balls as New Zealand reached their target from 15.3 overs. Phillips hit 34 off 16 balls at the end. This gave New Zealand a 3-2 series win.

AUSTRALIA

	Runs	Mins	Balls	6s	4s
J.R.Philippe lbw b Boult	2	11	8	-	-
A.J.Finch* c Santner b Sodhi	36	41	32	1	5
M.S.Wade† c Guptill b Boult	44	49	29	2	3
G.J.Maxwell c Boult b Chapman	1	3	2	-	-
M.P.Stoinis c Guptill b Sodhi	26	28	26	1	2
A.C.Agar c Guptill b Sodhi	6	14	7	-	-
M.R.Marsh b Southee	10	10	9	1	-
J.A.Richardson c Phillips b Southee	4	15	6	-	-
K.W.Richardson not out	2	3	2	-	-
A.Zampa					
R.P.Meredith					
Extras (lb 3, w 7, nb 1)	11				
TOTAL (20 overs) (8 wkts)	**142**	89			

NEW ZEALAND

	Runs	Mins	Balls	6s	4s
D.P.Conway c Agar b Meredith	36	53	28	1	3
M.J.Guptill c Marsh b Richardson J.A.	71	66	46	4	7
K.S.Williamson* lbw b Meredith	0	3	1	-	-
G.D.Phillips not out	34	18	16	2	5
M.S.Chapman not out	1	8	2	-	-
T.L.Seifert†					
J.D.S.Neesham					
M.J.Santner					
T.G.Southee					
I.S.Sodhi					
T.A.Boult					
Extras (w 1)	1				
TOTAL (15.3 overs) (3 wkts)	**143**	74			

Bowling	*O*	*M*	*R*	*W*
NEW ZEALAND				
Southee	4	0	38	2
Santner	4	0	21	0
Boult	4	0	26	2
Chapman	2	0	9	1
Sodhi	4	0	24	3
Phillips	2	0	21	0
AUSTRALIA				
Agar	4	0	26	0
Meredith	4	0	39	2
Richardson J.A.	3	0	19	1
Richardson K.W.	2	0	16	0
Zampa	2.3	0	43	0

Fall of Wickets	***A***	***NZ***
1st	8	106
2nd	74	106
3rd	77	124
4th	103	-
5th	122	-
6th	122	-
7th	139	-
8th	142	-
9th	-	-
10th	-	-

BANGLADESH IN NEW ZEALAND

Bangladesh made a six-match tour of New Zealand in March comprising three one-day internationals and three Twenty20 internationals. They struggled throughout and New Zealand won every match.

In the one-day internationals Mahmudullah, Mithun and Tamim scored fifties while Naim scored the only fifty in the shorter version. Mehedi got four wickets in Twenty20 games.

The touring party was: Tamim Iqbal *(captain)*, Mahmudullah *(vice-captain)*, Afif Hossain, Hasan Mahmud, Liton Das, Mehedi Hasan, Mohammad Mithun, Mohammad Naim, Mohammad Saifuddin, Mehidy Hasan, Mosaddek Hossain, Mushfiqur Rahim, Mustafizur Rahman, Nasum Ahmed, Rubel Hossain, Shoriful Islam, Soumya Sarkar, Taskin Ahmed. Coach, R.C. Domingo, Manager, Sabbir Khan.

New Zealand One-day International Averages

BATTING	*M*	*I*	*NO*	*HS*	*Agg*	*Ave*	*100s*	*50s*	*Ct*	*St*	*SR*
T.W.M. Latham	3	2	1	110*	128	128.00	1	-	3	1	90
D.P. Conway	3	3	0	126	225	75.00	1	1	3	-	88
H.M. Nicholls	3	3	1	49*	80	40.00	-	-	3	-	86
M.J. Guptill	3	3	0	38	84	28.00	-	-	2	-	118
J.D.S. Neesham	3	2	0	30	34	17.00	-	-	1	-	89
W.A. Young	2	2	1	11*	12	12.00	-	-	1	-	92
L.R.P.L. Taylor	1	1	0	7	7	7.00	-	-	-	-	50
D.J. Mitchell	3	2	2	100*	112	-	1	-	-	-	114
M.J. Santner	3	1	1	3*	3	-	-	-	3	-	300
T.A. Boult	3	-	-	-	-	-	-	-	3	-	-
M.J. Henry	3	-	-	-	-	-	-	-	-	-	-
K.A. Jamieson	3	-	-	-	-	-	-	-	-	-	-

BOWLING	*O*	*M*	*R*	*W*	*Ave*	*Best*	*R/O*
M.J. Henry	29	6	101	6	16.83	4-27	3.48
J.D.S. Neesham	24.4	2	127	7	18.14	5-27	5.15
M.J. Santner	21	0	81	4	20.25	2-23	3.86
T.A. Boult	28.5	1	113	5	22.60	4-27	3.92
K.A. Jamieson	26	3	91	2	45.50	1-30	3.50
D.J. Mitchell	5	0	33	0	-	-	6.60

Bangladesh One-day International Averages

BATTING	M	I	NO	HS	Agg	Ave	100s	50s	Ct	St	SR
Mahmudullah	3	3	1	76*	119	59.50	-	1	1	-	82
Mohammad Mithun	3	3	1	73*	88	44.00	-	1	-	-	71
Tamim Iqbal	3	3	0	78	92	30.66	-	1	-	-	69
Mushfiqur Rahim	3	3	0	34	78	26.00	-	-	2	-	51
Liton Das	3	3	0	21	40	13.33	-	-	3	-	65
Soumya Sarkar	3	3	0	32	33	11.00	-	-	1	-	60
Taskin Ahmed	3	2	0	10	19	9.50	-	-	-	-	33
Mehedi Hasan	3	3	0	14	24	8.00	-	-	-	-	72
Rubel Hossain	1	1	0	4	4	4.00	-	-	-	-	14
Mustafizur Rahman	3	2	1	1*	1	1.00	-	-	1	-	25
Hasan Mahmud	1	1	0	1	1	1.00	-	-	-	-	20
Mehidy Hasan	3	2	0	1	1	0.50	-	-	1	-	8
Mohammad Saifuddin	1	1	1	7*	7	-	-	-	-	-	175

BOWLING	O	M	R	W	Ave	Best	R/O
Rubel Hossain	10	1	70	3	23.33	3-70	7.00
Soumya Sarkar	9.3	0	49	1	49.00	1-37	5.16
Hasan Mahmud	4.2	0	49	1	49.00	1-49	11.32
Mehedi Hasan	23	1	105	2	52.50	2-42	4.57
Mustafizur Rahman	22.3	0	175	3	58.33	2-62	7.78
Taskin Ahmed	24	1	142	2	71.00	1-23	5.92
Mohammad Mithun	2	0	12	0	-	-	6.00
Mohammad Saifuddin	7.2	0	43	0	-	-	5.87
Mehidy Hasan	17	1	70	0	-	-	4.12

NEW ZEALAND v BANGLADESH First One-day International

at University of Otago Oval, Dunedin on 20 March, 2021
Toss : New Zealand. Umpires : C.B. Gaffaney & W.R. Knights
New Zealand won by 8 wickets

Conway, Young and Mitchell made their debuts for New Zealand while Mehedi made his debut for Bangladesh. Latham captained New Zealand and was playing his 100th one-day international. He won the toss and decided to bowl first.

Bangladesh lost two early wickets and never recovered, being 98-7 at one stage before making 131 from 41.5 overs. Boult took 4-27 while Neesham and Santner both took two wickets.

New Zealand's first fifty took 30 balls and with all batsmen scoring quickly they reached the target after just 21.2 overs. Nicholls, in his 50th one-day international, was one short of a fifty when the win came.

BANGLADESH

	Runs	Mins	Balls	6s	4s
Tamim Iqbal* lbw b Boult	13	16	15	1	1
Liton Das c Boult b Neesham	19	56	36	-	1
Soumya Sarkar c Conway b Boult	0	3	3	-	-
Mushfiqur Rahim† c Guptill b Neesham	23	75	49	-	2
Mohammad Mithun run out	9	49	27	-	1
Mahmudullah c Santner b Henry	27	83	54	1	1
Mehidy Hasan b Santner	1	16	10	-	-
Mehedi Hasan c Nicholls b Santner	14	17	20	1	1
Taskin Ahmed c Santner b Boult	10	48	32	-	1
Hasan Mahmud b Boult	1	5	5	-	-
Mustafizur Rahman not out	1	3	1	-	-
Extras (lb 3, w 9, nb 1)	13				
TOTAL (41.5 overs)	**131**	188			

NEW ZEALAND

	Runs	Mins	Balls	6s	4s
M.J.Guptill c Mushfiqur b Taskin	38	28	19	4	3
H.M.Nicholls not out	49	96	53	-	6
D.P.Conway c Mahmudullah b Mahmud	27	61	52	-	2
W.A.Young not out	11	6	6	-	2
T.W.M.Latham*†					
J.D.S.Neesham					
D.J.Mitchell					
K.A.Jamieson					
M.J.Santner					
M.J.Henry					
T.A.Boult					
Extras (b 1, lb 2, w 2, nb 2)	7				
TOTAL (21.2 overs) (2 wkts)	**132**	96			

Bowling	*O*	*M*	*R*	*W*
NEW ZEALAND				
Boult	8.5	0	27	4
Henry	9	1	26	1
Jamieson	8	1	25	0
Neesham	8	1	27	2
Santner	8	0	23	2
BANGLADESH				
Mustafizur	4	0	26	0
Mahmud	4.2	0	49	1
Taskin	4	0	23	1
Mehedi	6	0	17	0
Mehdiy	2	0	9	0
Sarkar	1	0	5	0

Fall of Wickets	***B***	***NZ***
1st	19	54
2nd	19	119
3rd	42	-
4th	69	-
5th	72	-
6th	78	-
7th	98	-
8th	125	-
9th	130	-
10th	131	-

NEW ZEALAND v BANGLADESH Second One-day International

at Hagley Oval, Christchurch on 23 March, 2021 (d/n)
Toss : New Zealand. Umpires : C.M. Brown & C.B. Gaffaney
New Zealand won by 5 wickets

New Zealand were unchanged while Saifuddin replaced Hasan for Bangladesh. New Zealand again won the toss and decided to field.

After losing Das in the second over Bangladesh recovered well with stands of 81, 48, 51 and 63 to reach 271-6. Tamim top scored with 78 (fifty from 84 balls) while Mithun made a career best score of 73 not out, with his fifty coming from 43 deliveries.

New Zealand were 53-3 when Latham joined Conway. They added 113 for the fourth wicket from 137 balls. Conway reached a maiden fifty from 73 balls while Latham needed 64 for his fifty and went to his fifth one-day hundred after a further 37 balls. New Zealand reached 275-5 with ten balls to spare.

BANGLADESH

	Runs	Mins	Balls	6s	4s
Tamim Iqbal* run out	78	136	108	-	11
Liton Das c Young b Henry	0	6	4	-	-
Soumya Sarkar st Latham b Santner	32	90	46	1	3
Mushfiqur Rahim† c Nicholls b Santner	34	61	59	-	3
Mohammad Mithun not out	73	89	57	2	6
Mahmudullah c Guptill b Jamieson	16	33	18	-	1
Mehedi Hasan c Nicholls b Boult	7	5	5	1	-
Mohammad Saifuddin not out	7	7	4	-	-
Mehidy Hasan					
Taskin Ahmed					
Mustafizur Rahman					
Extras (lb 6, w 17, nb 1)	24				
TOTAL (50 overs) (6 wkts)	**271**	226			

NEW ZEALAND

	Runs	Mins	Balls	6s	4s
M.J.Guptill c & b Mustafizur	20	22	24	1	3
H.M.Nicholls b Mehedi	13	38	18	-	1
D.P.Conway run out	72	113	93	-	7
W.A.Young b Mehedi	1	9	7	-	-
T.W.M.Latham*† not out	110	153	108	-	10
J.D.S.Neesham c Sarkar b Mustafizur	30	50	34	-	2
D.J.Mitchell not out	12	16	6	-	2
M.J.Santner					
K.A.Jamieson					
M.J.Henry					
T.A.Boult					
Extras (lb 4, w 13)	17				
TOTAL (48.2 overs) (5 wkts)	**275**	202			

Bowling	*O*	*M*	*R*	*W*
NEW ZEALAND				
Boult	10	0	49	1
Henry	10	3	48	1
Jamieson	10	2	36	1
Neesham	9	0	73	0
Santner	10	0	51	2
Mitchell	1	0	8	0
BANGLADESH				
Mustafizur	8.3	0	62	2
Taskin	10	0	67	0
Mehedi	10	1	42	2
Saifuddin	7.2	0	43	0
Mehdiy	10	1	38	0
Mithun	2	0	12	0
Sarkar	0.3	0	7	0

Fall of Wickets	***B***	***NZ***
1st	4	28
2nd	85	43
3rd	133	53
4th	184	166
5th	247	242
6th	258	-
7th	-	-
8th	-	-
9th	-	-
10th	-	-

NEW ZEALAND v BANGLADESH Third One-day International

at Basin Reserve, Wellington on 26 March, 2021
Toss : New Zealand. Umpires : C.B. Gaffaney & W.R. Knights
New Zealand won by 164 runs

Both sides made one change with Taylor coming in for Young in the New Zealand side while Rubel replaced Shaif for Bangladesh. The day was special for the visitors as it was the 50th anniversary of Bangladesh becoming a nation.

New Zealand decided to bat after winning the toss but were in some trouble at 57-3 despite a 44 run opening stand. Conway and Mitchell added 159 for the fifth wicket, a record for New Zealand against Bangladesh. Conway got his fifty from 52 balls and went to a maiden century after a further 43 deliveries. Mitchell scored his maiden fifty from 63 balls and reached his century off the last ball of the innings. It was New Zealand's highest one-day score at the Basin Reserve. Rubel took 3-70 as New Zealand made 318-6.

Bangladesh were soon 26-3 and never recovered, with only Mahmudullah passing 21. He scored his fifty off 64 balls as was undefeated on 76 when Bangladesh were dismissed for 154 after 42.4 overs. Neesham had career best figures with his second five wicket haul and Henry took 4-27. The 164 run win gave New Zealand a 3-0 win in the series.

NEW ZEALAND

	Runs	Mins	Balls	6s	4s
M.J.Guptill c Das b Rubel	26	43	28	-	2
H.M.Nicholls c Das b Taskin	18	37	21	-	2
D.P.Conway c sub (Afif Hossain) Mustafizur	126	172	110	-	17
L.R.P.L.Taylor c Mushfiqur b Rubel	7	14	11	-	1
T.W.M.Latham*† c Mehdiy b Sarkar	18	48	33	-	1
D.J.Mitchell not out	100	122	92	2	9
J.D.S.Neesham c Das b Rubel	4	7	4	-	-
M.J.Santner not out	3	8	1	-	-
K.A.Jamieson					
M.J.Henry					
T.A.Boult					
Extras (b 1, lb 2, w 10, nb 3)	16				
TOTAL (50 overs) (6 wkts)	**318**	227			

BANGLADESH

	Runs	Mins	Balls	6s	4s
Tamim Iqbal* c Latham b Henry	1	10	9	-	-
Liton Das c Boult b Henry	21	30	21	-	3
Soumya Sarkar c Boult b Henry	1	9	6	-	-
Mohammad Mithun c Santner b Jamieson	6	61	39	-	-
Mushfiqur Rahim† c & b Neesham	21	74	44	-	1
Mahmudullah not out	76	107	73	4	6
Mehidy Hasan c Conway b Neesham	0	2	2	-	-
Mehedi Hasan c Latham b Neesham	3	10	8	-	-
Taskin Ahmed c Conway b Henry	9	30	24	-	2
Rubel Hossain c Latham b Neesham	4	36	28	-	-
Mustafizur Rahman lbw b Neesham	0	4	3	-	-
Extras (b 1, w 10, nb 1)	12				
TOTAL (42.4 overs)	**154**	188			

Bowling	*O*	*M*	*R*	*W*
BANGLADESH				
Mustafizur	10	0	87	1
Taskin	10	1	52	1
Rubel	10	1	70	3
Mehedi	7	0	46	0
Mehdiy	5	0	23	0
Sarkar	8	0	37	1
NEW ZEALAND				
Henry	10	2	27	4
Boult	10	1	37	0
Jamieson	8	0	30	1
Neesham	7.4	1	27	5
Mitchell	4	0	25	0
Santner	3	0	7	0

Fall of Wickets	***NZ***	***B***
1st	44	10
2nd	49	18
3rd	57	26
4th	120	48
5th	279	77
6th	290	77
7th	-	82
8th	-	102
9th	-	154
10th	-	154

NEW ZEALAND v BANGLADESH First Twenty20 International

at Seddon Park, Hamilton on 28 March, 2021
Toss : New Zealand. Umpires : C.B. Gaffaney & S.B. Haig
New Zealand won by 66 runs

Allen and Young made their debuts for New Zealand while Nasum and Shoriful made their debuts for Bangladesh.

New Zealand won the toss and decided to bat but lost Allen in the first over. Conway and Young added 105 from 60 balls for the third wicket, Conway getting fifty off 37 balls while Young needed 28 for his half century. Conway and Phillips added an unbeaten 52 off 19 balls to get New Zealand to 210-3. Conway finished on 92 not out.

Bangladesh were soon in trouble and were 59-6 in the eighth over before Afif and Saif added 63 for the seventh wicket. The visitors eventually finished on 144-8, giving New Zealand a 66 run win. Sodhi equalled his best bowling figures.

NEW ZEALAND

	Runs	Mins	Balls	6s	4s
M.J.Guptill c Sarkar b Nasum	35	31	27	2	3
F.H.Allen b Nasum	0	2	1	-	-
D.P.Conway† not out	92	91	52	3	11
W.A.Young c Afif b Mehedi	53	45	30	4	2
G.D.Phillips not out	24	17	10	1	3
M.S.Chapman					
D.J.Mitchell					
T.G.Southee*					
I.S.Sodhi					
L.H.Ferguson					
H.K.Bennett					
Extras (lb 2, w 4)	6				
TOTAL (20 overs) (3 wkts)	**210**	94			

BANGLADESH

	Runs	Mins	Balls	6s	4s
Mohammad Naim lbw b Ferguson	27	23	18	-	5
Liton Das† c Sodhi b Southee	4	11	5	-	1
Soumya Sarkar c & b Sodhi	5	18	6	-	1
Mohammad Mithun b Sodhi	4	8	6	-	-
Mahmudullah* b Sodhi	11	9	9	-	1
Afif Hossain b Ferguson	45	45	33	1	5
Mehedi Hasan b Sodhi	0	1	1	-	-
Mohammad Saifuddin not out	34	54	34	1	3
Shoriful Islam c Guptill b Bennett	5	10	7	-	1
Nasum Ahmed not out	0	7	1	-	-
Mustafizur Rahman					
Extras (lb 2, w 7)	9				
TOTAL (20 overs) (8 wkts)	**144**	95			

Bowling	*O*	*M*	*R*	*W*
BANGLADESH				
Nasum	4	0	30	2
Saifuddin	4	0	43	0
Shoriful	4	0	50	0
Mustafizur	4	0	48	0
Mehedi	4	0	37	1
NEW ZEALAND				
Southee	4	0	34	1
Bennett	4	0	20	1
Ferguson	4	0	25	2
Sodhi	4	0	28	4
Chapman	1	0	9	0
Phillips	1	0	5	0
Mitchell	2	0	21	0

Fall of Wickets	***NZ***	***B***
1st	1	20
2nd	53	39
3rd	158	43
4th	-	44
5th	-	59
6th	-	59
7th	-	122
8th	-	133
9th	-	-
10th	-	-

NEW ZEALAND v BANGLADESH Second Twenty20 International

at McLean Park, Napier on 30 March, 2021 (d/n)
Toss : Bangladesh. Umpires : C.M. Brown & W.R. Knights
New Zealand won by 28 runs (D/L)

Milne replaced Ferguson in the New Zealand side while Taskin replaced Mustafizur in the Bangladesh team. Bangladesh decided to bowl first after winning the toss. New Zealand had steady partnerships before Phillips and Mitchell added an unbeaten 62 off 41 balls before rain ended the innings at 173-5 after 17.5 overs. Phillips scored his fifty from 27 balls.

Bangladesh had a revised target of 171 off 16 overs but lost Das in the second over. Naim and Sarkar scored 81 from 49 balls, with Sarkar getting fifty from 25 balls, but Bangladesh finished on 142-7. New Zealand won by 28 runs, winning their seventh series of the summer.

NEW ZEALAND

	Runs	Mins	Balls	6s	4s
M.J.Guptill c Taskin b Saifuddin	21	26	18	1	2
F.H.Allen c Naim b Taskin	17	16	10	1	2
D.P.Conway† c Mithun b Shoriful	15	13	9	-	2
G.D.Phillips not out	58	83	31	2	5
W.A.Young st Das b Mehedi	14	23	17	1	-
M.S.Chapman c & b Mehedi	7	31	8	-	1
D.J.Mitchell not out	34	24	16	-	6
T.G.Southee*					
A.F.Milne					
I.S.Sodhi					
H.K.Bennett					
Extras (b 1, lb 2, w 2, nb 2)	7				
TOTAL (17.5 overs) (5 wkts)	**173**	110			

BANGLADESH

	Runs	Mins	Balls	6s	4s
Mohammad Naim c Guptill b Phillips	38	64	35	-	4
Liton Das† c Phillips b Bennett	6	14	5	-	1
Soumya Sarkar c Milne b Southee	51	39	27	3	5
Mahmudullah* b Milne	21	16	12	-	4
Afif Hossain b Milne	2	8	4	-	-
Mohammad Mithun c Conway b Southee	1	4	2	-	-
Mehedi Hasan not out	12	12	6	1	-
Mohammad Saifuddin c Conway b Bennett	3	8	6	-	-
Taskin Ahmed not out	0	1	0	-	-
Shoriful Islam					
Nasum Ahmed					
Extras (b 1, lb 1, w 5, nb 1)	8				
TOTAL (16 overs) (7 wkts)	**142**	85			

Bowling	*O*	*M*	*R*	*W*
BANGLADESH				
Nasum	4	0	25	0
Saifuddin	3	0	35	1
Taskin	3.5	0	49	1
Shoriful	3	0	16	1
Mehedi	4	0	45	2
NEW ZEALAND				
Southee	4	0	21	2
Bennett	3	0	31	2
Milne	3	0	34	2
Sodhi	3	0	34	0
Phillips	3	0	20	1

Fall of Wickets	***NZ***	***B***
1st	36	13
2nd	55	94
3rd	55	110
4th	94	123
5th	111	124
6th	-	126
7th	-	137
8th	-	-
9th	-	-
10th	-	-

NEW ZEALAND v BANGLADESH Third Twenty20 International

at Eden Park, Auckland on 1 April, 2021 (d/n)
Toss : Bangladesh. Umpires : C.M. Brown & C.B. Gaffaney
New Zealand won by 65 runs

Ferguson and Astle replaced Bennett and Sodhi for New Zealand while Najmul, Saikat, and Rubel came into the Bangladesh side.

Rain throughout the day delayed the start and a 10 over game took place. Bangladesh again decided to bowl. Guptill and Allen had a first wicket stand of 85 off 34 balls with Allen getting a maiden international fifty from 18 balls. This equalled the second-fastest fifty by a New Zealand batsman in Twenty20 internationals. New Zealand finished on 141-4.

Bangladesh lost two wickets in the first over and never recovered, being dismissed for 76 off 9.3 overs. Astle had career best figures.

NEW ZEALAND

	Runs	Mins	Balls	6s	4s
M.J.Guptill c Afif b Mehedi	44	27	19	5	1
F.H.Allen c sub (Mehidy Hasan) b Taskin	71	50	29	3	10
G.D.Phillips c Sarkar b Shoriful	14	13	6	2	-
D.J.Mitchell run out	11	10	6	-	1
M.S.Chapman not out	0	1	0	-	-
D.P.Conway†					
W.A.Young					
T.G.Southee*					
A.F.Milne					
T.D.Astle					
L.H.Ferguson					
Extras (w 1)	1				
TOTAL (10 overs) (4 wkts)	**141**	52			

BANGLADESH

	Runs	Mins	Balls	6s	4s
Mohammad Naim c Chapman b Astle	19	17	13	2	1
Soumya Sarkar c & b Southee	10	4	4	-	2
Liton Das*† b Southee	0	1	1	-	-
Nazmul Hossain b Astle	8	15	6	-	1
Afif Hossain st Conway b Astle	8	13	6	1	-
Mossadek Hossain c Young b Southee	13	25	8	1	-
Mehedi Hasan c Phillips b Astle	0	1	2	-	-
Shoriful Islam b Milne	6	4	3	1	-
Taskin Ahmed b Ferguson	5	4	3	-	1
Rubel Hossain not out	3	11	6	-	-
Nasum Ahmed c Southee b Phillips	3	5	4	-	-
Extras (w 1)	1				
TOTAL (9.3 overs)	**76**	53			

Bowling	*O*	*M*	*R*	*W*
BANGLADESH				
Nasum	2	0	29	0
Taskin	2	0	24	1
Shoriful	2	0	21	1
Rubel	2	0	33	0
Mehedi	2	0	34	1
NEW ZEALAND				
Southee	2	0	15	3
Milne	2	0	24	1
Ferguson	2	0	13	1
Astle	2	0	13	4
Phillips	1.3	0	11	1

Fall of Wickets	***NZ***	***B***
1st	85	11
2nd	123	11
3rd	138	31
4th	141	37
5th	-	52
6th	-	52
7th	-	60
8th	-	65
9th	-	72
10th		76

NEW ZEALAND IN ENGLAND

New Zealand made a three test tour of England which included the first world test championship final. Prior to this game they played two tests against England winning the series 1-0 with a draw at Lord's and victory at Edgbaston. The final of the test championship was badly affected by rain before New Zealand secured their win on the sixth day.

Devon Conway was the batting star. He became the first player to score a double century on debut at Lord's and scored fifties in the other two games. He scored 379 runs, while Ross Taylor was next with 185. Kane Williamson, Henry Nicholls and Will Young all scored fifties.

Tim Southee was the leading wicket-taker with 12 wickets followed by Trent Boult (11). The test against India marked the retirement of wicketkeeper BJ Watling.

The touring squad was: K.S. Williamson, *(captain, Northern Districts)*, T.A. Blundell *(Wellington)*, T.A. Boult *(Northern Districts)*, D.A.J. Bracewell *(Central Districts)*, D.P. Conway *(Wellington)*, C. de Grandhomme *(Northern Districts)*, J.A. Duffy *(Otago)*, M.J. Henry *(Canterbury)*, K.A. Jamieson *(Auckland)*, T.W.M. Latham *(Canterbury)*, D.J. Mitchell *(Canterbury)*, H.M. Nicholls *(Canterbury)*, A.Y. Patel *(Central Districts)*, R. Ravindra *(Wellington)*, M.J. Santner *(Northern Districts)*, T.G. Southee *(Northern Districts)*, L.R.P.L. Taylor *(Central Districts)*, N. Wagner *(Northern Districts)*, B-J. Watling *(Northern Districts)*, W.A. Young *(Central Districts)*. Coach, G.R. Stead; Assistant coach, H. Malan (England tests); Batting coach, L. Ronchi; Bowling coach S.E. Jurgensen; Manager, M. Sandle; Logistics Manager, R. Muller; Trainer, C. Donaldson; Physiotherapists, T. Simsek, V. Vallabh (England tests). Bracewell, Duffy, Mitchell, Ravindra and Santner were the five players omitted from the test championship final squad.

New Zealand Test Averages

BATTING	*M*	*I*	*NO*	*HS*	*Agg*	*Ave*	*100s*	*50s*	*Ct*	*St*
D.P. Conway	3	6	0	200	379	63.16	1	2	-	-
L.R.P.L. Taylor	3	6	2	80	185	46.25	-	1	4	-
W.A. Young	1	2	0	82	90	45.00	-	1	-	-
K.S. Williamson	2	4	1	52*	115	38.33	-	1	-	-
T.A. Blundell	1	1	0	34	34	34.00	-	-	8	-
H.M. Nicholls	3	4	0	61	112	28.00	-	1	2	-
T.W.M. Latham	3	6	1	36	127	25.40	-	-	7	-
A.Y. Patel	1	1	0	20	20	20.00	-	-	-	-
T.G. Southee	2	2	0	30	38	19.00	-	-	2	-
K.A. Jamieson	2	2	0	21	30	15.00	-	-	1	-
M.J. Henry	1	1	0	12	12	12.00	-	-	-	-
N. Wagner	3	4	1	25*	35	11.66	-	-	-	-
C. de Grandhomme	2	3	1	13	22	11.00	-	-	1	-
B-J. Watling	2	3	1	15*	17	8.50	-	-	8	-
D.J. Mitchell	1	1	0	6	6	6.00	-	-	3	-
M.J. Santner	1	1	0	0	0	0.00	-	-	-	-
T.A. Boult	2	2	2	12*	19	-	-	-	-	-

BOWLING	*O*	*M*	*R*	*W*	*Ave*	*Best*	*5w*	*10w*
A.Y. Patel	23	8	59	4	14.75	2-25	-	-
T.G. Southee	83.1	19	192	12	16.00	6-43	1	-
K.A. Jamieson	87	36	174	10	17.40	5-31	1	-
T.A. Boult	75.2	14	205	11	18.63	4-85	-	-
M.J. Henry	38	9	114	6	19.00	3-36	-	-
N. Wagner	101	24	280	10	28.00	3-18	-	-
K.S. Williamson	3	0	12	0	-	-	-	-
D.J. Mitchell	11	2	23	0	-	-	-	-
C. de Grandhomme	34	14	68	0	-	-	-	-
M.J. Santner	23	7	68	0	-	-	-	-

New Zealand Test Averages

BATTING	M	I	NO	HS	Agg	Ave	100s	50s	Ct	St
D.P. Conway	2	4	0	200	306	76.50	1	1	-	-
W.A. Young	1	2	0	82	90	45.00	-	1	-	-
L.R.P.L. Taylor	2	4	1	80	127	42.33	-	1	1	-
H.M. Nicholls	2	3	0	61	105	35.00	-	1	1	-
T.A. Blundell	1	1	0	34	34	34.00	-	-	8	-
T.W.M. Latham	2	4	1	36	88	29.33	-	-	2	-
A.Y. Patel	1	1	0	20	20	20.00	-	-	-	-
N. Wagner	2	3	1	25*	35	17.50	-	-	-	-
B-J. Watling	1	2	1	15*	16	16.00	-	-	3	-
M.J. Henry	1	1	0	12	12	12.00	-	-	-	-
C. de Grandhomme	1	2	1	9*	9	9.00	-	-	1	-
K.A. Jamieson	1	1	0	9	9	9.00	-	-	1	-
T.G. Southee	1	1	0	8	8	8.00	-	-	1	-
K.S. Williamson	1	2	0	13	14	7.00	-	-	-	-
D.J. Mitchell	1	1	0	6	6	6.00	-	-	3	-
M.J. Santner	1	1	0	0	0	0.00	-	-	-	-
T.A. Boult	1	1	1	12*	12	-	-	-	-	-

BOWLING	O	M	R	W	Ave	Best	5w	10w
T.G. Southee	42.1	9	80	7	11.42	6-43	1	-
A.Y. Patel	23	8	59	4	14.75	2-25	-	-
M.J. Henry	38	9	114	6	19.00	3-36	-	-
T.A. Boult	39.1	8	119	6	19.83	4-85	-	-
N. Wagner	71	17	196	7	28.00	3-18	-	-
K.A. Jamieson	41	14	113	3	37.66	3-85	-	-
K.S. Williamson	3	0	12	0	-	-	-	-
D.J. Mitchell	11	2	23	0	-	-	-	-
C. de Grandhomme	22	8	36	0	-	-	-	-
M.J. Santner	23	7	68	0	-	-	-	-

England Test Averages

BATTING	M	I	NO	HS	Agg	Ave	100s	50s	Ct	St
R.J. Burns	2	4	0	132	238	59.50	1	1	1	-
O.E. Robinson	1	1	0	42	42	42.00	-	-	1	-
D.W. Lawrence	2	3	1	81*	81	40.50	-	1	-	-
D.P. Sibley	2	4	1	60*	103	34.33	-	1	1	-
O.J.D. Pope	2	4	1	23	84	28.00	-	-	1	-
J.E. Root	2	4	0	42	97	24.25	-	-	1	-
M.A. Wood	2	3	0	41	70	23.33	-	-	-	-
O.P. Stone	1	2	0	20	35	17.50	-	-	-	-
J.M. Anderson	2	3	2	8*	12	12.00	-	-	1	-
Z. Crawley	2	4	0	17	21	5.25	-	-	3	-
S.C.J. Broad	2	3	0	10	11	3.66	-	-	-	-
J.R. Bracey	2	3	0	8	8	2.66	-	-	6	-

BOWLING	O	M	R	W	Ave	Best	5w	10w
O.E. Robinson	42	11	101	7	14.42	4-75	-	-
D.W. Lawrence	3	0	16	1	16.00	1-16	-	-
S.C.J. Broad	66.1	15	174	6	29.00	4-48	-	-
O.P. Stone	25	5	97	3	32.33	2-92	-	-
M.A. Wood	59.5	11	205	6	34.16	3-81	-	-
J.M. Anderson	77.3	20	206	3	68.66	2-83	-	-
J.E. Root	31.4	4	99	1	99.00	1-16	-	-

ENGLAND v NEW ZEALAND — First Test

at Lord's on 2, 3, 4, 5, 6 June, 2021
Toss : New Zealand. Umpires : M.A. Gough & R.A. Kettleborough
Close of play: 1st day: NZ 246-3, Conway 136, Nicholls 46; 2nd day: England 111-2, Burns 59, Root 42
3rd day: no play; 4th day: NZ 62-2, Latham 30, Wagner 2
Match drawn

Conway made his test debut for New Zealand while Bracey and Robinson made their debuts for England. Williamson won the toss and decided to bat first.

Latham and Conway had a 58 run opening stand and were 114-3 before Conway and Nicholls broke the New Zealand fourth wicket record against England with a stand of 174 off 357 balls. Conway became the twelfth New Zealand batsman to score a century on debut needing 163 balls for the landmark. His hundred was New Zealand's 300th in test cricket.

Nicholls got fifty from 158 deliveries. When Nicholls departed New Zealand went from 288-3 to 294-7 but a last wicket stand of 40 saw the total reach 378. Conway became the second New Zealander to get a double century on debut, reaching his two hundred from 347 balls. His innings was the highest debut innings at Lord's. He was run out and the last man dismissed. Robinson got 4-75 and Wood 3-81.

England lost two early wickets before Burns and Root added 93. The third day's play was rained out and England went from 140-3 to 140-6 in 20 balls but Robinson helped Burns add 63 for the seventh wicket. Burns went to his third test hundred from 267 balls. England's last wicket put on 52 to get them to 275. Southee got his twelfth five wicket haul with 6-43.

With a lead of 103 New Zealand made 169-6 before declaring at lunch after a shower disrupted play. This meant England needed 279 from 75 overs. The openers put on 49 but two wickets fell quickly. England then batted out the rest of the game to be 170-3 when play was called off. Sibley got fifty from 161 balls.

NEW ZEALAND

FIRST INNINGS	Runs	Mins	Balls	6s	4s	*SECOND INNINGS*	Runs	Mins	Balls	6s	4s
T.W.M.Latham b Robinson	23	77	57	-	2	lbw b Broad	36	135	99	-	3
D.P.Conway run out	200	578	347	1	22	b Robinson	23	88	64	-	2
K.S.Williamson* b Anderson	13	46	33	-	2	lbw b Robinson	1	35	19	-	1
L.R.P.L.Taylor lbw b Robinson	14	59	38	-	1	(5) c Bracey b Wood	33	63	35	2	1
H.M.Nicholls c Robinson b Wood	61	267	175	-	4	(6) c Burns b Root	23	52	36	-	2
B-J.Watling† c Sibley b Wood	1	22	11	-	-	(7) not out	15	31	26	-	2
C.de Grandhomme lbw b Robinson	0	16	10	-	-	(8) not out	9	6	5	-	1
M.J.Santner c Anderson b Wood	0	9	6	-	-						
K.A.Jamieson c Crawley b Robinson	9	27	21	-	1						
T.G.Southee c Bracey b Anderson	8	29	19	-	-						
N.Wagner not out	25	30	21	1	3	(4) c Bracey b Robinson	10	32	39	-	2
Extras (b 7, lb 15, nb 2)	24					(b 6, lb 12, nb 1)	19				
TOTAL (122.4 overs)	**378**	578				(52.3 overs) (6 wkts dec)	**169**	211			

ENGLAND

	Runs	Mins	Balls	6s	4s		Runs	Mins	Balls	6s	4s
R.J.Burns c Watling b Southee	132	477	297	1	16	c Southee b Wagner	25	107	81	-	4
D.P.Sibley lbw b Jamieson	0	15	7	-	-	not out	60	312	207	-	3
Z.Crawley c Watling b Southee	2	17	10	-	-	c Nicholls b Southee	2	31	25	-	-
J.E.Root* c Taylor b Jamieson	42	169	113	-	5	lbw b Wagner	40	109	71	-	5
O.J.D.Pope lbw b Southee	22	44	32	-	5	not out	20	66	41	-	3
D.W.Lawrence c de Grandhomme b Southee	0	7	2	-	-						
J.R.Bracey† b Southee	0	13	6	-	-						
O.E.Robinson c Jamieson b Southee	42	119	101	-	5						
M.A.Wood c Watling b Jamieson	0	12	3	-	-						
S.C.J.Broad b Wagner	10	37	24	1	-						
J.M.Anderson not out	8	47	20	-	1						
Extras (b 4, lb 4, w 1, nb 8)	17					(b 8, lb 10, nb 5)	23				
TOTAL (101.1 overs)	**275**	477				(70 overs) (3 wkts)	**170**	312			

Bowling	O	M	R	W	O	M	R	W
ENGLAND								
Anderson	28	7	83	2	15.3	3	44	0
Broad	27	5	79	0	12	1	34	1
Robinson	28	6	75	4	14	5	26	3
Wood	27	8	81	3	7	0	31	1
Root	12.4	1	38	0	4	0	16	1
NEW ZEALAND								
Southee	25.1	8	43	6	17	1	37	1
Jamieson	26	8	85	3	15	6	28	0
de Grandhomme	15	5	24	0	7	3	12	0
Wagner	24	3	83	1	16	7	27	2
Santner	10	4	30	0	13	3	38	0
Williamson	1	0	2	0	2	0	10	0

Fall of Wickets

	NZ 1st	E 1st	NZ 2nd	E 2nd
1st	58	4	39	49
2nd	86	18	57	56
3rd	114	111	74	136
4th	288	140	105	-
5th	292	140	133	-
6th	293	140	159	-
7th	294	203	-	-
8th	317	207	-	-
9th	338	223	-	-
10th	378	275	-	-

ENGLAND v NEW ZEALAND — Second Test

at Edgbaston, Birmingham on 10, 11, 12, 13 June, 2021
Toss : England. Umpires : R.K. Illingworth & R.A. Kettleborough
Close of play: 1st day: England 258-7, Lawrence 67, Wood 16; 2nd day: NZ 229-3, Taylor 46
3rd day: England 122-9, Stone 15, Anderson 0
New Zealand won by 8 wickets

New Zealand made six changes from the first test with Young, Blundell, Patel, Mitchell, Henry and Boult replacing Williamson, Watling and Santner (all injured) and de Grandhomme, Jamieson and Southee. England replaced Robinson (who had been suspended) with Stone.

Root won the toss and decided to bat first. England had an opening stand of 72 but then lost wickets steadily. Burns got fifty from 141 balls. The home team were helped by an eighth wicket stand of 66 to help them reach 303. Lawrence had his highest test score, his fifty needing 75 deliveries. Boult took four wickets while Henry got three.

New Zealand lost Latham at 15 but then Conway and Young added 122 for the second wicket. Conway got fifty from 85 balls while Young reached his maiden half-century off 132 balls. Taylor scored an 80-ball fifty as New Zealand went from 292-3 to 388 all out.

England had a deficit of 85 and Burns went to the second ball of the innings. Wickets fell regularly and the eighth wicket was the only one to reach 30 runs. England were dismissed for 122 with the first ball of the third day. Henry and Wagner got three wickets each while Boult and Patel each got two. New Zealand got the required runs for the loss of two wickets to record their first series win in England since 1999.

ENGLAND

FIRST INNINGS	*Runs*	*Mins*	*Balls*	*6s*	*4s*	*SECOND INNINGS*	*Runs*	*Mins*	*Balls*	*6s*	*4s*
R.J.Burns c Latham b Boult	81	251	187	-	10	c Latham b Henry	0	3	2	-	-
D.P.Sibley c Blundell b Henry	35	122	84	-	5	c Mitchell b Henry	8	22	14	-	1
Z.Crawley c Mitchell b Wagner	0	6	4	-	-	lbw b Henry	17	42	27	-	2
J.E.Root* c Blundell b Henry	4	13	7	-	1	c Blundell b Patel	11	102	61	-	1
O.J.D.Pope c Blundell b Patel	19	71	49	-	1	lbw b Wagner	23	29	20	-	3
D.W.Lawrence not out	81	223	124	-	13	c Blundell b Wagner	0	6	2	-	-
J.R.Bracey† c Mitchell b Boult	0	7	1	-	-	b Patel	8	23	20	-	1
O.P.Stone lbw b Patel	20	68	52	-	2	c Blundell b Boult	15	76	54	-	2
M.A.Wood b Henry	41	80	80	-	7	c Blundell b Wagner	29	45	38	1	5
S.C.J.Broad c Blundell b Boult	0	7	4	-	-	b Boult	1	5	3	-	-
J.M.Anderson lbw b Boult	4	23	16	-	1	not out	0	9	7	-	-
Extras (b 5, lb 10, w 1, nb 2)	18					(b 5, lb 4, nb 1)	10				
TOTAL (101 overs)	**303**	444				(41.1 overs)	**122**	195			

NEW ZEALAND

	Runs	*Mins*	*Balls*	*6s*	*4s*		*Runs*	*Mins*	*Balls*	*6s*	*4s*
T.W.M.Latham* lbw b Broad	6	25	16	-	1	not out	23	52	32	-	3
D.P.Conway c Crawley b Broad	80	200	143	-	12	c Bracey b Broad	3	10	4	-	-
W.A.Young c Pope b Lawrence	82	306	204	-	11	b Stone	8	37	31	-	1
L.R.P.L.Taylor c Bracey b Stone	80	201	139	-	11	not out	0	6	0	-	-
H.M.Nicholls c Bracey b Wood	21	102	56	-	1						
T.A.Blundell† c Root b Broad	34	120	77	-	5						
D.J.Mitchell c Crawley b Stone	6	35	22	-	-						
N.Wagner b Anderson	0	5	3	-	-						
M.J.Henry lbw b Wood	12	24	14	-	3						
A.Y.Patel lbw b Broad	20	44	33	-	3						
T.A.Boult not out	12	19	9	-	3						
Extras (b 13, lb 21, nb 1)	35					(b 4, w 1, nb 2)	7				
TOTAL (119.1 overs)	**388**	540				(10.5 overs) (2 wkts)	**41**	52			

Bowling	*O*	*M*	*R*	*W*	*O*	*M*	*R*	*W*
NEW ZEALAND								
Boult	29	6	85	4	10.1	2	34	2
Henry	26	7	78	3	12	2	36	3
Wagner	21	6	68	1	10	1	18	3
Mitchell	11	2	23	0				
Patel	14	4	34	2	9	4	25	2
ENGLAND								
Anderson	29	9	68	1	5	1	11	0
Broad	23.1	8	48	4	4	1	13	1
Wood	25	3	85	2	0.5	0	8	0
Stone	24	5	92	2	1	0	5	1
Root	15	3	45	0				
Lawrence	3	0	16	1				

Fall of Wickets

	E *1st*	**NZ** *1st*	**E** *2nd*	**NZ** *2nd*
1st	72	15	0	6
2nd	73	137	17	33
3rd	85	229	30	-
4th	127	292	58	-
5th	169	312	58	-
6th	175	335	71	-
7th	222	336	76	-
8th	288	353	120	-
9th	289	361	121	-
10th	303	388	122	-

INDIA v NEW ZEALAND World Test Championship Final

at Rose Bowl, Southampton on 18, 19, 20, 21, 22, 23 June, 2021
Toss : New Zealand. Umpires : M.A. Gough & R.K. Illingworth
Close of play: 1st day: no play; 2nd day: India 146-3, Kohli 44, Rahane 29
3rd day: NZ 101-2, Williamson 12, Taylor 0, 4th day: no play
5th day: India 64-2, Pujara 12, Kohli 8
New Zealand won by 8 wickets

New Zealand won the toss and decided to bowl first after the first day's play was abandoned. India had an opening stand of 62 before losing both openers within four overs. Kohli and Rahane added 61 for the fourth wicket off 27.2 overs. India finished the day at 146-3 from 64.4 overs but then lost seven wickets for 81 on the third day, being dismissed for 217. Jamieson took his fifth five wicket bag getting 5-31.

New Zealand had a 70 run opening stand and finished the day at 101-2, with Conway being dismissed for 54 two balls before players went off the field for bad light for 54. His fifty came from 137 deliveries. The fourth day's play was washed out and on the fifth day New Zealand were bowled out for 249, giving them a 32 run lead. Shami took four wickets and Ishant three. India reached 64-2 by stumps.

Play went into the reserve day and India were all out for 170. Southee took 4-48 and Boult 3-39 as New Zealand needed 139 to become the first winners of the ICC World Test Championship. The openers went at 33 and 44 but Williamson and Taylor then had an unbroken third wicket stand of 96 to secure the win. Williamson scored fifty off 86 balls.

INDIA

FIRST INNINGS	*Runs*	*Mins*	*Balls*	*6s*	*4s*	*SECOND INNINGS*	*Runs*	*Mins*	*Balls*	*6s*	*4s*
R.G.Sharma c Southee b Jamieson	34	88	68	-	6	lbw b Southee	30	121	81	-	2
S.Gill c Watling b Wagner	28	108	64	-	3	lbw b Southee	8	48	33	-	-
C.A.Pujara lbw b Boult	8	85	54	-	2	c Taylor b Jamieson	15	129	80	-	2
V.Kohli* lbw b Jamieson	44	196	132	-	1	c Watling b Jamieson	13	43	29	-	-
A.M.Rahane c Latham b Wagner	49	190	117	-	5	c Watling b Boult	15	69	40	-	1
R.R.Pant† c Latham b Jamieson	4	31	22	-	1	c Nicholls b Boult	41	149	88	-	4
R.A.Jadeja c Watling b Boult	15	102	53	-	2	c Watling b Wagner	16	60	49	-	2
R.Ashwin c Latham b Southee	22	36	27	-	3	c Taylor b Boult	7	38	19	-	-
I.Sharma c Taylor b Jamieson	4	28	16	-	-	(10) not out	1	17	6	-	-
J.J.Bumrah lbw b Jamieson	0	3	1	-	-	(11) c Latham b Southee	0	6	4	-	-
Mohammad Shami not out	4	9	1	-	1	(9) c Latham b Southee	13	20	10	-	3
Extras (lb 3, nb 2)	5					(b 1, lb 8, w 1, nb 1)	11				
TOTAL (92.1 overs)	**217**	447				(73 overs)	**170**	359			

NEW ZEALAND

FIRST INNINGS	*Runs*	*Mins*	*Balls*	*6s*	*4s*	*SECOND INNINGS*	*Runs*	*Mins*	*Balls*	*6s*	*4s*
T.W.M.Latham c Kohli b Ashwin	30	158	104	-	3	st Pant b Ashwin	9	59	41	-	-
D.P.Conway c Shami b Sharma I.	54	222	153	-	6	lbw b Ashwin	19	80	47	-	4
K.S.Williamson* c Kohli b Sharma I.	49	294	177	-	7	not out	52	147	89	-	8
L.R.P.L.Taylor c Gill b Shami	11	81	37	-	2	not out	47	127	100	-	6
H.M.Nicholls c Sharma R.G. b Sharma I.	7	35	24	-	1						
B-J.Watling† b Shami	1	6	3	-	-						
C.de Grandhomme lbw b Shami	13	48	30	-	1						
K.A.Jamieson c Bumrah b Shami	21	30	16	1	-						
T.G.Southee b Jadeja	30	60	46	2	1						
N.Wagner c Rahane b Ashwin	0	12	5	-	-						
T.A.Boult not out	7	15	8	-	1						
Extras (b 4, lb 16, nb 6)	26					(lb 11, nb 2)	13				
TOTAL (99.2 overs)	**249**	489				(45.5 overs) (2 wkts)	**140**	207			

Bowling	*O*	*M*	*R*	*W*	*O*	*M*	*R*	*W*
NEW ZEALAND								
Southee	22	6	64	1	19	4	48	4
Boult	21.1	4	47	2	15	2	39	3
Jamieson	22	12	31	5	24	10	30	2
de Grandhomme	12	6	32	0				
Wagner	15	5	40	2	15	2	44	1
INDIA								
Sharma I.	25	9	48	3	6.2	2	21	0
Bumrah	26	9	57	0	10.4	2	35	0
Shami	26	8	76	4	10.5	3	31	0
Ashwin	15	5	28	2	10	5	17	2
Jadeja	7.2	2	20	1	8	1	25	0

Fall of Wickets

	I *1st*	*NZ* *1st*	*I* *2nd*	*NZ* *2nd*
1st	62	70	24	33
2nd	63	101	51	44
3rd	88	117	71	-
4th	149	134	72	-
5th	156	135	109	-
6th	182	162	142	-
7th	205	192	156	-
8th	213	221	156	-
9th	213	234	170	-
10th	217	249	170	-

T.A.Blundell (sub) kept wicket for the last four balls of India's second innings

INTERNATIONAL SUMMARY

2020/21

Test Matches

	Played	*Won*	*Lost*	*Drawn*
West Indies	2	2	–	–
Pakistan	2	2	–	–
England	2	1	–	1
India	1	1	–	–
TOTAL	**7**	**6**	**–**	**1**

New Zealand Test Averages

BATTING	*M*	*I*	*NO*	*HS*	*Agg*	*Ave*	*100s*	*50s*	*Ct*	*St*
K.S. Williamson	5	8	1	251	754	107.71	3	1	1	-
D.P. Conway	3	6	0	200	379	63.16	1	2	-	-
H.M. Nicholls	7	9	0	174	517	57.44	2	2	6	-
D.J. Mitchell	4	4	1	102*	159	53.00	1	-	4	-
L.R.P.L. Taylor	7	11	3	80	326	40.75	-	2	12	-
K.A. Jamieson	6	6	2	51*	163	40.75	-	1	2	-
W.A. Young	3	4	0	82	138	34.50	-	1	1	-
T.A. Boult	6	4	3	12*	33	33.00	-	-	1	-
T.W.M. Latham	7	11	1	86	330	33.00	-	2	14	-
N. Wagner	6	6	2	66*	120	30.00	-	1	-	-
T.A. Blundell	5	6	0	64	147	24.50	-	1	10	-
B-J. Watling	5	7	1	73	132	22.00	-	1	26	-
A.Y. Patel	1	1	0	20	20	20.00	-	-	-	-
T.G. Southee	6	5	1	30	60	15.00	-	-	8	-
M.J. Santner	2	3	1	19	25	12.50	-	-	2	-
M.J. Henry	2	1	0	12	12	12.00	-	-	1	-
C. de Grandhomme	2	3	1	13	22	11.00	-	-	1	-

BOWLING	*O*	*M*	*R*	*W*	*Ave*	*Best*	*5*	*10w*
K.A. Jamieson	230.2	89	505	37	13.64	6-48	4	1
A.Y. Patel	23	8	59	4	14.75	2-25	-	-
T.G. Southee	248.5	68	625	30	20.83	6-43	2	-
N. Wagner	208	50	566	23	24.60	4-66	-	-
T.A. Boult	232.5	50	696	25	27.84	4-85	-	-
K.S. Williamson	8	1	29	1	29.00	1-16	-	-
M.J. Henry	70	16	207	7	29.57	3-36	-	-
M.J. Santner	48.3	12	127	2	63.50	2-52	-	-
D.J. Mitchell	25	4	64	1	64.00	1-7	-	-
C. de Grandhomme	34	14	68	0	-	-	-	-

One-day Internationals

	Played	*Won*	*Lost*	*Tied*	*NR*
Bangladesh	3	3	–	–	–
TOTAL	**3**	**3**	**–**	**–**	**–**

New Zealand One-day International Averages

BATTING	*M*	*I*	*NO*	*HS*	*Agg*	*Ave*	*100s*	*50s*	*Ct*	*St*	*SR*
T.W.M. Latham	3	2	1	110*	128	128.00	1	-	3	1	90
D.P. Conway	3	3	0	126	225	75.00	1	1	3	-	88
H.M. Nicholls	3	3	1	49*	80	40.00	-	-	3	-	86
M.J. Guptill	3	3	0	38	84	28.00	-	-	2	-	118
J.D.S. Neesham	3	2	0	30	34	17.00	-	-	1	-	89
W.A. Young	2	2	1	11*	12	12.00	-	-	1	-	92
L.R.P.L. Taylor	1	1	0	7	7	7.00	-	-	-	-	50
D.J. Mitchell	3	2	2	100*	112	-	1	-	-	-	114
M.J. Santner	3	1	1	3*	3	-	-	-	3	-	300
T.A. Boult	3	-	-	-	-	-	-	-	3	-	-
M.J. Henry	3	-	-	-	-	-	-	-	-	-	-
K.A. Jamieson	3	-	-	-	-	-	-	-	-	-	-

BOWLING	*O*	*M*	*R*	*W*	*Ave*	*Best*	*R/O*
M.J. Henry	29	6	101	6	16.83	4-27	3.48
J.D.S. Neesham	24.4	2	127	7	18.14	5-27	5.15
M.J. Santner	21	0	81	4	20.25	2-23	3.86
T.A. Boult	28.5	1	113	5	22.60	4-27	3.91
K.A. Jamieson	26	3	91	2	45.50	1-30	3.50
D.J. Mitchell	5	0	33	0	-	-	6.60

Twenty20 Internationals

	Played	Won	Lost	Tied	NR
West Indies	3	2	–	–	1
Pakistan	3	2	1	–	–
Australia	5	3	2	–	–
Bangladesh	3	3	–	–	–
TOTAL	**14**	**10**	**3**	**–**	**1**

New Zealand Twenty20 International Averages

BATTING	M	I	NO	HS	Agg	Ave	100s	50s	Ct	St	SR
D.P. Conway	14	11	3	99*	473	59.12	-	4	7	1	151
D.J. Mitchell	4	2	1	34*	45	45.00	-	-	-	-	204
G.D. Phillips	14	12	3	108	366	40.66	1	1	8	-	184
J.D.S. Neesham	11	7	3	48*	139	34.75	-	-	4	-	185
W.A. Young	3	2	0	53	67	33.50	-	1	1	-	142
M.J. Guptill	14	13	0	97	403	31.00	-	2	11	-	152
T.L. Seifert	11	9	1	84*	238	29.75	-	2	9	1	122
F.H. Allen	3	3	0	71	88	29.33	-	1	-	-	220
M.J. Santner	8	5	3	31*	53	26.50	-	-	5	-	143
K.S. Williamson	7	7	1	57*	140	23.33	-	2	5	-	123
K.A. Jamieson	8	4	2	30	41	20.50	-	-	3	-	151
M.S. Chapman	6	5	2	34	60	20.00	-	-	3	-	150
S.C. Kuggeleijn	4	1	0	14	14	14.00	-	-	1	-	233
T.G. Southee	12	4	1	6*	23	7.66	-	-	8	-	121
I.S. Sodhi	12	2	0	1	1	0.50	-	-	6	-	25
L.R.P.L. Taylor	2	2	1	0*	0	0.00	-	-	-	-	0
T.A. Boult	7	2	2	6*	6	-	-	-	1	-	100
T.D. Astle	1	-	-	-	-	-	-	-	-	-	-
H.K. Bennett	4	-	-	-	-	-	-	-	-	-	-
A.F. Milne	2	-	-	-	-	-	-	-	1	-	-
J.A. Duffy	1	-	-	-	-	-	-	-	-	-	-
L.H. Ferguson	5	-	-	-	-	-	-	-	1	-	-
B.M. Tickner	1	-	-	-	-	-	-	-	1	-	-

BOWLING	O	M	R	W	Ave	Best	R/O
T.D. Astle	2	0	13	4	3.25	4-13	6.50
J.A. Duffy	4	0	33	4	8.25	4-33	8.25
L.H. Ferguson	15	0	94	10	9.40	5-21	6.27
I.S. Sodhi	38	0	309	20	15.45	4-28	8.13
T.G. Southee	44	0	351	21	16.71	4-21	7.98
M.S. Chapman	3	0	18	1	18.00	1-9	6.00
A.F. Milne	5	0	58	3	19.33	2-34	11.60
S.C. Kuggeleijn	11	0	100	5	20.00	3-27	9.09
M.J. Santner	25.3	0	191	8	23.87	4-31	7.49
G.D. Phillips	7.3	0	57	2	28.50	1-11	7.60
T.A. Boult	27	0	220	7	31.42	2-22	8.15
H.K. Bennett	9.5	0	101	3	33.66	2-31	10.27
J.D.S. Neesham	14.3	0	170	5	34.00	2-10	11.72
B.M. Tickner	4	0	35	1	35.00	1-35	8.75
K.A. Jamieson	28.4	0	281	4	70.25	2-15	9.80
D.J. Mitchell	2	0	21	0	-	-	10.50

PROVINCIAL SUMMARIES

AUCKLAND CRICKET ASSOCIATION

Formed 1883, affiliated 1894/95.

Selectors: H. Malan, D. Watson and K.P. Walmsley

Auckland had a disappointing season finishing fourth in the Plunket Shield and fifth in both limited over formats.

Robbie O'Donnell (546 runs) was their top scorer in the Plunket Shield while Glenn Phillips, Will O'Donnell and Ben Horne all scored over 300 runs. Kyle Jamieson was the leading wicket taker with 20 victims. Will O'Donnell (537 runs) was the competition's leading scorer in the Ford Trophy while Ross ter Braak took 13 wickets. Sean Solia (266 runs) led the way in the Super Smash while Will Somerville was the leading bowler with 12 wickets.

Ben Horne kept wicket throughout the season. Robbie O'Donnell captained the side in all formats. Heinrich Malan again coached the side with Doug Watson assisting.

Contracted players were: Graeme Beghin, Jamie Brown, Mark Chapman, Louis Delport, Danru Ferns, Ben Horne, Ben Lister, Matt McEwan, Colin Munro (replaced by Ryan Harrison), Robbie O'Donnell, Will O'Donnell, Glenn Phillips, Ollie Pringle, Sean Solia, Will Somerville and Ross ter Braak.

CANTERBURY CRICKET ASSOCIATION

Formed 1877, affiliated 1894/95.

Selectors: M.G. Croy, B.P. Donkers, P.G. Fulton and C.E. McConchie

Canterbury had an oustanding season winning both the Plunket Shield and Ford Trophy and being beaten finalists in the Super Smash.

Cameron Fletcher got 473 runs in the Plunket Shield while Leo Carter, Ken McClure and Tom Latham all scored over 300 runs. Will Williams was the leading bowler in the Plunket Shield competition with 31 wickets while Fraser Sheat got 27 and Ed Nuttall 21.

In the Ford Trophy McClure was their leading batsman with 480 runs and Williams was again the competition's leading bowler with 20 wickets. Sean Davey and Matt Henry both got 15 wickets. In the Super Smash Daryl Mitchell scored 374 runs and Henry took 14 wickets.

Fletcher was the regular keeper getting 26 victims in the first-class programme although Latham kept in some limited over games. McConchie was the regular captain but Carter led the side when he was on New Zealand A duty. Peter Fulton coached the side for the first time.

Contracted players were: Todd Astle, Chad Bowes, Jack Boyle, Leo Carter, Sean Davey, Cameron Fletcher, Andrew Hazeldine (replaced by Jackson Latham), Tyler Lortan, Ken McClure, Cole McConchie, Daryl Mitchell, Ed Nuttall, Fraser Sheat, Henry Shipley, Theo van Woerkom, Will Williams.

CENTRAL DISTRICTS CRICKET ASSOCIATION

Formed 1950, affiliated 1954/55.

Selectors: A.N. Smith and D.T. Meiring

Central Districts finished fifth in the Plunket Shield, last in the Ford Trophy and were beaten semi-finalists in the Super Smash.

Dane Cleaver was the top scorer in first-class cricket with 410 runs while Greg Hay made 395. Ben Tickner took 23 wickets and Ray Toole secured 22. In the Ford Trophy George Worker got 357 runs and Jayden Lennox took 12 wickets. Worker scored 424 runs in the Super Smash while Tickner was the competition's top wicket taker with 17.

Dane Cleaver kept wicket in the Plunket Shield and Bayley Wiggins deputised. Hay captained the side in the Plunket Shield while Tom Bruce and Worker led the side in white ball cricket. Aldin Smith again coached the side.

Contracted players were: Doug Bracewell, Tom Bruce, Josh Clarkson, Dane Cleaver, Greg Hay, Jayden Lennox, Christian Leopard, Adam Milne (replaced by Joey Field), Seth Rance, Brad Schmulian, Ben Smith, Blair Tickner, Ray Toole, Ben Wheeler, Bayley Wiggins, George Worker.

NORTHERN DISTRICTS CRICKET ASSOCIATION

Formed 1953, granted Plunket Shield status 1956/57

Selectors: P.J. Malcon, G.W. Aldridge and S. Krishnamurthy

Northern Districts finished second in both the Plunket Shield and Ford Trophy and fourth in the Super Smash.

In the Plunket Shield Joe Carter was the competition's top scorer with 590 runs while Jeet Raval got 547. Scott Kuggeleijn, Ish Sodhi and Neil Wagner all took 17 wickets. Raval (409 runs) and Henry Cooper (405) were their leading batsmen in the Ford Trophy. Brett Hampton took 18 wickets with Brett Randell getting 15.

The Super Smash saw Anton Devcich and Tim Seifert both score over 250 runs while Kuggeleijn got 12 wickets. Wicketkeeping duties were shared by BJ Watling, Seifert and Peter Bocock. Carter captained the side in the Plunket Shield and some Ford Trophy games while Anton Devcich also led the side. Graeme Aldridge coached the side for the first time.

Contracted players were: James Baker, Peter Bocock, Dean Brownlie, Joe Carter, Katene Clarke, Henry Cooper, Anton Devcich, Matthew Fisher, Zak Gibson, Brett Hampton, Scott Kuggeleijn, Brett Randell, Jeet Raval, Tim Seifert, Anurag Verma, Joe Walker.

OTAGO CRICKET ASSOCIATION

Formed 1876, affiliated 1894/95.

Selectors: S. Martin, R. Walter, and W.C. McSkimming

Otago finished third in the Plunket Shield, fourth in the Ford Trophy and last in the Super Smash. Hamish Rutherford scored 588 runs in the Plunket Shield with Nick Kelly getting 577. Michael Rae took 29 wickets while Jacob Duffy and Rippon got 22 each.

In the Ford Trophy Neil Broom and Rippon both reached 300 runs while Rae took 16 wickets. The Super Smash saw Broom lead the way with 292 runs and Mitchell McClenaghan took 12 wickets. Max Chu and Mitch Renwick were the keepers. Hamish Rutherford and Jacob Duffy both captained the team. Rob Walter again coached the side.

Contracted players were: Matt Bacon, Neil Broom, Max Chu, Jacob Duffy, Josh Finnie, Dean Foxcroft, Cam Hawkins, Nick Kelly, Anaru Kitchen, Jarrod McKay, Dale Phillips, Michael Rae, Mitch Renwick, Michael Rippon, Hamish Rutherford, Nathan Smith. Foxcroft was unable to return to New Zealand from South Africa because of Covid restrictions.

WELLINGTON CRICKET ASSOCIATION

Formed 1875, affiliated 1894/95.

Selectors: G.D. Pocknall and L.R. Dry

Wellington finished last in the Plunket Shield, third in the Ford Trophy but retained their title in the Super Smash.

In the Plunket Shield Michael Bracewell scored 560 runs while Devon Conway and Tom Blundell both scored over 400 runs. Iain McPeake was the leading bowler with 18 wickets. In the Ford Trophy Troy Johnson and Bracewell both scored over 300 runs while Peter Younghusband got 15 wickets. Finn Allen was the competition's top scorer in the Super Smash with 512 runs while Conway got 455. Hamish Bennett and Logan van Beek both took 13 wickets.

Blundell and Lauchie Johns kept wicket in first-class games. Bracewell captained the side in all formats but Fraser Colson and Troy Johnson led the side in some one-day games. The side was again coached by Glenn Pocknall.

Contracted players were: Finn Allen, Hamish Bennett, Jakob Bhula, Michael Bracewell, Fraser Colson, Andrew Fletcher, Jamie Gibson, Lauchie Johns, Troy Johnson, Iain McPeake, Ollie Newton, Rachin Ravindra, Ben Sears, Michael Snedden, Logan van Beek, Peter Younghusband.

PLUNKET SHIELD REVIEW 2020/21

The Plunket Shield was again played over eight rounds. Four rounds were played beginning on 19 October before the Ford Trophy started on 29 November. The Dream11 Super Smash took over from 24 December to 13 February with the Ford Trophy resuming on 19 February and ending on 6 March. The final four rounds of the Plunket Shield were played from 11 March to 6 April.

The final standings had some major differences from the previous year. Canterbury (previously fifth) and Northern Districts (who had been sixth) topped the table while Wellington, the winners in 2019/20, dropped to last place. Otago and Auckland remained third and fourth but Central Districts went from second place to fifth.

Canterbury were the dominant side throughout. They won their first three games and eventually claimed the title with two full rounds still to play. Canterbury and Auckland were both unbeaten while Wellington were the only side not gain at least one win.

Canterbury and Otago gained the maximum twenty points from a game while Otago and Northern Districts each took just one point in a game (for bowling).

Bonus points for batting and bowling were again available for the first 110 overs of the first innings. No points were awarded for a first innings lead. Playing time was six hours per day, although this was extended if the number of overs to be bowled in the day had not been completed. Teams were required to bowl 96 overs a day with no reduction for change of innings. Penalties for slow over rates were calculated round by round instead of over the whole season.

Points were awarded as follows:

a) twelve points for an outright win
b) six points for a tie
c) batting points at 200, 250, 300 and 350 runs
(available in first innings up to 110 overs)
d) bowling points at 3, 5, 7 and 9 wickets
(available in first innings up to 110 overs)

Final points and placings were:

	P	*OW*	*OL*	*Draw*	*Bat*	*Bowl*	TOTAL
Canterbury	8	5	–	3	19	30	109
Northern Districts	8	3	2	3	11	22	69
Otago	8	2	4	2	13	26	63
Auckland*	8	2	–	5	12	21	61
Central Districts*	8	2	4	1	7	21	56
Wellington	8	–	4	4	12	25	37

**Central Districts and Auckland were each awarded four points for their abandoned match*

NORTHERN DISTRICTS v CENTRAL DISTRICTS Plunket Shield

at Seddon Park, Hamilton on 19, 20, 21, 22 October, 2020
Toss : Central Districts. Umpires : B.F. Bowden & J.M. Dempsey
Close of play: 1st day: ND 81-0, Cooper 32, Raval 44; 2nd day: ND 121-0, Cooper 48, Raval 68
3rd day: ND 145-2, Carter 10, Clarke 4
***Central Districts won by 7 wickets.** Points: Central Districts 15 (3 bowl), Northern Districts 2 (2 bat)*

Rain caused disruptions on the first three days in which time just 41.3 overs were bowled and Northern had reached 145-2. Cooper and Raval (making his debut for Northern Districts) had put on 127 for the first wicket. Northern continued on the fourth day and declared at 253-8. Both teams then forfeited an innings, leaving Central 254 for victory.

Worker and Hay were undaunted by the Northern attack, which featured Southee, Wagner and de Grandhomme, and put on 177 before being parted. The two Central openers both fell in the 90s and Taylor was dismissed first ball but an unbeaten 43 from Young (off 40 balls) saw the visitors home.

NORTHERN DISTRICTS

FIRST INNINGS	*Runs*	*Mins*	*Balls*	*6s*	*4s*	*SECOND INNINGS*	*Runs*	*Mins*	*Balls*	*6s*	*4s*
H.R.Cooper c Bruce b Bracewell	58	169	108	1	6						
J.A.Raval c Taylor b Rance	68	163	115	-	8						
J.F.Carter* c Hay b Toole	26	86	65	-	4						
K.D.Clarke lbw b Bracewell	4	22	14	-	1						
C.de Grandhomme lbw b Schmulian	23	62	36	-	2						
S.C.Kuggeleijn b Rance	21	24	15	1	2						
P.D.Bocock† not out	36	42	25	5	1						
T.G.Southee c Hay b Schmulian	1	5	4	-	-						
N.Wagner c Bruce b Schmulian	0	13	2	-	-						
J.G.Walker not out	8	2	7	-	2						
J.D.Baker											
I.S.Sodhi											
Extras (lb 6, w 1, nb 1)	8										
TOTAL (65 overs) (8 wkts dec)	**253**	296				Innings forfeited					

CENTRAL DISTRICTS

G.H.Worker						c Kuggeleijn b Wagner	96	219	173	2	11
G.R.Hay*						lbw b Wagner	93	290	184	-	8
W.A.Young						not out	43	78	40	-	7
L.R.P.L.Taylor						lbw b Wagner	0	2	1	-	-
T.C.Bruce						not out	4	5	2	-	1
D.Cleaver†											
B.D.Schmulian											
D.A.J.Bracewell											
B.M.Tickner											
S.H.A.Rance											
R.L.Toole											
						(lb 5, w 12, nb 1)	18				
Innings forfeited						(66.3 overs) (3 wkts)	**254**	298			

Bowling	*O*	*M*	*R*	*W*	*O*	*M*	*R*	*W*
CENTRAL DISTRICTS								
Bracewell	23	2	60	2				
Rance	12.2	0	78	2				
Toole	14	4	55	1				
Tickner	9.4	3	38	0				
Schmulian	6	1	16	3				
NORTHERN DISTRICTS								
Southee					10	0	36	0
Wagner					17	0	65	3
de Grandhomme					12	3	42	0
Baker					16	1	60	0
Kuggeleijn					10.3	1	42	0
Walker					1	0	4	0

Fall of Wickets

	ND 1st	***CD 1st***	***ND 2nd***	***CD 2nd***
1st	127	-	-	177
2nd	135	-	-	248
3rd	146	-	-	248
4th	186	-	-	-
5th	188	-	-	-
6th	216	-	-	-
7th	233	-	-	-
8th	233	-	-	-
9th	-	-	-	-
10th	-	-	-	-

Walker replaced Sodhi as a Covid substitute on the 4th day

WELLINGTON v CANTERBURY — Plunket Shield

at Basin Reserve, Wellington on 19, 20, 21, 22 October, 2020
Toss : Canterbury. Umpires : C.M. Brown & A. Mehrotra
Close of play: 1st day: Wellington 46-2, Conway 22, Fletcher 2; 2nd day: Canterbury 148-5, Carter 18, Fletcher 4
3rd day: Canterbury 2-0, Latham 1, Bowes 1
***Canterbury won by 8 wickets.** Points: Canterbury 16 (4 bowl), Wellington 4 (4 bowl)*

Allen and Mitchell were making their debuts for their new provinces as Canterbury won the toss and decided to field on a day when just 19.1 overs were possible. Wellington finished on 46-2 but then lost their remaining wickets for just 19 in 15 overs the next day. Conway (31) scored more than half of the runs which came from the bat.

Canterbury did not have matters all their own way and were 148-5 at stumps and also collapsed when resuming the following day. However, they did lead by 91 runs.

Wellington again relied heavily on Conway when they batted again as he top scored with 81. Williams and Mitchell took four wickets apiece as Wellington were dismissed just before the end of the third day.

On the last day a brisk 86 from Latham made sure that Canterbury were untroubled to win their opening game of the season. In 162 games between the two sides, both teams had now won 59 games.

WELLINGTON

FIRST INNINGS	Runs	Mins	Balls	6s	4s	SECOND INNINGS	Runs	Mins	Balls	6s	4s
R.Ravindra c Fletcher b Williams	8	40	22	-	-	c Fletcher b Williams	20	109	74	-	2
T.A.Blundell† c Henry b Nuttall	2	15	10	-	-	c Latham b Williams	17	47	36	-	3
D.P.Conway c Latham b Mitchell	31	122	86	-	6	lbw b Mitchell	81	226	152	-	12
A.T.Fletcher lbw b Nuttall	2	60	33	-	-	c Latham b Nuttall	10	38	33	-	1
M.G.Bracewell* c Mitchell b Henry	7	21	24	-	1	b Mitchell	20	31	21	-	3
F.H.Allen c McClure b Henry	0	9	6	-	-	c Latham b Williams	0	35	29	-	-
J.D.Gibson b Henry	0	8	2	-	-	b Mitchell	5	21	13	-	1
L.V.van Beek c McClure b Mitchell	0	9	4	-	-	not out	21	108	72	-	1
O.R.Newton run out	2	13	10	-	-	c Fletcher b McConchie	7	19	13	-	-
I.G.McPeake lbw b Henry	0	14	5	-	-	lbw b Mitchell	8	24	20	-	1
H.K.Bennett not out	0	6	6	-	-	c McClure b Williams	10	27	22	-	2
Extras (lb 8, w 2, nb 3)	13					(lb 12, w 1)	13				
TOTAL (34.1 overs)	**65**	162				(80.5 overs)	**212**	345			

CANTERBURY

FIRST INNINGS	Runs	Mins	Balls	6s	4s	SECOND INNINGS	Runs	Mins	Balls	6s	4s
T.W.M.Latham b Gibson	14	61	42	-	2	lbw b Ravindra	86	122	95	2	12
C.J.Bowes c Allen b McPeake	34	169	111	-	4	c Gibson b Ravindra	29	128	77	-	3
K.J.McClure c Blundell b Newton	32	149	104	-	5	not out	0	8	5	-	-
C.E.McConchie* c Gibson b McPeake	16	94	67	-	2	not out	6	3	2	1	-
D.J.Mitchell b Bracewell	26	94	59	-	2						
L.J.Carter c Blundell b Bennett	20	84	69	-	2						
C.D.Fletcher† c Blundell b Newton	4	32	36	-	-						
T.F.van Woerkom c Blundell b Bennett	0	21	10	-	-						
M.J.Henry c Blundell b Bennett	0	5	5	-	-						
W.S.A.Williams c Allen b Bennett	3	16	10	-	-						
E.J.Nuttall not out	2	10	7	-	-						
Extras (lb 3, w 1, nb 1)	5					(b 1, lb 2, w 1, nb 1)	5				
TOTAL (86.3 overs)	**156**	369				(29.5 overs) (2 wkts)	**126**	131			

Bowling	O	M	R	W	O	M	R	W
CANTERBURY								
Henry	15.1	6	22	4	23	11	38	0
Nuttall	9	3	25	2	12	0	58	1
Williams	6	3	5	1	18.5	7	35	4
Mitchell	4	2	5	2	22	5	57	4
McConchie					3	1	6	1
van Woerkom					2	0	6	0
WELLINGTON								
Bennett	18.3	7	28	4	8	2	28	0
Newton	22	10	39	2	4	2	9	0
van Beek	3	1	3	0				
McPeake	17	7	31	2	4	0	19	0
Gibson	15	7	36	1	4	0	12	0
Bracewell	8	4	13	1	6	2	23	0
Ravindra	3	1	3	0	3.5	0	32	2

Fall of Wickets	W	C	W	C
	1st	1st	2nd	2nd
1st	8	23	26	119
2nd	30	79	66	120
3rd	51	91	95	-
4th	58	109	128	-
5th	62	140	136	-
6th	62	148	148	-
7th	62	150	171	-
8th	64	150	182	-
9th	65	153	200	-
10th	65	156	212	-

AUCKLAND v OTAGO — Plunket Shield

at Eden Park Outer Oval, Auckland on 20, 21, 22 October, 2020
Toss : Auckland. Umpires : W.R. Knights & T.J. Parlane
Close of play: 1st day: Auckland 79-3, Solia 16, Guptill 37; 2nd day: Otago 13-1, Kitchen 13, Rae 0
***Auckland won by an innings and 129 runs.** Points: Auckland 18 (2 bat, 4 bowl), Otago 3 (3 bowl)*

Otago's innings was dominated by Rippon's maiden century which came from 115 balls. Otago were in dire straits at 21-5 when he came to the crease and were soon 33-6 before Chu assisted in a stand of 107.

Auckland were also in trouble at 164-8 before Horne (his century from 183 balls and highest score) and Ferns (first fifty) put on 204 for the ninth wicket. This was an Auckland record for the ninth wicket against all teams.

Facing a deficit of 183, Otago collapsed completely. Their total of 54 was the lowest at the ground while Solia (5-8) had his first five wicket bag. Pringle, son of former Auckland player Martin, made his first-class debut in this game.

OTAGO

FIRST INNINGS	*Runs*	*Mins*	*Balls*	*6s*	*4s*	*SECOND INNINGS*	*Runs*	*Mins*	*Balls*	*6s*	*4s*
A.K.Kitchen c Phillips b Jamieson	14	39	34	-	2	lbw b Solia	30	122	73	-	4
C.T.Hawkins c Horne b Lister	1	14	8	-	-	lbw b Ferns	0	7	4	-	-
M.Renwick b Jamieson	0	13	8	-	-	(4) c Phillips b Jamieson	0	10	7	-	-
H.D.Rutherford* c Horne b Pringle	6	25	19	-	-	(5) c & b Jamieson	9	18	11	-	1
N.F.Kelly b Jamieson	0	2	1	-	-	(6) c Horne b Solia	1	11	7	-	-
N.G.Smith lbw b Ferns	0	11	7	-	-	(7) c Horne b Pringle	1	6	7	-	-
M.J.G.Rippon c Phillips b Jamieson	106	176	127	2	14	(8) c Guptill b Solia	6	9	7	1	-
M.W.Chu† b Ferns	42	121	84	-	8	(9) not out	4	39	21	-	1
J.A.Duffy c Horne b Ferns	3	13	14	-	-	(10) c Guptill b Solia	0	8	6	-	-
T.Muller not out	7	44	23	-	1	(11) b Solia	0	2	1	-	-
M.D.Rae b Jamieson	0	2	2	-	-	(3) c Guptill b Jamieson	0	30	18	-	-
Extras (lb 2, w 1, nb 4)	7					(lb 1, nb 2)	3				
TOTAL (53.5 overs)	**186**	232				(26.4 overs)	**54**	133			

AUCKLAND

	Runs	*Mins*	*Balls*	*6s*	*4s*
G.K.Beghin c Chu b Duffy	2	26	23	-	-
S.M.Solia c Renwick b Duffy	17	193	123	-	1
G.D.Phillips lbw b Smith	6	11	8	-	1
R.R.O'Donnell* c Chu b Rae	10	23	24	-	2
M.J.Guptill lbw b Smith	65	195	146	-	11
M.S.Chapman c & b Duffy	3	9	6	-	-
B.J.Horne† c Rutherford b Muller	162	314	236	3	18
K.A.Jamieson c Smith b Rippon	3	23	12	-	-
W.E.R.Somerville c Kitchen b Rippon	6	31	28	-	-
D.K.Ferns not out	63	213	155	1	7
O.M.R.Pringle not out	0	7	4	-	-
B.G.Lister					
Extras (b 6, lb 8, w 3, nb 15)	32				
TOTAL (125 overs) (9 wkts dec)	**369**	525			

Bowling	*O*	*M*	*R*	*W*	*O*	*M*	*R*	*W*
AUCKLAND								
Jamieson	12.5	2	39	5	8	4	6	3
Lister	11	2	40	1				
Ferns	10	1	44	3	6	3	27	1
Pringle	10	4	34	1	5	2	11	1
Solia	3	1	13	0	5.4	1	8	5
Somerville	7	1	14	0	2	1	1	0
OTAGO								
Duffy	28	10	60	3				
Smith	15	7	19	2				
Muller	19	4	62	1				
Rae	24	3	80	1				
Rippon	29	4	103	2				
Kitchen	10	4	31	0				

Fall of Wickets

	O	***A***	***O***
	1st	*1st*	*2nd*
1st	6	6	0
2nd	11	13	23
3rd	16	28	23
4th	16	88	37
5th	21	94	39
6th	33	131	41
7th	140	147	48
8th	152	164	54
9th	186	368	54
10th	186	-	54

Lister began the game as a Covid substitute for Chapman who subsequently replaced him

AUCKLAND v CENTRAL DISTRICTS — Plunket Shield

at Eden Park Outer Oval, Auckland on 28, 29, 30, 31 October, 2020
Toss : Auckland. Umpires : C.M. Brown & J.M. Dempsey
Close of play: 1st day: CD 81-3, Worker 26; 2nd day: Auckland 198-5, O'Donnell 13, Horne 18
3rd day: CD 210-8, Bracewell 65, Rance 0
***Auckland won by 25 runs.** Points: Auckland 16 (4 bowl), Central Districts 4 (4 bowl)*

Auckland decided to bat first but were soon 6-2 and they never recovered. Chapman top scored with 54 as all Central's bowlers were successful. Central were 81-3 at stumps but could post just 150 the following day. Jamieson took his second five wicket bag in successive games and performed the hat-trick, dismissing Bruce, Cleaver and Schmulian. Worker opened the batting and was last out.

Auckland made 269 in their second innings with fifties to Beghin and Phillips. Central needed 287 to win and were 210-8 at the close, with Bracewell on 65. Field (making his first-class debut) had shared a 102 run stand for the eighth wicket, Central's highest against Auckland.

Rance went at 220 the next day but Bracewell completed his hundred (from 131 balls) and found an ally in Toole. The pair had added 41 in 46 minutes before Bracewell was caught, giving Auckland a win by 25 runs. This was the 100th contest between the two sides.

AUCKLAND

FIRST INNINGS	*Runs*	*Mins*	*Balls*	*6s*	*4s*	*SECOND INNINGS*	*Runs*	*Mins*	*Balls*	*6s*	*4s*
G.K.Beghin c Cleaver b Bracewell	2	37	25	-	-	c & b Toole	55	129	101	-	7
S.M.Solia c Cleaver b Rance	0	8	8	-	-	lbw b Rance	2	16	7	-	-
G.D.Phillips c Cleaver b Bracewell	15	64	39	2	-	b Toole	66	140	79	1	11
M.S.Chapman lbw b Bracewell	54	149	93	-	9	c Bruce b Schmulian	6	66	50	-	-
M.J.Guptill b Rance	3	57	38	-	-	c Young b Bracewell	25	67	47	1	3
R.R.O'Donnell* c Cleaver b Rance	7	28	18	-	1	c Taylor b Bracewell	13	100	91	-	1
B.J.Horne† b Field	12	52	40	-	2	lbw b Toole	18	87	60	-	3
K.A.Jamieson c Young b Field	6	34	21	-	-	lbw b Bracewell	17	51	35	-	2
W.E.R.Somerville c Taylor b Toole	14	67	54	-	1	not out	22	96	56	-	3
D.K.Ferns c Worker b Schmulian	18	83	55	-	2	c Bruce b Bracewell	9	19	15	-	2
O.M.R.Pringle not out	19	25	24	-	4	c Cleaver b Toole	18	41	36	-	3
Extras (b 2, lb 5, w 2, nb 8)	17					(b 7, lb 3, w 1, nb 7)	18				
TOTAL (67.5 overs)	**167**	306				(95 overs)	**269**	409			

CENTRAL DISTRICTS

FIRST INNINGS	*Runs*	*Mins*	*Balls*	*6s*	*4s*	*SECOND INNINGS*	*Runs*	*Mins*	*Balls*	*6s*	*4s*
G.H.Worker c Phillips b Ferns	53	240	163	-	7	b Jamieson	5	17	13	-	1
G.R.Hay* c Guptill b Ferns	5	23	12	-	1	lbw b Pringle	17	87	55	-	3
W.A.Young lbw b Solia	9	39	19	-	2	lbw b Solia	23	50	37	-	4
L.R.P.L.Taylor c Phillips b Jamieson	27	40	28	2	2	c Jamieson b Pringle	21	40	25	-	5
T.C.Bruce c Guptill b Jamieson	8	16	13	1	-	c Guptill b Jamieson	1	14	10	-	-
D.Cleaver† b Jamieson	0	1	1	-	-	c Guptill b Solia	19	49	27	-	4
B.D.Schmulian b Jamieson	0	2	1	-	-	c Phillips b Somerville	17	45	33	-	2
D.A.J.Bracewell b Jamieson	20	47	28	-	4	c Chapman b Solia	102	197	137	5	7
J.F.A.Field b Solia	5	30	23	-	1	lbw b Solia	32	129	92	-	5
S.H.A.Rance c Solia b Pringle	0	10	3	-	-	c Guptill b Somerville	4	20	12	-	-
R.L.Toole not out	0	24	13	-	-	not out	6	46	34	-	1
Extras (b 6, lb 12, w 1, nb 4)	23					(b 4, lb 10)	14				
TOTAL (50 overs)	**150**	240				(79.1 overs)	**261**	350			

Bowling	*O*	*M*	*R*	*W*	*O*	*M*	*R*	*W*
CENTRAL DISTRICTS								
Bracewell	16	6	18	3	22	2	96	4
Rance	16	2	54	3	19	5	48	1
Toole	18	2	57	1	18	8	38	4
Field	11	3	18	2	15	5	44	0
Schmulian	6.5	1	13	1	18	9	25	1
Worker					2	0	4	0
Bruce					1	0	4	0
AUCKLAND								
Jamieson	17	7	41	5	18	6	46	2
Ferns	13	4	22	2	16	5	63	0
Pringle	9	4	19	1	10	1	43	2
Solia	9	1	29	2	14.1	2	41	4
Somerville	2	0	21	0	20	5	52	2
Phillips					1	0	2	0

Fall of Wickets

	A	*CD*	*A*	*CD*
	1st	*1st*	*2nd*	*2nd*
1st	2	8	4	8
2nd	6	33	116	43
3rd	33	81	135	52
4th	58	91	142	57
5th	77	91	163	69
6th	100	91	199	106
7th	108	124	201	106
8th	112	137	221	208
9th	139	138	236	220
10th	167	150	269	261

Phillips caught Worker in the first innings while keeping wicket. C.J.Briggs (sub) kept in Central's second innings

CANTERBURY v WELLINGTON — Plunket Shield

at Hagley Oval, Christchurch on 28, 29, 30, 31 October, 2020
Toss : Canterbury. Umpires : T.J. Parlane & D.J. Walker
Close of play: 1st day: Canterbury 146-4, Mitchell 22, Carter 42; 2nd day: Canterbury 315-5, Mitchell 81, Fletcher 57
3rd day: Wellington 220-6, Gibson 72, Newton 0
***Canterbury won by an innings and 19 runs.** Points: Canterbury 20 (4 bat, 4 bowl), Wellington 2 (2 bowl)*

Canterbury won the toss and bowled and were soon rewarded with the wickets of both Wellington openers. Conway (27) again top scored for Wellington as they were dismissed for 115 with Sheat claiming his first five wicket haul.

Canterbury had claimed the lead by stumps and carried on to make 410-6 after interruptions on the second day. Mitchell (241 balls) and Fletcher (190 balls) both hit hundreds.

Wellington's second innings saw more runs from Conway and a maiden hundred from Gibson (201 balls) but there was little else with eight batsmen being dismissed for single figure scores. Williams took his first five wicket bag as Canterbury wrapped up an innings win.

WELLINGTON

FIRST INNINGS	*Runs*	*Mins*	*Balls*	*6s*	*4s*	*SECOND INNINGS*	*Runs*	*Mins*	*Balls*	*6s*	*4s*
R.Ravindra c McClure b Nuttall	0	9	9	-	-	lbw b Williams	7	36	22	-	-
T.A.Blundell† c Mitchell b Nuttall	8	36	17	-	1	c Mitchell b Nuttall	1	5	2	-	-
D.P.Conway c Fletcher b Sheat	27	74	49	-	4	c Latham b Williams	94	285	210	1	13
A.T.Fletcher c McClure b Williams	9	80	53	-	-	c Latham b Williams	33	71	49	-	4
M.G.Bracewell* c Mitchell b Nuttall	19	69	52	-	2	lbw b Williams	0	9	7	-	-
F.H.Allen c Fletcher b Sheat	17	29	23	-	3	b Mitchell	3	11	3	-	-
J.D.Gibson c Nuttall b Sheat	24	58	30	1	2	not out	116	268	216	1	15
O.R.Newton c Bowes b Sheat	0	20	11	-	-	c Latham b Sheat	1	23	17	-	-
B.V.Sears c van Woerkom b Sheat	0	20	16	-	-	lbw b Nuttall	7	36	17	-	1
I.G.McPeake lbw b Williams	0	7	8	-	-	c McClure b Williams	0	11	5	-	-
H.K.Bennett not out	0	3	0	-	-	b Mitchell	3	34	22	-	-
Extras (b 1, lb 8, w 1, nb 1)	11					(lb 3, w 1, nb 7)	11				
TOTAL (44.3 overs)	**115**	205				(93.5 overs)	**276**	397			

CANTERBURY

	Runs	Mins	Balls	6s	4s
T.W.M.Latham lbw b Newton	45	123	84	1	7
C.J.Bowes lbw b McPeake	13	71	46	-	1
K.J.McClure c Blundell b McPeake	4	20	15	-	1
C.E.McConchie* c Bracewell b Newton	7	21	12	-	1
D.J.Mitchell c Ravindra b Newton	103	371	243	-	13
L.J.Carter c Ravindra b McPeake	87	131	84	5	8
C.D.Fletcher† not out	100	271	190	2	10
T.F.van Woerkom not out	28	43	33	2	1
W.S.A.Williams					
F.W.Sheat					
E.J.Nuttall					
Extras (b 4, lb 13, w 1, nb 5)	23				
TOTAL (117 overs) (6 wkts dec)	**410**	526			

Bowling	*O*	*M*	*R*	*W*	*O*	*M*	*R*	*W*
CANTERBURY								
Williams	12	6	16	2	26	9	58	5
Nuttall	12	3	48	3	16	1	69	2
Sheat	12.3	2	25	5	17	3	61	1
Mitchell	8	4	17	0	13.5	2	45	2
van Woerkom					10	2	28	0
McConchie					11	3	12	0
WELLINGTON								
Bennett	18	3	63	0				
Newton	24	4	91	3				
McPeake	32	12	74	3				
Sears	20	2	77	0				
Bracewell	4	0	33	0				
Gibson	16	7	44	0				
Ravindra	3	0	11	0				

Fall of Wickets	***W***	***C***	***W***
	1st	*1st*	*2nd*
1st	4	41	6
2nd	13	58	19
3rd	45	75	87
4th	54	86	87
5th	80	203	96
6th	84	357	218
7th	93	-	227
8th	112	-	245
9th	115	-	250
10th	115	-	276

NORTHERN DISTRICTS v OTAGO — Plunket Shield

at Bay Oval, Mt Maunganui on 28, 29, 30, 31 October, 2020
Toss : Northern Districts. Umpires : B.F. Bowden & W.R. Knights
Close of play: 1st day: ND 334-9, Carter 146, Wagner 1; 2nd day: ND 119-1, Cooper 58, Carter 37
3rd day: Otago 186-2, Hawkins 76, Rutherford 28
***Northern Districts won by 90 runs.** Points: Northern Districts 19 (3 bat, 4 bowl), Otago 4 (4 bowl)*

Northern Districts built a solid first innings after choosing to bat. Carter (century from 174 balls) held the innings together with de Grandhomme helping in a 121 run stand for the fifth wicket. Otago were bowled out for 179 on the second day and by stumps, Northern had extended their lead to 275.

Carter declared on the third day, leaving Otago 421 for victory. Kitchen and Hawkins (who went on to his highest score) responded with an opening stand of 109 and Otago had reached 186-2 by the close of play.

Rutherford was out with just two runs added on the last day and Smith soon followed. Hawkins fell ten short of his hundred and it was left to Kelly to put up some resistance. Rae helped in a last wicket stand of 83 but the stand was finally broken by Kuggeleijn, giving Northern a win by 90 runs.

NORTHERN DISTRICTS

FIRST INNINGS	*Runs*	*Mins*	*Balls*	*6s*	*4s*	*SECOND INNINGS*	*Runs*	*Mins*	*Balls*	*6s*	*4s*
H.R.Cooper c Duffy b Rae	12	31	23	-	2	(2) c Chu b Duffy	85	211	163	1	14
J.A.Raval c Chu b Duffy	9	26	18	-	1	(1) c Chu b Rae	15	50	32	1	-
J.F.Carter* not out	146	361	251	-	20	c Chu b Duffy	54	140	94	-	6
K.D.Clarke lbw b Muller	34	74	52	1	3	c Muller b Rae	20	33	18	-	4
B-J.Watling† c Chu b Duffy	25	83	67	-	3	c Kitchen b Smith	15	40	19	-	2
C.de Grandhomme c Duffy b Kitchen	60	99	63	2	7	c Chu b Rae	23	11	9	3	-
S.C.Kuggeleijn c Duffy b Rippon	8	20	20	-	1	c Rippon b Smith	9	6	8	-	2
T.G.Southee c Chu b Rae	13	15	20	-	3	not out	19	35	13	1	1
I.S.Sodhi lbw b Rae	2	20	11	-	-						
J.G.Walker c Kitchen b Duffy	9	28	23	-	1						
N.Wagner lbw b Duffy	2	14	13	-	-	(9) not out	14	27	17	-	3
Extras (b 4, lb 4, w 6, nb 1)	15					(b 5, lb 3, w 1, nb 1)	10				
TOTAL (93 overs)	**335**	387				(62 overs) (7 wkts dec)	**264**	279			

OTAGO

	Runs	*Mins*	*Balls*	*6s*	*4s*		*Runs*	*Mins*	*Balls*	*6s*	*4s*
A.K.Kitchen lbw b Southee	0	1	1	-	-	b Sodhi	63	122	100	-	8
C.T.Hawkins c Raval b Southee	11	34	17	-	2	b Walker	90	296	211	-	7
M.Renwick lbw b Wagner	12	28	20	-	2	c Clarke b Sodhi	11	41	27	-	1
H.D.Rutherford* c de Grandhomme b Southee	4	10	3	-	-	c Watling b Southee	28	56	47	-	3
N.F.Kelly c Watling b Wagner	23	81	43	-	3	(6) not out	82	216	168	1	11
N.G.Smith c Cooper b Wagner	27	89	71	-	2	(5) c Sodhi b Southee	3	24	20	-	-
M.J.G.Rippon c Watling b Southee	44	78	45	1	5	c Watling b Kuggeleijn	3	6	4	-	-
M.W.Chu† b Wagner	28	108	68	-	4						
J.A.Duffy c Watling b Southee	4	15	12	-	1	(8) c Carter b Kuggeleijn	2	12	11	-	-
T.Muller not out	11	32	25	-	1	(9) lbw b Sodhi	6	30	22	-	-
M.D.Rae c Watling b Kuggeleijn	5	5	5	-	1	c Southee b Kuggeleijn	28	113	69	-	6
M.B.Bacon						(10) lbw b Sodhi	0	2	2	-	-
Extras (b 5, lb 3, nb 2)	10					(b 5, lb 3, w 3, nb 3)	14				
TOTAL (51.2 overs)	**179**	243				(113.1 overs)	**330**	462			

Bowling	*O*	*M*	*R*	*W*	*O*	*M*	*R*	*W*
OTAGO								
Duffy	20	6	52	4	13	2	53	2
Smith	10	3	23	0	10	2	46	2
Rae	20	3	105	3	18	1	102	3
Rippon	23	3	85	1	11	2	34	0
Muller	10	4	28	1	6	0	16	0
Kitchen	10	1	34	1	4	1	5	0
NORTHERN DISTRICTS								
Southee	14	0	42	5	22	5	55	2
Wagner	15	2	69	4	5	0	19	0
de Grandhomme	5	3	6	0	11	1	40	0
Kuggeleijn	10.2	1	31	1	20.1	4	46	3
Sodhi	7	1	23	0	31	6	89	4
Walker					24	5	73	1

Fall of Wickets

	ND	***O***	***ND***	***O***
	1st	*1st*	*2nd*	*2nd*
1st	21	0	41	109
2nd	21	22	153	137
3rd	83	30	176	188
4th	149	31	190	194
5th	270	79	217	221
6th	284	86	226	228
7th	300	139	233	236
8th	312	153	-	247
9th	333	174	-	247
10th	335	179	-	330

Bacon was a concussion substitute for Chu in Otago's second innings

CANTERBURY v NORTHERN DISTRICTS — Plunket Shield

at MainPower Oval, Rangiora on 5, 6, 7 November, 2020
Toss : Canterbury. Umpires : J.A.K. Bromley & T.J. Parlane
Close of play: 1st day: ND 7-0, Cooper 1, Raval 4; 2nd day: ND 39-3, Cooper 17, Watling 0
***Canterbury won by an innings and 32 runs.** Points: Canterbury 18 (2 bat, 4 bowl), Northern Districts 4 (4 bowl)*

Canterbury chose to bat and were dismissed just before the close of play. Carter made 50 and Sheat scored 36 out of a last wicket stand of 37 with Davey (first-class debut) with the other run being an extra.

Sheat was again prominent the following day as he and Williams (best bowling) took nine wickets between them as Northern were bowled out for just 113, after an opening stand of 52. Forced to follow on, Northern lost three more wickets before the close.

Northern's resistance did not last long on the third day as they were dismissed for 121, to give Canterbury an innings win. Sheat took 5-31, giving him match figures of 9-63.

CANTERBURY

FIRST INNINGS	*Runs*	*Mins*	*Balls*	*6s*	*4s*
C.J.Bowes c Carter b Randell	16	48	41	-	1
J.C.T.Boyle c Clarke b Hampton	27	118	82	-	3
K.J.McClure c Cooper b Sodhi	45	142	92	1	5
C.E.McConchie* lbw b Baker	2	35	24	-	-
D.J.Mitchell lbw b Kuggeleijn	30	116	76	1	-
L.J.Carter c Raval b Kuggeleijn	50	71	59	1	6
C.D.Fletcher† c Carter b Randell	17	101	71	-	2
T.F.van Woerkom lbw b Hampton	12	59	59	-	-
W.S.A.Williams c Cooper b Baker	11	41	25	-	1
S.B.Davey not out	0	24	5	-	-
F.W.Sheat c Cooper b Kuggeleijn	36	18	21	-	7
Extras (b 1, lb 8, w 1, nb 10)	20				
TOTAL (90.5 overs)	**266**	388			

NORTHERN DISTRICTS

	Runs	Mins	Balls	6s	4s		Runs	Mins	Balls	6s	4s
H.R.Cooper c Mitchell b Sheat	18	130	101	-	2	(2) c Fletcher b Sheat	22	140	86	-	1
J.A.Raval lbw b Sheat	23	108	70	-	1	(1) c Boyle b Sheat	2	37	28	-	-
J.F.Carter* c Mitchell b Sheat	0	3	2	-	-	c Boyle b Mitchell	9	29	19	-	-
K.D.Clarke b Mitchell	25	73	54	-	2	c van Woerkom b Mitchell	7	19	14	-	1
B-J.Watling† c McConchie b Williams	23	128	80	-	3	lbw b Williams	0	13	9	-	-
S.C.Kuggeleijn b Williams	4	23	14	-	1	c Mitchell b Sheat	16	13	10	2	-
B.R.Hampton lbw b Williams	0	4	3	-	-	b Sheat	3	31	24	-	-
I.S.Sodhi c Bowes b Williams	5	25	11	-	1	lbw b Davey	17	36	18	1	1
J.G.Walker lbw b Sheat	1	16	16	-	-	c Mitchell b Sheat	15	16	13	-	2
B.G.Randell lbw b Williams	0	6	4	-	-	c Carter b Mitchell	12	36	28	-	1
J.D.Baker not out	0	2	0	-	-	not out	12	21	15	1	-
Extras (b 1, lb 10, w 1, nb 2)	14					(lb 3, w 2, nb 1)	6				
TOTAL (59 overs)	**113**	261				(43.5 overs)	**121**	198			

Bowling	*O*	*M*	*R*	*W*	*O*	*M*	*R*	*W*
NORTHERN DISTRICTS								
Kuggeleijn	15.5	2	44	3				
Baker	23	7	57	2				
Randell	16	2	58	2				
Hampton	14	5	40	2				
Sodhi	7	0	40	1				
Walker	15	7	18	0				
CANTERBURY								
Williams	18	8	26	5	14	5	39	1
Sheat	16	5	32	4	16	7	31	5
Mitchell	13	5	25	1	5.5	2	10	3
Davey	12	4	19	0	8	0	38	1

Fall of Wickets	***C***	***ND***	***ND***
	1st	*1st*	*2nd*
1st	28	52	4
2nd	73	52	25
3rd	81	57	39
4th	112	80	39
5th	182	92	58
6th	183	92	63
7th	203	108	64
8th	226	111	86
9th	229	113	105
10th	266	113	121

CENTRAL DISTRICTS v AUCKLAND — Plunket Shield

at Saxton Oval, Nelson on 5, 6, 7, 8 November, 2020
***Abandoned without a ball being bowled.** Points: Central Districts 4, Auckland 4*

WELLINGTON v OTAGO — Plunket Shield

at Basin Reserve, Wellington on 5, 6, 7, 8 November, 2020
Toss : Wellington. Umpires : C.M. Brown & S.B. Haig
Close of play: 1st day: Wellington 48-1, Blundell 31; 2nd day: Otago 36-1, Hawkins 21, Phillips 4
3rd day: Wellington 185-7, Blundell 101, Fletcher 8
***Otago won by 84 runs.** Points: Otago 18 (2 bat, 4 bowl), Wellington 5 (1 bat, 4 bowl)*

Otago were asked to bat and lost an early wicket. Phillips (maiden fifty) and Rutherford scored half-centuries and the visitors reached 265 and took the wicket of Ravindra before the close.

Wellington struggled on the second day and it was only a last wicket stand of 61 between Sears and Bennett which took them past 200. Phillips (highest score) and Rutherford again scored fifties when Otago batted again and Wellington were left with 279 to win.

The home side were 185-7 at the close with Blundell dominating with 101 not out. The next morning he was given out obstructing the field, without addition, when he used his hand to stop the ball from hitting his stumps. The last two wickets soon followed to give Otago a comfortable win.

OTAGO

FIRST INNINGS	Runs	Mins	Balls	6s	4s	*SECOND INNINGS*	Runs	Mins	Balls	6s	4s
A.K.Kitchen b Newton	5	15	10	-	1	c Sears b Newton	6	39	24	-	1
C.T.Hawkins c Johns b Sears	24	100	61	-	2	c Gibson b Bennett	21	92	62	-	4
D.N.Phillips b Newton	65	117	82	-	11	not out	83	207	151	-	14
H.D.Rutherford* c Allen b Sears	57	130	99	-	10	lbw b Allen	69	131	87	1	12
N.F.Kelly c Johns b McPeake	24	82	43	-	4	not out	24	22	22	-	5
M.Renwick† b Gibson	7	28	19	-	1						
N.G.Smith c Bracewell b Newton	11	66	51	-	2						
M.J.G.Rippon c Johns b Newton	30	68	49	-	7						
J.A.Duffy not out	20	53	34	-	3						
T.Muller c Ravindra b Sears	16	32	33	-	3						
M.D.Rae c Gibson b Sears	0	5	2	-	-						
Extras (lb 5, w 1)	6					(b 6, lb 7, w 2)	15				
TOTAL (80.3 overs)	**265**	350				(57.4 overs) (3 wkts dec)	**218**	246			

WELLINGTON

	Runs	Mins	Balls	6s	4s		Runs	Mins	Balls	6s	4s
R.Ravindra c Muller b Rippon	9	51	31	-	1	b Muller	14	63	43	-	1
T.A.Blundell c Phillips b Duffy	31	71	59	-	7	obstructing the field	101	245	147	-	12
D.P.Conway b Duffy	4	15	11	-	-	c & b Duffy	16	45	32	-	4
M.G.Bracewell* c Phillips b Duffy	37	137	83	-	5	c Renwick b Duffy	1	11	11	-	-
F.H.Allen c Rutherford b Smith	3	27	20	-	-	c Kitchen b Rae	17	69	53	-	-
J.D.Gibson c Renwick b Muller	19	55	36	-	3	c Renwick b Rae	0	2	1	-	-
L.R.Johns† c Rippon b Rae	9	12	11	-	2	run out	0	4	1	-	-
O.R.Newton c Kitchen b Rae	4	17	11	-	1	b Duffy	11	11	11	-	2
B.V.Sears c Hawkins b Muller	41	194	154	-	5						
I.G.McPeake c Phillips b Duffy	0	14	10	-	-	c Kitchen b Duffy	0	23	12	-	-
H.K.Bennett not out	20	158	106	-	2	not out	2	8	6	-	-
A.T.Fletcher						c Kitchen b Smith	15	53	44	-	2
Extras (b 23, lb 3, w 2)	28					(b 6, lb 3, w 6, nb 2)	17				
TOTAL (88.4 overs)	**205**	378				(59.5 overs)	**194**	255			

Bowling	O	M	R	W	O	M	R	W
WELLINGTON								
Bennett	15	3	50	0	8	5	12	1
Newton	23	8	62	4	13	5	26	1
Gibson	10	3	27	1	5	1	24	0
McPeake	14	0	61	1	6	0	31	0
Sears	12.3	4	46	4	8	1	27	0
Ravindra	6	1	14	0	9	4	32	0
Bracewell					2.4	0	18	0
Allen					3	0	15	1
Blundell					3	0	20	0
OTAGO								
Duffy	28	10	52	4	19.5	1	69	4
Smith	17	10	34	1	15	3	26	1
Rae	19	5	53	2	12	0	57	2
Rippon	4	0	8	1	4	0	11	0
Muller	14.4	5	20	2	8	2	21	1
Kitchen	6	1	12	0	1	0	1	0

Fall of Wickets

	O 1st	W 1st	O 2nd	W 2nd
1st	6	48	23	54
2nd	82	52	42	92
3rd	112	53	174	94
4th	168	64	-	152
5th	182	103	-	152
6th	188	112	-	156
7th	222	122	-	167
8th	229	142	-	186
9th	265	144	-	192
10th	265	205	-	194

Fletcher was a concussion substitute for Sears in Wellington's second innings

CENTRAL DISTRICTS v NORTHERN DISTRICTS Plunket Shield

at Saxton Oval, Nelson on 14, 15, 16, 17 November, 2020
Toss : Northern Districts. Umpires : C.M. Brown & K.D. Cotton
Close of play: 1st day: ND 223-6, Hampton 21, Southee 16; 2nd day: CD 161-4, Bruce 29, Cleaver 6
3rd day: ND 158-4, Watling 19, Kuggeleijn 15
***Northern Districts won by 40 runs.** Points: Northern Districts 17 (2 bat, 3 bowl), Central Districts 4 (2 bat, 2 bowl)*

Northern decided to bat but were in trouble at 31-3. Carter and Watling combined for a century stand for the fourth wicket and the visitors got through to 347, with some useful contributions from Hampton, Southee and Sodhi.

Central had eight batsmen reach double figures with Schmulian's 49 being the highest score. Hay declared 66 runs in arrears and Northern ran up 233-7 before they declared on the last day. Raval and Watling made fifties.

Central needed 300 to win but were soon 17-2. Young played an excellent innings, reaching three figures from 179 balls, but could not find sufficient support. Cleaver made 48 and Taylor 32 but it was not enough as Central were dismissed for 259, leaving Young unbeaten on 110.

NORTHERN DISTRICTS

FIRST INNINGS	*Runs*	*Mins*	*Balls*	*6s*	*4s*	*SECOND INNINGS*	*Runs*	*Mins*	*Balls*	*6s*	*4s*
H.R.Cooper c Cleaver b Toole	11	67	47	-	2	(2) c Cleaver b Rance	3	18	11	-	-
J.A.Raval c Taylor b Rance	5	27	22	-	1	(1) c Cleaver b Rance	63	151	119	-	10
J.F.Carter* lbw b Schmulian	66	258	184	-	7	lbw b Toole	44	166	90	-	6
K.D.Clarke c Worker b Toole	0	8	3	-	-	c sub (J.F.A.Field) b Toole	11	57	44	-	2
B-J.Watling† c Bruce b Tickner	77	303	214	-	10	not out	62	120	75	2	7
S.C.Kuggeleijn run out	10	29	29	1	-	b Bracewell	16	48	42	1	1
B.R.Hampton lbw b Rance	59	174	132	2	7	c Taylor b Bracewell	1	17	10	-	-
T.G.Southee c Taylor b Rance	36	93	59	-	5	c Bruce b Toole	27	33	24	1	2
I.S.Sodhi c Taylor b Rance	42	78	59	1	6	not out	1	4	2	-	-
J.G.Walker not out	12	79	50	-	2						
J.D.Baker lbw b Rance	0	18	13	-	-						
Extras (b 5, lb 11, w 4, nb 9)	29					(lb 2, nb 3)	5				
TOTAL (133.5 overs)	**347**	569				(69 overs) (7 wkts dec)	**233**	305			

CENTRAL DISTRICTS

	Runs	*Mins*	*Balls*	*6s*	*4s*		*Runs*	*Mins*	*Balls*	*6s*	*4s*
G.H.Worker b Walker	11	52	49	-	1	lbw b Southee	6	19	16	-	1
G.R.Hay* c Watling b Sodhi	39	118	84	-	5	b Southee	11	30	21	-	2
W.A.Young c Raval b Sodhi	14	56	38	-	2	not out	110	273	182	1	16
L.R.P.L.Taylor lbw b Baker	45	86	62	2	4	c Raval b Sodhi	32	52	39	-	7
T.C.Bruce lbw b Southee	41	124	80	-	5	b Walker	17	25	20	1	2
D.Cleaver† lbw b Southee	32	137	112	1	1	c Southee b Hampton	48	97	65	-	8
B.D.Schmulian c Watling b Southee	49	110	87	-	6	c Watling b Walker	13	32	22	-	2
D.A.J.Bracewell not out	28	55	29	2	2	b Southee	2	5	4	-	-
B.M.Tickner c Raval b Walker	5	22	17	-	1	(10) c Walker b Sodhi	11	28	25	-	2
S.H.A.Rance not out	9	13	8	1	-	(9) b Southee	2	8	5	-	-
R.L.Toole						b Sodhi	5	10	7	-	-
Extras (lb 6, nb 2)	8					(lb 2)	2				
TOTAL (94 overs) (8 wkts dec)	**281**	388				(67.4 overs)	**259**	292			

Bowling	*O*	*M*	*R*	*W*	*O*	*M*	*R*	*W*
CENTRAL DISTRICTS								
Bracewell	25	8	41	0	16	2	49	2
Rance	26.5	5	64	5	11	4	18	2
Toole	26	12	55	2	17	3	42	3
Tickner	24	6	73	1	8	0	31	0
Schmulian	29	8	81	1	11	2	68	0
Worker	2	0	10	0	6	2	23	0
Bruce	1	0	7	0				
NORTHERN DISTRICTS								
Southee	21	7	50	3	15	3	53	4
Baker	16	2	54	1	5	0	18	0
Walker	27	4	83	2	22	2	94	2
Kuggeleijn	9	0	23	0	9	0	34	0
Sodhi	21	3	65	2	9.4	0	39	3
Hampton					7	1	19	1

Fall of Wickets

	ND *1st*	***CD*** *1st*	***ND*** *2nd*	***CD*** *2nd*
1st	9	29	13	12
2nd	29	68	108	17
3rd	31	71	122	70
4th	147	148	127	103
5th	161	165	161	197
6th	207	226	173	218
7th	281	241	220	221
8th	294	260	-	225
9th	345	-	-	243
10th	347	-	-	259

OTAGO v CANTERBURY

Plunket Shield

at Molyneux Park, Alexandra on 14, 15, 16, 17 November, 2020
Toss : Otago. Umpires : S.B. Haig & D.J. Walker
Close of play: 1st day: Canterbury 96-0, Latham 45, McClure 43; 2nd day: Canterbury 424-4, Mitchell 28, Carter 24
3rd day: Otago 157-4, Rutherford 26, Smith 21
***Match drawn.** Points: Canterbury 8 (4 bat, 4 bowl), Otago 1 (1 bowl)*

Otago won the toss and batted but it was not a successful move with Kitchen out in the first over, Phillips in the fourth and when Chu was dismissed it was 85-7. Kelly and Duffy did their best but Otago could tally just 168. Canterbury replied with 96-0 by the close of the day.

The Canterbury openers duly reached their century stand the next morning and McClure carried on to reach a hundred from 196 balls. Nicholls helped McClure add 198 for the second wicket and the visitors finally declared at 499-7 on the third day.

Otago were 331 in arrears and had reached 157-4 at stumps. Smith went early on the last day and when Duffy was dismissed Otago were 246-8. Muller stayed with Chu for almost two hours before he was caught and Otago were nine down. Chu could not be moved and Rae stayed for 75 minutes as Otago saved the game. Mitchell achieved his first five wicket haul.

OTAGO

FIRST INNINGS	Runs	Mins	Balls	6s	4s	SECOND INNINGS	Runs	Mins	Balls	6s	4s
A.K.Kitchen b Williams	4	2	3	-	1	b Mitchell	59	118	88	1	6
C.T.Hawkins c Mitchell b Williams	16	55	43	-	1	lbw b Mitchell	21	89	51	-	2
D.N.Phillips c Mitchell b Nuttall	9	15	10	-	2	b van Woerkom	2	5	5	-	-
H.D.Rutherford* c Fletcher b Sheat	6	50	23	-	1	c Fletcher b Mitchell	72	293	207	1	7
N.F.Kelly lbw b Nuttall	50	13	102	-	5	c Mitchell b McConchie	23	42	38	-	4
N.G.Smith c Mitchell b Sheat	10	11	9	-	2	b Mitchell	23	75	60	-	4
M.J.G.Rippon b Nuttall	11	23	11	-	2	c Fletcher b Williams	19	89	74	-	1
M.W.Chu† c Mitchell b McConchie	2	40	28	-	-	not out	41	271	229	-	6
J.A.Duffy c McClure b Sheat	43	86	48	-	7	b Mitchell	6	16	15	-	1
T.Muller st Fletcher b van Woerkom	13	63	46	-	2	c Nicholls b McConchie	46	116	97	1	5
M.D.Rae not out	0	21	15	-	-	not out	13	75	56	-	1
Extras (lb 2, nb 2)	4					(b 1, lb 8, nb 3)	12				
TOTAL (56 overs)	**168**	251				(153 overs) (9 wkts)	**337**	597			

CANTERBURY

	Runs	Mins	Balls	6s	4s
T.W.M.Latham c & b Rippon	63	168	130	-	7
K.J.McClure c Kelly b Smith	165	440	322	1	19
H.M.Nicholls b Muller	87	214	144	-	12
C.E.McConchie* c Rippon b Duffy	30	112	84	-	3
D.J.Mitchell c Rae b Kitchen	36	114	66	-	2
L.J.Carter c Kitchen b Duffy	49	56	60	-	7
T.F.van Woerkom c Muller b Smith	18	29	24	-	2
C.D.Fletcher† not out	20	30	21	-	2
W.S.A.Williams not out	2	2	1	-	-
F.W.Sheat					
E.J.Nuttall					
Extras (b 7, lb 14, w 2, nb 6)	29				
TOTAL (141 overs) (7 wkts dec)	**499**	585			

Bowling	*O*	*M*	*R*	*W*	*O*	*M*	*R*	*W*
CANTERBURY								
Williams	14	4	37	2	19	2	63	1
Nuttall	16	2	42	3	20	7	41	0
Sheat	14	3	48	3	12	4	40	0
Mitchell	9	1	39	0	28	10	44	5
McConchie	1	1	0	1	35	14	56	2
van Woerkom	2	2	0	1	37	9	82	1
McClure					2	0	2	0
OTAGO								
Duffy	25	3	80	2				
Rae	22	3	87	0				
Smith	22	5	72	2				
Muller	19	3	65	1				
Rippon	22	4	70	1				
Kitchen	31	7	104	1				

Fall of Wickets

	O	*C*	*O*
	1st	*1st*	*2nd*
1st	4	121	76
2nd	19	319	79
3rd	36	346	93
4th	40	394	124
5th	50	457	164
6th	63	457	212
7th	85	496	240
8th	130	-	246
9th	158	-	304
10th	168	-	-

WELLINGTON v AUCKLAND — Plunket Shield

at Basin Reserve, Wellington on 14, 15, 16, 17 November, 2020
Toss : Wellington. Umpires : W.R. Knights & A. Mehrotra
Close of play: 1st day: Wellington 27-1, Ravindra 17, Conway 7; 2nd day: Wellington 312-2, Conway 149, Bracewell 123
3rd day: Auckland 109-2, Beghin 55, Chapman 29
***Match drawn.** Points: Wellington 7 (3 bat, 4 bowl), Auckland 3 (2 bat, 1 bowl)*

Wellington decided to bowl first and had the wickets of the Auckland openers within three overs. Phillips and Chapman responded with fifties and Horne and Jamieson did the same later in the innings. Curiously, the other seven Auckland batsmen all made single figure scores.

Wellington also lost an early wicket but Conway (hundred from 191 balls) and Bracewell (253 balls) made amends with the highest Wellington third wicket partnership of all time. The home side reached 446, giving them a lead of 167.

Auckland were 109-2 by stumps and batted through until tea on the last day when the game was called off. Beghin reached his century from 227 balls.

AUCKLAND

FIRST INNINGS	*Runs*	*Mins*	*Balls*	*6s*	*4s*	*SECOND INNINGS*	*Runs*	*Mins*	*Balls*	*6s*	*4s*
G.K.Beghin lbw b McPeake	1	8	7	-	-	c & b Bracewell	108	302	238	3	13
S.M.Solia c Johns b Newton	1	16	7	-	-	b Newton	1	11	9	-	-
G.D.Phillips c Johns b Snedden	54	92	60	5	4	c sub (J.W.Hartshorn) b McPeake	19	88	61	1	3
M.S.Chapman c Conway b Gibson	95	189	125	1	16	c Johns b Snedden	60	250	185	1	7
M.J.Guptill c Johns b Newton	5	30	21	-	1	c Younghusband b Snedden	29	86	60	-	4
R.R.O'Donnell* c Conway b Snedden	4	22	17	-	1	not out	39	116	85	-	7
B.J.Horne† b McPeake	57	181	147	-	9	not out	24	77	62	-	3
K.A.Jamieson lbw b Gibson	51	99	77	1	6						
W.E.R.Somerville b McPeake	8	44	41	-	-						
D.K.Ferns c Bracewell b McPeake	0	9	7	-	-						
O.M.R.Pringle not out	0	6	2	-	-						
Extras (lb 2, w 1)	3					(lb 10, w 3, nb 4)	17				
TOTAL (85.1 overs)	**279**	349				(116 overs) (5 wkts)	**297**	467			

WELLINGTON

	Runs	*Mins*	*Balls*	*6s*	*4s*
R.Ravindra c Chapman b Jamieson	23	73	54	-	4
T.A.Blundell c Ferns b Jamieson	2	11	4	-	-
D.P.Conway c Ferns b Somerville	157	475	325	3	18
M.G.Bracewell* c Horne b Solia	142	393	296	3	16
F.J.Colson c Beghin b Ferns	2	25	16	-	-
J.D.Gibson c Horne b Jamieson	15	77	55	-	-
P.F.Younghusband c Guptill b Somerville	41	189	102	1	5
L.R.Johns† c Beghin b Jamieson	0	34	9	-	-
O.R.Newton c Horne b Jamieson	14	40	19	1	1
I.G.McPeake c Guptill b Ferns	20	28	18	1	3
M.W.Snedden not out	4	14	8	-	1
Extras (b 1, lb 9, w 7, nb 9)	26				
TOTAL (149.3 overs)	**446**	682			

Bowling	*O*	*M*	*R*	*W*	*O*	*M*	*R*	*W*
WELLINGTON								
Newton	23	3	61	2	24	8	59	1
McPeake	19.1	6	53	4	12	6	15	1
Snedden	16	1	63	2	22	6	52	2
Gibson	13	2	61	2				
Bracewell	13	1	34	0	28	7	74	1
Younghusband	1	0	5	0	14	3	46	0
Ravindra					15	7	36	0
Blundell					1	0	5	0
AUCKLAND								
Jamieson	31	5	85	5				
Pringle	19	2	69	0				
Solia	19	4	54	1				
Ferns	25	4	84	2				
Somerville	51.3	16	137	2				
O'Donnell	1	0	2	0				
Phillips	3	1	5	0				

Fall of Wickets

	A *1st*	**W** *1st*	**A** *2nd*
1st	1	11	5
2nd	3	51	34
3rd	102	338	190
4th	125	348	213
5th	134	349	237
6th	177	375	-
7th	262	379	-
8th	276	397	-
9th	278	430	-
10th	279	446	-

CANTERBURY v OTAGO

Plunket Shield

at Hagley Oval, Christchurch on 11, 12, 13, 14 March, 2021
Toss : Otago. Umpires : J.A.K. Bromley & T.J. Parlane
Close of play: 1st day: Canterbury 435-5, Carter 140, Fletcher 114; 2nd day: Otago 218-3, Kelly 50, Phillips 24
3rd day: Otago 15-0, Rutherford 7, Kitchen 8
***Canterbury won by 188 runs.** Points: Canterbury 18 (4 bat, 2 bowl), Otago 6 (3 bat, 3 bowl)*

Canterbury were asked to bat and by the end of the day were 435-5. Carter (89 balls) and Fletcher (113 balls and highest score) had both reached hundreds and scored 219 runs in the last session off 35 overs. They carried on next morning with their stand finally being worth 305, the highest sixth wicket partnership by any team against Otago.

The visitors made a valiant reply with eight batsmen scoring over thirty and declared at 375-6. Canterbury responded with 209 in 35.3 overs before setting Otago a target of 352. Latham's hundred came from just 80 deliveries.

Otago were 15-0 by stumps and 82-0 the next day but fell apart once the opening stand was broken. Otago were all out for just another 81 runs, with Smith absent, giving Canterbury a win by 188 runs.

CANTERBURY

FIRST INNINGS	*Runs*	*Mins*	*Balls*	*6s*	*4s*	*SECOND INNINGS*	*Runs*	*Mins*	*Balls*	*6s*	*4s*
T.W.M.Latham c Chu b Rae	32	74	60	-	5	c Muller b Rippon	106	140	82	2	15
K.J.McClure c Chu b Muller	15	66	46	-	3	c Phillips b Rae	0	2	2	-	-
H.M.Nicholls run out	72	174	107	-	11	c Phillips b Kitchen	33	84	31	-	6
C.E.McConchie* b Muller	2	13	6	-	-	b Rippon	0	4	2	-	-
D.J.Mitchell b Rippon	56	137	98	-	8	c Rutherford b Rippon	37	63	49	1	5
L.J.Carter c Smith b Rippon	169	241	163	2	27	not out	18	33	34	-	1
C.D.Fletcher† c & b Muller	157	244	172	2	23	not out	11	19	13	-	-
M.J.Henry c Rae b Rippon	5	13	9	-	1						
S.B.Davey c Chu b Muller	0	13	4	-	-						
W.S.A.Williams not out	3	11	9	-	-						
F.W.Sheat c Phillips b Muller	2	3	3	-	-						
Extras (b 1, lb 3)	4					(b 4)	4				
TOTAL (112.5 overs)	**517**	497				(35.3 overs) (5 wkts dec)	**209**	174			

OTAGO

	Runs	*Mins*	*Balls*	*6s*	*4s*		*Runs*	*Mins*	*Balls*	*6s*	*4s*
H.D.Rutherford* b Davey	60	172	127	-	5	c Sheat b McConchie	39	169	116	-	5
A.K.Kitchen b Henry	33	81	57	-	5	lbw b McConchie	45	115	93	1	3
M.Renwick b Williams	42	121	83	-	7	b McConchie	9	10	11	-	1
N.F.Kelly c Fletcher b Henry	62	179	153	-	10	c Nicholls b Henry	0	24	18	-	-
D.N.Phillips c Nicholls b Sheat	55	212	147	-	9	b Henry	0	3	2	-	-
N.G.Smith retired hurt	34	80	53	-	6	absent hurt					
M.J.G.Rippon not out	34	96	79	-	4	(6) c Carter b Sheat	24	57	45	1	3
M.W.Chu† b Williams	8	38	22	-	1	(7) c Carter b Davey	18	70	56	-	4
T.Muller not out	31	42	40	-	6	(8) b Davey	19	42	33	-	3
M.D.Rae						not out	1	8	1	-	-
J.A.Duffy						(9) c Latham b Henry	1	5	4	-	-
Extras (lb 5, w 6, nb 5)	16					(lb 1, w 5, nb 1)	7				
TOTAL (126 overs) (6 wkts dec)	**375**	512				(63 overs)	**163**	253			

Bowling	*O*	*M*	*R*	*W*	*O*	*M*	*R*	*W*
OTAGO								
Duffy	8	3	22	0				
Smith	24	7	62	0				
Muller	24.5	1	131	5	7	1	46	0
Rae	25	3	124	1	9	0	60	1
Kitchen	7	0	47	0	7	0	39	1
Rippon	20	0	105	3	12.3	1	60	3
Phillips	4	1	22	0				
CANTERBURY								
Henry	26	4	76	2	15	3	42	3
Williams	26	8	43	2	11	1	20	0
Sheat	16	0	88	1	6	1	26	1
Davey	21	5	64	1	7	4	10	2
Mitchell	11	1	38	0	7	0	20	0
McConchie	25	5	57	0	17	9	44	3
Carter	1	0	4	0				

Fall of Wickets

	C	*O*	*C*	*O*
	1st	*1st*	*2nd*	*2nd*
1st	45	55	1	82
2nd	50	135	79	92
3rd	57	153	83	94
4th	174	240	166	94
5th	188	299	182	100
6th	493	334	-	132
7th	506	-	-	153
8th	512	-	-	156
9th	515	-	-	163
10th	517	-	-	-

Smith retired hurt at 305-5

CENTRAL DISTRICTS v WELLINGTON — Plunket Shield

at Nelson Park, Napier on 11, 12, 13, 14 March, 2021
Toss : Wellington. Umpires : A. Mehrotra & D.J. Walker
Close of play: 1st day: no play; 2nd day: Wellington 60-5, Bracewell 11, Younghusband 2
3rd day: Wellington 2-0, Georgeson 1, Blundell 1
***Central Districts won by 60 runs.** Points: Central Districts 16 (4 bowl), Wellington 4 (4 bowl),*

There was no play on the first day and then fifteen wickets fell on the second. Worker went first ball of the innings while Cleaver (63) top scored in Central's total of 175. Wellington fared no better and by stumps were 60-5 and all out for 104 the next day. Conway (27) was the top scorer.

Central fared better in their second knock and declared just before the close, meaning fourteen wickets had fallen on the third day. Patel, batting at number eight, top scored for Central with his first fifty. Wellington thus needed 317 to win and were 2-0 by the close.

Blundell went early on the last day and, despite fifties from Bracewell and Gibson, could total just 256, giving Central a win by 60 runs. Georgeson made his first-class debut in this game.

CENTRAL DISTRICTS

FIRST INNINGS	*Runs*	*Mins*	*Balls*	*6s*	*4s*	*SECOND INNINGS*	*Runs*	*Mins*	*Balls*	*6s*	*4s*
G.H.Worker lbw b McPeake	0	1	1	-	-	b Gibson	49	118	85	-	7
G.R.Hay* c Johns b Snedden	18	84	55	-	1	c Gibson b Georgeson	5	35	24	-	-
W.A.Young lbw b van Beek	10	33	23	-	1	lbw b van Beek	3	23	19	-	-
L.R.P.L.Taylor c Conway b Gibson	4	15	11	-	1	c Conway b Georgeson	50	98	45	2	6
T.C.Bruce c Younghusband b Georgeson	37	146	103	-	2	c Johns b Georgeson	1	11	4	-	-
D.Cleaver† c Johns b van Beek	63	164	94	-	8	c & b Gibson	14	63	36	-	3
J.A.Clarkson c Johnson b Snedden	10	18	12	-	2	c Johnson b Bracewell	35	112	80	-	6
A.Y.Patel c McPeake b Georgeson	2	21	16	-	-	c Bracewell b Younghusband	52	91	66	1	4
B.M.Tickner c Johnson b Snedden	19	75	55	-	2	(10) not out	6	9	3	-	1
S.H.A.Rance c Snedden b McPeake	3	12	9	-	-	(9) c Gibson b Bracewell	13	9	7	2	-
R.L.Toole not out	2	50	43	-	-	not out	1	2	1	-	-
Extras (lb 5, nb 2)	7					(b 1, lb 5, w 1, nb 9)	16				
TOTAL (70 overs)	**175**	311				(60.2 overs) (9 wkts dec)	**245**	288			

WELLINGTON

FIRST INNINGS	*Runs*	*Mins*	*Balls*	*6s*	*4s*	*SECOND INNINGS*	*Runs*	*Mins*	*Balls*	*6s*	*4s*
L.I.Georgeson b Rance	1	12	10	-	-	c Taylor b Toole	36	164	119	-	3
T.A.Blundell b Rance	10	30	17	-	1	lbw b Rance	2	32	25	-	-
D.P.Conway c Cleaver b Toole	27	55	42	-	4	c Cleaver b Clarkson	19	84	53	1	1
M.G.Bracewell* c Taylor b Rance	11	76	51	-	-	lbw b Patel	56	122	89	-	7
T.M.Johnson lbw b Clarkson	1	7	7	-	-	c Worker b Clarkson	30	119	89	-	3
J.D.Gibson c Cleaver b Toole	0	5	5	-	-	run out	56	142	93	2	3
P.F.Younghusband c Bruce b Tickner	17	101	66	-	-	c Cleaver b Tickner	0	2	3	-	-
L.V.van Beek c Bruce b Rance	7	49	31	-	-	c sub (D.D.Ebrahim) b Tickner	39	74	60	1	3
L.R.Johns† c Taylor b Tickner	20	48	35	-	3	c Bruce b Tickner	5	3	4	-	1
I.G.McPeake lbw b Tickner	0	11	9	-	-	lbw b Tickner	6	7	5	-	-
M.W.Snedden not out	0	8	4	-	-	not out	1	9	3	-	-
Extras (lb 4, w 2, nb 4)	10					(lb 2, w 1, nb 3)	6				
TOTAL (45.3 overs)	**104**	203				(90 overs)	**256**	381			

Bowling	*O*	*M*	*R*	*W*	*O*	*M*	*R*	*W*
WELLINGTON								
McPeake	18	8	32	2	12	1	73	0
van Beek	21	6	48	2	14	4	34	1
Gibson	10	1	32	1	6	0	18	2
Snedden	10	0	37	3	9	2	50	0
Georgeson	8	2	20	2	11	3	39	3
Bracewell	3	2	1	0	4.2	1	12	2
Younghusband					4	1	13	1
CENTRAL DISTRICTS								
Rance	14	0	47	4	13	2	30	1
Tickner	9.3	5	10	3	19	1	73	4
Toole	13	3	23	2	21	6	50	1
Clarkson	9	3	20	1	12	2	34	2
Patel					25	7	67	1

Fall of Wickets

	CD *1st*	***W*** *1st*	***CD*** *2nd*	***W*** *2nd*
1st	0	8	25	5
2nd	15	18	37	43
3rd	24	53	79	90
4th	41	54	92	140
5th	114	57	120	175
6th	135	61	148	176
7th	148	81	211	232
8th	150	98	231	238
9th	159	102	240	246
10th	175	104	-	256

NORTHERN DISTRICTS v AUCKLAND — Plunket Shield

at Cobham Oval, Whangarei on 11, 12, 13, 14 March, 2021
Toss : Northern Districts. Umpires : B.F. Bowden & J.M. Dempsey
Close of play: 1st day: no play; 2nd day: ND 112-2, Raval 63, Carter 2
3rd day: no play
Match drawn. *Points: Northern Districts 6 (2 bat, 4 bowl), Auckland 3 (3 bowl)*

In a match ruined by rain, there was no play at all on the first and third days. On the second day Auckland were bowled out for just 141 with Kuggeleijn taking career best figures, which were also the best by any bowler at Cobham Oval. Northern were 112-2 by the close.

When play resumed on the fourth day, Delport achieved a hat-trick by dismissing Hampton, Sodhi and Watling, on his way to career best figures. Northern declared at 281-8 but there was little likelihood of a result. Will O'Donnell took the chance to record a maiden fifty. This was ter Braak's first-class debut.

AUCKLAND

FIRST INNINGS	*Runs*	*Mins*	*Balls*	*6s*	*4s*
S.M.Solia c Baker b Kuggeleijn	0	6	8	-	-
W.T.O'Donnell c Walker b Wagner	5	24	12	-	1
G.D.Phillips c Wagner b Kuggeleijn	28	46	30	1	5
M.S.Chapman c Carter b Walker	57	147	70	-	9
R.R.O'Donnell* c Watling b Kuggeleijn	2	13	7	-	-
B.J.Horne† c Seifert b Kuggeleijn	8	12	7	-	2
R.M.ter Braak c Carter b Wagner	17	88	79	-	1
W.E.R.Somerville c Seifert b Kuggeleijn	9	39	32	-	1
D.K.Ferns not out	10	53	30	-	1
O.M.R.Pringle c Seifert b Kuggeleijn	1	10	10	-	-
L.J.Delport c Seifert b Kuggeleijn	0	9	5	-	-
Extras (b 1, lb 1, w 1, nb 1)	4				
TOTAL (48.1 overs)	**141**	225			

SECOND INNINGS	*Runs*	*Mins*	*Balls*	*6s*	*4s*
lbw b Sodhi	25	120	85	-	2
not out	51	261	200	-	3
c Carter b Sodhi	31	91	60	1	2
not out	19	50	51	-	2
(b 5, lb 3, w 5, nb 2)	15				
(65.4 overs) (2 wkts)	**141**	261			

NORTHERN DISTRICTS

	Runs	*Mins*	*Balls*	*6s*	*4s*
H.R.Cooper c Pringle b Somerville	35	96	69	-	5
J.A.Raval c Chapman b Delport	91	230	176	-	10
T.L.Seifert† b Delport	9	46	31	-	1
J.F.Carter* c Horne b Delport	49	74	54	4	5
B-J.Watling c O'Donnell R.R. b Delport	37	64	41	-	4
S.C.Kuggeleijn c & b Delport	46	34	25	3	3
B.R.Hampton c Solia b Delport	4	8	6	-	-
I.S.Sodhi c ter Braak b Delport	0	5	1	-	-
N.Wagner not out	1	4	3	-	-
J.G.Walker not out	0	3	5	-	-
J.D.Baker					
Extras (lb 4, w 2, nb 3)	9				
TOTAL (68 overs) (8 wkts dec)	**281**	282			

Bowling	*O*	*M*	*R*	*W*	*O*	*M*	*R*	*W*
NORTHERN DISTRICTS								
Wagner	13	2	39	2	14	1	37	0
Kuggeleijn	11.1	0	45	7	8	0	31	0
Baker	4	0	24	0	4	2	2	0
Hampton	4	0	6	0				
Sodhi	4	1	7	0	21	6	39	2
Walker	12	4	18	1	18.4	10	24	0
AUCKLAND								
ter Braak	8	3	32	0				
Pringle	12	1	44	0				
Ferns	11	2	41	0				
Delport	17	4	88	7				
Somerville	20	4	72	1				

Fall of Wickets

	A *1st*	**ND** *1st*	**A** *2nd*
1st	2	70	58
2nd	10	105	114
3rd	38	186	-
4th	45	199	-
5th	65	270	-
6th	116	279	-
7th	120	279	-
8th	139	279	-
9th	141	-	-
10th	141	-	-

NORTHERN DISTRICTS v WELLINGTON — Plunket Shield

at Bay Oval, Mt Maunganui on 18, 19, 20, 21 March, 2021
Toss : Northern Districts. Umpires : C.A. Black & D.J. Walker
Close of play: 1st day: Wellington 31-0, Georgeson 19, Blundell 11;
2nd day: Welllington 282-5, Johnson 79, Younghusband 33; 3rd day: ND 179-4, Carter 16, Kuggeleijn 11
***Match drawn.** Points: Wellington 6 (2 bat, 4 bowl), Northern Districts 3 (1 bat, 2 bowl)*

Northern decided to bat first but lost wickets at regular intervals. The last two wickets added 82 to take the total to 246 and some respectability. Wellington were 31-0 at stumps and 282-5 by the close of the second day. On the third day Johnson (previous highest score 33) went to his maiden hundred off 247 balls and Wellington finished with a lead of 149.

Northern fared much better in their second innings and reached 379-5 before declaring. Carter scored his hundred off 220 balls and Hampton made his highest score. Wellington batted out the remainder of the game with Bhula hitting his maiden fifty.

NORTHERN DISTRICTS

FIRST INNINGS	Runs	Mins	Balls	6s	4s	SECOND INNINGS	Runs	Mins	Balls	6s	4s
H.R.Cooper b McPeake	19	28	27	1	2	(2) lbw b Bracewell	73	143	100	-	11
J.A.Raval c van Beek b Gibson	42	117	80	-	6	(1) b Younghusband	40	94	79	-	3
T.L.Seifert† c van Beek b Sears	14	35	25	-	2	lbw b Bracewell	19	69	55	-	2
J.F.Carter* c Bhula b Sears	27	87	58	1	1	not out	103	278	222	2	12
B-J.Watling lbw b Sears	23	113	73	-	4	st Johns b Bracewell	11	18	16	-	2
S.C.Kuggeleijn c Johns b Gibson	8	32	29	-	-	st Johns b Bracewell	51	195	158	-	4
B.R.Hampton b van Beek	4	30	19	-	-	not out	63	43	44	4	5
I.S.Sodhi c Gibson b Sears	33	90	69	-	5						
N.Wagner c Gibson b Bracewell	17	19	19	-	3						
J.G.Walker not out	41	85	59	-	4						
Z.N.Gibson c Johns b Gibson	10	31	26	-	1						
Extras (b 5, lb 2, w 1)	8					(b 12, lb 4, w 1, nb 2)	19				
TOTAL (80.4 overs)	**246**	336				(112 overs) (5 wkts dec)	**379**	422			

WELLINGTON

FIRST INNINGS	Runs	Mins	Balls	6s	4s	SECOND INNINGS	Runs	Mins	Balls	6s	4s
L.I.Georgeson c Raval b Hampton	28	92	63	-	4	c Sodhi b Kuggeleijn	2	6	8	-	-
T.A.Blundell lbw b Wagner	30	123	95	-	5	c Raval b Kuggeleijn	6	19	8	-	1
J.J.N.P.Bhula b Gibson	17	72	43	-	3	c Seifert b Walker	55	154	110	1	5
M.G.Bracewell* b Wagner	31	126	92	-	2	b Walker	11	39	32	-	1
T.M.Johnson c Raval b Wagner	114	374	271	-	11	c Seifert b Wagner	3	49	40	-	-
J.D.Gibson b Wagner	46	86	79	-	6	not out	10	68	74	-	1
P.F.Younghusband c Kuggeleijn b Sodhi	72	208	178	-	9	not out	6	15	22	-	1
L.V.van Beek st Seifert b Walker	5	6	7	-	1						
L.R.Johns† c Watling b Kuggeleijn	25	83	56	-	4						
I.G.McPeake c Raval b Sodhi	4	19	16	-	-						
B.V.Sears not out	0	3	2	-	-						
Extras (lb 4, w 1, nb 18)	23					(b 2, lb 1, nb 12)	15				
TOTAL (147.2 overs)	**395**	629				(47 overs) (5 wkts)	**108**	176			

Bowling	O	M	R	W	O	M	R	W
WELLINGTON								
McPeake	17	4	36	1	9	1	28	0
van Beek	19	5	39	1	15	1	45	0
Georgeson	3	0	14	0				
Sears	16	3	55	4	12	1	48	0
Bracewell	9	1	37	1	41	13	133	4
Gibson	13.4	3	40	3	5	1	24	0
Younghusband	3	0	18	0	30	6	85	1
NORTHERN DISTRICTS								
Wagner	23	6	58	4	9	2	21	1
Kuggeleijn	28.2	7	75	1	8	3	25	2
Walker	30	7	68	1	17	8	19	2
Sodhi	24	5	56	2	10	2	33	0
Gibson	23	5	87	1				
Hampton	19	2	47	1				
Cooper					2	0	6	0
Watling					1	0	1	0

Fall of Wickets	ND 1st	W 1st	ND 2nd	W 2nd
1st	24	51	72	4
2nd	48	71	133	17
3rd	91	97	145	40
4th	114	150	159	69
5th	122	218	287	98
6th	133	345	-	-
7th	145	350	-	-
8th	164	389	-	-
9th	213	395	-	-
10th	246	395	-	-

OTAGO v AUCKLAND — Plunket Shield

at Queen's Park, Invercargill on 18, 19, 20, 21 March, 2021
Toss : Auckland. Umpires : J.A.K. Bromley & G.A. Stirrat
Close of play: 1st day: Auckland 273-6, R.R.O'Donnell 92, Somerville 2; 2nd day: Otago 39-1, Rutherford 22, Renwick 2
3rd day: Otago 259-5, Rippon 40, Chu 29
Match drawn. *Points: Auckland 6 (4 bat, 2 bowl), Otago 5 (2 bat, 3 bowl)*

Auckland won the toss and batted throughout a shortened first day. Robbie O'Donnell was 92 at the close (Phillips having been earlier dismissed for that score) and went to his hundred off 176 balls the next day, when just 42.2 overs were bowled.

Otago reached 259-5 by the end of the third day with Rutherford making 63 and three other batsmen reaching 40. No play was possible on the fourth day. Briggs and McKenzie made their first-class debuts in this game.

AUCKLAND

FIRST INNINGS	*Runs*	*Mins*	*Balls*	*6s*	*4s*
S.M.Solia c McKenzie b Muller	29	91	63	-	5
W.T.O'Donnell b Rae	5	34	20	-	-
G.D.Phillips c Kelly b Rae	92	106	64	5	11
R.R.O'Donnell* run out	128	308	199	2	19
C.J.Briggs c Kitchen b McKenzie	30	117	95	-	5
B.J.Horne† c Kelly b Rae	15	28	25	-	2
R.M.ter Braak c Phillips b Kitchen	1	13	13	-	-
W.E.R.Somerville c Rippon b Rae	23	67	63	-	3
D.K.Ferns not out	9	40	28	-	1
O.M.R.Pringle not out	11	7	8	-	2
L.J.Delport					
Extras (w 2, nb 6)	8				
TOTAL (95.2 overs) (8 wkts dec)	**351**	407			

OTAGO

	Runs	*Mins*	*Balls*	*6s*	*4s*
H.D.Rutherford* c O'Donnell W.T. b Delport	63	172	121	1	5
A.K.Kitchen lbw b Somerville	13	71	39	-	2
M.Renwick c Briggs b Somerville	49	119	103	1	7
N.F.Kelly lbw b Phillips	43	87	70	-	8
D.N.Phillips c Somerville b Phillips	15	34	20	-	2
M.J.G.Rippon not out	40	107	76	-	5
M.W.Chu† not out	29	73	58	-	3
A.W.McKenzie					
T.Muller					
M.B.Bacon					
M.D.Rae					
Extras (b 4, w 1, nb 2)	7				
TOTAL (80.5 overs) (5 wkts)	**259**	333			

Bowling	*O*	*M*	*R*	*W*
OTAGO				
Rae	27	4	89	4
McKenzie	13	3	47	1
Bacon	16	1	76	0
Muller	18	1	73	1
Rippon	5.2	2	26	0
Kitchen	16	5	40	1
AUCKLAND				
Ferns	8	0	27	0
Pringle	9	1	18	0
ter Braak	8	2	23	0
Somerville	23	5	79	2
Delport	21	1	69	1
Phillips	10.5	2	33	2
O'Donnell W.T.	1	0	6	0

Fall of Wickets

	A	**O**
	1st	*1st*
1st	15	28
2nd	87	120
3rd	143	140
4th	234	176
5th	262	200
6th	264	-
7th	308	-
8th	339	-
9th	-	-
10th	-	-

CANTERBURY v CENTRAL DISTRICTS — Plunket Shield

at MainPower Oval, Rangiora on 19, 20, 21 March, 2021
Toss : Central Districts. Umpires : A. Mehrotra & T.J. Parlane
Close of play: 1st day: Canterbury 61-3, McConchie 8; 2nd day: CD 69-4, Hay 31, Cleaver 22
***Canterbury won by 9 wickets.** Points: Canterbury 18 (2 bat, 4 bowl), Central Districts 4 (4 bowl)*

Central Districts won the toss and batted but lost Worker in the first over. Bracewell came in at 76-5 and hit 52 to help Central reach 149. Davey had his first five wicket bag. Canterbury lost three wickets before the close but recovered to reach 281 the next day. McConchie and Fletcher top scored with seventies.

Central faced a deficit of 132 and were soon 37-4. Hay and Cleaver then added 89 but once the stand was broken there was little resistance and Central were all out for 170. Canterbury lost one wicket chasing their small total and won with more than a day to spare and secured the Plunket Shield for 2020/21 with two rounds remaining. Lennox made his first-class debut in this game.

CENTRAL DISTRICTS

FIRST INNINGS	*Runs*	*Mins*	*Balls*	*6s*	*4s*	*SECOND INNINGS*	*Runs*	*Mins*	*Balls*	*6s*	*4s*
G.H.Worker c Davey b Nuttall	0	4	6	-	-	c Fletcher b Sheat	8	38	25	-	-
G.R.Hay* c Fletcher b Nuttall	38	101	72	-	5	b van Woerkom	55	237	156	-	6
B.S.Smith lbw b Williams	3	19	9	-	-	c Fletcher b Sheat	0	8	5	-	-
B.D.Schmulian c Fletcher b Williams	17	137	84	-	1	lbw b Davey	1	12	8	-	-
T.C.Bruce c Bowes b Davey	4	14	10	-	1	c van Woerkom b Sheat	5	15	12	-	-
D.Cleaver† c Fletcher b Sheat	5	31	26	-	-	c Sheat b van Woerkom	60	196	153	-	7
D.A.J.Bracewell c McClure b Davey	52	177	119	-	5	c Sheat b van Woerkom	7	20	19	-	-
J.A.Clarkson c Fletcher b Davey	11	43	32	-	2	st Fletcher b van Woerkom	7	23	21	-	1
B.M.Tickner b Davey	2	43	37	-	-	c McClure b Sheat	16	67	66	-	1
J.R.Lennox c Bowes b Davey	6	62	45	-	1	b Davey	0	18	5	-	-
R.L.Toole not out	0	14	16	-	-	not out	5	38	30	-	-
Extras (b 4, lb 2, nb 5)	11					(b 1, lb 2, w 1, nb 2)	6				
TOTAL (75.1 overs)	**149**	325				(83 overs)	**170**	339			

CANTERBURY

	Runs	*Mins*	*Balls*	*6s*	*4s*		*Runs*	*Mins*	*Balls*	*6s*	*4s*
J.C.T.Boyle lbw b Bracewell	4	27	22	-	-	(2) c Bruce b Tickner	12	31	29	-	3
C.J.Bowes run out	46	79	55	-	7	(1) not out	25	45	27	-	3
K.J.McClure c Clarkson b Toole	0	8	3	-	-	not out	2	14	9	-	-
C.E.McConchie* c Cleaver b Tickner	75	200	130	2	4						
L.J.Carter c & b Bracewell	10	23	18	-	1						
C.D.Fletcher† c Cleaver b Clarkson	78	188	133	1	10						
T.F.van Woerkom c Bruce b Tickner	20	102	67	-	3						
S.B.Davey c Bracewell b Clarkson	0	7	2	-	-						
W.S.A.Williams c Toole b Tickner	19	48	40	1	2						
F.W.Sheat c Clarkson b Tickner	13	20	16	1	1						
E.J.Nuttall not out	0	10	4	-	-						
Extras (b 4, lb 9, w 2, nb 1)	16						0				
TOTAL (81.3 overs)	**281**	358				(10.5 overs) (1 wkt)	**39**	45			

Bowling	*O*	*M*	*R*	*W*	*O*	*M*	*R*	*W*
CANTERBURY								
Nuttall	18	2	54	2	9	2	51	0
Williams	17	9	24	2	19	13	13	0
Sheat	18	7	36	1	15	5	28	4
Davey	16.1	6	19	5	16	5	34	2
McConchie	2	1	3	0	6	1	15	0
van Woerkom	4	0	7	0	18	7	26	4
CENTRAL DISTRICTS								
Bracewell	21	6	49	2	5	0	12	0
Toole	17	3	55	1				
Tickner	21.3	5	89	4	5	0	22	1
Clarkson	11	2	28	2	0.5	0	5	0
Lennox	11	2	47	0				

Fall of Wickets

	CD *1st*	**C** *1st*	**CD** *2nd*	**C** *2nd*
1st	0	18	29	24
2nd	11	23	29	-
3rd	60	61	30	-
4th	67	82	37	-
5th	76	193	126	-
6th	78	232	136	-
7th	98	234	145	-
8th	108	267	147	-
9th	146	270	152	-
10th	149	281	170	-

OTAGO v CENTRAL DISTRICTS — Plunket Shield

at University of Otago Oval, Dunedin on 26, 27, 28, 29 March, 2021
Toss : Otago. Umpires : E.D. Sanders & D.J. Walker
Close of play: 1st day: Otago 321-5, Phillips 134, Chu 21; 2nd day: CD 212-4, Schmulian 73, Cleaver 51
3rd day: Otago 222-4, Kelly 69, Rippon 9
***Otago won by 44 runs.** Points: Otago 20 (4 bat, 4 bowl), Central Districts 6 (4 bat, 2 bowl)*

Otago decided to bat first but were 28-3 after 17 overs. Phillips came to the rescue, reaching his maiden hundred off 191 balls and was well supported by Kelly, Rippon and Chu, who made his first fifty.

Otago finished with 393 and Central replied strongly, declaring at 353-9 on the third day. Schmulian reached his hundred from 169 deliveries while Cleaver was caught for 99. Rae performed the hat-trick by dismissing Cleaver, Clarkson and Tickner. All three batsmen were caught by Phillips, who also equalled the Otago record for catches in an innings.

Rutherford reached three figures from 119 balls when Otago batted again and he declared at 292-7, leaving Central 333 to win. Hay, Schmulian and Bruce all hit fifties but it was not quite enough as Rippon claimed career best figures in Otago's 44 run win. McKay made his Otago debut in this game.

OTAGO

FIRST INNINGS	*Runs*	*Mins*	*Balls*	*6s*	*4s*	*SECOND INNINGS*	*Runs*	*Mins*	*Balls*	*6s*	*4s*
H.D.Rutherford* c Hay b Tickner	3	16	14	-	-	c Smith b Schmulian	111	205	128	2	14
A.K.Kitchen c & b Bracewell	4	23	13	-	1	c Cleaver b Toole	15	46	36	-	1
M.Renwick c Cleaver b Clarkson	16	59	40	-	2	c Cleaver b Tickner	4	15	11	-	1
N.F.Kelly lbw b Lennox	57	115	88	-	8	c Lennox b Toole	74	201	141	1	5
D.N.Phillips lbw b Bracewell	149	361	257	1	22	c Cleaver b Clarkson	8	21	17	-	1
M.J.G.Rippon b Tickner	79	229	160	2	9	not out	43	87	51	1	4
M.W.Chu† c Hay b Toole	53	112	83	-	8	b Tickner	0	6	3	-	-
A.W.McKenzie c Smith b Toole	15	51	35	1	1	c sub (J.F.A.Field) b Tickner	8	16	13	-	1
M.B.Bacon c Hay b Toole	7	24	17	-	1	not out	20	28	22	-	2
M.D.Rae c & b Lennox	2	16	13	-	-						
J.D.McKay not out	0	1	1	-	-						
Extras (lb 4, w 4)	8					(b 1, lb 3, w 3, nb 2)	9				
TOTAL (120.2 overs)	**393**	506				(70 overs) (7 wkts dec)	**292**	314			

CENTRAL DISTRICTS

	Runs	*Mins*	*Balls*	*6s*	*4s*		*Runs*	*Mins*	*Balls*	*6s*	*4s*
G.H.Worker c Renwick b Rae	13	60	40	-	-	c Rippon b Rae	21	87	61	-	4
G.R.Hay* c Bacon b McKenzie	5	16	15	-	1	lbw b Rippon	58	157	111	1	8
B.S.Smith c McKay b Bacon	14	60	42	-	2	c Chu b Rae	2	9	9	-	-
B.D.Schmulian c Chu b McKenzie	127	296	212	1	15	c Renwick b McKenzie	64	107	83	1	7
T.C.Bruce c Chu b McKenzie	49	81	58	-	7	not out	81	141	76	1	10
D.Cleaver† c Phillips b Rae	99	220	168	3	7	lbw b Rae	10	28	12	-	2
D.A.J.Bracewell not out	29	49	30	1	4	(8) lbw b Rippon	16	10	10	1	2
J.A.Clarkson c Phillips b Rae	0	1	1	-	-	(7) b Rippon	22	39	25	-	2
B.M.Tickner c Phillips b Rae	0	2	1	-	-	c Kitchen b Rippon	0	3	3	-	-
J.R.Lennox c Phillips b Rae	6	21	13	-	-	c Kelly b Rippon	2	8	8	-	-
R.L.Toole not out	0	3	0	-	-	lbw b Rippon	0	2	1	-	-
Extras (b 4, lb 2, w 3, nb 2)	11					(lb 8, w 4)	12				
TOTAL (96.2 overs) (9 wkts dec)	**353**	407				(66.3 overs)	**288**	298			

Bowling	*O*	*M*	*R*	*W*	*O*	*M*	*R*	*W*
CENTRAL DISTRICTS								
Bracewell	29	10	60	2	2	0	8	0
Tickner	29	7	104	2	20	0	64	3
Toole	23.2	6	77	3	23	2	86	2
Clarkson	10	0	77	1	9	0	51	1
Lennox	24	5	56	2	10	0	45	0
Schmulian	5	0	15	0	6	0	34	1
OTAGO								
Rae	23	6	62	5	14	2	72	3
McKenzie	21	5	77	3	14	4	39	1
Bacon	13	3	49	1	14	3	67	0
McKay	13.2	0	74	0	6	1	34	0
Kitchen	15	3	42	0	2	0	2	0
Rippon	11	2	43	0	16.3	0	66	6

Fall of Wickets	***O***	***CD***	***O***	***CD***
	1st	*1st*	*2nd*	*2nd*
1st	7	8	31	64
2nd	7	32	38	66
3rd	28	34	185	127
4th	96	123	202	181
5th	280	310	235	228
6th	356	322	239	268
7th	383	322	253	286
8th	388	322	-	286
9th	391	349	-	288
10th	393	-	-	288

AUCKLAND v CANTERBURY — Plunket Shield

at Eden Park Outer Oval, Auckland on 27, 28, 29, 30 March, 2021
Toss : Auckland. Umpires : B.F. Bowden & G.A. Stirrat
Close of play: 1st day: Canterbury 23-0, Bowes 21, McClure 0; 2nd day: Auckland 131-2, Beghin 32, R.R.O'Donnell 11; 3rd day: Canterbury 83-2, Chamberlain 20, McConchie 16
***Match drawn.** Points: Auckland 5 (1 bat, 4 bowl), Canterbury 4 (4 bowl)*

Auckland decided to bat first but lost Will O'Donnell in the first over. His brother, Robbie, held the innings together with 93 and he was assisted by ter Braak, who made a maiden fifty. Canterbury, with the Plunket Shield already secured, collapsed from 60-1 to 131 all out on the second day, giving Auckland an unexpected lead of 104 runs.

Auckland extended their lead to 421 before declaring late on the third day. Will O'Donnell made his highest score and his brother hit a century from 197 balls. With time lost on the last day there was never any possibility of a result and the match was drawn. Harrison and Chamberlain made their first-class debuts in this game.

AUCKLAND

FIRST INNINGS	*Runs*	*Mins*	*Balls*	*6s*	*4s*	*SECOND INNINGS*	*Runs*	*Mins*	*Balls*	*6s*	*4s*
S.M.Solia b Davey	21	71	51	-	1	b McConchie	33	120	98	1	2
W.T.O'Donnell b Nuttall	0	4	1	-	-	lbw b van Woerkom	60	108	82	1	6
G.K.Beghin c Fletcher b Nuttall	11	94	69	-	-	c Fletcher b Nuttall	83	225	180	1	11
R.R.O'Donnell* lbw b Davey	93	237	156	3	12	not out	107	280	202	2	10
C.J.Briggs c Fletcher b Davey	22	47	46	-	2	not out	22	65	32	-	4
B.J.Horne† c van Woerkom b Davey	4	17	13	-	1						
R.M.ter Braak c Bowes b Williams	58	178	134	2	9						
W.E.R.Somerville lbw b Williams	5	43	30	-	-						
R.D.Harrison b Williams	2	19	16	-	-						
O.M.R.Pringle c McClure b Nuttall	0	15	11	-	-						
LJ.Delport not out	0	5	3	-	-						
Extras (b 4, lb 3, w 2, nb 10)	19					(lb 5, w 1, nb 6)	12				
TOTAL (86.4 overs)	**235**	369				(98 overs) (3 wkts dec)	**317**	401			

CANTERBURY

	Runs	*Mins*	*Balls*	*6s*	*4s*		*Runs*	*Mins*	*Balls*	*6s*	*4s*
C.J.Bowes c Beghin b ter Braak	21	29	30	-	4	c Harrison b ter Braak	6	26	21	-	1
K.J.McClure run out	28	118	73	1	4	c O'Donnell W.T. b Delport	35	86	73	-	7
H.J.Chamberlain c Delport b O'Donnell R.R.	6	33	23	-	-	c & b Somerville	25	177	129	-	2
C.E.McConchie* c Horne b Pringle	24	68	56	-	4	c Somerville b Harrison	72	199	166	1	7
L.J.Carter c Horne b Pringle	0	5	3	-	-						
T.F.van Woerkom c Harrison b Delport	9	55	49	-	1						
S.B.Davey c Pringle b Delport	17	75	73	1	-						
C.D.Fletcher† c Pringle b Somerville	2	8	8	-	-	(6) not out	32	51	36	-	6
W.S.A.Williams c Briggs b Somerville	8	39	23	-	1						
F.W.Sheat c O'Donnell W.T. b Delport	1	6	9	-	-						
E.J.Nuttall not out	0	13	8	-	-						
J.C.T.Boyle						not out	13	134	110	-	1
Extras (b 1, lb 8, w 3, nb 3)	15					(lb 6, w 2, nb 1)	9				
TOTAL (58.4 overs)	**131**	229				(89 overs) (4 wkts)	**192**	339			

Bowling	*O*	*M*	*R*	*W*	*O*	*M*	*R*	*W*
CANTERBURY								
Nuttall	19.4	4	90	3	11	0	50	1
Williams	19	7	32	3	18	4	44	0
Davey	19	7	45	4	14	3	50	0
Sheat	15	5	32	0	12	4	21	0
van Woerkom	12	5	27	0	31	7	94	1
McConchie	2	1	2	0	12	0	53	1
AUCKLAND								
Pringle	11	3	29	2				
ter Braak	7	1	35	1	15	5	26	1
Solia	1	0	2	0	3	1	11	0
O'Donnell R.R.	10	5	9	1	3	1	6	0
Harrison	5	2	13	0	8	3	29	1
Somerville	12.4	4	23	2	30	14	50	1
Delport	12	7	11	3	29	8	62	1
O'Donnell W.T.					1	0	2	0

Fall of Wickets

	A	*C*	*A*	*C*
	1st	*1st*	*2nd*	*2nd*
1st	5	23	95	17
2nd	37	60	107	59
3rd	49	84	262	125
4th	89	85	-	148
5th	97	89	-	-
6th	218	103	-	-
7th	233	108	-	-
8th	234	121	-	-
9th	234	122	-	-
10th	235	131	-	-

Boyle was a concussion substitute for Carter after 76 overs in Auckland's second innings

WELLINGTON v NORTHERN DISTRICTS — Plunket Shield

at Basin Reserve, Wellington on 27, 28, 29, 30 March, 2021
Toss : Northern Districts. Umpires : J.A.K. Bromley & T.J. Parlane
Close of play: 1st day: Wellington 237-3, Bhula 3, Blundell 0; 2nd day: ND 97-4, Watling 8, Kuggeleijn 0
3rd day: no play
***Match drawn.** Points: Wellington 4 (3 bat, 1 bowl), Northern Districts 1 (1 bowl)*

Northern Districts decided to bowl first but Wellington had 226 runs on the board by the time the first wicket fell. Georgeson hit his first fifty while Ravindra (hundred from 168 balls) registered his highest score. Blundell (hundred from 142 balls) and Johnson shared an unbroken fifth wicket stand of 158 (a Wellington record against Northern) before Bracewell declared at 414.

Northern were 97-4 at the end of the second day but no play was possible on the last two days. Fisher made his first-class debut in this match.

WELLINGTON

FIRST INNINGS	*Runs*	*Mins*	*Balls*	*6s*	*4s*
L.I.Georgeson c Bocock b Walker	70	337	261	-	7
R.Ravindra c Wagner b Walker	138	320	212	6	14
J.J.N.P.Bhula b Baker	13	68	46	-	2
M.G.Bracewell* c Popli b Wagner	1	6	6	-	-
T.A.Blundell† not out	103	203	142	1	14
T.M.Johnson not out	58	158	105	1	7
J.D.Gibson					
P.F.Younghusband					
L.V.van Beek					
I.G.McPeake					
M.W.Snedden					
Extras (b 9, lb 6, w 6, nb 10)	31				
TOTAL (127 overs) (4 wkts dec)	**414**	546			

NORTHERN DISTRICTS

	Runs	*Mins*	*Balls*	*6s*	*4s*
H.R.Cooper c Ravindra b Snedden	10	65	51	-	-
J.A.Raval b van Beek	4	20	12	-	1
B.Popli c Blundell b McPeake	50	147	117	-	8
J.F.Carter* c Johnson b McPeake	13	91	55	-	1
B-J.Watling not out	8	29	28	-	1
S.C.Kuggeleijn not out	0	18	9	-	-
P.D.Bocock†					
N.Wagner					
J.G.Walker					
J.D.Baker					
M.J.Fisher					
Extras (lb 9, nb 3)	12				
TOTAL (45 overs) (4 wkts dec)	**97**	187			

Bowling	*O*	*M*	*R*	*W*
NORTHERN DISTRICTS				
Wagner	24	7	34	1
Kuggeleijn	25	2	111	0
Baker	32	9	88	1
Fisher	20	3	88	0
Walker	25	7	68	2
Raval	1	0	10	0
WELLINGTON				
McPeake	13	7	14	2
van Beek	11	3	19	1
Gibson	5	1	21	0
Snedden	8	0	17	1
Bracewell	4	2	2	0
Georgeson	3	0	10	0
Younghusband	1	0	5	0

Fall of Wickets

	W	***ND***
	1st	*1st*
1st	226	10
2nd	236	33
3rd	237	88
4th	256	89
5th	-	-
6th	-	-
7th	-	-
8th	-	-
9th	-	-
10th	-	-

AUCKLAND v WELLINGTON

Plunket Shield

at Eden Park Outer Oval, Auckland on 3, 4, 5, 6 April, 2021
Toss : Wellington. Umpires : W.R. Knights, T.J. Parlane & A. Stanley
Close of play: 1st day: Wellington 278-6, Johnson 6, Younghusband 1;
2nd day: Auckland 220-1, W.T.O'Donnell 79, R.R.O'Donnell 100;
3rd day: Wellington 130-3, Georgeson 36, Bracewell 56
***Match drawn.** Points: Auckland 6 (3 bat, 3 bowl), Wellington 5 (3 bat, 2 bowl)*

Wellington decided to bat first but lost three wickets in the first eight overs. Bracewell and Blundell (who both scored hundreds from 213 balls) transformed the game with a Wellington fourth wicket record against Auckland. The visitors were able to reach 342 and Auckland replied in similar vein. Will O'Donnell reached his maiden hundred from 239 while Robbie took 151 deliveries for his hundred as the brothers shared a second wicket partnership of 232.

The runs continued when Wellington batted again with Bracewell scoring his second century of the match from just 78 balls. His declaration left Auckland with 273 to win.

Will O'Donnell emulated Bracewell in scoring his second hundred of the game (from 171 balls) and went on to his highest score. Somerville hit a maiden fifty but Auckland finished just short of their target.

On the third day, umpire Tim Parlane left the field ill and Wayne Knights stood at both ends with match referee Gary Troup as temporary square leg umpire. Allen Stanley (making his first-class debut) then joined Knights as replacement umpire for the remainder of the game.

WELLINGTON

FIRST INNINGS	*Runs*	*Mins*	*Balls*	*6s*	*4s*	*SECOND INNINGS*	*Runs*	*Mins*	*Balls*	*6s*	*4s*
L.I.Georgeson b ter Braak	2	37	24	-	-	c Briggs b Ferns	54	186	130	1	6
R.Ravindra c Horne b ter Braak	4	8	5	-	1	c Briggs b Ferns	8	32	21	-	2
J.J.N.P.Bhula c Harrison b ter Braak	6	16	11	-	1	c Horne b Somerville	11	72	53	-	2
M.G.Bracewell* c O'Donnell R.R. b Ferns	105	299	231	1	12	(5) lbw b Somerville	119	133	93	5	10
T.A.Blundell† lbw b Ferns	113	308	226	2	12	(6) c O'Donnell R.R. b Harrison	19	35	20	-	1
T.M.Johnson not out	46	200	124	-	5	(7) not out	39	54	29	2	3
J.D.Gibson c Harrison b Somerville	23	24	19	-	5	(8) b Delport	17	15	12	2	-
P.F.Younghusband c Briggs b ter Braak	15	81	60	-	1	(9) not out	11	15	5	1	1
L.V.van Beek c Briggs b Somerville	1	28	22	-	-	(4) c Somerville b Delport	13	6	7	2	-
B.V.Sears st Horne b Somerville	3	40	33	-	-						
I.G.McPeake c Ferns b Somerville	2	3	3	-	-						
Extras (b 5, lb 6, w 8, nb 3)	22					(b 1, lb 4, w 1, nb 1)	7				
TOTAL (125.5 overs)	**342**	517				(61.3 overs) (7 wkts dec)	**298**	275			

AUCKLAND

FIRST INNINGS	*Runs*	*Mins*	*Balls*	*6s*	*4s*	*SECOND INNINGS*	*Runs*	*Mins*	*Balls*	*6s*	*4s*
G.D.Phillips c Sears b Ravindra	36	52	38	3	3	c van Beek b Ravindra	43	78	59	2	5
W.T.O'Donnell c Blundell b van Beek	117	345	257	2	13	not out	137	295	210	4	14
R.R.O'Donnell* c Gibson b McPeake	142	332	208	3	15	run out	1	10	6	-	-
C.J.Briggs c & b Sears	13	44	22	-	3	lbw b Younghusband	4	51	38	-	-
B.J.Horne† c van Beek b Ravindra	24	113	67	-	2	lbw b Ravindra	1	6	8	-	-
R.M.ter Braak c Johnson b Sears	4	9	7	-	1	c Johnson b Sears	12	55	47	-	2
W.E.R.Somerville c Ravindra b McPeake	5	13	12	-	-	c Younghusband b Ravindra	59	82	54	2	5
R.D.Harrison c Georgeson b Gibson	12	93	70	-	1	run out	1	4	2	-	-
D.K.Ferns c Bracewell b Ravindra	0	1	1	-	-	not out	1	5	3	-	-
L.J.Delport not out	1	6	1	-	-						
S.M.Solia absent hurt											
Extras (b 4, lb 3, w 7)	14					(b 6, lb 1, nb 1)	8				
TOTAL (123.5 overs)	**368**	507				(71 overs) (7 wkts)	**267**	295			

Bowling	*O*	*M*	*R*	*W*	*O*	*M*	*R*	*W*
AUCKLAND								
Ferns	23	9	88	2	14	4	56	2
ter Braak	23	2	67	4	9	2	44	0
Harrison	12	1	45	0	5	0	33	1
O'Donnell R.R.	6	3	5	0				
Delport	16	2	49	0	9.3	2	55	2
Somerville	39.5	16	61	4	22	6	89	2
Phillips	6	0	16	0	2	0	16	0
WELLINGTON								
van Beek	27	6	61	1	16	4	55	0
McPeake	18	6	47	2	8	3	20	0
Ravindra	13	2	47	3	21	2	77	3
Sears	17	4	52	2	9	1	40	1
Gibson	13.5	4	35	1	2	0	10	0
Bracewell	26	6	82	0	8	1	31	0
Younghusband	9	1	37	0	7	3	27	1

Fall of Wickets

	W 1st	*A 1st*	*W 2nd*	*A 2nd*
1st	4	49	14	68
2nd	12	281	41	72
3rd	13	316	54	97
4th	230	317	163	99
5th	241	323	210	135
6th	274	330	244	258
7th	307	366	270	262
8th	318	366	-	-
9th	340	368	-	-
10th	342	-	-	-

CENTRAL DISTRICTS v CANTERBURY — Plunket Shield

at McLean Park, Napier on 3, 4, 5, 6 April, 2021
Toss : Canterbury. Umpires : B.F. Bowden & J.M. Dempsey
Close of play: 1st day: Canterbury 2-0, Latham 1, McClure 1; 2nd day: Canterbury 302-4, Chamberlain 93, Fletcher 52
3rd day: CD 125-2, Smith 9, Schmulian 7
***Match drawn.** Points: Canterbury 7 (3 bat, 4 bowl), Central Districts 3 (1 bat, 2 bowl)*

Canterbury decided to field first and had early success. Their bowlers continued to strike regularly and it was only Smith (hundred from 208 balls) who offered any major resistance. He came in at number three and was unbeaten on 111 when the innings ended.

Canterbury made a solid reply and reached 391. Chamberlain, playing just his second game, reached his maiden fifty and then his first century from 218 balls. McConchie and Fletcher assisted with fifties.

Central were 184 runs in arrears and had reached 125-2 by stumps on the third day. On the last day they batted resolutely with everyone reaching double figures. With no result possible, the game was called off at tea.

CENTRAL DISTRICTS

FIRST INNINGS	*Runs*	*Mins*	*Balls*	*6s*	*4s*	*SECOND INNINGS*	*Runs*	*Mins*	*Balls*	*6s*	*4s*
G.H.Worker b Williams	13	85	65	-	2	c & b van Woerkom	64	151	129	1	10
G.R.Hay* c Fletcher b Williams	7	67	50	-	1	b Henry	44	118	84	-	6
B.S.Smith not out	111	300	210	-	17	b Nuttall	47	240	183	-	8
B.D.Schmulian c Williams b Henry	1	12	5	-	-	c Fletcher b McConchie	23	77	59	-	2
T.C.Bruce c Chamberlain b Nuttall	12	30	21	-	2	c Fletcher b Sheat	15	42	30	-	2
D.Cleaver† c Fletcher b Sheat	6	47	33	-	-	not out	54	179	124	-	6
C.K.Leopard c Latham b Williams	16	32	16	-	2	not out	34	91	76	-	6
J.A.Clarkson c van Woerkom b Nuttall	4	13	18	-	-						
A.Y.Patel c McConchie b Nuttall	5	18	18	-	1						
B.M.Tickner b Henry	26	85	76	-	3						
R.L.Toole c Fletcher b Henry	1	42	30	-	-						
Extras (lb 4, nb 1)	5					(b 11, lb 4, w 2, nb 1)	18				
TOTAL (90.1 overs)	**207**	367				(114 overs) (5 wkts)	**299**	450			

CANTERBURY

	Runs	Mins	Balls	6s	4s
T.W.M.Latham lbw b Toole	19	72	48	-	2
K.J.McClure lbw b Tickner	41	91	78	3	3
H.M.Nicholls c Bruce b Toole	37	103	68	-	6
C.E.McConchie* lbw b Patel	54	172	123	-	4
H.J.Chamberlain lbw b Tickner	132	373	267	1	18
C.D.Fletcher† c Schmulian b Tickner	52	138	109	1	5
T.F.van Woerkom c Patel b Schmulian	22	105	98	-	2
M.J.Henry c Clarkson b Schmulian	10	26	34	-	2
W.S.A.Williams c Patel b Tickner	6	30	18	-	-
F.W.Sheat c Bruce b Tickner	8	20	13	-	1
E.J.Nuttall not out	0	5	4	-	-
Extras (b 4, lb 3, w 2, nb 1)	10				
TOTAL (143.1 overs)	**391**	570			

Bowling	*O*	*M*	*R*	*W*	*O*	*M*	*R*	*W*
CANTERBURY								
Henry	27.1	12	45	3	21	6	54	1
Nuttall	18	6	48	3	14	1	63	1
Williams	22	8	38	3	16	5	35	0
Sheat	18	3	71	1	16	8	26	1
van Woerkom	5	4	1	0	31	10	56	1
McConchie					16	3	50	1
CENTRAL DISTRICTS								
Tickner	34.1	6	80	5				
Toole	26	7	53	2				
Leopard	14	3	56	0				
Clarkson	20	6	43	0				
Patel	35	5	114	1				
Schmulian	14	3	38	2				

Fall of Wickets	***CD***	***C***	***CD***
	1st	*1st*	*2nd*
1st	20	51	98
2nd	23	64	112
3rd	24	124	158
4th	47	179	181
5th	70	302	219
6th	92	348	-
7th	97	367	-
8th	105	379	-
9th	170	386	-
10th	207	391	-

OTAGO v NORTHERN DISTRICTS — Plunket Shield

at University of Otago Oval, Dunedin on 3, 4, 5, 6 April, 2021
Toss : Northern Districts. Umpires : J.A.K. Bromley & S.B. Haig
Close of play: 1st day: ND 14-0, Cooper 6, Raval 8; 2nd day: Otago 82-2, Kitchen 33, Kelly 40
3rd day: ND 45-0, Raval 27, Cooper 15
***Northern Districts won by 3 wickets.** Points: Northern Districts 17 (1 bat, 4 bowl), Otago 6, (2 bat, 4 bowl)*

Otago were asked to bat and lost Kitchen in the sixth over. Rutherford hit fifty and with the next six batsmen scoring twenties or thirties, the home side reached 272. This proved more than enough as Northern were dismissed for 222 on the second day, after they had been 149-8 at one stage.

Otago were bowled out a second time near the end of the third day with Kelly scoring 94 and Baker taking 5-55 in what turned out to be his last game before he announced his retirement. He also reached 200 wickets in first-class cricket.

Northern needed 317 to win and Raval (hundred from 231 balls) made sure this was achieved and he was unbeaten on 161 when the winning runs came. It was his first century for Northern Districts.

OTAGO

FIRST INNINGS	*Runs*	*Mins*	*Balls*	*6s*	*4s*	*SECOND INNINGS*	*Runs*	*Mins*	*Balls*	*6s*	*4s*
H.D.Rutherford* c Bocock b Walker	54	189	106	-	6	c Bocock b Baker	7	13	8	-	1
A.K.Kitchen c Hampton b Baker	3	23	18	-	-	c Bocock b Hampton	39	166	111	-	3
M.Renwick c Hampton b Wagner	31	88	69	-	5	c Bocock b Baker	0	3	4	-	-
N.F.Kelly c Carter b Walker	22	39	34	-	4	st Bocock b Walker	94	270	199	1	13
D.N.Phillips c Raval b Wagner	25	66	61	-	3	c Bocock b Baker	8	70	45	-	1
M.J.G.Rippon c Wagner b Walker	34	103	76	-	5	c Cooper b Sodhi	24	75	61	-	4
M.W.Chu† c & b Sodhi	25	99	68	-	2	run out	26	102	77	-	2
A.W.McKenzie not out	34	66	45	-	6	c Bocock b Hampton	13	70	56	-	2
T.Muller c Bocock b Sodhi	2	8	8	-	-	not out	26	54	28	-	6
J.A.Duffy c Wagner b Baker	14	23	20	-	3	b Baker	23	40	37	1	3
M.D.Rae lbw b Baker	7	10	13	-	1	c Sodhi b Baker	0	7	3	-	-
Extras (b 9, lb 9, nb 3)	21					(lb 2, w 2, nb 2)	6				
TOTAL (85.5 overs)	**272**	359				(104.3 overs)	**266**	437			

NORTHERN DISTRICTS

	Runs	*Mins*	*Balls*	*6s*	*4s*		*Runs*	*Mins*	*Balls*	*6s*	*4s*
H.R.Cooper c Phillips b Rae	10	17	12	-	2	(2) run out	15	95	57	-	1
J.A.Raval c Phillips b Duffy	24	46	34	-	6	(1) not out	161	475	341	-	20
B.Popli c Kitchen b Muller	38	95	72	-	6						
J.F.Carter* c Rutherford b Rae	40	165	101	-	4	c Renwick b McKenzie	13	41	28	-	2
B-J.Watling c Kitchen b Duffy	0	20	15	-	-	lbw b Rippon	4	20	15	-	1
B.R.Hampton b Rae	0	6	4	-	-	b Rippon	23	31	24	-	5
P.D.Bocock† c Chu b Muller	14	34	28	-	3	(3) c Chu b Duffy	22	57	47	-	3
I.S.Sodhi c Kitchen b Rae	10	25	20	-	2	(7) lbw b Rippon	40	124	91	2	4
N.Wagner lbw b Rippon	32	36	18	2	4	(8) c Kelly b Rippon	0	9	8	-	-
J.G.Walker st Chu b Kitchen	27	60	52	-	3	(9) not out	24	86	86	-	3
J.D.Baker not out	18	36	29	-	3						
Extras (lb 5, w 3, nb 1)	9					(b 6, lb 5, w 1, nb 3)	15				
TOTAL (64 overs)	**222**	273				(115.4 overs) (7 wkts)	**317**	475			

Bowling	*O*	*M*	*R*	*W*	*O*	*M*	*R*	*W*
NORTHERN DISTRICTS								
Wagner	23	4	79	2	28	10	60	0
Baker	15.5	3	35	3	27.3	10	55	5
Hampton	10	2	44	0	13	0	51	2
Sodhi	19	4	48	2	16	2	42	1
Walker	18	4	48	3	20	4	56	1
OTAGO								
Kitchen	4	1	7	1	9	1	18	0
Rippon	7	0	39	1	35.4	4	117	4
Rae	16	3	55	4	18	3	49	0
Duffy	15	6	53	2	26	10	49	1
Muller	12	4	39	2	11	0	50	0
McKenzie	10	1	24	0	16	8	23	1

Fall of Wickets

	O *1st*	***ND*** *1st*	***O*** *2nd*	***ND*** *2nd*
1st	14	22	15	45
2nd	74	49	15	84
3rd	110	90	93	121
4th	137	98	120	128
5th	164	101	167	154
6th	202	125	183	246
7th	227	140	215	248
8th	233	149	215	-
9th	264	189	258	-
10th	272	222	266	-

2020/21 FIRST-CLASS STATISTICS

REGISTER OF PLAYERS

The following players appeared in first-class cricket for New Zealand teams during the 2020/21 season.

		Born	*At*	*Type*			*First-class debut*	
Allen Finnley Hugh	W	22. 4.99	Auckland	RHB		WK	A v CD	17/18
Bacon Matthew Boyce	O	13. 4.93	Auckland	RHB	RM		W v O	15/16
Baker James David	ND	16. 2.88	Tokoroa	RHB	RM		ND v A	10/11
Beghin Graeme Kenneth	A	10.12.89	Cape Town, S.Africa	RHB	RM		A v W	18/19
Bennett Hamish Kyle	W	22. 2.87	Timaru	LHB	RFM		C v W	05/06
Bhula Jakob Jarrod Naran Patel	W	12.12.98	Wellington	RHB	ROB		W v ND	18/19
Blundell Thomas Ackland	W, NZ	1. 9.90	Wellington	RHB	ROB	WK	W v A	12/13
Bocock Peter David	ND	12. 4.91	Te Awamutu	RHB		WK	ND v O	17/18
Boult Trent Alexander	NZ	22. 7.89	Rotorua	RHB	LFM		NZ A v India A	08/09
Bowes Chad Jayson	C	19.10.92	Benoni, S. Africa	RHB	RFM		KZN v FS	10/11
Boyle John Christopher Thwaites	C	24. 3.96	Christchurch	RHB	ROB		C v A	16/17
Bracewell Douglas Andrew John	CD	28. 9.90	Tauranga	RHB	RM		CD v A	08/09
Bracewell Michael Gordon	W	14. 2.91	Masterton	LHB		WK	O v CD	10/11
Briggs Cole Jeffery	A	20. 8.97	Pretoria, S.Africa	RHB		WK	A v O	20/21
Bruce Thomas Charles	CD	2. 8.91	Te Kuiti	RHB	ROB		CD v O	14/15
Carter Joseph Franklyn	ND	17.12.92	Hemel Hempstead, Eng	RHB	ROB		ND v A	13/14
Carter Leo James	C	10.12.94	Wellington	LHB	RLB		C v ND	14/15
Chamberlain Harry John	C	16.11.95	Christchurch	RHB	RM		C v A	20/21
Chapman Mark Sinclair	A	27. 6.94	Hong Kong (China)	LHB	SLA		A v ND	15/16
Chu Max Wilkie	O	21. 3.00	Dunedin	LHB		WK	O v CD	18/19
Clarke Katene Dalton	ND	21. 9.99	Pukekohe	RHB	RSM		ND v CD	19/20
Clarkson Joshua Andrew	CD	21. 1.97	Christchurch	RHB	RM		CD v O	15/16
Cleaver Dane	CD	1. 1.92	Auckland	RHB		WK	CD v ND	10/11
Colson Fraser John	W	19. 3.90	Lower Hutt	RHB	ROB		W v CD	13/14
Conway Devon Philip	W, NZ	8. 7.91	Johannesburg, S.Africa	LHB	RM	WK	Gaut v East	08/09
Cooper Henry Ross	ND	20. 5.93	Whangarei	RHB	ROB		ND v CD	16/17
Davey Sean Benjamin	C	8. 4.93	Tauranga	RHB	RM		C v ND	20/21
de Grandhomme Colin	ND, NZ	22. 7.86	Harare, Zimbabwe	RHB	RM		Zim A v Kenya	05/06
Delport Louis Johannes	A	12. 2.88	Nelspruit, S.Africa	LHB	SLA		WP v Boland	14/15
Duffy Jacob Andrew	O	2. 8.94	Lumsden	RHB	RFM		O v W	11/12
Ferns Daniel Kruger	A	23. 2.94	Pretoria, S.Africa	RHB	RM		A v O	17/18
Field Joseph Francis Alexander	CD	19.12.00	Hamilton	RHB	RM		CD v A	20/21
Fisher Matthew John	ND	10.11.99	Auckland	RHB	RM		ND v W	20/21
Fletcher Andrew Townsend	W	29. 3.93	Somerset W, S.Africa	RHB			W v A	18/19
Fletcher Cameron Dean	C	1. 3.93	Auckland	RHB		WK	ND v CD	12/13
Georgeson Luke Ian	W	14. 4.99	Wellington	LHB	RM		W v CD	20/21
Gibson James David	W	29. 4.93	Greytown	RHB	RM		W v C	19/20
Gibson Zakary Neil	ND	19. 3.97	Hamilton	RHB	RM		ND v CD	15/16
Guptill Martin John	A	30. 9.86	Auckland	RHB	ROB		A v W	05/06
Hampton Brett Raymond	ND	30. 4.91	Tauranga	RHB	RM		ND v A	15/16
Harrison Ryan David	A	10.10.99	Auckland	RHB	RM		A v C	20/21
Hawkins Camden Thomas	O	6.12.94	Christchurch	RHB	RLBG		O v CD	18/19
Hay Gregory Robert	CD	14. 7.84	Rotorua	RHB	ROB		CD v W	06/07
Henry Matthew James	C, NZ	14.12.91	Christchurch	RHB	RFM		C v W	10/11
Horne Benjamin James	A	4. 3.93	Auckland	RHB	SLA	WK	A v CD	16/17
Jamieson Kyle Alex	A, NZ	30.12.94	Auckland	RHB	RFM		C v W	14/15
Johns Lauchlan Ritchie	W	1. 7.96	Wellington	RHB		WK	W v CD	17/18
Johnson Troy Manning	W	1.10.97	Lower Hutt	RHB	ROB		W v C	19/20
Kelly Nicholas Fred	O	25. 7.93	Melbourne, Australia	LHB	SLA		ND v A	15/16
Kitchen Anaru Kyle	O	21. 2.84	Auckland	RHB	SLA		A v ND	08/09
Kuggeleijn Scott Christopher	ND	3. 1.92	Hamilton	RHB	RFM		W v CD	11/12
Latham Thomas William Maxwell	C, NZ	2. 4.92	Christchurch	LHB	RM	WK	C v ND	10/11
Lennox Jayden Richard	CD	14.12.94	Napier	LHB	SLA		CD v C	20/21
Leopard Christian Kevin	CD	17. 9.97	Hastings	RHB	RM		CD v O	16/17
Lister Benjamin George	A	1. 1.96	Auckland	RHB	LFM		A v O	17/18
McClure Kenneth James	C	25.10.94	Christchurch	RHB	RLB		C v A	15/16
McConchie Cole Edward	C	12. 1.92	Christchurch	RHB	ROB		C v O	12/13
McKay Jarrod Douglas	O	8. 6.00	Nelson	RHB	RM		CD v ND	19/20
McPeake Iain Geoffrey	W	24. 5.91	Lower Hutt	RHB	RM		W v ND	15/16
McKenzie Angus William	O	17. 7.98	Wellington	LHB	RM		O v A	20/21
Mitchell Daryl Joseph	C, NZ	20. 5.91	Hamilton	RHB	RM		ND v A	11/12

		Born	At	Type			First-class debut	
Muller Travis	O	4. 3.93	Cape Town, S.Africa	RHB	RFM		WP v Namibia	11/12
Neesham James Douglas Sheehan	W	17. 9.90	Auckland	LHB	RFM		A v C	09/10
Newton Oliver Robert	W	22. 8.88	Dunedin	LHB	RM		W v A	17/18
Nicholls Henry Michael	C, NZ	15.11.91	Christchurch	LHB	ROB		C v O	11/12
Nuttall Edward James	C	15. 7.93	Christchurch	LHB	LFM		C v O	11/12
O'Donnell Robert Roux	A	12. 9.94	Kimberley, S.Africa	RHB	ROB		A v CD	14/15
O'Donnell William Taylor	A	29. 9.97	Randburg, S.Africa	RHB	ROB		A v O	18/19
Patel Ajaz Yunus	CD, NZ	21.10.88	Bombay, India	LHB	SLA		CD v W	12/13
Phillips Dale Nathan	O	15.10.98	Johannesburg, S.Africa	RHB	RM		O v W	19/20
Phillips Glenn Dominic	A	6.12.96	East London, S.Africa	RHB	ROB	WK	A v C	16/17
Popli Bharat	ND	30. 5.90	New Delhi, India	RHB	RLB		ND v A	13/14
Pringle Oliver Morgan Reynolds	A	27. 5.92	Auckland	LHB	RM		A v O	20/21
Rae Michael David	O	13. 6.95	Dunedin	RHB	RFM		O v ND	14/15
Rance Seth Hayden Arnold	CD	23. 8.87	Wellington	RHB	RM		CD v W	08/09
Randell Brett Graham	ND	20. 5.95	Auckland	RHB	RM		ND v W	16/17
Raval Jeet Ashok	A	22. 5.88	Ahmedabad, India	LHB	RLB		A v WI	08/09
Ravindra Rachin	W	18.11.99	Wellington	LHB	SLA		NZ A v Pak A	18/19
Renwick Mitchell	O	23. 2.93	Palmerston North	RHB	RLB		CD v W	15/16
Rippon Michael James Gratton	O	14. 9.91	Cape Town, S.Africa	RHB	SLC		WP v KZN	11/12
Rutherford Hamish Duncan	O	27. 4.89	Dunedin	LHB	SLA		O v ND	08/09
Santner Mitchell Josef	NZ	5. 2.92	Hamilton	LHB	SLA		ND v O	11/12
Schmulian Bradley Dean	CD	3. 8.90	Cape Town, S.Africa	RHB	RLB		CD v ND	17/18
Sears Benjamin Vincent	W	11. 2.98	Lower Hutt	RHB	RFM		W v ND	18/19
Seifert Tim Louis	ND	14.12.94	Wanganui	RHB		WK	ND v O	14/15
Sheat Fraser William	C	29. 4.98	Christchurch	RHB	RM		C v O	17/18
Smith Benjamin Seth	CD	7. 1.91	Hamilton	RHB	ROB		CD v W	10/11
Smith Nathan Gregory	O	15. 7.98	Dunedin	RHB	RFM		O v ND	15/16
Snedden Michael Warwick	W	20. 9.92	Auckland	RHB	RM		W v C	19/20
Sodhi Inderbir Singh	ND	31.10.92	Ludhiana, India	RHB	RLB		ND v O	12/13
Solia Sean Mikaele	A	15.12.92	Auckland	LHB	RM		A v C	16/17
Somerville William Edgar Richard	A	9. 8.84	Wellington	RHB	ROB		O v W	04/05
Southee Timothy Grant	ND, NZ	11.12.88	Whangarei	RHB	RFM		ND v O	06/07
Taylor Luteru Ross Poutoa Lote	CD, NZ	8. 3.84	Lower Hutt	RHB	ROB		CD v C	02/03
ter Braak Ross Matthew	A	5. 6.97	Auckland	RHB	LM		A v ND	20/21
Tickner Blair Marshall	CD	13.10.93	Napier	RHB	RFM		CD v A	14/15
Toole Raymond Lawrence	CD	30.10.97	Johannesburg, S.Africa	LHB	LM		CD v ND	19/20
van Beek Logan Verjus	W	7. 9.90	Christchurch	RHB	RFM		C v CD	09/10
van Woerkom Theo Francis	C	26. 7.93	Christchurch	RHB	SLA		C v A	15/16
Wagner Neil	ND, NZ	13. 3.86	Pretoria, S.Africa	LHB	LFM		NW v Nthns	05/06
Walker Josef Grant	ND	6. 9.92	Hamilton	RHB	ROB		ND v C	10/11
Watling Bradley-John	ND, NZ	9. 7.85	Durban, S.Africa	RHB		WK	ND v A	04/05
Williams William Salter Austen	C	6.10.92	Christchurch	RHB	RM		C v O	12/13
Williamson Kane Stuart	NZ	8. 8.90	Tauranga	RHB	ROB		ND v A	07/08
Worker George Herrick	CD	23. 8.89	Palmerston North	LHB	SLA		CD v W	07/08
Young William Alexander	CD, NZ	22.11.92	New Plymouth	RHB	ROB		CD v A	11/12
Younghusband Peter Francis	W	17. 2.90	Harare, Zimbabwe	RHB	RLBG		W v C	16/17

Key

RHB	right-hand batsman	*LM*	left medium	*RLB*	right leg-break	*RSM*	right slow-medium
LHB	left-hand batsman	*SLA*	slow left-arm	*ROB*	right off-break	*LFM*	left fast-medium
RM	right medium	*SLC*	left-arm chinaman	*RFM*	right fast-medium	*LSM*	left slow-medium
						WK	wicketkeeper

FIRST-CLASS UMPIRES

2020/21

Nineteen umpires officiated in international, first-class and limited overs games. ICC elite panel umpire Chris Gaffaney umpired all four test matches at home while Wayne Knights and Chris Brown made test debuts. There were no exchange programmes this season. Brown, Knights and Shaun Haig were again on the ICC International Panel and Kim Cotton was on the ICC Associate Panel. She made her first-class debut during the season.

Black, Cory Alan *(Wellington)*. Age 40. Made his debut in 2019/20 and has now umpired one first-class game, five one-day matches and two Twenty20 fixtures.

Bowden, Brent Fraser *(Auckland)*. Age 58. Debut in 1992/93and has now umpired 187 first-class games including 84 Tests, 333 one-day games, which include 200 one-day internationals, and 150 Twenty20 games, of which 24 were internationals.

Bromley, John Arthur Kinneir *(South Canterbury)*. Age 53. Debut in 2013/14 and has now stood in 23 first-class games, 30 one-day fixtures and 26 Twenty20 games.

Brown, Christopher Mark, *(Auckland)*. Age 48. Former first-class player with Auckland from 1993 to 1997. Made his umpiring debut in 2012/13. Has now umpired 40 first-class games, including two tests, 47 one-day matches, including 18 internationals, and 72 Twenty20 fixtures, including 35 internationals

Cotton, Kim Diane *(Canterbury)*. Age 43. Made her debut in 2019/20 and has now umpired one first-class match, two one-day matches and three Twenty20 games. Has also umpired eight women's one-day internationals and 30 women's Twenty20 internationals.

Dempsey, John Michael *(Counties-Manukau)*. Age 55. Made his debut in 2015/16 and has now officiated in 22 first-class matches, 25 one-day games and 19 Twenty20 games.

Gaffaney, Christopher Blair *(Otago)*. Age 45. Former Otago player who made his umpiring debut in 2007/08. Member of ICC Elite Panel and has now umpired 68 first-class games, including 37 tests. Also stood in 98 one-day games which include 71 internationals and 130 Twenty20 games, including 28 internationals.

Haig, Shaun Barry *(Otago)*. Age 39. Played first-class cricket for Otago from 2005 to 2011. Made his umpiring debut in 2015/16. Has now stood in 20 first-class fixtures, 24 one-day games, including six internationals, and 59 Twenty20 matches, which include 25 internationals.

Jagannathan, Kannan Sudarsanam *(Otago)*. Age 34. Made his debut in 2019/20 and has now umpired four one-day matches and two Twenty20 games.

Knights, Wayne Roger *(Auckland)*. Age 50. Made his debut in 2001/02 and has now officiated in 72 first-class games, including two tests. Has also umpired 77 one-day games, including 17 internationals, and 83 Twenty20 games, including 24 internationals.

Mehrotra, Ashley *(Counties-Manukau)*. Age 51. Debut in 2012/13 and has now stood in 47 first-class games, 37 one-day matches and 35 Twenty20 games.

Morrow, Damian Ross *(Hamilton)*. Age 40. Debut in 2015/16 and has now umpired one first-class match, 14 one-day games and four Twenty20 fixtures.

Parlane, Timothy James *(Canterbury)*. Age 63. Made his debut in 2001/02. Has umpired 111 first-class games, 116 one-day matches and 85 Twenty20 matches.

Pasco, Peter John *(Southland)*. Age 50. Made his debut this season standing in one one-day match.

Sanders, Eugene Dalaine *(Canterbury)*. Age 48. Made his debut in 2016/17 and has now stood in four first-class fixtures, 11 one-day matches and five Twenty20 games.

Stanley, Allen *(Auckland)*. Age 37. Debut this season standing in one first-class game as a substitute.

Stirrat, Garth Andrew *(Wellington)*. Age 52. Debut in 2015/16 and has now officiated in nine first-class games, 17 one-day fixtures and 12 Twenty20 matches.

Walker, Derek John *(North Otago)*. Age 61. Played first-class cricket for Otago and made his umpiring debut in 2004/05. Has now umpired 107 first-class games, 107 one-day matches, including nine internationals, and 111 Twenty20 games, including eight internationals

Walklin, Glen Michael *(Hawke's Bay)*. Age 47. Made his debut in 2018/19 and has now umpired four one-day matches and one Twenty20 game.

COMPLETE AVERAGES

Averages for West Indies, West Indies A and Pakistan are on pages 40, 48 and 55

	M	In	NO	HS	Runs	Ave	100	50	Ct	St	O	M	R	W	Ave	5WI	10WM	Best
F.H.Allen	3	6	0	17	40	6.66	-	-	3	-	3	0	15	1	15.00	-	-	1-15
M.B.Bacon	3	3	1	20*	27	13.50	-	-	1	-	43	7	192	1	192.00	-	-	1-49
J.D.Baker	6	4	3	18*	30	30.00	-	-	1	-	143.2	34	393	12	32.75	1	-	5-55
G.K.Beghin	4	7	0	108	262	37.42	1	2	3	-								
H.K.Bennett	3	6	4	20*	35	17.50	-	-	-	-	67.3	20	181	5	36.20	-	-	4-28
J.J.N.P.Bhula	3	5	0	55	102	20.40	-	1	1	-								
T.A.Blundell	12	19	1	113	558	31.00	3	1	10	-	4	0	25	0	-	-	-	-
P.D.Bocock	3	3	1	36*	72	36.00	-	-	8	1								
T.A.Boult	4	2	1	8*	14	14.00	-	-	1	-	157.3	36	491	14	35.07	-	-	3-43
C.J.Bowes	5	8	1	46	190	27.14	-	-	5	-								
J.C.T.Boyle	3	4	1	27	56	18.66	-	-	2	-								
D.A.J.Bracewell	7	11	2	102	302	33.55	1	1	5	-	210	44	569	24	23.70	1	-	6-42
M.G.Bracewell	10	18	0	142	725	40.27	4	1	9	-	175	42	590	10	59.00	-	-	4-133
C.J.Briggs	3	5	1	30	91	22.75	-	-	6	-								
T.C.Bruce	7	13	2	81*	275	25.00	-	1	13	-	2	0	11	0	-	-	-	-
J.F.Carter	11	17	2	146*	657	43.80	2	2	11	-								
L.J.Carter	7	8	1	169	403	57.57	1	2	3	-	1	0	4	0	-	-	-	-
H.J.Chamberlain	2	3	0	132	163	54.33	1	-	1	-								
M.S.Chapman	6	10	1	95	424	47.11	-	4	4	-								
M.W.Chu	7	12	3	53	276	30.66	-	1	17	1								
K.D.Clarke	4	7	0	34	101	14.42	-	-	2	-								
J.A.Clarkson	4	7	0	35	89	12.71	-	-	3	-	71.5	13	258	7	36.85	-	-	2-28
D.Cleaver	9	14	1	99	505	38.84	-	5	24	-								
F.J.Colson	1	1	0	2	2	2.00	-	-	-	-								
D.P.Conway	5	9	0	157	456	50.66	1	2	4	-								
H.R.Cooper	10	16	0	85	426	26.62	-	4	7	-	2	0	6	0	-	-	-	-
S.B.Davey	4	4	1	17	17	5.66	-	-	1	-	113.1	34	279	15	18.60	1	-	5-19
C.de Grandhomme	2	3	0	60	106	35.33	-	1	1	-	28	7	88	0	-	-	-	-
L.J.Delport	4	3	2	1*	1	1.00	-	-	2	-	104.3	24	334	14	23.85	1	-	7-88
J.A.Duffy	7	11	2	43	116	12.88	-	-	6	-	211	58	564	28	20.14	-	-	-4-47
D.K.Ferns	6	8	4	63*	110	27.50	-	1	3	-	126	32	452	12	37.66	-	-	3-44
J.F.A.Field	1	2	0	32	37	18.50	-	-	-	-	26	8	62	2	31.00	-	-	2-18
M.J.Fisher	1	-	-	-	-	-	-	-	-	-	20	3	88	0	-	-	-	-
A.T.Fletcher	3	5	0	33	69	13.80	-	-	-	-								
C.D.Fletcher	10	14	5	157	586	65.11	2	3	33	3								
L.I.Georgeson	4	7	0	70	193	27.57	-	2	1	-	25	5	83	5	16.60	-	-	3-39
J.D.Gibson	8	13	2	116*	331	30.09	1	1	10	-	118.3	30	384	11	34.90	-	-	3-40
Z.N.Gibson	1	1	0	10	10	10.00	-	-	-	-	23	5	87	1	87.00	-	-	1-87
M.J.Guptill	3	5	0	65	127	25.40	-	1	10	-								
B.R.Hampton	5	9	1	63*	157	19.62	-	2	2	-	67	10	207	6	34.50	-	-	2-40
R.D.Harrison	2	3	0	12	15	5.00	-	-	4	-	30	6	120	2	60.00	-	-	1-29
C.T.Hawkins	4	8	0	90	184	23.00	-	1	1	-								
G.R.Hay	7	13	0	93	395	30.38	-	3	5	-								
M.J.Henry	5	5	0	10	30	6.00	-	-	2	-	203.5	58	477	21	22.71	1	-	6-53
B.J.Horne	7	10	1	162	325	36.11	1	1	13	1								
K.A.Jamieson	7	8	2	51*	210	35.00	-	2	3	-	230.1	77	548	47	11.65	6	1	6-48
L.R.Johns	4	6	0	25	59	9.83	-	-	12	2								
T.M.Johnson	4	7	3	114	291	72.75	1	1	6	-								
N.F.Kelly	8	15	2	94	579	44.53	-	6	5	-								
A.K.Kitchen	8	15	0	63	333	22.20	-	2	13	-	122	24	382	5	76.40	-	-	1-7
S.C.Kuggeleijn	9	13	2	51	236	21.45	-	1	4	-	204.2	32	643	22	29.22	1	-	7-45
T.W.M.Latham	9	12	0	106	568	47.33	1	4	16	-								
J.R.Lennox	2	4	0	6	14	3.50	-	-	2	-	45	7	148	2	74.00	-	-	2-56
C.K.Leopard	1	2	1	34*	50	50.00	-	-	-	-	14	3	56	0	-	-	-	-
B.G.Lister	1	-	-	-	-	-	-	-	-	-	11	2	40	1	40.00	-	-	1-40
K.J.McClure	10	15	2	165	433	33.30	1	-	12	-	2	0	2	0	-	-	-	-
C.E.McConchie	10	13	2	124*	420	38.18	1	3	4	-	174.1	42	486	12	40.50	-	-	3-44
J.D.McKay	1	1	1	0*	0	-	-	-	1	-	19.2	1	108	0	-	-	-	-
A.W.McKenzie	3	4	1	34*	70	23.33	-	-	1	-	74	21	210	6	35.00	-	-	3-77
I.G.McPeake	8	11	0	20	40	3.63	-	-	1	-	199.1	61	534	18	29.66	-	-	4-53
D.J.Mitchell	8	9	1	103	441	55.12	2	1	14	-	135.4	34	341	18	18.94	1	-	5-44
T.Muller	7	11	4	46	177	25.28	-	-	5	-	149.3	25	551	14	39.35	1	-	5-131
J.D.S.Neesham	1	2	0	38	48	24.00	-	-	-	-	11	4	35	0	-	-	-	-

	M	In	NO	HS	Runs	Ave	100	50	Ct	St	O	M	R	W	Ave	5WI	10WM	Best
O.R.Newton	4	7	0	14	39	5.57	-	-	-	-	133	40	347	13	26.69	-	-	4-62
H.M.Nicholls	7	9	0	174	634	70.44	2	3	7	-								
E.J.Nuttall	7	6	6	24*	40	-	-	-	1	-	196 .4	33	710	27	26.29	1	-	5-54
R.R.O'Donnell	7	11	2	142	546	60.66	3	1	3	-	20	9	22	1	22.00	-	-	1-9
W.T.O'Donnell	4	7	2	137*	375	75.00	2	2	3	-	2	0	8	0	-	-	-	-
A.Y.Patel	2	3	0	52	59	19.66	-	1	2	-	60	12	181	2	90.50	-	-	1-67
D.N.Phillips	6	11	1	149	419	41.90	1	3	13	-	4	1	22	0	-	-	-	-
G.D.Phillips	8	13	0	136	548	42.15	1	3	8	-	30 .5	3	110	2	55.00	-	-	2-33
B.Popli	2	2	0	50	88	44.00	-	1	1	-								
O.M.R.Pringle	6	7	4	19*	49	16.33	-	-	3	-	85	18	267	7	38.14	-	-	2-29
M.D.Rae	10	13	3	28	60	6.00	-	-	3	-	308	45	1216	34	35.76	1	-	5-62
S.H.A.Rance	4	6	1	13	31	6.20	-	-	-	-	112 .1	18	339	18	18.83	1	-	5-64
B.G.Randell	1	2	0	12	12	6.00	-	-	-	-	16	2	58	2	29.00	-	-	2-58
J.A.Raval	8	13	1	161*	547	45.58	1	3	10	-	1	0	10	0	-	-	-	-
R.Ravindra	9	15	1	144*	536	38.28	2	2	6	-	154 .2	26	549	16	34.31	1	-	6-89
M.Renwick	7	12	0	49	181	15.08	-	-	7	-								
M.J.G.Rippon	9	16	3	106	504	38.76	1	1	6	-	219	26	819	23	35.60	1	-	6-66
H.D.Rutherford	8	15	0	111	588	39.20	1	6	4	-								
M.J.Santner	1	2	1	19	25	25.00	-	-	2	-	25 .3	5	59	2	29.50	-	-	2-52
B.D.Schmulian	6	10	0	127	312	31.20	1	1	1	-	95 .5	24	290	9	32.22	-	-	3-16
B.V.Sears	5	6	1	41	56	11.20	-	-	4	-	115 .3	16	421	12	35.08	-	-	4-46
T.L.Seifert	4	6	0	111	226	37.66	1	1	8	1								
F.W.Sheat	7	5	0	36	60	12.00	-	-	3	-	203 .3	57	565	27	20.92	2	-	5-25
B.S.Smith	3	6	1	111*	177	35.40	1	-	2	-								
N.G.Smith	7	11	1	76	270	27.00	-	1	3	-	160	49	393	16	24.56	-	-	3-29
M.W.Snedden	3	3	3	4*	5	-	-	-	1	-	65	9	219	8	27.37	-	-	3-37
I.S.Sodhi	9	10	1	42	156	17.33	-	-	6	-	205 .4	34	610	19	32.10	-	-	4-89
S.M.Solia	8	11	0	33	129	11.72	-	-	2	-	68 .5	10	201	12	16.75	1	-	5-8
W.E.R.Somerville	7	9	1	59	151	18.87	-	1	4	-	230	72	599	16	37.43	-	-	4-61
T.G.Southee	7	8	2	36	118	19.66	-	-	8	-	247 .4	64	669	32	20.90	2	-	5-32
L.R.P.L.Taylor	8	12	1	70	320	29.09	-	2	18	-								
R.M.ter Braak	4	5	0	58	92	18.40	-	1	1	-	70	15	227	6	37.83	-	-	4-67
B.M.Tickner	8	10	2	26	98	12.25	-	-	1	-	234 .2	43	759	28	27.10	1	-	5-80
R.L.Toole	7	10	7	6*	20	6.66	-	-	2	-	216 .2	56	591	22	26.86	-	-	4-38
L.V.van Beek	5	7	1	39	86	14.33	-	-	4	-	126	30	304	6	50.66	-	-	2-48
T.F.van Woerkom	7	7	1	28*	109	18.16	-	-	6	-	152	46	327	8	40.87	-	-	4-26
N.Wagner	9	9	3	66*	151	25.16	-	1	4	-	278	60	767	30	25.56	-	-	4-58
J.G.Walker	8	9	5	41*	137	34.25	-	-	2	-	229 .4	62	573	15	38.20	-	-	3-48
B-J.Watling	10	16	2	77	400	28.57	-	3	29	-	1	0	1	0	-	-	-	-
W.S.A.Williams	8	7	2	19	52	10.40	-	-	1	-	275 .5	99	528	31	17.03	2	-	5-26
K.S.Williamson	3	4	0	251	639	159.75	3	-	1	-	5	1	17	1	17.00	-	-	1-16
G.H.Worker	7	13	0	96	339	26.07	-	3	3	-	10	2	37	0	-	-	-	-
W.A.Young	7	10	2	133	393	49.12	2	-	4	-								
P.F.Younghusband	5	7	2	72	162	32.40	-	1	3	-	69	14	236	3	78.66	-	-	1-13

WICKETKEEPING DISMISSALS

The following New Zealand players who appeared in 2020/21 have made at least one dismissal in first-class cricket while keeping wicket.

	ct	st	total
B-J.Watling	407	10	417
C.D.Fletcher *	209	11	220
D.Cleaver	162	11	173
T.A.Blundell	142	6	150
T.L.Seifert	111	7	118
B.J. Horne *	115	3	118
T.W.M.Latham	38	1	39
M.Renwick	27	1	28
L.R.Johns *	33	2	35
M.W.Chu *	28	1	29
P.D.Bocock *	25	1	26
D.P.Conway	19	–	19
B.S.Smith	15	2	17
M.G.Bracewell	3	–	3
J.F.Carter	1	–	1
G.D.Phillips	1	–	1

** no further catches taken as fielder*

LEADING AVERAGES

BATTING *(top 20, qualification six innings)*

	M	I	NO	HS	Runs	Ave	100s	50s
W.T. O'Donnell	4	7	2	137*	375	75.00	2	2
T.M. Johnson	4	7	3	114	291	72.75	1	1
H.M. Nicholls	7	9	0	174	634	70.44	2	3
C.D. Fletcher	10	14	5	157	586	65.11	2	3
R.R. O'Donnell	7	11	2	142	546	60.66	3	1
L.J. Carter	7	8	1	169	403	57.57	1	2
D.J. Mitchell	8	9	1	103	441	55.12	2	1
D.P. Conway	5	9	0	157	456	50.66	1	2
W.A. Young	7	10	2	133	393	49.12	2	-
T.W.M. Latham	9	12	0	106	568	47.33	1	4
M.S. Chapman	6	10	1	95	424	47.11	-	4
J.A. Raval	8	13	1	161*	547	45.58	1	3
Fawad Alam	3	6	0	139	271	45.16	2	-
N.F. Kelly	8	15	2	94	579	44.53	-	6
J.F. Carter	11	17	2	146*	657	43.80	2	2
Azhar Ali	3	6	0	93	260	43.33	-	2
G.D. Phillips	8	13	0	136	548	42.15	1	3
D.N. Phillips	6	11	1	149	419	41.90	1	3
M.G. Bracewell	10	18	0	142	725	40.27	4	1
H.D. Rutherford	8	15	0	111	588	39.20	1	6

BOWLING *(top 20, qualification 10 wickets)*

	Overs	Mdns	Runs	Wkts	Ave	5WI	10WM	Best
K.A. Jamieson	230.1	77	548	47	11.65	6	1	6-48
S.M. Solia	68.5	10	201	12	16.75	1	-	5-8
W.S.A. Williams	275.5	99	528	31	17.03	2	-	5-26
S.B. Davey	113.1	34	279	15	18.60	1	-	5-19
S.H.A. Rance	112.1	18	339	18	18.83	1	-	5-64
D.J. Mitchell	135.4	34	341	18	18.94	1	-	5-44
J.A. Duffy	211	58	564	28	20.14	-	-	4-47
T.G. Southee	247.4	64	669	32	20.90	2	-	5-32
F.W. Sheat	203.3	57	565	27	20.92	2	-	5-25
M.J. Henry	203.5	58	477	21	22.71	1	-	6-53
D.A.J. Bracewell	210	44	569	24	23.70	1	-	6-42
L.J. Delport	104.3	24	334	14	23.85	1	-	7-88
N.G. Smith	160	49	393	16	24.56	-	-	3-29
N. Wagner	278	60	767	30	25.56	-	-	4-58
E.J. Nuttall	196.4	33	710	27	26.29	1	-	5-54
O.R. Newton	133	40	347	13	26.69	-	-	4-62
R.L. Toole	216.2	56	591	22	26.86	-	-	4-38
B.M. Tickner	234.2	43	759	28	27.10	1	-	5-80
S.C. Kuggeleijn	204.2	32	643	22	29.22	1	-	7-45
I.G. McPeake	199.1	61	534	18	29.66	-	-	4-53

CENTURIES

There were 53 centuries scored in first-class cricket in 2020/21 compared to 41 the previous season and the record of 84 in 2008/09. Thirty-six players scored hundreds during the season, with M.G. Bracewell making four and T. A. Blundell, K.S. Williamson and R.R. O'Donnell each scoring three.

The fastest hundred of the season was scored by M.G. Bracewell from 78 balls for Wellington against Auckland at Auckland.

251	K.S. Williamson	New Zealand v West Indies *(First Test)*	Hamilton
246	K.C. Brathwaite	West Indies v New Zealand A	Queenstown
238	K.S. Williamson	New Zealand v Pakistan *(Second Test)*	Christchurch
174	H.M. Nicholls	New Zealand v West Indies *(Second Test)*	Wellington
169	L.J. Carter	Canterbury v Otago	Christchurch
165	K.J. McClure	Canterbury v Otago	Alexandra
162	B.J. Horne	Auckland v Otago	Auckland
161*	J.A. Raval	Northern Districts v Otago	Dunedin
157	H.M. Nicholls	New Zealand v Pakistan *(Second Test)*	Christchurch
157	D.P. Conway	Wellington v Auckland	Wellington
157	C.D. Fletcher	Canterbury v Otago	Christchurch
†149	D.N. Phillips	Otago v Central Districts	Dunedin
146*	J.F. Carter	Northern Districts v Otago	Mt Maunganui
144*	R. Ravindra	New Zealand A v West Indies A	Nelson
142	M.G. Bracewell	Wellington v Auckland	Wellington
142	R.R. O'Donnell	Auckland v Wellington	Auckland
139	Fawad Alam	Pakistan A v New Zealand A	Whangarei
138	R. Ravindra	Wellington v Northern Districts	Wellington
137*	W.T. O'Donnell	Auckland v Wellington	Auckland
136	G.D. Phillips	New Zealand A v West Indies A	Mt Maunganui
135	M.G. Bracewell	New Zealand A v West Indies A	Nelson
†133	R. Shepherd	West Indies A v New Zealand A	Mt Maunganui
133	W.A. Young	New Zealand A v West Indies	Queenstown
†132	H.J. Chamberlain	Canterbury v Central Districts	Napier
129	K.S. Williamson	New Zealand v Pakistan *(First Test)*	Mt Maunganui
128	R.R. O'Donnell	Auckland v Otago	Invercargill
127	B.D. Schmulian	Central Districts v Otago	Dunedin
124*	C.E. McConchie	New Zealand A v West Indies	Queenstown
119	M.G. Bracewell	Wellington v Auckland	Auckland
†117	W.T. O'Donnell	Auckland v Wellington	Auckland
†116*	J.D. Gibson	Wellington v Canterbury	Christchurch
†114	T.M. Johnson	Wellington v Northern Districts	Mt Maunganui
113	T.A. Blundell	Wellington v Auckland	Auckland
111	T.L. Seifert	New Zealand A v West Indies A	Mt Maunganui
111	H.D. Rutherford	Otago v Central Districts	Dunedin
111*	B.S. Smith	Central Districts v Canterbury	Napier
110	S.A.R. Moseley	West Indies A v New Zealand A	Nelson
110*	W.A. Young	Central Districts v Northern Districts	Nelson
108	G.K. Beghin	Auckland v Wellington	Wellington
107*	R.R. O'Donnell	Auckland v Canterbury	Auckland
†106	M.J.G. Rippon	Otago v Auckland	Auckland
106	T.W.M. Latham	Canterbury v Otago	Christchurch
105	M.G. Bracewell	Wellington v Auckland	Auckland
104	J. Blackwood	West Indies v New Zealand *(First Test)*	Hamilton
103*	J.F. Carter	Northern Districts v Wellington	Mt Maunganui
103*	T.A. Blundell	Wellington v Northern Districts	Wellington
103	D.J. Mitchell	Canterbury v Wellington	Christchurch

102*	D.J. Mitchell	New Zealand v Pakistan *(Second Test)*	Christchurch
102	Fawad Alam	Pakistan v New Zealand *(First Test)*	Mt Maunganui
102	D.A.J. Bracewell	Central Districts v Auckland	Auckland
101	T.A. Blundell	Wellington v Otago	Wellington
100*	C.D. Fletcher	Canterbury v Wellington	Christchurch
100	Rohail Nazir	Pakistan A v New Zealand A	Whangarei

† *maiden first-class century*

CENTURY PARTNERSHIPS

There were 57 century partnerships in 2020/21 compared to 42 the previous season and the record of 92 in 2009/10.

FIRST WICKET

226	G.D.Phillips & T.L.Seifert	New Zealand A v West Indies A	Mt Maunganui
226	L.I.Georgeson & R.Ravindra	Wellington v Northern Districts	Wellington
177	G.H.Worker & G.R.Hay	Central Districts v Northern Districts	Hamilton
127	H.R.Cooper & J.A.Raval	Northern Districts v Central Districts	Hamilton
121	T.W.M.Latham & K.J.McClure	Canterbury v Otago	Alexandra
119	T.W.M.Latham & C.J.Bowes	Canterbury v Wellington	Wellington
111	T.W.M.Latham & T.A.Blundell	New Zealand v Pakistan *(First Test)*	Mt Maunganui
111	K.C.Brathwaite & J.D.Campbell	West Indies v New Zealand A	Queenstown
109	A.K.Kitchen & C.T.Hawkins	Otago v Northern Districts	Mt Maunganui
100	H.R.Cooper & R.Ravindra	New Zealand A v West Indies	Queenstown

SECOND WICKET

232	W.T.O'Donnell & R.R.O'Donnell	Auckland v Wellington	Auckland
198	K.J.McClure & H.M.Nicholls	Canterbury v Otago	Alexandra
189	K.C.Brathwaite & D.M.Bravo	West Indies v New Zealand A	Queenstown
154	T.W.M.Latham & K.S.Williamson	New Zealand v West Indies *(First Test)*	Hamilton
112	G.K.Beghin & G.D.Phillips	Auckland v Central Districts	Auckland
112	H.R.Cooper & J.F.Carter	Northern Districts v Otago	Mt Maunganui

THIRD WICKET

287	D.P.Conway & M.G.Bracewell	Wellington v Auckland	Wellington
156	G.K.Beghin & M.S.Chapman	Auckland v Wellington	Wellington
155	G.K.Beghin & R.R.O'Donnell	Auckland v Canterbury	Auckland
147	H.D.Rutherford & N.F.Kelly	Otago v Central Districts	Dunedin
132	D.N.Phillips & H.D.Rutherford	Otago v Wellington	Wellington
120	K.S.Williamson & L.R.P.L.Taylor	New Zealand v Pakistan *(First Test)*	Mt Maunganui

FOURTH WICKET

369	K.S.Williamson & H.M.Nicholls	New Zealand v Pakistan *(Second Test)*	Christchurch
217	M.G.Bracewell & T.A.Blundell	Wellington v Auckland	Auckland
133	K.S.Williamson & H.M.Nicholls	New Zealand v Pakistan *(First Test)*	Mt Maunganui
117	H.M.Nicholls & L.J.Carter	Canterbury v Otago	Christchurch
116	J.F.Carter & B-J. Watling	Northern Districts v Central Districts	Nelson
109	L.I.Georgeson & M.G.Bracewell	Wellington v Auckland	Auckland
107	K.C.Brathwaite v J.Blackwood	West Indies v New Zealand A	Queenstown

FIFTH WICKET

215	Fawad Alam & Rohail Nazir	Pakistan A v New Zealand A	Whangarei
187	B.D.Schmulian & D.Cleaver	Central Districts v Otago	Dunedin
184	D.N.Phillips & M.J.G.Rippon	Otago v Central Districts	Dunedin
170	W.A.Young & C.E.McConchie	New Zealand A v West Indies	Queenstown
165	Fawad Alam & Mohammad Rizwan	Pakistan v New Zealand *(First Test)*	Mt Maunganui
161	M.G.Bracewell & R.Ravindra	New Zealand A v West Indies A	Nelson
158*	T.A.Blundell & T.M.Johnson	Wellington v Northern Districts	Wellington
128	J.F.Carter & S.C.Kuggeleijn	Northern Districts v Wellington	Mt Maunganui
123	H.J.Chamberlain & C.D.Fletcher	Canterbury v Central Districts	Napier
121	J.F.Carter & C.de Grandhomme	Northern Districts v Otago	Mt Maunganui
117	D.J.Mitchell & L.J.Carter	Canterbury v Wellington	Christchurch
111	C.E.McConchie & C.D.Fletcher	Canterbury v Central Districts	Rangiora

SIXTH WICKET

305	L.J.Carter & C.D.Fletcher	Canterbury v Otago	Christchurch
154	D.J.Mitchell & C.D.Fletcher	Canterbury v Wellington	Christchurch

133	K.S.Williamson & D.J.Mitchell	New Zealand v Pakistan *(Second Test)*	Christchurch
127	T.M.Johnson & P.F.Younghusband	Wellington v Northern Districts	Mt Maunganui
123	W.T.O'Donnell & W.E.R.Somerville	Auckland v Wellington	Auckland
122	D.P.Conway & J.D.Gibson	Wellington v Canterbury	Christchurch
121	W.T.O'Donnell & R.M.ter Braak	Auckland v Canterbury	Auckland
107	R.Ravindra & C.D.Fletcher	New Zealand A v West Indies A	Nelson

SEVENTH WICKET

155	J.Blackwood & A.S.Joseph	West Indies v New Zealand *(First Test)*	Hamilton
115	S.A.R.Moseley & R.Shepherd	West Indies A v New Zealand A	Nelson
107	M.J.G.Rippon & M.W.Chu	Otago v Auckland	Auckland
107	Mohammad Rizwan & Faheem Ashraf	Pakistan v New Zealand *(First Test)*	Mt Maunganui
106	D.Cleaver & N.G.Smith	New Zealand A v West Indies A	Mt Maunganui

EIGHTH WICKET

199	R.A.Reifer & R.Shepherd	West Indies A v New Zealand A	Mt Maunganui
102	D.A.J.Bracewell & J.F.A.Field	Central Districts v Auckland	Auckland

NINTH WICKET

204	B.J.Horne & D.K.Ferns	Auckland v Otago	Auckland

BOWLING PERFORMANCES

There were 27 instances of bowlers taking five wickets or more in an innings in 2020/21 compared with 15 in 2019/20. Nineteen players achieved the feat with K.A. Jamieson doing it on six occasions, while W.S.A. Williams, F.W. Sheat and T.G. Southee did it twice. There were three hat-tricks recorded during the season.

FIVE WICKETS IN AN INNINGS

7-45	S.C. Kuggeleijn	Northern Districts v Auckland	Whangarei
7-88	L.J. Delport	Auckland v Northern Districts	Whangarei
6-42	D.A.J. Bracewell	New Zealand A v West Indies A	Nelson
6-48	K.A. Jamieson	New Zealand v Pakistan *(Second Test)*	Christchurch
6-53	M.J. Henry	New Zealand A v Pakistan A	Whangarei
6-66	M.J.G. Rippon	Otago v Central Districts	Dunedin
6-89	R. Ravindra	New Zealand A v West Indies A	Nelson
5-8	S.M. Solia	Auckland v Otago	Auckland
5-19	S.B. Davey	Canterbury v Central Districts	Rangiora
5-25	F.W. Sheat	Canterbury v Wellington	Christchurch
5-26	W.S.A. Williams	Canterbury v Northern Districts	Rangiora
5-31	F.W. Sheat	Canterbury v Northern Districts	Rangiora
5-32	T.G. Southee	New Zealand v West Indies *(Second Test)*	Wellington
5-34	K.A. Jamieson	New Zealand v West Indies *(Second Test)*	Wellington
5-39	K.A. Jamieson	Auckland v Otago	Auckland
5-41	K.A. Jamieson	Auckland v Central Districts	Auckland
5-42	T.G. Southee	Northern Districts v Otago	Mt Maunganui
5-44	D.J. Mitchell	Canterbury v Otago	Alexandra
5-54	E.J. Nuttall	New Zealand A v Pakistan A	Whangarei
5-55	J.D. Baker	Northern Districts v Otago	Dunedin
5-58	W.S.A. Williams	Canterbury v Wellington	Christchurch
5-62	M.D. Rae	Otago v Central Districts	Dunedin
5-64	S.H.A. Rance	Central Districts v Northern Districts	Nelson
5-69	K.A. Jamieson	New Zealand v Pakistan *(Second Test)*	Christchurch
5-80	B.M. Tickner	Central Districts v Canterbury	Napier
5-85	K.A. Jamieson	Auckland v Wellington	Wellington
5-131	T. Muller	Otago v Canterbury	Christchurch

TEN WICKETS IN A MATCH

11-117	K.A. Jamieson	New Zealand v Pakistan *(Second Test)*	Christchurch

CAREER AVERAGES

as at 1 July, 2021 for players active during the 2020/21 season

	M	In	NO	HS	Runs	Ave	100	50	Ct	St	Wkts	Runs	Ave	5WI	10WM	Best
F.H.Allen	12	20	2	66	343	19.05	-	3	12	-	1	15	15.00	-	-	1-15
M.B.Bacon	19	27	7	43	202	10.10	-	-	9	-	53	1663	31.37	1	1	6-73
J.D.Baker	76	94	43	41*	592	11.60	-	-	24	-	201	5961	29.65	7	1	6-72
G.K.Beghin	13	21	1	140	636	31.80	2	4	8	-						
H.K.Bennett	79	90	44	30*	446	9.69	-	-	17	-	261	7437	28.49	8	1	7-50
J.J.N.P.Bhula	5	8	0	55	122	15.25	-	1	5	-						
T.A.Blundell	72	121	15	153	3856	36.40	10	16	155	6	1	65	65.00	-	-	1-15
P.D.Bocock	9	14	1	56	266	20.46	-	1	25	1						
T.A.Boult	108	128	52	61	1140	15.00	-	2	55	-	408	10,997	26.95	16	1	6-30
C.J.Bowes	72	117	8	155	2962	27.17	4	11	45	-	1	129	129.00	-	-	1-22
J.C.T.Boyle	19	33	1	108	603	18.84	1	1	15	-	1	4	4.00	-	-	1-4
D.A.J.Bracewell	109	163	23	105	3778	26.98	3	19	51	-	334	10,804	32.34	10	-	7-35
M.G.Bracewell	91	161	13	190	5072	34.27	11	21	89	-	20	881	44.05	1	-	5-43
C.J.Briggs	3	5	1	30	91	18.20	-	-	6	-						
T.C.Bruce	51	19	13	166*	3101	39.75	4	22	78	-	21	692	32.95	-	-	2-17
J.F.Carter	52	92	3	169	2924	32.85	6	14	38	-						
L.J.Carter	35	59	3	226*	1934	34.53	3	11	31	-	0	4	-	-	-	-
M.S.Chapman	30	50	2	146	2031	42.31	4	12	24	-	1	222	222.00	-	-	1-60
H.J.Chamberlain	2	3	0	132	166	54.33	1	-	1	-						
M.W.Chu	10	17	3	53	347	24.78	-	1	28	1						
K.D.Clarke	7	13	1	41	242	20.16	-	-	5	-						
J.A.Clarkson	7	11	1	35	154	15.40	-	-	5	-	12	442	36.83	-	-	2-28
D.Cleaver	59	97	10	201	3598	41.35	6	25	163	11						
F.J.Colson	25	44	2	97	872	20.76	-	5	20	-						
D.P.Conway	111	180	23	327*	7509	47.82	19	32	96	-	9	467	51.88	-	-	3-36
H.R.Cooper	35	61	2	149	2108	35.72	5	12	17	-	2	56	28.00	-	-	1-8
S.B.Davey	4	4	1	17	17	5.66	-	-	1	-	15	279	18.60	1	-	5-19
C.de Grandhomme	114	184	24	144*	5821	36.38	12	35	106	-	180	5541	30.78	2	-	6-24
L.J.Delport	12	12	5	53*	136	19.42	-	1	5	-	41	1159	28.26	2	-	7-88
J.A.Duffy	69	94	30	71	830	12.96	-	1	31	-	197	6295	31.95	8	-	7-89
D.K.Ferns	15	21	8	63*	193	14.84	-	1	6	-	35	1189	33.97	-	-	4-33
J.F.A.Field	1	2	0	32	37	18.50	-	-	-	-	2	62	31.20	-	-	2-18
M.J.Fisher	1	-	-	-	-	-	-	-	-	-	0	88	-	-	-	-
A.T.Fletcher	9	16	1	50*	220	14.66	-	1	2	-						
C.D.Fletcher	65	101	20	157	2815	34.75	5	13	209	11						
L.I.Georgeson	4	7	0	70	193	27.57	-	2	1	-	5	83	16.60	-	-	3-39
J.D.Gibson	14	22	3	116*	580	30.52	1	2	14	-	18	626	34.77	-	-	3-36
Z.N.Gibson	15	15	8	31*	95	13.57	-	-	5	-	19	1187	62.47	-	-	4-62
M.J.Guptill	115	208	13	227	7389	37.89	16	39	130	-	11	674	61.27	-	-	3-11
B.R.Hampton	14	23	6	63*	454	26.70	-	4	7	-	21	760	36.19	-	-	4-78
R.D.Harrison	2	3	0	12	15	5.00	-	-	4	-	2	120	60.00	-	-	1-29
C.T.Hawkins	14	27	0	90	680	25.18	-	5	10	-	0	10	-	-	-	-
G.R.Hay	87	153	11	226	5964	42.00	13	31	46	-	2	201	100.50	-	-	1-8
M.J.Henry	74	95	16	81	1562	19.77	-	5	32	-	314	7906	25.17	15	3	7-42
B.J.Horne	35	56	10	162	1472	32.00	2	8	115	3						
K.A.Jamieson	36	46	8	67	803	21.13	-	5	7	-	138	2881	20.87	11	2	8-74
L.R.Johns	11	16	1	40	201	13.40	-	-	33	2						
T.M.Johnson	7	11	3	114	362	45.25	1	1	7	-						
N.F.Kelly	27	47	4	118	1305	30.34	1	7	21	-	0	55	-	-	-	-
A.K.Kitchen	88	160	13	207	5119	34.82	10	26	71	-	34	1726	50.76	-	-	3-19
S.C.Kuggeleijn	83	128	21	142*	3043	28.43	3	16	31	-	266	8474	31.85	9	-	7-45
T.W.M.Latham	126	216	14	264*	8668	42.91	20	48	163	1	1	18	18.00	-	-	1-7
J.R.Lennox	2	4	0	6	14	3.50	-	-	2	-	2	148	74.00	-	-	2-56
C.K.Leopard	4	7	2	52	203	40.60	-	1	1	-	2	124	62.00	-	-	1-21
B.G.Lister	19	23	8	19*	124	8.26	-	-	10	-	47	1205	25.63	1	-	5-29
K.J.McClure	41	68	7	210	2285	37.45	5	8	28	-	0	2	-	-	-	-
C.E.McConchie	43	67	6	162	2078	34.06	5	9	17	-	35	1297	37.05	-	-	4-46
J.D.McKay	2	3	1	0*	0	0.00	-	-	3	-	2	185	92.50	-	-	1-27
A.W.McKenzie	3	4	1	34*	70	23.33	-	-	1	-	6	210	35.00	-	-	3-77
I.G.McPeake	43	58	13	48	528	11.73	-	-	10	-	120	3595	29.95	3	1	5-21
D.J.Mitchell	79	125	17	170*	4144	38.37	10	22	88	-	80	2522	31.52	1	-	5-44
T.Muller	51	59	21	48	661	17.39	-	-	18	-	135	3544	26.25	6	-	6-54
J.D.S.Neesham	65	110	9	147	3239	32.06	5	17	66	-	118	3940	33.38	2	-	5-65

	M	In	NO	HS	Runs	Ave	100	50	Ct	St	Wkts	Runs	Ave	5WI	10WM	Best
O.R.Newton	20	28	3	68	327	13.08	-	1	1	-	50	1506	30.12	-	-	4-26
H.M.Nicholls	91	147	11	174	5436	39.97	12	29	70	-	0	24	-	-	-	-
E.J.Nuttall	35	31	21	24*	128	12.80	-	-	9	-	105	3394	32.32	4	-	6-35
R.R.O'Donnell	55	96	6	167	3049	33.87	5	17	67	-	8	408	51.00	-	-	3-74
W.T.O'Donnell	6	11	2	137*	421	46.77	2	2	5	-	1	47	47.00	-	-	1-39
A.Y.Patel	67	96	25	52	972	13.69	-	1	47	-	248	8012	32.30	18	3	6-48
D.N.Phillips	9	16	1	149	460	30.66	1	3	19	-	0	40	-	-	-	-
G.D.Phillips	37	62	4	138*	2331	40.18	6	14	30	-	22	926	42.09	-	-	4-70
B.Popli	49	83	4	172	2889	36.56	3	20	47	-	0	16	-	-	-	-
O.M.R.Pringle	6	7	4	19*	49	16.33	-	-	3	-	7	267	38.17	-	-	2-29
M.D.Rae	40	53	14	36	315	8.07	-	-	10	-	114	3876	34.00	2	-	5-18
S.H.A.Rance	48	66	15	71	907	17.78	-	4	15	-	146	4083	27.96	7	-	6-26
B.G.Randell	12	21	4	56	174	10.23	-	1	3	-	21	836	39.80	-	-	3-50
J.A.Raval	126	221	11	256	7832	37.29	17	37	134	-	23	1084	47.13	-	-	2-10
R.Ravindra	26	42	4	144*	1470	38.68	3	9	13	-	22	1283	58.31	1	-	6-89
M.Renwick	33	61	2	131	1375	23.30	1	5	38	1						
M.J.G.Rippon	36	63	6	106	1731	30.36	1	8	14	-	86	2903	33.75	3	-	6-66
H.D.Rutherford	111	192	3	239	6830	36.13	15	35	73	-	0	81	-	-	-	-
M.J.Santner	54	81	5	126	2152	28.31	3	12	45	-	84	3981	47.39	-	-	4-111
B.D.Schmulian	22	37	2	203	1352	38.62	2	9	12	-	21	634	30.19	-	-	4-34
B.V.Sears	10	11	4	41	77	11.00	-	-	7	-	28	764	27.28	1	-	6-43
T.L.Seifert	51	86	6	167*	2912	36.40	6	14	124	7						
F.W.Sheat	17	22	11	36	167	15.18	-	-	9	-	63	1429	22.68	2	-	5-25
B.S.Smith	62	107	7	244	3313	33.13	6	17	39	2	1	59	59.00	-	-	1-17
N.G.Smith	29	47	8	114	1110	28.46	1	4	14	-	50	1892	37.84	1	-	5-56
M.W.Snedden	6	5	3	6	11	5.50	-	-	5	-	12	376	31.33	-	-	3-37
I.S.Sodhi	84	123	18	82*	2259	21.51	-	11	38	-	264	9105	34.48	14	2	7-30
S.M.Solia	34	55	5	81	1327	26.54	-	11	14	-	53	1502	28.33	-	-	5-8
W.E.R.Somerville	37	47	8	59	693	17.76	-	-	14	-	113	3340	29.55	4	-	8-136
T.G.Southee	119	159	16	156	2539	17.75	1	7	72	-	472	12,392	26.25	22	1	8-27
L.R.P.L.Taylor	188	316	27	290	12,250	42.38	27	65	246	-	6	378	63.00	-	-	2-4
R.M.ter Braak	4	5	0	58	92	18.40	-	1	1	-	6	227	37.83	-	-	4-67
B.M.Tickner	52	55	21	30*	354	10.41	-	-	23	-	148	5357	36.19	3	-	5-23
R.L.Toole	11	17	11	17*	44	7.33	-	-	3	-	30	857	28.56	-	-	4-38
L.V.van Beek	61	83	18	111*	1479	22.75	1	7	42	-	155	5004	32.28	6	1	6-46
T.F.van Woerkom	24	27	7	63*	397	19.85	-	3	8	-	36	1304	36.22	-	-	4-26
N.Wagner	184	241	53	70	3139	16.69	-	9	55	-	762	20,314	26.65	36	2	7-39
J.G.Walker	35	45	14	87	608	19.61	-	1	17	-	62	2650	42.74	3	-	5-25
B-J.Watling	178	297	36	205	10,034	38.44	18	59	450	10	0	9	-	-	-	-
W.S.A.Williams	33	46	11	38	435	12.42	-	-	15	-	91	2119	23.28	2	-	5-26
K.S.Williamson	153	261	21	284*	12,041	50.17	34	60	136	-	86	3709	43.12	1	-	5-75
G.H.Worker	105	189	7	210	5228	28.72	9	26	99	-	58	3878	66.86	-	-	4-58
W.A.Young	86	142	13	162	5506	42.68	12	29	45	-	0	8	-	-	-	-
P.F.Younghusband	12	18	5	97	482	37.07	-	2	10	-	10	578	57.80	1	-	5-89

NEW ZEALANDERS IN OVERSEAS CRICKET

Matt Quinn *(Essex)* was the only New Zealand player to appear in county cricket in 2020. The details are:

	M	I	NO	HS	Runs	Ave	100	50	ct/st
M.R. Quinn	2	2	0	13	13	6.50	-	-	-

	O	M	R	W	Ave	5WI	10WM	Best
M.R. Quinn	55.3	10	156	3	52.00	-	-	1-19

FORD TROPHY

2020/21

Canterbury won the Ford Trophy for the first time since 2016/17 when they defeated Northern Districts in the final. Northern had earlier beaten Wellington in the elimination play-off.

The leading run scorers were Will O'Donnell *(Auckland)* with 537 while Ken McClure *(Canterbury)* totalled 480. They were followed by the Northern Districts pair of Jeet Raval (409) and Henry Cooper (405). There were 16 centuries recorded with Tom Blundell's 151 for Wellington against Otago the highest.

Finn Allen scored the fastest century with a 50-ball hundred (equalling Peter Fulton's New Zealand one-day record) also for Wellington against Otago. The fastest fifty was scored by Hamish Rutherford from 21 balls for Otago against Central Districts.

The leading wicket-takers were Will Williams *(Canterbury)* with 20, Brett Hampton *(Northern Districts)* 18 and Michael Rae *(Otago)* 16. There were five instances of bowlers taking five wickets in an innings. Rae had the season's best figures of 7-35 against Auckland.

Final points were:

	P	*W*	*L*	*T*	*NR*	*Bonus*	*Points*
Canterbury	10	7	3	–	–	3	31
Northern Districts	10	6	4	–	–	2	26
Wellington	10	5	4	–	1	–	22
Otago	10	5	5	–	–	–	20
Auckland	10	4	6	–	–	2	18
Central Districts	10	2	7	–	1	2	12

First Round

Harrison and Pringle *(Auckland)*, Davey *(Canterbury)*, Field *(Central Districts)* and Johnson and Hartshorn *(Wellington)* made their debuts. Rodden made his Auckland debut while Raval made his Northern debut.

Wellington were in some trouble against Canterbury, being 39-3, before Bracewell scored 62 and they reached 119. Davey took 6-30 on debut, the second best bowling figures by a Canterbury bowler. Boyle and Nicholls both scored forties as Canterbury got the required runs off 22.4 overs.

Rain delayed the start of Central's game with Otago and reduced it to 20 overs per side. Otago decided to bowl. Wiggins top scored with 44 as many batsmen got starts and Central reached 183-6. Otago captain Rutherford scored fifty from 30 balls and was dismissed for 97 as Otago reached its target with ten balls to spare.

Auckland were 35-2 after 11.2 overs when rain stopped play and the game was reduced to 27 overs. Beghin and Rodden both scored forties. Randell had career best figures of 5-22. Auckland finished with 138-9. Northern had a revised target of 143 and had an opening stand of 95. Clarke had a 27-ball fifty as he got to 63. Northern reached their target off 19.3 overs.

CANTERBURY v WELLINGTON — Ford Trophy

at Hagley Oval, Christchurch on 29 November, 2020
Toss : Wellington. Umpires : T.J. Parlane & G.M. Walklin
Canterbury won by 7 wickets. *Points: Canterbury 5, Wellington 0*

WELLINGTON

	Runs	Mins	Balls	6s	4s
A.T.Fletcher c Williams b Sheat	2	22	11	-	-
L.R.Johns† b Sheat	23	32	28	-	4
J.J.N.P.Bhula c Fletcher b Sheat	5	20	9	-	1
M.G.Bracewell* c Fletcher b Davey	62	118	81	-	8
T.M.Johnson c Fletcher b Nuttall	13	52	28	-	2
F.J.Colson b Davey	3	12	11	-	-
J.D.Gibson c Boyle b Davey	0	10	5	-	-
P.F.Younghusband c Fletcher b Davey	6	9	9	-	1
I.G.McPeake c Williams b Davey	1	8	6	-	-
M.W.Snedden not out	1	18	11	-	-
J.W.Hartshorn c Astle b Davey	0	4	5	-	-
Extras (lb 2, w 1)	3				
TOTAL (34 overs)	**119**	154			

CANTERBURY

	Runs	Mins	Balls	6s	4s
C.J.Bowes b Gibson	19	45	18	-	3
J.C.T.Boyle b Gibson	41	73	61	-	5
H.M.Nicholls not out	43	52	40	-	9
T.W.M.Latham c Gibson b Bracewell	16	21	16	-	3
L.J.Carter* not out	0	2	1	-	-
T.D.Astle					
C.D.Fletcher†					
S.B.Davey					
W.S.A.Williams					
F.W.Sheat					
E.J.Nuttall					
Extras (lb 1, w 3)	4				
TOTAL (22.4 overs) (3 wkts)	**123**	97			

Bowling	*O*	*M*	*R*	*W*
CANTERBURY				
Nuttall	8	2	34	1
Sheat	7	2	22	3
Williams	5	0	19	0
Davey	10	1	30	6
Astle	4	0	12	0
WELLINGTON				
Hartshorn	4	0	31	0
McPeake	5	0	18	0
Snedden	6	0	21	0
Gibson	5	0	31	2
Bhula	1.4	0	15	0
Bracewell	1	0	6	1

Fall of Wickets

	W	*C*
1st	15	58
2nd	30	77
3rd	39	119
4th	83	-
5th	88	-
6th	90	-
7th	98	-
8th	102	-
9th	119	-
10th	119	-

CENTRAL DISTRICTS v OTAGO **Ford Trophy**

at Pukekura Park, New Plymouth on 29 November, 2020
Toss : Otago. Umpires : J.A.K. Bromley & G.A Stirrat
***Otago won by 6 wickets.** Points: Oago 4, Central Districts 0*

CENTRAL DISTRICTS

	Runs	Mins	Balls	6s	4s
G.H.Worker b Bacon	33	39	24	2	3
B.L.Wiggins† c Phillips b Finnie	44	48	28	3	4
C.K.Leopard c Kelly b Muller	19	21	14	1	2
T.C.Bruce* c Rutherford b Kitchen	39	25	19	3	2
B.S.Smith run out	24	35	23	1	1
J.A.Clarkson c Kelly b Duffy	6	6	5	-	1
B.D.Schmulian not out	10	14	8	-	1
J.F.A.Field					
J.R.Lennox					
S.H.A.Rance					
L.R.Dudding					
Extras (lb 1, w 6, nb 1)	8				
TOTAL (20 overs) (6 wkts)	**183**	95			

OTAGO

	Runs	Mins	Balls	6s	4s
H.D.Rutherford* b Rance	97	89	59	3	13
N.T.Broom b Clarkson	17	29	10	1	2
M.Renwick† c Schmulian b Leopard	15	27	16	1	-
J.L.Finnie c Field b Clarkson	21	16	12	1	3
A.K.Kitchen not out	30	18	13	2	3
N.F.Kelly not out	0	3	1	-	-
M.J.G.Rippon					
J.A.Duffy					
T.Muller					
M.B.Bacon					
D.N.Phillips					
Extras (lb 4, w 2, nb 1)	7				
TOTAL (18.2 overs) (4 wkts)	**187**	93			

Bowling	*O*	*M*	*R*	*W*
OTAGO				
Kitchen	4	0	34	1
Duffy	4	0	28	1
Bacon	4	0	34	1
Muller	2	0	31	1
Rippon	4	0	32	0
Finnie	2	0	23	1
CENTRAL DISTRICTS				
Dudding	3	0	26	0
Rance	4	0	37	1
Field	3.2	0	40	0
Lennox	2	0	26	0
Clarkson	4	0	31	2
Leopard	2	0	23	1

Fall of Wickets	***CD***	***O***
1st	73	68
2nd	86	107
3rd	123	146
4th	148	179
5th	155	-
6th	183	-
7th	-	-
8th	-	-
9th	-	-
10th	-	-

NORTHERN DISTRICTS v AUCKLAND **Ford Trophy**

at Cobham Oval, Whangarei on 29 November, 2020
Toss : Northern Districts. Umpires : J.M. Dempsey & A. Mehrotra
***Northern Districts won by 6 wickets (D/L).** Points: Northern Districts 5, Auckland 0*

AUCKLAND

	Runs	Mins	Balls	6s	4s
G.K.Beghin c Raval b Hampton	47	101	67	-	5
C.Munro c Popli b Verma	7	17	12	-	1
W.T.O'Donnell c Watling b Randell	5	25	20	-	1
R.R.O'Donnell* c Watling b Walker	12	24	15	-	1
B.J.Horne† c Walker b Randell	11	11	12	-	1
B.P.Rodden c Wagner b Randell	41	42	28	1	3
R.D.Harrison b Verma	1	9	4	-	-
W.E.R.Somerville c Clarke	6	4	-	-	
b Randell	5	1	2	-	-
D.K.Ferns c Clarke b Randell	2	1	0	-	-
O.M.R.Pringle not out	0				
B.G.Lister					
Extras (lb 3, w 2, nb 2)	7				
TOTAL (27 overs) (9 wkts)	**138**	122			

NORTHERN DISTRICTS

	Runs	Mins	Balls	6s	4s
K.D.Clarke run out	63	48	38	2	7
J.A.Raval c Horne b Harrison	43	68	45	1	3
B.Popli c Horne b Harrison	0	3	1	-	-
B-J.Watling† not out	23	35	28	-	2
D.G.Brownlie lbw b Somerville	0	4	1	-	-
A.P.Devcich* not out	4	14	6	-	-
B.R.Hampton					
A.Verma					
N.Wagner					
J.G.Walker					
B.G.Randell					
Extras (lb 4, w 4, nb 2)	10				
TOTAL (19.3 overs) (4 wkts)	**143**	87			

Bowling	*O*	*M*	*R*	*W*
NORTHERN DISTRICTS				
Wagner	6	0	17	0
Verma	5	1	27	2
Randell	6	0	22	5
Hampton	5	0	38	1
Walker	5	0	31	1
AUCKLAND				
Lister	4	0	34	0
Ferns	2	0	18	0
Pringle	3	0	26	0
Somerville	6	0	39	1
Harrison	4.3	0	22	2

Fall of Wickets	***A***	***ND***
1st	18	95
2nd	33	96
3rd	52	121
4th	73	127
5th	104	-
6th	125	-
7th	135	-
8th	138	-
9th	138	-
10th	-	-

Second Round

Ter Braak *(Auckland)*, Lortan and Matt Hay *(Canterbury)* and McKay *(Otago)* made their debuts.

Wellington decided to bowl first after the game had been reduced to 40 overs and looked to have been successful but then Carter and Astle added 130 for the fourth wicket. Carter got fifty from 47 balls, three faster than Astle who equalled his highest score of 83. Canterbury ended with 236-5. Wellington were in trouble at 25-4 but a 98 run stand between Bracewell and Colson gave some respectability. Bracewell got fifty from 47 balls but Wellington were dismissed for 205 off 37.3 overs.

Rain again delayed the Central and Otago game reducing it to 24 overs. Central decided to bowl but Otago had a 91 run opening stand. Rutherford scored fifty from 21 balls and was assisted by Broom who made 69. Field had best bowling figures. Central opener Worker was the star of the day getting his 12th hundred off 65 balls. He added 99 off 63 balls with Clarkson but Central then collapsed. They went from 197-4 to lose four wickets in six balls. Muller had career best figures as Central finished at 202-8.

Auckland decided to bat and made 202-7 with Will O'Donnell top scoring with his maiden fifty from 90 balls. Auckland were indebted to an unbroken eighth wicket stand of 80 from 79 balls. Gibson took 3-56. Northern had three fifty plus stands in their innings. Popli got fifty from 84 balls as Northern reached their target with 6.4 overs to spare.

CANTERBURY v WELLINGTON — Ford Trophy

at MainPower Oval, Rangiora on 1 December, 2020
Toss : Wellington. Umpires : T.J. Parlane & E.D. Sanders
Canterbury won by 31 runs. *Points: Canterbury 4, Wellington 0*

CANTERBURY

	Runs	Mins	Balls	6s	4s
J.C.T.Boyle st Johns b Younghusband	24	80	52	-	1
C.J.Bowes c Colson b Snedden	16	34	27	-	2
T.M.Lortan c Johns b Bracewell	12	36	29	-	1
L.J.Carter* c Bracewell b McPeake	60	83	52	3	2
T.D.Astle c Younghusband b Hartshorn	83	86	69	1	7
M.W.Hay not out	20	16	11	1	1
C.D.Fletcher† not out	4	2	1	-	1
S.B.Davey					
W.S.A.Williams					
M.J.Henry					
E.J.Nuttall					
Extras (lb 6, w 10, nb 1)	17				
TOTAL (40 overs) (5 wkts)	**236**	170			

WELLINGTON

	Runs	Mins	Balls	6s	4s
A.T.Fletcher c Boyle b Nuttall	7	31	25	-	1
L.R.Johns† c Fletcher b Nuttall	5	12	3	-	1
J.J.N.P.Bhula lbw b Henry	3	6	8	-	-
M.G.Bracewell* lbw b Astle	55	83	49	1	6
T.M.Johnson lbw b Williams	3	5	5	-	-
F.J.Colson c Fletcher b Hay	43	68	54	-	5
J.D.Gibson c Nuttall b Williams	39	35	41	1	4
P.F.Younghusband not out	29	54	25	-	1
I.G.McPeake c Bowes b Henry	6	14	7	-	-
M.W.Snedden b Henry	0	2	1	-	-
J.W.Hartshorn b Williams	5	6	7	-	-
Extras (lb 2, w 8)	10				
TOTAL (37.3 overs)	**205**	160			

Bowling	*O*	*M*	*R*	*W*
CENTRAL DISTRICTS				
McPeake	8	1	46	1
Hartshorn	7	0	47	1
Snedden	7	0	38	1
Gibson	2	0	11	0
Younghusband	8	0	49	1
Bracewell	8	0	39	1
CANTERBURY				
Henry	7	1	27	3
Nuttall	6	0	33	2
Williams	7.3	0	37	3
Davey	4	0	32	0
Astle	8	0	48	1
Hay	5	0	26	1

Fall of Wickets	***C***	***W***
1st	25	9
2nd	61	12
3rd	71	22
4th	201	25
5th	231	123
6th	-	123
7th	-	177
8th	-	200
9th	-	200
10th	-	205

CENTRAL DISTRICTS v OTAGO — Ford Trophy

at Pukekura Park, New Plymouth on 1 December, 2020
Toss : Central Districts. Umpires : J.A.K. Bromley & G.A. Stirrat
***Otago won by 10 runs.** Points: Otago 4, Central Districts 0*

OTAGO

	Runs	Mins	Balls	6s	4s
H.D.Rutherford* c Bruce b Lennox	62	39	27	5	5
N.T.Broom c Leopard b Dudding	69	74	47	3	8
N.F.Kelly c Wiggins b Dudding ...	1	3	3	-	-
J.L.Finnie c Schmulian b Field .	11	10	8	-	2
M.Renwick† not out	41	64	31	-	6
A.K.Kitchen c Leopard b Field	3	6	4	-	-
M.J.G.Rippon c Leopard b Field .	4	7	5	-	-
D.N.Phillips c Bruce b Clarkson .	8	9	8	-	1
T.Muller c Wiggins b Field	4	10	6	-	-
M.B.Bacon not out	5	9	5	-	-
J.D.McKay					
Extras (lb 1, w 3)	4				
TOTAL (24 overs) (8 wkts) .	**212**	117			

CENTRAL DISTRICTS

	Runs	Mins	Balls	6s	4s
G.H.Worker c Kelly b Muller ...	125	114	79	6	11
B.L.Wiggins† st Renwick b Kitchen	11	9	8	1	1
B.S.Smith c Bacon b Rippon	4	13	6	-	-
T.C.Bruce* b Muller	3	12	5	-	-
C.K.Leopard c Renwick b Muller	12	21	14	-	1
J.A.Clarkson c Finnie b Bacon .	30	53	27	1	-
B.D.Schmulian b Muller	0	5	2	-	-
J.F.A.Field not out	4	6	1	-	1
J.R.Lennox lbw b Muller	0	2	2	-	-
L.R.Dudding not out	1	2	1	-	-
R.L.Toole					
Extras (lb 2, w 9, nb 1)	12				
TOTAL (24 overs) (8 wkts) .	**202**	121			

Bowling	*O*	*M*	*R*	*W*
CENTRAL DISTRICTS				
Dudding	5	0	33	2
Toole	4	0	53	0
Field	5	0	42	4
Clarkson	5	0	39	1
Lennox	5	0	44	1
OTAGO				
Rippon	5	0	43	1
Bacon	5	0	23	1
Kitchen	5	0	47	1
Muller	5	0	34	5
McKay	3	0	41	0
Finnie	1	0	12	0

Fall of Wickets	***O***	***CD***
1st	91	19
2nd	92	34
3rd	114	54
4th	154	98
5th	160	197
6th	167	197
7th	182	197
8th	195	197
9th	-	-
10th	-	-

NORTHERN DISTRICTS v AUCKLAND — Ford Trophy

at Cobham Oval, Whangarei on 1 December, 2020
Toss : Auckland. Umpires : J.M. Dempsey & A. Mehrotra
***Northern Districts won by 4 wickets.** Points: Northern Districts 4, Auckland 0*

AUCKLAND

	Runs	Mins	Balls	6s	4s
G.K.Beghin c Popli b Gibson	1	4	7	-	-
C.Munro c Bocock b Gibson	4	24	9	-	-
W.T.O'Donnell b Walker J.G. ...	50	117	91	-	4
R.R.O'Donnell* b Gibson	1	19	13	-	-
B.J.Horne† c Devcich b Randell	18	27	25	1	2
B.P.Rodden c Brownlie b Hampton	17	57	37	-	-
R.D.Harrison c Popli b Randell .	15	32	27	-	1
W.E.R.Somerville not out	39	79	52	-	3
R.M.ter Braak not out	42	53	43	1	2
L.J.Delport					
B.G.Lister					
Extras (lb 7, w 4, nb 4)	15				
TOTAL (50 overs) (7 wkts) .	**202**	209			

NORTHERN DISTRICTS

	Runs	Mins	Balls	6s	4s
J.A.Raval c O'Donnell W.T. b Delport	13	63	37	-	1
K.D.Clarke c Lister b Somerville	42	39	40	-	6
B.Popli not out	57	141	95	-	4
D.G.Brownlie c & b Delport	2	8	7	-	-
A.P.Devcich* c O'Donnell R.R. b Harrison	40	66	60	1	1
B.R.Hampton c Lister b Harrison	32	36	18	-	5
P.D.Bocock† b O'Donnell R.R. ...	0	3	2	-	-
J.M.Gibson not out	5	3	4	-	1
J.G.Walker					
F.L.Walker					
B.G.Randell					
Extras (b 1, lb 3, w 7, nb 3)	14				
TOTAL (43.2 overs) (6 wkts)	**205**	181			

Bowling	*O*	*M*	*R*	*W*
NORTHERN DISTRICTS				
Randell	10	0	33	2
Gibson	10	1	56	3
Walker F.L.	10	2	37	0
Hampton	10	1	38	1
Walker J.G.	10	0	31	1
AUCKLAND				
ter Braak	6	1	39	0
Lister	6	0	41	0
Delport	10	2	26	2
Somerville	10	0	47	1
Munro	5	0	20	0
Harrison	5.2	0	26	2
O'Donnell R.R.	1	0	2	1

Fall of Wickets	***A***	***ND***
1st	2	52
2nd	15	71
3rd	29	75
4th	57	140
5th	101	199
6th	105	200
7th	122	-
8th	-	-
9th	-	-
10th	-	-

Third Round

Otago decided to field first against Auckland. The O'Donnell brothers both scored fifties. Will made his highest score with a 66-ball fifty while Robbie needed 51 deliveries. The highlight of the innings was Rae taking 7-35. These were the third-best figures in New Zealand limited-overs cricket and the best by an Otago bowler. Auckland were dismissed for 246. Otago started disastrously being 18-5 and only Phillips reached 20. Ter Braak had career best figures with Somerville getting three wickets as Auckland won by 133 runs after bowling out Otago for 113.

Canterbury decided to bat and had a 200 run stand for the second wicket. Bowes reached his fourth century from 102 balls while McClure had his maiden hundred off 93 balls. Canterbury made 346-8 with Gibson taking 3-63. Clarke went in the third over of Northern's innings and, despite fifties from Brownlie and Hampton, they always struggled. Williams and Nuttall both took three wickets as Northern were all out for 209.

Central won the toss and decided to bat and had a 69 run stand for the second wicket. Worker got fifty from 66 balls, 11 faster than Smith. Younghusband was the best of the bowlers with 3-42 as Central finished with 261-9. Wellington's first three partnerships were all over 50 runs. Fletcher got fifty from 70 balls, two fewer than Bhula who finished unbeaten on 97 as Wellington reached the target with ten balls to spare.

AUCKLAND v OTAGO — Ford Trophy

at Eden Park Outer Oval, Auckland on 6 December, 2020
Toss : Otago. Umpires : B.F. Bowden & D.R. Morrow
***Auckland won by 133 runs.** Points: Auckland 5, Otago 0*

AUCKLAND

	Runs	Mins	Balls	6s	4s
M.J.Guptill c Muller b Rippon	36	74	48	1	3
S.M.Solia b Muller	25	44	33	1	1
W.T.O'Donnell c Renwick b Bacon	61	126	76	2	4
G.K.Beghin b Rae	20	42	36	-	1
R.R.O'Donnell* b Rae	52	73	53	-	5
B.J.Horne† lbw b Rae	27	42	24	-	2
R.D.Harrison c Renwick b Rae	1	3	2	-	-
W.E.R.Somerville c Broom b Rae	0	1	1	-	-
R.M.ter Braak lbw b Rae	7	7	7	-	1
L.J.Delport not out	3	11	7	-	-
B.G.Lister b Rae	0	2	2	-	-
Extras (lb 6, w 7, nb 1)	14				
TOTAL (48 overs)	**246**	215			

OTAGO

	Runs	Mins	Balls	6s	4s
N.F.Kelly* b ter Braak	4	24	7	-	-
M.Renwick† lbw b Lister	0	2	4	-	-
N.T.Broom lbw b ter Braak	0	4	2	-	-
A.K.Kitchen lbw b ter Braak	0	2	2	-	-
J.L.Finnie c Guptill b Lister	9	30	27	-	1
M.J.G.Rippon c Horne b Solia	19	49	34	1	2
D.N.Phillips c sub O.M.R.Pringle) b ter Braak	41	89	61	-	6
A.W.McKenzie c Guptill b Somerville	1	9	10	-	-
T.Muller c Harrison b Somerville	11	22	27	-	1
M.B.Bacon not out	15	33	39	-	1
M.D.Rae c Guptill b Somerville	5	9	6	-	1
Extras (lb 3, w 5)	8				
TOTAL (36.3 overs)	**113**	139			

Bowling	*O*	*M*	*R*	*W*
OTAGO				
Kitchen	7	0	44	0
Bacon	8	1	42	1
Muller	8	0	38	1
Rae	10	1	35	7
Rippon	9	0	49	1
McKenzie	4	0	19	0
Finnie	2	0	13	0
AUCKLAND				
Lister	6	1	13	2
ter Braak	8	0	27	4
Delport	10	2	22	0
Solia	3	0	22	1
Somerville	9.3	0	26	3

Fall of Wickets	***A***	***O***
1st	56	2
2nd	80	3
3rd	125	3
4th	192	13
5th	223	18
6th	225	49
7th	225	55
8th	239	71
9th	246	103
10th	246	113

CANTERBURY v NORTHERN DISTRICTS — Ford Trophy

at Hagley Oval, Christchurch on 6 December, 2020
Toss : Canterbury. Umpires : K.D. Cotton & D.J. Walker
***Canterbury won by 137 runs.** Points: Canterbury 5, Northern Districts 0*

CANTERBURY

	Runs	Mins	Balls	6s	4s
C.J.Bowes c Verma b Randell	110	177	110	1	10
J.C.T.Boyle c Clarke b Verma ..	13	26	26	-	2
K.J.McClure c Randell b Gibson	107	128	100	2	10
L.J.Carter* c Bocock b Randell	22	34	21	1	1
T.D.Astle c Bocock b Verma	9	9	6	-	-
C.D.Fletcher† not out	40	33	19	1	5
M.W.Hay run out	2	5	2	-	-
S.B.Davey c Hampton b Gibson .	9	8	8	-	2
M.J.Henry c Devcich b Gibson .	21	9	9	2	1
W.S.A.Williams not out	2	6	1	-	-
E.J.Nuttall					
Extras (lb 3, w 6, nb 2)	11				
TOTAL (50 overs) (8 wkts) .	**346**	220			

NORTHERN DISTRICTS

	Runs	Mins	Balls	6s	4s
K.D.Clarke lbw b Nuttall	3	10	5	-	-
J.A.Raval c Fletcher b Williams	45	62	48	-	7
D.G.Brownlie c Astle b Davey ..	53	105	68	1	3
H.R.Cooper lbw b Astle	2	5	4	-	-
A.P.Devcich* c Fletcher b Astle .	2	10	8	-	-
B.R.Hampton c Carter b Williams	53	84	69	1	3
P.D.Bocock† c Bowes b Davey ..	7	17	14	-	-
A.Verma c Astle b Nuttall	13	37	20	-	1
J.M.Gibson b Williams	7	14	10	1	-
J.G.Walker c Carter b Nuttall	2	14	4	-	-
B.G.Randell not out	3	7	4	-	-
Extras (b 2, lb 3, w 6, nb 3, p 5)	19				
TOTAL (41.5 overs)	**209**	185			

Bowling	O	M	R	W
NORTHERN DISTRICTS				
Verma	10	0	77	2
Gibson	10	0	63	3
Randell	10	0	76	2
Raval	5	0	23	0
Cooper	1	0	13	0
Walker	7	0	40	0
Hampton	7	0	51	0
CANTERBURY				
Nuttall	9.5	0	58	3
Henry	8	0	40	0
Astle	10	0	52	2
Williams	8	0	26	3
Davey	6	0	23	2

Fall of Wickets	C	ND
1st	26	12
2nd	226	81
3rd	253	88
4th	265	94
5th	271	133
6th	278	148
7th	293	188
8th	320	191
9th	-	198
10th	-	209

CENTRAL DISTRICTS v WELLINGTON — Ford Trophy

at Fitzherbert Park, Palmerston North on 6 December, 2020
Toss : Central Districts. Umpires : J.A.K. Bromley & G.A. Stirrat
***Wellington won by 5 wickets.** Points: Wellington 4, Central Districts 0*

CENTRAL DISTRICTS

	Runs	Mins	Balls	6s	4s
G.H.Worker c Bracewell b Younghusband	52	105	71	1	7
B.L.Wiggins† c Bracewell b Sears	30	47	25	1	4
B.S.Smith c Johnson b Younghusband	79	138	105	1	6
B.D.Schmulian st Johns b Bracewell	14	17	17	-	1
T.C.Bruce* b Younghusband	11	31	26	-	1
C.K.Leopard c Johns b McPeake	1	5	7	-	-
J.A.Clarkson c Younghusband b Sears	39	39	29	-	5
J.F.A.Field run out	2	7	4	-	-
L.R.Dudding not out	19	18	11	-	3
S.H.A.Rance c Johnson b McPeake	2	6	4	-	-
J.R.Lennox not out	1	7	1	-	-
Extras (lb 3, w 8)	11				
TOTAL (50 overs) (9 wkts) .	**261**	212			

WELLINGTON

	Runs	Mins	Balls	6s	4s
A.T.Fletcher b Lennox	53	95	73	-	7
L.R.Johns† run out	22	27	16	-	4
J.J.N.P.Bhula not out	97	177	114	-	5
M.G.Bracewell* c Rance b Worker	30	40	34	-	3
T.M.Johnson c Clarkson b Worker	2	10	9	-	-
F.J.Colson b Lennox	23	33	28	-	3
J.D.Gibson not out	27	25	18	2	2
P.F.Younghusband					
I.G.McPeake					
H.K.Bennett					
B.V.Sears					
Extras (lb 4, w 4, nb 2)	10				
TOTAL (48.2 overs) (5 wkts)	**264**	205			

Bowling	O	M	R	W
WELLINGTON				
McPeake	10	1	62	2
Bennett	3	0	23	0
Sears	10	1	49	2
Gibson	7	0	27	0
Bracewell	10	0	55	1
Younghusband	10	0	42	3
CENTRAL DISTRICTS				
Rance	9	0	49	0
Dudding	4	0	35	0
Field	8	0	49	0
Clarkson	8.2	0	44	0
Lennox	10	1	28	2
Schmulian	4	0	23	0
Worker	5	0	32	2

Fall of Wickets	CD	W
1st	54	51
2nd	123	116
3rd	142	169
4th	168	173
5th	171	222
6th	210	-
7th	225	-
8th	237	-
9th	242	-
10th	-	-

Fourth Round

Fisher *(Northern Districts)* made his debut.

Otago decided to bowl first and dismissed Auckland for 225. Will O'Donnell had another highest score getting 85, with his fifty needing 71 balls. Rae took another three wickets and McKenzie had career best figures. Kelly and Broom led the way for Otago getting fifties from 52 and 53 balls respectively as their team reached the target off 43.1 overs.

Canterbury decided to bat and had a 105 run stand for the third wicket. McClure scored his second successive century as they reached 266-8. Randell took three wickets. Northern had a 93 run opening stand. Clarke got fifty from 63 balls, ten faster than Raval. Raval went to his fourth century off 116 balls and was assisted by Cooper (fifty from 60 balls) but Northern went from 239-2 to 262-7 in 18 balls with three run outs. However, they still won the match with a ball to spare.

The match between Central Districts and Wellington was abandoned without a ball being bowled due to heavy rain.

AUCKLAND v OTAGO — Ford Trophy

at Eden Park Outer Oval, Auckland on 8 December, 2020
Toss : Otago. Umpires : B.F. Bowden & D.R. Morrow
***Otago won by 6 wickets.** Points: Otago 4, Auckland 0*

AUCKLAND	Runs	Mins	Balls	6s	4s
M.J.Guptill c Renwick b Rae	40	56	31	-	6
S.M.Solia c Muller b Bacon	19	33	28	-	1
W.T.O'Donnell c Phillips b Rae	85	178	110	-	6
R.R.O'Donnell* c & b McKenzie	9	40	33	-	-
B.J.Horne† c Phillips b McKenzie	11	14	11	-	1
B.P.Rodden lbw b Rippon	1	5	4	-	-
R.D.Harrison lbw b Rippon	7	28	22	-	-
W.E.R.Somerville c Renwick b Kitchen	12	23	18	-	1
R.M.ter Braak b Kitchen	31	30	24	1	4
L.J.Delport c Kitchen b Rae	1	5	5	-	-
B.G.Lister not out	3	8	5	-	-
Extras (b 1, w 5)	6				
TOTAL (48.3 overs)	**225**	212			

OTAGO	Runs	Mins	Balls	6s	4s
N.F.Kelly* c Horne b Delport	61	97	68	-	7
M.Renwick† b Somerville	40	79	55	1	4
N.T.Broom not out	68	98	73	1	6
A.K.Kitchen c ter Braak b Harrison	32	52	45	1	3
J.L.Finnie lbw b Delport	8	5	4	-	2
M.J.G.Rippon not out	18	22	14	-	3
D.N.Phillips					
A.W.McKenzie					
M.B.Bacon					
M.D.Rae					
T.Muller					
Extras (w 2)	2				
TOTAL (43.1 overs) (4 wkts)	**229**	178			

Bowling	*O*	*M*	*R*	*W*
OTAGO				
Muller	7	0	45	0
Bacon	7	1	30	1
Rae	9.3	1	65	3
McKenzie	9	0	22	2
Rippon	10	2	36	2
Kitchen	6	1	26	2
AUCKLAND				
Lister	8	0	41	0
ter Braak	6.1	1	38	0
Somerville	10	0	45	1
Solia	2	0	15	0
Delport	10	0	51	2
Harrison	7	0	39	1

Fall of Wickets	***A***	***O***
1st	47	97
2nd	71	119
3rd	92	184
4th	112	194
5th	113	-
6th	133	-
7th	162	-
8th	210	-
9th	213	-
10th	225	-

CANTERBURY v NORTHERN DISTRICTS

Ford Trophy

at Hagley Oval, Christchurch on 8 December, 2020
Toss : Canterbury. Umpires : J.M. Dempsey & D.J. Walker
***Northern Districts won by 3 wickets.** Points: Northern Districts 4, Canterbury 0*

CANTERBURY

	Runs	Mins	Balls	6s	4s
J.C.T.Boyle c Bocock b Randell	6	16	14	-	1
C.J.Bowes c Verma b Fisher	7	31	14	-	1
K.J.McClure b Randell	105	133	103	2	13
L.J.Carter* c Bocock b Randell	40	94	52	-	3
T.D.Astle b Hampton	10	33	19	-	1
C.D.Fletcher† not out	39	76	39	-	3
M.W.Hay b Walker	4	17	16	-	-
S.B.Davey c Walker b Verma	22	29	31	-	3
M.J.Henry run out	23	19	16	-	2
W.S.A.Williams					
E.J.Nuttall					
Extras (lb 1, w 5, nb 4)	10				
TOTAL (50 overs) (8 wkts)	**266**	225			

NORTHERN DISTRICTS

	Runs	Mins	Balls	6s	4s
K.D.Clarke run out	56	84	73	-	5
J.A.Raval c Henry b Williams	105	198	122	1	6
D.G.Brownlie c Boyle b Davey	18	25	25	-	2
H.R.Cooper c Fletcher b Henry	52	79	65	1	4
A.P.Devcich* run out	1	4	3	-	-
P.D.Bocock† run out	1	8	1	-	-
B.R.Hampton not out	20	15	11	1	1
A.Verma run out	2	9	2	-	-
J.G.Walker not out	0	2	0	-	-
B.G.Randell					
M.J.Fisher					
Extras (lb 3, w 6, nb 3)	12				
TOTAL (49.5 overs) (7 wkts)	**267**	213			

Bowling	*O*	*M*	*R*	*W*
NORTHERN DISTRICTS				
Fisher	10	0	60	1
Randell	10	0	65	3
Verma	10	0	52	1
Hampton	10	0	53	1
Walker	10	1	35	1
CANTERBURY				
Henry	10	0	59	1
Nuttall	6	0	39	0
Davey	7	0	40	1
Williams	9.5	0	38	1
Astle	10	0	52	0
Hay	7	0	36	0

Fall of Wickets

	C	***ND***
1st	16	93
2nd	38	120
3rd	143	239
4th	175	241
5th	182	243
6th	199	245
7th	228	262
8th	266	-
9th	-	-
10th	-	-

CENTRAL DISTRICTS v WELLINGTON

Ford Trophy

at Fitzherbert Park, Palmerston North on 8 December, 2020
***Abandoned without a ball being bowled.** Points:Central Districts 2, Wellington 2*

Fifth Round

Allen made his Wellington debut.

Wellington decided to bowl first against Auckland and had immediate success dismissing Guptill in the first over. Will O'Donnell went to his fourth fifty and was in a 75 run stand with Solia. O'Donnell got his fifty from 63 balls but Auckland went from 163-3 to 255-9. Younghusband took three wickets. All the Wellington batsmen reached double figures with Johnson leading the way with his maiden fifty from 64 balls. Wellington reached their target with nine balls and four wickets to spare.

Canterbury decided to bowl against Central Districts. Wiggins and Smith added 87 for the second wicket. The former got fifty from 64 balls. Clarkson scored a half-century off 49 deliveries as Central were dismissed for 213. Henry took 3-28. Canterbury had a good start with Bowes getting fifty off 48 balls and McClure and Carter added an unbeaten 98 for the fourth wicket. Carter had his highest score as Canterbury won by seven wickets with 8.3 overs to spare.

Otago decided to bowl but Northern got on top to reach 323-9. There were fifties to Clarke (49 balls), Devcich (41) and Cooper (59) the latter reaching his highest score. Smith took three wickets. Otago had a 45 run opening stand but then lost five wickets for fifty to be 95-5. Smith and Rippon added 132 from 111 balls with both getting fifties. Smith made his highest score but Otago were bowled out for 283 from 47.3 overs.

AUCKLAND v WELLINGTON — Ford Trophy

at Eden Park Outer Oval, Auckland on 13 December, 2020
Toss : Wellington. Umpires : B.F. Bowden & D.R. Morrow
***Wellington won by 4 wickets.** Points: Wellington 4, Auckland 0*

AUCKLAND

	Runs	Mins	Balls	6s	4s
M.J.Guptill run out	0	9	2	-	-
S.M.Solia c Colson b Snedden	42	68	45	-	7
W.T.O'Donnell c Bhula b Younghusband	62	114	79	2	7
R.R.O'Donnell* c McPeake b Bhula	40	73	50	-	5
B.J.Horne† c Johnson b Snedden	32	44	37	-	4
B.P.Rodden c Fletcher b McPeake	26	51	36	-	2
W.E.R.Somerville lbw b Younghusband	7	20	15	-	-
D.K.Ferns c Bhula b Younghusband	20	18	17	-	2
R.M.ter Braak c Johnson b McPeake	6	17	9	-	-
L.J.Delport not out	6	9	7	-	-
B.G.Lister not out	3	6	3	-	-
Extras (lb 1, w 10)	11				
TOTAL (50 overs) (9 wkts)	**255**	216			

WELLINGTON

	Runs	Mins	Balls	6s	4s
A.T.Fletcher lbw b ter Braak	17	23	16	-	4
L.R.Johns† c Horne b ter Braak	21	15	13	2	2
J.J.N.P.Bhula c Horne b Ferns	40	57	35	-	5
F.H.Allen c O'Donnell W.T. b Somerville	30	59	40	1	2
T.M.Johnson not out	80	127	89	-	9
F.J.Colson* c O'Donnell R.R. b Delport	11	13	12	-	2
J.D.Gibson c Lister b Ferns	31	70	65	-	3
P.F.Younghusband not out	20	34	18	1	1
I.G.McPeake					
M.W.Snedden					
J.W.Hartshorn					
Extras (lb 3, w 3)	6				
TOTAL (48.3 overs) (6 wkts)	**256**	200			

Bowling	O	M	R	W
WELLINGTON				
McPeake	10	0	37	2
Hartshorn	6	0	34	0
Snedden	10	0	53	2
Gibson	8	0	42	0
Younghusband	10	0	57	3
Bhula	3	0	18	1
Allen	3	0	13	0
AUCKLAND				
Lister	10	0	57	0
ter Braak	7	0	50	2
Ferns	10	0	52	2
Somerville	10	1	39	1
Delport	10	1	39	1
Solia	1.3	0	16	0

Fall of Wickets	A	W
1st	3	34
2nd	78	41
3rd	139	107
4th	163	115
5th	198	130
6th	218	199
7th	220	-
8th	245	-
9th	246	-
10th	-	-

CENTRAL DISTRICTS v CANTERBURY — Ford Trophy

at Pukekura Park, New Plymouth on 13 December, 2020
Toss : Canterbury. Umpires : C.A. Black & A. Mehrotra
***Canterbury won by 7 wickets.** Points: Canterbury 4, Central Districts 0*

CENTRAL DISTRICTS

	Runs	Mins	Balls	6s	4s
G.H.Worker b Henry	4	19	14	-	-
B.L.Wiggins b Henry	59	124	75	4	2
B.S.Smith run out	44	78	67	-	5
T.C.Bruce* c Williams b McConchie	18	21	23	1	1
D.Cleaver† c Hay b Henry	9	15	13	-	1
J.A.Clarkson run out	51	74	50	2	4
C.K.Leopard run out	4	18	14	-	-
J.F.A.Field b Astle	10	21	20	-	1
S.H.A.Rance c Hay b Williams	0	3	2	-	-
J.R.Lennox c Hay b Williams	4	10	8	-	1
R.L.Toole not out	0	13	6	-	-
Extras (lb 5, w 5)	10				
TOTAL (49 overs)	**213**	199			

CANTERBURY

	Runs	Mins	Balls	6s	4s
C.J.Bowes c Cleaver b Toole	59	74	59	-	12
J.C.T.Boyle c Cleaver b Toole	18	44	25	-	2
K.J.McClure not out	61	131	83	1	8
C.E.McConchie* c Cleaver b Leopard	13	21	18	-	2
L.J.Carter not out	63	78	65	3	7
T.D.Astle					
M.W.Hay†					
S.B.Davey					
M.J.Henry					
W.S.A.Williams					
F.W.Sheat					
Extras (lb 1, w 1, nb 1)	3				
TOTAL (41.3 overs) (3 wkts)	**217**	175			

Bowling	O	M	R	W
CANTERBURY				
Henry	10	0	28	3
Sheat	8	0	39	0
Williams	8	1	37	2
Davey	7	0	32	0
Astle	10	0	42	1
McConchie	6	0	30	1
CENTRAL DISTRICTS				
Rance	8	2	21	0
Field	6	0	41	0
Clarkson	4	0	25	0
Toole	10	2	53	2
Lennox	8	0	33	0
Leopard	5.3	0	43	1

Fall of Wickets	***CD***	***C***
1st	10	56
2nd	97	94
3rd	129	119
4th	132	-
5th	141	-
6th	154	-
7th	185	-
8th	186	-
9th	192	-
10th	213	-

OTAGO v NORTHERN DISTRICTS — Ford Trophy

at University of Otago Oval, Dunedin on 13 December, 2020
Toss : Otago. Umpires : J.A.K. Bromley & S.J. Kannan
***Northern Districts won by 40 runs.** Points: Northern Districts 4, Otago 0*

NORTHERN DISTRICTS

	Runs	Mins	Balls	6s	4s
J.A.Raval c Bacon b Smith	8	23	13	-	1
K.D.Clarke b Kitchen	58	85	65	-	9
D.G.Brownlie c Broom b Bacon	33	88	57	-	2
A.P.Devcich* run out	51	64	43	2	3
H.R.Cooper c Phillips b Duffy	88	106	73	4	4
B.R.Hampton c Duffy b Bacon	47	48	35	2	5
P.D.Bocock† c Kelly b Smith	11	15	9	-	2
J.M.Gibson c Finnie b Smith	0	2	1	-	-
A.Verma run out	5	5	4	-	-
J.G.Walker not out	1	3	1	-	-
B.G.Randell					
Extras (lb 6, w 14, nb 1)	21				
TOTAL (50 overs) (9 wkts)	**323**	221			

OTAGO

	Runs	Mins	Balls	6s	4s
N.F.Kelly run out	47	75	46	-	6
M.Renwick† c & b Randell	15	36	25	-	3
N.T.Broom b Verma	0	3	3	-	-
A.K.Kitchen b Walker	4	16	12	-	-
J.L.Finnie c Brownlie b Hampton	17	34	27	-	2
N.G.Smith c Raval b Hampton	81	103	69	-	10
M.J.G.Rippon c Raval b Randell	57	79	57	1	4
D.N.Phillips c Brownlie b Verma	14	35	15	-	1
J.A.Duffy* c Verma b Cooper	22	13	16	-	3
M.B.Bacon c Raval b Cooper	14	16	14	-	1
M.D.Rae not out	0	3	1	-	-
Extras (lb 1, w 11)	12				
TOTAL (47.3 overs)	**283**	209			

Bowling	O	M	R	W
OTAGO				
Duffy	10	0	72	1
Smith	10	1	58	3
Rae	5	0	36	0
Bacon	10	0	63	2
Rippon	10	1	62	0
Kitchen	5	0	26	1
NORTHERN DISTRICTS				
Verma	9	0	40	2
Randell	10	0	68	2
Walker	9	0	54	1
Cooper	9.3	0	60	2
Hampton	10	0	60	2

Fall of Wickets	***ND***	***O***
1st	18	45
2nd	97	46
3rd	147	60
4th	180	78
5th	274	95
6th	316	227
7th	317	236
8th	320	261
9th	323	279
10th	-	283

Sixth Round

Mitchell Hay *(Canterbury)* made his debut.

Auckland decided to bowl first and had Wellington 41-4. Fletcher had reached 1000 runs when on 19 before Wellington record stands against Auckland for the fifth and sixth wickets got them to 283-6. Johnson made his maiden century from 111 balls and Gibson equalled his top score including a 30-ball fifty. Lister and Pringle (best bowling) took three wickets each. The O'Donnell brothers had a 132 run stand for the third wicket for Auckland. Will scored his maiden hundred from 115 balls while Robbie got fifty off 70 balls. Auckland eventually reached 284-5 from 47.5 overs.

Central decided to bowl and dismissed Canterbury for 158 in 41.1 overs. Matt Hay had his highest score and Lennox and Leopard had best bowling figures. Clarkson and Bruce added 88 from 97 balls to ensure a Central victory. Williams took three wickets but Central reached their target four down and with 19 overs to spare.

Northern decided to bat and had four players reaching forties as they made 243. Hampton reached 1000 runs and Kitchen took three wickets. Otago were 57-5 and never threatened. Muller had his highest score while Fisher had his best bowling figures. Otago were all out for 177 after 45.2 overs.

AUCKLAND v WELLINGTON — Ford Trophy

at Eden Park Outer Oval, Auckland on 15 December, 2020
Toss : Auckland. Umpires : B.F. Bowden & D.R. Morrow
***Auckland won by 5 wickets.** Points: Auckland 4, Wellington 0*

WELLINGTON

	Runs	Mins	Balls	6s	4s
A.T.Fletcher c O'Donnell W.T. b Lister	26	43	27	-	6
L.R.Johns† c O'Donnell W.T. b Lister	7	13	11	-	1
J.J.N.P.Bhula c O'Donnell R.R. b Lister	0	10	9	-	-
F.H.Allen lbw b Pringle	6	13	7	-	1
T.M.Johnson c Delport b Pringle	113	167	116	4	10
F.J.Colson* c Horne b Pringle	45	120	88	1	4
J.D.Gibson not out	64	51	38	2	5
P.F.Younghusband not out	6	9	7	-	-
I.G.McPeake					
M.W.Snedden					
J.W.Hartshorn					
Extras (b 1, lb 2, w 10, nb 3)	16				
TOTAL (50 overs) (6 wkts)	**283**	216			

AUCKLAND

	Runs	Mins	Balls	6s	4s
G.K.Beghin c Gibson b Hartshorn	10	15	13	-	2
S.M.Solia lbw b Younghusband	34	56	35	-	6
W.T.O'Donnell c Allen b Bhula	106	153	120	2	12
R.R.O'Donnell* c Snedden b Bhula	59	131	78	1	3
B.J.Horne† not out	38	41	25	-	6
B.P.Rodden c Bhula b McPeake	21	16	15	2	-
W.E.R.Somerville not out	5	5	2	-	-
O.M.R.Pringle					
R.M.ter Braak					
B.G.Lister					
L.J.Delport					
Extras (lb 2, w 8, nb 1)	11				
TOTAL (47.5 overs) (5 wkts)	**284**	211			

Bowling	O	M	R	W
AUCKLAND				
ter Braak	6	0	45	0
Lister	10	3	56	3
Pringle	10	0	70	3
Solia	4	0	17	0
Delport	10	1	42	0
Somerville	10	0	50	0
WELLINGTON				
McPeake	9	0	64	1
Hartshorn	9	0	52	1
Snedden	9	1	47	0
Younghusband	7.5	0	37	1
Allen	2	0	15	0
Gibson	6	0	39	0
Bhula	5	0	28	2

Fall of Wickets	W	A
1st	17	22
2nd	21	73
3rd	41	205
4th	41	233
5th	165	271
6th	264	-
7th	-	-
8th	-	-
9th	-	-
10th	-	-

CENTRAL DISTRICTS v CANTERBURY — Ford Trophy

at Pukekura Park, New Plymouth on 15 December, 2020
Toss : Central Districts. Umpires : C.A. Black & A. Mehrotra
***Central Districts won by 6 wickets.** Points: Central Districts 5, Canterbury 0*

CANTERBURY

	Runs	Mins	Balls	6s	4s
J.C.T.Boyle lbw b Lennox	42	104	75	-	5
C.J.Bowes c Cleaver b Toole	13	24	17	-	1
C.E.McConchie* c Cleaver b Clarkson	17	27	22	1	1
L.J.Carter c Lennox b Leopard	7	11	10	-	1
H.B.Shipley b Lennox	2	18	12	-	-
M.W.Hay run out	49	70	52	1	5
M.J.Hay† c Wiggins b Lennox	3	8	6	-	-
T.F.van Woerkom run out	9	43	27	-	1
S.B.Davey c Field b Leopard	8	19	19	1	-
W.S.A.Williams c & b Worker	0	5	5	-	-
F.W.Sheat not out	0	9	3	-	-
Extras (lb 1, w 6, nb 1)	8				
TOTAL (41.1 overs)	**158**	172			

CENTRAL DISTRICTS

	Runs	Mins	Balls	6s	4s
G.H.Worker lbw b Williams	1	10	6	-	-
B.L.Wiggins c Shipley b Davey	35	27	16	1	6
B.S.Smith c Boyle b Williams	9	36	27	-	1
T.C.Bruce* not out	42	100	74	-	7
D.Cleaver† c van Woerkom b Williams	15	19	17	1	1
J.A.Clarkson not out	56	61	46	2	8
C.K.Leopard					
J.F.A.Field					
B.D.Schmulian					
J.R.Lennox					
R.L.Toole					
Extras (lb 3, w 1)	4				
TOTAL (31 overs) (4 wkts)	**162**	128			

Bowling	*O*	*M*	*R*	*W*
CENTRAL DISTRICTS				
Toole	8	0	24	1
Field	7	0	32	0
Leopard	9.1	2	22	2
Clarkson	3	0	21	1
Lennox	9	0	30	3
Schmulian	2	0	22	0
Worker	3	0	6	1
CANTERBURY				
Williams	10	2	24	3
Sheat	5	0	49	0
Davey	8	0	52	1
van Woerkom	5	0	22	0
McConchie	3	1	12	0

Fall of Wickets	***C***	***CD***
1st	19	22
2nd	46	38
3rd	57	50
4th	72	74
5th	102	-
6th	116	-
7th	147	-
8th	148	-
9th	149	-
10th	158	-

OTAGO v NORTHERN DISTRICTS — Ford Trophy

at University of Otago Oval, Dunedin on 15 December, 2020
Toss : Northern Districts. Umpires : S.J. Kannan & T.J. Parlane
***Northern Districts won by 66 runs.** Points: Northern Districts 5, Otago 0*

NORTHERN DISTRICTS

	Runs	Mins	Balls	6s	4s
J.A.Raval b Bacon	42	82	55	-	6
K.D.Clarke c & b Bacon	9	35	20	-	1
B.Popli c & b Kitchen	40	74	54	-	3
D.G.Brownlie lbw b Finnie	23	41	31	-	3
A.P.Devcich* b Kitchen	1	8	3	-	-
B.R.Hampton b McKenzie	43	67	41	1	5
P.D.Bocock† st Renwick b Kitchen	5	14	14	-	-
A.Verma not out	47	80	58	1	3
J.G.Walker c Kitchen b McKay	0	5	4	-	-
F.L.Walker run out	9	18	14	-	1
M.J.Fisher c McKay b Muller	2	9	6	-	-
Extras (lb 4, w 18)	22				
TOTAL (50 overs)	**243**	218			

OTAGO

	Runs	Mins	Balls	6s	4s
H.D.Rutherford* c Verma b Fisher	8	10	6	-	2
M.Renwick† b Walker J.G.	48	108	69	-	6
N.T.Broom c Raval b Fisher	2	15	8	-	-
N.F.Kelly c Bocock b Walker J.G.	4	7	6	-	1
J.L.Finnie c Bocock b Hampton	0	12	8	-	-
A.K.Kitchen c Clarke b Hampton	5	14	16	-	-
D.N.Phillips c Bocock b Fisher	35	50	43	-	3
A.W.McKenzie c Raval b Hampton	22	55	42	1	-
T.Muller c Walker J.G. b Walker F.L.	34	75	58	-	5
M.B.Bacon b Fisher	3	10	7	-	-
J.D.McKay not out	4	12	10	-	-
Extras (lb 5, w 6, nb 1)	12				
TOTAL (45.2 overs)	**177**	186			

Bowling	*O*	*M*	*R*	*W*
OTAGO				
Muller	10	0	44	1
Bacon	10	0	44	2
McKay	9	0	52	1
McKenzie	8	0	46	1
Kitchen	10	1	25	3
Finnie	3	0	28	1
NORTHERN DISTRICTS				
Fisher	10	1	34	4
Verma	8	0	25	0
Walker J.G.	10	0	32	2
Walker F.L.	9.2	0	51	1
Hampton	8	1	30	3

Fall of Wickets	***ND***	***O***
1st	27	18
2nd	83	26
3rd	116	30
4th	123	42
5th	127	57
6th	154	107
7th	203	107
8th	206	151
9th	226	162
10th	243	177

Seventh Round

Briggs *(Auckland)* and Chu *(Otago)* made their debuts. McClenaghan made his Otago debut.

Central Districts decided to bat against Auckland and had a 120 run opening stand, a record for them against Auckland. Worker and Cleaver scored fifties from 56 and 72 balls respectively. Bruce and Clarkson added 85 for the fifth wicket. Bruce went to fifty off 40 deliveries. Field made his highest score and Delport took three wickets as Central made 309-7. Auckland had a record opening stand against all comers with Solia and Briggs putting on 226. Solia made his third century off 95 balls and Briggs got his hundred on debut off 100 balls. Auckland got to their target for the loss of four wickets with 17 balls to spare. Young was playing his 50th match.

Canterbury decided to bat first against Otago but lost two quick wickets. Latham made 63 and the other middle order batsmen all got good starts. Fletcher reached 1000 runs. Duffy took four wickets and Kitchen three as Canterbury were dismissed for 271 after 49.2 overs. Otago also lost two early wickets but Broom and Kitchen added 135 off 165 deliveries. Both got fifties with Broom needing 67 balls, six more than Kitchen. Once the stand was broken Otago went from 144-2 to 217 all out from 45.1 overs. Henry was the best bowler with 3-34.

Wellington decided to bowl and Northern Districts were in a good position at 168-4. Raval had made 69 but then in the space of 14 overs Northern were dismissed for 205. Newton and Sears both took three wickets. Wellington were in trouble at 24-4 but a 109 run stand between new captain Johnson and Colson swung the game. Johnson got fifty from 68 balls, 11 faster than Colson who went on to register his highest score. Kuggeleijn took four wickets as Wellington won by one wicket with nine balls to spare.

AUCKLAND v CENTRAL DISTRICTS — Ford Trophy

at Eden Park Outer Oval, Auckland on 19 February, 2021
Toss : Central Districts. Umpires : J.M. Dempsey & W.R. Knights
***Auckland won by 6 wickets.** Points: Auckland 4, Central Districts 0*

CENTRAL DISTRICTS

	Runs	Mins	Balls	6s	4s
G.H.Worker c Lister b Delport	59	96	68	1	6
D.Cleaver† lbw b Somerville	56	121	87	-	5
W.A.Young c ter Braak b Delport	7	5	7	-	1
L.R.P.L.Taylor c Beghin b Delport	0	9	8	-	-
T.C.Bruce* not out	96	97	62	2	9
J.A.Clarkson c Somerville b Lister	35	46	38	2	1
B.M.Wheeler c Delport b Lister	4	10	7	-	-
J.F.A.Field c O'Donnell W.T. b Harrison	31	28	23	2	-
A.Y.Patel not out	0	1	0	-	-
B.M.Tickner					
J.R.Lennox					
Extras (lb 7, w 14)	21				
TOTAL (50 overs) (7 wkts)	**309**	210			

AUCKLAND

	Runs	Mins	Balls	6s	4s
S.M.Solia c Tickner b Lennox	121	179	119	2	15
C.J.Briggs c Taylor b Clarkson	101	153	104	4	7
W.T.O'Donnell c Worker b Tickner	0	6	4	-	-
R.R.O'Donnell* c & b Lennox	31	29	24	1	4
B.J.Horne† not out	29	31	22	-	3
G.K.Beghin not out	8	20	11	-	1
R.D.Harrison					
W.E.R.Somerville					
R.M.ter Braak					
L.J.Delport					
B.G.Lister					
Extras (lb 5, w 14, nb 1)	20				
TOTAL (47.1 overs) (4 wkts)	**310**	211			

Bowling	*O*	*M*	*R*	*W*
AUCKLAND				
ter Braak	8	0	56	0
Lister	10	0	66	2
Solia	7	0	38	0
Harrison	5	0	35	1
Delport	10	0	50	3
Somerville	10	0	57	1
CENTRAL DISTRICTS				
Tickner	10	0	65	1
Wheeler	6	0	35	0
Field	6.1	0	54	0
Patel	9	0	73	0
Lennox	10	0	48	2
Clarkson	6	1	30	1

Fall of Wickets

	CD	***A***
1st	120	226
2nd	128	228
3rd	133	253
4th	139	274
5th	224	-
6th	239	-
7th	302	-
8th	-	-
9th	-	-
10th	-	-

OTAGO v CANTERBURY — Ford Trophy

at John Davies Oval, Queenstown on 19 February, 2021
Toss : Canterbury. Umpires : S.B. Haig & D.J. Walker
***Canterbury won by 54 runs.** Points: Canterbury 4, Otago 0*

CANTERBURY

	Runs	Mins	Balls	6s	4s
C.J.Bowes c Kitchen b Smith ...	11	22	19	-	1
K.J.McClure c Chu b Duffy	0	10	5	-	-
T.W.M.Latham† c Rippon b Kitchen	63	125	75	1	5
C.E.McConchie* c Kelly b Rippon	31	73	47	-	3
L.J.Carter c Rutherford b Duffy	29	58	41	1	2
C.D.Fletcher lbw b Duffy	45	82	49	-	3
T.F.van Woerkom c Duffy b Smith	31	40	40	1	3
S.B.Davey c Smith b Duffy	22	13	11	1	3
M.J.Henry c Broom b Kitchen ...	11	12	6	1	-
W.S.A.Williams c Phillips b Kitchen	7	3	3	1	-
E.J.Nuttall not out	0	1	0	-	-
Extras (b 4, lb 10, w 7)	21				
TOTAL (49.2 overs)	**271**	222			

OTAGO

	Runs	Mins	Balls	6s	4s
H.D.Rutherford c Nuttall b Henry	4	15	10	-	1
N.F.Kelly c Bowes b Henry	1	11	7	-	-
N.T.Broom c Latham b van Woerkom	83	157	107	-	6
A.K.Kitchen c Carter b Nuttall ...	69	109	84	2	5
M.J.G.Rippon lbw b Williams	8	24	18	-	-
D.N.Phillips c Henry b van Woerkom	5	17	13	-	-
N.G.Smith b Henry	17	26	11	-	2
M.W.Chu† run out	11	12	9	-	1
M.J.McClenaghan c Latham b Davey	2	5	5	-	-
J.A.Duffy* not out	2	10	4	-	-
M.D.Rae c McConchie b Davey .	5	4	3	-	1
Extras (lb 1, w 9)	10				
TOTAL (45.1 overs)	**217**	198			

Bowling	*O*	*M*	*R*	*W*
OTAGO				
Duffy	10	0	53	4
Smith	7	0	48	2
Rae	9	0	51	0
McClenaghan	10	0	36	0
Rippon	6	0	38	1
Kitchen	7.2	1	31	3
CANTERBURY				
Henry	10	0	34	3
Nuttall	8	0	41	1
Williams	8	0	34	1
Davey	5.1	0	26	2
McConchie	6	0	36	0
van Woerkom	8	0	45	2

Fall of Wickets	*C*	*O*
1st	7	8
2nd	14	9
3rd	91	144
4th	130	165
5th	156	179
6th	213	179
7th	243	203
8th	264	206
9th	271	212
10th	271	217

WELLINGTON v NORTHERN DISTRICTS — Ford Trophy

at Basin Reserve, Wellington on 19 February, 2021
Toss : Wellington. Umpires : J.A.K. Bromley & C.M. Brown
***Wellington won by 1 wicket.** Points: Wellington 4, Northern Districts 0*

NORTHERN DISTRICTS

	Runs	Mins	Balls	6s	4s
J.A.Raval c & b Younghusband	69	121	89	-	6
K.D.Clarke c Blundell b Sears ..	20	59	38	-	2
J.F.Carter* c & b Bracewell	10	28	20	-	1
B-J.Watling† c Gibson b Younghusband	5	11	11	-	1
C.de Grandhomme c Sears b van Beek	43	58	40	3	4
H.R.Cooper c Johnson b Newton	11	27	17	-	1
B.R.Hampton c Bhula b Newton .	0	2	1	-	-
S.C.Kuggeleijn c Colson b Sears	2	20	14	-	-
A.Verma c Gibson b Newton	11	51	29	-	-
J.G.Walker b Sears	19	39	34	-	1
B.G.Randell not out	1	3	2	-	-
Extras (lb 4, w 10)	14				
TOTAL (49.1 overs)	**205**	212			

WELLINGTON

	Runs	Mins	Balls	6s	4s
F.H.Allen lbw b Kuggeleijn	0	1	3	-	-
T.A.Blundell† c Clarke b Kuggeleijn	16	34	25	-	2
J.J.N.P.Bhula c Clarke b Kuggeleijn	1	19	7	-	-
M.G.Bracewell lbw b Verma	1	5	4	-	-
T.M.Johnson* b Walker	66	108	85	-	8
F.J.Colson not out	80	184	115	-	8
J.D.Gibson c Cooper b Randell ..	5	22	14	-	-
L.V.van Beek c Walker b Kuggeleijn	15	29	20	-	2
P.F.Younghusband c Carter b Verma	6	18	12	-	-
O.R.Newton b Hampton	5	9	6	-	-
B.V.Sears not out	0	4	0	-	-
Extras (lb 3, w 9)	12				
TOTAL (48.3 overs) (9 wkts)	**207**	219			

Bowling	*O*	*M*	*R*	*W*
WELLINGTON				
van Beek	10	1	42	1
Newton	10	2	23	3
Bracewell	7	1	29	1
Sears	9.1	0	40	3
Younghusband	10	1	50	2
Gibson	3	0	17	0
NORTHERN DISTRICTS				
Kuggeleijn	10	1	41	4
Verma	9.3	0	47	2
de Grandhomme	4	0	14	0
Randell	10	2	50	1
Walker	10	1	31	1
Hampton	5	0	21	1

Fall of Wickets	*ND*	*W*
1st	58	0
2nd	90	11
3rd	105	12
4th	125	24
5th	168	133
6th	169	148
7th	170	183
8th	174	194
9th	203	201
10th	205	-

Eighth Round

Morrison *(Auckland)* made his debut.

Auckland batted first against Central Districts and again had a century opening stand with 106 runs. Briggs and Will O'Donnell added 130 for the second wicket. All the top three batsmen got fifties with Solia taking 46 balls, Briggs 59 and O'Donnell 61. Briggs was out stumped one run short of becoming the first player to get centuries in his first two games. Four bowlers took two wickets as Auckland made 311-9. Young was the backbone of the Central innings getting 79 (fifty from 48 balls) but they lost wickets at regular intervals being all out for 218 off 39.3 overs. Delport and ter Braak both got three wickets.

Otago decided to bat but lost an early wicket. Kelly and Rippon both got half-centuries from 72 and 62 deliveries respectively as Otago reached 263-9. Five Canterbury batsmen scored between 28 and 45 but they struggled to get the required runs. Davey made his highest score. Rae took four wickets while Duffy, playing in his 50th game, took three as Canterbury made 232 off 48.5 overs.

Wellington won the toss and decided to bat first. Bhula and Bracewell added 72 for the third wicket but Wellington went from 115-2 to 145-7 before eventually making 188 off 46.5 overs. Bracewell top scored with an unbeaten 64. Fisher and Hampton both got three wickets. Northern lost wickets regularly with no one able to get to forty. They were bowled out for 171 off 48.4 overs. Bhula had career best bowling figures. Verma was playing his 50th game.

AUCKLAND v CENTRAL DISTRICTS — Ford Trophy

at Eden Park Outer Oval, Auckland on 21 February, 2021
Toss : Auckland. Umpires : J.M. Dempsey & D.R. Morrow
Auckland won by 93 runs. *Points: Auckland 5, Central Districts 0*

AUCKLAND

	Runs	Mins	Balls	6s	4s
S.M.Solia c Leopard b Patel	57	78	54	2	6
C.J.Briggs st Cleaver b Clarkson	99	165	104	1	11
W.T.O'Donnell c sub (J.F.A.Field) b Leopard	81	132	92	4	5
R.R.O'Donnell* lbw b Patel	18	17	16	2	-
G.K.Beghin lbw b Lennox	2	5	3	-	-
A.R.Morrison† run out	1	4	2	-	-
R.D.Harrison lbw b Clarkson	0	1	1	-	-
W.E.R.Somerville b Lennox	6	6	9	-	1
R.M.ter Braak c Wheeler b Leopard	18	18	14	1	-
L.J.Delport not out	3	11	4	-	-
B.G.Lister not out	3	2	2	-	-
Extras (lb 6, w 16, nb 1)	23				
TOTAL (50 overs) (9 wkts)	**311**	222			

CENTRAL DISTRICTS

	Runs	Mins	Balls	6s	4s
G.H.Worker c Morrison b ter Braak	17	23	18	-	2
D.Cleaver† run out	39	43	34	-	8
W.A.Young b Delport	79	122	75	1	9
L.R.P.L.Taylor c ter Braak b Delport	9	15	10	-	2
T.C.Bruce* c O'Donnell R.R. b Harrison	12	27	15	-	1
J.A.Clarkson b Delport	18	23	23	-	2
C.K.Leopard c Harrison b Solia	0	5	3	-	-
B.M.Wheeler not out	31	56	42	-	4
A.Y.Patel c Somerville b ter Braak	1	9	4	-	-
J.R.Lennox c Beghin b ter Braak	5	17	13	-	-
B.M.Tickner absent hurt					
Extras (lb 2, w 5)	7				
TOTAL (39.3 overs)	**218**	172			

Bowling	*O*	*M*	*R*	*W*
CENTRAL DISTRICTS				
Wheeler	7	0	55	0
Tickner	1	0	4	0
Leopard	10	0	65	2
Lennox	10	0	50	2
Patel	10	0	51	2
Clarkson	10	0	59	2
Worker	2	0	21	0
AUCKLAND				
Lister	7	0	49	0
ter Braak	6.3	0	45	3
Delport	10	1	45	3
Solia	6	0	24	1
Somerville	7	0	27	0
Harrison	3	0	26	1

Fall of Wickets	***A***	***CD***
1st	106	39
2nd	236	75
3rd	266	95
4th	273	122
5th	276	158
6th	276	159
7th	283	194
8th	290	202
9th	306	218
10th	-	-

OTAGO v CANTERBURY — Ford Trophy

at John Davies Oval, Queenstown on 21 February, 2021
Toss : Otago. Umpires : P.J. Pasco & D.J. Walker
***Otago won by 31 runs.** Points: Otago 4, Canterbury 0*

OTAGO

	Runs	Mins	Balls	6s	4s
H.D.Rutherford c Latham b Nuttall	1	15	15	-	-
N.F.Kelly c Davey b Henry	76	136	99	2	7
N.T.Broom c Latham b Nuttall	25	58	39	1	1
A.K.Kitchen lbw b Astle	11	34	26	-	-
M.J.G.Rippon c Bowes b Williams	77	103	73	3	2
D.N.Phillips c Nuttall b Davey	31	44	31	-	2
N.G.Smith run out	0	2	0	-	-
M.W.Chu† lbw b Henry	19	11	10	-	3
M.J.McClenaghan c Davey b Henry	10	9	7	-	1
J.A.Duffy* not out	3	7	3	-	-
M.D.Rae					
Extras (lb 2, w 5, nb 3)	10				
TOTAL (50 overs) (9 wkts)	**263**	211			

CANTERBURY

	Runs	Mins	Balls	6s	4s
H.M.Nicholls c Kitchen b Rae	33	77	50	-	4
C.J.Bowes c Smith b Duffy	13	27	19	-	1
K.J.McClure c Kelly b Rae	9	42	26	-	1
T.W.M.Latham† c Chu b Rae	36	81	43	-	2
C.E.McConchie* c Smith b Rae	45	59	56	-	3
C.D.Fletcher c Phillips b McClenaghan	28	76	46	-	-
T.D.Astle c Phillips b McClenaghan	6	12	10	-	-
S.B.Davey b Duffy	43	53	39	-	4
M.J.Henry c Phillips b Duffy	0	8	2	-	-
W.S.A.Williams run out	0	5	2	-	-
E.J.Nuttall not out	0	1	0	-	-
Extras (b 3, lb 5, w 11)	19				
TOTAL (48.5 overs)	**232**	222			

Bowling	*O*	*M*	*R*	*W*
CANTERBURY				
Henry	10	0	37	3
Nuttall	10	2	38	2
Williams	6	1	40	1
Davey	5	0	37	1
Astle	10	0	52	1
McConchie	9	0	57	0
OTAGO				
Duffy	9.5	0	48	3
Smith	5	0	27	0
McClenaghan	9	1	32	2
Rae	10	0	39	4
Kitchen	10	0	46	0
Rippon	5	0	32	0

Fall of Wickets	*O*	*C*
1st	3	32
2nd	60	59
3rd	97	62
4th	137	140
5th	201	153
6th	201	161
7th	229	226
8th	247	231
9th	263	232
10th	-	232

WELLINGTON v NORTHERN DISTRICTS — Ford Trophy

at Basin Reserve, Wellington on 21 February, 2021
Toss : Wellington. Umpires : T.J. Parlane & G.A Stirrat
***Wellington won by 17 runs.** Points: Wellington 4, Northern Districts 0*

WELLINGTON

	Runs	Mins	Balls	6s	4s
F.H.Allen c & b Verma	7	17	12	-	1
T.A.Blundell† c Raval b Fisher	29	50	34	-	5
J.J.N.P.Bhula c Carter b Hampton	47	90	62	-	5
M.G.Bracewell not out	64	161	82	1	1
T.M.Johnson* c Clarke b Hampton	6	8	9	-	1
F.J.Colson c Kuggeleijn b Verma	5	36	27	-	-
J.D.Gibson c Watling b Fisher	1	5	3	-	-
L.V.van Beek lbw b Fisher	0	2	2	-	-
P.F.Younghusband c Carter b Hampton	14	35	34	-	-
B.V.Sears c Watling b Kuggeleijn	5	13	12	-	-
I.G.McPeake lbw b Kuggeleijn	0	3	4	-	-
Extras (b 1, lb 4, w 5)	10				
TOTAL (46.5 overs)	**188**	212			

NORTHERN DISTRICTS

	Runs	Mins	Balls	6s	4s
K.D.Clarke c Younghusband b McPeake	13	24	21	-	2
J.A.Raval lbw b Bracewell	37	92	61	-	5
J.F.Carter* c Gibson b McPeake	5	9	6	-	1
B-J.Watling† b van Beek	13	25	16	-	1
C.de Grandhomme b Younghusband	19	24	16	-	4
H.R.Cooper c Younghusband b Bhula	31	114	82	-	1
B.R.Hampton run out	11	9	14	-	2
S.C.Kuggeleijn c Allen b Bhula	3	11	12	-	-
A.Verma c Johnson b Younghusband	10	43	35	-	1
J.G.Walker c Younghusband b Bhula	16	39	30	-	2
M.J.Fisher not out	0	2	0	-	-
Extras (w 12, nb 1)	13				
TOTAL (48.4 overs)	**171**	199			

Bowling	*O*	*M*	*R*	*W*
NORTHERN DISTRICTS				
Kuggeleijn	8.5	0	32	2
Verma	8	0	30	2
Fisher	10	1	26	3
Hampton	10	0	39	3
Walker	8	0	40	0
Raval	2	0	16	0
WELLINGTON				
van Beek	9	0	45	1
McPeake	6	0	31	2
Sears	8	1	27	0
Bracewell	10	0	35	1
Younghusband	10	0	20	2
Bhula	5.4	0	13	3

Fall of Wickets	*W*	*ND*
1st	11	27
2nd	43	33
3rd	115	56
4th	122	91
5th	143	95
6th	145	106
7th	145	114
8th	173	141
9th	188	171
10th	188	171

Ninth Round

Auckland decided to bowl and Canterbury had a record second wicket stand for their team against Auckland. Nicholls scored his fifth hundred from 118 balls and McClure got 96. Canterbury finished with 313-4. Auckland struggled from the start. Only two players reached 20 as Auckland were dismissed for 97 off 26.3 overs. Three players took two wickets. The 216 run margin was Auckland's heaviest defeat.

Central decided to bowl first against Northern and had immediate success. Carter and Watling added 87 for the third wicket with both players scoring fifties but Northern went from 107-2 to 144-7 and eventually made 194 from 48.3 overs. Clarkson took 3-30. Worker went to the first ball of the innings but Taylor and Clarkson won the match with an unbeaten 89 run stand from 79 balls. Central won with six wickets in hand and 15.3 overs to spare. Kuggeleijn's sole wicket was his 100th domestic one-day wicket.

Otago decided to bowl and got Blundell early. Bhula and Bracewell added 119 off 122 balls for the third wicket. Their fifties came from 59 and 56 balls respectively. Johnson scored a 48-ball fifty as Wellington reached 340-8. McClenaghan took five wickets for the fourth time. Otago had a good start with Rutherford and Kelly getting 125 from 124 balls for the first wicket. Their fifties came from 52 and 61 balls. There were further half-centuries from Broom (53 balls) and Kitchen (35 balls) while Rutherford got his seventh century for Otago. Rippon reached 1000 runs. Otago got to 342-4 after 49.1 overs.

CANTERBURY v AUCKLAND — Ford Trophy

at MainPower Oval, Rangiora on 26 February, 2021
Toss : Auckland. Umpires : J.A.K. Bromley & D.J. Walker
***Canterbury won by 216 runs.** Points: Canterbury 5, Auckland 0*

CANTERBURY

	Runs	Mins	Balls	6s	4s
H.M.Nicholls b Somerville	113	165	127	2	10
C.J.Bowes c O'Donnell R.R. b Delport	31	60	40	-	5
K.J.McClure c Beghin b ter Braak	96	136	101	-	12
T.W.M.Latham† c Briggs b ter Braak	30	40	25	1	2
D.J.Mitchell not out	10	13	6	-	1
M.J.Henry not out	12	4	4	-	3
C.E.McConchie*					
T.D.Astle					
S.B.Davey					
W.S.A.Williams					
E.J.Nuttall					
Extras (b 5, lb 6, w 7, nb 3)	21				
TOTAL (50 overs) (4 wkts)	**313**	211			

AUCKLAND

	Runs	Mins	Balls	6s	4s
G.K.Beghin run out	10	14	9	-	2
C.J.Briggs b Williams	23	57	41	-	3
W.T.O'Donnell c Henry b Williams	8	24	21	-	1
R.R.O'Donnell* b Henry	1	4	2	-	-
B.J.Horne† lbw b Astle	21	50	31	-	3
R.D.Harrison c McClure b Nuttall	3	15	9	-	-
R.M.ter Braak c sub (C.D.Fletcher) b Davey	4	26	16	-	-
W.E.R.Somerville b Astle	0	8	5	-	-
O.M.R.Pringle run out	1	13	8	-	-
L.J.Delport not out	16	15	15	-	3
B.G.Lister c Mitchell b Davey	0	7	2	-	-
Extras (lb 7, w 3)	10				
TOTAL (26.3 overs)	**97**	119			

Bowling	O	M	R	W
AUCKLAND				
ter Braak	8	1	59	2
Lister	9	0	52	0
Delport	10	0	55	1
Pringle	5	0	32	0
Somerville	10	0	49	1
O'Donnell W.T.	8	0	55	0
CANTERBURY				
Henry	6	1	14	1
Nuttall	7	1	32	1
Williams	6	2	15	2
Astle	4	1	22	2
Davey	3.3	1	7	2

Fall of Wickets	***C***	***A***
1st	66	16
2nd	230	32
3rd	278	34
4th	299	48
5th	-	59
6th	-	79
7th	-	79
8th	-	79
9th	-	85
10th	-	97

NORTHERN DISTRICTS v CENTRAL DISTRICTS — Ford Trophy

at Seddon Park, Hamilton on 26 February, 2021
Toss : Central Districts. Umpires : J.M. Dempsey & D.R. Morrow
***Central Districts won by 6 wickets.** Points: Central Districts 5, Northern Districts 0*

NORTHERN DISTRICTS

	Runs	Mins	Balls	6s	4s
J.A.Raval c Young b Wheeler	0	1	2	-	-
K.D.Clarke c Cleaver b Rance	4	26	12	-	1
J.F.Carter* lbw b Lennox	58	114	89	1	5
B-J.Watling† c Leopard b Field	68	158	103	1	5
C.de Grandhomme c Cleaver b Clarkson	12	11	11	1	-
H.R.Cooper c Cleaver b Clarkson	4	9	10	-	-
B.R.Hampton c Leopard b Clarkson	2	12	9	-	-
S.C.Kuggeleijn c Cleaver b Rance	2	10	7	-	-
A.Verma not out	28	52	35	1	-
J.G.Walker c Taylor b Wheeler	0	7	6	-	-
B.G.Randell c Leopard b Field	6	17	8	-	1
Extras (w 9, nb 1)	10				
TOTAL (48.3 overs)	**194**	210			

CENTRAL DISTRICTS

	Runs	Mins	Balls	6s	4s
G.H.Worker lbw b Kuggeleijn	0	1	1	-	-
D.Cleaver† c Kuggeleijn b Hampton	29	46	30	-	6
W.A.Young b Verma	13	63	38	-	2
L.R.P.L.Taylor not out	68	109	72	3	6
T.C.Bruce* c Watling b Hampton	17	37	24	-	2
J.A.Clarkson not out	55	54	42	3	7
C.K.Leopard					
J.F.A.Field					
B.M.Wheeler					
S.H.A.Rance					
J.R.Lennox					
Extras (lb 12, w 2)	14				
TOTAL (34.3 overs) (4 wkts)	**196**	155			

Bowling	*O*	*M*	*R*	*W*
CENTRAL DISTRICTS				
Wheeler	8	0	34	2
Rance	9	1	26	2
Leopard	6	1	24	0
Field	5.3	0	38	2
Lennox	10	0	42	1
Clarkson	10	1	30	3
NORTHERN DISTRICTS				
Kuggeleijn	8.3	1	42	1
Verma	5	0	34	1
Randell	7	0	41	0
Hampton	7	0	26	2
Walker	7	0	41	0

Fall of Wickets	***ND***	***CD***
1st	0	0
2nd	20	45
3rd	107	63
4th	120	107
5th	126	-
6th	130	-
7th	144	-
8th	168	-
9th	171	-
10th	194	-

WELLINGTON v OTAGO — Ford Trophy

at Basin Reserve, Wellington on 26 February, 2021
Toss : Otago. Umpires : C.A. Black & T.J Parlane
***Otago won by 6 wickets.** Points: Otago 4, Wellington 0*

WELLINGTON

	Runs	Mins	Balls	6s	4s
F.H.Allen c Chu b McClenaghan	46	39	21	2	7
T.A.Blundell† c Smith b McClenaghan	2	16	7	-	-
J.J.N.P.Bhula c Smith b Kitchen	60	115	74	-	7
M.G.Bracewell c Kelly b Kitchen	82	117	87	-	12
T.M.Johnson* b Rae	58	62	52	2	5
F.J.Colson c Kelly b McClenaghan	46	54	31	2	4
J.D.Gibson b McClenaghan	2	9	7	-	-
L.V.van Beek not out	33	18	17	2	1
P.F.Younghusband c Rippon b McClenaghan	2	10	4	-	-
O.R.Newton					
I.G.McPeake					
Extras (w 9)	9				
TOTAL (50 overs) (8 wkts)	**340**	222			

OTAGO

	Runs	Mins	Balls	6s	4s
H.D.Rutherford c McPeake b Younghusband	102	133	91	4	8
N.F.Kelly b Bracewell	56	82	64	2	6
N.T.Broom c Blundell b Bracewell	55	83	57	-	6
A.K.Kitchen not out	72	83	46	3	6
M.J.G.Rippon c Gibson b van Beek	39	42	35	-	6
D.N.Phillips not out	4	6	3	-	1
N.G.Smith					
M.W.Chu†					
M.J.McClenaghan					
J.A.Duffy*					
M.D.Rae					
Extras (lb 2, w 11, nb 1)	14				
TOTAL (49.1 overs) (4 wkts)	**342**	216			

Bowling	*O*	*M*	*R*	*W*
OTAGO				
Duffy	10	0	72	0
McClenaghan	9	0	73	5
Smith	6	0	32	0
Rae	7	1	52	1
Rippon	9	0	58	0
Kitchen	9	0	53	2
WELLINGTON				
van Beek	9	1	64	1
Newton	8.1	0	67	0
McPeake	7	0	50	0
Bracewell	10	0	51	2
Bhula	2	0	17	0
Gibson	6	0	46	0
Younghusband	7	0	45	1

Fall of Wickets	***W***	***O***
1st	27	125
2nd	59	199
3rd	178	258
4th	215	331
5th	294	-
6th	300	-
7th	317	-
8th	340	-
9th	-	-
10th	-	-

Tenth Round

Due to Covid restrictions these games were played without spectators.

Canterbury decided to bat first and made 238-5 with Latham scoring his third hundred from 63 balls. He finished on 118 not out. There was a 63 run stand for the sixth wicket off 35 balls. Will O'Donnell top scored for Auckland. He got fifty off 37 deliveries and finished with 79 but Auckland went from 100-1 to 112-5 in three overs. Astle took 3-32 as Auckland made 225-8.

Northern decided to bowl first as Central had a 112 run opening stand. There were fifties to Worker and Cleaver from 58 and 60 balls. Patel got 45 which was a career best. Hampton took his 50th wicket in his 3-35. Central finished with 253. Northern had a 102 run stand for the third wicket with Carter and Cooper getting fifties from 66 and 72 balls. Northern reached 257-5 with 16 balls to spare.

Wellington decided to bat first and a run feast developed. They made 427-8, the highest one-day total in New Zealand. Allen hit his maiden century from just 50 balls which equalled Peter Fulton's record for the fastest century in New Zealand one-day cricket. The first wicket put on 191 from 123 balls. Blundell went to his maiden century from 112 balls. Otago lost three early wickets but Rippon and Phillips added 138 for the fifth wicket. Both got fifties from 46 and 43 balls and both had their highest scores. The tenth wicket set an Otago record with 67 from 41 balls. Smith got fifty from 28 balls while Rae had his highest score. Otago were eventually bowled out for 345 from 41.2 overs.

CANTERBURY v AUCKLAND — Ford Trophy

at MainPower Oval, Rangiora on 28 February, 2021
Toss : Canterbury. Umpires : J.A.K. Bromley & D.J. Walker
Canterbury won by 13 runs. *Points: Canterbury 4, Auckland 0*

CANTERBURY

	Runs	*Mins*	*Balls*	*6s*	*4s*
H.M.Nicholls b Pringle	49	53	36	1	6
C.J.Bowes c Beghin b Lister	0	6	3	-	-
K.J.McClure c O'Donnell W.T. b ter Braak	10	21	20	-	1
T.W.M.Latham† not out	118	107	75	2	12
D.J.Mitchell c ter Braak b Somerville	20	26	17	1	1
C.E.McConchie* b ter Braak	13	27	13	1	-
T.D.Astle not out	17	26	13	-	2
S.B.Davey					
M.J.Henry					
W.S.A.Williams					
E.J.Nuttall					
Extras (lb 2, w 6, nb 3)	11				
TOTAL (29 overs) (5 wkts)	**238**	135			

AUCKLAND

	Runs	*Mins*	*Balls*	*6s*	*4s*
G.K.Beghin c Bowes b McConchie	42	45	31	-	7
C.J.Briggs b Astle	29	32	21	2	3
W.T.O'Donnell c Henry b Williams	79	81	59	2	5
R.R.O'Donnell* c Bowes b Nuttall	5	6	6	-	-
B.J.Horne† b Astle	4	6	5	-	-
A.R.Morrison b Astle	0	1	1	-	-
R.M.ter Braak c Henry b Williams	32	43	27	1	3
W.E.R.Somerville not out	9	24	12	-	-
O.M.R.Pringle c sub (C.D.Fletcher) b Henry	13	10	9	1	-
L.J.Delport not out	6	2	3	-	1
B.G.Lister					
Extras (b 1, lb 3, w 2)	6				
TOTAL (29 overs) (8 wkts)	**225**	128			

Bowling	*O*	*M*	*R*	*W*
AUCKLAND				
Delport	6	1	33	0
Lister	6	0	57	1
ter Braak	6	0	50	2
Somerville	6	0	45	1
Pringle	2	0	19	1
O'Donnell W.T.	3	0	32	0
CANTERBURY				
Henry	6	0	48	1
Nuttall	3	0	27	1
Williams	6	0	45	2
McConchie	5	0	44	1
Astle	6	0	32	3
Davey	3	0	25	0

Fall of Wickets	***C***	***A***
1st	4	65
2nd	32	100
3rd	83	107
4th	125	112
5th	175	112
6th	-	190
7th	-	202
8th	-	218
9th	-	-
10th	-	-

C.D.Fletcher (sub) kept wicket for Canterbury

NORTHERN DISTRICTS v CENTRAL DISTRICTS Ford Trophy

at Seddon Park, Hamilton on 28 February, 2021
Toss : Northern Districts. Umpires : J.M. Dempsey & D.R. Morrow
***Northern Districts won by 5 wickets.** Points: Northern Districts 4, Central Districts 0*

CENTRAL DISTRICTS

	Runs	Mins	Balls	6s	4s
G.H.Worker b Walker	66	125	87	2	5
D.Cleaver† run out	57	90	64	2	6
W.A.Young c Kuggeleijn b Walker	20	22	15	-	3
L.R.P.L.Taylor c Raval b Fisher	2	5	4	-	-
T.C.Bruce* c Kuggeleijn b Hampton	12	21	17	1	-
J.A.Clarkson c Watling b Fisher	18	59	28	-	3
C.K.Leopard c Carter b Hampton	3	10	8	-	-
J.F.A.Field c Watling b Verma	5	16	10	-	-
A.Y.Patel c Raval b Hampton	45	61	44	1	6
J.R.Lennox run out	5	22	13	-	-
R.L.Toole not out	2	20	6	-	-
Extras (b 1, lb 2, w 14, nb 1)	18				
TOTAL (49.1 overs)	**253**	228			

NORTHERN DISTRICTS

	Runs	Mins	Balls	6s	4s
J.A.Raval c Cleaver b Field	9	29	16	-	2
K.D.Clarke c Bruce b Toole	31	22	19	2	2
J.F.Carter* b Toole	71	132	92	-	6
H.R.Cooper c Patel b Clarkson	51	80	73	1	5
B-J.Watling† not out	43	80	56	-	4
C.de Grandhomme lbw b Lennox	29	28	19	-	4
B.R.Hampton not out	15	8	9	2	-
S.C.Kuggeleijn					
A.Verma					
J.G.Walker					
M.J.Fisher					
Extras (lb 4, w 4)	8				
TOTAL (47.2 overs) (5 wkts)	**257**	191			

Bowling	*O*	*M*	*R*	*W*
NORTHERN DISTRICTS				
Kuggeleijn	10	1	56	0
Verma	10	1	38	1
Fisher	10	0	73	2
Hampton	9.1	0	35	3
Walker	10	0	48	2
CENTRAL DISTRICTS				
Field	6	0	47	1
Toole	9	0	45	2
Leopard	3	0	18	0
Lennox	10	0	43	1
Patel	9.2	0	53	0
Clarkson	10	0	47	1

Fall of Wickets	*CD*	*ND*
1st	112	37
2nd	146	43
3rd	150	145
4th	162	194
5th	167	241
6th	171	-
7th	186	-
8th	201	-
9th	221	-
10th	253	-

WELLINGTON v OTAGO Ford Trophy

at Basin Reserve, Wellington on 28 February, 2021
Toss : Wellington. Umpires : T.J. Parlane & G.A. Stirrat
***Wellington won by 82 runs** Points: Wellington 4, Otago 0*

WELLINGTON

	Runs	Mins	Balls	6s	4s
F.H.Allen c Chu b Rae	128	101	59	11	9
T.A.Blundell† b McClenaghan	151	214	140	1	17
J.J.N.P.Bhula b Rippon	20	29	20	-	3
M.G.Bracewell c Broom b Rippon	47	52	45	1	4
J.D.Gibson run out	44	27	21	4	2
L.V.van Beek c Smith b McClenaghan	13	14	7	1	-
T.M.Johnson* c Phillips b McClenaghan	12	13	9	1	-
F.J.Colson run out	0	2	0	-	-
P.F.Younghusband not out	0	1	0	-	-
B.V.Sears					
I.G.McPeake					
Extras (w 11, nb 1)	12				
TOTAL (50 overs) (8 wkts)	**427**	228			

OTAGO

	Runs	Mins	Balls	6s	4s
H.D.Rutherford b van Beek	7	7	8	-	1
N.F.Kelly c Blundell b McPeake	23	24	11	1	4
N.T.Broom lbw b van Beek	9	9	7	-	2
A.K.Kitchen c Gibson b Sears	40	51	41	1	5
M.J.G.Rippon run out	84	112	68	4	5
D.N.Phillips b van Beek	62	70	48	2	7
N.G.Smith not out	50	51	28	5	2
M.W.Chu† c van Beek b Sears	2	7	5	-	-
M.J.McClenaghan c Gibson b Bracewell	8	8	5	1	-
J.A.Duffy* b Sears	4	3	3	-	1
M.D.Rae c Sears b Bracewell	33	30	24	2	2
Extras (b 4, lb 7, w 12)	23				
TOTAL (41.2 overs)	**345**	187			

Bowling	*O*	*M*	*R*	*W*
AUCKLAND				
Duffy	10	1	79	0
McClenaghan	9	0	78	3
Rae	7	0	75	1
Smith	6	0	62	0
Kitchen	9	0	81	0
Rippon	9	0	52	2
WELLINGTON				
McPeake	5	0	46	1
van Beek	8	0	48	3
Younghusband	8	0	64	0
Sears	8	0	75	3
Bracewell	9.2	0	61	2
Gibson	3	0	40	0

Fall of Wickets	*W*	*O*
1st	191	13
2nd	236	23
3rd	313	49
4th	393	104
5th	400	242
6th	425	242
7th	427	250
8th	427	274
9th	-	278
10th	-	345

NORTHERN DISTRICTS v WELLINGTON — Elimination final

at Seddon Park, Hamilton on 3 March, 2021
Toss : Wellington. Umpires : B.F. Bowden & T.J. Parlane
Northern Districts won by 138 runs (D/L)

The game was reduced to 42 overs due to rain. Wellington decided to bowl but Northern batted positively getting 351-8. Carter and Cooper added 136 off 87 balls for the third wicket. Carter got fifty from 57 balls while Cooper got his fifty from 33 balls and then reached his maiden hundred off 67 balls as he made 146 not out. Sears took three wickets.

Wellington had no partnerships of note and only Blundell with an unbeaten 80 (fifty from 52 balls) had any real contribution. Rain came again after 26.1 overs with Wellington 145-7. Northern were well ahead on the Duckworth/Lewis calculation, winning by 138 runs and proceeding to the final against top qualifiers Canterbury.

NORTHERN DISTRICTS

	Runs	Mins	Balls	6s	4s
J.A.Raval c Gibson b Younghusband	33	61	43	-	5
K.D.Clarke b van Beek	6	9	4	1	-
J.F.Carter* c Allen b Younghusband	75	112	71	2	7
H.R.Cooper not out	146	130	94	7	11
B.R.Hampton c Gibson b Sears	34	15	13	4	2
C.de Grandhomme c Younghusband b Sears	0	2	1	-	-
B-J.Watling† c Colson b Sears	16	16	12	1	1
S.C.Kuggeleijn c Blundell b van Beek	16	16	9	-	2
A.Verma run out	3	17	5	-	-
J.G.Walker					
M.J.Fisher					
Extras (lb 4, w 18)	22				
TOTAL (42 overs) (8 wkts)	**351**	192			

WELLINGTON

	Runs	Mins	Balls	6s	4s
F.H.Allen c Raval b Kuggeleijn	24	37	29	1	2
T.A.Blundell† not out	80	126	74	1	9
J.J.N.P.Bhula lbw b Hampton	2	16	7	-	-
M.G.Bracewell c de Grandhomme b Fisher	3	5	3	-	-
T.M.Johnson* c Watling b Kuggeleijn	17	35	1	1	-
F.J.Colson c Fisher b Walker	11	15	11	-	1
J.D.Gibson c Fisher b Verma	0	4	5	-	-
L.V.van Beek c de Grandhomme b Walker	1	3	4	-	-
P.F.Younghusband not out	1	8	5	-	-
B.V.Sears					
O.R.Newton					
Extras (lb 2, w 4)	6				
TOTAL (26.1 overs) (7 wkts)	**145**	126			

Bowling	*O*	*M*	*R*	*W*
WELLINGTON				
van Beek	9	0	79	2
Newton	2	0	2	0
Sears	9	0	74	3
Gibson	6	0	51	0
Bracewell	6	0	60	0
Younghusband	6	0	56	2
Bhula	4	0	25	0
NORTHERN DISTRICTS				
Kuggeleijn	7	1	38	2
Verma	6	0	44	1
Hampton	5	0	32	1
Fisher	4	0	18	1
Walker	4.1	1	11	2

Fall of Wickets	***ND***	***W***
1st	16	47
2nd	77	61
3rd	213	64
4th	254	106
5th	255	127
6th	280	128
7th	319	130
8th	351	-
9th	-	-
10th	-	-

CANTERBURY v NORTHERN DISTRICTS — Final

at Hagley Oval, Christchurch on 6 March, 2021 (d/n)
Toss : Northern Districts. Umpires : T.J. Parlane & D.J. Walker
Canterbury won by 8 wickets

Northern decided to bat first and lost Raval early. Clarke and Carter then put on 125 for the second wicket, with Clarke (fifty off 62 balls) making his highest score. Carter took 61 balls for his fifty and de Grandhomme reached a half-century from 34 balls to get Northern to 289-7.

Canterbury had a 113 run opening stand off 111 balls and a 150 run second wicket partnership from 138 deliveries. Nicholls, after getting fifty from 54 balls, got his sixth hundred from 114 balls. McClure scored fifty from 44 balls as Canterbury reached 292-2 in 45 overs to win the Ford Trophy for the first time since 2016/17.

NORTHERN DISTRICTS

	Runs	Mins	Balls	6s	4s
J.A.Raval c & b Williams	5	30	18	-	-
K.D.Clarke c McClure b Astle	82	131	104	1	7
J.F.Carter* c Latham b Nuttall	70	125	86	-	3
H.R.Cooper c Latham b Nuttall	20	32	24	-	2
B-J.Watling† c McClure b Williams	31	52	28	-	3
C.de Grandhomme c Bowes b Mitchell	57	52	37	2	5
B.R.Hampton c Bowes b Mitchell	2	10	4	-	-
S.C.Kuggeleijn not out	5	3	2	-	1
A.Verma					
J.G.Walker					
M.J.Fisher					
Extras (lb 3, w 11, nb 3)	17				
TOTAL (50 overs) (7 wkts)	**289**	218			

CANTERBURY

	Runs	Mins	Balls	6s	4s
H.M.Nicholls not out	127	195	144	-	12
C.J.Bowes lbw b Walker	42	80	40	-	5
K.J.McClure c Carter b Raval	92	99	74	4	8
T.W.M.Latham† not out	17	15	12	-	3
D.J.Mitchell					
C.E.McConchie*					
C.D.Fletcher					
T.D.Astle					
M.J.Henry					
W.S.A.Williams					
E.J.Nuttall					
Extras (lb 8, w 6)	14				
TOTAL (45 overs) (2 wkts)	**292**	195			

Bowling	*O*	*M*	*R*	*W*
CANTERBURY				
Henry	10	1	52	0
Nuttall	10	0	58	2
Williams	9	0	46	2
Mitchell	5	0	37	2
Astle	10	0	52	1
McConchie	6	0	41	0
NORTHERN DISTRICTS				
Kuggeleijn	9	0	67	0
Verma	6	0	45	0
Hampton	7	0	35	0
Fisher	9	0	69	0
Walker	10	0	44	1
Raval	4	0	24	1

Fall of Wickets	***ND***	***C***
1st	32	113
2nd	157	263
3rd	184	-
4th	189	-
5th	271	-
6th	283	-
7th	289	-
8th	-	-
9th	-	-
10th	-	-

2020/21 FORD TROPHY AVERAGES

	M	*In*	*NO*	*HS*	*Runs*	*Ave*	*100s*	*50s*	*Ct*	*St*	*O*	*M*	*R*	*W*	*Ave*	*R/O*	*Best*
F.H.Allen	7	7	0	128	241	34.42	1	-	3	-	5	0	28	0	-	5.60	-
T.D.Astle	9	5	1	83	125	31.25	-	1	3	-	72	1	364	11	33.09	5.06	3-32
M.B.Bacon	6	4	2	15*	37	18.50	-	-	3	-	44	2	236	8	29.50	5.36	2-44
G.K.Beghin	8	8	1	47	140	20.00	-	-	4	-							
H.K.Bennett	1	-	-	-	-	-	-	-	-	-	3	0	23	0	-	7.67	-
J.J.N.P.Bhula	10	10	1	97*	275	30.55	-	2	4	-	21.2	0	116	6	19.33	5.44	3-13
T.A.Blundell	5	5	1	151	278	69.50	1	1	4	-							
P.D.Bocock	5	5	0	11	24	4.80	-	-	8	-							
C.J.Bowes	11	11	0	110	321	29.18	1	1	8	-							
J.C.T.Boyle	6	6	0	42	144	24.00	-	-	4	-							
M.G.Bracewell	8	8	1	82	344	49.14	-	4	4	-	61.2	1	336	9	37.33	5.48	2-51
C.J.Briggs	4	4	0	101	252	63.00	1	1	1	-							
N.T.Broom	10	10	1	83	328	36.44	-	4	4	-							
D.G.Brownlie	6	6	0	53	129	21.50	-	1	3	-							
T.C.Bruce	9	9	2	96*	250	35.71	-	1	3	-							
J.F.Carter	6	6	0	75	289	48.16	-	4	5	-							
L.J.Carter	7	7	2	63*	221	44.20	-	2	3	-							
M.W.Chu	4	3	0	19	32	10.66	-	-	4	-							
K.D.Clarke	12	12	0	82	387	32.25	-	4	7	-							
J.A.Clarkson	9	9	2	56*	308	44.00	-	3	1	-	60.2	2	326	11	29.63	5.40	3-30
D.Cleaver	6	6	0	57	205	34.16	-	2	10	1							
F.J.Colson	10	10	1	80*	267	29.66	-	1	4	-							
H.R.Cooper	9	9	1	146*	405	50.62	1	3	1	-	10.3	0	73	2	36.50	6.95	2-60
S.B.Davey	10	5	0	43	104	20.80	-	-	2	-	58.4	2	304	15	20.26	5.18	6-30
C.de Grandhomme	6	6	0	57	160	26.66	-	1	2	-	4	0	14	0	-	3.50	-
L.J.Delport	9	6	5	16*	35	35.00	-	-	3	-	86	8	363	12	30.25	4.22	3-45
A.P.Devcich	6	6	1	51	99	19.80	-	1	2	-							
L.R.Dudding	3	2	2	19*	20	-	-	-	-	-	12	0	94	2	47.00	7.83	2-33
J.A.Duffy	6	4	2	22	31	15.50	-	-	2	-	53.5	1	352	9	39.11	6.54	4-53
D.K.Ferns	2	2	0	20	22	11.00	-	-	-	-	12	0	70	2	35.00	5.83	2-52
J.F.A.Field	8	5	1	31	52	13.00	-	-	2	-	47	0	343	7	49.00	7.30	4-42
J.L.Finnie	6	6	0	21	66	11.00	-	-	2	-	8	0	76	2	38.00	9.50	1-23
M.J.Fisher	6	2	1	2	2	2.00	-	-	2	-	53	2	280	11	25.45	5.28	4-34
A.T.Fletcher	5	5	0	53	105	21.00	-	1	1	-							
C.D.Fletcher	7	5	3	45	156	78.00	-	-	9	-							
J.D.Gibson	10	10	2	64*	213	26.62	-	1	10	-	46	0	304	2	152.00	6.61	2-31
J.M.Gibson	3	3	1	7	12	6.00	-	-	-	-	20	1	119	6	19.83	5.95	3-56
M.J.Guptill	3	3	0	40	76	25.33	-	-	3	-							
B.R.Hampton	12	11	2	53	259	28.77	-	1	1	-	93.1	2	458	18	25.44	4.92	3-30
R.D.Harrison	7	6	0	15	27	4.50	-	-	2	-	24.5	0	148	7	21.14	5.96	2-22
J.W.Hartshorn	4	2	0	5	5	2.50	-	-	-	-	26	0	164	2	82.00	6.31	1-47
M.J.Hay	1	1	0	3	3	3.00	-	-	-	-							
M.W.Hay	5	4	1	49	75	25.00	-	-	3	-	12	0	62	1	62.00	5.17	1-26
M.J.Henry	9	5	1	23	67	16.75	-	-	5	-	77	3	339	15	22.60	4.40	3-27
B.J.Horne	9	9	2	38*	191	27.28	-	-	7	-							
L.R.Johns	5	5	0	23	78	15.60	-	-	2	2							
T.M.Johnson	10	10	1	113	370	41.11	1	3	6	-							
N.F.Kelly	10	10	1	76	273	30.33	-	3	8	-							
A.K.Kitchen	10	10	2	72*	266	33.25	-	2	5	-	72.2	3	413	13	31.76	5.71	3-25
S.C.Kuggeleijn	6	5	1	16	28	7.00	-	-	4	-	53.2	4	276	9	30.66	5.18	4-41
T.W.M.Latham	6	6	2	118*	280	70.00	1	1	6	-							
J.R.Lennox	9	5	1	5	15	3.75	-	-	2	-	74	1	344	12	28.66	4.65	3-30
C.K.Leopard	8	6	0	19	39	6.50	-	-	7	-	35.4	3	195	6	32.50	5.47	2-22
B.G.Lister	10	5	3	3*	9	4.50	-	-	4	-	76	4	466	8	58.25	6.13	3-56
T.M.Lortan	1	1	0	12	12	12.00	-	-	-	-							
M.J.McClenaghan	4	3	0	10	20	6.66	-	-	-	-	37	1	219	10	21.90	5.92	5-73
K.J.McClure	8	8	1	107	480	68.57	2	3	3	-							
C.E.McConchie	7	5	0	45	119	23.80	-	-	1	-	35	1	220	2	110.00	6.29	1-30
J.D.McKay	2	1	1	4*	4	-	-	-	1	-	12	0	93	1	93.00	7.75	1-52
A.W.McKenzie	3	2	0	22	23	11.50	-	-	1	-	21	0	87	3	29.00	4.14	2-22
I.G.McPeake	8	3	0	6	7	2.33	-	-	2	-	60	2	354	9	39.33	5.90	2-31
D.J.Mitchell	3	2	1	20	30	30.00	-	-	1	-	5	0	37	2	18.50	7.40	2-37
A.R.Morrison	2	2	0	1	1	0.50	-	-	1	-							
T.Muller	5	3	0	34	49	16.33	-	-	2	-	32	0	192	8	24.00	6.00	5-34
C.Munro	2	2	0	7	11	5.50	-	-	-	-	5	0	20	0	-	4.00	-

	M	In	NO	HS	Runs	Ave	100s	50s	Ct	St	O	M	R	W	Ave	R/O	Best
O.R.Newton	3	1	0	5	5	5.00	-	-	-	-	20.1	2	92	3	30.66	4.56	3-23
H.M.Nicholls	5	5	2	127*	365	121.66	2	-	-	-							
E.J.Nuttall	9	2	2	0*	0	-	-	-	3	-	67.5	5	360	13	27.69	5.31	3-58
R.R.O'Donnell	10	10	0	59	228	22.80	-	2	5	-	1	0	2	1	2.00	2.00	1-2
W.T.O'Donnell	10	10	0	106	537	53.70	1	6	6	-	11	0	87	0	-	7.91	-
A.Y.Patel	3	3	1	45	46	23.00	-	-	1	-	28.2	0	177	2	88.50	6.25	2-51
D.N.Phillips	10	8	1	62	200	28.57	-	1	9	-							
B.Popli	3	3	1	57*	97	48.50	-	1	3	-							
O.M.R.Pringle	4	3	1	13	14	7.00	-	-	-	-	20	0	147	4	36.75	7.35	3-70
M.D.Rae	7	4	1	33	43	14.33	-	-	-	-	57.3	3	353	16	22.06	6.14	7-35
S.H.A.Rance	4	2	0	2	2	1.00	-	-	1	-	30	3	133	3	44.33	4.43	2-26
B.G.Randell	7	3	2	6	10	10.00	-	-	2	-	63	2	355	15	23.66	5.63	5-22
J.A.Raval	12	12	0	105	409	34.08	1	1	10	-	11	0	63	1	63.00	5.73	1-24
M.Renwick	6	6	1	48	159	31.80	-	-	5	2							
M.J.G.Rippon	9	8	1	84	306	43.71	-	3	2	-	67	3	402	7	57.42	6.00	2-36
B.P.Rodden	5	5	0	41	106	21.20	-	-	-	-							
H.D.Rutherford	7	7	0	102	281	40.14	1	2	2	-							
B.D.Schmulian	4	3	1	14	24	12.00	-	-	2	-	6	0	45	0	-	7.50	-
B.V.Sears	5	2	1	5	5	5.00	-	-	2	-	44.1	2	265	11	24.09	6.00	3-40
F.W.Sheat	3	1	1	0*	0	-	-	-	-	-	20	2	110	3	36.66	5.50	3-22
H.B.Shipley	1	1	0	2	2	2.00	-	-	1	-							
B.S.Smith	5	5	0	79	160	32.00	-	1	-	-							
N.G.Smith	5	4	1	81	148	49.33	-	2	6	-	34	1	227	5	45.40	6.68	3-58
M.W.Snedden	4	2	1	1*	1	1.00	-	-	1	-	32	1	159	3	53.00	4.97	2-53
S.M.Solia	6	6	0	121	298	49.66	1	1	-	-	23.3	0	132	2	66.00	5.62	1-22
W.E.R.Somerville	10	9	3	39*	83	13.83	-	-	2	-	88.3	1	424	10	42.40	4.79	3-26
L.R.P.L.Taylor	4	4	1	68*	79	26.33	-	1	2	-							
R.M.ter Braak	9	7	1	42*	140	23.33	-	-	4	-	61.4	3	409	13	31.46	6.63	4-27
B.M.Tickner	2	-	-	-	-	-	-	-	1	-	11	0	69	1	69.00	6.27	1-65
R.L.Toole	4	2	2	2*	2	-	-	-	-	-	31	2	175	5	35.00	5.65	2-45
L.V.van Beek	5	5	1	33*	62	15.50	-	-	1	-	45	2	278	8	34.75	6.18	3-48
T.F.van Woerkom	2	2	0	31	40	20.00	-	-	1	-	13	0	67	2	33.50	5.15	2-45
A.Verma	11	8	2	47*	119	19.83	-	-	5	-	86.3	2	459	14	32.78	5.31	2-27
N.Wagner	1	-	-	-	-	-	-	-	1	-	6	0	17	0	-	2.83	-
F.L.Walker	2	1	0	9	9	9.00	-	-	-	-	19.2	2	88	1	88.00	4.55	1-51
J.G.Walker	12	7	2	19	38	7.60	-	-	4	-	100.1	3	438	12	36.50	4.37	2-11
B-J.Watling	7	7	2	68	199	39.80	-	1	8	-							
B.M.Wheeler	3	2	1	31*	35	35.00	-	-	1	-	21	0	124	2	62.00	5.90	2-34
B.L.Wiggins	5	5	0	59	179	35.80	-	1	3	-							
W.S.A.Williams	11	4	1	7	9	3.00	-	-	4	-	83.2	6	361	20	18.05	4.33	3-24
G.H.Worker	9	9	0	125	357	39.66	1	3	2	-	10	0	59	3	19.66	5.90	2-32
W.A.Young	4	4	0	79	119	29.75	-	1	1	-							
P.F.Younghusband	10	9	5	29*	84	21.00	-	-	7	-	76.5	1	420	15	28.00	5.47	3-42

HIGHEST STRIKE RATES *(qualification 150 runs)*

		Runs	Balls	S/R
F.H.Allen	W	241	171	140
H.D.Rutherford	O	281	216	130
C.de Grandhomme	ND	160	124	129
B.L.Wiggins	CD	179	152	117
B.R.Hampton	ND	259	224	115
T.W.M.Latham	C	280	246	113
J.A.Clarkson	CD	308	288	106
G.H.Worker	CD	357	348	102
C.D.Fletcher	C	156	154	101
M.J.G.Rippon	O	306	304	100

MOST ECONOMICAL BOWLING *(qualification 30 overs)*

		O	M	R	W	Ave	R/O
L.J.Delport	A	86	8	363	12	30.25	4.22
W.S.A.Williams	C	83.2	6	361	20	18.05	4.33
J.G.Walker	ND	100.1	3	438	12	36.50	4.37
M.J.Henry	C	77	3	339	15	22.60	4.40
S.H.A.Rance	CD	30	3	133	3	44.33	4.43
J.R.Lennox	CD	74	1	344	12	28.66	4.65
W.E.R.Somerville	A	88.3	1	424	10	42.40	4.79
B.R.Hampton	ND	93.1	2	458	18	25.44	4.92
M.W.Snedden	W	32	1	159	3	53.00	4.97
T.D.Astle	C	72	1	364	11	33.09	5.06

CAREER RECORDS

	M	In	NO	HS	Runs	Ave	100s	50s	Ct	St	O	M	R	W	Ave	R/O	Best
F.H.Allen	18	18	0	128	400	22.22	1	-	8	-	27	0	157	1	157.00	5.81	1-32
T.D.Astle	75	58	12	83	1576	34.26	-	13	23	-	550.5	11	2893	78	37.08	5.25	4-36
M.B.Bacon	26	14	5	21*	97	10.77	-	-	9	-	182.5	4	1127	29	38.86	6.16	3-35
G.K.Beghin	23	23	4	69	477	25.10	-	2	9	-							
H.K.Bennett	77	26	15	20*	73	6.63	-	-	11	-	557.3	33	2854	108	26.42	5.12	6-45
J.J.N.P.Bhula	24	23	1	99	485	22.04	-	3	13	-	37.2	0	182	10	18.20	4.88	3-13
T.A.Blundell	40	34	1	151	1048	31.75	1	5	31	4							
P.D.Bocock	20	18	2	57*	371	23.18	-	3	27	1							
C.J.Bowes	47	47	4	114*	1570	36.51	4	6	24	-							
J.C.T.Boyle	28	28	1	126	1112	41.18	3	5	11	-							
M.G.Bracewell	96	91	5	120	2780	32.32	1	23	51	-	111	3	586	15	39.06	5.28	3-30
C.J.Briggs	4	4	0	101	252	63.00	1	1	1	-							
N.T.Broom	130	120	13	164	4455	41.63	9	28	45	-	51.2	1	306	4	76.50	5.96	1-10
D.G.Brownlie	72	70	5	118	2310	35.53	3	18	43	-							
T.C.Bruce	45	45	5	100	1421	35.52	1	13	20	-	18	0	130	2	65.00	7.22	1-13
J.F.Carter	37	35	4	102*	1061	34.22	1	7	19	-							
L.J.Carter	27	22	4	63*	367	20.38	-	2	7	-							
M.W.Chu	4	3	0	19	32	10.66	-	-	4	-							
K.D.Clarke	21	21	0	82	673	32.04	-	6	11	-							
J.A.Clarkson	44	41	7	111	1257	36.97	2	6	11	-	81.2	2	454	14	32.42	5.58	3-30
D.Cleaver	56	48	4	124*	1351	30.70	2	8	60	9							
F.J.Colson	14	13	2	80*	346	31.45	-	2	4	-							
H.R.Cooper	27	27	2	146*	892	35.68	1	7	8	-	25.3	1	157	5	31.40	6.16	2-9
S.B.Davey	10	5	0	43	104	20.80	-	-	2	-	58.4	2	304	15	20.26	5.18	6-30
C.de Grandhomme	81	76	9	115	1725	25.74	1	6	43	-	343	8	1866	45	41.46	5.44	4-37
L.J.Delport	16	9	5	16*	51	12.75	-	-	4	-	153	8	674	23	29.30	4.41	3-41
A.P.Devcich	73	70	7	101*	1937	30.74	1	17	31	-	368.5	5	2011	42	47.88	5.45	5-46
L.R.Dudding	6	4	3	19*	32	32.00	-	-	-	-	38	3	260	5	52.00	6.84	3-67
J.A.Duffy	52	30	14	39	183	11.43	-	-	14	-	424.4	21	2308	99	23.31	5.43	6-35
D.K.Ferns	17	13	6	35*	129	18.42	-	-	8	-	123.2	10	699	22	31.77	5.67	4-35
J.F.A.Field	8	5	1	31	52	13.00	-	-	2	-	47	0	343	7	49.00	7.30	4-42
J.L.Finnie	38	35	5	73*	767	25.56	-	5	10	-	46	0	313	4	78.25	6.80	1-14
M.J.Fisher	6	2	1	2	2	2.00	-	-	2	-	53	2	280	11	25.45	5.28	4-34
A.T.Fletcher	27	27	1	132*	1007	38.73	3	7	10	-							
C.D.Fletcher	62	48	14	73	1048	30.82	-	3	67	9							
J.D.Gibson	22	21	5	64*	410	25.62	-	2	13	-	76	1	505	5	101.00	6.64	2-31
J.M.Gibson	5	5	1	7	18	4.50	-	-	-	-	34.5	2	178	12	14.83	5.11	5-31
M.J.Guptill	45	44	2	156	1846	43.95	8	6	25	-							
B.R.Hampton	58	50	12	95	1083	28.50	-	4	19	-	346.4	9	1850	51	36.27	5.34	4-30
R.D.Harrison	7	6	0	15	27	4.50	-	-	2	-	24.5	0	148	7	21.14	5.96	2-22
J.W.Hartshorn	4	2	0	5	5	2.50	-	-	-	-	26	0	164	2	82.00	6.31	1-47
M.J.Hay	1	1	0	3	3	3.00	-	-	-	-							
M.W.Hay	5	4	1	49	75	25.00	-	-	3	-	12	0	62	1	62.00	5.17	1-26
M.J.Henry	47	32	8	37*	337	14.04	-	-	21	-	383.5	32	1918	78	24.58	5.00	6-45
B.J.Horne	39	36	5	101	886	28.58	1	5	43	7							
L.R.Johns	22	18	3	25*	219	14.60	-	-	32	4							
T.M.Johnson	10	10	1	113	370	41.11	1	3	6	-							
N.F.Kelly	48	46	2	120	1496	34.00	3	11	26	-	8	0	60	2	30.00	7.50	2-55
A.K.Kitchen	107	103	10	143*	2988	32.12	4	15	47	-	344.2	8	1868	46	40.60	5.43	4-23
S.C.Kuggeleijn	66	54	11	85*	888	20.65	-	3	24	-	552.5	32	3132	102	30.70	5.67	5-24
T.W.M.Latham	48	45	6	130	1730	44.35	3	9	52	5							
J.R.Lennox	13	6	2	5	17	4.25	-	-	2	-	97	1	493	13	37.92	5.08	3-30
C.K.Leopard	21	18	1	29	163	9.58	-	-	13	-	55.2	4	294	8	36.75	5.31	2-22
T.M.Lortan	1	1	0	12	12	12.00	-	-	-	-							
G.R.Loveridge	18	16	3	50*	185	14.23	-	1	-	-	99.1	7	424	16	26.50	4.28	4-25
M.J.McClenaghan	44	23	7	23	170	10.62	-	-	9	-	365	21	2052	89	23.05	5.62	6-41
K.J.McClure	21	17	3	107	637	45.50	2	3	4	-							
C.E.McConchie	51	39	5	90	904	26.58	-	5	13	-	224	4	1274	29	43.93	5.69	3-28
J.D.McKay	2	1	1	4*	4	-	-	-	1	-	12	0	93	1	93.00	7.75	1-52
A.W.McKenzie	5	3	1	22	33	16.50	-	-	2	-	28	0	139	3	46.33	4.96	2-22
I.G.McPeake	34	15	5	19*	73	7.30	-	-	9	-	261.1	18	1402	42	33.38	5.37	5-40
D.J.Mitchell	69	65	8	126*	2261	39.66	3	17	35	-	234.4	4	1461	44	33.20	6.23	3-34
A.R.Morrison	2	2	0	1	1	0.50	-	-	1	-							
T.Muller	6	4	0	34	53	13.25	-	-	2	-	41	0	258	8	32.25	6.29	5-34
C.Munro	62	58	9	174*	2464	50.28	8	11	22	-	169.1	1	932	16	58.25	5.51	3-45
O.R.Newton	22	16	7	35*	150	16.66	-	-	2	-	178.4	9	835	40	20.87	4.67	5-46

	M	In	NO	HS	Runs	Ave	100s	50s	Ct	St	O	M	R	W	Ave	R/O	Best
H.M.Nicholls	56	51	4	178	2456	52.25	6	16	26	-	2	0	17	0	-	8.50	-
E.J.Nuttall	33	12	7	2*	5	1.00	-	-	9	-	247.2	17	1363	52	26.21	5.51	4-50
R.R.O'Donnell	51	50	4	78	1387	30.15	-	9	27	-	51	0	281	8	35.12	5.51	2-19
W.T.O'Donnell	18	18	0	106	653	36.27	1	6	11	-	27	0	193	1	193.00	7.15	1-54
A.Y.Patel	28	17	7	45	179	17.90	-	-	12	-	232.1	6	1255	27	46.48	5.41	3-43
D.N.Phillips	16	14	2	62	303	25.25	-	1	10	-	4.1	0	41	0	-	9.84	-
B.Popli	15	14	1	69	394	30.30	-	3	5	-							
O.M.R.Pringle	4	3	1	13	14	7.00	-	-	-	-	20	0	147	4	36.75	7.35	3-70
M.D.Rae	13	9	4	33	76	15.20	-	-	2	-	101.2	6	627	22	28.50	6.19	7-35
S.H.A.Rance	52	33	11	41*	216	9.81	-	-	8	-	402.3	33	2027	83	24.42	5.04	4-32
B.G.Randell	25	13	6	25	72	10.28	-	-	10	-	204	11	1077	46	23.41	5.28	5-22
J.A.Raval	65	65	0	149	1955	30.07	4	8	38	-	23	0	133	3	44.33	5.78	2-8
M.Renwick	28	28	1	75	743	27.51	-	3	29	5							
M.J.G.Rippon	40	37	7	84	1138	37.93	-	7	17	-	331	14	1754	49	35.79	5.30	5-21
B.P.Rodden	8	7	1	41	119	19.83	-	-	-	-							
H.D.Rutherford	58	56	3	155	1990	37.54	7	5	20	-	7	0	33	1	33.00	4.71	1-4
B.D.Schmulian	10	8	3	61*	201	40.20	-	1	2	-	42.2	1	293	1	293.00	6.92	1-44
B.V.Sears	15	6	3	11	18	6.00	-	-	9	-	124	7	679	25	27.16	5.48	3-40
F.W.Sheat	8	6	5	35*	53	53.00	-	-	3	-	57	2	312	7	44.57	5.47	3-22
H.B.Shipley	25	16	3	51*	242	18.61	-	1	8	-	171.4	7	1023	18	56.83	5.96	4-60
B.S.Smith	58	57	4	149*	1690	31.88	2	8	18	-							
N.G.Smith	29	26	5	81	502	23.90	-	3	16	-	224.4	8	1248	38	32.84	5.55	3-21
M.W.Snedden	7	3	2	18*	19	19.00	-	-	1	-	58	1	351	7	50.14	6.05	3-61
S.M.Solia	39	39	4	152	1491	42.60	3	8	9	-	148.1	2	901	30	30.03	6.08	4-38
W.E.R.Somerville	19	16	4	50	207	17.25	-	1	7	-	178.3	2	881	24	36.70	4.94	4-48
L.R.P.L.Taylor	41	41	5	132*	1711	47.52	4	13	26	-	31	0	140	2	70.00	4.52	1-13
R.M.ter Braak	9	7	1	42*	140	23.33	-	-	4	-	61.4	3	409	13	31.46	6.63	4-27
B.M.Tickner	27	9	8	24*	56	56.00	-	-	9	-	218	4	1227	33	37.18	5.63	4-43
R.L.Toole	10	6	3	5	8	2.66	-	-	1	-	59	2	340	7	48.57	5.76	2-31
L.V.van Beek	59	36	6	53	376	12.53	-	1	30	-	383.5	15	2166	61	35.50	5.64	4-23
T.F.van Woerkom	14	7	1	31	57	9.50	-	-	2	-	118.1	1	601	12	50.08	5.09	2-31
A.Verma	54	36	13	58	561	24.39	-	2	28	-	405.4	19	2331	76	30.67	5.75	5-44
N.Wagner	66	41	9	42	455	14.21	-	-	12	-	549.4	38	3007	106	28.36	5.47	5-34
F.L.Walker	5	2	1	9	10	10.00	-	-	1	-	32.2	2	182	1	182.00	5.63	1-51
J.G.Walker	29	19	7	31*	170	14.16	-	-	4	-	219.1	4	1098	24	45.75	5.01	3-35
B-J.Watling	90	89	11	145*	3288	42.15	7	22	63	3							
B.M.Wheeler	32	24	6	80*	378	21.00	-	3	9	-	240.1	12	1305	40	32.62	5.43	4-24
B.L.Wiggins	9	8	0	103	383	47.87	1	2	4	-							
W.S.A.Williams	35	19	7	19*	115	9.58	-	-	16	-	265.5	18	1357	47	28.87	5.10	4-34
G.H.Worker	107	106	7	194	4397	44.41	12	26	37	-	356.4	6	1974	54	36.55	5.53	4-22
W.A.Young	53	53	4	106*	1649	33.65	3	11	22	-							
P.F.Younghusband	34	26	7	52*	300	15.78	-	1	21	-	265.4	2	1436	34	42.23	5.41	3-42

DREAM11 SUPER SMASH

2020/21

Wellington became the first side since Auckland in 2011/12 to win the Twenty20 title in successive seasons. They beat Canterbury in the final in a thrilling game after being the dominant team throughout the competition where they lost just one match. Central Districts finished second in the table but lost the elimination play off to Canterbury.

A total of 26 games were shown on Spark Sport with some on free-to-air television. No overseas players appeared in the tournament. The Wellington pair of Finn Allen (512 runs) and Devon Conway (455) were the leading scorers. George Worker made 424 runs while Daryl Mitchell scored 374. Three centuries were registered with Anton Devcich, Worker and Will Young all reaching three figures.

The fastest hundred was by Young who needed just 46 balls in the elimination play-off. The fastest fifty was scored by Allen off 16 balls against Central Districts. He also had the next two fastest fifties (both from 20 balls).

Blair Tickner was the leading wicket-taker with 17 followed by Matt Henry (14) and the Wellington duo of Logan van Beek and Hamish Bennett with 13.

Final points were:

	P	*W*	*L*	*NR*	*Points*
Wellington	10	9	1	–	36
Central Districts	10	6	4	–	24
Canterbury	10	6	4	–	24
Northern Districts	10	5	5	–	20
Auckland	10	2	8	–	8
Otago	10	2	8	–	8

WELLINGTON v AUCKLAND — Super Smash

at Basin Reserve, Wellington on 24 December, 2020
Toss : Wellington. Umpires : B.F. Bowden & K.D. Cotton
***Wellington won by 4 wickets.** Points: Wellington 4, Auckland 0*

AUCKLAND

	Runs	*Mins*	*Balls*	*6s*	*4s*
G.K.Beghin c van Beek b Snedden	32	33	23	1	5
S.M.Solia c Johns b Bennett	75	87	56	2	6
W.T.O'Donnell c Johnson b Younghusband	29	37	24	-	3
R.R.O'Donnell* not out	27	20	15	1	3
B.J.Horne† not out	4	4	2	-	1
B.P.Rodden					
W.E.R.Somerville					
O.M.R.Pringle					
R.D.Harrison					
B.G.Lister					
D.K.Ferns					
Extras (b 1, lb 1, w 7)	9				
TOTAL (20 overs) (3 wkts)	**176**	92			

WELLINGTON

	Runs	*Mins*	*Balls*	*6s*	*4s*
F.H.Allen c Lister b Pringle	53	28	23	1	9
R.Ravindra b Somerville	3	10	6	-	-
T.M.Johnson not out	50	83	44	2	2
M.G.Bracewell* c Solia b O'Donnell R.R.	1	5	4	-	-
F.J.Colson c Beghin b Somerville	22	20	17	-	4
J.D.Gibson c O'Donnell W.T. b Ferns	24	26	14	2	-
L.V.van Beek c O'Donnell W.T. b Ferns	1	4	3	-	-
L.R.Johns† not out	11	8	7	1	1
P.F.Younghusband					
H.K.Bennett					
M.W.Snedden					
Extras (lb 2, w 8, nb 3)	13				
TOTAL (19.1 overs) (6 wkts)	**178**	94			

Bowling	*O*	*M*	*R*	*W*
WELLINGTON				
Bennett	4	0	28	1
Snedden	4	0	36	1
van Beek	4	0	36	0
Ravindra	3	0	36	0
Younghusband	4	0	25	1
Bracewell	1	0	13	0
AUCKLAND				
Somerville	4	0	34	2
Lister	4	0	45	0
Ferns	4	0	39	2
Pringle	3	0	23	1
O'Donnell R.R.	4	0	30	1
Harrison	0.1	0	5	0

Fall of Wickets	*A*	*W*
1st	62	21
2nd	138	68
3rd	166	71
4th	-	106
5th	-	157
6th	-	160
7th	-	-
8th	-	-
9th	-	-
10th	-	-

CENTRAL DISTRICTS v WELLINGTON — Super Smash

at McLean Park, Napier on 27 December, 2020 (d/n)
Toss : Central Districts. Umpires : B.F. Bowden & G.A. Stirrat
***Wellington won by 39 runs.** Points: Wellington 4, Central Districts 0*

WELLINGTON

	Runs	Mins	Balls	6s	4s
D.P.Conway† c Bruce b Field	67	75	51	2	5
F.H.Allen c Worker b Tickner	11	12	8	-	2
R.Ravindra run out	4	13	6	-	-
J.D.S.Neesham c Field b Tickner	9	18	13	-	-
M.G.Bracewell* c Leopard b Noema-Barnett	35	19	21	2	2
J.D.Gibson c Bruce b Field	20	15	12	2	-
F.J.Colson c Leopard b Bracewell	7	7	4	-	1
T.M.Johnson not out	5	6	2	-	1
L.V.van Beek not out	12	3	2	1	1
P.F.Younghusband					
H.K.Bennett					
Extras (lb 2, w 3)	5				
TOTAL (20 overs) (7 wkts)	**175**	86			

CENTRAL DISTRICTS

	Runs	Mins	Balls	6s	4s
G.H.Worker c van Beek b Younghusband	27	38	29	-	3
B.L.Wiggins c Bennett b van Beek	17	22	13	-	3
D.Cleaver† b Bennett	29	35	23	1	1
T.C.Bruce* b Ravindra	1	3	3	-	-
J.A.Clarkson run out	30	41	30	1	-
K.Noema-Barnett c Younghusband b Ravindra	6	11	9	-	-
D.A.J.Bracewell c van Beek b Bennett	2	6	3	-	-
C.K.Leopard run out	7	10	4	1	-
A.Y.Patel not out	5	5	5	-	1
J.F.A.Field b Neesham	0	3	1	-	-
B.M.Tickner					
Extras (lb 9, w 3)	12				
TOTAL (20 overs) (9 wkts)	**136**	88			

Bowling	O	M	R	W
CENTRAL DISTRICTS				
Patel	4	0	32	0
Bracewell	4	0	40	1
Tickner	4	0	30	2
Field	4	0	32	2
Bruce	2	0	22	0
Noema-Barnett	2	0	17	1
WELLINGTON				
Bennett	4	0	20	2
van Beek	4	0	28	1
Neesham	4	0	28	1
Younghusband	4	0	29	1
Ravindra	4	0	22	2

Fall of Wickets	W	CD
1st	20	38
2nd	42	61
3rd	74	64
4th	124	97
5th	150	107
6th	154	116
7th	163	125
8th	-	131
9th	-	136
10th	-	-

OTAGO v AUCKLAND — Super Smash

at Molyneux Park, Alexandra on 28 December, 2020
Toss : Auckland. Umpires : J.A.K. Bromley & S.J. Kannan
***Otago won by 45 runs.** Points: Otago 4, Auckland 0*

OTAGO

	Runs	Mins	Balls	6s	4s
H.D.Rutherford c Lister b Pringle	25	17	13	2	3
N.T.Broom c Lister b Somerville	30	28	13	1	5
N.F.Kelly lbw b Phillips	27	32	18	-	4
L.C.Johnson c Phillips b Ferns	72	67	4	7	2
A.K.Kitchen lbw b Phillips	2	9	3	-	-
M.Renwick† c O'Donnell R.R. b Ferns	42	28	22	3	1
M.J.G.Rippon c Beghin b Ferns	10	10	7	-	2
D.N.Phillips not out	5	3	2	-	1
J.A.Duffy* not out	0	1	0	-	-
M.B.Bacon					
M.J.McClenaghan					
Extras (lb 1, w 3, nb 2)	6				
TOTAL (20 overs) (7 wkts)	**219**	99			

AUCKLAND

	Runs	Mins	Balls	6s	4s
G.K.Beghin c Phillips b Bacon	4	14	9	-	-
S.M.Solia c Kitchen b Bacon	30	52	29	-	2
W.T.O'Donnell c Kelly b Rippon	23	21	15	1	2
G.D.Phillips c Phillips b Kitchen	1	3	2	-	-
R.R.O'Donnell* c Kitchen b McClenaghan	18	25	12	1	1
B.J.Horne† run out	63	49	35	3	5
B.P.Rodden run out	6	19	7	-	-
W.E.R.Somerville not out	6	35	5	-	-
O.M.R.Pringle run out	1	4	1	-	-
D.K.Ferns c & b Duffy	0	8	1	-	-
B.G.Lister c Rippon b Bacon	1	4	3	-	-
Extras (b 1, lb 5, w 15)	21				
TOTAL (19.5 overs)	**174**	119			

Bowling	O	M	R	W
AUCKLAND				
Ferns	4	0	43	3
Somerville	4	0	51	1
Lister	4	0	52	0
Pringle	3	0	35	1
Phillips	4	0	22	2
O'Donnell R.R.	1	0	15	0
OTAGO				
Duffy	4	0	38	1
McClenaghan	4	0	50	1
Bacon	3.5	0	18	3
Kitchen	4	0	23	1
Rippon	4	0	39	1

Fall of Wickets	O	A
1st	41	15
2nd	67	61
3rd	98	65
4th	114	85
5th	191	106
6th	210	146
7th	214	169
8th	-	171
9th	-	171
10th	-	174

OTAGO v CANTERBURY — Super Smash

at Molyneux Park, Alexandra on 29 December, 2020
Toss : Canterbury. Umpires : J.A.K. Bromley & S.J. Kannan
***Canterbury won by 61 runs.** Points: Canterbury 4, Otago 0*

CANTERBURY

	Runs	Mins	Balls	6s	4s
C.J.Bowes b Rippon	72	68	48	3	6
K.J.McClure run out	40	37	26	1	4
J.C.T.Boyle c sub (D.N.Phillips) b Bacon	4	11	8	-	-
C.E.McConchie* c Johnson b McClenaghan	9	13	7	-	-
L.J.Carter not out	12	30	15	-	-
C.D.Fletcher† not out	35	25	18	2	3
M.W.Hay					
M.J.Henry					
T.D.Astle					
W.S.A.Williams					
E.J.Nuttall					
Extras (b 3, lb 3, w 5, nb 2)	13				
TOTAL (20 overs) (4 wkts)	**185**	93			

OTAGO

	Runs	Mins	Balls	6s	4s
N.T.Broom c Fletcher b Astle	41	44	28	1	3
H.D.Rutherford c Williams b Henry	13	8	8	1	1
N.F.Kelly c Fletcher b Nuttall	2	12	9	-	-
L.C.Johnson c Astle b McConchie	6	12	9	-	-
M.Renwick† c Boyle b Henry	22	30	25	-	-
A.K.Kitchen c Fletcher b Nuttall	6	8	6	-	1
M.J.G.Rippon c Carter b Nuttall	17	16	11	-	2
J.L.Finnie c McConchie b Henry	6	17	8	-	-
M.J.McClenaghan b Williams	8	5	4	-	-
M.B.Bacon run out	1	3	3	-	-
J.A.Duffy* not out	1	3	1	-	-
Extras (w 1)	1				
TOTAL (18.4 overs)	**124**	81			

Bowling	O	M	R	W
OTAGO				
Duffy	4	0	28	0
McClenaghan	3	0	29	1
Bacon	4	0	48	1
Kitchen	4	0	35	0
Rippon	4	0	22	1
Finnie	1	0	17	0
CANTERBURY				
McConchie	4	0	36	1
Henry	3.4	0	25	3
Nuttall	4	0	18	3
Williams	3	0	22	1
Astle	4	0	23	1

Fall of Wickets	*C*	*O*
1st	77	22
2nd	94	33
3rd	131	49
4th	135	73
5th	-	85
6th	-	103
7th	-	110
8th	-	120
9th	-	122
10th	-	124

CENTRAL DISTRICTS v NORTHERN DISTRICTS — Super Smash

at Pukekura Park, New Plymouth on 30 December, 2020
Toss : Central Districts. Umpires : J.M. Dempsey & A. Mehrotra
***Central Districts won by 45 runs.** Points: Central Districts 4, Northern Districts 0*

CENTRAL DISTRICTS

	Runs	Mins	Balls	6s	4s
G.H.Worker b Kuggeleijn	71	67	42	3	7
B.L.Wiggins c Seifert b Randell	1	5	2	-	-
D.Cleaver† c Gibson b Walker	27	26	21	2	2
T.C.Bruce* c Fisher b Walker	2	8	3	-	-
J.A.Clarkson b Fisher	25	13	13	1	3
D.A.J.Bracewell not out	55	39	25	4	4
K.Noema-Barnett c Gibson b Randell	12	17	10	-	2
C.K.Leopard not out	18	7	6	2	1
J.F.A.Field					
A.Y.Patel					
B.M.Tickner					
Extras (lb 5, w 5, nb 2)	12				
TOTAL (20 overs) (6 wkts)	**223**	93			

NORTHERN DISTRICTS

	Runs	Mins	Balls	6s	4s
K.D.Clarke b Field	6	18	8	-	1
T.L.Seifert† c Field b Tickner	11	14	15	-	2
D.G.Brownlie c Patel b Bracewell	7	9	7	-	1
A.P.Devcich* run out	102	72	49	9	7
H.R.Cooper c Cleaver b Field	5	19	11	-	1
B.R.Hampton c Bruce b Noema-Barnett	1	4	4	-	-
S.C.Kuggeleijn c Bruce b Noema-Barnett	18	19	12	1	2
Z.N.Gibson c Worker b Noema-Barnett	4	2	2	-	1
J.G.Walker run out	16	18	11	1	1
B.G.Randell not out	1	5	1	-	-
M.J.Fisher not out	1	2	1	-	-
Extras (lb 2, w 3, nb 1)	6				
TOTAL (20 overs) (9 wkts)	**178**	94			

Bowling	O	M	R	W
NORTHERN DISTRICTS				
Randell	4	0	34	2
Kuggeleijn	4	0	56	1
Fisher	4	0	54	1
Gibson	4	0	44	0
Walker	4	0	30	2
CENTRAL DISTRICTS				
Bracewell	4	0	32	1
Tickner	4	0	35	1
Field	4	0	26	2
Patel	4	0	46	0
Noema-Barnett	4	0	37	3

Fall of Wickets	*CD*	*ND*
1st	8	18
2nd	65	24
3rd	75	30
4th	114	55
5th	152	56
6th	198	103
7th	-	108
8th	-	171
9th	-	176
10th	-	-

CENTRAL DISTRICTS v AUCKLAND — Super Smash

at Pukekura Park, New Plymouth on 31 December, 2020
Toss : Central Districts. Umpires : K.D. Cotton & J.M. Dempsey
***Central Districts won by 70 runs.** Points: Central Districts 4, Auckland 0*

CENTRAL DISTRICTS

	Runs	Mins	Balls	6s	4s
G.H.Worker c Horne b Lister	79	69	46	4	7
B.L.Wiggins c O'Donnell W.T. b Somerville	0	3	2	-	-
D.Cleaver† c Rodden b Lister	9	10	10	-	2
T.C.Bruce* c Horne b Somerville	21	27	16	1	-
J.A.Clarkson run out	78	53	31	6	5
K.Noema-Barnett b Lister	7	13	8	-	1
D.A.J.Bracewell c O'Donnell R.R. b Phillips	13	6	5	1	1
C.K.Leopard not out	6	7	4	1	-
A.Y.Patel run out	1	2	1	-	-
J.F.A.Field not out	2	1	1	-	-
B.M.Tickner					
Extras (lb 4, w 2, nb 4)	10				
TOTAL (20 overs) (8 wkts) .	**226**	97			

AUCKLAND

	Runs	Mins	Balls	6s	4s
G.K.Beghin c Bracewell b Field ..	9	12	8	1	-
S.M.Solia b Tickner	8	7	5	1	-
W.T.O'Donnell c Worker b Patel	28	44	30	1	3
G.D.Phillips c Clarkson b Tickner	42	35	22	2	6
R.R.O'Donnell* c Tickner b Worker	39	24	21	1	6
B.J.Horne† run out	2	3	4	-	-
B.P.Rodden c Clarkson b Field ..	5	12	4	-	1
W.E.R.Somerville c Tickner b Leopard	12	11	6	1	1
O.M.R.Pringle not out	2	14	5	-	-
D.K.Ferns b Leopard	2	3	2	-	-
B.G.Lister b Clarkson	5	5	3	-	1
Extras (w 2)	2				
TOTAL (18.4 overs)	**156**	86			

Bowling	O	M	R	W
AUCKLAND				
Somerville	4	0	21	2
Lister	4	0	21	3
Pringle	2	0	37	0
Ferns	4	0	63	0
Phillips	4	0	51	1
Solia	2	0	29	0
CENTRAL DISTRICTS				
Bracewell	3	1	19	0
Tickner	3	0	23	2
Field	4	0	37	2
Noema-Barnett	2	0	24	0
Patel	3	0	27	1
Worker	1	0	12	1
Clarkson	1.4	0	10	1
Leopard	1	0	4	2

Fall of Wickets	CD	A
1st	1	16
2nd	19	22
3rd	92	88
4th	160	91
5th	190	93
6th	207	130
7th	223	136
8th	224	148
9th	-	151
10th	-	156

NORTHERN DISTRICTS v WELLINGTON — Super Smash

at Bay Oval, Mt Maunganui on 1 January, 2021 (d/n)
Toss : Wellington. Umpires : D.R. Morrow & T.J. Parlane
***Wellington won by 9 wickets.** Points: Wellington 4, Northern Districts 0*

NORTHERN DISTRICTS

	Runs	Mins	Balls	6s	4s
K.D.Clarke c Johnson b Neesham	7	18	5	-	1
T.L.Seifert† c Bracewell b Ravindra	46	59	46	1	4
D.G.Brownlie c Bennett b Neesham	8	14	11	-	1
A.P.Devcich* c Bracewell b van Beek	19	19	12	1	2
H.R.Cooper c Ravindra b Younghusband	9	16	10	-	-
B.R.Hampton c Allen b Bennett	28	28	22	-	3
S.C.Kuggeleijn not out	18	22	13	1	-
Z.N.Gibson not out	1	4	2	-	-
J.G.Walker					
B.G.Randell					
F.L.Walker					
Extras (b 1, lb 1, w 9, nb 1)	12				
TOTAL (20 overs) (6 wkts) .	**148**	92			

WELLINGTON

	Runs	Mins	Balls	6s	4s
D.P.Conway† c Gibson b Kuggeleijn	13	21	15	-	1
F.H.Allen not out	91	70	50	5	7
R.Ravindra not out	40	48	31	2	3
J.D.S.Neesham					
M.G.Bracewell*					
J.D.Gibson					
T.M.Johnson					
L.V.van Beek					
P.F.Younghusband					
B.V.Sears					
H.K.Bennett					
Extras (lb 7, w 1)	8				
TOTAL (16 overs) (1 wkt) ...	**152**	70			

Bowling	O	M	R	W
AUCKLAND				
Bennett	4	0	34	1
Sears	2	0	21	0
van Beek	4	0	31	1
Neesham	4	0	23	2
Younghusband	4	0	21	1
Ravindra	2	0	16	1
NORTHERN DISTRICTS				
Walker F.L.	4	0	29	0
Randell	2	0	27	0
Kuggeleijn	4	0	21	1
Gibson	2	0	30	0
Walker J.G.	3	0	31	0
Hampton	1	0	7	0

Fall of Wickets	ND	W
1st	29	42
2nd	45	-
3rd	82	-
4th	90	-
5th	114	-
6th	138	-
7th	-	-
8th	-	-
9th	-	-
10th	-	-

NORTHERN DISTRICTS v OTAGO — Super Smash

at Bay Oval, Mt Maunganui on 2 January, 2021 (d/n)
Toss : Otago. Umpires : T.J. Parlane & G.A Stirrat
***Otago won by 2 wickets.** Points: Otago 4, Northern Districts 0*

NORTHERN DISTRICTS

	Runs	Mins	Balls	6s	4s
K.D.Clarke st Renwick b Rippon	26	33	21	-	4
T.L.Seifert† c McClenaghan b Bacon	74	81	58	3	5
D.G.Brownlie c McClenaghan b Bacon	2	4	4	-	-
H.R.Cooper c Bacon b McClenaghan	3	10	5	-	-
A.P.Devcich* b Kitchen	4	9	7	-	-
B.R.Hampton c Renwick b Rippon	8	8	7	-	1
S.C.Kuggeleijn c Kelly b Bacon	14	18	10	1	-
F.L.Walker not out	3	9	4	-	-
Z.N.Gibson not out	3	6	4	-	-
J.G.Walker					
M.J.Fisher					
Extras (b 2, lb 4, w 10)	16				
TOTAL (20 overs) (7 wkts)	**153**	90			

OTAGO

	Runs	Mins	Balls	6s	4s
H.D.Rutherford run out	49	48	28	2	6
N.T.Broom c Walker F.L. b Kuggeleijn	6	15	7	-	1
L.C.Johnson c Seifert b Gibson	17	22	16	-	3
N.F.Kelly c Walker F.L. b Kuggeleijn	13	33	17	-	1
A.K.Kitchen c Seifert b Fisher	3	7	5	-	-
M.Renwick† run out	14	24	13	-	1
M.J.G.Rippon c Devcich b Gibson	6	9	6	-	1
D.N.Phillips not out	10	22	11	-	1
J.A.Duffy c Seifert b Gibson	0	2	3	-	-
M.J.McClenaghan not out	14	18	13	-	1
M.B.Bacon*					
Extras (lb 8, w 15, nb 1)	24				
TOTAL (19.4 overs) (8 wkts)	**156**	102			

Bowling	*O*	*M*	*R*	*W*
OTAGO				
Duffy	4	0	35	0
McClenaghan	4	0	29	1
Bacon	4	0	35	3
Kitchen	4	0	29	1
Rippon	4	0	19	2
NORTHERN DISTRICTS				
Kuggeleijn	4	0	45	2
Fisher	4	0	35	1
Walker F.L.	2	0	15	0
Walker J.G.	3	0	20	0
Gibson	4	0	17	3
Hampton	2.4	0	16	0

Fall of Wickets	***ND***	***O***
1st	84	29
2nd	87	79
3rd	96	85
4th	105	90
5th	116	123
6th	136	131
7th	144	132
8th	-	132
9th	-	-
10th	-	-

AUCKLAND v CANTERBURY — Super Smash

at Eden Park Outer Oval, Auckland on 3 January, 2021
Toss : Canterbury. Umpires : J.A.K. Bromley & A. Mehrotra
***Canterbury won by 10 wickets.** Points: Canterbury 4, Auckland 0*

AUCKLAND

	Runs	Mins	Balls	6s	4s
G.D.Phillips c Carter b Nuttall	1	3	2	-	-
M.S.Chapman c Carter b Williams	25	20	13	1	2
R.R.O'Donnell* c Williams b Davey	4	6	4	-	-
B.J.Horne† not out	13	18	7	1	-
S.M.Solia b Sheat	5	7	4	-	-
W.T.O'Donnell					
W.E.R.Somerville					
R.M.ter Braak					
L.J.Delport					
B.G.Lister					
D.K.Ferns					
Extras (lb 1, w 3)	4				
TOTAL (5 overs) (4 wkts)	**52**	28			

CANTERBURY

	Runs	Mins	Balls	6s	4s
K.J.McClure not out	15	22	13	1	1
C.J.Bowes not out	39	22	14	4	2
C.E.McConchie*					
L.J.Carter					
C.D.Fletcher†					
M.W.Hay					
S.B.Davey					
T.D.Astle					
W.S.A.Williams					
E.J.Nuttall					
F.W.Sheat					
Extras (w 1)	1				
TOTAL (4.3 overs) (0 wkts)	**55**	22			

Bowling	*O*	*M*	*R*	*W*
CANTERBURY				
Nuttall	1	0	9	1
Davey	1	0	8	1
Astle	1	0	15	0
Williams	1	0	9	1
Sheat	1	0	10	1
AUCKLAND				
Lister	1	0	2	0
ter Braak	1	0	15	0
Delport	1	0	10	0
Somerville	1	0	17	0
Ferns	0.3	0	11	0

Fall of Wickets	***A***	***C***
1st	7	-
2nd	16	-
3rd	37	-
4th	52	-
5th	-	-
6th	-	-
7th	-	-
8th	-	-
9th	-	-
10th	-	-

NORTHERN DISTRICTS v CENTRAL DISTRICTS Super Smash

at Seddon Park, Hamilton on 4 January, 2021 (d/n)
Toss : Northern Districts. Umpires : J.M. Dempsey & G.M. Walklin
***Northern Districts won by 6 wickets.** Points: Northern Districts 4, Central Districts 0*

CENTRAL DISTRICTS

	Runs	Mins	Balls	6s	4s
G.H.Worker* c Devcich b Walker J.G.	23	41	22	-	3
C.K.Leopard c Walker F.L. b Gibson	23	25	21	-	3
D.Cleaver† c Seifert b Hampton	17	27	20	-	2
J.A.Clarkson c Brownlie b Walker F.L.	0	5	5	-	-
D.A.J.Bracewell c Kuggeleijn b Hampton	9	24	13	-	1
K.Noema-Barnett c Seifert b Hampton	4	9	8	-	-
B.S.Smith not out	22	24	22	-	2
A.Y.Patel c Hampton b Walker F.L.	6	8	6	-	1
J.F.A.Field c Walker J.G. b Cooper	1	3	2	-	-
B.M.Tickner c Seifert b Cooper	0	3	1	-	-
J.R.Lennox					
Extras (b 7, lb 1, w 4)	12				
TOTAL (20 overs) (9 wkts)	**117**	87			

NORTHERN DISTRICTS

	Runs	Mins	Balls	6s	4s
K.D.Clarke c Worker b Tickner	24	14	12	-	5
T.L.Seifert† b Lennox	22	37	25	-	4
D.G.Brownlie c Worker b Lennox	0	5	3	-	-
H.R.Cooper c Smith b Tickner	23	36	28	-	1
A.P.Devcich* not out	35	36	22	2	3
B.R.Hampton not out	15	17	17	1	-
S.C.Kuggeleijn					
Z.N.Gibson					
J.G.Walker					
F.L.Walker					
M.J.Fisher					
Extras (lb 2, nb 1)	3				
TOTAL (17.4 overs) (4 wkts)	**122**	74			

Bowling	*O*	*M*	*R*	*W*
NORTHERN DISTRICTS				
Fisher	2	0	14	0
Kuggeleijn	2	0	16	0
Hampton	4	0	21	3
Gibson	2	0	10	1
Walker F.L.	4	0	20	2
Walker J.G.	4	0	14	1
Cooper	2	0	14	2
CENTRAL DISTRICTS				
Bracewell	1	0	12	0
Tickner	4	0	35	2
Patel	4	0	19	0
Lennox	4	0	17	2
Worker	1.4	0	18	0
Field	2	0	10	0
Noema-Barnett	1	0	9	0

Fall of Wickets	*CD*	*ND*
1st	41	32
2nd	60	36
3rd	63	63
4th	73	83
5th	85	-
6th	92	-
7th	104	-
8th	106	-
9th	117	-
10th	-	-

OTAGO v CENTRAL DISTRICTS Super Smash

at University of Otago Oval, Dunedin on 8 January, 2021
Toss : Otago. Umpires : J.A.K. Bromley & D.J. Walker
***Central Districts won by 53 runs.** Points: Central Districts 4, Otago 0*

CENTRAL DISTRICTS

	Runs	Mins	Balls	6s	4s
G.H.Worker* c McClenaghan b Bacon	106	86	58	8	6
B.L.Wiggins c Kelly b Rae	16	21	13	-	2
W.A.Young c Kitchen b McClenaghan	50	37	25	4	2
D.Cleaver† b Rippon	1	5	3	-	-
J.A.Clarkson b Duffy	33	28	17	3	1
D.A.J.Bracewell not out	6	7	3	-	1
C.K.Leopard not out	1	1	1	-	-
K.Noema-Barnett					
J.F.A.Field					
A.Y.Patel					
B.M.Tickner					
Extras (b 2, lb 1, w 7)	10				
TOTAL (20 overs) (5 wkts)	**223**	93			

OTAGO

	Runs	Mins	Balls	6s	4s
H.D.Rutherford c Wiggins b Bracewell	25	29	15	1	3
N.T.Broom c Young b Field	15	11	7	1	1
L.C.Johnson c Young b Patel	17	23	16	-	3
N.F.Kelly run out	75	61	54	3	7
M.Renwick† c Field b Bracewell	5	12	6	-	-
A.K.Kitchen b Patel	15	20	11	1	-
M.J.McClenaghan c Wiggins b Patel	0	1	1	-	-
M.J.G.Rippon c Cleaver b Tickner	5	11	7	-	-
J.A.Duffy* not out	6	9	3	-	1
M.B.Bacon					
M.D.Rae					
Extras (b 1, w 6)	7				
TOTAL (20 overs) (8 wkts)	**170**	90			

Bowling	*O*	*M*	*R*	*W*
OTAGO				
Kitchen	2	0	34	0
Duffy	4	0	44	1
McClenaghan	4	0	31	1
Bacon	3	0	42	1
Rae	3	0	34	1
Rippon	4	0	35	1
CENTRAL DISTRICTS				
Bracewell	4	0	41	2
Tickner	4	0	34	1
Field	4	0	30	1
Clarkson	2	0	12	0
Patel	4	0	34	3
Noema-Barnett	2	0	18	0

Fall of Wickets	*CD*	*O*
1st	48	28
2nd	135	59
3rd	141	65
4th	195	89
5th	222	132
6th		132
7th	-	154
8th	-	170
9th	-	-
10th	-	-

WELLINGTON v NORTHERN DISTRICTS — Super Smash

at Basin Reserve, Wellington on 9 January, 2021
Toss : Northern Districts. Umpires : B.F. Bowden & T.J. Parlane
Wellington won by 80 runs. *Points: Wellington 4, Northern Districts 0*

WELLINGTON

	Runs	Mins	Balls	6s	4s
F.H.Allen b Hampton	75	48	39	2	10
D.P.Conway st Seifert b Walker	45	61	35	-	5
T.A.Blundell† c Clarke b Kuggeleijn	22	33	20	1	-
J.D.S.Neesham c Hampton b Walker	5	8	5	-	1
M.G.Bracewell* c Devcich b Kuggeleijn	6	8	7	-	-
J.D.Gibson b Fisher	13	18	8	1	1
R.Ravindra run out	6	11	4	-	1
T.M.Johnson not out	1	4	1	-	-
L.V.van Beek not out	2	1	1	-	-
P.F.Younghusband					
H.K.Bennett					
Extras (lb 3, w 7)	10				
TOTAL (20 overs) (7 wkts)	**185**	98			

NORTHERN DISTRICTS

	Runs	Mins	Balls	6s	4s
K.D.Clarke b Bennett	0	2	2	-	-
T.L.Seifert† c Bracewell b Neesham	53	66	41	3	1
J.A.Raval c Gibson b Neesham	10	16	11	-	2
J.F.Carter c Blundell b Neesham	5	11	6	-	1
A.P.Devcich* c Johnson b Bracewell	8	10	6	1	-
M.J.Santner c Johnson b Bracewell	1	3	2	-	-
B.R.Hampton c van Beek b Bracewell	3	6	5	-	-
S.C.Kuggeleijn c Conway b Bracewell	2	5	5	-	-
Z.N.Gibson c Bennett b Ravindra	9	15	8	-	1
J.G.Walker c Bracewell b Bennett	5	8	7	-	-
M.J.Fisher not out	0	3	0	-	-
Extras (lb 2, w 7)	9				
TOTAL (15.2 overs)	**105**	74			

Bowling	O	M	R	W
NORTHERN DISTRICTS				
Kuggeleijn	4	0	36	2
Fisher	3	0	28	1
Santner	4	0	44	0
Gibson	2	0	21	0
Hampton	3	0	28	1
Walker	4	0	25	2
WELLINGTON				
Bennett	2.2	0	13	2
van Beek	2	0	18	0
Neesham	3	0	11	3
Younghusband	1	0	11	0
Bracewell	3	0	28	4
Ravindra	4	0	22	1

Fall of Wickets	W	ND
1st	117	0
2nd	133	19
3rd	143	32
4th	160	48
5th	161	51
6th	181	65
7th	183	68
8th	-	93
9th	-	103
10th	-	105

CANTERBURY v CENTRAL DISTRICTS — Super Smash

at Hagley Oval, Christchurch on 10 January, 2021 (d/n)
Toss : Central Districts. Umpires : J.M. Dempsey & D.J. Walker
Central Districts won by 18 runs. *Points: Central Districts 4, Canterbury 0*

CENTRAL DISTRICTS

	Runs	Mins	Balls	6s	4s
G.H.Worker* c Fletcher b Henry	32	45	31	-	3
D.Cleaver† c & b Henry	0	8	5	-	-
W.A.Young c Bowes b Nuttall	68	58	43	2	7
L.R.P.L.Taylor c Henry b Mitchell	10	9	7	1	-
J.A.Clarkson run out	26	33	15	1	1
D.A.J.Bracewell not out	37	27	16	2	3
K.Noema-Barnett not out	4	6	4	-	-
C.K.Leopard					
J.F.A.Field					
A.Y.Patel					
B.M.Tickner					
Extras (lb 2, w 6, nb 1)	9				
TOTAL (20 overs) (5 wkts)	**186**	94			

CANTERBURY

	Runs	Mins	Balls	6s	4s
C.J.Bowes c Taylor b Bracewell	0	2	1	-	-
K.J.McClure c Leopard b Bracewell	0	5	2	-	-
J.C.T.Boyle run out	15	19	13	-	2
D.J.Mitchell c Field b Clarkson	71	67	46	1	8
C.E.McConchie* c Field b Tickner	28	43	27	-	2
L.J.Carter not out	23	29	19	-	2
C.D.Fletcher† c Worker b Bracewell	17	19	11	-	2
M.J.Henry not out	7	2	2	1	-
T.D.Astle					
W.S.A.Williams					
E.J.Nuttall					
Extras (lb 2, w 4, nb 1)	7				
TOTAL (20 overs) (6 wkts)	**168**	94			

Bowling	O	M	R	W
CANTERBURY				
Nuttall	3	0	30	1
Henry	4	0	32	2
Williams	3	0	29	0
Mitchell	4	0	42	1
Astle	4	0	38	0
McConchie	2	0	13	0
CENTRAL DISTRICTS				
Bracewell	4	0	38	3
Patel	4	0	37	0
Field	3	0	27	0
Tickner	4	0	23	1
Noema-Barnett	3	0	30	0
Clarkson	2	0	11	1

Fall of Wickets	CD	C
1st	3	0
2nd	82	0
3rd	96	26
4th	124	117
5th	168	120
6th	-	158
7th	-	-
8th	-	-
9th	-	-
10th	-	-

CANTERBURY v AUCKLAND — Super Smash

at Hagley Oval, Christchurch on 11 January, 2021 (d/n)
Toss : Canterbury. Umpires : K.D. Cotton & D.J. Walker
Canterbury won by 6 runs. *Points: Canterbury 4, Auckland 0*

CANTERBURY

	Runs	Mins	Balls	6s	4s
K.J.McClure c O'Donnell R.R. b ter Braak	17	19	14	-	2
C.J.Bowes c Phillips b Delport	9	11	10	-	1
J.C.T.Boyle c O'Donnell W.T. b Ferns	44	56	34	-	2
D.J.Mitchell c Phillips b ter Braak	13	24	15	-	-
C.E.McConchie* lbw b Somerville	10	9	6	-	2
L.J.Carter c Horne b Ferns	42	36	28	2	1
C.D.Fletcher† not out	13	27	11	-	1
M.J.Henry not out	1	3	2	-	-
T.D.Astle					
W.S.A.Williams					
E.J.Nuttall					
Extras (lb 2, w 3)	5				
TOTAL (20 overs) (6 wkts)	**154**	94			

AUCKLAND

	Runs	Mins	Balls	6s	4s
M.J.Guptill c Boyle b Henry	6	7	7	-	1
S.M.Solia run out	55	55	42	-	6
G.D.Phillips c Boyle b Nuttall	4	6	6	-	1
W.T.O'Donnell not out	50	71	44	1	2
R.R.O'Donnell* c Boyle b Mitchell	2	6	4	-	-
B.J.Horne† b Mitchell	27	21	16	2	1
W.E.R.Somerville not out	1	1	1	-	-
R.M.ter Braak					
L.J.Delport					
B.G.Lister					
D.K.Ferns					
Extras (w 3)	3				
TOTAL (20 overs) (5 wkts)	**148**	85			

Bowling	*O*	*M*	*R*	*W*
AUCKLAND				
ter Braak	4	0	24	2
Lister	4	0	35	0
Delport	4	0	29	1
Somerville	4	0	38	1
Ferns	4	0	26	2
CANTERBURY				
Nuttall	3	0	31	1
Henry	4	0	26	1
McConchie	4	0	21	0
Astle	4	0	29	0
Mitchell	3	0	21	2
Williams	2	0	20	0

Fall of Wickets	***C***	***A***
1st	17	15
2nd	29	20
3rd	69	97
4th	82	106
5th	102	147
6th	148	-
7th	-	-
8th	-	-
9th	-	-
10th	-	-

OTAGO v WELLINGTON — Super Smash

at University of Otago Oval, Dunedin on 14 January, 2021
Toss : Otago. Umpires : C.M. Brown & S.B. Haig
Wellington won by 5 wickets. *Points: Wellington 4, Otago 0*

OTAGO

	Runs	Mins	Balls	6s	4s
H.D.Rutherford c Younghusband b Neesham	9	11	9	-	2
N.T.Broom c Bracewell b van Beek	57	78	48	1	5
N.F.Kelly c Gibson b Neesham	1	11	5	-	-
L.C.Johnson run out	6	4	3	-	1
M.Renwick† c Gibson b Younghusband	11	16	12	-	1
A.K.Kitchen not out	57	52	32	5	2
M.J.G.Rippon not out	16	18	11	-	3
M.B.Bacon					
M.J.McClenaghan					
J.A.Duffy*					
M.D.Rae					
Extras (lb 5, w 5)	10				
TOTAL (20 overs) (5 wkts)	**167**	96			

WELLINGTON

	Runs	Mins	Balls	6s	4s
F.H.Allen not out	92	83	43	8	5
D.P.Conway b McClenaghan	18	24	15	1	3
R.Ravindra c sub (D.N.Phillips) b Bacon	13	7	6	1	1
T.A.Blundell† c Kelly b Rippon	8	14	10	-	-
J.D.S.Neesham c Renwick b McClenaghan	2	6	4	-	-
M.G.Bracewell* c Kelly b Rippon	26	24	16	-	4
J.D.Gibson not out	3	5	5	-	-
L.V.van Beek					
P.F.Younghusband					
B.V.Sears					
H.K.Bennett					
Extras (lb 1, w 5)	6				
TOTAL (16.3 overs) (5 wkts)	**168**	83			

Bowling	*O*	*M*	*R*	*W*
WELLINGTON				
Bennett	4	0	31	0
van Beek	4	0	24	1
Neesham	4	0	38	2
Ravindra	2	0	21	0
Younghusband	4	0	38	1
Sears	2	0	10	0
OTAGO				
McClenaghan	4	0	37	2
Duffy	3	0	36	0
Rae	1.3	0	31	0
Bacon	3	0	32	1
Rippon	4	0	23	2
Kitchen	1	0	8	0

Fall of Wickets	***O***	***W***
1st	18	59
2nd	30	72
3rd	41	99
4th	68	106
5th	137	162
6th	-	-
7th	-	-
8th	-	-
9th	-	-
10th	-	-

CANTERBURY v NORTHERN DISTRICTS — Super Smash

at Hagley Oval, Christchurch on 15 January, 2021
Toss : Northern Districts. Umpires : J.A.K. Bromley & T.J. Parlane
***Canterbury won by 6 wickets.** Points: Canterbury 4, Northern Districts 0*

NORTHERN DISTRICTS

	Runs	Mins	Balls	6s	4s
J.A.Raval c Williams b Mitchell	70	87	55	2	6
T.L.Seifert c Mitchell b Henry	1	9	4	-	-
A.P.Devcich* st Fletcher b McConchie	35	23	22	1	4
J.F.Carter c Williams b Astle	2	5	4	-	-
B.R.Hampton c Carter b Astle	7	13	12	-	-
M.J.Santner c Nuttall b Williams	23	30	19	1	1
P.D.Bocock† c Astle b Mitchell	2	7	3	-	-
S.C.Kuggeleijn not out	2	5	2	-	-
A.Verma not out	1	2	1	-	-
J.G.Walker					
F.L.Walker					
Extras (b 3, lb 1, w 1, nb 2)	7				
TOTAL (20 overs) (7 wkts)	**150**	92			

CANTERBURY

	Runs	Mins	Balls	6s	4s
C.J.Bowes c Carter b Walker F.L.	0	1	2	-	-
K.J.McClure c Devcich b Kuggeleijn	8	16	6	-	1
J.C.T.Boyle c Hampton b Walker F.L.	3	8	8	-	-
D.J.Mitchell c Hampton b Walker F.L.	69	75	47	1	2
C.E.McConchie* not out	56	71	48	1	4
L.J.Carter not out	4	2	1	-	1
C.D.Fletcher†					
M.J.Henry					
T.D.Astle					
W.S.A.Williams					
E.J.Nuttall					
Extras (w 12)	12				
TOTAL (18.5 overs) (4 wkts)	**152**	87			

Bowling	O	M	R	W
CANTERBURY				
Nuttall	1	0	8	0
Henry	4	0	33	1
McConchie	4	0	29	1
Mitchell	4	0	30	2
Williams	3	0	34	1
Astle	4	0	12	2
NORTHERN DISTRICTS				
Walker F.L.	3.5	0	20	3
Verma	3	0	27	0
Kuggeleijn	4	0	35	1
Santner	4	0	38	0
Walker J.G.	2	0	10	0
Hampton	2	0	22	0

Fall of Wickets

	ND	C
1st	9	0
2nd	61	8
3rd	66	15
4th	89	148
5th	144	-
6th	146	-
7th	148	-
8th	-	-
9th	-	-
10th	-	-

CANTERBURY v WELLINGTON — Super Smash

at Hagley Oval, Christchurch on 16 January, 2021
Toss : Wellington. Umpires : J.A.K. Bromley & T.J. Parlane
***Canterbury won by 4 wickets.** Points: Canterbury 4, Wellington 0*

WELLINGTON

	Runs	Mins	Balls	6s	4s
F.H.Allen c Bowes b Henry	27	27	16	2	2
D.P.Conway b McConchie	0	3	3	-	-
R.Ravindra b McConchie	4	11	3	-	1
T.A.Blundell† c Bowes b Henry	6	12	8	-	1
J.D.S.Neesham c Bowes b Williams	49	54	38	2	2
M.G.Bracewell* retired hurt	31	36	32	-	2
J.D.Gibson c Mitchell b Coburn	0	6	1	-	-
T.M.Johnson c Williams b Mitchell	3	15	3	-	-
L.V.van Beek not out	29	12	10	1	4
P.F.Younghusband not out	2	3	2	-	-
H.K.Bennett					
B.V.Sears					
Extras (lb 1, w 2)	3				
TOTAL (20 overs) (7 wkts)	**154**	90			

CANTERBURY

	Runs	Mins	Balls	6s	4s
K.J.McClure c Allen b Bennett	4	3	4	-	1
C.J.Bowes c Blundell b van Beek	7	12	7	-	1
J.C.T.Boyle c Sears b Ravindra	39	60	33	-	3
D.J.Mitchell lbw b Sears	34	29	23	1	4
C.E.McConchie* not out	48	56	34	-	5
L.J.Carter c Blundell b Bennett	6	14	8	-	-
C.D.Fletcher† run out	10	19	9	-	1
M.J.Henry not out	0	1	0	-	-
T.D.Astle					
W.S.A.Williams					
B.P.Coburn					
Extras (lb 1, w 6)	7				
TOTAL (19.4 overs) (6 wkts)	**155**	98			

Bowling	O	M	R	W
CANTERBURY				
McConchie	4	0	14	2
Henry	4	0	46	2
Mitchell	3	0	33	1
Astle	4	0	25	0
Coburn	4	0	26	1
Williams	1	0	9	1
WELLINGTON				
Bennett	4	0	29	2
Ravindra	3	0	29	1
van Beek	4	0	26	1
Neesham	3.4	0	30	0
Allen	1	0	8	0
Younghusband	2	0	19	0
Sears	2	0	13	1

Fall of Wickets

	W	C
1st	5	5
2nd	33	17
3rd	39	78
4th	40	109
5th	108	128
6th	121	154
7th	146	-
8th	-	-
9th	-	-
10th	-	-

Bracewell retired hurt at 108-4 and was replaced by Sears (concussion substitute)

AUCKLAND v NORTHERN DISTRICTS — Super Smash

at Eden Park Outer Oval, Auckland on 17 January, 2021
Toss : Northern Districts. Umpires : C.M. Brown & W.R. Knights
***Northern Districts won by 5 wickets (D/L).** Points: Northern Districts 4, Auckland 0*

AUCKLAND

	Runs	Mins	Balls	6s	4s
M.J.Guptill c de Grandhomme b Southee	9	5	6	-	2
S.M.Solia c Southee b Santner	10	30	11	-	1
G.D.Phillips c Seifert b Kuggeleijn	68	43	3	8	1
W.T.O'Donnell b Verma	4	6	3	-	1
R.R.O'Donnell* not out	20	36	13	1	1
B.J.Horne† c Seifert b Kuggeleijn	4	3	3	-	-
K.A.Jamieson b Southee	18	16	14	1	-
W.E.R.Somerville not out	1	3	1	-	-
R.M.ter Braak					
L.J.Delport					
B.G.Lister					
Extras (lb 2, w 4)	6				
TOTAL (14 overs) (6 wkts)	**140**	73			

NORTHERN DISTRICTS

	Runs	Mins	Balls	6s	4s
J.A.Raval lbw b Somerville	14	16	11	1	1
T.L.Seifert† c Jamieson b ter Braak	14	12	7	1	2
A.P.Devcich* c Jamieson b Somerville	4	16	5	-	-
C.de Grandhomme c Guptill b Somerville	12	2	3	2	-
J.F.Carter c Guptill b Jamieson	14	22	15	-	-
M.J.Santner not out	39	21	16	3	2
S.C.Kuggeleijn not out	5	8	3	-	1
T.G.Southee					
A.Verma					
J.G.Walker					
T.A.Boult					
Extras (b 1, lb 2, w 3, nb 1)	7				
TOTAL (9.5 overs) (5 wkts)	**109**	49			

Bowling	*O*	*M*	*R*	*W*
NORTHERN DISTRICTS				
Boult	3	0	21	0
Southee	3	0	30	2
Verma	3	0	29	1
Santner	2	0	17	1
Kuggeleijn	3	0	41	2
AUCKLAND				
Jamieson	2	0	23	1
Lister	2	0	28	0
ter Braak	1.5	0	20	1
Somerville	2	0	18	3
Delport	2	0	17	0

Fall of Wickets	***A***	***ND***
1st	13	28
2nd	61	34
3rd	69	46
4th	99	56
5th	103	84
6th	136	-
7th	-	-
8th	-	-
9th	-	-
10th	-	-

CENTRAL DISTRICTS v OTAGO — Super Smash

at Pukekura Park, New Plymouth on 18 January, 2021
Toss : Central Districts. Umpires : S.B. Haig & E.D. Sanders
***Central Districts won by 5 wickets (D/L).** Points: Central Districts 4, Otago 0*

OTAGO

	Runs	Mins	Balls	6s	4s
H.D.Rutherford c Bracewell b Tickner	4	9	6	-	-
N.T.Broom c Field b Patel	42	38	30	2	4
N.F.Kelly c Bruce b Clarkson	27	31	18	1	4
L.C.Johnson c Cleaver b Clarkson	0	4	2	-	-
A.K.Kitchen run out	41	32	22	2	4
M.Renwick† lbw b Tickner	5	11	8	-	-
M.J.G.Rippon c Young b Tickner	10	14	10	-	1
N.G.Smith c Field b Bracewell	5	6	3	-	1
M.J.McClenaghan not out	1	5	3	-	-
J.A.Duffy* run out	0	2	0	-	-
M.D.Rae					
Extras (b 6, lb 1, w 3)	10				
TOTAL (17 overs) (9 wkts)	**145**	78			

CENTRAL DISTRICTS

	Runs	Mins	Balls	6s	4s
G.H.Worker c Rutherford b Smith	20	14	15	1	3
D.Cleaver† b Smith	19	23	11	-	3
W.A.Young c Johnson b Rippon	27	27	14	1	3
L.R.P.L.Taylor not out	48	56	27	3	3
T.C.Bruce* c Duffy b Smith	6	8	6	-	1
J.A.Clarkson c Duffy b Smith	31	26	19	1	5
D.A.J.Bracewell not out	1	4	2	-	-
K.Noema-Barnett					
J.F.A.Field					
A.Y.Patel					
B.M.Tickner					
Extras (lb 3, w 3)	6				
TOTAL (15.4 overs) (5 wkts)	**158**	79			

Bowling	*O*	*M*	*R*	*W*
CENTRAL DISTRICTS				
Bracewell	4	0	33	1
Tickner	4	0	23	3
Field	2	0	31	0
Patel	3	0	11	1
Clarkson	3	0	30	2
Worker	1	0	10	0
OTAGO				
McClenaghan	3.4	0	36	0
Duffy	3	0	34	0
Smith	4	0	32	4
Rippon	2	0	20	1
Rae	2	0	23	0
Kitchen	1	0	10	0

Fall of Wickets	***O***	***CD***
1st	15	27
2nd	77	46
3rd	77	80
4th	78	89
5th	105	149
6th	133	-
7th	136	-
8th	142	-
9th	145	-
10th	-	-

NORTHERN DISTRICTS v CANTERBURY — Super Smash

at Seddon Park, Hamilton on 21 January, 2021 (d/n)
Toss : Northern Districts. Umpires : J.M. Dempsey & S.B. Haig
***Northern Districts won by 8 wickets (D/L).** Points: Northern Districts 4, Canterbury 0*

CANTERBURY

	Runs	Mins	Balls	6s	4s
K.J.McClure c Devcich b Verma	10	20	12	-	2
C.J.Bowes b Southee	12	9	7	1	1
J.C.T.Boyle c Seifert b Boult	1	4	5	-	-
D.J.Mitchell c Seifert b Walker	8	18	7	-	1
C.E.McConchie* c Hampton b Kuggeleijn	28	50	30	-	3
L.J.Carter c & b Walker	1	3	2	-	-
C.D.Fletcher† c Seifert b Boult	0	3	2	-	-
T.D.Astle c Clarke b Verma	36	25	22	1	5
M.J.Henry c Hampton b Kuggeleijn	6	13	7	-	-
W.S.A.Williams not out	8	19	12	-	-
E.J.Nuttall c Southee b Hampton	5	10	9	-	-
Extras (lb 1, w 2)	3				
TOTAL (19.1 overs)	**118**	90			

NORTHERN DISTRICTS

	Runs	Mins	Balls	6s	4s
T.L.Seifert† b Mitchell	24	39	18	1	3
K.D.Clarke c Astle b Nuttall	16	13	8	1	2
K.S.Williamson not out	34	41	27	-	5
C.de Grandhomme not out	14	14	9	1	1
A.P.Devcich*					
B.R.Hampton					
S.C.Kuggeleijn					
T.G.Southee					
A.Verma					
J.G.Walker					
T.A.Boult					
Extras (lb 1, w 4)	5				
TOTAL (10.2 overs) (2 wkts)	**93**	54			

Bowling	O	M	R	W
NORTHERN DISTRICTS				
Southee	4	0	18	1
Boult	4	0	29	2
Verma	4	0	21	2
Kuggeleijn	4	0	26	2
Walker	3	0	23	2
Hampton	0.1	0	0	1
CANTERBURY				
Nuttall	3	0	23	1
Henry	2	0	25	0
Astle	2	0	16	0
McConchie	1	0	12	0
Mitchell	2	0	12	1
Williams	0.2	0	4	0

Fall of Wickets	C	ND
1st	18	28
2nd	19	70
3rd	24	-
4th	44	-
5th	46	-
6th	47	-
7th	95	-
8th	100	-
9th	108	-
10th	118	-

AUCKLAND v CENTRAL DISTRICTS — Super Smash

at Eden Park Outer Oval, Auckland on 23 January, 2021
Toss : Central Districts. Umpires : C.M. Brown & W.R. Knights
***Auckland won by 17 runs.** Points: Auckland 4, Central Districts 0*

AUCKLAND

	Runs	Mins	Balls	6s	4s
M.J.Guptill c Cleaver b Tickner	29	52	31	2	-
S.M.Solia c Cleaver b Tickner	21	21	13	-	5
G.D.Phillips c Field b Bracewell	1	5	5	-	-
M.S.Chapman c Field b Bracewell	73	58	34	3	9
R.R.O'Donnell* c Bruce b Clarkson	61	42	34	3	5
B.J.Horne† c Bracewell b Clarkson	2	10	3	-	-
K.A.Jamieson not out	0	1	0	-	-
R.M.ter Braak					
W.E.R.Somerville					
L.J.Delport					
B.G.Lister					
Extras (lb 4, w 8)	12				
TOTAL (20 overs) (6 wkts)	**199**	95			

CENTRAL DISTRICTS

	Runs	Mins	Balls	6s	4s
G.H.Worker c Guptill b Delport	11	20	11	-	1
D.Cleaver† b Delport	11	16	10	-	2
W.A.Young c Lister b Somerville	37	50	29	3	-
L.R.P.L.Taylor run out	2	9	3	-	-
T.C.Bruce* c Lister b ter Braak	52	42	35	1	7
J.A.Clarkson run out	3	9	3	-	-
K.Noema-Barnett lbw b ter Braak	9	10	6	1	-
D.A.J.Bracewell not out	32	26	14	3	2
A.Y.Patel not out	7	20	10	-	-
J.F.A.Field					
B.M.Tickner					
Extras (lb 6, w 11, nb 1)	18				
TOTAL (20 overs) (7 wkts)	**182**	103			

Bowling	O	M	R	W
CENTRAL DISTRICTS				
Bracewell	4	0	22	2
Patel	4	0	37	0
Tickner	4	0	32	2
Field	3	0	44	0
Clarkson	4	0	46	2
Noema-Barnett	1	0	14	0
AUCKLAND				
ter Braak	4	0	31	2
Jamieson	4	0	25	0
Lister	4	0	49	0
Delport	4	0	28	2
Somerville	4	0	43	1

Fall of Wickets	A	CD
1st	41	24
2nd	42	27
3rd	96	39
4th	181	115
5th	199	122
6th	199	124
7th	-	135
8th	-	-
9th	-	-
10th	-	-

WELLINGTON v OTAGO — Super Smash

at Basin Reserve, Wellington on 24 January, 2021
Toss : Wellington. Umpires : C.A. Black & T.J. Parlane
***Wellington won by 4 wickets.** Points: Wellington 4, Otago 0*

OTAGO

	Runs	Mins	Balls	6s	4s
H.D.Rutherford c Gibson b Sears	10	13	9	-	1
N.T.Broom c Blundell b Sears	6	15	8	-	1
N.F.Kelly run out	11	34	15	-	2
J.L.Finnie c Gibson b Sears	10	10	6	1	1
D.N.Phillips c Blundell b Sears ...	2	10	5	-	-
A.K.Kitchen c Blundell b Younghusband	28	29	22	2	1
M.J.G.Rippon c Gibson b van Beek	22	33	23	-	1
N.G.Smith c Gibson b Ravindra	16	21	16	-	-
M.W.Chu† not out	21	19	12	-	3
M.J.McClenaghan run out	4	12	4	-	-
J.A.Duffy*					
Extras (b 4, w 3)	7				
TOTAL (20 overs) (9 wkts) .	**137**	102			

WELLINGTON

	Runs	Mins	Balls	6s	4s
F.H.Allen b McClenaghan	4	2	3	-	1
D.P.Conway c Rutherford b McClenaghan	9	13	5	-	2
R.Ravindra run out	29	44	20	2	2
T.A.Blundell† c Finnie b McClenaghan	19	15	11	-	4
M.G.Bracewell* not out	47	62	43	1	3
J.D.Gibson c Smith b Duffy	6	18	10	-	-
T.M.Johnson c Duffy b Smith	2	14	7	-	-
L.V.van Beek not out	17	11	10	-	3
P.F.Younghusband					
B.V.Sears					
H.K.Bennett					
Extras (b 2, w 4, nb 1)	7				
TOTAL (18 overs) (6 wkts) .	**140**	91			

Bowling	*O*	*M*	*R*	*W*
WELLINGTON				
Bennett	4	0	27	0
van Beek	4	0	33	1
Sears	4	0	21	4
Ravindra	3	0	22	1
Bracewell	2	0	14	0
Younghusband	3	0	16	1
OTAGO				
McClenaghan	4	0	36	3
Smith	4	0	36	1
Duffy	3	0	24	1
Kitchen	2	0	18	0
Rippon	4	0	17	0
Finnie	1	0	7	0

Fall of Wickets	**O**	**W**
1st	16	4
2nd	16	19
3rd	28	51
4th	38	82
5th	51	106
6th	82	118
7th	105	-
8th	112	-
9th	137	-
10th	-	-

WELLINGTON v CANTERBURY — Super Smash

at Basin Reserve, Wellington on 25 January, 2021
Toss : Wellington. Umpires : T.J. Parlane & D.J. Walker
***Wellington won by 7 wickets.** Points: Wellington 4, Canterbury 0*

CANTERBURY

	Runs	Mins	Balls	6s	4s
C.J.Bowes c Ravindra b Sears .	44	45	29	-	8
K.J.McClure c Blundell b Bennett	36	28	15	3	3
J.C.T.Boyle c Conway b Sears .	14	32	18	-	-
D.J.Mitchell c Blundell b Bennett	11	26	16	-	-
C.E.McConchie* c Blundell b Sears	0	3	3	-	-
L.J.Carter run out	19	37	18	1	-
C.D.Fletcher† c Younghusband b Bracewell	3	8	5	-	-
T.D.Astle not out	17	23	15	-	1
M.J.Henry not out	1	1	1	-	-
W.S.A.Williams					
E.J.Nuttall					
Extras (b 1, lb 1, w 6)	8				
TOTAL (20 overs) (7 wkts) .	**153**	104			

WELLINGTON

	Runs	Mins	Balls	6s	4s
F.H.Allen c Henry b Nuttall	4	18	9	-	-
D.P.Conway c Boyle b Henry ...	50	50	40	-	7
T.A.Blundell† not out	62	76	42	16	
T.M.Johnson c Henry b Astle ...	24	30	22	-	2
M.G.Bracewell* not out	5	13	5	-	-
R.Ravindra					
J.D.Gibson					
L.V.van Beek					
P.F.Younghusband					
B.V.Sears					
H.K.Bennett					
Extras (b 2, lb 3, w 4)	9				
TOTAL (19.4 overs) (3 wkts)	**154**	**94**			

Bowling	*O*	*M*	*R*	*W*
WELLINGTON				
Bennett	4	0	32	2
van Beek	4	0	26	0
Sears	4	0	34	3
Ravindra	2	0	18	0
Younghusband	3	0	16	0
Bracewell	3	0	25	1
CANTERBURY				
Henry	4	0	22	1
McConchie	4	0	24	0
Nuttall	3	0	27	1
Mitchell	3.4	0	32	0
Astle	3	0	22	1
Williams	2	0	22	0

Fall of Wickets	**C**	**W**
1st	59	21
2nd	90	81
3rd	107	134
4th	109	-
5th	118	-
6th	125	-
7th	150	-
8th	-	-
9th	-	-
10th	-	-

NORTHERN DISTRICTS v AUCKLAND — Super Smash

at Seddon Park, Hamilton on 29 January, 2021
Toss : Northern Districts. Umpires : B.F. Bowden & J.M. Dempsey
Northern Districts won by 3 wickets. *Points: Northern Districts 4, Auckland 0*

AUCKLAND

	Runs	Mins	Balls	6s	4s
M.J.Guptill c Devcich b Boult	2	7	6	-	-
S.M.Solia c Seifert b Verma	18	27	13	-	3
G.D.Phillips b Southee	4	4	2	-	1
M.S.Chapman c Seifert b Southee	69	60	51	4	6
R.R.O'Donnell* not out	42	63	33	2	1
B.J.Horne† not out	19	18	15	1	1
K.A.Jamieson					
W.E.R.Somerville					
D.K.Ferns					
L.J.Delport					
R.M.ter Braak					
Extras (lb 7, w 1)	8				
TOTAL (20 overs) (4 wkts)	**162**	91			

NORTHERN DISTRICTS

	Runs	Mins	Balls	6s	4s
T.L.Seifert† c Ferns b ter Braak	13	14	10	-	3
K.D.Clarke c sub (J.R.M.Bassett-Graham) b Jamieson	6	19	6	-	1
K.S.Williamson not out	79	88	55	3	5
C.de Grandhomme c Chapman b Ferns	19	13	8	2	1
A.P.Devcich* c O'Donnell b Ferns	4	7	6	-	-
M.J.Santner b ter Braak	7	16	8	-	1
S.C.Kuggeleijn c sub (B.G.Lister) b Ferns	10	13	9	-	1
T.G.Southee c Horne b ter Braak	24	27	15	2	1
A.Verma not out	0	1	0	-	-
I.S.Sodhi					
T.A.Boult					
Extras (b 1, w 2, nb 1)	4				
TOTAL (20 overs) (7 wkts)	**166**	99			

Bowling	O	M	R	W
NORTHERN DISTRICTS				
Southee	4	0	29	2
Boult	4	0	28	1
Kuggeleijn	1	0	11	0
Verma	3	0	31	1
Sodhi	4	0	24	0
Santner	4	0	32	0
AUCKLAND				
Delport	3	0	32	0
Jamieson	4	0	32	1
ter Braak	4	0	26	3
Ferns	4	0	39	3
Somerville	3	0	21	0
Phillips	2	0	15	0

Fall of Wickets	*A*	*ND*
1st	9	16
2nd	13	24
3rd	44	57
4th	133	64
5th	-	81
6th	-	112
7th	-	162
8th	-	-
9th	-	-
10th	-	-

CANTERBURY v OTAGO — Super Smash

at Hagley Oval, Christchurch on 30 January, 2021 (d/n)
Toss : Canterbury. Umpires : J.A.K. Bromley & D.J. Walker
Canterbury won by 6 wickets. *Points: Canterbury 4, Otago 0*

OTAGO

	Runs	Mins	Balls	6s	4s
H.D.Rutherford c Mitchell b Williams	23	19	15	-	4
N.T.Broom c Boyle b Astle	48	58	37	-	7
N.F.Kelly c Bowes b Astle	1	10	3	-	-
J.L.Finnie c Nuttall b Henry	26	16	15	1	2
A.K.Kitchen c Bowes b Williams	36	38	30	1	3
D.N.Phillips not out	22	30	19	-	1
M.J.G.Rippon not out	4	3	1	-	1
M.W.Chu†					
J.A.Duffy*					
M.J.McClenaghan					
N.G.Smith					
Extras (lb 1, w 1)	2				
TOTAL (20 overs) (5 wkts)	**162**	89			

CANTERBURY

	Runs	Mins	Balls	6s	4s
C.J.Bowes c McClenaghan b Kitchen	31	34	19	-	5
K.J.McClure run out	33	22	19	1	5
J.C.T.Boyle c Broom b Rippon	14	25	19	-	-
D.J.Mitchell st Chu b Kitchen	10	24	11	-	-
C.E.McConchie* not out	50	46	36	2	3
L.J.Carter not out	16	35	10	-	2
C.D.Fletcher†					
M.J.Henry					
T.D.Astle					
W.S.A.Williams					
E.J.Nuttall					
Extras (lb 4, w 5)	9				
TOTAL (19 overs) (4 wkts)	**163**	94			

Bowling	O	M	R	W
CANTERBURY				
Henry	4	0	29	1
Nuttall	4	0	40	0
Mitchell	3	0	30	0
Williams	2	0	18	2
Astle	4	0	18	2
McConchie	3	0	26	0
OTAGO				
Duffy	4	0	28	0
McClenaghan	4	0	29	0
Smith	3	0	38	0
Kitchen	4	0	38	2
Rippon	4	0	26	1

Fall of Wickets	*O*	*C*
1st	42	45
2nd	53	74
3rd	91	88
4th	108	100
5th	155	-
6th	-	-
7th	-	-
8th	-	-
9th	-	-
10th	-	-

WELLINGTON v CENTRAL DISTRICTS — Super Smash

at Basin Reserve, Wellington on 31 January, 2021
Toss : Central Districts. Umpires : C.M. Brown & T.J. Parlane
***Wellington won by 8 wickets.** Points: Wellington 4, Central Districts 0*

CENTRAL DISTRICTS	Runs	Mins	Balls	6s	4s
G.H.Worker c van Beek b Bracewell	49	75	45	-	6
D.Cleaver† c Sears b van Beek	10	16	9	-	2
W.A.Young c Bennett b van Beek	1	5	2	-	-
L.R.P.L.Taylor c Blundell b Bennett	0	6	1	-	-
T.C.Bruce* c Johnson b Gibson	5	12	8	-	-
J.A.Clarkson c van Beek b Sears	27	21	19	1	2
D.A.J.Bracewell not out	53	34	27	3	4
A.Y.Patel c Blundell b van Beek	4	13	6	-	-
J.F.A.Field not out	8	8	3	-	2
B.M.Tickner					
J.R.Lennox					
Extras (b 1, w 6)	7				
TOTAL (20 overs) (7 wkts)	**164**	96			

WELLINGTON	Runs	Mins	Balls	6s	4s
F.H.Allen b Lennox	66	42	27	3	9
D.P.Conway not out	69	75	50	1	11
T.A.Blundell† c Young b Field	24	20	14	-	4
T.M.Johnson not out	7	7	11	-	1
M.G.Bracewell*					
J.D.Gibson					
F.J.Colson					
L.V.van Beek					
P.F.Younghusband					
B.V.Sears					
H.K.Bennett					
Extras (w 4)	4				
TOTAL (16.2 overs) (2 wkts)	**170**	75			

Bowling	O	M	R	W
WELLINGTON				
Bennett	4	0	44	1
van Beek	4	0	35	3
Sears	4	1	18	1
Gibson	2	0	20	1
Younghusband	2	0	20	0
Bracewell	4	0	26	1
CENTRAL DISTRICTS				
Bracewell	3	0	29	0
Tickner	3	0	41	0
Field	2	0	22	1
Patel	3.2	0	37	0
Lennox	3	0	15	1
Clarkson	2	0	26	0

Fall of Wickets	*CD*	*W*
1st	19	107
2nd	27	148
3rd	27	-
4th	41	-
5th	87	-
6th	105	-
7th	132	-
8th	-	-
9th	-	-
10th	-	-

AUCKLAND v OTAGO — Super Smash

at Eden Park Outer Oval, Auckland on 1 February, 2021
Toss : Auckland. Umpires : B.F. Bowden & D.J. Walker
***Auckland won by 103 runs.** Points: Auckland 4, Otago 0*

AUCKLAND	Runs	Mins	Balls	6s	4s
S.M.Solia c & b Smith	27	12	15	1	4
G.D.Phillips c Kelly b Rippon	20	31	17	2	-
W.T.O'Donnell c Duffy b McClenaghan	40	48	30	2	2
M.S.Chapman c Rippon b Rae	36	39	23	1	4
R.R.O'Donnell* c Kitchen b Smith	21	19	14	1	1
B.J.Horne† c Rutherford b McClenaghan	12	15	9	1	-
K.A.Jamieson not out	21	13	12	1	1
W.E.R.Somerville run out	0	5	0	-	-
R.M.ter Braak not out	0	1	0	-	-
D.K.Ferns					
L.J.Delport					
Extras (w 6)	6				
TOTAL (20 overs) (7 wkts)	**183**	95			

OTAGO	Runs	Mins	Balls	6s	4s
H.D.Rutherford b Jamieson	4	4	6	-	1
N.T.Broom c Horne b ter Braak	0	6	1	-	-
N.F.Kelly b Somerville	38	43	29	2	4
J.L.Finnie c Ferns b ter Braak	3	9	4	-	-
A.K.Kitchen c O'Donnell W.T. b Delport	4	7	4	-	1
M.J.G.Rippon c O'Donnell W.T. b Ferns	8	16	8	-	1
N.G.Smith run out	0	2	0	-	-
M.W.Chu† not out	8	17	12	-	1
M.J.McClenaghan c Horne b Jamieson	8	5	6	1	-
J.A.Duffy* b Somerville	1	4	3	-	-
M.D.Rae c Solia b Jamieson	4	4	2	-	1
Extras (lb 2)	2				
TOTAL (12.3 overs)	**80**	62			

Bowling	O	M	R	W
OTAGO				
Duffy	4	0	30	0
McClenaghan	4	0	36	2
Smith	3	0	29	2
Rippon	3	0	39	1
Kitchen	3	0	19	0
Rae	3	0	30	1
AUCKLAND				
Jamieson	3.3	0	18	3
ter Braak	2	0	8	2
Delport	2	0	15	1
Ferns	2	0	13	1
Somerville	3	0	24	2

Fall of Wickets	*A*	*O*
1st	29	4
2nd	57	4
3rd	120	14
4th	138	24
5th	154	51
6th	163	57
7th	181	59
8th	-	68
9th	-	71
10th	-	80

CENTRAL DISTRICTS v CANTERBURY **Super Smash**

at McLean Park, Napier on 5 February, 2021 (d/n)
Toss : Canterbury. Umpires :C.M. Brown & J.M. Dempsey
***Central Districts won by 30 runs.** Points: Central Districts 4, Canterbury 0*

CENTRAL DISTRICTS

	Runs	Mins	Balls	6s	4s
D.Cleaver† c Fletcher b Williams	33	56	32	-	4
G.H.Worker run out	2	5	2	-	-
W.A.Young c Fletcher b Mitchell	13	13	10	1	1
L.R.P.L.Taylor c Williams b Astle	65	54	36	7	2
T.C.Bruce* c Williams b Henry	39	55	35	-	5
J.A.Clarkson not out	21	22	13	-	2
D.A.J.Bracewell run out	2	2	2	-	-
J.F.A.Field not out	0	2	0	-	-
A.Y.Patel					
B.M.Tickner					
J.R.Lennox					
Extras (b 1, lb 3, w 4)	8				
TOTAL (20 overs) (6 wkts)	**183**	96			

CANTERBURY

	Runs	Mins	Balls	6s	4s
C.J.Bowes c Cleaver b Tickner	19	20	15	2	1
K.J.McClure b Field	7	13	10	-	1
J.C.T.Boyle c Clarkson b Lennox	21	30	19	-	3
D.J.Mitchell c Bracewell b Patel	35	45	30	1	2
L.J.Carter run out	1	9	5	-	-
C.E.McConchie* c Field b Lennox	18	21	11	1	1
C.D.Fletcher† not out	39	26	21	2	4
M.J.Henry c Field b Lennox	0	2	2	-	-
T.D.Astle not out	5	14	7	-	-
W.S.A.Williams					
E.J.Nuttall					
Extras (b 2, lb 3, w 3)	8				
TOTAL (20 overs) (7 wkts)	**153**	92			

Bowling	*O*	*M*	*R*	*W*
CANTERBURY				
McConchie	2	0	14	0
Henry	4	0	32	1
Nuttall	3	0	31	0
Mitchell	3	0	34	1
Astle	4	0	35	1
Williams	4	0	33	1
CENTRAL DISTRICTS				
Bracewell	4	0	31	0
Tickner	4	0	35	1
Field	3	0	30	1
Patel	4	0	24	1
Lennox	4	0	20	3
Clarkson	1	0	8	0

Fall of Wickets	***CD***	***C***
1st	11	21
2nd	36	31
3rd	106	73
4th	132	76
5th	172	94
6th	176	116
7th	-	117
8th	-	-
9th	-	-
10th	-	-

OTAGO v NORTHERN DISTRICTS **Super Smash**

at University of Otago Oval, Dunedin on 6 February, 2021
Toss : Northern Districts. Umpires : J.A.K. Bromley & D.J. Walker
***Northern Districts won by 36 runs.** Points: Northern Districts 4, Otago 0*

NORTHERN DISTRICTS

	Runs	Mins	Balls	6s	4s
T.L.Seifert† c Smith b Duffy	23	17	15	1	2
K.D.Clarke run out	23	32	16	1	2
J.F.Carter lbw b Kitchen	11	12	9	-	2
C.de Grandhomme c Broom b Rae	6	11	12	-	-
A.P.Devcich* not out	75	69	40	6	4
M.J.Santner c Rutherford b McClenaghan	3	12	5	-	-
S.C.Kuggeleijn run out	41	45	25	3	1
T.G.Southee not out	0	1	0	-	-
I.S.Sodhi					
T.A.Boult					
J.G.Walker					
Extras (w 7, nb 2)	9				
TOTAL (20 overs) (6 wkts)	**191**	101			

OTAGO

	Runs	Mins	Balls	6s	4s
H.D.Rutherford c Kuggeleijn b Southee	4	2	4	-	1
N.T.Broom c Southee b Santner	47	60	34	2	3
D.N.Phillips c Sodhi b Southee	21	9	9	1	3
A.K.Kitchen c Boult b Kuggeleijn	37	37	26	3	3
M.J.G.Rippon c Kuggeleijn b Walker	1	5	5	-	-
N.G.Smith c Carter b Southee	9	15	9	-	-
M.W.Chu† st Seifert b Walker	1	4	2	-	-
M.J.McClenaghan run out	7	3	4	1	-
J.A.Duffy* not out	9	15	10	1	-
M.D.Rae c Seifert b Boult	16	13	10	-	3
N.F.Kelly absent hurt					
Extras (w 3)	3				
TOTAL (18.5 overs)	**155**	84			

Bowling	*O*	*M*	*R*	*W*
OTAGO				
Duffy	4	0	44	1
McClenaghan	4	0	39	1
Smith	3	0	38	0
Rae	4	0	37	1
Kitchen	1	0	5	1
Rippon	4	0	28	0
NORTHERN DISTRICTS				
Southee	4	0	41	3
Boult	3.5	0	29	1
Santner	4	0	33	1
Kuggeleijn	2	0	17	1
Sodhi	3	0	21	0
Walker	2	0	14	2

Fall of Wickets	***ND***	***O***
1st	38	4
2nd	60	33
3rd	60	107
4th	68	108
5th	83	115
6th	189	119
7th	-	128
8th	-	130
9th	-	155
10th	-	-

AUCKLAND v WELLINGTON — Super Smash

at Eden Park Outer Oval, Auckland on 7 February, 2021
Toss : Wellington. Umpires : B.F. Bowden & D.R. Morrow
***Wellington won by 39 runs.** Points: Wellington 4, Auckland 0*

WELLINGTON

	Runs	Mins	Balls	6s	4s
F.H.Allen c ter Braak b Solia	73	51	35	4	8
D.P.Conway not out	91	103	58	4	7
T.A.Blundell† c O'Donnell R.R. b ter Braak	46	41	23	3	5
J.D.S.Neesham not out	6	10	5	-	1
T.M.Johnson					
M.G.Bracewell*					
J.D.Gibson					
F.J.Colson					
L.V.van Beek					
P.F.Younghusband					
H.K.Bennett					
Extras (lb 3, w 10, nb 1)	14				
TOTAL (20 overs) (2 wkts)	**230**	103			

AUCKLAND

	Runs	Mins	Balls	6s	4s
S.M.Solia c Bracewell b Bennett	17	26	9	1	2
G.D.Phillips c Neesham b van Beek	15	9	7	1	2
W.T.O'Donnell c Younghusband b Gibson	38	33	24	3	2
M.S.Chapman c Gibson b Younghusband	16	24	14	1	1
R.R.O'Donnell* c Conway b Bennett	20	23	12	1	1
B.J.Horne† c & b Younghusband	17	25	18	1	-
K.A.Jamieson b Neesham	17	21	12	-	1
W.E.R.Somerville c Allen b Neesham	26	16	9	3	1
R.M.ter Braak c Johnson b Neesham	0	1	1	-	-
D.K.Ferns c Bracewell b van Beek	13	11	10	-	2
L.J.Delport not out	3	9	4	-	-
Extras (lb 4, w 5)	9				
TOTAL (20 overs)	**191**	101			

Bowling	*O*	*M*	*R*	*W*
AUCKLAND				
Jamieson	4	0	43	0
ter Braak	4	0	46	1
Delport	3	0	33	0
Somerville	2	0	31	0
Ferns	2	0	42	0
Solia	4	0	23	1
Phillips	1	0	9	0
WELLINGTON				
Bennett	4	0	28	2
van Beek	4	0	42	2
Neesham	4	0	41	3
Bracewell	1	0	24	0
Younghusband	4	0	33	2
Gibson	3	0	19	1

Fall of Wickets	***W***	***A***
1st	105	22
2nd	207	51
3rd	-	87
4th	-	90
5th	-	120
6th	-	133
7th	-	173
8th	-	173
9th	-	175
10th	-	191

CENTRAL DISTRICTS v CANTERBURY — Elimination Final

at Eden Park Outer Oval, Auckland on 11 February, 2021
Toss : Central Districts. Umpires : B.F. Bowden & J.M. Dempsey
Canterbury won by 4 wickets

CENTRAL DISTRICTS

	Runs	Mins	Balls	6s	4s
G.H.Worker c Bowes b Nuttall	4	7	5	-	1
D.Cleaver† c McClure b Mitchell	21	24	20	-	3
W.A.Young run out	101	91	47	10	1
L.R.P.L.Taylor c Fletcher b Mitchell	0	2	2	-	-
T.C.Bruce* c Williams b Henry	17	19	17	1	-
J.A.Clarkson c Shipley b Astle	6	13	11	-	-
D.A.J.Bracewell c Williams b Henry	13	20	13	-	1
J.F.A.Field not out	7	18	6	-	-
A.Y.Patel					
B.M.Tickner					
J.R.Lennox					
Extras (lb 1, w 9, nb 1)	11				
TOTAL (20 overs) (7 wkts)	**180**	99			

CANTERBURY

	Runs	Mins	Balls	6s	4s
C.J.Bowes run out	1	2	3	-	-
K.J.McClure c Field b Tickner	5	8	4	-	1
D.J.Mitchell c Taylor b Tickner	88	81	58	4	7
C.E.McConchie* c Bruce b Field	7	15	7	-	1
L.J.Carter c Tickner b Patel	0	2	1	-	-
C.D.Fletcher† run out	72	63	42	5	4
M.J.Henry not out	3	10	3	-	-
H.B.Shipley not out	1	3	1	-	-
T.D.Astle					
W.S.A.Williams					
E.J.Nuttall					
Extras (lb 2, w 2)	4				
TOTAL (19.5 overs) (6 wkts)	**181**	95			

Bowling	*O*	*M*	*R*	*W*
CANTERBURY				
Henry	4	0	30	2
Nuttall	3	0	23	1
Williams	3	0	44	0
Mitchell	3	0	28	2
Astle	4	0	27	1
McConchie	3	0	27	0
CENTRAL DISTRICTS				
Bracewell	3.5	0	44	0
Tickner	4	0	38	2
Field	2	0	18	1
Patel	4	0	31	1
Lennox	4	0	30	0
Clarkson	2	0	18	0

Fall of Wickets	***CD***	***C***
1st	7	2
2nd	42	7
3rd	42	37
4th	84	38
5th	103	170
6th	140	179
7th	180	-
8th	-	-
9th	-	-
10th	-	-

WELLINGTON v CANTERBURY **Final**

at Basin Reserve, Wellington on 13 February, 2021
Toss : Wellington. Umpires : C.M. Brown & W.R. Knights
Wellington won by 5 wickets

CANTERBURY

	Runs	Mins	Balls	6s	4s
C.J.Bowes c Johnson b Younghusband	37	38	23	-	7
K.J.McClure c Sears b van Beek	12	8	8	1	1
D.J.Mitchell c Conway b Younghusband	35	48	24	2	2
C.E.McConchie* c Bennett b van Beek	44	62	39	1	2
L.J.Carter c Neesham b Bracewell	3	7	4	-	-
C.D.Fletcher† c & b Bracewell	0	1	1	-	-
H.B.Shipley c Bracewell b Neesham	29	24	15	2	2
M.J.Henry c Johnson b van Beek	4	11	5	-	-
T.D.Astle not out	1	2	1	-	-
W.S.A.Williams not out	0	1	0	-	-
E.J.Nuttall					
Extras (lb 4, w 6)	10				
TOTAL (20 overs) (8 wkts)	**175**	103			

WELLINGTON

	Runs	Mins	Balls	6s	4s
F.H.Allen c Carter b McConchie	16	19	11	-	3
D.P.Conway not out	93	99	63	1	11
T.A.Blundell† c Bowes b Nuttall	0	3	2	-	-
T.M.Johnson c Shipley b Astle	28	22	15	2	2
J.D.S.Neesham c Fletcher b Williams	18	21	12	1	1
M.G.Bracewell* c Bowes b Nuttall	4	10	5	-	-
J.D.Gibson not out	16	23	10	-	2
L.V.van Beek					
P.F.Younghusband					
B.V.Sears					
H.K.Bennett					
Extras (lb 1, w 2)	3				
TOTAL (19.4 overs) (5 wkts)	**178**	99			

Bowling	*O*	*M*	*R*	*W*
WELLINGTON				
Bennett	4	0	42	0
van Beek	4	0	28	3
Sears	4	0	34	0
Neesham	4	0	39	1
Younghusband	3	0	25	2
Bracewell	1	0	3	2
CANTERBURY				
Henry	4	0	45	0
Nuttall	4	0	32	2
McConchie	4	0	43	1
Mitchell	1	0	4	0
Astle	4	0	34	1
Williams	2.4	0	19	1

Fall of Wickets

	C	*W*
1st	14	32
2nd	79	32
3rd	106	90
4th	115	130
5th	115	145
6th	159	-
7th	174	-
8th	174	-
9th	-	-
10th	-	-

2020/21 DREAM11 SUPER SMASH AVERAGES

	M	In	NO	HS	Runs	Ave	100s	50s	Ct	St	O	M	R	W	Ave	R/O	Best
F.H.Allen	11	11	2	92*	512	56.88	-	6	3	-	1	0	8	0	-	8.00	-
T.D.Astle	12	4	3	36	59	59.00	-	-	3	-	42	0	294	9	32.66	7.00	2-12
M.B.Bacon	5	1	0	1	1	1.00	-	-	1	-	17.5	0	175	9	19.44	9.81	3-18
G.K.Beghin	3	3	0	32	45	15.00	-	-	2	-							
H.K.Bennett	11	-	-	-	-	-	-	-	5	-	42.2	0	328	13	25.23	7.75	2-13
T.A.Blundell	8	8	1	62*	187	26.71	-	1	11	-							
P.D.Bocock	1	1	0	2	2	2.00	-	-	-	-							
T.A.Boult	4	-	-	-	-	-	-	-	1	-	14.5	0	107	4	26.75	7.21	2-29
C.J.Bowes	12	12	1	72	271	24.63	-	1	9	-							
J.C.T.Boyle	9	9	0	44	155	17.22	-	-	6	-							
D.A.J.Bracewell	11	11	6	55*	223	44.60	-	2	4	-	38.5	1	341	10	34.10	8.78	3-38
M.G.Bracewell	11	8	3	47*	155	31.00	-	-	9	-	15	0	133	8	16.62	8.87	4-28
N.T.Broom	10	10	0	57	292	29.20	-	1	2	-							
D.G.Brownlie	4	4	0	8	17	4.25	-	-	1	-							
T.C.Bruce	8	8	0	52	143	17.87	-	1	7	-	2	0	22	0	-	11.00	-
J.F.Carter	4	4	0	14	32	8.00	-	-	2	-							
L.J.Carter	12	11	4	42	127	18.14	-	-	5	-							
M.S.Chapman	5	5	0	73	219	43.80	-	2	1	-							
M.W.Chu	4	3	2	21*	30	30.00	-	-	-	1							
K.D.Clarke	8	8	0	26	108	13.50	-	-	2	-							
J.A.Clarkson	11	11	1	78	280	28.00	-	1	3	-	17.4	0	161	6	26.83	9.17	2-30
D.Cleaver	11	11	0	33	177	16.09	-	-	6	-							
B.P.Coburn	1	-	-	-	-	-	-	-	-	-	4	0	26	1	26.00	6.50	1-26
F.J.Colson	4	2	0	22	29	14.50	-	-	-	-							
D.P.Conway	10	10	3	93*	455	65.00	-	5	4	-							
H.R.Cooper	4	4	0	23	40	10.00	-	-	-	-	2	0	14	2	7.00	7.00	2-14
S.B.Davey	1	-	-	-	-	-	-	-	-	-	1	0	8	1	8.00	8.00	1-8
C.de Grandhomme	4	4	1	19	51	17.00	-	-	1	-							
L.J.Delport	7	1	1	3*	3	-	-	-	-	-	19	0	164	4	41.00	8.63	2-28
A.P.Devcich	10	9	2	102	286	40.85	1	1	6	-							
J.A.Duffy	10	7	4	9*	17	5.66	-	-	5	-	37	0	341	4	85.25	9.22	1-24
D.K.Ferns	8	3	0	13	15	5.00	-	-	2	-	24.3	0	276	11	25.09	11.27	3-39
J.F.A.Field	11	6	4	8*	18	9.00	-	-	12	-	33	0	307	10	30.70	9.30	2-26
J.L.Finnie	4	4	0	26	45	11.25	-	-	1	-	2	0	24	0	-	12.00	-
M.J.Fisher	4	2	2	1*	1	-	-	-	1	-	13	0	131	3	43.66	10.08	1-28
C.D.Fletcher	12	9	3	72	189	31.50	-	1	8	1							
J.D.Gibson	11	7	2	24	82	16.40	-	-	8	-	5	0	39	2	19.50	7.80	1-19
Z.N.Gibson	5	4	2	9	17	8.50	-	-	3	-	14	0	122	4	30.50	8.71	3-17
M.J.Guptill	4	4	0	29	46	11.50	-	-	3	-							
B.R.Hampton	7	6	1	28	62	12.40	-	-	6	-	12.5	0	94	5	18.80	7.32	3-21
R.D.Harrison	1	-	-	-	-	-	-	-	-	-	0.1	0	5	0	-	-	-
M.W.Hay	2	-	-	-	-	-	-	-	-	-							
M.J.Henry	11	8	5	7*	22	7.33	-	-	4	-	41.4	0	345	14	24.64	8.28	3-25
B.J.Horne	10	10	3	63	163	23.28	-	1	6	-							
K.A.Jamieson	5	4	2	21*	56	28.00	-	-	2	-	17.3	0	141	5	28.20	8.06	3-18
L.R.Johns	1	1	1	11*	11	-	-	-	1	-							
L.C.Johnson	6	6	0	72	118	19.66	-	1	2	-							
T.M.Johnson	10	8	4	50*	120	30.00	-	1	8	-							
N.F.Kelly	10	9	0	75	195	21.66	-	1	6	-							
A.K.Kitchen	10	10	1	57*	229	25.44	-	1	4	-	26	0	219	5	43.80	8.42	2-38
S.C.Kuggeleijn	10	8	3	41	110	22.00	-	-	3	-	32	0	304	12	25.33	9.50	2-26
J.R.Lennox	4	-	-	-	-	-	-	-	-	-	15	0	82	6	13.66	5.47	3-20
C.K.Leopard	6	5	3	23	55	27.50	-	-	3	-	1	0	4	2	2.00	4.00	2-4
B.G.Lister	7	2	0	5	6	3.00	-	-	5	-	23	0	232	3	77.33	10.09	3-21
M.J.McClenaghan	10	7	2	14*	42	8.40	-	-	4	-	38.4	0	352	12	29.33	9.11	3-36
K.J.McClure	12	12	1	40	187	17.00	-	-	1	-							
C.E.McConchie	12	11	3	56*	298	37.25	-	2	1	-	35	0	259	5	51.80	7.40	2-14
D.J.Mitchell	10	10	0	88	374	37.40	-	3	3	-	29.4	0	266	10	26.60	8.97	2-21
J.D.S.Neesham	7	6	1	49	89	17.80	-	-	2	-	26.4	0	210	12	17.50	7.88	3-11
K.Noema-Barnett	8	6	1	12	42	8.40	-	-	-	-	15	0	149	4	37.25	9.93	3-37
E.J.Nuttall	11	1	0	5	5	5.00	-	-	2	-	32	0	272	11	24.72	8.50	3-18
R.R.O'Donnell	10	10	3	61	254	36.28	-	1	5	-	5	0	45	1	45.00	9.00	1-30
W.T.O'Donnell	8	7	1	50*	212	35.33	-	1	6	-							
A.Y.Patel	11	5	2	7*	23	7.66	-	-	1	-	41.2	0	335	7	47.85	8.11	3-34
D.N.Phillips	5	5	3	22*	60	30.00	-	-	2	-							
G.D.Phillips	9	9	0	68	156	17.33	-	1	3	-	11	0	97	3	32.33	8.82	2-22

	M	In	NO	HS	Runs	Ave	100s	50s	Ct	St	O	M	R	W	Ave	R/O	Best
O.M.R.Pringle	3	2	1	2*	3	3.00	-	-	-	-	8	0	95	2	47.50	11.88	1-23
M.D.Rae	5	2	0	16	20	10.00	-	-	-	-	13.3	0	155	3	51.66	11.48	1-30
B.G.Randell	2	1	1	1*	1	-	-	-	-	-	6	0	61	2	30.50	10.17	2-34
J.A.Raval	3	3	0	70	94	31.33	-	1	-	-							
R.Ravindra	8	7	1	40*	99	16.50	-	-	2	-	23	0	186	6	31.00	8.09	2-22
M.Renwick	6	6	0	42	99	16.50	-	-	2	1							
M.J.G.Rippon	10	10	2	22	99	12.37	-	-	2	-	37	0	268	10	26.80	7.24	2-19
B.P.Rodden	3	2	0	6	11	5.50	-	-	1	-							
H.D.Rutherford	10	10	0	49	166	16.60	-	-	4	-							
M.J.Santner	5	5	1	39*	73	18.25	-	-	-	-	18	0	164	2	82.00	9.11	1-17
B.V.Sears	7	-	-	-	-	-	-	-	3	-	22	1	151	9	16.77	6.86	4-21
T.L.Seifert	10	10	0	74	281	28.10	-	2	15	2							
F.W.Sheat	1	0	0	0	0	-	-	-	-	-	1	0	10	1	10.00	10.00	1-10
H.B.Shipley	2	2	1	29	30	30.00	-	-	2	-							
B.S.Smith	1	1	1	22*	22	-	-	-	1	-							
N.G.Smith	5	4	0	16	30	7.50	-	-	3	-	17	0	173	7	24.71	10.18	4-32
M.W.Snedden	1	-	-	-	-	-	-	-	-	-	4	0	36	1	36.00	9.00	1-36
I.S.Sodhi	2	-	-	-	-	-	-	-	1	-	7	0	45	0	-	6.43	-
S.M.Solia	10	10	0	75	266	26.60	-	2	2	-	6	0	52	1	52.00	8.67	1-23
W.E.R.Somerville	10	6	3	26	46	15.33	-	-	-	-	31	0	298	12	24.83	9.61	3-18
T.G.Southee	4	2	1	24	24	24.00	-	-	3	-	15	0	118	8	14.75	7.87	3-41
L.R.P.L.Taylor	6	6	1	65	125	25.00	-	1	2	-							
R.M.ter Braak	7	2	1	0*	0	0.00	-	-	1	-	20.5	0	170	11	15.45	8.16	3-26
B.M.Tickner	11	1	0	0	0	0.00	-	-	3	-	42	0	349	17	20.52	8.31	3-23
L.V.van Beek	11	5	4	29*	61	61.00	-	-	6	-	42	0	327	13	25.15	7.79	3-28
A.Verma	4	2	2	1*	1	-	-	-	-	-	13	0	108	4	27.00	8.31	2-21
F.L.Walker	4	1	1	3*	3	-	-	-	3	-	13.5	0	84	5	16.80	6.07	3-20
J.G.Walker	9	2	0	16	21	10.50	-	-	2	-	25	0	167	9	18.55	6.68	2-14
B.L.Wiggins	4	4	0	17	34	8.50	-	-	2	-							
W.S.A.Williams	12	2	2	8*	8	-	-	-	9	-	27	0	263	8	32.87	9.74	2-18
K.S.Williamson	2	2	2	79*	113	-	-	1	-	-							
G.H.Worker	11	11	0	106	424	38.54	1	2	6	-	3.4	0	40	1	40.00	10.93	1-12
W.A.Young	7	7	0	101	297	42.42	1	2	4	-							
P.F.Younghusband	11	1	1	2*	2	-	-	-	5	-	34	0	253	9	28.11	7.44	2-25

HIGHEST STRIKE RATES *(qualification 100 runs)*

		Runs	Balls	S/R
F.H.Allen	W	512	264	193
D.A.J.Bracewell	CD	223	123	181
W.A.Young	CD	297	170	174
A.P.Devcich	ND	286	169	169
L.R.P.L.Taylor	CD	125	76	164
G.D.Phillips	A	156	96	162
M.S.Chapman	A	219	135	162
J.A.Clarkson	CD	280	176	159
C.D.Fletcher	C	189	120	157
R.R.O'Donnell	A	254	162	156

MOST ECONOMICAL BOWLING *(qualification 20 overs)*

		O	M	R	W	Ave	R/O
J.G.Walker	ND	25	0	167	9	18.55	6.68
B.V.Sears	W	22	1	151	9	16.77	6.86
T.D.Astle	C	42	0	294	9	32.66	7.00
M.J.G.Rippon	O	37	0	268	10	26.80	7.24
C.E.McConchie	C	35	0	259	5	51.80	7.40
P.F.Younghusband	W	34	0	253	9	28.11	7.44
H.K.Bennett	W	42.2	0	328	13	25.23	7.75
L.V.van Beek	W	42	0	327	13	25.15	7.79
J.D.S.Neesham	W	26.4	0	210	12	17.50	7.88
R.Ravindra	W	23	0	186	6	31.00	8.09

CAREER RECORDS

	M	In	NO	HS	Runs	Ave	100s	50s	Ct	St	O	M	R	W	Ave	R/O	Best
F.H.Allen	12	12	2	92*	517	51.70	-	6	3	-	1	0	8	0	-	8.00	-
T.D.Astle	67	36	18	37*	345	19.16	-	-	27	-	198	1	1388	46	30.17	7.01	3-18
M.B.Bacon	12	3	1	1	1	0.50	-	-	3	-	42.5	1	368	20	18.40	8.59	4-31
G.K.Beghin	6	4	0	32	46	11.50	-	-	2	-							
H.K.Bennett	63	12	8	12*	25	6.25	-	-	13	-	206.4	1	1579	59	26.76	7.64	3-18
T.A.Blundell	47	42	3	79	970	24.87	-	8	32	2	0.1	0	4	0	-	-	-
P.D.Bocock	18	14	5	29*	141	15.66	-	-	11	1							
T.A.Boult	32	8	6	4	16	8.00	-	-	13	-	106.2	2	841	26	32.34	7.91	3-35
C.J.Bowes	49	49	2	95	1309	27.85	-	9	23	-							
J.C.T.Boyle	19	19	1	69*	386	21.44	-	1	8	-							
D.A.J.Bracewell	44	36	14	55*	688	31.27	-	2	20	-	136.5	2	1131	44	25.70	8.27	3-21
M.G.Bracewell	89	79	17	80*	1693	27.30	-	8	55	1	24	0	196	13	15.07	8.17	4-28
N.T.Broom	114	112	11	96*	2839	28.10	-	18	49	-	25	0	241	8	30.12	9.64	2-19
D.G.Brownlie	89	85	4	99	1922	23.72	-	7	49	-							
T.C.Bruce	56	55	6	88*	1501	30.63	-	10	37	1	9.1	0	83	3	27.66	9.06	1-11
J.F.Carter	18	16	2	55	174	12.42	-	1	6	-							
L.J.Carter	42	37	9	70*	471	16.82	-	1	13	-							
M.S.Chapman	47	41	6	101	1153	32.94	1	9	17	-	44	0	332	14	23.71	7.55	3-22
M.W.Chu	13	4	3	21*	31	31.00	-	-	2	1							
K.D.Clarke	8	8	0	26	108	13.50	-	-	2	-							
J.A.Clarkson	60	55	15	78	1087	27.17	-	4	21	-	25	0	223	8	27.87	8.92	2-21
D.Cleaver	65	61	6	81	1089	19.80	-	3	50	5							
B.P.Coburn	8	2	0	9	14	7.00	-	-	1	-	25	0	223	7	31.85	8.92	4-17
F.J.Colson	12	7	1	37	120	20.00	-	-	4	-							
D.P.Conway	37	36	9	105*	1526	56.51	2	11	16	1							
H.R.Cooper	4	4	0	23	40	10.00	-	-	-	-	2	0	14	2	7.00	7.00	2-14
S.B.Davey	4	2	1	3	3	3.00	-	-	-	-	9	0	65	1	65.00	7.22	1-8
C.de Grandhomme	88	81	19	72*	1646	26.54	-	6	37	-	110.4	0	1020	38	26.84	9.22	3-22
L.J.Delport	8	1	1	3*	3	-	-	-	-	-	22	0	190	4	47.50	8.64	2-28
A.P.Devcich	102	93	8	102	2189	25.75	1	14	34	-	211.3	0	1570	66	23.78	7.42	4-12
J.A.Duffy	75	28	17	13*	103	9.36	-	-	16	-	251.3	3	2190	83	26.38	8.71	5-18
D.K.Ferns	8	3	0	13	15	5.00	-	-	2	-	24.3	0	276	11	25.09	11.27	3-39
J.F.A.Field	11	6	4	8*	18	9.00	-	-	12	-	33	0	307	10	30.70	9.30	2-26
J.L.Finnie	50	39	7	71*	574	17.93	-	1	20	-	31	0	288	6	48.00	9.29	4-11
M.J.Fisher	6	4	4	1*	2	-	-	-	1	-	18	0	196	4	49.00	10.89	1-28
C.D.Fletcher	69	59	22	74*	1268	34.27	-	5	40	13							
J.D.Gibson	22	13	2	28	168	15.27	-	-	11	-	5	0	39	2	19.50	7.80	1-19
Z.N.Gibson	11	7	3	9	30	7.50	-	-	7	-	28	0	250	8	31.25	8.93	3-17
M.J.Guptill	62	58	10	120*	1964	40.91	1	13	44	-	1	0	8	0	-	8.00	-
B.R.Hampton	43	37	3	64	534	15.70	-	3	25	-	23.4	0	209	7	29.85	8.83	3-21
R.D.Harrison	1	-	-	-	-	-	-	-	-	-	0.1	0	5	0	-	-	-
M.W.Hay	2	-	-	-	-	-	-	-	-	-							
M.J.Henry	50	31	17	29	178	12.71	-	-	18	-	165.3	2	1335	51	26.17	8.07	4-43
B.J.Horne	28	26	7	63	369	19.42	-	1	18	4	6	0	66	3	22.00	11.00	2-46
K.A.Jamieson	31	15	9	33*	192	32.00	-	-	4	-	115.4	1	952	49	19.42	8.23	6-7
L.R.Johns	3	3	1	19	30	15.00	-	-	3	-							
L.C.Johnson	9	9	0	72	136	15.11	-	1	4	-							
T.M.Johnson	14	11	4	50*	141	20.14	-	1	9	-							
N.F.Kelly	49	41	5	85	927	25.75	-	6	24	-	4	0	38	1	38.00	9.50	1-22
A.K.Kitchen	117	106	9	66	2034	20.96	-	6	55	-	163	0	1298	25	51.92	7.96	3-24
S.C.Kuggeleijn	81	56	24	41	590	18.43	-	-	32	-	274	3	2392	80	29.90	8.73	4-18
J.R.Lennox	4	-	-	-	-	-	-	-	-	-	15	0	82	6	13.66	5.47	3-20
C.K.Leopard	20	19	4	52	281	18.73	-	1	7	-	1	0	4	2	2.00	4.00	2-4
B.G.Lister	24	6	3	5	9	3.00	-	-	9	-	81	0	705	23	30.65	8.70	3-21
M.J.McClenaghan	56	17	6	16	76	6.90	-	-	16	-	191.3	2	1633	74	22.06	8.53	3-18
K.J.McClure	15	15	1	40	216	15.42	-	-	1	-							
C.E.McConchie	63	49	8	83	899	21.92	-	4	22	-	158	0	1184	41	28.87	7.49	3-18
D.J.Mitchell	86	75	21	88*	1919	35.53	-	8	43	-	118.3	0	1059	43	24.62	8.94	4-32
J.D.S.Neesham	50	42	11	59*	864	27.87	-	1	17	-	127.5	1	1104	55	20.07	8.64	4-24
K.Noema-Barnett	89	83	10	58	1241	17.00	-	4	14	-	139	0	1240	39	31.79	8.92	3-10
E.J.Nuttall	56	13	11	13*	29	14.50	-	-	15	-	184.1	2	1505	49	30.71	8.17	3-13
R.R.O'Donnell	42	34	16	61	782	43.44	-	4	20	-	5	0	45	1	45.00	9.00	1-30
W.T.O'Donnell	8	7	1	50*	212	35.33	-	1	6	-							
A.Y.Patel	52	19	10	12*	92	10.22	-	-	11	-	180.1	1	1446	58	24.93	8.03	3-20
D.N.Phillips	8	7	4	25*	88	29.33	-	-	4	-	1	0	20	0	-	20.00	-

	M	In	NO	HS	Runs	Ave	100s	50s	Ct	St	O	M	R	W	Ave	R/O	Best
G.D.Phillips	47	45	4	116*	1075	26.21	2	6	26	4	11	0	97	3	32.33	8.82	2-22
O.M.R.Pringle	3	2	1	2*	3	3.00	-	-	-	-	8	0	95	2	47.50	11.88	1-23
M.D.Rae	20	5	2	16	33	11.00	-	-	5	-	61	0	547	21	26.04	8.97	3-14
B.G.Randell	17	3	2	1*	1	1.00	-	-	5	-	53	0	488	19	25.68	9.21	3-29
J.A.Raval	36	35	1	70	770	22.64	-	4	11	-							
R.Ravindra	22	18	1	40*	291	17.11	-	-	6	-	71	0	566	19	29.78	7.97	3-32
M.Renwick	10	8	0	42	110	13.75	-	-	2	2							
S.J.Rhodes	9	9	2	75*	201	28.71	-	1	3	-	6	0	51	1	51.00	8.50	1-23
M.J.G.Rippon	32	26	10	28	282	17.62	-	-	9	-	114.4	0	898	23	39.04	7.83	2-19
B.P.Rodden	6	5	0	14	47	9.40	-	-	1	-							
H.D.Rutherford	90	88	3	106	2109	24.81	1	9	31	-	1	0	11	0	-	11.00	-
B.V.Sears	12	2	1	12	14	14.00	-	-	6	-	37	2	260	15	17.33	7.03	4-16
T.L.Seifert	66	59	6	107	1421	26.81	1	7	56	10							
F.W.Sheat	1	-	-	-	-	-	-	-	-	-	1	0	10	1	10.00	10.00	1-10
H.B.Shipley	18	10	1	29	147	16.33	-	-	5	-	33	1	295	5	59.00	8.94	2-24
B.S.Smith	26	23	2	59*	345	16.42	-	1	13	-							
N.G.Smith	22	10	2	22	69	8.62	-	-	5	-	72.2	1	657	28	23.46	9.08	5-14
M.W.Snedden	1	-	-	-	-	-	-	-	-	-	4	0	36	1	36.00	9.00	1-36
I.S.Sodhi	57	17	8	51	108	12.00	-	1	11	-	198.5	1	1475	49	30.10	7.42	3-12
S.M.Solia	35	31	7	75	582	24.25	-	2	11	-	37.3	0	361	10	36.10	9.63	2-16
W.E.R.Somerville	28	11	7	37*	140	35.00	-	-	3	-	86.4	0	737	26	28.34	8.50	3-18
T.G.Southee	43	23	4	35*	181	9.52	-	-	17	-	153.1	2	1246	52	23.96	8.13	3-15
L.R.P.L.Taylor	36	36	7	111*	1331	45.89	1	8	23	-	29	0	256	8	32.00	8.83	3-28
R.M.ter Braak	10	3	2	1*	1	1.00	-	-	2	-	30.5	0	262	13	20.15	8.50	3-26
B.M.Tickner	48	9	7	3*	7	3.50	-	-	11	-	173	2	1471	79	18.62	8.50	5-19
L.V.van Beek	76	42	15	29*	293	10.85	-	-	40	-	226.3	2	1960	73	26.84	8.65	3-15
A.Verma	42	18	5	18*	82	6.30	-	-	13	-	134	1	1193	48	24.85	8.90	4-27
F.L.Walker	4	1	1	3*	3	-	-	-	3	-	13.5	0	84	5	16.80	6.07	3-20
J.G.Walker	12	3	0	16	22	7.33	-	-	3	-	32.2	0	230	11	20.90	7.11	2-14
B.L.Wiggins	5	5	1	17	42	10.50	-	-	2	-							
W.S.A.Williams	33	11	8	12*	46	15.33	-	-	25	-	71.1	0	681	26	26.19	9.57	5-12
K.S.Williamson	26	21	4	79*	417	24.52	-	3	9	-	58	1	388	10	38.80	6.69	3-33
G.H.Worker	112	107	8	106	2798	28.26	1	14	39	-	109.4	1	922	35	26.34	8.41	5-10
W.A.Young	71	67	4	101	1703	27.03	1	9	33	-							
P.F.Younghusband	17	5	3	6	13	6.50	-	-	8	-	48	0	369	11	33.54	7.69	2-16

NATIONAL UNDER 19 TOURNAMENT

The National Under 19 tournament was held at Lincoln from 17 to 23 December 2020. The tournament consisted of four rounds of fifty-over matches and three rounds of Twenty20 games. Final positions were: Canterbury, Central Districts, Wellington, Auckland, Northern Districts, Otago.

FIRST ROUND

CANTERBURY v AUCKLAND *Canterbury won by 8 runs*

Canterbury 235 (R.A. Mariu 54, N.J. Lidstone 43, Z.G. Foulkes 34, J.J.A. Frew 31, Y.B. Zeb 3-37)

Auckland 227-9 (J.J. McKenzie 70, N.S. Perera 49)

CENTRAL DISTRICTS v WELLINGTON *Central Districts won by 14 runs*

Central Districts 256-7 (C.G. Heaphy 60, T.T. Sutherland 37*, S.R Ferguson 36, B.M. Foote 32)

Wellington 242 (S.J. French 89, T.B. Robinson 68, R.D.W. Vekony 35, T.A. Findlay 3-30)

NORTHERN DISTRICTS v OTAGO *Northern Districts won by 37 runs*

Northern Districts 302-9 (N.J. Dovey 106, J.M. Parker 49, L.J. Marconi 42, P.C. Spencer 39, B.R. Seavill 3-53)

Otago 265 (B.R. Wheeler-Greenall 94, T.M. Dempster 42, N.J. Parkes 4-52)

SECOND ROUND

AUCKLAND v NORTHERN DISTRICTS *Auckland won by 134 runs*

Auckland 215 (N.S. Perera 79, J.W.P. Stephan 36, M.W. Marconi 3-21, N.J. Parkes 3-23)

Northern Districts 81 (Mohammad Abbas 3-21, A. Ashok 3-27)

CANTERBURY v WELLINGTON *Wellington won by 83 runs*

Wellington 211-7 (T.B. Robinson 68, C.A.J. Montague 62, R.N. Sheahan 3-26)

Canterbury 128 (M.W.T. Boyle 29)

CENTRAL DISTRICTS v OTAGO *Central Districts won by 93 runs*

Central Districts 290-8 (B.M. Foote 56, T.T. Sutherland 51, S. Lauderdale-Smith 50, C.G. Heaphy 49)

Otago 197 (J.R. Murray 69, J.I. Mockford 54*, T.A. Findlay 3-17)

THIRD ROUND

AUCKLAND v OTAGO *Auckland won by 4 wickets*

Otago 291 (B.J. Culhane 123, B.R. Wheeler-Greenall 44, T.M. Dempster 32, A. Ashok 3-46)

Auckland 293-6 (N.A.J. Robinson 66, J.W.P. Stephan 48, J.J. McKenzie 44, B. Jacobs 41, A. Ashok 30*)

CANTERBURY v CENTRAL DISTRICTS *Canterbury won by 1 wicket*

Central Districts 221-8 (S. Lauderdale-Smith 51, J.T.R. Gard 50, T.T. Sutherland 41*, A.H. Sidey 3-21)

Canterbury 225-9 (J.J.A. Frew 63, M.W.T. Boyle 33)

NORTHERN DISTRICTS v WELLINGTON *Wellington won by 2 wickets*

Northern Districts 216-9 (N.J. Dovey 50, J.M. Parker 49, B. Gandhi 3-39, J.C. Vandenberg 3-40)

Wellington 217-8 (P. Bonar 76, T.B. Robinson 59, O.T. Jackson 35*, P.C. Spencer 4-53)

FOURTH ROUND

AUCKLAND v CENTRAL DISTRICTS *Auckland won by 5 wickets*

Central Districts 122-8 (C.G. Heaphy 64*)

Auckland 123-5 (J.W.P Stephan 31, J.T.R. Gard 3-27)

CANTERBURY *v* **NORTHERN DISTRICTS** *Canterbury won by 7 wickets*

Northern Districts 197-9 (J.M. Parker 41, P.C. Spencer 31, Z.G. Foulkes 3-34)

Canterbury 201-3 (R.A. Mariu 71, M.W.T. Boyle 51, N.J. Lidstone 37)

OTAGO v WELLINGTON *Wellington won by 7 wickets (D/L)*

Otago 118 (J.M. Cumming 58, J.I. Mockford 40*, M.Z.T. Scoble 3-15)

Wellington 118-3 (T.B. Robinson 71*, M.S.M. Conroy 36*)

FIFTH ROUND

AUCKLAND v WELLINGTON *Wellington won by 1 wicket*

Auckland 139-7 (B. Jacobs 50, N.A.J. Robinson 41, J.C. Vandenberg 5-23)

Wellington 143-9 (T.B. Robinson 54, N.S. Perera 3-23)

CANTERBURY v OTAGO *Canterbury won by 87 runs*

Canterbury 210-6 (R.A. Mariu 49, N.J. Lidstone 35, M.W.T. Boyle 31)

Otago 123-9 (J.I. Mockford 33)

CENTRAL DISTRICTS v NORTHERN DISTRICTS *Central Districts won by 10 runs*

Central Districts 171-4 (F.P. Raxworthy 48, S. Lauderdale-Smith 44, W.J. Clark 39*

Northern Districts 161-5 (K.R.S. Price 44*, L.J. Marconi 36, J.T.R. Gard 3-35)

SIXTH ROUND

CANTERBURY v AUCKLAND *Canterbury won by 3 wickets*

Auckland 155-5 (J.W.P. Stephan 46*, B. Jacobs 42)

Canterbury 157-7 (R.A. Mariu 74, J.J.A. Frew 30)

CENTRAL DISTRICTS v WELLINGTON *Central Districts won by 6 wickets*
Wellington 150-8 (C.A.J. Montague 46, J.C. Vandenberg 41, L.T. McCarthy 3-25)
Central Districts 154-4 (C.G. Heaphy 34*, W.J. Clark 32)

NORTHERN DISTRICTS v OTAGO *Northern Districts won by 4 wickets*
Otago 143-4 (B.J. Culhane 59, J.M. Cumming 49, P.C. Spencer 3-49)
Northern Districts 145-6 (L.R. Trigg 50, T.J. Hart 3-25)

SEVENTH ROUND

AUCKLAND v WELLINGTON *Auckland won by 3 wickets*
Wellington 124 (W.J. Stevenson 35, C.A.J. Montague 32, Mohammad Abbas 3-11)
Auckland 127-7 (N.A.J. Robinson 33*)

NORTHERN DISTRICTS v CANTERBURY *Canterbury won by 58 runs*
Canterbury 173-5 (A. Bhagwat 32)
Northern Districts 115 (L.J Marconi 36, K.R.S. Price 31, J.J.A. Frew 5-11, O.D. Curtis 3-15)

CENTRAL DISTRICTS v OTAGO *Central Districts won by 50 runs*
Central Districts 148-6 (C.G. Heaphy 53*, S.R. Ferguson 32, G.T. Ross 3-29)
Otago 98 (C.I.G. Logan 3-16)

HAWKE CUP

The major competition for the District (formerly Minor) Associations reverted to the Hawke Cup from 1999/00. The Fuji Xerox Cup since 1995/96, it was renamed the National District Championship in 1998/99. The competition was for the U-Bix Cup from 1985/86 to 1994/95.

Apart from tournaments in 1910/11, 1912/13 and 2000/01, the competition has always been on a challenge basis. To reduce the number of challenges received by the holders it was decided to pair off all the Minor Associations. This scheme commenced in the 1924/25 season, when the first three elimination matches were played. Since then numerous elimination matches have been staged to determine the right to challenge the holders of the cup.

At the end of 1999/00 it was decided to exclude the teams from the four major centres who had taken part in the tournament from 1995/96. As Dunedin Metropolitan held the trophy at the time, a national zonal tournament was held to find a new holder in 2000/01 and the challenge format resumed in 2001/02.

Holders

Southland, 1910/11; won the tournament of six matches.
Southland, March 14, 1911, to March 25, 1913; resisted one challenge.
South Auckland, 1912/13; won the tournament of four matches.

	Challenges resisted
Wanganui, December 26, 1913, to March 28, 1919	5
Poverty Bay, March 28, 1919, to February 15, 1921	4
Wairarapa, February 15, 1921, to December 26, 1921	1
Rangitikei, December 26, 1921, to January 3, 1922	—
Nelson, January 3, 1922, to April 1, 1922	2
Wanganui, April 1, 1922, to January 22, 1924	7
Nelson, January 22, 1924, to February 2, 1926	7
Wanganui, February 2, 1926, to December 6, 1926	2
Taranaki, December 6, 1926, to December 20, 1927	3
Wanganui, December 20, 1927, to February 23, 1928	2
Manawatu, February 23, 1928, to March 29, 1930	9
Rangitikei, March 29, 1930, to December 15, 1930	—
Waikato, December 15, 1930, to January 2, 1933	11
Nelson, January 2, 1933, to December 27, 1933	2
Taranaki, December 27, 1933, to December 27, 1934	3
Manawatu, December 27, 1934, to February 14, 1938	15
Waikato, February 14, 1938, to January 30, 1940	7
Manawatu, January 30, 1940, to April 7, 1947	9
Hawke's Bay, April 7, 1947, to February 14, 1948	1
Wanganui, February 14, 1948, to December 13, 1948	1
Hutt Valley, December 13, 1948, to April 11, 1950	7
Hawke's Bay, April 11, 1950, to January 3, 1951	2
Wairarapa, January 3, 1951, to March 12, 1951	1
Waikato, March 12, 1951, to December 10, 1951	—
Nelson, December 10, 1951, to December 30, 1952	6
Wanganui, December 30, 1952, to December 28, 1955	13
Hutt Valley, December 28, 1955, to January 2, 1956	—
Northland, January 2, 1956, to December 8, 1956	2
Waikato, December 8, 1956, to December 8, 1958	9
Nelson, December 8, 1958, to February 1, 1965	28
Manawatu, February 1, 1965, to January 24, 1967	9
North Canterbury, January 24, 1967, to February 27, 1967	—
Nelson, February 27, 1967, to December 17, 1967	—
Hutt Valley, December 17, 1967, to January 7, 1968	1
Marlborough, January 7, 1968, to March 3, 1968	1
Hawke's Bay, March 3, 1968, to February 23, 1969	4

	Challenges resisted
Waikato, February 23, 1969, to February 7, 1970	3
Southland, February 7, 1970, to December 29, 1970	1
Taranaki, December 29, 1970, to March 12, 1973	12
Southland, March 12, 1973, to February 27, 1977	14
Wairarapa, February 27, 1977, to February 5, 1979	6
Nelson, February 5, 1979, to February 21, 1983	14
Northland, February 21, 1983, to March 14, 1983	2
Hawke's Bay, March 14, 1983, to February 20, 1984	2
Northland, February 20, 1984, to February 27, 1984	—
Nelson, February 27, 1984, to February 24, 1986	8
Hawke's Bay, February 24, 1986, to March 18, 1986	1
Bay of Plenty, March 18, 1986, to February 23, 1987	2
Hawke's Bay, February 23, 1987, to March 16, 1987	—
Bay of Plenty, March 16, 1987, to March 23, 1987	—
Southland, March 23, 1987, to March 15, 1988	4
North Canterbury, March 15, 1988, to March 22, 1988	—
Taranaki, March 22, 1988, to February 13, 1989	—
Northland, February 13, 1989, to February 27, 1989	—
Southland, February 27, 1989, to February 24, 1992	15
Northland, February 24, 1992, to March 23, 1992	1
Nelson, March 23, 1992, to March 15, 1993	3
Canterbury Country, March 15, 1993, to March 29, 1993	—
Manawatu, March 29, 1993, to February 28, 1994	2
Marlborough, February 28, 1994 to March 14, 1994	—
Taranaki, March 14, 1994 to January 29, 1996	7
Central Otago, January 29, 1996 to February 12, 1996	—
Nelson, February 12, 1996 to February 26, 1996	—
Hutt Valley, February 26, 1996 to January 20, 1997	2
Nelson, January 20, 1997 to February 17, 1997	1
Auckland-Manukau, February 17, 1997 to March 3, 1997	—
Bay of Plenty, March 3, 1997 to January 26, 1998	1
Wellington City, January 26, 1998 to February 9, 1998	—
Manawatu, February 9, 1998 to February 23, 1998	—
Auckland-Waitakere, February 23, 1998 to March 9, 1998	—
Northland, March 9, 1998 to February 8, 1999	2
Wellington City, February 8, 1999 to February 22, 1999	—
Canterbury Country, February 22, 1999 to January 24, 2000	2
South Canterbury, January 24, 2000 to February 7, 2000	—
Dunedin Metropolitan, February 7, 2000 to March 26, 2001	3
Hamilton, March 26, 2001 to March 25, 2002	4
Manawatu, March 25, 2002 to February 17, 2003	—
Hawke's Bay, February 17, 2003 to 3 March, 2003	—
Northland, 3 March, 2003 to 16 February, 2004	2
Mid-Canterbury, 16 February, 2004 to 7 February, 2005	1
Canterbury Country, 7 February, 2005 to 7 March, 2005	1
Hamilton, 7 March, 2005 to 12 March, 2007	5
Taranaki, 12 March, 2007 to 18 February, 2008	—
Canterbury Country, 18 February 2008 to 17 March, 2008	1
Hamilton, 17 March, 2008 to 16 February, 2009	—
Hawke's Bay, 16 February, 2009 to 8 February, 2010	2
Manawatu, 8 February, 2010 to 15 March, 2010	2
North Otago, 15 March, 2010 to 30 January, 2011	—
Otago Country, 30 January, 2011 to 13 February, 2011	—
Marlborough, 13 February, 2011 to 13 March, 2011	1
Hamilton, 13 March, 2011 to 27 January, 2013	4
Bay of Plenty, 27 January, 2013 to 9 February, 2014	4

	Challenges resisted
Manawatu, 9 February, 2014 to 1 March, 2015	4
Canterbury Country, 1 March, 2015 to 31 January, 2016	1
Buller, 31 January, 2016 to 14 February, 2016	—
North Otago, 14 February, 2016 to 27 February, 2016	—
Hawke's Bay, 27 February, 2016 to 13 March, 2016	—
Bay of Plenty, 13 March, 2016 to 29 January, 2018	4
Counties-Manukau, 29 January, 2018 to 11 March, 2018	2
Southland, 11 March 2018 to 17 February, 2019	1
Nelson, 17 February, 2019 to 3 March, 2019	—
Hawke's Bay, 3 March, 2019 to 17 March, 2019	—
Hamilton, 17 March, 2019 to 1 March, 2020	2
Canterbury Country, 1 March 2020 to 31 January 2021	1
Nelson, 31 January 2021 to 14 February 2021	—
North Otago, 14 February 2021 to 27 February 2021	—
Hawke's Bay, 27 February 2021	1

Career Aggregates

BATTING	*M*	*I*	*NO*	*HS*	*Runs*	*Ave*
Leggat I.B. *(Nelson),* 1948-68	38	56	1	130	1968	35.78
Reade L.B. *(Nelson),* 1958-73	35	57	2	117	1951	35.47
Lowans G.E. *(Nelson),* 1958-73	30	48	1	148	1811	38.53
Anderson R.W. *(Northland and Southland),* 1970-77	16	31	6	255	1773	70.92
McVicar C.C. *(Manawatu),* 1935-54	28	44	1	180	1754	40.79
Spence D.V. *(Hawkes Bay and Nelson),* 1949-67	34	51	8	151	1574	36.60
Hoskin R.N.*(Southland and Central Otago),* 1978-96	31	35	4	162	1429	46.09
Pierce R.A. *(Nelson),* 1969-89	24	31	2	150	1426	49.17
Congdon B.E. *(Nelson),* 1959-65	19	28	2	133	1413	54.34
Gallichan N. *(Manawatu),* 1925-47	29	48	5	142	1409	32.76
Hampton B.L. *(Nelson),* 1960-75	21	32	3	236	1391	49.26
Hodgson W.G. *(Nelson),* 1978-86	24	29	2	265	1348	49.92
Norris W.E. *(Manawatu),* 1926-47	42	61	6	84	1242	22.58
Orton R.W. *(Rangitikei and Wanganui),* 1911-26	20	33	1	204	1222	38.18
Hayward R.E. *(Nelson),* 1979-89	23	26	2	113	1115	46.45
Holland C.A. *(Wanganui),* 1912-28	24	38	4	111	1060	31.17
Robinson G.G. *(Hamilton),* 2000-09	11	16	1	268	1039	69.26
Edwards G.N. *(Nelson),* 1972-86	24	30	2	236	1038	37.07
Toynbee M.H. *(Nelson),* 1974-81	13	17	3	200*	1031	73.64

BOWLING	*M*	*Runs*	*Wkts*	*Ave*
Holland C.A. *(Wanganui),* 1912-28	24	2202	189	11.65
Gallichan N. *(Manawatu),* 1925-47	29	2053	177	11.59
Leggat I.B. *(Nelson),* 1948-68	38	2149	134	16.03
Spence D.V. *(Hawkes Bay and Nelson),* 1949-67	34	1697	110	15.42
Alabaster G.D. *(Thames Valley and Southland),* 1961-79	20	1508	102	14.78
Newman J. *(Nelson),* 1922-46	20	1348	97	13.89
Alabaster J.C. *(Southland),* 1955-74	14	1223	92	13.29
Bernau E.H.L. *(Wanganui and Hawkes Bay),* 1912-28	14	1009	90	11.21

Highest Individual Innings

272*	Kinzett C.A.	Nelson v Marlborough	Nelson	1933/34
268	Robinson G.G.	Hamilton v Northland	Hamilton	2005/06
265	Hodgson W.G.	Nelson v Taranaki	Nelson	1983/84
264	Everest J.K.	Waikato v Manawatu	Hamilton	1956/57
255	Anderson R.W.	Southland v Ashburton County	Invercargill	1976/77
242	Edmondson M.J.	Hawke's Bay v Nelson	Nelson	2018/19
236	Hampton B.L.	Nelson v Waikato	Nelson	1963/64
236	Edwards G.N.	Nelson v North Canterbury	Nelson	1984/85
229	Douglas M.W.	Nelson v Southland	Nelson	1992/93

Best Bowling in an Innings

10-35	Holland C.A.	Wanganui v South Taranaki	Wanganui	1922/23
9-38	Williams W.S.A.	Canterbury Country v Buller	Rangiora	2015/16
9-103	Jordan A.B.	Taranaki v Hutt Valley	New Plymouth	1971/72
8-9	Clough R.	Waikato v Bay of Plenty	Hamilton	1938/39
8-20	Andrews S.L.	Hamilton v Northland	Hamilton	2001/02
8-25	Smith J.D.	Waikato v Horowhenua	Hamilton	1969/70
8-25	Jordan A.B.	Taranaki v Franklin	New Plymouth	1971/72
8-26	Haycock R.S.	Nelson v Marlborough	Nelson	1924/25

Best Bowling in a Match

14-79	Holland C.A.	Wanganui v South Taranaki	Wanganui	1922/23
14-89	Jordan A.B.	Taranaki v Franklin	New Plymouth	1971/72
14-133	Upston I.A.	Hutt Valley v Wanganui	Wanganui	1955/56
14-149	Sulzberger G.P.	Taranaki v Manawatu	New Plymouth	1994/95

CANTERBURY COUNTRY v NELSON

Hawke Cup

at MainPower Oval, Rangiora on 29, 30, 31 January, 2021
Toss : Nelson. Umpires : A. Mehrotra & G.M. Walklin
Close of play: 1st day: Nelson 247-4, Clark 121, O'Connor 93;
2nd day: Canterbury Country 147-7, Williams 21, Foulkes 22
Match drawn

NELSON

FIRST INNINGS	Runs	Mins	Balls	6s	4s	SECOND INNINGS	Runs	Mins	Balls	6s	4s
N.C.Clark† c Williams b Foulkes	172	490	354	-	12	b Sheat	4	9	7	-	1
T.A.D.Zohrab b Sheat	9	39	91	-	1						
G.R.Hay c Gruijters b Chamberlain S.G.	10	14	13	-	-	not out	31	71	58	-	3
H.J.Visavadiya c Hamilton b Chamberlain S.G.	3	27	19	-	-						
F.P.Raxworthy c Chamberlain S.G. b Foulkes	1	5	2	-	-	(2) not out	19	80	73	-	1
J.M.O'Connor c Hamilton b Foulkes	120	387	316	1	11						
D.L.D.Zohrab not out	23	65	53	-	1						
F.J.M.Murray b Foulkes	5	19	12	-	1						
B.M.Hodgson* c Hamilton b Foulkes	0	8	6	-	-						
D.J.Eginton lbw b Foulkes	0	2	1		-						
J.N.Newport lbw b Mariu	4	19	11	-	1						
Extras (b 10, lb 2, w 3, nb 3)	18										
TOTAL (133.5 overs)	**365**	541				(23 overs) (1 wkt)	**54**	80			

CANTERBURY COUNTRY

	Runs	Mins	Balls	6s	4s
R.A.Mariu lbw b O'Connor	21	51	46	-	1
R.P.Young b Newport	3	27	14	-	-
J.J.A.Frew c Clark b Newport	5	37	21	-	-
H.J.Chamberlain* lbw b Newport	3	10	6	-	-
H.B.Shipley run out	5	14	14	-	1
T.G.J.Gruijters c Clark b Zohrab T.A.D.	23	110	68	-	2
W.L.V.Hamilton† b Zohrab T.A.D.	19	56	52	-	1
J.H.S.Williams c Clark b Newport	28	136	92	-	2
Z.G.Foulkes c Hodgson b Zohrab T.A.D.	92	287	255	1	6
F.W.Sheat c Visavadiya b Zohrab T.A.D.	76	112	85	1	8
S.G.Chamberlain not out	20	81	63	-	2
Extras (b 12, lb 7, w 6, nb 5)	30				
TOTAL (118.4 overs)	**325**	463			

Bowling	*O*	*M*	*R*	*W*				
CANTERBURY COUNTRY								
Sheat	24	4	87	1	5	0	17	1
Foulkes	27	3	88	6	7	3	9	0
Chamberlain S.G.	25	8	62	2	3	1	4	0
Gruijters	4	1	10	0	2	1	4	0
Frew	16	5	31	0				
Mariu	25.5	6	45	1	2	0	8	0
Williams	12	4	30	0	4	1	12	0
NELSON								
Newport	30	5	74	4				
Eginton	11	1	54	0				
O'Connor	13	2	40	1				
Zohrab T.A.D.	29.4	9	48	4				
Visavadiya	18	6	44	0				
Raxworthy	2	0	9	0				
Murray	14	3	36	0				
Zohrab D.L.D.	1	0	1	0				

Fall of Wickets

	N *1st*	***CC*** *1st*	***N*** *2nd*
1st	23	21	6
2nd	38	39	-
3rd	54	46	-
4th	57	47	-
5th	328	52	-
6th	340	85	-
7th	348	111	-
8th	352	162	-
9th	352	279	-
10th	365	325	-

NELSON v NORTH OTAGO — Hawke Cup

at Saxton Oval, Nelson on 12, 13, 14 February, 2021
Toss : North Otago. Umpires : J.A.K. Bromley & T.J. Parlane
Close of play: 1st day: Nelson 81-7, Smith 0, R.J. Restieaux 5; 2nd day: North Otago 241-7, J.B. Smith 17, Kitto 2
North Otago won by 250 runs

NORTH OTAGO

FIRST INNINGS	Runs	Mins	Balls	6s	4s	SECOND INNINGS	Runs	Mins	Balls	6s	4s
J.H.Shields b Newport	0	1	1	-	-	c & b O'Connor	44	63	57	-	9
S.F.Grobler lbw b Newport	5	31	16	-	-	c Clark b Zohrab T.A.D.	9	72	49	-	1
L.C.Kingan*† b Newport	0	2	2		-	b Zohrab D.L.D.	54	206	180	-	7
L.C.Johnson c Visavadiya b Restieaux R.J.	10	21	18	-	1	c Restieaux F.D. b Zohrab D.L.D.	60	182	153	-	6
T.M.Dempster c Clark b Visavadiya	43	97	77	-	7	b Restieaux R.J.	40	70	51	-	6
N.G.Smith c Hay b O'Connor	22	48	41	-	2	c Hay b Zohrab T.A.D.	0	10	7	-	-
B.H.Donkers lbw b Newport	49	113	78	-	4	c Clark b Restieaux R.J.	2	17	13	-	-
J.B.Smith c Jones-Allen b Newport	12	49	43	1	-	b Newport	25	71	55	-	4
S.C.Kitto b Visavadiya	2	20	13	-	-	c Restieaux R.J. b Visavadiya	4	40	27	-	-
B.G.James c Hay b Visavadiya	5	18	11	-	1	not out	13	63	66	-	1
C.N.Grubb not out	14	16	12	-	1	c Zohrab T.A.D. b Visavadiya	46	60	47	-	9
Extras (lb 5, w 1)	6					(b 7, lb 4, w 1, nb 5)	17				
TOTAL (52 overs)	**168**	209				(116.4 overs)	**314**	430			

NELSON

FIRST INNINGS	Runs	Mins	Balls	6s	4s	SECOND INNINGS	Runs	Mins	Balls	6s	4s
N.C.Clark† c Kingan b Grubb	10	35	28	-	1	c Shields b Smith J.B.	28	57	48	-	6
T.A.D.Zohrab b Smith N.G.	17	117	85	-	1	(6) c Smith N.G. b Grobler	21	47	32	-	1
G.R.Hay c Kingan b Smith N.G.	16	63	31	-	3	lbw b Grubb	6	30	17	-	1
H.J.Visavadiya c Kingan b Smith N.G.	3	32	21	-	-	(5) c Kingan b Smith J.B.	7	22	15	-	1
D.L.D.Zohrab b Grobler	6	44	29	-	-	(7) st Kingan b Grobler	16	50	41	-	1
J.M.O'Connor c Johnson b Grobler	15	39	24		3	(2) c Kingan b Smith N.G.	1	9	3	-	-
F.D.Restieaux c Donkers b Smith J.B.	1	5	4	-	-	(4) c Smith N.G. b Smith J.B.	14	31	21	-	4
J.Smith c Kingan b Smith N.G.	0	32	25	-	-	lbw b James	2	23	8	-	-
R.J.Restieaux not out	24	48	41	-	2	not out	16	24	17	-	2
J.N.Newport c Donkers b Smith N.G.	2	9	6	-	-	st Kingan b Grobler	0	3	3	-	-
O.W.Jones-Allen* run out	6	12	4	-	1	c Kitto b James	6	6	5	1	-
Extras (lb 3, w 3, nb 3)	9					(lb 5, w 1)	6				
TOTAL (49.1 overs)	**109**	220				(35 overs)	**123**	154			

Bowling	O	M	R	W	O	M	R	W
NELSON								
Newport	17	2	65	5	20	7	71	1
Restieaux R.J.	7	0	25	1	8	2	30	2
O'Connor	6	2	11	1	16	6	39	1
Zohrab T.A.D.	9	3	17	0	27	13	47	2
Visavadiya	13	3	45	3	9.4	5	23	2
Jones-Allen					18	4	47	0
Restieaux F.D.					2	0	26	0
Zohrab D.L.D.					16	6	20	2
NORTH OTAGO								
Smith N.G.	14	1	32	5	7	3	13	1
Smith J.B.	13.1	7	21	1	11	0	45	3
Grubb	10	6	17	1	8	1	25	1
James	2	1	4	0	3	1	19	2
Donkers	2	0	12	0				
Grobler	8	3	20	2	6	1	16	3

Fall of Wickets

	NO 1st	N 1st	NO 2nd	N 2nd
1st	0	13	53	9
2nd	0	43	53	29
3rd	13	49	175	49
4th	17	52	188	60
5th	58	74	193	61
6th	89	75	203	94
7th	125	75	224	99
8th	148	82	251	105
9th	148	93	251	106
10th	168	109	314	123

NORTH OTAGO v HAWKE'S BAY

Hawke Cup

at Whitestone Contracting Stadium, Oamaru on 26, 27 February, 2021
Toss : Hawke's Bay. Umpires : L.R. Els & A. Stanley
Close of play: 1st day: Hawke's Bay 147-4, Schmulian 52, Thompson 0
Hawke's Bay won by an innings and 52 runs

NORTH OTAGO

FIRST INNINGS	Runs	Mins	Balls	6s	4s	SECOND INNINGS	Runs	Mins	Balls	6s	4s
J.H.Shields lbw b Dudding	12	45	32	-	2	c Dudding b Watson	40	69	55	-	8
S.F.Grobler c Wiggins b Stoyanoff	3	32	20	-	-	c Edmondson b Watson	37	75	48	-	6
N.R.Johnson b Stoyanoff	17	97	69	-	2	c Watson b Stoyanoff	9	44	31	-	1
L.C.Johnson lbw b Schmulian	28	71	51	-	4	c Edmondson b Watson	13	17	15	1	1
T.M.Dempster c Wiggins b Stoyanoff	26	72	65	-	3	b Watson	0	2	2	-	-
B.H.Donkers b Schmulian	0	4	4	-	-	c & b Schmulian	0	2	1	-	-
L.C.Kingan*† lbw b Schmulian	11	33	30	-	2	not out	12	50	37	-	2
J.B.Smith c Wiggins b Schaw	20	57	42	-	2	c Wiggins b Dudding	3	23	10	-	-
S.C.Kitto c Edmondson b Dudding	2	15	7	-	-	c Wiggins b Dudding	0	3	3	-	-
B.G.James c Thompson b Dudding	5	34	25	-	1	c Wiggins b Dudding	0	3	2	-	-
C.N.Grubb not out	7	13	7	1	-	run out	0	5	0	-	-
Extras (lb 8, w 5, nb 1)	14					(b 1, lb 3, w 2)	6				
TOTAL (58.3 overs)	**145**	240				(34 overs)	**120**				

HAWKE'S BAY

	Runs	Mins	Balls	6s	4s
M.J.Edmondson lbw b Donkers	21	43	33	1	2
B.L.Wiggins† b Donkers	17	26	20	-	4
B.D.Schmulian c Kingan b Donkers	53	128	103	-	7
G.D.Tryon c Johnson L.C. b Grobler	8	18	15	-	1
I.D.Lange c Dempster b Smith	39	71	46	-	7
D.R.Thompson c Kingan b Smith	0	33	15	-	-
A.R.Schaw* b Smith	129	219	185	3	17
T.J.Watson c Kingan b James	7	71	58	-	-
W.J.Clark c & b Kitto	9	72	64	-	1
L.R.Dudding c Kingan b Smith	8	49	21	-	1
B.P.Stoyanoff not out	0	13	6	-	-
Extras (b 8, lb 5, w 8, nb 5)	26				
TOTAL (93.3 overs)	**317**	374			

Bowling	O	M	R	W	O	M	R	W
HAWKE'S BAY								
Dudding	11.3	1	28	3	10	1	37	3
Stoyanoff	15	5	42	3	10	2	42	1
Clark	5	3	3	0				
Watson	5	0	17	0	7	3	23	4
Schmulian	16	7	37	3	7	1	14	1
Schaw	6	2	10	1				
NORTH OTAGO								
Grubb	21	5	69	0				
Smith	25.3	8	94	4				
Donkers	22	4	73	3				
Grobler	9	4	18	1				
James	10	2	36	1				
Kitto	6	1	14	1				

Fall of Wickets	**NO**	**HB**	**NO**
	1st	*1st*	*2nd*
1st	11	35	79
2nd	17	47	80
3rd	64	59	96
4th	74	139	96
5th	75	148	97
6th	93	160	102
7th	105	197	115
8th	120	234	115
9th	136	293	116
10th	145	317	120

HAWKE'S BAY v HAMILTON

at Nelson Park, Napier on 12, 13, 14 March, 2021
Toss : Hawke's Bay. Umpires : C.M. Brown & W.R. Knights
Close of play: 1st day: Hawke's Bay 111-3, Schmulian 30, Leopard 0; 2nd day: Hamilton 166-6, Parker 22, Walker 39
Hawke's Bay won by 8 wickets

HAMILTON

FIRST INNINGS	*Runs*	*Mins*	*Balls*	*6s*	*4s*	*SECOND INNINGS*	*Runs*	*Mins*	*Balls*	*6s*	*4s*
R.Clinton b Lennox	24	135	86	-	-	c Wiggins b Dudding	10	61	39	-	1
E.H.Santner lbw b Dudding	1	20	17	-	-	b Dudding	9	28	21	-	-
S.N.Dhambagolla lbw b Dudding	4	16	9	-	-	c Wiggins b Stoyanoff	2	6	6	-	-
A.Desai c & b Leopard	14	31	28	-	1	lbw b Lennox	45	132	88	-	6
P.D.Bocock† c Stoyanoff b Dudding	19	72	52	-	1	b Watson	9	28	14	-	1
A.P.Devcich c Edmondson b Lennox	20	35	24	1	1	c Tryon b Dudding	16	40	24	-	2
J.M.Parker c Wiggins b Lennox	0	4	2	-	-	lbw b Tryon	43	128	104	-	4
F.L.Walker* c & b Lennox	21	35	25	-	5	b Watson	61	96	76	1	8
J.H.Brown c Lennox b Dudding	5	6	5	-	1	not out	53	72	46	2	7
N.W.Farrell c Watson b Dudding	1	8	6	-	-	lbw b Schmulian	14	59	55	-	2
C.B.Rowell not out	0	5	3	-	-	c Tryon b Schmulian	0	8	2	-	-
Extras (b 1, lb 1, nb 2)	4					(b 8, lb 6, w 4)	18				
TOTAL (42.5 overs)	**113**	186				(79.1 overs)	**280**	331			

HAWKE'S BAY

FIRST INNINGS	*Runs*	*Mins*	*Balls*	*6s*	*4s*	*SECOND INNINGS*	*Runs*	*Mins*	*Balls*	*6s*	*4s*
J.D.Whitley c Devcich b Farrell	39	196	167	-	2	c sub (K.R.S.Price) b Farrell	35	124	114	-	4
B.L.Wiggins† lbw b Farrell	3	20	17	-	-	not out	107	160	115	3	12
M.J.Edmondson c Devcich b Farrell	27	88	69	-	3	c Bocock b Walker	13	21	15	-	1
B.D.Schmulian lbw b Farrell	70	194	171	-	6	not out	1	13	10	-	-
C.K.Leopard c Bocock b Rowell	35	111	86	-	2						
G.D.Tryon c Brown b Farrell	0	11	5	-	-						
I.D.Lange c Desai b Rowell	0	4	5	-	-						
T.J.Watson c Parker b Rowell	1	19	12	-	-						
J.R.Lennox* c Santner b Rowell	11	48	27	-	-						
L.R.Dudding not out	14	46	30	-	1						
B.P.Stoyanoff c Walker b Brown	5	14	15	-	1						
Extras (b 8, lb 8, w 1, nb 10)	27					(lb 4, nb 4)	8				
TOTAL (99 overs)	**232**	378				(41.4 overs) (2 wkts)	**164**	160			

Bowling	*O*	*M*	*R*	*W*	*O*	*M*	*R*	*W*
HAWKE'S BAY								
Dudding	15.5	5	46	5	18	4	55	3
Stoyanoff	6	2	12	0	12	2	56	1
Leopard	7	2	19	1	8	1	30	0
Watson	6	0	19	0	14	3	51	2
Lennox	8	5	15	4	17	3	49	1
Schmulian					3.1	2	2	2
Tryon					7	1	23	1
HAMILTON								
Rowell	23	4	58	4	5.4	1	25	0
Farrell	20	6	46	5	4.2	0	25	1
Walker	35	9	59	0	15.4	2	51	1
Brown	13	2	35	1	7	2	13	0
Santner	2	1	4	0	2	0	21	0
Clinton	6	0	14	0	7	1	25	0

Fall of Wickets

	HAM	***HB***	***HAM***	***HB***
	1st	*1st*	*2nd*	*2nd*
1st	3	9	21	101
2nd	8	56	24	151
3rd	27	111	39	-
4th	64	194	59	-
5th	64	194	90	-
6th	68	194	118	-
7th	106	194	209	-
8th	112	203	209	-
9th	113	216	264	-
10th	113	232	280	-

WOMEN'S CRICKET

Compiled by Catherine Campbell

Despite the global impact of the coronavirus pandemic, and the rescheduling of the Women's World Cup to 2022, New Zealand still had a busy 2020/21 summer with 18 matches scheduled.

The White Ferns went to Australia in September, losing the Twenty20 series 2-1 and the one-day series 3-0. They then played England at home, losing the one-day series 2-1 and the Twenty20 series 3-0 before finishing the summer hosting Australia. The visitors won the one-day series 3-0 but the Twenty20 series finished level with the deciding game washed out.

Fran Jonas, a 16-year-old left-arm spinner from Auckland and Brooke Halliday, left-hand bat and right-arm medium-pace bowler from Northern Districts, made their White Ferns debuts during the summer.

Canterbury won the Hallyburton Johnstone Shield beating Auckland at Eden Park Outer Oval, with Frances Mackay top scoring with an unbeaten 94 and putting on a 166 run second wicket partnership with Amy Satterthwaite to ensure a comprehensive victory in the 38th over. Kate Ebrahim was the leading run scorer in the competition with 480 runs and Sarah Asmussen took the most wickets (19), both players from Canterbury.

Canterbury also won the Super Smash Twenty20 competition final against Wellington at the Basin Reserve after being 60-6 but winning with two balls to spare after an unbroken seventh wicket partnership between Ebrahim and Lea Tahuhu. Sophie Devine was the leading scorer in the Super Smash competition (434 runs) and Mackay took the most wickets (20).

Auckland won the national under 19 tournament played at Lincoln University, Christchurch Girls' High School won the Gillette Venus Cup and Heaton Normal Intermediate continued their dominance by winning the ANZ Primary School Cup.

Contracted players were: Auckland: Jane Barnett, Sarah Carnachan, Amie Hucker, Arlene Kelly, Tariel Lamb, Regina Lili'i, Roz McNeill, Jesse Prasad, Saachi Shahri.

Canterbury: Sarah Asmussen, Missy Banks, Natalie Cox, Kate Ebrahim, Laura Hughes, Allie Mace-Cochrane, Frances Mackay, Jess Simmons, Gabby Sullivan.

Central Districts: Georgia Atkinson, Emily Cunningham, Claudia Green, Mikaela Greig, Melissa Hansen, Ashtuti Kumar, Monique Rees, Kerry Tomlinson, Anlo van Deventer.

Northern Districts: Kate Anderson, Lucy Boucher, Brooke Halliday, Lauren Heaps, Felicity Leydon-Davis, Olivia Lobb, Lily Mulivai, Eimear Richardson, Charlotte Sarsfield.

Otago: Gemma Adams, Emma Black, Caitlin Blakely, Millie Cowan, Bhagya Herath, Polly Inglis, Bella James, Marina Lamplough, Sophie Oldershaw.

Wellington: Olivia Boivin, Dee Doughty, Xara Jetly, Caitlin King, Jess McFadyen, Beth Molony, Thamsyn Newton, Georgia Plimmer, Maneka Singh.

PLAYER OF THE YEAR

Amy Satterthwaite is the Player of the Year. She was the second highest run scorer in the Twenty20 competition with 364 runs at a strike rate of 131 and took eight wickets with her best figures being in the final where she took 3-13. In the Hallyburton Johnstone Shield she scored 264 runs at 52.80, took nine wickets and scored 73 and took 4-27 in the final.

On the White Ferns tour to Australia Satterthwaite was the team's leading run scorer and in the home series against England she scored an unbeaten 119 in the third one-day international at Dunedin, to lead the team to their only win and was the team's leading run scorer in both the one-day and Twenty20 matches against England.

PROMISING PLAYER

Brooke Halliday is the Promising Player of the Year. Halliday scored 331 runs in the Hallyburton Johnstone Shield with a top score of 101 not out and an average of 47.28 while she also took ten wickets. She scored 175 runs in the Super Smash at a strike rate of 87 and took nine wickets.

Halliday was selected for the New Zealand XI against England in two matches at Queenstown, scoring 26 and 79. She was then selected for the White Ferns and made her debut in the first one-day game against England at Hagley Oval, Christchurch where she scored 50 runs batting at number seven. She followed this up with 60 in the second match at Dunedin.

NEW ZEALAND IN AUSTRALIA

The White Ferns toured Australia in September 2020 to play three Twenty20s and three one-day internationals. The team was based in Brisbane and all the games played at Allan Border Field with the team operating in a bio-secure environment throughout the tour which also included a practice match against Australia.

Australia won the first two Twenty20s with New Zealand fighting back to win the third with Amelia Kerr and Hayley Jensen seeing the team home with three balls to spare. Australia secured a clean sweep in the one-day series, with captain Meg Lanning scoring an unbeaten 101 in the second game, and they then crushed New Zealand to win by 232 runs in the third match. Suzie Bates suffered a season ending injury in the first one-day game with a serious shoulder injury.

To cover for any possible Covid issues, seventeen players travelled. The uncapped Deanna Doughty from Wellington was selected for the tour but she and Jess Watkin did not feature during the series.

The New Zealand squad was: Sophie Devine *(captain)*, Deanna Doughty, Maddy Green, Amelia Kerr, Jess Kerr *(Wellington)*, Lauren Down, Holly Huddleston, Katie Perkins *(Auckland)*, Natalie Dodd, Rosemary Mair, Hannah Rowe, Jess Watkin *(Central Districts)*, Amy Satterthwaite, Lea Tahuhu *(Canterbury)*, Suzie Bates, Hayley Jensen, Katey Martin *(Otago)*.

Coach, Bob Carter; Batting coach, Rob Nicol; Bowling coach, Jacob Oram; Manager, Belinda Muller; Trainer, Scott Wrenn; Physiotherapist, Zoe Russell.

New Zealand One-day International Averages

BATTING	*M*	*I*	*NO*	*HS*	*Agg*	*Ave*	*100s*	*50s*	*Ct*	*St*	*SR*
A.E. Satterthwaite	3	3	0	69	111	37.00	-	1	-	-	85
S.F.M. Devine	3	3	0	79	90	30.00	-	1	1	-	64
M.L. Green	3	3	0	35	78	26.00	-	-	1	-	92
K.T. Perkins	3	3	1	32	43	21.50	-	-	2	-	53
N.C. Dodd	3	3	0	34	58	19.33	-	-	-	-	59
K.J. Martin	3	3	0	26	50	16.66	-	-	1	1	68
S.W. Bates	1	1	0	14	14	14.00	-	-	1	-	46
H.N.K. Jensen	3	3	0	21	27	9.00	-	-	-	-	75
A.C. Kerr	3	3	0	11	128	6.00	-	-	2	-	36
R.A. Mair	3	3	1	7	11	5.50	-	-	-	-	57
H.M. Rowe	2	2	0	3	4	2.00	-	-	1	-	44
H.R. Huddleston	1	1	0	0	0	0.00	-	-	-	-	0
L.M.M. Tahuhu	2	2	2	1*	1	-	-	-	-	-	50

BOWLING	*O*	*M*	*R*	*W*	*Ave*	*Best*	*R/O*
A.C. Kerr	26	1	136	6	22.66	3-47	5.23
H.R. Huddleston	10	1	62	2	31.00	2-62	6.20
H.N.K. Jensen	14.3	0	106	2	53.00	1-20	7.31
S.F.M. Devine	23	3	125	2	62.50	2-50	5.43
R.A. Mair	27	3	132	2	66.00	2-21	4.89
H.M. Rowe	7	0	47	0	-	-	6.71
L.M.M. Tahuhu	8.4	0	66	0	-	-	7.62
M.L. Green	12.4	0	81	0	-	-	6.39

Australia One-day International Averages

BATTING	*M*	*I*	*NO*	*HS*	*Agg*	*Ave*	*100s*	*50s*	*Ct*	*St*	*SR*
R.L. Haynes	3	3	0	96	222	74.00	-	2	-	1	87
A.J. Healy	3	3	0	87	134	44.66	-	1	1	1	100
A.J. Sutherland	3	2	0	35	52	26.00	-	-	3	-	60
B.L. Mooney	3	3	1	29*	51	25.50	-	-	1	-	98
A.K. Gardner	3	2	0	34	34	17.00	-	-	5	-	161
S.G. Molineux	3	3	1	18*	34	17.00	-	-	2	-	75
M.M. Lanning	2	2	2	101*	163	-	1	1	1	-	98
T.M. McGrath	1	1	1	29*	29	-	-	-	-	-	263
N.J. Carey	3	1	1	5*	5	-	-	-	1	-	71
J.L. Jonassen	3	-	-	-	-	-	-	-	-	-	-
M.L. Schutt	3	-	-	-	-	-	-	-	-	-	-
G.L. Wareham	3	-	-	-	-	-	-	-	1	-	-

BOWLING	*O*	*M*	*R*	*W*	*Ave*	*Best*	*R/O*
J.L. Jonassen	24.1	0	81	8	10.12	4-36	3.35
A.K. Gardner	5	0	26	2	13.00	2-11	5.20
S.G. Molineux	20	3	79	6	13.16	2-2	3.95
M.L. Schutt	25	4	115	5	23.00	2-25	4.60
G.L. Wareham	24	2	84	3	28.00	2-23	3.50
N.J. Carey	13	1	61	2	30.50	1-27	4.69
A.J. Sutherland	15	1	73	2	36.50	1-16	4.87

AUSTRALIA v NEW ZEALAND
At Allan Border Field, Brisbane 24 September, 2020

Australia 247-8 (B.L. Mooney 80, S.G. Molineux 57, R.L. Haynes 54) **defeated New Zealand** 236 (S.F.M. Devine 89, A.E. Satterthwaite 48, S.G. Molineux 5-29) by 11 runs

AUSTRALIA v NEW ZEALAND — First Twenty20 International

at Allan Border Field, Brisbane on 26 September, 2020
Toss : New Zealand. Umpires : D.M. Koch & B.N.J. Oxenford
Australia won by 17 runs

New Zealand won the toss in their first game of the season and decided to field. Mair removed Mooney in the second over and Healy soon followed. Gardner dominated the remainder of the innings, hitting three sixes in her 61. Australia finished on 138-6 with Devine taking 3-18.

Devine and Bates top scored for New Zealand but struggled to score at the required rate. Martin hit 21 off 16 balls but the later batsmen were left with too much to do and the New Zealand innings ended at 121-7. Schutt took 4-23.

AUSTRALIA

	Runs	Mins	Balls	6s	4s
A.J.Healy† c Bates b Devine	6	24	9	-	1
B.L.Mooney c Green b Mair	2	9	4	-	-
M.M.Lanning* c Martin b Tahuhu	24	30	28	-	3
R.L.Haynes c Kerr b Devine	23	35	18	-	3
A.K.Gardner c Green b Bates	61	43	41	3	6
S.G.Molineux c Bates b Devine	0	3	2	-	-
N.J.Carey not out	7	26	12	-	-
G.L.Wareham not out	9	7	6	-	1
J.L.Jonassen					
M.L.Schutt					
D.M.Kimmince					
Extras (lb 1, w 5)	6				
TOTAL (20 overs) (6 wkts)	**138**	83			

NEW ZEALAND

	Runs	Mins	Balls	6s	4s
S.F.M.Devine* st Healy b Kimmince	29	36	34	1	3
M.L.Green c Schutt b Kimmince	5	20	9	-	-
S.W.Bates c Mooney b Schutt	33	54	38	-	2
A.E.Satterthwaite c Healy b Jonassen	9	17	12	-	1
K.J.Martin† c Lanning b Schutt	21	20	16	-	3
A.C.Kerr c Carey b Schutt	5	8	5	-	-
H.N.K.Jensen c Gardner b Schutt	4	9	4	-	1
L.R.Down not out	6	3	4	-	1
K.T.Perkins not out	0	1	0	-	-
R.A.Mair					
L.M.M.Tahuhu					
Extras (b 1, lb 2, w 4, nb 2)	9				
TOTAL (20 overs) (7 wkts)	**121**	81			

Bowling	*O*	*M*	*R*	*W*
NEW ZEALAND				
Tahuhu	4	0	30	1
Mair	4	0	22	1
Jensen	3	0	26	0
Devine	4	0	18	3
Kerr	4	0	35	0
Bates	1	0	6	1
AUSTRALIA				
Schutt	4	0	23	4
Jonassen	4	0	20	1
Molineux	4	0	22	0
Kimmince	4	0	24	2
Wareham	2	0	15	0
Gardner	1	0	8	0
Carey	1	0	6	0

Fall of Wickets	***A***	***NZ***
1st	5	27
2nd	25	43
3rd	46	65
4th	81	105
5th	82	105
6th	126	115
7th	-	116
8th	-	-
9th	-	-
10th	-	-

AUSTRALIA v NEW ZEALAND Second Twenty20 International

at Allan Border Field, Brisbane on 27 September, 2020
Toss : New Zealand. Umpires : M.W. Graham-Smith & B.N.J. Oxenford
Australia won by 8 wickets

New Zealand won the toss and batted in the second game but soon lost their openers. Bates and Satterthwaite put on 49 for the third wicket but New Zealand could not last their twenty overs and were all out for 128. Wareham and Kimmince took three wickets apiece.

In reply, Healy and Mooney raced to fifty inside five overs and, following their dismissals, Lanning and Hayes shared an unbroken stand of 65 to see Australia to a 2-0 series lead.

NEW ZEALAND

	Runs	Mins	Balls	6s	4s
S.F.M.Devine* c & b Molineux	9	10	9	-	1
M.L.Green run out	7	14	7	-	1
S.W.Bates c Jonassen b Kimmince	22	49	28	-	1
A.E.Satterthwaite st Healy b Wareham	30	29	25	-	5
H.N.K.Jensen b Wareham	7	10	6	-	1
L.R.Down c Healy b Wareham	12	13	9	-	1
K.J.Martin† b Molineux	3	11	4	-	-
A.C.Kerr c Carey b Kimmince	11	16	11	-	1
K.T.Perkins not out	15	20	13	-	1
L.M.M.Tahuhu c Carey b Kimmince	4	4	3	-	1
R.A.Mair c Lanning b Carey	0	4	1	-	-
Extras (b 4, lb 1, w 3)	8				
TOTAL (19.2 overs)	**128**	84			

AUSTRALIA

	Runs	Mins	Balls	6s	4s
A.J.Healy† c Bates b Tahuhu	33	21	17	1	5
B.L.Mooney c Satterthwaite b Kerr	24	32	21	-	4
M.M.Lanning* not out	26	48	32	1	-
R.L.Haynes not out	40	36	31	-	5
A.K.Gardner					
N.J.Carey					
J.L.Jonassen					
D.M.Kimmince					
S.G.Molineux					
M.L.Schutt					
G.L.Wareham					
Extras (b 1, lb 1, w 3, nb 1)	6				
TOTAL (16.4 overs) (2 wkts)	**129**	67			

Bowling	*O*	*M*	*R*	*W*
AUSTRALIA				
Jonassen	3	0	20	0
Schutt	2	0	23	0
Molineux	4	0	17	2
Gardner	2	0	11	0
Kimmince	3	0	21	3
Wareham	4	0	26	3
Carey	1.2	0	5	1
NEW ZEALAND				
Mair	3.4	0	19	0
Tahuhu	3	0	20	1
Devine	2	0	20	0
Bates	1	0	22	0
Kerr	3	0	19	1
Jensen	1	0	3	0
Green	3	0	24	0

Fall of Wickets

	NZ	*A*
1st	16	51
2nd	19	64
3rd	68	-
4th	80	-
5th	85	-
6th	96	-
7th	100	-
8th	121	-
9th	126	-
10th	128	-

AUSTRALIA v NEW ZEALAND Third Twenty20 International

at Allan Border Field, Brisbane on 30 September, 2020
Toss : New Zealand. Umpires : M.W. Graham-Smith & D.M. Koch
New Zealand won by 5 wickets

New Zealand won their third toss in a row and bowled first. Gardner made 29 off 21 balls but none of the other batsmen could get on top of the bowling and Australia finished on 123-7.

Devine hit 25 off 22 balls and Satterthwaite made 30 from 25 before she was fifth out at 98 with 26 needed off 3.4 overs. Jensen and Kerr kept their heads and New Zealand hit the winning runs with three balls to spare.

AUSTRALIA

	Runs	Mins	Balls	6s	4s
A.J.Healy† c Perkins b Tahuhu	8	31	14	1	-
B.L.Mooney c Martin b Devine	11	16	9	-	2
M.M.Lanning* c Huddleston b Kerr A.C.	21	28	23	-	4
R.L.Haynes c Satterthwaite b Kerr A.C.	3	4	7	-	-
A.K.Gardner st Martin b Jensen	29	24	21	-	5
S.G.Molineux c & b Green	18	24	17	-	3
N.J.Carey not out	10	22	12	-	-
G.L.Wareham c Bates b Tahuhu	11	11	12	-	1
J.L.Jonassen not out	6	3	5	-	1
M.L.Schutt					
D.M.Kimmince					
Extras (b 1, lb 2, w 3)	6				
TOTAL (20 overs) (7 wkts)	**123**	78			

NEW ZEALAND

	Runs	Mins	Balls	6s	4s
S.F.M.Devine* st Healy b Wareham	25	29	22	1	1
M.L.Green c Gardner b Kimmince	10	18	17	-	1
S.W.Bates run out	3	14	8	-	-
A.E.Satterthwaite b Jonassen	30	39	25	-	3
K.J.Martin† b Wareham	23	31	24	1	1
H.N.K.Jensen not out	10	18	11	-	1
A.C.Kerr not out	18	14	10	-	3
K.T.Perkins					
H.R.Huddleston					
L.M.M.Tahuhu					
J.M.Kerr					
Extras (lb 1, w 5)	6				
TOTAL (19.3 overs) (5 wkts)	**125**	78			

Bowling	O	M	R	W
NEW ZEALAND				
Kerr J.M.	3	1	15	0
Huddleston	1	0	7	0
Tahuhu	4	0	29	2
Devine	4	0	28	1
Kerr A.C.	4	0	18	2
Jensen	2	0	17	1
Green	2	0	6	1
AUSTRALIA				
Jonassen	4	0	15	1
Schutt	3.3	0	27	0
Molineux	4	0	31	0
Kimmince	2	0	17	1
Carey	2	0	10	0
Wareham	3	0	19	2
Gardner	1	0	5	0

Fall of Wickets	***A***	***NZ***
1st	20	27
2nd	43	40
3rd	46	44
4th	57	96
5th	84	98
6th	100	-
7th	116	-
8th	-	-
9th	-	-
10th	-	-

AUSTRALIA v NEW ZEALAND — First One-day International

at Allan Border Field, Brisbane on 3 October, 2020
Toss : Australia. Umpires : M.W. Graham-Smith & B.N.J. Oxenford
Australia won by 7 wickets

Australia won their first toss of the summer and asked New Zealand to bat. The visitors had slumped to 83-6 in the 28th over before Perkins and Green added 62 for the seventh wicket. Jensen chimed in with 21 but New Zealand could muster just 180, being bowled out in the fiftieth over.

Healy and Haynes gave Australia a good start with 41 in 8.3 overs before Lanning (fifty off 62 balls) took Australia through to a comfortable win with 16.2 overs to spare. Bates was injured while fielding and did not play again for the remainder of the season.

NEW ZEALAND

	Runs	Mins	Balls	6s	4s
N.C.Dodd c Gardner b Schutt	19	19	21	1	2
S.W.Bates c Gardner b Wareham	14	50	30	-	1
A.E.Satterthwaite c Lanning b Sutherland	1	7	8	-	-
S.F.M.Devine* c Gardner b Jonassen	11	34	23	-	1
K.J.Martin† b Molinuex	21	46	44	-	2
A.C.Kerr c Mooney b Wareham	7	40	32	-	-
K.T.Perkins b Carey	32	70	51	-	3
M.L.Green b Molinuex	35	56	49	3	-
H.N.K.Jensen c Carey b Jonassen	21	30	24	-	2
R.A.Mair run out	7	17	12	-	-
L.M.M.Tahuhu not out	1	5	1	-	-
Extras (b 1, lb 3, w 7)	11				
TOTAL (49.1 overs)	**180**	183			

AUSTRALIA

	Runs	Mins	Balls	6s	4s
R.L.Haynes c Perkins b Jensen	44	84	62	1	5
A.J.Healy† c Kerr b Mair	26	33	27	-	5
M.M.Lanning* not out	62	100	70	2	5
B.L.Mooney c Bates b Mair	16	30	25	-	1
S.G.Molineux not out	18	21	19	-	3
A.K.Gardner					
A.J.Sutherland					
N.J.Carey					
J.L.Jonassen					
G.L.Wareham					
M.L.Schutt					
Extras (lb 1, w 13, nb 1)	15				
TOTAL (33.4 overs) (3 wkts)	**181**	133			

Bowling	*O*	*M*	*R*	*W*
AUSTRALIA				
Schutt	9	1	36	1
Sutherland	5	1	33	1
Wareham	10	1	23	2
Jonassen	9.1	0	29	2
Molinuex	10	3	28	2
Carey	6	0	27	1
NEW ZEALAND				
Tahuhu	6	0	40	0
Mair	7	2	21	2
Jensen	3	0	20	1
Devine	5	1	27	0
Kerr	6	0	39	0
Green	6.4	0	33	0

Fall of Wickets	***NZ***	***A***
1st	23	41
2nd	24	106
3rd	51	149
4th	60	-
5th	83	-
6th	83	-
7th	145	-
8th	153	-
9th	177	-
10th	180	-

AUSTRALIA v NEW ZEALAND Second One-day International

at Allan Border Field, Brisbane on 5 October, 2020
Toss : Australia. Umpires : B.N.J. Oxenford & D.M. Koch
Australia won by 4 wickets

Australia again won the toss and again bowled first. Dodd and Devine (fifty off 67 balls) put on 75 for the first wicket and then Satterthwaite (fifty off 58 balls) helped her captain add 93 for the second wicket. Martin and Green had a useful stand and New Zealand reached 252-9.

Healy went at 37 in Australia's reply but then Haynes (fifty off 54 balls) and Lanning put on 117 for the second wicket. The Australian captain reached fifty off 61 balls and her hundred just 35 balls later. She was still there at the finish as Australia won with 4.5 overs to spare and won yet another series.

NEW ZEALAND

	Runs	Mins	Balls	6s	4s
N.C.Dodd b Molinuex	34	59	59	-	5
S.F.M.Devine* c Healy b Jonassen	79	134	115	-	7
A.E.Satterthwaite c & b Molinuex	69	97	73	-	9
A.C.Kerr c Sutherland b Carey	11	18	16	-	1
K.J.Martin† b Jonassen	26	24	14	1	3
M.L.Green c Gardner b Jonassen	21	15	13	1	2
H.N.K.Jensen c Wareham b Jonassen	0	5	2	-	-
H.M.Rowe st Haynes b Schutt	1	6	3	-	-
K.T.Perkins not out	5	6	3	-	1
R.A.Mair c Sutherland b Schutt	0	1	1	-	-
L.M.M.Tahuhu not out	0	3	1	-	-
Extras (lb 2, w 4)	6				
TOTAL (50 overs) (9 wkts)	**252**	181			

AUSTRALIA

	Runs	Mins	Balls	6s	4s
A.J.Healy† b Devine	21	25	19	1	3
R.L.Haynes c Perkins b Devine	82	103	89	1	13
M.M.Lanning* not out	101	153	96	3	9
B.L.Mooney lbw b Kerr	6	12	8	-	-
S.G.Molineux st Martin b Kerr	14	26	23	-	2
A.K.Gardner c Martin b Kerr	0	2	1	-	-
A.J.Sutherland c Green b Jensen	17	31	30	-	2
N.J.Carey not out	5	6	7	-	1
J.L.Jonassen					
G.L.Wareham					
M.L.Schutt					
Extras (lb 3, w 4, nb 2)	9				
TOTAL (45.1 overs) (6 wkts)	**255**	178			

Bowling	*O*	*M*	*R*	*W*
AUSTRALIA				
Schutt	10	2	54	2
Sutherland	5	0	24	0
Jonassen	10	0	36	4
Wareham	8	1	38	0
Molinuex	8	0	49	2
Gardner	2	0	15	0
Carey	7	1	34	1
NEW ZEALAND				
Tahuhu	2.4	0	26	0
Mair	10	1	41	0
Devine	10	1	50	2
Kerr	10	0	47	3
Jensen	6.3	0	45	1
Green	3	0	25	0
Rowe	3	0	18	0

Fall of Wickets	***NZ***	***A***
1st	75	37
2nd	168	154
3rd	193	166
4th	203	196
5th	245	196
6th	245	245
7th	246	-
8th	247	-
9th	247	-
10th	-	-

NZC

AUSTRALIA v NEW ZEALAND Third One-day International

at Allan Border Field, Brisbane on 7 October, 2020
Toss : Australia. Umpires : M.W. Graham-Smith & D.M. Koch
Australia won by 232 runs

New Zealand won their first toss of the one-day series and fielded first only to see Haynes (fifty from 67 balls) and Healy (fifty off 63 balls) put on 144 for the first wicket. Sutherland, Gardner, Mooney and McGrath all made contributions as Australia amassed 325-5.

New Zealand lost Devine for a duck in reply and, apart from Satterthwaite and Green, no one was able to reach double figures. New Zealand were dismissed for just 93, with all six Australian bowlers being successful.

AUSTRALIA

	Runs	Mins	Balls	6s	4s
R.L.Haynes* lbw b Kerr	96	161	104	2	10
A.J.Healy† c Rowe b Kerr	87	98	87	1	13
A.J.Sutherland b Kerr	35	55	56	1	2
A.K.Gardner c Kerr b Huddleston	34	22	20	2	3
B.L.Mooney not out	29	36	19	1	3
S.G.Molineux c Devine b Huddleston	2	11	3	-	-
T.M.McGrath not out	29	12	11	1	4
N.J.Carey					
J.L.Jonassen					
G.L.Wareham					
M.L.Schutt					
Extras (lb 2, w 11)	13				
TOTAL (50 overs) (5 wkts)	**325**	196			

NEW ZEALAND

	Runs	Mins	Balls	6s	4s
N.C.Dodd c Gardner b Sutherland	5	24	18	-	-
S.F.M.Devine* c Molinuex b Schutt	0	4	1	-	-
A.E.Satterthwaite c Sutherland b Jonassen	41	57	49	-	6
A.C.Kerr b Schutt	0	5	1	-	-
K.J.Martin† b Jonassen	3	20	15	-	-
K.T.Perkins st Healy b Wareham	6	31	26	-	-
M.L.Green lbw b Gardner	22	27	22	-	4
H.N.K.Jensen b Molinuex	6	12	10	-	1
H.M.Rowe lbw b Gardner	3	8	6	-	-
H.R.Huddleston b Molinuex	0	8	8	-	-
R.A.Mair not out	4	5	6	-	-
Extras (w 3)	3				
TOTAL (27 overs)	**93**	97			

Bowling	*O*	*M*	*R*	*W*
NEW ZEALAND				
Mair	10	0	70	0
Huddleston	10	1	62	2
Devine	8	1	48	0
Kerr	10	1	50	3
Green	3	0	23	0
Jensen	5	0	41	0
Rowe	4	0	29	0
AUSTRALIA				
Schutt	6	1	25	2
Sutherland	5	0	16	1
Jonassen	5	0	16	2
Wareham	6	0	23	1
Gardner	3	0	11	2
Molinuex	2	0	2	2

Fall of Wickets	*A*	*NZ*
1st	144	1
2nd	222	27
3rd	237	28
4th	257	42
5th	292	54
6th	-	73
7th	-	85
8th	-	89
9th	-	89
10th	-	93

ENGLAND IN NEW ZEALAND

England arrived in New Zealand in February 2021 and underwent 14 days managed isolation ahead of a camp in Queenstown. They played two warm-up matches against a New Zealand XI in Queenstown before starting the one-day series at Hagley Oval in Christchurch. Women's international cricket returned to Dunedin after a long absence for the second and third one-day games.

After winning the first two one-day games batting second, England chose to bat first in the third match but, led by Amy Satterthwaite's unbeaten 119, the White Ferns won in the 46th over. The focus then shifted to the Twenty20 series. Due to a change in Covid alert levels all three games were played at Sky Stadium in Wellington with England completing a clean sweep with comfortable victories in all three matches. Left-arm spinner Fran Jonas, aged 16, and left-hand bat Brooke Halliday both made their debuts during the series.

The New Zealand squad was: Sophie Devine *(captain)*, Maddy Green, Amelia Kerr, Jess Kerr *(Wellington)*, Fran Jonas *(Auckland)*, Brooke Halliday *(Northern Districts)*, Natalie Dodd, Hannah Rowe *(Central Districts)*, Frances Mackay, Amy Satterthwaite, Lea Tahuhu *(Canterbury)*, Hayley Jensen, Katey Martin *(Otago)*.

Coach, Bob Carter; Batting coach, Rob Nicol; Bowling coach, Jacob Oram; Manager, Belinda Muller; Trainer, Scott Wrenn; Physiotherapist, Helen Littleworth.

New Zealand One-day International Averages

BATTING	*M*	*I*	*NO*	*HS*	*Agg*	*Ave*	*100s*	*50s*	*Ct*	*St*	*SR*
A.E. Satterthwaite	3	3	1	119*	135	67.50	1	-	2	-	75
B.M. Halliday	3	2	0	60	110	55.00	-	2	-	-	82
A.C. Kerr	3	3	1	72*	87	43.50	-	1	1	-	68
H.M. Rowe	3	2	1	29*	29	29.00	-	-	-	-	63
J.M. Kerr	2	1	0	28	28	28.00	-	-	1	-	93
H.N.K. Jensen	3	3	0	53	61	20.33	-	1	-	-	76
K.J. Martin	3	2	0	17	31	15.50	-	-	3	-	43
M.L. Green	2	1	0	14	14	14.00	-	-	1	-	38
S.F.M. Devine	3	3	0	16	37	12.33	-	-	-	-	63
L.M.M. Tahuhu	1	1	0	8	8	8.00	-	-	-	-	66
F.L. Mackay	2	1	0	5	5	5.00	-	-	-	-	31
N.C. Dodd	3	3	0	8	13	4.33	-	-	1	-	26
F.C. Jonas	2	2	1	1*	1	1.00	-	-	-	-	9

BOWLING	*O*	*M*	*R*	*W*	*Ave*	*Best*	*R/O*
J.M. Kerr	14	0	50	3	16.66	2-27	3.57
B.M. Halliday	8	1	40	2	20.00	1-17	5.00
S.F.M. Devine	13	0	56	2	28.00	2-26	4.31
A.C. Kerr	24.3	1	112	4	28.00	4-42	4.57
H.N.K. Jensen	14	0	75	2	37.50	1-18	5.36
L.M.M. Tahuhu	6	0	38	1	38.00	1-38	6.33
A.E. Satterthwaite	1.4	0	13	0	-	-	7.80
F.L. Mackay	11	0	64	0	-	-	5.82
F.C. Jonas	11	1	70	0	-	-	6.36
H.M. Rowe	16	0	72	0	-	-	4.50

England One-day International Averages

BATTING	*M*	*I*	*NO*	*HS*	*Agg*	*Ave*	*100s*	*50s*	*Ct*	*St*	*SR*
T.T. Beaumont	3	3	2	88*	231	231.00	-	3	2	-	74
H.C. Knight	3	3	1	67*	135	67.50	-	2	1	-	84
A.E. Jones	3	2	1	46*	61	61.00	-	-	3	-	91
N.R. Sciver	3	3	1	63	96	48.00	-	1	1	-	100
L. Winfield	1	1	0	11	11	11.00	-	-	-	-	68
S. Glenn	3	1	0	11	11	11.00	-	-	1	-	100
D.N. Wyatt	3	3	0	17	18	6.00	-	-	1	-	60
F.C. Wilson	3	1	0	6	6	6.00	-	-	1	-	66
S. Ecclestone	3	1	0	3	3	3.00	-	-	2	-	30
F.R. Davies	2	1	0	2	2	2.00	-	-	-	-	33
K.L. Cross	2	1	0	0	0	0.00	-	-	-	-	0
K.H. Brunt	2	-	-	-	-	-	-	-	-	-	-
N.E. Farrant	2	-	-	-	-	-	-	-	1	-	-

BOWLING	*O*	*M*	*R*	*W*	*Ave*	*Best*	*R/O*
N.R. Sciver	23.4	2	83	5	16.60	3-26	3.51
K.H. Brunt	16.5	1	60	3	20.00	2-34	3.56
K.L. Cross	14	0	63	2	31.50	1-23	4.50
F.R. Davies	15	0	63	2	31.50	1-30	4.20
N.E. Farrant	14	0	64	2	32.00	2-31	4.57
S. Glenn	19.1	1	97	3	32.33	2-37	5.06
H.C. Knight	9	0	42	1	42.00	1-14	4.67
S. Ecclestone	30	2	114	2	57.00	2-36	3.80

NEW ZEALAND XI v ENGLAND
At John Davies Oval, Queenstown 14 February, 2021

England 299-9 (N.R. Sciver 75, K.H. Brunt 41, D.N. Wyatt 35) **defeated New Zealand XI** 279-6 (L.R. Down 97) by 20 runs

NEW ZEALAND XI v ENGLAND
At John Davies Oval, Queenstown 16 February, 2021

New Zealand XI 316-5 (N.C. Dodd 91, B.M. Halliday 79, H.N.K. Jensen 47, K.J. Martin 31*, L.R. Down 30) **defeated England** 286 (D.N. Wyatt 54, S. Ecclestone 52, H.C. Knight 51, C.L. Green 5-56) by 30 runs

NEW ZEALAND v ENGLAND — First One-day International

at Hagley Oval, Christchurch on 23 February, 2021 (d/n)
Toss : New Zealand. Umpires : B.F. Bowden & K.D. Cotton
England won by 8 wickets

Halliday and 16-year-old Jonas made their New Zealand debuts as Devine won the toss and batted first. Promoted to open Jensen made her maiden fifty off 53 balls and Halliday made 50 before being run out to end the innings at 178. All seven England bowlers took wickets.

England's reply was dominated by a 94 run stand between Beaumont (fifty off 67 balls) and Knight (fifty off 58 balls). England won by eight wickets with 16.2 overs to spare.

NEW ZEALAND

	Runs	Mins	Balls	6s	4s
N.C.Dodd c Wyatt b Brunt	8	23	24	-	-
H.N.K.Jensen b Glenn	53	98	58	-	8
A.E.Satterthwaite c Sciver b Farrant	3	14	12	-	-
S.F.M.Devine* c Glenn b Sciver	16	34	24	-	1
A.C.Kerr c Ecclestone b Davies	13	40	27	-	1
K.J.Martin† c Ecclestone b Knight	14	36	35	-	-
B.M.Halliday run out	50	75	54	-	5
F.L.Mackay lbw b Ecclestone	5	18	16	-	-
H.M.Rowe lbw b Ecclestone	0	1	1	-	-
L.M.M.Tahuhu c Beaumont b Farrant	8	19	12	-	-
F.C.Jonas not out	1	14	8	-	-
Extras (lb 1, w 6)	7				
TOTAL (45.1 overs)	**178**	188			

ENGLAND

	Runs	Mins	Balls	6s	4s
T.T.Beaumont c Martin b Tahuhu	71	102	86	-	11
D.N.Wyatt c Satterthwaite b Jensen	17	28	21	-	2
H.C.Knight* not out	67	103	69	1	7
N.R.Sciver not out	21	29	26	-	3
A.E.Jones†					
F.C.Wilson					
K.H.Brunt					
S.Ecclestone					
S.Glenn					
N.E.Farrant					
F.R.Davies					
Extras (lb 3, w 2)	5				
TOTAL (33.4 overs) (2 wkts)	**181**	132			

Bowling	*O*	*M*	*R*	*W*
ENGLAND				
Brunt	7	0	26	1
Farrant	7	0	31	2
Davies	7	0	30	1
Ecclestone	10	1	36	2
Sciver	5	0	22	1
Glenn	6.1	1	18	1
Knight	3	0	14	1
NEW ZEALAND				
Tahuhu	6	0	38	1
Rowe	6	0	32	0
Jensen	5	0	18	1
Kerr	7.4	0	42	0
Mackay	2	0	12	0
Jonas	5	1	31	0
Halliday	2	0	5	0

Fall of Wickets

	NZ	*E*
1st	24	42
2nd	34	136
3rd	73	-
4th	94	-
5th	104	-
6th	126	-
7th	145	-
8th	145	-
9th	172	-
10th	178	-

NEW ZEALAND v ENGLAND Second One-day International

at University of Otago Oval, Dunedin on 26 February, 2021
Toss : New Zealand. Umpires : B.F. Bowden & K.D. Cotton
England won by 7 wickets

New Zealand again won the toss and batted but lost both openers within three overs. The score had reached 76-6 before Halliday, who reached her second fifty in a row (from 63 balls) put on 48 with Green. Rowe and Jess Kerr added some useful runs but New Zealand were all out for 192 in 49.5 overs.

Beaumont (fifty off 93 balls) was again in form in England's reply and was assisted by Sciver (fifty off 48 balls) and Jones, who made 46 not out. The latter two shared an unbroken partnership of 79 as England won with 12.2 overs remaining.

NEW ZEALAND

	Runs	Mins	Balls	6s	4s
N.C.Dodd b Brunt	2	12	7	-	-
H.N.K.Jensen c Jones b Brunt	0	3	2	-	-
A.E.Satterthwaite c Jones b Cross	13	55	38	-	1
S.F.M.Devine* c Farrant b Sciver	6	11	9	-	-
A.C.Kerr b Sciver	2	12	12	-	-
K.J.Martin† c Beaumont b Glenn	17	59	37	-	1
B.M.Halliday c Jones b Sciver	60	97	80	-	6
M.L.Green run out	14	47	36	-	-
H.M.Rowe not out	29	52	45	-	2
J.M.Kerr c Wilson b Glenn	28	33	30	1	2
F.C.Jonas run out	0	6	3	-	-
Extras (lb 6, w 15)	21				
TOTAL (49.5 overs)	**192**	195			

ENGLAND

	Runs	Mins	Balls	6s	4s
T.T.Beaumont not out	72	150	112	-	7
D.N.Wyatt b Kerr J.M.	0	1	2	-	-
H.C.Knight* run out	8	10	9	-	1
N.R.Sciver c Kerr A.C. b Halliday	63	82	61	1	5
A.E.Jones† not out	46	55	45	-	8
F.C.Wilson					
K.H.Brunt					
S.Ecclestone					
S.Glenn					
N.E.Farrant					
K.L.Cross					
Extras (w 2, nb 3)	5				
TOTAL (37.4 overs) (3 wkts)	**194**	150			

Bowling	*O*	*M*	*R*	*W*
ENGLAND				
Brunt	9.5	1	34	2
Sciver	9	0	26	3
Farrant	7	0	33	0
Cross	6	0	23	1
Glenn	8	0	37	2
Ecclestone	10	1	33	0
NEW ZEALAND				
Kerr J.M.	6	0	23	1
Devine	5	0	30	0
Rowe	4	0	18	0
Kerr A.C.	8	1	28	0
Jensen	3	0	25	0
Jonas	6	0	39	0
Halliday	4	1	18	1
Satterthwaite	1.4	0	13	0

Fall of Wickets

	NZ	*E*
1st	2	1
2nd	9	12
3rd	21	115
4th	27	-
5th	34	-
6th	76	-
7th	124	-
8th	137	-
9th	190	-
10th	192	-

NEW ZEALAND v ENGLAND — Third One-day International

at University of Otago Oval, Dunedin on 28 February, 2021
Toss : England. Umpires : B.F. Bowden & A. Mehrotra
New Zealand won by 7 wickets

England won the toss for the first time and batted. Wyatt went early but Beaumont reached her third consecutive fifty (68 balls) in a century stand with Knight (fifty from 70 balls). England were all out in the 48th over for 220 with Amelia Kerr taking 4-42.

New Zealand lost their openers cheaply in reply and Devine at 51. Satterthwaite was then joined by Amelia Kerr and the pair added an unbroken 172 to take New Zealand to an eight wicket victory. Satterthwaite reached fifty from 60 balls and her century 60 balls later while Kerr took 66 balls for her fifty.

ENGLAND

	Runs	Mins	Balls	6s	4s
T.T.Beaumont not out	88	193	113	-	7
D.N.Wyatt c Martin b Kerr J.M.	1	6	7	-	-
H.C.Knight* lbw b Kerr A.C.	60	94	82	-	7
N.R.Sciver c Dodd b Halliday	12	13	9	-	2
A.E.Jones† c & b Kerr J.M.	15	20	22	1	1
F.C.Wilson b Devine	6	8	9	-	1
L.Winfield c Green b Devine	11	14	16	-	1
S.Ecclestone c Martin b Jensen	3	11	10	-	-
S.Glenn c Satterthwaite b Kerr A.C.	11	11	11	-	1
F.R.Davies b Kerr A.C.	2	11	6	-	-
K.L.Cross lbw b Kerr A.C.	0	3	3	-	-
Extras (b 2, lw 8, nb 1)	11				
TOTAL (47.5 overs)	**220**	193			

NEW ZEALAND

	Runs	Mins	Balls	6s	4s
N.C.Dodd c Knight b Davies	3	21	19	-	-
H.N.K.Jensen b Sciver	8	27	20	-	1
A.E.Satterthwaite not out	119	150	128	2	10
S.F.M.Devine* lbw b Cross	15	37	25	-	2
A.C.Kerr not out	72	106	88	-	7
K.J.Martin†					
B.M.Halliday					
M.L.Green					
F.L.Mackay					
H.M.Rowe					
J.M.Kerr					
Extras (w 6)	6				
TOTAL (46.4 overs) (3 wkts)	**223**	171			

Bowling	*O*	*M*	*R*	*W*
NEW ZEALAND				
Mackay	9	0	52	0
Kerr J.M.	8	0	27	2
Rowe	6	0	22	0
Devine	8	0	26	2
Jensen	6	0	32	1
Kerr A.C.	8.5	0	42	4
Halliday	2	0	17	1
ENGLAND				
Sciver	9.4	2	35	1
Davies	8	0	33	1
Cross	8	0	40	1
Ecclestone	10	0	45	0
Glenn	5	0	42	0
Knight	6	0	28	0

Fall of Wickets	***E***	***NZ***
1st	6	13
2nd	115	15
3rd	140	51
4th	161	-
5th	169	-
6th	183	-
7th	190	-
8th	215	-
9th	220	-
10th	220	-

NEW ZEALAND v ENGLAND — First Twenty20 International

at Sky Stadium, Wellington on 3 March, 2021
Toss : England. Umpires : K.D. Cotton & J.M. Dempsey
England won by 7 wickets

England bowled first after winning the toss and soon had the wickets of Devine and Satterthwaite. Martin 36 off 32) was the only player to reach twenty as New Zealand folded for 96 in 19.4 overs

With England's top three of Beaumont, Wyatt and Sciver in form, the visitors won comfortably with four overs and seven wickets in hand. Halliday made her Twenty20 international debut in this game.

NEW ZEALAND

	Runs	Mins	Balls	6s	4s
S.F.M.Devine* c Dunkley b Sciver	2	5	6	-	-
H.N.K.Jensen c Villiers b Glenn	13	31	20	-	1
A.E.Satterthwaite c Davies b Sciver	2	9	6	-	-
A.C.Kerr c & b Ecclestone	14	19	17	-	2
K.J.Martin† st Jones b Brunt	36	44	32	-	5
B.M.Halliday st Jones b Ecclestone	1	9	7	-	-
M.L.Green b Glenn	3	9	7	-	-
T.M.M.Newton c & b Brunt	2	7	6	-	-
L.M.Kasperek c Dunkley b Villiers	4	6	5	-	-
J.M.Kerr run out	10	12	11	-	1
R.A.Mair not out	1	3	1	-	-
Extras (b 3, lb 4, w 1)	8				
TOTAL (19.4 overs)	**96**	79			

ENGLAND

	Runs	Mins	Balls	6s	4s
T.T.Beaumont c Green b Kasperek	25	45	31	-	3
D.N.Wyatt c Devine b Kasperek	33	35	26	-	4
N.R.Sciver not out	26	32	25	-	3
H.C.Knight* run out	0	3	2	-	-
A.E.Jones† not out	12	18	14	-	1
S.I.R.Dunkley					
K.H.Brunt					
S.Ecclestone					
S.Glenn					
M.K.Villiers					
F.R.Davies					
Extras (lb 1, nb 2)	3				
TOTAL (16 overs) (3 wkts)	**99**	68			

Bowling	*O*	*M*	*R*	*W*
ENGLAND				
Brunt	3.4	0	13	2
Sciver	4	0	28	2
Davies	1	0	3	0
Ecclestone	4	1	18	2
Glenn	4	1	11	2
Villiers	3	0	16	1
NEW ZEALAND				
Kerr J.M.	3	0	21	0
Mair	3	0	18	0
Kerr A.C.	4	0	21	0
Devine	2	0	14	0
Kasperek	4	0	24	2

Fall of Wickets	***NZ***	***E***
1st	5	59
2nd	10	66
3rd	37	67
4th	38	-
5th	48	-
6th	61	-
7th	67	-
8th	78	-
9th	95	-
10th	96	-

NEW ZEALAND v ENGLAND Second Twenty20 International

at Sky Stadium, Wellington on 5 March, 2021
Toss : England. Umpires : J.M. Dempsey & A. Mehrotra
England won by 6 wickets

England again bowled first after winning the toss. Devine and Jensen went cheaply but Satterthwaite and Amelia Kerr then added 56 for the third wicket.The later batsmen, apart from Halliday, contributed little, however, and the innings ended on 123-9. Davies took 4-23.

With another half-century from Beaumont (from 39 balls) and 39 from Knight, England were able to reach their target in the eighteenth over and won by six wickets with 16 balls remaining.

NEW ZEALAND

	Runs	Mins	Balls	6s	4s
S.F.M.Devine* lbw b Ecclestone	8	11	10	-	1
H.N.K.Jensen c Dunkley b Davies	12	18	16	-	1
A.E.Satterthwaite b Davies	49	44	30	-	7
A.C.Kerr st Jones b Glenn	25	24	22	-	3
K.J.Martin† st Jones b Glenn	0	3	2	-	-
B.M.Halliday not out	16	35	20	-	2
M.L.Green c Jones b Davies	0	2	3	-	-
K.E.Ebrahim b Davies	2	8	6	-	-
L.M.Kasperek b Sciver	5	10	8	-	-
J.M.Kerr b Sciver	0	1	1	-	-
R.A.Mair not out	2	3	2	-	-
Extras (lb 2, w 2)	4				
TOTAL (20 overs) (9 wkts)	**123**	81			

ENGLAND

	Runs	Mins	Balls	6s	4s
T.T.Beaumont c Satterthwaite b Kasperek	63	62	53	1	7
D.N.Wyatt b Mair	9	10	6	1	-
N.R.Sciver c Martin b Mair	0	6	2	-	-
H.C.Knight* c Green b Jensen	39	50	39	-	3
A.E.Jones† not out	7	6	5	-	1
S.I.R.Dunkley not out	0	1	0	-	-
M.K.Villiers					
S.Ecclestone					
S.Glenn					
N.E.Farrant					
F.R.Davies					
Extras (w 5, nb 1)	6				
TOTAL (17.2 overs) (4 wkts)	**124**	69			

Bowling	*O*	*M*	*R*	*W*
ENGLAND				
Farrant	4	0	17	0
Sciver	4	0	25	2
Ecclestone	4	0	14	1
Davies	4	0	23	4
Glenn	3	0	27	2
Villiers	1	0	15	0
NEW ZEALAND				
Kerr J.M.	2	0	19	0
Kasperek	4	0	26	1
Mair	3	0	22	2
Devine	1	0	11	0
Jensen	3.2	0	20	1
Kerr A.C.	4	0	26	0

Fall of Wickets

	NZ	***E***
1st	14	19
2nd	28	30
3rd	84	113
4th	84	122
5th	98	-
6th	98	-
7th	108	-
8th	120	-
9th	120	-
10th	-	-

NEW ZEALAND v ENGLAND — Third Twenty20 International

at Sky Stadium, Wellington on 7 March, 2021 (d/n)
Toss : New Zealand. Umpires : K.D. Cotton & J.M. Dempsey
England won by 32 runs

New Zealand won their first toss of the Twenty20 series and bowled first. The England top three went cheaply and it was left to Wilson (31 not out off 23 balls) to see the team to a reasonable score. The innings closed at 128-9 with Devine taking 3-30.

This turned out to be more than enough as New Zealand were bowled out for 96 in eighteen overs. The openers, Devine and Jensen, went in the first over and the home side never recovered and were 63-9 before Green and Mair added 33 for the last wicket. Villiers took 3-10.

ENGLAND

	Runs	Mins	Balls	6s	4s
T.T.Beaumont c Kerr A.C. b Devine	14	23	17	-	2
D.N.Wyatt c Kerr A.C. b Mair	3	12	8	-	-
N.R.Sciver* run out	9	18	10	-	2
S.I.R.Dunkley c Satterthwaite b Kerr A.C.	26	33	29	1	-
A.E.Jones† c & b Devine	15	21	13	-	1
F.C.Wilson not out	31	37	23	-	2
K.H.Brunt st Martin b Halliday	3	6	3	-	-
S.Ecclestone st Martin b Kasperek	9	8	8	-	1
S.Glenn c Kasperek b Devine	7	5	6	-	1
M.K.Villiers run out	1	11	2	-	-
F.R.Davies not out	1	1	1	-	-
Extras (b 4, lb 2, w 3)	9				
TOTAL (20 overs) (9 wkts)	**128**	89			

NEW ZEALAND

	Runs	Mins	Balls	6s	4s
S.F.M.Devine* lbw b Brunt	0	2	2	-	-
H.N.K.Jensen lbw b Brunt	0	6	1	-	-
A.E.Satterthwaite st Jones b Glenn	25	28	26	-	4
A.C.Kerr st Jones b Ecclestone	18	30	19	-	1
K.J.Martin† c Davies b Villiers	3	9	4	-	-
B.M.Halliday b Davies	7	12	8	-	1
M.L.Green c Ecclestone b Sciver	20	37	23	-	1
K.E.Ebrahim b Villiers	0	3	2	-	-
L.M.Kasperek st Jones b Villiers	0	1	1	-	-
J.M.Kerr b Ecclestone	3	4	7	-	-
R.A.Mair not out	13	20	15	-	1
Extras (w 7)	7				
TOTAL (18 overs)	**96**	78			

Bowling	O	M	R	W
NEW ZEALAND				
Kasperek	4	0	24	1
Kerr J.M.	2	0	12	0
Mair	4	0	17	1
Devine	4	0	30	3
Kerr A.C.	4	0	28	1
Halliday	2	0	11	1
ENGLAND				
Brunt	4	0	19	2
Sciver	3	0	20	1
Ecclestone	4	0	19	2
Davies	2	0	7	1
Glenn	3	0	21	1
Villiers	2	0	10	3

Fall of Wickets	E	NZ
1st	12	0
2nd	24	1
3rd	34	37
4th	70	45
5th	77	48
6th	84	58
7th	104	59
8th	114	60
9th	125	63
10th	-	96

AUSTRALIA IN NEW ZEALAND

Australia arrived in New Zealand in mid-March to play the White Ferns in a return series. The Twenty20s were played first and Australia had an easy win in Hamilton with New Zealand bouncing back for an exciting last-ball win at McLean Park thanks to an unbeaten 30 run partnership between Hannah Rowe and Maddy Green. The deciding match at Eden Park was reduced to 13 overs per side but was abandoned due to rain after 2.5 overs leaving the series tied at one-all.

All three one-day games were played at Bay Oval, Mt Maunganui. Lauren Down scored 90 in the first game but Australia won by six wickets in the 39th over. Batting first in the second game, all the Australian players reached double figures as the total reached 271 and Australia then bowled New Zealand out for 200 in 45 overs. The third match was reduced to 25 overs and, again batting first, Australia continued their dominance winning by 21 runs.

The New Zealand squad was: Sophie Devine *(captain)*, Maddy Green, Leigh Kasperek, Amelia Kerr, Jess Kerr, Thamsyn Newton *(Wellington)*, Lauren Down, Fran Jonas *(Auckland)*, Brooke Halliday *(Northern Districts)*, Rosemary Mair, Hannah Rowe *(Central Districts)*, Hayley Jensen, Katey Martin *(Otago)*, Frankie Mackay, Amy Satterthwaite, Lea Tahuhu *(Canterbury)*.

Coach, Bob Carter; Batting coach, Rob Nicol; Bowling coach, Jacob Oram; Manager, Belinda Muller; Trainer, Scott Wrenn; Physiotherapist, Helen Littleworth.

Sophie Devine made herself unavailable after the first game while Kate Anderson *(Northern Districts)* and Molly Penfold *(Auckland)* were called into the squad as cover.

New Zealand One-day International Averages

BATTING	*M*	*I*	*NO*	*HS*	*Agg*	*Ave*	*100s*	*50s*	*Ct*	*St*	*SR*
L.R. Down	3	3	0	90	106	35.33	-	1	2	-	68
A.C. Kerr	3	3	0	47	84	28.00	-	-	2	-	69
B.M. Halliday	3	3	0	32	60	20.00	-	-	-	-	65
A.E. Satterthwaite	3	3	0	32	58	19.33	-	-	2	-	72
M.L. Green	3	3	0	23	43	14.33	-	-	3	-	66
H.N.K. Jensen	3	3	0	28	41	13.66	-	-	-	-	58
K.J. Martin	3	3	0	20	26	8.66	-	-	4	1	52
J.M. Kerr	3	3	0	17	26	8.66	-	-	-	-	136
H.M. Rowe	2	2	0	13	13	6.50	-	-	-	-	54
L.M. Kasperek	2	2	1	6*	6	6.00	-	-	2	-	40
R.A. Mair	3	3	1	6	7	3.50	-	-	1	-	77
L.M.M. Tahuhu	2	2	2	21*	22	-	-	-	-	-	137

BOWLING	*O*	*M*	*R*	*W*	*Ave*	*Best*	*R/O*
L.M. Kasperek	15	1	70	9	7.77	6-46	4.67
A.E. Satterthwaite	9	0	50	2	25.00	1-10	5.56
L.M.M. Tahuhu	10	0	67	2	33.50	2-30	6.70
H.M. Rowe	7	0	49	1	49.00	1-31	7.00
J.M. Kerr	23	2	103	2	51.50	1-22	4.48
A.C. Kerr	22.3	0	133	2	66.50	1-32	5.91
H.N.K. Jensen	5	0	25	0	-	-	5.00
R.A. Mair	22	1	131	0	-	-	5.95

Australia One-day International Averages

BATTING	***M***	***I***	***NO***	***HS***	***Agg***	***Ave***	***100s***	***50s***	***Ct***	***St***	***SR***
A.J. Healy	3	3	0	65	155	51.66	-	1	1	3	122
E.A. Perry	3	3	1	56*	85	42.50	-	1	1	-	72
A.K. Gardner	3	3	1	53*	73	36.50	-	1	3	-	121
R.L. Haynes	3	3	0	87	101	33.66	-	1	4	-	80
M.M. Lanning	3	3	0	49	69	23.00	-	-	2	-	80
B.L. Mooney	3	3	0	28	66	22.00	-	-	-	-	98
N.J. Carey	3	2	0	14	27	13.50	-	-	1	-	79
G.L. Wareham	3	2	2	18*	29	-	-	-	-	-	111
J.L. Jonassen	3	2	2	9*	10	-	-	-	-	-	111
M.L. Schutt	3	-	-	-	-	-	-	-	1	-	-
T.J. Vlaeminck	2	-	-	-	-	-	-	-	1	-	-
D.R. Brown	1	-	-	-	-	-	-	-	1	-	-

BOWLING	***O***	***M***	***R***	***W***	***Ave***	***Best***	***R/O***
M.L. Schutt	22	1	92	7	13.14	4-32	4.18
J.L. Jonassen	21	1	77	4	19.25	3-29	3.67
N.J. Carey	19.5	0	81	4	20.25	3-34	4.08
G.L. Wareham	20	0	100	4	25.00	2-25	5.00
A.K. Gardner	18	0	78	2	39.00	1-26	4.33
T.J. Vlaeminck	11	1	46	1	46.00	1-21	4.18
D.R. Brown	1	0	6	0	-	-	6.00
E.A. Perry	6	0	31	0	-	-	5.17

NEW ZEALAND v AUSTRALIA First Twenty20 International

at Seddon Park, Hamilton on 28 March, 2021 (d/n)
Toss : Australia. Umpires : K.D. Cotton & J.M. Dempsey
Australia won by 6 wickets

Australia won the toss and decided to bowl first. New Zealand reached 33 without loss before both openers went. Satterthwaite and Amelia Kerr added 58 for the third wicket as the total reached 130-6 after the twenty overs.

Good bowling from Jess Kerr and a wicket to Mackay had Australia in trouble at 14-3. Lanning went at 62 but Gardner (fifty off 37 balls) took the game away from New Zealand, sharing an unbroken stand of 71 with Perry. Australia won with two overs to spare.

NEW ZEALAND

	Runs	Mins	Balls	6s	4s
S.F.M.Devine* c Gardner b Jonassen	17	20	22	-	3
H.N.K.Jensen c Healy b Jonassen	14	22	14	-	2
A.E.Satterthwaite c Perry b Carey	40	37	31	1	5
A.C.Kerr c Haynes b Wareham	20	41	29	-	-
K.J.Martin† lbw b Jonassen	1	2	2	-	-
M.L.Green b Schutt	15	14	11	1	1
B.M.Halliday not out	11	16	8	-	1
F.L.Mackay not out	3	5	4	-	-
H.M.Rowe					
J.M.Kerr					
R.A.Mair					
Extras (b 4, lb 2, w 2, nb 1)	9				
TOTAL (20 overs) (6 wkts)	**130**	80			

AUSTRALIA

	Runs	Mins	Balls	6s	4s
A.J.Healy† c Satterthwaite b Mackay	2	3	6	-	-
B.L.Mooney c Mackay b Kerr J.M.	0	5	1	-	-
M.M.Lanning* c Green b Kerr A.C.	28	43	28	1	2
R.L.Haynes c Devine b Kerr J.M.	3	10	9	-	-
A.K.Gardner not out	73	55	48	3	6
E.A.Perry not out	23	24	16	-	3
N.J.Carey					
G.L.Wareham					
J.L.Jonassen					
M.L.Schutt					
T.J.Vlaeminck					
Extras (lb 1, w 3)	4				
TOTAL (18 overs) (4 wkts)	**133**	70			

Bowling	*O*	*M*	*R*	*W*
AUSTRALIA				
Vlaeminck	4	1	26	0
Schutt	4	0	26	1
Jonassen	4	0	26	3
Gardner	1	0	8	0
Carey	3	0	20	1
Wareham	4	0	18	1
NEW ZEALAND				
Mackay	4	0	29	1
Kerr J.M.	4	0	17	2
Mair	3	0	18	0
Kerr A.C.	3	0	34	1
Devine	3	0	22	0
Jensen	1	0	12	0

Fall of Wickets	*NZ*	*A*
1st	33	3
2nd	35	3
3rd	93	14
4th	95	62
5th	97	-
6th	122	-
7th	-	-
8th	-	-
9th	-	-
10th	-	-

NEW ZEALAND v AUSTRALIA Second Twenty20 International

at McLean Park, Napier on 30 March, 2021
Toss : New Zealand. Umpires : K.D. Cotton & J.M. Dempsey
New Zealand won by 4 wickets

New Zealand won the toss and bowled first and removed Healy at 19. Mooney (fifty from 43 balls) was assisted by Lanning and Haynes and Australia reached 129-4 from their twenty overs.

Jensen and Satterthwaite went cheaply in New Zealand's reply but Mackay, who had suffered an injury while fielding, hit out and made 46 from 39 balls. Amelia Kerr made 36 before being sixth out at 101 before Green and Rowe saw New Zealand home with an unbroken stand. Green hit the winning runs from the last possible ball to level the series at 1-1.

AUSTRALIA

	Runs	Mins	Balls	6s	4s
A.J.Healy† c Martin b Kerr J.M.	4	15	11	-	-
B.L.Mooney not out	61	80	54	-	6
M.M.Lanning* run out	27	29	25	1	2
R.L.Haynes c Kerr J.M. b Mackay	29	27	25	-	3
A.K.Gardner c Martin b Mackay	3	3	3	-	-
E.A.Perry not out	2	5	2	-	-
N.J.Carey					
G.L.Wareham					
J.L.Jonassen					
M.L.Schutt					
D.R.Brown					
Extras (lb 2, w 1)	3				
TOTAL (20 overs) (4 wkts)	**129**	80			

NEW ZEALAND

	Runs	Mins	Balls	6s	4s
F.L.Mackay c Mooney b Brown	46	47	39	2	3
H.N.K.Jensen c Lanning b Perry	3	11	12	-	-
A.E.Satterthwaite* c Mooney b Carey	6	12	6	-	1
A.C.Kerr b Schutt	36	41	33	-	4
K.J.Martin† c Carey b Wareham	5	12	11	-	-
B.M.Halliday c Healy b Schutt	1	4	2	-	-
M.L.Green not out	16	14	8	-	3
H.M.Rowe not out	14	13	10	-	2
J.M.Kerr					
R.A.Mair					
T.M.M.Newton					
Extras (lb 1, w 2, nb 1)	4				
TOTAL (20 overs) (6 wkts)	**131**	79			

Bowling	O	M	R	W
NEW ZEALAND				
Mackay	4	0	20	2
Kerr J.M.	4	0	28	1
Mair	4	0	26	0
Rowe	2	0	16	0
Kerr A.C.	4	0	26	0
Satterthwaite	2	0	11	0
AUSTRALIA				
Schutt	4	0	24	2
Brown	4	0	26	1
Perry	1	0	8	1
Carey	3	0	24	1
Wareham	4	0	26	1
Jonassen	4	0	22	0

Fall of Wickets	***A***	***NZ***
1st	19	14
2nd	69	27
3rd	118	81
4th	122	97
5th	-	101
6th	-	101
7th	-	-
8th	-	-
9th	-	-
10th	-	-

NEW ZEALAND v AUSTRALIA Third Twenty20 International

at Eden Park, Auckland on 1 April, 2021
Toss : New Zealand. Umpires : K.D. Cotton & J.M. Dempsey
No result

With the series level, New Zealand won the toss and decided to field in a game reduced to 13 overs-a-side. Only 2.5 overs were possible, however, before rain returned and the game was eventually abandoned.

AUSTRALIA	Runs	Mins	Balls	6s	4s	NEW ZEALAND
A.J.Healy† not out	8	14	11	-	2	H.N.K.Jensen
B.L.Mooney c Down b Mair	4	7	4	-	-	K.J.Martin†
M.M.Lanning* not out	0	6	2	-	-	A.E.Satterthwaite*
R.L.Haynes						A.C.Kerr
A.K.Gardner						M.L.Green
E.A.Perry						B.M.Halliday
N.J.Carey						H.M.Rowe
G.L.Wareham						L.R.Down
J.L.Jonassen						T.M.M.Newton
M.L.Schutt						J.M.Kerr
T.J.Vlaeminck						R.A.Mair
Extras (w 2)	2					
TOTAL (2.5 overs) (1 wkt)	**14**	14				

Bowling	O	M	R	W
NEW ZEALAND				
Kerr J.M.	1.5	0	9	0
Mair	1	0	5	1

Fall of Wickets	A
1st	8
2nd	-
3rd	-
4th	-
5th	-
6th	-
7th	-
8th	-
9th	-
10th	-

NEW ZEALAND v AUSTRALIA — First One-day International

at Bay Oval, Mt Maunganui on 4 April, 2021
Toss : Australia. Umpires : C.M. Brown & K.D. Cotton
Australia won by 6 wickets

Australia won the toss in the first one-day international and sent New Zealand in. Jensen went for a first-ball duck in the second over but Down and Satterthwaite then added 69. Amelia Kerr helped Down add a further 90 runs and Down was fifth out at 168 after posting her maiden fifty from 90 balls. New Zealand were all out in the 49th over for 212.

Healy (57 balls), Perry (73 balls) and Gardner (41 balls) all made fifties for Australia with the latter two sharing an unbroken 79 run partnership. Australia won with 11.3 overs remaining.

NEW ZEALAND

	Runs	Mins	Balls	6s	4s
L.R.Down c & b Carey	90	153	134	-	8
H.N.K.Jensen b Schutt	0	4	1	-	-
A.E.Satterthwaite* c Schutt b Carey	32	71	50	-	3
A.C.Kerr st Healy b Schutt	33	66	46	-	4
K.J.Martin† run out	1	8	5	-	-
M.L.Green b Schutt	12	25	15	1	-
B.M.Halliday st Healy b Gardner	13	11	13	1	1
H.M.Rowe b Carey	13	24	20	-	-
J.M.Kerr c Haynes b Schutt	3	7	6	-	-
L.M.M.Tahuhu not out	1	9	3	-	-
R.A.Mair run out	1	2	1	-	-
Extras (b 1, lb 3, w 8, nb 1)	13				
TOTAL (48.5 overs)	**212**	193			

AUSTRALIA

	Runs	Mins	Balls	6s	4s
A.J.Healy† c & b Kerr A.C.	65	85	68	2	6
R.L.Haynes c Martin b Kerr J.M.	14	23	19	-	2
M.M.Lanning* c Martin b Rowe	5	11	12	-	-
E.A.Perry not out	56	114	79	-	7
B.L.Mooney c Green b Satterthwaite	12	11	13	-	1
A.K.Gardner not out	53	51	41	3	3
N.J.Carey					
J.L.Jonassen					
G.L.Wareham					
M.L.Schutt					
T.J.Vlaeminck					
Extras (lb 5, w 4, nb 1)	10				
TOTAL (38.3 overs) (4 wkts)	**215**	149			

Bowling	*O*	*M*	*R*	*W*
AUSTRALIA				
Vlaeminck	6	1	25	0
Schutt	9	0	32	4
Perry	3	0	15	0
Jonassen	7	0	34	0
Gardner	8	0	32	1
Carey	9.5	0	34	3
Wareham	6	0	36	0
NEW ZEALAND				
Kerr J.M.	8	0	30	1
Mair	8	1	32	0
Rowe	5	0	31	1
Tahuhu	5	0	37	0
Kerr A.C.	7.3	0	60	1
Jensen	3	0	10	0
Satterthwaite	2	0	10	1

Fall of Wickets

	NZ	*A*
1st	0	23
2nd	69	37
3rd	159	115
4th	166	136
5th	168	-
6th	185	-
7th	197	-
8th	205	-
9th	211	-
10th	212	-

NEW ZEALAND v AUSTRALIA Second One-day International

at Bay Oval, Mt Maunganui on 7 April, 2021 (d/n)
Toss : New Zealand. Umpires : K.D. Cotton & E.D. Sanders
Australia won by 71 runs

New Zealand won the toss and put Australia in on this occasion but Haynes (fifty off 72 balls) and Healy put on 82 before being separated. Lanning fell one short of her half-century and some other useful contributions saw Australia reach 271-7. Kasperek achieved career best figures of 6-46.

New Zealand lost Down in the first over and Satterthwaite in the second and the other players found it hard to accelerate their scoring. Wickets began to fall and the task became too much for the lower order with New Zealand bowled out for 200 after 45 overs to give Australia another series win.

AUSTRALIA

	Runs	Mins	Balls	6s	4s
R.L.Haynes c Down b Kasperek	87	134	105	-	8
A.J.Healy† c Satterthwaite b Kasperek	44	66	50	-	7
M.M.Lanning* c Down b Satterthwaite	49	59	51	-	6
E.A.Perry c Mair b Kasperek	16	34	24	-	1
A.K.Gardner c Martin b Kasperek	19	17	14	1	-
B.L.Mooney c Satterthwaite b Kasperek	26	40	28	-	2
N.J.Carey c Green b Kasperek	14	22	17	-	1
G.L.Wareham not out	11	12	9	-	-
J.L.Jonassen not out	1	2	2	-	-
M.L.Schutt					
T.J.Vlaeminck					
Extras (w 4)	4				
TOTAL (50 overs) (7 wkts)	**271**	195			

NEW ZEALAND

	Runs	Mins	Balls	6s	4s
L.R.Down c Lanning b Vlaeminck	0	2	5	-	-
H.N.K.Jensen c Vlaeminck b Wareham	28	56	40	-	2
A.E.Satterthwaite* c Healy b Schutt	6	4	3	-	1
A.C.Kerr c Gardner b Jonassen	47	89	70	-	5
B.M.Halliday run out	32	61	56	-	2
M.L.Green st Healy b Jonassen	23	46	33	-	1
K.J.Martin† c Haynes b Wareham	20	37	31	-	1
H.M.Rowe run out	0	3	4	-	-
J.M.Kerr c Haynes b Jonassen	6	5	5	-	1
L.M.Kasperek not out	6	14	15	-	-
R.A.Mair run out	6	11	8	-	-
Extras (b 9, lb 10, w 7)	26				
TOTAL (45 overs)	**200**	166			

Bowling	*O*	*M*	*R*	*W*
NEW ZEALAND				
Kerr J.M.	10	2	51	0
Mair	9	0	60	0
Rowe	2	0	18	0
Kerr A.C.	10	0	41	0
Kasperek	10	0	46	6
Satterthwaite	7	0	40	1
Jensen	2	0	15	0
AUSTRALIA				
Vlaeminck	5	0	21	1
Schutt	8	0	38	1
Perry	3	0	16	0
Jonassen	9	1	29	3
Wareham	10	0	39	2
Gardner	5	0	20	0
Carey	5	0	18	0

Fall of Wickets

	A	*NZ*
1st	82	0
2nd	180	7
3rd	187	76
4th	213	120
5th	220	144
6th	255	174
7th	267	175
8th	-	183
9th	-	184
10th	-	200

NEW ZEALAND v AUSTRALIA — Third One-day International

at Bay Oval, Mt Maunganui on 10 April, 2021 (d/n)
Toss : New Zealand. Umpires : C.M. Brown & E.D. Sanders
Australia won by 21 runs

The match was reduced to 25-overs-a-side and New Zealand again sent Australia in after winning the toss but once more were thwarted by the Australian openers, who put on 73. Healy top scored with 46 and Australia reached 149-7.

New Zealand promoted Martin to open but she went cheaply. No New Zealand player was able to put together a substantial innings and it was left to Tahuhu, who hit out at the end, to make the top score. New Zealand went down by 21 runs, with Australia winning the series 3-0 and winning their 24th successive one-day international. Brown made her one-day international debut in this game.

AUSTRALIA

	Runs	Mins	Balls	6s	4s
A.J.Healy† c Kerr A.C. b Kasperek	46	50	39	-	6
B.L.Mooney c Kasperek b Tahuhu	28	44	26	-	2
A.K.Gardner st Martin b Kasperek	1	7	5	-	-
M.M.Lanning* c Green b Tahuhu	15	29	23	-	-
R.L.Haynes b Kasperek	0	1	1	-	-
E.A.Perry c Kasperek b Kerr A.C.	13	17	15	-	1
N.J.Carey c Martin b Kerr J.M.	13	26	17	-	-
G.L.Wareham not out	18	25	17	-	1
J.L.Jonassen not out	9	6	7	-	1
M.L.Schutt					
D.R.Brown					
Extras (lb 2, w 4)	6				
TOTAL (25 overs) (7 wkts)	**149**	105			

NEW ZEALAND

	Runs	Mins	Balls	6s	4s
K.J.Martin† c Perry b Schutt	5	12	14	-	1
H.N.K.Jensen c Brown b Wareham	13	32	29	-	1
A.E.Satterthwaite* c Lanning b Gardner	20	31	27	-	1
A.C.Kerr run out	4	7	5	-	-
B.M.Halliday c Gardner b Wareham	15	20	22	1	-
M.L.Green c Gardner b Jonassen	8	23	17	-	-
L.R.Down c Haynes b Schutt	16	24	15	-	2
J.M.Kerr b Carey	17	8	8	1	2
L.M.M.Tahuhu not out	21	12	13	2	1
L.M.Kasperek run out	0	1	0	-	-
R.A.Mair not out	0	1	0	-	-
Extras (b 4, lb 2, w 3)	9				
TOTAL (25 overs) (9 wkts)	**128**	88			

Bowling	O	M	R	W
NEW ZEALAND				
Kerr J.M.	5	0	22	1
Mair	5	0	39	0
Kasperek	5	1	24	3
Tahuhu	5	0	30	2
Kerr A.C.	5	0	32	1
AUSTRALIA				
Brown	1	0	6	0
Schutt	5	1	22	2
Jonassen	5	0	14	1
Carey	5	0	29	1
Gardner	5	0	26	1
Wareham	4	0	25	2

Fall of Wickets	A	NZ
1st	73	13
2nd	80	36
3rd	80	49
4th	80	51
5th	103	73
6th	113	77
7th	136	100
8th	-	126
9th	-	127
10th	-	

HALLYBURTON JOHNSTONE SHIELD

2020/21

The Hallyburton Johnstone Shield was won by Canterbury who defeated Auckland by eight wickets in the final at Eden Park's outer oval.

Canterbury's Kate Edrahim was the leading scorer with 480 runs followed by team mate Frances Mackay (455) and Wellington's Jess McFadyen (397). Ebrahim (2), Mackay, McFadyen, Lauren Down, Brooke Halliday, Katey Martin and Natalie Dodd scored centuries.

Canterbury's Sarah Asmussen topped the wicket takers with 19 victims followed by Eimear Richardson with 17. Jacinta Savage had the season's best figures of 6-18 for Canterbury against Northern Districts.

Final points were:

	P	*W*	*L*	*T*	*NR*	*Bonus*	*Points*
Canterbury	10	7	3	–	–	5	33
Auckland	10	7	3	–	–	5	33
Central Districts	10	7	3	–	–	4	32
Northern Districts	10	5	5	–	–	4	24
Wellington	10	4	6	–	–	3	19
Otago	10	–	10	–	–	–	0

CENTRAL DISTRICTS v AUCKLAND — One-day Competition

at Pukekura Park, New Plymouth on 21 November, 2020
Toss : Central Districts. Umpires : D.R. Morrow & A. Stanley
***Central Districts won by 7 wickets.** Points: Central Districts 5, Auckland 0*

AUCKLAND

	Runs	Mins	Balls	6s	4s
S.Shahri c Rees b Rowe	7	25	27	-	1
Y.Kareem c Dodd b Green	4	35	22	-	-
B.G.Armstrong lbw b Green	1	2	2	-	-
R.S.M.Lili'i* b Green	1	9	6	-	-
J.E.I.Prasad b Green	1	9	8	-	-
T.I.Lamb† c Tomlinson b Rees	6	20	20	-	1
S.E.Bowden b Rees	5	25	16	-	1
R.H.McNeill c Greig b Watkin	0	6	4	-	-
M.M.Penfold b Rees	0	7	2	-	-
F.C.Jonas not out	1	14	13	-	-
J.L.Barnett b Rowe	0	13	8	-	-
Extras (lb 3, w 19, nb 1)	23				
TOTAL (21.1 overs)	**49**	78			

CENTRAL DISTRICTS

	Runs	Mins	Balls	6s	4s
N.C.Dodd† b Prasad	17	28	21	-	2
E.G.Cunningham c Lamb b Penfold	3	18	13	-	-
J.M.Watkin not out	22	14	11	1	4
A.van Deventer* c Shahri b Prasad	0	1	1	-	-
K.A.Tomlinson not out	1	2	1	-	-
H.M.Rowe					
M.J.Greig					
M.J.Hansen					
M.S.Rees					
G.K.Atkinson					
C.L.Green					
Extras (b 1, lb 1, w 6, nb 1)	9				
TOTAL (7.4 overs) (3 wkts)	**52**	38			

Bowling	*O*	*M*	*R*	*W*
CENTRAL DISTRICTS				
Rowe	4.1	2	3	2
Green	8	0	20	4
Watkin	5	1	8	1
Rees	4	0	15	3
AUCKLAND				
Bowden	1	0	8	0
Penfold	3.4	0	13	1
McNeill	1	0	10	0
Jonas	1	0	19	0
Prasad	1	1	0	2

Fall of Wickets

	A	*CD*
1st	10	24
2nd	12	24
3rd	18	46
4th	19	-
5th	22	-
6th	33	-
7th	37	-
8th	42	-
9th	43	-
10th	49	-

OTAGO v CANTERBURY One-day Competition

at Centennial Park, Oamaru on 21 November, 2020
Toss : Otago. Umpires : S.J. Kannan & D.J. Walker
***Canterbury won by 91 runs (D/L).** Points: Canterbury 5, Otago 0*

CANTERBURY

	Runs	Mins	Balls	6s	4s
F.L.Mackay* c Lamplough b Carson	142	188	157	-	22
A.C.Mace-Cochrane b Black	1	10	8	-	-
E.K.Kench lbw b Wilson	26	29	24	-	5
K.E.Ebrahim not out	106	160	109	2	12
N.B.Cox b Wilson	2	9	4	-	-
J.L.Savage not out	0	1	2	-	-
L.E.V.Hughes†					
G.E.S.Sullivan					
S.R.Asmussen					
J.A.Simmons					
G.E.Edge					
Extras (b 4, lb 4, w 32, nb 4)	44				
TOTAL (50 overs) (4 wkts)	**321**	200			

OTAGO

	Runs	Mins	Balls	6s	4s
G.R.Adams c Hughes b Savage	11	22	18	-	2
M.R.Cowan b Savage	26	32	26	-	5
C.G.Blakely run out	78	132	117	1	7
P.M.Inglis† c Cox b Mackay	39	66	61	-	4
I.R.James* b Mackay	4	11	8	-	-
O.N.Gain b Asmussen	5	10	9	-	-
S.I.Gray c Asmussen b Sullivan	2	22	15	-	-
S.R.Wilson not out	4	26	14	-	-
E.J.Black c Sullivan b Simmons	1	5	3	-	-
E.J.Carson not out	10	6	5	-	2
M.B.Lamplough					
Extras (b 5, lb 1, w 24, nb)	33				
TOTAL (46 overs) (8 wkts)	**213**	167			

Bowling	*O*	*M*	*R*	*W*
OTAGO				
Black	10	1	62	1
Lamplough	8	0	62	0
Adams	10	0	76	0
Wilson	10	0	49	2
Carson	10	0	45	1
Blakely	2	0	19	0
CANTERBURY				
Savage	7	1	47	2
Simmons	8	0	29	1
Sullivan	7	0	31	1
Edge	5	0	20	0
Mackay	8	0	31	2
Asmussen	7	0	31	1
Ebrahim	4	0	18	0

Fall of Wickets	***C***	***O***
1st	12	41
2nd	62	55
3rd	302	126
4th	321	144
5th	-	161
6th	-	176
7th	-	194
8th	-	196
9th	-	-
10th	-	-

WELLINGTON v NORTHERN DISTRICTS One-day Competition

at Basin Reserve, Wellington on 21 November, 2020
Toss : Northern Districts. Umpires : C.A. Black & G.A. Stirrat
***Northern Districts won by 2 wickets.** Points: Northern Districts 4, Wellington 0*

WELLINGTON

	Runs	Mins	Balls	6s	4s
J.T.McFadyen† lbw b Leydon-Davis	23	26	47	-	3
R.M.Burns c Lobb b Sarsfield	39	32	59	-	6
C.R.King c Heaps b Templeton	20	56	47	-	1
T.M.M.Newton* b Sarsfield	0	5	2	-	-
G.E.Plimmer run out	0	9	8	-	-
M.P.Singh c Halliday b Sarsfield	32	61	45	-	3
X.A.R.Jetly c & b Halliday	10	15	20	-	-
O.A.Boivin not out	12	25	19	-	1
B.C.Molony not out	9	14	13	-	-
N.E.Codyre					
A.S.Hamilton					
Extras (b 1, lb 3, w 18, nb 2)	24				
TOTAL (43 overs) (7 wkts)	**169**	124			

NORTHERN DISTRICTS

	Runs	Mins	Balls	6s	4s
C.A.Gurrey c McFadyen b Molony	41	64	59	-	7
B.M.Halliday lbw b Singh	13	13	11	-	3
F.C.Leydon-Davis* c Plimmer b Molony	14	58	44	-	1
M.B.Templeton run out	21	64	52	-	2
E.A.J.Richardson lbw b Newton	11	13	10	-	2
O.R.Lobb† c Hamilton b Jetly	19	61	38	-	2
L.F.Boucher not out	36	39	32	1	4
N.H.Patel c Hamilton b Molony	0	4	4	-	-
C.R.Sarsfield c Newton b Jetly	2	3	3	-	-
L.H.Heaps not out	2	13	3	-	-
K.A.Knight					
Extras (b 1, lb 1, w 11)	13				
TOTAL (42.4 overs) (8 wkts)	**172**	168			

Bowling	*O*	*M*	*R*	*W*
NORTHERN DISTRICTS				
Knight	6	2	25	0
Heaps	3	0	19	0
Richardson	5	0	25	0
Leydon-Davis	9	1	31	1
Sarsfield	9	2	29	3
Halliday	7	1	21	1
Templeton	4	0	15	1
WELLINGTON				
Jetly	8	0	50	2
Singh	7	1	28	1
Codyre	6	0	15	0
Molony	9	2	25	3
Boivin	6	0	26	0
Newton	6.4	1	26	1

Fall of Wickets	***W***	***ND***
1st	73	27
2nd	78	72
3rd	80	76
4th	82	91
5th	114	124
6th	139	146
7th	151	148
8th	-	153
9th	-	-
10th	-	-

CENTRAL DISTRICTS v AUCKLAND — One-day Competition

at Pukekura Park, New Plymouth on 22 November, 2020
Toss : Central Districts. Umpires : D.R. Morrow & A. Stanley
***Central Districts won by 10 wickets.** Points: Central Districts 5, Auckland 0*

AUCKLAND

	Runs	Mins	Balls	6s	4s
S.Shahri c Rees b Green	4	21	18	-	-
Y.Kareem c & b Watkin	10	67	58	-	1
B.G.Armstrong lbw b Green	0	8	10	-	-
R.S.M.Lili'i* c Green b Rees	0	13	12	-	-
J.E.I.Prasad lbw b Rees	4	7	5	-	1
T.I.Lamb† c Watkin b Rees	2	5	3	-	-
S.E.Bowden c van Deventer b Hansen	27	57	42	-	3
R.H.McNeill st Dodd b Atkinson	18	36	35	-	3
M.M.Penfold c Rowe b Hansen	0	5	4	-	-
F.C.Jonas c Rees b Atkinson	3	15	14	-	-
J.L.Barnett not out	3	10	12	-	-
Extras (lb 1, w 14)	15				
TOTAL (35.3 overs)	**86**	124			

CENTRAL DISTRICTS

	Runs	Mins	Balls	6s	4s
J.M.Watkin not out	68	37	33	4	8
N.C.Dodd† not out	14	37	22	1	-
A.van Deventer*					
K.A.Tomlinson					
H.M.Rowe					
M.J.Greig					
M.J.Hansen					
M.S.Rees					
A.Kumar					
G.K.Atkinson					
C.L.Green					
Extras (lb 4, w 4, nb 1)	9				
TOTAL (9 overs) (0 wkts)	**91**	37			

Bowling	*O*	*M*	*R*	*W*
CENTRAL DISTRICTS				
Green	8	1	19	2
Hansen	8	3	14	2
Watkin	7	3	6	1
Rees	4	0	15	3
Greig	4	0	24	0
Atkinson	4.3	1	7	2
AUCKLAND				
Bowden	2	0	15	0
Penfold	2	0	25	0
Prasad	1	0	18	0
Jonas	2	0	11	0
McNeill	2	0	18	0

Fall of Wickets	***A***	***CD***
1st	9	-
2nd	11	-
3rd	18	-
4th	24	-
5th	26	-
6th	30	-
7th	75	-
8th	76	-
9th	80	-
10th	86	-

OTAGO v CANTERBURY — One-day Competition

at Whitestone Contracting Stadium, Oamaru on 22 November, 2020
Toss : Canterbury. Umpires : S.J. Kannan & D.J. Walker
***Canterbury won by 133 runs.** Points: Canterbury 5, Otago 0*

CANTERBURY

	Runs	Mins	Balls	6s	4s
F.L.Mackay* c Inglis b Black	6	16	16	-	-
A.C.Mace-Cochrane b Wilson	9	35	29	-	-
E.K.Kench lbw b Oldershaw	17	65	54	-	-
K.E.Ebrahim c Carson b Adams	62	96	80	-	7
J.L.Savage c Gain b Black	24	70	56	-	1
L.E.V.Hughes† b Black	30	36	25	-	5
G.E.Edge not out	10	33	21	-	-
M.J.Banks run out	8	13	8	-	1
G.E.S.Sullivan run out	6	1	7	-	-
K.M.Sims not out	4	3	5	-	-
S.R.Asmussen					
Extras (b 6, lb 7, w 32, nb 1)	46				
TOTAL (50 overs) (8 wkts)	**222**	187			

OTAGO

	Runs	Mins	Balls	6s	4s
G.R.Adams lbw b Sims	2	1	4	-	-
M.R.Cowan c Hughes b Sims	2	5	8	-	-
C.G.Blakely run out	6	25	14	-	1
P.M.Inglis† b Savage	9	11	12	-	2
I.R.James* b Sims	5	19	16	-	1
O.N.Gain c Asmussen b Mackay	13	25	25	-	2
S.R.Wilson not out	23	59	43	-	2
E.J.Black b Asmussen	3	23	22	-	-
E.J.Carson b Asmussen	6	15	19	-	-
M.B.Lamplough st Hughes b Asmussen	0	1	1	-	-
S.A.Oldershaw b Asmussen	0	4	2	-	-
Extras (b 4, w 16)	20				
TOTAL (28 overs)	**89**	28			

Bowling	*O*	*M*	*R*	*W*
OTAGO				
Black	9	0	50	3
Lamplough	8	1	25	0
Adams	9	0	38	1
Wilson	7	0	31	1
Oldershaw	9	0	24	1
Carson	8	0	41	0
CANTERBURY				
Sims	6	1	25	3
Savage	5	1	17	1
Banks	5	0	15	0
Mackay	8	1	19	1
Asmussen	4	1	9	4

Fall of Wickets	***C***	***O***
1st	13	2
2nd	23	12
3rd	71	22
4th	131	25
5th	162	42
6th	191	56
7th	202	69
8th	211	89
9th	-	89
10th	-	89

WELLINGTON v NORTHERN DISTRICTS One-day Competition

at Basin Reserve, Wellington on 22 November, 2020
Toss : Northern Districts. Umpires : C.A. Black & G.A. Stirrat
***Northern Districts won by 8 wickets.** Points: Northern Districts 5, Wellington 0*

WELLINGTON

	Runs	Mins	Balls	6s	4s
J.T.McFadyen c Halliday b Richardson	107	180	134	-	11
R.M.Burns st Lobb b Heaps	21	61	47	-	3
C.R.King b Leydon-Davis	4	20	19	-	-
T.M.M.Newton* b Templeton	19	29	28	-	3
G.E.Plimmer c Lobb b Sarsfield	4	9	15	-	-
M.P.Singh b Sarsfield	14	28	25	-	1
X.A.R.Jetly c & b Richardson	10	19	20	-	-
O.A.Boivin c & b Richardson	6	8	6	-	1
B.C.Molony not out	4	8	5	-	-
N.E.Codyre run out	1	5	2	-	-
A.S.Hamilton†					
Extras (lb 4, w 19, nb 1)	24				
TOTAL (50 overs) (9 wkts)	**214**	185			

NORTHERN DISTRICTS

	Runs	Mins	Balls	6s	4s
C.A.Gurrey c Newton b Codyre	55	163	82	-	5
B.M.Halliday not out	101	222	115	-	10
F.C.Leydon-Davis* lbw b Newton	28	53	33	-	2
E.A.J.Richardson not out	7	4	2	-	1
M.B.Templeton					
O.R.Lobb†					
L.F.Boucher					
G.A.Harris					
C.R.Sarsfield					
L.H.Heaps					
K.A.Knight					
Extras (b 1, w 23)	24				
TOTAL (38.3 overs) (2 wkts)	**215**	222			

Bowling	*O*	*M*	*R*	*W*
NORTHERN DISTRICTS				
Boucher	6	0	24	0
Knight	5	0	28	0
Richardson	6	0	34	3
Halliday	10	1	39	0
Heaps	5	0	17	1
Leydon-Davis	4	0	19	1
Sarsfield	10	1	34	2
Templeton	4	0	15	1
WELLINGTON				
Codyre	7.3	0	46	1
Molony	6	0	40	0
Jetly	7	0	43	0
Newton	8	0	38	1
Singh	7	0	26	0
Boivin	3	0	21	0

Fall of Wickets	***W***	***ND***
1st	75	126
2nd	90	202
3rd	128	-
4th	136	-
5th	164	-
6th	190	-
7th	204	-
8th	210	-
9th	214	-
10th	-	-

NORTHERN DISTRICTS v CANTERBURY One-day Competition

at Cobham Oval, Whangarei on 5 December, 2020
Toss : Northern Districts. Umpires : L.R. Els & A. Stanley
***Canterbury won by 84 runs.** Points: Canterbury 5, Northern Districts 0*

CANTERBURY

	Runs	Mins	Balls	6s	4s
F.L.Mackay* b Hyde	16	35	28	-	1
E.K.Kench b Knight	11	47	33	-	2
K.E.Ebrahim c Leydon-Davis b Knight	14	25	16	-	2
N.B.Cox b Templeton	37	62	46	2	2
J.L.Savage c Lobb b Boucher	59	101	81	-	7
K.F.G.Nation c Richardson b Boucher	23	45	31	-	3
L.E.V.Hughes† c Richardson b Sarsfield	4	9	9	-	-
G.E.S.Sullivan c Gurrey b Sarsfield	6	9	11	-	-
M.J.Banks run out	2	8	4	-	-
K.M.Sims not out	18	21	23	-	1
S.R.Asmussen run out	8	19	19	-	-
Extras (lb 6, w 30, nb 2)	38				
TOTAL (49.5 overs)	**236**	195			

NORTHERN DISTRICTS

	Runs	Mins	Balls	6s	4s
C.A.Gurrey b Savage	1	5	6	-	-
B.M.Halliday c Hughes b Savage	16	46	32	-	3
F.C.Leydon-Davis* lbw b Sims	1	6	6	-	-
K.G.Anderson lbw b Savage	16	31	27	-	3
M.B.Templeton c Cox b Ebrahim	15	41	47	-	2
O.R.Lobb† c Mackay b Asmussen	32	72	55	-	3
E.A.J.Richardson b Savage	35	54	39	-	3
L.F.Boucher c Ebrahim b Asmussen	0	2	1	-	-
M.N.Hyde c Sullivan b Savage	12	15	10	-	2
C.R.Sarsfield b Savage	3	6	6	-	-
K.A.Knight not out	0	4	1	-	-
Extras (lb 2, w 18, nb 1)	21				
TOTAL (38.1 overs)	**152**	145			

Bowling	*O*	*M*	*R*	*W*
NORTHERN DISTRICTS				
Hyde	7	0	28	1
Boucher	7	0	27	2
Knight	5	1	25	2
Richardson	10	1	44	0
Sarsfield	7	0	39	2
Templeton	4	0	24	1
Leydon-Davis	6	0	30	0
Halliday	3.5	0	13	0
CANTERBURY				
Sims	4	0	26	1
Savage	7.1	1	18	6
Banks	3	1	14	0
Mackay	9	1	29	0
Sullivan	5	0	18	0
Ebrahim	5	1	22	1
Asmussen	5	0	23	2

Fall of Wickets	***C***	***ND***
1st	33	1
2nd	46	9
3rd	59	49
4th	134	50
5th	191	81
6th	197	131
7th	201	132
8th	209	149
9th	209	149
10th	236	152

OTAGO v AUCKLAND — One-day Competition

at Queen's Park, Invercargill on 5 December, 2020
Toss : Auckland. Umpires : S.J. Kannan & P.J. Pasco
Auckland won by 5 wickets. *Points: Auckland 5, Otago 0*

OTAGO	Runs	Mins	Balls	6s	4s
M.R.Cowan b Prasad	18	29	25	-	3
G.R.Adams lbw b Penfold	0	6	2	-	-
C.G.Blakely not out	44	84	62	-	6
I.R.James* lbw b Barnett	9	23	19	-	-
P.M.Inglis† run out	22	18	19	-	2
O.N.Gain c Perkins b Prasad	2	7	11	-	-
S.R.Wilson not out	4	12	7	-	-
E.J.Black					
E.J.Carson					
S.A.Oldershaw					
B.J.Herath					
M.B.Lamplough					
Extras (lb 1, w 15, nb 1)	17				
TOTAL (24 overs) (5 wkts)	**116**	91			

AUCKLAND	Runs	Mins	Balls	6s	4s
S.Shahri c Inglis b Black	7	16	13	-	1
L.R.Down* c Blakely b Wilson	40	55	34	-	7
B.G.Armstrong not out	62	53	48	1	9
K.T.Perkins not out	5	14	11	-	-
R.S.M.Lili'i					
J.E.I.Prasad					
S.E.Bowden					
T.I.Lamb†					
M.M.Penfold					
F.C.Jonas					
J.L.Barnett					
Extras (b 2, w 5)	7				
TOTAL (17.4 overs) (2 wkts)	**121**	70			

Bowling	O	M	R	W
AUCKLAND				
Bowden	2	0	15	0
Penfold	4	0	26	1
Prasad	5	1	12	2
Jonas	5	0	23	0
Armstrong	5	0	25	0
Barnett	3	0	14	1
OTAGO				
Herath	4	0	23	0
Lamplough	3	0	25	0
Black	3	0	8	1
Carson	2	0	15	0
Oldershaw	2	0	14	0
Wilson	3.4	0	34	1

Fall of Wickets	***O***	***A***
1st	7	28
2nd	38	91
3rd	63	-
4th	95	-
5th	99	-
6th	-	-
7th	-	-
8th	-	-
9th	-	-
10th	-	-

Lamplough was a concussion substitute for Adams

WELLINGTON v CENTRAL DISTRICTS — One-day Competition

at Donnelly Park, Levin on 5 December, 2020
Toss : Central Districts. Umpires : C.A. Black & T.S. Shirriffs
Central Districts won by 8 wickets. *Points: Central Districts 5, Wellington 0*

WELLINGTON	Runs	Mins	Balls	6s	4s
J.T.McFadyen† b Hansen	25	58	49	-	2
R.M.Burns c Watkin b Rees	24	39	27	-	4
C.R.King c Rowe b Watkin	18	47	41	-	2
T.M.M.Newton* b Watkin	20	81	43	-	1
G.E.Plimmer c Dodd b Atkinson	0	19	27	-	-
M.P.Singh c Greig b Watkin	0	4	4	-	-
X.A.R.Jetly c Atkinson b Watkin	1	6	9	-	-
O.A.Boivin c Green b Greig	0	6	8	-	-
B.C.Molony c Hansen b Greig	0	20	14	-	-
N.E.Codyre not out	0	5	2	-	-
K.M.Chandler run out	0	3	4	-	-
Extras (b 5, lb 3, w 13, nb 2)	23				
TOTAL (38.4 overs)	**111**	143			

CENTRAL DISTRICTS	Runs	Mins	Balls	6s	4s
N.C.Dodd† not out	37	88	86	-	4
E.G.Cunningham hit wicket b Jetly	15	32	26	-	1
J.M.Watkin st McFadyen b Jetly	29	25	27	1	3
A.van Deventer* not out	21	30	25	-	3
K.A.Tomlinson					
H.M.Rowe					
M.J.Greig					
M.J.Hansen					
G.K.Atkinson					
M.S.Rees					
C.L.Green					
Extras (lb 2, w 8)	10				
TOTAL (27.2 overs) (2 wkts)	**112**	88			

Bowling	O	M	R	W
CENTRAL DISTRICTS				
Rowe	3	1	18	0
Green	4	0	17	0
Rees	5	1	15	1
Hansen	5	1	16	1
Atkinson	10	1	19	1
Watkin	8.4	2	13	4
Greig	3	0	5	2
WELLINGTON				
Singh	5	2	16	0
Codyre	6	0	17	0
Molony	5.2	0	24	0
Jetly	8	0	41	2
Newton	2	0	7	0
Chandler	1	0	5	0

Fall of Wickets	***W***	***CD***
1st	49	30
2nd	65	67
3rd	88	-
4th	98	-
5th	99	-
6th	102	-
7th	104	-
8th	110	-
9th	110	-
10th	111	-

NORTHERN DISTRICTS v CANTERBURY One-day Competition

aat Cobham Oval, Whangarei on 6 December, 2020
Toss : Canterbury. Umpires : L.R. Els & A. Stanley
***Canterbury won by 35 runs.** Points: Canterbury 4, Northern Districts 0*

CANTERBURY

	Runs	Mins	Balls	6s	4s
F.L.Mackay* b Knight	1	4	5	-	-
E.K.Kench b Knight	5	17	10	-	1
K.E.Ebrahim c Halliday b Richardson	63	145	107	-	6
N.B.Cox c Anderson b Sarsfield	45	78	64	-	5
J.L.Savage c Lobb b Halliday	26	50	32	-	2
K.F.G.Nation c Lobb b Halliday	0	6	4	-	-
L.E.V.Hughes† run out	1	11	7	-	-
G.E.S.Sullivan run out	7	11	13	-	1
M.J.Banks c sub (L.H.Heaps) b Halliday	45	41	33	-	6
J.A.Simmons b Leydon-Davis	12	21	14	-	1
S.R.Asmussen not out	4	15	8	-	-
Extras (b 1, lb 5, w 34)	40				
TOTAL (49.3 overs)	**249**	204			

NORTHERN DISTRICTS

	Runs	Mins	Balls	6s	4s
C.A.Gurrey b Asmussen	49	96	70	-	6
B.M.Halliday c Ebrahim b Sullivan	77	109	82	-	14
F.C.Leydon-Davis* lbw b Asmussen	16	51	45	-	1
E.A.J.Richardson c Hughes b Asmussen	2	11	13	-	-
L.F.Boucher run out	11	22	15	-	1
M.B.Templeton c Ebrahim b Savage	11	26	14	-	1
O.R.Lobb† c Kench b Savage	1	5	6	-	-
K.G.Anderson c & b Mackay	2	4	5	-	-
M.N.Hyde c Sullivan b Simmons	8	25	20	-	-
C.R.Sarsfield b Sullivan	0	3	2	-	-
K.A.Knight not out	2	10	6	-	-
Extras (b 2, lb 9, w 24)	35				
TOTAL (46.2 overs)	**214**	184			

Bowling	*O*	*M*	*R*	*W*
NORTHERN DISTRICTS				
Hyde	5	0	26	0
Knight	5	0	29	2
Halliday	8.3	1	28	3
Leydon-Davis	5	0	28	1
Richardson	10	1	32	1
Templeton	4	0	36	0
Sarsfield	9	0	48	1
Boucher	3	0	16	0
CANTERBURY				
Simmons	4.2	0	14	1
Savage	10	1	23	2
Ebrahim	3	0	21	0
Banks	3	0	21	0
Mackay	10	1	49	1
Asmussen	10	1	41	3
Sullivan	6	0	34	2

Fall of Wickets

	C	***ND***
1st	1	143
2nd	13	162
3rd	120	169
4th	173	187
5th	173	188
6th	173	190
7th	181	194
8th	183	206
9th	218	206
10th	249	214

OTAGO v AUCKLAND One-day Competition

at Queen's Park, Invercargill on 6 December, 2020
Toss : Auckland. Umpires : S.J. Kanna & P.J. Pasco
***Auckland won by 3 wickets.** Points: Auckland 5, Otago 0*

OTAGO

	Runs	Mins	Balls	6s	4s
M.R.Cowan c Lamb b Penfold	8	18	13	-	1
S.R.Wilson lbw b Jonas	3	37	21	-	-
C.G.Blakely lbw b Jonas	5	26	26	-	-
I.R.James* c Armstrong b Barnett	13	64	49	-	1
P.M.Inglis† c Bowden b Barnett	23	49	31	1	2
O.N.Gain c Prasad b McNeill	12	31	26	-	-
E.J.Carson Perkins b Prasad	17	47	36	-	1
B.J.Herath c Prasad b Barnett	8	39	31	-	-
E.J.Black st Lamb b Barnett	8	26	29	-	-
M.E.Loe not out	6	21	18	-	-
S.A.Oldershaw b Armstrong	10	9	14	-	2
Extras (b 4, lb 1, w 35, nb 1)	41				
TOTAL (48.5 overs)	**154**	186			

AUCKLAND

	Runs	Mins	Balls	6s	4s
L.R.Down* b Carson	24	48	37	-	3
B.G.Armstrong c Carson b Loe	0	8	7	-	-
K.T.Perkins c Oldershaw b Loe	39	81	59	-	3
R.S.M.Lili'i c Blakely b Oldershaw	45	81	73	-	4
J.E.I.Prasad b Oldershaw	12	22	19	-	2
S.E.Bowden st Inglis b Black	13	22	25	-	2
R.H.McNeill not out	1	6	2	-	-
T.I.Lamb† b Black	0	1	1	-	-
M.M.Penfold not out	0	1	0	-	-
F.C.Jonas					
J.L.Barnett					
Extras (lb 4, w 17)	21				
TOTAL (37.1 overs) (7 wkts)	**155**	137			

Bowling	*O*	*M*	*R*	*W*
AUCKLAND				
Penfold	7	1	18	1
McNeill	8	0	14	1
Jonas	10	2	28	2
Prasad	8	2	17	1
Barnett	8	0	31	4
Bowden	1	0	16	0
Armstrong	6.5	1	25	1
OTAGO				
Black	9	1	27	2
Loe	7	0	27	2
Carson	10	1	48	1
Herath	4	1	20	0
Oldershaw	7.1	0	29	2

Fall of Wickets

	O	***A***
1st	16	6
2nd	26	51
3rd	29	97
4th	83	119
5th	89	150
6th	112	154
7th	127	154
8th	132	-
9th	140	-
10th	154	-

WELLINGTON v CENTRAL DISTRICTS One-day Competition

at Donnelly Park, Levin on 6 December, 2020
Toss : Central Districts. Umpires : C.A. Black & T.S. Shirriffs
***Wellington won by 2 wickets.** Points: Wellington 4, Central Districts 0*

CENTRAL DISTRICTS

	Runs	Mins	Balls	6s	4s
J.M.Watkin c Burns b Singh	0	2	5	-	-
N.C.Dodd† c Newton b Chandler	22	52	45	-	1
A.van Deventer* c Burns b Jetly	12	33	24	-	1
K.A.Tomlinson c McFadyen b Chandler	4	36	27	-	-
H.M.Rowe lbw b Molony	62	130	101	-	5
M.J.Greig st McFadyen b Chandler	4	11	9	-	-
M.J.Hansen c Chandler b Singh	0	5	7	-	-
G.K.Atkinson c & b Newton	58	80	72	-	7
M.S.Rees c McFadyen b Molony	1	4	3	-	-
A.Kumar not out	4	11	5	-	-
C.L.Green run out	0	1	1	-	-
Extras (b 2, lb 2, w 16)	20				
TOTAL (49.5 overs)	**187**	184			

WELLINGTON

	Runs	Mins	Balls	6s	4s
R.M.Burns b Watkin	33	77	68	-	6
G.E.Plimmer c Greig b Green	0	13	9	-	-
T.M.M.Newton* run out	7	36	27	-	1
C.R.King b Atkinson	22	46	43	-	4
J.T.McFadyen† not out	63	102	71	1	4
J.M.Kerr c van Deventer b Atkinson	2	5	4	-	-
M.P.Singh c & b Greig	6	20	27	-	-
X.A.R.Jetly lbw b Watkin	23	28	28	-	2
B.C.Molony st Dodd b Greig	5	18	9	-	-
N.E.Codyre not out	5	9	9	-	-
K.M.Chandler					
Extras (lb 2, w 18, nb 2)	22				
TOTAL (48.5 overs) (8 wkts)	**188**	179			

Bowling	*O*	*M*	*R*	*W*
WELLINGTON				
Singh	10	0	20	2
Codyre	6	0	21	0
Molony	4.5	0	29	2
Jetly	10	1	37	1
Chandler	10	0	39	3
Newton	9	1	37	1
CENTRAL DISTRICTS				
Rowe	6	1	36	0
Green	5	2	9	1
Rees	6	0	30	0
Watkin	10	3	23	2
Hansen	4	0	15	0
Atkinson	6	0	35	2
Greig	8.5	0	30	2
Kumar	3	0	8	0

Fall of Wickets	***CD***	***W***
1st	0	12
2nd	26	38
3rd	42	58
4th	54	83
5th	63	89
6th	64	105
7th	175	149
8th	176	177
9th	187	-
10th	187	-

AUCKLAND v NORTHERN DISTRICTS One-day Competition

at Eden Park Outer Oval, Auckland on 19 December, 2020
Toss : Northern Districts. Umpires : A. Stanley & G.M. Walklin
***Auckland won by 12 runs.** Points: Auckland 4, Northern Districts 0*

AUCKLAND

	Runs	Mins	Balls	6s	4s
A.M.Peterson c Leydon-Davis b Richardson	32	65	46	-	4
L.R.Down* c Sarsfield b Knight	1	7	4	-	-
A.N.Kelly b Boucher	6	16	13	-	1
K.T.Perkins c Lobb b Leydon-Davis	45	95	56	-	3
B.G.Armstrong c Leydon-Davis b Richardson	4	13	16	-	-
R.S.M.Lili'i c & b Heaps	10	19	21	-	-
J.E.I.Prasad c Lobb b Heaps	8	9	9	-	1
R.H.McNeill c Sarsfield b Heaps	2	7	9	-	-
T.I.Lamb† c & b Heaps	0	9	4	-	-
M.M.Penfold b Leydon-Davis	6	17	18	-	1
F.C.Jonas not out	0	11	6	-	-
Extras (lb 1, w 22, nb 1)	24				
TOTAL (33.3 overs)	**138**	137			

NORTHERN DISTRICTS

	Runs	Mins	Balls	6s	4s
C.A.Gurrey b Jonas	11	29	21	-	1
B.M.Halliday c Kelly b Peterson	34	74	45	-	3
F.C.Leydon-Davis* c Prasad b Armstrong	8	25	27	-	1
K.G.Anderson st Lamb b Jonas	33	47	39	-	4
E.A.J.Richardson lbw b Prasad	2	10	6	-	-
L.F.Boucher b Kelly	3	13	11	-	-
M.B.Templeton c Penfold b Jonas	2	13	12	-	-
O.R.Lobb† b Peterson	12	37	22	-	1
C.R.Sarsfield c Kelly b Jonas	1	17	6	-	-
L.H.Heaps b Prasad	6	36	33	-	-
K.A.Knight not out	0	24	15	-	-
Extras (b 1, lb 4, w 9)	14				
TOTAL (41.1 overs)	**126**	165			

Bowling	*O*	*M*	*R*	*W*
NORTHERN DISTRICTS				
Boucher	6	1	23	1
Knight	4	0	32	1
Richardson	8	0	31	2
Heaps	10	1	34	4
Leydon-Davis	4.3	1	16	2
Halliday	1	0	1	0
AUCKLAND				
Penfold	3	0	16	0
McNeill	3	0	6	0
Peterson	10	0	26	2
Jonas	10	0	41	4
Armstrong	2	0	12	1
Prasad	7.1	2	15	2
Kelly	6	2	5	1

Fall of Wickets	***A***	***ND***
1st	9	24
2nd	27	54
3rd	78	80
4th	90	90
5th	113	99
6th	125	101
7th	131	104
8th	131	117
9th	137	120
10th	138	126

CANTERBURY v WELLINGTON — One-day Competition

at Hagley Oval, Christchurch on 19 December, 2020
Toss : Wellington. Umpires : K.D. Cotton & L.R. Els
***Wellington won by 8 wickets.** Points: Wellington 5, Canterbury 0*

CANTERBURY

	Runs	Mins	Balls	6s	4s
F.L.Mackay* c McFadyen b Molony	11	25	20	-	1
E.K.Kench c McFadyen b Newton	20	77	56	-	-
A.E.Satterthwaite c Chandler b Kerr	1	10	8	-	-
K.E.Ebrahim c McFadyen b Chandler	48	105	67	-	6
N.B.Cox c McFadyen b Jetly	23	40	43	-	3
L.M.M.Tahuhu c Kerr b Chandler	6	21	14	-	-
L.E.V.Hughes† c Newton b Chandler	12	21	17	-	1
M.J.Banks c King b Molony	14	32	25	-	1
G.E.S.Sullivan c Burns b Chandler	8	25	16	-	1
K.M.Sims st McFadyen b Chandler	0	4	6	-	-
S.R.Asmussen not out	0	6	5	-	-
Extras (lb 1, w 11)	12				
TOTAL (46.1 overs)	**155**	186			

WELLINGTON

	Runs	Mins	Balls	6s	4s
R.M.Burns c Banks b Sullivan	26	53	46	-	4
C.R.King not out	53	114	86	1	6
T.M.M.Newton* b Mackay	61	58	58	-	11
J.T.McFadyen† not out	1	2	3	-	-
G.E.Plimmer					
J.M.Kerr					
M.P.Singh					
X.A.R.Jetly					
D.M.Doughty					
B.C.Molony					
K.M.Chandler					
Extras (b 1, lb 2, w 12)	15				
TOTAL (32.1 overs) (2 wkts)	**156**	114			

Bowling	O	M	R	W
WELLINGTON				
Singh	7	1	12	0
Molony	9	0	25	2
Kerr	6	0	18	1
Jetly	10	1	33	1
Newton	5	0	25	1
Chandler	9.1	2	41	5
CANTERBURY				
Tahuhu	6	0	20	0
Banks	3	1	11	0
Mackay	6	0	22	1
Sims	3	0	9	0
Asmussen	7	1	45	0
Sullivan	3	0	19	1
Satterthwaite	3	0	18	0
Ebrahim	1.1	0	9	0

Fall of Wickets

	C	W
1st	18	49
2nd	19	153
3rd	51	-
4th	89	-
5th	117	-
6th	117	-
7th	139	-
8th	153	-
9th	153	-
10th	155	-

OTAGO v CENTRAL DISTRICTS — One-day Competition

at University of Otago Oval, Dunedin on 19 December, 2020
Toss : Otago. Umpires : J.A.K. Bromley & P.J. Pasco
***Central Districts won by 9 wickets (D/L).** Points: Central Districts 5, Otago 0*

OTAGO

	Runs	Mins	Balls	6s	4s
M.R.Cowan c Rowe b Hansen	16	29	25	-	2
G.R.Adams c Dodd b Hansen	10	40	35	-	-
C.G.Blakely lbw b Rowe	62	125	103	-	4
K.J.Martin† st Dodd b Greig	19	32	23	-	3
I.R.James* c Tomlinson b Greig	30	49	56	-	3
P.M.Inglis c & b Atkinson	14	23	21	-	1
E.J.Carson c Cunningham b Watkin	15	16	11	1	1
E.J.Black b Rowe	2	1	2	-	-
B.J.Herath b Rowe	3	8	6	-	-
M.B.Lamplough c van Deventer b Rowe	1	11	9	-	-
S.A.Oldershaw not out	4	7	7	-	1
Extras (lb 2, w 18)	20				
TOTAL (49.4 overs)	**196**	173			

CENTRAL DISTRICTS

	Runs	Mins	Balls	6s	4s
N.C.Dodd† not out	50	72	56	-	7
E.G.Cunningham lbw b Carson	42	61	49	1	3
J.M.Watkin not out	33	11	9	4	2
A.van Deventer*					
K.A.Tomlinson					
H.M.Rowe					
M.J.Greig					
G.K.Atkinson					
M.J.Hansen					
M.S.Rees					
C.L.Green					
Extras (b 1, lb 3, w 6)	10				
TOTAL (19 overs) (1 wkt)	**135**	72			

Bowling	O	M	R	W
CENTRAL DISTRICTS				
Rowe	6.4	0	23	4
Green	3	0	14	0
Hansen	9	1	47	2
Watkin	10	1	33	1
Rees	4	1	17	0
Greig	10	0	29	2
Atkinson	7	0	31	1
OTAGO				
Herath	4	1	33	0
Black	3	1	19	0
Adams	3	0	17	0
Oldershaw	3	0	15	0
Carson	3	0	20	1
Lamplough	3	0	27	0

Fall of Wickets

	O	CD
1st	34	95
2nd	37	-
3rd	79	-
4th	132	-
5th	164	-
6th	183	-
7th	185	-
8th	188	-
9th	189	-
10th	196	-

AUCKLAND v NORTHERN DISTRICTS One-day Competition

at Eden Park Outer Oval, Auckland on 20 December, 2020
Toss : Auckland. Umpires : A. Stanley & G.M. Walkin
***Auckland won by 46 runs.** Points: Auckland 5, Northern Districts 0*

AUCKLAND

	Runs	Mins	Balls	6s	4s
A.M.Peterson b Boucher	2	9	9	-	-
L.R.Down* c Heaps b Richardson	16	51	33	-	1
B.G.Armstrong c Halliday b Boucher	8	18	14	-	-
K.T.Perkins c Patel b Leydon-Davis	63	118	82	-	9
R.S.M.Lili'i st Lobb b Richardson	10	32	24	-	-
S.Shahri c Hyde b Halliday	65	86	67	-	5
H.R.Huddleston c Sarsfield b Halliday	3	14	12	-	-
J.E.I.Prasad c Lobb b Halliday	3	18	12	-	-
R.H.McNeill c Lobb b Halliday	1	7	2	-	-
S.J.Carnachan† not out	6	24	22	-	-
F.C.Jonas c Anderson b Leydon-Davis	6	22	20	-	-
Extras (lb 12, w 26, nb 1)	39				
TOTAL (49.2 overs)	**222**	201			

NORTHERN DISTRICTS

	Runs	Mins	Balls	6s	4s
C.A.Gurrey lbw b McNeill	13	31	23	-	2
B.M.Halliday c Carnachan b McNeill	23	38	30	-	3
F.C.Leydon-Davis* lbw b Jonas	19	49	32	-	2
K.G.Anderson lbw b Armstrong	55	115	68	-	4
N.H.Patel lbw b Huddleston	3	18	24	-	-
O.R.Lobb† c Peterson b Prasad	8	23	21	-	-
E.A.J.Richardson c Lili'i b Armstrong	26	43	27	-	3
L.F.Boucher c Carnachan b Jonas	0	8	3	-	-
M.N.Hyde b Prasad	6	19	9	-	1
C.R.Sarsfield c Down b Jonas	1	10	16	-	-
L.H.Heaps not out	1	5	3	-	-
Extras (b 1, lb 6, w 14)	21				
TOTAL (42.4 overs)	**176**	181			

Bowling	*O*	*M*	*R*	*W*
NORTHERN DISTRICTS				
Boucher	9	1	45	2
Hyde	4	0	21	0
Richardson	7	1	26	2
Heaps	6	0	27	0
Sarsfield	4	0	27	0
Halliday	10	0	33	4
Leydon-Davis	9.2	0	31	2
AUCKLAND				
Huddleston	7	1	34	1
McNeill	7	0	35	2
Armstrong	6	0	30	2
Jonas	9	1	22	3
Peterson	8	0	30	0
Prasad	5.4	1	18	2

Fall of Wickets	***A***	***ND***
1st	10	34
2nd	28	38
3rd	43	88
4th	75	99
5th	180	119
6th	199	153
7th	209	165
8th	210	165
9th	211	170
10th	222	176

CANTERBURY v WELLINGTON One-day Competition

at Hagley Oval, Christchurch on 20 December, 2020
Toss : Canterbury. Umpires : K.D. Cotton & L.R. Els
***Canterbury won by 139 runs.** Points: Canterbury 5, Wellington 0*

CANTERBURY

	Runs	Mins	Balls	6s	4s
F.L.Mackay* c McFadyen b Kerr	68	141	104	-	7
E.K.Kench b Singh	9	41	39	-	1
A.E.Satterthwaite c & b Chandler	81	119	87	-	11
K.E.Ebrahim b Molony	35	43	28	1	3
N.B.Cox not out	42	39	31	1	2
K.F.G.Nation not out	15	15	11	-	-
L.E.V.Hughes†					
M.J.Banks					
G.E.S.Sullivan					
K.M.Sims					
S.R.Asmussen					
Extras (lb 4, w 21)	25				
TOTAL (50 overs) (4 wkts)	**275**	200			

WELLINGTON

	Runs	Mins	Balls	6s	4s
J.T.McFadyen† b Mackay	25	52	47	-	4
R.M.Burns b Sims	1	8	7	-	-
C.R.King b Mackay	34	65	52	-	4
T.M.M.Newton* c Banks b Satterthwaite	34	68	58	-	1
G.E.Plimmer c Satterthwaite b Mackay	7	16	25	-	-
M.P.Singh c Banks b Sims	21	44	34	-	4
J.M.Kerr c Kench b Sims	0	5	5	-	-
X.A.R.Jetly c Sullivan b Asmussen	2	14	7	-	-
B.C.Molony not out	6	15	16	-	-
N.E.Codyre b Satterthwaite	0	3	1	-	-
K.M.Chandler c Mackay b Banks	0	5	5	-	-
Extras (lb 2, w 4)	6				
TOTAL (42.5 overs)	**136**	150			

Bowling	*O*	*M*	*R*	*W*
WELLINGTON				
Molony	10	0	56	1
Singh	10	1	31	1
Codyre	3	0	13	0
Newton	7	0	39	0
Kerr	6	0	31	1
Chandler	6	0	43	1
Jetly	8	0	58	0
CANTERBURY				
Sims	8	2	19	3
Sullivan	7	1	29	0
Banks	4.5	0	22	1
Mackay	10	1	18	3
Asmussen	9	0	33	1
Satterthwaite	4	0	13	2

Fall of Wickets	***C***	***W***
1st	27	6
2nd	154	53
3rd	182	72
4th	234	84
5th	-	122
6th	-	122
7th	-	129
8th	-	131
9th	-	135
10th	-	136

OTAGO v CENTRAL DISTRICTS — One-day Competition

at University of Otago Oval, Dunedin on 20 December, 2020
Toss : Central Districts. Umpires : J.A.K. Bromley & P.J. Pasco
***Central Districts won by 4 wickets.** Points: Central Districts 4, Otago 0*

OTAGO

	Runs	Mins	Balls	6s	4s
G.R.Adams lbw b Watkin	2	11	15	-	-
M.R.Cowan c Hansen b Watkin	4	9	7	-	-
C.G.Blakely lbw b Hansen	10	23	26	-	1
K.J.Martin† c Rowe b Rees	105	138	104	2	10
I.R.James* lbw b Greig	36	62	63	-	4
P.M.Inglis c Greig b Hansen	53	60	45	2	5
E.J.Carson not out	9	12	5	-	1
E.J.Black not out	5	6	5	-	-
S.A.Oldershaw					
B.J.Herath					
M.B.Lamplough					
Extras (lb 1, w 6)	7				
TOTAL (45 overs) (6 wkts)	**231**	163			

CENTRAL DISTRICTS

	Runs	Mins	Balls	6s	4s
N.C.Dodd† not out	108	161	132	1	11
E.G.Cunningham b Carson	46	55	51	-	7
J.M.Watkin c Inglis b Black	16	27	21	-	3
A.van Deventer* b Carson	29	37	27	-	4
K.A.Tomlinson b Lamplough	6	21	19	-	-
H.M.Rowe b Herath	4	9	9	-	-
M.J.Greig run out	1	3	1	-	-
G.K.Atkinson not out	8	6	5	1	-
M.J.Hansen					
M.S.Rees					
A.Kumar					
Extras (b 2, lb 1, w 13, nb 2)	18				
TOTAL (43.5 overs) (6 wkts)	**236**	161			

Bowling	O	M	R	W
CENTRAL DISTRICTS				
Rowe	7	1	27	0
Watkin	6	1	35	2
Greig	9	0	48	1
Hansen	9	0	43	2
Atkinson	4	0	22	0
Rees	8	0	46	1
Kumar	2	0	9	0
OTAGO				
Black	8	0	40	1
Herath	7	1	36	1
Oldershaw	5	0	30	0
Adams	6	0	38	0
Lamplough	9	0	51	1
Carson	8.5	1	38	2

Fall of Wickets

	O	CD
1st	6	83
2nd	6	108
3rd	25	173
4th	99	198
5th	200	211
6th	217	216
7th	-	-
8th	-	-
9th	-	-
10th	-	-

CANTERBURY v CENTRAL DISTRICTS — One-day Competition

at MainPower Oval, Rangiora on 20 February, 2021
Toss : Central Districts. Umpires : K.D. Cotton & S.J. Kannan
***Canterbury won by 78 runs.** Points: Canterbury 5, Central Districts 0*

CANTERBURY

	Runs	Mins	Balls	6s	4s
K.E.Ebrahim not out	102	208	150	-	7
E.K.Kench lbw b Gaging A.M.	33	101	83	-	2
J.Dean b Hansen	1	13	9	-	-
N.B.Cox lbw b Green	9	11	12	-	2
K.F.G.Nation run out	16	38	23	-	2
M.J.Banks c van Deventer b Atkinson	1	9	4	-	-
L.E.V.Hughes† run out	13	19	15	-	1
G.E.S.Sullivan* run out	4	14	8	-	-
K.M.Sims not out	0	1	0	-	-
S.R.Asmussen					
J.A.Simmons					
Extras (b 1, lb 6, w 38, nb 4)	49				
TOTAL (50 overs) (7 wkts)	**228**	208			

CENTRAL DISTRICTS

	Runs	Mins	Balls	6s	4s
J.M.Watkin b Simmons	2	9	7	-	-
E.G.Cunningham lbw b Sullivan	20	65	42	-	1
A.van Deventer* lbw b Simmons	16	24	24	1	1
K.A.Tomlinson lbw b Asmussen	22	60	45	-	-
M.J.Greig c Hughes b Banks	5	18	11	-	-
K.L.Gaging† st Hughes b Asmussen	13	25	31	-	-
G.K.Atkinson c & b Dean	4	6	9	-	-
M.J.Hansen st Hughes b Simmons	5	17	11	-	-
M.S.Rees not out	24	54	47	-	1
C.L.Green c Sullivan b Sims	16	34	24	-	1
A.M.Gaging c Hughes b Sullivan	5	10	11	-	-
Extras (lb 1, w 17)	18				
TOTAL (43.4 overs)	**150**	164			

Bowling	O	M	R	W
CENTRAL DISTRICTS				
Green	8	0	29	1
Gaging A.M.	5	0	37	1
Hansen	9	0	41	1
Rees	8	1	33	0
Watkin	10	1	32	0
Atkinson	10	1	49	1
CANTERBURY				
Simmons	10	2	32	3
Sims	6	1	27	1
Banks	6	0	20	1
Sullivan	6.4	0	27	2
Asmussen	10	1	31	2
Dean	5	1	12	1

Fall of Wickets

	C	CD
1st	90	8
2nd	99	35
3rd	111	62
4th	158	74
5th	166	90
6th	196	95
7th	226	101
8th	-	106
9th	-	140
10th	-	150

NORTHERN DISTRICTS v OTAGO — One-day Competition

at Seddon Park, Hamilton on 20 February, 2021
Toss : Otago. Umpires : L.R. Els & C. High
***Northern Districts won by 72 runs.** Points: Northern Districts 5, Otago 0*

NORTHERN DISTRICTS

	Runs	Mins	Balls	6s	4s
C.A.Gurrey b Carson	37	58	66	-	6
O.R.Lobb† st Inglis b Carson	51	122	71	-	2
K.G.Anderson run out	47	42	36	-	8
F.C.Leydon-Davis* c James b Oldershaw	32	66	53	-	1
E.A.J.Richardson c Lamplough b Loe	72	67	48	-	10
L.F.Boucher b Carson	0	5	3	-	-
M.B.Templeton lbw b Oldershaw	7	8	9	-	1
N.H.Patel not out	16	14	13	-	1
M.N.Hyde not out	7	6	3	-	1
S.R.Naidu					
C.R.Sarsfield					
Extras (w 18, nb 2)	20				
TOTAL (50 overs) (7 wkts)	**289**	195			

OTAGO

	Runs	Mins	Balls	6s	4s
S.R.Wilson st Lobb b Richardson	14	35	21	-	2
I.R.James* c Gurrey b Templeton	50	59	53	-	7
C.G.Blakely c & b Richardson	12	27	23	-	1
P.M.Inglis† lbw b Sarsfield	13	16	15	-	2
O.N.Gain lbw b Templeton	3	9	5	-	-
E.J.Carson c Sarsfield b Richardson	16	49	38	-	-
E.J.Black lbw b Richardson	7	36	22	-	-
G.R.Adams c Lobb b Boucher	0	5	5	-	-
M.B.Lamplough c sub (G.A.Harris) b Patel	7	24	16	-	-
S.A.Oldershaw not out	36	65	58	-	4
M.E.Loe run out	16	45	40	-	1
Extras (b 2, lb 5, w 36)	43				
TOTAL (49.2 overs)	**217**	187			

Bowling	*O*	*M*	*R*	*W*
OTAGO				
Loe	9	0	34	1
Black	8	0	50	0
Lamplough	5	0	33	0
Oldershaw	10	0	59	2
Adams	6	0	31	0
Carson	10	0	69	3
Wilson	2	0	13	0
NORTHERN DISTRICTS				
Naidu	8	0	38	0
Hyde	5	0	41	0
Patel	7.2	1	31	1
Richardson	10	1	37	4
Templeton	10	1	22	2
Sarsfield	4	0	19	1
Boucher	5	0	22	1

Fall of Wickets

	ND	***O***
1st	65	56
2nd	133	84
3rd	159	91
4th	239	101
5th	244	101
6th	260	145
7th	275	147
8th	-	149
9th	-	164
10th	-	217

WELLINGTON v AUCKLAND — One-day Competition

at Karori Park, Wellington on 20 February, 2021
Toss : Wellington. Umpires : C.A. Black & T.R. Davies
***Auckland won by 110 runs.** Points: Auckland 5, Wellington 0*

AUCKLAND

	Runs	Mins	Balls	6s	4s
L.R.Down* c McFadyen b Newton	69	99	79	-	12
A.M.Peterson lbw b Singh	24	32	26	-	3
A.N.Kelly c McFadyen b Newton	23	44	40	1	2
K.T.Perkins c Jetly b Molony	30	60	47	1	3
H.R.Huddleston c sub (O.A.Boivin) b Newton	31	58	46	-	3
B.G.Armstrong st McFadyen b Jetly	10	15	10	-	2
R.S.M.Lili'i not out	24	35	21	-	2
J.E.I.Prasad st McFadyen b Codyre	36	27	28	-	4
M.M.Penfold not out	4	2	3	-	1
R.H.McNeill					
T.I.Lamb†					
Extras (b 4, lb 8, w 22)	34				
TOTAL (50 overs) (7 wkts)	**285**	188			

WELLINGTON

	Runs	Mins	Balls	6s	4s
J.T.McFadyen† b McNeill	75	148	93	1	10
R.M.Burns lbw b Peterson	14	37	24	-	3
C.R.King b Penfold	7	15	14	-	1
T.M.M.Newton* lbw b McNeill	7	14	17	-	1
G.E.Plimmer c Prasad b Kelly	29	45	39	-	2
M.P.Singh c Down b Kelly	0	4	4	-	-
X.A.R.Jetly run out	14	24	22	-	3
N.E.Codyre not out	3	19	11	-	-
B.C.Molony c Armstrong b Peterson	7	10	15	-	1
K.M.Chandler b Peterson	0	2	1	-	-
L.M.Kasperek absent hurt					
Extras (b 1, lb 6, w 12)	19				
TOTAL (39.4 overs)	**175**	160			

Bowling	*O*	*M*	*R*	*W*
WELLINGTON				
Codyre	9	1	52	1
Singh	8	0	29	1
Kasperek	4	0	29	0
Molony	9	0	58	1
Jetly	9	0	41	1
Newton	7	0	36	3
Chandler	4	0	28	0
AUCKLAND				
Kelly	8	2	25	2
Huddleston	7	0	23	0
Peterson	7.4	0	43	3
McNeill	9	1	29	2
Penfold	3	0	17	1
Armstrong	3	0	15	0
Prasad	2	0	16	0

Fall of Wickets

	A	***W***
1st	43	27
2nd	108	44
3rd	139	62
4th	189	128
5th	209	128
6th	214	154
7th	279	165
8th	-	174
9th	-	175
10th	-	

CANTERBURY v CENTRAL DISTRICTS One-day Competition

at MainPower Oval, Rangiora on 21 February, 2021
Toss : Central Districts. Umpires : K.D. Cotton & S.J. Kannan
***Central Districts won by 2 wickets.** Points: Central Districts 4, Canterbury 0*

CANTERBURY

	Runs	Mins	Balls	6s	4s
K.E.Ebrahim b Hansen	12	35	40	-	1
E.K.Kench b Rees	11	42	29	-	-
A.G.Gerken c Kumar b Rees	9	41	25	-	-
N.B.Cox st Gaging b Atkinson	34	60	51	-	3
K.F.G.Nation c & b Atkinson	0	3	3	-	-
M.J.Banks b Atkinson	2	8	6	-	-
L.E.V.Hughes† c Hansen b Watkin	51	80	68	-	5
G.E.S.Sullivan* c Green b Watkin	27	68	48	-	2
K.M.Sims c Greig b Watkin	0	9	7	-	-
J.A.Simmons b Atkinson	0	1	1	-	-
S.R.Asmussen not out	2	5	2	-	-
Extras (b 1, lb 6, w 27)	34				
TOTAL (46.4 overs)	**182**	176			

CENTRAL DISTRICTS

	Runs	Mins	Balls	6s	4s
J.M.Watkin c Hughes b Asmussen	66	96	68	3	5
E.G.Cunningham lbw b Simmons	4	21	18	-	-
A.van Deventer* lbw b Sullivan	18	23	18	-	1
K.A.Tomlinson c Nation b Asmussen	16	32	32	-	2
M.J.Greig c Nation b Sullivan	27	72	60	-	1
K.L.Gaging† b Simmons	10	49	31	-	-
G.K.Atkinson run out	2	18	13	-	-
M.J.Hansen c Sullivan b Simmons	0	5	2	-	-
M.S.Rees not out	3	10	9	-	-
C.L.Green not out	0	1	0	-	-
A.Kumar					
Extras (b 1, lb 2, w 34)	37				
TOTAL (41.5 overs) (8 wkts)	**183**	166			

Bowling	*O*	*M*	*R*	*W*
CENTRAL DISTRICTS				
Green	10	1	27	0
Watkin	8.4	2	17	3
Hansen	6	0	31	1
Rees	5	0	28	2
Atkinson	10	0	50	4
Kumar	7	0	22	0
CANTERBURY				
Simmons	9.5	1	35	3
Sims	5	0	39	0
Banks	5	1	24	0
Sullivan	10	1	26	2
Asmussen	10	1	46	2
Ebrahim	2	0	10	0

Fall of Wickets	***C***	***CD***
1st	31	22
2nd	36	64
3rd	67	100
4th	72	124
5th	81	172
6th	95	172
7th	178	176
8th	178	181
9th	178	-
10th	182	-

NORTHERN DISTRICTS v OTAGO One-day Competition

at Seddon Park, Hamilton on 21 February, 2021
Toss : Northern Districts. Umpires : L.R. Els & C. High
***Northern Districts won by 76 runs.** Points: Northern Districts 5, Otago 0*

NORTHERN DISTRICTS

	Runs	Mins	Balls	6s	4s
C.A.Gurrey c Lamplough b Carson	26	67	57	-	4
O.R.Lobb† c Oldershaw b Wilson	41	61	58	-	4
K.G.Anderson c Lamplough b Carson	47	68	46	-	5
F.C.Leydon-Davis* lbw b Oldershaw	88	118	93	-	8
E.A.J.Richardson c Lamplough b Oldershaw	55	46	34	-	8
L.F.Boucher c James b Black	1	4	2	-	-
M.N.Hyde st Inglis b Black	7	9	6	-	-
M.B.Templeton not out	2	6	2	-	-
N.H.Patel not out	5	2	3	-	-
S.R.Naidu					
C.R.Sarsfield					
Extras (lb 2, w 17, nb 1)	20				
TOTAL (50 overs) (7 wkts)	**292**	192			

OTAGO

	Runs	Mins	Balls	6s	4s
S.R.Wilson c Leydon-Davis b Naidu	20	29	29	-	3
I.R.James* c Patel b Hyde	6	24	12	-	-
C.G.Blakely lbw b Richardson	25	50	44	-	-
P.M.Inglis† lbw b Richardson	22	34	31	-	2
O.N.Gain c Naidu b Richardson	12	20	24	-	-
S.I.Gray c Leydon-Davis b Boucher	13	41	29	-	1
E.J.Carson b Boucher	4	13	10	-	-
E.J.Black c Richardson b Boucher	13	23	17	-	1
M.B.Lamplough c & b Patel	43	59	46	-	5
S.A.Oldershaw b Richardson	16	22	17	-	3
M.E.Loe not out	7	31	23	-	-
Extras (b 4, lb 2, w 28, nb 1)	35				
TOTAL (46.5 overs)	**216**	175			

Bowling	*O*	*M*	*R*	*W*
OTAGO				
Loe	10	0	47	0
Black	10	0	51	2
Oldershaw	10	0	70	2
Carson	10	0	57	2
Lamplough	3	0	23	0
Wilson	2	0	14	1
Blakely	5	0	28	0
NORTHERN DISTRICTS				
Naidu	6	1	23	1
Hyde	3	0	20	1
Patel	5.5	1	32	1
Sarsfield	6	0	30	0
Templeton	9	1	28	0
Richardson	10	0	21	4
Boucher	6	0	52	3
Anderson	1	0	4	0

Fall of Wickets	***ND***	***O***
1st	72	35
2nd	80	35
3rd	180	83
4th	268	92
5th	273	100
6th	279	113
7th	286	130
8th	-	139
9th	-	174
10th	-	216

WELLINGTON v AUCKLAND

One-day Competition

at Karori Park, Wellington on 21 February, 2021
Toss : Wellington. Umpires : C.A. Black & T.R. Davies
***Auckland won by 8 wickets.** Points: Auckland 5, Wellington 0*

WELLINGTON

	Runs	Mins	Balls	6s	4s
J.T.McFadyen† c McNeill b Armstrong	52	109	63	-	6
R.M.Burns b Huddleston	17	40	31	-	3
C.R.King b Huddleston	0	2	1	-	-
T.M.M.Newton* c Armstrong b Huddleston	2	8	9	-	-
G.E.Plimmer b Peterson	9	13	12	-	1
M.P.Singh b Huddleston	18	57	58	-	1
X.A.R.Jetly c Perkins b Peterson	30	77	68	-	3
O.A.Boivin c Lili'i b Prasad	13	35	21	-	1
N.E.Codyre b Penfold	0	2	1	-	-
B.C.Molony run out	31	30	33	-	5
K.M.Chandler not out	2	2	3	-	-
Extras (b 5, lb 8, w 12, nb 1)	26				
TOTAL (50 overs)	**200**	190			

AUCKLAND

	Runs	Mins	Balls	6s	4s
A.M.Peterson b Singh	0	1	3	-	-
L.R.Down* not out	104	141	124	-	11
A.N.Kelly st McFadyen b Jetly	65	126	102	-	6
K.T.Perkins not out	12	12	8	-	2
H.R.Huddleston					
B.G.Armstrong					
R.S.M.Lili'i					
J.E.I.Prasad					
R.H.McNeill					
T.I.Lamb†					
M.M.Penfold					
Extras (lb 1, w 19, nb 1)	21				
TOTAL (39.2 overs) (2 wkts)	**202**	141			

Bowling	*O*	*M*	*R*	*W*
AUCKLAND				
Kelly	8	0	50	0
Huddleston	10	1	29	4
McNeill	5	1	20	0
Penfold	7	0	28	1
Peterson	10	2	27	2
Armstrong	4	1	16	1
Prasad	6	0	17	1
WELLINGTON				
Singh	9	2	34	1
Codyre	4.2	0	27	0
Molony	6	0	29	0
Newton	6	0	37	0
Jetly	4	0	21	1
Boivin	4	0	17	0
Chandler	6	0	36	0

Fall of Wickets

	W	*A*
1st	45	0
2nd	46	180
3rd	50	-
4th	67	-
5th	106	-
6th	114	-
7th	151	-
8th	151	-
9th	197	-
10th	200	-

AUCKLAND v CANTERBURY

One-day Competition

at Eden Park Outer Oval, Auckland on 13 March, 2021
Toss : Canterbury. Umpires : K. Hogue & P.J. Pasco
***Canterbury won by 24 runs.** Points: Canterbury 4, Auckland 0*

CANTERBURY

	Runs	Mins	Balls	6s	4s
F.L.Mackay* c Kelly b Armstrong	75	150	111	-	6
K.E.Ebrahim b Jonas	18	72	50	-	-
A.E.Satterthwaite c & b Jonas	13	16	18	-	3
N.B.Cox b Armstrong	52	68	55	1	7
K.F.G.Nation c Armstrong b Peterson	17	25	22	-	2
E.K.Kench c Perkins b Prasad	8	12	10	-	-
M.J.Banks c Kelly b Peterson	0	2	3	-	-
L.E.V.Hughes† b Peterson	7	7	8	-	-
G.E.S.Sullivan not out	7	13	7	-	1
J.A.Simmons b Peterson	0	1	3	-	-
S.R.Asmussen lbw b Peterson	0	5	2	-	-
Extras (lb 2, w 5)	7				
TOTAL (48.1 overs)	**204**	190			

AUCKLAND

	Runs	Mins	Balls	6s	4s
A.M.Peterson c Satterthwaite b Simmons	20	27	23	-	4
L.R.Down* c Cox b Sullivan	3	7	3	-	-
A.N.Kelly c Nation b Sullivan	3	16	12	-	-
K.T.Perkins c Sullivan b Mackay	69	144	99	-	4
H.R.Huddleston lbw b Satterthwaite	24	57	52	-	2
B.G.Armstrong c Ebrahim b Asmussen	1	3	5	-	-
R.S.M.Lili'i lbw b Satterthwaite	23	43	48	-	1
J.E.I.Prasad lbw b Sullivan	0	4	3	-	-
T.I.Lamb† c Ebrahim b Sullivan	0	7	7	-	-
M.M.Penfold c Banks b Ebrahim	9	9	9	-	1
F.C.Jonas not out	1	11	10	-	-
Extras (lb 2, w 25)	27				
TOTAL (45.1 overs)	**180**	168			

Bowling	*O*	*M*	*R*	*W*
AUCKLAND				
Huddleston	6	2	23	0
Kelly	6	1	25	0
Penfold	3	0	16	0
Armstrong	10	1	47	2
Jonas	10	1	35	2
Peterson	7.1	1	30	5
Prasad	6	1	26	1
CANTERBURY				
Simmons	5	1	21	1
Sullivan	9	0	51	4
Banks	2	0	15	0
Mackay	7.1	1	28	1
Asmussen	10	0	36	1
Satterthwaite	10	1	24	2
Ebrahim	2	0	3	1

Fall of Wickets

	C	*A*
1st	63	13
2nd	81	32
3rd	162	33
4th	173	96
5th	189	97
6th	190	151
7th	190	153
8th	198	159
9th	198	173
10th	204	180

CENTRAL DISTRICTS v NORTHERN DISTRICTS One-day

at Pukekura Park, New Plymouth on 13 March, 2021
Toss : Northern Districts. Umpires : R.C.R. Combe & T.S. Shirriffs
***Northern Districts won by 8 wickets.** Points: Northern Districts 5, Central Districts 0*

CENTRAL DISTRICTS

	Runs	Mins	Balls	6s	4s
J.M.Watkin c Richardson b Naidu	4	17	16	-	-
E.G.Cunningham run out	4	13	8	-	1
A.van Deventer* b Naidu	18	36	28	-	1
K.A.Tomlinson b Anderson	57	127	107	-	8
M.J.Greig c Lobb b Templeton	3	15	14	-	-
K.L.Gaging† c Naidu b Sarsfield	4	10	9	-	1
R.A.Mair b Templeton	0	5	4	-	-
G.K.Atkinson c Leydon-Davis b Halliday	31	57	48	-	4
M.S.Rees c Richardson b Halliday	11	27	28	-	1
M.J.Hansen b Richardson	21	31	27	-	3
C.L.Green not out	3	8	6	-	-
Extras (b 3, lb 4, w 13)	20				
TOTAL (49.1 overs)	**176**	176			

NORTHERN DISTRICTS

	Runs	Mins	Balls	6s	4s
C.A.Gurrey c Watkin b Rees	30	72	60	-	2
B.M.Halliday* b Hansen	59	117	83	-	8
K.G.Anderson not out	47	63	42	1	6
F.C.Leydon-Davis not out	25	19	21	-	5
E.A.J.Richardson					
L.F.Boucher					
M.B.Templeton					
O.R.Lobb†					
N.H.Patel					
C.R.Sarsfield					
S.R.Naidu					
Extras (lb 2, w 14)	16				
TOTAL (34.2 overs) (2 wkts)	**177**	136			

Bowling	*O*	*M*	*R*	*W*
NORTHERN DISTRICTS				
Naidu	8	0	29	2
Patel	7	0	19	0
Richardson	5.1	1	22	1
Templeton	10	2	31	2
Sarsfield	8	0	27	1
Anderson	4	0	18	1
Halliday	7	1	23	2
CENTRAL DISTRICTS				
Green	6	0	25	0
Mair	6	1	14	0
Hansen	7	2	31	1
Watkin	10	0	57	0
Rees	3	0	25	1
Atkinson	2.2	0	23	0

Fall of Wickets

	CD	*ND*
1st	8	70
2nd	11	147
3rd	37	-
4th	55	-
5th	66	-
6th	68	-
7th	131	-
8th	135	-
9th	169	-
10th	176	-

WELLINGTON v OTAGO One-day Competition

at Basin Reserve, Wellington on 13 March, 2021
Toss : Wellington. Umpires : T.R. Davies & A. Stanley
***Wellington won by 8 wickets.** Points: Wellington 5, Otago 0*

OTAGO

	Runs	Mins	Balls	6s	4s
I.R.James* b Singh	19	42	34	-	3
H.N.K.Jensen b Singh	1	6	4	-	-
C.G.Blakely b Kerr A.C.	26	72	52	-	3
K.J.Martin c Newton b Jetly	70	95	80	-	8
P.M.Inglis† b Kerr A.C.	3	7	7	-	-
O.N.Gain c McFadyen b Kasperek	0	5	4	-	-
S.R.Wilson c Jetly b Kasperek	0	7	4	-	-
E.J.Black c Kasperek b Jetly	5	26	19	-	-
M.B.Lamplough c Newton b Kasperek	14	43	31	-	1
E.J.Carson b Kasperek	25	39	40	-	3
M.E.Loe not out	1	7	9	-	-
Extras (b 1, lb 3, w 12)	16				
TOTAL (47.2 overs)	**180**	177			

WELLINGTON

	Runs	Mins	Balls	6s	4s
J.T.McFadyen† c Inglis b Jensen	15	31	23	-	3
S.F.M.Devine c Jensen b Black	97	74	54	6	10
A.C.Kerr not out	54	68	44	-	7
M.L.Green not out	10	25	21	-	1
L.M.Kasperek					
T.M.M.Newton*					
J.M.Kerr					
G.E.Plimmer					
M.P.Singh					
X.A.R.Jetly					
B.C.Molony					
Extras (w 7)	7				
TOTAL (23.4 overs) (2 wkts)	**183**	100			

Bowling	*O*	*M*	*R*	*W*
WELLINGTON				
Molony	5	0	25	0
Singh	8	2	25	2
Devine	7	1	25	0
Kerr J.M.	8	1	18	0
Kerr A.C.	7	0	33	2
Kasperek	7.2	0	28	4
Newton	2	0	9	0
Jetly	3	0	13	2
OTAGO				
Black	7	0	37	1
Loe	4	0	42	0
Jensen	7	0	29	1
Carson	3	0	40	0
Lamplough	2	0	27	0
Wilson	0.4	0	8	0

Fall of Wickets

	O	*W*
1st	2	51
2nd	42	142
3rd	77	-
4th	89	-
5th	91	-
6th	98	-
7th	130	-
8th	136	-
9th	176	-
10th	180	-

AUCKLAND v CANTERBURY — One-day Competition

at Eden Park Outer Oval, Auckland on 14 March, 2021
Toss : Auckland. Umpires : K. Hogue & P.J. Pasco
***Auckland won by 10 runs.** Points: Auckland 4, Canterbury 0*

AUCKLAND

	Runs	Mins	Balls	6s	4s
S.Shahri c & b Satterthwaite	60	94	83	-	7
L.R.Down* b Mackay	75	150	111	-	6
A.N.Kelly lbw b Asmussen	2	8	14	-	-
K.T.Perkins b Ebrahim	27	43	44	-	1
A.M.Peterson b Ebrahim	6	18	8	-	1
H.R.Huddleston b Mackay	0	2	4	-	-
B.G.Armstrong c Banks b Mackay	0	5	1	-	-
R.S.M.Lili'i not out	11	19	13	-	1
J.E.I.Prasad lbw b Mackay	5	7	5	-	-
T.I.Lamb† lbw b Mackay	0	1	2	-	-
F.C.Jonas run out	2	8	10	-	-
Extras (lb 7, w 21)	28				
TOTAL (49.1 overs)	**216**	178			

CANTERBURY

	Runs	Mins	Balls	6s	4s
F.L.Mackay* c Lamb b Kelly	42	88	73	-	5
K.E.Ebrahim c Kelly b Jonas	16	43	36	-	1
A.E.Satterthwaite b Prasad	96	153	96	-	9
N.B.Cox c Peterson b Kelly	1	9	6	-	-
E.K.Kench c Perkins b Prasad	17	37	40	-	-
K.F.G.Nation b Huddleston	2	11	13	-	-
M.J.Banks b Jonas	1	5	6	-	-
L.E.V.Hughes† c Jonas b Prasad	23	39	29	-	2
G.E.S.Sullivan not out	0	4	0	-	-
J.A.Simmons not out	2	1	1	-	-
S.R.Asmussen					
Extras (lb 1, w 5)	6				
TOTAL (50 overs) (8 wkts)	**206**	199			

Bowling	*O*	*M*	*R*	*W*
CANTERBURY				
Simmons	3	0	21	0
Sullivan	7	0	40	0
Mackay	9	0	40	5
Banks	3	0	12	0
Ebrahim	10	1	44	2
Asmussen	10	0	29	1
Satterthwaite	7.1	0	23	1
AUCKLAND				
Huddleston	10	0	44	1
Kelly	7	0	26	2
Jonas	10	1	25	2
Peterson	10	1	35	0
Armstrong	5	0	28	0
Prasad	8	0	47	3

Fall of Wickets	*A*	*C*
1st	117	38
2nd	123	82
3rd	185	94
4th	185	127
5th	186	130
6th	196	133
7th	196	200
8th	206	204
9th	206	-
10th	216	-

CENTRAL DISTRICTS v NORTHERN DISTRICTS — One-day

at Pukekura Park, New Plymouth on 14 March, 2021
Toss : Northern Districts. Umpires : R.C.R. Combe & T.S. Shirriffs
***Central Districts won by 13 runs.** Points: Central Districts 4, Northern Districts 0*

CENTRAL DISTRICTS

	Runs	Mins	Balls	6s	4s
J.M.Watkin c Templeton b Patel	27	21	20	2	2
G.K.Atkinson b Sarsfield	28	75	57	-	3
A.van Deventer* c Lobb b Patel	2	11	3	-	-
K.A.Tomlinson c Sarsfield b Templeton	5	30	23	-	-
H.M.Rowe lbw b Anderson	43	96	70	-	2
M.J.Greig lbw b Templeton	0	5	5	-	-
K.L.Gaging† lbw b Templeton	16	22	27	-	2
R.A.Mair c & b Patel	27	31	34	-	2
M.J.Hansen c Anderson b Sarsfield	11	13	15	-	1
A.Kumar b Sarsfield	2	6	10	-	-
C.L.Green not out	0	3	2	-	-
Extras (w 5)	5				
TOTAL (44.2 overs)	**166**	160			

NORTHERN DISTRICTS

	Runs	Mins	Balls	6s	4s
C.A.Gurrey c Green b Atkinson	43	98	61	-	5
F.C.Leydon-Davis c Hansen b Green	6	22	20	-	1
K.G.Anderson lbw b Rowe	15	18	16	-	2
M.B.Templeton c Mair b Kumar	3	11	9	-	-
N.H.Patel not out	53	122	87	-	5
B.M.Halliday* run out	8	15	11	-	-
E.A.J.Richardson c & b Kumar	2	8	6	-	-
L.F.Boucher c Gaging b Mair	1	4	5	-	-
O.R.Lobb† c van Deventer b Kumar	1	4	4	-	-
S.R.Naidu run out	7	19	14	-	-
C.R.Sarsfield c Watkin b Hansen	5	23	31	-	1
Extras (b 1, w 8)	9				
TOTAL (44 overs)	**153**	174			

Bowling	*O*	*M*	*R*	*W*
NORTHERN DISTRICTS				
Naidu	3	0	21	0
Patel	10	0	36	3
Halliday	4	1	9	0
Sarsfield	10	1	31	3
Templeton	10	0	36	3
Richardson	2	0	14	0
Anderson	5.2	0	19	1
CENTRAL DISTRICTS				
Green	5	0	21	1
Mair	6	1	23	1
Rowe	6	1	14	1
Kumar	9	0	28	3
Watkin	9	1	27	0
Atkinson	3	0	16	1
Hansen	6	0	23	1

Fall of Wickets	*CD*	*ND*
1st	38	16
2nd	42	40
3rd	62	48
4th	75	97
5th	79	108
6th	107	118
7th	146	119
8th	164	120
9th	166	140
10th	166	153

WELLINGTON v OTAGO — One-day Competition

at Basin Reserve, Wellington on 14 March, 2021
Toss : Wellington. Umpires : T.R. Davies & A. Stanley
***Wellington won by 175 runs.** Points: Wellington 5, Otago 0*

WELLINGTON

	Runs	Mins	Balls	6s	4s
J.T.McFadyen† c Blakely b Carson	11	47	38	-	1
S.F.M.Devine c Jensen b Oldershaw	74	56	44	3	9
A.C.Kerr c Martin b Oldershaw	26	38	38	-	2
M.L.Green c sub (M.E.Loe) b Black	62	87	61	1	5
L.M.Kasperek b Oldershaw	27	42	31	-	3
T.M.M.Newton* c & b Black	6	21	15	-	-
J.M.Kerr c Blakely b Carson	58	49	39	-	8
G.E.Plimmer st Inglis b Black	21	36	29	-	2
M.P.Singh not out	5	8	5	-	1
X.A.R.Jetly not out	2	1	1	-	-
B.C.Molony					
Extras (b 3, lb 7, w 18, nb 1)	29				
TOTAL (50 overs) (8 wkts)	**321**	194			

OTAGO

	Runs	Mins	Balls	6s	4s
I.R.James* b Singh	3	6	6	-	-
P.M.Inglis† b Devine	13	29	17	-	3
C.G.Blakely c McFadyen b Singh	1	8	4	-	-
K.J.Martin c Kerr J.M. b Kerr A.C.	64	93	62	-	7
H.N.K.Jensen b Newton	11	33	25	-	-
O.N.Gain b Kerr A.C.	27	32	38	-	4
S.R.Wilson b Kasperek	8	33	26	-	1
E.J.Black c Kerr A.C. b Kerr J.M.	4	15	14	-	-
M.B.Lamplough b Kerr J.M.	0	1	1	-	-
E.J.Carson not out	1	8	3	-	-
S.A.Oldershaw b Kerr J.M.	0	4	6	-	-
Extras (b 4, w 10)	14				
TOTAL (33.4 overs)	**146**	134			

Bowling	*O*	*M*	*R*	*W*
OTAGO				
Black	10	0	58	3
Jensen	5	0	34	0
Carson	10	0	58	2
Oldershaw	10	0	57	3
Lamplough	7	0	40	0
Wilson	6	0	49	0
Blakely	2	0	15	0
WELLINGTON				
Molony	6	0	18	0
Singh	5	0	21	2
Devine	3	0	21	1
Kerr J.M.	4.4	1	9	3
Kasperek	5	1	21	1
Newton	2	0	18	1
Kerr A.C.	6	0	20	2
Jetly	2	0	14	0

Fall of Wickets

	W	O
1st	86	4
2nd	103	11
3rd	135	27
4th	206	81
5th	226	129
6th	228	134
7th	302	145
8th	319	145
9th	-	145
10th	-	146

CANTERBURY v AUCKLAND — One-day Final

at Eden Park Outer Oval, Auckland on 21 March, 2021
Toss : Auckland. Umpires : K.D. Cotton & P.J. Pasco
Canterbury won by 8 wickets

AUCKLAND

	Runs	Mins	Balls	6s	4s
L.R.Down* c Hughes b Sullivan	19	36	32	-	2
S.Shahri c Cox b Ebrahim	14	48	32	-	-
A.N.Kelly lbw b Sullivan	6	17	13	-	1
K.T.Perkins c & b Satterthwaite	52	75	64	-	4
H.R.Huddleston c Hughes b Asmussen	7	35	24	-	-
A.M.Peterson c Kench b Asmussen	19	18	20	-	1
B.G.Armstrong c Mackay b Ebrahim	10	19	16	-	1
R.S.M.Lili'i not out	29	45	43	-	2
J.E.I.Prasad c Hughes b Satterthwaite	7	16	13	-	-
T.I.Lamb† b Satterthwaite	7	16	19	-	-
F.C.Jonas c Mackay b Satterthwaite	0	6	11	-	-
Extras (w 15)	15				
TOTAL (47.5 overs)	**185**	170			

CANTERBURY

	Runs	Mins	Balls	6s	4s
F.L.Mackay* not out	94	148	112	-	10
E.K.Kench b Kelly	6	21	26	-	-
A.E.Satterthwaite c Lili'i b Peterson	73	117	80	-	9
K.E.Ebrahim not out	4	8	8	-	1
N.B.Cox					
K.F.G.Nation					
M.J.Banks					
L.E.V.Hughes†					
G.E.S.Sullivan					
J.A.Simmons					
S.R.Asmussen					
Extras (lb 2, w 9)	11				
TOTAL (37.4 overs) (2 wkts)	**188**	148			

Bowling	*O*	*M*	*R*	*W*
CANTERBURY				
Simmons	6	0	23	0
Banks	3	0	15	0
Sullivan	8	0	30	2
Ebrahim	8	0	25	2
Mackay	9	0	31	0
Asmussen	5	0	34	2
Satterthwaite	8.5	2	27	4
AUCKLAND				
Huddleston	7	0	40	0
Kelly	8	1	30	1
Peterson	7.4	0	30	1
Jonas	7	0	38	0
Armstrong	4	0	30	0
Prasad	4	1	18	0

Fall of Wickets

	A	C
1st	35	13
2nd	46	179
3rd	52	-
4th	87	-
5th	126	-
6th	141	-
7th	141	-
8th	163	-
9th	183	-
10th	185	-

REGISTER OF PLAYERS

		Born	At	Type	
Adams Gemma Rose	A	15. 2.02	Auckland	RHB	RM
Anderson Kate Georgia	ND	6. 5.96	Invercargill	RHB	ROB
Armstrong Bella Grace	A	16.11.99	Auckland	RHB	RM
Asmussen Sarah Renee	C	15. 7.00	Christchurch	RHB	RLB
Atkinson Georgia Kate	CD	23. 4.00	Masterton	RHB	RLBG
Banks Melissa Jane	C	2.11.01	Christchurch	RHB	RM
Barnett Jane Louise	A	7. 7.93	Palmerston North	RHB	RLB
Bartlett Ocean Jade Sadlier	CD	27. 6.03	Hamilton	RHB	RLBG
Black Emma Jordan	O	8. 8.01	Dunedin	RHB	RM
Blakely Caitlin Grace	O	7. 1.96	Dunedin	RHB	RM
Boivin Olivia Ann	W	18. 4.99	Lower Hutt	RHB	RM
Boucher Lucy Frances	ND	23.10.01	Hamilton	RHB	RM
Bowden Skye Elizabeth	A	23. 7.01	Palmerston North	RHB	RM
Burns Rebecca Maureen	W	30. 9.94	Wellington	RHB	ROB
Carnachan Sarah Jane	A	10.12.91	Auckland	RHB	WK
Carson Eden Jean	O	8. 8.01	Dunedin	RHB	ROB
Chandler Ella Reseigh	C	19.10.00	Frimley, England	RHB	ROB
Codyre Natasha Emma	W	29.10.03	Lower Hutt	RHB	RM
Cowan Millie Rose	O	7. 7.93	Dunedin	RHB	RM
Cox Natalie Bridget	C	21. 8.94	Dunedin	RHB	
Cunningham Emily Grace	CD	5. 7.97	Bury St Edmunds, England	RHB	RLB
Dean Jodie	C	7. 5.02	Christchurch	RHB	RM
Devine Sophie Frances Monique	W, NZ	1. 9.89	Wellington	RHB	RM
Dodd Natalie Claire	CD, NZ	22.11.92	Hamilton	RHB	ROB
Doughty Deanna Mary	W	7.12.93	Porirua	RHB	RLB
Down Lauren Renee	A, NZ	7. 5.95	Auckland	RHB	RM
Ebrahim Kate Ellen	C	11.11.91	New Plymouth	RHB	RM
Edge Georgia Elizabeth	C	8.10.03	Christchurch	LHB	LM
Ewart Annie May	ND	27. 1.01	Auckland	RHB	WK
Gaging Anna Megan	CD	19. 7.01	Ashford, England	RHB	RM
Gaging Kate Jane	CD	19. 7.01	Ashford, England	RHB	WK
Gain Olivia Nicole	O	2. 1.02	Dunedin	RHB	WK
Gerken Abigale Grace	C	12. 5.02	Christchurch	RHB	RM
Gray Sophie Isabella	O	9.12.99	Christchurch	RHB	WK
Green Claudia Lauren	CD	6.12.97	Nelson	RHB	RM
Green Madeline Lee	W, NZ	20.10.92	Auckland	RHB	ROB
Greig Mikaela Jane	CD	22. 4.95	Palmerston North	RHB	ROB
Gurrey Caitlin Ann	ND	3. 8.95	Wellington	RHB	
Halliday Brooke Maree	ND, NZ	30.10.95	Hamilton	LHB	RM
Hamilton Antonia Shu-Mei	W	15. 4.04	Lower Hutt	RHB	WK
Hansen Melissa Jane	CD	2. 5.96	Masterton	RHB	RM
Harris Georgina Ann	ND	10.12.01	Wellington	RHB	SLA
Havill Kirsty Jane	C	10.12.96	Greymouth	RHB	RLBG
Heaps Lauren Heather	ND	13. 1.90	Auckland	RHB	SLA
Herath Bhagya Janethri	O	2.11.00	Colombo, Sri Lanka	RHB	SLA
Huddleston Holly Rachael	A, NZ	11.10.87	Springs, South Africa	RHB	RM
Hughes Laura Ellen Victoria	C	16.10.92	Palmerston North	RHB	WK
Hyde Mereana Natasha	ND	23 .9.95	Waikari	RHB	RM
Inglis Polly Margot	O	31. 5.96	Dunedin	RHB	WK
James Isabela Rose	O	27. 1.99	Timaru	RHB	
Jensen Hayley Nicole Kayla	O, NZ	7.10.92	Christchurch	RHB	RM
Jetly Xara Ange Rose	W	29. 8.01	Lower Hutt	RHB	ROB
Jonas Frances Cecilia	A, NZ	8. 4.04	Auckland	RHB	SLA
Kareem Yazmeen	A	8. 9.99	Auckland	LHB	RM
Kasperek Leigh Megan	W, NZ	15. 2.92	Edinburgh, Scotland	RHB	ROB
Kelly Arlene Nora	A	8. 1.94	Auckland	RHB	RM
Kench Emma Kate	C	3. 7.99	Christchurch	RHB	RM
Kerr Amelia Charlotte	W, NZ	13.10.00	Wellington	RHB	RLBG
Kerr Jessica Mackenzie	W, NZ	18. 1.98	Wellington	RHB	RM
King Caitlin Rose	W	5. 9.96	Hastings	RHB	RM
Knight Kayley Alona	ND	20.10.03	Gisborne	RHB	RM
Kumar Ashtuti	CD	14.12.94	Suva, Fiji	RHB	RM
Lamb Tariel Iris	A	21. 5.99	Auckland	RHB	WK
Lamplough Marina Buonocore Antonia	O	28. 9.99	Hong Kong (China)	RHB	RM
Leydon-Davis Felicity Carol	ND	22. 6.94	Hamilton	RHB	RM

		Born	At	Type	
Lili'i Regina Sela Monika	ND	3.10.86	Apia, Samoa	RHB	RM
Lobb Olivia Rosemary	ND	7. 4.98	Whangarei	RHB	WK
Loe Molly Elizabeth	O	25. 6.03	Christchurch	RHB	RM
Mair Rosemary Alison	CD, NZ	7.11.98	Napier	RHB	RM
Martin Katey Jane	O, NZ	7. 2.85	Dunedin	RHB	WK
Mace-Cochrane Alexandra Christine	C	27. 8.97	Christchurch	RHB	ROB
McFadyen Jessica Toihi	W	5.10.91	Wellington	RHB	WK
Mackay Frances Louise	C, NZ	1. 6.90	Christchurch	RHB	ROB
McNeill Rosalind Helen	A	13. 8.90	Auckland	RHB	RM
Matthews Naomi	ND	4. 6.97	Belfast, Ireland	RHB	ROB
Molony Bethany Clare	W	31.10.00	Wellington	RHB	RM
Naidu Shriya Ramesh	ND	26.11.95	Dubai	RHB	RM
Nation Kirsten Frances Glasson	C	23.12.95	Christchurch	RHB	RM
Newton Thamsyn Michelle Moupia	W, NZ	3. 6.95	Paraparaumu	RHB	RM
Oldershaw Sophie Alice	O	20. 5.98	Auckland	RHB	RLB
Patel Nensi Hiteshkumar	ND	27. 5.02	Bharuch, India	RHB	RM
Penfold Molly Mae	A	15. 6.01	London, England	RHB	RM
Perkins Katie Teresa	A, NZ	7. 7.88	Auckland	RHB	RM
Peterson Anna Michelle	A	12. 9.90	Auckland	RHB	ROB
Plimmer Georgia Ellen	W	8. 2.04	Wellington	RHB	RSM
Prasad Jesse Ellen Indira	A	19. 1.99	Auckland	RHB	RM
Rees Monique Sarah	CD	29. 9.00	Wellington	RHB	RM
Richardson Eimear Ann Jermyn	ND	14. 9.86	Dublin, Ireland	RHB	ROB
Rout Alisha Jane	ND	17. 7.95	Morrinsville	RHB	RM
Rowe Hannah Maree	CD	3.10.96	Palmerston North	RHB	RM
Sarsfield Charlotte Rose	ND	22. 6.93	Auckland	RHB	ROB
Satterthwaite Amy Ella	C, NZ	7.11.86	Christchurch	LHB	RM
Savage Jacinta Lynn	C	17. 6.95	Christchurch	RHB	RM
Shahri Saachi	A	7.11.97	Mumbai, India	RHB	RLB
Simmons Jessica Ann	C	29. 4.00	Christchurch	RHB	RM
Sims Gemma	CD	27. 7.01	Masterton	RHB	WK
Sims Kate Margaret	C	27. 7.01	Masterton	RHB	RM
Singh Maneka Pushpanjali	W	18. 2.96	Dunedin	RHB	LM
Sullivan Gabrielle Eileen Suzanne	C	28. 7.98	Christchurch	RHB	RM
Tahuhu Lea-Marie Maureen	C, NZ	23. 9.90	Christchurch	RHB	RFM
Templeton Makayla Belle	ND	10.10.02	Redhill, England	RHB	RLB
Tomlinson Kerry-Anne	CD	19. 1.90	Gisborne	RHB	RM
van Deventer Anlo	CD	23.11.93	Worcester, S. Africa	RHB	
Watkin Jessica Marie	CD	7. 5.98	Wanganui	RHB	ROB
Wilson Saffron Rose	O	5.12.01	Christchurch	RHB	RM

2020/21 ONE-DAY AVERAGES

	M	*In*	*NO*	*HS*	*Runs*	*Ave*	*100s*	*50s*	*ct*	*st*	*O*	*M*	*R*	*W*	*Ave*	*R/O*	*Best*
G.R.Adams	6	6	0	11	25	4.16	-	-	-	-	34	0	200	1	200.00	5.88	1-38
K.G.Anderson	8	8	1	55	262	37.42	-	1	3	-	10.2	0	41	2	20.50	3.97	1-18
B.G.Armstrong	11	10	1	62*	96	10.66	-	1	4	-	45.5	3	228	7	32.57	4.97	2-30
S.R.Asmussen	11	5	3	8	14	7.00	-	-	2	-	87	5	358	19	18.84	4.11	4-9
G.K.Atkinson	10	6	1	58	131	26.20	-	1	3	-	56.5	3	252	12	21.00	4.43	4-50
M.J.Banks	10	8	0	45	73	9.12	-	-	5	-	37.5	3	169	2	84.50	4.47	1-20
J.L.Barnett	4	2	1	3*	3	3.00	-	-	-	-	11	0	45	5	9.00	4.09	4-31
E.J.Black	10	9	1	13	48	6.00	-	-	1	-	77	3	402	14	28.71	5.22	3-50
C.G.Blakely	10	10	1	78	269	29.88	-	2	4	-	9	0	62	0	-	6.89	-
O.A.Boivin	4	4	1	13	31	10.33	-	-	-	-	13	0	64	0	-	4.92	-
L.F.Boucher	10	8	1	36*	52	7.42	-	-	-	-	42	2	209	9	23.22	4.98	3-52
S.E.Bowden	4	3	0	27	45	15.00	-	-	1	-	6	0	54	0	-	9.00	-
R.M.Burns	8	8	0	39	175	21.87	-	-	3	-							
S.J.Carnachan	1	1	1	6*	6	-	-	-	2	-							
E.J.Carson	10	9	3	25	103	17.16	-	-	2	-	74.5	2	431	12	35.91	5.76	3-69
K.M.Chandler	6	4	1	2*	2	0.66	-	-	3	-	36.1	2	192	9	21.33	5.31	5-41
N.E.Codyre	7	6	3	5*	9	3.00	-	-	-	-	41.5	1	191	2	95.50	4.57	1-46
M.R.Cowan	6	6	0	26	74	12.33	-	-	-	-							
N.B.Cox	10	9	1	52	245	30.62	-	1	4	-							
E.G.Cunningham	7	7	0	46	134	19.14	-	-	1	-							
J.Dean	1	1	0	1	1	1.00	-	-	1	-	5	1	12	1	12.00	2.40	1-12
S.F.M.Devine	2	2	0	97	171	85.50	-	2	-	-	10	1	46	1	46.00	4.60	1-21
N.C.Dodd	6	6	4	108*	248	124.00	1	1	3	3							
D.M.Doughty	1	-	-	-	-	-	-	-	-	-							
L.R.Down	9	9	1	104*	351	43.87	1	2	2	-							
K.E.Ebrahim	11	11	3	106*	480	60.00	2	2	5	-	35.1	2	152	6	25.33	4.32	2-25
G.E.Edge	2	1	1	10*	10	-	-	-	-	-	5	0	20	0	-	4.00	-
A.M.Gaging	1	1	0	5	5	5.00	-	-	-	-	5	0	37	1	37.00	7.40	1-37
K.L.Gaging	4	4	0	16	43	10.75	-	-	1	1							
O.N.Gain	8	8	0	27	74	9.25	-	-	1	-							
A.G.Gerken	1	1	0	9	9	9.00	-	-	-	-							
S.I.Gray	2	2	0	13	15	7.50	-	-	-	-							
C.L.Green	9	5	3	16	19	9.50	-	-	4	-	57	4	181	9	20.11	3.18	4-20
M.L.Green	2	2	1	62	72	72.00	-	1	-	-							
M.J.Greig	10	6	0	27	40	6.66	-	-	6	-	34.5	0	136	7	19.42	3.90	2-5
C.A.Gurrey	10	10	0	55	306	30.60	-	1	2	-							
B.M.Halliday	8	8	1	101*	331	47.28	1	2	5	-	51.2	5	167	10	16.70	3.25	4-33
A.S.Hamilton	2	-	-	-	-	-	-	-	2	-							
M.J.Hansen	10	5	0	21	37	7.40	-	-	4	-	63	7	261	11	23.72	4.14	2-14
G.A.Harris	1	-	-	-	-	-	-	-	-	-							
L.H.Heaps	4	3	2	6	9	9.00	-	-	4	-	24	1	97	5	19.40	4.04	4-34
B.J.Herath	4	2	0	8	11	5.50	-	-	-	-	19	3	112	1	112.00	5.89	1-36
H.R.Huddleston	6	5	0	31	65	13.00	-	-	-	-	47	4	193	6	32.16	4.11	4-29
L.E.V.Hughes	11	8	0	51	141	17.62	-	1	10	3							
M.N.Hyde	5	5	1	12	40	10.00	-	-	1	-	24	0	136	2	68.00	5.67	1-20
P.M.Inglis	10	10	0	53	211	21.10	-	1	4	4							
I.R.James	10	10	0	50	175	17.50	-	1	2	-							
H.N.K.Jensen	2	2	0	11	12	6.00	-	-	2	-	12	0	63	1	63.00	5.25	1-29
X.A.R.Jetly	10	8	1	30	92	13.14	-	-	2	-	69	2	351	10	35.10	5.09	2-13
F.C.Jonas	9	7	3	6	13	3.25	-	-	2	-	64	5	242	13	18.61	3.78	4-41
Y.Kareem	2	2	0	10	14	7.00	-	-	-	-							
L.M.Kasperek	3	1	0	27	27	27.00	-	-	1	-	16.2	1	78	5	15.60	4.78	4-28
A.N.Kelly	6	6	0	65	105	17.50	-	1	5	-	43	6	161	6	26.83	3.74	2-25
E.K.Kench	11	11	0	33	163	14.81	-	-	3	-							
A.C.Kerr	2	2	1	54*	80	80.00	-	1	1	-	13	0	53	4	13.25	4.08	2-20
J.M.Kerr	5	3	0	58	60	20.00	-	1	2	-	24.4	2	76	5	15.20	3.08	3-9
C.R.King	8	8	1	53*	158	22.57	-	1	1	-							
K.A.Knight	5	3	3	2*	2	-	-	-	-	-	25	3	139	5	27.80	5.56	2-25
A.Kumar	5	2	1	4*	6	6.00	-	-	2	-	21	0	67	3	22.33	3.19	3-28
T.I.Lamb	10	7	0	7	15	2.14	-	-	3	2							
M.B.Lamplough	9	6	0	43	65	10.83	-	-	5	-	48	1	313	1	313.00	6.52	1-51
F.C.Leydon-Davis	10	10	1	88	237	26.33	-	1	6	-	37.5	2	155	7	22.14	4.10	2-16
R.S.M.Lili'i	11	9	3	45	153	25.50	-	-	3	-							
O.R.Lobb	10	8	0	51	165	20.62	-	1	12	3							
M.E.Loe	4	4	3	16	30	30.00	-	-	-	-	30	0	150	3	50.00	5.00	2-27

	M	In	NO	HS	Runs	Ave	100s	50s	ct	st	O	M	R	W	Ave	R/O	Best
A.C.Mace-Cochrane	2	2	0	9	10	5.00	-	-	-	-							
F.L.Mackay	9	9	1	142	455	56.87	1	3	5	-	76.1	5	267	14	19.07	3.51	5-40
R.A.Mair	2	2	0	27	27	13.50	-	-	1	-	12	2	37	1	37.00	3.08	1-23
K.J.Martin	4	4	0	105	258	64.50	1	2	1	-							
J.T.McFadyen	10	10	2	107	397	49.62	1	3	12	6							
R.H.McNeill	7	5	1	18	22	5.50	-	-	1	-	35	2	132	5	26.40	3.77	2-29
B.C.Molony	10	7	3	31	62	15.50	-	-	-	-	70.1	2	329	9	36.55	4.69	3-25
S.R.Naidu	4	1	0	7	7	7.00	-	-	2	-	25	1	111	3	37.00	4.44	2-29
K.F.G.Nation	8	7	1	23	73	12.16	-	-	3	-							
T.M.M.Newton	10	9	0	61	156	17.33	-	1	7	-	54.4	2	272	8	34.00	4.98	3-36
S.A.Oldershaw	8	6	2	36*	66	16.50	-	-	2	-	56.1	0	298	10	29.80	5.31	3-57
N.H.Patel	6	5	3	53*	77	38.50	-	1	4	-	30.1	2	118	5	23.60	3.91	3-36
M.M.Penfold	8	6	2	9	19	4.75	-	-	1	-	32.4	1	159	5	31.80	4.87	1-13
K.T.Perkins	9	9	2	69	342	48.85	-	3	5	-							
A.M.Peterson	7	7	0	32	103	14.71	-	-	2	-	60.3	4	221	13	17.00	3.65	5-30
G.E.Plimmer	10	8	0	29	70	8.75	-	-	1	-							
J.E.I.Prasad	11	9	0	36	76	8.44	-	-	4	-	53.5	9	204	14	14.57	3.79	3-47
M.S.Rees	9	4	2	24*	39	19.50	-	-	3	-	47	3	224	11	20.36	4.77	3-15
E.A.J.Richardson	10	9	1	72	212	26.50	-	2	8	-	73.1	5	286	17	16.82	3.91	4-21
H.M.Rowe	7	3	0	62	109	36.33	-	1	4	-	32.5	6	121	7	17.28	3.69	4-23
C.R.Sarsfield	10	6	0	5	12	2.00	-	-	5	-	67	4	284	13	21.84	4.24	3-29
A.E.Satterthwaite	5	5	0	96	264	52.80	-	3	4	-	33	3	105	9	11.66	3.18	4-27
J.L.Savage	4	4	1	59	109	36.33	-	1	-	-	29.1	4	105	11	9.54	3.60	6-18
S.Shahri	6	6	0	65	157	26.16	-	2	1	-							
J.A.Simmons	7	4	1	12	14	4.66	-	-	-	-	46.1	4	175	9	19.44	3.79	3-32
K.M.Sims	6	5	3	18*	22	11.00	-	-	-	-	32	4	145	8	18.12	4.53	3-19
M.P.Singh	10	8	1	32	96	13.71	-	-	-	-	76	9	242	10	24.20	3.18	2-20
G.E.S.Sullivan	11	8	2	27	65	10.83	-	-	7	-	68.4	2	305	14	21.78	4.44	4-51
L.M.M.Tahuhu	1	1	0	6	6	6.00	-	-	-	-	6	0	20	0	-	3.33	-
M.B.Templeton	9	7	1	21	61	10.16	-	-	1	-	55	4	207	10	20.70	3.76	3-36
K.A.Tomlinson	10	7	1	57	111	18.50	-	1	2	-							
A.van Deventer	10	8	1	29	116	16.57	-	-	5	-							
J.M.Watkin	10	10	3	68*	267	38.14	-	2	5	-	84.2	15	251	14	17.92	2.98	4-13
S.R.Wilson	8	8	3	23*	76	15.20	-	-	-	-	31.2	0	198	5	39.60	6.32	2-49

HIGHEST STRIKE RATES *(qualification 100 runs)*

		Runs	Balls	S/R
S.F.M.Devine	*W*	171	98	174
J.M.Watkin	*CD*	267	217	123
E.A.J.Richardson	*ND*	212	185	114
K.J.Martin	*O*	258	269	95
K.G.Anderson	*ND*	262	279	93
A.E.Satterthwaite	*C*	264	289	91
P.M.Inglis	*O*	211	259	81
B.M.Halliday	*ND*	331	409	80
L.E.V.Hughes	*C*	141	178	79
N.B.Cox	*C*	245	312	78

MOST ECONOMICAL BOWLING *(qualification 30 overs)*

		O	M	R	W	Ave	R/O
J.M.Watkin	*CD*	84.2	15	251	14	17.92	2.98
C.L.Green	*CD*	57	4	181	9	20.11	3.18
A.E.Satterthwaite	*C*	33	3	105	9	11.66	3.18
M.P.Singh	*W*	76	9	242	10	24.20	3.18
B.M.Halliday	*ND*	51.2	5	167	10	16.70	3.25
F.L.Mackay	*C*	76.1	5	267	14	19.07	3.51
A.M.Peterson	*A*	60.3	4	221	13	17.00	3.65
H.M.Rowe	*CD*	32.5	6	121	7	17.28	3.69
A.N.Kelly	*A*	43	6	161	6	26.83	3.74
M.B.Templeton	*ND*	55	4	207	10	20.70	3.76

CAREER RECORDS

	M	In	NO	HS	Runs	Ave	100s	50s	ct	st	O	M	R	W	Ave	R/O	Best
G.R.Adams	8	8	0	15	42	5.25	-	-	-	-	34	0	200	1	200.00	5.88	1-38
K.G.Anderson	59	55	9	160*	1309	28.45	2	3	18	-	285.2	7	1465	50	29.30	5.13	5-30
B.G.Armstrong	48	25	6	62*	200	10.52	-	1	11	-	293.5	25	1169	59	19.81	3.98	7-18
S.R.Asmussen	24	7	3	8	18	4.50	-	-	4	-	168.1	9	816	35	23.31	4.85	4-9
G.K.Atkinson	35	17	2	58	210	14.00	-	1	9	-	163.5	4	784	30	26.13	4.79	4-24
M.J.Banks	34	22	7	46*	195	13.00	-	-	10	-	164.4	12	785	15	52.33	4.77	2-5
J.L.Barnett	8	3	2	4	8	8.00	-	-	1	-	31	1	149	11	13.54	4.81	4-31
E.J.Black	32	24	4	36	156	7.80	-	-	3	-	233.2	11	1139	37	30.78	4.88	3-34
C.G.Blakely	74	67	7	78	1071	17.85	-	5	18	-	21	0	126	2	63.00	6.00	1-2
O.A.Boivin	5	5	2	13	36	12.00	-	-	-	-	13	0	64	0	-	4.92	-
L.F.Boucher	13	10	1	36*	79	8.77	-	-	2	-	46	2	223	9	24.77	4.85	3-52
S.E.Bowden	14	7	0	27	86	12.28	-	-	1	-	49.4	2	231	7	33.00	4.65	4-37
R.M.Burns	62	58	2	72*	1349	24.08	-	8	26	-	51	4	237	8	29.62	4.65	2-33
S.J.Carnachan	38	22	9	23	138	10.61	-	-	33	8							
E.J.Carson	28	23	6	51*	229	13.47	-	1	5	-	167.4	4	925	22	42.04	5.52	3-69
K.M.Chandler	6	4	1	2*	2	0.66	-	-	3	-	36.1	2	192	9	21.33	5.31	5-41
N.E.Codyre	11	8	3	10	19	3.80	-	-	1	-	61.4	1	297	5	59.40	4.82	3-50
M.R.Cowan	64	55	5	105	675	13.50	1	1	8	-	110.5	2	590	18	32.77	5.32	4-31
N.B.Cox	62	45	10	65	773	22.08	-	4	14	-							
E.G.Cunningham	24	20	1	46	350	18.42	-	-	3	-	3	0	22	0	-	7.33	-
J.Dean	4	3	1	5*	11	5.50	-	-	2	-	18	1	70	3	23.33	3.89	1-12
S.F.M.Devine	104	85	17	162*	2859	42.04	6	14	23	-	764.1	92	2733	129	21.18	3.58	5-15
N.C.Dodd	119	110	17	142	4243	45.62	10	23	50	7	177.3	7	792	22	36.00	4.46	2-22
D.M.Doughty	79	38	11	26	152	5.62	-	-	11	-	640.4	71	2484	102	24.35	3.88	5-26
L.R.Down	76	66	5	108	1866	30.59	2	12	27	-	126.3	8	548	18	30.44	4.33	3-38
K.E.Ebrahim	123	111	21	115*	3235	35.94	5	22	45	-	882.4	100	3264	125	26.11	3.70	4-11
G.E.Edge	3	1	1	10*	10	-	-	-	-	-	6	0	31	0	-	5.17	-
A.M.Gaging	1	1	0	5	5	5.00	-	-	-	-	5	0	37	1	37.00	7.40	1-37
K.L.Gaging	4	4	0	16	43	10.75	-	-	1	1							
O.N.Gain	27	27	1	60	275	10.57	-	1	4	-							
A.G.Gerken	1	1	0	9	9	9.00	-	-	-	-							
S.I.Gray	10	10	0	36	86	8.60	-	-	3	2							
C.L.Green	20	8	5	16	33	11.00	-	-	5	-	102.2	5	393	17	23.11	3.84	4-20
M.L.Green	83	77	13	105*	1915	29.92	1	11	31	-	129.5	3	566	28	20.21	4.36	5-45
M.J.Greig	57	37	4	27	286	8.66	-	-	21	-	240.4	5	1178	46	25.60	4.89	7-56
C.A.Gurrey	61	60	4	123	1726	30.82	3	6	18	-							
B.M.Halliday	57	47	5	101*	857	20.40	1	3	21	-	134	8	641	19	33.73	4.78	4-33
A.S.Hamilton	2	-	-	-	-	-	-	-	2	-							
M.J.Hansen	56	43	7	62	448	12.44	-	1	13	-	249.2	14	1112	37	30.05	4.46	4-29
G.A.Harris	4	2	0	17	20	10.00	-	-	-	-	6	0	36	0	-	6.00	-
L.H.Heaps	13	6	5	6	9	9.00	-	-	5	-	84	3	354	14	25.28	4.21	4-34
B.J.Herath	12	10	1	17	43	4.77	-	-	-	-	58.2	4	312	3	104.00	5.35	1-27
H.R.Huddleston	135	90	20	64	1404	20.05	-	2	26	1	841.2	90	3313	122	27.15	3.94	4-22
L.E.V.Hughes	48	31	5	51	305	11.73	-	1	31	8							
M.N.Hyde	45	24	6	49	195	10.83	-	-	6	-	182.1	13	936	23	40.69	5.14	3-21
P.M.Inglis	71	63	3	83*	971	16.18	-	4	38	11							
I.R.James	43	38	2	60	465	12.91	-	2	14	-							
H.N.K.Jensen	64	55	8	83	1090	23.19	-	7	14	-	375	34	1496	59	25.35	3.99	5-40
X.A.R.Jetly	20	15	4	30	136	12.36	-	-	4	-	138	8	630	17	37.05	4.57	3-35
F.C.Jonas	15	9	3	6	17	2.83	-	-	3	-	102.5	6	390	20	19.50	3.79	4-41
Y.Kareem	2	2	0	10	14	7.00	-	-	-	-							
L.M.Kasperek	64	58	3	95*	1554	28.25	-	11	24	-	493.2	47	2036	102	19.96	4.13	6-8
A.N.Kelly	76	47	8	110	733	18.79	1	2	21	-	541.3	68	2055	56	36.69	3.80	4-34
E.K.Kench	24	21	2	33	215	11.31	-	-	6	-							
A.C.Kerr	45	38	7	119	903	29.12	1	5	17	-	381.5	20	1550	70	22.14	4.06	4-8
J.M.Kerr	37	28	7	58	408	19.42	-	2	10	-	242.3	16	1023	41	24.95	4.22	5-44
C.R.King	30	22	2	53*	293	14.65	-	1	7	-							
K.A.Knight	5	3	3	2*	2	-	-	-	-	-	25	3	139	5	27.80	5.56	2-25
A.Kumar	6	3	1	4*	8	4.00	-	-	4	-	25	0	95	3	31.66	3.80	3-28
T.I.Lamb	32	15	2	20	91	7.00	-	-	20	6							
M.B.Lamplough	18	14	4	43	136	13.60	-	-	9	-	94.3	2	577	2	288.50	6.11	1-15
F.C.Leydon-Davis	86	75	17	131*	1645	28.36	2	4	27	-	454.3	26	2094	73	28.68	4.61	5-18
R.S.M.Lili'i	72	45	13	63	617	19.28	-	2	16	-	312.2	31	1333	45	29.62	4.27	4-16
O.R.Lobb	27	21	3	51	330	18.33	-	1	22	6							
M.B.Loe	9	8	6	16	39	19.50	-	-	2	-	51	0	273	4	68.25	5.35	2-27

	M	In	NO	HS	Runs	Ave	100s	50s	ct	st	O	M	R	W	Ave	R/O	Best
A.C.Mace-Cochrane	32	26	5	84	363	17.28	-	2	6	-	31	2	148	4	37.00	4.77	2-18
F.L.Mackay	115	110	12	145	4788	48.85	13	22	42	-	902.1	72	3144	154	20.41	3.48	5-15
R.A.Mair	43	28	9	36*	306	16.10	-	-	9	-	291	27	1105	46	24.02	3.80	3-21
K.J.Martin	164	156	15	118*	4349	30.84	6	26	105	68	1	0	7	1	7.00	7.00	1-7
J.T.McFadyen	48	42	10	153*	1153	36.03	2	5	41	20							
R.H.McNeill	66	29	17	18	88	7.33	-	-	16	-	388.5	25	1585	62	25.56	4.08	4-20
B.C.Molony	31	16	7	31	92	10.22	-	-	1	-	171.1	5	766	17	45.05	4.48	3-25
S.R.Naidu	8	3	0	7	7	2.33	-	-	3	-	32	1	151	3	50.33	4.72	2-29
K.F.G.Nation	50	41	4	40	482	13.02	-	-	15	-	8.4	0	71	0	-	8.19	-
T.M.M.Newton	82	65	9	64	1107	19.76	-	6	34	-	325.3	14	1553	40	38.82	4.77	3-23
S.A.Oldershaw	22	17	5	36*	102	8.50	-	-	3	-	125.1	4	635	24	26.45	5.07	5-19
N.H.Patel	25	18	7	53*	137	12.45	-	1	6	-	156	10	633	18	35.16	4.06	3-36
M.M.Penfold	8	6	2	9	19	4.75	-	-	1	-	32.4	1	159	5	31.80	4.87	1-13
K.T.Perkins	117	108	28	101*	2865	35.81	3	18	52	-	13	0	96	1	96.00	7.38	1-26
A.M.Peterson	96	81	8	102*	1685	23.08	1	9	30	-	503.3	31	2008	78	25.74	3.99	5-20
G.E.Plimmer	15	13	2	29	137	12.45	-	-	1	-							
J.E.I.Prasad	19	12	0	52	161	13.41	-	1	5	-	92	10	389	20	19.45	4.23	3-47
M.S.Rees	26	14	7	24*	106	15.14	-	-	3	-	132.1	10	592	26	22.76	4.48	5-14
E.A.J.Richardson	94	83	4	102*	1875	23.73	1	11	30	-	655.2	33	2899	87	33.32	4.42	4-21
H.M.Rowe	77	59	14	62	1024	22.75	-	1	22	-	528.1	48	2143	87	24.63	4.06	4-17
C.R.Sarsfield	24	13	2	20	42	3.81	-	-	10	-	121	5	562	17	33.05	4.64	3-29
A.E.Satterthwaite	146	127	30	136	4499	46.38	7	32	59	-	807	73	3245	138	23.51	4.02	5-27
J.L.Savage	72	52	8	59	900	20.45	-	4	35	4	196.3	14	955	29	32.93	4.86	6-18
S.Shahri	39	35	3	89	730	22.81	-	5	5	-							
J.A.Simmons	36	14	6	12	31	3.87	-	-	2	-	235.5	20	1048	33	31.75	4.44	3-17
K.M.Sims	11	7	5	18*	27	13.50	-	-	2	-	42	4	206	9	22.88	4.90	3-19
M.P.Singh	49	32	10	47*	254	11.54	-	-	1	-	354.5	33	1375	43	31.97	3.88	4-11
G.E.S.Sullivan	41	23	8	27	138	9.20	-	-	13	-	206.1	17	863	33	26.15	4.19	4-51
L.M.M.Tahuhu	72	40	16	56	480	20.00	-	2	25	-	511.4	43	2161	73	29.60	4.22	4-17
M.B.Templeton	13	9	1	21	85	10.62	-	-	2	-	72	5	271	13	20.84	3.76	3-36
K.A.Tomlinson	118	102	13	67	1892	21.25	-	8	35	3	72.5	4	396	3	132.00	5.44	1-20
A.van Deventer	75	66	8	169*	1550	26.72	2	8	26	-	0.5	0	6	0	-	-	-
J.M.Watkin	72	69	3	158	1599	24.22	1	10	24	-	550.4	59	2084	83	25.10	3.78	4-13
S.R.Wilson	8	8	3	23*	76	15.20	-	-	-	-	31.2	0	198	5	39.60	6.32	2-49

UNDER 19 DEVELOPMENT TEAM

The under 19 development side played three matches against a New Zealand Police team in February. Three games against a New Zealand Provincial XI set down for 29, 30 March and 1 April at St Paul's Collegiate Ground in Hamilton were rained off.

NEW ZEALAND UNDER 19 v NEW ZEALAND POLICE
At Burnside Park, Christchurch 15 February, 2021
New Zealand Police 150-7 (O.R. Gregory 38*, S.K. Wynands 33, G.A. Guy 24) lost to **New Zealand Under 19** 152-8 (G.E. Plimmer 25, E.M. Bermingham 3-30) by 2 wickets

NEW ZEALAND UNDER 19 v NEW ZEALAND POLICE
At Burnside Park, Christchurch 16 February, 2021
New Zealand Under 19 255-7 (O.N. Gain 50, G.E. Plimmer 46, I.C. Gaze 45, M.J. Banks 27*, E.M. Bermingham 4-42) defeated **New Zealand Police** 136 (E.M. Bermingham 22, W.J. Campbell 22, G.A. Harris 3-20) by 119 runs

NEW ZEALAND UNDER 19 v NEW ZEALAND POLICE
At Burnside Park, Christchurch 17 February, 2021
New Zealand Under 19 273-7 (E. Irwin 66, G.R. Adams 46, M.J. Banks 23, N.E. Codyre 21*, M.L. Tuapawa 4-41) defeated **New Zealand Police** 151 (E.M. Bermingham 52, K.T. Perkins 38, G.A. Harris 3-19, M.E. Loe 3-22) by 122 runs

PROVINCIAL COMPETITIONS

The symbol of supremacy in women's provincial cricket has been the Hallyburton Johnstone Shield (1935/36 to 1981/82), Hansells Cup (1982/83 to 1989/90), Pub Charities National Tournament (1990/91 to 1997/98), State Insurance Cup (1998/99 to 2000/01), State League (2001/02 to 2008/09), One-day Competition (2009/10 and from 2012/13 to 2016/17) and Action Cricket Cup (2010/11 to 2011/12). The Hallyburton Johnstone Shield was reinstated in 2017/18.

WINNERS

1935/36	Wellington	1964/65	Auckland	1993/94	Canterbury
1936/37	Wellington	1965/66	Auckland	1994/95	Canterbury
1937/38	Wellington	1966/67	Canterbury	1995/96	Canterbury
1938/39	Wellington	1967/68	Wellington	1996/97	Canterbury
1939/40	Auckland	1968/69	North Shore	1997/98	Canterbury
1940/41	Auckland	1969/70	Wellington	1998/99	Canterbury
1941/42	no competition	1970/71	North Shore	1999/00	Auckland
1942/43	Auckland	1971/72	North Shore	2000/01	Auckland
1943/44	Canterbury	1972/73	Canterbury	2001/02	Auckland
1944/45	Canterbury	1973/74	Wellington	2002/03	Auckland
1945/46	Canterbury	1974/75	Wellington	2003/04	Canterbury
1946/47	Auckland	1975/76	Canterbury	2004/05	Canterbury/Wellington
1947/48	Auckland	1976/77	Wellington	2005/06	Central Districts
1948/49	Auckland	1977/78	Wellington	2006/07	Canterbury
1949/50	Wellington	1978/79	Canterbury	2007/08	Canterbury
1950/51	Wellington	1979/80	Canterbury	2008/09	Canterbury
1951/52	Auckland	1980/81	Canterbury	2009/10	Central Districts
1952/53	Wellington	1981/82	Canterbury	2010/11	Canterbury
1953/54	Wellington	1982/83	Canterbury	2011/12	Auckland
1954/55	Auckland	1983/84	Canterbury	2012/13	Canterbury
1955/56	Canterbury	1984/85	Canterbury	2013/14	Otago
1956/57	Auckland	1985/86	Canterbury	2014/15	Auckland
1957/58	Auckland	1986/87	Canterbury	2015/16	Auckland
1958/59	Wellington	1987/88	Canterbury	2016/17	Canterbury
1959/60	Wellington	1988/89	Canterbury	2017/18	Auckland
1960/61	Canterbury	1989/90	Wellington	2018/19	Central Districts
1961/62	Canterbury	1990/91	Canterbury	2019/20	Auckland
1962/63	Otago	1991/92	Canterbury	2020/21	Canterbury
1963/64	Canterbury	1992/93	Canterbury		

The women's Twenty20 competition was introduced in 2007/08 as the State League Twenty20 to 2008/09, Twenty20 Competition (2009/10 and from 2012/13 to 2017/18), Action Cricket Twenty20 (2010/11 to 2011/12) and Burger King Super Smash from 2018/19.

WINNERS

2007/08	Canterbury	2012/13	Wellington	2017/18	Wellington
2008/09	Wellington	2013/14	Auckland	2018/19	Wellington
2009/10	Central Districts	2014/15	Wellington	2019/20	Wellington
2010/11	Canterbury	2015/16	Canterbury	2020/21	Canterbury
2011/12	Canterbury	2016/17	Otago		

TEAM RECORDS

Highest Totals

339-9	Wellington v Northern Districts	Wellington	2015/16
339-2	Central Districts v Otago	Palmerston North	2018/19
332-4	Otago v Wellington	Lincoln	2012/13
329-5	Wellington v Otago	Dunedin	2019/20
325-7	Wellington v Northern Districts	Wellington	2013/14
322-4	Wellington v Northern Districts	Mt Maunganui	2012/13
322-8	Auckland v Wellington	Wellington	2014/15
322-5	Auckland v Northern Districts	Hamilton	2019/20
321-4	Canterbury v Otago	Oamaru	2020/21
321-8	Wellington v Otago	Wellington	2020/21

Lowest Totals

41	Otago v Wellington	Upper Hutt	2010/11
43	Central Districts v Auckland	Wanganui	1999/00
46	Northern Districts v Wellington	Wellington	1999/00
49	Auckland v Central Districts	New Plymouth	2020/21
51	Northern Districts v Otago	Dunedin	2004/05

INDIVIDUAL RECORDS

Highest Scores

183*	S.W. Bates	Otago v Auckland	Auckland	2005/06
169*	A. van Deventer	Central Districts v Otago	Palmerston North	2018/19
164*	S.W. Bates	Otago v Wellington	Lincoln	2012/13
162*	S.F.M. Devine	Wellington v Northern Districts	Wellington	2015/16
160*	S.W. Bates	Otago v Canterbury	Rangiora	2012/13
160*	K.G. Anderson	Northern Districts v Canterbury	Christchurch	2018/19
158	J.M. Watkin	Central Districts v Wellington	Wellington	2019/20
153*	K.L. Pulford	Central Districts v Canterbury	Christchurch	1999/00
153*	J.T. McFadyen	Wellington v Otago	Dunedin	2019/20
150*	M.L.Lynch	Auckland v Canterbury	Auckland	2009/10
150*	S.W. Bates	Otago v Central Districts	Lincoln	2014/15

Most Wickets in an Innings

9-4-18-7	B.G. Armstrong	Auckland v Otago	Auckland	2019/20
7.1-1-19-7	M.F. Tunupopo	Auckland v Central Districts	Wanganui	1999/00
9-0-56-7	M.J. Greig	Central Districts v Canterbury	Hastings	2015/16
10-6-8-6	R.J. Steele	Canterbury v Auckland	Auckland	2005/06
5.1-3-8-6	L.M. Kasperek	Otago v Canterbury	Mosgiel	2013/14
10-6-9-6	A.E. Cooper	Wellington v Otago	Wellington	2008/09
10-3-18-6	N. Scripps	Auckland v Northern Districts	Auckland	2003/04
7.1-1-18-6	J.L. Savage	Canterbury v Northern Districts	Whangarei	2020/21
9.2-2-19-6	N. Scripps	Auckland v Wellington	Auckland	2002/03
9-1-20-6	D.M. Trow	Central Districts v Northern Districts	Wanganui	2003/04
9.5-1-31-6	B.H. McNeill	Canterbury v Auckland	Auckland	2001/02

RECORD PARTNERSHIPS

AUCKLAND

1st	187	R.J. Rolls & R.J. Kember	v Otago	Auckland	2005/06
2nd	180	L.R. Down & A.N. Kelly	v Wellington	Wellington	2020/21
3rd	151*	R.J. Rolls & I. Cronin-Knight	v Otago	Dunedin	2006/07
	151*	A.N. Kelly & R.S.M. Lili'i	v Central Districts	Auckland	2019/20
4th	† 198*	K.T. Perkins & A.M. Peterson	v Wellington	Wellington	2019/20
5th	120	R.J. Rolls & K. Perkins	v Northern Districts	Auckland	2006/07
6th	101*	V.J. Lind & H.R. Huddleston	v Central Districts	Masterton	2009/10
7th	90	K.A. Ramel & A. Soma	v Wellington	Auckland	1998/99
8th	60	H.R. Huddleston & R.S.M. Lili'i	v Northern Districts	Whangarei	2016/17
9th	35	E.C. Drumm & S.E.M. Cowlrick	v Canterbury	Christchurch	1998/99
10th	57*	K.T. Perkins & N. Scripps	v Northern Districts	Whangarei	2008/09

CANTERBURY

1st	181	F.L. Mackay & A.E. Satterthwaite	v Otago	Christchurch	2015/16
2nd	227	D.A. Hockley & N. Payne	v Wellington	Christchurch	1999/00
3rd	240	F.L. Mackay & K.E. Ebrahim	v Otago	Oamaru	2020/21
4th	167	E.M. Bermingham & H.N.K. Jensen	v Otago	Alexandra	2016/17
5th	127	K.E. Ebrahim & A.C. Mace-Cochrane	v Northern Districts	Hamilton	2018/19
6th	114*	A.E. Satterthwaite & L.M.M. Tahuhu	v Northern Districts	Hamilton	2014/15
7th	† 128	E.M. Bermingham & L.M.M. Tahuhu	v Central Districts	Rangiora	2014/15
8th	53	H.M. Tiffen & E.M. Bermingham	v Northern Districts	Mt Maunganui	2007/08
9th	44*	N.B. Cox & K.F.G. Nation	v Northern Districts	Rangiora	2013/14
10th	53	L.M.M. Tahuhu & G.E.S. Sullivan	v Otago	Christchurch	2015/16

CENTRAL DISTRICTS

1st	† 216	J.M. Watkin & N.C. Dodd	v Wellington	Wellington	2019/20
2nd	† 328	N.C. Dodd & A. van Deventer	v Otago	P. North	2018/19
3rd	143	N.M. Thessman & A.L. Mason	v Wellington	Wanganui	2005/06
4th	152	S.J. McGlashan & A.L. Mason	v Auckland	P. North	2007/08
5th	112	A.L. Mason & Z.A. McWilliams	v Wellington	New Plymouth	2007/08
6th	120	K.C.R. Rangi & H.M. Rowe	v Northern Districts	Whangarei	2015/16
7th	111	H.M. Rowe & G.K. Atkinson	v Wellington	Levin	2020/21
8th	70	R.H. Priest & M.A. Frey	v Northern Districts	Mt Maunganui	2008/09
9th	67*	N.M. Thessman & K.M. Sutherland	v Otago	Dunedin	2001/02
10th	† 66	H.M. Rowe & K.E. Baxter	v Otago	New Plymouth	2016/17

NORTHERN DISTRICTS

1st	164	K.L. Pulford & N.C. Dodd	v Otago	Mt Maunganui	2007/08
2nd	154	N.C. Dodd & E.J. Parker	v Auckland	Whangarei	2016/17
3rd	† 308*	F.C. Leydon-Davis & K.G. Anderson	v Canterbury	Hamilton	2018/19
4th	137	E.C. Drumm & N.J. Browne	v Canterbury	Hamilton	2005/06
5th	101	N.C. Dodd & F.C. Leydon-Davis	v Canterbury	Hamilton	2014/15
6th	138*	N.J. Browne & L.E. Milliken	v Auckland	Auckland	2005/06
7th	122	R.F. Vincent & M.J.G. Nielsen	v Otago	Lincoln	2011/12
8th	† 81	L.S. Mulivai & B.M. Perry	v Central Districts	New Plymouth	2018/19
9th	69	N.J. Browne & K.A. Tomlinson	v Wellington	Wellington	2007/08
10th	52	H.R. Huddleston & M.A. Taylor	v Otago	Mt Maunganui	2007/08

OTAGO

1st	199	E.J. Scurr & P.B. Flannery	v Auckland	Queenstown	2004/05
2nd	214	S.E Bates & L.M. Kasperek	v Northern Districts	Alexandra	2014/15
3rd	168	K.J. Martin & L.M. Kasperek	v Central Districts	Alexandra	2013/14
4th	143	S.W. Bates & V.L. Abbott	v Auckland	Auckland	2013/14
5th †	166	L.M. Kasperek & B.A. Langston	v Central Districts	Oamaru	2017/18
6th	101	K.J. Martin & V.L. Holden	v Auckland	Lincoln	2016/17
7th	106	E.J. Scurr & S.W. Bates	v Auckland	Auckland	2003/04
8th	80	C.E. Taylor & K.M. Spence	v Northern Districts	Hamilton	2005/06
9th	56	S.K. Helmore & A.L. Kane	v Auckland	Auckland	2003/04
10th	53	S.A. Oldershaw & M.E. Loe	v Northern Districts	Hamilton	2020/21

WELLINGTON

1st	153	L.R. Doolan & R.J.M Moffitt	v Central Districts	Hastings	2013/14
2nd	173*	L.R.V.S. Harford & M.A.M. Lewis	v Auckland	Wellington	2003/04
3rd	185	R.H. Priest & S.F.M. Devine	v Canterbury	Wellington	2014/15
4th	141	L.R. Doolan & S.F.M Devine	v Northern Districts	Wellington	2009/10
5th	144*	E.C. Perry & J.T. McFadyen	v Otago	Wellington	2018/19
6th †	144*	M.A.M. Lewis & M.G. Wakefield	v Auckland	Auckland	2002/03
7th	92	L.M. Kasperek & M.P. Singh	v Canterbury	Wellington	2019/20
8th	55	A.E. Cooper & S.F.M Devine	v Auckland	Auckland	2006/07
9th †	97	A.C. Stockwell & M.D. Bunkall	v Canterbury	Wellington	2012/13
10th	44	A.M. Corbin & A.J. Green	v Central Districts	Lower Hutt	2000/01

† record for all teams

Wicketkeeping

MOST DISMISSALS IN AN INNINGS

	(ct/st)				
6	(6/0)	S.J. Hill	Wellington v Northern Districts	Hamilton	2006/07
5	(2/3)	R.J. Rolls	Auckland v Canterbury	Christchurch	2000/01
5	(4/1)	R.C. Milburn	Canterbury v Auckland	Auckland	2003/04
5	(0/5)	K.J. Martin	Otago v Wellington	Dunedin	2007/08
5	(5/0)	A.C. Stockwell	Wellington v Auckland	Auckland	2008/09
5	(3/2)	A.C. Stockwell	Wellington v Northern Districts	Upper Hutt	2011/12
5	(5/0)	K.C.R. Rangi	Central Districts v Northern Districts	Hastings	2014/15
5	(5/0)	B.M. Bezuidenhout	Northern Districts v Central Districts	Napier	2016/17
5	(5/0)	S.J. Carnachan	Auckland v Otago	Auckland	2017/18
5	(5/0)	T.I. Lamb	Auckland v Otago	Auckland	2019/20
5	(4/1)	J.T. McFadyen	Wellington v Canterbury	Christchurch	2020/21

Fielding

MOST CATCHES IN AN INNINGS

4	M.M. Graham	Central Districts v Northern Districts	Wanganui	1999/00
4	S.J. Tsukigawa	Otago v Canterbury	Dunedin	2003/04
4	E.C. Drumm	Auckland v Central Districts	Auckland	2004/05

WICKETKEEPING	*ct*	*st*	*Total*
K.J. Martin	98	68	166
R.J. Rolls	86	48	134
R.H. Priest	94	38	132
R.C. Milburn	76	36	112
V.J. Lind	59	16	75
A.C. Stockwell	44	14	58
S.J. Hill	35	21	56
J.T. McFadyen	36	18	54

FIELDING	*ct*
A.E. Satterthwaite	59
E.C. Perry	56
K.T. Perkins	52
H.M. Tiffen	49
A.L. Watkins	49
N.J. Browne	49
K.E. Ebrahim	45

CAREER RECORDS

BATTING	M	In	NO	HS	Runs	Ave	100s	50s
F.L. Mackay	115	110	12	145	4788	48.85	13	22
S.J. McGlashan	146	137	21	125	4553	39.25	5	31
A.E. Satterthwaite	146	127	30	136	4499	46.38	7	32
K.J. Martin	164	156	15	118*	4349	30.84	6	26
S.W. Bates	115	110	14	183*	4329	45.09	8	25
N.C. Dodd	119	110	17	142	4243	45.62	10	23
N.J. Browne	133	123	22	115	3893	38.54	4	28
K.E. Ebrahim	123	111	21	115*	3235	35.94	5	22
R.H. Priest	127	121	14	136*	3172	29.64	4	14
E.C. Drumm	80	78	16	118	2993	48.27	5	17
K.T. Perkins	117	108	28	101*	2865	35.81	3	18
S.F.M. Devine	104	85	17	162*	2859	42.04	6	14
H.M. Tiffen	104	96	25	97	2692	37.91	-	15
R.J. Rolls	90	88	7	118	2591	31.98	4	14
E.C. Perry	136	110	25	114	2543	29.91	2	16
V.J. Lind	118	107	14	91	2538	27.29	-	14
L.R. Doolan	98	96	4	102*	2396	26.04	2	1
K.L. Pulford	89	86	11	153*	2395	31.93	3	15
S.J. Tsukigawa	123	115	16	117*	2381	24.05	2	12
A.L. Watkins	105	97	14	116	2361	28.44	1	10
S.R.H. Curtis	103	93	9	95*	2234	26.59	-	16
M.C. Godliman	77	72	3	139	2223	32.21	1	18
M.G. Wakefield	91	83	11	120	2124	29.50	1	13
M.F. Fahey	96	90	11	91	2050	25.94	-	16

BOWLING	M	O	M	R	W	Ave	R/O	Best
N. Scripps	91	767.3	111	2499	158	15.81	3.26	6-18
F.L. Mackay	115	902.1	72	3144	154	20.41	3.48	5-15
N.J. Browne	133	1020	81	4246	144	29.48	4.16	5-31
A.E. Satterthwaite	146	807	73	3245	138	23.51	4.02	5-27
S.F.M. Devine	104	764.1	92	2733	129	21.18	3.58	5-15
K.E. Ebrahim	123	882.4	100	3264	125	26.11	3.70	4-11
B.H. McNeill	94	714.2	95	2541	122	20.82	3.56	6-31
H.R. Huddleston	135	841.2	90	3313	122	27.15	3.94	4-22
E.M. Campbell	71	548.1	49	2018	120	16.81	3.68	5-8
A.L. Watkins	105	812.4	97	2840	119	23.86	3.49	5-25
L.R. Doolan	98	689.4	54	2752	119	23.12	3.99	5-38
S.W. Bates	115	883.1	94	3602	117	30.78	4.08	4-20
A.E. Cooper	104	587.3	80	2204	114	19.33	3.75	6-9
A.K. Burrows	109	805.1	90	2908	112	25.96	3.61	5-39
H.M. Watson	101	732.5	130	2263	110	20.57	3.09	5-18
P.A. Gruber	96	697.3	66	2361	106	22.27	3.38	4-15
S.J. Tsukigawa	123	728.3	83	2809	104	27.00	3.86	5-13
S.K. Burke	97	737.3	105	2528	103	24.54	3.43	4-28
D.M. Doughty	79	640.4	71	2484	102	24.35	3.88	5-26
L.M. Kasperek	64	493.2	47	2036	102	19.96	4.13	6-8
E.M. Bermingham	102	713.3	71	2755	101	27.27	3.86	4-19

UNDER 19 TOURNAMENT

The Under 19 Tournament was held at Lincoln from 6 to 12 January, 2021. The tournament was made up of four rounds of fifty-over games, followed by three rounds of Twenty20 matches. The tournament was won by Auckland.

FIRST ROUND

Auckland 187 defeated **Northern District**s 108 by 79 runs
Central Districts 168 defeated **Canterbury** 109 by 59 runs
Otago 278-5 defeated **Wellington** 188 by 90 runs

SECOND ROUND

Canterbury 100 lost to **Auckland** 102-3 by 7 wickets
Central Districts 162 defeated **Otago** 128 by 34 runs
Northern Districts 199 defeated **Wellington** 103 by 96 runs

THIRD ROUND

Wellington 118-9 lost to **Auckland** 119-8 by 2 wickets
Canterbury 178-8 defeated **Otago** 107 by 71 runs
Northern Districts 205-2 lost to **Central District**s 206-9 by 1 wicket

FOURTH ROUND

Auckland 198 lost to **Central District**s 199-9 by 1 wicket
Wellington 223-9 defeated **Canterbury** 177 by 46 runs
Otago 277-5 lost to **Northern Districts** 278-9 by 1 wicket

FIFTH ROUND

Auckland 117-8 lost to **Otago** 118-6 by 4 wickets
Northern Districts 148-3 defeated **Canterbury** 146-6 by 2 runs
Wellington 155-7 defeated **Central Districts** 147-8 by 8 runs

SIXTH ROUND

Northern Districts 119-7 lost to **Auckland** 122-4 by 6 wickets
Canterbury 118-5 defeated **Central Districts** 116-6 by 2 runs
Wellington 182-5 defeated **Otago** 167-9 by 15 runs

SEVENTH ROUND

Central Districts 108-8 lost to **Auckland** 109-7 by 3 wickets
Wellington 84 lost to **Canterbury** 87-7 by 3 wickets
Otago 85 lost to **Northern District**s 86-5 by 5 wickets

Final points: Auckland 20, Central Districts 18, Northern Districts 15, Canterbury 11, Wellington 11, Otago 8.

TEST CAREER RECORDS

	M	In	NO	HS	Runs	Ave	100	50	Ct	st	Wkts	Runs	Ave	5WI	10WM	Best
E.P.N.Allan	4	6	4	29*	87	43.50	-	-	1	-	5	138	27.60	-	-	3-38
T.L.Anderson	2	3	0	63	108	36.00	-	1	-	-						
E.A.Badham	3	6	1	42	121	24.20	-	-	7	-	10	275	27.50	-	-	4-46
D.L.Bailey	1	2	0	5	6	3.00	-	-	-	-						
H.R.Bastion	1	-	-	-	-	-	-	-	-	-	0	59	-	-	-	-
K.E.Batty	4	7	1	24	67	11.16	-	-	6	-	2	78	39.00	-	-	1-18
L.I.Bayliss	1	-	-	-	-	-	-	-	-	-	5	70	14.00	1	-	5-28
B.L.Bevege	5	10	1	100*	400	44.44	1	2	3	-	0	70	-	-	-	-
M.C.Bishop	1	2	0	27	27	13.50	-	-	2	-	0	33	-	-	-	-
E.E.Blackie	1	2	1	13*	21	21.00	-	-	3	1						
P.Blackler	12	21	0	68	371	17.66	-	1	5	-	18	527	29.27	-	-	4-2
B.A.Brentnall	10	16	2	84*	301	21.50	-	1	16	12						
K.D.Brown	3	2	2	50*	52	-	-	1	4	-	7	160	22.85	-	-	3-4
S.H.Brown	6	9	3	19	59	9.83	-	-	1	-	9	432	48.00	-	-	3-6
N.A.Browne	1	2	2	5*	5	-	-	-	1	-	0	77	-	-	-	-
N.J.Browne	2	2	0	24	23	12.00	-	-	2	-	1	83	83.00	-	-	1-4
D.K.Brownlee	1	2	0	12	17	8.50	-	-	-	-						
H.E.Buck	1	2	0	16	16	8.00	-	-	-	-						
S.K.Burke	1	1	1	1*	1	-	-	-	-	-	1	57	57.00	-	-	1-5
J.A.Burley	6	9	0	46	110	12.22	-	-	3	-	21	553	26.33	1	-	7-4
V.E.Burt	3	5	0	15	40	8.00	-	-	-	-	0	28	-	-	-	-
V.L.Burtt	4	8	0	39	101	12.62	-	-	5	-						
C.A.Campbell	9	5	1	29	55	13.75	-	-	2	-	18	720	40.00	-	-	4-9
P.F.Carrick	7	11	3	21	63	7.87	-	-	4	-	21	489	23.28	1	-	6-2
J.Clark	11	18	0	79	482	26.77	-	2	7	-	0	5	-	-	-	-
A.L.Clough	1	1	0	0	0	0.00	-	-	-	-	1	70	70.00	-	-	1-7
W.J.Coe	3	5	1	34	83	20.75	-	-	-	-	6	222	37.00	-	-	2-3
M.C.Corby	1	2	0	12	13	6.50	-	-	-	-	0	36	-	-	-	-
D.A.Costello	1	1	0	0	0	0.00	-	-	-	-	2	104	52.00	-	-	2-7
J.M.Coulston	5	8	1	24	76	10.85	-	-	3	-	19	341	17.94	-	-	4-3
V.R.Coutts	6	11	0	41	136	12.36	-	-	1	-						
S.D.Cowles	7	14	0	46	324	23.14	-	-	6	-	0	13	-	-	-	-
M.J.Currie	3	5	2	3*	7	2.33	-	-	2	-	3	170	56.66	-	-	3-3
E.J.Dickson	2	4	0	65	114	28.50	-	1	-	-						
J.D.Doull	11	22	4	103	779	43.27	1	5	6	-	0	34	-	-	-	-
E.C.Drumm	5	6	3	161*	433	144.33	2	2	-	-	2	175	87.50	-	-	1-2
B.M.Duncan	2	3	3	1*	1	-	-	-	1	-	2	115	57.50	-	-	1-3
M.H.Dunlop	2	2	0	5	5	2.50	-	-	-	-	3	123	41.00	-	-	1-5
J.R.Dunning	6	12	2	71	320	32.00	-	2	5	-	6	170	28.33	-	-	2-1
A.E.Ell	1	2	0	1	2	1.00	-	-	-	-	0	55	-	-	-	-
M.F.Fahey	2	4	1	60*	125	41.66	-	1	1	-						
V.H.M.Farrell	3	4	0	5	12	3.00	-	-	5	3						
P.B.Flannery	1	2	0	46	64	32.00	-	-	-	-	0	5	-	-	-	-
K.E.Flavell	6	7	0	204	473	67.57	1	2	2	-						
J.W.Francis	5	7	1	19	46	7.66	-	-	2	-	14	362	25.85	-	-	4-7
L.M.Fraser	3	-	-	-	-	-	-	-	-	-	4	210	52.50	-	-	2-6
M.K.Fruin	6	8	0	80	188	23.50	-	2	3	1						
J.A.Fryer	3	1	1	7*	7	-	-	-	1	-	5	154	30.80	-	-	4-3
M.J.Fulford	1	2	0	10	12	6.00	-	-	-	-	2	46	23.00	-	-	2-4
S.M.Gilchrist	5	3	2	7*	12	12.00	-	-	5	-	14	384	27.42	-	-	3-4
G.P.Gooder	1	2	0	11	11	5.50	-	-	-	-	8	73	9.12	1	-	6-4
K.V.Gunn	9	12	0	49	194	16.16	-	-	6	1	11	429	39.00	-	-	3-4
J.E.Harris	10	7	3	9	26	6.50	-	-	1	-	15	691	46.06	-	-	4-1
J.C.Hatcher	4	7	0	23	79	11.28	-	-	-	-						
C.E.Henshilwood	1	2	0	41	48	24.00	-	-	-	-	0	14	-	-	-	-
D.A.Hockley	19	29	4	126*	1301	52.04	4	7	9	-	5	146	29.20	-	-	2-9
M.Hollis	1	2	0	24	26	13.00	-	-	-	-	1	81	81.00	-	-	1-8
S.L.Illingworth	6	7	3	40*	120	30.00	-	-	5	5						
I.C.P.Jagersma	9	13	5	52	271	33.87	-	1	10	2	4	38	9.50	-	-	4-3
Y.J.Kainuku	1	1	1	23*	23	-	-	-	-	-	1	50	50.00	-	-	1-5
K.M.Keenan	5	3	2	26*	32	32.00	-	-	4	-	15	348	23.20	1	-	6-7
P.D.Kinsella	6	8	0	53	131	16.37	-	1	3	-						
I.M.Lamason	4	6	2	37*	86	21.50	-	-	-	-	2	136	68.00	-	-	2-2
J.G.Lamason	4	8	0	24	87	10.87	-	-	-	-	8	264	33.00	-	-	4-5
B.J.Legg	3	4	1	26	30	10.00	-	-	-	-	4	149	37.25	-	-	2-5
M.A.M.Lewis	9	12	0	65	252	21.00	-	2	6	-						

	M	In	NO	HS	Runs	Ave	100	50	Ct	st	Wkts	Runs	Ave	5WI	10WM	Best
J.Lord	15	22	3	39*	258	13.57	-	-	5	-	55	1049	19.07	4	1	6-119
E.J.Maker	3	4	0	5	10	2.50	-	-	1	-	5	156	31.20	-	-	3-34
C.E.Marett	7	13	4	49	304	33.77	-	-	3	-	9	268	29.77	-	-	2-16
M.E.Marks	2	4	1	23	30	10.00	-	-	-	-						
K.J.Martin	1	2	0	46	49	24.50	-	-	-	-						
A.L.Mason	2	2	0	14	15	7.50	-	-	2	-	3	105	35.00	-	-	2-68
K.L.McDonald	1	1	0	1	1	1.00	-	-	-	-						
S.J.McGlashan	2	2	0	14	20	10.00	-	-	-	-						
P.F.McKelvey	15	26	2	155*	699	29.12	2	1	8	-						
A.McKenna	7	14	1	97*	465	35.76	-	3	7	-	0	6	-	-	-	-
R.U.McKenzie	7	13	0	61	295	22.69	-	2	3	-	8	214	26.75	-	-	4-18
S.McLauchlan	4	4	0	4	4	1.00	-	-	1	-	2	83	41.50	-	-	1-7
E.L.Miller	3	6	0	32	92	15.33	-	-	1	-						
H.Miller	1	2	0	11	11	5.50	-	-	-	-	1	77	77.00	-	-	1-77
L.E.Milliken	2	2	0	6	10	5.00	-	-	-	-	2	73	36.50	-	-	2-49
K.S.Molloy	2	1	1	1*	1	-	-	-	2	-	5	91	18.20	-	-	2-24
P.N.Moore	2	3	1	47*	80	40.00	-	-	3	-	0	31	-	-	-	-
L.J.Murdoch	6	10	0	72	253	25.30	-	1	1	-						
K.J.Musson	1	-	-	-	-	-	-	-	-	-						
C.M.Nicholson	4	5	0	46	140	28.00	-	-	1	-	5	170	34.00	-	-	2-25
A.M.O'Leary	1	1	0	27	27	27.00	-	-	1	-						
J.B.Olson	1	1	0	0	0	0.00	-	-	-	-	0	48	-	-	-	-
C.M.Oyler	5	8	2	67*	212	35.33	-	1	2	-						
E.A.Paton	4	8	1	77*	180	25.71	-	1	4	-	9	160	17.77	-	-	4-35
K.V.Plummer	4	6	0	13	28	4.66	-	-	2	-						
I.J.Powell	7	13	2	63	272	24.72	-	1	9	1						
L.M.Powell	5	9	0	66	188	20.88	-	1	2	-	0	8	-	-	-	-
K.L.Pulford	1	2	0	0	0	0.00	-	-	1	-	2	15	7.50	-	-	2-15
S.J.Rattray	9	17	2	59	412	27.46	-	4	1	-	19	461	24.26	1	-	5-76
D.M.M.Robinson	1	1	1	2*	2	-	-	-	-	-	1	16	16.00	-	-	1-16
R.J.Rolls	1	2	1	71	71	71.00	-	1	1	-						
E.F.Rouse	1	2	0	35	36	18.00	-	-	-	-						
M.T.Rouse	2	4	2	15*	18	9.00	-	-	-	-						
J.A.Russell	1	1	0	39	39	39.00	-	-	-	-	1	37	37.00	-	-	1-14
E.M.Ryan	5	8	4	10	38	9.50	-	-	3	11						
J.M.Saulbrey	11	16	4	62	198	16.50	-	1	6	-	35	951	27.17	1	-	5-32
P.H.Savin	1	2	0	15	18	9.00	-	-	-	-						
N.Scripps	1	1	1	10*	10	-	-	-	-	-	0	57	-	-	-	-
E.A.Signal	6	6	2	55*	82	20.50	-	1	3	-	8	325	40.62	-	-	2-34
R.J.Signal	1	2	1	8*	8	8.00	-	-	-	-	0	21	-	-	-	-
L.J.Simpson	1	2	0	4	6	3.00	-	-	-	-						
E.M.Sinclair	2	4	1	10	26	8.66	-	-	2	-						
C.M.Sinton	1	2	0	10	14	7.00	-	-	-	-						
J.E.Stead	9	18	2	95	433	27.06	-	3	3	-						
R.J.Steele	2	3	0	12	16	5.33	-	-	3	-	8	141	17.62	1	-	5-79
J.M.Stonell	4	8	0	47	127	15.87	-	-	2	-						
G.A.Sutherland	3	6	0	22	66	11.00	-	-	1	-	2	86	43.00	-	-	1-29
R.E.Symons	1	1	0	5	5	5.00	-	-	1	-	2	71	35.50	-	-	2-71
M.J.Taylor	1	2	0	3	3	1.50	-	-	-	-	1	62	62.00	-	-	1-62
H.M.Thompson	1	2	1	17*	17	17.00	-	-	1	-	0	18	-	-	-	-
B.I.Thorner	3	6	1	37	76	15.20	-	-	-	-	4	78	19.50	-	-	2-33
H.M.Tiffen	2	4	3	66*	124	124.00	-	1	1	-						
J.A.Turner	6	8	1	11*	30	4.28	-	-	2	-	19	469	24.68	-	-	3-42
N.J.Turner	6	9	2	65*	208	29.71	-	2	1	-						
M.A.Webb	4	8	0	42	110	13.75	-	-	-	-	6	66	11.00	-	-	3-32
E.G.White	3	5	0	17	33	6.60	-	-	-	-	2	85	42.50	-	-	1-5
J.K.Wickham	2	4	0	34	40	10.00	-	-	-	-	3	76	25.33	-	-	2-33
N.M.Williams	4	5	1	35*	70	17.50	-	-	1	-	3	158	52.66	-	-	2-19
T.L.Woodbury	2	3	3	7*	7	-	-	-	-	-	4	100	25.00	-	-	2-29

TEAM RECORDS

Highest Totals

517-8	v England	Scarborough	1996
403-8d	v India	Nelson	1994/95
362-5d	v England	Guildford	1996
359	v Australia	Wellington	1974/75
335	v Australia	Melbourne	1971/72

Lowest Totals

44	v England	Christchurch	1934/35
61	v England	Auckland	1948/49
63	v England	Worcester	1954
78	v Australia	Adelaide	1978/79
87	v Australia	Wellington	1947/48

INDIVIDUAL RECORDS

Centuries

204	K.E. Flavell v England at Scarborough	1996
161*	E.C. Drumm v Australia at Christchurch	1994/95
155*	P.F. McKelvey v England at Wellington	1968/69
126*	D.A. Hockley v Australia at Auckland	1989/90
117*	P.F. McKelvey v South Africa at Cape Town	1971/72
115	D.A. Hockley v England at Worcester	1996
112*	E.C. Drumm v England at Guildford	1996
107*	D.A. Hockley v England at Canterbury	1984
107	D.A. Hockley v India at Nelson	1994/95
103	J.D. Doull v England at Christchurch	1968/69
100*	B.L. Bevege v India at Dunedin	1976/77

Five Wickets in an Innings

7-41	J.A. Burley v England at The Oval	1966
6-29	P.F. Carrick v Australia at Melbourne	1971/72
6-42	G.P. Gooder v England at Auckland	1948/49
6-73	K.M. Keenan v England at Worcester	1996
6-119	J. Lord v Australia at Melbourne	1978/79
5-24	J. Lord v South Africa at Durban	1971/72
5-28	L.I. Bayliss v Australia at Dunedin	1960/61
5-32	J.M. Saulbrey v South Africa at Durban	1971/72
5-40	J. Lord v India at Dunedin	1976/77
5-76	S.J. Rattray v India at Cuttack	1984/85
5-78	J. Lord v Australia at Adelaide	1978/79
5-79	R.J. Steele v India at Vapi	2003/04

Ten Wickets in a Match

10-137	J. Lord v Australia at Melbourne	1978/79

Wicketkeeping

DISMISSALS IN AN INNINGS

	(ct/st)				
6	(2/4)	B.A. Brentnall	v South Africa	Johannesburg	1971/72
5	(3/2)	B.A. Brentnall	v England	Auckland	1968/69
4	(1/3)	V.H.M. Farrell	v England	Worcester	1954
4	(4/0)	V.H.M. Farrell	v England	The Oval	1954
4	(1/3)	E.M. Ryan	v Australia	Melbourne	1978/79

DISMISSALS IN A MATCH

	(ct/st)				
7	(3/4)	B.A. Brentnall	v South Africa	Johannesburg	1971/72
7	(2/5)	E.M. Ryan	v Australia	Melbourne	1978/79
6	(4/2)	B.A. Brentnall	v England	Auckland	1968/69
5	(3/2)	B.A. Brentnall	v South Africa	Durban	1971/72
5	(2/3)	S.L. Illingworth	v England	Guildford	1996

Fielding

CATCHES IN AN INNINGS

3	K.E. Batty	v England	Auckland	1948/49
3	P. N.Moore	v England	The Oval	1966
3	E.A. Badham	v Australia	Sydney	1978/79
3	M.A.M. Lewis	v England	Wanganui	1991/92
3	D.A. Hockley	v England	Scarborough	1996

CATCHES IN A MATCH

4	S.M. Gilchrist	v India	Ahmedabad	1984/85
4	M.A.M. Lewis	v England	Wanganui	1991/92

RECORD PARTNERSHIPS

1st	150	M.K. Fruin & D.A. Hockley	v England	Guildford	1996
2nd	146	M.K. Fruin & K.E. Flavell	v England	Scarborough	1996
3rd	106	K.E. Flavell & E.C. Drumm	v England	Guildford	1996
4th	94	I.J. Powell & R.U. McKenzie	v Australia	Dunedin	1960/61
5th	94*	E.C. Drumm & D.A. Hockley	v England	Guildford	1996
6th	83	D.A. Hockley & K.V. Gunn	v Australia	Christchurch	1989/90
7th	90	B.A. Brentnall & J.A. Burley	v England	Birmingham	1966
8th	87	C.E. Marett & J.M. Saulbrey	v Australia	Wellington	1974/75
9th	60*	K.E. Flavell & K.D. Brown	v England	Scarborough	1996
10th	55*	C.M. Oyler & J. Lord	v England	The Oval	1966

SUMMARY OF TEST CAREER RECORDS

Most Matches

D.A. Hockley	19	P. Blackler	12	J. Clark	11
P.F. McKelvey	15	J.D. Doull	11	J.E. Harris	10
J. Lord	15	J.M. Saulbrey	11	B.A. Brentnall	10

Most Runs

D.A. Hockley	1301	K.E. Flavell	473	J.E. Stead	433
J.D. Doull	779	A. McKenna	465	S.J. Rattray	412
P.F. McKelvey	699	E.C. Drumm	433	B.L. Bevege	400
J. Clark	482				

Most Wickets

J. Lord	55	J.M. Coulston	19	P. Blackler	18
J.M. Saulbrey	35	J.A. Turner	19	K.M. Keenan	15
J.A. Burley	21	S.J. Rattray	19	J.E. Harris	15
P.F. Carrick	21	C.A. Campbell	18		

Most Wicketkeeping Dismissals

	Ct	*St*	*Total*
B.A. Brentnall	15	12	27
E.M. Ryan	3	11	14
I.C.P. Jagersma	10	2	12
S.L. Illingworth	5	5	10

Most Catches

D.A. Hockley	9
P.F. McKelvey	8
E.A. Badham	7
A. McKenna	7
J. Clark	7

ONE-DAY INTERNATIONAL CAREER RECORDS

	M	In	NO	HS	Runs	Ave	100s	50s	Ct	st	O	M	R	W	Ave	R/O	Best
E.P.N.Allan	7	6	1	17	42	8.40	-	-	2	-	59	8	162	3	54.00	2.75	1-22
K.S.Anderson	6	5	2	9*	22	7.33	-	-	-	-	38	2	187	5	37.40	4.92	3-45
T.L.Anderson	26	25	0	85	440	17.60	-	2	9	-							
L.M.Astle	1	-	-	-	-	-	-	-	-	-							
E.A.Badham	13	10	1	30	86	9.55	-	-	5	-	135.3	33	290	12	24.16	2.14	2-14
H.R.Bastion	3	-	-	-	-	-	-	-	1	-	20	2	57	2	28.50	2.85	1-12
S.W.Bates	125	119	12	168	4548	42.50	10	27	66	-	502.5	31	2488	75	33.17	4.95	4-7
E.M.Bermingham	34	21	5	35	187	11.68	-	-	10	-	260.5	19	1047	43	24.34	4.01	4-16
B.L.Bevege	16	16	1	101	488	32.53	1	3	3	-	22.2	7	48	3	16.00	2.15	3-17
B.M.Bezuidenhout	9	7	1	43	123	20.50	-	-	6	1							
J.C.Brehaut	3	3	1	23*	40	20.00	-	-	3	-							
B.A.Brentnall	5	3	0	18	40	13.33	-	-	3	3							
K.D.Brown	14	6	3	9*	19	6.33	-	-	4	-	86.4	14	252	10	25.20	2.91	2-8
S.H.Brown	18	9	4	17*	59	11.80	-	-	5	-	170	63	308	19	16.21	1.81	2-3
N.J.Browne	125	102	28	63	2002	27.05	-	10	33	-	761.5	66	3005	88	34.14	3.94	4-20
S.K.Burke	36	18	9	10*	73	8.11	-	-	3	-	256	27	1019	25	40.76	3.98	3-17
J.A.Burley	2	1	0	7	7	7.00	-	-	-	-	13	3	28	0	-	2.15	-
A.K.Burrows	9	5	5	3*	5	-	-	-	2	-	56.1	3	267	7	38.14	4.75	3-27
V.L.Burtt	9	8	0	46	168	21.00	-	-	4	-	6	0	31	2	15.50	5.17	2-31
S.D.Caird	4	4	1	45	72	24.00	-	-	-	-							
C.A.Campbell	85	30	15	12	69	4.60	-	-	15	-	753	150	2018	78	25.87	2.68	3-15
E.A.Campbell	2	2	1	8*	14	14.00	-	-	2	-	14	0	69	2	34.50	4.93	1-19
R.H.Candy	18	11	7	8	27	6.75	-	-	3	-	120	12	551	18	30.61	4.59	5-19
P.F.Carrick	3	2	1	6*	7	7.00	-	-	1	-	29	1	106	6	17.66	3.66	3-43
S.E.Charteris	5	3	1	20*	20	10.00	-	-	-	-	16	0	102	1	102.00	6.38	1-32
J.Clark	31	31	1	85	875	29.16	-	7	5	-							
D.A.Costello	7	2	1	1	1	1.00	-	-	1	-	56.4	8	139	2	69.50	2.45	2-37
S.D.Cowles	5	5	0	46	93	18.60	-	-	2	-	5	0	24	0	-	4.80	-
S.R.H.Curtis	20	18	3	55*	346	23.06	-	2	5	-	10	0	54	2	27.00	5.40	1-15
I.Cronin-Knight	3	3	0	36	41	13.66	-	-	-	-							
S.F.M.Devine	111	98	11	145	2697	31.00	5	13	32	-	642.5	50	2803	75	37.37	4.36	3-24
A.M.Dodd	31	20	11	20*	155	17.22	-	-	10	-	207.1	24	755	28	26.96	3.64	3-13
N.C.Dodd	18	17	0	52	224	13.17	-	1	6	-							
L.R.Doolan	40	36	5	76	674	21.74	-	1	18	-	214.3	21	1003	32	31.34	4.68	3-7
J.D.Doull	5	5	0	42	64	12.80	-	-	2	-							
L.R.Down	14	13	0	90	181	13.92	-	1	5	-							
E.C.Drumm	101	94	13	116	2844	35.11	2	19	24	-	257	53	778	37	21.02	3.03	4-31
J.R.Dunning	22	21	4	89	346	20.35	-	1	4	-	157	12	527	13	40.53	3.36	3-29
K.E.Ebrahim	31	25	8	24	181	10.64	-	-	7	-	183.1	18	735	20	36.75	4.01	3-33
M.F.Fahey	54	53	2	91	1403	27.50	-	14	15	-							
P.B.Flannery	17	17	2	49*	258	17.20	-	-	3	-							
K.E.Flavell	38	33	9	54	719	29.95	-	2	5	-	70	15	156	7	22.28	2.23	2-5
D.L.Ford	3	2	0	35	46	23.00	-	-	1	-	6	0	32	0	-	5.33	-
F.E.Fraser	5	3	2	54*	94	94.00	-	1	1	-							
L.M.Fraser	13	7	1	8	31	5.16	-	-	2	-	117	20	294	12	24.50	2.51	3-21
M.K.Fruin	23	23	4	51	385	20.26	-	1	4	1							
J.A.Fryer	7	1	1	1*	1	-	-	-	-	-	33	9	115	10	11.50	3.48	3-8
S.M.Gilchrist	8	5	1	12	19	4.75	-	-	4	-	77	21	202	7	28.85	2.62	3-20
A.J.Green	14	8	5	17*	23	7.66	-	-	3	-	108.3	17	392	12	32.66	3.61	5-15
M.L.Green	37	32	1	121	587	18.93	1	1	16	-	18.4	0	118	1	118.00	6.32	1-30
P.A.Gruber	2	1	0	0	0	0.00	-	-	-	-	10	3	35	0	-	3.50	-
K.V.Gunn	45	34	9	52	461	18.44	-	1	14	-	458.5	110	1113	53	21.00	2.43	5-22
G.A.Guy	7	5	4	2*	2	2.00	-	-	1	-	48.1	5	177	9	19.66	3.67	3-23
K.A.Hadlee	1	1	0	14	14	14.00	-	-	-	-							
B.M.Halliday	6	5	0	60	170	34.00	-	2	-	-	8	1	40	2	20.00	5.00	1-17
L.R.V.S.Harford	3	3	0	9	20	6.66	-	-	-	-	7	0	30	0	-	4.29	-
J.E.Harris	45	24	12	19*	99	8.25	-	-	9	-	414.2	98	1124	61	18.42	2.71	4-8
S.A.Harris	2	1	1	1*	1	-	-	-	-	-	3	0	19	0	-	6.33	-
C.E.Henshilwood	2	1	1	15*	15	-	-	-	-	-							
D.A.Hockley	118	115	18	117	4064	41.89	4	34	41	-	253.4	41	853	20	42.65	3.36	3-49
H.R.Huddleston	36	18	7	16*	67	6.09	-	-	2	-	254.3	22	1118	46	24.30	4.39	5-25
S.L.Illingworth	37	29	7	51	342	15.54	-	1	27	21							
I.C.P.Jagersma	34	27	4	58*	453	19.69	-	2	24	9	22	5	48	4	12.00	2.18	2-14
H.N.K.Jensen	20	17	1	53	224	14.00	-	1	-	-	102.4	5	491	12	40.91	4.78	2-26
F.C.Jonas	2	2	1	1*	1	1.00	-	-	-	-	11	1	70	0	-	6.36	-
Y.Kainuku	2	2	0	4	4	2.00	-	-	-	-	12	0	49	0	-	4.08	-

	M	In	NO	HS	Runs	Ave	100s	50s	Ct	st	O	M	R	W	Ave	R/O	Best
L.M.Kasperek	35	23	8	113	274	18.26	1	-	10	-	286.2	31	1126	60	18.76	3.93	6-46
K.M.Keenan	55	36	9	57*	348	12.88	-	1	9	-	452	72	1253	70	17.90	2.77	4-5
R.J.Kember	10	10	0	64	155	15.50	-	1	3	-							
A.C.Kerr	41	30	7	232*	686	29.82	1	2	20	-	341.4	15	1524	60	25.40	4.46	5-17
J.M.Kerr	7	6	0	28	54	9.00	-	-	1	-	44	4	193	7	27.57	4.39	2-27
F.S.King	15	10	3	31	81	11.57	-	-	2	-	108.1	14	404	21	19.23	3.73	4-24
P.D.Kinsella	20	20	3	57	443	26.05	-	2	-	-							
K.Le Comber	15	14	4	135*	442	44.20	1	2	2	-							
B.J.Legg	18	13	3	17	79	7.90	-	-	2	-	199.4	62	394	20	19.70	1.97	3-4
M.A.M.Lewis	78	73	12	105	1372	22.49	1	4	30	-	5	0	32	0	-	6.40	-
F.C.Leydon-Davis	1	1	1	10*	10	-	-	-	-	-	8.2	1	18	5	3.60	2.16	5-18
V.J.Lind	8	8	0	68	178	22.25	-	1	5	-							
L.R.Lindsay	2	1	0	27	27	27.00	-	-	-	-	13	0	42	2	21.00	3.23	2-26
J.Lord	15	13	0	25	101	7.76	-	-	2	-	132.3	25	318	25	12.72	2.40	6-10
M.L.Lynch	6	6	0	29	105	17.50	-	-	-	-							
F.L.Mackay	21	16	1	39*	243	16.20	-	-	10	-	94.4	8	424	13	32.61	4.48	2-18
R.A.Mair	11	10	5	7	23	4.60	-	-	1	-	81	6	420	4	105.00	5.19	2-21
C.E.Marett	14	12	2	24	149	14.90	-	-	-	-	126.5	24	310	16	19.37	2.44	3-14
K.J.Martin	86	80	12	81	1481	21.77	-	6	43	16							
E.T.McDonald	3	-	-	-	-	-	-	-	1	-	24	4	50	5	10.00	2.08	2-17
K.L.McDonald	6	6	0	34	80	13.33	-	-	1	-							
S.J.McGlashan	134	125	16	97*	2438	22.36	-	11	37	-							
P.F.McKelvey	15	14	4	42	214	21.40	-	-	2	-							
A.McKenna	14	13	0	39	214	16.46	-	-	-	-							
S.McLauchlan	29	21	5	34*	137	8.56	-	-	6	-	227.5	47	665	19	35.00	2.92	2-6
B.H.McNeill	23	18	8	88*	193	19.30	-	1	8	-	175.1	20	680	23	29.56	3.88	6-32
R.C.Milburn	15	14	1	71	237	18.23	-	1	7	5							
L.E.Milliken	48	18	8	21	110	11.00	-	-	13	-	370	45	1409	59	23.88	3.81	5-25
K.S.Molloy	5	2	1	0*	0	0.00	-	-	2	-	36	8	99	4	24.75	2.75	2-16
S.R.M.Morris	8	1	0	5	5	5.00	-	-	-	-	69	12	175	7	25.00	2.54	2-13
L.J.Murdoch	25	22	3	69	417	21.94	-	1	4	-							
K.J.Musson	13	10	2	31	86	10.75	-	-	3	-	87.2	12	253	10	25.30	2.90	3-22
T.M.M.Newton	10	7	1	18*	56	9.33	-	-	5	-	64	5	275	11	25.00	4.30	5-31
C.M.Nicholson	35	22	10	73*	195	16.25	-	1	13	-	272.4	62	707	38	18.60	2.59	4-18
M.J.G.Nielsen	52	25	5	20	121	6.05	-	-	7	-	392	54	1418	53	26.75	3.62	5-21
A.M.O'Leary	19	18	3	91*	497	33.13	-	3	3	-							
J.B.Olson	4	4	1	9*	17	5.66	-	-	-	-	27	9	52	4	13.00	1.93	3-16
G.L.Page	2	1	0	5	5	5.00	-	-	-	-	17.2	3	46	6	7.66	2.65	6-20
N.Payne	65	64	7	93	1178	20.66	-	4	17	-	158	48	407	20	20.35	2.58	3-20
K.T.Perkins	73	57	13	78	1198	27.22	-	4	35	-							
E.C.Perry	17	13	4	70	201	22.33	-	1	4	-	8	0	50	0	-	6.25	-
M.H.Peters	16	12	5	24	79	11.28	-	-	3	-	155.5	63	291	19	15.31	1.87	2-3
A.M.Peterson	32	21	4	46	279	16.41	-	-	9	-	137.4	13	482	27	17.85	3.50	4-25
K.V.Plummer	11	10	1	32	100	11.11	-	-	2	-	10	0	36	0	-	3.60	-
L.M.Powell	5	4	0	70	73	18.25	-	1	1	-							
R.H.Priest	87	74	14	157	1694	28.23	2	9	73	20							
K.L.Pulford	46	40	0	95	743	18.57	-	3	9	-	199.3	16	782	30	26.06	3.92	4-5
R.J.Pullar	51	32	11	27*	253	12.04	-	-	14	-	430.1	80	1215	74	16.41	2.82	5-7
K.A.Ramel	47	37	7	41	519	17.30	-	-	13	-	204.3	26	729	35	20.82	3.56	3-26
S.J.Rattray	15	15	7	60*	305	38.12	-	1	1	-	123.1	16	399	11	36.27	3.24	2-33
R.J.Rolls	104	91	3	114	2201	25.01	2	12	90	43							
E.F.Rouse	3	3	0	48	90	30.00	-	-	-	-							
H.M.Rowe	26	14	4	29*	108	10.80	-	-	4	-	155.2	14	639	20	31.95	4.11	3-22
S.E.A.Ruck	27	12	8	12*	48	12.00	-	-	3	-	213.1	28	786	24	32.75	3.69	4-31
J.A.Russell	5	4	1	8*	8	2.66	-	-	-	-	26	3	84	1	84.00	3.23	1-20
E.M.Ryan	15	5	1	6*	17	4.25	-	-	13	8							
J.M.Saulbrey	5	5	3	22*	75	37.50	-	-	-	-	43	12	100	4	25.00	2.33	2-32
A.E.Satterthwaite	128	122	16	137*	4125	38.91	7	22	51	-	294.4	19	1330	45	29.55	4.51	4-13
N.Scripps	7	3	3	9*	12	-	-	-	-	-	50.2	6	206	6	34.33	4.09	2-17
V.S.Sexton	2	2	0	9	12	6.00	-	-	-	-							
E.A.Signal	19	12	5	28*	79	11.28	-	-	5	-	130.3	23	496	7	70.85	3.80	2-26
R.J.Signal	6	3	1	8	12	6.00	-	-	2	-	27	2	89	2	44.50	3.30	1-10
L.J.Simpson	12	11	1	23*	95	9.50	-	-	1	-							
R.J.Steele	32	12	6	8*	41	6.83	-	-	6	-	293	57	831	34	24.44	2.84	3-10
L.M.M.Tahuhu	71	43	15	26	251	8.96	-	-	20	-	529.2	36	2358	73	32.30	4.45	4-27
H.M.Tiffen	117	111	16	100	2919	30.72	1	18	32	-	276	43	955	49	19.48	3.46	4-43
E.A.Travers	3	-	-	-	-	-	-	-	-	-							
D.M.Trow	2	1	1	1*	1	-	-	-	1	-	12	3	18	4	4.50	1.50	3-8
S.J.Tsukigawa	42	39	6	78*	730	22.12	-	2	9	-	255.5	19	1121	35	32.02	4.38	4-43
M.F.Tunupopo	3	-	-	-	-	-	-	-	2	-	18	4	57	0	-	3.17	-

	M	In	NO	HS	Runs	Ave	100s	50s	Ct	st	O	M	R	W	Ave	R/O	Best
J.A.Turner	30	14	2	15	54	4.50	-	-	6	-	265.2	42	695	28	24.82	2.62	5-5
N.J.Turner	28	26	2	114	624	26.00	1	2	4	-							
J.M.Watkin	6	5	0	62	86	17.20	-	1	-	-	29.3	2	113	6	18.83	3.83	2-30
A.L.Watkins	103	94	7	111	1889	21.71	2	6	37	-	732	67	2860	92	31.08	3.91	4-2
H.M.Watson	66	48	10	115*	580	15.26	1	-	21	-	414.3	67	1287	54	23.83	3.10	3-14
N.M.Williams	19	13	2	21*	80	7.27	-	-	1	-	110.5	19	374	15	24.93	3.37	3-37

TEAM RECORDS

Highest Totals

490-4	v Ireland	Dublin	2018
455-5	v Pakistan	Christchurch	1996/97
440-3	v Ireland	Dublin	2018
418	v Ireland	Dublin	2018
373-7	v Pakistan	Sydney	2008/09

Lowest Totals

58	v Australia	Melbourne	1984/85
59	v West Indies	Kingston	2013/14
61	v Australia	Wellington	1998/99
69	v West Indies	Basseterre	2014/15
72	v England	Blackpool	2007

INDIVIDUAL RECORDS

Centuries

232*	A,C. Kerr v Ireland at Dublin	2018
168	S.W. Bates v Pakistan at Sydney	2008/09
157	R.H. Priest v Sri Lanka at Lincoln	2015/16
151	S.W. Bates v Ireland at Dublin	2018
145	S.F.M. Devine v South Africa at Cuttack	2012/13
137*	A.E. Satterthwaite v Pakistan at Lincoln	2016/17
135*	K. LeComber v Ireland at Dublin	1996
123	A.E. Satterthwaite v Pakistan at Nelson	2016/17
122*	S.W. Bates v Australia at Sydney	2012/13
122	S.W. Bates v India at Chennai	2006/07
121	M.L. Green v Ireland at Dublin	2018
119*	A.E. Satterthwaite v England at Dunedin	2020/21
117	D.A. Hockley v England at Chester-le-Street	1996
116	E.C. Drumm v England at Oamaru	2000/01
115*	H.M. Watson v Ireland at Dublin	2004
115*	A.E. Satterthwaite v Pakistan at Lincoln	2016/17
114	N.J. Turner v Netherlands at Sydney	1988/89
114	R.J. Rolls v Australia at Lincoln	2001/02
113	L.M. Kasperek v Ireland at Dublin	2018
111	A.L. Mason v England at Blackpool	2007
110	S.W. Bates v West Indies at Kingston	2013/14
110	S.W. Bates v Australia at Mt Maunganui	2015/16
109	A.E. Satterthwaite v Australia at Sydney	2012/13
108*	E.C. Drumm v South Africa at Lincoln	2000/01
108	R.H. Priest v Sri Lanka at Lincoln	2015/16

108	S.F.M. Devine v West Indies at Lincoln	2017/18
108	S.F.M. Devine v Ireland at Dublin	2018
106*	S.W. Bates v Sri Lanka at Bristol	2017
106	S.W. Bates v England at Mt Maunganui	2014/15
105	M.A.M. Lewis v Pakistan at Christchurch	1996/97
104*	R.J. Rolls v Australia at Chennai	2006/07
103	A.E. Satterthwaite v England at Mumbai	2012/13
103	S.F.M. Devine v Pakistan at Sharjah	2017/18
102*	A.E. Satterthwaite v Australia at Auckland	2016/17
102	A.L. Mason v Australia at Darwin	2007/08
102	S.W. Bates v Australia at Cuttack	2012/13
101*	S.W. Bates v West Indies at Lincoln	2017/18
101	B.L. Bevege v International XI at Auckland	1981/82
100*	D.A. Hockley v Sri Lanka at Chandigarh	1997/98
100	D.A. Hockley v West Indies at Chandigarh	1997/98
100	D.A. Hockley v Australia at Melbourne	1999/00
100	H.M. Tiffen v Pakistan at Sydney	2008/09

Five Wickets in an Innings

6-10	J. Lord v India at Auckland	1981/82
6-20	G.L. Page v Trinidad & Tobago at St Albans	1973
6-32	B.H. McNeill v England at Lincoln	2007/08
6-46	L.M. Kasperek v Australia at Mt Maunganui	2020/21
5-5	J.A. Turner v Netherlands at Lindfield	1993
5-7	R.J. Pullar v South Africa at Hamilton	1998/99
5-10	R.J. Pullar v India at St Saviour	2002
5-15	A.J Green v Ireland at Dublin	2004
5-17	A.C Kerr v Ireland at Dublin	2018
5-18	F.C. Leydon-Davis v West Indies at Lincoln	2013/14
5-19	R.H. Candy v Pakistan at Cuttack	2012/13
5-21	M.J.G. Nielsen v Sri Lanka at Lincoln	2015/16
5-22	K.V. Gunn v Australia at Wellington	1989/90
5-25	L.E. Milliken v India, Pretoria	2004/05
5-25	H.R. Huddleston v South Africa at Kimberley	2016/17
5-31	T.M.M. Newton v Pakistan at Nelson	2016/17
5-35	H.R. Huddleston v Sri Lanka at Bristol	2017
5-36	H.R. Huddleston v West Indies at Lincoln	2013/14
5-39	M.J.G. Nielsen v South Africa at Kimberley	2016/17
5-39	L.M. Kasperek v England at Leicester	2018

Hat-tricks

7.1-1-18-3	J.E. Harris	v West Indies	Chiswick	1993
8-2-22-3	E.C. Drumm	v Australia	Adelaide	1995/96

Most Economical Bowling

10-7-3-0	C.A. Campbell	v Netherlands	Christchurch	2000/01
12-9-4-3	B.J. Legg	v Netherlands	Melbourne	1988/89
12-9-5-3	J.E. Harris	v Netherlands	Lindfield	1993
11.2-7-5-5	J.A. Turner	v Netherlands	Lindfield	1993
10-6-5-4	K.M. Keenan	v West Indies	Chandigarh	1997/98

Most Expensive Bowling

10-0-70-0	R.A. Mair	v Australia	Brisbane	2020/21
10-1-69-1	S.E.A. Ruck	v Australia	Sydney	2012/13
9-1-68-1	L.E. Milliken	v Australia	Auckland	2003/04
10-0-67-0	R.H. Candy	v Australia	Sydney	2012/13
10-0-67-0	L.M.M. Tahuhu	v Australia	Mt Maunganui	2016/17
10-0-65-0	L.R. Doolan	v England	Lincoln	2011/12
10-0-65-2	A.E. Satterthwaite	v Pakistan	Lincoln	2016/17

Wicketkeeping

DISMISSALS IN AN INNINGS

	(ct/st)				
6	(4/2)	S.L. Illingworth	v Australia	Beckenham	1993
5	(4/1)	R.H. Priest	v Australia	Auckland	2016/17
4	(2/2)	E.M. Ryan	v International XI	Auckland	1981/82
4	(2/2)	I.C.P. Jagersma	v Netherlands	Sydney	1988/89
4	(3/1)	S.L. Illingworth	v India	Ealing	1993
4	(3/1)	R.J. Rolls	v England	Oamaru	2000/01
4	(2/2)	R.J. Rolls	v England	Lincoln	2000/01
4	(4/0)	R.J. Rolls	v Australia	Lincoln	2001/02
4	(4/0)	R.J. Rolls	v India	Durham	2002
4	(4/0)	R.J. Rolls	v Sri Lanka	Pretoria	2004/05
4	(3/1)	R.J. Rolls	v Ireland	Pretoria	2004/05
4	(2/2)	R.J. Rolls	v India	Lincoln	2005/06
4	(4/0)	R.H. Priest	v South Africa	Paarl	2016/17
4	(3/1)	K.J. Martin	v England	Leeds	2018

Fielding

CATCHES IN AN INNINGS

3	S.H. Brown	v England	Hastings	1984
3	S.M. Gilchrist	v India	Indore	1984/85
3	D.A. Hockley	v Australia	Melbourne	1990/91
3	K.A. Ramel	v Netherlands	Ghaziabad	1997/98
3	D.A. Hockley	v Sri Lanka	Chandigarh	1997/98
3	H.M. Watson	v Netherlands	Christchurch	2000/01
3	H.M. Tiffen	v England	Lincoln	2002/03
3	S.W. Bates	v England	Taunton	2007
3	S.J. Tsukigawa	v England	Lincoln	2007/08
3	M.F. Fahey	v Ireland	Kibworth	2010
3	L.R. Doolan	v Australia	Brisbane	2010/11
3	A.L. Watkins	v India	Aston Rowant	2011
3	S.W. Bates	v Australia	Sydney	2012/13
3	F.L. Mackay	v West Indies	Kingston	2013/14
3	A.E. Satterthwaite	v Australia	Mt Maunganui	2015/16
3	K.T. Perkins	v South Africa	Kimberley	2016/17
3	A.C. Kerr	v Pakistan	Nelson	2016/17
3	A.E. Satterthwaite	v England	Derby	2017
3	S.W. Bates	v West Indies	Lincoln	2017/18
3	A.M. Peterson	v West Indies	Christchurch	2017/18

SUMMARY OF ONE-DAY INTERNATIONAL CAREER RECORDS

Most Matches

S.J. McGlashan	134	R.J. Rolls	104	K.T. Perkins	73
A.E. Satterthwaite	128	A.L. Watkins	103	L.M.M.Tahuhu	71
N.J. Browne	125	E.C. Drumm	101	H.M. Watson	66
S.W. Bates	125	R.H. Priest	87	K.M. Keenan	55
D.A. Hockley	118	K.J. Martin	86	M.F. Fahey	54
H.M. Tiffen	117	C.A. Campbell	85	M.J.G. Nielsen	52
S.F.M. Devine	111	M.A.M. Lewis	78	R.J. Pullar	51

Most Runs

S.W. Bates	4548	S.J. McGlashan	2438	K.J. Martin	1481
A.E. Satterthwaite	4125	R.J. Rolls	2201	M.F. Fahey	1403
D.A. Hockley	4064	N.J. Browne	2002	M.A.M. Lewis	1372
H.M. Tiffen	2919	A.L. Watkins	1889	K.T. Perkins	1198
E.C. Drumm	2844	R.H. Priest	1694	N. Payne	1178
S.F.M. Devine	2697				

Most Wickets

A.L. Watkins	92	R.J. Pullar	74	A.C Kerr	60
N.J. Browne	88	L.M.M.Tahuhu	73	L.E. Milliken	59
C.A. Campbell	78	K.M. Keenan	70	H.M. Watson	54
S.W. Bates	75	J.E. Harris	61	K.V. Gunn	53
S.F.M. Devine	75	L.M. Kasperek	60	M.J.G. Nielsen	53

Most Wicketkeeping Dismissals

	Ct	*St*	*Total*
R.J. Rolls	90	43	133
R.H. Priest	73	20	93
K.J. Martin	36	16	52
S.L. Illingworth	26	21	47
I.C.P. Jagersma	24	9	33
E.M. Ryan	13	8	21

Most Catches

S.W. Bates	67
A.E.Satterthwaite	50
D.A. Hockley	41
A.L. Watkins	37
S.J. McGlashan	36
K.T. Perkins	35
N.J. Browne	33
H.M. Tiffen	32
S.F.M. Devine	32
M.A.M. Lewis	30

RECORD PARTNERSHIPS

1st	196	S.W. Bates & R.H. Priest	v Sri Lanka	Lincoln	2015/16
2nd	295	A.C. Kerr & L.M. Kasperek	v Ireland	Dublin	2018
3rd	150	A.E.Satterthwaite & K.J. Martin	v Pakistan	Lincoln	2016/17
4th	172*	A.E.Satterthwaite & A.C Kerr	v England	Dunedin	2020/21
5th	108*	R.J. Rolls & S.J. Tsukigawa	v Australia	Chennai	2006/07
6th	139*	S.J. McGlashan & N.J. Browne	v South Africa	Bowral	2008/09
7th	104*	S.J. Tsukigawa & N.J. Browne	v England	Chennai	2006/07
8th	74	A.E.Satterthwaite & L.R.Doolan	v Australia	Whangarei	2008/09
9th	58	K.V. Gunn & S. McLauchlan	v Australia	Wellington	1991/92
10th	33	E.C. Drumm & C.A. Campbell	v Australia	Wellington	1996/97

TWENTY20 INTERNATIONAL CAREER RECORDS

	M	In	NO	HS	Runs	Ave	100s	50s	Ct	St	O	M	R	W	Ave	R/O	Best
K.S.Anderson	2	1	1	1*	1	-	-	-	-	-	4	0	17	3	5.66	4.25	3-17
S.W.Bates	122	119	9	124*	3302	30.01	1	21	66	-	189.3	1	1276	50	25.52	6.73	4-26
E.M.Bermingham	31	17	4	20	74	5.69	-	-	3	-	105	3	569	33	17.24	5.42	2-12
B.M.Bezuidenhout	9	7	2	20*	35	7.00	-	-	3	2							
N.J.Browne	54	46	12	34*	547	16.08	-	-	24	-	146	4	814	47	17.31	5.58	4-15
S.M.Bullen	3	-	-	-	-	-	-	-	-	-	9	0	57	3	19.00	6.33	2-20
S.K.Burke	7	2	1	3*	6	6.00	-	-	-	-	23	1	149	7	21.28	6.48	3-15
R.H.Candy	10	4	2	9*	14	7.00	-	-	3	-	33	1	213	7	30.42	6.45	2-24
S.E.Charteris	2	1	1	5*	5	-	-	-	1	-	4	0	17	1	17.00	4.25	1-17
S.R.H.Curtis	8	4	0	8	13	3.25	-	-	-	-							
S.F.M.Devine	98	95	12	105	2474	29.80	1	14	33	-	258	7	1631	94	17.35	6.32	4-22
N.C.Dodd	6	4	1	14	26	8.66	-	-	-	-							
L.R.Doolan	33	23	3	41	194	9.70	-	-	5	-	100	2	602	28	21.50	6.02	3-16
L.R.Down	5	4	1	12	35	11.66	-	-	4	-							
K.E.Ebrahim	39	20	9	27*	91	8.27	-	-	8	-	96.4	3	595	22	27.04	6.16	3-9
M.F.Fahey	8	7	1	43	134	22.33	-	-	1	-							
P.B.Flannery	1	1	0	18	18	18.00	-	-	-	-							
A.J.Green	1	1	0	3	3	3.00	-	-	-	-	4	0	20	2	10.00	5.00	2-20
M.L.Green	57	45	8	29	440	11.89	-	-	19	-	9	0	58	1	58.00	6.44	1-6
C.A.Gurrey	2	2	0	15	19	9.50	-	-	-	-							
G.A.Guy	6	2	1	2	2	2.00	-	-	-	-	18	0	100	3	33.33	5.56	1-14
B.M.Halliday	6	5	2	16*	36	12.00	-	-	-	-	2	0	11	1	11.00	5.50	1-11
K.A.Heffernan	2	-	-	-	-	-	-	-	-	-	6	0	29	1	29.00	4.83	1-14
H.R.Huddleston	16	3	1	10	15	7.50	-	-	7	-	44	4	238	13	18.30	5.41	2-9
H.N.K.Jensen	36	21	6	19	128	8.53	-	-	10	-	93	1	630	25	25.20	6.77	3-11
L.M.Kasperek	43	21	5	19	104	6.50	-	-	11	-	156.2	2	961	69	13.92	6.15	4-7
R.J.Kember	3	3	0	15	22	7.33	-	-	-	-							
A.C.Kerr	41	23	9	36	217	15.50	-	-	20	-	146.3	1	867	39	22.23	5.92	3-16
J.M.Kerr	10	3	0	10	13	4.33	-	-	1	-	26.5	1	161	5	32.20	6.00	2-17
M.A.M.Lewis	1	1	0	25	25	25.00	-	-	-	-							
F.C.Leydon-Davis	8		-	-	-	-	-	-	2	-	22	0	120	4	30.00	5.45	2-15
V.J.Lind	2	2	0	20	29	14.50	-	-	-	-							
F.L.Mackay	30	22	5	51	332	19.52	-	1	6	-	87.4	1	576	25	23.04	6.57	3-18
R.A.Mair	17	5	4	13*	18	18.00	-	-	-	-	48.2	0	321	13	24.69	6.64	2-17
K.J.Martin	91	73	19	65	960	17.77	-	4	32	22							
S.J.McGlashan	76	73	9	84	1164	18.18	-	2	30	-							
B.H.McNeill	2	-	-	-	-	-	-	-	-	-	5	0	30	0	-	6.00	-
R.C.Milburn	2	1	1	1*	1	-	-	-	-	1							
L.E.Milliken	1	-	-	-	-	-	-	-	-	-	4	0	28	1	28.00	7.00	1-28
T.M.M.Newton	12	6	3	3*	8	2.66	-	-	6	-	23	0	126	9	14.00	5.48	3-9
M.J.G.Nielsen	44	13	8	21*	60	12.00	-	-	6	-	156.5	4	753	41	18.36	4.80	4-10
K.T.Perkins	55	42	16	34	448	17.23	-	-	15	-							
E.C.Perry	31	29	7	50*	369	16.77	-	1	11	-							
A.M.Peterson	33	18	3	15	92	6.13	-	-	8	-	62	0	427	18	23.72	6.89	3-2
R.H.Priest	75	64	12	60	873	16.78	-	1	39	33							
K.L.Pulford	12	8	2	29	66	11.00	-	-	1	-	39	1	186	11	16.90	4.77	2-21
R.J.Rolls	2	2	0	41	80	40.00	-	-	2	1							
H.M.Rowe	21	8	5	14*	37	12.33	-	-	6	-	34	1	226	10	22.60	6.65	3-18
S.E.A.Ruck	37	9	5	6	16	4.00	-	-	5	-	125	5	688	40	17.20	5.50	3-12
A.E.Satterthwaite	108	97	17	71*	1717	21.46	-	1	36	-	76.4	0	539	24	22.45	7.03	6-17
R.J.Steele	1	-	-	-	-	-	-	-	2	-	4	0	14	0	-	3.50	-
L.M.M.Tahuhu	60	16	6	16	62	6.20	-	-	16	-	183.3	5	1097	52	21.09	5.98	3-17
H.M.Tiffen	9	8	1	30	121	17.28	-	-	6	-							
S.J.Tsukigawa	19	16	2	22	129	9.21	-	-	2	-	25	0	170	5	34.00	6.80	2-19
J.M.Watkin	9	8	1	77*	118	16.85	-	1	2	-	20.3	0	132	7	18.85	6.44	3-9
A.L.Watkins	36	36	3	89*	772	23.39	-	3	14	-	84.3	0	519	22	23.59	6.14	3-8
H.M.Watson	8	3	2	9*	16	16.00	-	-	2	-	28	2	152	7	21.71	5.43	3-13

Highest Totals

216-1	v South Africa	Taunton	2018
188-3	v Sri Lanka	Christchurch	2015/16
186-7	v South Africa	Taunton	2007
185-3	v West Indies	Mt Maunganui	2017/18
180-5	v West Indies	Gros Islet	2009/10

Highest Individual Scores

124*	S.W. Bates v South Africa at Taunton	2018
105	S.F.M. Devine v South Africa at Wellington	2019/20
94*	S.W. Bates v Pakistan at Sylhet	2013/14
89*	A.L. Watkins v India at Nottingham	2009
84	S.J. McGlashan v West Indies at Gros Islet	2009/10
82	S.W. Bates v Ireland at Mohali	2015/16
77*	J.M. Watkin v Ireland at Dublin	2018
77	S.W. Bates v Australia at Brisbane	2018/19
77	S.F.M. Devine v South Africa at Wellington	2019/20
75*	S.F.M. Devine v Sri Lanka at Perth	2019/20

Best Bowling in an Innings

6-17	A.E. Satterthwaite v England at Taunton	2007
4-7	L.M. Kasperek v Australia at Wellington	2015/16
4-10	M.J.G. Nielsen v England at Invercargill	2011/12
4-15	N.J. Browne v Pakistan at Basseterre	2009/10
4-22	S.F.M. Devine v West Indies at Mumbai	2015/16
4-24	A.E. Satterthwaite v West Inides at Kingstown	2014/15
4-26	S.W. Bates v Australia at Invercargill	2010/11

Hat-trick

1-0-2-3	A.N. Peterson	v Australia	Geelong	2016/17

RECORD PARTNERSHIPS

1st	182	S.W. Bates & S.F.M. Devine	v South Africa	Taunton	2018
2nd	142	S.F.M. Devine & S.W. Bates	v South Africa	Wellington	2019/20
3rd	124	K.J. Martin & A.E. Satterthwaite	v West Indies	Mt Maunganui	2017/18
4th	116*	K.J. Martin & A.E. Satterthwaite	v West Indies	Hamilton	2017/18
5th	62	K.J. Martin & E.C. Perry	v India	Clifton	2011
6th	42*	K.J. Martin & B.M.Bezuidenhout	v Australia	Sydney	2018/19
7th	37	K.J. Martin & L.M. Kasperek	v India	Providence	2018/19
8th	27	L.M.M. Tahuhu & A.C. Kerr	v Pakistan	Nelson	2016/17
9th	32*	K.J. Martin & M.J.G. Nielsen	v Australia	Sydney	2011/12
10th	33	M.L. Green & R.A. Mair	v England	Wellington	2020/21

DREAM11 SUPER SMASH

2020/21

Canterbury won the Twenty20 competition after finishing last the previous season. They defeated Wellington in the final. Wellington, who were aiming for their fourth win in a row, defeated Auckland in the elimination final. Wellington's Sophie Devine was the leading run scorer with 434, followed by Amy Satterthwaite (364), Amelia Kerr (361) and Natalie Dodd (301). Canterbury's Frances Mackay was the top wicket-taker with 20, followed by Holly Huddleston (16) and Amelia Kerr (14).

Final points were:

	P	*W*	*L*	*NR*	*Points*
Canterbury	10	7	2	1	30
Auckland	10	7	2	1	30
Wellington	10	7	3	–	28
Northern Districts	10	3	7	–	12
Otago	10	3	7	–	12
Central Districts	10	2	8	–	8

WELLINGTON v AUCKLAND — Super Smash

at Basin Reserve, Wellington on 24 December, 2020
Toss : Wellington. Umpires : B.F. Bowden & A. Stanley
***Wellington won by 9 wickets.** Points: Wellington 4, Auckland 0*

AUCKLAND

	Runs	*Mins*	*Balls*	*6s*	*4s*
L.R.Down* c Singh b Kerr J.M.	8	17	12	-	-
A.M.Peterson lbw b Singh	0	2	1	-	-
K.T.Perkins run out	15	28	17	-	2
B.G.Armstrong c Kerr J.M. b Singh	2	8	6	-	-
S.Shahri c Kerr A.C. b Newton	29	40	27	-	4
H.R.Huddleston c McFadyen b Kerr A.C.	4	9	9	-	-
R.S.M.Lili'i c McFadyen b Green	11	15	15	-	1
A.N.Kelly c Kerr J.M. b Kerr A.C.	4	6	6	-	-
J.E.I.Prasad b Kerr A.C.	4	2	4	-	1
S.J.Carnachan† not out	5	14	12	-	-
F.C.Jonas not out	5	12	11	-	-
Extras (lb 1, w 4)	5				
TOTAL (20 overs) (9 wkts)	**92**	78			

WELLINGTON

	Runs	*Mins*	*Balls*	*6s*	*4s*
R.M.Burns c Lili'i b Peterson	3	8	9	-	-
M.L.Green* not out	30	38	21	1	4
A.C.Kerr not out	58	29	34	-	12
J.T.McFadyen†					
T.M.M.Newton					
C.R.King					
J.M.Kerr					
X.A.R.Jetly					
G.E.Plimmer					
M.P.Singh					
B.C.Molony					
Extras (lb 2, w 1)	3				
TOTAL (10.4 overs) (1 wkt)	**94**	38			

Bowling	*O*	*M*	*R*	*W*
WELLINGTON				
Singh	4	0	13	2
Kerr J.M.	4	0	13	1
Newton	4	0	26	1
Kerr A.C.	4	0	11	3
Green	2	0	16	1
Molony	2	0	12	0
AUCKLAND				
Kelly	3	1	17	0
Huddleston	1	0	7	0
Peterson	2	0	17	1
Jonas	2	0	21	0
Armstrong	2	0	22	0
Prasad	0.4	0	8	0

Fall of Wickets

	A	*W*
1st	1	8
2nd	16	-
3rd	27	-
4th	28	-
5th	43	-
6th	69	-
7th	77	-
8th	81	-
9th	81	-
10th	-	-

CENTRAL DISTRICTS v WELLINGTON — Super Smash

at McLean Park, Napier on 27 December, 2020
Toss : Wellington. Umpires : G.A. Stirrat & G.M. Walklin
***Wellington won by 9 wickets.** Points: Wellington 4, Central Districts 0*

CENTRAL DISTRICTS

	Runs	Mins	Balls	6s	4s
J.M.Watkin* c Newton b Kerr A.C.	12	21	15	-	1
E.G.Cunningham c Jetly b Newton	6	17	18	-	-
N.C.Dodd† c Newton b Green ..	20	29	27	-	1
A.van Deventer c Burns b Newton	7	12	8	-	1
H.M.Rowe b Green	8	18	13	-	-
M.J.Greig b Kerr A.C.	4	9	10	-	-
R.A.Mair b Kerr J.M.	7	15	9	-	-
G.K.Atkinson run out	7	9	7	-	-
M.J.Hansen not out	9	9	7	-	1
M.S.Rees c & b Newton	2	5	6	-	-
C.L.Green not out	0	1	0	-	-
Extras (lb 1, w 5)	6				
TOTAL (20 overs) (9 wkts) ...	**88**	74			

WELLINGTON

	Runs	Mins	Balls	6s	4s
R.M.Burns c Dodd b Hansen	42	38	42	2	3
M.L.Green* not out	22	50	25	-	-
A.C.Kerr not out	20	12	12	-	2
J.T.McFadyen†					
T.M.M.Newton					
C.R.King					
J.M.Kerr					
X.A.R.Jetly					
G.E.Plimmer					
M.P.Singh					
B.C.Molony					
Extras (lb 3, w 2)	5				
TOTAL (13.1 overs) (1 wkt) ..	**89**	50			

Bowling	O	M	R	W
WELLINGTON				
Kerr J.M.	4	0	14	1
Singh	3	0	19	0
Newton	4	0	23	3
Kerr A.C.	4	0	10	2
Green	3	0	12	2
Jetly	2	0	9	0
CENTRAL DISTRICTS				
Watkin	3	0	24	0
Mair	3	0	17	0
Green	2	0	7	0
Rowe	2	0	10	0
Atkinson	1	0	9	0
Hansen	1	0	7	1
Rees	1.1	0	12	0

Fall of Wickets	***CD***	***W***
1st	19	62
2nd	21	-
3rd	40	-
4th	56	-
5th	61	-
6th	64	-
7th	77	-
8th	81	-
9th	86	-
10th	-	-

OTAGO v AUCKLAND — Super Smash

at Molyneux Park, Alexandra on 28 December, 2020
Toss : Otago. Umpires : J.A.K. Bromley & P.J. Pasco
***Auckland won by 37 runs.** Points: Auckland 4, Otago 0*

AUCKLAND

	Runs	Mins	Balls	6s	4s
A.M.Peterson st Martin b Black	68	59	50	1	9
L.R.Down* c Inglis b Adams	10	25	16	-	-
K.T.Perkins lbw b Herath	25	40	24	-	3
B.G.Armstrong not out	15	21	18	-	-
S.Shahri not out	19	15	12	-	3
H.R.Huddleston					
R.S.M.Lili'i					
A.N.Kelly					
J.E.I.Prasad					
S.J.Carnachan†					
F.C.Jonas					
Extras (b 1, lb 2, w 16)	19				
TOTAL (20 overs) (3 wkts) .	**156**	81			

OTAGO

	Runs	Mins	Balls	6s	4s
M.R.Cowan b Kelly	5	3	4	-	1
P.M.Inglis b Jonas	62	62	61	1	7
K.J.Martin*† b Huddleston	0	5	2	-	-
H.N.K.Jensen c Perkins b Huddleston	12	16	8	-	2
C.G.Blakely b Armstrong	0	4	3	-	-
I.R.James c Huddleston b Prasad	4	15	10	-	-
G.R.Adams c Kelly b Prasad	8	9	7	-	1
E.J.Carson b Kelly	4	23	8	-	-
E.J.Black run out	10	21	11	-	1
B.J.Herath c Huddleston b Kelly	2	3	4	-	-
M.E.Loe not out	1	2	1	-	-
Extras (b 3, lb 1, w 7)	11				
TOTAL (19.5 overs)	**119**	84			

Bowling	O	M	R	W
OTAGO				
Black	4	0	44	1
Loe	4	0	19	0
Adams	4	0	16	1
Jensen	2	0	10	0
Carson	2	0	28	0
Herath	4	0	36	1
AUCKLAND				
Kelly	3.5	0	26	3
Huddleston	4	0	17	2
Armstrong	3	0	18	1
Peterson	2	0	17	0
Jonas	4	0	18	1
Prasad	3	0	19	2

Fall of Wickets	***A***	***O***
1st	39	6
2nd	113	9
3rd	120	38
4th	-	39
5th	-	65
6th	-	82
7th	-	100
8th	-	109
9th	-	113
10th	-	119

OTAGO v CANTERBURY **Super Smash**

at Molyneux Park, Alexandra on 29 December, 2020
Toss : Otago. Umpires : J.A.K. Bromley & P.J. Pasco
***Canterbury won by 8 wickets.** Points: Canterbury 4, Otago 0*

OTAGO

	Runs	Mins	Balls	6s	4s
M.R.Cowan b Tahuhu	9	14	12	-	2
P.M.Inglis st Hughes b Havill	21	26	22	-	4
K.J.Martin*† c Cox b Tahuhu	3	9	5	-	-
H.N.K.Jensen lbw b Mackay	14	20	17	-	2
C.G.Blakely c Havill b Mackay	18	25	21	-	1
I.R.James run out	24	33	19	-	2
E.J.Carson c Ebrahim b Sullivan	10	10	14	-	-
G.R.Adams b Sullivan	2	5	3	-	-
E.J.Black b Sullivan	3	3	4	-	-
S.A.Oldershaw b Tahuhu	0	4	2	-	-
M.E.Loe not out	0	2	1	-	-
Extras (lb 5, w 3)	8				
TOTAL (20 overs)	**112**	78			

CANTERBURY

	Runs	Mins	Balls	6s	4s
F.L.Mackay* lbw b Loe	0	1	1	-	-
N.B.Cox c Cowan b Oldershaw	29	40	32	-	2
A.E.Satterthwaite not out	56	60	40	-	9
K.E.Ebrahim not out	22	21	20	-	3
L.E.V.Hughes†					
G.E.S.Sullivan					
K.F.G.Nation					
M.J.Banks					
K.M.Sims					
L.M.M.Tahuhu					
K.J.Havill					
Extras (lb 1, w 5)	6				
TOTAL (15.3 overs) (2 wkts)	**113**	61			

Bowling	O	M	R	W
CANTERBURY				
Satterthwaite	2	0	12	0
Tahuhu	4	0	11	3
Sullivan	4	0	19	3
Sims	2	0	11	0
Havill	3	0	25	1
Mackay	4	0	18	2
Ebrahim	1	0	11	0
OTAGO				
Loe	3	0	22	1
Black	2.3	0	18	0
Jensen	2	0	20	0
Adams	3	0	17	0
Carson	2	0	14	0
Oldershaw	3	0	21	1

Fall of Wickets

	O	C
1st	19	0
2nd	30	74
3rd	34	-
4th	65	-
5th	74	-
6th	91	-
7th	102	-
8th	106	-
9th	111	-
10th	112	-

CENTRAL DISTRICTS v NORTHERN DISTRICTS **Super Smash**

at Pukekura Park, New Plymouth on 30 December, 2020
Toss : Central Districts. Umpires : A. Mehrotra & A. Stanley
***Northern Districts won by 17 runs.** Points: Northern Districts 4, Central Districts 0*

NORTHERN DISTRICTS

	Runs	Mins	Balls	6s	4s
K.G.Anderson lbw b Green	17	16	9	-	4
B.M.Halliday* b Mair	7	11	10	-	1
C.A.Gurrey c Greig b Hansen	57	65	40	1	8
E.A.J.Richardson b Rowe	20	23	14	1	1
F.C.Leydon-Davis c Dodd b Watkin	42	29	31	1	4
L.F.Boucher c & b Watkin	0	1	1	-	-
A.J.Rout not out	9	12	8	1	-
N.H.Patel not out	4	5	7	-	-
C.R.Sarsfield					
O.R.Lobb†					
L.H.Heaps					
Extras (b 1, lb 1, w 3)	5				
TOTAL (20 overs) (6 wkts)	**161**	82			

CENTRAL DISTRICTS

	Runs	Mins	Balls	6s	4s
J.M.Watkin* c Anderson b Heaps	1	5	4	-	-
E.G.Cunningham c Anderson b Leydon-Davis	17	18	15	-	3
N.C.Dodd† lbw b Patel	49	45	40	-	7
A.van Deventer c Boucher b Richardson	35	41	29	-	2
H.M.Rowe b Richardson	3	6	5	-	-
M.J.Greig c Halliday b Sarsfield	9	8	7	-	1
R.A.Mair c Anderson b Richardson	12	9	7	-	2
G.K.Atkinson run out	0	7	0	-	-
M.J.Hansen c Heaps b Leydon-Davis	3	4	4	-	-
M.S.Rees not out	4	5	5	-	-
C.L.Green not out	5	3	4	-	-
Extras (w 5, nb 1)	6				
TOTAL (20 overs) (9 wkts)	**144**	78			

Bowling	O	M	R	W
CENTRAL DISTRICTS				
Mair	4	1	24	1
Rowe	3	0	28	1
Green	2	0	13	1
Watkin	3	0	17	2
Rees	2	0	19	0
Greig	2	0	17	0
Atkinson	3	0	38	0
Hansen	1	0	3	1
NORTHERN DISTRICTS				
Leydon-Davis	4	0	23	2
Heaps	4	0	29	1
Halliday	1	0	14	0
Boucher	2	0	22	0
Richardson	4	0	27	3
Sarsfield	4	0	22	1
Patel	1	0	7	1

Fall of Wickets

	ND	CD
1st	21	3
2nd	25	34
3rd	64	102
4th	133	111
5th	133	112
6th	150	121
7th	-	132
8th	-	134
9th	-	136
10th	-	-

CENTRAL DISTRICTS v AUCKLAND — Super Smash

at Pukekura Park, New Plymouth on 31 December, 2020
Toss : Auckland. Umpires : K.D. Cotton & A. Stanley
***Auckland won by 8 runs.** Points: Auckland 4, Central Districts 0*

AUCKLAND

	Runs	Mins	Balls	6s	4s
L.R.Down* not out	63	77	64	-	6
A.M.Peterson c Rowe b Watkin	41	37	22	2	4
K.T.Perkins c Greig b Watkin	20	14	12	-	2
B.G.Armstrong not out	29	25	22	-	3
S.Shahri					
H.R.Huddleston					
R.S.M.Lili'i					
A.N.Kelly					
J.E.I.Prasad					
S.J.Carnachan†					
M.M.Penfold					
Extras (lb 1, w 4)	5				
TOTAL (20 overs) (2 wkts)	**158**	77			

CENTRAL DISTRICTS

	Runs	Mins	Balls	6s	4s
J.M.Watkin* c Perkins b Kelly	3	10	7	-	-
E.G.Cunningham b Huddleston	14	16	13	-	2
N.C.Dodd† st Carnachan b Prasad	28	44	28	-	2
A.van Deventer lbw b Kelly	4	3	3	-	1
H.M.Rowe run out	44	48	46	-	3
M.J.Greig c Shahri b Kelly	18	19	14	-	3
R.A.Mair c Huddleston b Kelly	6	6	4	-	1
K.A.Tomlinson not out	5	6	2	-	1
G.K.Atkinson b Huddleston	8	4	5	-	2
M.J.Hansen					
C.L.Green					
Extras (lb 2, w 17, nb 1)	20				
TOTAL (20 overs) (8 wkts)	**150**	81			

Bowling	*O*	*M*	*R*	*W*
CENTRAL DISTRICTS				
Mair	4	0	34	0
Green	2	0	15	0
Watkin	4	0	27	2
Rowe	4	0	34	0
Hansen	3	0	23	0
Greig	2	0	17	0
Atkinson	1	0	7	0
AUCKLAND				
Kelly	4	0	28	4
Huddleston	4	0	38	2
Peterson	4	0	16	0
Armstrong	3	0	29	0
Penfold	1	0	12	0
Prasad	4	0	25	1

Fall of Wickets

	A	***CD***
1st	80	20
2nd	112	30
3rd	-	35
4th	-	96
5th	-	123
6th	-	137
7th	-	137
8th	-	150
9th	-	-
10th	-	-

NORTHERN DISTRICTS v WELLINGTON — Super Smash

at Bay Oval, Mt Maunganui on 1 January, 2021
Toss : Wellington. Umpires : L.R. Els & D.R. Morrow
***Northern Districts won by 5 wickets.** Points: Northern Districts 4, Wellington 0*

WELLINGTON

	Runs	Mins	Balls	6s	4s
R.M.Burns c Halliday b Leydon-Davis	17	21	21	-	3
M.L.Green* c Hyde b Halliday	6	12	8	-	1
A.C.Kerr run out	60	55	43	-	7
J.T.McFadyen† run out	8	14	13	-	1
T.M.M.Newton b Patel	12	22	13	-	1
L.M.Kasperek b Leydon-Davis	17	19	11	-	2
J.M.Kerr not out	14	13	9	-	2
C.R.King run out	0	2	1	-	-
X.A.R.Jetly not out	1	2	1	-	-
M.P.Singh					
G.E.Plimmer					
Extras (lb 1, w 3)	4				
TOTAL (20 overs) (7 wkts)	**139**	81			

NORTHERN DISTRICTS

	Runs	Mins	Balls	6s	4s
K.G.Anderson b Kerr J.M.	50	58	47	-	6
B.M.Halliday* run out	7	19	14	-	-
C.A.Gurrey run out	13	23	13	-	1
E.A.J.Richardson c Burns b Kasperek	17	9	10	-	3
F.C.Leydon-Davis not out	13	35	17	-	-
N.H.Patel run out	25	27	18	-	3
M.N.Hyde not out	4	2	1	-	1
A.J.Rout					
C.R.Sarsfield					
O.R.Lobb†					
L.H.Heaps					
Extras (b 1, lb 2, w 8)	11				
TOTAL (20 overs) (5 wkts)	**140**	88			

Bowling	*O*	*M*	*R*	*W*
NORTHERN DISTRICTS				
Patel	4	0	17	1
Heaps	4	0	30	0
Leydon-Davis	3	0	23	2
Halliday	4	0	28	1
Richardson	3	0	28	0
Sarsfield	2	0	12	0
WELLINGTON				
Singh	4	0	17	0
Kerr J.M.	4	0	23	1
Kasperek	2	0	20	1
Kerr A.C.	4	0	28	0
Newton	4	0	34	0
Green	2	0	15	0

Fall of Wickets

	W	***ND***
1st	19	22
2nd	38	63
3rd	58	84
4th	98	94
5th	113	135
6th	134	-
7th	135	-
8th	-	-
9th	-	-
10th	-	-

NORTHERN DISTRICTS v OTAGO — Super Smash

at Bay Oval, Mt Maunganui on 2 January, 2021
Toss : Otago. Umpires : L.R. Els & G.A. Stirrat
***Otago won by 6 wickets (D/L).** Points: Otago 4, Northern Districts 0*

NORTHERN DISTRICTS

	Runs	Mins	Balls	6s	4s
K.G.Anderson b Black	1	5	6	-	-
B.M.Halliday* st Martin b Carson	37	35	31	-	7
C.A.Gurrey c Blakely b Oldershaw	22	35	19	-	4
E.A.J.Richardson not out	20	20	15	-	3
F.C.Leydon-Davis run out	3	12	5	-	-
M.N.Hyde not out	5	2	3	-	1
N.H.Patel					
A.J.Rout					
O.R.Lobb†					
C.R.Sarsfield					
L.H.Heaps					
Extras (lb 2, w 7)	9				
TOTAL (13 overs) (4 wkts)	**97**	56			

OTAGO

	Runs	Mins	Balls	6s	4s
M.R.Cowan c Anderson b Leydon-Davis	5	7	9	-	1
P.M.Inglis run out	14	13	12	1	-
K.J.Martin*† c Lobb b Halliday	11	13	8	-	1
H.N.K.Jensen c Leydon-Davis b Heaps	32	28	17	1	4
C.G.Blakely not out	32	31	24	-	5
I.R.James not out	3	9	4	-	-
G.R.Adams					
E.J.Carson					
E.J.Black					
S.A.Oldershaw					
M.E.Loe					
Extras (b 1, w 5)	6				
TOTAL (12.2 overs) (4 wkts)	**103**	52			

Bowling	O	M	R	W
OTAGO				
Loe	3	0	21	0
Black	1	0	9	1
Jensen	3	0	25	0
Oldershaw	3	0	22	1
Carson	2	0	9	1
Adams	1	0	9	0
NORTHERN DISTRICTS				
Heaps	2.2	0	15	1
Patel	2	0	17	0
Leydon-Davis	3	0	24	1
Richardson	2	0	23	0
Halliday	2	0	14	1
Sarsfield	1	0	9	0

Fall of Wickets	ND	O
1st	7	10
2nd	61	20
3rd	68	33
4th	91	85
5th	-	-
6th	-	-
7th	-	-
8th	-	-
9th	-	-
10th	-	-

AUCKLAND v CANTERBURY — Super Smash

at Eden Park Outer Oval, Auckland on 3 January, 2021
Toss : Auckland. Umpires : J.A.K. Bromley & A. Stanley
***No result.** Points: Auckland 2, Canterbury 2*

CANTERBURY

	Runs	Mins	Balls	6s	4s
F.L.Mackay* not out	5	5	5	-	1
N.B.Cox not out	1	5	5	-	-
G.E.S.Sullivan					
L.E.V.Hughes†					
A.E.Satterthwaite					
K.F.G.Nation					
M.J.Banks					
K.E.Ebrahim					
L.M.M.Tahuhu					
K.J.Havill					
J.L.Savage					
Extras	0				
TOTAL (1.4 overs) (0 wkts)	**6**	5			

AUCKLAND

L.R.Down*
A.M.Peterson
K.T.Perkins
B.G.Armstrong
S.Shahri
H.R.Huddleston
R.S.M.Lili'i
A.N.Kelly
J.E.I.Prasad
S.J.Carnachan†
F.C.Jonas

Bowling	O	M	R	W
AUCKLAND				
Kelly	1	0	6	0
Huddleston	0.4	0	0	0

Fall of Wickets	C
1st	-
2nd	-
3rd	-
4th	-
5th	-
6th	-
7th	-
8th	-
9th	-
10th	-

NORTHERN DISTRICTS v CENTRAL DISTRICTS Super Smash

at Seddon Park, Hamilton on 4 January, 2021
Toss : Northern Districts. Umpires : J.M. Dempsey & L.R. Els
***Northern Districts won by 9 wickets.** Points: Northern Districts 4, Central Districts 0*

CENTRAL DISTRICTS

	Runs	Mins	Balls	6s	4s
J.M.Watkin* st Ewart b Heaps	0	1	1	-	-
G.K.Atkinson c Heaps b Halliday	1	8	5	-	-
N.C.Dodd† not out	38	43	30	-	4
A.van Deventer not out	24	36	25	-	3
H.M.Rowe					
K.A.Tomlinson					
R.A.Mair					
M.J.Greig					
M.J.Hansen					
M.S.Rees					
C.L.Green					
Extras (b 1, w 3, nb 1)	5				
TOTAL (10 overs) (2 wkts) ...	**68**	44			

NORTHERN DISTRICTS

	Runs	Mins	Balls	6s	4s
K.G.Anderson st Dodd b Greig .	18	24	13	1	1
B.M.Halliday* not out	27	43	30	-	2
C.A.Gurrey not out	24	18	16	-	3
E.A.J.Richardson					
F.C.Leydon-Davis					
N.H.Patel					
A.J.Rout					
M.N.Hyde					
A.M.Ewart†					
C.R.Sarsfield					
L.H.Heaps					
Extras (w 3)	3				
TOTAL (9.5 overs) (1 wkt)	**72**	43			

Bowling	*O*	*M*	*R*	*W*
NORTHERN DISTRICTS				
Heaps	2	0	9	1
Halliday	2	0	12	1
Leydon-Davis	1	0	9	0
Patel	1	0	7	0
Sarsfield	2	0	17	0
Richardson	2	0	13	0
CENTRAL DISTRICTS				
Mair	1	0	7	0
Watkin	2	0	14	0
Green	1	0	8	0
Hansen	2	0	12	0
Rowe	1.5	0	15	0
Greig	2	0	16	1

Fall of Wickets	***CD***	***ND***
1st	0	39
2nd	4	-
3rd	-	-
4th	-	-
5th	-	-
6th	-	-
7th	-	-
8th	-	-
9th	-	-
10th	-	-

OTAGO v CENTRAL DISTRICTS Super Smash

at University of Otago Oval, Dunedin on 8 January, 2021
Toss : Otago. Umpires : P.J. Pasco & D.J. Walker
***Otago won by 7 wickets.** Points: Otago 4, Central Districts 0*

CENTRAL DISTRICTS

	Runs	Mins	Balls	6s	4s
J.M.Watkin* c Cowan b Jensen ..	7	11	13	-	1
G.K.Atkinson b Carson	21	38	24	-	1
N.C.Dodd† b Black	26	51	41	-	-
H.M.Rowe st Martin b Black	4	10	8	-	-
K.A.Tomlinson run out	20	19	15	-	2
K.L.Gaging c James b Jensen	9	11	10	-	-
M.J.Hansen c Blakely b Oldershaw	3	7	4	-	-
M.S.Rees not out	3	3	4	-	-
C.L.Green not out	1	1	1	-	-
O.J.S.Bartlett					
A.Kumar					
Extras (b 2, lb 2, w 4)	8				
TOTAL (20 overs) (7 wkts) .	**102**	77			

OTAGO

	Runs	Mins	Balls	6s	4s
M.R.Cowan b Green	20	16	18	-	4
P.M.Inglis not out	43	58	38	-	5
K.J.Martin*† b Rees	13	16	14	-	1
H.N.K.Jensen c Atkinson b Watkin	17	19	15	-	2
C.G.Blakely not out	9	5	7	-	1
I.R.James					
G.R.Adams					
E.J.Carson					
E.J.Black					
M.B.Lamplough					
S.A.Oldershaw					
Extras (w 3)	3				
TOTAL (15.2 overs) (3 wkts)	**105**	58			

Bowling	*O*	*M*	*R*	*W*
OTAGO				
Jensen	4	0	22	2
Black	4	0	26	2
Adams	4	0	15	0
Oldershaw	4	0	14	1
Carson	4	0	21	1
CENTRAL DISTRICTS				
Green	3	0	21	1
Hansen	3	0	20	0
Watkin	3.2	0	20	1
Rowe	3	0	19	0
Rees	2	0	13	1
Kumar	1	0	12	0

Fall of Wickets	***CD***	***O***
1st	13	32
2nd	48	55
3rd	59	92
4th	76	-
5th	89	-
6th	98	-
7th	99	-
8th	-	-
9th	-	-
10th	-	-

WELLINGTON v NORTHERN DISTRICTS — Super Smash

at Basin Reserve, Wellington on 9 January, 2021
Toss : Northern Districts. Umpires : T.R. Davies & T.J. Parlane
***Wellington won by 5 wickets.** Points: Wellington 4, Northern Districts 0*

NORTHERN DISTRICTS

	Runs	Mins	Balls	6s	4s
K.G.Anderson c Kerr A.C. b Kerr J.M.	17	14	12	-	4
B.M.Halliday* c Kerr J.M. b Kasperek	3	18	11	-	-
C.A.Gurrey c Burns b Kasperek	11	35	22	-	-
E.A.J.Richardson run out	30	45	38	-	3
L.F.Boucher st McFadyen b Green	11	11	7	-	2
N.H.Patel st McFadyen b Kasperek	3	13	7	-	-
A.J.Rout st McFadyen b Kasperek	7	14	16	-	-
M.N.Hyde not out	7	8	5	-	1
A.M.Ewart† b Kerr J.M.	0	2	1	-	-
C.R.Sarsfield not out	1	2	2	-	-
L.H.Heaps					
Extras (lb 3, w 6, nb 1)	10				
TOTAL (20 overs) (8 wkts)	**100**	83			

WELLINGTON

	Runs	Mins	Balls	6s	4s
A.C.Kerr c Heaps b Patel	4	2	3	-	1
M.L.Green* c Anderson b Boucher	23	39	23	-	3
R.M.Burns c Sarsfield b Heaps	24	14	15	-	5
L.M.Kasperek not out	20	51	30	-	2
T.M.M.Newton c Sarsfield b Boucher	20	25	28	-	2
J.T.McFadyen† lbw b Boucher	0	2	1	-	-
J.M.Kerr not out	4	1	1	-	1
X.A.R.Jetly					
M.P.Singh					
B.C.Molony					
D.M.Doughty					
Extras (b 2, lb 1, w 4)	7				
TOTAL (17 overs) (5 wkts)	**102**	68			

Bowling	*O*	*M*	*R*	*W*
WELLINGTON				
Singh	1	0	12	0
Kerr J.M.	4	0	21	2
Kasperek	4	0	16	4
Kerr A.C.	4	0	16	0
Green	3	0	10	1
Doughty	2	0	13	0
Newton	2	0	9	0
NORTHERN DISTRICTS				
Patel	2	0	7	1
Heaps	2	0	18	1
Halliday	4	0	18	0
Richardson	2	0	11	0
Boucher	3	0	21	3
Sarsfield	4	1	24	0

Fall of Wickets	***ND***	***W***
1st	21	4
2nd	21	33
3rd	59	58
4th	80	98
5th	81	98
6th	91	-
7th	94	-
8th	95	-
9th	-	-
10th	-	-

CANTERBURY v CENTRAL DISTRICTS — Super Smash

at Hagley Oval, Christchurch on 10 January, 2021
Toss : Canterbury. Umpires : J.M. Dempsey & G.M. Walklin
***Canterbury won by 8 wickets.** Points: Canterbury 4,. Central Districts 0*

CENTRAL DISTRICTS

	Runs	Mins	Balls	6s	4s
J.M.Watkin* c Havill b Sullivan	15	24	17	-	3
E.G.Cunningham st Kench b Sims	0	3	2	-	-
N.C.Dodd† lbw b Mackay	21	33	22	-	3
A.van Deventer c Cox b Mackay	12	17	15	-	1
H.M.Rowe run out	7	16	11	-	-
K.A.Tomlinson lbw b Mackay	2	7	5	-	-
K.L.Gaging c Satterthwaite b Savage	28	31	27	-	3
G.K.Atkinson st Hughes b Mackay	0	2	4	-	-
M.J.Hansen not out	9	24	14	-	-
M.S.Rees run out	1	2	1	-	-
C.L.Green					
Extras (w 5)	5				
TOTAL (20 overs) (9 wkts)	**100**	81			

CANTERBURY

	Runs	Mins	Balls	6s	4s
F.L.Mackay* c Dodd b Green	48	37	33	-	9
N.B.Cox b Watkin	6	23	12	-	-
A.E.Satterthwaite not out	29	32	20	-	5
K.E.Ebrahim not out	15	18	13	-	1
E.K.Kench					
L.E.V.Hughes†					
G.E.S.Sullivan					
K.F.G.Nation					
K.M.Sims					
K.J.Havill					
J.L.Savage					
Extras (w 3)	3				
TOTAL (13 overs) (2 wkts)	**101**	56			

Bowling	*O*	*M*	*R*	*W*
CANTERBURY				
Sims	2	1	5	1
Savage	3	0	29	1
Satterthwaite	4	0	18	0
Sullivan	4	0	20	1
Havill	2	0	9	0
Mackay	4	0	10	4
Ebrahim	1	0	9	0
CENTRAL DISTRICTS				
Green	4	0	26	1
Rowe	3	0	24	0
Watkin	4	0	33	1
Rees	1	0	14	0
Hansen	0.2	0	0	0
Cunningham	0.4	0	4	0

Fall of Wickets	***CD***	***C***
1st	4	50
2nd	31	61
3rd	52	-
4th	53	-
5th	59	-
6th	62	-
7th	63	-
8th	99	-
9th	100	-
10th	-	-

CANTERBURY v AUCKLAND — Super Smash

at Hagley Oval, Christchurch on 11 January, 2021
Toss : Canterbury. Umpires : K.D. Cotton & L.R. Els
Auckland won by 20 runs. *Points: Auckland 4, Canterbury 0*

AUCKLAND

	Runs	Mins	Balls	6s	4s
L.R.Down* run out	33	52	39	-	2
A.M.Peterson c Satterthwaite b Savage	8	8	5	-	2
K.T.Perkins b Sims	1	5	3	-	-
B.G.Armstrong c Sullivan b Mackay	39	32	29	1	4
S.Shahri not out	30	32	28	-	4
H.R.Huddleston not out	18	25	16	-	1
R.S.M.Lili'i					
A.N.Kelly					
J.E.I.Prasad					
S.J.Carnachan†					
F.C.Jonas					
Extras (lb 1, w 8)	9				
TOTAL (20 overs) (4 wkts)	**138**	78			

CANTERBURY

	Runs	Mins	Balls	6s	4s
F.L.Mackay* c Lili'i b Peterson	6	19	12	-	1
N.B.Cox b Kelly	5	14	9	-	-
A.E.Satterthwaite st Carnachan b Jonas	32	34	33	-	4
K.E.Ebrahim c Prasad b Armstrong	31	45	35	-	4
K.F.G.Nation run out	10	26	9	-	1
L.E.V.Hughes† b Prasad	4	3	4	-	1
J.L.Savage c Down b Prasad	4	2	2	-	1
E.K.Kench c Down b Huddleston	0	1	1	-	-
G.E.S.Sullivan c Down b Huddleston	11	9	10	-	2
K.J.Havill c Armstrong b Huddleston	2	7	3	-	-
K.M.Sims not out	0	1	0	-	-
Extras (b 1, lb 2, w 8, nb 2)	13				
TOTAL (19.2 overs)	**118**	83			

Bowling	O	M	R	W
CANTERBURY				
Sims	3	0	23	1
Savage	3	0	21	1
Sullivan	4	0	21	0
Havill	2	0	18	0
Mackay	4	0	19	1
Satterthwaite	3	0	25	0
Ebrahim	1	0	10	0
AUCKLAND				
Huddleston	3.2	0	8	3
Kelly	3	1	17	1
Peterson	4	1	14	1
Jonas	4	0	27	1
Armstrong	2	0	21	1
Prasad	3	0	28	2

Fall of Wickets	A	C
1st	12	16
2nd	17	16
3rd	80	74
4th	92	97
5th	-	101
6th	-	105
7th	-	105
8th	-	106
9th	-	118
10th	-	118

OTAGO v WELLINGTON — Super Smash

at University of Otago Oval, Dunedin on 14 January, 2021
Toss : Otago. Umpires : C.M. Brown & S.J. Kannan
Wellington won by 10 wickets. *Points: Wellington 4, Otago 0*

OTAGO

	Runs	Mins	Balls	6s	4s
M.R.Cowan c McFadyen b Kasperek	29	32	29	-	4
P.M.Inglis b Kerr A.C.	19	37	27	-	1
K.J.Martin*† run out	27	37	29	-	3
H.N.K.Jensen b Kasperek	35	36	26	-	4
C.G.Blakely run out	1	6	1	-	-
I.R.James not out	2	9	3	-	-
O.N.Gain c McFadyen b Kerr J.M.	5	4	4	-	1
E.J.Black c Kasperek b Kerr J.M.	0	2	3	-	-
E.J.Carson					
M.B.Lamplough					
S.A.Oldershaw					
Extras (b 1, lb 3, w 4, nb 2)	10				
TOTAL (20 overs) (7 wkts)	**128**	83			

WELLINGTON

	Runs	Mins	Balls	6s	4s
S.F.M.Devine not out	108	39	38	9	9
M.L.Green* not out	20	39	15	1	1
A.C.Kerr					
L.M.Kasperek					
T.M.M.Newton					
J.T.McFadyen†					
R.M.Burns					
J.M.Kerr					
C.R.King					
M.P.Singh					
G.E.Plimmer					
Extras (w 2, nb 1)	3				
TOTAL (8.4 overs) (0 wkts)	**131**	39			

Bowling	O	M	R	W
WELLINGTON				
Singh	3	0	14	0
Kerr J.M.	4	0	15	2
Kasperek	4	0	20	2
Green	3	0	33	0
Kerr A.C.	4	0	22	1
Newton	2	0	20	0
OTAGO				
Jensen	2	0	36	0
Black	2.4	0	36	0
Oldershaw	2	0	23	0
Carson	1	0	16	0
Lamplough	1	0	20	0

Fall of Wickets	O	W
1st	46	-
2nd	50	-
3rd	113	-
4th	121	-
5th	123	-
6th	128	-
7th	128	-
8th	-	-
9th	-	-
10th	-	-

CANTERBURY v NORTHERN DISTRICTS — Super Smash

at Hagley Oval, Christchurch on 15 January, 2021 (d/n)
Toss : Canterbury. Umpires : D.R. Morrow & T.J Parlane
***Canterbury won by 53 runs.** Points: Canterbury 4, Northern Districts 0*

CANTERBURY

	Runs	Mins	Balls	6s	4s
F.L.Mackay* lbw b Halliday	17	11	11	-	3
N.B.Cox lbw b Patel	6	18	6	-	1
A.E.Satterthwaite c Leydon-Davis b Richardson	14	20	15	-	2
K.E.Ebrahim not out	84	65	65	-	8
J.L.Savage run out	5	8	6	-	-
K.F.G.Nation not out	21	44	17	-	2
L.E.V.Hughes†					
G.E.S.Sullivan					
S.R.Asmussen					
L.M.M.Tahuhu					
M.J.Banks					
Extras (lb 1, w 6)	7				
TOTAL (20 overs) (4 wkts)	**154**	84			

NORTHERN DISTRICTS

	Runs	Mins	Balls	6s	4s
K.G.Anderson run out	38	37	31	-	6
B.M.Halliday* st Hughes b Sullivan	2	6	4	-	-
C.A.Gurrey b Asmussen	29	44	34	-	4
E.A.J.Richardson run out	0	4	0	-	-
L.F.Boucher b Mackay	0	3	4	-	-
F.C.Leydon-Davis c Mackay b Satterthwaite	11	15	14	-	-
N.Matthews c Cox b Asmussen	1	5	5	-	-
N.H.Patel b Banks	12	14	12	-	1
A.M.Ewart† run out	1	4	4	-	-
C.R.Sarsfield not out	2	12	4	-	-
L.H.Heaps run out	3	6	7	-	-
Extras (w 2)	2				
TOTAL (19.5 overs)	**101**	77			

Bowling	*O*	*M*	*R*	*W*
NORTHERN DISTRICTS				
Boucher	1	0	12	0
Heaps	3	0	24	0
Halliday	3	0	32	1
Patel	3	0	23	1
Richardson	4	0	14	1
Leydon-Davis	4	0	36	0
Sarsfield	2	0	12	0
CANTERBURY				
Tahuhu	3	0	23	0
Sullivan	2.5	0	12	1
Savage	3	0	20	0
Mackay	4	0	14	1
Asmussen	4	0	21	2
Satterthwaite	2	0	9	1
Banks	1	0	2	1

Fall of Wickets	*C*	*ND*
1st	21	6
2nd	32	61
3rd	44	64
4th	54	66
5th	-	74
6th	-	78
7th	-	85
8th	-	87
9th	-	97
10th	-	101

CANTERBURY v WELLINGTON — Super Smash

at Hagley Oval, Christchurch on 16 January, 2021
Toss : Canterbury. Umpires : J.A.K. Bromley & A. Mehrotra
***Wellington won by 7 wickets.** Points: Wellington 4, Canterbury 0*

CANTERBURY

	Runs	Mins	Balls	6s	4s
F.L.Mackay* c Green b Kerr J.M.	0	2	5	-	-
N.B.Cox c Jetly b Kasperek	4	15	10	-	1
A.E.Satterthwaite c Burns b Jetly	52	49	28	-	10
K.E.Ebrahim c Newton b Green	34	57	44	-	2
J.L.Savage c Burns b Green	6	12	8	-	-
L.M.M.Tahuhu c Kerr J.M. b Green	9	8	9	-	1
K.F.G.Nation c Devine b Kasperek	5	6	4	-	1
M.J.Banks c Burns b Kasperek	1	3	3	-	-
L.E.V.Hughes† c Devine b Kasperek	1	3	2	-	-
G.E.S.Sullivan not out	1	4	2	-	-
S.R.Asmussen c Newton b Green	1	2	2	-	-
Extras (w 3)	3				
TOTAL (19.3 overs)	**117**	83			

WELLINGTON

	Runs	Mins	Balls	6s	4s
S.F.M.Devine c Sullivan b Asmussen	59	29	26	1	12
M.L.Green* c Hughes b Asmussen	25	42	28	-	3
A.C.Kerr not out	20	27	19	-	1
R.M.Burns c Sullivan b Mackay	0	5	4	-	-
T.M.M.Newton not out	3	8	3	-	-
L.M.Kasperek					
J.T.McFadyen†					
J.M.Kerr					
X.A.R.Jetly					
G.E.Plimmer					
M.P.Singh					
Extras (b 1, lb 2, w 8)	11				
TOTAL (13.2 overs) (3 wkts)	**118**	56			

Bowling	*O*	*M*	*R*	*W*
WELLINGTON				
Kerr J.M.	3	0	25	1
Singh	4	1	15	0
Kasperek	4	0	22	4
Newton	1	0	16	0
Kerr A.C.	4	0	21	0
Jetly	1	0	9	1
Green	2.3	0	9	4
CANTERBURY				
Tahuhu	2	0	16	0
Sullivan	1.2	0	17	0
Satterthwaite	1	0	13	0
Savage	1	0	11	0
Mackay	4	0	30	1
Asmussen	4	0	28	2

Fall of Wickets	*C*	*W*
1st	0	83
2nd	18	105
3rd	78	106
4th	96	-
5th	108	-
6th	108	-
7th	110	-
8th	115	-
9th	115	-
10th	117	-

AUCKLAND v NORTHERN DISTRICTS — Super Smash

at Eden Park Outer Oval, Auckland on 17 January, 2021
Toss : Northern Districts. Umpires : C.M. Brown & A. Stanley
***Auckland won by 6 wickets.** Points: Auckland 4, Northern Districts 0*

NORTHERN DISTRICTS

	Runs	Mins	Balls	6s	4s
K.G.Anderson c Perkins b Kelly	1	2	4	-	-
B.M.Halliday* c Perkins b Huddleston	1	5	2	-	-
C.A.Gurrey c Perkins b Prasad	28	48	36	-	3
E.A.J.Richardson c Prasad b Huddleston	0	2	1	-	-
F.C.Leydon-Davis b Prasad	25	41	33	-	3
L.F.Boucher run out	1	6	4	-	-
N.Matthews c & b Prasad	0	1	1	-	-
N.H.Patel c Kelly b Huddleston	17	18	15	-	2
A.M.Ewart† run out	8	20	13	-	-
C.R.Sarsfield not out	3	10	7	-	-
L.H.Heaps not out	3	5	4	-	-
Extras (lb 1, w 9)	10				
TOTAL (20 overs) (9 wkts)	**97**	82			

AUCKLAND

	Runs	Mins	Balls	6s	4s
L.R.Down* st Ewart b Patel	4	1	3	-	1
B.G.Armstrong c Gurrey b Patel	0	3	1	-	-
K.T.Perkins not out	52	67	48	-	5
S.Shahri c Boucher b Patel	5	14	15	-	-
H.R.Huddleston c Boucher b Richardson	25	48	39	-	-
R.S.M.Lili'i not out	0	1	0	-	-
A.N.Kelly					
J.E.I.Prasad					
R.H.McNeill					
T.I.Lamb†					
F.C.Jonas					
Extras (lb 8, w 6)	14				
TOTAL (17.4 overs) (4 wkts)	**100**	68			

Bowling	*O*	*M*	*R*	*W*
AUCKLAND				
Kelly	4	0	14	1
Huddleston	4	1	14	3
Prasad	4	0	19	3
McNeill	4	0	27	0
Jonas	4	0	22	0
NORTHERN DISTRICTS				
Patel	4	0	19	3
Heaps	3	0	14	0
Halliday	2	0	15	0
Richardson	3.4	0	22	1
Leydon-Davis	1	0	6	0
Sarsfield	3	0	11	0
Boucher	1	0	5	0

Fall of Wickets	***ND***	***A***
1st	2	4
2nd	6	5
3rd	6	17
4th	61	96
5th	62	-
6th	62	-
7th	62	-
8th	88	-
9th	91	-
10th	-	-

CENTRAL DISTRICTS v OTAGO — Super Smash

at Pukekura Park, New Plymouth on 18 January, 2021
Toss : Otago. Umpires : E.D. Sanders & T.S. Shirriffs
***Central Districts won by 6 runs (D/L).** Points: Central Districts 4, Otago 0*

CENTRAL DISTRICTS

	Runs	Mins	Balls	6s	4s
J.M.Watkin* run out	26	28	17	1	2
E.G.Cunningham b Jensen	1	10	9	-	-
N.C.Dodd† c Cowan b Black	2	10	9	-	-
A.van Deventer not out	63	46	40	2	4
H.M.Rowe not out	25	39	27	1	-
K.A.Tomlinson					
K.L.Gaging					
G.K.Atkinson					
M.S.Rees					
C.L.Green					
A.M.Gaging					
Extras (lb 5, w 4)	9				
TOTAL (17 overs) (3 wkts)	**126**	67			

OTAGO

	Runs	Mins	Balls	6s	4s
M.R.Cowan c Gaging A.M. b Watkin	6	6	7	-	1
P.M.Inglis c Gaging K.L. b Rowe	1	15	8	-	-
K.J.Martin*† not out	33	30	24	1	3
H.N.K.Jensen run out	4	10	5	-	-
C.G.Blakely not out	10	11	4	-	1
I.R.James					
O.N.Gain					
G.R.Adams					
E.J.Carson					
E.J.Black					
S.A.Oldershaw					
Extras (b 1, lb 3, w 1)	5				
TOTAL (8 overs) (3 wkts)	**59**	36			

Bowling	*O*	*M*	*R*	*W*
OTAGO				
Jensen	4	0	22	1
Black	4	1	27	1
Adams	3	0	31	0
Oldershaw	3	0	20	0
Carson	3	0	21	0
CENTRAL DISTRICTS				
Gaging A.M.	1	0	6	0
Watkin	2	0	14	1
Green	2	0	8	0
Rowe	2	1	16	1
Rees	1	0	11	0

Fall of Wickets	***CD***	***O***
1st	19	8
2nd	28	14
3rd	38	28
4th	-	-
5th	-	-
6th	-	-
7th	-	-
8th	-	-
9th	-	-
10th	-	-

NORTHERN DISTRICTS v CANTERBURY — Super Smash

at Seddon Park, Hamilton on 21 January, 2021
Toss : Canterbury. Umpires : J.M. Dempsey & L.R. Els
***Canterbury won by 6 wickets.** Points: Canterbury 4, Northern Districts 0*

NORTHERN DISTRICTS

	Runs	Mins	Balls	6s	4s
K.G.Anderson c Satterthwaite b Mackay	35	47	38	1	1
B.M.Halliday* c Sullivan b Satterthwaite	35	45	35	-	3
E.A.J.Richardson c Hughes b Mackay	1	4	3	-	-
C.A.Gurrey not out	27	22	18	1	3
L.F.Boucher c Satterthwaite b Mackay	13	10	12	-	1
F.C.Leydon-Davis lbw b Mackay	0	1	1	-	-
N.H.Patel not out	6	8	7	-	-
A.M.Ewart†					
C.R.Sarsfield					
L.H.Heaps					
M.B.Templeton					
Extras (b 2, lb 2, w 3)	7				
TOTAL (19 overs) (5 wkts)	**124**	69			

CANTERBURY

	Runs	Mins	Balls	6s	4s
F.L.Mackay* b Halliday	28	44	29	-	3
N.B.Cox c Richardson b Sarsfield	31	17	16	3	1
A.E.Satterthwaite c Halliday b Templeton	38	36	27	-	6
K.E.Ebrahim not out	12	23	14	-	1
J.L.Savage b Templeton	8	11	12	-	1
K.F.G.Nation not out	4	1	1	-	1
L.E.V.Hughes†					
G.E.S.Sullivan					
S.R.Asmussen					
L.M.M.Tahuhu					
M.J.Banks					
Extras (lb 1, w 7)	8				
TOTAL (16.3 overs) (4 wkts)	**129**	67			

Bowling	*O*	*M*	*R*	*W*
CANTERBURY				
Tahuhu	3	0	14	0
Savage	3	0	21	0
Sullivan	3	0	19	0
Asmussen	2	0	14	0
Mackay	4	0	17	4
Satterthwaite	4	0	35	1
NORTHERN DISTRICTS				
Patel	3	0	11	0
Heaps	1	0	8	0
Halliday	3	0	17	1
Richardson	1	0	17	0
Sarsfield	3	0	39	1
Boucher	1	0	12	0
Leydon-Davis	1	0	9	0
Templeton	3.3	0	15	2

Fall of Wickets	***ND***	***C***
1st	76	40
2nd	77	88
3rd	77	109
4th	102	125
5th	103	-
6th	-	-
7th	-	-
8th	-	-
9th	-	-
10th	-	-

AUCKLAND v CENTRAL DISTRICTS — Super Smash

at Eden Park Outer Oval, Auckland on 23 January, 2021
Toss : Auckland. Umpires : C.M. Brown & D.R. Morrow
***Central Districts won by 9 wickets.** Points: Central Districts 4, Auckland 0*

AUCKLAND

	Runs	Mins	Balls	6s	4s
A.M.Peterson b Kumar	1	2	3	-	-
L.R.Down* lbw b Green	1	8	3	-	-
K.T.Perkins c Dodd b Rowe	34	61	37	-	2
B.G.Armstrong c van Deventer b Rowe	7	6	9	-	1
S.Shahri st Dodd b Atkinson	16	25	25	-	1
H.R.Huddleston not out	37	40	32	-	2
R.S.M.Lili'i not out	17	16	12	-	2
A.N.Kelly					
J.E.I.Prasad					
T.I.Lamb†					
F.C.Jonas					
Extras (lb 2, w 5)	7				
TOTAL (20 overs) (5 wkts)	**120**	80			

CENTRAL DISTRICTS

	Runs	Mins	Balls	6s	4s
J.M.Watkin* not out	68	59	48	3	7
E.G.Cunningham c Peterson b Huddleston	1	9	6	-	-
N.C.Dodd† not out	49	49	45	1	5
A.van Deventer					
H.M.Rowe					
K.A.Tomlinson					
M.J.Hansen					
A.Kumar					
M.S.Rees					
G.K.Atkinson					
C.L.Green					
Extras (lb 1, w 3)	4				
TOTAL (16.3 overs) (1 wkt)	**122**	59			

Bowling	*O*	*M*	*R*	*W*
CENTRAL DISTRICTS				
Kumar	4	0	23	1
Green	2	0	6	1
Watkin	4	0	20	0
Rowe	4	0	26	2
Atkinson	3	0	19	1
Cunningham	1	0	6	0
Rees	1	0	8	0
Hansen	1	0	10	0
AUCKLAND				
Huddleston	3	0	27	1
Kelly	2	0	16	0
Peterson	3	0	18	0
Prasad	3	0	22	0
Jonas	4	0	21	0
Armstrong	1.3	0	17	0

Fall of Wickets	***A***	***CD***
1st	3	13
2nd	6	-
3rd	14	-
4th	45	-
5th	85	-
6th	-	-
7th	-	-
8th	-	-
9th	-	-
10th	-	-

WELLINGTON v OTAGO — Super Smash

at Basin Reserve, Wellington on 24 January, 2021
Toss : Wellington. Umpires : C.A. Black & E.D. Sanders
Wellington won by 122 runs. *Points: Wellington 4, Otago 0*

WELLINGTON

	Runs	Mins	Balls	6s	4s
S.F.M.Devine c Gain b Carson	80	62	44	4	7
M.L.Green* run out	14	18	13	-	2
A.C.Kerr c Black b Oldershaw	66	59	43	-	9
L.M.Kasperek not out	20	25	14	-	2
T.M.M.Newton b Oldershaw	0	1	1	-	-
J.T.McFadyen† run out	8	6	4	-	1
J.M.Kerr not out	2	1	1	-	-
C.R.King					
G.E.Plimmer					
X.A.R.Jetly					
M.P.Singh					
Extras (b 1, lb 1, w 4)	6				
TOTAL (20 overs) (5 wkts)	**196**	87			

OTAGO

	Runs	Mins	Balls	6s	4s
M.R.Cowan c Newton b Singh	8	4	6	-	2
P.M.Inglis b Singh	24	41	25	-	3
K.J.Martin*† c Jetly b Kasperek	7	14	11	-	1
C.G.Blakely c McFadyen b Jetly	18	29	16	-	2
I.R.James st McFadyen b Jetly	2	6	4	-	-
O.N.Gain c Kasperek b Jetly	1	9	8	-	-
G.R.Adams c & b Jetly	0	1	2	-	-
E.J.Carson b Newton	1	9	5	-	-
E.J.Black c McFadyen b Newton	0	5	4	-	-
S.A.Oldershaw c Green b Newton	6	10	10	-	1
M.E.Loe not out	0	8	2	-	-
Extras (b 1, lb 2, w 4)	7				
TOTAL (15.3 overs)	**74**	70			

Bowling	O	M	R	W
OTAGO				
Adams	3	0	36	0
Black	4	0	32	0
Loe	4	0	52	0
Carson	4	0	39	1
Oldershaw	4	0	24	2
Blakely	1	0	11	0
WELLINGTON				
Singh	4	0	20	2
Kerr J.M.	2	0	10	0
Devine	1	0	6	0
Kasperek	2	0	12	1
Newton	3.3	0	14	3
Jetly	3	0	9	4

Fall of Wickets	W	O
1st	34	8
2nd	144	25
3rd	182	59
4th	182	62
5th	194	63
6th	-	63
7th	-	65
8th	-	67
9th	-	68
10th	-	74

WELLINGTON v CANTERBURY — Super Smash

at Basin Reserve, Wellington on 25 January, 2021
Toss : Canterbury. Umpires : T.R. Davies & D.J. Walker
Canterbury won by 9 wickets. *Points: Canterbury 4, Wellington 0*

WELLINGTON

	Runs	Mins	Balls	6s	4s
S.F.M.Devine c Mackay b Tahuhu	13	22	15	-	2
M.L.Green* c & b Savage	21	31	20	-	2
A.C.Kerr c Satterthwaite b Sullivan	9	19	14	-	1
L.M.Kasperek b Tahuhu	39	35	32	-	6
T.M.M.Newton lbw b Mackay	22	33	26	-	1
J.M.Kerr c Banks b Mackay	9	11	6	-	1
J.T.McFadyen† run out	3	8	3	-	-
C.R.King b Satterthwaite	0	2	1	-	-
G.E.Plimmer b Satterthwaite	4	3	5	-	-
X.A.R.Jetly not out	0	1	0	-	-
M.P.Singh					
Extras (b 2, lb 1, w 7, nb 2)	12				
TOTAL (20 overs) (9 wkts)	**132**	84			

CANTERBURY

	Runs	Mins	Balls	6s	4s
F.L.Mackay* run out	8	22	12	-	1
N.B.Cox not out	48	73	49	1	5
A.E.Satterthwaite not out	71	51	50	2	9
K.E.Ebrahim					
L.E.V.Hughes†					
G.E.S.Sullivan					
K.F.G.Nation					
J.L.Savage					
S.R.Asmussen					
L.M.M.Tahuhu					
M.J.Banks					
Extras (lb 1, w 5, nb 1)	7				
TOTAL (18.2 overs) (1 wkt)	**134**	73			

Bowling	O	M	R	W
CANTERBURY				
Tahuhu	4	0	22	2
Savage	3	0	31	1
Sullivan	4	0	13	1
Mackay	4	0	25	2
Ebrahim	3	0	24	0
Asmussen	1	0	9	0
Satterthwaite	1	0	5	2
WELLINGTON				
Singh	3	0	13	0
Kerr J.M.	4	0	25	0
Kasperek	3.2	0	21	0
Jetly	2	0	27	0
Kerr A.C.	4	0	27	0
Green	2	0	20	0

Fall of Wickets	W	C
1st	35	30
2nd	42	-
3rd	58	-
4th	102	-
5th	122	-
6th	127	-
7th	127	-
8th	132	-
9th	132	-
10th	-	-

NORTHERN DISTRICTS v AUCKLAND — Super Smash

at Seddon Park, Hamilton on 29 January, 2021 (d/n)
Toss : Northern Districts. Umpires : J.M. Dempsey & A. Stanley
***Auckland won by 6 wickets.** Points: Auckland 4, Northern Districts 0*

NORTHERN DISTRICTS

	Runs	Mins	Balls	6s	4s
K.G.Anderson c Huddleston b Kelly	11	16	11	-	2
B.M.Halliday* st Lamb b Peterson	34	50	40	-	3
C.A.Gurrey c Lili'i b Jonas	18	29	29	-	-
F.C.Leydon-Davis c Down b Jonas	3	10	5	-	-
E.A.J.Richardson c Lili'i b Kelly	18	13	10	-	3
N.H.Patel not out	7	24	18	-	-
L.F.Boucher c Perkins b Prasad .	2	7	4	-	-
A.M.Ewart† run out	0	2	0	-	-
M.B.Templeton not out	2	6	3	-	-
C.R.Sarsfield					
L.H.Heaps					
Extras (b 1, lb 2, w 10)	13				
TOTAL (20 overs) (7 wkts) .	**108**	80			

AUCKLAND

	Runs	Mins	Balls	6s	4s
L.R.Down* c Halliday b Heaps ...	5	4	6	-	1
A.M.Peterson c Ewart b Halliday	16	19	16	-	3
K.T.Perkins c Heaps b Halliday	45	50	37	-	6
B.G.Armstrong st Ewart b Sarsfield	2	8	5	-	-
H.R.Huddleston not out	29	43	31	-	3
R.S.M.Lili'i not out	7	17	14	-	-
S.Shahri					
A.N.Kelly					
J.E.I.Prasad					
T.I.Lamb†					
F.C.Jonas					
Extras (lb 1, w 6)	7				
TOTAL (18.1 overs) (4 wkts)	**111**	71			

Bowling	*O*	*M*	*R*	*W*
AUCKLAND				
Huddleston	4	0	21	0
Kelly	4	0	17	2
Peterson	4	0	17	1
Prasad	4	0	32	1
Jonas	4	0	18	2
NORTHERN DISTRICTS				
Patel	3	0	18	0
Heaps	3.1	1	20	1
Halliday	4	0	22	2
Richardson	2	0	12	0
Templeton	4	0	21	0
Sarsfield	1	0	7	1
Boucher	1	0	10	0

Fall of Wickets	***ND***	***A***
1st	22	9
2nd	70	35
3rd	73	44
4th	81	88
5th	94	-
6th	100	-
7th	101	-
8th	-	-
9th	-	-
10th	-	-

CANTERBURY v OTAGO — Super Smash

at Hagley Oval, Christchurch on 30 January, 2021
Toss : Otago. Umpires : J.A.K. Bromley & D.R. Morrow
***Canterbury won by 3 runs.** Points: Canterbury 4, Otago 0*

CANTERBURY

	Runs	Mins	Balls	6s	4s
J.L.Savage b Loe	0	1	1	-	-
N.B.Cox lbw b Black	8	9	4	-	2
K.E.Ebrahim c Carson b Loe	22	47	31	-	2
A.E.Satterthwaite c Oldershaw b Carson	36	44	30	-	5
K.F.G.Nation c Inglis b Oldershaw	13	15	16	-	1
F.L.Mackay* not out	26	32	20	-	4
L.E.V.Hughes† c Oldershaw b Adams	9	12	12	-	2
L.M.M.Tahuhu c Blakely b Oldershaw	3	5	3	-	-
G.E.S.Sullivan run out	6	6	3	-	1
S.R.Asmussen					
K.M.Sims					
Extras (lb 1, w 8)	9				
TOTAL (20 overs) (8 wkts) .	**132**	86			

OTAGO

	Runs	Mins	Balls	6s	4s
I.R.James run out	7	37	18	-	1
P.M.Inglis c Ebrahim b Tahuhu ..	4	11	8	-	-
K.J.Martin*† c Hughes b Savage	42	42	36	-	6
M.R.Cowan st Hughes b Ebrahim	50	40	37	2	5
C.G.Blakely b Savage	0	5	6	-	-
O.N.Gain c Ebrahim b Mackay ...	7	24	12	-	1
G.R.Adams c Satterthwaite b Mackay	1	4	3	-	-
E.J.Carson not out	0	2	0	-	-
E.J.Black					
S.A.Oldershaw					
M.E.Loe					
Extras (lb 7, w 11)	18				
TOTAL (20 overs) (7 wkts) .	**129**	84			

Bowling	*O*	*M*	*R*	*W*
OTAGO				
Loe	4	0	25	2
Black	4	0	36	1
Adams	4	0	20	1
Carson	4	0	30	1
Oldershaw	4	0	20	2
CANTERBURY				
Tahuhu	4	0	10	1
Sims	2	0	22	0
Sullivan	4	0	20	0
Savage	4	0	28	2
Mackay	4	0	23	2
Asmussen	1	0	12	0
Ebrahim	1	0	7	1

Fall of Wickets	***C***	***O***
1st	0	10
2nd	13	47
3rd	73	89
4th	77	91
5th	93	126
6th	114	129
7th	120	129
8th	132	-
9th	-	-
10th	-	-

WELLINGTON v CENTRAL DISTRICTS — Super Smash

at Basin Reserve, Wellington on 31 January, 2021
Toss : Wellington. Umpires : C.M. Brown & T.R. Davies
***Wellington won by 37 runs.** Points: Wellington 4, Central Districts 0*

WELLINGTON

Batsman	Runs	Mins	Balls	6s	4s
S.F.M.Devine c sub (M.S.Rees) b Hansen	88	70	58	-	12
M.L.Green* c Rowe b Atkinson	16	36	22	-	1
A.C.Kerr c Atkinson b Rowe	38	40	29	-	3
L.M.Kasperek not out	6	14	5	-	-
T.M.M.Newton run out	0	1	0	-	-
J.T.McFadyen† run out	10	6	6	-	1
J.M.Kerr					
G.E.Plimmer					
C.R.King					
X.A.R.Jetly					
M.P.Singh					
Extras (w 4)	4				
TOTAL (20 overs) (5 wkts)	**162**	85			

CENTRAL DISTRICTS

Batsman	Runs	Mins	Balls	6s	4s
E.G.Cunningham run out	4	4	6	-	1
G.K.Atkinson c Jetly b Devine	10	19	12	1	1
N.C.Dodd† not out	61	74	55	-	5
A.van Deventer run out	0	4	0	-	-
H.M.Rowe st McFadyen b Kasperek	39	41	38	-	4
C.L.Green st McFadyen b Kerr A.C.	2	4	5	-	-
K.A.Tomlinson run out	4	4	2	-	1
K.L.Gaging not out	2	5	3	-	-
J.M.Watkin*					
A.Kumar					
M.J.Hansen					
Extras (lb 1, w 1, nb 1)	3				
TOTAL (20 overs) (6 wkts)	**125**	78			

Bowling	*O*	*M*	*R*	*W*
CENTRAL DISTRICTS				
Green	4	0	32	0
Rowe	4	0	30	1
Watkin	2	0	17	0
Kumar	2	0	23	0
Hansen	4	0	34	1
Atkinson	4	0	26	1
WELLINGTON				
Singh	2	0	11	0
Kerr J.M.	3	0	23	0
Devine	3	0	22	1
Kasperek	4	0	19	1
Kerr A.C.	4	0	23	1
Newton	2	0	14	0
Green	2	0	12	0

Fall of Wickets	*W*	*CD*
1st	73	4
2nd	135	26
3rd	148	27
4th	149	102
5th	162	105
6th	-	114
7th	-	-
8th	-	-
9th	-	-
10th	-	-

AUCKLAND v OTAGO — Super Smash

at Eden Park Outer Oval, Auckland on 1 February, 2021
Toss : Otago. Umpires : S.J. Kannan & D.J. Walker
***Auckland won by 27 runs.** Points: Auckland 4, Otago 0*

AUCKLAND

Batsman	Runs	Mins	Balls	6s	4s
A.M.Peterson lbw b Carson	31	36	26	-	5
L.R.Down* lbw b Black	0	6	2	-	-
K.T.Perkins b Carson	23	19	17	-	5
B.G.Armstrong b Black	19	27	25	-	2
H.R.Huddleston c Martin b Adams	23	26	17	2	1
S.Shahri b Black	1	3	2	-	-
R.S.M.Lili'i b Oldershaw	3	8	3	-	-
A.N.Kelly c Cowan b Black	9	15	10	-	1
J.E.I.Prasad b Oldershaw	0	1	2	-	-
T.I.Lamb† b Adams	2	7	5	-	-
F.C.Jonas not out	0	1	0	-	-
Extras (lb 4, w 8)	12				
TOTAL (18.1 overs)	**123**	79			

OTAGO

Batsman	Runs	Mins	Balls	6s	4s
I.R.James lbw b Jonas	9	22	15	-	1
P.M.Inglis b Huddleston	1	6	6	-	-
K.J.Martin*† c Lili'i b Jonas	44	60	42	1	3
M.R.Cowan run out	10	22	13	-	-
C.G.Blakely b Armstrong	7	3	5	-	1
O.N.Gain lbw b Peterson	2	5	9	-	-
G.R.Adams c Huddleston b Peterson	7	8	7	-	1
E.J.Carson run out	3	11	6	-	-
E.J.Black b Huddleston	7	12	11	-	-
S.A.Oldershaw b Peterson	1	2	2	-	-
M.E.Loe not out	1	2	2	-	-
Extras (lb 3, w 1)	4				
TOTAL (19.4 overs)	**96**	80			

Bowling	*O*	*M*	*R*	*W*
OTAGO				
Loe	3	0	30	0
Black	3.1	0	14	4
Oldershaw	4	0	21	2
Adams	4	0	32	2
Carson	4	0	22	2
AUCKLAND				
Kelly	3	0	13	0
Huddleston	3.4	1	8	2
Jonas	4	0	21	2
Prasad	3	0	16	0
Peterson	4	0	23	3
Armstrong	2	0	12	1

Fall of Wickets	*A*	*O*
1st	12	7
2nd	49	20
3rd	66	55
4th	88	62
5th	91	65
6th	105	83
7th	108	84
8th	108	92
9th	123	94
10th	123	96

CENTRAL DISTRICTS v CANTERBURY — Super Smash

at McLean Park, Napier on 5 February, 2021
Toss : Canterbury. Umpires : C.M. Brown & G.M. Walklin
***Canterbury won by 30 runs.** Points: Canterbury 4, Central Districts 0*

CANTERBURY

	Runs	Mins	Balls	6s	4s
F.L.Mackay* b Atkinson	46	49	45	-	5
N.B.Cox b Green	16	18	15	2	-
A.E.Satterthwaite run out	36	53	28	1	1
K.E.Ebrahim c Cunningham b Rowe	27	28	26	-	3
K.F.G.Nation run out	3	9	3	-	-
L.M.M.Tahuhu not out	4	3	3	-	-
E.K.Kench					
L.E.V.Hughes†					
G.E.S.Sullivan					
S.R.Asmussen					
M.J.Banks					
Extras (b 1, lb 2, w 2)	5				
TOTAL (20 overs) (5 wkts)	**137**	81			

CENTRAL DISTRICTS

	Runs	Mins	Balls	6s	4s
E.G.Cunningham c Hughes b Satterthwaite	25	32	30	1	1
G.K.Atkinson c Cox b Tahuhu	4	6	5	-	1
N.C.Dodd† lbw b Asmussen	7	19	12	-	1
A.van Deventer c Satterthwaite b Mackay	29	30	27	-	2
H.M.Rowe* c Ebrahim b Tahuhu	26	31	22	-	2
K.A.Tomlinson b Banks	2	5	4	-	-
G.Sims c Satterthwaite b Sullivan	2	7	5	-	-
C.L.Green b Mackay	6	9	6	-	1
M.J.Hansen b Sullivan	0	1	1	-	-
M.S.Rees b Sullivan	0	1	2	-	-
A.Kumar not out	3	3	3	-	-
Extras (w 3)	3				
TOTAL (19.4 overs)	**107**	73			

Bowling	O	M	R	W
CENTRAL DISTRICTS				
Kumar	3	0	26	0
Green	4	0	18	1
Rowe	4	0	26	1
Atkinson	4	0	25	1
Hansen	2	0	15	0
Rees	3	0	24	0
CANTERBURY				
Mackay	3.4	0	18	2
Tahuhu	4	0	13	2
Banks	3	0	18	1
Sullivan	3	0	26	3
Asmussen	4	0	21	1
Satterthwaite	2	0	11	1

Fall of Wickets	***C***	***CD***
1st	34	6
2nd	85	36
3rd	118	42
4th	132	91
5th	137	96
6th	-	98
7th	-	102
8th	-	103
9th	-	103
10th	-	107

OTAGO v NORTHERN DISTRICTS — Super Smash

at University of Otago Oval, Dunedin on 6 February, 2021
Toss : Northern Districts. Umpires : P.J. Pasco & D.J. Walker
***Otago won by 42 runs.** Points: Otago 4, Northern Districts 0*

OTAGO

	Runs	Mins	Balls	6s	4s
P.M.Inglis c Boucher b Sarsfield	28	52	32	-	3
H.N.K.Jensen c & b Patel	11	14	11	-	2
K.J.Martin*† lbw b Halliday	85	59	58	2	11
M.R.Cowan b Sarsfield	0	2	1	-	-
C.G.Blakely c Gurrey b Halliday	12	23	13	-	1
I.R.James run out	0	2	2	-	-
E.J.Carson not out	7	6	5	-	1
G.R.Adams not out	2	4	2	-	-
E.J.Black					
S.A.Oldershaw					
M.E.Loe					
Extras (b 1, w 5, nb 2)	8				
TOTAL (20 overs) (6 wkts)	**153**	82			

NORTHERN DISTRICTS

	Runs	Mins	Balls	6s	4s
K.G.Anderson st Martin b Oldershaw	15	31	19	-	1
C.A.Gurrey c Martin b Jensen	17	20	21	-	2
B.M.Halliday* c Blakely b Black	22	36	22	-	3
M.B.Templeton b Carson	31	45	30	-	1
E.A.J.Richardson c Inglis b Carson	11	18	10	1	-
L.F.Boucher c Loe b Black	0	5	3	-	-
G.A.Harris b Carson	1	6	3	-	-
A.M.Ewart† c Blakely b Loe	5	8	6	-	1
C.R.Sarsfield run out	1	5	5	-	-
S.R.Naidu not out	0	1	0	-	-
N.H.Patel not out	2	1	1	-	-
Extras (lb 1, w 5)	6				
TOTAL (20 overs) (9 wkts)	**111**	90			

Bowling	O	M	R	W
NORTHERN DISTRICTS				
Naidu	3	0	16	0
Patel	4	0	17	1
Richardson	3	0	37	0
Halliday	2	0	18	2
Templeton	3	0	23	0
Boucher	1	0	13	0
Sarsfield	4	0	28	2
OTAGO				
Loe	4	0	28	1
Black	4	0	10	2
Adams	2	0	12	0
Jensen	2	0	18	1
Carson	4	1	18	3
Oldershaw	4	0	24	1

Fall of Wickets	***O***	***ND***
1st	21	25
2nd	96	39
3rd	97	77
4th	144	100
5th	144	102
6th	144	102
7th	-	103
8th	-	109
9th	-	109
10th	-	-

AUCKLAND v WELLINGTON — Super Smash

at Eden Park Outer Oval, Auckland on 7 February, 2021
Toss : Auckland. Umpires : L.R. Els & D.R. Morrow
***Auckland won by 7 runs.** Points: Auckland 4, Wellington 0*

AUCKLAND

	Runs	Mins	Balls	6s	4s
L.R.Down* c McFadyen b Kerr J.M.	1	3	3	-	-
A.M.Peterson c Green b Devine	6	8	5	-	1
K.T.Perkins b Kerr A.C.	29	53	40	-	2
B.G.Armstrong c Green b Devine	3	6	5	-	-
H.R.Huddleston b Kerr A.C.	16	27	17	-	2
R.S.M.Lili'i c Green b Jetly	17	18	19	-	2
A.N.Kelly run out	7	18	9	-	-
J.E.I.Prasad not out	18	23	17	-	1
T.I.Lamb† c Kerr A.C. b Kerr J.M.	2	2	2	-	-
M.M.Penfold c & b Devine	1	5	3	-	-
F.C.Jonas b Devine	0	1	1	-	-
Extras (lb 3, w 13, nb 1)	17				
TOTAL (20 overs)	**117**	84			

WELLINGTON

	Runs	Mins	Balls	6s	4s
S.F.M.Devine c Perkins b Peterson	6	11	8	-	-
M.L.Green* c Peterson b Prasad	33	46	34	-	4
A.C.Kerr lbw b Peterson	1	6	2	-	-
R.M.Burns c Lamb b Kelly	2	12	6	-	-
T.M.M.Newton run out	16	24	15	-	1
J.T.McFadyen† run out	14	27	17	-	-
J.M.Kerr c Kelly b Prasad	6	7	10	-	1
G.E.Plimmer c Lamb b Huddleston	0	3	1	-	-
X.A.R.Jetly b Huddleston	0	1	2	-	-
C.R.King not out	13	16	15	-	1
M.P.Singh run out	6	9	4	-	1
Extras (b 2, lb 1, w 10)	13				
TOTAL (19 overs)	**110**	83			

Bowling	*O*	*M*	*R*	*W*
WELLINGTON				
Kerr J.M.	4	0	25	2
Devine	4	0	21	4
Green	2	0	16	0
Singh	2	0	7	0
Newton	1	0	6	0
Kerr A.C.	4	0	20	2
Jetly	3	0	19	1
AUCKLAND				
Kelly	2	0	16	1
Huddleston	3	0	24	2
Peterson	4	0	12	2
Penfold	2	0	15	0
Jonas	4	0	16	0
Prasad	4	0	24	2

Fall of Wickets	***A***	***W***
1st	6	24
2nd	11	31
3rd	16	45
4th	59	65
5th	85	79
6th	91	87
7th	108	87
8th	111	87
9th	117	94
10th	117	110

AUCKLAND v WELLINGTON — Elimination Final

at Eden Park Outer Oval, Auckland on 11 February, 2021
Toss : Wellington. Umpires : C.A. Black & E.D. Sanders
Wellington won by 35 runs

WELLINGTON

	Runs	Mins	Balls	6s	4s
S.F.M.Devine lbw b Jonas	33	28	29	-	5
M.L.Green* st Lamb b Jonas	32	52	29	-	3
A.C.Kerr not out	54	58	44	-	6
R.M.Burns c Down b Peterson	8	7	8	-	1
J.M.Kerr run out	0	2	0	-	-
T.M.M.Newton b Huddleston	11	17	9	-	1
J.T.McFadyen† run out	2	3	2	-	-
C.R.King not out	0	1	0	-	-
G.E.Plimmer					
X.A.R.Jetly					
M.P.Singh					
Extras (lb 6, w 3, nb 1)	10				
TOTAL (20 overs) (6 wkts)	**150**	87			

AUCKLAND

	Runs	Mins	Balls	6s	4s
A.M.Peterson b Devine	0	1	1	-	-
L.R.Down* c Green b Singh	13	15	11	-	3
K.T.Perkins run out	46	69	57	-	3
B.G.Armstrong c Kerr J.M. b Green	33	36	27	-	4
H.R.Huddleston c McFadyen b Kerr A.C.	6	16	9	-	-
A.N.Kelly st McFadyen b Kerr J.M.	3	10	5	-	-
M.M.Penfold c Devine b Kerr A.C.	0	1	2	-	-
R.S.M.Lili'i not out	7	8	7	-	-
J.E.I.Prasad not out	1	1	1	-	-
T.I.Lamb†					
F.C.Jonas					
Extras (b 1, lb 1, w 4)	6				
TOTAL (20 overs) (7 wkts)	**115**	79			

Bowling	*O*	*M*	*R*	*W*
AUCKLAND				
Kelly	4	0	18	0
Huddleston	3	0	29	1
Penfold	2	0	14	0
Peterson	4	0	33	1
Jonas	4	0	23	2
Prasad	3	0	27	0
WELLINGTON				
Devine	4	0	16	1
Kerr J.M.	4	0	29	1
Singh	4	0	21	1
Kerr A.C.	4	0	16	2
Green	2	0	18	1
Newton	2	0	13	0

Fall of Wickets	***W***	***A***
1st	52	0
2nd	94	18
3rd	103	83
4th	104	103
5th	145	103
6th	149	103
7th	-	113
8th	-	-
9th	-	-
10th	-	-

WELLINGTON v CANTERBURY — Final

at Basin Reserve, Wellington on 13 February, 2021
Toss : Canterbury. Umpires : B.F. Bowden & K.D. Cotton
Canterbury won by 4 wickets

WELLINGTON

	Runs	Mins	Balls	6s	4s
S.F.M.Devine b Banks	47	57	45	-	4
M.L.Green* c Sullivan b Mackay	22	36	22	-	3
A.C.Kerr run out	31	39	25	-	3
L.M.Kasperek st Hughes b Satterthwaite	2	7	5	-	-
R.M.Burns lbw b Satterthwaite	0	1	1	-	-
T.M.M.Newton run out	0	5	3	-	-
J.T.McFadyen† not out	8	17	11	-	-
J.M.Kerr c Hughes b Satterthwaite	0	3	1	-	-
C.R.King run out	4	11	7	-	-
G.E.Plimmer					
M.P.Singh					
Extras (lb 2, w 9)	11				
TOTAL (20 overs) (8 wkts)	**125**	90			

CANTERBURY

	Runs	Mins	Balls	6s	4s
F.L.Mackay* b Kerr A.C.	24	45	30	-	4
N.B.Cox run out	3	10	9	-	-
A.E.Satterthwaite c Green b Kerr J.M.	0	10	5	-	-
K.E.Ebrahim not out	45	69	40	-	4
K.F.G.Nation b Kerr A.C.	0	1	1	-	-
E.K.Kench b Kerr A.C.	0	1	1	-	-
M.J.Banks c Devine b Singh	3	14	12	-	-
L.M.M.Tahuhu not out	38	27	20	3	1
L.E.V.Hughes†					
G.E.S.Sullivan					
S.R.Asmussen					
Extras (b 4, lb 2, w 7)	13				
TOTAL (19.4 overs) (6 wkts)	**126**	90			

Bowling	O	M	R	W
CANTERBURY				
Tahuhu	4	0	21	0
Banks	2	0	18	1
Sullivan	4	0	31	0
Mackay	4	0	17	1
Asmussen	1	0	11	0
Ebrahim	1	0	12	0
Satterthwaite	4	0	13	3
WELLINGTON				
Devine	4	0	20	0
Kerr J.M.	4	1	32	1
Singh	3	0	17	1
Kerr A.C.	4	0	19	3
Kasperek	3.4	0	20	0
Newton	1	0	12	0

Fall of Wickets

	W	C
1st	62	14
2nd	100	18
3rd	106	40
4th	106	40
5th	111	40
6th	114	60
7th	114	-
8th	125	-
9th	-	-
10th	-	-

A.C.Kerr took a hat-trick when she dismissed Mackay, Nation and Kench

2020/21 DREAM11 SUPER SMASH AVERAGES

	M	In	NO	HS	Runs	Ave	100s	50s	Ct	St	O	M	R	W	Ave	R/O	Best
G.R.Adams	9	6	1	8	20	4.00	-	-	-	-	28	0	188	4	47.00	6.71	2-32
K.G.Anderson	10	10	0	50	203	20.30	-	1	5	-							
B.G.Armstrong	11	10	2	39	149	18.62	-	-	1	-	13.3	0	119	3	39.66	8.81	1-12
S.R.Asmussen	7	1	0	1	1	1.00	-	-	-	-	17	0	116	5	23.20	6.82	2-21
G.K.Atkinson	10	8	0	21	51	6.37	-	-	2	-	16	0	124	3	41.33	7.75	1-19
M.J.Banks	8	2	0	3	4	2.00	-	-	1	-	6	0	38	3	12.66	6.33	1-2
O.J.S.Bartlett	1	-	-	-	-	-	-	-	-	-							
E.J.Black	10	5	0	10	20	4.00	-	-	1	-	33.2	1	252	12	21.00	7.56	4-14
C.G.Blakely	10	10	3	32*	107	15.28	-	-	5	-	1	0	11	0	-	11.00	-
L.F.Boucher	7	7	0	13	27	3.85	-	-	4	-	10	0	95	3	31.66	9.50	3-21
R.M.Burns	9	8	0	42	96	12.00	-	-	6	-							
S.J.Carnachan	5	1	1	5*	5	-	-	-	-	2							
E.J.Carson	10	6	2	10	25	6.25	-	-	1	-	30	1	218	9	24.22	7.27	3-18
M.R.Cowan	10	10	0	50	142	14.20	-	1	4	-							
N.B.Cox	11	11	2	48*	157	17.44	-	-	4	-							
E.G.Cunningham	8	8	0	25	68	8.50	-	-	1	-	1.4	0	10	0	-	6.00	-
S.F.M.Devine	8	8	1	108*	434	62.00	1	3	5	-	16	0	85	6	14.16	5.31	4-21
N.C.Dodd	10	10	3	61*	301	43.00	-	1	4	2							
D.M.Doughty	1	-	-	-	-	-	-	-	-	-	2	0	13	0	-	6.50	-
L.R.Down	11	10	1	63*	138	15.33	-	1	5	-							
K.E.Ebrahim	11	9	5	84*	292	73.00	-	1	4	-	8	0	73	1	73.00	9.13	1-7
A.M.Ewart	7	5	0	8	14	2.80	-	-	1	3							
A.M.Gaging	1	-	-	-	-	-	-	-	1	-	1	0	6	0	-	6.00	-
K.L.Gaging	4	3	1	28	39	19.50	-	-	1	-							
O.N.Gain	5	4	0	7	15	3.75	-	-	1	-							
C.L.Green	10	5	3	6	14	7.00	-	-	-	-	26	0	154	5	30.80	5.92	1-6
M.L.Green	12	12	3	33	264	29.33	-	-	7	-	23.3	0	161	9	17.88	6.85	4-9
M.J.Greig	4	3	0	18	31	10.33	-	-	2	-	6	0	50	1	50.00	8.33	1-16
C.A.Gurrey	10	10	2	57	246	30.75	-	1	2	-							
B.M.Halliday	10	10	1	37	175	19.44	-	-	4	-	27	0	190	9	21.11	7.04	2-18
M.J.Hansen	9	5	2	9*	24	8.00	-	-	-	-	17.2	0	124	3	41.33	7.16	1-3
G.A.Harris	1	1	0	1	1	1.00	-	-	-	-							
K.J.Havill	4	1	0	2	2	2.00	-	-	2	-	7	0	52	1	52.00	7.43	1-25
L.H.Heaps	9	2	1	3*	6	6.00	-	-	4	-	24.3	1	167	5	33.40	6.82	1-9
B.J.Herath	1	1	0	2	2	2.00	-	-	-	-	4	0	36	1	36.00	9.00	1-36
H.R.Huddleston	11	8	3	37*	158	31.60	-	-	5	-	33.4	2	193	16	12.06	5.73	3-8
L.E.V.Hughes	11	3	0	9	14	4.66	-	-	5	5							
M.N.Hyde	4	3	3	7*	16	-	-	-	1	-							
P.M.Inglis	10	10	1	62	217	24.11	-	1	3	-							
I.R.James	10	8	2	24	51	8.50	-	-	1	-							
H.N.K.Jensen	7	7	0	35	125	17.85	-	-	-	-	19	0	153	4	38.25	8.05	2-22
X.A.R.Jetly	10	3	2	1*	1	1.00	-	-	5	-	11	0	73	6	12.16	6.64	4-9
F.C.Jonas	10	3	2	5*	5	5.00	-	-	-	-	34	0	187	8	23.37	5.50	2-18
L.M.Kasperek	8	6	3	39	104	34.66	-	-	2	-	27	0	150	13	11.53	5.56	4-16
A.N.Kelly	11	4	0	9	23	5.75	-	-	3	-	33.5	2	188	12	15.66	5.56	4-28
E.K.Kench	4	2	0	0	0	0.00	-	-	-	1							
A.C.Kerr	12	11	4	66	361	51.57	-	4	3	-	44	0	213	14	15.21	4.84	3-11
J.M.Kerr	12	7	3	14*	35	8.75	-	-	5	-	44	1	255	12	21.25	5.80	2-15
C.R.King	10	5	2	13*	17	5.66	-	-	-	-							
A.Kumar	4	1	1	3*	3	-	-	-	-	-	10	0	84	1	84.00	8.40	1-23
T.I.Lamb	6	2	0	2	4	2.00	-	-	2	2							
M.B.Lamplough	2	-	-	-	-	-	-	-	-	-	1	0	20	0	-	20.00	-
F.C.Leydon-Davis	8	7	1	42	97	16.16	-	-	2	-	17	0	130	5	26.00	7.65	2-23
R.S.M.Lili'i	11	7	4	17*	62	20.66	-	-	5	-							
O.R.Lobb	3	-	-	-	-	-	-	-	1	-							
M.E.Loe	7	4	4	1*	2	-	-	-	1	-	25	0	197	4	49.25	7.88	2-25
F.L.Mackay	11	11	2	48	208	23.11	-	-	2	-	39.4	0	191	20	9.55	4.82	4-10
R.A.Mair	4	3	0	12	25	8.33	-	-	-	-	12	1	82	1	82.00	6.83	1-24
K.J.Martin	10	10	1	85	265	29.44	-	1	2	4							
N.Matthews	2	2	0	1	1	0.50	-	-	-	-							
J.T.McFadyen	12	8	1	14	53	7.57	-	-	8	7							
R.H.McNeill	1	-	-	-	-	-	-	-	-	-	4	0	27	0	-	6.75	-
B.C.Molony	3	-	-	-	-	-	-	-	-	-	2	0	12	0	-	6.00	-
S.R.Naidu	1	1	1	0*	0	-	-	-	-	-	3	0	16	0	-	5.33	-
K.F.G.Nation	11	7	2	21*	56	11.20	-	-	-	-							
T.M.M.Newton	12	9	1	22	84	10.50	-	-	6	-	26.3	0	187	7	26.71	7.06	3-14

	M	In	NO	HS	Runs	Ave	100s	50s	Ct	St	O	M	R	W	Ave	R/O	Best
S.A.Oldershaw	9	3	0	6	7	2.33	-	-	2	-	31	0	189	10	18.90	6.10	2-20
N.H.Patel	10	8	4	25	76	19.00	-	-	1	-	27	0	143	8	17.87	5.30	3-19
M.M.Penfold	3	2	0	1	1	0.50	-	-	-	-	5	0	41	0	-	8.20	-
K.T.Perkins	11	10	1	52*	290	32.22	-	1	7	-							
A.M.Peterson	10	9	0	68	171	19.00	-	1	2	-	31	1	167	9	18.55	5.39	3-23
G.E.Plimmer	11	2	0	4	4	2.00	-	-	-	-							
J.E.I.Prasad	11	4	2	18*	23	11.50	-	-	3	-	31.4	0	220	11	20.00	6.95	3-19
M.S.Rees	8	5	2	4*	10	3.33	-	-	-	-	11.1	0	101	1	101.00	9.05	1-13
E.A.J.Richardson	10	9	1	30	117	14.62	-	-	1	-	26.4	0	204	5	40.80	7.65	3-27
A.J.Rout	5	2	1	9*	16	16.00	-	-	-	-							
H.M.Rowe	10	8	1	44	156	22.28	-	-	2	-	30.5	1	228	6	38.00	7.40	2-26
C.R.Sarsfield	10	4	3	3*	7	7.00	-	-	2	-	26	1	181	5	36.20	6.96	2-28
A.E.Satterthwaite	11	10	3	71*	364	52.00	-	3	8	-	23	0	141	8	17.62	6.13	3-13
J.L.Savage	8	5	0	8	23	4.60	-	-	1	-	20	0	161	5	32.20	8.05	2-28
S.Shahri	9	6	2	30*	100	25.00	-	-	1	-							
G.Sims	1	1	0	2	2	2.00	-	-	-	-							
K.M.Sims	4	1	1	0*	0	-	-	-	-	-	9	1	61	2	30.50	6.78	1-5
M.P.Singh	12	1	0	6	6	6.00	-	-	1	-	37	1	179	6	29.83	4.84	2-13
G.E.S.Sullivan	11	3	1	11	18	9.00	-	-	5	-	34.1	0	198	9	22.00	5.80	3-19
L.M.M.Tahuhu	9	4	2	38*	54	27.00	-	-	-	-	28	0	130	8	16.25	4.64	3-11
M.B.Templeton	3	2	1	31	33	33.00	-	-	-	-	10.3	0	59	2	29.50	5.62	2-15
K.A.Tomlinson	8	5	1	20	33	8.25	-	-	-	-							
A.van Deventer	9	8	2	63*	174	29.00	-	1	1	-							
J.M.Watkin	9	8	1	68*	132	18.85	-	1	1	-	27.2	0	186	7	26.57	6.81	2-17

HIGHEST STRIKE RATES *(qualification 100 runs)*

		Runs	Balls	S/R
S.F.M.Devine	*W*	434	263	165
A.C.Kerr	*W*	361	268	134
A.M.Peterson	*A*	171	129	132
A.E.Satterthwaite	*C*	364	276	131
H.N.K.Jensen	*O*	125	99	126
A.van Deventer	*CD*	174	148	117
K.J.Martin	*O*	265	227	116
E.A.J.Richardson	*ND*	117	101	115
J.M.Watkin	*CD*	132	122	108
L.M.Kasperek	*W*	104	97	107

MOST ECONOMICAL BOWLING *(qualification 20 overs)*

		O	M	R	W	Ave	R/O
L.M.M.Tahuhu	*C*	28	0	130	8	16.25	4.64
F.L.Mackay	*C*	39.4	0	191	20	9.55	4.82
M.P.Singh	*W*	37	1	179	6	29.83	4.84
A.C.Kerr	*W*	44	0	213	14	15.21	4.84
N.H.Patel	*ND*	27	0	143	8	17.87	5.30
A.M.Peterson	*A*	31	1	167	9	18.55	5.39
F.C.Jonas	*A*	34	0	187	8	23.37	5.50
L.M.Kasperek	*W*	27	0	150	13	11.53	5.56
A.N.Kelly	*A*	33.5	2	188	12	15.66	5.56
H.R.Huddleston	*A*	33.4	2	193	16	12.06	5.73

CAREER RECORDS

	M	In	NO	HS	Runs	Ave	100s	50s	Ct	St	O	M	R	W	Ave	R/O	Best
G.R.Adams	9	6	1	8	20	4.00	-	-	-	-	28	0	188	4	47.00	6.71	2-32
K.G.Anderson	52	43	4	50	517	13.25	-	1	16	-	75	0	514	19	27.05	6.85	3-22
B.G.Armstrong	41	29	9	39	256	12.80	-	-	10	-	119.3	1	756	31	24.38	6.33	3-18
S.R.Asmussen	15	4	1	2*	4	1.33	-	-	-	-	27	0	219	6	36.50	8.11	2-21
G.K.Atkinson	30	16	3	21	84	6.46	-	-	3	-	42	0	316	9	35.11	7.52	2-20
M.J.Banks	30	9	4	8*	28	5.60	-	-	8	-	40.1	0	295	13	22.69	7.34	2-21
O.J.S.Bartlett	1	-	-	-	-	-	-	-	-	-							
E.J.Black	33	12	3	13*	41	4.55	-	-	6	-	98.1	1	697	32	21.78	7.10	4-14
C.G.Blakely	39	30	10	32*	209	10.45	-	-	9	-	4.3	0	33	2	16.50	7.33	1-1
L.F.Boucher	12	12	1	41*	96	8.72	-	-	4	-	13	0	123	3	41.00	9.46	3-21
R.M.Burns	54	46	4	62	608	14.47	-	2	22	-	15	0	100	4	25.00	6.67	2-22
S.J.Carnachan	19	5	1	5*	12	3.00	-	-	1	10							
E.J.Carson	25	14	7	17*	49	7.00	-	-	1	-	68.4	1	486	23	21.13	7.08	5-18
M.R.Cowan	52	45	4	61	564	13.75	-	4	16	-	30	0	210	9	23.33	7.00	2-17
N.B.Cox	48	34	8	48*	334	12.84	-	-	11	-							
E.G.Cunningham	27	27	0	45	301	11.14	-	-	5	-	1.4	0	10	0	-	6.00	-
S.F.M.Devine	71	68	16	112	2491	47.90	3	15	33	-	200	3	1221	62	19.69	6.11	4-21
N.C.Dodd	89	81	14	70*	1633	24.37	-	5	30	6	11	0	65	6	10.83	5.91	3-16
D.M.Doughty	64	4	2	6	6	3.00	-	-	6	-	224.4	4	1167	67	17.41	5.19	4-13
L.R.Down	59	48	7	92*	739	18.02	-	2	18	-	31.2	0	220	9	24.44	7.02	2-17
K.E.Ebrahim	86	70	22	84*	1487	30.97	-	6	15	-	245.4	6	1374	51	26.94	5.59	3-8
A.M.Ewart	7	5	0	8	14	2.80	-	-	1	3							
A.M.Gaging	1	-	-	-	-	-	-	-	1	-	1	0	6	0	-	6.00	-
K.L.Gaging	4	3	1	28	39	19.50	-	-	1	-							
O.N.Gain	5	4	0	7	15	3.75	-	-	1	-							
C.L.Green	25	12	8	6	26	6.50	-	-	2	-	64.2	0	394	9	43.77	6.09	1-6
M.L.Green	83	77	17	74	1427	23.78	-	5	32	-	43.3	0	314	15	20.93	7.22	4-9
M.J.Greig	40	30	7	39*	238	10.34	-	-	6	-	79.2	0	596	19	31.36	7.51	3-33
C.A.Gurrey	50	48	6	106*	1338	31.85	1	9	6	-							
B.M.Halliday	46	37	8	43	452	15.58	-	-	11	-	49	0	346	15	23.06	7.06	2-3
M.J.Hansen	43	30	14	31*	148	9.25	-	-	6	-	66.3	0	480	8	60.00	7.22	2-15
G.A.Harris	1	1	0	1	1	1.00	-	-	-	-							
K.J.Havill	4	1	0	2	2	2.00	-	-	2	-	7	0	52	1	52.00	7.43	1-25
L.H.Heaps	18	3	2	3*	7	7.00	-	-	5	-	45.3	1	327	13	25.15	7.19	3-32
B.J.Herath	4	2	1	3*	5	5.00	-	-	-	-	9	0	71	2	35.50	7.89	1-18
H.R.Huddleston	91	62	19	55*	827	19.23	-	1	22	-	246.2	12	1405	58	24.22	5.70	3-8
L.E.V.Hughes	43	14	0	16	105	7.50	-	-	18	12							
M.N.Hyde	29	7	4	9	32	10.66	-	-	8	-	53	0	421	7	60.14	7.94	2-14
P.M.Inglis	45	39	7	62	501	15.65	-	1	11	-							
I.R.James	31	19	4	24	134	8.93	-	-	10	-							
H.N.K.Jensen	59	40	8	55	562	17.56	-	1	8	-	158.2	4	963	36	26.75	6.08	3-14
X.A.R.Jetly	13	3	2	1*	1	1.00	-	-	5	-	16	0	90	7	12.85	5.63	4-9
F.C.Jonas	19	3	2	5*	5	5.00	-	-	1	-	64.2	0	388	14	27.71	6.03	2-18
L.M.Kasperek	58	47	13	54*	691	20.32	-	1	13	-	197.3	0	1144	66	17.33	5.70	4-16
A.N.Kelly	57	29	9	41*	223	11.15	-	-	7	-	194.5	6	1120	50	22.40	5.75	4-28
E.K.Kench	9	5	2	11	19	6.33	-	-	-	1							
A.C.Kerr	56	40	15	66	907	36.28	-	5	11	-	206.4	2	1084	79	13.72	5.25	4-4
J.M.Kerr	45	19	7	20*	138	11.50	-	-	12	-	136	2	783	44	17.79	5.76	4-13
C.R.King	21	8	4	13*	25	6.25	-	-	3	-							
A.Kumar	5	1	1	3*	3	-	-	-	2	-	10	0	84	1	84.00	8.40	1-23
T.I.Lamb	10	2	0	2	4	2.00	-	-	3	2							
M.B.Lamplough	6	-	-	-	-	-	-	-	-	-	6	0	46	0	-	7.67	-
F.C.Leydon-Davis	72	58	13	54	723	16.06	-	1	25	-	185.4	4	1363	32	42.59	7.34	3-21
R.S.M.Lili'i	69	38	17	36	263	12.52	-	-	24	-	108.3	1	733	24	30.54	6.76	3-26
O.R.Lobb	15	8	6	33	69	34.50	-	-	5	1							
M.E.Loe	7	4	4	1*	2	-	-	-	1	-	25	0	197	4	49.25	7.88	2-25
F.L.Mackay	94	87	20	97	2337	34.88	-	13	25	-	326.2	8	1683	97	17.35	5.16	4-10
R.A.Mair	38	27	9	36*	206	11.44	-	-	-	-	108.2	6	620	25	24.80	5.72	2-6
K.J.Martin	91	91	9	94	2338	28.51	-	17	34	27							
N.Matthews	2	2	0	1	1	0.50	-	-	-	-							
J.T.McFadyen	38	20	4	28	173	10.81	-	-	13	18							
R.H.McNeill	38	3	3	1*	2	-	-	-	3	-	109.3	1	689	14	49.21	6.29	2-12
B.C.Molony	13	1	0	3	3	3.00	-	-	-	-	7	0	54	0	-	7.71	-
S.R.Naidu	3	1	1	0*	0	-	-	-	-	-	5	0	37	0	-	7.40	-
K.F.G.Nation	46	34	4	91	451	15.03	-	1	8	-							

	M	In	NO	HS	Runs	Ave	100s	50s	Ct	St	O	M	R	W	Ave	R/O	Best
T.M.M.Newton	66	38	14	50*	327	13.62	-	1	22	-	99.2	1	699	24	29.12	7.04	3-13
S.A.Oldershaw	19	4	1	6	7	2.33	-	-	2	-	40.3	0	263	12	21.91	6.49	2-20
N.H.Patel	19	9	4	25	77	15.40	-	-	1	-	44.1	0	254	17	14.94	5.75	4-19
M.M.Penfold	3	2	0	1	1	0.50	-	-	-	-	5	0	41	0	-	8.20	-
K.T.Perkins	92	82	24	75*	1894	32.65	-	8	33	-							
A.M.Peterson	85	80	9	68	1324	18.64	-	4	24	-	231.3	4	1441	72	20.01	6.22	4-11
G.E.Plimmer	11	2	0	4	4	2.00	-	-	-	-							
J.E.I.Prasad	16	4	2	18*	23	11.50	-	-	3	-	31.4	0	220	11	20.00	6.95	3-19
M.S.Rees	18	9	3	7	17	2.83	-	-	3	-	21.1	0	201	4	50.25	9.50	2-40
E.A.J.Richardson	77	58	13	54*	611	13.57	-	1	14	-	229.3	5	1404	59	23.79	6.12	5-17
A.J.Rout	29	6	3	9*	27	9.00	-	-	5	-	41.2	0	260	12	21.66	6.29	3-15
H.M.Rowe	62	50	12	45	579	15.23	-	-	17	-	194.4	4	1351	39	34.64	6.94	3-27
C.R.Sarsfield	20	8	5	3*	11	3.66	-	-	3	-	48	1	372	14	26.57	7.75	3-19
A.E.Satterthwaite	83	79	17	80*	2236	36.06	-	14	38	-	187	1	1154	56	20.60	6.17	4-14
J.L.Savage	57	24	5	42	221	11.63	-	-	11	6	92.1	0	621	30	20.70	6.74	4-26
S.Shahri	27	20	5	40*	256	17.06	-	-	2	-							
G.Sims	1	1	0	2	2	2.00	-	-	-	-							
K.M.Sims	6	2	1	0*	0	0.00	-	-	-	-	10	1	72	2	36.00	7.20	1-5
M.P.Singh	46	5	4	6	13	13.00	-	-	4	-	139.4	5	781	34	22.97	5.59	4-26
G.E.S.Sullivan	36	11	5	11	34	5.66	-	-	11	-	88.1	1	594	30	19.80	6.74	3-19
L.M.M.Tahuhu	67	33	17	38*	242	15.12	-	-	11	-	206.4	7	1175	52	22.59	5.69	3-6
M.B.Templeton	3	2	1	31	33	33.00	-	-	-	-	10.3	0	59	2	29.50	5.62	2-15
K.A.Tomlinson	75	63	5	47	743	12.81	-	-	17	5	12	0	95	6	15.83	7.92	3-11
A.van Deventer	56	52	6	63*	738	16.04	-	1	9	-	1	0	7	0	-	7.00	-
J.M.Watkin	53	50	4	95	967	21.02	-	5	8	-	165.4	4	1041	35	29.74	6.28	4-22

NEW ZEALAND FIRST-CLASS RECORDS

to 1 July, 2021

FIRST-CLASS MATCH DEFINED

The six countries represented at Imperial Cricket Conference on 19 May 1947 reached agreement in regard to definition of a first-class match. This did not have effect retrospectively.

A match of three or more days' duration between two sides of eleven players officially adjudged first-class shall be regarded as a first-class fixture. Matches in which either team has more than eleven players or which are scheduled for less than three days shall not be regarded as first-class. The governing body in each country shall decide the status of teams.

The records have been compiled on the following basis:

(1) Otago and Canterbury from 1863/64 to date
(2) Wellington and Auckland from 1873/74 to date
(3) Nelson from 1873/74 to 1891/92 inclusive
(4) West Coast (North Island) 1879/80
(5) Taranaki from 1882/83 to 1897/98 inclusive
(6) Hawke's Bay from 1883/84 to 1920/21 inclusive
(7) Southland from 1914/15 to 1920/21 inclusive
(8) Central Districts from 1950/51 to date
(9) Northern Districts from 1956/57 to date

Notes:

- Games played by the Melbourne Cricket Club teams of 1899/1900, 1905/1906 and 1926/27, are not treated as first-class in accordance with a decision of the New Zealand Cricket Council.
- Although set down for only two days each, the return matches played by A. Sims' Australian XI in 1913/14 against Canterbury and Wellington are included in these records; so is the match An Australian XI v Minor Associations, 1920/21, and MCC v Wellington, 1932/33.
- From 1933/34 season onwards, only games for which at least three days have been set down are treated as first-class.
- There have now been 2501 first-class matches in New Zealand.
- Unless otherwise stated, the first-class records relate to first-class matches in New Zealand and by New Zealand touring teams overseas. Apart from the games which have taken place in New Zealand, there are a further 631 played by New Zealand overseas as follows:

in Australia	1898/99 to 2019/20	96
in England	1927 to 2021	311
in South Africa	1953/54 to 2016/17	59
in Pakistan	1955/56 to 2001/02	33
in India	1955/56 to 2016/17	52
in West Indies	1971/72 to 2014	32
in Sri Lanka	1983/84 to 2019/20	24
in Zimbabwe	1992/93 to 2016/17	15
in Bangladesh	2004/05 to 2013/14	6
in United Arab Emirates	2014/15 to 2018/19	6

plus four games by Young New Zealand in Zimbabwe in 1984/85, three games by New Zealand Young Internationals in Zimbabwe 1988/89, one match by Wellington in Australia 1990/91, one match by Canterbury in South Africa 1993/94, three matches by New Zealand Academy in South Africa 1997/98, seven games by New Zealand A in England 2000 and 2014, three matches by New Zealand A in South Africa in 2004/05, five matches by New Zealand A in Sri Lanka in 2005/06 and 2013/14, one match by New Zealand White in Australia 2006/07, six matches by New Zealand A in India in 2008/09, 2013/14 and 2017/18, three games by New Zealand A in Zimbabwe in 2010/11 and two games by New Zealand A in United Arab Emirates in 2018/19.

GROUNDS

Ground	No of matches	First and most recent match		Highest and lowest team totals				Highest Innings Best Bowling			
South Dunedin	9	O v C	1863/64	C	272	v O	1875/76	75	H.W. Moore	C v O	1877/78
Recreation Ground		O v C	1877/78	MCC	34	v O	1863/64	8-28	W. Hendley	O v C	1869/70
Hagley Park *(old)*	1	C v O	1864/65	C	80	v O	1864/65	22	J. Fulton	O v C	1864/65
Christchurch		only match		O	61	v C	1864/65	5-17	J.W. Stevens	C v O	1864/65
Hagley Park *(new)* *	67	C v O	1866/67	NZ	659-6d	v P	2020/21	301*	P.G. Fulton	C v A	2002/03
Christchurch		C v O	2020/21	C	25	v O	1866/67	10-28	A.E. Moss	C v W	1889/90
Basin Reserve	453	W v A	1873/74	NZ	680-8d	v I	2013/14	327*	D.P. Conway	W v C	2019/20
Wellington		W v ND	2020/21	W	22	v C	1903/04	9-43	T. Eden	N v W	1875/76
Victory Square	7	N v W	1874/75	N	150	v A	1882/83	31	C.A. Knapp	W v N	1874/75
Nelson		N v W	1887/88	W	19	v N	1885/86	8-26	F.H. Cooke	N v W	1887/88
Domain	33	A v C	1877/78	A	579	v O	1909/10	151*	Harold B. Lusk	C v A	1910/11
Auckland		A v C	1912/13	A	13	v C	1877/78	9-75	R. Neill	A v C	1891/92
Caledonian Ground	4	O v C	1879/80	O	297	v W	1904/05	88	H.G. Seideberg	O v W	1904/05
Dunedin		O v W	1904/05	A	48	v O	1889/90	8-36	A.W. Rees	A v O	1889/90
Lancaster Park §	334	C v A	1882/83	C	777	v O	1996/97	385	B. Sutcliffe	O v C	1952/53
Christchurch		NZ v SL	2006/07	O	35	v A	1884/85	9-72	F.H. Cooke	O v C	1884/85
Botanical Gardens	1	N v W	1883/84	N	56	v W	1883/84	17	L. Fowler	N v W	1883/84
Nelson		only match		W	30	v N	1883/84	5-10	G. Fowler	N v W	1883/84
Carisbrook	252	O v Tas	1883/84	NSW	752-8d	v O	1923/24	355	B. Sutcliffe	O v A	1949/50
Dunedin		O v C	2007/08	C	27	v O	1896/97	9-50	A.H. Fisher	O v Q'ld	1896/97
Recreation Ground	20½	HB v W	1884/85	MCC	394	v HB	1906/07	188	C.G. Wilson	O v HB	1908/09
Napier		HB v A	1912/13	HB	42	v C	1897/98	9-47	T.H. Dent	HB v W	1900/01
Farndon Park	4½	HB v T	1891/92	Q'ld	492	v HB	1896/97	135	O.W. Cowley	Q'ld v HB	1896/97
Napier		HB v Q'ld	1896/97	T	39	v HB	1891/92	8-14	S.W. Austin	NSW v HB	1893/94
King Edward Park	2	T v HB	1891/92	T	135	v Fiji	1894/95	62	Hugh B. Lusk	HB v T	1891/92
Hawera		T v Fiji	1894/95	T	29	v HB	1891/92	7-?	C.R. Smith	HB v T	1891/92
Bayly Park	2	T v HB	1896/97	C	260	v T	1897/98	106	W.J. Crawshaw	T v HB	1896/97
Hawera		T v C	1897/98	HB	100	v T	1896/97	6-43	D. Reese	C v T	1897/98
Victoria Park	3	A v C	1908/09	A	470	v HB	1910/11	88	W. Carlton	C v A	1909/10
Auckland		A v HB	1910/11	HB	28	v A	1910/11	7-42	A.E. Relf	A v C	1908/09
Nelson Cricket Ground	3	HB v W	1913/14	C	337	v HB	1914/15	111	V.S. Ransford	Aust v HB	1913/14
Hastings		HB v C	1914/15	HB	89	v C	1914/15	8-51	A.A. Mailey	Aust v HB	1913/14
Eden Park	237	A v Aust	1913/14	A	693-9d	v C	1939/40	336*	W.R. Hammond	E v NZ	1932/33
Auckland		NZ v E	2017/18	NZ	26	v E	1954/55	9-36	A.F. Wensley	A v O	1929/30
Rugby Park	5	S v O	1914/15	Aust	195	v S	1920/21	71	A. Galland	O v S	1919/20
Invercargill		S v Aust	1920/21	C	37	v S	1920/21	8-84	D.J. McBeath	S v C	1920/21
Nelson Park	23	HB v W	1919/20	A	668-7d	v CD	2014/15	281	C. Munro	A v CD	2014/15
Napier		CD v ND	2017/18	CD	99	v ND	2017/18	7-48	S.C. Kuggeleijn	ND v CD	2017/18
Wellington College	1	W v A	1923/24	W	569	v A	1923/24	163	J.S. Hiddleston	W v A	1923/24
Ground		only match		A	280	v W	1923/24	6-172	S.G. Smith	A v W	1923/24
Sportsground †	51	CD v C	1950/51	W	590-8d	v CD	2004/05	236	J.D. Ryder	W v CD	2004/05
Palmerston North		CD v W	2007/08	A	71	v CD	2001/02	7-31	H.B. Cave	CD v A	1952/53
Pukekura Park	55	CD v A	1950/51	ND	556-9d	v CD	2014/15	334	D.G. Brownlie	ND v CD	2014/15
New Plymouth		CD v W	2014/15	CD	59	v A	1958/59	9-100	B.W. Yuile	CD v C	1965/66
McLean Park	90	CD v O	1951/52	O	624	v CD	2006/07	265	M.D. Bell	W v CD	2007/08
Napier		CD v C	2020/21	Zim	51	v NZ	2011/12	8-148	T.D. Astle	C v CD	2013/14
Trafalgar Park	28	N v W	1891/92	CD	448-3d	v O	1968/69	202*	B.E. Congdon	CD v O	1968/69
Nelson		CD v ND	1996/97	CD	65	v W	1995/96	7-23	B.A. Bolton	C v CD	1961/62
Cook's Gardens	17	CD v WI	1955/56	MCC	376-7d	v CD	1960/61	138	M.G. Burgess	A v CD	1976/77
Wanganui		CD v YNZ	1979/80	CD	71	v ND	1962/63	8-37	D.B. Clarke	ND v CD	1962/63

§ was Jade Stadium and later AMI Stadium *† now Fitzherbert Park* ** now Hagley Oval*

	Ground	No of matches	First and most recent match		Highest and lowest team totals				Highest Innings Best Bowling			
26	Seddon Park Hamilton	192	ND v A NZ v WI	1956/57 2020/21	NZ ND	715-6d 32	v Ban v A	2018/19 1996/97	251 9-48	K.S. Williamson A.R. Tait	NZ v WI ND v A	2020/21 1996/97
27	Tauranga Domain Tauranga *(Inner)*	1	ND v CD only match	1965/66	CD ND	232 163	v ND v CD	1965/66 1965/66	64 5-41	G.V. Giles B.W. Yuile	ND v CD CD v ND	1965/66 1965/66
28	Tauranga Domain Tauranga *(Outer)*	6	ND v C ND v A	1978/79 1985/86	ND O	370 90	v O v ND	1982/83 1982/83	127 6-75	J.G. Gibson D.A. Stirling	ND v C CD v ND	1978/79 1981/82
29	Cobham Oval Whangarei	11	ND v A ND v C	1966/67 2000/01	ND ND	363 127	v CD v A	1983/84 1966/67	195 7-30	J.M. Parker R.S. Cunis	ND v C A v ND	1972/73 1966/67
30	Queen Elizabeth Park Masterton	12	CD v A CD v W	1966/67 2002/03	CD CD	414-7d 86	v A v A	1998/99 1966/67	189 6-33	M.S. Sinclair A.J. Penn	CD v W W v CD	1996/97 2002/03
31	Smallbone Park Rotorua	17	ND v O ND v CD	1968/69 1995/96	CD A	456 72	v ND v ND	1995/96 1991/92	237* 7-74	R.T. Latham G.D. Alabaster	C v ND O v ND	1990/91 1968/69
32	Cornwall Park Auckland	3	A v U23 A v W	1970/71 2000/01	A A A	274-8d 274-9d 75	v U23 v U23 v W	1970/71 1976/77 2000/01	102 8-75	R.W. Morgan H.J. Howarth	A v U23 A v U23	1970/71 1976/77
33	Horton Park Blenheim	10	CD v ND CD v A	1972/73 2002/03	CD ND	538 100	v C v CD	2000/01 2001/02	212* 7-36	D.P. Kelly A.M. Schwass	CD v C CD v ND	2000/01 2001/02
34	Harry Barker Reserve Gisborne	28	ND v O ND v C	1974/75 2013/14	ND O	516 77	v CD v ND	2006/07 1999/00	161* 6-32	V.R. Brown S.B. Styris	C v ND ND v O	1986/87 1999/00
35	Eden Park No. 2 † Auckland	130	A v CD A v C	1975/76 2020/21	A O	662-5d 54	v C v A	2008/09 2020/21	269* 7-27	C. Munro N.A. Mallender	A v W O v A	2012/13 1984/85
36	Queen's Park Invercargill	22	O v CD O v A	1975/76 2020/21	W O	487 68	v O v C	2013/14 1977/78	196 8-31	A.M. Ellis D.G. Sewell	C v O O v CD	2016/17 1996/97
37	Bledisloe Park Pukekohe	2	ND v A ND v W	1976/77 1989/90	W ND	297-5d 152	v ND v W	1989/90 1989/90	123 5-27	R.H. Vance G.R. Larsen	W v ND W v ND	1989/90 1989/90
38	Hutt Recreation Ground Lower Hutt	14	W v ND W v C	1976/77 1985/86	W W	316 93	v O v WI	1983/84 1979/80	145* 8-24	J.G. Wright E.J. Chatfield	ND v W W v ND	1978/79 1979/80
39	Logan Park Dunedin	3	O v U23 O v C	1977/78 1979/80	O O	313 127	v U23 v C	1977/78 1979/80	106 6-44	J.M. Parker P.J. Petherick	ND v O O v U23	1978/79 1977/78
40	Temuka Oval Temuka	1	YNZ v E only match	1977/78	E YNZ	310 139	v YNZ v E	1977/78 1977/78	104 6-71	D.W. Randall G. Miller	E v YNZ E v YNZ	1977/78 1977/78
41	Molyneux Park Alexandra	31	O v CD O v C	1978/79 2020/21	CD O	511-6d 81	v O v CD	2018/19 2001/02	226 8-27	G.R. Hay J.T.C. Vaughan	CD v O A v O	2018/19 1996/97
42	University Oval * Dunedin	64	O v Pak O v ND	1978/79 2020/21	O O A	651-9d 46 46	v W v Pak v O	2012/13 1978/79 2010/11	239 7-46	H.D. Rutherford N. Wagner	O v W O v W	2011/12 2011/12
43	Maidstone Park Upper Hutt	1	W v CD only match	1979/80	W CD	216 50	v CD v W	1979/80 1979/80	63 6-17	B.R. Taylor J.V. Coney	W v CD W v CD	1979/80 1979/80
44	Dudley Park Rangiora	15	C v W C v W	1984/85 2002/03	C C	543-8d 62	v CD v A	1996/97 1998/99	251* 7-17	C.Z. Harris S.J. Maguiness	C v CD W v C	1996/97 1984/85
45	Centennial Park Oamaru	9	O v CD O v W	1984/85 1998/99	O C	430 94	v CD v O	1984/85 1994/95	182 6-36	K.R. Rutherford S.W. Duff	O v W CD v O	1987/88 1985/86
46	Levin Domain Levin	3	CD v C CD v W	1985/86 1987/88	W C	435-5d 68	v CD v CD	1987/88 1985/86	205* 6-28	E.B. McSweeney P.J. Visser	W v CD CD v C	1987/88 1985/86
47	Recreational Ground Morrinsville	2	ND v CD ND v W	1986/87 1988/89	CD ND	368-3d 198	v ND v CD	1986/87 1986/87	151 5-71	M.D. Crowe K.W. Martin	CD v ND CD v ND	1986/87 1986/87
48	Albert Park Te Awamutu	1	ND v CD only match	1987/88	ND CD	259 135	v CD v ND	1987/88 1987/88	94 4-41	B.A. Young B.J. Barrett	ND v CD ND v CD	1987/88 1987/88
49	Victoria Park Wanganui	11	CD v ND CD v O	1990/91 2002/03	W CC	506-4d 103	v CD v SC	1993/94 1997/98	203* 6-20	M.S. Sinclair B.C. Strang	CD v ND Z v NZ XI	1998/9 1995/96
50	Burnside Park Christchurch	1	C v CD only match	1991/92	C C	189-7 124	v CD v CD	1991/92 1991/92	63 6-67	T.E. Blain D.J. Leonard	CD v C CD v C	1991/9 1991/9
51	Petone Recreation Ground, Lower Hutt	2	W v O W v A	1991/92 1998/99	O W	300-8d 142	v W v O	1991/92 1991/92	107 5-37	E.B. McSweeney N.A. Mallender	W v O O v W	1991/9 1991/9
52	Sunnyvale Dunedin	1	O v A only match	1992/93	O A	193 105	v A v O	1992/93 1992/93	51 4-21	I.S. Billcliff N.A. Mallender	O v A O v A	1992/9 1992/9

† now Eden Park Outer Oval   ** now University of Otago Oval*

	Ground	No of matches	First and most recent match		Highest and lowest team totals			Highest Innings Best Bowling			
53	Lincoln Green	5	NZA v B	1997/98	NZA	459-8d v PkA	1998/99	190	M.E. Parlane	NZA v B	1997/98
	Lincoln		NZA v SA	1998/99	B	130 v NZA	1997/98	6-69	Fazal-e-Akber	Pk A v NZA	1998/99
54	Aorangi Park	4	C v Z	1997/98	Z	422-8d v C	1997/98	196	A.D.R. Campbell	Z v C	1997/98
	Timaru		C v O	2003/04	C	100 v Z	1997/98	6-56	M.J. Mason	CD v C	2002/03
55	Owen Delany Park	6	ND v O	1998/99	WI	450 v NZ A	1999/00	216*	S. Chanderpaul	WI v NZ A	1999/00
	Taupo		ND v W	2002/03	A	131 v ND	1999/00	7-33	B.P. Martin	ND v A	1999/00
56	Colin Maiden Park	28	A v ND	1998/99	A	635-6d v CD	2009/10	210	J.M. Brodie	W v A	2011/12
	Auckland		A v W	2019/20	O	63 v A	2011/12	8-23	M.J. McClenaghan	A v O	2011/12
57	Queen Elizabeth II Park	31	C v O	1998/99	W	614-8 v C	2006/07	235	J.A.H. Marshall	ND v C	2001/02
	Christchurch		C v A	2010/11	C	114 v O	1998/99	9-13	P.J. Wiseman	C v CD	2004/05
58	BIL Oval †	15	NI v E A	1999/00	A	627-7d v O	2006/07	205	T.G. McIntosh	A v O	2006/07
	Lincoln		NZA v IA	2019/20	O	63 v CD	2011/12	6-20	M.J. Mason	CD v O	2011/12
59	Queenstown Events	18	O v E	2001/02	NZ A	597-9d v SL A	2003/04	246	K.C. Brathwaite	WI v NZA	2020/21
	Centre #		NZ A v WI	2020/21	C	114 v O	2005/06	6-32	J.S. Patel	W v O	2004/05
60	North Harbour Stadium	1	A v O	2002/03	A	289 v O	2002/03	157	T.G. McIntosh	A v O	2002/03
	Auckland		only match		O	185 v A	2002/03	4-34	S.B. O'Connor	O v A	2002/03
61	Rangiora Recreation *	35	C v CD	2003/04	ND	726 v C	2009/10	226*	L.J. Carter	C v W	2019/20
	Ground		C v CD	2020/21	C	61 v ND	2011/12	8-74	K.A. Jamieson	C v A	2016/17
62	Cobham Oval *(new)*	23	ND v A	2008/09	O	576-8d v ND	2009/10	192	K.S. Williamson	ND v A	2009/10
	Whangarei		ND v A	2020/21	ND	93 v C	2010/11	7-45	S.C. Kuggeleijn	ND v A	2020/21
63	Lincoln No.3	1	ND v W	2011/12	ND	608-9d v W	2011/12	284*	K.S. Williamson	ND v W	2011/12
	Lincoln		only match		W	162 v N	2011/12	7-37	T.G. Southee	ND v W	2011/12
64	Saxton Oval	17	CD v C	2011/12	NZA	481-7d v WIA	2020/21	210	G.H. Worker	CD v W	2015/16
	Nelson		NZA v WIA	2020/21	CD	118 v C	2011/12	6-42	D.A.J. Bracewell	NZA v WIA	2020/21
65	Karori Park	6	W v CD	2011/12	W	501-6d v CD	2011/12	241*	T.W.M. Latham	W v C	2013/14
	Wellington		W v O	2014/15	ND	206 v W	2012/13	5-69	T.G. Southee	ND v W	2012/13
66	Bay Oval	14	ND v C	2014/15	NZ	615-9d v E	2019/20	205	B-J. Watling	NZ v E	2019/20
	Mt Maunganui		ND v W	2020/21	A	98 v ND	2015/16	6-35	E.J. Nuttall	C v ND	2014/15
67	Westpac Stadium §	1	W v O	2016/17	W	302-8d v O	2016/17	118	S.R. Wells	O v W	2016/17
	Wellington		only match		O	98 v W	2016/17	4-19	H.K. Bennett	O v W	2016/17

† now Bert Sutcliffe Oval ** now MainPower Oval* *§ now Sky Stadium* *# now John Davies Oval*

PROVINCIAL CAREER RECORDS

Performances for the following teams are not included in the Provincial Career Records:

Team	Opponent	
D. Reese's Canterbury XI	Wellington	1913/14
Canterbury/Otago	MCC	1936/37
Auckland/Wellington	MCC	1936/37
Auckland XI	New Zealand	1957/58
Northern Districts/Central Districts	MCC	1958/59
Otago Invitation XI	MCC	1962/63
Canterbury XI	New Zealand Touring Team	1967/68

Most Games for One Province

202 players have now represented their province on 50 or more occasions in first-class cricket.

143	Woodcock L.J.	W
134	Patel J.S.	W
127	Marshall J.A.H.	ND
121	Fulton P.G.	C
120	Gray E.J.	W
120	Yovich J.A.F.	ND
119	Vance R.H.	W
119	Sinclair M.S.	CD
119	Aldridge G.W.	ND
115	Bradburn G.E.	ND
108	Lees W.K.	O
106	Nevin C.J.	W
105	Ellis A.M.	C
105	Astle T.D.	C
104	Roberts A.D.G.	ND
103	McEwan P.E.	C
102	McSweeney E.B.	W
102	McIntosh T.G.	A
101	Latham R.T.	C
101	Broom N.T.	O
100	Flynn D.R.	ND
99	White D.J.	ND
99	de Boorder D.C.	O
97	Shrimpton M.J.F.	CD
97	Young R.A.	A
96	Bell M.D.	W
96*	Stewart S.L.	C
95	Hart M.N.	ND
95	Papps M.H.W.	C
95	Cumming C.D.	O
93	Young B.A.	ND
92	How J.M.	CD
91	Watling B-J.	ND
90	Blair B.R.	O
90*	Dickeson C.W.	ND
90	Morgan R.W.	A
90	McGregor S.N.	O
90	O'Sullivan D.R.	CD
89	Morrison J.F.M.	W
88	Boock S.L.	O
88	Franklin T.J.	A
88	Priest M.W.	C
88	Stead G.R.	C
87	Edgar B.A.	W
85	Duff S.W.	CD
85	Hart R.G.	ND
85	Parlane M.E.	ND
85	Nicol R.J.	A
85	Hay G.R.	CD
84	Chatfield E.J.	W
84	Harris C.Z.	C
83	Blain T.E.	CD
82	Dunning B.	ND
82	Hadlee B.G.	C
82	Kuggeleijn C.M.	ND
82	Griggs B.B.J.	CD
82	Gillespie M.R.	W
81	Blair W.L.	O
81	Briasco P.S.	CD
80	Howarth H.J.	A
80	Hoskin R.N.	O
80	Franklin J.E.C.	W
79	Larsen G.R.	W
79	Jones R.A.	A
79	Parlane N.R.	W
79	Mason M.J.	CD
78	Mallender N.A.	O
78	Robertson G.K.	CD
78	Bailey M.D.	ND
78	Wilson B.S.	ND
77	McIntyre J.M.	A
77	Stead D.W.	C
77	Martin B.P.	ND
77	Ingram P.J.	CD
77	de Grandhomme C.	A
76	Germon L.K.	C
76	Douglas M.W.	CD
76	Marshall H.J.H.	ND
76	Murdoch S.J.	W
76*	Baker J.D.	ND
75	Parker J.M.	ND
75*	McCullum S.J.	O
75	Gaffaney C.B.	O
74	Coney J.V.	W
74	Sulzberger G.P.	CD
74	Redmond A.J.	O
74	Worker G.H.	CD
73	Sparling J.T.	A
73	Barnes A.C.	A
73	Raval J.A.	A
72	Hastings B.F.	C
72	Troup G.B.	A
72	Wells J.D.	W
69	Alabaster G.D.	O
69	Reid J.F.	A
69*	Boyle D.J.	C
69	Papps M.H.W.	W
68	Burgess M.G.	A
68	Cameron F.J.	O
68	Sinclair B.W.	W
68	Rutherford K.R.	O
68*	Bates M.D.	A
67	Edwards G.N.	CD
67	Harris R.M.	A
67	Patel D.N.	A
67	McSkimming W.C.	O
67	Young W.A.	CD
66	Puna N.	ND
66	Lawson R.A.	O
65	Alabaster J.C.	O
65	Brown V.R.	C
65	Hunt A.J.	A
65	Webb P.N.	A
65*	Wright M.J.E.	ND
64	Murray B.A.G.	W
64	Mitchell D.J.	ND
64	Rutherford H.D.	O
63	Rutherford I.A.	O
63*	Stott L.W.	A
63	Wagner N.	O
63	Duffy J.A.	O
62	Cunis R.S.	A
62	Hadlee R.J.	C

62*	Smith C.J.P.	CD
62*	Cooper B.G.	ND
62	McCullum N.L.	O
62	Arnel B.J.	ND
62	Bracewell D.A.J.	CD
62*	Smith B.S.	CD
61	Yuile B.W.	CD
61	Campbell K.O.	O
61	Greatbatch M.J.	CD
61	Walker B.G.K.	A
61	Wells S.R.	O
60	Milburn B.D.	O
60	Newdick G.A.	W
60	Parsons A.E.W.	A
60	Sutcliffe B.	O
60	Roberts S.J.	C
59	Blair R.W.	W
59	Crowe J.J.	A
59	Smith I.D.S.	CD
59	Turner G.M.	O
59	Hartland B.R.	C
59	Smith L.D.	O
59	McGlashan P.D.	ND
59	Kuggeleijn S.C.	ND
58	Dowling G.T.	C
58	Howarth G.P.	ND
58	Patrick W.R.	C
58	Reid J.R.	W
58	Ritchie T.D.	W
58	Thomson K.	C
58	Vivian G.E.	A
57	Bull C.L.	C
57	Burns K.J.	O
57	Petrie E.C.	ND
57	Hamilton L.J.	CD
57	Elliott G.D.	W
57*	Fletcher C.D.	C
57	Blundell T.A.	W
56	Brice A.W.S.	W
56	Motz R.C.	C
56	Canning T.K.	A
56	Adams A.R.	A
56*	McMillan J.M.	O
56	Sodhi I.S.	ND
55	Bradburn W.P.	ND
55	Congdon B.E.	CD
55	Jordan A.B.	CD
55	Mills G.H.	O
55	Snedden M.C.	A
55	Sewell D.G.	O
55	Hopkins G.J.	A
55	Bracewell M.G.	O
55*	O'Donnell R.R.	A
54	Bilby G.P.	W
54*	Crocker L.M.	ND
54	Cromb I.B.	C
54	McGirr H.M.	W
54	Moir A.M.	O
54	Sutton R.E.	A
54	Ward J.T.	C
54	Dobbs P.W.	O
54	Patel A.Y.	CD
53	Colquhoun I.A.	CD
53*	Pierce R.A.	CD
53*	Schofield R.M.	CD
53	Toynbee M.H.	CD
53	Watson W.	A
53	Devcich A.P.	ND
53	Cleaver D.	CD
52*	Cederwall B.W.	W
51*	Knight A.R.	O
51	Brown S.W.	A
51	Thomson S.A.	ND
51	Thompson E.P.	CD
51	Kitchen A.K.	A
50	Boxshall C.	C
50	Butler L.C.	W
50	Horne M.J.	A
50	Mills K.D.	A

** entire first-class career*

Most Runs for One Province

	Province	*M*	*In*	*NO*	*HS*	*Runs*	*Ave*	*100*
Sinclair M.S.	CD	119	203	26	243*	9148	51.68	27
Fulton P.G.	C	121	224	22	301*	8719	43.16	16
Woodcock L.J.	W	143	246	30	220*	7719	35.73	11
Papps M.H.W.	C	95	172	14	192	6663	42.17	19
Cumming C.D.	O	95	167	15	173	6589	43.34	21
Bell M.D.	W	96	168	11	265	6565	41.81	20
Edgar B.A.	W	87	160	3	162	6494	44.17	15
Vance R.H.	W	119	205	18	254*	6440	34.43	12
Marshall J.A.H.	ND	127	214	16	235	6418	32.41	11
Flynn D.R.	ND	100	175	9	241	6265	37.74	20
Broom N.T.	O	101	172	22	203*	6085	40.56	15
Sutcliffe B.	O	60	110	8	385*	6028	59.09	17
McIntosh T.G.	A	102	176	15	268	5980	37.14	17
McEwan P.E.	C	103	185	11	155	5940	34.13	11
Latham R.T.	C	101	176	17	237*	5919	37.22	8
Hay G.R.	CD	85	149	11	226	5866	42.50	13
Stewart S.L.	C	96	173	18	227*	5693	36.72	7
How J.M.	CD	92	167	16	207*	5680	37.61	13
Roberts A.D.G.	ND	104	192	35	128*	5533	35.24	7
Watling B-J.	ND	91	162	12	176	5479	36.52	9
Harris C.Z.	C	84	125	31	251*	5442	57.89	13
Ingram P.J.	CD	77	140	8	247	5378	40.74	17
Ellis A.M.	C	105	167	21	171	5179	35.47	9
Blair B.R.	O	90	154	5	143	5057	33.93	7
Franklin T.J.	A	88	157	14	181	5051	35.25	12
Rutherford K.R.	O	68	121	7	226*	5051	44.30	14

Highest Averages

2000 RUNS/45.00 AVE	Province	M	In	NO	HS	Runs	Ave	100
Hick G.A.	ND	17	30	4	211*	2055	79.03	10
Crowe M.D.	CD	32	55	7	242	3299	68.72	13
Conway D.P.	W	22	39	8	327*	2054	66.25	5
Scott V.J.	A	44	74	15	204	3546	60.10	11
Sutcliffe B.	O	60	110	8	385	6028	59.09	17
Harris C.Z.	C	84	125	31	251*	5442	57.89	13
Munro C.	A	42	64	4	281	3440	57.33	13
Jones A.H.	W	39	67	11	181*	2978	53.17	7
van Wyk C.F.K.	CD	45	73	19	131	2854	52.85	3
Myburgh J.G.	C	25	46	4	199	2172	51.71	7
Sinclair M.S.	CD	119	203	26	243*	9148	51.68	27
Wallace W.M.	A	47	73	5	211	3409	50.13	9
Crowe J.J.	A	59	95	9	156	4245	49.36	11
Reid J.R.	W	58	102	8	296	4538	48.27	13
Turner G.M.	O	59	109	14	186*	4439	46.72	13
Hopkins G.J.	A	55	82	12	201	3228	46.40	9
Brownlie D.G.	C	35	65	8	171	2635	46.22	6
Hiddleston J.S.	W	41	75	1	212	3413	46.12	8
Guptill M.J.	A	39	67	6	195*	2804	45.96	8
Ryder J.D.	W	40	67	3	236	2908	45.43	8

Most Wickets for One Province

	Province	M	Wkts	Runs	Ave	5WI	10WM	Best
Chatfield E.J.	W	84	403	7531	18.68	23	7	8-24
Boock S.L.	O	88	399	8235	20.63	28	5	8-57
O'Sullivan D.R.	CD	90	392	9560	24.38	21	3	6-40
Gray E.J.	W	120	357	9778	27.38	13	3	8-37
Aldridge G.W.	ND	119	355	10,052	28.31	14	1	6-41
Gillespie M.R.	W	82	344	9389	27.29	16	2	6-38
Patel J.S.	W	134	333	12,592	37.81	12	1	7-105
Howarth H.J.	A	80	332	7361	22.17	18	4	8-75
Blair R.W.	W	59	330	5004	15.16	30	10	9-72
Astle T.D.	C	105	303	9505	31.36	12	1	8-148
Priest M.W.	C	88	290	8501	29.31	12	3	9-95
Downes A.D.	O	44	287	3902	13.59	33	13	8-35
Hadlee R.J.	C	62	285	4600	16.14	19	2	7-49
Moir A.M.	O	54	282	5926	21.01	20	5	8-37
Dickeson C.W.	ND	90	282	8242	29.22	9	2	7-79
Wagner N.	O	63	277	7307	26.37	16	1	7-46
Mallender N.A.	O	78	268	5433	20.27	14	3	7-27
Alabaster J.C.	O	65	264	5738	21.73	14	3	6-39
Mason M.J.	CD	78	263	6387	24.28	12	1	6-20
Cameron F.J.	O	68	258	5204	20.17	9	—	6-21
Yovich J.A.F.	ND	110	255	8579	33.64	8	1	7-64
Adams A.R.	A	56	251	4729	18.84	14	3	6-25

Most Centuries for One Province

	Province	100s		Province	100s		Province	100s
Sinclair M.S.	CD	27	Reid J.R.	W	13	Murdoch S.J.	W	12
Cumming C.D.	O	21	Turner G.M.	O	13	Scott V.J.	A	11
Bell M.D.	W	20	Crowe M.D.	CD	13	Crowe J.J.	A	11
Flynn D.R.	ND	20	Harris C.Z.	C	13	McEwan P.E.	C	11
Papps M.H.W.	C	19	How J.M.	CD	13	Parlane N.R.	W	11
Sutcliffe B.	O	17	Franklin J.E.C	W	13	Redmond A.J.	O	11
McIntosh T.G.	A	17	Munro C.	A	13	Marshall J.A.H.	ND	11
Ingram P.J.	CD	17	Papps M.H.W.	W	13	Woodcock L.J.	W	11
Fulton P.G.	C	16	Raval J.A.	A	13	Hadlee W.A.	C	10
Edgar B.A.	W	15	Hay G.R.	CD	13	Burgess M.G.	A	10
Broom N.T.	O	15	Vance R.H.	W	12	Hick G.A.	ND	10
Greatbatch M.J.	CD	14	Franklin T.J.	A	12	Stead G.R.	C	10
Rutherford K.R.	O	14	Jones R.A.	A	12			

Most Dismissals for One Province

WICKETKEEPING	Province	M	Caught	Stumped	Total
de Boorder D.C.	O	99	322	22	344
McSweeney E.B.	W	102	289	39	328
Nevin C.J.	W	106	289	9	298
Young R.A.	A	97	245	5	250
Lees W.K.	O	108	208	36	244
Hart R.G.	ND	85	228	15	243
Germon L.K.	C	76	217	21	238
Griggs B.B.J	CD	82	225	7	232
Fletcher C.D.	C	57	181	10	191
Young B.A.	ND	93	179	11	190
McGlashan P.D.	ND	59	175	12	187
Hopkins G.J.	A	55	165	7	172
Milburn B.D.	O	60	148	17	165
Cleaver D.	CD	53	145	11	156
Ward J.T.	C	54	136	17	153
Kelly P.J.	A	48	140	12	152
van Wyk C.F.K.	CD	45	140	5	145
Blain T.E.	CD	83	124	19	143
Blundell T.A.	W	57	130	5	135
Croy M.G.	O	42	127	4	131
Watling B-J.	ND	91	129	2	131
Colquhoun I.A.	CD	53	102	28	130
Smith I.D.S.	CD	59	119	11	130
Sigley M.A.	CD	44	124	4	128
Schofield R.M.	CD	53	107	15	122
Robinson S.A.	O	45	117	5	122
Wright M.J.E.	ND	65	104	17	121
Horne B.L.	A	35	115	3	118
Seifert T.L.	ND	41	109	7	116
Hopkins G.J.	O	33	111	3	114
Petrie E.C.	ND	57	90	22	112
Mills G.H.	O	55	78	29	107
Boxshall C.	C	50	70	36	106
van Wyk C.F.K.	C	35	101	5	106
Cachopa B.	A	43	101	4	105
Hopkins G.J.	C	41	91	10	101
Therkleson I.J.	W	39	93	7	100

Represented Most Provinces

5	Guy J.W.	CD, C, O, W, ND
4	Anderson R.W.	C, ND, O, CD
	Congdon B.E.	CD, W, O, C
	Crawshaw W.J.	O, C, W, T
	Hopkins G.J.	ND, C, O, A
	Hounsell A.R.	C, W, A, ND
	Howell L.G.	C, CD, A, ND
	McGregor P.B.	A, ND, W, CD
	Worker R.V. de R.	A, C, O, W
3	Alabaster G.D.	O, C, ND
	Allcott C.F.W.	HB, A, O
	Alpe S.	A, C, W
	Andrews B.	C, CD, O
	Beard D.D.	W, CD, ND
	Billcliff I.S.	O, W, A
	Bracewell B.P.	CD, O, ND
	Cairns B.L.	CD, O, ND
	Clark L.A.	W, O, A
	Collinge R.O.	CD, W, ND
	Crowe M.D.	A, CD, W
	D'Arcy J.W.	C, O, W
	Frith W.	C, O, W
	Hastings B.F.	W, CD, C
	Holland P.J.	CD, ND, W
	Hussey J.M.	HB, O, A
	Jones A.H.	CD, O, W
	King R.T.	O, A, CD
	Lane M.E.L.	W, CD, C
3	Lusk Harold B.	A, C, W
	McBeath D.J.	O, C, S
	McEwan M.B.	C, W, A
	McGlashan P.D.	CD, O, ND
	Macleod D.N.	CD, W, C
	Mills G.	A, HB, O
	Moloney D.A.R.	O, W, C
	Neesham. J.D.S.	A, O, W
	Neutze P.S.	O, A, ND
	Nicol R.J.	A, C, O
	Parlane N.R.	ND, W, A
	Paterson J.L.	C, HB, A
	Raval J.A.	A, CD, ND
	Riley J.D.	C, W, A
	Ryder J.D.	CD, W, O
	Sampson H.C.	CD, O, C
	Salmon W.J.	W, HB, T
	Sherlock R.R.	CD, C, A
	Stephenson F.C.	O, W, C
	Sutcliffe B.	A, O, ND
	Todd G.R.	CD, O, A
	Tracy S.R.	A, C, O
	Twose R.G.	ND, CD, W
	Uttley K.F.M.	O, C, W
	Watson H.C.	O, C, W
	Wiseman P.J.	A, O, C
	Wright E.	A, W, C
	Wright J.G.	ND, C, A

T *Taranaki* S *Southland* HB *Hawke's Bay*

Longest Careers for One Province

Seasons			
34	Read R.J.	Canterbury	1904/05-1937/38
31	Reese T.W.	Canterbury	1887/88-1917/18
29	Luckie M.M.F.	Wellington	1891/92-1919/20
27	Fowke J.N.	Canterbury	1880/81-1906/07
27	Downes A.D.	Otago	1887/88-1913/14
27	Dempster C.S.	Wellington	1921/22-1947/48
26	Reese D.	Canterbury	1895/96-1920/21
26	Knight A.R.	Otago	1918/19-1943/44

PROVINCIAL RECORDS

MOST WINS IN SUCCESSION

8	Canterbury	1873/74 to 1880/81
7	Canterbury	1912/13 to 1913/14
7	Wellington	1960/61 to 1961/62
6	Canterbury	1910/11 to 1911/12
6	Auckland	1939/40 to 1943/44
6	Wellington	1962/63 to 1963/64
6	Canterbury	1996/97

MOST LOSSES IN SUCCESSION

10	Otago	1961/62 to 1963/64
8	Otago	1929/30 to 1931/32
7	Otago	1874/75 to 1880/81
7	Otago	1920/21 to 1922/23
7	Otago	1926/27 to 1927/28
7	Auckland	1997/98 to 1998/99
7	Otago	2001/02

MOST DRAWS IN SUCCESSION

9	ND	1974/75 to 1975/76
8	Wellington	1974/75 to 1975/76
7	ND	1968/69 to 1969/70
7	CD	1991/92 to 1992/93
7	Wellington	1992/93

MOST GAMES WITHOUT A WIN

38	CD	1973/74 to 1978/79
36	Otago	1960/61 to 1965/66
24	ND	1972/73 to 1975/76
21	ND	1966/67 to 1970/71

MOST GAMES WITHOUT A LOSS

24	Wellington	1984/85 to 1986/87
23	Auckland	1978/79 to 1981/82
22	Auckland	1934/35 to 1943/44
21	Central Districts	2016/17 to 2018/19
18	Auckland	1961/62 to 1964/65
18	Canterbury	1966/67 to 1969/70

MOST GAMES WITHOUT A DRAW

42	Canterbury	1896/97 to 1909/10
30	Otago	1894/95 to 1907/08
22	Canterbury	1869/70 to 1883/84
20	Canterbury	1919/20 to 1924/25

Highest Individual Innings

for and against the major sides in NZ

	For		Against	
Auckland	290	W.N. Carson v Otago at Dunedin, 1936/37	355	B. Sutcliffe for Otago at Dunedin, 1949/50
Canterbury	301*	P.G. Fulton v Auckland at Christchurch, 2002/03	385	B. Sutcliffe for Otago at Christchurch, 1952/53
Central Dist.	247	P.J. Ingram v ND at Hamilton, 2008/09	334	D.G. Brownlie for ND at New Plymouth, 2014/15
Northern Dist.	334	D.G. Brownlie v CD at New Plymouth, 2014/15	296	J.R. Reid for Wellington at Wellington, 1962/63
Otago	385	B. Sutcliffe v Canterbury at Christchurch, 1952/53	290	W.N. Carson for Auckland at Dunedin, 1936/37
Wellington	327*	D.P. Conway v Canterbury at Wellington, 2019/20	284*	K.S. Williamson v Wellington at Lincoln, 2011/12
MCC/England	336*	W.R. Hammond v NZ at Auckand, 1932/33	222	N.J. Astle for NZ at Christchurch, 2001/02
Australia	293	V.T. Trumper v Canterbury at Christchurch 1913/14	198	W.A. Hadlee for Otago at Dunedin, 1945/46
South Africa	275*	D.J. Cullinan v NZ at Auckland, 1998/99	176	K.S. Williamson for NZ at Hamilton, 2016/17
West Indies	258	S.M. Nurse v NZ at Christchurch, 1968/69	251	K.S. Williamson for NZ at Hamilton, 2020/21
Pakistan	271	Javed Miandad v NZ at Auckland, 1988/89	238	K.S. Williamson for NZ at Christchurch, 2020/21
India	192	M. Azharuddin v NZ at Auckand, 1989/90	302	B.B. McCullum v India at Wellington, 2013/14
Sri Lanka	267	P.A. de Silva v NZ at Wellington, 1990/91	299	M.D. Crowe for NZ at Wellington, 1990/91
New Zealand	302	B.B. McCullum v India at Wellington, 2013/14	336*	W.R. Hammond for England at Auckland, 1932/33
Zimbabwe	196	A.D.R. Campbell v Canterbury at Timaru, 1997/98	157	M.J. Horne for NZ at Auckland, 1997/98
Bangladesh	217	Shakib Al Hasan v NZ at Wellington, 2016/17	200*	K.S. Williamson for NZ at Hamilton, 2018/19
			200	L.R.P.L. Taylor for NZ at Wellington, 2018/19

Best Bowling

for and against the major sides in NZ

	For		Against	
Auckland	9-36	A.F. Wensley v Otago at Auckland, 1929/30	9-48	A.R. Tait v Auckland at Hamilton, 1996/97
Canterbury	10-28	A.E. Moss v Wellington at Christchurch, 1889/90	9-72	F.H. Cooke for Otago at Christchurch, 1884/85
Central Dist.	9-100	B.W. Yuile v Canterbury at New Plymouth, 1965/66	9-13	P.J. Wiseman for Canterbury at Christchurch, 2004/05
Northern Dist.	9-48	A.R. Tait v Auckland at Hamilton, 1996/97	9-93	P.J. Petherick for Otago at Dunedin, 1975/76
Otago	9-50	A.H. Fisher v Queensland at Dunedin, 1896/97	9-36	A.E. Wensley for Auckland at Auckland, 1929/30
Wellington	9-67	A.W.S. Brice v Auckland at Wellington, 1918/19	10-28	A.E. Moss for Canterbury at Christchurch, 1889/90
MCC/England	8-45	F.S. Trueman v Otago at Dunedin, 1958/59	7-50	H.W. Monaghan for Wellington at Wellington, 1906/07
Australia	8-27	W.J. Whitty v Auckland at Auckland, 1909/10	8-66	G.O. Rabone for Auckland at Auckland, 1956/57
South Africa	6-40	K.A. Maharaj v NZ at Wellington, 2016/17	7-75	C.F.W. Allcott for Auckland at Auckland, 1931/32
West Indies	7-37	C.A. Walsh v NZ at Wellington, 1994/95	7-27	C.L. Cairns for NZ at Hamilton, 1999/00
Pakistan	7-16	Farooq Hamid v Wellington at Wellington, 1964/65	7-95	N.A. Huxford for Wellington at Wellington, 1964/65
India	8-76	E.A.S. Prasanna v NZ at Auckland, 1975/76	7-23	R.J. Hadlee for NZ at Wellington, 1975/76
Sri Lanka	6-79	C.P.H. Ramanayake v Wellington at Wellington, 1990/91	7-130	D.L. Vettori for New Zealand at Wellington, 2006/07
New Zealand	8-100	G.F. Cresswell v Australia B at Dunedin, 1949/50	8-33	H.S.T.L. Hendry for NSW at Wellington, 1923/24
Zimbabwe	6-20	B.C. Strang v NZ XI at Wanganui, 1995/96	6-26	C.S. Martin for NZ at Napier, 2011/12
Bangladesh	6-143	Hasibul Hussain v Northern at Hamilton, 1997/98	7-53	C.L. Cairns for NZ at Hamilton, 2001/02

Highest Totals

for and against the major sides in NZ

	For		Against	
Auckland	693-9 dec	v Canterbury at Auckland, 1939/40	658	by Australians at Auckland, 1913/14
Canterbury	777	v Otago at Christchurch, 1996/97	726	by Northern Districts at Rangiora, 2009/10
Central Dist.	650-8 dec	v Otago at Napier, 2015/16	668-7 dec	by Auckland at Napier, 2014/15
Northern Dist.	726	v Canterbury at Rangiora, 2009/10	608-9 dec	by Wellington at Hamilton, 1998/99
Otago	651-9 dec	v Wellington at Dunedin, 2012/13	777	by Canterbury at Christchurch, 1996/97
Wellington	614-8	v Canterbury at Christchurch, 2006/07	658-9 dec	by Auckland at Auckland, 2012/13
MCC/England	653-5 dec	v New Zealand at Dunedin, 1935/36	615-9 dec	by New Zealand at Mt Maunganui, 2019/20
Australia	663	v New Zealand at Auckland, 1920/21	484	by New Zealand at Wellington, 1973/74
South Africa	621-5 dec	v New Zealand at Auckland, 1998/99	595	by New Zealand at Auckland, 2003/04
West Indies	660-5 dec	v New Zealand at Wellington, 1994/95	609-9 dec	by New Zealand at Dunedin, 2013/14
Pakistan	616-5 dec	v New Zealand at Auckland, 1988/89	659-6 dec	by New Zealand at Christchurch, 2020/21
India	520	v New Zealand at Hamilton, 2008/09	680-8 dec	by New Zealand at Wellington, 2013/14
Sri Lanka	498	v New Zealand at Napier, 2004/05	671-4	by New Zealand at Wellington, 1990/91
New Zealand	715-6 dec	v Bangladesh at Hamilton, 2018/19	663	by Australia at Auckland, 1920/21
Zimbabwe	422-8 dec	v Canterbury at Timaru, 1997/98	495-7 dec	by New Zealand at Napier, 2011/12
Bangladesh	595-8 dec	v New Zealand at Wellington, 2016/17	715-6 dec	by New Zealand at Hamilton, 2018/19

Lowest Totals

for and against the major sides in NZ

	For		Against	
Auckland	13	v Canterbury at Auckland, 1877/78	28	by Hawke's Bay at Auckland, 1910/11
Canterbury	25	v Otago at Christchurch, 1866/67	13	by Auckland at Auckland, 1877/78
Central Dist.	50	v Wellington at Upper Hutt, 1979/80	63	by Otago at Lincoln, 2011/12
Northern Dist.	32	v Auckland at Hamilton, 1996/97	51	by Central Dist. at Hamilton, 1957/58
Otago	34	v Wellington at Dunedin, 1956/57	25	by Canterbury at Christchurch, 1866/67
Wellington	19	v Nelson at Nelson, 1885/86	32	by Hawke's Bay at Wellington, 1883/84
MCC/England	58	v New Zealand at Auckland, 2017/18	26	by New Zealand at Auckland, 1954/55
Australia	103	v New Zealand at Auckland, 1985/86	42	by New Zealand at Wellington, 1945/46
South Africa	165	v NZ Academy XI at Nelson, 1994/95	73	by Canterbury at Christchurch, 1963/64
West Indies	77	v New Zealand at Auckland, 1955/56	74	by New Zealand at Dunedin, 1955/56
Pakistan	100	v New Zealand A at Lincoln, 2000/01	46	by Otago at Dunedin, 1978/79
India	81	v New Zealand at Wellington, 1975/76	94	by New Zealand at Hamilton, 2002/03
Sri Lanka	93	v New Zealand at Wellington, 1982/83	109	by New Zealand at Napier, 1994/95
New Zealand	26	v England at Auckland, 1954/55	58	by England at Auckland, 2017/18
Zimbabwe	51	v New Zealand at Napier, 2011/12	100	by Canterbury at Timaru, 1997/98
Bangladesh	108	v New Zealand at Hamilton, 2001/02	311	by Central at Wellington, 1997/98

AUCKLAND

Highest Totals

693-9 dec	v Canterbury	Auckland	1939/40
668-7 dec	v Central Districts	Napier	2014/15
662-5 dec	v Central Districts	Auckland	2008/09
658-9 dec	v Wellington	Auckland	2012/13
643	v Canterbury	Auckland	1919/20
635-6 dec	v Central Districts	Auckland	2009/10
627-7 dec	v Otago	Lincoln	2006/07
598	v Wellington	Wellington	2015/16
590	v Canterbury	Auckland	1937/38
587-7 dec	v West Indies	Auckland	2008/09

Lowest Totals

13	v Canterbury	Auckland	1877/78
46	v Otago	Dunedin	2010/11
48	v Otago	Dunedin	1889/90
48	v Wellington	Wellington	1889/90
53	v Wellington	Wellington	1873/74
55	v Otago	Dunedin	1900/01
56	v Canterbury	Auckland	1931/32
62	v Wellington	Wellington	2017/18
69	v Northern Districts	Auckland	1963/64

Most Appearances

102	McIntosh T.G.
97	Young R.A.
90	Morgan R.W.
88	Franklin T.J.
85	Nicol R.J.
80	Howarth H.J.
79	Jones R.A.
77	McIntyre J.M.
77	de Grandhomme C.
73	Sparling J.T.
73	Barnes A.C.
73	Raval J.A.
72	Troup G.B.
69	Reid J.F.
68	Burgess M.G.
68	Bates M.D.
67	Harris R.M.
67	Patel D.N.
65	Hunt A.J.
65	Webb P.N.
63	Stott L.W.
62	Cunis R.S.
61	Walker B.G.K.
60	Parsons A.E.W.
59	Crowe J.J.
58	Vivian G.E.
56	Canning T.K.
56	Adams A.R.
55	Snedden M.C.
55	Hopkins G.J.
55	O'Donnell R.R.
54	Sutton R.E.
53	Watson W.
51	Brown S.W.
51	Kitchen A.K.
50	Horne M.J.
50	Mills K.D.

Longest Careers

Seasons		
25	Garrard D.R.	1917/18-1941/42
24	Wallace W.M.	1933/34-1956/57
22	Anthony A.	1909/10-1930/31
22	McIntyre J.M.	1961/62-1982-83
21	Yates R.J.	1873/74-1893/94
21	Cleverley D.C.	1930/31-1950/51
20	Stemson W.I.	1889/90-1908/09
20	Horspool E.	1909/10-1928/29
20	Weir G.L.	1927/28-1946/47
20	Morgan R.W.	1957/58-1976/77

Benefits

Troup G.B.	1986/87
Snedden M.C.	1989/90
Crowe J.J.	1990/91
Franklin T.J.	1991/92
Hunt A.J.	1992/93
Watson W.	1994/95
Patel D.N.	1995/96
Morrison D.K.	1996/97
Pringle C.	1998/99
Barnes A.C.	2002/03

Batting

2000 RUNS	Career	M	In	NO	HS	Runs	Ave	100
McIntosh T.G.	1998/99-2013/14	102	176	15	268	5980	37.14	17
Franklin T.J.	1980/81-1992/93	88	157	14	181	5051	35.25	12
Raval J.A.	2008/09-2019/20	73	131	6	256	4796	38.36	13
Jones R.A.	1993/94-2009/10	79	137	8	201	4721	36.59	12
Crowe J.J.	1982/83-1991/92	59	95	9	156	4245	49.36	11
Burgess M.G.	1966/67-1979/80	68	116	13	146	4228	41.04	10
Nicol R.J.	2001/02-2016/17	85	136	15	160	4227	34.93	7
Morgan R.W.	1957/58-1976/77	90	154	8	166	4162	28.50	7
de Grandhomme C.	2006/07-2017/18	77	125	18	144*	3980	37.19	9
Reid J.F.	1975/76-1987/88	69	117	17	173	3733	37.33	5
Patel D.N.	1985/86-1994/95	67	102	9	204	3648	39.22	8
Harris R.M.	1955/56-1973/74	67	119	4	157	3598	31.28	3
Scott V.J.	1937/38-1952/53	44	74	15	204	3546	60.10	11
Munro C.	2006/07-2017/18	42	64	4	281	3440	57.33	13
Wallace W.M.	1933/34-1956/57	47	73	5	211	3409	50.13	9
Webb P.N.	1976/77-1986/87	65	114	18	136	3307	34.44	5
Hopkins G.J.	2007/08-2013/14	55	82	12	201	3228	46.40	9
Horne M.J.	1992/93-2005/06	50	80	4	209*	3184	41.89	9
Young R.A.	1998/99-2012/13	97	132	22	126*	3056	27.78	5
O'Donnell R.R.	2014/15-2020/21	55	96	6	167	3049	33.87	5
Sparling J.T.	1956/57-1970/71	73	123	17	105	2977	28.08	2
Barnes A.C.	1993/94-2004/05	73	113	10	134*	2893	28.08	4
Kitchen A.K.	2008/09-2014/15	51	90	11	132	2893	36.62	6
Parsons A.E.W.	1973/74-1982/83	60	113	8	132	2820	26.85	3
Guptill M.J.	2005/06-2020/21	39	67	6	195*	2804	45.96	8
Hemus L.G.	1904/05-1921/22	39	71	4	148	2701	40.31	8
Weir G.L.	1927/28-1946/47	42	67	6	191	2625	43.03	7
Whitelaw P.E.	1928/29-1946/47	42	68	4	195	2417	37.76	5
Jarvis T.W.	1964/65-1976/77	46	80	3	118*	2403	31.20	2
Horne P.A.	1979/80-1990/91	40	67	6	209	2380	39.01	4
Vincent L.	1997/98-2012/13	45	70	6	185*	2345	36.64	4
Vivian G.E.	1966/67-1978/79	58	98	16	111*	2327	28.37	2
Guptill-Bunce M.L.	2012/13-2018/19	38	71	1	189	2290	32.71	3
Cachopa B.	2010/11-2016/17	43	75	10	135*	2278	35.04	3
Vaughan J.T.C.	1989/90-1996/97	48	81	14	127	2269	33.86	2
Gedye S.G.	1956/57-1964/65	40	73	4	104	2169	31.43	3
Mills J.E.	1925/26-1937/38	35	63	1	185	2126	34.29	3
Hunt A.J.	1981/82-1992/93	65	99	15	102*	2069	24.63	1
Canning T.K.	1999/00-2006/07	56	82	10	115	2067	28.70	3
Redmond R.E.	1969/70-1975/76	29	55	4	141*	2004	39.29	4

CENTURY ON DEBUT FOR PROVINCE

† 112*	Brook-Smith W.	v Hawke's Bay	Auckland	1904/05
157	Relf A.E.	v Canterbury	Christchurch	1907/08
† 119	Snedden C.A.	v Hawke's Bay	Auckland	1920/21
† 122	Scott V.J.	v Canterbury	Auckland	1937/38
† 122	Kerr A.C.	v Wellington	Auckland	1941/42
174	Patel D.N.	v Canterbury	Christchurch	1985/86
† 106* & 1	Vaughan J.T.C.	v Wellington	Wellington	1989/90
† 141* & 4	Hakaraia D.N.	v Northern Districts	Hamilton	2012/13

† indicates player was making his first-class debut

MOST RUNS IN A SEASON

		Runs	Ave
Crowe J.J.	1991/92	1063	62.52
Jones R.A.	2009/10	953	59.56
Munro C.	2014/15	899	56.18
Raval J.	2014/15	876	48.66
Guptill-Bunce M.L.	2015/16	859	45.21
McIntosh T.G.	2002/03	820	58.57
Cachopa Craig	2012/13	795	49.68
Cachopa B.	2014/15	783	71.18
Cachopa Craig	2013/14	781	55.78
Raval J.A.	2015/16	780	55.71
Crowe M.D.	1982/83	736	52.57
Patel D.N.	1986/87	723	55.61
O'Donnell R.R.	2015/16	721	40.05
Jones R.A.	2008/09	703	46.86

HIGHEST INDIVIDUAL INNINGS

290	Carson W.N.	v Otago	Dunedin	1936/37
281	Munro C.	v Central Districts	Napier	2014/15
269*	Munro C.	v Wellington	Auckland	2012/13
268	McIntosh T.G.	v Canterbury	Auckland	2007/08
256	Smith S.G.	v Canterbury	Auckland	1919/20
256	Raval J.A.	v Central Districts	Auckland	2008/09
211	Wallace W.M.	v Canterbury	Auckland	1939/40
209*	Brown S.W.	v Canterbury	Christchurch	1990/91
209*	Horne M.J.	v Northern Districts	Auckland	2003/04
209	Horne P.A.	v Northern Districts	Auckland	1988/89
205	McIntosh T.G.	v Otago	Lincoln	2006/07
204	Scott V.J.	v Otago	Dunedin	1947/48
204	Patel D.N.	v Northern Districts	Auckland	1991/92
203	Cachopa C.	v Wellington	Auckland	2013/14
202*	Raval J.A.	v Otago	Auckland	2015/16
201	Jones R.A.	v West Indies	Auckland	2008/09
201	Hopkins G.J.	v Central Districts	Auckland	2009/10

MOST CENTURIES IN A SEASON

4	Franklin T.J.	1987/88
4	Crowe J.J.	1991/92
4	Jones R.A.	2009/10
4	Munro C.	2016/17

TOTAL NUMBER OF CENTURIES		**386**
Most in one season	18	2008/09
1st	Mills G. 106* v Wellington	1895/96
100th	Playle W.R. 102* v Central Districts	1957/58
200th	Crowe J.J. 102 v Otago	1991/92
300th	Jones R.A. 123 v Central Districts	2009/10

Bowling

150 WICKETS	Career	M	Wkts	Runs	Ave	5WI	10WM	Best
Howarth H.J.	1963/64-1978/79	80	332	7361	22.17	18	4	8-75
Adams A.R.	1997/98-2011/12	56	251	4729	18.84	14	3	6-25
Sparling J.T.	1956/57-1970/71	73	248	5327	21.47	17	3	7-49
McIntyre J.M.	1961/62-1982/83	77	238	5447	22.88	8	1	6-84
Cunis R.S.	1960/61-1973/74	62	229	4603	20.10	14	2	7-29
Snedden M.C.	1977/78-1989/90	55	217	4631	21.34	10	2	7-49
Stott L.W.	1969/70-1983/84	63	214	5341	24.95	8	—	6-68
Troup G.B.	1974/75-1986/87	72	200	5213	26.06	4	—	6-48
Canning T.K.	1999/00-2006/07	56	196	4822	24.60	6	—	6-44
Bates M.D.	2003/04-2015/16	68	193	5681	29.43	5	—	6-55
Patel D.N.	1985/86-1994/95	67	184	4298	23.35	8	2	7-83
Watson W.	1984/85-1994/95	53	176	4110	23.35	7	—	7-60

	Career	M	Wkts	Runs	Ave	5WI	10WM	Best
Bracewell J.G.	1982/83-1989/90	42	168	4189	24.93	8	2	7-65
Morrison D.K.	1985/86-1996/97	49	168	4034	24.01	7	—	7-82
Nethula T.S.	2008/09-2017/18	46	156	5483	35.14	7	2	6-36
Cowie J.	1932/33-1949/50	34	154	3379	21.94	6	—	6-44
Sutton R.E.	1958/59-1973/74	54	152	3364	22.13	6	—	7-64

MOST WICKETS IN A SEASON

		Wkts	Ave
Canning T.K.	2002/03	46	21.97
Bracewell J.G.	1986/87	43	20.90
Nethula T.S.	2016/17	43	30.06
Hayes J.A.	1957/58	42	11.38
Lankham W.	1882/83	41	6.31

BEST IN AN INNINGS

9-36	Wensley A.F.	v Otago	Auckland	1929/30
9-75	Neill R.	v Canterbury	Auckland	1891/92
9-86	Neill R.	v Canterbury	Auckland	1897/98
8-23	McClenaghan M.J.	v Otago	Auckland	2011/12
8-27	Vaughan J.T.C.	v Otago	Alexandra	1996/97
8-36	Rees A.W.	v Otago	Dunedin	1889/90
8-51	Neill R.	v Wellington	Auckland	1895/96
8-51	Garrard D.R.	v Canterbury	Auckland	1921/22
8-55	Smith S.G.	v Wellington	Auckland	1919/20
8-65	Smith S.G.	v Otago	Auckland	1923/24
8-66	Rabone G.O.	v Australia	Auckland	1956/57
8-75	Cleverley D.C.	v Wellington	Wellington	1945/46
8-75	Howarth H.J.	v NZ Under 23 XI	Auckland	1976/77

BEST IN A MATCH

14-63	Rees A.W.	v Otago	Dunedin	1889/90
14-65	Hayes J.A.	v Wellington	Auckland	1957/58
14-94	Howarth H.J.	v Otago	Dunedin	1973/74
14-119	Pringle C.	v Otago	Dunedin	1993/94
13-35	Lankham W.	v Taranaki	Auckland	1882/83
13-85	Cunis R.S.	v Canterbury	Christchurch	1963/64
13-104	Oliff C.	v Wellington	Auckland	1912/13
13-107	Smith S.G.	v Wellington	Auckland	1919/20

Wicketkeeping

100 DISMISSALS	Career	M	Caught	Stumped	Total
Young R.A.	1998/99-2009/10	97	245	5	250
Hopkins G.J.	2007/08-2013/14	55	165	7	172
Kelly P.J.	1981/82-1988/89	48	140	12	152
Horne B.J.	2016/17-2020/21	35	115	3	118
Cachopa B.	2010/11-2016/17	43	101	4	105

MOST DISMISSALS IN A SEASON

45	(44ct/1st)	Cachopa B.	2015/16
39	(39ct)	Cachopa B.	2014/15
35	(33ct/2st)	Young R.A.	2001/02
35	(35ct)	Young R.A.	2002/03
35	(34ct/1st)	Hopkins G.J.	2012/13

MOST DISMISSALS IN A MATCH

9	(9ct)	Horne B.J. v Central Districts	Auckland	2018/19
8	(2ct/6st)	Kent L.A.W. v Wellington	Wellington	1944/45
8	(8ct)	Smith I.D.S. v Central Districts	Nelson	1988/89
8	(8ct)	Vincent L. v Central Districts	Palmerston North	2000/01
8	(8ct)	Hopkins G.J. v Canterbury	Auckland	2010/11
8	(8ct)	Hopkins G.J. v Otago	Dunedin	2013/14
8	(8ct)	Cachopa B. v Otago	Auckland	2014/15
8	(8ct)	Cachopa B. v Otago	Dunedin	2015/16
8	(8ct)	Cachopa B. v Wellington	Wellington	2015/16
8	(8ct)	Horne B.J. v Northern Districts	Auckland	2017/18
8	(8ct)	Horne B.J. v Central Districts	Auckland	2019/20

MOST DISMISSALS IN AN INNINGS

6	(6ct)	Young R.A.v Wellington	Wellington	2002/03
6	(6ct)	Hopkins G.J. v Northern Districts	Whangarei	2011/12
6	(6ct)	Hopkins G.J. v Otago	Auckland	2011/12
6	(6ct)	Cachopa B. v Wellington	Wellington	2015/16
6	(6ct)	Horne B.J. v Central Districts	Auckland	2018/19

MOST CATCHES IN A MATCH

9	Horne B.J. v Central Districts	Auckland	2018/19
8	Smith I.D.S. v Central Districts	Nelson	1988/89
8	Vincent L. v Central Districts	Palmerston North	2000/01
8	Hopkins G.J. v Canterbury	Auckland	2010/11
8	Hopkins G.J. v Otago	Dunedin	2013/14
8	Cachopa B. v Otago	Auckland	2014/15
8	Cachopa B. v Otago	Dunedin	2015/16
8	Cachopa B. v Wellington	Wellington	2015/16
8	Horne B.J. v Northern Districts	Auckland	2017/18
8	Horne B.J. v Central Districts	Auckland	2019/20

MOST CATCHES IN AN INNINGS

6	Young R.A.v Wellington	Wellington	2002/03
6	Hopkins G.J. v Northern Districts	Whangarei	2011/12
6	Hopkins G.J. v Otago	Auckland	2011/12
6	Cachopa B. v Wellington	Wellington	2015/16
6	Horne B.J. v Central Districts	Auckland	2018/19

Fielding

MOST CATCHES IN A SEASON

18	Raval J.A.	2014/15

MOST CATCHES IN A MATCH

6	Williams N.T. v Hawke's Bay	Napier	1894/95
6	Jarvis T.W. v Northern Districts	Hamilton	1968/69
6	de Grandhomme C. v Canterbury	Christchurch	2010/11

MOST CATCHES IN AN INNINGS

5	Williams N.T. v Hawkes Bay	Napier	1894/95
5	Crowe J.J. v Canterbury	Auckland	1988/89

Record Partnerships

FOR

Wicket	*Score*	*Batsmen*	*Against*	*At*	*Date*
1st	286	B. Sutcliffe & D.D. Taylor	Canterbury	Auckland	1948/49
2nd	241	T.J. Franklin & J.J. Crowe	Wellington	Wellington	1988/89
3rd	445	P.E. Whitelaw & W.N. Carson	Otago	Dunedin	1936/37
4th	280	J.J. Crowe & D.N. Patel	ND	Auckland	1991/92
5th	347*	M.J. Horne & A.C. Barnes	ND	Auckland	2003/04
6th	377	C. Munro & Craig Cachopa	Wellington	Auckland	2012/13
7th	224	V.J. Scott & A.M. Matheson	Canterbury	Auckland	1937/38
8th	189	W.N. Carson & A.M. Matheson	Wellington	Auckland	1938/39
9th	204	B.J. Horne & D.K. Ferns	Otago	Auckland	2020/21
10th	139	M.J. McClenaghan & R.S. Sandhu	ND	Auckland	2016/17

AGAINST

Wicket	*Score*	*Batsmen*	*For*	*At*	*Date*
1st	432	M.H.W. Papps & L.J. Woodcock	Wellington	Wellington	2017/18
2nd	301	D.R. Flynn & B.S. Wilson	ND	Hamilton	2012/13
3rd	287	D.P. Conway & M.G. Bracewell	Wellington	Wellington	2020/21
4th	252	S.A. Thomson & B.A. Young	ND	Auckland	1990/91
5th	282	J.E.C. Franklin & L.J. Woodcock	Wellington	Auckland	2008/09
6th	220	M.H. Toynbee & I.D.S. Smith	CD	Napier	1982/83
7th	165	R.K. Brown & M.E.L. Lane	CD	Palmerston Nth	1993/94
8th	166	R.J. Hadlee & D.R. Hadlee	Canterbury	Christchurch	1983/84
9th	208	W.C. McSkimming & B.E. Scott	Otago	Auckland	2004/05
10th	133	G.A. Bartlett & I.A. Colquhoun	CD	Auckland	1959/60

CANTERBURY

Highest Totals

777	v Otago	Christchurch	1996/97
613-7 dec	v Wellington	Christchurch	2006/07
582	v Central Districts	Napier	2013/14
570-8 dec	v Wellington	Rangiora	2019/20
559	v Central Districts	Christchurch	1993/94
558-4 dec	v Northern Districts	Rangiora	2009/10
551-5 dec	v Central Districts	New Plymouth	2009/10
549	v Northern Districts	Christchurch	1996/97
547-5 dec	v Wellington	Christchurch	1953/54
543-8 dec	v Central Districts	Rangiora	1996/97

Lowest Totals

25	v Otago	Christchurch	1886/87
27	v Otago	Dunedin	1896/97
32	v Otago	Christchurch	1866/67
34	v Otago	Dunedin	1863/64
37	v Southland	Invercargill	1920/21
37	v Wellington	Wellington	1925/26
38	v Otago	Dunedin	1873/74
42	v Otago	Dunedin	1863/64
42	v Otago	Dunedin	1992/93
44	v Otago	Dunedin	1883/84

Most Appearances

121	Fulton P.G.	82	Hadlee B.G.	58	Patrick W.R.
105	Ellis A.M.	77	Stead D.W.	58	Dowling G.T.
105	Astle T.D.	76	Germon L.K.	58	Thomson K.
103	McEwan P.E.	72	Hastings B.F.	57	Bull C.L.
101	Latham R.T.	69	Boyle D.J.	57	Fletcher C.D.
96	Stewart S.L.	65	Brown V.R.	56	Motz R.C.
95	Papps M.H.W.	62	Hadlee R.J.	54	Cromb I.B.
88	Stead G.R.	60	Roberts S.J.	54	Ward J.T.
88	Priest M.W.	59	Hartland B.R.	50	Boxshall C.
84	Harris C.Z.				

Longest Careers

Seasons			*Seasons*		
34	Read R.J.	1904/05-1937/38	21	Stevens E.C.J.	1863/64-1883/84
31	Reese T.W.	1887/88-1917/18	21	Wilding F.	1881/82-1901/02
27	Fowke J.N.	1880/81-1906/07	21	Ridley A.E.	1889/90-1909/10
26	Reese D.	1895/96-1920/21	21	Harris C.Z.	1989/90-2009/10
25	Moorhouse H.M.	1883/84-1907/08	20	Harman T.D.	1882/83-1901/02
22	Wheatley J.	1882/83-1903/04	20	Hadlee B.G.	1961/62-1980/81
22	Patrick W.R.	1905/06-1926/27			

Benefits

McEwan P.E.	1988/89	Germon L.K./Priest M.W.	1997/98
Hadlee R.J.	1989/90	Harris C.Z.	1998/99
Latham R.T.	1992/93	Cairns C.L.	1999/00

Batting

2000 RUNS	*Career*	*M*	*In*	*NO*	*HS*	*Runs*	*Ave*	*100*
Fulton P.G.	2000/01-2016/17	121	224	22	301*	8719	43.16	16
Papps M.H.W.	1998/99-2010/11	95	172	14	192	6663	42.17	19
McEwan P.E.	1977/78-1990/91	103	185	11	155	5940	34.13	11
Latham R.T.	1980/81-1994/95	101	176	17	237*	5919	37.22	8
Stewart S.L.	2001/02-2013/14	96	173	18	227*	5693	36.72	7
Harris C.Z.	1989/90-2009/10	84	125	31	251*	5442	57.89	13
Ellis A.M.	2002/03-2017/18	105	167	21	171	5179	35.47	9
Hadlee B.G.	1961/62-1980/81	82	151	11	163*	4429	31.63	6
Stead G.R.	1993/94-2005/06	88	146	10	190	4410	32.42	10
Astle T.D.	2005/06-2019/20	105	172	20	195	4077	26.82	2
Dowling G.T.	1958/59-1971/72	58	100	7	206	3690	39.67	8
Hastings B.F.	1961/62-1976/77	72	122	8	226	3540	31.05	7
Priest M.W.	1984/85-1998/99	88	130	21	119	3457	31.71	4
Boyle D.J.	1980/81-1994/95	69	121	12	149	3216	29.50	3
Hadlee W.A.	1933/34-1951/52	44	80	7	194	3183	43.60	10
Stead D.W.	1969/70-1985/86	77	133	11	193*	3169	25.97	1
Cromb I.B.	1929/30-1946/47	54	96	5	171	2986	32.81	3
Latham T.W.M.	2010/11-2020/21	43	72	4	261	2907	42.75	5
Brown V.R.	1978/79-1986/87	65	111	11	161*	2872	28.72	5
Patrick W.R.	1905/06-1926/27	58	108	7	129*	2803	27.75	2
Hartland B.R.	1986/87-1996/97	59	103	8	150	2771	29.16	5
Nicholls H.M.	2011/12-2020/21	46	81	4	119	2703	35.10	3
Brownlie D.G.	2009/10-2013/14	35	65	8	171	2635	46.22	6
Coman P.G.	1968/69-1977/78	44	78	4	104	2603	35.17	2
Thomson K.	1959/60-1973/74	58	103	11	136*	2543	27.64	4
Fletcher C.D.	2014/15-2020/21	57	88	17	157	2518	35.46	4

	Career	M	In	NO	HS	Runs	Ave	100
Page M.L.	1920/21-1936/37	41	75	2	206	2424	33.20	2
Leggat J.G.	1944/45-1955/56	35	66	6	166	2391	39.85	5
Chapple M.E.	1949/50-1960/61	44	79	9	165	2364	33.77	3
Germon L.K.	1987/88-1997/98	76	101	25	160*	2336	30.73	3
McMillan C.D.	1994/95-2006/07	40	65	9	159	2332	41.64	6
Kerr J.L.	1929/30-1939/40	32	61	3	196	2228	38.41	3
McClure K.J.	2015/16-2020/21	39	65	7	210	2219	38.25	5
Guillen S.C.	1952/53-1960/61	42	73	5	197	2186	32.14	3
Myburgh J.G.	2007/08-2009/10	25	46	4	199	2172	51.71	7
Reese D.	1895/96-1920/21	47	85	4	111	2066	25.50	2
Ryan M.L.	1965/66-1978/79	45	78	8	129	2041	29.15	2
Hadlee R.J.	1971/72-1988/89	62	100	22	93	2012	25.79	—
Roberts A.W.	1927/28-1940/41	35	60	8	181	2004	38.53	2

CENTURY ON DEBUT FOR PROVINCE

† 175	Watson G.	v Otago	Christchurch	1880/81
† 108 & 18	Wood B.B.	v Wellington	Wellington	1907/08
† 105	Talbot R.O.	v Otago	Dunedin	1922/23
5 & 112*	Newman J.A.	v Otago	Christchurch	1927/28
149	Hastings B.F.	v Central Districts	Nelson	1961/62
8 & 135	Parker N.M.	v Wellington	Wellington	1973/74
115	Hopkins G.J.	v Central Districts	Christchurch	1998/99
102	Dravid R.S.	v Central Districts	Rangiora	2008/09
† 102	McCone R.J.	v Otago	Christchurch	2008/09
† 112*	Brownlie D.G.	v Northern Districts	Rangiora	2009/10

† indicates player was making his first-class debut

HIGHEST INDIVIDUAL INNINGS

301*	Fulton P.G.	v Auckland	Christchurch	2002/03
261	Latham T.W.M.	v Central Districts	Napier	2013/14
251*	Harris C.Z.	v Central Districts	Rangiora	1996/97
241*	Latham T.W.M.	v Wellington	Wellington	2013/14
237*	Latham R.T.	v Northern Districts	Rotorua	1990/91
227*	Stewart S.L.	v Central Districts	New Plymouth	2009/10
226*	Carter L.J.	v Wellington	Rangiora	2019/20
226	Hastings B.F.	v NZ Under 23 XI	Christchurch	1964/65
224	Latham T.W.M.	v Wellington	Wellington	2019/20
221*	Fulton P.G.	v Otago	Dunedin	2004/05
210	McClure K.J.	v Auckland	Rangiora	2017/18
209*	Fulton P.G.	v Central Districts	Christchurch	2014/15
206	Page M.L.	v Wellington	Wellington	1931/32
206	Dowling G.T.	v Wellington	Christchurch	1962/63
206	Harris C.Z.	v Central Districts	Blenheim	1996/97
204	Cox A.	v Otago	Christchurch	1925/26

MOST RUNS IN A SEASON

		Runs	Ave
Papps M.H.W.	2006/07	1005	91.36
Latham T.W.M.	2013/14	948	79.00
Papps M.H.W.	2009/10	927	48.78
Fulton P.G.	2012/13	902	56.37
Fulton P.G.	2014/15	879	54.93
Ellis A.M.	2014/15	853	53.31
Stead G.R.	2000/01	852	50.11
Fulton P.G.	2004/05	828	69.00
Wright J.G.	1986/87	780	60.00
Nicholls H.M.	2014/15	778	43.22
McEwan P.E.	1988/89	758	44.58
Myburgh J.G.	2009/10	758	50.53
Latham R.T.	1988/89	757	58.23
Harris C.Z.	1996/97	748	187.00
Brownlie D.G.	2012/13	743	43.70
Myburgh J.G.	2008/09	739	61.58

		Runs	Ave
Broom N.T.	2014/15	820	45.55
Stewart S.L.	2009/10	812	73.81
McMillan C.D.	1996/97	809	73.54
Papps M.H.W.	2001/02	793	52.86
Brownlie D.G.	2013/14	733	40.72
Englefield J.I.	2000/01	724	38.10
Papps M.H.W.	2008/09	719	59.91
McEwan P.E.	1983/84	713	59.41

MOST CENTURIES IN A SEASON

4	Papps M.H.W.	2006/07
4	Papps M.H.W.	2009/10

TOTAL NUMBER OF CENTURIES		**366**
Most in one season	14	2009/10
1st	Watson G. 175 v Otago	1880/81
100th	Hastings B.F. 136 v Auckland	1964/65
200th	Germon L.K. 114 v Central Districts	1993/94
300th	Brownlie D.G. 153* v Auckland	2010/11

Bowling

150 WICKETS	*Career*	*M*	*Wkts*	*Runs*	*Ave*	*5WI*	*10WM*	*Best*
Astle T.D.	2005/06-2019/20	105	303	9505	31.36	12	1	8-148
Priest M.W.	1984/85-1998/99	88	290	8501	29.31	12	3	9-95
Hadlee R.J.	1971/72-1988/89	62	285	4600	16.14	19	2	7-49
Ellis A.M.	2003/04-2017/18	105	249	7356	29.54	6	—	6-35
Burtt T.B.	1943/44-1954/55	46	241	4991	20.70	16	3	8-35
Motz R.C.	1957/58-1968/69	56	239	4589	19.20	12	3	8-61
Bennett J.H.	1898/99-1919/20	40	205	3367	16.43	17	4	7-35
Hadlee D.R.	1969/70-1983/84	49	195	3918	20.09	10	3	7-55
Roberts S.J.	1985/86-1995/96	60	193	5738	29.73	6	–	5-56
Read R.J.	1904/05-1937/38	44	184	4704	25.56	11	1	7-24
Reese D.	1895/96-1920/21	48	168	3040	18.09	10	1	6-43
Stead D.W.	1969/70-1985/86	77	167	5009	29.99	6	—	7-99
Henry M.J.	2010/11-2020/21	38	160	3897	24.35	7	—	5-21
Brown V.R.	1978/79-1986/87	65	159	4393	27.62	4	2	7-28
Merritt W.E.	1926/27-1935/36	24	154	3559	23.11	15	4	8-105
Wisneski W.A.	1996/97-2003/04	44	154	4092	26.57	7	—	7-151
Bennett H.K.	2005/06-2015/16	48	154	4942	32.09	3	—	7-50
Martin C.S.	1997/98-2009/10	49	152	4445	29.24	3	—	5-40

BEST IN AN INNINGS

10-28	Moss A.E.	v Wellington	Christchurch	1889/90
9-13	Wiseman P.J.	v Central Districts	Christchurch	2004/05
9-56	McBeath D.J.	v Auckland	Christchurch	1918/19
9-95	Priest M.W.	v Otago	Dunedin	1989/90
9-98	Robertson W.	v Wellington	Christchurch	1894/95
8-18	Frith W.	v Otago	Christchurch	1880/81
8-33	Callaway S.T.	v Hawkes Bay	Napier	1903/04
8-35	Burtt T.B.	v Otago	Dunedin	1953/54
8-41	Callaway S.T.	v Otago	Dunedin	1900/01
8-59	Robertson W.	v Auckland	Christchurch	1893/94
8-61	Mulcock E.	v Otago	Christchurch	1937/38
8-61	Motz R.C.	v Wellington	Christchurch	1966/67
8-74	Jamieson K.A.	v Auckland	Rangiora	2016/17
8-75	Edser H.	v Wellington	Wellington	1883/84
8-96	McBeath D.J.	v Auckland	Auckland	1921/22
8-99	Thomas A.W.	v Auckland	Auckland	1914/15

8-105	Merritt W.E.	v Auckland	Auckland	1931/32
8-148	Astle T.D.	v Central Districts	Napier	2013/14

BEST IN A MATCH

15-60	Callaway S.T.	v Hawkes Bay	Napier	1903/04
15-168	McBeath D.J.	v Auckland	Christchurch	1918/19
14-59	Read R.J.	v Southland	Invercargill	1920/21
14-107	Robertson W.	v Auckland	Christchurch	1893/94
14-234	Astle T.D.	v Central Districts	Napier	2013/14
13-72	Moss A.E.	v Wellington	Christchurch	1889/90
13-82	Howell W.B.	v Wellington	Christchurch	1902/03
13-90	Frankish F.S.	v Wellington	Wellington	1901/02
13-140	Edser H.	v Wellington	Wellington	1883/84
13-163	Robertson W.	v Wellington	Christchurch	1894/95
13-181	Merritt W.E.	v Otago	Wellington	1935/36

MOST WICKETS IN A SEASON

		Wkts	*Ave*			*Wkts*	*Ave*
Boock S.L.	1977/78	56	15.66	Hadlee R.J.	1981/82	45	14.31
Callaway S.T.	1903/04	47	8.49	Hadlee R.J.	1986/87	45	12.91

Wicketkeeping

100 DISMISSALS	*Career*	*M*	*Caught*	*Stumped*	*Total*
Germon L.K.	1987/88-1997/98	76	217	21	238
Fletcher C.D.	2014/15-2020/21	57	181	10	191
Ward J.T.	1957/58-1970/71	54	136	17	153
Boxshall C.	1897/98-1914/15	50	70	36	106
van Wyk C.F.K.	2006/07-2009/10	35	101	5	106
Hopkins G.J.	1998/99-2002/03	41	91	10	101

MOST DISMISSALS IN A SEASON

39	(37ct/2st)	Fletcher C.D.	2015/16
34	(31ct/3st)	Germon L.K.	1991/92

MOST DISMISSALS IN A MATCH

9	(9ct)	Germon L.K. v Northern Districts	Christchurch	1992/93

MOST DISMISSALS IN AN INNINGS

6	(6ct)	Germon L.K. v Northern Districts	Christchurch	1992/93
6	(5ct/1st)	Papps M.H.W. v Northern Districts	Gisborne	2004/05

MOST CATCHES IN A MATCH

9	Germon L.K. v Northern Districts	Christchurch	1992/93

MOST CATCHES IN AN INNINGS

6	Germon L.K. v Northern Districts	Christchurch	1992/93

Fielding

MOST CATCHES IN A SEASON

20	Fulton P.G.	2014/15

MOST CATCHES IN A MATCH

6	Cromb I.B. v Otago	Christchurch	1937/38
6	MacDonald G.K. v Pakistan	Christchurch	1984/85
6	Latham R.T. v Otago	Oamaru	1994/95
6	Myburgh J.G. v Auckland	Rangiora	2008/09

MOST CATCHES IN AN INNINGS

5	MacDonald G.K. v Pakistan	Christchurch	1984/85
5	Harris C.Z. v England	Christchurch	2001/02
5	Myburgh J.G. v Auckland	Rangiora	2008/09

Record Partnerships

FOR

Wicket	*Score*	*Batsmen*	*Against*	*At*	*Date*
1st	306	L.A. Cuff & J.D. Lawrence	Auckland	Christchurch	1893/94
2nd	254*	M.H.W. Papps & J.G. Myburgh	CD	Napier	2007/08
3rd	394*	P.G. Kennedy & R.T. Latham	ND	Rotorua	1990/91
4th	278	M.L. Page & A.W. Roberts	Wellington	Wellington	1931/32
5th	290	G.R. Stead & C.Z. Harris	CD	Blenheim	1996/97
6th	379*	S.L. Stewart & C.F.K. van Wyk	CD	New Plymouth	2009/10
7th	265	J.L. Powell & N. Dorreen	Otago	Christchurch	1929/30
8th	220	P.J. Wiseman & B.C. Hiini	ND	Hamilton	2005/06
9th	182*	L.K. Germon & R.M. Ford	Wellington	Christchurch	1989/90
10th	160	L.K. Germon & W.A. Wisneski	ND	Rangiora	1997/98

AGAINST

Wicket	*Score*	*Batsmen*	*For*	*At*	*Date*
1st	286	B. Sutcliffe & D.D. Taylor	Auckland	Auckland	1948/49
2nd	317	R.T. Hart & P.S. Briasco	CD	New Plymouth	1983/84
3rd	278	T.J. Franklin & D.N. Patel	Auckland	Christchurch	1985/86
4th	282	W.A.C. Wilkinson & A.P.F. Chapman	MCC	Christchurch	1922/23
5th	235*	G.P. Sulzberger & J.D. Ryder	CD	Napier	2002/03
6th	211	M.J. Guptill & C. de Grandhomme	Auckland	Rangiora	2011/12
7th	261	A.D.R. Campbell & P.A. Strang	Zimbabwe	Timaru	1997/98
8th	433	A. Sims & V.T. Trumper	Australia	Christchurch	1913/14
9th	134	J.W. Wilson & N.A. Mallender	Otago	Christchurch	1992/93
10th	184	R.C. Blunt & W. Hawksworth	Otago	Christchurch	1931/32

CENTRAL DISTRICTS

Highest Totals

650-8 dec	v Otago	Napier	2015/16
594-8 dec	v Auckland	Auckland	1995/96
584-8 dec	v Otago	Napier	2018/19
549-8 dec	v Canterbury	Christchurch	1998/99
542-4 dec	v Canterbury	Napier	2002/03
538	v Canterbury	Blenheim	2000/01
531-7 dec	v Northern Districts	Napier	2009/10
526	v Otago	Napier	1995/96
524	v Auckland	Auckland	2017/18
523	v Wellington	Wellington	2008/09

Lowest Totals

50	v Wellington	Upper Hutt	1979/80
51	v Northern Districts	Hamilton	1957/58
59	v Auckland	New Plymouth	1958/59
61	v Auckland	Auckland	1996/97
61	v Auckland	Auckland	2007/08
63	v Wellington	Napier	2003/04

65	v Wellington	Nelson	1995/96
71	v Northern Districts	Wanganui	1962/63
72	v Auckland	Palmerston North	2001/02
74	v Otago	Invercargill	1996/97

Most Appearances

119	Sinclair M.S.	77	Ingram P.J.	59	Smith I.D.S.
97	Shrimpton M.J.F.	76	Douglas M.W.	57	Hamilton L.J.
92	How J.M.	74	Sulzberger G.P.	55	Congdon B.E.
90	O'Sullivan D.R.	74	Worker G.H.	55	Jordan A.B.
85	Duff S.W.	67	Edwards G.N.	54	Patel A.Y.
85	Hay G.R.	67	Young W.A.	53	Colquhoun I.A.
83	Blain T.E.	62	Smith C.J.P.	53	Toynbee M.H.
82	Griggs B.B.J.	62	Smith B.S.	53	Schofield R.M.
81	Briasco P.S.	62	Bracewell D.A.J.	53	Pierce R.A.
79	Mason M.J.	61	Greatbatch M.J.	53	Cleaver D.
78	Robertson G.K.	61	Yuile B.W.	51	Thompson E.P.

Longest Careers

Seasons			*Seasons*		
19	Shrimpton M.J.F.	1961/62-1979/80	16	Snook I.R.	1972/73-1987/88
19	Taylor L.R.P.L.	2002/03-2020/21	16	Ryder J.D.	2002/03-2017/18
18	Sinclair M.S.	1995/96-2012/13	15	Coutts P.J.C.	1958/59-1972/73
17	Jones A.H.	1979/80-1995/96	15	Mason M.J.	1997/98-2011/12
16	Chapple M.E.	1950/51-1965/66	15	How J.M.	2000/01-2014/15
16	Schofield R.M.	1959/60-1974/75	15	Hay G.R.	2006/07-2020/21

Benefits

O'Sullivan D.R.	1984/85	Duff S.W.	1995/96
Robertson G.K.	1989/90	Greatbatch M.J.	1996/97
Briasco P.S.	1991/92	Douglas M.W.	2000/01
Blain T.E.	1994/95	Sinclair M.S.	2009/10

Batting

2000 RUNS	*Career*	*M*	*In*	*NO*	*HS*	*Runs*	*Ave*	*100*
Sinclair M.S.	1995/96-2012/13	119	203	26	243*	9148	51.68	27
Hay G.R.	2006/07-2020/21	85	149	11	226	5866	42.50	13
How J.M.	2000/01-2014/15	92	167	16	207*	5680	37.61	13
Ingram P.J.	2001/02-2011/12	77	140	8	247	5378	40.74	17
Shrimpton M.J.F.	1961/62-1979/80	97	171	15	150	4551	29.17	5
Blain T.E.	1982/83-1994/95	83	145	15	161	4547	34.97	7
Young W.A.	2011/12-2020/21	67	116	12	162	4454	42.82	8
Greatbatch M.J.	1986/87-1999/00	61	107	8	202*	4363	44.07	14
Briasco P.S.	1982/83-1991/92	81	146	16	157	4301	33.08	6
Douglas M.W.	1987/88-2000/01	76	132	19	144	3838	33.96	7
Worker G.H.	2007/08-2020/21	74	129	4	210	3730	29.84	7
Edwards G.N.	1973/74-1984/85	67	122	5	177*	3709	31.70	5
Sulzberger G.P.	1995/96-2004/05	74	120	12	159	3505	32.45	8
Smith C.J.P.	1983/84-1990/91	62	118	9	160*	3499	32.10	7
Smith B.S.	2010/11-2020/21	62	107	7	244	3313	33.13	6
Crowe M.D.	1983/84-1989/90	32	55	7	242	3299	68.72	13
Cleaver D.	2010/11-2020/21	53	90	10	201	3197	39.96	5
Griggs B.B.J	2000/01-2009/10	82	129	16	143	3144	27.82	2
Duff S.W.	1985/86-1995/96	85	129	29	164*	3079	30.79	1
Bruce T.C.	2014/15-2020/21	49	87	12	166*	3061	40.81	4

	Career	M	In	NO	HS	Runs	Ave	100
Spearman C.M.	1996/97-2003/04	44	76	3	144	2951	40.42	5
van Wyk C.F.K.	2010/11-2015/16	45	73	19	131	2854	52.85	3
Congdon B.E.	1960/61-1970/71	55	93	8	202*	2807	33.02	3
Taylor L.R.P.L.	2002/03-2020/21	48	75	1	217	2783	37.60	4
Weston T.I.	2005/06-2010/11	46	75	11	152	2577	40.26	2
Bracewell D.A.J.	2008/09-2020/21	62	93	15	105	2518	32.28	2
Payton D.H.	1965/66-1976/77	49	92	4	145	2459	27.94	3
Pierce R.A.	1971/72-1984/85	53	98	5	100*	2296	24.68	1
Smith I.D.S.	1977/78-1986/87	59	95	12	145	2265	27.28	3
Hart R.T.	1982/83-1990/91	37	68	3	207	2222	34.18	5
Yuile B.W.	1959/60-1971/72	61	90	10	146	2190	27.37	1
Noema-Barnett K.	2008/09-2018/19	47	73	9	108	2053	32.07	4

CENTURY ON DEBUT FOR PROVINCE

† 117	Macleod D.N.	v Wellington	Wanganui	1956/57
† 25 & 119	Sampson H.C.	v Wellington	Wellington	1970/71
119 & 0	Crowe M.D.	v Northern Districts	Whangarei	1983/84
112 & 21	Wilson S.W.J.	v Otago	Blenheim	1990/91
124 & 7*	Smith B.F.	v Otago	Wanganui	2000/01
† 203 & 4	Schmulian B.D.	v Northern Districts	Mt Maunganui	2017/18

† indicates player was making his first-class debut

HIGHEST INDIVIDUAL INNINGS

247	Ingram P.J.	v Northern Districts	Hamilton	2008/09
245*	Ingram P.J.	v Wellington	Wellington	2009/10
244	Smith B.S.	v Otago	Napier	2015/16
243*	Sinclair M.S.	v Otago	Napier	2007/08
242	Crowe M.D.	v Otago	New Plymouth	1989/90
226	Hay G.R.	v Otago	Alexandra	2018/19
217	Taylor L.R.P.L.	v Otago	Napier	2006/07
212*	Kelly D.P.	v Canterbury	Blenheim	2000/01
210	Worker G.H.	v Wellington	Nelson	2015/16
207*	How J.M.	v Otago	Nelson	2013/14
207	Hart R.T.	v Wellington	Wellington	1985/86
203*	Sinclair M.S.	v Northern Districts	Wanganui	1998/99
203	Schmulian B.D.	v Northern Districts	Mt Maunganui	2017/18
202*	Congdon B.E.	v Otago	Nelson	1968/69
202*	Greatbatch M.J.	v Otago	Palmerston North	1988/89
202*	Hay G.R.	v Canterbury	Rangiora	2013/14
202	Greatbatch M.J.	v Northern Districts	Rotorua	1995/96
201*	Smith B.F.	v Canterbury	New Plymouth	2001/02
201	Cleaver D.	v Northern Districts	Napier	2019/20

MOST RUNS IN A SEASON

		Runs	Ave
Crowe M.D.	1986/87	1348	103.69
Smith B.F.	2000/01	939	58.68
Smith B.S.	2015/16	917	61.13
Young W.A.	2014/15	909	53.47
Sinclair M.S.	2008/09	904	75.33
Ingram P.J.	2008/09	884	63.14
Ingram P.J.	2010/11	858	50.47
Ingram P.J.	2009/10	855	77.72
Sinclair M.S.	2011/12	809	53.93
Cachopa C.	2012/13	807	47.47
Hay G.R.	2017/18	786	60.46
Sinclair M.S.	2009/10	778	59.64
Raval J.A.	2012/13	750	44.11
Young W.A.	2015/16	733	45.81
van Wyk C.F.K.	2013/14	725	55.76
Sinclair M.S.	2005/06	723	51.64
Sinclair M.S.	1996/97	722	48.13
Douglas M.W.	1991/92	714	44.62
Briasco P.S.	1990/91	708	41.64
How J.M.	2012/13	706	41.52
How J.M.	2002/03	704	44.00

MOST CENTURIES IN A SEASON

6 Crowe M.D. 1986/87

TOTAL NUMBER OF CENTURIES		**288**
Most in one season	12	2008/09, 2011/12
1st	Hunter A.A. 108 v Otago	1951/52
100th	Blain T.E. 103* v Otago	1990/91
200th	Hay G.R. 131* v Canterbury	2008/09

Bowling

150 WICKETS	*Career*	*M*	*Wkts*	*Runs*	*Ave*	*5WI*	*10WM*	*Best*
O'Sullivan D.R.	1972/73-1984/85	90	392	9560	24.38	21	3	6-40
Mason M.J.	1997/98-2011/12	78	263	6387	24.28	12	1	6-20
Yuile B.W.	1959/60-1971/72	61	233	4485	19.24	11	2	9-100
Robertson G.K.	1979/80-1989/90	78	228	6573	28.78	8	1	6-47
Patel A.Y.	2012/13-2020/21	54	217	6722	30.97	16	3	6-48
Beard D.D.	1950/51-1960/61	49	213	4531	21.27	8	2	7-56
Duff S.W.	1985/86-1995/96	85	208	6856	32.96	4	2	6-36
Hamilton L.J.	1996/97-2006/07	57	198	5104	25.77	7	—	6-32
Bracewell D.A.J.	2008/09-2019/20	57	188	5825	30.98	6	—	7-35
Thompson E.P.	2000/01-2009/10	51	171	5140	30.05	6	1	7-55
Jordan A.B.	1968/69-1979/80	55	157	4431	28.22	7	—	7-82
Cave H.B.	1950/51-1958/59	37	150	2962	19.74	7	1	7-31

BEST IN AN INNINGS

9-100	Yuile B.W.	v Canterbury	New Plymouth	1965/66
7-28	Yuile B.W.	v Northern Districts	Hamilton	1967/68
7-35	Bracewell D.A.J.	v Canterbury	Rangiora	2012/13
7-31	Cave H.B.	v Auckland	Palmerston North	1952/53
7-33	Cave H.B.	v Northern Districts	New Plymouth	1956/57
7-36	Yuile B.W.	v Otago	Nelson	1962/63
7-36	Schwass A.M.	v Northern Districts	Blenheim	2001/02

BEST IN A MATCH

13-64	Cave H.B.	v Auckland	Palmerston North	1952/53
11-99	Beard D.D.	v Otago	Dunedin	1956/57
11-115	Mason M.J.	v Canterbury	Timaru	2002/03
11-134	Robertson G.K.	v Northern Districts	Nelson	1986/87
11-138	Kay D.J.	v Canterbury	Palmerston North	1976/77

MOST WICKETS IN A SEASON

		Wkts	*Ave*
O'Sullivan D.R.	1978/79	52	19.01
Patel A.Y.	2017/18	48	21.52
Schwass A.M.	2001/02	45	14.73
O'Sullivan D.R.	1977/78	44	20.22
Patel A.Y	2016/17	44	30.81
Patel A.Y.	2015/16	43	33.69
Blair R.W.	1955/56	42	17.28
Hamilton L.J.	2001/02	42	18.40
O'Sullivan D.R.	1980/81	40	22.00
Mason M.J.	2002/03	40	19.67

Wicketkeeping

100 DISMISSALS	*Career*	*M*	*Caught*	*Stumped*	*Total*
Griggs B.B.J	2000/01-2009/10	82	225	7	232
Cleaver D.	2010/11-2020/21	53	145	11	156
van Wyk C.F.K.	2010/11-2015/16	45	140	5	145
Blain T.E.	1982/83-1994/95	83	124	19	143
Colquhoun I.A.	1953/54-1963/64	53	102	28	130

100 DISMISSALS	Career	M	Caught	Stumped	Total
Smith I.D.S.	1977/78-1986/87	59	119	11	130
Sigley M.A.	1994/95-2002/03	44	124	4	128
Schofield R.M.	1959/60-1974/75	53	107	15	122

MOST DISMISSALS IN A SEASON

40	(39ct/1st))	van Wyk C.F.K.	2014/15
36	(35ct/1st))	Griggs B.B.J.	2005/06

MOST DISMISSALS IN A MATCH

10	(10ct)	van Wyk C.F.K. v Otago	Napier	2014/15

MOST DISMISSALS IN AN INNINGS

7	(7ct)	Schofield R.M. v Wellington	Wellington	1964/65
7	(7ct)	Griggs B.B.J. v Northern Districts	Hamilton	2007/08

MOST CATCHES IN A MATCH

10	van Wyk C.F.K. v Otago	Napier	2014/15

MOST CATCHES IN AN INNINGS

7	Schofield R.M. v Wellington	Wellington	1964/65
7	Griggs B.B.J. v Northern Districts	Hamilton	2007/08

Fielding

MOST CATCHES IN A SEASON

22	Bruce T.C.	2015/16

MOST CATCHES IN A MATCH

5	Congdon B.E.v Wellington	Wellington	1964/65
5	Congdon B.E. v Otago	New Plymouth	1970/71
5	Smith I.D.S. v Auckland	New Plymouth	1978/79
5	Edwards G.N. v Otago	Palmerston North	1979/80
5	Briasco P.S. v Canterbury	Christchurch	1984/85
5	Douglas M.W. v Otago	Palmerston North	1988/89
5	How J.M. v Canterbury	Palmerston North	2003/04
5	Sinclair M.S. v Canterbury	Napier	2010/11
5	Sinclair M.S. v Wellington	Wellington	2010/11
5	Sinclair M.S. v Auckland	Napier	2012/13
5	How J.M. v Wellington	Napier	2013/14

MOST CATCHES IN AN INNINGS

5	Sinclair M.S. v Wellington	Wellington	2010/11

Record Partnerships

FOR

Wicket	Score	Batsmen	Against	At	Date
1st	428	P.J. Ingram & J.M. How	Wellington	Wellington	2009/10
2nd	317	R.T. Hart & P.S. Briasco	Canterbury	New Plymouth	1983/84
3rd	264	P.J. Ingram & M.S. Sinclair	ND	Hamilton	2008/09
4th	276*	M.D. Crowe & P.S. Briasco	Canterbury	Christchurch	1986/87
5th	301	J.I. Englefield & L.R.P.L. Taylor	Wellington	P. North	2004/05
6th	235	M.S. Sinclair & B.B.J. Griggs	Wellington	Wellington	2008/09
7th	219	B.W. Yuile & B.L. Hampton	Canterbury	Napier	1967/68
8th	173	I.D.S. Smith & G.K. Robertson	ND	Hamilton	1982/83
9th	239	H.B. Cave & I.B. Leggat	Otago	Dunedin	1952/53
10th	134	G.H. Worker & A.W. Mathieson	Wellington	Nelson	2015/16

AGAINST

Wicket	Score	Batsmen	For	At	Date
1st	316	M.H. Austen & R.T. Hart	Wellington	Wanganui	1993/94
2nd	254*	M.H.W. Papps & J.G. Myburgh	Canterbury	Napier	2007/08
3rd	306	S.B. Haig & N.T. Broom	Otago	Napier	2009/10
4th	310	J.D. Ryder & N.R. Parlane	Wellington	P. North	2004/05
5th	341	G.R. Larsen & E.B. McSweeney	Wellington	Levin	1987/88
6th	379*	S.L. Stewart & C.F.K. van Wyk	Canterbury	New Plymouth	2009/10
7th	192	S.W. Brown & A.C. Parore	Auckland	Auckland	1990/91
8th	143	C.M. Presland & C.W. Dickeson	ND	Whangarei	1983/84
9th	225	L.J. Woodcock & M.J. Tugaga	Wellington	Wellington	2009/10
10th	89	M.J.E. Wright & S.J. Scott	ND	Wanganui	1978/79

NORTHERN DISTRICTS

Highest Totals

726	v Canterbury	Rangiora	2009/10
614-7 dec	v Auckland	Hamilton	2012/13
608-9 dec	v Wellington	Lincoln	2011/12
559-9 dec	v Otago	Hamilton	2010/11
556-9 dec	v Central Districts	New Plymouth	2014/15
546	v Wellington	Whangarei	2008/09
533-6 dec	v Otago	Hamilton	2012/13
523-7 dec	v Otago	Hamilton	2006/07
520-8 dec	v Otago	Hamilton	1987/88
518-4 dec	v Canterbury	Christchurch	1996/97

Lowest Totals

32	v Auckland	Hamilton	1996/97
52	v Canterbury	Hamilton	1966/67
57	v Wellington	Hamilton	1961/62
59	v Canterbury	Hamilton	1960/61
64	v Otago	Dunedin	1971/72
64	v Auckland	Auckland	1987/88
69	v Australia	Hamilton	1973/74
69	v England	Hamilton	1996/97
77	v Auckland	Auckland	2000/01
79	v Auckland	Auckland	1989/90

Most Appearances

127	Marshall J.A.H.
120	Yovich J.A.F.
119	Aldridge G.W.
115	Bradburn G.E.
104	Roberts A.D.G.
100	Flynn D.R.
99	White D.J.
95	Hart M.N.
93	Young B.A.
91	Watling B-J.
90	Dickeson C.W.
85	Parlane M.E.
85	Hart R.G.
82	Kuggeleijn C.M.
82	Dunning B.
78	Bailey M.D.
78	Wilson B.S.
77	Martin B.P.
76	Marshall H.J.H.
76	Baker J.D.
75	Parker J.M.
66	Puna N.
65	Wright M.J.E.
64	Mitchell D.J.
62	Arnel B.J.
62	Cooper B.G.
59	McGlashan P.D.
59	Kuggeleijn S.C.
58	Howarth G.P.
57	Petrie E.C.
56	Sodhi I.S.
55	Bradburn W.P.
54	Crocker L.M.
53	Devcich A.P.
51	Thomson S.A.

Longest Careers

Seasons		
19	Parlane M.E.	1992/93-2010/11
18	Vettori D.L.	1996/97-2013/14
17	Dunning B.	1961/62-1977/78
17	Roberts A.D.G.	1967/68-1983/84
17	Bradburn G.E.	1985/86-2001/02
17	Yovich J.A.F.	1996/97-2012/13
17	Aldridge G.W.	1998/99-2014/15
17	Watling B-J.	2004/05-2020/21
16	Kuggeleijn C.M.	1975/76-1990/91
16	Marshall J.A.H.	1997/98-2012/13
16	Flynn D.R.	2004/05-2019/20
15	Giles G.V.	1961/62-1975/76
15	Cooper B.G.	1980/81-1994/95
15	Young B.A.	1983/84-1997/98
15	Hart M.N.	1990/91-2004/05
15	Devcich A.P.	2004/05-2018/19
15	Southee T.G.	2006/07-2020/21

Benefits

Kuggeleijn C.M.	1990/91
White D.J.	1992/93
Cooper B.G.	1995/96
Young B.A.	1997/98

Batting

2000 RUNS	*Career*	*M*	*In*	*NO*	*HS*	*Runs*	*Ave*	*100*
Marshall J.A.H.	1997/98-2012/13	127	214	16	235	6418	32.41	11
Flynn D.R.	2004/05-2019/20	100	175	9	241	6265	37.74	20
Roberts A.D.G.	1967/68-1983/84	104	192	35	128*	5533	35.24	7
Watling B-J.	2004/05-2020/21	91	162	12	176	5479	36.52	9
Yovich J.A.F.	1996/97-2012/13	120	189	29	144	4839	30.24	6
White D.J.	1979/80-1992/93	99	173	15	209	4656	29.46	7
Bradburn G.E.	1985/86-2001/02	115	188	23	148*	4614	27.96	4
Parker J.M.	1972/73-1983/84	75	139	19	195	4611	38.42	7
Parlane M.E.	1992/93-2010/11	85	146	13	146	4258	32.01	7
Wilson B.S.	2004/05-2014/15	78	143	7	165	4171	30.66	8
Marshall H.J.H.	1998/99-2011/12	76	130	9	170	4093	33.82	6
Dunning B.	1961/62-1977/78	82	148	10	142	3898	28.24	3
Young B.A.	1983/84-1997/98	93	148	36	138*	3853	34.40	5
Bailey M.D.	1989/90-2001/02	78	122	8	180*	3468	30.42	6
Kuggeleijn C.M.	1975/76-1990/91	82	138	12	116	3457	27.43	3
Mitchell D.J.	2011/12-2019/20	64	107	14	170*	3429	36.87	7
Hart M.N.	1990/91-2004/05	95	140	15	201*	3398	27.18	4
Wright J.G.	1975/76-1983/84	43	84	3	145*	3301	40.75	5
Howarth G.P.	1974/75-1985/86	58	105	6	151	3122	31.53	5
Cooper B.G.	1980/81-1994/95	62	110	4	116*	2982	28.13	4
Popli B.	2013/14-2020/21	48	83	4	172	2889	36.56	3
Carter J.F.	2013/14-2020/21	49	88	3	169	2857	33.61	6
Crocker L.M.	1982/83-1988/89	54	100	3	126	2663	27.45	2
Wright M.J.E.	1972/73-1983/84	65	114	10	115	2632	25.30	1
Devcich A.P.	2004/05-2018/19	53	95	5	132	2606	28.95	4
Gibson J.G.	1968/69-1980/81	49	92	5	128	2580	29.65	4
Thomson S.A.	1987/88-1996/97	51	80	20	167	2530	42.16	5
McGlashan P.D.	2004/05-2011/12	59	85	6	115	2482	31.41	2
Seifert T.L.	2014/15-2020/21	41	71	4	167*	2424	36.17	5
Aldridge G.W.	1998/99-2014/15	119	157	42	75	2327	20.23	—
Kuggeleijn S.C.	2013/14-2020/21	59	98	18	112	2312	28.90	2
Brownlie D.G.	2014/15-2019/20	33	60	3	334	2224	39.01	5
Hart R.G.	1992/93-2003/04	85	119	19	102*	2135	21.35	1
Hick G.A.	1987/88-1988/89	17	30	4	211*	2055	79.03	10
Wealleans K.A.	1988/89-1994/95	43	74	4	112*	2053	29.33	4

	Career	M	In	NO	HS	Runs	Ave	100
Cooper H.R.	2016/17-2020/21	33	58	2	149	2053	36.66	5
Williamson K.S.	2007/08-2019/20	25	41	4	284*	2021	54.62	6
Bradburn W.P.	1957/58-1968/69	55	103	5	107	2015	20.56	1
Horsley N.K.W.	2002/03-2007/08	35	60	3	159	2003	35.14	2

CENTURY ON DEBUT FOR PROVINCE

118	McGregor P.B.	v Auckland	Hamilton	1962/63
† 127*	Mitchell W.J.	v Pakistan	Hamilton	1964/65
14 & 153*	Maynard M.P.	v Auckland	Hamilton	1990/91

† indicates player was making his first-class debut

HIGHEST INDIVIDUAL INNINGS

334	Brownlie D.G.	v Central Districts	New Plymouth	2014/15
284*	Williamson K.S.	v Wellington	Lincoln	2011/12
241	Flynn D.R.	v Otago	Hamilton	2010/11
235	Marshall J.A.H.	v Canterbury	Christchurch	2001/02
212*	Styris S.B.	v Otago	Hamilton	2001/02
211*	Hick G.A.	v Auckland	Auckland	1988/89
209	White D.J.	v Central Districts	Hamilton	1985/86
201*	Hart M.N.	v Auckland	Auckland	2002/03

MOST RUNS IN A SEASON

		Runs	Ave
Hick G.A.	1988/89	1228	94.46
Popli B.	2015/16	1149	67.58
Maynard M.P.	1991/92	893	68.69
Hick G.A.	1987/88	827	63.61
Flynn D.R.	2013/14	775	43.05
Marshall H.J.H.	2006/07	766	54.71
Flynn D.R.	2015/16	764	42.44
Devcich A.P.	2014/15	744	49.60
Wilson B.S.	2010/11	733	48.86
Bradburn G.E.	1989/90	726	36.30
Wealleans K.A.	1989/90	721	36.05
Mitchell D.J.	2012/13	709	54.53
Williamson K.S.	2008/09	707	54.38
Marshall J.A.H.	2001/02	706	39.22
Seifert T.L.	2017/18	703	50.21

MOST CENTURIES IN A SEASON

6 Hick G.A. 1988/89

TOTAL NUMBER OF CENTURIES		237
Most in one season	12	2012/13
1st	Everest J.K. 104 v Canterbury	1956/57
100th	Parlane M.E. 132* v Canterbury	1995/96
200th	Santner M.J. 101 v Central Districts	2014/15

Bowling

150 WICKETS	Career	M	Wkts	Runs	Ave	5WI	10WM	Best
Aldridge G.W.	1998/99-2014/15	119	355	10052	28.31	14	1	6-41
Dickeson C.W.	1973/74-1986/87	90	282	8242	29.22	9	2	7-79
Yovich J.A.F.	1996/97-2012/13	110	255	8579	33.64	8	1	7-64
Bradburn G.E.	1985/86-2001/02	115	231	7302	31.61	3	—	6-56
Arnel B.J.	2005/06-2017/18	62	229	5432	23.97	10	1	6-18
Puna N.	1956/57-1968/69	66	224	5314	23.72	11	—	6-25
Kuggeleijn S.C.	2013/14-2020/21	59	205	6121	29.85	8	—	7-45
Baker J.D.	2010/11-2020/21	76	201	5961	29.65	7	1	6-72
Sodhi I.S.	2012/13-2020/21	56	201	6003	29.26	13	2	7-30
Martin B.P.	1999/00-2009/10	77	192	6889	35.88	12	2	7-33
de Groen R.P.	1990/91-1995/96	38	157	3320	21.14	8	2	7-50

BEST IN AN INNINGS

9-48	Tait A.R.	v Auckland	Hamilton	1996/97
8-21	Langdon M.C.	v Auckland	Auckland	1963/64
8-27	Southee T.G.	v Wellington	Hamilton	2009/10
8-30	Alabaster G.D.	v NZ Under 23 XI	Hamilton	1962/63
8-37	Clarke D.B.	v Central Districts	Wanganui	1962/63
8-49	Kennedy K.D.	v Central Districts	Hamilton	1969/70

BEST IN A MATCH

16-130	Tait A.R.	v Auckland	Hamilton	1996/97
13-99	de Groen R.P.	v Otago	Alexandra	1992/93
12-55	Martin B.P.	v Auckland	Taupo	1999/00
12-62	Sodhi I.S.	v Wellington	Wellington	2017/18
12-109	Lissette A.F.	v Otago	Dunedin	1959/60

MOST WICKETS IN A SEASON

		Wkts	*Ave*
Tait A.R.	1996/97	53	16.32
de Groen R.P.	1992/93	46	16.84
Arnel B.J.	2012/13	45	24.84
Aldridge G.W.	2009/10	42	23.04
Yovich J.A.F.	2001/02	40	26.45
Sodhi I.S.	2016/17	40	25.92

Wicketkeeping

100 DISMISSALS	*Career*	*M*	*Caught*	*Stumped*	*Total*
Hart R.G.	1992/93-2003/04	85	228	15	243
Young B.A.	1983/84-1997/98	93	179	11	190
McGlashan P.D.	2004/05-2011/12	59	175	12	187
Watling B-J.	2004/05-2020/21	91	129	2	131
Wright M.J.E.	1972/73-1983/84	65	104	17	121
Seifert T.L.	2014/15-2020/21	41	109	7	116
Petrie E.C.	1956/57-1966/67	57	90	22	112

MOST DISMISSALS IN A SEASON

41 (37ct/4st) McGlashan P.D. 2009/10

MOST DISMISSALS IN A MATCH

12 (12ct) McGlashan P.D. v Central Districts Whangarei 2009/10

MOST DISMISSALS IN AN INNINGS

7 (7ct) Young B.A. v Canterbury Christchurch 1986/87

MOST CATCHES IN A MATCH

12 McGlashan P.D. v Central Districts Whangarei 2009/10

MOST CATCHES IN AN INNINGS

7 Young B.A. v Canterbury Christchurch 1986/87

Fielding

MOST CATCHES IN A SEASON

15 Mitchell D.J. 2014/15 15 Brownlie D.G. 2015/16

MOST CATCHES IN A MATCH

6	Young B.A. v Wellington	Wellington	1995/96
6	Vettori D.L. v Canterbury	Rangiora	2011/12
6	Anderson C.J. v Auckland	Auckland	2015/16
6	Brownlie D.G. v Canterbury	Christchurch	2018/19

MOST CATCHES IN AN INNINGS

4	Pairaudeau B.H. v Central Districts	Wanganui	1962/63
4	Harris S.J. (sub) v Otago	Dunedin	1965/66
4	Barton P.H. v Canterbury	Hamilton	1974/75
4	Young B.A. v Wellington	Wellington	1995/96
4	Bailey M.D. v Otago	Alexandra	1996/97
4	Vettori D.L. v Canterbury	Rangiora	2011/12
4	Mitchell D.J. v Auckland	Whangarei	2014/15
4	Brownlie D.G. v Canterbury	Christchurch	2018/19

Record Partnerships

FOR

Wicket	*Score*	*Batsmen*	*Against*	*At*	*Date*
1st	278	D.R. Flynn & H.R. Cooper	Canterbury	Whangarei	2017/18
2nd	317	D.R. Flynn & B.S. Wilson	Auckland	Hamilton	2012/13
3rd	261*	M.P. Maynard & S.A. Thomson	Auckland	Hamilton	1990/91
4th	283	D.R. Flynn & C.J. Anderson	Otago	Hamilton	2012/13
5th	226	D.J. Mitchell & T.L. Seifert	Otago	Dunedin	2016/17
6th	322	M.G. Orchard & J.A.F. Yovich	CD	Napier	2005/06
7th	174	B. Popli & M.J. Santner	Wellington	Gisborne	2013/14
8th	163	P.D.McGlashan & G.W.Aldridge	Canterbury	Hamilton	2008/09
9th	188	N.R. Parlane & D.R. Tuffey	Wellington	Wellington	1999/00
10th	113*	P.D. McGlashan & G.W. Aldridge	Wellington	Wellington	2005/06

AGAINST

Wicket	*Score*	*Batsmen*	*For*	*At*	*Date*
1st	310	R.H. Vance & B.A. Edgar	Wellington	Wellington	1988/89
2nd	263	M.J. Greatbatch & M.D. Crowe	CD	Morrinsville	1986/87
3rd	394*	P.G. Kennedy & R.T. Latham	Canterbury	Rotorua	1990/91
4th	280	J.J. Crowe & D.N. Patel	Auckland	Auckland	1991/92
5th	347*	M.J. Horne & A.C. Barnes	Auckland	Auckland	2003/04
6th	224	B.D. Schmulian & D.A.J. Bracewell	CD	Mt Maunganui	2017/18
7th	205	L.K. Germon & M.W. Priest	Canterbury	Christchurch	1991/92
8th	220	P.J. Wiseman & B.C. Hiini	Canterbury	Hamilton	2005/06
9th	151	R.A. Young & G.J. Morgan	Auckland	Auckland	2007/08
10th	160	L.K. Germon & W.A. Wisneski	Canterbury	Rangiora	1997/98

OTAGO

Highest Totals

651-9 dec	v Wellington	Dunedin	2012/13
624	v Central Districts	Napier	2006/07
602-8 dec	v Canterbury	Dunedin	1928/29
601-9 dec	v Canterbury	Christchurch	2006/07
589	v Canterbury	Christchurch	1931/32
576-8 dec	v Northern Districts	Whangarei	2009/10
571-8	v Central Districts	Napier	1995/96
569-8 dec	v Auckland	Dunedin	2012/13
558-8 dec	v Auckland	Dunedin	1949/50
548-7 dec	v Auckland	Dunedin	1996/97

Lowest Totals

34	v Wellington	Dunedin	1956/57
35	v Auckland	Christchurch	1884/85
36	v New South Wales	Dunedin	1889/90
40	v Canterbury	Dunedin	1869/70
41	v Auckland	Dunedin	1873/74
42	v Canterbury	Dunedin	1871/72
43	v Canterbury	Christchurch	1872/73
44	v Canterbury	Dunedin	1904/05
46	v Pakistan	Dunedin	1978/79
47	v Canterbury	Christchurch	1888/89

Most Appearances

108	Lees W.K.	69	Alabaster G.D.	60	Sutcliffe B.
101	Broom N.T.	68	Cameron F.J.	60	Milburn B.D.
99	de Boorder D.C.	68	Rutherford K.R.	59	Smith L.D.
95	Cumming C.D.	67	McSkimming W.C.	59	Turner G.M.
90	Blair B.R.	66	Lawson R.A.	57	Burns K.J.
90	McGregor S.N.	65	Alabaster J.C.	56	McMillan J.M.
88	Boock S.L.	64	Rutherford H.D.	55	Mills G.H.
81	Blair W.L.	63	Rutherford I.A.	55	Sewell D.G.
80	Hoskin R.N.	63	Wagner N.	55	Bracewell M.G.
78	Mallender N.A.	63	Duffy J.A.	54	Moir A.M.
75	McCullum S.J.	62	McCullum N.L.	54	Dobbs P.W.
75	Gaffaney C.B.	61	Campbell K.O.	51	Knight A.R.
74	Redmond A.J.	61	Wells S.R.		

Longest Careers

Seasons			*Seasons*		
27	Downes A.D.	1887/88-1913/14	22	McGregor S.N.	1947/48-1968/69
26	Knight A.R.	1918/19-1943/44	21	Groves L.J.	1929/30-1949/50
24	Siedeberg H.G.	1898/99-1921/22	21	Alabaster G.D.	1955/56-1975/76
24	Blair W.L.	1967/68-1990/91	20	Fisher A.H.	1890/91-1909/10
23	Torrance R.C.	1905/06-1927/28	20	Watt L.	1943/44-1962/63
23	Smith L.D.	1934/35-1956/57	20	Milburn B.D.	1963/64-1982/83
23	Mills G.H.	1935/36-1957/58			

Benefits

Lees W.K.	1987/88	Boock S.L.	1989/90	Mallender N.A.	1992/93

Batting

2000 RUNS	*Career*	*M*	*In*	*NO*	*HS*	*Runs*	*Ave*	*100*
Cumming C.D.	2000/01-2011/12	95	167	15	173	6589	43.34	21
Broom N.T.	2005/06-2019/20	101	172	22	203*	6085	40.56	15
Sutcliffe B.	1946/47-1961/62	60	110	8	385	6028	59.09	17
Blair B.R.	1977/78-1989/90	90	154	5	143	5057	33.93	7
Rutherford K.R.	1982/83-1994/95	68	121	7	226*	5051	44.30	14
Redmond A.J.	2004/05-2014/15	74	130	8	154	4795	39.30	11
de Boorder D.C.	2007/08-2017/18	99	154	25	146	4695	36.39	4
Turner G.M.	1964/65-1982/83	59	109	14	186*	4439	46.72	13
Rutherford H.D.	2008/09-2020/21	64	116	0	239	4434	38.22	10
Gaffaney C.B.	1995/96-2004/05	75	138	11	194	4326	34.06	7
McGregor S.N.	1947/48-1968/69	90	167	13	114*	4259	27.65	3
Lees W.K.	1972/73-1987/88	108	179	31	124	3754	25.36	4
Blair W.L.	1967/68-1990/91	81	149	9	140	3654	26.10	2

	Career	M	In	NO	HS	Runs	Ave	100
Hoskin R.N.	1980/81-1992/93	80	138	6	157	3573	27.06	6
Bracewell M.G.	2010/11-2016/17	55	98	7	190	3266	35.89	7
McCullum S.J.	1976/77-1990/91	75	131	1	134	3174	24.41	2
Rutherford I.A.	1974/75-1983/84	63	115	3	222	3122	27.87	4
Richardson M.H.	1992/93-2000/01	49	89	10	166	3089	39.10	8
Lawson R.A.	1992/93-2003/04	66	120	5	200	2890	25.13	2
Todd G.R.	2004/05-2009/10	45	79	10	165	2774	40.20	4
Burns K.J.	1980/81-1991/92	57	98	6	136	2699	29.33	3
Campbell K.O.	1963/64-1978/79	61	108	17	111	2613	28.71	3
Dobbs P.W.	1988/89-1994/95	54	99	6	144*	2606	28.02	3
Wells S.R.	2007/08-2016/17	61	95	10	118	2588	30.44	4
Alabaster G.D.	1955/56-1975/76	69	108	16	108	2340	25.43	3
Smith L.D.	1934/35-1956/57	59	108	16	109	2277	24.75	1
McCullum N.L.	1999/00-2015/16	62	97	9	106*	2270	25.79	1
Knight A.R.	1918/19-1943/44	51	97	3	152	2245	23.88	1
Kitchen A.K.	2015/16-2020/21	37	70	2	207	2226	32.73	4
Wilson B.S.	2015/16-2018/19	33	61	2	126	2112	35.79	6

CENTURY ON DEBUT FOR PROVINCE

107 & 38	Patrick W.R.	v Canterbury	Christchurch	1917/18
† 157*	McMullan J.J.M.	v Southland	Dunedin	1917/18
172 & 16	Worker R.V.de R.	v Canterbury	Christchurch	1923/24
35 & 133	Blamires E.O.	v Canterbury	Christchurch	1923/24
† 15 & 105	Watt D.G.	v Canterbury	Christchurch	1943/44
157	Hadlee W.A.	v Auckland	Dunedin	1945/46
197 & 128	Sutcliffe B.	v MCC	Dunedin	1946/47
124 & 90	Horne M.J.	v Central Districts	Wanganui	1996/97
† 119	Broom D.J.	v Northern Districts	Whangarei	2009/10
118 & 54*	ten Doeschate R.N.	v Central Districts	Dunedin	2012/13
117 & 28	Ryder J.D.	v Wellington	Wellington	2013/14

† indicates player was making his first-class debut

HIGHEST INDIVIDUAL INNINGS

385	Sutcliffe B.	v Canterbury	Christchurch	1952/53
355	Sutcliffe B.	v Auckland	Dunedin	1949/50
338*	Blunt R.C.	v Canterbury	Christchurch	1931/32
275	Sutcliffe B.	v Auckland	Auckland	1950/51
264	Sutcliffe B.	v Central Districts	Dunedin	1959/60
241	Horne M.J.	v Auckland	Auckland	1997/98
239	Rutherford H.D.	v Wellington	Dunedin	2011/12
226*	Rutherford K.R.	v India	Dunedin	1989/90
222	Rutherford I.A.	v Central Districts	New Plymouth	1978/79
221	Blunt R.C.	v Canterbury	Dunedin	1928/29
207	Kitchen A.K.	v Northern Districts	Dunedin	2016/17
203*	Broom N.T.	v Northern Districts	Queenstown	2010/11
201	Reid J.R.	v Canterbury	Dunedin	1957/58
201	Sutcliffe B.	v Northern Districts	Hamilton	1960/61
200	Lawson R.A.	v Central Districts	Napier	1995/96

MOST RUNS IN A SEASON

		Runs	Ave
Turner G.M.	1975/76	1027	85.58
Redmond A.J.	2012/13	941	55.35
Cumming C.D.	2009/10	924	61.60
Wilson B.S.	2015/16	886	46.63
Bracewell M.G.	2013/14	845	52.81
Cumming C.D.	2008/09	784	65.33
Ryder J.D.	2013/14	776	59.69
Blair B.R.	1989/90	759	47.43
Cumming C.D.	2002/03	751	46.93
Rutherford K.R.	1989/90	747	67.90
Wilson B.S.	2016/17	730	45.62
Bracewell M.G.	2014/15	726	42.70
Cumming C.D.	2010/11	714	51.00
Sutcliffe B.	1952/53	709	78.77
Turner G.M.	1974/75	703	78.11

MOST CENTURIES IN A SEASON

4	Turner G.M.	1974/75
4	Turner G.M.	1975/76
4	Cumming C.D.	2008/09
4	Cumming C.D	2009/10
4	Ryder J.D.	2013/14
4	Bracewell M.G.	2013/14
4	Kitchen A.K.	2016/17

TOTAL NUMBER OF CENTURIES		**302**
Most in one season	14	2013/14
1st	Baker J.C. 103 v Hawke's Bay	1901/02
100th	Cairns B.L. 110 v Wellington	1979/80
200th	Hopkins G.J. 139* v Auckland	2006/07
300th	Rippon M.J.G. 106 v Auckland	2020/21

Bowling

150 WICKETS	Career	M	Wkts	Runs	Ave	5WI	10WM	Best
Boock S.L.	1973/74-1989/90	88	399	8235	20.63	28	5	8-57
Downes A.D.	1887/88-1913/14	44	287	3902	13.59	33	13	8-35
Moir A.M.	1949/50-1961/62	54	282	5926	21.01	20	5	8-37
Wagner N.	2008/09-2017/18	63	277	7307	26.37	16	1	7-46
Mallender N.A.	1983/84-1992/93	78	268	5433	20.27	14	3	7-27
Alabaster J.C.	1956/57-1971/72	65	264	5738	21.73	14	3	6-39
Cameron F.J.	1953/54-1966/67	68	258	5204	20.17	9	—	6-21
McSkimming W.C.	1999/00-2011/12	67	238	5808	24.40	11	2	6-39
Alabaster G.D.	1955/56-1975/76	69	205	4774	23.28	13	1	7-74
Duffy J.A.	2011/12-2020/21	63	187	5941	31.77	8	—	7-89
Sewell D.G.	1995/96-2005/06	55	178	5198	29.20	7	1	8-31
Fisher A.H.	1890/91-1909/10	40	176	2766	15.71	9	1	9-50
O'Connor S.B.	1994/95-2002/03	35	160	3321	20.75	11	2	6-31
Scott B.E.	2000/01-2015/16	49	158	3982	25.20	5	—	6-20

BEST IN AN INNINGS

9-50	Fisher A.H.	v Queensland	Dunedin	1896/97
9-72	Cooke F.H.	v Canterbury	Christchurch	1884/85
9-93	Petherick P.J.	v Northern Districts	Dunedin	1975/76
8-28	Hendley W.	v Canterbury	Dunedin	1869/70
8-31	Sewell D.G.	v Central Districts	Invercargill	1996/97
8-35	Downes A.D.	v Canterbury	Dunedin	1891/92
8-37	Moir A.M.	v Northern Districts	Hamilton	1958/59
8-46	Cairns B.L.	v Wellington	Invercargill	1978/79
8-55	Moir A.M.	v Canterbury	Dunedin	1951/52
8-57	Boock S.L.	v Auckland	Dunedin	1989/90
8-59	Boock S.L.	v Wellington	Invercargill	1978/79

8-61	Cooke F.H.	v Canterbury	Christchurch	1882/83
8-66	Wiseman P.J.	v Wellington	Wellington	1996/97
8-70	Hay W.A.	v Southland	Dunedin	1917/18
8-99	Blunt R.C.	v Auckland	Dunedin	1930/31
8-119	Moir A.M.	v Central Districts	New Plymouth	1953/54
8-136	Shacklock F.J.	v Canterbury	Christchurch	1903/04

BEST IN A MATCH

15-94	Cooke F.H.	v Canterbury	Christchurch	1882/83
15-104	Boock S.L.	v Auckland	Dunedin	1989/90
15-203	Moir A.M.	v Central Districts	New Plymouth	1953/54
14-93	Torrance R.C.	v Hawke's Bay	Napier	1908/09
14-103	Downes A.D.	v Hawke's Bay	Dunedin	1893/94
14-126	Moir A.M.	v Canterbury	Dunedin	1951/52
13-111	Downes A.D.	v Hawke's Bay	Dunedin	1901/02
13-144	Boock S.L.	v Northern Districts	Whangarei	1980/81

MOST WICKETS IN A SEASON

		Wkts	*Ave*
Boock S.L.	1978/79	54	18.51
Wagner N.	2010/11	51	18.15
Mallender N.A.	1991/92	49	12.30
Boock S.L.	1986/87	48	15.48
Wagner N.	2011/12	46	26.32
Petherick P.J.	1977/78	45	17.15
Duffy J.A.	2014/15	45	24.06
Petherick P.J.	1975/76	42	20.16
O'Connor S.B.	2002/03	42	18.71
Moir A.M.	1953/54	41	17.58
Boock S.L.	1980/81	41	18.46
Boock S.L.	1987/88	41	21.82
Webb M.G.	1973/74	40	14.65
Cairns B.L.	1978/79	40	22.70

Wicketkeeping

100 DISMISSALS	*Career*	*M*	*Caught*	*Stumped*	*Total*
de Boorder D.C.	2007/08-2017/18	99	322	22	344
Lees W.K.	1972/73-1987/88	108	208	36	244
Milburn B.D.	1963/64-1982/83	60	148	17	165
Croy M.G.	1994/95-2001/02	42	127	4	131
Robinson S.A.	1984/85-1996/97	45	117	5	122
Hopkins G.J.	2003/04-2006/07	33	111	3	114
Mills G.H.	1935/36-1957/58	55	78	29	107

MOST DISMISSALS IN A SEASON

44 (43ct/1st) de Boorder D.C. 2012/13

MOST DISMISSALS IN A MATCH

10 (10ct) Hopkins G.J. v Canterbury Dunedin 2004/05

MOST DISMISSALS IN AN INNINGS

8 (8ct) de Boorder D.C. v Wellington Wellington 2009/10

MOST CATCHES IN A MATCH

10 Hopkins G.J. v Canterbury Dunedin 2004/05

MOST CATCHES IN AN INNINGS

8 de Boorder D.C. v Wellington Wellington 2009/10

Fielding

MOST CATCHES IN A SEASON

15 Blair W.L. 1978/79

MOST CATCHES IN A MATCH

6	McCullum N.L. v Central Districts	Napier	2006/07

MOST CATCHES IN AN INNINGS

4	Geddes A.E. v Canterbury	Christchurch	1903/04
4	Watson E.A. v Canterbury	Dunedin	1953/54
4	Campbell K.O. v Auckland	Dunedin	1969/70
4	Blair W.L. v Canterbury	Invercargill	1977/78
4	Blair W.L. v Northern Districts	Dunedin	1978/79
4	McCullum S.J. v Auckland	Dunedin	1987/88
4	Dobbs P.W. v India	Dunedin	1989/90
4	Burns K.J. v Northern Districts	Dunedin	1990/91
4	Gaffaney C.B. v Wellington	Wellington	1996/97
4	McCullum N.L. v Auckland	Dunedin	2004/05
4	McCullum N.L. v Central Districts	Napier	2006/07
4	Hicks S. v Auckland	Auckland	2018/19
4	Phillips D.N. v Central Districts	Dunedin	2020/21

Record Partnerships

FOR

Wicket	*Score*	*Batsmen*	*Against*	*At*	*Date*
1st	373	B. Sutcliffe & L. Watt	Auckland	Auckland	1950/51
2nd	254	K.J. Burns & K.R. Rutherford	Wellington	Oamaru	1987/88
3rd	306	S.B. Haig & N.T. Broom	CD	Napier	2009/10
4th	239	N.B. Beard & N.T. Broom	Auckland	Dunedin	2012/13
5th	266	B. Sutcliffe & W.S. Haig	Auckland	Dunedin	1949/50
6th	216	H.D. Rutherford & D.C. de Boorder	Wellington	Dunedin	2011/12
7th	190	N.G. Smith & M.J.G. Rippon	ND	Dunedin	2019/20
8th	165*	J.N. Crawford & A.G. Eckhold	Wellington	Wellington	1914/15
9th	208	W.C. McSkimming & B.E. Scott	Auckland	Auckland	2004/05
10th	184	R.C. Blunt & W. Hawksworth	Canterbury	Christchurch	1931/32

AGAINST

Wicket	*Score*	*Batsmen*	*For*	*At*	*Date*
1st	299	M.D. Bell & R.A. Jones	Wellington	Dunedin	2001/02
2nd	279	M.D. Bell & M.E. Parlane	Wellington	Dunedin	2006/07
3rd	445	P.E. Whitelaw & W.N. Carson	Auckland	Dunedin	1936/37
4th	283	D.R. Flynn & C.J. Anderson	ND	Hamilton	2012/13
5th	258	C.E. McConchie & A.M. Ellis	Canterbury	Invercargill	2016/17
6th	305	L.J. Carter & C.D. Fletcher	Canterbury	Christchurch	2020/21
7th	265	J.L. Powell & N. Dorreen	Canterbury	Christchurch	1929/30
8th	215	J.R. Murray & A.C. Cummins	West Indies	Dunedin	1994/95
9th	239	H.B. Cave & I.B. Leggat	CD	Dunedin	1952/53
10th	138	K.C. James & A.W.S. Brice	Wellington	Wellington	1926/27

WELLINGTON

Highest Totals

614-8	v Canterbury	Christchurch	2006/07
608-9 dec	v Northern Districts	Hamilton	1998/99
595	v Auckland	Wellington	1927/28
590-8 dec	v Central Districts	Palmerston North	2004/05
575-7 dec	v Otago	Wellington	1951/52
569	v Auckland	Wellington	1923/24
560	v Otago	Dunedin	1923/24
553	v Canterbury	Wellington	1931/32
553-3 dec	v Auckland	Wellington	2017/18
547-8 dec	v Auckland	Wellington	2005/06

Lowest Totals

19	v Nelson	Nelson	1885/86
22	v Canterbury	Wellington	1903/04
29	v Nelson	Nelson	1879/80
30	v Nelson	Nelson	1883/84
31	v Nelson	Nelson	1887/88
34	v Canterbury	Wellington	1886/87
35	v Auckland	Wellington	1873/74
36	v Nelson	Nelson	1885/86
37	v Nelson	Nelson	1876/77
42	v New South Wales	Wellington	1895/96
42	v Otago	Wellington	1945/46

Most Appearances

143	Woodcock L.J.
134	Patel J.S.
120	Gray E.J.
119	Vance R.H.
106	Nevin C.J.
102	McSweeney E.B.
96	Bell M.D.
89	Morrison J.F.M.
87	Edgar B.A.
84	Chatfield E.J.
82	Gillespie M.R.
80	Franklin J.E.C.
79	Larsen G.R.
79	Parlane N.R.
76	Murdoch S.J.
74	Coney J.V.
72	Wells J.D.
69	Papps M.H.W.
68	Sinclair B.W.
64	Murray B.A.G.
60	Newdick G.A.
59	Blair R.W.
58	Reid J.R.
58	Ritchie T.D.
57	Elliott G.D.
57	Blundell T.A.
56	Brice A.W.S.
54	Bilby G.P.
54	McGirr H.M.
52	Cederwall B.W.
50	Butler L.C.

Longest Careers

Seasons		
29	Luckie M.M.F.	1891/92-1919/20
27	Dempster C.S.	1921/22-1947/48
25	Tucker K.H.	1895/96-1919/20
24	James K.C.	1923/24-1946/47
22	Hutchings J.H.	1903/04-1924/25
22	Collins D.C.	1905/06-1926/27
22	Reaney T.P.L.	1927/28-1948/49
20	McGirr H.M.	1913/14-1932/33
20	Lamason J.R.	1927/28-1946/47
20	Patel J.S.	1999/00-2018/19

Benefits

Morrison J.F.M.	1983/84
Chatfield E.J.	1985/86
Coney J.V.	1986/87
Edgar B.A.	1987/88
Gray E.J.	1989/90
Vance R.H.	1990/91
McSweeney E.B.	1991/92
Larsen G.R.	1996/97

Batting

2000 RUNS	Career	M	In	NO	HS	Runs	Ave	100
Woodcock L.J.	2001/02-2018/19	143	246	30	220*	7719	35.73	11
Bell M.D.	1997/98-2010/11	96	168	11	265	6565	41.81	20
Edgar B.A.	1975/76-1989/90	87	160	13	162	6494	44.17	15
Vance R.H.	1976/77-1990/91	119	205	18	254*	6440	34.43	12
Nevin C.J.	1995/96-2009/10	106	163	26	143*	4882	35.63	4
Murdoch S.J.	2009/10-2017/18	76	140	6	171	4847	36.17	12
Papps M.H.W.	2011/12-2017/18	69	128	9	316*	4837	40.64	13
Morrison J.F.M.	1967/68-1983/84	89	160	22	180*	4694	34.01	6
Parlane N.R.	2002/03-2010/11	79	128	11	193	4654	39.77	11
Franklin J.E.C.	1998/99-2014/15	80	122	18	219	4595	44.18	13
Reid J.R.	1947/48-1964/65	58	102	8	296	4538	48.27	13
McSweeney E.B.	1981/82-1993/94	102	153	23	205*	4296	33.04	5
Gray E.J.	1975/76-1991/92	120	181	38	128*	4228	29.56	5
Murray B.A.G.	1958/59-1972/73	64	116	9	213	3753	35.07	3
Sinclair B.W.	1955/56-1970/71	68	116	14	148	3583	35.12	2
Hiddleston J.S.	1913/14-1928/29	41	75	1	212	3413	46.12	8
Coney J.V.	1971/72-1986/87	74	126	21	120*	3251	30.96	4
Newdick G.A.	1970/71-1980/81	60	112	6	143	3236	30.52	4
Blundell T.A.	2012/13-2020/21	57	98	13	153	3157	37.14	8
McGirr H.M.	1913/14-1932/33	54	97	4	141	3032	32.60	5
Wells J.D.	1989/90-2000/01	72	113	18	115	3016	31.74	5
Jones A.H.	1985/86-1993/94	39	67	11	181*	2978	53.17	7
Larsen G.R.	1984/85-1998/99	79	118	25	161	2938	31.59	2
Ryder J.D.	2004/05-2012/13	40	67	3	236	2908	45.43	8
Elliott G.D.	2005/06-2013/14	57	91	6	196*	2907	34.20	7
Bilby G.P.	1962/63-1976/77	54	95	11	161	2852	33.95	3
Patel J.S.	1999/00-2018/19	134	174	42	99	2691	20.38	—
Dempster C.S.	1921/22-1947/48	40	76	3	154	2602	35.64	5
Ritchie T.D.	1982/83-1990/91	58	92	14	106	2494	31.97	3
Tindill E.W.T.	1932/33-1949/50	39	73	5	149	2442	35.91	6
Parlane M.E.	2003/04-2007/08	40	69	3	203	2598	38.20	7
Jones R.A.	2000/01-2003/04	36	63	4	188	2343	39.71	7
Pollard M.A.	2009/10-2016/17	45	85	7	166	2317	29.70	3
Brodie J.M.	2007/08-2013/14	42	73	2	210	2266	31.91	4
Conway D.P.	2017/18-2020/21	22	39	8	327*	2054	66.25	5
Burnett G.P.	1987/88-1992/93	44	80	13	203*	2029	30.28	1

CENTURY ON DEBUT FOR PROVINCE

163	Williams A.B.	v Canterbury	Christchurch	1896/97
110 & 5*	Crawford J.N.	v Auckland	Auckland	1917/18
113 & 53	Kortlang H.H.L.	v Auckland	Wellington	1922/23
117 & 6	Bernau E.H.L.	v Auckland	Wellington	1922/23
† 106 & 0	Tindill E.W.T.	v Auckland	Auckland	1932/33
† 110	Ongley J.A.	v Otago	Wellington	1938/39
† 27 & 141*	Smith K.F.H.	v Central Districts	Wellington	1953/54
† 132 & 2*	Bilby G.P.	v Central Districts	Wellington	1962/63
† 39 & 156*	Aiken J.M.	v Canterbury	Christchurch	1989/90
115	Fleming S.P.	v Central Districts	Wellington	2001/02
† 142* & 1	Rhodes S.J.	v Otago	Queenstown	2009/10
111	Ronchi L.	v Central Districts	Wellington	2011/12
102 & 0	Borthwick S.G.	v Otago	Queenstown	2015/16
179 & 6	Nofal M.J.	v Central Districts	Wellington	2017/18

† indicates player was making his first-class debut

HIGHEST INDIVIDUAL INNINGS

327*	Conway D.P.	v Canterbury	Wellington	2019/20
316*	Papps M.H.W.	v Auckland	Wellington	2017/18
296	Reid J.R.	v Northern Districts	Wellington	1962/63
283	Reid J.R.	v Otago	Wellington	1951/52
265	Bell M.D.	v Central Districts	Napier	2007/08
254*	Vance R.H.	v Northern Districts	Wellington	1988/89
236	Ryder J.D.	v Central Districts	Palmerston North	2004/05
222*	Midlane F.A.	v Otago	Wellington	1914/15
220*	Woodcock L.J.	v Central Districts	Wellington	2009/10
219	Bell M.D.	v Northern Districts	Hamilton	1998/99
219	Franklin J.E.C.	v Auckland	Auckland	2008/09
216	Bell M.D.	v Auckland	Auckland	1997/98
214*	Kortlang H.H.L.	v Auckland	Wellington	1921/26
213	Murray B.A.G.	v Otago	Dunedin	1968/69
212	Hiddleston J.S.	v Canterbury	Wellington	1925/26
210	Brodie J.M.	v Auckland	Auckland	2011/12
208	Franklin J.E.C.	v Auckland	Wellington	2005/06
206*	Papps M.H.W.	v Canterbury	Rangiora	2012/13
205*	McSweeney E.B.	v Central Districts	Levin	1987/88
204	Hiddleston J.S.	v Auckland	Wellington	1925/26
203*	Burnett G.P.	v Northern Districts	Hamilton	1991/92
203*	Woodcock L.J.	v Auckland	Auckland	2016/17
203*	Conway D.P.	v Otago	Wellington	2018/19
203	Parlane M.E.	v Auckland	Auckland	2004/05
202	Austen M.H.	v Central Districts	Wanganui	1993/94

MOST RUNS IN A SEASON

		Runs	*Ave*
Murdoch S.J.	2014/15	998	52.52
Woodcock L.J.	2009/10	988	65.86
Ronchi L.	2012/13	898	64.14
Vance R.H.	1988/89	888	80.72
Jones R.A.	2000/01	849	47.16
Bell M.D.	2000/01	844	52.75
Papps M.H.W.	2013/14	841	64.69
Murdoch S.J.	2015/16	824	43.36
Papps M.H.W.	2017/18	814	50.87
Papps M.H.W.	2012/13	810	45.00
Parlane N.R.	2007/08	809	57.78
Merchant C.J.	2009/10	764	40.21
Parlane N.R.	2009/10	763	40.15
Edgar B.A.	1988/89	762	63.50
Blundell T.A.	2015/16	761	44.76
Woodcock L.J.	2015/16	739	38.89
Papps M.H.W.	2014/15	738	39.60
Bell M.D.	2007/08	731	73.10
Edgar B.A.	1978/79	728	45.50
Jones R.A.	2002/03	726	45.37
Ryder J.D.	2012/13	723	51.64
Franklin T.J.	2013/14	721	65.54
Edgar B.A.	1989/90	720	40.00
Twose R.G.	1994/95	720	80.00
Jones A.H.	1988/89	701	87.62
Conway D.P.	2019/20	701	87.62

MOST CENTURIES IN A SEASON

5 Bell M.D. 2000/01

TOTAL NUMBER OF CENTURIES 381

Most in one season	12	2012/13
1st	Heenan G.C. 146* v Hawke's Bay	1886/87
100th	Sinclair B.W. 102* v Northern Districts	1963/64
200th	Chandler P.J.B. 177 v Auckland	1996/97
300th	Murdoch S.J. 103 v Central Districts	2011/12

Bowling

150 WICKETS	Career	M	Wkts	Runs	Ave	5WI	10WM	Best
Chatfield E.J.	1973/74-1989/90	84	403	7531	18.68	23	7	8-24
Gray E.J.	1975/76-1991/92	120	357	9778	27.38	13	3	8-37
Gillespie M.R.	1999/00-2014/15	82	344	9389	27.29	16	2	6-38
Patel J.S.	1999/00-2018/19	134	333	12,592	37.81	12	1	7-105
Blair R.W.	1951/52-1964/65	59	330	5004	15.16	30	10	9-72
Brice A.W.S.	1902/03-1927/28	56	229	4684	20.45	17	7	9-67
Upham E.F.	1892/93-1909/10	40	227	3393	14.94	17	2	7-24
Franklin J.E.C.	1998/99-2014/15	80	206	5103	24.77	6	1	7-30
O'Brien I.E.	2000/01-2009/10	45	179	3976	22.21	10	1	8-55
Reid J.R.	1947/48-1964/65	58	172	3115	18.11	10	—	7-29
McGirr H.M.	1913/14-1932/33	54	166	4326	26.06	7	1	7-45
Morrison B.D.	1953/54-1964/65	45	163	3858	23.66	7	2	7-42

BEST IN AN INNINGS

9-67	Brice A.W.S.	v Auckland	Wellington	1918/19
9-72	Blair R.W.	v Auckland	Wellington	1956/57
9-75	Blair R.W.	v Canterbury	Wellington	1956/57
8-13	Firth J.P.	v Hawke's Bay	Wellington	1883/84
8-21	Penn A.J.	v Canterbury	Wellington	2001/02
8-24	Chatfield E.J.	v Northern Districts	Lower Hutt	1979/80
8-34	Fisher F.E.	v Canterbury	Wellington	1952/53
8-36	Blair R.W.	v Otago	Dunedin	1952/53
8-37	Gray E.J.	v Canterbury	Lower Hutt	1985/86
8-50	Butler L.C.	v NZ Under 23 XI	Wellington	1965/66
8-55	O'Brien I.E.	v Auckland	Wellington	2006/07
8-58	Ashbolt F.L.	v Hawke's Bay	Napier	1897/98
8-59	Hiddleston J.S.	v Canterbury	Christchurch	1918/19
8-64	Collinge R.O.	v Auckland	Auckland	1967/68
8-78	Gray E.J.	v Auckland	Wellington	1989/90
8-83	Chatfield E.J.	v Otago	Dunedin	1986/87

BEST IN A MATCH

14-136	Blair R.W.	v Canterbury	Wellington	1956/57
14-151	Gray E.J.	v Canterbury	Lower Hutt	1985/86
13-58	Salmon I.J.	v Nelson	Wellington	1873/74
13-86	Chatfield E.J.	v West Indies	Lower Hutt	1979/80
13-91	Gore A.H.	v Hawke's Bay	Napier	1886/87
13-92	Middleton F.S.	v Hawke's Bay	Wellington	1919/20
13-97	Ashbolt F.L.	v Hawke's Bay	Napier	1897/98
13-117	O'Brien I.E.	v Auckland	Wellington	2006/07
13-157	Tucker K.H.	v Auckland	Wellington	1900/01
13-176	Brice A.W.S.	v Auckland	Wellington	1920/21

MOST WICKETS IN A SEASON

		Wkts	Ave
Chatfield E.J.	1979/80	49	10.51
Gray E.J.	1984/85	48	21.75
Chatfield E.J.	1981/82	47	16.87
Blair R.W.	1956/57	46	9.47
Walker M.D.J.	2002/03	45	18.00
Gillespie M.R.	2012/13	45	31.37
Gillespie M.R.	2005/06	43	23.16
Gillespie M.R.	2013/14	42	32.90
Saunders J.V.	1913/14	41	17.58
Chatfield E.J.	1976/77	41	19.48
O'Brien I.E.	2000/01	41	19.68
Penn A.J.	2001/02	40	18.30
van Beek L.V.	2017/18	40	14.47

Wicketkeeping

100 DISMISSALS	*Career*	*M*	*Caught*	*Stumped*	*Total*
McSweeney E.B.	1981/82-1993/94	102	289	39	328
Nevin C.J.	1995/95-2009/10	106	289	9	298
Blundell T.A.	2012/13-2020/21	57	130	5	135
Therkleson I.J.	1966/67-1973/74	39	93	7	100

MOST DISMISSALS IN A SEASON

46 (46ct) Nevin C.J. 2000/01

MOST DISMISSALS IN A MATCH

10	(10ct)	Nevin C.J. v Otago	Dunedin	1995/96
10	(10ct)	Blundell T.A. v Canterbury	Wellington	2017/18

MOST DISMISSALS IN AN INNINGS

6	(6ct)	Vance R.H. v Otago	Wellington	1977/78
6	(5ct 1st)	Nevin C.J. v Central Districts	Nelson	1995/96
6	(6ct)	Austin-Smellie J. v Central Districts	Napier	2010/11
6	(6ct)	Ronchi L. v Northern Districts	Wellington	2012/13
6	(6ct)	Ronchi L. v Canterbury	Christchurch	2016/17
6	(6ct)	Blundell T.A. v Canterbury	Wellington	2017/18

MOST CATCHES IN A MATCH

10	Nevin C.J. v Otago	Dunedin	1995/96
10	Blundell T.A. v Canterbury	Wellington	2017/18

MOST CATCHES IN AN INNINGS

6	Vance R.H. v Otago	Wellington	1977/78
6	Austin-Smellie J. v Central Districts	Napier	2010/11
6	Ronchi L. v Northern Districts	Wellington	2012/13
6	Ronchi L. v Canterbury	Christchurch	2016/17
6	Blundell T.A. v Canterbury	Wellington	2017/18

Fielding

MOST CATCHES IN A SEASON

18 Coney J.V. 1977/78

MOST CATCHES IN A MATCH

7	Morrison J.F.M. v Northern Districts	Wellington	1980/81

MOST CATCHES IN AN INNINGS

5	Lamason J.R. v Otago	Dunedin	1937/38
5	Morrison J.F.M. v Northern Districts	Wellington	1980/81
5	Brodie J.M. v Otago	Wellington	2008/09
5	Bell M.D. v Northern Districts	Hamilton	2009/10

Record Partnerships

FOR

Wicket	*Score*	*Batsmen*	*Against*	*At*	*Date*
1st	432	M.H.W. Papps & L.J. Woodcock	Wellington	Wellington	2017/18
2nd	287	M.D. Bell & J.D. Wells	Auckland	Auckland	1997/98
3rd	346	G.P. Burnett & R.A. Verry	ND	Hamilton	1991/92
4th	310	J.D. Ryder & N.R. Parlane	CD	P. North	2004/05
5th	341	G.R. Larsen & E.B. McSweeney	CD	Levin	1987/88
6th	247	L.J. Woodcock & M.J. Nofal	CD	Wellington	2017/18
7th	250	C.J. Nevin & M.D.J. Walker	Otago	Wellington	2003/04
8th	180	R.G. Twose & M.C. Goodson	Otago	Dunedin	1994/95
9th	225	L.J. Woodcock & M.J. Tugaga	CD	Wellington	2009/10
10th	138	K.C. James & A.W.S. Brice	Otago	Wellington	1926/27

AGAINST

Wicket	*Score*	*Batsmen*	*For*	*At*	*Date*
1st	428	P.J. Ingram & J.M. How	CD	Wellington	2009/10
2nd	254	K.J. Burns & K.R. Rutherford	Otago	Oamaru	1987/88
3rd	291	M.G. Bracewell & N.T. Broom	Otago	Dunedin	2012/13
4th	278	A.W. Roberts & M.L. Page	Canterbury	Wellington	1931/32
5th	301	J.I. Englefield & L.R.P.L. Taylor	CD	P. North	2004/05
6th	377	C. Munro & Craig Cachopa	Auckland	Auckland	2012/13
7th	241	N.J. Astle & M.W. Priest	Canterbury	Christchurch	1994/95
8th	189	W.N. Carson & A.M. Matheson	Auckland	Auckland	1938/39
9th	188	N.R. Parlane & D.R. Tuffey	ND	Wellington	1999/00
10th	134	G.H. Worker & A.W. Mathieson	CD	Nelson	2015/16

INTER-PROVINCIAL RECORDS

AUCKLAND v CANTERBURY

First match	*Played*	*Won by Auckland*	*Won by Canterbury*	*Drawn*
1873/74	147	53	47	47

Highest totals	**A**	693-9 dec		Auckland	1939/40
	C	514-6 dec		Christchurch	2002/03
Lowest totals	**A**	13		Auckland	1877/78
	C	62		Rangiora	1998/99
Highest innings	**A**	268	T.G. McIntosh	Auckland	2007/08
	C	301*	P.G. Fulton	Christchurch	2002/03
Best bowling *(innings)*	**A**	9-75	R. Neill	Auckland	1891/92
	C	9-56	D.J. McBeath	Christchurch	1918/19
Best bowling *(match)*	**A**	13-85	R.S. Cunis	Christchurch	1963/64
	C	15-168	D.J. McBeath	Christchurch	1918/19

Record Partnerships

AUCKLAND

1st	286	B. Sutcliffe & D.D. Taylor	Auckland	1948/49
2nd	197	T.G. McIntosh & R.A. Young	Rangiora	2008/09
3rd	278	T.J. Franklin & D.N. Patel	Christchurch	1985/86
4th	241*	R.A. Jones & R.A. Young	Auckland	2009/10
5th	161*	B. Sutcliffe & D.D. Taylor	Auckland	1946/47
6th	211	M.J. Guptill & C. de Grandhomme	Rangiora	2011/12
7th	224	V.J. Scott & A.M. Matheson	Auckland	1937/38
8th	153	R.J. Nicol & R.A. Young	Auckland	2001/02
9th	96	C. Pringle & D.K. Morrison	Rangiora	1995/96
10th	83	S.W. Brown & C. Pringle	Christchurch	1990/91

CANTERBURY

1st	306	L.A. Cuff & J.D. Lawrence	Christchurch	1893/94
2nd	179	B.G. Hadlee & N.M. Parker	Auckland	1978/79
3rd	183	G.R. Stead & C.Z. Harris	Christchurch	2000/01
4th	200	K.J. McClure & C.E. McConchie	Rangiora	2017/18
5th	183	K.J. McClure & A.M. Ellis	Auckland	2016/17
6th	185	K.J. McClure & C.D. Fletcher	Rangiora	2017/18
7th	142	G.J. Hopkins & P.J. Wiseman	Auckland	2002/03
8th	166	R.J. Hadlee & D.R. Hadlee	Christchurch	1983/84
9th	115	G.J. Hopkins & A.M. Ellis	Auckland	2002/03
10th	83	H.C. Wilson & H.W. Monaghan	Christchurch	1913/14
	83	M. Graham & A.P. Cobden	Auckland	1935/36

AUCKLAND v CENTRAL DISTRICTS

First match	*Played*	*Won by Auckland*	*Won by Central Districts*	*Drawn*
1950/51	100	35	29	36

Highest totals	**A**	668-7 dec	Napier	2014/15
	CD	594-8 dec	Auckland	1995/96
Lowest totals	**A**	71	Palmerston North	2001/02
	CD	59	New Plymouth	1958/59
Highest innings	**A**	281 C. Munro	Napier	2014/15
	CD	175 J.D. Ryder	Nelson	2017/18
Best bowling *(innings)*	**A**	7-29 R.S. Cunis	Auckland	1961/62
	CD	7-31 H.B. Cave	Palmerston North	1952/53
Best bowling *(match)*	**A**	12-146 K.W. Hough	Auckland	1959/60
	CD	13-64 H.B. Cave	Palmerston North	1952/53

Record Partnerships

AUCKLAND

1st	172	R.A. Jones & M.J. Horne	Auckland	2004/05
2nd	196	J.A. Raval & R.R. O'Donnell	Auckland	2015/16
3rd	184	R.A. Jones & A.K. Kitchen	Lincoln	2008/09
4th	214	C. Munro & R.R. O'Donnell	Napier	2014/15
5th	234*	V.J. Scott & J.B. Morris	Auckland	1951/52
6th	165	J.J. Crowe & J.G. Bracewell	Auckland	1987/88
7th	192	S.W. Brown & A.C. Parore	Auckland	1990/91
8th	133	C. Munro & M.D. Bates	Napier	2012/13
9th	104*	R.A. Young & C.J. Drum	Auckland	2000/01
10th	86*	L.J. Shaw & A.J. McKay	Auckland	2007/08

CENTRAL DISTRICTS

1st	173	J.M. How & J.A. Raval	Auckland	2012/13
2nd	207*	R.G. Twose & M.W. Douglas	Auckland	1991/92
3rd	224	M.S. Sinclair & C.M. Spearman	Auckland	2003/04
4th	155	R.T. Hart & T.E. Blain	Masterton	1989/90
5th	168	B.B.J. Griggs & T.I. Weston	Auckland	2006/07
6th	220	M.H. Toynbee & I.D.S. Smith	Napier	1982/83
7th	165	R.K. Brown & M.E.L. Lane	Palmerston North	1993/94
8th	102	D.A.J. Bracewell & J.F.A. Field	Auckland	2020/21
9th	82	R.J. Schaw & G.J.T. Hegglun	Auckland	2006/07
10th	133	G.A. Bartlett & I.A. Colquhoun	Auckland	1959/60

AUCKLAND v NORTHERN DISTRICTS

First match	Played	Won by Auckland	Won by Northern Districts	Drawn
1956/57	95	37	21	37

Highest totals	**A**	547-8 dec	Auckland	2000/01
	ND	492	Auckland	1990/91
Lowest totals	**A**	69	Auckland	1963/64
	ND	32	Hamilton	1996/97
Highest innings	**A**	209 P.A. Horne	Auckland	1988/89
		209* M.J. Horne	Auckland	2003/04
	ND	211* G.A. Hick	Auckland	1988/89
Best bowling *(innings)*	**A**	7-28 K.P. Walmsley	Hamilton	2004/05
	ND	9-48 A.R. Tait	Hamilton	1996/97
Best bowling *(match)*	**A**	11-71 J.A. Hayes	Auckland	1957/58
	ND	16-130 A.R. Tait	Hamilton	1996/97

Record Partnerships

AUCKLAND

1st	197	T.J. Franklin & P.A. Horne	Auckland	1985/86
2nd	190	M.J. Guptill & S.M. Solia	Whangarei	2018/19
3rd	152	T.J. Franklin & J.J. Crowe	Rotorua	1983/84
4th	280	J.J. Crowe & D.N. Patel	Auckland	1991/92
5th	347*	M.J. Horne & A.C. Barnes	Auckland	2003/04
6th	205	M.S. Chapman & B.J. Horne	Auckland	2019/20
7th	168	Craig Cachopa & B.P. Martin	Auckland	2012/13
8th	93	G.J. Hopkins & R.M. Hira	Gisborne	2007/08
9th	151	R.A. Young & G.J. Morgan	Auckland	2007/08
10th	139	M.J. McClenaghan & R.S. Sandhu	Auckland	2016/17

NORTHERN DISTRICTS

1st	156	J.A.H. Marshall & N.K.W. Horsley	Auckland	2003/04
2nd	301	D.R. Flynn & B.S. Wilson	Hamilton	2012/13
3rd	261*	M.P. Maynard & S.A. Thomson	Hamilton	1990/91
4th	252	S.A. Thomson & B.A. Young	Auckland	1990/91
5th	142	M.P. Maynard & B.A. Young	Auckland	1991/92
6th	146*	G.A. Hick & S.A. Thomson	Auckland	1988/89
7th	127	C.M. Kuggeleijn & S.A. Thomson	Auckland	1988/89
8th	113*	S.C. Kuggeleijn & B.R. Hampton	Auckland	2015/16
9th	185	M.P. Maynard & S.B. Doull	Auckland	1991/92
10th	82	S.B. Doull & B.P. Martin	Taupo	1999/00

AUCKLAND v OTAGO

First match	Played	Won by Auckland	Won by Otago	Drawn
1873/74	139	68	33	38

Highest totals	A	627		Lincoln	2006/07
	O	569-8 dec		Dunedin	2012/13
Lowest totals	A	46		Dunedin	2010/11
	O	35		Christchurch	1884/85
Highest innings	A	290	W.N. Carson	Dunedin	1936/37
	O	355	B. Sutcliffe	Dunedin	1949/50
Best bowling *(innings)*	A	9-36	A.F. Wensley	Auckland	1929/30
	O	8-57	S.L. Boock	Dunedin	1989/90
Best bowling *(match)*	A	14-63	A.W. Rees	Dunedin	1889/90
	O	15-104	S.L. Boock	Dunedin	1989/90

Record Partnerships

AUCKLAND

1st	240	T.G. McIntosh & M.J. Horne	Dunedin	2001/02
2nd	170	L.G. Hemus & A.E. Relf	Auckland	1909/10
3rd	445	P.E. Whitelaw & W.N. Carson	Dunedin	1936/37
4th	273	T.G. McIntosh & R.J. Nicol	Lincoln	2006/07
5th	197	C.C.R. Dacre & C.F.W. Allcott	Dunedin	1926/27
6th	209*	A.C. Parore & A.P. O'Dowd	Dunedin	1991/92
7th	177*	A.C. Barnes & J.M. Mills	Alexandra	1995/96
8th	140	J.G. Kemp & J.M. McIntyre	Dunedin	1969/70
9th	204	B.J. Horne & D.K. Ferns	Auckland	2020/21
10th	119	W.N. Carson & J. Cowie	Auckland	1937/38

OTAGO

1st	373	B. Sutcliffe & L. Watt	Auckland	1950/51
2nd	227	P.W. Dobbs & M.J. Lamont	Dunedin	1990/91
3rd	199	W.S. Haig & B. Sutcliffe	Auckland	1954/55
4th	239	N.B. Beard & N.T. Broom	Dunedin	2012/13
5th	266	B. Sutcliffe & W.S. Haig	Dunedin	1949/50
6th	162*	N.T. Broom & L.J. Morgan	Auckland	2009/10
7th	164	A. Galland & A.R. Knight	Auckland	1925/26
8th	93	A.K. Kitchen & C. Viljoen	Dunedin	2016/17
9th	208	W.C. McSkimming & B.E. Scott	Auckland	2004/05
10th	63	R.M. Phillips & J.A. Duffy	Auckland	2014/15

AUCKLAND v WELLINGTON

First match	*Played*	*Won by Auckland*	*Won by Wellington*	*Drawn*
1873/74	158	61	42	55

Highest totals	**A**	658-9d		Auckland	2012/13
	W	595		Wellington	1927/28
Lowest totals	**A**	48		Wellington	1889/90
	W	35		Wellington	1873/74
Highest innings	**A**	269*	C. Munro	Auckland	2012/13
	W	316*	M.H.W. Papps	Wellington	2017/18
Best bowling *(innings)*	**A**	8-51	R. Neill	Auckland	1895/96
	W	9-67	A.W.S. Brice	Wellington	1918/19
Best bowling *(match)*	**A**	14-65	J.A. Hayes	Auckland	1957/58
	W	13-117	I.E. O'Brien	Wellington	2006/07

Record Partnerships

AUCKLAND

1st	215	M.L. Guptill-Bunce & J.A. Raval	Wellington	2015/16
2nd	241	T.J. Franklin & J.J. Crowe	Wellington	1988/89
3rd	203*	B.A. Pocock & A.C. Parore	Auckland	1997/98
4th	180	A.N.C. Snedden & C.C.R. Dacre	Wellington	1922/23
5th	174	R.W. Morgan & J.G. Kemp	Auckland	1967/68
6th	377	C. Munro & Craig Cachopa	Auckland	2012/13
7th	131	G.L. Weir & C.C.R. Dacre	Wellington	1927/28
8th	189	W.N. Carson & A.M. Matheson	Auckland	1938/39
9th	122	H.T. Schuster & R.S. Cunis	Wellington	1964/65
10th	97	A.C. Kerr & H.C. Nottman	Auckland	1941/42

WELLINGTON

1st	432	M.H.W. Papps & L.J. Woodcock	Wellington	2017/18
2nd	287	M.D. Bell & J.D. Wells	Auckland	1997/98
3rd	287	D.P. Conway & M.G. Bracewell	Wellington	2020/21
4th	217	M.G. Bracewell & T.A. Blundell	Auckland	2020/21
5th	282	J.E.C. Franklin & L.J. Woodcock	Auckland	2008/09
6th	199	J.E.C. Franklin & T.A. Blundell	Wellington	2013/14
7th	144	J.R. Reid & P.T. Barton	Auckland	1959/60
8th	137	F.L.H. Mooney & F.E. Fisher	Wellington	1952/53
9th	127	F.L.H. Mooney & R.A. Buchan	Wellington	1943/44
10th	113	F.L.H. Mooney & E.C.V. Knapp	Wellington	1943/44

CANTERBURY v CENTRAL DISTRICTS

First match	*Played*	*Won by Canterbury*	*Won by Central Districts*	*Drawn*
1950/51	103	35	29	39

Highest totals	**C**	582		Napier	2013/14
	CD	549-8 dec		Christchurch	1998/99
Lowest totals	**C**	68		Levin	1985/86
	CD	86		Christchurch	2016/17
Highest innings	**C**	261	T.W.M. Latham	Napier	2013/14
	CD	212*	D.P. Kelly	Blenheim	2000/01
Best bowling *(innings)*	**C**	9-13	P.J. Wiseman	Christchurch	2004/05
	CD	9-100	B.W. Yuile	New Plymouth	1965/66
Best bowling *(match)*	**C**	14-234	T.D. Astle	Napier	2013/14
	CD	11-115	M.J. Mason	Timaru	2002/03

Record Partnerships

CANTERBURY

1st	185	B.R. Hartland & D.J. Murray	Palmerston North	1994/95
2nd	254*	M.H.W. Papps & J.G. Myburgh	Napier	2007/08
3rd	208	M.H.W. Papps & C.D. McMillan	Christchurch	2006/07
4th	204	T.W. Jarvis & K. Thomson	Wanganui	1969/70
5th	290	C.Z. Harris & G.R. Stead	Blenheim	1996/97
6th	379*	S.L. Stewart & C.F.K. van Wyk	New Plymouth	2009/10
7th	184*	C.L. Bull & B.P. Isherwood	Nelson	1971/72
8th	136	G.R. Stead & C.J. Anderson	Christchurch	2000/01
9th	113	G.J. Hopkins & S.J. Cunis	Christchurch	1998/99
10th	85	G.T. Dowling & A.F. Rapley	Christchurch	1958/59

CENTRAL DISTRICTS

1st	188	G.H. Worker & G.R. Hay	Christchurch	2017/18
2nd	317	R.T. Hart & P.S. Briasco	New Plymouth	1983/84
3rd	197	M.J. Greatbatch & M.D. Crowe	New Plymouth	1986/87
4th	276*	M.D. Crowe & P.S. Briasco	Christchurch	1986/87
5th	235*	G.P. Sulzberger & J.D. Ryder	Napier	2002/03
6th	142	M.S. Sinclair & C.F.K. van Wyk	Napier	2012/13
7th	219	B.W. Yuile & B.L. Hampton	Napier	1967/68
8th	159	B.J. Diamanti & R.R. Sherlock	Napier	2007/08
9th	89	S.W. Duff & D.J. Leonard	Christchurch	1993/94
10th	98	I.A. Rutherford & D.J. Kay	Napier	1977/78

CANTERBURY v NORTHERN DISTRICTS

First match	Played	Won by Canterbury	Won by Northern Districts	Drawn
1956/57	94	36	21	37

Highest totals	**C**	558-4 dec		Rangiora	2009/10
	ND	726		Rangiora	2009/10
Lowest totals	**C**	73		Gisborne	2013/14
	ND	52		Hamilton	1966/67
Highest innings	**C**	237*	R.T. Latham	Rotorua	1990/91
	ND	235	J.A.H. Marshall	Christchurch	2001/02
Best bowling	**C**	7-24	J.W.F. Kiddey	Hamilton	1960/61
(innings)	**ND**	7-58	R.P. de Groen	Hamilton	1995/96
Best bowling	**C**	12-81	R.J. Hadlee	Christchurch	1986/87
(match)	**ND**	11-129	R.P. de Groen	Hamilton	1995/96

Record Partnerships

CANTERBURY

1st	214	B.A. Bolton & G.T. Dowling	Christchurch	1959/60
2nd	243	M.H.W. Papps & S.L. Stewart	Hamilton	2006/07
3rd	394*	P.G. Kennedy & R.T. Latham	Rotorua	1990/91
4th	182	H.M. Nicholls & C.E. McConchie	Christchurch	2019/20
5th	252*	R.T. Latham & M.W. Priest	Christchurch	1988/89
6th	175	S.P. Fleming & L.K. Germon	Hamilton	1993/94
7th	205	L.K. Germon & M.W. Priest	Christchurch	1991/92
8th	220	P.J. Wiseman & B.C. Hiini	Hamilton	2005/06
9th	76	C.R.W. Dickel & K.I. Ferries	Hamilton	1974/75
10th	160	L.K. Germon & W.A. Wisneski	Rangiora	1997/98

NORTHERN DISTRICTS

1st	278	D.R. Flynn & H.R. Cooper	Whangarei	2017/18
2nd	237	J.G. Gibson & C.M. Kuggeleijn	Hamilton	1980/81
3rd	198	K.S. Williamson & H.J.H. Marshall	Rangiora	2009/10
4th	259	G.E. Bradburn & M.E. Parlane	Christchurch	1996/97
5th	155*	J.A.H. Marshall & N.K.W. Horsley	Hamilton	2005/06
6th	180	S.A. Thomson & M.N. Hart	Hamilton	1992/93
7th	174	B. Popli & M.J. Santner	Gisborne	2013/14
8th	163	P.D. McGlashan & G.W. Aldridge	Hamilton	2008/09
9th	69	M.N. Hart & S.B. Doull	Rangiora	2000/01
10th	80	D.J. Mitchell & T.C. Goodin	Hamilton	2015/16

CANTERBURY v OTAGO

First match	*Played*	*Won by Canterbury*	*Won by Otago*	*Drawn*
1863/64	192	86	68	38

Highest totals	**C**	777		Christchurch	1996/97
	O	602-8 dec		Dunedin	1928/29
Lowest totals	**C**	25		Christchurch	1866/67
	O	40		Dunedin	1869/70
Highest innings	**C**	221*	P.G. Fulton	Dunedin	2004/05
	O	385	B. Sutcliffe	Christchurch	1952/53
Best bowling *(innings)*	**C**	9-95	M.W. Priest	Dunedin	1989/90
	O	9-72	F.H. Cooke	Christchurch	1884/85
Best bowling *(match)*	**C**	13-181	W.E. Merritt	Christchurch	1935/36
	O	15-94	F.H. Cooke	Christchurch	1882/83

Record Partnerships

CANTERBURY

1st	226*	W.A. Hadlee & J.G. Leggat	Christchurch	1948/49
2nd	210	W.A. Hadlee & F.P. O'Brien	Christchurch	1940/41
3rd	216*	P.G. Fulton & K.J. McClure	Christchurch	2015/16
4th	187	P.G. Fulton & J.G. Myburgh	Christchurch	2007/08
5th	258	C.E. McConchie & A.M. Ellis	Invercargill	2016/17
6th	305	L.J. Carter & C.D. Fletcher	Christchurch	2020/21
7th	265	J.L. Powell & N. Dorreen	Christchurch	1929/30
8th	167	C.F.K. van Wyk & R.J. McCone	Christchurch	2008/09
9th	112	A.M. Ellis & R.J. McCone	Queenstown	2010/11
10th	104	L.V. van Beek & W.S.A. Williams	Christchurch	2015/16

OTAGO

1st	209	B. Sutcliffe & L. Watt	Dunedin	1947/48
2nd	170	C.C. Hopkins & G.G. Austin	Christchurch	1911/12
3rd	221	R.C. Blunt & J.J.M. McMullan	Dunedin	1928/29
4th	185*	N.T. Broom & S.R. Wells	Dunedin	2013/14
5th	147	K.J. Burns & D.J. Walker	Christchurch	1985/86
6th	121	J.D.S. Neesham & M.J.G. Rippon	Dunedin	2017/18
7th	182	B. Sutcliffe & A.W. Gilbertson	Christchurch	1952/53
8th	146	M.H. Austen & P.J. Wiseman	Christchurch	1996/97
9th	134	J.W. Wilson & N.A. Mallender	Christchurch	1992/93
10th	184	R.C. Blunt & W. Hawksworth	Christchurch	1931/32

CANTERBURY v WELLINGTON

First match	Played	Won by Canterbury	Won by Wellington	Drawn	Tied
1883/84	163	60	59	43	1

Highest totals	**C**	613-7 dec	Christchurch	2006/07
	W	614-8	Christchurch	2006/07
Lowest totals	**C**	37	Wellington	1925/26
	W	22	Wellington	1903/04
Highest innings	**C**	241* T.W.M. Latham	Wellington	2013/14
	W	327* D.P. Conway	Wellington	2019/20
Best bowling *(innings)*	**C**	10-28 A.E. Moss	Christchurch	1889/90
	W	9-75 R.W. Blair	Wellington	1956/57
Best bowling *(match)*	**C**	13-72 A.E. Moss	Christchurch	1889/90
	W	14-136 R.W. Blair	Wellington	1956/57

Record Partnerships

CANTERBURY

1st	287	B.R. Hartland & G.R. Stead	Christchurch	1994/95
2nd	174	G.T. Dowling & J.W. Burtt	Wellington	1967/68
3rd	187*	C.D. McMillan & R.T. Latham	Christchurch	1994/95
4th	278	M.L. Page & A.W. Roberts	Wellington	1931/32
5th	183	C.Z. Harris & C.D. McMillan	Christchurch	1996/97
6th	209	C.Z. Harris & A.J. Redmond	Rangiora	2001/02
7th	241	N.J. Astle & M.W. Priest	Christchurch	1994/95
8th	114	A.W. Thomas & H.B. Whitta	Christchurch	1919/20
9th	182*	L.K. Germon & R.M. Ford	Christchurch	1989/90
10th	85	A.W. Hart & C.H. Thiele	Rangiora	1984/85

WELLINGTON

1st	239	C.S. Dempster & W.H. Dustin	Wellington	1931/32
2nd	209*	A.H. Jones & M.D. Crowe	Christchurch	1992/93
3rd	206	A.H. Preston & J.E.F. Beck	Christchurch	1955/56
4th	187	H.M. McGirr & T.C. Lowry	Christchurch	1930/31
5th	139	M.H.W. Papps & L.J. Woodcock	Rangiora	2013/14
6th	184	G.D. Elliott & S.M. Mills	Christchurch	2006/07
7th	176	S.M. Mills & C.J. Nevin	Christchurch	2006/07
	176	T.A. Blundell & P.F. Younghusband	Christchurch	2016/17
8th	154	K.C. James & F.T. Badcock	Christchurch	1926/27
9th	125	S.G. Borthwick & I.G. McPeake	Christchurch	2015/16
10th	113	A.J. McKay & M.R. Gillespie	Rangiora	2012/13

CENTRAL DISTRICTS v NORTHERN DISTRICTS

First match	*Played*	*Won by Central Districts*	*Won by Northern Districts*	*Drawn*
1956/57	95	28	28	39

Highest totals	**CD**	531-7 dec		Napier	2009/10
	ND	556-9 dec		New Plymouth	2014/15
Lowest totals	**CD**	51		Hamilton	1957/58
	ND	86		New Plymouth	1956/57
Highest innings	**CD**	247	P.J. Ingram	Hamilton	2008/09
	ND	334	D.G. Brownlie	New Plymouth	2014/15
Best bowling *(innings)*	**CD**	7-28	B.W. Yuile	Hamilton	1967/68
	ND	8-37	D.B. Clarke	Wanganui	1962/63
Best bowling *(match)*	**CD**	11-134	G.K. Robertson	Nelson	1986/87
	ND	11-145	G.W. Aldridge	Whangarei	2009/10

Record Partnerships

CENTRAL DISTRICTS

1st	215	J.M. How & M.S. Sinclair	Napier	2004/05
	215	J.M. How & J.A. Raval	Nelson	2012/13
2nd	263	M.J. Greatbatch & M.D. Crowe	Morrinsville	1986/87
3rd	264	P.J. Ingram & M.S. Sinclair	Hamilton	2008/09
4th	176	T.C. Bruce & D. Cleaver	Napier	2016/17
5th	222	M.S. Sinclair & C.F.K van Wyk	Gisborne	2011/12
6th	224	B.D. Schmulian & D.A.J. Bracewell	Mt Maunganui	2017/18
7th	179	B.B.J. Griggs & C.J.M. Furlong	Hamilton	2001/02
8th	173	I.D.S. Smith & G.K. Robertson	Hamilton	1982/83
9th	116	V. Pollard & R.O. Collinge	Palmerston North	1964/65
10th	55	B.S. Smith & A.F. Milne	Gisborne	2012/13

NORTHERN DISTRICTS

1st	167	M.E. Parlane & M.D. Bell	New Plymouth	1994/95
2nd	199	R.E.W. Mawhinney & D.J. White	Hamilton	1985/86
3rd	258	D.R. Flynn & B. Popli	Hamilton	2015/16
4th	169	D.J. White & B.S. Oxenham	Wanganui	1990/91
5th	155	C.J. Anderson & J.A.H. Marshall	Nelson	2012/13
6th	322	M.G. Orchard & J.A.F. Yovich	Napier	2005/06
7th	136	D.J. Nash & A.R. Tait	Masterton	1997/98
8th	143	C.M. Presland & C.W. Dickeson	Whangarei	1983/84
9th	107	R.G. Hart & A.R. Tait	Rotorua	1995/96
10th	89	M.J.E. Wright & S.J. Scott	Wanganui	1978/79

CENTRAL DISTRICTS v OTAGO

First match	Played	Won by Central Districts	Won by Otago	Drawn
1950/51	99	34	26	39

Highest totals	CD	650-8 dec		Napier	2015/16
	O	624		Napier	2006/07
Lowest totals	CD	74		Invercargill	1996/97
	O	63		Lincoln	2011/12
Highest innings	CD	244	B.S. Smith	Napier	2015/16
	O	264	B. Sutcliffe	Dunedin	1959/60
Best bowling (innings)	CD	7-36	B.W. Yuile	Nelson	1962/63
	O	8-31	D.G. Sewell	Invercargill	1996/97
Best bowling (match)	CD	11-99	D.D. Beard	Dunedin	1956/57
	O	15-203	A.M. Moir	New Plymouth	1953/54

Record Partnerships

CENTRAL DISTRICTS

1st	202	G.H. Worker & G.R. Hay	Napier	2018/19
2nd	242*	J.M. How & M.S. Sinclair	New Plymouth	2005/06
3rd	223	C.J.P. Smith & S.W.J. Wilson	Blenheim	1990/91
4th	234	B.S. Smith & G.H. Worker	Napier	2015/16
5th	205	G.R. Hay & K. Noema-Barnett	Alexandra	2018/19
6th	184*	M.S. Sinclair & T.I. Lythe	Napier	2007/08
7th	123	I.D.S. Smith & S.J. Gill	Napier	1981/82
8th	133	T.S. Nethula & A.F. Milne	Napier	2012/13
9th	239	H.B. Cave & I.B. Leggat	Dunedin	1952/53
10th	60*	B.L. Cairns & A.B. Jordan	Wanganui	1975/76

OTAGO

1st	305	R.A. Lawson & M.G. Croy	Napier	1995/96
2nd	169	G.M. Turner & R.W. Anderson	Dunedin	1974/75
3rd	306	S.B. Haig & N.T. Broom	Napier	2009/10
4th	200	B.R. Blair & G.J. Dawson	Dunedin	1982/83
5th	192	M.H. Richardson & I.S. Billcliff	Napier	1994/95
6th	182	J.L. Finnie & A.K. Kitchen	Dunedin	2016/17
7th	121*	W.K. Lees & B. Abernethy	Napier	1981/82
8th	119	M.D. Craig & N. Wagner	Dunedin	2012/13
9th	92	D.E.C. McKechnie & B.L. Cairns	Dunedin	1976/77
10th	78	C.B. Gaffaney & D.G. Sewell	Palmerston North	1999/00

CENTRAL DISTRICTS v WELLINGTON

First match	*Played*	*Won by Central Districts*	*Won by Wellington*	*Drawn*
1950/51	98	21	34	43

Highest totals	**CD**	523		Wellington	2008/09
	W	590-8 dec		Palmerston North	2004/05
Lowest totals	**CD**	50		Upper Hutt	1979/80
	W	88		Wellington	1991/92
Highest innings	**CD**	245*	P.J. Ingram	Wellington	2009/10
	W	265	M.D. Bell	Napier	2007/08
Best bowling *(innings)*	**CD**	7-55	E.P. Thompson	Napier	2003/04
	W	7-30	J.E.C. Franklin	Wellington	2005/06
Best bowling *(match)*	**CD**	11-149	E.P. Thompson	Napier	2003/04
	W	10-103	B.D. Morrison	Wellington	1955/56

Record Partnerships

CENTRAL DISTRICTS

1st	428	P.J. Ingram & J.M. How	Wellington	2009/10
2nd	204	P.J. Ingram & B.S. Smith	Wellington	2010/11
3rd	224	C. Cachopa & M.S. Sinclair	Napier	2012/13
4th	172*	P.S. Briasco & M.W. Douglas	Palmerston North	1990/91
5th	301	J.I. Englefield & L.R.P.L. Taylor	Palmerston North	2004/05
6th	235	M.S. Sinclair & B.B.J. Griggs	Wellington	2008/09
7th	187	C.F.K. van Wyk & D.A.J. Bracewell	Napier	2010/11
8th	84	P.M. Blackbourn & G.K. Robertson	Palmerston North	1983/84
9th	73	G.R. Hay & E.J. McInnis	Napier	2007/08
10th	134	G.H. Worker & A.W. Mathieson	Nelson	2015/16

WELLINGTON

1st	316	M.H. Austen & R.T. Hart	Wanganui	1993/94
2nd	215	M.D. Bell & M.E. Parlane	Napier	2004/05
3rd	256	M.H.W. Papps & J.D. Ryder	Wellington	2012/13
4th	310	J.D. Ryder & N.R. Parlane	Palmerston North	2004/05
5th	341	G.R. Larsen & E.B. McSweeney	Levin	1987/88
6th	247	L.J. Woodcock & M.J. Nofal	Wellington	2017/18
7th	161	S.P. Fleming & M.D.J. Walker	Wellington	2001/02
8th	135	G.R. Larsen & J.E.C. Franklin	Wellington	1998/99
9th	225	L.J. Woodcock & M.J. Tugaga	Wellington	2009/10
10th	81	L.C. Butler & R.E. Reid	Wanganui	1959/60

NORTHERN DISTRICTS v OTAGO

First match	Played	Won by Northern Districts	Won by Otago	Drawn
1956/57	91	32	23	36

Highest totals	**ND**	559-9 dec		Hamilton	2010/11
	O	576-8 dec		Whangarei	2009/10
Lowest totals	**ND**	64		Dunedin	1971/72
	O	77		Gisborne	1999/00
Highest innings	**ND**	241	D.R. Flynn	Hamilton	2010/11
	O	207	A.K. Kitchen	Dunedin	2016/17
Best bowling	**ND**	7-42	K. Treiber	Hamilton	1985/86
(innings)	**O**	9-93	P.J. Petherick	Dunedin	1975/76
Best bowling	**ND**	13-99	R.P. de Groen	Alexandra	1992/93
(match)	**O**	13-144	S.L. Boock	Whangarei	1980/81

Record Partnerships

NORTHERN DISTRICTS

1st	214	D.G. Brownlie & B.S. Wilson	Hamilton	2014/15
2nd	222	L.M. Crocker & C.M. Kuggeleijn	Hamilton	1983/84
3rd	199	B-J. Watling & B. Popli	Whangarei	2015/16
4th	283	D.R. Flynn & C.J. Anderson	Hamilton	2012/13
5th	226	D.J. Mitchell & T.L. Seifert	Dunedin	2016/17
6th	191	S.B. Styris & R.G. Hart	Hamilton	2001/02
7th	131	D.R. Flynn & P.D. McGlashan	Gisborne	2005/06
8th	102	J.A.F. Yovich & B.P. Martin	Dunedin	2005/06
9th	112	J.A.F. Yovich & B.E. Scott	Dunedin	2009/10
10th	97	R.G. Hart & G.L. West	Hamilton	2002/03

OTAGO

1st	260	R.A. Lawson & Mohammad Wasim	Dunedin	2002/03
2nd	247	C.D. Cumming & D.J. Broom	Whangarei	2009/10
3rd	150	K.B.K. Ibadulla & K.J. Burns	Gisborne	1989/90
4th	235	K.J. Burns & R.N. Hoskin	Hamilton	1987/88
5th	252	N.T. Broom & D.J. Broom	Queenstown	2010/11
6th	146	G.J. Hopkins & N.L. McCullum	Dunedin	2006/07
7th	190	N.G. Smith & M.J.G. Rippon	Dunedin	2019/20
8th	149	N.T. Broom & M.D. Craig	Hamilton	2012/13
9th	85	D.C. de Boorder & N.B. Beard	Queenstown	2010/11
10th	102	M.D. Craig & J.A. Duffy	Dunedin	2014/15

NORTHERN DISTRICTS v WELLINGTON

First match	Played	Won by Northern Districts	Won by Wellington	Drawn
1956/57	95	23	38	34

Highest totals	**ND**	608-9 dec		Lincoln	2011/12
	W	608-9 dec		Hamilton	1998/99
Lowest totals	**ND**	57		Hamilton	1961/62
	W	58		Hamilton	2014/15
Highest innings	**ND**	284*	K.S. Williamson	Lincoln	2011/12
	W	296	J.R. Reid	Wellington	1962/63
Best bowling *(innings)*	**ND**	8-27	T.G. Southee	Hamilton	2009/10
	W	8-24	E.J. Chatfield	Lower Hutt	1979/80
Best bowling *(match)*	**ND**	12-62	I.S. Sodhi	Wellington	2017/18
	W	12-39	E.J. Chatfield	Lower Hutt	1979/80

Record Partnerships

NORTHERN DISTRICTS

1st	274	B.S. Wilson & B-J. Watling	Whangarei	2010/11
2nd	177	B.S. Wilson & K.S. Williamson	Lincoln	2011/12
3rd	169	J.M. Parker & A.D.G. Roberts	Wellington	1983/84
4th	208	S.A. Thomson & M.P. Maynard	Hamilton	1991/92
5th	180	B. Popli & B-J. Watling	Hamilton	2015/16
6th	170	E.C. Petrie & R.J. McPherson	Hamilton	1959/60
7th	166	D.J. Mitchell & T.G. Southee	Wellington	2012/13
8th	152	J.A.H. Marshall & M.G. Orchard	Hamilton	2006/07
9th	188	N.R. Parlane & D.R. Tuffey	Wellington	1999/00
10th	113*	P.D. McGlashan & G.W. Aldridge	Wellington	2005/06

WELLINGTON

1st	310	B.A. Edgar & R.H. Vance	Wellington	1988/89
2nd	215	M.D. Bell & J.D. Wells	Hamilton	1998/99
3rd	346	G.P. Burnett & R.A. Verry	Hamilton	1991/92
4th	179	P.T. Barton & J.R. Reid	Wellington	1964/65
5th	158*	T.A. Blundell & T.M. Johnson	Wellington	2020/21
6th	139	J.F.M. Morrison & R.W. Smith	Wellington	1972/73
7th	165	G.D. Elliott & H.K.P. Boam	Wellington	2010/11
8th	102	L. Ronchi & J.S. Patel	Wellington	2012/13
9th	87	I.J. Therkleson & R.O. Collinge	Whangarei	1973/74
10th	81*	D.S. Hutchinson & B.J. Arnel	Hamilton	2015/16

OTAGO v WELLINGTON

First match	Played	Won by Otago	Won by Wellington	Drawn
1892/93	135	36	62	37

Highest totals	**O**	651-9 dec		Dunedin	2012/13
	W	575-7 dec		Wellington	1951/52
Lowest totals	**O**	34		Dunedin	1956/57
	W	42		Wellington	1945/46
Highest innings	**O**	239	H.D. Rutherford	Dunedin	2011/12
	W	283	J.R. Reid	Wellington	1951/52
Best bowling *(innings)*	**O**	8-46	B.L. Cairns	Invercargill	1978/79
	W	8-36	R.W. Blair	Dunedin	1952/53
Best bowling *(match)*	**O**	12-277	A.W. Alloo	Dunedin	1923/24
	W	12-87	E.J. Chatfield	Wellington	1973/74

Record Partnerships

OTAGO

1st	193	M.H. Richardson & M.J. Horne	Wellington	2000/01
2nd	254	K.J. Burns & K.R. Rutherford	Oamaru	1987/88
3rd	291	M.G. Bracewell & N.T. Broom	Dunedin	2012/13
4th	211*	K.J. Burns & A.H. Jones	Wellington	1984/85
5th	134	C.B. Gaffaney & G.J. Hopkins	Dunedin	2003/04
6th	216	H.D. Rutherford & D.C. de Boorder	Dunedin	2011/12
7th	159	D.C. de Boorder & M.D. Craig	Wellington	2013/14
8th	165*	J.N. Crawford & A.G. Eckhold	Wellington	1914/15
9th	130*	D.C. de Boorder & W.C. McSkimming	Queenstown	2010/11
10th	90	B.L. Cairns & G.B. Thomson	Lower Hutt	1979/80

WELLINGTON

1st	299	M.D. Bell & R.A. Jones	Dunedin	2001/02
2nd	279	M.D. Bell & M.E. Parlane	Dunedin	2006/07
3rd	246	B.A.G. Murray & J.F.M. Morrison	Dunedin	1968/69
4th	274	R.A. Jones & S.R. Mather	Wellington	2000/01
5th	255	B.R. Taylor & J.V. Coney	Dunedin	1972/73
6th	184	H.M. McGirr & D.C. Collins	Dunedin	1923/24
7th	250	C.J. Nevin & M.D.J. Walker	Wellington	2003/04
8th	180	R.G. Twose & M.C. Goodson	Dunedin	1994/95
9th	72	F.T. Badcock & K.C. James	Wellington	1926/27
10th	138	K.C. James & A.W.S. Brice	Wellington	1926/27

PROVINCIAL COMPETITION

Plunket Shield

1921/22 – 1974/75

Awarded by the Governor of New Zealand, Lord Plunket, the Shield was given to Canterbury as the association with the best record in the 1906/07 season. From 1907/08 to 1920/21 the trophy was competed for under a challenge system but thereafter on a competition basis.

HOLDERS	*Tenure*	*Challenges resisted*
Canterbury	17 December, 1907	—
Auckland	17 December, 1907 to 1 February, 1911	7
Canterbury	1 February, 1911 to 12 February, 1912	2
Auckland	12 February, 1912 to 31 January, 1913	1
Canterbury	31 January, 1913 to 27 December, 1918	9
Wellington	27 December, 1918 to 24 January, 1919	—
Canterbury	24 January, 1919 to 4 January, 1920	2
Auckland	4 January, 1920 to 10 January, 1921	3
Wellington	10 January, 1921	—

Shell Series

1975/76-2000/01

In 1975/76, a new competition, sponsored by Shell, was established. For the first four seasons this was played under a two-stage system — the first round of 15 games (all teams playing each other) was for the Shell Cup*, while the second round (on a knock-out basis culminating in a final) carried the season's major prize, the Shell Trophy.

From 1979/80, only the Shell Trophy was competed for. The Shell Cup was reallocated to the limited-over competition in 1980/81, while the Plunket Shield was reserved for matches between the North and South Islands.

WINNERS

1921/22	Auckland
1922/23	Canterbury
1923/24	Wellington
1924/25	Otago
1925/26	Wellington
1926/27	Auckland
1927/28	Wellington
1928/29	Auckland
1929/30	Wellington
1930/31	Canterbury
1931/32	Wellington
1932/33	Otago
1933/34	Auckland
1934/35	Canterbury
1935/36	Wellington
1936/37	Auckland
1937/38	Auckland
1938/39	Auckland
1939/40	Auckland
1945/46	Canterbury
1946/47	Auckland
1947/48	Otago
1948/49	Canterbury
1949/50	Wellington
1950/51	Otago
1951/52	Canterbury
1952/53	Otago
1953/54	Central Districts
1954/55	Wellington
1955/56	Canterbury
1956/57	Wellington
1957/58	Otago
1958/59	Auckland
1959/60	Canterbury
1960/61	Wellington
1961/62	Wellington
1962/63	Northern Districts
1963/64	Auckland
1964/65	Canterbury
1965/66	Wellington
1966/67	Central Districts
1967/68	Central Districts
1968/69	Auckland
1969/70	Otago
1970/71	Central Districts
1971/72	Otago
1972/73	Wellington
1973/74	Wellington
1974/75	Otago
1975/76	Canterbury *Canterbury**
1976/77	Otago *Northern Districts**
1977/78	Auckland *Canterbury**
1978/79	Otago *Otago**
1979/80	Northern Districts
1980/81	Auckland
1981/82	Wellington
1982/83	Wellington
1983/84	Canterbury
1984/85	Wellington
1985/86	Otago
1986/87	Central Districts
1987/88	Otago
1988/89	Auckland
1989/90	Wellington
1990/91	Auckland
1991/92	Central Districts & Northern Districts
1992/93	Northern Districts
1993/94	Canterbury
1994/95	Auckland
1995/96	Auckland
1996/97	Canterbury
1997/98	Canterbury
1998/99	Central Districts
1999/00	Northern Districts
2000/01	Wellington

State Championship

from 2001/02

State Insurance took over the sponsorship of the competition in 2001/02.

WINNERS

2001/02	Auckland	2002/03	Auckland	2003/04	Wellington
2004/05	Auckland	2005/06	Central Districts	2006/07	Northern Districts
2007/08	Canterbury	2008/09	Auckland		

Plunket Shield

from 2009/10

The Plunket Shield was reinstated at the conclusion of State Insurance's sponsorship term.

WINNERS

2009/10	Northern Districts	2010/11	Canterbury	2011/12	Northern Districts
2012/13	Central Districts	2013/14	Canterbury	2014/15	Canterbury
2015/16	Auckland	2016/17	Canterbury	2017/18	Central Districts
2018/19	Central Districts	2019/20	Wellington	2020/21	Canterbury

TEAM RECORDS

Playing Record of the First-class Sides in New Zealand

	P	W	L	D
Canterbury	752	279	253	220*
Wellington	732	259	235	238†
Otago	713	199	308	206
Auckland	696	268	193	235
Central Districts	522	144	166	212*
Northern Districts	490	126	174	190
New Zealand	282	77	85	120
England/MCC	140	63	12	65*
Australia	113	63	7	43
Pakistan	61	22	11	28
Hawke's Bay	53	9	34	10
West Indies	49	11	16	22
India	40	11	11	18
New Zealand A	30	12	2	16
South Africa	28	11	1	16
Sri Lanka	28	4	12	12
New South Wales	24	16	2	6
Nelson	17	9	6	2*
North Island	16	6	5	5
Fiji	15	5	8	2
South Island	15	4	8	3
Bangladesh	14	—	14	—
New Zealand U23 XI	12	—	9	3
Zimbabwe	11	2	4	5
President's XI	9	—	3	6
NZ Academy XI	9	3	3	3
Southland	8	1	5	2
Taranaki	8	1	6	1
Southern	8	4	1	3
Sri Lanka A	8	—	6	2
Northern	7	2	1	4
Central	7	2	3	2
England A	7	3	—	4
NZ XI	7	1	3	3

	P	W	L	D
India A	7	—	—	7
The Rest	6	1	3	2
Victoria	6	1	1	4
Pakistan A	6	1	1	4
Young New Zealand	5	—	2	3
Queensland	5	3	1	1
Tasmania	4	—	3	1
Shell XI	3	1	1	1
Emerging Players	3	—	1	2
Governor General's XI	2	1	1	—
Commonwealth XI	2	2	—	—
D.H. Robins' XI	2	—	—	2
NZ Major Association XI	2	—	—	2
West Indies A	2	—	2	—
U-Bix XI	1	—	—	1
West Coast (NI)	1	1	—	—
D. Reese's XI	1	—	1	—
Minor Associations	1	—	1	—
Sir Julien Cahn's XI	1	—	—	1
South Island Army	1	1	—	—
North Island Army	1	—	1	—
New Zealand Army	1	1	—	—
New Zealand Air Force	1	—	1	—
New Zealand Services	1	—	—	1
Canterbury/Otago	1	—	—	1
Auckland/Wellington	1	—	1	—
ND/CD	1	—	—	1
Auckland XI	1	—	—	1
Otago Invitation XI	1	—	1	—
Canterbury XI	1	—	—	1
Board XI	1	—	1	—
Australian Academy XI	1	1	—	—
Western Australia	1	—	—	1
TOTALS	**5002**	**1629**	**1629**	**1744**

** includes a tie   † includes two ties*

Highest Match Aggregates

Runs-Wickets			
1945-18	Canterbury v Wellington	Christchurch	1994/95
1905-40	Otago v Wellington	Dunedin	1923/24
1567-37	Auckland v Wellington	Auckland	1936/37
1554-40	Wellington v Auckland	Wellington	1922/23
1549-34	Central Districts v Canterbury	New Plymouth	2009/10
1549-36	Auckland v Central Districts	Auckland	2015/16
1531-39	Wellington v Auckland	Wellington	1923/24
1521-17	Auckland v Northern Districts	Auckland	2013/14
1513-34	Central Districts v Otago	Napier	2006/07
1511-31	New Zealand v Bangladesh	Wellington	2016/17
1505-25	New Zealand v India	Auckland	1989/90
1501-37	Canterbury v Otago	Christchurch	1931/32
1501-32	New Zealand v Bangladesh	Hamilton	2009/10
1501-31	Central Districts v Northern Districts	Napier	2009/10
1500-32	Wellington v Canterbury	Wellington	2019/20

Highest Team Totals

777	Canterbury v Otago at Christchurch	1996/97
752-8 dec	NSW v Otago at Dunedin	1923/24
726	Northern Districts v Canterbury at Rangiora	2009/10
715-6 dec	New Zealand v Bangladesh at Hamilton	2018/19
693-9 dec	Auckland v Canterbury at Auckland	1939/40
680-8 dec	New Zealand v India at Wellington	2013/14
671-4	New Zealand v Sri Lanka at Wellington	1990/91
668-7 dec	Auckland v Central Districts at Napier	2014/15
663	Australia v New Zealand at Auckland	1920/21
662-5 dec	Auckland v Central Districts at Auckland	2008/09
660-5 dec	West Indies v New Zealand at Wellington	1994/95
659-6 dec	New Zealand v Pakistan at Christchurch	2020/21
658	Australians v Auckland at Auckland	1913/14
658-9 dec	Auckland v Wellington at Auckland	2012/13
653-5 dec	MCC v New Zealand at Dunedin	1935/36
653	Australians v Canterbury at Christchurch	1913/14
651-9 dec	Otago v Wellington at Dunedin	2012/13
650-8 dec	Central Districts v Otago at Napier	2015/16
643	Auckland v Canterbury at Auckland	1919/20
635-6 dec	Auckland v Central Districts at Auckland	2009/10
627-7 dec	Auckland v Otago at Lincoln	2006/07
624	Otago v Central Districts at Napier	2006/07
621-5 dec	South Africa v New Zealand at Auckland	1998/99
619-9 dec	New Zealand v India at Napier	2008/09
616-5 dec	Pakistan v New Zealand at Auckland	1988/89
615-9 dec	New Zealand v England at Mt Maunganui	2019/20
614-8	Wellington v Canterbury at Christchurch	2006/07
614-7 dec	Northern Districts v Auckland at Hamilton	2012/13
613-7 dec	Canterbury v Wellington at Christchurch	2006/07
610-6 dec	Australia v New Zealand at Auckland	1913/14
609-9 dec	New Zealand v West Indies at Dunedin	2013/14
608-9 dec	Wellington v Northern Districts at Hamilton	1998/99
608-9 dec	Northern Districts v Wellington at Lincoln	2011/12
602-8 dec	Otago v Canterbury at Dunedin	1928/29
601-9 dec	Otago v Canterbury at Christchurch	2006/07

Most Runs in a Match by One Side

Runs-Wickets				
1025-20	560 & 465	Wellington v Otago	Dunedin	1923/24
973-6	498-2d & 475-4	Wellington v Canterbury	Christchurch	1994/95
972-12	496 & 476-2d	Canterbury v Wellington	Christchurch	1994/95
971-14	511-6d & 460-8	Australia v New Zealand	Wellington	1973/74
948-20	569 & 379	Wellington v Auckland	Wellington	1923/24
903-17	534-9d & 369-8d	Otago v Wellington	Wellington	2013/14

Lowest Match Aggregates

completed matches, i.e. not drawn

Runs-Wickets			
151-30	Canterbury v Otago	Christchurch	1866/67
153-31	Otago v Canterbury	Dunedin	1896/97
156-30	Nelson v Wellington	Nelson	1885/86
159-31	Nelson v Wellington	Nelson	1887/88
176-32	Otago v Tasmania	Dunedin	1883/84
183-40	Nelson v Wellington	Nelson	1883/84
192-30	Taranaki v Hawke's Bay	Hawera	1891/92

The lowest aggregates since 1900 are:

Runs-Wickets			
241-30	Otago v Southland	Dunedin	1919/20
278-40	Southland v Otago	Invercargill	1918/19
295-28	New Zealand v Australia	Wellington	1945/46

Lowest Match Aggregates by One Side

55	36 & 19	Wellington v Nelson	Nelson	1885/86
57	25 & 32	Canterbury v Otago	Christchurch	1866/67
64	35 & 29	Taranaki v Hawke's Bay	Hawera	1891/92
72	30 & 42	Wellington v Nelson	Nelson	1883/84
76	34 & 42	Canterbury v Otago	Dunedin	1863/64
76	27 & 49	Canterbury v Otago	Dunedin	1896/97
79	31 & 48	Wellington v Nelson	Nelson	1887/88
80	51 & 29	Wellington v Nelson	Nelson	1879/80
87	40 & 47	Tasmania v Otago	Dunedin	1883/84
95	43 & 52	Otago v Canterbury	Christchurch	1872/73
96	41 & 55	Southland v Otago	Invercargill	1918/19
96	42 & 54	New Zealand v Australia	Wellington	1945/46
97	37 & 60	Wellington v Nelson	Christchurch	1876/77
99	65 & 34	Wellington v Canterbury	Wellington	1886/87

Lowest Team Totals

by any first-class team in New Zealand

13	Auckland v Canterbury at Auckland (included 8 extras)	1877/78
19	Wellington v Nelson at Nelson	1885/86
22	Wellington v Canterbury at Wellington	1903/04
25	Canterbury v Otago at Christchurch	1866/67
26	NZ v England at Auckland	1954/55
27	Canterbury v Otago at Dunedin	1896/97
28	Hawke's Bay v Auckland at Auckland (included 13 extras)	1910/11
29	Wellington v Nelson at Nelson	1879/80
29	Taranaki v Hawke's Bay at Hawera	1891/92

Highest Second Innings Totals

680-8 dec	New Zealand v India	Wellington	2013/14
671-4	New Zealand v Sri Lanka	Wellington	1990/91
602-8	Otago v Canterbury	Dunedin	1928/29
598	Auckland v Wellington	Wellington	2015/16
589	Otago v Canterbury	Christchurch	1931/32
585-4 dec	New Zealand v Sri Lanka	Christchurch	2018/19
575-7 dec	Wellington v Otago	Wellington	1951/52
571-8	Otago v Central Districts	Napier	1995/96
551-5 dec	Canterbury v Central Districts	New Plymouth	2009/10
539	Auckland v Otago	Dunedin	1926/27
537	Auckland v Canterbury	Christchurch	1930/31
537	New Zealand v England	Wellington	1983/84
533-6 dec	Northern Districts v Otago	Hamilton	2012/13
531-7 dec	Central Districts v Northern Districts	Napier	2009/10
526-8 dec	Canterbury v Wellington	Wellington	1931/32
524-5 dec	New Zealand v Sri Lanka	Wellington	2014/15
519	Canterbury v Wellington	Christchurch	1930/31
517	Central Districts v Otago	Napier	2009/10
511-8 dec	Australia v New Zealand	Hamilton	2009/10
507	West Indies v New Zealand	Dunedin	2013/14

Highest Fourth Innings Totals

495	lost 145 runs	Otago v Wellington	Dunedin	1923/24
475-4	and won	Wellington v Canterbury	Christchurch	1994/95
474	lost 27 runs	Otago v Northern Districts	Dunedin	2014/15
473-6	and won	Canterbury v Auckland	Christchurch	1930/31
459	lost 10 runs	Wellington v Canterbury	Rangiora	2013/14
458	lost 276 runs	Auckland v Wellington	Wellington	1927/28
453-8	and won	Northern Districts v Wellington	Wellington	1995/96
451	lost 98 runs	New Zealand v England	Christchurch	2001/02
450-7	and won	Central Districts v Canterbury	New Plymouth	2008/09
445-1	and won	Central Districts v Wellington	Wellington	2009/10
431	lost 121 runs	New Zealand v England	Napier	2007/08
429-8	and won	Northern Districts v Central Districts	Lincoln	2006/07
411-4	and won	Northern Districts v Central Districts	Napier	2009/10
409-4	and won	Auckland v Northern Districts	Auckland	2013/14
400-9	and won	Northern Districts v Central Districts	Napier	2004/05

Highest Fourth Innings Totals without Loss for Victory

226-0	Canterbury v Otago	Christchurch	1948/49
175-0	Otago v Central Districts	Masterton	1971/72
174-0	Otago v Northern Districts	Alexandra	1985/86
147-0	Wellington v Otago	Dunedin	2005/06
138-0	Auckland v Otago	Auckland	1937/38
130-0	Wellington v Otago	Wellington	1921/22
130-0	Canterbury v Auckland	Christchurch	1951/52

Large Victories

BY AN INNINGS AND

364 runs	Sims' Australian XI defeated Canterbury	Christchurch	1913/14
358 runs	Australia defeated New Zealand	Wellington	1904/05
356 runs	Australia defeated Otago	Dunedin	1949/50
354 runs	Auckland defeated Hawke's Bay	Auckland	1920/21
332 runs	Wellington defeated Canterbury	Wellington	1925/26
327 runs	NSW defeated Otago	Dunedin	1923/24
322 runs	Wellington defeated Hawkes Bay	Wellington	1905/06
322 runs	West Indies defeated New Zealand	Wellington	1994/95

BY A RUNS MARGIN

512 runs	Wellington defeated Auckland	Wellington	1925/26
446 runs	Wellington defeated Otago	Wellington	1926/27
438 runs	Auckland defeated Wellington	Auckland	1934/35
425 runs	Central Districts defeated Otago	Alexandra	2001/02
423 runs	New Zealand defeated Sri Lanka	Christchurch	2018/19
395 runs	Northern Districts defeated Wellington	Hamilton	2014/15
382 runs	Auckland defeated Canterbury	Christchurch	1920/21
365 runs	Wellington defeated Auckland	Wellington	1923/24
355 runs	Wellington defeated Canterbury	Christchurch	1926/27

Tied Matches

Wellington v Nelson	Wellington	1873/74
New Zealand v T.N. Pearce's XI	Scarborough	1958
Central Districts v England XI	New Plymouth	1977/78
Victoria v New Zealand	Melbourne	1982/83
Wellington v Canterbury	Wellington	1988/89

Close Finishes

VICTORY BY 1 WICKET

Canterbury defeated Tasmania	Christchurch	1883/84
Otago defeated Canterbury	Christchurch	1890/91
Wellington defeated Nelson	Nelson	1891/92
Auckland defeated Wellington	Wellington	1893/94
Canterbury defeated Wellington	Wellington	1899/00
Auckland defeated Wellington	Wellington	1911/12
Canterbury defeated Auckland	Auckland	1914/15
Wellington defeated Otago	Wellington	1924/25
Auckland defeated Otago	Auckland	1946/47
Fiji defeated Wellington	Wellington	1947/48
Otago defeated Wellington	Dunedin	1948/49
Auckland defeated Canterbury	Auckland	1950/51
Central Districts defeated Wellington	Wellington	1951/52
Otago defeated Wellington	Dunedin	1952/53
MCC defeated Canterbury	Christchurch	1960/61
Auckland defeated Canterbury	Christchurch	1963/64
Wellington defeated NZ Under-23 XI	Wellington	1965/66
Canterbury defeated Auckland	Auckland	1974/75
Northern Districts defeated Central Districts	Gisborne	1979/80
New Zealand defeated West Indies	Dunedin	1979/80
Otago defeated Wellington	Alexandra	1980/81
Otago defeated Canterbury	Christchurch	1990/91

Otago defeated Wellington	Dunedin	1991/92
Central Districts defeated Auckland	Auckland	1994/95
Canterbury defeated Northern Districts	Christchurch	1994/95
Southern defeated Central	Wanganui	1997/98
Wellington defeated Northern Districts	Hamilton	2001/02
Northern Districts defeated Central Districts	Napier	2004/05
Central Districts defeated Canterbury	New Plymouth	2009/10
Central Districts defeated Northern Districts	Napier	2018/19
Auckland defeated Northern Districts	Auckland	2019/20

VICTORY BY 10 RUNS OR LESS

1 run	Northern Districts defeated Central Districts	Rotorua	1989/90
2 runs	Auckland defeated Canterbury	Auckland	1903/04
	Wellington defeated Canterbury	Wellington	1935/36
3 runs	Otago defeated Wellington	Wellington	1953/54
	Central Districts defeated Wellington	Wellington	1970/71
	Central Districts defeated Otago	New Plymouth	1970/71
	Canterbury defeated Central Districts	Napier	1979/80
	Auckland defeated Otago	Dunedin	2004/05
4 runs	Auckland defeated Nelson	Nelson	1882/83
	Canterbury defeated Otago	Christchurch	1882/83
	Auckland defeated Wellington	Auckland	1977/78
	New Zealand defeated Pakistan	Abu Dhabi	2018/19
5 runs	Central Districts defeated Otago	New Plymouth	1953/54
	Northern Districts defeated Central Districts	Napier	1976/77
6 runs	Canterbury defeated Tasmania	Christchurch	1883/84
	Auckland defeated Canterbury	Auckland	1952/53
	South Island XI defeated North Island XI	Wellington	1957/58
	Northern Districts defeated Central Districts	Hamilton	1977/78
	Northern Districts defeated Otago	Dunedin	1978/79
	Central Districts defeated Northern Districts	Napier	1988/89
	Canterbury defeated Auckland	Auckland	2006/07
7 runs	Auckland defeated Canterbury	Christchurch	1873/74
8 runs	Auckland defeated Wellington	Wellington	1945/46
	Auckland defeated Northern Districts	Auckland	1963/64
	Central Districts defeated Auckland	Napier	1982/83
	Auckland defeated Central Districts	Auckland	1999/00
	Canterbury defeated Northern Districts	Rangiora	2017/18
9 runs	Central Districts defeated Auckland	Nelson	1983/84
10 runs	Northern Districts defeated Canterbury	Hamilton	1960/61
	Wellington defeated Central Districts	New Plymouth	1973/74
	Otago defeated Auckland	Dunedin	1975/76
	Canterbury defeated Wellington	Rangiora	2013/14
	Auckland defeated Otago	Dunedin	2015/16
	Canterbury defeated Auckland	Rangiora	2016/17

Victory after Follow-on

Auckland (180 & 302)	beat Canterbury (392 & 84)	Auckland	1952/53
Northern Districts (165 & 275)	beat Otago (320-9d & 105)	Dunedin	1961/62
Auckland (69 & 303)	beat Northern Districts (224 & 140)	Auckland	1963/64
Canterbury (166 & 360)	beat Auckland (351-9d & 149)	Christchurch	1973/74
Auckland (101 & 278)	beat Otago (268 & 108)	Dunedin	2004/05

Longest Matches in New Zealand

before 1900

FOUR DAYS

Otago v Canterbury	Dunedin	1875/76
Canterbury v Tasmania	Christchurch	1883/84
Otago v Canterbury	Dunedin	1884/85

since 1900

SIX DAYS

New Zealand v England	Christchurch	1974/75
New Zealand v India	Christchurch	1975/76
* New Zealand v England	Auckland	1977/78
New Zealand v Pakistan	Napier	1978/79
New Zealand v West Indies	Auckland	1979/80
New Zealand v India	Christchurch	1980/81

** the only match where play took place on all six days*
The other instances involved the rest day being used after a day's play was lost

FIVE DAYS

Canterbury v Otago	Christchurch	1911/12
Canterbury v Wellington	Christchurch	1922/23
Otago v Wellington	Dunedin	1923/24
Canterbury v Auckland	Christchurch	1924/25
Wellington v Otago	Wellington	1926/27
Northern Districts v Auckland	Taupo	1999/00
Auckland v Wellington	Auckland	2004/05
Wellington v Central Districts	Wellington	2005/06
Northern Districts v Canterbury	Hamilton	2006/07
Wellington v Canterbury	Wellington	2007/08
Auckland v Central Districts	Lincoln	2008/09

All other matches of five days duration since 1926/27 have been test matches. A complete list of these up to 1993/94 is on pages 288 and 289 of the 1994 Almanack. *The 1998/99 Shell Trophy final between Central Districts and Otago at Napier was scheduled for five days but completed in three.*

Matches Abandoned without a Ball Being Bowled

these matches are not included in any first-class records

Hawke's Bay v Australia	Napier	1909/10
Central Districts v Northern Districts	Napier	1970/71
† Wellington v Australia	Wellington	1973/74
Central Districts v Australia	Napier	1973/74
† New Zealand v Pakistan	Dunedin	1988/89
† New Zealand President's XI v Australia	Nelson	1992/93
New Zealand A v Sri Lanka	Gisborne	1996/97
Wellington v Canterbury	Wellington	1996/97
† Northern v Pakistan A	Auckland	1998/99
† New Zealand v India	Dunedin	1998/99
Wellington v Canterbury	Wellington	2010/11
Wellington v Central Districts	Wellington	2010/11
New Zealand v Bangladesh	Christchurch	2018/19
Wellington v Canterbury	Wellington	2018/19
Otago v Auckland	Dunedin	2019/20
Central Districts v Auckland	Nelson	2020/21

† replaced with a limited-overs match

The match between New Zealand A and Pakistan at Nelson, 2016/17 was abandoned without any play but as the toss had been made it counts as an official game and is included in all records.

Matches Completed in One Day

Otago v Canterbury	Dunedin	11. 2.1868
Wellington v Auckland	Wellington	29.11.1874
Nelson v Wellington	Nelson	26.12.1887
Otago v Auckland	Dunedin	27.12.1889
Hawke's Bay v Taranaki	Napier	9. 1.1892
Auckland v New South Wales*	Auckland	20. 1.1894
Ireland v New Zealand	Dublin	11. 9.1937
Auckland v Fiji†	Auckland	9. 3.1954

** no play on first day* *† after no play on first two days and three declarations on third*

Most Extras in an Innings

Extras	*B*	*LB*	*NB*	*W*				
67	26	34	6	1	New Zealand (523)	v England	Lord's	2015
† 66	2	9	54	1	NZ Academy XI (459-8d)	v Pakistan A	Lincoln	1998/99
64	27	8	12	17	New Zealand (659-6d)	v Pakistan	Christchurch	2020/21
62	25	21	13	3	England (562)	v New Zealand	Leeds	2004
† 60	18	17	20	5	Central Districts (460-4d)	v Wellington	Wellington	1997/98
58	41	14	3	—	Wellington (380-5)	v Auckland	Wellington	1929/30
†58	6	14	30	8	Auckland (322-4d)	v Wellington	Auckland	1993/94
58	4	12	33	9	New Zealand (563)	v Pakistan	Hamilton	2003/04
57	31	16	10	—	New Zealand (387)	v England	Auckland	1929/30
54	35	14	1	4	Auckland (200-8d)	v Wellington	Auckland	1973/74
54	5	16	33	—	New Zealand A (597-9d)	v Sri Lanka A	Queenstown	2003/04
53	26	10	17	—	Canterbury (473-6)	v Auckland	Christchurch	1930/31
†53	4	2	46	1	Wellington (498-2d)	v Canterbury	Christchurch	1994/95
52					Wellington (370)	v Canterbury	Christchurch	1922/23
52	12	7	33	—	New Zealand (468)	v Pakistan	Karachi	1976/77
52	1	27	33	1	Auckland (423-7d)	v Wellington	Wellington	1992/93
† 52	1	15	32	4	Canterbury (537)	v Central Districts	Blenheim	1996/97
52	21	28	3	1	New Zealand (630-6d)	v India	Mohali	2003/04
52	7	9	28	8	Central Districts (499)	v Canterbury	N.Plymouth	2004/05
52	7	15	7	23	Central Districts (476)	v Otago	Napier	2012/13
51	10	11	30	—	Auckland (369)	v West Indies	Auckland	1999/00
51	5	23	13	10	New Zealand (393)	v Bangladesh	Wellington	2007/08
51	7	16	15	13	Northern Districts (334)	v Auckland	Auckland	2016/17
50					Otago (602-8d)	v Canterbury	Dunedin	1928/29
50	13	24	11	2	Wellington (356)	v Canterbury	Wellington	1981/82
† 50	3	11	36	—	Southern (554)	v Pakistan A	Christchurch	1998/99
50	12	22	9	7	Northern Districts (438)	v Auckland	Auckland	2019/20

† no balls counted as two extras, regardless of whether runs were scored from the bat

INDIVIDUAL RECORDS

BATTING

Highest Individual Scores

385	Sutcliffe B.	Otago v Canterbury	Christchurch	1952/53
355	Sutcliffe B.	Otago v Auckland	Dunedin	1949/50
338*	Blunt R.C.	Otago v Canterbury	Christchurch	1931/32
336*	Hammond W.R.	England v New Zealand	Auckland	1932/33
334	Brownlie D.G.	Northern Districts v Central Districts	New Plymouth	2014/15
327*	Conway D.P.	Wellington v Canterbury	Wellington	2019/20
317	Rutherford K.R.	New Zealand v D.B. Close's XI	Scarborough	1986
316*	Papps M.H.W.	Wellington v Auckland	Wellington	2017/18
306	Richardson M.H.	New Zealand v Zimbabwe A	Kwekwe	2000/01
302	McCullum B.B.	New Zealand v India	Wellington	2013/14
301*	Fulton P.G.	Canterbury v Auckland	Christchurch	2002/03
299	Crowe M.D.	New Zealand v Sri Lanka	Wellington	1990/91
296	Reid J.R.	Wellington v Northern Districts	Wellington	1962/63
293	Trumper V.T.	Sims' Australian XI v Canterbury	Christchurch	1913/14
290	Carson W.N.	Auckland v Otago	Dunedin	1936/37
290	Taylor L.R.P.L.	New Zealand v Australia	Perth	2015/16
284*	Williamson K.S.	Northern Districts v Wellington	Lincoln	2011/12
284	Woodfull W.M.	Australia v New Zealand	Auckland	1927/28
283	Reid J.R.	Wellington v Otago	Wellington	1951/52
281	Munro C.	Auckland v Central Districts	Napier	2014/15
275*	Cullinan D.J.	South Africa v New Zealand	Auckland	1998/99
275	Sutcliffe B.	Otago v Auckland	Auckland	1950/51
274*	Fleming S.P.	New Zealand v Sri Lanka	Colombo	2002/03
271	Javed Miandad	Pakistan v New Zealand	Auckland	1988/89
269*	Munro C.	Auckland v Wellington	Auckland	2012/13
268	Sinclair M.S.	New Zealand A v South Africa A	Potchefstroom	2004/05
268	McIntosh T.G.	Auckland v Canterbury	Auckland	2007/08
267*	Young B.A.	New Zealand v Sri Lanka	Dunedin	1996/97
267	de Silva P.A.	Sri Lanka v New Zealand	Wellington	1990/91
265	Bell M.D.	Wellington v Central Districts	Napier	2007/08
264*	Latham T.W.M.	New Zealand v Sri Lanka	Wellington	2018/19
264	Sutcliffe B.	Otago v Central Districts	Dunedin	1959/60
262	Fleming S.P.	New Zealand v South Africa	Cape Town	2005/06
261	Latham T.W.M.	Canterbury v Central Districts	Napier	2013/14
259	Turner G.M.	New Zealand v Guyana	Georgetown	1971/72
259	Turner G.M.	New Zealand v West Indies	Georgetown	1971/72
258	Nurse S.M.	West Indies v New Zealand	Christchurch	1968/69
256	Smith S.G.	Auckland v Canterbury	Auckland	1919/20
256	Raval J.A.	Auckland v Central Districts	Auckland	2008/09
255*	McGlew D.J.	South Africa v New Zealand	Wellington	1952/53
254*	Vance R.H.	Wellington v Northern Districts	Wellington	1988/89
251*	Harris C.Z.	Canterbury v Central Districts	Rangiora	1996/97
251	Williamson K.S.	New Zealand v West Indies	Hamilton	2020/21
250	Walters K.D.	Australia v New Zealand	Christchurch	1976/77
247*	Chappell G.S.	Australia v New Zealand	Wellington	1973/74
247	Ingram P.J.	Central Districts v Northern Districts	Hamilton	2008/09
246	Brathwaite K.C.	West Indies v New Zealand A	Queenstown	2020/21
245*	Ingram P.J.	Central Districts v Wellington	Wellington	2009/10
244	Smith B.S.	Central Districts v Otago	Napier	2015/16
243*	Sinclair M.S.	Central Districts v Otago	Napier	2007/08

243	Sutcliffe B.	New Zealand v Essex	Southend	1949
242*	Crowe M.D.	New Zealand v South Australia	Adelaide	1985/86
242*	Williamson K.S.	New Zealand v Sri Lanka	Wellington	2014/15
242	Crowe M.D.	Central Districts v Otago	New Plymouth	1989/90
241*	Latham T.W.M.	Canterbury v Wellington	Wellington	2013/14
241	Horne M.J.	Otago v Auckland	Auckland	1997/98
241	Flynn D.R.	Northern Districts v Otago	Hamilton	2010/11
239	Dowling G.T.	New Zealand v India	Christchurch	1967/68
239	Rutherford H.D.	Otago v Wellington	Dunedin	2011/12
239	Voges A.C.	Australia v New Zealand	Wellington	2015/16
238	Williamson K.S.	New Zealand v Pakistan	Christchurch	2020/21
237*	Latham R.T.	Canterbury v Northern Districts	Rotorua	1990/91
236	Ryder J.D.	Wellington v Central Districts	Palmerston North	2004/05
235	Marshall J.A.H.	Northern Districts v Canterbury	Christchurch	2001/02
230*	Sutcliffe B.	New Zealand v India	New Delhi	1955/56
227*	Stewart S.L.	Canterbury v Central Districts	New Plymouth	2009/10
227	Hammond W.R.	England v New Zealand	Christchurch	1932/33
226*	Rutherford K.R.	Otago v India	Dunedin	1989/90
226*	Carter L.J.	Canterbury v Wellington	Rangiora	2019/20
226	Hastings B.F.	Canterbury v NZ Under 23 XI	Christchurch	1964/65
226	Hay G.R.	Central Districts v Otago	Alexandra	2018/19
226	Root J.E.	England v New Zealand	Hamilton	2019/20
225*	Blunt R.C.	New Zealand v Gentlemen	Eastbourne	1931
225	McCullum B.B.	New Zealand v India	Hyderabad	2010/11
224	Vincent L.	New Zealand v Sri Lanka	Wellington	2004/05
224	McCullum B.B.	New Zealand v India	Auckland	2013/14
224	Latham T.W.M.	Canterbury v Wellington	Wellington	2019/20
223*	Turner G.M.	New Zealand v West Indies	Kingston	1971/72
223	Astle N.J.	New Zealand v Queensland	Brisbane	2001/02
222*	Midlane F.A.	Wellington v Otago	Wellington	1914/15
222	Rutherford I.A.	Otago v Central Districts	New Plymouth	1978/79
222	Astle N.J.	New Zealand v England	Christchurch	2001/02
221*	Fulton P.G.	Canterbury v Otago	Dunedin	2004/05
221	Macartney C.G.	NSW v Canterbury	Christchurch	1923/24
221	Blunt R.C.	Otago v Canterbury	Dunedin	1928/29
220*	Woodcock L.J.	Wellington v Central Districts	Wellington	2009/10
219	Bell M.D.	Wellington v Northern Districts	Hamilton	1998/99
219	Franklin J.E.C.	Wellington v Auckland	Auckland	2008/09
218	Bravo D.M.	West Indies v New Zealand	Dunedin	2013/14
217*	Taylor L.R.P.L.	New Zealand v West Indies	Dunedin	2013/14
217	Taylor L.R.P.L.	Central Districts v Otago	Napier	2006/07
217	Shakib Al Hasan	Bangladesh v New Zealand	Wellington	2016/17
216	Fletcher K.W.R.	England v New Zealand	Auckland	1974/75
216	Bell M.D.	Wellington v Auckland	Auckland	1997/98
216*	Chanderpaul S.	West Indies v New Zealand A	Taupo	1999/00
214*	Kortlang H.H.L.	Wellington v Auckland	Wellington	1925/26
214*	Booth B.C.	Australia B v Central Districts	Palmerston North	1966/67
214	Sinclair M.S.	New Zealand v West Indies	Wellington	1999/00
213	Murray B.A.G.	Wellington v Otago	Dunedin	1968/69
213	Trimble S.C.	Australia B v New Zealand	Wellington	1969/70
213	Greenidge C.G.	West Indies v New Zealand	Auckland	1986/87
212*	Woodfull W.M.	Victoria v Canterbury	Christchurch	1924/25
212*	Richardson M.H.	New Zealand A v Sussex	Hove	2000
212*	Kelly D.P.	Central Districts v Canterbury	Blenheim	2000/01
212*	Styris S.B.	Northern Districts v Otago	Hamilton	2001/02
212	Hiddleston J.S.	Wellington v Canterbury	Wellington	1925/26

212	Dempster C.S.	New Zealand v Essex	Leyton	1931
211*	Hick G.A.	Northern Districts v Auckland	Auckland	1988/89
211*	Gibbs H.H.	South Africa v New Zealand	Christchurch	1998/99
211	Warner P.F.	Lord Hawke's XI v Otago	Dunedin	1902/03
211	Wallace W.M.	Auckland v Canterbury	Auckland	1939/40
210	Brodie J.M.	Wellington v Auckland	Auckland	2011/12
210	Worker G.H.	Central Districts v Wellington	Nelson	2015/16
210	McClure K.J.	Canterbury v Auckland	Rangiora	2017/18
209*	Brown S.W.	Auckland v Canterbury	Christchurch	1990/91
209*	Horne M.J.	Auckland v Northern Districts	Auckland	2003/04
209*	Fulton P.G.	Canterbury v Central Districts	Christchurch	2014/15
209	White D.J.	Northern Districts v Central Districts	Hamilton	1985/86
209	Horne P.A.	Auckland v Northern Districts	Auckland	1988/89
208*	Sutcliffe B.	North Island v South Island	Dunedin	1947/48
208	Franklin J.E.C.	Wellington v Auckland	Wellington	2005/06
207*	How J.M.	Central Districts v Otago	Nelson	2013/14
207	Hart R.T.	Central Districts v Wellington	Wellington	1985/86
207	Kitchen A.K.	Otago v Northern Districts	Dunedin	2016/17
206*	Papps M.H.W.	Wellington v Canterbury	Rangiora	2012/13
206	Page M.L.	Canterbury v Wellington	Wellington	1931/32
206	Donnelly M.P.	New Zealand v England	Lord's	1949
206	Dowling G.T.	Canterbury v Wellington	Christchurch	1962/63
206	Harris C.Z	Canterbury v Central Districts	Blenheim	1996/97
205*	Lloyd C.H.	West Indies v South Island	Dunedin	1968/69
205*	McSweeney E.B.	Wellington v Central Districts	Levin	1987/88
205	McIntosh T.G.	Auckland v Otago	Lincoln	2006/07
205	Watling B-J.	New Zealand v England	Mt Maunganui	2019/20
204*	Sinclair M.S.	New Zealand v Pakistan	Christchurch	2000/01
204*	Gill S.	India A v New Zealand A	Christchurch	2019/20
204	Cox A.	Canterbury v Otago	Christchurch	1925/26
204	Hiddleston J.S.	Wellington v Auckland	Wellington	1925/26
204	Scott V.J.	Auckland v Otago	Dunedin	1947/48
204	Patel D.N.	Auckland v Northern Districts	Auckland	1991/92
203*	Burnett G.P.	Wellington v Northern Districts	Hamilton	1991/92
203*	Sinclair M.S.	Central Districts v Northern Districts	Wanganui	1998/99
203*	Broom N.T.	Otago v Northern Districts	Queenstown	2010/11
203*	Woodcock L.J.	Wellington v Auckland	Auckland	2016/17
203*	Conway D.P.	Wellington v Otago	Wellington	2018/19
203	Scott V.J.	New Zealand v Combined Services	Gillingham	1949
203	Reid J.R.	New Zealand v Western Province	Cape Town	1961/62
203	Edgar B.A.	Young New Zealand v Zimbabwe	Bulawayo	1984/85
203	Parlane M.E.	Wellington v Auckland	Auckland	2004/05
203	Cachopa C.	Auckland v Wellington	Auckland	2013/14
203	Sangakkara K.C.	Sri Lanka v New Zealand	Wellington	2014/15
203	Schmulian B.D. †	Central Districts v Northern Districts	Mt Maunganui	2017/18
202*	Congdon B.E.	Central Districts v Otago	Nelson	1968/69
202*	Greatbatch M.J.	Central Districts v Otago	Palmerston North	1988/89
202*	Hay G.R.	Central Districts v Canterbury	Rangiora	2013/14
202*	Raval J.A.	Auckland v Otago	Auckland	2015/16
202	Turner G.M.	New Zealand v President's XI	Montego Bay	1971/72
202	Austen M.H.	Wellington v Central Districts	Wanganui	1993/94
202	Greatbatch M.J.	Central Districts v Northern Districts	Rotorua	1995/96
202	Fleming S.P.	New Zealand v Bangladesh	Chittagong	2004/05
202	McCullum B.B.	New Zealand v Pakistan	Sharjah	2014/15
201*	Hart M.N.	Northern Districts v Auckland	Auckland	2002/03
201*	Smith B.F.	Central Districts v Canterbury	New Plymouth	2001/02

201	Reid J.R.	Otago v Canterbury	Dunedin	1957/58
201	Sutcliffe B.	Otago v Northern Districts	Hamilton	1960/61
201	Mushtaq Mohammad	Pakistan v New Zealand	Dunedin	1972/73
201	Jones R.A.	Auckland v West Indies	Auckland	2008/09
201	Ryder J.D.	New Zealand v India	Napier	2008/09
201	Hopkins G.J.	Auckland v Central Districts	Auckland	2009/10
201	Cleaver D.	Central Districts v Northern Districts	Napier	2019/20
200*	MacLaren A.C.	MCC v New Zealand	Wellington	1922/23
200*	Bardsley W.	NSW v Auckland	Auckland	1923/24
200*	Thorpe G.P.	England v New Zealand	Christchurch	2001/02
200*	Williamson K.S.	New Zealand v Bangladesh	Hamilton	2018/19
200	Lawson R.A.	Otago v Central Districts	Napier	1995/96
200	Taylor L.R.P.L.	New Zealand v Bangladesh	Wellington	2018/19
200	Conway D.P.	New Zealand v England	Lord's	2021

† on first-class debut

Most Runs in a Season in New Zealand

		M	I	NO	HS	Runs	Ave	100
Crowe M.D.	1986/87	11	21	3	175*	1676	93.11	8
Fulton P.G.	2012/13	12	23	2	136	1249	59.47	5
Turner G.M.	1975/76	11	20	4	177*	1244	77.75	5
Hick G.A.	1988/89	8	16	3	211*	1228	94.46	6
Popli B.	2015/16	10	17	0	172	1149	67.58	3
Bell M.D.	2000/01	13	21	0	134	1092	52.00	6
Rutherford H.D.	2012/13	13	23	0	171	1077	46.82	2
Crowe J.J.	1991/92	10	19	2	142*	1063	62.52	4
Brownlie D.G.	2012/13	16	28	2	135*	1057	40.65	4
Vance R.H.	1988/89	10	18	2	254*	1037	64.81	4
Richardson M.H.	2000/01	11	19	2	166	1035	60.88	2
Wright J.G.	1986/87	11	21	2	192	1019	53.63	3
Bell M.D.	2007/08	12	21	2	265	1016	53.47	3
Raval J.A.	2015/16	10	19	2	202*	1016	59.76	4
Papps M.H.W.	2006/07	7	11	0	188	1005	91.36	4
Sinclair M.S.	1999/00	14	26	2	214	1004	41.83	3

Most Runs in a Season for New Zealand

		M	I	NO	HS	Runs	Ave	100
Sutcliffe B.	1949	29	49	5	243	2627	59.70	7
Donnelly M.P.	1949	29	45	8	206	2287	61.81	5
Reid J.R.	*1961/62	20	36	2	203	2083	61.26	7

** includes South Africa & Australia*

Most Runs in Season of First-class Debut

			M	I	NO	HS	Runs	Ave
Carter J.F.	*ND*	2013/14	9	16	1	95	674	44.93
McClure K.J.	*Canterbury*	2015/16	8	13	2	193*	667	60.63
Bruce T.C.	*CD*	2014/15	7	12	1	112*	632	57.45
Hay G.R.	*CD*	2006/07	8	14	1	106	593	45.61
Cooper B.G.	*ND*	1980/81	7	13	0	105	520	40.00
Briasco P.S.	*CD*	1982/83	8	15	1	95	519	37.07
Cachopa B.	*Auckland*	2010/11	10	18	1	71	509	29.94
Carson W.N.	*Auckland*	1936/37	3	4	0	290	500	125.00

Highest Average in a Season in New Zealand

		M	I	NO	HS	Runs	Ave	100
Hammond W.R.	1932/33	3	3	1	336*	621	310.50	2
Woodfull W.M.	1924/25	6	9	5	212*	710	177.50	3
Williamson K.S.	2020/21	3	4	0	251	639	159.75	3
Greatbatch M.J.	1995/96	5	6	2	202	623	155.75	4
Javed Miandad	1988/89	4	5	1	271	597	149.25	3
Harris C.Z.	1996/97	5	7	1	251*	835	139.16	3
Woodfull W.M.	1927/28	6	9	3	284	781	130.16	3
Carson W.N.	1936/37	3	4	0	290	500	125.00	2
Bardsley W.	1923/24	6	7	2	200*	623	124.60	1
Munro C.	2012/13	4	6	1	269*	623	124.60	3
Cullinan D.J.	1998/99	5	7	2	275*	553	110.60	3
Hiddleston J.S.	1925/26	3	5	0	212	537	107.40	2
Weekes E. de C.	1955/56	8	10	1	156	940	104.44	6
Williamson K.S.	2011/12	5	7	2	284*	517	103.40	2
Sutcliffe B.	1946/47	6	8	1	197	722	103.14	3
Parker J.M.	1981/82	7	13	7	117	618	103.00	2
Sutcliffe B.	1947/48	5	10	1	208*	911	101.22	4

minimum 500 runs

Centuries

George Watson registered the first century in New Zealand first-class cricket on 24 February, 1881 when he made 175 for Canterbury v Otago at Hagley Park, Christchurch.

To date, 2659 centuries have been scored in New Zealand with 92 in 2009/10 being the record for one season. A further 424 have been recorded for New Zealand teams overseas. The following New Zealand players have made 20 or more centuries during their first-class careers:

Turner G.M.	103	Howarth G.P.	32	Donnelly M.P.	23
Crowe M.D.	71	Marshall H.J.H.	31	Congdon B.E.	23
Wright J.G.	59	Spearman C.M.	30	Cumming C.D.	23
Sutcliffe B.	44	Taylor L.R.P.L.	27	Crowe J.J.	22
Reid J.R.	39	Patel D.N.	26	Parker J.M.	21
Sinclair M.S.	36	Ryder J.D.	25	Franklin J.E.C.	21
Dempster C.S.	35	Dacre C.C.R.	24	Flynn D.R.	21
Rutherford K.R.	35	Edgar B.A.	24	Burgess M.G.	20
Fleming S.P.	35	Greatbatch M.J.	24	Richardson M.H.	20
Williamson K.S.	34	Horne M.J.	24	Latham T.W.M.	20
Papps M.H.W.	33	Bell M.D.	24		

Most Centuries in a Season in New Zealand

8	Crowe M.D.	1986/87	6	Bell M.D.	2000/01
6	Weekes E. de C.	1955/56	5	Turner G.M.	1975/76
6	Hick G.A.	1988/89	5	Fulton P.G.	2012/13

Five Centuries in Consecutive Innings

Weekes E. de C.	156	West Indies v Auckland	Auckland	1955/56
	148	West Indies v Canterbury	Auckland	
	123	West Indies v New Zealand	Dunedin	
	119*	West Indies v Wellington	Wellington	
	103	West Indies v New Zealand	Christchurch	

Three Centuries in Consecutive Innings

Macartney C.G.	120	NSW v Wellington	Wellington	1923/24
	120	NSW v Otago	Dunedin	
	221	NSW v Canterbury	Christchurch	
Sutcliffe B.	103	Otago v Auckland	Auckland	1947/48
	118 125	Otago v Canterbury	Dunedin	
Sutcliffe B.	141 135	Auckland v Canterbury	Auckland	1948/49
	140	New Zealand XI v The Rest	Christchurch	
Reid J.R.	101 118*	New Zealand v Orange Free State	Bloemfontein	1961/62
	165	New Zealand v South African Colts XI	East London	
Chappell I.M.	128	Australia v Northern Districts	Hamilton	1973/74
	145 121	Australia v New Zealand	Wellington	
Crowe M.D.	151	Central Districts v Northern Districts	Morrinsville	1986/87
	144 151	Central Districts v Canterbury	New Plymouth	
Hick G.A.	211*	Northern Districts v Auckland	Auckland	1988/89
	144 132	Northern Districts v Wellington	Morrinsville	

Jones A.H.	186	New Zealand v Sri Lanka	Wellington	1990/91
	122 } 100* }	New Zealand v Sri Lanka	Hamilton	
Maynard M.P.	142	Northern Districts v Otago	Hamilton	1991/92
	195 } 110 }	Northern Districts v Auckland	Auckland	
Greatbatch M.J.	115	Central Districts v Canterbury	Christchurch	1995/96
	202	Central Districts v Northern Districts	Rotorua	
	162*	Central Districts v Auckland	Auckland	
Campbell S.L.	112 } 109* }	West Indies v Auckland	Auckland	1999/00
	170	West Indies v New Zealand	Hamilton	
Wells J.D.	143	Wellington v Canterbury	Wellington	1999/00
	107 } 132* }	Wellington v Central Districts	New Plymouth	
How J.M.	105 } 108* }	Central Districts v Otago	Queenstown	2004/05
	121	Central Districts v Northern Districts	Napier	
Sinclair M.S.	121 } 103* }	Central Districts v Otago	New Plymouth	2005/06
	101	Central Districts v Auckland	Palmerston North	
Ingram P.J.	119 } 166* }	Central Districts v Canterbury	Christchurch	2006/07
	105	Central Districts v Auckland	Napier	
Franklin J.E.C.	116	Wellington v Otago	Invercargill	2013/14
	108*	Wellington v Canterbury	Wellington	
	120*	Wellington v Auckland	Wellington	
Ryder J.D.	109*	Central Districts v Canterbury	Nelson	2016/17
	175 } 106* }	Central Districts v Auckland	Nelson	2017/18

Century on First-class Debut

† Watson G.	175	Canterbury v Otago	Christchurch	1880/81
Brook-Smith W.	112*	Auckland v Hawke's Bay	Auckland	1904/05
† Wood B.B.	108 & 18	Canterbury v Wellington	Wellington	1907/08
McMullan J.J.M.	157*	Otago v Southland	Dunedin	1917/18
† Snedden C.A.	119	Auckland v Hawke's Bay	Auckland	1920/21
Talbot R.O.	105	Canterbury v Otago	Dunedin	1922/23
Tindill E.W.T.	106 & 0	Wellington v Auckland	Auckland	1932/33
Scott V.J.	122	Auckland v Canterbury	Auckland	1937/38
† Ongley J.A.	110	Wellington v Otago	Wellington	1938/39
† Kerr A.C.	122	Auckland v Wellington	Auckland	1941/42
† Watt D.G.	15 & 105	Otago v Canterbury	Christchurch	1943/44
Smith K.F.H.	27 & 141*	Wellington v Central Districts	Wellington	1953/54
Macleod D.N.	117	Central Districts v Wellington	Wanganui	1956/57
Bilby G.P.	132 & 2*	Wellington v Central Districts	Wellington	1962/63
† Mitchell W.J.	127*	Northern Districts v Pakistan	Hamilton	1964/65
† Sampson H.C.	25 & 119	Central Districts v Wellington	Wellington	1970/71
Vaughan J.T.C.	106* & 1	Auckland v Wellington	Wellington	1989/90
Aiken J.M.	39 & 156*	Wellington v Canterbury	Christchurch	1989/90
† McCone R.J.	102	Canterbury v Otago	Christchurch	2008/09
Rhodes S.J.	142* & 1	Wellington v Otago	Queenstown	2009/10
Brownlie D.G.	112*	Canterbury v Northern Districts	Rangiora	2009/10
Broom D.J.	119	Otago v Northern Districts	Whangarei	2009/10

† Hakaraia D.N.	141* & 4	Auckland v Northern Districts	Hamilton	2012/13
Schmulian B.D.	203 & 4	Central Districts v Northern Districts	Mt Maunganui	2017/18

† only century in first-class cricket

B.R. Williams scored 103 in his fourth first-class match, not having batted in his first three matches, for Wellington v Central Districts at Wellington, 1989/90.*

Century on First-class Debut in Other Countries

In ENGLAND

Dacre C.C.R.	107	New Zealand v MCC	Lord's	1927
Crowe M.D.	104	D.B. Close's XI v Pakistan	Scarborough	1982
Horne M.J.	133	New Zealand v British Universities	Oxford	1999
Spearman C.M.	111	Gloucestershire v Worcestershire	Worcester	2002
Adams A.R.	124	Essex v Leicestershire	Leicester	2004
Marshall H.J.H.	102	Gloucestershire v Worcestershire	Bristol	2006
Conway D.P.	200	New Zealand v England	Lord's	2021

J.D.P. Oram scored 103 for New Zealand v Worcestershire at Worcester in 2004 in his first innings in England after not batting in his first game*

In AUSTRALIA

Sutcliffe B.	142	New Zealand v Western Australia	Perth	1953/54
Miller L.S.M.	142	New Zealand v South Australia	Adelaide	1953/54
Patel D.N.	105	New Zealand v Western Australia	Perth	1987/88
How J.M.	170	New Zealand v New South Wales	Sydney	2008/09
Blundell T.A.	121	New Zealand v Australia	Melbourne	2019/20

In SOUTH AFRICA

Reid J.R.	111	New Zealand v Western Province	Cape Town	1953/54
Kasper R.J.	122*	Natal B v Transvaal B	Pietermaritzburg	1970/71
Harris C.Z.	118*	Canterbury v Eastern Province	Grahamstown	1993/94
Richardson M.H.	173*	New Zealand v Boland	Paarl	2000/01
McCullum B.B.	101	New Zealand v Rest of South Africa	Benoni	2005/06
Brownlie D.G.	109	New Zealand v South Africa	Cape Town	2012/13

In WEST INDIES

Hastings B.F.	100*	New Zealand v Jamaica	Kingston	1971/72
Crowe M.D.	118	New Zealand v Shell Award XI	Kingston	1984/85
Styris S.B.	107	New Zealand v West Indies	St George's	2001/02
Neesham J.D.S.	107	New Zealand v West Indies	Kingston	2014

In INDIA

Taylor B.R.	105	New Zealand v India	Calcutta	1964/65
Burgess M.G.	102	Prime Minister's XI v President's XI	Bombay	1967/68
Parker J.M.	104	New Zealand v India	Bombay	1976/77
Wright J.G.	104	New Zealand v West Zone	Rajkot	1988/89
Crowe M.D.	101*	New Zealand v President's XI	Rajkot	1995/96
Oram J.D.P.	101*	New Zealand v India A	Rajkot	2003/04
Ryder J.D.	103	New Zealand v India	Ahmedabad	2010/11
Williamson K.S.	131	New Zealand v India	Ahmedabad	2010/11
Anderson C.J.	100	New Zealand A v India A	Visakhapatnam	2013/14
Devcich A.P.	115	New Zealand A v India A	Visakhapatnam	2013/14

M.H. Richardson scored 128 for New Zealand v India at Rajkot in 2003/04 in his first innings in India after not batting in his first game.*

In PAKISTAN

Reid J.R.	105*	NZ v Chief Commissioner's XI	Karachi	1955/56
Anderson R.W.	103*	NZ v NWFP Chief Minister's XI	Peshawar	1976/77

In SRI LANKA

Dempster C.S.	112*	Sir Julien Cahn's XI v Ceylon	Colombo	1936/37
Rutherford K.R.	108	New Zealand v Board President's XI	Galle	1986/87
Fulton P.G.	101	New Zealand A v Sri Lanka A	Kandy	2005/06
Cachopa Carl	104	New Zealand A v Sri Lanka A	Pallekele	2013/14

In ZIMBABWE

Franklin T.J.	153*	Young New Zealand v Zimbabwe	Harare	1984/85
Horne M.J.	181	New Zealand v Mashonaland	Harare	1997/98
Sinclair M.S.	100*	New Zealand v President's XI	Mutare	2000/01
Flynn D.R.	162	New Zealand A v Zimbabwe A	Harare	2010/11
Latham T.W.M.	105	New Zealand v Zimbabwe	Bulawayo	2016/17

In BANGLADESH

McCullum B.B.	143	New Zealand v Bangladesh	Dhaka	2004/05
Williamson K.S.	114	New Zealand v Bangladesh	Chittagong	2013/14
Watling B-J.	103	New Zealand v Bangladesh	Chittagong	2013/14

In UNITED ARAB EMIRATES

Latham T.W.M.	103	New Zealand v Pakistan	Abu Dhabi	2014/15

Century in Last First-class Match

† Phillips J.	110*	Canterbury v Wellington	Christchurch	1898/99
Midlane F.A.	126 & 4	Auckland v Wellington	Wellington	1918/19
† Beechey E.M.	180 & 5	Wellington vAuckland	Wellington	1918/19
† Watt D.G.	15 & 105	Otago v Canterbury	Christchurch	1943/44
Redmond R.E.	103 & 22	Auckland v Otago	Auckland	1975/76
Wadsworth K.J.	117	Canterbury v Otago	Christchurch	1975/76
Parker J.M.	1* & 100	Northern Districts v Wellington	Wellington	1983/84
† Snook I.R.	100*	Central Dists v Northern Dists	Palmerston North	1987/88
Dempsey D.A.	121 & 44	Canterbury v Otago	Dunedin	1987/88
Reid J.F.	112	Auckland v Northern Districts	Hamilton	1987/88
Mawhinney R.E.W.	9* & 108	Otago v Canterbury	Christchurch	1990/91
Twose R.G.	108 & 6	Wellington v Auckland	Wellington	2000/01
Nash D.J.	118 & 11*	Auckland v Otago	Dunedin	2001/02
Jones R.A.	89 & 170*	Auckland v Canterbury	Auckland	2009/10
Ingram P.J.	39 & 139	Central Districts v Auckland	Auckland	2011/12
Marshall J.A.H.	54 & 156*	Northern Dists v Central Dists	Nelson	2012/13
McCullum B.B.	145 & 25	New Zealand v Australia	Christchurch	2015/16
Marshall H.J.H.	25 & 105*	Wellington v Canterbury	Christchurch	2016/17

† *only first-class century of career. D.G. Watt was making his only appearance in first-class cricket.*
J. Phillips was playing his 124th first-class match and 203rd innings.
J.D. Riley scored 34, 121, 26 and 94 (run out) in his final two first-class matches, for Auckland in 1976/77.*

Century in Each Innings of a Match

Dacre C.C.R.	127* & 101*	Auckland v Victoria	Auckland	1924/25
† Whitelaw P.E.	115 & 155	Auckland v Wellington	Auckland	1934/35
Uttley K.F.M.	132 & 138	Otago v Auckland	Auckland	1937/38
Sutcliffe B.	197 & 128	Otago v MCC	Dunedin	1946/47
Sutcliffe B.	118 & 125	Otago v Canterbury	Dunedin	1947/48
Sutcliffe B.	141 & 135	Auckland v Canterbury	Auckland	1948/49
Sutcliffe B.	243 & 100*	New Zealand v Essex	Southend	1949

Reid J.R.	101 & 118*	New Zealand v Orange Free State	Bloemfontein	1961/62
† Gedye S.G.	104 & 101	Auckland v Central Districts	Auckland	1963/64
† Thomson K.	102 & 102*	Canterbury v Otago	Dunedin	1966/67
Chappell G.S.	247* & 133	Australia v New Zealand	Wellington	1973/74
Chappell I.M.	145 & 121	Australia v New Zealand	Wellington	1973/74
Turner G.M.	101 & 110*	New Zealand v Australia	Christchurch	1973/74
Turner G.M.	135 & 108	Otago v Northern Districts	Gisborne	1974/75
Turner G.M.	105 & 186*	Otago v Central Districts	Dunedin	1974/75
Howarth G.P.	122 & 102	New Zealand v England	Auckland	1977/78
Wright J.G.	113 & 105	Northern Districts v Auckland	Auckland	1981/82
Parker J.M.	117 & 102*	Northern Districts v Central Districts	Tauranga	1981/82
Rutherford K.R.	105 & 104*	Otago v Northern Districts	Alexandra	1985/86
Border A.R.	140 & 114*	Australia v New Zealand	Christchurch	1985/86
Cooper B.G.	105 & 100	Northern Districts v Canterbury	Gisborne	1986/87
Crowe M.D.	144 & 151	Central Districts v Canterbury	New Plymouth	1986/87
Vance R.H.	116* & 123	Wellington v Central Districts	New Plymouth	1988/89
Hick G.A.	144 & 132	Northern Districts v Wellington	Morrinsville	1988/89
Jones A.H.	122 & 100*	New Zealand v Sri Lanka	Hamilton	1990/91
Gurusinha A.P.	119 & 102	Sri Lanka v New Zealand	Hamilton	1990/91
Maynard M.P.	195 & 110	Northern Districts v Auckland	Auckland	1991/92
Crowe M.D.	152 & 137*	Wellington v Canterbury	Christchurch	1992/93
Dravid R.S.	190 & 103*	India v New Zealand	Hamilton	1998/99
Rhodes J.N.	101* & 106*	South Africa v New Zealand A	Lincoln	1998/99
Campbell S.L.	112 & 109*	West Indies v Auckland	Auckland	1999/00
Wells J.D.	107 & 132*	Wellington v Central Districts	New Plymouth	1999/00
Spearman C.M.	100 & 115	New Zealand v North West	Potchefstroom	2000/01
Hopkins G.J.	113 & 175*	Canterbury v Auckland	Auckland	2002/03
Horne M.J.	118 & 209*	Auckland v Northern Districts	Auckland	2003/04
How J.M.	105 & 108*	Central Districts v Otago	Queenstown	2004/05
Sinclair M.S.	121 & 103*	Central Districts v Otago	New Plymouth	2005/06
Ingram P.J.	119 & 166*	Central Districts v Canterbury	Christchurch	2006/07
Jones R.A.	143 & 120	Auckland v Central Districts	Auckland	2006/07
Todd G.R.	110 & 165	Otago v Wellington	Wellington	2007/08
Myburgh J.G.	199 & 101*	Canterbury v Central Districts	New Plymouth	2008/09
Papps M.H.W.	104 & 180	Canterbury v Auckland	Auckland	2009/10
Cumming C.D.	127* & 127	Otago v Canterbury	Queenstown	2010/11
Redmond A.J.	122 & 115	Otago v Northern Districts	Hamilton	2010/11
Ingram P.J.	135 & 143	Central Districts v Wellington	Wellington	2010/11
† Rutherford H.D.	107 & 118	Otago v Northern Districts	Hamilton	2011/12
Redmond A.J.	133 & 123	Otago v Canterbury	Rangiora	2012/13
Ryder J.D.	117* & 174	Wellington v Central Districts	Napier	2012/13
Fulton P.G.	102 & 108	Canterbury v Otago	Dunedin	2012/13
Ronchi L.	113 & 108	Wellington v Northern Districts	Wellington	2012/13
Fulton P.G.	136 & 110	New Zealand v England	Auckland	2012/13
Wilson B.S.	111 & 117*	Otago v Central Districts	Nelson	2016/17
Munro C.	146 & 142	Auckland v Central Districts	Auckland	2016/17
Ryder J.D.	175 & 106*	Central Districts v Auckland	Nelson	2017/18
Carter J.F.	169 & 120	Northern Districts v Auckland	Auckland	2019/20
Chapman M.S.	143 & 146	Auckland v Northern Districts	Auckland	2019/20
Bracewell M.G.	105 & 119	Wellington v Auckland	Auckland	2020/21
† O'Donnell W.T.	117 & 137*	Auckland v Wellington	Auckland	2020/21

† *maiden first-class century*

Highest Maiden Centuries

301*	Fulton P.G.	Canterbury v Auckland	Christchurch	2002/03
290	Carson W.N.	Auckland v Otago	Dunedin	1936/37
256	Raval J.A.	Auckland v Central Districts	Auckland	2008/09
209	White D.J.	Northern Districts v Central Districts	Hamilton	1985/86
204	Cox A.	Canterbury v Otago	Christchurch	1925/26
203*	Burnett G.P.	Wellington v Northern Districts	Hamilton	1991/92
203	Schmulian B.D.	Central Districts v Northern Districts	Mt Maunganui	2017/18
196	Kerr J.L.	Canterbury v Wellington	Christchurch	1932/33
194	Gaffaney C.B.	Otago v Auckland	Dunedin	1996/97
193*	Stead D.W.	Canterbury v Central Districts	Christchurch	1980/81
193*	McClure K.J.	Canterbury v Otago	Invercargill	2015/16
190	Moloney D.A.R.	Wellington v Auckland	Auckland	1936/37
190	Bracewell M.G.	Otago v Wellington	Dunedin	2012/13
189	Sinclair M.S.	Central Districts v Wellington	Masterton	1996/97
188	Beard N.B.	Otago v Auckland	Dunedin	2012/13
184	Taylor L.R.P.L.	Central Districts v Wellington	Palmerston North	2004/05
183	Gillespie H.D.	Auckland v Canterbury	Auckland	1929/30
182	McIntosh T.G.	Auckland v Canterbury	Christchurch	2000/01
180	Beechey E.M.	Wellington v Auckland	Wellington	1918/19
180	Dempster C.S.	New Zealand v Warwickshire	Birmingham	1927
180	Mooney F.L.H.	Wellington v Auckland	Wellington	1943/44
180*	Andrew G.M.	Canterbury v Auckland	Auckland	2012/13
179	Ormiston R.W.	Wellington v Central Districts	New Plymouth	1982/83
179	Nofal M.J.	Wellington v Central Districts	Wellington	2017/18
177	Chandler P.J.B.	Wellington v Auckland	Wellington	1996/97
176	Cuff L.A.	Canterbury v Auckland	Christchurch	1893/94
175	Watson G.	Canterbury v Otago	Christchurch	1880/81
175	Astle N.J.	Canterbury v Northern Districts	Hamilton	1994/95
175	Orchard M.G.	Northern Districts v Central Districts	Napier	2005/06
172	Worker R.V. de R.	Otago v Canterbury	Dunedin	1923/24
172	Englefield J.I.	Canterbury v Central Districts	Blenheim	2000/01
171	Mills S.M.	Wellington v Canterbury	Christchurch	2006/07
167*	Hart R.T.	Central Districts v Canterbury	New Plymouth	1983/84
167	Lawrence J.D.	Canterbury v Auckland	Christchurch	1893/94
167	Anderson C.J.	Northern Districts v Otago	Hamilton	2012/13
167	O'Donnell R.R.	Auckland v Wellington	Auckland	2015/16
166	Cachopa C.	Auckland v Wellington	Auckland	2012/13
165	Redgrave W.P.	Wellington v Hawkes Bay	Wellington	1905/06
165	Chapple M.E.	Canterbury v South Africans	Christchurch	1952/53
165	Truscott P.B.	NZ Under-23 v Auckland	Auckland	1963/64
164*	Duff S.W.	Central Districts v Auckland	Wanganui	1991/92
164	Powell J.L.	Canterbury v Otago	Christchurch	1929/30
163*	How J.M.	Central Districts v Northern Districts	Hamilton	2002/03
163	Menzies R.E.J.	Canterbury v Wellington	Christchurch	1938/39
163	Williams A.B.	Wellington v Canterbury	Christchurch	1896/97
163	Reade L.B.	Central Districts v Northern Districts	Palmerston North	1960/61
161	Larsen G.R.	Wellington v Central Districts	Levin	1987/88
159*	Kennedy P.G.	Canterbury v Northern Districts	Rotorua	1990/91
159	Vincent L.	Auckland v Northern Districts	Auckland	1998/99
158*	Papps M.H.W.	Canterbury v Otago	Christchurch	2001/02
158	Harford N.S.	New Zealand v Oxford University	Oxford	1958
157*	McMullan J.J.M.	Otago v Southland	Dunedin	1917/18
157	Briasco P.S.	Central Districts v Canterbury	New Plymouth	1983/84
156*	Aiken J.M.	Wellington v Canterbury	Christchurch	1989/90
156	Southee T.G.	Northern Districts v Wellington	Wellington	2012/13

155*	James V.	Canterbury v Otago	Dunedin	1940/41
155*	Parore A.C.	Auckland v Otago	Dunedin	1991/92
155	Badcock F.T.	Wellington v Canterbury	Christchurch	1926/27
155	Oram J.D.P.	Central Districts v Canterbury	Christchurch	1998/99
154	Meuli E.M.	Central Districts v Auckland	Palmerston North	1952/53
153	Watling B-J.	Northern Districts v Otago	Dunedin	2006/07
152	Knight A.R.	Otago v Canterbury	Dunedin	1940/41
152	Kemp R.J.	Wellington v Auckland	Auckland	1947/48
152	Coutts P.J.C.	Central Districts v Canterbury	Christchurch	1966/67
152	Lees W.K.	New Zealand v Pakistan	Karachi	1976/77
152	Brown S.W.	Auckland v Central Districts	Auckland	1990/91
152	Weston T.I.	Central Districts v Auckland	Auckland	2006/07
151	Petrie E.C.	Auckland v Wellington	Auckland	1953/54
151*	Cleaver D.	Central Districts v Wellington	Napier	2015/16
150	Crowe M.D.	Auckland v Central Districts	New Plymouth	1981/82

Watson, McMullan and Aiken scored their centuries on their debut in first-class cricket. Beechey was playing in his last first-class game. Carson (aged 20 years 168 days) and Cox (21 years 19 days) were both playing only their second first-class innings and remain the youngest players to score a double-century in New Zealand first-class cricket.

One Hundred Runs before Lunch

	Runs	*Mins*					
*	110	120		Smith S.G.	Auckland v Canterbury	Auckland	1919/20
	100	120		Richardson V.Y.	Australia v New Zealand	Auckland	1920/21
*	106	120		Blunt R.C.	Canterbury v MCC	Christchurch	1922/23
	112	113		Macartney C.G.	NSW v Wellington	Wellington	1923/24
*	116	120	†	Punch A.T.E.	NSW v Otago	Dunedin	1923/24
*	101	91		Macartney C.G.	NSW v Otago	Dunedin	1923/24
*	108	120		Macartney C.G.	NSW v Canterbury	Christchurch	1923/24
*	100	120		Bardsley W.	NSW v Auckland	Auckland	1923/24
	103	110		Hiddleston J.S.	Wellington v Canterbury	Wellington	1925/26
	105	102		Dacre C.C.R.	Auckland v Otago	Dunedin	1926/27
	103	103	†	Vorrath W.	Otago v Wellington	Dunedin	1927/28
*	106	120		Blunt R.C.	Otago v Canterbury	Christchurch	1928/29
	164	130	†	Powell J.L.	Canterbury v Otago	Christchurch	1929/30
	105	105		Badcock F.T.	Otago v Canterbury	Christchurch	1931/32
*	111	120		Hammond W.R.	England v New Zealand	Auckland	1932/33
	102	120		Whitelaw P.E.	Auckland v Wellington	Auckland	1934/35
	115	110		Wallace W.M.	New Zealand v Somerset	Taunton	1937
*	110	120		Wallace W.M.	New Zealand v Sussex	Hove	1937
*	103	120		Smith F.B.	Canterbury v Auckland	Auckland	1948/49
	100	117		Sutcliffe B.	New Zealand v Essex	Southend	1949
*	100	120		Reid J.R.	Wellington v Otago	Wellington	1951/52
*	122	111		Guillen S.C.	Canterbury v Fiji	Christchurch	1953/54
*	100	126		Smith K.F.H.	Central Districts v Wellington	Wanganui	1959/60
*	108	131		Sutcliffe B.	Otago v Central Districts	Dunedin	1959/60
*	100	140		Sutcliffe B.	Otago v Northern Districts	Hamilton	1960/61
*	174	140		Reid J.R.	Wellington v Northern Districts	Wellington	1962/63
	120	125		Reid J.R.	Wellington v Northern Districts	Wellington	1964/65
	103	120		Murray B.A.G.	New Zealand v President's XI	Rawalpindi	1969/70
*	109	141		Dunning B.	Northern Dist. v Central Dist.	Blenheim	1972/73
	111	150		Dempsey D.A.	Canterbury v Otago	Christchurch	1980/81
	102	147	†	Crowe M.D.	Auckland v Central Districts	New Plymouth	1981/82
*	100	107		Chappell G.S.	Australia v New Zealand	Christchurch	1981/82
*	100	150		Crowe J.J.	Auckland v Northern Districts	Rotorua	1983/84
	101	103		Rutherford K.R.	New Zealand v DB Close's XI	Scarborough	1986
*	101	144		Jones A.H.	Wellington v Otago	Wellington	1986/87
*	112	149		McSweeney E.B.	Wellington v Central Districts	Levin	1987/88

Runs	Mins				
* 122	150	Crowe J.J.	Auckland v Wellington	Wellington	1988/89
* 117	160	Greatbatch M.J.	Central Districts v Otago	Palmerston North	1988/89
101	127	Blain T.E.	Central Districts v Wellington	New Plymouth	1988/89
107	136	† Reid R.B.	Auckland v Central Districts	Masterton	1989/90
* 116	136	Thomson S.A.	Northern Districts v Auckland	Auckland	1990/91
141	144	Maynard M.P.	Northern Districts v Auckland	Auckland	1991/92
* 139	92	Patel D.N.	Auckland v Northern Districts	Auckland	1991/92
104	140	Spearman C.M.	Central Districts v Wellington	Wellington	1997/98
101	137	Cairns C.L.	Southern v Central	Wellington	1998/99
103	140	How J.M.	Central Districts v Northern Districts	Napier	2004/05
105	140	Fulton P.G.	Canterbury v Otago	Christchurch	2004/05
106	122	Taylor L.R.P.L.	Central Districts v Northern Districts	Napier	2007/08
* 100	120	Watling B-J.	Northern Districts v Auckland	Auckland	2009/10
* 104	150	Sinclair M.S.	Central Districts v Otago	Invercargill	2009/10
104	120	Papps M.H.W.	Canterbury v Auckland	Auckland	2009/10
121	120	Munro C.	Auckland v Central Districts	Auckland	2016/17

** batsman had been not out overnight*

† maiden first-class hundred. Punch, Vorrath, Powell and Reid did not score another century in first-class cricket

Scores of Ninety-nine

	Johnson P.R.	MCC v New Zealand	Christchurch	1906/07
†	Snedden A.N.C.	Auckland v Canterbury	Auckland	1921/22
§	Elmes C.J.	New Zealand v MCC	Auckland	1935/36
*	Whitelaw P.E.	Auckland/Wellington v MCC	Auckland	1936/37
	Sutcliffe B.	Otago v Auckland	Dunedin	1947/48
	Taylor D.D.	Auckland v Canterbury	Auckland	1948/49
†	Leggat J.G.	Canterbury v Auckland	Christchurch	1951/52
	Rae A.F.	West Indies v New Zealand	Auckland	1951/52
	O'Malley P.W.	Canterbury v Wellington	Christchurch	1953/54
†	Beck J.E.F.	New Zealand v South Africa	Cape Town	1953/54
	Hunter A.A.	Central Districts v Auckland	Auckland	1953/54
†	Leggat J.G.	Canterbury v MCC	Christchurch	1954/55
	Sutcliffe B.	Rest v New Zealand XI	Christchurch	1957/58
	Sutcliffe B.	New Zealand v Sussex	Hove	1958
§*	Bartlett G.A.	Central Districts v Auckland	Auckland	1959/60
	McGregor S.N.	Otago v Canterbury	Christchurch	1963/64
†	Cunis R.S.	Auckland v Wellington	Wellington	1966/67
	Surti R.F.	India v New Zealand	Auckland	1967/68
	Turner G.M.	New Zealand v Tasmania	Hobart	1969/70
	Burtt J.W.	Canterbury v Central Districts	Christchurch	1970/71
	Dowling G.T.	Canterbury v Northern Districts	Hamilton	1970/71
	Murray B.A.G.	Wellington v Northern Districts	Wellington	1970/71
	Dowling G.T.	New Zealand v Western Australia	Perth	1970/71
§*	O'Keeffe K.J.	Australia v Auckland	Auckland	1973/74
	Edwards G.N.	Central Districts v Australia	Nelson	1976/77
	Blair W.L.	Otago v Auckland	Auckland	1978/79
	Crowe M.D.	Auckland v Northern Districts	Auckland	1981/82
	Hadlee R.J.	New Zealand v England	Christchurch	1983/84
†	Lees W.K.	Otago v Northern Districts	Hamilton	1983/84
	Vance R.H.	Wellington v Canterbury	Wellington	1984/85
	Coney J.V.	New Zealand v President's XI	St Lucia	1984/85
	Jones A.H.	Wellington v Auckland	Auckland	1985/86
§*	Robertson G.K.	Central Districts v Otago	Oamaru	1985/86
	Wright J.G.	New Zealand v Australia	Melbourne	1987/88

	Crocker L.M.	Northern Districts v Wellington	Hamilton	1987/88
	Moxon M.D.	England v New Zealand	Auckland	1987/88
	McEwan P.E.	Canterbury v Wellington	Christchurch	1988/89
	Hart R.T.	Central Districts v Auckland	Masterton	1989/90
	Wright J.G.	New Zealand v Worcestershire	Worcester	1990
†	Patel D.N.	New Zealand v England	Christchurch	1991/92
+	Wright J.G.	New Zealand v England	Christchurch	1991/92
	Douglas M.W.	Central Districts v Auckland	Wanganui	1991/92
	McSweeney E.B.	Wellington v Canterbury	Wellington	1993/94
	Twose R.G.	Central Districts v Auckland	Palmerston North	1993/94
†	Jones R.A.	Auckland v Otago	Dunedin	1996/97
*	Sinclair M.S.	Central Districts v Northern Districts	Hamilton	1996/97
	Twose R.G.	Wellington v India	Wellington	1998/99
	Yovich J.A.F.	Northern Districts v Auckland	Taupo	1999/00
	Richardson M.H.	New Zealand v Zimbabwe	Harare	2000/01
	Fleming S.P.	New Zealand v South Africa	Bloemfontein	2000/01
	Gaffaney C.B.	Otago v Auckland	Auckland	2000/01
	Nevin C.J.	Wellington v Otago	Wellington	2000/01
	Sinclair M.S.	Central Districts v South Africa	Napier	2003/04
	Gaffaney C.B.	Otago v Wellington	Wellington	2004/05
	McCullum B.B.	New Zealand v Sri Lanka	Napier	2004/05
	Redmond A.J.	Otago v Northern Districts	Gisborne	2005/06
	Guptill M.J.	Auckland v Wellington	Auckland	2005/06
	Marshall H.J.H.	Northern Districts v Auckland	Auckland	2006/07
	Marshall J.A.H.	Northern Districts v Central Districts	Gisborne	2006/07
	Vettori D.L.	New Zealand v SA Inviation XI	Bloemfontein	2007/08
	Marshall J.A.H.	Northern Districts v Central Districts	Hamilton	2007/08
	Hay G.R.	Central Districts v Northern Districts	Hamilton	2007/08
	Hopkins G.J.	Auckland v Northern Districts	Gisborne	2007/08
	Vettori D.L.	New Zealand v Pakistan	Dunedin	2009/10
	Merchant C.J.	Wellington v Canterbury	Wellington	2009/10
	Misbah-ul-Haq	Pakistan v New Zealand	Wellington	2010/11
	Watling B-J.	Northern Districts v Central Districts	Whangarei	2010/11
	Weston T.I.	Central Districts v Northern Districts	Whangarei	2010/11
	Patel J.S.	Wellington v Northern Districts	Whangarei	2010/11
	Stewart S.L.	Canterbury v Wellington	Rangiora	2010/11
	Rutherford H.D.	New Zealand A v India A	Lincoln	2012/13
*	de Grandhomme C.	Auckland v Wellington	Wellington	2012/13
	Young W.A.	Central Districts v Otago	Dunedin	2013/14
	Grobbelaar D.J.	Auckland v Canterbury	Rangiora	2014/15
	Jayasundera M.D.U.S.	Sri Lanka A v New Zealand A	Christchurch	2015/16
	McConchie C.E.	Canterbury v Auckland	Rangiora	2017/18
	Rutherford H.D.	Otago v Central Districts	Napier	2018/19
	Cleaver D.	Central Districts v Otago	Dunedin	2020/21

** not out   † batsman was run out   + batsman was stumped   § highest score in first-class cricket*

Carried Bat Through a Complete Innings

		Score	Total			
	Harris L.M.	41*	65	Otago v Tasmania	Dunedin	1883/84
	Gatehouse G.H.	54*	146	Tasmania v Otago	Dunedin	1883/84
	Mills I.	88*	156	Auckland v Otago	Dunedin	1893/94
†	Collins J.C.	128*	187	Fiji v Hawke's Bay	Napier	1894/95
	Cobcroft L.T.	85*	239	NSW v Wellington	Wellington	1895/96
	Mills G.	106*	235	Auckland v Wellington	Auckland	1895/96
	Collins D.C.	53*	131	Wellington v Canterbury	Christchurch	1906/07

Score	Total				
§ Midlane F.A.	14*	60	Wellington v Canterbury	Christchurch	1910/11
Gibbes W.R.L.	75*	193	Wellington v Canterbury	Christchurch	1911/12
† Midlane F.A.	222*	498	Wellington v Otago	Wellington	1914/15
Blunt R.C.	137*	336	Canterbury v Wellington	Wellington	1919/20
† Bardsley W.	200*	352	NSW v Auckland	Auckland	1923/24
Blunt R.C.	131*	204	Otago v Canterbury	Dunedin	1926/27
Dempster C.S.	167*	345	New Zealand v Glamorgan	Cardiff	1927
Kerr J.L.	146*	243	Canterbury v MCC	Christchurch	1935/36
Whitelaw P.E.	99*	183	Auckland/Wellington v MCC	Auckland	1936/37
Tindill E.W.T.	47*	111	Wellington v Otago	Dunedin	1946/47
† Miller L.S.M.	81*	154	Wellington v Otago	Dunedin	1956/57
Playle W.R.	89*	139	Auckland v Northern Districts	Auckland	1959/60
Bradburn W.P.	45*	87	Northern Districts v Wellington	Wellington	1960/61
Bradburn W.P.	37*	57	Northern Districts v Wellington	Hamilton	1961/62
Holloway R.A.	61*	122	Otago v Central Districts	Nelson	1962/63
Turner G.M.	43*	131	New Zealand v England	Lord's	1969
Turner G.M.	223*	386	New Zealand v West Indies	Kingston	1971/72
Redpath I.R.	159*	346	Australia v New Zealand	Auckland	1973/74
Wettimuny S.	63*	144	Sri Lanka v New Zealand	Christchurch	1982/83
† Franklin T.J.	153*	311	Young NZ v Zimbabwe	Harare	1984/85
Rutherford K.R.	89*	241	Otago v Auckland	Dunedin	1984/85
Boon D.C.	58*	103	Australia v New Zealand	Auckland	1985/86
Wright J.G.	149*	307	Canterbury v Auckland	Auckland	1988/89
Smith C.J.P.	90*	154	Central Dists v Northern Dists	Rotorua	1989/90
Murray D.J.	106*	233	Canterbury v Northern Dists	Hamilton	1992/93
Dobbs P.W.	81*	177	Otago v Canterbury	Oamaru	1994/95
Atherton M.A.	94*	228	England v New Zealand	Christchurch	1996/97
Kelly D.P.	212*	538	Central Districts v Canterbury	Blenheim	2000/01
Ingram P.J.	105*	201	Central Districts v Auckland	Auckland	2003/04
† How J.M. §	190*	430	New Zealand A v England Lions	Queenstown	2008/09
Imran Farhat	117*	223	Pakistan v New Zealand	Napier	2009/10
† Cumming C.D.	106*	199	Otago v Canterbury	Rangiora	2010/11
Guptill M.J.	195*	381	Auckland v Canterbury	Rangiora	2011/12
Papps M.H.W.	183*	459	Wellington v Canterbury	Rangiora	2013/14
Duffy R.M.	90*	177	Otago v Auckland	Dunedin	2015/16
† Latham T.W.M.	264*	578	New Zealand v Sri Lanka	Wellington	2018/19

† player was on the field for every ball of the match   § one man absent

Longest Individual Batting in a Match

Mins	Runs				
954	274* & 69*	Fleming S.P.	New Zealand v Sri Lanka	Colombo	2002/03
876	76 & 146*	Greatbatch M.J.	New Zealand v Australia	Perth	1989/90
835	122 & 102	Howarth G.P.	New Zealand v England	Auckland	1977/78
828	75 & 138	Wright J.G.	New Zealand v West Indies	Wellington	1986/87
818	8 & 302	McCullum B.B.	New Zealand v India	Wellington	2013/14
813	93 & 101	Richardson M.H.	New Zealand v England	Lord's	2004
811	69 & 242*	Williamson K.S.	New Zealand v Sri Lanka	Wellington	2014/15
772	140 & 89	Elgar D.	South Africa v New Zealand	Dunedin	2016/17
770	166* & 82	Congdon B.E.	New Zealand v West Indies	Port-of-Spain	1971/72

Longest Individual Innings

Mins	*Runs*				
775	302	McCullum B.B.	New Zealand v India	Wellington	2013/14
741	306	Richardson M.H.	New Zealand v Zimbabwe A	Kwekwe	2000/01
720	163	Shoaib Mohammad	Pakistan v New Zealand	Wellington	1988/89
704	259	Turner G.M.	New Zealand v West Indies	Georgetown	1971/72
694	264*	Latham T.W.M.	New Zealand v Sri Lanka	Wellington	2018/19
685	180	Reid J.F.	New Zealand v Sri Lanka	Colombo	1983/84
671	212*	Richardson M.H.	New Zealand A v Sussex	Hove	2000
667	205	Watling B-J.	England v New Zealand	Mt Maunganui	2019/20
659	211*	Gibbs H.H.	South Africa v New Zealand	Christchurch	1998/99
658	275*	Cullinan D.J.	South Africa v New Zealand	Auckland	1998/99
655	146*	Greatbatch M.J.	New Zealand v Australia	Perth	1989/90
655	274*	Fleming S.P.	New Zealand v Sri Lanka	Colombo	2002/03
648	158	Radley C.T.	England v New Zealand	Auckland	1977/78
647	251*	Harris C.Z.	Canterbury v Central Districts	Rangiora	1996/97
643	137	Gambhir G.	India v New Zealand	Napier	2008/09
636	170*	Jones A.H.	New Zealand v India	Auckland	1989/90
635	226	Root J.E.	England v New Zealand	Hamilton	2019/20
625	222	Rutherford I.A.	Otago v Central Districts	New Plymouth	1978/79
624	251	Williamson K.S.	New Zealand v West Indies	Hamilton	2020/21
623	242*	Williamson K.S.	New Zealand v Sri Lanka	Wellington	2014/15
621	226	Hay G.R.	Central Districts v Otago	Alexandra	2018/19
610	299	Crowe M.D.	New Zealand v Sri Lanka	Wellington	1990/91
609	120*	Crowe J.J.	New Zealand v Sri Lanka	Colombo	1986/87
606	241*	Latham T.W.M.	Canterbury v Wellington	Wellington	2013/14
605	267*	Young B.A.	New Zealand v Sri Lanka	Dunedin	1996/97
603	259	Turner G.M.	New Zealand v Guyana	Georgetown	1971/72
603	256	Raval J.A.	Auckland v Central Districts	Auckland	2008/09

Fastest Centuries

Mins	*Balls*				
52	45	Cairns B.L.	Otago v Wellington	Lower Hutt	1979/80
52	66	Cooper B.G.	Northern Districts v Canterbury	Gisborne	1986/87
53	63	Motz R.C.	Canterbury v Otago	Christchurch	1967/68

Slowest Centuries

Mins	*Balls*				
516	331	Crowe J.J.	New Zealand v Sri Lanka	Colombo	1986/87
487	397	Radley C.T.	England v New Zealand	Auckland	1977/78
464	390	Austen M.H.	Otago v Canterbury	Christchurch	1996/97
462	341	Greatbatch M.J.	New Zealand v Australia	Perth	1989/90
461	265	Crowe M.D.	New Zealand v Pakistan	Lahore	1990/91
458	341	Astle N.J.	New Zealand v Zimbabwe	Wellington	2000/01
455	307	Howarth G.P.	New Zealand v England	Auckland	1977/78

Most Boundaries in an Innings

	6s	4s		Runs			
53	8	45	Rutherford K.R.	317	New Zealand v D.B. Close's XI	Scarborough	1986
53	5	48	Conway D.P.	327*	Wellington v Canterbury	Wellington	2019/20
52	1	51	Papps M.H.W.	316*	Wellington v Auckland	Wellington	2017/18
50	15	35	Reid J.R.	296	Wellington v Northern Districts	Wellington	1962/63
49	3	46	Sutcliffe B.	385	Otago v Canterbury	Christchurch	1952/53
48	3	45	Fulton P.G.	301*	Canterbury v Auckland	Christchurch	2002/03
48	8	40	Brownlie D.G.	334	Northern Districts v Central Districts	New Plymouth	2014/15
47	3	44	Trumper V.T.	293	Sims' Australian XI v Canterbury	Christchurch	1913/14
45	2	43	Raval J.A.	256	Auckland v Central Districts	Auckland	2008/09
43	10	33	Hammond W.R.	336*	England v New Zealand	Auckland	1932/33
43	–	43	Richardson M.H.	306	New Zealand v Zimbabwe A	Kwekwe	2000/01
43	3	40	McIntosh T.G.	268	Auckland v Canterbury	Auckland	2007/08
43	–	43	Taylor L.R.P.L.	290	New Zealand v Australia	Perth	2015/16
42	1	41	Reid J.R.	283	Wellington v Otago	Wellington	1951/52
42	1	41	Crowe M.D.	242*	New Zealand v South Australia	Adelaide	1985/86
42	3	39	Crowe M.D.	242	Central Districts v Otago	New Plymouth	1989/90
41	–	41	Blunt R.C.	338*	Otago v Canterbury	Christchurch	1931/32
41	14	27	Munro C.	269*	Auckland v Wellington	Auckland	2012/13
40	–	40	de Silva P.A.	267	Sri Lanka v New Zealand	Wellington	1990/91
40	23	17	Munro C.	281	Auckland v Central Districts	Napier	2014/15

Most Sixes in an Innings

Sixes		Runs			
23	Munro C.	281	Auckland v Central Districts	Napier	2014/15
16	Ryder J.D.	175	New Zealand v Australia A	Brisbane	2011/12
15	Reid J.R.	296	Wellington v Northern Districts	Wellington	1962/63
14	Munro C.	269*	Auckland v Wellington	Auckland	2012/13
12	Patel D.N.	204	Auckland v Northern Districts	Auckland	1991/92
11	Astle N.J.	222	New Zealand v England	Christchurch	2001/02
11	Spearman C.M.	133	Central Districts v Auckland	Auckland	2003/04
11	McCullum B.B.	202	New Zealand v Pakistan	Sharjah	2014/15
11	McCullum B.B.	195	New Zealand v Sri Lanka	Christchurch	2014/15
10	Hammond W.R.	336*	England v New Zealand	Auckland	1932/33
10	Robinson R.T.	166	England XI v Northern Districts	Hamilton	1987/88
10	Styris S.B.	212*	Northern Districts v Otago	Hamilton	2001/02
9	Cairns B.L.	110	Otago v Wellington	Lower Hutt	1979/80
9	Botham I.T.	80	England XI v Central Districts	Palmerston North	1983/84
9	Cairns C.L.	120	New Zealand v Zimbabwe	Auckland	1995/96
9	Southee T.G.	77*	New Zaland v England	Napier	2007/08
9	Flynn D.R.	241	Northern Districts v Otago	Hamilton	2010/11
9	Cachopa C.	203	Auckland v Wellington	Auckland	2013/14
9	Kitchen A.K.	207	Otago v Northern Districts	Dunedin	2016/17
8	Taylor L.R.P.L.	152	Central Districts v Northern Districts	Napier	2007/08
8	Dacre C.C.R.	176	New Zealand v Derbyshire	Derby	1927
8	Bula I.L.	102	Fiji v Canterbury	Christchurch	1953/54
8	Rutherford K.R.	317	New Zealand v DB Close's XI	Scarborough	1986
8	Germon L.K.	160*	Canterbury v Wellington	Christchurch	1989/90
8	Parore A.C.	111*	Auckland v Wellington	Auckland	1997/98
8	Horne M.J.	209*	Auckland v Northern Districts	Auckland	2003/04
8	Adams A.R.	117*	Auckland v Otago	Lincoln	2006/07
8	Franklin J.E.C.	219	Wellington v Auckland	Auckland	2008/09
8	Fulton P.G.	122	Canterbury v Northern Districts	Christchurch	2008/09

8	de Grandhomme C.	103*	Auckland v Central Districts	Auckland	2008/09
8	Brownlie D.G.	334	Northern Districts v Central Districts	New Plymouth	2014/15
8	Ellis A.M.	143	Canterbury v Northern Districts	Hamilton	2015/16
8	Cleaver D.	201	Central Districts v Northern Districts	Napier	2019/20

Five Sixes off Consecutive Balls

Germon L.K.	off Vance R.H.	Canterbury v Wellington	Christchurch	1989/90

(Full tosses and deliberate no-balls were provided for him to hit).

Four Sixes off Consecutive Balls

Rutherford K.R.	off Doshi D.R.	New Zealand v DB Close's XI	Scarborough	1986

Three Sixes off Consecutive Balls

Hill C.	off Ollivier K.M.	Australia v New Zealand	Wellington	1904/05
Hammond W.R.	off Newman J.	England v New Zealand	Auckland	1932/33
McRae D.A.N.	off Burke C.	Canterbury v Auckland	Auckland	1937/38
Pritchard T.L.	off Groves L.J.	Wellington v Otago	Dunedin	1937/38
Edwards R.M.	off Carew M.C.	Governor General's XI v West Indies	Auckland	1968/69
Burgess M.G.	off Anderson R.W.	Auckland v Central Districts	Wanganui	1977/78
Stirling D.A.	off Brown V.R.	Central Districts v Canterbury	New Plymouth	1986/87
Thomson S.A.	off Bracewell J.G.	Northern Districts v Auckland	Auckland	1987/88
Hick G.A.	off Duff S.W.	England XI v Central Districts	New Plymouth	1991/92
Astle N.J.	off Wells J.D.	Canterbury v Wellington	Christchurch	1994/95
Vincent L.	off Vettori D.L.	Auckland v Northern Districts	Auckland	1998/99
Astle N.J.	off Caddick A.R.	New Zealand v England	Christchurch	2001/02
Spearman C.M.	off Nicol R.J.	Central Districts v Auckland	Auckland	2003/04
Adams A.R.	off Bowden D.J.	Auckland v Wellington	Wellington	2005/06
Nicol R.J.	off Worker G.H.	Auckland v Central Districts	Auckland	2008/09
Taylor L.R.P.L.	off Hauritz N.M.	New Zealand v Australia	Hamilton	2009/10
Southee T.G.	off Zulfiqar Babar	New Zealand v Pakistan	Dubai	2014/15
Boult T.A.	off Craig M.D.	Northern Districts v Otago	Mt Maunganui	2018/19
de Grandhomme C.	off Rae M.D.	Northern Districts v Otago	Mt Maunganui	2020/21
Shepherd R.*	off McConchie C.E.	West Indies A v New Zealand A	Mt Maunganui	2020/21

** Shepherd had also hit a six from the previous ball he had faced (from I.S. Sodhi)*

Most Ducks in Succession

5	Hayes J.A.	(C, NZ 1954/55)	17,0 / dnb / 0,0 / 0,0
5	Bateman S.N.	(C 1982/83)	5*,0 / 0,0 / 0,0
4	Frith W.	(C 1882/83-1887/88)	0,0 / 0,0
4	Silver R.C.D.	(O 1936/37-1937/38)	12,0 / 0,0 / 0,11
*4	Langdon M.C.	(ND 1957/58)	25,0 / 0,0 / 0,5
4	Hastings B.F.	(C 1963/64)	1,0 / 0,0 / 0,35
4	Steele H.K.C.	(A 1974/75)	0,0 / 0,0
4	Bracewell B.P.	(NZ 1978)	0 / dnb / 0,0 / 0,0*
4	Bradburn G.E.	(ND 1987/88)	0 / 0,0 / 0
4	Morrison D.K.	(NZ 1993/94)	0 / 0,0 / 0,20*
4	Davis H.T.	(NZ, W 1997/98)	7*,0 / 0,0 / 0,21
4	Young R.A.	(A 1999/00)	0,0 / 0,0
4	Martin C.S.	(C NZ 2000/01)	5,0 / 0,0 / 0
4	Gaffaney C.B.	(O 2001/02)	31,0 / 0,0 / 0,56
4	Hamilton L.J.	(CD 2004/05)	11,0 / 0,0 / 0,2
4	Astle T.D.	(C 2008/09)	18,0 / 0,0 / 0,1
4	McPeake I.G.	(W 2020/21)	0,0 / 0,0

** first three games in first-class cricket*

Most Scoreless Innings in Succession

10	Visser P.J.	(CD 1984/85-1985/86)	0 / 0,0 / dnb / 0*,0 / dnb / 0*,0* 0,0 / dnb / 0
7	Hamilton L.J.	(CD 1999/00)	0,0* / 0 / 0*,0 / 0 / 0
7	Martin C.S.	(NZ 2008, NZ 2008/09))	0*,dnb / 0,0* / 0*,0 / 0*,0*
6	Hayes J.A.	(C, NZ 1954/55-1955/56)	17,0 / dnb / 0,0 / 0,0 / 0*
6	de Groen R.P.	(A 1988/89-1989/90)	1,0* / dnb / 0,0 / 0* / 0*,0*
6	Martin C.S.	(NZ, NZ A 2008/09))	0,0 / 0*,0* / 0*,0*
6	Martin C.S.	(NZ, A 2011/12-2012/13)	4*,0* / 0,0 / 0*,0 / 0,1
5	Frith W.	(O, C 1881/82-1887/8)	1,0* / 0,0 / 0,0
*5	Moss A.E.	(C 1889/90)	0,0* / 0,0 / 0*,4*
5	Burrows J.T.	(C 1932/33)	0*,0* / 0* / 0*,0*
5	Hill J.	(O 1961/62-1962/63)	0*,0* / 0* / 0*,0*
5	Unka H.	(ND 1968/69-1971/72)	0* / 0*,0* / dnb / 0*,0
5	Bracewell B.P.	(NZ 1978)	0 / dnb / 0,0 / 0,0*
5	Webb R.J.	(O 1980/81)	1,0 / dnb,0 / 0*,dnb / 0,0*
5	Troup G.B.	(A, NZ 1980/81-1981/82)	0,0* / 0,0 / dnb / 0
5	Bateman S.N.	(C 1982/83)	5*,0 / 0,0 / 0,0
5	Arnel B.J.	(ND 2012/13)	0*,0 / 0,dnb / 0*,dnb / 0,4*
5	McMillan J.M.	(O 2012/13-2013/14)	0,dnb / 0,dnb / 0*,dnb / 0*,dnb / 0,dnb

** first five innings in first-class cricket*

UNUSUAL DISMISSALS

HANDLED THE BALL

Benson E.T.	MCC v Auckland	Auckland	1929/30
Gilbertson A.W.	Otago v Auckland	Auckland	1952/53
Vaughan J.T.C.	NZ Emerging Players v England XI	Hamilton	1991/92
Williams W.S.A.	Canterbury v Otago	Dunedin	2012/13

OBSTRUCTING THE FIELD

Hayes J.A.	Canterbury v Central Districts	Christchurch	1954/55
Blundell T.A.	Wellington v Otago	Wellington	2020/21

(prior to a change in the laws in 2017, Blundell would have been given out handled the ball)

RUN OUT BY THE BOWLER *(while backing up before the ball had been bowled)*

Reese T.W. by Downes A.D.	Canterbury v Otago	Christchurch	1894/95
Smith J. by Allen R.	Canterbury v Wellington	Wellington	1943/44
Randall D.W. by Chatfield E.J.	England v New Zealand	Christchurch	1977/78

STUMPED BY A SUBSTITUTE

Pervez Sajjad by Congdon B.E.	Pakistan v New Zealand	Lahore	1964/65
Congdon B.E. by Burge P.J.P.	Central Districts v Australia	Palmerston North	1966/67

RETIRED (out)

Ransford V.S.	Australia v Hawke's Bay	Napier	1920/21
Chappell G.S.	Australia v Wellington	Wellington	1976/77
Saeed Anwar	Pakistan v New Zealand XI	Napier	1993/94
Basit Ali	Pakistan v New Zealand XI	Napier	1993/94
Inzamam-ul-Haq	Pakistan v New Zealand XI	Napier	1993/94
Spearman C.M.	New Zealand v North West	Potchefstroom	2000/01
Strauss A.J.	England v Major Association XI	Dunedin	2007/08
Taylor L.R.P.L.	New Zealand v Northamptonshire	Northampton	2008
How J.M.	Central Districts v Northern Districts	Napier	2009/10

REPRESENTED TWO PROVINCES IN ONE SEASON

Sutcliffe B.	Auckland and Otago	1946/47
Sutcliffe B.	Otago and Auckland	1947/48
Clark L.A.	Otago and Auckland	1959/60
Andrews B.	Canterbury and Central Districts	1966/67

On each occasion, the second province was represented in a match against a non-provincial side. No player has played for two provinces in inter-provincial matches in the same season.

REPLACEMENT PLAYERS

Substitute	*Player replaced*			
Lawrence —	Bell A.	Wellington v Nelson	Wellington	1873/74
Cotterill C.N.	White G.	Hawke's Bay v NSW	Napier	1893/94
unknown	Ratu Epeli	Fiji v Auckland	Auckland	1894/95
Kilgour W.A.	*Wilson C.G.	Otago v Auckland	Auckland	1907/08
Bryden J.S.	*Siedeberg H.G.	Otago v Canterbury	Dunedin	1913/14
Graham W.H.	Middleton F.S.	Auckland v Wellington	Wellington	1917/18
Whitta H.B.	*Foster P.S.	Canterbury v Wellington	Christchurch	1919/20
Samuels B.	*Brice A.W.S.	Wellington v Auckland	Auckland	1919/20
Wilson E.S.	Eastman L.C.	Otago v Wellington	Wellington	1927/28
Kubunavanua P.	Logavatu I.T.	Fiji v Canterbury	Christchurch	1947/48
Abernethy B.	Webb R.J.	Otago v Auckland	Dunedin	1982/83
Neutze P.S.	Brown V.R.	Auckland v Wellington	Auckland	1987/88
Brown R.K.	Greatbatch M.J.	Central Districts v Otago	Palmerston North	1991/92
Lee C.D.	Larsen G.R.	Wellington v Northern Dists	Hamilton	1991/92
Fleming S.P.	Harris C.Z.	Canterbury v Auckland	Auckland	1991/92
Lee C.D.	*Patel D.N.	Auckland v Otago	Dunedin	1994/95
Garner C.D.	Spearman C.M.	Central Dists v Northern Dists	Nelson	1996/97
Cooper D.M.	Howell L.G.	Central Dists v Northern Dists	Nelson	1996/97
Lamont M.J.	Horne M.J.	Otago v Auckland	Dunedin	1996/97
Morland N.D.	Wiseman P.J.	Otago v Auckland	Dunedin	1996/97
Sewell D.G.	Kennedy R.J.	Otago v Auckland	Dunedin	1996/97
Irving R.J.R.	Mills J.M.	Auckland v Otago	Dunedin	1996/97
Weenink S.W.	Chandler P.J.B.	Wellington v Canterbury	Christchurch	1996/97
Jonas G.R.	Davis H.T.	Wellington v Canterbury	Christchurch	1996/97
Hartland B.R.	Murray D.J.	Canterbury v Wellington	Christchurch	1996/97
Frew R.M.	Harris C.Z.	Canterbury v Wellington	Christchurch	1996/97
Sharpe M.F.	Allott G.I.	Canterbury v Wellington	Christchurch	1996/97
Hotter S.J.	Davis H.T.	Wellington v Central Districts	Masterton	1996/97
Muir G.A.	Priest M.W.	Canterbury v Zimbabwe	Timaru	1997/98
Pawson S.J.	Priest M.W.	Canterbury v Otago	Dunedin	1997/98
Dry L.R.	Bell M.D.	Wellington v Northern Dists	Hamilton	1998/99
Morland N.D.	*Wiseman P.J.	Otago v Auckland	Dunedin	1999/00
Spearman C.M.	Sinclair M.S.	Central Districts v Otago	Palmerston North	1999/00
Todd G.R.	Oram J.D.P.	Central Districts v Wellington	Napier	2000/01
McCullum N.L.	Wiseman P.J.	Otago v Canterbury	Alexandra	2000/01
Robinson G.G.	*Marshall J.A.H.	Northern Dists v Canterbury	Gisborne	2004/05
O'Brien I.E.	Rasmussen S.	Wellington v Otago	Dunedin	2006/07
Hitchcock P.A.	*Hopkins G.J.	Auckland v Wellington	Auckland	2008/09
Houghton M.V.	Patel J.S.	Wellington v Auckland	Auckland	2008/09
Shaw L.J.	McIntosh T.G.	Auckland v West Indies	Auckland	2008/09
Boult J.J.	Martin B.P.	Northern Districts v Auckland	Whangarei	2008/09
Robertson I.A.	Thompson E.P.	N.Zealand A v England Lions	Lincoln	2008/09
Raval J.A.	McIntosh T.G.	Auckland v Otago	Queenstown	2008/09
Shaw L.J.	Martin C.S.	Auckland v Otago	Queenstown	2008/09
Davis T.T.	Arnel B.J.	Northern Dists v Canterbury	Christchurch	2008/09
Scott B.E.	Flynn D.R.	Northern Dists v Canterbury	Christchurch	2008/09
Boam H.K.P.	Franklin J.E.C.	Wellington v Central Districts	Napier	2008/09
Croft S.J.	Mills K.D.	Auckland v Central Districts	Auckland	2008/09
Patel J.S.	Burns M.	Wellington v Northern Dists	Hamilton	2009/10
Milne A.F.	*Mason M.J.	Central Districts v Canterbury	New Plymouth	2009/10
van Beek L.V.	Stewart S.L.	Canterbury v Central Districts	New Plymouth	2009/10
Kitchen A.K.	*Hopkins G.J.	Auckland v Otago	Dunedin	2009/10
Gillespie M.R.	Patel J.S.	Wellington v Central Districts	Napier	2009/10

Substitute	*Player replaced*			
Astle T.D.	Martin C.S.	Canterbury v Otago	Queenstown	2009/10
Tuffey D.R.	Munro C.	Auckland v Canterbury	Christchurch	2010/11
van Beek L.V.	*Lonsdale W.M.	Canterbury v Auckland	Christchurch	2010/11
Styris S.B.	Scott B.E.	Northern Districts v Otago	Queenstown	2010/11
McCullum N.L.	Butler I.G.	Otago v Northern Districts	Queenstown	2010/11
Henry M.J.	Ellis A.M.	Canterbury v Wellington	Rangiora	2010/11
Latham T.W.M.	Astle T.D.	Canterbury v Wellington	Rangiora	2010/11
Verma A.	Watling B-J.	Northern Districts v Otago	Dunedin	2011/12
Johnston T.G.	Latham T.W.M.	Canterbury v Northern Dists	Rangiora	2011/12
Tuffey D.R.	Martin C.S.	Auckland v Central Districts	Napier	2011/12
Young W.A.	*Taylor L.R.P.L.	Central Districts v Auckland	Napier	2011/12
de Terte J.W.	van Wyk C.F.K.	Central Districts v Auckland	Napier	2011/12
Devcich A.P.	Vettori D.L.	Northern Districts v Otago	Hamilton	2011/12
Hiini B.C.	*Arnel B.J.	Northern Districts v Otago	Hamilton	2011/12
Santner M.J.	*Boult T.A.	Northern Districts v Otago	Hamilton	2011/12
Arnel B.J.	Boult T.A.	Northern Districts v Auckland	Auckland	2011/12
Mitchell D.J.	Flynn D.R.	Northern Districts v Auckland	Auckland	2011/12
Wagner N.	Duffy J.A.	Otago v Auckland	Auckland	2012/13
Martin C.S.	Bartlett D.J.	Auckland v Otago	Auckland	2012/13
Astle T.D.	*Hira R.M.	Canterbury v Northern Dists	Hamilton	2012/13
Wagner N.	Soper B.E.	Otago v Northern Districts	Queenstown	2012/13
Elliott G.D.	Boam H.K.P.	Wellington v Canterbury	Wellington	2012/13
Boam H.K.P.	Ronchi L.	Wellington v Canterbury	Wellington	2012/13
Fulton D.H.	Latham T.W.M.	Canterbury v Wellington	Wellington	2012/13
Bates M.D.	*Ferguson L.H.	Auckland v Wellington	Wellington	2012/13
Ronchi L.	Blundell T.A.	Wellington v Auckland	Wellington	2012/13
Latham T.W.M.	Fulton D.H.	Canterbury v Northern Dists	Christchurch	2012/13
Walker J.G.	Sodhi I.S.	Northern Dists v Central Dists	Napier	2015/16
van Beek L.V.	Henry M.J.	Canterbury v Auckland	Rangiora	2016/17
Cooper H.R.	Brownlie D.G.	Northern Dists v Central Dists	Napier	2016/17
Rance S.H.A.	Bracewell D.A.J.	Central Dists v Northern Dists	Napier	2016/17
Younghusband P.F.	Patel J.S.	Wellington v Canterbury	Wellington	2016/17
Ronchi L.	Taylor M.J.	Wellington v Otago	Wellington	2016/17
Hampton B.R.	Kuggeleijn S.C.	Northern Districts v Wellington	Mt Maunganui	2016/17
Rae M.D.	*Hicks S.	Otago v Wellington	Dunedin	2017/18
Conway D.P.	Blundell T.A.	Wellington v Otago	Dunedin	2017/18
Ridley A.D.	Woodcock L.J.	Wellington v Central Districts	Wellington	2017/18
van Woerkom T.F.	McClure K.J.	Canterbury v Northern Dists	Christchurch	2018/19
Brown J.A.	McEwan M.B.	Auckland v Northern Dists	Auckland	2018/19
Astle T.D.	*van Woerkom T.F.	Canterbury v Auckland	Rangiora	2018/19
Young W.A.	Smith B.S.	Central Dists v Northern Dists	Napier	2018/19
Kuggeleijn S.C	Rutherford H.D.	New Zealand A v England	Whangarei	2019/20
Rae M.D.	Tickner B.M.	New Zealand A v India A	Lincoln	2019/20
Lister B.G.	Sodhi I.S.	New Zealand A v India A	Lincoln	2019/20
Walker J.G.	*Sodhi I.S.	Northern Dists v Central Dists	Hamilton	2020/21
Lister B.G.	†Chapman M.S.	Auckland v Otago	Auckland	2020/21
Bacon M.B.	Chu M.W.	Otago v Northern Districts	Mt Maunganui	2020/21
Fletcher A.T.	Sears B.V.	Wellington v Otago	Wellington	2020/21
Boyle J.C.T.	Carter L.J.	Canterbury v Auckland	Auckland	2020/21

** indicates player did not bat or bowl before being replaced*

† Lister began the game as a Covid subsitute for Chapman who subsequently replaced him

BOWLING

Ten Wickets in an Innings

	Overs	Maidens	Runs	Wickets			
* Moss A.E.	21.3	10	28	10	Canterbury v Wellington	Christchurch	1889/90

** on debut – the only instance in first-class cricket*

Nine Wickets in an Innings

	Overs	Maidens	Runs	Wickets			
Wiseman P.J.	16.4	9	13	9	Canterbury v Central Districts	Christchurch	2004/05
Wensley A.F.	24	13	36	9	Auckland v Otago	Auckland	1929/30
Eden T.	15.2	0	43	9	Nelson v Wellington	Wellington	1875/76
Dent T.H.	28	11	47	9	Hawke's Bay v Wellington	Napier	1900/01
Tait A.R.	24.5	8	48	9	Northern Districts v Auckland	Hamilton	1996/97
Fisher A.H.	25.2	4	50	9	Otago v Queensland	Dunedin	1896/97
Hadlee R.J.	23.4	4	52	9	New Zealand v Australia	Brisbane	1985/86
Hadlee R.J.	24	5	55	9	New Zealand v West Zone	Rajkot	1988/89
McBeath D.J.	24	7	56	9	Canterbury v Auckland	Christchurch	1918/19
Brice A.W.S.	25.5	5	67	9	Wellington v Auckland	Wellington	1918/19
Blair R.W.	35	9	72	9	Wellington v Auckland	Wellington	1956/57
Cooke F.H.	56	24	73	9	Otago v Canterbury	Christchurch	1884/85
Neill R.	31	7	75	9	Auckland v Canterbury	Auckland	1891/92
Blair R.W.	29.5	9	75	9	Wellington v Canterbury	Wellington	1956/57
Neill R.	24.2	1	86	9	Auckland v Canterbury	Auckland	1897/98
Petherick P.J.	35	10	93	9	Otago v Northern Districts	Dunedin	1975/76
Priest M.W.	28.5	5	95	9	Canterbury v Otago	Dunedin	1989/90
Robertson W.	39.3	8	98	9	Canterbury v Wellington	Christchurch	1894/95
Yuile B.W.	45	19	100	9	Central Districts v Canterbury	New Plymouth	1965/66

Sixteen Wickets in a Match

16-130	Tait A.R.	24.5-8-48-9/38.4-13-82-7	Northern Dists v Auckland, Hamilton	1996/97

Fifteen Wickets in a Match

15-60	Callaway S.T.	23.3-10-33-8/17-7-27-7	Canterbury v Hawke's Bay, Napier	1903/04
15-94	Cooke F.H.	40.3-16-61-8/33.3-14-33-7	Otago v Canterbury, Christchurch	1882/83
15-104	Boock S.L.	29.3-13-47-7/34.3-16-57-8	Otago v Auckland, Dunedin	1989/90
15-123	Hadlee R.J.	23.4-4-52-9/28.5-9-71-6	New Zealand v Australia, Brisbane	1985/86
15-168	McBeath D.J.	24-7-56-9/37-4-112-6	Canterbury v Auckland, Christchurch	1918/19
15-175	Callaway S.T.	35-14-77-7/43.4-11-98-8	NSW v New Zealand, Christchurch	1895/96
15-203	Moir A.M.	24.1-4-84-7/35.1-3-119-8	Otago v Central Dists, New Plymouth	1953/54

Fourteen Wickets in a Match

14-59	Read R.J.	13-3-35-7/14-5-24-7	Canterbury v Southland, Invercargill	1920/21
14-63	Eden T.	15.2-0-43-9/15.5-7-20-5	Nelson v Wellington, Wellington	1875/76
* 14-63	Rees A.W.	13-4-27-6/15.3-3-36-8	Auckland v Otago, Dunedin	1889/90
14-65	Callaway S.T.	36.3-18-47-7/18.2-7-18-7	NSW v Wellington, Wellington	1895/96
14-65	Hayes J.A.	18.2-6-28-7/12.1-3-37-7	Auckland v Wellington, Auckland	1957/58
14-93	Torrance R.C.	23-6-51-7/19-5-42-7	Otago v Hawke's Bay, Napier	1908/09
14-94	Howarth H.J.	22.1-5-42-7/23-6-52-7	Auckland v Otago, Dunedin	1973/74
14-103	Downes A.D.	30-12-32-7/30-8-71-7	Otago v Hawke's Bay, Dunedin	1893/94
* 14-107	Robertson W.	28.2-8-59-8/20.4-7-48-6	Canterbury v Auckland, Christchurch	1893/94
14-119	Pringle C.	27.4-10-63-7/23.5-5-56-7	Auckland v Otago, Dunedin	1993/94

14-126	Moir A.M.	18-1-55-8/25-6-71-6	Otago v Canterbury, Dunedin	1951/52
14-136	Blair R.W.	29.5-9-75-9/26-8-61-5	Wellington v Canterbury, Wellington	1956/57
14-151	Gray E.J.	50-19-114-6/26.1-12-37-8	Wellington v Canterbury, Lower Hutt	1985/86
14-234	Astle T.D.	51.4-9-148-8/35-7-86-6	Canterbury v Central Districts, Napier	2013/14

** on debut*

Four Wickets with Consecutive Balls

Downes A.D.	Otago v Auckland	Dunedin	1893/94
Wagner N.	Otago v Wellington	Queenstown	2010/11

** Wagner achieved the unique feat of taking five wickets in one over*

Hat Tricks

Salmon I.J.	Wellington v Nelson	Wellington	1873/74
Lankham W.	Auckland v Taranaki	Auckland	1882/83
Frith C.	Otago v Canterbury	Dunedin	1884/85
Fannin H.A.	Hawkes Bay v Taranaki	Napier	1897/98
Barclay F.	Auckland v Canterbury	Auckland	1903/04
Orchard S.A.	Canterbury v Auckland	Auckland	1909/10
Bennett J.H.	Canterbury v Wellington	Wellington	1911/12
Olliff C.	Auckland v Wellington	Auckland	1912/13
Middleton F.S.	Wellington v Hawke's Bay	Wellington	1919/20
Allom M.J.C.*	England v New Zealand	Christchurch	1929/30
Mulcock E.	Canterbury v Otago	Christchurch	1937/38
Overton G.W.F.	Otago v Canterbury	Christchurch	1946/47
Murray R.M.	Wellington v Otago	Wellington	1949/50
Moir A.M.	Otago v Canterbury	Christchurch	1950/51
Jones J.F.	Wellington v Central Districts	Wellington	1953/54
Reid R.E.	Wellington v Otago	Dunedin	1958/59
Bartlett G.A.	Central Districts v Northern Districts	Hamilton	1959/60
Cameron F.J.	Otago v Northern Districts	Hamilton	1962/63
Blair R.W.	Wellington v Northern Districts	Wellington	1962/63
Alabaster G.D.	Northern Districts v Canterbury	Hamilton	1962/63
Furlong B.D.M.	NZ Under 23 XI v Canterbury	Christchurch	1964/65
Hadlee R.J.	Canterbury v Central Districts	Nelson	1971/72
Petherick P.J.	New Zealand v Pakistan	Lahore	1976/77
Toynbee M.H.	Central Districts v Northern Districts	Gisborne	1979/80
Visser P.J.	Central Districts v Auckland	Nelson	1983/84
Maguiness S.J.	Wellington v Northern Districts	Wellington	1983/84
Beard D.A.	Northern Districts v Central Districts	Nelson	1989/90
Gale A.J.	Otago v Canterbury	Dunedin	1992/93
Harris C.Z.	New Zealand v Orange Free State	Bloemfontein	1994/95
Hayes R.L.	Northern Districts v Central Districts	Rotorua	1995/96
Hotter S.J.	Wellington v Otago	Wellington	1996/97
Anderson T.R.	Central Districts v Auckland	Masterton	1998/99
Canning T.K.	Auckland v Central Districts	Auckland	1999/00
Orchard M.G.	Northern Districts v Canterbury	Gisborne	2003/04
Franklin J.E.C.	New Zealand v Bangladesh	Dhaka	2004/05
Sidebottom R.J.	England v New Zealand	Hamilton	2007/08
McClenaghan M.J.	Central Districts v Canterbury	Rangiora	2008/09
Aldridge G.W.	Northern Districts v Central Districts	Whangarei	2010/11
Noema-Barnett K.	Central Districts v Otago	Nelson	2013/14
Hutchinson D.S.	Wellington v Northern Districts	Hamilton	2015/16
Tickner B.M.	Central Districts v Wellington	Nelson	2017/18
van Beek L.V.†	Wellington v Canterbury	Christchurch	2017/18
McEwan M.B.†	Auckland v Northern Districts	Auckland	2017/18

Lister B.G.	Auckland v Otago	Auckland	2018/19
Jamieson K.A.	Auckland v Central Districts	Auckland	2020/21
Delport L.J.	Auckland v Northern Districts	Whangarei	2020/21
Rae M.D.	Otago v Central Districts	Dunedin	2020/21

** Allom took 4 wickets with 5 balls in the same over † van Beek and McEwan performed their hat-tricks on the same day*

Most Wickets in a Single Day's Play in New Zealand

14	Rees A.W.	Auckland v Otago	Dunedin	1889/90
13	Lankham W.	Auckland v Taranaki	Auckland	1882/83
13	Smith C.R.	Hawke's Bay v Taranaki	Hawera	1891/92
13	Cave H.B.	Central Districts v Auckland	Palmerston North	1952/53

Outstanding Analyses

TEN WICKETS IN AN INNINGS

21.3	11	28	10	Moss A.E.	Canterbury v Wellington	Christchurch	1889/90

NINE WICKETS IN AN INNINGS

16.4	9	13	9	Wiseman P.J.	Canterbury v Central Districts	Christchurch	2004/05
24	13	36	9	Wensley A.F.	Auckland v Otago	Auckland	1929/30
15.2	0	43	9	Eden T.	Nelson v Wellington	Wellington	1875/76
28	11	47	9	Dent T.H.	Hawke's Bay v Wellington	Napier	1900/01

EIGHT WICKETS IN AN INNINGS

13	6	13	8	Firth J.P.	Wellington v Hawke's Bay	Wellington	1883/84
19	12	14	8	Austin S.W.	NSW v Hawke's Bay	Napier	1893/94
29	21	18	8	Frith W.	Canterbury v Otago	Christchurch	1880/81
14.5	7	19	8	Fannin H.A.	Hawke's Bay v Auckland	Auckland	1897/98

SEVEN WICKETS IN AN INNINGS

10.1	6	9	7	Bracewell J.G.	Otago v Canterbury	Dunedin	1981/82
13	9	11	7	Fisher A.H.	Otago v Canterbury	Christchurch	1896/97
25.3	16	12	7	Downes A.D.	Otago v Canterbury	Dunedin	1896/97
16	8	12	7	Tuffey D.R.	Northern Districts v Wellington	Hamilton	2000/01
32.1	24	13	7	Lankham W.	Auckland v Taranaki	Auckland	1882/83
10.4	5	16	7	Farooq Hamid	Pakistan v Wellington	Wellington	1964/65
17	10	17	7	Armstrong W.W.	Australia v Wellington	Wellington	1913/14
14.2	7	17	7	Maguiness S.J.	Wellington v Canterbury	Rangiora	1984/85
18.2	7	18	7	Callaway S.T.	NSW v Wellington	Wellington	1895/96

SIX WICKETS IN AN INNINGS

8	5	3	6	Cowie J.	New Zealand v Ireland	Dublin	1937
8	5	4	6	Callaway S.T.	Canterbury v Wellington	Wellington	1903/04
9.2	3	5	6	Bennett A.P.	Nelson v Wellington	Nelson	1885/86
16	11	6	6	Haskell W.J.R.	Wellington v Otago	Wellington	1967/68
14	10	7	6	Dunlop D.	Canterbury v Wellington	Wellington	1886/87
18	14	7	6	Hampton B.L.	Central Districts v Otago	Dunedin	1963/64
15	10	8	6	Downes W.F.	Otago v Canterbury	Christchurch	1866/67
11.2	6	9	6	Fowler G.	Nelson v Wellington	Nelson	1887/88
9.3	6	10	6	Pearson F.A.	Auckland v Hawke's Bay	Auckland	1910/11

FIVE WICKETS IN AN INNINGS

15.2	13	2	5	Ashby D.A.	Canterbury v Auckland	Auckland	1877/78
5	3	3	5	Allcott C.F.W.	New Zealand v Somerset	Taunton	1927
10.3	6	5	5	Bright R.J.	Australia v Central Districts	Nelson	1976/77
9	6	6	5	Parker T.S.	Otago v Canterbury	Christchurch	1866/67
21	18	8	5	Frith C.	Otago v Tasmania	Dunedin	1883/84
4	2	8	5	Burnup C.J.	Lord Hawke's XI v NZ	Wellington	1902/03
8	4	8	5	McBeath D.J.	Southland v Canterbury	Invercargill	1920/21

5.4	1	8	5	Solia S.M.	Auckland v Otago	Auckland	2020/21
9	3	9	5	Bennett J.H.	Canterbury v Wellington	Christchurch	1910/11
12	5	9	5	Butterfield L.A.	South Island v North Island	Auckland	1944/45
9.1	5	9	5	Boock S.L.	New Zealand v Middlesex	Lord's	1978
FOUR WICKETS IN AN INNINGS							
3.2	2	1	4	Snedden C.A.	Auckland v Hawke's Bay	Auckland	1920/21
6.4	5	2	4	Puna N.	Northern Dists v Central Dists	Hamilton	1957/58
7	6	3	4	Carrington S.M.	Northern Districts v Otago	Tauranga	1982/83
6.5	5	3	4	Woodcock L.J.	Wellington v Otago	Wellington	2001/02
THREE WICKETS IN AN INNINGS							
3	3	0	3	Smith K.F.H.	Central Districts v Canterbury	Nelson	1959/60
2.1	2	0	3	Barnes S.G.	Australia v Canterbury	Christchurch	1945/46
5	5	0	3	Gray E.J.	Wellington v Canterbury	Christchurch	1985/86
1.4	0	1	3	Bolton B.A.	Canterbury v Central Districts	Christchurch	1958/59
2	1	1	3	Thomson S.A.	Northern Districts v Canterbury	Christchurch	1992/93
1.4	0	2	3	Anthony A.	Canterbury v Wellington	Christchurch	1908/09
3.3	1	2	3	Thomas A.W.	Canterbury v Otago	Christchurch	1917/18
4	2	2	3	Sparling J.T.	Auckland v Wellington	Auckland	1957/58
5	4	2	3	Bennett H.K.	Wellington v Auckland	Wellington	2017/18
5	2	3	3	Cowlishaw W.P.	Canterbury v Otago	Christchurch	1864/65
15	12	3	3	Frith W.	Canterbury v Auckland	Auckland	1877/78
2.3	1	3	3	Richardson G.	Nelson v Wellington	Wellington	1886/87
3	2	3	3	Dowson E.M.	Lord Hawke's XI v Otago	Dunedin	1902/03
5	2	3	3	Pollard V.	New Zealand v England	Auckland	1965/66

Seven Wickets in an Innings on First-class Debut

10-28	Moss A.E.	Canterbury v Wellington	Christchurch	1889/90
8-35	Wilson R.	Queensland v Auckland	Auckland	1896/97
† 8-36	Rees A.W.	Auckland v Otago	Dunedin	1889/90
8-37	Hole H.	Nelson v Wellington	Nelson	1874/75
8-48	O'Connell W.J.	Hawke's Bay v Wellington	Wellington	1919/20
8-59	Robertson W.	Canterbury v Auckland	Christchurch	1893/94
8-70	Hay W.A.	Otago v Southland	Dunedin	1917/18
7-31	Lynch D.	Auckland v Canterbury	Auckland	1877/78
7-36	Mills G.	Auckland v Wellington	Auckland	1886/87
7-39	Lankham W.	Auckland v Canterbury	Christchurch	1882/83
† 7-42	Morrison B.D.	Wellington v Otago	Wellington	1953/54
† 7-46	Stephens W.B.	Auckland v Otago	Auckland	1899/00
7-46	Doig J.A.	Southland v Otago	Invercargill	1914/15
† 7-50	Badcock F.T.	Wellington v Canterbury	Christchurch	1924/25
† 7-54	Turnbull J.A.	Auckland v Central Districts	Auckland	1955/56
7-61	Merrin R.C.	Canterbury XI v NZ Touring Team	Christchurch	1967/68
† 7-95	Noonan D.J.	New South Wales v Canterbury	Christchurch	1895/96
7-95	Huxford N.A.	Wellington v Pakistan	Wellington	1964/65

† 2nd innings

Ten Wickets in a Match on First-class Debut

14-63	Rees A.W.	Auckland v Otago	Dunedin	1889/90
14-107	Robertson W.	Canterbury v Auckland	Christchurch	1893/94
13-72	Moss A.E.	Canterbury v Wellington	Christchurch	1889/90
12-18	Bennett A.P.	Nelson v Wellington	Nelson	1885/86
12-90	Mills W.	Taranaki v Fiji	Hawera	1894/95
12-118	Hay W.A.	Otago v Southland	Dunedin	1917/18
11-43	Fuller E.T.A.	Canterbury v Otago	Christchurch	1872/73
11-97	Wilson R.	Queensland v Auckland	Auckland	1896/97

11-99	Lankham W.	Auckland v Canterbury	Christchurch	1882/83
11-112	Morrison B.D.	Wellington v Otago	Wellington	1953/54
11-126	Noonan D.J.	New South Wales v Canterbury	Christchurch	1895/96
10-30	Lawson H.	Wellington v Nelson	Nelson	1883/84
10-31	MacDonald F.	Otago v Canterbury	Dunedin	1863/64
10-39	Holderness H.V.A.	Otago v Southland	Invercargill	1918/19
10-61	Hole H.	Nelson v Wellington	Nelson	1874/75
10-70	Mills G.	Auckland v Wellington	Auckland	1886/87
10-71	Lawton J.C.	Otago v Canterbury	Christchurch	1890/91
10-90	Brown C.M.	Auckland v Canterbury	Rangiora	1993/94
10-105	Frame W.D.	Otago v Canterbury	Dunedin	1955/56
10-122	Badcock F.T.	Wellington v Canterbury	Christchurch	1924/25
10-133	Leonard D.J.	Central Districts v Northern Districts	Rotorua	1989/90

Ten Wickets in Last First-class Match

† 10-31	MacDonald F.	Otago v Canterbury	Dunedin	1863/64
† 10-61	Hole H.	Nelson v Wellington	Nelson	1874/75
10-91	Downes W.F.	Otago v Canterbury	Dunedin	1875/76
12-114	Lankham W.	Auckland v Canterbury	Auckland	1883/84
13-140	Edser H.	Canterbury v Wellington	Wellington	1883/84
11-25	Fowler G.	Nelson v Wellington	Nelson	1887/88
11-77	Carson W.	Otago v Canterbury	Dunedin	1887/88
† 10-39	Holderness H.V.A.	Otago v Southland	Invercargill	1918/19
10-108	Vivian H.G.	Auckland v Wellington	Auckland	1938/39
11-129	de Groen R.P.	Northern Districts v Canterbury	Hamilton	1995/96

† this was the players only first-class appearance

Most Wickets in a Season

		Matches	*Wkts*	*Runs*	*Ave*	*5WI*	*10WM*	*Best*
Boock S.L.	1977/78	13	66	1088	16.48	6	—	7-57
Hadlee R.J.	1986/87	11	62	935	15.08	8	1	7-49
Hadlee R.J.	1981/82	10	59	867	14.69	7	—	6-26
Boock S.L.	1978/79	12	58	1238	21.34	4	1	8-59
Thompson G.J.	1902/03	7	57	668	11.71	6	3	8-124
Boock S.L.	1986/87	10	55	920	16.72	6	1	6-62
Callaway S.T.	1903/04	5	54	474	8.77	8	4	8-33
Blair R.W.	1956/57	8	53	784	14.79	6	4	9-72
Tait A.R.	1996/97	9	53	865	16.32	4	1	9-48
Drum C.J.	2001/02	9	53	827	15.60	3	2	6-34
Martin C.S.	2003/04	12	53	1144	21.58	6	1	6-76
Austin S.W.	1893/94	7	52	606	11.65	6	1	8-14
Armstrong W.W.	1913/14	8	52	789	15.17	7	1	7-17
O'Sullivan D.R.	1978/79	9	52	989	19.01	3	—	6-51
Arnel B.J.	2012/13	12	52	1341	25.78	2	—	5-55
Chatfield E.J.	1981/82	10	51	868	17.01	2	—	5-29
Wagner N.	2010/11	9	51	926	18.15	4	1	6-36
Wagner N.	2012/13	12	51	1454	28.50	1	—	5-54
Douglas J.W.H.T.	1906/07	9	50	663	13.26	5	1	7-49
Hadlee R.J.	1978/79	10	50	909	18.18	4	—	6-28
Gillespie M.R.	2012/13	10	50	1611	32.22	2	1	6-83

Most Wickets in a Season for New Zealand Overseas

		Matches	*Wkts*	*Runs*	*Ave*	*5WI*	*10WM*	*Best*
Burtt T.B.	1949	27	128	2929	22.28	11	2	7-102
Cowie J.	1937	24	114	2275	19.95	6	1	6-3
Merritt W.E.	1927	25	107	2530	23.64	5	1	6-38

Most Wickets in a Season of First-class Debut

			Overs	Mdns	Runs	Wkts	Ave
Robertson W.	*Canterbury & NZ*	1893/94	*1534	balls	570	47	12.12
Gillespie S.R.	*Northern Districts*	1979/80	384.5	98	998	45	22.17
Petherick P.J.	*Otago*	1975/76	286	57	847	42	20.16
Lankham W.	*Auckland*	1882/83	†1006	balls	259	41	6.31
O'Brien I.E.	*Wellington*	2000/01	319.1	81	807	41	19.68

** Robertson bowled 222.2 6-ball overs and 40 5-ball overs † Lankham bowled 96.2 5-ball overs and 131 4-ball overs*

Most Balls Bowled in an Innings

444	Howarth H.J.	74-24-138-2	New Zealand v West Indies	Bridgetown	1971/72
426	Tufnell P.C.R.	71-22-147-2	England v New Zealand	Wellington	1991/92
426	Vettori D.L.	71-24-171-2	New Zealand v India	Mohali	1999/00
420	Howarth H.J.	70-24-144-4	New Zealand v England	Lord's	1973
420	Boock S.L.	70-10-229-1	New Zealand v Pakistan	Auckland	1988/89
417†	O'Sullivan D.R.	52.1-15-125-4	Central Districts v Otago	New Plymouth	1978/79
414	Doshi D.R.	69-34-79-2	India v New Zealand	Auckland	1980/81
414	Tauseef Ahmed	69-28-106-1	Pakistan v New Zealand	Auckland	1988/89
414	Hick G.A.	69-27-126-4	England v New Zealand	Wellington	1991/92
414	Donnelly J.P.T.	69-10-257-4	Canterbury v Northern Dists	Rangiora	2009/10
408†	Morgan H.A.	51-16-108-3	Wellington v Otago	Dunedin	1968/69
408	Wiseman P.J.	68-21-123-4	Otago v Northern Districts	Hamilton	1995/96
407	Boock S.L.	67.5-31-75-4	Otago v Central Districts	Alexandra	1988/89
399	Cook N.G.B.	66.3-26-153-3	England v New Zealand	Wellington	1983/84
396	Puna N.	66-23-131-4	Northern Dists v Auckland	Hamilton	1964/65
396	Nadkarni R.G.	66-34-114-2	India v New Zealand	Christchurch	1967/68
390	Chatfield E.J.	65-14-158-1	New Zealand v Pakistan	Auckland	1988/89

† eight-ball overs

Most Balls Bowled in a Match

629	Badcock F.T.	104.5-44-178-9	Otago v Canterbury	Christchurch	1933/34
624	Dickeson C.W.	104-45-142-11	Northern Dists v Wellington	Hamilton	1979/80
618	Gray E.J.	103-39-214-6	Wellington v Otago	Wellington	1984/85
600†	Allcott C.F.W.	75-23-161-5	Auckland v Canterbury	Christchurch	1924/25
600	Butler L.C.	100-46-122-4	Wellington v Auckland	Auckland	1965/66

† eight-ball overs

Most Runs Conceded in a Match

304	2-173, 0-131	Dickinson G.R.	Otago v Wellington	Dunedin	1923/24
300	6-172, 4-128	Smith S.G.	Auckland v Wellington	Wellington	1923/24
277	6-136, 6-141	Alloo A.W.	Otago v Wellington	Dunedin	1923/24
266	6-185, 2-81	Merritt W.E.	New Zealand v Kent	Canterbury	1927
266	1-104, 2-162	Southee T.G.	New Zealand v England	Lord's	2015
257	4-257	Donnelly J.P.T.	Canterbury v Northern Districts	Rangiora	2009/10
251	1-105, 1-146	Schaw R.J.	Central Districts v Canterbury	Napier	2007/08
246	2-246	Mehidy Hasan	Bangladesh v New Zealand	Hamilton	2018/19
243	6-128, 7-115	Grimmett C.V.	Australia v Canterbury	Christchurch	1927/28
243	1-58, 3-185	Lythe T.I.	Central Districts v Wellington	Napier	2007/08
241	2-99, 5-142	Brice A.W.S.	Wellington v Otago	Dunedin	1923/24
241	3-123, 1-118	Prabhakar M.	India v New Zealand	Auckland	1989/90
240	1-90, 4-150	Donnelly J.P.T.	Canterbury v Central Districts	New Plymouth	2009/10
239	6-112, 3-127	McBeath D.J.	Otago v Auckland	Dunedin	1922/23
239	1-60, 4-179	Lambert H.N.	Wellington v Canterbury	Wellington	1931/32
237	0-99, 0-138	Bracewell J.G.	New Zealand v Sussex	Hove	1990

237	4-158, 0-79	Vettori D.L.	New Zealand v South Africa	Hamilton	2003/04
236	2-83, 2-153	Newman J.A.	Canterbury v Otago	Dunedin	1928/29
234	3-86, 4-148	Merritt W.E.	Canterbury v Otago	Dunedin	1928/29
234	4-165, 2-69	Vettori D.L.	New Zealand v Zimbabwe	Bulawayo	1997/98
234	8-148, 6-86	Astle T.D.	Canterbury v Central Districts	Napier	2013/14

Most Runs Conceded in an Innings

69	10	257	4	Donnelly J.P.T.	Canterbury v Northern Districts	Rangiora	2009/10
49	2	246	2	Mehidy Hasan	Bangladesh v New Zealand	Hamilton	2018/19
56	6	230	3	Martin B.P.	Auckland v Northern Districts	Hamilton	2012/13
70	10	229	1	Boock S.L.	New Zealand v Pakistan	Auckland	1988/89
23.2	0	218	5	Merritt W.E.	New Zealand v NSW	Sydney	1927/28
34	1	206	1	Alloo A.W.	Otago v NSW	Dunedin	1923/24
59	12	204	4	Furlong C.J.M.	Central Districts v Canterbury	Palmerston Nth	1994/95
42	3	204	3	Worker G.H.	Central Districts v Auckland	Auckland	2009/10
57	5	200	4	Vettori D.L.	New Zealand v India	Ahmedabad	1999/00
51.2	11	198	5	Pringle C.	Auckland v Central Districts	Auckland	1995/96
41	3	194	3	Callaway S.T.	New Zealand v Australia	Wellington	1904/05
59	8	187	6	Martin B.P.	Auckland v Wellington	Auckland	2011/12
32	1	186	2	Torrance R.C.	Otago v NSW	Dunedin	1923/24
43.1	1	185	6	Merritt W.E.	New Zealand v Kent	Canterbury	1927
38.3	6	185	3	Lythe T.I.	Central Districts v Wellington	Napier	2007/08
46	4	181	0	Hart M.N.	New Zealand v West Indies	Wellington	1994/95
34	2	180	5	O'Connell W.J.	Hawke's Bay v Auckland	Auckland	1920/21

ALL ROUND CRICKET

500 Runs and 25 Wickets in the Same Season

		Runs	Ave	Wkts	Ave
Reid J.R.	1954/55	505	38.84	30	16.53
Sparling J.T.	1959/60	705	37.11	36	19.50
Reid J.R.	1960/61	549	34.31	37	14.78
Pollard V.	1967/68	537	31.58	31	24.74
Taylor B.R.	1968/69	518	39.84	30	28.06
Cairns B.L.	1975/76	538	41.38	27	25.66
Hadlee R.J.	1981/82	500	33.33	59	14.69
Brown V.R.	1984/85	540	38.57	31	31.35
Gray E.J.	1985/86	545	49.54	34	22.00
Priest M.W.	1988/89	603	43.07	28	40.14
Bradburn G.E.	1989/90	842	38.27	30	30.93
Patel D.N.	1990/91	679	52.23	41	28.09
Patel D.N.	1991/92	574	44.15	32	26.78
Duff S.W.	1991/92	559	46.58	28	27.64
Styris S.B.	2001/02	662	44.13	28	17.03
Wiseman P.J.	2003/04	535	38.21	31	31.00
de Grandhomme C.	2013/14	629	48.38	30	20.80
Ellis A.M.	2014/15	853	53.31	29	32.93
Ellis A.M.	2015/16	518	37.00	33	18.57
Ellis A.M	2016/17	652	40.75	27	24.59
Astle T.D.	2016/17	522	37.28	31	26.87

A Century and Five Wickets in Each Innings of the Same Match

Armstrong W.W.	126*	5-27 & 5-25	Australia v New Zealand	Christchurch	1904/05
Crawford J.N.	110 & 4*	5-90 & 5-53	Wellington v Auckland	Auckland	1917/18

A Century and Ten Wickets in the Same Match

but not five in each innings

Woolley F.E.	132	6-50 & 4-38	MCC v Otago	Dunedin	1929/30
Patel D.N.	6 & 204	6-117 & 4-116	Auckland v ND	Auckland	1991/92

A Century and Five Wickets in One Innings of the Same Match

Wilding F.	104	6-55 & 0-4	Canterbury v Auckland	Christchurch	1884/85
Redgrave W.P.	165	5-37	Wellington v Hawke's Bay	Wellington	1905/06
Relf A.E.	157	6-64 & 2-48	Auckland v Canterbury	Christchurch	1907/08
Armstrong W.W.	110*	6-47 & 0-25	Australia v New Zealand	Auckland	1913/14
Crawford J.N.	6 & 178*	5-149	Otago v Wellington	Wellington	1914/15
Snedden A.N.C.	139	5-13 & 2-21	Auckland v Hawke's Bay	Auckland	1920/21
Andrews T.J.E.	111*	5-41	NSW v Canterbury	Christchurch	1923/24
McGirr H.M.	106	5-17 & 0-22	Wellington v Canterbury	Wellington	1925/26
Bellamy F.W.J.	113 & 22*	5-31 & 1-39	Canterbury v Wellington	Christchurch	1934/35
Cromb I.B.	171	5-66 & 0-56	Canterbury v Wellington	Wellington	1939/40
Reid J.R.	0 & 283	5-35 & 1-34	Wellington v Otago	Wellington	1951/52
Reid J.R.	150*	7-28 & 1-15	NZ v Chief Comm XI	Karachi	1955/56
Sutcliffe B.	152*	5-102	Otago v ND	Hamilton	1956/57
Sparling J.T.	105 & 51	7-98 & 2-13	Auckland v Canterbury	Christchurch	1959/60
Reid J.R.	165	5-50 & 1-28	Wellington v Auckland	Auckland	1959/60
Butler L.C.	101*	5-34	Wellington v CD	New Plymouth	1961/62
Alabaster G.D.	108 & 35	1-34 & 5-49	Otago v CD	Wanganui	1964/65
Taylor B.R.	105 & 0*	5-86	New Zealand v India	Calcutta	1964/65

Pollard V.	146 & 16*	3-66 & 6-53	CD v Otago	Dunedin	1967/68
Motz R.C.	103*	3-41 & 6-57	Canterbury v Otago	Christchurch	1967/68
Yuile B.W.	146	6-68 & 1-13	CD v Canterbury	Napier	1967/68
Inverarity R.J.	108	5-28	Australia B v Otago	Dunedin	1969/70
Morgan R.W.	102 & 52	5-42 & 3-48	Auckland v NZ U23 XI	Auckland	1970/71
Taylor B.R.	10 & 129*	5-37 & 2-34	Wellington v Canterbury	Wellington	1971/72
Mushtaq Mohammad	201	2-15 & 5-49	Pakistan v New Zealand	Dunedin	1972/73
Morrison J.F.M.	8 & 106	0-4 & 5-69	Wellington v Auckland	Auckland	1977/78
Botham I.T.	103 & 30*	5-73 & 3-38	England v New Zealand	Christchurch	1977/78
Hadlee R.J.	48 & 103	5-61 & 1-76	New Zealand v Queensland	Brisbane	1980/81
Stead D.W.	2 & 193*	6-79 & 1-67	Canterbury v CD	New Plymouth	1980/81
Crowe M.D.	17 & 151	0-20 & 5-18	CD v Auckland	Auckland	1983/84
Botham I.T.	138	5-59 & 1-137	England v New Zealand	Wellington	1983/84
Crowe M.D.	20 & 143	1-54 & 5-51	CD v ND	New Plymouth	1984/85
Gray E.J.	108	5-54 & 4-52	NZ v Minor Counties	Norwich	1986
Rutherford K.R.	11 & 146	5-72	Otago v Wellington	Wellington	1989/90
Astle N.J.	160	6-22 & 0-45	Canterbury v Otago	Christchurch	1996/97
Nash D.J.	135* & 62	7-39 & 0-22	New Zealand v Hampshire	Southampton	1999
Bradburn G.E.	35 & 104	5-114	ND v Wellington	Wellington	2000/01
Canning T.K.	115	6-44 & 2-28	Auckland v ND	Hamilton	2004/05
Diamanti B.J.	0 & 135*	5-74	CD v Canterbury	Rangiora	2008/09
Southee T.G.	156	5-69 & 2-75	ND v Wellington	Wellington	2012/13
Wells S.R.	7 & 100*	2-46 & 5-74	Otago v Canterbury	Dunedin	2013/14
van Beek L.V.	111*	2-13 & 6-57	Canterbury v Otago	Christchurch	2015/16
Ravindra R.	144* & 22	0-56 & 6-89	NZ A v West Indies A	Nelson	2020/21

WICKETKEEPING

Most Dismissals in a Season

49	49/0	Nevin C.J.	2000/01
45	44/1	Cachopa B.	2015/16
44	43/1	de Boorder D.C.	2012/13
43	41/2	Watling B-J.	2013/14
41	31/10	McSweeney E.B.	1984/85
41	35/6	McSweeney E.B.	1989/90
41	37/4	McGlashan P.D.	2009/10
41	39/2	Fletcher C.D.	2015/16
41	39/2	Blundell T.A.	2017/18
40	39/1	van Wyk C.F.K.	2014/15
39	37/2	Ronchi L.	2012/13
39	39/0	Cachopa B.	2014/15
38	37/1	Hopkins G.J.	2004/05
38	36/2	de Boorder D.C.	2011/12
38	38/0	Watling B-J.	2016/17
38	38/0	Watling B-J.	2019/20
37	36/1	de Boorder D.C.	2014/15
37	36/1	de Boorder D.C.	2015/16
36	32/4	Smith I.D.S.	1990/91
36	35/1	Griggs B.B.J.	2005/06
36	35/1	Watling B-J.	2014/15
36	34/2	de Boorder D.C	2017/18
36	33/3	Fletcher C.D.	2020/21
35	30/5	Smith I.D.S.	1979/80
35	33/2	Young R.A.	2001/02
35	35/0	Young R.A.	2002/03
35	33/2	Griggs B.B.J.	2007/08
35	31/4	de Boorder D.C.	2009/10
35	34/1	Hopkins G.J.	2012/13
35	33/2	van Wyk C.F.K.	2013/14
35	33/2	Cleaver D.	2019/20

Most Dismissals in a Match

12	12/0	McGlashan P.D., Northern Districts v Central Districts	Whangarei	2009/10
10	10/0	Nevin C.J., Wellington v Otago	Wellington	1995/96
	10/0	Gilchrist A.C., Australia v New Zealand	Hamilton	1999/00
	10/0	Hopkins G.J., Otago v Canterbury	Dunedin	2004/05
	8/2	Hopkins G.J., New Zealand A v Sri Lanka A	Kandy	2005/06
	9/1	McCullum B.B., New Zealand v S.African Invitation XI	Bloemfontein	2007/08
	9/1	de Boorder D.C., Otago v Wellington	Wellington	2009/10

	10/0	McGlashan P.D., Northern Districts v Auckland	Auckland	2010/11
	10/0	van Wyk C.F.K., Central Districts v Otago	Napier	2014/15
	10/0	Blundell T.A., Wellington v Canterbury	Wellington	2017/18
9	9/0	Schofield R.M., Central Districts v Wellington	Wellington	1964/65
	9/0	Vance R.H., Wellington v Otago	Wellington	1977/78
	8/1	McSweeney E.B., Wellington v Otago	Lower Hutt	1983/84
	9/0	Young B.A., Northern Districts v Canterbury	Christchurch	1986/87
	9/0	Germon L.K., Canterbury v Northern Districts	Christchurch	1992/93
	9/0	Rashid Latif., Pakistan v New Zealand	Auckland	1993/94
	9/0	Hopkins G.J., Otago v Wellington	Queenstown	2004/05
	9/0	Hopkins G.J., Otago v Northern Districts	Dunedin	2005/06
	9/0	de Boorder D.C., Otago v Northern Districts	Hamilton	2012/13
	9/0	Watling B-J., New Zealand v India	Auckland	2013/14
	9/0	Watling B.J., New Zealand v Sri Lanka	Dunedin	2015/16
	9/0	Ronchi L., Wellington v Canterbury	Christchurch	2016/17
	9/0	de Boorder D.C., Otago v Auckland	Auckland	2017/18
	9/0	Horne B.J., Auckland v Central Districts	Auckland	2018/19
	8/1	Cleaver D., Central Districts v Northern Districts	Napier	2019/20
8	3/5	James K.C., New Zealand v Derbyshire	Derby	1927
	1/7	Jackman C.K.Q., Canterbury v Wellington	Wellington	1935/36
	2/6	Kent L.A.W., Auckland v Wellington	Wellington	1944/45
	8/0	Curtis W.M., North Island XI v South Island XI	Wellington	1957/58
	8/0	Petrie E.C., New Zealand v Sussex	Hove	1958
	5/3	Dick A.E., NZ v Griqualand West	Kimberley	1961/62
	8/0	Parks J.M., England v New Zealand	Christchurch	1965/66
	7/1	Therkleson, I.J., Wellington v Northern Districts	Whangarei	1973/74
	8/0	Marsh R.W., Australia v New Zealand	Christchurch	1976/77
	8/0	Lees W.K., New Zealand v Sri Lanka	Wellington	1982/83
	4/4	McSweeney E.B., Wellington v Northern Districts	Wellington	1984/85
	8/0	Smith I.D.S., Auckland v Central Districts	Nelson	1988/89
	8/0	Smith I.D.S., New Zealand v Sri Lanka	Hamilton	1990/91
	7/1	Hart R.G., Northern Districts v Canterbury	Hamilton	1994/95
	7/1	Germon L.K., Canterbury v Central Districts	Palmerston North	1994/95
	7/1	Nevin C.J., Wellington v Central Districts	Nelson	1995/96
	8/0	Vincent L., Auckland v Central Districts	Palmerston North	2000/01
	8/0	Howell G.A., Wellington v Northern Districts	Hamilton	2001/02
	7/1	McCullum B.B., Canterbury v Northern Districts	Christchurch	2003/04
	7/1	Papps M.W.H., Canterbury v Northern Districts	Gisborne	2004/05
	8/0	van Wyk C.F.K., Canterbury v Auckland	Auckland	2006/07
	8/0	McGlashan P.D., Northern Districts v Auckland	Auckland	2006/07
	8/0	Griggs B.B.J., Central Districts v Northern Districts	Hamilton	2007/08
	8/0	Griggs B.B.J., Central Districts v Canterbury	Rangiora	2009/10
	8/0	Hopkins G.J., Auckland v Canterbury	Auckland	2010/11
	8/0	Adnan Akmal, Pakistan v New Zealand	Wellington	2010/11
	8/0	Ronchi L., Wellington v Northern Districts	Wellington	2012/13
	8/0	Watling B-J., Northern Districts v Canterbury	Christchurch	2012/13
	8/0	Latham T.W.M., Canterbury v Auckland	Christchurch	2012/13
	8/0	Watling B-J., New Zealand v West Indies	Hamilton	2013/14
	8/0	Fletcher C.D., Northern Districts v Otago	Whangarei	2013/14
	8/0	Hopkins G.J., Auckland v Otago	Dunedin	2013/14
	8/0	Watling B-J., New Zealand v West Indies	Kingston	2014
	8/0	Cachopa B., Auckland v Otago	Auckland	2014/15
	8/0	de Boorder D.C., Otago v Northern Districts	Dunedin	2015/16
	8/0	Cachopa B., Auckland v Otago	Dunedin	2015/16
	8/0	Cachopa B., Auckland v Wellington	Wellington	2015/16
	7/1	Fletcher C.D., Canterbury v Northern Districts	Christchurch	2015/16

	8/0	Fletcher C.D., Canterbury v Wellington	Wellington	2015/16
	8/0	Horne B.J., Auckland v Northern Districts	Auckland	2017/18
	7/1	Cleaver D., Central Districts v Canterbury	Napier	2017/18
	7/1	Blundell T.A., Wellington v Auckland	Auckland	2017/18
	8/0	Cleaver D., Central Districts v Northern Districts	Napier	2018/19
	8/0	Horne B.J., Auckland v Central Districts	Auckland	2019/20
	8/0	Watling B-J., New Zealand v Pakistan	Mt Maunganui	2020/21
	7/1	Bocock P.D., Northern Districts v Otago	Dunedin	2020/21
	8/0	Blundell T.A., New Zealand v England	Birmingham	2021

Most Dismissals in an Innings

8	8/0	de Boorder D.C., Otago v Wellington	Wellington	2009/10
7	7/0	Schofield R.M., Central Districts v Wellington	Wellington	1964/65
	7/0	Wasim Bari, Pakistan v New Zealand	Auckland	1978/79
	7/0	Young B.A., Northern Districts v Canterbury	Christchurch	1986/87
	7/0	Smith I.D.S., New Zealand v Sri Lanka	Hamilton	1990/91
	7/0	Croy M.G., Otago v Auckland	Auckland	2001/02
	7/0	Hopkins G.J., New Zealand A v South Africa A	Centurion	2004/05
	5/2	Hopkins G.J., New Zealand A v Sri Lanka A	Kandy	2005/06
	7/0	Griggs B.B.J., Central Districts v Northern Districts	Hamilton	2007/08
6	4/2	Mooney F.L.H., New Zealand v Warwickshire	Birmingham	1949
	5/1	Wadsworth K.J., New Zealand v Surrey	The Oval	1973
	6/0	Downes L.W., Central Districts v Canterbury	Nelson	1975/76
	5/1	Kirmani S.M.H., India v New Zealand	Christchurch	1975/76
	6/0	Vance R.H., Wellington v Otago	Wellington	1977/78
	6/0	Downton P.R., England XI v Otago	Dunedin	1977/78
	6/0	Germon L.K., Canterbury v Northern Districts	Christchurch	1992/93
	5/1	Hart R.G., Northern Districts v Canterbury	Hamilton	1994/95
	5/1	Nevin C.J., Wellington v Central Districts	Nelson	1995/96
	6/0	Parore A.C., New Zealand A v Pakistan A	Hamilton	1998/99
	6/0	Young R.A., Auckland v Wellington	Wellington	2002/03
	6/0	Hopkins G.J., Otago v Canterbury	Dunedin	2004/05
	5/1	Papps M.H.W., Canterbury v Northern Districts	Gisborne	2004/05
	6/0	McGlashan P.D., Northern Districts v Auckland	Auckland	2006/07
	6/0	Watling B-J., Northern Districts v Central Districts	Gisborne	2006/07
	6/0	Dhoni M.S., India v New Zealand	Wellington	2008/09
	6/0	McGlashan P.D., Northern Districts v Central Districts	Whangarei	2009/10
	6/0	McGlashan P.D., Northern Districts v Central Districts	Whangarei	2009/10
	6/0	Austin-Smellie J., Wellington v Central Districts	Napier	2010/11
	6/0	McGlashan P.D., Northern Districts v Auckland	Auckland	2010/11
	6/0	Adnan Akmal, Pakistan v New Zealand	Wellington	2010/11
	6/0	Hopkins G.J., Auckland v Northern Districts	Whangarei	2011/12
	6/0	Hopkins G.J., Auckland v Otago	Auckland	2011/12
	6/0	de Boorder D.C., Otago v Northern Districts	Hamilton	2012/13
	6/0	Ronchi L.,Wellington v Northern Districts	Wellington	2012/13
	6/0	Watling B-J., New Zealand v India	Auckland	2013/14
	6/0	van Wyk C.F.K., Central Districts v Otago	Napier	2014/15
	6/0	Cachopa B., Auckland v Wellington	Wellington	2015/16
	6/0	Watling B-J., New Zealand v Sri Lanka	Dunedin	2015/16
	6/0	Ronchi L., Wellington v Canterbury	Christchurch	2016/17
	6/0	Blundell T.A., Wellington v Canterbury	Wellington	2017/18
	6/0	Horne B.J., Auckland v Central Districts	Auckland	2018/19
	5/1	Bocock P.D., Northern Districts v Otago	Dunedin	2020/21

Most Catches in a Season

49	Nevin C.J.	2000/01	37	Hopkins G.J.	2004/05
44	Cachopa B.	2015/16	37	McGlashan P.D.	2009/10
43	de Boorder D.C.	2012/13	37	Ronchi L.	2012/13
41	Watling B-J.	2013/14	37	de Boorder D.C.	2015/16
41	Fletcher C.D.	2015/16	36	de Boorder D.C.	2011/12
39	van Wyk C.F.K.	2014/15	36	de Boorder D.C.	2014/15
39	Cachopa B.	2014/15	35	McSweeney E.B.	1989/90
39	Blundell T.A.	2017/18	35	Young R.A.	2002/03
38	Watling B-J	2016/17	35	Griggs B.B.J.	2005/06
38	Watling B-J	2019/20	35	Watling B-J.	2014/15

Most Catches in a Match

12	McGlashan P.D., Northern Districts v Central Districts	Whangarei	2009/10
10	Nevin C.J., Wellington v Otago	Wellington	1995/96
	Gilchrist A.C., Australia v New Zealand	Hamilton	1999/00
	Hopkins G.J., Otago v Canterbury	Dunedin	2004/05
	McGlashan P.D., Northern Districts v Auckland	Auckland	2010/11
	van Wyk C.F.K., Central Districts v Otago	Napier	2014/15
	Blundell T.A., Wellington v Canterbury	Wellington	2017/18
9	Schofield R.M., Central Districts v Wellington	Wellington	1964/65
	Vance R.H., Wellington v Otago	Wellington	1977/78
	Young B.A., Northern Districts v Canterbury	Christchurch	1986/87
	Germon L.K., Canterbury v Northern Districts	Christchurch	1992/93
	Rashid Latif., Pakistan v New Zealand	Auckland	1993/94
	Hopkins G.J., Otago v Wellington	Queenstown	2004/05
	Hopkins G.J., Otago v Northern Districts	Dunedin	2005/06
	McCullum B.B., New Zealand v South African Invitation XI	Bloemfontein	2007/08
	de Boorder D.C., Otago v Wellington	Wellington	2009/10
	de Boorder D.C., Otago v Northern Districts	Hamilton	2012/13
	Watling B-J., New Zealand v India	Auckland	2013/14
	de Boorder D.C., Otago v Auckland	Auckland	2017/18
	Horne B.J., Auckland v Central Districts	Auckland	2018/19
8	Curtis W.M., North Island XI v South Island XI	Wellington	1957/58
	Petrie E.C., New Zealand v Sussex	Hove	1958
	Parks J.M., England v New Zealand	Christchurch	1965/66
	Marsh R.W., Australia v New Zealand	Christchurch	1976/77
	Lees W.K., New Zealand v Sri Lanka	Wellington	1982/83
	McSweeney E.B., Wellington v Otago	Lower Hutt	1983/84
	Smith I.D.S., Auckland v Central Districts	Nelson	1988/89
	Smith I.D.S., New Zealand v Sri Lanka	Hamilton	1990/91
	Vincent L., Auckland v Central Districts	Palmerston North	2000/01
	Howell G.A., Wellington v Northern Districts	Hamilton	2001/02
	Hopkins G.J., New Zealand A v Sri Lanka A	Kandy	2005/06
	van Wyk C.F.K., Canterbury v Auckland	Auckland	2006/07
	McGlashan P.D., Northern Districts v Auckland	Auckland	2006/07
	Griggs B.B.J., Central Districts v Northern Districts	Hamilton	2007/08
	Griggs B.B.J., Central Districts v Canterbury	Rangiora	2009/10
	Hopkins G.J., Auckland v Canterbury	Auckland	2010/11
	Adnan Akmal, Pakistan v New Zealand	Wellington	2010/11
	Ronchi L., Wellington v Northern Districts	Wellington	2012/13
	Watling B-J., Northern Districts v Canterbury	Christchurch	2012/13

	Latham T.W.M., Canterbury v Auckland	Christchurch	2012/13
	Watling B-J., New Zealand v West Indies	Hamilton	2013/14
	Fletcher C.D., Northern Districts v Otago	Whangarei	2013/14
	Hopkins G J., Auckland v Otago	Dunedin	2013/14
	Watling B-J., New Zealand v West Indies	Kingston	2014
	Cachopa B., Auckland v Otago	Auckland	2014/15
	de Boorder D.C., Otago v Northern Districts	Dunedin	2015/16
	Cachopa B., Auckland v Otago	Dunedin	2015/16
	Cachopa B., Auckland v Wellington	Wellington	2015/16
	Fletcher C.D., Canterbury v Wellington	Wellington	2015/16
	Ronchi L., Wellington v Canterbury	Wellington	2016/17
	Horne B.J., Auckland v Northern Districts	Auckland	2017/18
	Cleaver D., Central Districts v Northern Districts	Napier	2018/19
	Cleaver D., Central Districts v Northern Districts	Napier	2019/20
	Horne B.J., Auckland v Central Districts	Auckland	2019/20
	Watling B-J., New Zealand v Pakistan	Mt Maunganui	2020/21
	Blundell T.A., New Zealand v England	Birmingham	2021

Most Catches in an Innings

8	de Boorder D.C., Otago v Wellington	Wellington	2009/10
7	Schofield R.M., Central Districts v Wellington	Wellington	1964/65
	Wasim Bari, Pakistan v New Zealand	Auckland	1978/79
	Young B.A., Northern Districts v Canterbury	Christchurch	1986/87
	Smith I.D.S., New Zealand v Sri Lanka	Hamilton	1990/91
	Croy M.G., Otago v Auckland	Auckland	2001/02
	Hopkins G.J., New Zealand A v South Africa A	Centurion	2004/05
	Griggs B.B.J., Central Districts v Northern Districts	Hamilton	2007/08
6	Downes L.W., Central Districts v Canterbury	Nelson	1975/76
	Vance R.H., Wellington v Otago	Wellington	1977/78
	Downton P.R., England XI v Otago	Dunedin	1977/78
	Germon L.K., Canterbury v Northern Districts	Christchurch	1992/93
	Parore A.C., New Zealand A v Pakistan A	Hamilton	1998/99
	Young R.A., Auckland v Wellington	Wellington	2002/03
	Hopkins G.J., Otago v Canterbury	Dunedin	2004/05
	McGlashan P.D., Northern Districts v Auckland	Auckland	2006/07
	Watling B-J., Northern Districts v Central Districts	Gisborne	2006/07
	Dhoni M.S., India v New Zealand	Wellington	2008/09
	McGlashan P.D., Northern Districts v Central Districts *(1st)*	Whangarei	2009/10
	McGlashan P.D., Northern Districts v Central Districts *(2nd)*	Whangarei	2009/10
	Austin-Smellie J., Wellington v Central Districts	Napier	2010/11
	McGlashan P.D., Northern Districts v Auckland	Auckland	2010/11
	Adnan Akmal, Pakistan v New Zealand	Wellington	2010/11
	Hopkins G.J., Auckland v Northern Districts	Whangarei	2011/12
	Hopkins G.J., Auckland v Otago	Auckland	2011/12
	de Boorder D.C., Otago v Northern Districts	Hamilton	2012/13
	Ronchi L.,Wellington v Northern Districts	Wellington	2012/13
	Watling B-J., New Zealand v India	Auckland	2013/14
	van Wyk C.F.K., Central Districts v Otago	Napier	2014/15
	Cachopa B., Auckland v Wellington	Wellington	2015/16
	Watling B-J., New Zealand v Sri Lanka	Dunedin	2015/16
	Ronchi L., Wellington v Canterbury	Wellington	2016/17
	Blundell T.A., Wellington v Canterbury	Wellington	2017/18
	Horne B.J., Auckland v Central Districts	Auckland	2018/19

Most Stumpings in a Season

13	Jackman C.K.Q.	1935/36	13	Kent L.A.W.	1944/45

Most Stumpings in a Match

7	Jackman C.K.Q., Canterbury v Wellington	Wellington	1935/36
6	Kent L.A.W., Auckand v Wellington	Wellington	1944/45
5	James K.C., NZ v Surrey	The Oval	1927
	James K.C., NZ v Derbyshire	Derby	1927
	Burns R.C., Canterbury v Otago	Dunedin	1928/29
	Mills A.S., Otago v Fiji	Dunedin	1947/48

Most Stumpings in an Innings

4	Jackman C.K.Q., Canterbury v Wellington	Wellington	1935/36
	Tindill E.W.T., NZ v Glamorgan	Cardiff	1937
	Kent L.A.W., Auckland v Wellington	Wellington	1944/45
	Mills A.S., Otago v Fiji	Dunedin	1947/48
	McSweeney E.B., Wellington v Northern Districts	Wellington	1984/85

FIELDING

Most Catches in a Season

23	Murray B.A.G.	1967/68	18	Brownlie D.G.	2015/16
22	Coney J.V.	1977/78	18	Fulton P.G.	2016/17
22	Bruce T.C.	2015/16	18	Taylor L.R.P.L.	2020/21
20	Howarth H.J.	1973/74	17	Blair W.L.	1978/79
20	Fulton P.G.	2014/15	17	Crowe M.D.	1986/87
19	Fulton P.G.	2015/16	17	Boyle D.J.	1990/91
18	Sinclair M.S.	2001/02	17	Parlane N.R.	2002/03
18	Sinclair M.S.	2008/09	17	Raval J.A.	2012/13
18	Sinclair M.S.	2010/11	17	Brownlie D.G.	2012/13
18	Raval J.A.	2014/15	17	Papps M.H.W.	2014/15

Most Catches in a Match

7	Morrison J.F.M., Wellington v Northern Districts	Wellington	1980/81
	Fleming S.P., New Zealand v Zimbabwe	Harare	1997/98
6	Marchant J.W.A., Wellington v Nelson	Wellington	1873/74
	Williams N.T., Auckland v Hawke's Bay	Napier	1894/95
	Cromb I.B., Canterbury v Otago	Christchurch	1937/38
	Ikin J.T., MCC v Auckland	Auckland	1946/47
	Reid J.R., New Zealand v South Zone	Bangalore	1955/56
	Jarvis T.W., Auckland v Northern Districts	Hamilton	1968/69
	Anderson R.W., Rest v New Zealand	New Plymouth	1974/75
	MacDonald G.K., Canterbury v Pakistan	Christchurch	1984/85
	Young B.A., New Zealand v Pakistan	Auckland	1993/94
	Latham R.T., Canterbury v Otago	Oamaru	1994/95
	Young B.A., Northern Districts v Wellington	Wellington	1995/96
	Chandler P.J.B., New Zealand A v England	Wanganui	1996/97
	McHardy D.S., Wellington v Northern Districts	Hamilton	1996/97
	Fleming S.P., New Zealand v Australia	Brisbane	1997/98
	Bell M.D., Wellington v Canterbury	Wellington	2003/04

	Fleming S.P., New Zealand v West Indies	Wellington	2005/06
	McCullum N.L., Otago v Central Districts	Napier	2006/07
	Myburgh J.G., Canterbury v Auckland	Rangiora	2008/09
	de Grandhomme C., Auckland v Canterbury	Christchurch	2010/11
	Vettori D.L., Northern Districts v Canterbury	Rangiora	2011/12
	Sinclair M.S., Central Districts v Auckland	Napier	2012/13
	de Grandhomme C., Auckland v Otago	Auckland	2012/13
	Papps M.H.W., Wellington v Otago	Invercargill	2013/14
	Anderson C.J., Northern Districts v Auckland	Auckland	2015/16
	Papps M.H.W., Wellington v Auckland	Wellington	2015/16
	Brownlie D.G., Northern Districts v Canterbury	Christchurch	2018/19

Most Catches in an Innings

5	Williams N.T., Auckand v Hawke's Bay	Napier	1894/95
	Lamason J.R., Wellington v Otago	Dunedin	1937/38
	Lamason J.R., North Island Army v South Island Army	Wellington	1942/43
	Ikin J.T., MCC v Auckland	Auckland	1946/47
	Rabone G.O., New Zealand v Oxford University	Oxford	1949
	Reid J.R., New Zealand v South Zone	Bangalore	1955/56
	Morrison J.F.M., Wellington v Northern Districts	Wellington	1980/81
	MacDonald G.K., Canterbury v Pakistan	Christchurch	1984/85
	Crowe J.J., Auckland v Canterbury	Auckland	1988/89
	Fleming S.P., New Zealand v Zimbabwe	Harare	1997/98
	Harris C.Z., Canterbury v England	Christchurch	2001/02
	Myburgh J.G., Canterbury v Auckland	Rangiora	2008/09
	Brodie J.M., Wellington v Otago	Wellington	2008/09
	Bell M.D. Wellington v Northern Districts	Hamilton	2009/10
	Sinclair M.S., Central Districts v Wellington	Wellington	2010/11

OLDEST PLAYERS

AGE Years/days			
52/189	Boxshall C.	Canterbury v Wellington	1914/15
51/216	Read R.J.	Canterbury v Auckland	1937/38
51/203	Lyttelton C.J. †	Governor-General's XI v MCC	1960/61
51/87	Wilson C.G.	Wellington v Hawke's Bay	1919/20
51/32	MacLaren A.C.	MCC v New Zealand	1922/23
50/284	Wilson E.S.	Otago v Wellington	1927/28
50/269	Hay T.D.B.	New Zealand v Royal Navy	1927
50/184	Reese T.W.	Canterbury v Otago	1917/18
50/86	Dufaur F.E.	Auckland v Wellington	1882/83
49/88	Allcott C.F.W.	Otago v Auckland	1945/46
49/48	Wilding F.	Canterbury v Hawke's Bay	1901/02
48/96	Hartley J.C.	MCC v Auckland	1922/23
48/40	Hallamore R.G.	Southland v Otago	1918/19
48/26	Badcock F.T.	New Zealanders v H.D.G. Leveson-Gower's XI	1945
47/357	Board J.H.	Hawke's Bay v Wellington	1914/15
47/325	Rowntree R.W.	Auckland v South Africa	1931/32
47/177	Fox R.H.	New Zealand v Civil Service	1927
47/151	Jones S.P.	Auckland v Otago	1908/09
47/114	Hughes W.J.	Hawke's Bay v Wellington	1905/06
47/98	Brice A.W.S.	Wellington v Australia	1927/28
47/70	Fowke J.N.	Canterbury v MCC	1906/07
46/319	Kortlang H.H.L.	Wellington v Auckland	1926/27
46/149	Stevens E.C.J.	Canterbury v Otago	1883/84
46/125	Allen R.	Wellington v Fiji	1953/54
46/14	Downes A.D.	Otago v Canterbury	1913/14
45/364	Blackie D.D.	Australia v New Zealand	1927/28
45/292	Handford A.	Southland v Otago	1914/15
45/270	Wynyard E.G.	MCC v Wellington	1906/07
45/241	Blamires E.O.	Otago v Canterbury	1926/27
45/39	Smith S.G.	Auckland v Wellington	1925/26
45/6	Beard D.D.	Northern Districts v Wellington	1964/65
44/349	Levers W.C.S.	Hawke's Bay v Wellington	1908/09
44/338	Knight A.R.	Otago v Canterbury	1943/44
44/308	Chadwick C.S.	Otago v Auckland	1924/25
44/226	Tucker K.H.	Wellington v Hawke's Bay	1919/20
44/182	Anthony A.	Auckland v Wellington	1930/31
44/178	Siedeberg H.G.	Otago v Wellington	1921/22
44/126	Garrard D.R.	Auckland v Wellington	1941/42
44/105	Newman J.A.	Canterbury v Otago	1928/29
44/75	Cate W.A.	New Zealand v MCC	1922/23
44/70	Wallace W.M.	Governor General's XI v MCC	1960/61
44/59	Dempster C.S.	Wellington v Auckland	1947/48
44/7	Wheatley J.	Canterbury v Hawke's Bay	1903/04

† Lord Cobham

YOUNGEST PLAYERS

AGE Years/days			
15/224	Dacre C.C.R.	Auckland v Wellington	1914/15
15/272	Midlane F.A.	Wellington v Hawke's Bay	1898/99
15/319	Ollivier A.M.	Canterbury v Otago	1866/67
16/36	Hartland J.F.	Canterbury v Otago	1877/78
16/84	Broad C.H.	Nelson v Wellington	1888/89
16/86	McGregor S.N.	Otago v Fiji	1947/48
16/87	Dacre L.M.	Auckland v Wellington	1912/13
16/89	Anderson C.J.	Canterbury v Central Districts	2006/07
16/130	Coutts H.D.	Taranaki v Auckland	1882/83
16/147	Puna K.N.	New Zealand Under 23 XI v Otago	1971/72
16/173	Aaqib Javed	Pakistan v President's XI	1988/89
16/242	Collins J.U.	Nelson v Wellington	1884/85
16/250	Taylor L.G.	Auckland v Hawke's Bay	1910/11
16/273	Tendulkar S.R.	India v President's XI	1989/90
16/285	Reese D.	Canterbury v Wellington	1895/96
16/311	Hale H.	Tasmania v Otago	1883/84
16/325	Morgan R.W.	Auckland v Northern Districts	1957/58
16/330	Maunder P.A.	Central Districts v Auckland	1961/62
17/4	Wallace W.M.	Auckland v Wellington	1933/34
17/5	Frater R.E.	Auckland v Wellington	1918/19
17/12	Bell M.D.	Northern Districts v New Zealand Academy XI	1993/94
17/49	Williams A.B.	Otago v Canterbury	1886/87
17/52	Blunt R.C.	Canterbury v Otago	1917/18
17/65	Mitchell W.J.	Northern Districts v Pakistan	1964/65
17/66	Wilding A.F.	Canterbury v Auckland	1900/01
17/77	Clarke D.B.	Auckland v Central Districts	1950/51
17/93	Hay T.D.B.	Auckland v Wellington	1893/94
17/107	Rutherford K.R.	Otago v Auckland	1982/83
17/110	Cooke F.H.	Otago v Canterbury	1879/80
17/112	Barron J.R.	Otago v Canterbury	1917/18
17/119	Crowe M.D.	Auckland v Canterbury	1979/80
17/124	MacNeil H.	Otago v Canterbury	1877/78
17/124	Williamson K.S.	Northern Districts v Auckland	2007/08
17/152	Butler L.C.	Wellington v Auckland	1951/52
17/174	McIntyre J.M.	Auckland v Canterbury	1961/62
17/179	Rutherford I.A.	Otago v Canterbury	1974/75
17/182	Robin T.P.	Central Districts v Canterbury	1999/00
17/185	Robinson S.A.	Otago v Northern Districts	1984/85
17/213	Turner G.M.	Otago v Canterbury	1964/65
17/222	Hemi R.C.	Auckland v Wellington	1950/51
17/237	Duffy J.A.	Otago v Wellington	2011/12
17/244	Ghulam Abbas	Pakistan v Auckland	1964/65
17/258	Rose G.A.	Central Districts v Northern Districts	1958/59
17/259	Smith N.G.	Otago v Northern Districts	2015/16
17/268	Snedden A.N.C.	Auckland v Wellington	1909/10
17/268	Beuth J.A.	Northern Districts v New Zealand Under 23 XI	1962/63
17/274	Ashbolt F.L.	Wellington v Auckland	1893/94
17/276	Collinge R.O.	Central Districts v Auckland	1963/64
17/278	Nicholls J.G.	Otago v Canterbury	1876/77
17/286	Hickmott R.G.	Canterbury v Wellington	1911/12
17/291	Bennett J.H.	Canterbury v Otago	1898/99

Years/days			
17/294	Cairns A.E.	Otago v Canterbury	1867/68
17/305	Gill M.F.	Central Districts v Wellington	1974/75
17/307	Currie E.W.	Otago v New South Wales	1893/94
17/307	Hastings B.F.	Wellington v Canterbury	1957/58
17/325	Bartlett G.A.	Central Districts v Northern Districts	1958/59
17/326	Milne A.F.	Central Districts v Canterbury	2009/10
17/328	Cushen J.A.J.	Otago v Canterbury	1967/68
17/329	West R.M.	Central Districts v Northern Districts	1996/97
17/332	Gadsdon S.R.	Northern Districts v Auckland	2008/09
17/336	Lambert H.N.	Wellington v Canterbury	1917/18
17/352	Motz R.C.	Canterbury v Northern Districts	1957/58
17/355	Tarrant D.R.	Central Districts v Auckland	1954/55
17/362	Vettori D.L.	Northern Districts v England	1996/97

CAREER RECORDS

The following career records cover the complete first-class careers of New Zealand players. Matches for other than New Zealand teams e.g. county sides, are included.
To qualify for inclusion a player must have appeared in first-class cricket in New Zealand while a bona fide resident of the country — professional coaches and the like thus being excluded.

Batting

3000 RUNS	*Career*	*M*	*In*	*NO*	*HS*	*Runs*	*Ave*	*100*
Turner G.M.	1964/65-1982/83	455	792	101	311*	34,346	49.70	103
Wright J.G.	1975/76-1992/93	366	636	44	192	25,073	42.35	59
Crowe M.D.	1979/80-1995/96	247	412	62	299	19,608	56.02	71
Sutcliffe B.	1941/42-1965/66	233	407	39	385	17,447	47.41	44
Howarth G.P.	1968/69-1985/86	338	584	42	183	17,294	31.90	32
Fleming S.P.	1991/92-2007/08	247	406	32	274*	16,409	43.87	35
Reid J.R.	1947/48-1965	246	418	28	296	16,128	41.35	39
Patel D.N.	1976-1996/97	358	558	51	204	15,188	29.95	26
Marshall H.J.H.	1998/99-2016/17	264	434	29	170	14,820	36.59	31
Rutherford K.R.	1982/83-1999/00	220	383	33	317	13,974	39.92	35
Sinclair M.S.	1995/96-2012/13	188	319	37	268	13,717	48.64	36
Congdon B.E.	1960/61-1978	241	416	40	202*	13,101	34.84	23
Spearman C.M.	1993/94-2009	201	360	16	341	13,021	37.85	30
Hitchcock R.E.	1947/48-1964	323	519	71	153*	12,473	27.84	13
Papps M.H.W.	1998/99-2017/18	188	344	26	316*	12,294	38.66	33
Taylor L.R.P.L.	2002/03-2021	188	316	27	290	12,250	42.38	27
Dacre C.C.R.	1914/15-1936	269	439	20	223	12,230	29.18	24
Dempster C.S.	1921/22-1947/48	184	306	36	212	12,145	44.98	35
Hadlee R.J.	1971/72-1990	342	473	93	210*	12,052	31.71	14
Williamson K.S.	2007/08-2021	153	261	21	284*	12,041	50.17	34
Edgar B.A.	1975/76-1989/90	175	307	26	203	11,304	40.22	24
Parker J.M.	1971-1983/84	207	362	39	195	11,254	34.84	21
Smith S.G.	1899/00-1925/26	211	379	30	256	10,920	31.28	14
Cairns C.L.	1988-2005/06	217	341	38	158	10,702	35.32	13
Fulton P.G.	2000/01-2016/17	162	288	23	301*	10,569	39.88	19
Burgess M.G.	1963/64-1980/81	192	322	35	146	10,281	35.82	20
Crowe J.J.	1977/78-1991/92	180	304	34	159	10,233	37.90	22
Watling B-J.	2004/05-2021	178	297	36	205	10,034	38.44	18
Richardson M.H.	1989/90-2004/05	157	264	31	306	9994	42.89	20
Greatbatch M.J.	1982/83-1999/00	170	292	31	202*	9890	37.89	24
Bell M.D.	1993/94-2010/11	171	293	18	265	9881	35.93	24
Twose R.G.	1989-2000/01	178	300	35	277*	9802	36.98	18
Franklin J.E.C.	1998/99-2017	206	321	46	219	9780	35.56	22
Lowry T.C.	1917/18-1937/38	198	322	20	181	9421	31.19	18
Dowling G.T.	1958/59-1971/72	158	282	13	239	9399	34.94	16
Astle N.J.	1991/92-2006/07	171	272	24	223	9321	37.58	19
Donnelly M.P.	1936/37-1960/61	131	221	26	208*	9250	47.43	23
McCullum B.B.	1999/00-2015/16	150	261	13	302	9210	37.13	17
Jones A.H.	1979/80-1995/96	145	254	33	186	9180	41.53	16
Cumming C.D.	1995/96-2011/12	147	260	21	187	9142	38.25	23
Ryder J.D.	2002/03-2017/18	131	214	19	236	8784	45.04	25
Latham T.W.M.	2010/11-2021	126	216	14	264*	8668	42.91	20
Horne M.J.	1992/93-2005/06	128	219	11	241	8501	40.87	24
Broom N.T.	2002/03-2019/20	149	252	26	203*	8457	37.42	18
Arnold P.A.	1953/54-1960	174	306	15	122	8013	27.53	7
Blunt R.C.	1917/18-1935	123	209	15	338*	7953	40.99	15

	Career	M	In	NO	HS	Runs	Ave	100
Coney J.V.	1970/71-1986/87	165	272	48	174*	7872	35.14	8
Raval J.A.	2008/09-2020/21	126	221	11	256	7832	37.29	17
McMillan C.D.	1994/95-2007	138	226	27	168*	7817	39.28	16
Flynn D.R.	2004/05-2019/20	135	238	15	241	7815	35.04	21
Woodcock L.J.	2001/02-2018/19	147	250	31	220*	7811	35.66	11
Franklin T.J.	1980/81-1992/93	148	254	20	181	7794	33.30	15
Wallace W.M.	1933/34-1960/61	121	192	17	211	7757	44.32	17
Hastings B.F.	1957/58-1976/77	163	273	32	226	7685	31.89	15
How J.M.	2000/01-2014/15	131	231	20	207*	7647	36.24	16
Hopkins G.J.	1997/98-2013/14	158	245	39	201	7550	36.65	17
Hadlee W.A.	1933/34-1951/52	117	203	17	198	7523	40.44	18
Conway D.P.	2008/09-2021	111	180	23	327*	7509	47.82	19
Young B.A.	1983/84-1998/99	163	276	43	267*	7489	32.14	10
Marshall J.A.H.	1997/98-2012/13	148	250	17	235	7422	31.85	13
Guptill M.J.	2005/06-2020/21	115	208	13	227	7389	37.89	16
Harris C.Z.	1989/90-2009/10	131	204	42	251*	7377	45.53	15
Parlane M.E.	1992/93-2010/11	139	238	16	203	7354	33.12	15
Jones R.A.	1993/94-2009/10	124	215	12	201	7254	35.73	19
Redmond A.J.	1999/00-2014/15	129	225	13	154	7248	34.18	15
McIntosh T.G.	1998/99-2013/14	131	229	19	268	7169	33.58	19
Vance R.H.	1976/77-1990/91	135	230	18	254*	6955	32.80	12
Myburgh J.G.	1997/98-2016	108	190	23	203	6841	40.53	16
Rutherford H.D.	2008/09-2020/21	111	192	3	239	6830	36.13	15
Parore A.C.	1988/89-2001/02	163	252	43	155*	6826	32.66	10
van Wyk C.F.K.	2000/01-2015/16	138	217	47	178*	6733	39.60	7
Vettori D.L.	1996/97-2014/15	174	257	31	140	6695	29.62	9
McEwan P.E.	1976/77-1990/91	115	206	15	155	6677	34.95	12
McGregor S.N.	1947/48-1968/69	148	274	16	114*	6573	25.47	5
Patel J.S.	1999/00-2019	289	385	77	120	6573	21.34	3
James K.C.	1923/24-1946/47	204	330	41	109*	6413	22.19	7
Nicol R.J.	2001/02-2017/18	130	218	25	160	6319	32.74	10
Latham R.T.	1980/81-1994/95	108	189	19	237*	6298	37.05	9
Wilson B.S.	2004/05-2018/19	111	204	9	165	6283	32.22	14
Murray B.A.G.	1958/59-1972/73	102	187	11	213	6257	35.55	6
Brownlie D.G.	2009/10-2019/20	94	169	14	334	6208	40.05	14
Morrison J.F.M.	1965/66-1983/84	126	225	25	180*	6142	30.71	7
Sinclair B.W.	1955/56-1970/71	118	204	18	148	6114	32.87	6
Styris S.B.	1994/95-2010/11	128	213	20	212*	6048	31.33	10
Blair B.R.	1977/78-1989/90	110	190	6	143	5995	32.58	7
Hay G.R.	2006/07-2020/21	87	153	11	226	5964	42.00	13
Morgan R.W.	1957/58-1976/77	136	229	13	166	5940	27.50	8
Roberts A.D.G.	1967/68-1983/84	112	206	37	128*	5865	34.70	7
Page M.L.	1920/21-1942/43	132	213	17	206	5857	29.88	9
de Grandhomme C.	2005/06-2021	114	184	24	144*	5821	36.38	12
Shrimpton M.J.F.	1961/62-1979/80	122	218	23	150	5812	29.80	7
Blain T.E.	1982/83-1994/95	118	199	30	161	5749	34.02	8
Stewart S.L.	2001/02-2013/14	96	173	18	227*	5693	36.72	7
Reid J.F.	1975/76-1987/88	101	170	22	180	5650	38.17	11
Ingram P.J.	2001/02-2011/12	82	149	8	247	5623	39.87	17
Scott V.J.	1937/38-1952/53	80	130	17	204	5620	49.73	16
Ronchi L.	2002/03-2016/17	100	158	15	148	5614	39.25	16
Anderson R.W.	1967/68-1981/82	111	197	14	155	5609	30.65	8
Parlane N.R.	1996/97-2011/12	103	170	14	193	5602	35.91	12
Smith I.D.S.	1977/78-1991/92	178	250	42	173	5570	26.77	6
Murdoch S.J.	2009/10-2019/20	87	158	9	171	5551	37.25	13

	Career	M	In	NO	HS	Runs	Ave	100
Young W.A.	2011/12-2021	86	142	13	162	5506	42.68	12
Gray E.J.	1975/76-1991/92	162	241	51	128*	5472	28.80	6
Nicholls H.M.	2011/12-2021	91	147	11	174	5436	39.97	12
Chapple M.E.	1949/50-1971/72	119	201	16	165	5344	28.88	4
Pollard V.	1964/65-1974/75	130	207	33	146	5314	30.54	6
Worker G.H.	2007/08-2020/21	105	189	7	210	5228	28.72	9
Ellis A.M.	2002/03-2017/18	106	169	21	196	5221	35.27	9
Vincent L.	1997/98-2012/13	98	162	12	224	5184	34.56	10
Kitchen A.K.	2008/09-2020/21	88	160	13	207	5119	34.82	10
Bracewell M.G.	2010/11-2020/21	91	161	13	190	5072	34.27	11
Nevin C.J.	1995/96-2009/10	112	172	26	143*	5058	34.64	4
Mills J.E.	1925/26-1937/38	97	161	8	185	5025	32.84	11
Graham H.	1892/93-1906/07	113	200	9	124	5023	26.29	7
Weir G.L.	1927/28-1946/47	107	172	16	191	5022	32.19	10
Stead G.R.	1991/92-2005/06	101	165	10	190	4984	32.15	10
Bradburn G.E.	1985/86-2001/02	127	206	27	148*	4978	27.81	4
McSweeney E.B.	1979/80-1993/94	121	177	30	205*	4947	33.65	6
Lees W.K.	1970/71-1987/88	146	243	43	152	4932	24.66	5
Pairaudeau B.H.	1946/47-1966/67	89	159	5	163	4930	32.01	11
White D.J.	1979/80-1993/94	106	187	17	209	4926	28.98	7
de Boorder D.C.	2007/08-2017/18	103	160	28	146	4858	36.80	4
Yovich J.A.F.	1996/97-2012/13	121	190	29	144	4839	30.05	6
Kerr J.L.	1929/30-1942/43	89	157	7	196	4829	32.19	8
Douglas M.W.	1987/88-2000/01	94	160	23	144	4808	35.09	9
Miller L.S.M.	1950/51-1959/60	82	142	15	144	4777	37.61	5
Grimmett C.V.	1911/12-1940/41	248	321	54	71*	4720	17.67	—
Gaffaney C.B.	1995/96-2004/05	83	152	11	194	4711	33.41	8
Pocock B.A.	1990/91-2000/01	100	176	16	167	4699	29.36	10
Jarvis T.W.	1964/65-1976/77	97	167	8	182	4666	29.34	6
Young R.A.	1998/99-2012/13	126	183	30	126*	4633	30.28	8
Sparling J.T.	1956/57-1970/71	127	215	26	105	4606	24.11	2
Edwards G.N.	1973/74-1984/85	92	164	8	177*	4589	29.41	5
Taylor B.R.	1963/64-1979/80	141	210	25	173	4579	24.75	4
Adams A.R.	1997/98-2015	173	237	24	124	4540	21.31	3
Hadlee B.G.	1961/62-1980/81	84	155	11	163*	4539	31.52	6
Vivian H.G.	1930/31-1938/39	85	143	15	165	4443	34.71	6
Hart M.N.	1990/91-2004/05	135	198	26	201*	4418	25.68	4
Briasco P.S.	1982/83-1991/92	83	148	16	157	4390	33.25	6
Bracewell J.G.	1978/79-1990	149	208	40	110*	4354	25.91	4
Astle T.D.	2005/06-2019/20	119	190	22	195	4345	25.86	2
Wiseman P.J.	1991/92-2008	186	254	51	130	4254	20.95	2
Thomson S.A.	1987/88-1996/97	90	148	38	167	4209	38.26	6
Cairns B.L.	1971/72-1988	148	226	25	110	4165	20.72	1
Mitchell D.J.	2011/12-2021	79	125	17	170*	4144	38.37	10
McGirr H.M.	1913/14-1932/33	88	146	7	141	3992	28.71	5
Oram J.D.P.	1997/98-2009/10	85	136	18	155	3992	33.83	8
Cromb I.B.	1929/30-1946/47	88	148	12	171	3950	29.04	3
Priest M.W.	1984/85-1998/99	109	154	25	119	3945	30.58	4
Dunning B.	1961/62-1977/78	83	150	10	142	3929	28.06	3
Guy J.W.	1953/54-1972/73	90	165	13	115	3923	25.80	3
Elliott G.D.	1996/97-2013/14	83	134	7	196*	3883	30.57	8
Bailey M.D.	1989/90-2001/02	89	138	9	180*	3882	30.09	8
Harris R.M.	1955/56-1973/74	73	130	5	157	3863	30.90	3
Blundell T.A.	2012/13-2021	72	121	15	153	3856	36.40	10
Yuile B.W.	1959/60-1971/72	123	187	31	146	3850	24.67	1

	Career	M	In	NO	HS	Runs	Ave	100
Parsons A.E.W.	1971/72-1982/83	82	156	10	141	3847	26.34	4
Sulzberger G.P.	1995/96-2004/05	83	135	12	159	3836	31.18	8
Hiddleston J.S.	1909/10-1928/29	52	97	1	212	3818	39.77	8
Rutherford I.A.	1974/75-1983/84	79	144	4	222	3794	27.10	5
Bracewell D.A.J.	2008/09-2020/21	109	163	23	105	3778	26.98	3
Taylor D.D.	1946/47-1960/61	95	168	6	143	3772	23.28	1
Hartland B.R.	1986/87-1996/97	83	150	8	150	3753	26.42	5
Kuggeleijn C.M.	1975/76-1990/91	89	151	15	116	3747	27.55	4
MacGibbon A.R.	1947/48-1961/62	124	206	20	94	3699	19.88	—
Blair W.L.	1967/68-1990/91	82	151	9	140	3698	26.04	2
Webb P.N.	1976/77-1986/87	75	130	19	136	3671	33.07	5
Wadsworth K.J.	1968/69-1975/76	118	164	23	117	3664	25.98	2
Roberts A.W.	1927/28-1950/51	84	135	17	181	3645	30.88	3
Leggat J.G.	1944/45-1955/56	57	106	9	166	3634	37.46	7
Austen M.H.	1982/83-1996/97	66	120	8	202*	3619	32.31	6
Munro C.	2006/07-2017/18	48	74	4	281	3611	51.58	13
Cleaver D.	2010/11-2020/21	59	97	10	201	3598	41.35	6
Howell L.G.	1990/91-2004/05	83	143	16	181	3586	28.23	3
Hoskin R.N.	1980/81-1992/93	81	140	7	157	3580	26.91	6
Nash D.J.	1990/91-2001/02	120	168	37	135*	3555	27.13	5
Patrick W.R.	1905/06-1926/27	74	138	8	143	3536	27.20	4
Smith C.J.P.	1983/84-1990/91	62	118	9	160*	3499	32.10	7
Motz R.C.	1957/58-1969	142	225	21	103*	3494	17.12	1
Larsen G.R.	1984/85-1998/99	103	157	35	161	3491	28.61	2
Brown V.R.	1978/79-1989/90	83	136	17	161*	3485	29.28	6
Rabone G.O.	1940/41-1960/61	82	135	14	125	3425	28.30	3
Todd G.R.	2000/01-2011/12	64	114	15	165	3368	34.02	4
Pritchard T.L.	1937/38-1956	200	293	41	81	3363	13.34	—
Smith B.S.	2010/11-2020/21	62	107	7	244	3313	33.13	6
Newdick G.A.	1970/71-1980/81	61	114	6	143	3292	30.48	4
Lawson R.A.	1992/93-2003/04	73	133	6	200	3278	25.81	3
Vivian G.E.	1964/65-1978/79	88	140	25	137*	3259	28.33	3
Noema-Barnett K.	2008/09-2018/19	87	131	19	108	3243	28.95	4
Neesham J.D.S.	2009/10-2020/21	65	110	9	147	3239	32.06	5
Moloney D.A.R.	1929/30-1940/41	64	119	7	190	3219	28.74	2
Boyle D.J.	1980/81-1994/95	69	121	12	149	3216	29.50	3
Stead D.W.	1968/69-1985/86	80	139	11	193*	3205	25.03	1
Alabaster G.D.	1955/56-1975/76	96	154	20	108	3200	23.88	3
Reese D.	1895/96-1920/21	72	134	8	148	3186	25.28	4
McCullum S.J.	1976/77-1990/91	75	131	1	134	3174	24.41	2
Duff S.W.	1985/86-1995/96	88	134	29	164*	3167	30.16	1
Vaughan J.T.C.	1989/90-1996/97	70	120	20	127	3159	31.59	2
Griggs B.B.J.	2000/01-2009/10	83	130	16	143	3155	27.67	2
Harford N.S.	1953/54-1966/67	74	122	8	158	3149	27.62	3
Merritt W.E.	1926/27-1946	125	191	33	87	3147	19.91	—
Mooney F.L.H.	1941/42-1954/55	91	150	14	180	3143	23.11	2
Wagner N.	2005/06-2021	184	241	53	70	3136	16.69	—
Redmond R.E.	1963/64-1975/76	53	100	7	141*	3134	33.69	5
Thomson K.	1959/60-1973/74	71	125	14	136*	3134	28.23	5
Tindill E.W.T.	1932/33-1949/50	69	116	13	149	3127	30.35	6
Harris P.G.Z.	1949/50-1964/65	69	120	9	118	3126	28.16	5
Germon L.K.	1987/88-2001/02	103	142	35	160*	3123	29.18	4
Englefield J.I.	1998/99-2005/06	55	97	7	172	3113	34.58	3
Bruce T.C.	2014/15-2020/21	51	19	13	166*	3101	39.75	4
Wells J.D.	1989/90-2000/01	73	115	18	143	3058	31.52	5

	Career	M	In	NO	HS	Runs	Ave	100
O'Donnell R.R.	2014/15-2020/21	55	96	6	167	3049	33.87	5
Kuggeleijn S.C.	2011/12-2020/21	83	128	21	142*	3043	28.43	3
Ryan M.L.	1965/66-1978/79	66	113	9	129	3023	29.06	3
Barnes A.C.	1993/94-2004/05	78	121	10	134*	3006	27.08	4

Bowling

200 WICKETS	Career	M	Wkts	Runs	Ave
Hadlee R.J.	1971/72-1990	342	1490	26,998	18.11
Grimmett C.V.	1911/12-1940/41	248	1424	31,740	22.28
Smith S.G.	1899/00-1925/26	211	955	17,272	18.08
Patel J.S.	1999/00-2019	293	892	29,239	32.77
Pritchard T.L.	1937/38-1956	200	818	19,062	23.30
Wagner N.	2005/06-2021	184	762	20,314	26.65
Adams A.R.	1997/98-2015	173	692	16,581	23.96
Patel D.N.	1976-1996/97	358	654	21,737	33.23
Cairns C.L.	1988-2005/06	217	647	18,322	28.31
Boock S.L.	1973/74-1989/90	164	640	14,314	22.36
Martin C.S.	1997/98-2012/13	192	599	19,070	31.83
Chatfield E.J.	1973/74-1989/90	157	587	13,429	22.87
Vettori D.L.	1996/97-2014/15	174	565	17,981	31.82
Saunders J.V.	1899/00-1913/14	107	553	12,065	21.81
Howarth H.J.	1962/63-1978/79	145	541	13,674	25.27
Blair R.W.	1951/52-1964/65	119	537	9961	18.54
Merritt W.E.	1926/27-1946	125	536	13,669	25.50
Collinge R.O.	1963/64-1978	163	524	12,793	24.41
O'Sullivan D.R.	1971-1984/85	136	523	13,554	25.91
Bracewell J.G.	1978/79-1990	149	522	13,919	26.66
Motz R.C.	1957/58-1969	142	518	11,769	22.72
Alabaster J.C.	1955/56-1971/72	143	500	12,688	25.37
Franklin J.E.C.	1998/99-2017	206	479	13,504	28.19
Cairns B.L.	1971/72-1988	148	473	12,544	26.52
Southee T.G.	2006/07-2021	119	472	12,392	26.25
Reid J.R.	1947/48-1965	246	466	10,535	22.60
Wiseman P.J.	1991/92-2008	186	466	15,727	33.74
Cameron F.J.	1952/53-1966/67	119	447	9658	21.60
Gray E.J.	1975/76-1991/92	162	444	12,522	28.20
Morrison D.K.	1985/86-1996/97	142	440	13,298	30.22
Taylor B.R.	1963/64-1979/80	141	422	10,605	25.13
Burtt T.B.	1943/44-1954/55	84	408	9054	22.19
Boult T.A.	2008/09-2021	108	408	10,997	26.95
Arnel B.J	2005/06-2017/18	111	394	10,598	26.89
Snedden M.C.	1977/78-1990	118	387	9918	25.62
Cunis R.S.	1960/61-1976/77	132	386	10,287	26.65
Gillespie M.R.	1999/00-2014/15	94	385	10,769	27.97
Yuile B.W.	1959/60-1971/72	123	375	8209	21.89
Moir A.M.	1949/50-1961/62	97	368	9040	24.56
Aldridge G.W.	1998/99-2014/15	123	364	10,299	28.29
Cave H.B.	1945/46-1958/59	117	362	8663	23.93
Cowie J.	1932/33-1949/50	86	359	8002	22.28
MacGibbon A.R.	1947/48-1961/62	124	356	9301	26.12
Martin B.P.	1999/00-2013/14	131	355	13,345	37.59
Hadlee D.R.	1966/67-1983/84	111	351	8853	25.22
McIntyre J.M.	1961/62-1982/83	113	336	7917	23.56

	Career	*M*	*Wkts*	*Runs*	*Ave*
Astle T.D.	2005/06-2019/20	119	334	10,746	32.17
Bracewell D.A.J.	2008/09-2020/21	109	334	10,804	32.34
Priest M.W.	1984/85-1998/99	109	329	10,478	31.84
O'Brien I.E.	2000/01-2010	91	322	8392	26.06
Callaway S.T.	1888/89-1906/07	62	320	5460	17.06
Sparling J.T.	1956/57-1970/71	127	318	7226	22.72
Henry M.J.	2010/11-2021	74	314	7906	25.17
Downes A.D.	1888/89-1913/14	51	311	4564	14.67
Hayes J.A.	1946/47-1960/61	78	292	6759	23.14
Tuffey D.R.	1996/97-2011/12	91	288	7705	26.75
Mason M.J.	1997/98-2011/12	91	288	7240	25.13
Dickeson C.W.	1973/74-1986/87	90	282	8242	29.22
Beard D.D.	1945/46-1964/65	66	278	6000	21.58
O'Connor S.B.	1994/95-2002/03	73	278	6582	23.67
Alabaster G.D.	1955/56-1975/76	96	275	6388	23.22
Troup G.B.	1974/75-1986/87	100	272	7541	27.72
Watson W.	1984/85-1994/95	93	272	7485	27.52
Kuggeleijn S.C.	2011/12-2020/21	83	266	8474	31.85
Upham E.F.	1892/93-1909/10	49	265	4414	16.65
Sodhi I.S.	2012/13-2020/21	84	264	9105	34.48
Bennett H.K.	2005/06-2020/21	79	261	7437	28.49
Nash D.J.	1990/91-2001/02	120	255	7165	28.09
Yovich J.A.F.	1996/97-2012/13	102	255	8579	33.64
Walmsley K.P	1994/95-2005/06	67	253	6302	24.90
Robertson G.K.	1979/80-1989/90	88	252	7469	29.59
Penn A.J.	1994/95-2003/04	66	252	5806	23.03
Bradburn G.E.	1985/86-2001/02	127	250	8174	32.69
Doull S.B.	1989/90-2001/02	99	250	7233	28.93
Ellis A.M.	2002/03-2017/18	106	249	7416	29.78
Wisneski W.A.	1992/93-2003/04	71	248	6467	26.07
Patel A.Y.	2012/13-2021	67	248	8012	32.30
Brice A.W.S.	1902/03-1927/28	61	247	5260	21.29
Nethula T.S.	2008/09-2017/18	80	245	9040	36.89
Bennett J.H.	1898/99-1919/20	52	241	4476	18.58
McSkimming W.C.	1999/00-2011/12	69	240	5850	24.37
McGirr H.M.	1913/14-1932/33	88	239	6571	27.49
Puna N.	1956/57-1968/69	70	229	5597	24.44
Dunning J.A.	1923/24-1937/38	60	228	6290	27.58
Bond S.E.	1996/97-2009/10	60	225	5478	24.34
Viljoen C.	2009/10-2018/19	80	225	6075	27.00
Pollard V.	1964/65-1974/75	130	224	6931	30.94
Vivian H.G.	1930/31-1938/39	85	223	6160	27.62
Cromb I.B.	1929/30-1946/47	88	222	6152	27.71
Badcock F.T.	1924/25-1945	53	221	5211	23.57
Allcott C.F.W.	1920/21-1945/46	82	220	5882	26.73
Sewell D.G.	1995/96-2005/06	67	218	6260	28.71
Duff S.W.	1985/86-1995/96	88	217	7051	32.49
Davis H.T.	1991/92-2003/04	71	215	6693	31.13
Blunt R.C.	1917/18-1935	123	214	6638	31.01
Stott L.W.	1969/70-1983/84	63	214	5341	24.95
Hart M.N.	1990/91-2004/05	135	212	7424	35.01
Hamilton L.J.	1996/97-2006/07	60	212	5391	25.42
de Groen R.P.	1987/88-1995/96	60	210	5266	25.07
Stirling D.A.	1981/82-1991/92	84	206	6948	33.72

	Career	M	Wkts	Runs	Ave
Canning T.K.	1998/99-2006/07	61	206	5042	24.47
Congdon B.E.	1960/61-1978	241	204	6125	30.02
Styris S.B.	1994/95-2010/11	128	204	6440	31.56
Mills K.D.	1998/99-2013/14	76	204	6083	29.81
Butler I.G.	2001/02-2014	72	204	6315	30.95
Roberts S.J.	1985/86-1995/96	63	203	6001	29.56
Baker J.D.	2010/11-2020/21	76	201	5961	29.65

Leading Career Averages

BATTING *(qualification 3000 runs)*	*M*	*In*	*NO*	*HS*	*Runs*	*Ave*
Crowe M.D.	247	412	62	299	19,608	56.02
Munro C.	48	74	4	281	3611	51.58
Williamson K.S.	153	261	21	284*	12,041	50.17
Scott V.J.	80	130	17	204	5620	49.73
Turner G.M.	455	792	101	311*	34,346	49.70
Sinclair M.S.	188	319	37	268	13,717	48.64
Conway D.P.	111	180	23	327*	7509	47.82
Sutcliffe B.	233	407	39	385	17,447	47.41
Harris C.Z.	131	204	42	251*	7377	45.53
Ryder J.D.	131	214	19	236	8784	45.04
Dempster C.S.	184	306	36	212	12,145	44.98
Wallace W.M.	121	192	17	211	7757	44.32
Fleming S.P.	247	406	32	274*	16,409	43.87
Latham T.W.M.	126	216	14	264*	8668	42.91
Richardson M.H.	157	264	31	306	9994	42.89
Young W.A.	86	142	13	162	5506	42.68
Taylor L.R.P.L.	188	316	27	290	12,250	42.38
Wright J.G.	366	636	44	192	25,073	42.35
Hay G.R.	87	153	11	226	5964	42.00
Jones A.H.	145	254	33	186	9180	41.53
Reid J.R.	246	418	28	296	16,128	41.35
Cleaver D.	59	97	10	201	3598	41.35
Blunt R.C.	123	209	15	338*	7953	40.99
Horne M.J.	128	219	11	241	8501	40.87
Myburgh J.G.	108	190	23	203	6841	40.53
Hadlee W.A.	117	203	17	198	7523	40.44
Broom N.T.	116	197	22	203*	7060	40.34
Edgar B.A.	175	307	26	203	11,304	40.22
Brownlie D.G.	94	169	14	334	6208	40.05

BOWLING *(qualification 200 wickets)*	*M*	*Wkts*	*Runs*	*Ave*
Downes A.D.	51	311	4564	14.67
Upham E.F.	49	265	4414	16.65
Callaway S.T.	62	320	5460	17.06
Smith S.G.	211	955	17,272	18.08
Hadlee R.J.	342	1490	26,998	18.11
Blair R.W.	119	537	9961	18.54
Bennett J.H.	52	241	4476	18.58

(C.J. Drum took 199 wickets at 19.46)

Wicketkeeping

100 DISMISSALS	*Career*	*M*	*Caught*	*Stumped*	*Total*
Hopkins G.J.	1997/98-2013/14	158	429	26	455
van Wyk C.F.K.	2000/01-2015/16	138	414	21	435
Smith I.D.S.	1977/78-1991/92	178	390	36	426
James K.C.	1923/24-1946/47	204	310	112	422
Watling B-J.	2004/05-2021	178	407	10	417
McSweeney E.B.	1979/80-1993/94	121	340	45	385
Parore A.C.	1988/89-2001/02	163	358	24	382
Ronchi L.	2002/03-2016/17	100	339	17	356
de Boorder D.C.	2007/08-2017/18	103	332	22	354
Lees W.K.	1970/71-1987/88	146	292	44	336
Young R.A.	1998/99-2012/13	126	315	5	320
Hart R.G.	1992/93-2003/04	110	298	17	315
Nevin C.J.	1995/96-2009/10	112	299	9	308
Wadsworth K.J.	1968/69-1975/76	118	256	26	282
Germon L.K.	1987/88-2001/02	103	256	26	282
McCullum B.B.	1999/00-2015/16	150	259	19	278
Ward J.T.	1957/58-1970/71	95	227	27	254
Griggs B.B.J.	2000/01-2009/10	83	231	7	238
Petrie E.C.	1950/51-1966/67	115	194	37	231
Fletcher C.D.	2012/13-2020/21	65	209	11	220
Mooney F.L.H.	1941/42-1954/55	91	164	54	218
Blain T.E.	1982/83-1994/95	118	190	26	216
McGlashan P.D.	2000/01-2011/12	71	194	13	207
Croy M.G.	1994/95-2001/02	65	183	14	197
Young B.A.	1983/84-1997/98	163	185	11	196
Milburn B.D.	1963/64-1982/83	75	176	19	195
Cleaver D.	2010/11-2020/21	59	162	11	173
Dick A.E.	1956/57-1968/69	78	133	21	154
Kelly P.J.	1980/81-1988/89	49	140	13	153
Blundell T.A.	2012/13-2021	72	144	6	150
Cachopa B.	2010/11-2016/17	58	131	7	138
Colquhoun I.A.	1953/54-1963/64	57	108	28	136
Guillen S.C.	1947/48-1960/61	66	100	34	134
Sigley M.A.	1994/95-2002/03	44	124	4	128
Boxshall C.	1897/98-1914/15	65	81	43	124
Schofield R.M.	1964/65-1974/75	53	107	15	122
Robinson S.A.	1984/85-1996/97	45	117	5	122
Wright M.J.E.	1972/73-1983/84	65	104	17	121
Mills G.H.	1935/36-1957/58	59	85	34	119
Tindill E.W.T.	1932/33-1949/50	69	85	33	118
Horne B.J.	2016/17-2020/21	35	115	3	118
Seifert T.L.	2014/15-2020/21	51	111	7	118
Edwards G.N.	1973/74-1984/85	92	88	16	104
Therkleson I.J.	1966/67-1973/74	39	93	7	100

HIGHEST PARTNERSHIPS

FIRST WICKET

432	Papps M.H.W.	Woodcock L.J.	Wellington v Auckland	Wellington	2017/18
428	Ingram P.J.	How J.M.	Central Districts v Wellington	Wellington	2009/10
387	Turner G.M.	Jarvis T.W.	New Zealand v West Indies	Georgetown	1971/72
373	Sutcliffe B.	Watt L.	Otago v Auckland	Auckland	1950/51
333	Edgar B.A.	Jones A.H.	Wellington v Auckland	Wellington	1988/89
316	Austen M.H.	Hart R.T.	Wellington v Central Districts	Wanganui	1993/94
310	Edgar B.A.	Vance R.H.	Wellington v Northern Districts	Wellington	1988/89
306	Cuff L.A.	Lawrence J.D.	Canterbury v Auckland	Christchurch	1893/94
305	Lawson R.A.	Croy M.G.	Otago v Central Districts	Napier	1995/96
299	Bell M.D.	Jones R.A.	Wellington v Otago	Dunedin	2001/02
287	Hartland B.R.	Stead G.R.	Canterbury v Wellington	Christchurch	1994/95
286	Sutcliffe B.	Taylor D.D.	Auckland v Canterbury	Auckland	1948/49
278	Flynn D.R.	Cooper H.R.	Northern Districts v Canterbury	Whangarei	2017/18
276	Dempster C.S.	Mills J.E.	New Zealand v England	Wellington	1929/30
276	Griffith A.F.G.	Campbell S.L.	West Indies v New Zealand	Hamilton	1999/00
274	Wilson B.S.	Watling B-J.	Northern Districts v Wellington	Whangarei	2010/11
268	Turner G.M.	Dowling G.T.	New Zealand v President's XI	Montego Bay	1971/72
260	Lawson R.A.	Mohammad Wasim	Otago v Northern Districts	Dunedin	2002/03
259	Austen M.H.	Aiken J.M.	Wellington v Otago	Wellington	1994/95
254	Raval J.A.	Latham T.W.M.	New Zealand v Bangladesh	Hamilton	2018/19
253	Bell M.D.	Woodcock L.J.	Wellington v Central Districts	Napier	2007/08
252	Sutcliffe B.	Scott V.J.	New Zealand v Rest	Christchurch	1948/49
250	Hart R.T.	Smith C.J.P.	Central Districts v Wellington	Wellington	1985/86
247	Sutcliffe B.	Scott V.J.	New Zealand v Combined Services	Gillingham	1949
244	Richardson M.H.	Papps M.H.W.	New Zealand v Kent	Canterbury	2004
240	McIntosh T.G.	Horne M.J.	Auckland v Otago	Dunedin	2001/02
239	Dempster C.S.	Dustin W.H.	Wellington v Canterbury	Wellington	1931/32
239	Smith D.	Parks J.H.	MCC v Otago	Dunedin	1935/36
236	Brodie J.M.	Papps M.H.W.	Wellington v Auckland	Auckland	2011/12
235	Hadlee W.A.	Page M.L.	Canterbury v Wellington	Christchurch	1936/37
235	Woodcock L.J.	Papps M.H.W.	Wellington v Otago	Wellington	2015/16
231	Richardson M.H.	Vincent L.	New Zealand v India	Mohali	2003/04
231	Cook A.N.	Compton N.R.D.	England v New Zealand	Dunedin	2012/13
230	Murray B.A.G.	Turner G.M.	New Zealand v President's XI	Rawalpindi	1969/70
229	Sutcliffe B.	Scott V.J.	New Zealand v Surrey	Oval	1949
227	Rutherford H.D.	Wilson B.S.	Otago v Central Districts	Nelson	2016/17
226*	Hadlee W.A.	Leggat J.G.	Canterbury v Otago	Christchurch	1948/49
226	Phillips G.D.	Seifert T.L.	New Zealand A v West Indies A	Mt Maunganui	2020/21
226	Georgeson L.I.	Ravindra R.	Wellington v Northern Districts	Wellington	2020/21
225	Richardson P.E.	Watson W.	MCC v Wellington	Wellington	1958/59
225	Greenidge C.G.	Haynes D.L.	West Indies v New Zealand	Christchurch	1979/80
220	Sutcliffe B.	Taylor D.D.	Auckland v Canterbury	Auckland	1948/49
220	Bell M.D.	Jones R.A.	Wellington v Canterbury	Christchurch	2000/01
219*	Edgar B.A.	Vance R.H.	Wellington v Central Districts	Wellington	1987/88
218	Hadlee W.A.	Leggat J.G.	Canterbury v Wellington	Christchurch	1947/48
218	Dempsey D.A.	Hadlee B.G.	Canterbury v Otago	Christchurch	1980/81
215	Sinclair M.S.	How J.M.	Central Districts v Northern Districts	Napier	2004/05
215	Raval J.A.	How J.M.	Central Districts v Northern Districts	Nelson	2012/13
215	Guptill-Bunce M.L.	Raval J.A.	Auckland v Wellington	Wellington	2015/16
214	Woodfull W.M.	Ponsford W.H.	Australia v Otago	Dunedin	1927/28
214	Bolton B.A.	Dowling G.T.	Canterbury v Northern Districts	Christchurch	1959/60
214	Spearman C.M.	Twose R.G.	New Zealand v Zimbabwe	Auckland	1995/96
214	Brownlie D.G.	Wilson B.S.	Northern Districts v Otago	Hamilton	2014/15
213	Lawson R.A.	Bell M.D.	NZ Academy XI v Zimbabwe	Whangarei	1995/96
213	Gaffaney C.B.	Parlane M.E.	NZ Academy XI v Bangladesh	Christchurch	1997/98
211	Turner G.M.	Parker J.M.	New Zealand v MCC	Lord's	1973
211	Bell M.D.	Donaldson G.T.	Wellington v Central Districts	Wellington	2003/04
211	Brodie J.M.	Papps M.H.W.	Wellington v Canterbury	Rangiora	2012/13
209	Sutcliffe B.	Watt L.	Otago v Canterbury	Dunedin	1947/48

209	Harris B.Z.	Boyle D.J.	Canterbury v Otago	Christchurch	1991/92
208	Blunt R.C.	Worker R.V. de R.	Canterbury v MCC	Christchurch	1922/23
208	Athey C.W.J.	Robinson R.T.	England XI v Northern Districts	Hamilton	1987/88
207	Sadiq Mohammad	Zaheer Abbas	Pakistan v Wellington	Wellington	1972/73
202	Worker G.H.	Hay G.R.	Central Districts v Otago	Napier	2018/19
201	Anthony A.	Horspool E.	Auckland v Wellington	Auckland	1924/25
201	Astle T.D.	Papps M.H.W.	Canterbury v Wellington	Christchurch	2006/07

SECOND WICKET

317	Hart R.T.	Briasco P.S.	Central Districts v Canterbury	New Plymouth	1983/84
315*	Gibbs H.H.	Kallis J.H.	South Africa v New Zealand	Christchurch	1998/99
303	Dempster C.S.	Allcott C.F.W.	New Zealand v Warwickshire	Birmingham	1927
301	Flynn D.R.	Wilson B.S.	Northern Districts v Auckland	Hamilton	2012/13
287	Bell M.D.	Wells J.D.	Wellington v Auckland	Auckland	1997/98
279	Bell M.D.	Parlane M.E.	Wellington v Otago	Dunedin	2006/07
263	Greatbatch M.J.	Crowe M.D.	Central Districts v Northern Districts	Morrinsville	1986/87
256	Anderson R.W.	Edgar B.A.	New Zealand v Scotland	Dundee	1978
254*	Papps M.H.W.	Myburgh J.G.	Canterbury v Central Districts	Napier	2007/08
254	Burns K.J.	Rutherford K.R.	Otago v Wellington	Oamaru	1987/88
252	Baker W.A.	Beechey E.M.	Wellington v Auckland	Wellington	1918/19
251	Parlane N.R.	Merchant C.J.	Wellington v Otago	Wellington	2009/10
250	Bell M.D.	Sinclair M.S.	New Zealand A v Sri Lanka A	Queenstown	2003/04
248	Horne M.J.	Fleming S.P.	Southern v Pakistan A	Christchurch	1998/99
247	Cumming C.D.	Broom D.J.	Otago v Northern Districts	Whangarei	2009/10
245	Horne M.J.	Fleming S.P.	New Zealand v British Universities	Oxford	1999
244	Spearman C.M.	Sinclair M.S.	Central Districts v Northern Districts	Wanganui	1998/99
243	Papps M.H.W.	Stewart S.L.	Canterbury v Northern Districts	Hamilton	2006/07
242*	How J.M.	Sinclair M.S.	Central Districts v Otago	New Plymouth	2005/06
241	Franklin T.J.	Crowe J.J.	Auckland v Wellington	Wellington	1988/89
241	Wright J.G.	Jones A.H.	New Zealand v England	Wellington	1991/92
237	Gibson J.G.	Kuggeleijn C.M.	Northern Districts v Canterbury	Hamilton	1980/81
232	O'Donnell W.T.	O'Donnell R.R.	Auckland v Wellington	Auckland	2020/21
231	Carew M.C.	Nurse S.M.	West Indies v New Zealand	Christchurch	1968/69
229	Hemus L.G.	Midlane F.A.	Auckland v Wellington	Wellington	1918/19
227	Baker W.A.	Kortlang H.H.L.	Wellington v Otago	Dunedin	1923/24
227	Dobbs P.W.	Lamont M.J.	Otago v Auckland	Dunedin	1990/91
223	McIntosh T.G.	Jones R.A.	Auckland v West Indies	Auckland	2008/09
222	Warner P.F.	Fane F.L.	Lord Hawke's XI v Otago	Dunedin	1902/03
222	Crocker L.M.	Kuggeleijn C.M.	Northern Districts v Otago	Hamilton	1983/84
222	McCullum B.B.	Cumming C.D.	Otago v Auckland	Dunedin	2001/02
220	Macartney C.G.	Punch A.T.E.	NSW v Otago	Dunedin	1923/24
220	Richardson M.H.	Cumming C.D.	Otago v Northern Districts	Hamilton	2000/01
217	Redmond A.J.	Bracewell M.G.	Otago v Wellington	Wellington	2013/14
215	Bell M.D.	Wells J.D.	Wellington v Northern Districts	Hamilton	1998/99
215	Bell M.D.	Parlane M.E.	Wellington v Central Districts	Napier	2004/05
213	Barnett G.E.F.	Sinclair M.S.	Central Districts v Otago	New Plymouth	2005/06
212	Horspool E.	Snedden A.N.C.	Auckland v Victoria	Auckland	1924/25
212	McIntosh T.G.	Jones R.A.	Auckland v Wellington	Auckland	2009/10
212	Flynn D.R.	Carter J.F.	Northern Districts v Auckland	Auckland	2013/14
210	Hadlee W.A.	O'Brien F.P.	Canterbury v Otago	Christchurch	1940/41
210	Howarth G.P.	Crowe J.J.	New Zealand v West Indies	Kingston	1984/85
210	Compton N.R.D.	Trott I.J.L.	England v New Zealand	Wellington	2012/13
209*	Jones A.H.	Crowe M.D.	Wellington v Canterbury	Christchurch	1992/93
209	Wilson B.S.	Flynn D.R.	Northern Districts v Canterbury	Christchurch	2008/09
207*	Twose R.G.	Douglas M.W.	Central Districts v Auckland	Auckland	1991/92
207	Mills J.E.	Blunt R.C.	New Zealand v H.D.G.Leveson-Gower's XI	Scarborough	1927
207	Vaughan M.P.	Hussain N.	England v Canterbury	Christchurch	2001/02
206	Raman W.V.	Gursharan Singh	India v Otago	Dunedin	1989/90
204	Gavaskar S.M.	Amarnath S.	India v New Zealand	Auckland	1975/76
204	Ingram P.J.	Smith B.S.	Central Districts v Wellington	Wellington	2010/11
202	Naushad Ali	Saeed Ahmed	Pakistan v Canterbury	Christchurch	1964/65
200	Smith R.W.	Bilby G.P.	Wellington v Northern Districts	Whangarei	1973/74

THIRD WICKET

467	Jones A.H.	Crowe M.D.	New Zealand v Sri Lanka	Wellington	1990/91
445	Whitelaw P.E.	Carson W.N.	Auckland v Otago	Dunedin	1936/37
394*	Kennedy P.G.	Latham R.T.	Canterbury v Northern Districts	Rotorua	1990/91
346	Burnett G.P.	Verry R.A.	Wellington v Northern Districts	Hamilton	1991/92
306	Haig S.B.	Broom N.T.	Otago v Central Districts	Napier	2009/10
291	Bracewell M.G.	Broom N.T.	Otago v Wellington	Dunedin	2012/13
289	Burns J.A.	Smith S.P.D.	Australia v New Zealand	Christchurch	2015/16
287	Conway D.P.	Bracewell M.G.	Wellington v Auckland	Wellington	2020/21
278	Franklin T.J.	Patel D.N.	Auckland v Canterbury	Christchurch	1985/86
265	Horne M.J.	Barnes A.C.	Auckland v Bangladesh	Auckland	2001/02
264	Chappell I.M.	Chappell G.S.	Australia v New Zealand	Wellington	1973/74
264	Ingram P.J.	Sinclair M.S.	Central Districts v Northern Districts	Hamilton	2008/09
261*	Maynard M.P.	Thomson S.A.	Northern Districts v Auckland	Hamilton	1990/91
259	Papps M.H.W.	Fulton P.G.	Canterbury v Northern Districts	Christchurch	2008/09
258	Flynn D.R.	Popli B.	Northern Districts v Central Districts	Hamilton	2015/16
256	Papps M.H.W.	Ryder J.D.	Wellington v Central Districts	Wellington	2012/13
255	Lloyd C.H.	Davis C.A.	West Indies v South Island	Dunedin	1968/69
252*	Howarth G.P.	Roberts A.D.G.	Northern Districts v Pakistan	Gisborne	1978/79
248	Shoaib Mohammad	Javed Miandad	Pakistan v New Zealand	Auckland	1988/89
246	Rabone G.O.	Reid J.R.	New Zealand v Nottinghamshire	Nottingham	1949
246	Murray B.A.G.	Morrison J.F.M.	Wellington v Otago	Dunedin	1968/69
246	Parlane N.R.	Elliott G.D.	Wellington v Auckland	Auckland	2007/08
246	McIntosh T.G.	Raval J.A.	Auckland v Otago	Dunedin	2013/14
245	Crowe M.D.	Coney J.V.	New Zealand v South Australia	Adelaide	1985/86
244	Nicol R.J.	Vincent L.	Auckland v Otago	Auckland	2004/05
241	Wright J.G.	Crowe M.D.	New Zealand v West Indies	Wellington	1986/87
229	Miller L.S.M.	Sutcliffe B.	New Zealand v South Australia	Adelaide	1953/54
227	Rutherford K.R.	Blair B.R.	Otago v Central Districts	Alexandra	1988/89
226	Haynes D.L.	Richardson R.B.	West Indies v Shell XI	Napier	1986/87
224	Reid J.F.	Crowe M.D.	New Zealand v Australia	Brisbane	1985/86
224	Sinclair M.S.	Spearman C.M.	Central Districts v Auckland	Auckland	2003/04
224	Cachopa Carl	Sinclair M.S.	Central Districts v Wellington	Napier	2012/13
223	Smith C.J.P.	Wilson S.W.J.	Central Districts v Otago	Blenheim	1990/91
222*	Sutcliffe B.	Reid J.R.	New Zealand v India	New Delhi	1955/56
222	Snedden A.N.C.	Smith S.G.	Auckland v Hawke's Bay	Auckland	1920/21
221	Blunt R.C.	McMullan J.J.M.	Otago v Canterbury	Dunedin	1928/29
221	Lara B.C.	Adams J.C.	West Indies v New Zealand	Wellington	1994/95
220	Shoaib Mohammad	Javed Miandad	Pakistan v New Zealand	Wellington	1988/89
218	Woodfull W.M.	Schneider K.J.	Australia v New Zealand	Auckland	1927/28
217	Dobbs P.W.	Rutherford K.R.	Otago v Central Districts	Blenheim	1990/91
216*	Fulton P.G.	McClure K.J.	Canterbury v Otago	Christchurch	2015/16
216	Hemus L.G.	Smith S.G.	Auckland v Canterbury	Auckland	1919/20
214	Anthony A.	Gillespie H.D.	Auckland v Canterbury	Auckland	1929/30
213*	Williamson K.S.	Taylor L.R.P.L.	New Zealand v England	Hamilton	2019/20
213	Turner G.M.	Congdon B.E.	Otago v Wellington	Dunedin	1972/73
213	Jones A.H.	Crowe M.D.	New Zealand v Australia	Adelaide	1987/88
212	Booth B.C.	Burge P.J.P.	Australia B v New Zealand	Auckland	1966/67
211	McIntosh T.G.	Kitchen A.K.	Auckland v Canterbury	Auckland	2011/12
210	Howarth G.P.	Crowe M.D.	New Zealand v Essex	Chelmsford	1983
210	Edgar G.A.	Crowe M.D.	New Zealand v England	Lord's	1986
210	Smith B.F.	Douglas M.W.	Central Districts v Northern Districts	Taupo	2000/01
209	McCosker R.G.	Chappell G.S.	Australia v Wellington	Wellington	1976/77
208	Papps M.H.W.	McMillan C.D.	Canterbury v Central Districts	Christchurch	2006/07
206	Preston A.H.	Beck J.E.F.	Wellington v Canterbury	Christchurch	1955/56
204	Harford N.S.	Reid J.R.	New Zealand v Oxford University	Oxford	1958
204	Twose R.G.	Crowe M.D.	New Zealand v Indian Colts XI	Hyderabad	1995/96
204	Fleming S.P.	Styris S.B.	New Zealand v Bangladesh	Chittagong	2004/05
204	Wilson B.S.	Broom N.T.	Otago v Central Districts	Napier	2015/16
203*	Pocock B.A.	Parore A.C.	Auckland v Wellington	Auckland	1997/98
201	McLeod E.G.	Lamason J.R.	Wellington v Auckland	Wellington	1935/36
201	Raval J.A.	Munro C.	Auckland v Wellington	Auckland	2014/15

200	Smith G.C.	Kallis J.H.	South Africa v New Zealand	Dunedin	2011/12
200	Petersen A.N.	Duminy J.P.	South Africa v New Zealand	Wellington	2011/12

FOURTH WICKET

369	Williamson K.S.	Nicholls H.M.	New Zealand v Pakistan	Christchurch	2020/21
350	Mushtaq Mohammad	Asif Iqbal	Pakistan v New Zealand	Dunedin	1972/73
324	Reid J.R.	Wallace W.M.	New Zealand v Cambridge University	Cambridge	1949
310	Ryder J.D.	Parlane N.R.	Wellington v Central Districts	Palmerston North	2004/05
299	Wallace W.M.	Donnelly M.P.	New Zealand v Leicestershire	Leicester	1949
283	Flynn D.R.	Anderson C.J.	Northern Districts v Otago	Hamilton	2012/13
282	Wilkinson W.A.C.	Chapman A.P.F.	MCC v Canterbury	Christchurch	1922/23
280	Crowe J.J.	Patel D.N.	Auckland v Northern Districts	Auckland	1991/92
278	Roberts A.W.	Page M.L.	Canterbury v Wellington	Wellington	1931/32
276*	Crowe M.D.	Briasco P.S.	Central Districts v Canterbury	Christchurch	1986/87
274*	Mendis B.K.G.	Mathews A.D.	Sri Lanka v New Zealand	Wellington	2018/19
274	Jones R.A.	Mather S.R.	Wellington v Otago	Wellington	2000/01
273	McIntosh T.G.	Nicol R.J.	Auckland v Otago	Lincoln	2006/07
271	Taylor L.R.P.L.	Ryder J.D.	New Zealand v India	Napier	2008/09
266	Denness M.H.	Fletcher K.W.R.	England v New Zealand	Auckland	1974/75
259	Bradburn G.E.	Parlane M.E.	Northern Districts v Canterbury	Christchurch	1996/97
254	Reid J.R.	Miller L.S.M.	New Zealand v Natal	Durban	1953/54
252	Thomson S.A.	Young B.A.	Northern Districts v Auckland	Auckland	1990/91
243	Horne M.J.	Astle N.J.	New Zealand v Zimbabwe	Auckland	1997/98
241*	Jones R.A.	Young R.A.	Auckland v Canterbury	Auckland	2009/10
240	Fleming S.P.	McMillan C.D.	New Zealand v Sri Lanka	Colombo	1997/98
239	Beard N.B.	Broom N.T.	Otago v Auckland	Dunedin	2012/13
238	Pollard M.A.	Franklin J.E.C.	Wellington v Otago	Invercargill	2013/14
235	Burns K.J.	Hoskin R.N.	Otago v Northern Districts	Hamilton	1987/88
234	Smith B.S.	Worker G.H.	Central Districts v Otago	Napier	2015/16
229	Congdon B.E.	Hastings B.F.	New Zealand v Australia	Wellington	1973/74
222*	Gill S.	Vihari G.H.	India A v New Zealand A	Christchurch	2019/20
221	Williamson K.S.	McCullum B.B.	New Zealand v India	Auckland	2013/14
221	McClure K.J.	Carter L.J.	Canterbury v Wellington	Rangiora	2019/20
219	Vivian H.G.	Page M.L.	New Zealand v Oxford University	Oxford	1931
218	Crowe J.J.	Coney J.V.	New Zealand v Glamorgan	Swansea	1986
217	Bracewell M.G.	Blundell T.A.	Wellington v Auckland	Auckland	2020/21
216	Taylor L.R.P.L.	Nicholls H.M.	New Zealand v Bangladesh	Wellington	2018/19
214	Ransford V.S.	Lampard A.W.	Australia v New Zealand	Auckland	1920/21
214*	Papps M.H.W.	Kuggeleijn S.C.	Wellington v Central Districts	Wellington	2012/13
214	Munro C.	O'Donnell R.R.	Auckland v Central Districts	Napier	2014/15
214	Latham T.W.M.	Nicholls H.M.	New Zealand v Sri Lanka	Christchurch	2018/19
211*	Jones A.H.	Burns K.J.	Otago v Wellington	Wellington	1984/85
211	White D.J.	Young B.A.	Northern Districts v Auckland	Auckland	1992/93
210	Nicol R.J.	Munro C.	Auckland v Central Districts	Auckland	2016/17
208	Thomson S.A.	Maynard M.P.	Northern Districts v Wellington	Hamilton	1991/92
207	Midlane F.A.	Richardson C.A.	Wellington v Otago	Wellington	1899/00
207	Badcock F.T.	Lowry T.C.	Wellington v Auckland	Wellington	1927/28
207	Sulzberger G.P.	Penn A.J.	Central Districts v Otago	Napier	1995/96
206	McCullum S.J.	Dawson G.J.	Otago v Northern Districts	Dunedin	1983/84
206	Stewart A.J.	Hussain N.	England v New Zealand XI	Palmerston North	1996/97
206	McIntosh T.G.	Vincent L.	Auckland v Canterbury	Christchurch	2000/01
204	Harvey R.N.	Simpson R.B.	Australia B v Otago	Dunedin	1956/57
204	Jarvis T.W.	Thomson K.	Canterbury v Central Districts	Wanganui	1969/70
204	Redmond A.J.	Broom N.T.	Otago v Northern Districts	Hamilton	2006/07
203	Thomson S.A.	Maynard M.P.	Northern Districts v Otago	Hamilton	1991/92
200	Blair B.R.	Dawson G.J.	Otago v Central Districts	Dunedin	1982/83
200	McClure K.J.	McConchie C.E.	Canterbury v Auckland	Rangiora	2017/18

FIFTH WICKET

359	Shakib Al Hasan	Mushfiqur Rahim	Bangladesh v New Zealand	Wellington	2016/17
347*	Horne M.J.	Barnes A.C.	Auckland v Northern Districts	Auckland	2003/04
341	Larsen G.R.	McSweeney E.B.	Wellington v Central Districts	Levin	1987/88

319	Rutherford K.R.	Gray E.J.	NZ v DB Close's XI	Scarborough	1986
318	Mandeep Singh	Menaria A.L.	India A v New Zealand A	Lincoln	2012/13
301	Englefield J.I.	Taylor L.R.P.L.	Central Districts v Wellington	Palmerston North	2004/05
290	Harris C.Z.	Stead G.R.	Canterbury v Central Districts	Blenheim	1996/97
282	Franklin J.E.C.	Woodcock L.J.	Wellington v Auckland	Auckland	2008/09
266	Sutcliffe B.	Haig W.S.	Otago v Auckland	Dunedin	1949/50
258	Salim Malik	Inzamam-ul-Haq	Pakistan v New Zealand	Wellington	1993/94
258	McConchie C.E.	Ellis A.M.	Canterbury v Otago	Invercargill	2016/17
255	Taylor B.R.	Coney J.V.	Wellington v Otago	Dunedin	1972/73
253	Clarke M.J.	North M.J.	Australia v New Zealand	Wellington	2009/10
252*	Latham R.T.	Priest M.W.	Canterbury v Northern Districts	Christchurch	1988/89
252	Broom N.T.	Broom D.J.	Otago v Northern Districts	Queenstown	2010/11
244	Reid J.R.	Chapple M.E.	New Zealand v Western Province	Cape Town	1962/63
242	Hammond W.R.	Ames L.E.G.	England v New Zealand	Christchurch	1932/33
236*	Stewart S.L.	Brownlie D.G.	Canterbury v Northern Districts	Rangiora	2009/10
236	Harris C.Z.	Astle N.J.	Canterbury v Otago	Christchurch	1996/97
235*	Woodfull W.M.	Ransford V.S.	Victoria v New Zealand	Christchurch	1924/25
235*	Sulzberger G.P.	Ryder J.D.	Central Districts v Canterbury	Napier	2002/03
235	McClure K.J.	Ellis A.M.	Canterbury v Northern Districts	Hamilton	2015/16
235	Soumya Sarkar	Mahmudullah	Bangladesh v New Zealand	Hamilton	2018/19
234*	Scott V.J.	Morris J.B.	Auckland v Central Districts	Auckland	1951/52
233	Moloney D.A.R.	Kerr J.L.	New Zealand v England XI	Folkestone	1937
228	Raval J.A.	Hopkins G.J.	Auckland v Central Districts	Auckland	2008/09
226	Mitchell D.J.	Seifert T.L.	Northern Districts v Otago	Dunedin	2016/17
222	Astle N.J.	McMillan C.D.	New Zealand v Zimbabwe	Wellington	2000/01
222	Sinclair M.S.	van Wyk C.F.K.	Central Districts v Northern Districts	Gisborne	2011/12
219	Broom N.T.	Hopkins G.J.	Otago v Auckland	Lincoln	2006/07
216	Parlane N.R.	Franklin J.E.C.	Wellington v Auckland	Wellington	2005/06
215	Fawad Alam	Rohail Nazir	Pakistan A v New Zealand A	Whangarei	2020/21
213	Ritchie G.M.	Matthews G.R.J.	Australia v New Zealand	Wellington	1985/86
213	de Boorder D.C.	Kitchen A.K.	Otago v Northern Districts	Dunedin	2016/17
206	Hopkins G.J.	Kitchen A.K.	Auckland v Central Districts	Auckland	2009/10
205	Hay G.R.	Noema-Barnett K.	Central Districts v Otago	Alexandra	2018/19
203	Booth B.C.	Davies G.R.	Australia B v Central Districts	Palmerston North	1966/67
201	Alexander W.C.	Richardson V.Y.	Australia v Auckland	Auckland	1927/28
201	Burgess M.G.	Jarvis T.W.	Auckland v Central Districts	Auckland	1971/72

SIXTH WICKET

379*	Stewart S.L.	van Wyk C.F.K.	Canterbury v Central Districts	New Plymouth	2009/10
377	Munro C.	Cachopa Craig	Auckland v Wellington	Auckland	2012/13
365*	Williamson K.S.	Watling B-J.	New Zealand v Sri Lanka	Wellington	2014/15
352	McCullum B.B.	Watling B-J.	New Zealand v India	Wellington	2013/14
339	Guptill M.J.	McCullum B.B.	New Zealand v Bangladesh	Hamilton	2009/10
322	Orchard M.G.	Yovich J.A.F.	Northern Districts v Central Districts	Napier	2005/06
305	Carter L.J.	Fletcher C.D.	Canterbury v Otago	Christchurch	2020/21
293*	Fulton P.G.	Broom N.T.	Canterbury v Otago	Dunedin	2004/05
281	Thorpe G.P.	Flintoff A.	England v New Zealand	Christchurch	2001/02
269	Trumper V.T.	Hill C.	Australia v New Zealand	Wellington	1904/05
268	Chapman M.S.	Cleaver D.	New Zealand A v India A	Christchurch	2019/20
256	Martyn D.R.	Gilchrist A.C.	Australia v New Zealand	Wellington	2004/05
247	Cachopa Craig	Hopkins G.J.	Auckland v Wellington	Auckland	2013/14
247	Woodcock L.J.	Nofal M.J.	Wellington v Central Districts	Wellington	2017/18
246*	Crowe J.J.	Hadlee R.J.	New Zealand v Sri Lanka	Colombo	1986/87
240	Parfitt P.H.	Knight B.R.	England v New Zealand	Auckland	1962/63
238	McDonald R.	Cowley O.W.	Queensland v Hawke's Bay	Napier	1896/97
235	Sinclair M.S.	Griggs B.B.J.	Central Districts v Wellington	Wellington	2008/09
233	Crawford J.N.	Armstrong W.W.	Australia v New Zealand	Auckland	1913/14
232	Botham I.T.	Randall D.W.	England v New Zealand	Wellington	1983/84
230	Worker G.H.	Cleaver D.	Central Districts v Wellington	Napier	2015/16
226	Gray E.J.	Ormiston R.W.	Wellington v Central Districts	Wellington	1981/82
224	Schmulian B.D.	Bracewell D.A.J.	Central Districts v Northern Districts	Mt Maunganui	2017/18
220	Turner G.M.	Wadsworth K.J.	New Zealand v West Indies	Kingston	1971/72

220	Toynbee M.H.	Smith I.D.S.	Central Districts v Auckland	Napier	1982/83
218	Trego P.D.	van Wyk C.F.K.	Central Districts v Auckland	Napier	2013/14
217	Brownlie D.G.	Santner M.J.	Northern Districts v Central Districts	New Plymouth	2014/15
216	Hart M.N.	Marshall H.J.H.	Northern Districts v Central Districts	Napier	2004/05
216	Rutherford H.D.	de Boorder D.C.	Otago v Wellington	Dunedin	2011/12
212*	McMillan C.D.	Parore A.C.	New Zealand v President's XI	Jodhpur	1999/00
211	Guptill M.J.	de Grandhomme C.	Auckland v Canterbury	Rangiora	2011/12
209*	Parore A.C.	O'Dowd A.P.	Auckland v Otago	Dunedin	1991/92
209	Harris C.Z.	Redmond A.J.	Canterbury v Wellington	Rangiora	2001/02
205	Chapman M.S.	Horne B.J.	Auckland v Northern Districts	Auckland	2019/20
203	Ormiston R.W.	Coney J.V.	Wellington v Central Districts	New Plymouth	1982/83
202	de Grandhomme C.	Munro C.	Auckland v Canterbury	Auckland	2011/12
201	Harris C.Z.	Parore A.C	New Zealand v Orange Free State	Bloemfontein	1994/95
201	Tendulkar S.R.	Mongia N.R.	India v Central Districts	Napier	1998/99
201	Neesham J.D.S.	Watling B-J.	New Zealand v West Indies	Kingston	2014
200	Chanderpaul S.	Ramdin D.	West Indies v New Zealand	Hamilton	2013/14

SEVENTH WICKET

265	Powell J.L.	Dorreen N.	Canterbury v Otago	Christchurch	1929/30
261	Watling B-J.	Santner M.J.	New Zealand v England	Mt Maunganui	2019/20
261	Campbell A.D.R.	Strang P.A.	Zimbabwe v Canterbury	Timaru	1997/98
250	Nevin C.J.	Walker M.D.J.	Wellington v Otago	Wellington	2003/04
248	Yousuf Youhana	Saqlain Mushtaq	Pakistan v New Zealand	Christchurch	2000/01
246	McGlew D.J.	Murray A.R.A.	South Africa v New Zealand	Wellington	1952/53
244	Patrick W.R.	Allcott C.F.W.	New Zealand v NSW	Sydney	1925/26
241	Astle N.J.	Priest M.W.	Canterbury v Wellington	Christchurch	1994/95
229	Schneider K.J.	Oldfield W.A.S.	Australia v Canterbury	Christchurch	1927/28
225	Cairns C.L.	Oram J.D.P.	New Zealand v South Africa	Auckland	2003/04
224	Scott V.J.	Matheson A.M.	Auckland v Canterbury	Auckland	1937/38
219	Yuile B.W.	Hampton B.L.	Central Districts v Canterbury	Napier	1967/68
217	Walters K.D.	Gilmour G.J.	Australia v New Zealand	Christchurch	1976/77
212	Katich S.M.	Gilchrist A.C.	Australia v New Zealand	Christchurch	2004/05
205	Germon L.K.	Priest M.W.	Canterbury v Northern Districts	Christchurch	1991/92
205*	Hay G.R.	Diamanti B.J.	Central Districts v Canterbury	Rangiora	2008/09
192	Brown S.W.	Parore A.C.	Auckland v Central Districts	Auckland	1990/91
191	Wright J.G.	Smith I.D.S.	New Zealand v Western Australia	Perth	1989/90
190	Smith N.G.	Rippon M.J.G.	Otago v Northern Districts	Dunedin	2019/20
187	vanWyk C.F.K.	Bracewell D.A.J.	Central Districts v Wellington	Napier	2010/11
186	Lees W.K.	Hadlee R.J.	New Zealand v Pakistan	Karachi	1976/77
186	Leggat R.I.	Hadlee D.R.	Canterbury v Sri Lanka	Christchurch	1982/83
186	Ryder J.D.	Vettori D.L.	New Zealand v India	Hamilton	2008/09
184*	Bull C.L.	Isherwood B.P.	Canterbury v Central Districts	Nelson	1971/72
183	Oram J.D.P.	Vettori D.L.	New Zealand v South Africa	Centurion	2005/06
182	Sutcliffe B.	Gilbertson A.W.	Otago v Canterbury	Christchurch	1952/53
182	Weston T.I.	Thompson E.P.	Central Districts v Canterbury	Christchurch	2005/06
179	Griggs B.B.J.	Furlong C.J.M.	Central Districts v Northern Districts	Hamilton	2001/02
179	McCullum B.B.	Neesham J.D.S.	New Zealand v India	Wellington	2013/14
178	Ellis A.M.	Anderson F.G.	Canterbury v Wellington	Wellington	2014/15
177*	Barnes A.C.	Mills J.M.	Auckland v Otago	Alexandra	1995/96
177	Bruce T.C.	Small B.J.	Central Districts v Northern Districts	Hamilton	2015/16
176	Rabone G.O.	Mooney F.L.H.	New Zealand v MCC	Lord's	1949
176	Mills S.M.	Nevin C.J.	Wellington v Canterbury	Christchurch	2006/07

EIGHTH WICKET

433†	Trumper V.T.	Sims A.	Sims' Australian XI v Canterbury	Christchurch	1913/14
256	Fleming S.P.	Franklin J.E.C.	New Zealand v South Africa	Cape Town	2005/06
253	Astle N.J.	Parore A.C.	New Zealand v Australia	Perth	2001/02
220	Wiseman P.J.	Hiini B.C.	Canterbury v Northern Districts	Hamilton	2005/06
215	Murray J.R.	Cummins A.C.	West Indies v Otago	Dunedin	1994/95
210	Stead G.R.	Bond S.E.	Canterbury v Northern Districts	Christchurch	2004/05
199	Reifer R.A.	Shepherd R.	West Indies A v New Zealand A	Mt Maunganui	2020/21
190*	Mills J.E.	Allcott C.F.W.	New Zealand v Civil Service	Chiswick	1927

189	Carson W.N.	Matheson A.M.	Auckland v Wellington	Auckland	1938/39
185	Nash D.J.	Mills K.D.	Auckland v Wellington	Wellington	2000/01
180	Twose R.G.	Goodson M.C.	Wellington v Otago	Dunedin	1994/95
173	Smith I.D.S.	Robertson G.K.	Central Districts v Northern Districts	Hamilton	1982/83
172*	Walker B.G.K.	Mills K.D.	Auckland v Wellington	Auckland	1999/00
167	van Wyk C.F.K.	McCone R.J.	Canterbury v Otago	Christchurch	2008/09
166	Hadlee R.J.	Hadlee D.R.	Canterbury v Auckland	Christchurch	1983/84
165*	Eckhold A.G.	Crawford J.N.	Otago v Wellington	Wellington	1914/15
163	McGlashan P.D.	Aldridge G.W.	Northern Districts v Canterbury	Hamilton	2008/09
161	McSweeney E.B.	Snedden M.C.	Shell XI v West Indies	Napier	1986/87
159	Diamanti B.J.	Sherlock R.R.	Central Districts v Canterbury	Napier	2007/08
157	McLaren A.C.	McLean J.F.	MCC v New Zealand	Wellington	1922/23
154	James K.C.	Badcock F.T.	Wellington v Canterbury	Christchurch	1926/27
153	Nicol R.J.	Young R.A.	Auckland v Canterbury	Auckland	2001/02
152	Bradburn G.E.	Doull S.B.	Northern Districts v Canterbury	Christchurch	1991/92
152	Marshall J.A.H.	Orchard M.G.	Northern Districts v Wellington	Hamilton	2006/07

† *world record*

NINTH WICKET

239	Cave H.B.	Leggat I.B.	Central Districts v Otago	Dunedin	1952/53
225	Woodcock L.J.	Tugaga M.J.	Wellington v Central Districts	Wellington	2009/10
209	Wiseman P.J.	Martin B.P.	New Zealand A v Sri Lanka A	Christchurch	2003/04
208	McSkimming W.C.	Scott B.E.	Otago v Auckland	Auckland	2004/05
204	Horne B.J.	Ferns D.K.	Auckland v Otago	Auckland	2020/21
188	Parlane N.R.	Tuffey D.R.	Northern Districts v Wellington	Wellington	1999/00
185	Maynard M.P.	Doull S.B.	Northern Districts v Auckland	Auckland	1991/92
182*	Germon L.K.	Ford R.M.	Canterbury v Wellington	Christchurch	1989/90
170*	Hart M.N.	Yovich J.A.F.	Northern Districts v South Africa	Hamilton	1998/99
163*	Cowdrey M.C.	Smith A.C.	England v New Zealand	Wellington	1962/63
162	Bracewell D.A.J.	Sodhi I.S.	New Zealand A v India A	Visakhapatnam	2013/14
151	Young R.A.	Morgan G.J.	Auckland v Northern Districts	Auckland	2007/08
139	Hart R.G.	Tait A.R.	Northern Districts v Wellington	Gisborne	1996/97
136	Smith I.D.S.	Snedden M.C.	New Zealand v India	Auckland	1989/90
135	Hart R.G.	Penn A.J.	Central v Northern	Rangiora	1998/99
134	Wilson J.W.	Mallender N.A.	Otago v Canterbury	Christchurch	1992/93
130*	de Boorder D.C.	McSkimming W.C.	Otago v Wellington	Queenstown	2010/11
127	Mooney F.L.H.	Buchan R.A.	Wellington v Auckland	Wellington	1943/44
125	Borthwick S.G.	McPeake I.G.	Wellington v Canterbury	Christchurch	2015/16
122	Schuster H.T.	Cunis R.S.	Auckland v Wellington	Wellington	1964/65
121	Cheetham J.E.	Murray A.R.A.	South Africa v Canterbury	Christchurch	1952/53
118	Coney J.V.	Cairns B.L.	New Zealand v England	Wellington	1983/84
116	Nevin C.J.	Davis H.T.	Wellington v Auckland	Auckland	1995/96
115	Robertson G.K.	Hart R.T.	Central Districts v Otago	Oamaru	1985/86
115	Hopkins G.J.	Ellis A.M.	Canterbury v Auckland	Auckland	2002/03

TENTH WICKET

184	Blunt R.C.	Hawksworth W.	Otago v Canterbury	Christchurch	1931/32
160	Germon L.K.	Wisneski W.A.	Canterbury v Northern Districts	Rangiora	1997/98
151	Hastings B.F.	Collinge R.O.	New Zealand v Pakistan	Auckland	1972/73
139	McClenaghan M.J.	Sandhu R.S.	Auckland v Northern Districts	Auckland	2016/17
138	James K.C.	Brice A.W.S.	Wellington v Otago	Wellington	1926/27
134	Worker G.H.	Mathieson A.M.	Central Districts v Wellington	Nelson	2015/16
133	Bartlett G.A.	Colquhoun I.A.	Central Districts v Auckland	Auckland	1959/60
127	Watling B-J.	Boult T.A.	New Zealand v Bangladesh	Chittagaong	2013/14
124	Bracewell J.G.	Boock S.L.	New Zealand v Australia	Sydney	1985/86
123	Brice A.W.S.	Beard T.	Wellington v Otago	Wellington	1927/28
119	Carson W.N.	Cowie J.	Auckland v Otago	Auckland	1937/38
118	Astle N.J.	Cairns C.L.	New Zealand v England	Christchurch	2001/02
113*	McGlashan P.D.	Aldridge G.W.	Northern Districts v Wellington	Wellington	2005/06
113	Mooney F.L.H.	Knapp E.C.V.	Wellington v Auckland	Wellington	1943/44
113	McKay A.J.	Gillespie M.R.	Wellington v Canterbury	Rangiora	2012/13
107	Motz R.C.	Cameron F.J.	New Zealand v Worcestershire	Worcester	1965

106*	Astle N.J.	Morrison D.K.	New Zealand v England	Auckland	1996/97
105	Cherry R.W.	Torrance R.C.	Otago v Canterbury	Christchurch	1925/26
104	James K.C.	Massey H.B.	Wellington v Australia	Wellington	1927/28
104	van Beek L.V.	Williams W.S.A.	Canterbury v Otago	Christchurch	2015/16
103	Kelly P.J.	Troup G.B.	Auckland v Northern Districts	Auckland	1985/86
102	Craig M.D.	Duffy J.A.	Otago v Northern Districts	Dunedin	2014/15
101	Astle N.J.	Owens M.B.	Canterbury v Northern Districts	Hamilton	1994/95

Hundred Partnership for the First Wicket in Both Innings

154 & 155	Shepherd J.S.F.	Worker R.V. de.R.	Otago v Wellington	Dunedin	1923/24
220 & 286	Taylor D.D.	Sutcliffe B.	Auckland v Canterbury	Auckland	1948/49
102 & 155	Blair W.L.	Turner G.M.	Otago v Auckland	Auckland	1972/73
172 & 148	Briasco P.S.	Smith C.J.P.	Central Districts v Auckland	New Plymouth	1985/86
107	Broad B.C.	Moxon M.D.	England XI v Northern Districts	Hamilton	1987/88
208	Athey C.W.J.	Robinson R.T.			
109 & 111	Wealleans K.A.	White D.J.	Northern Districts v India	Hamilton	1989/90
116 & 102	Greatbatch M.J.	Latham R.T.	New Zealand v Zimbabwe	Bulawayo	1992/93
145 & 131	Lawson R.A.	Gaffaney C.B.	Otago v Wellington	Wellington	1996/97
118* & 179	Twose R.G.	Bell M.D.	Wellington v Central Districts	Wellington	1997/98
102 & 112	Spearman C.M.	Kelly D.P.	Central Districts v Wellington	New Plymouth	1999/00
220	Bell M.D.	Jones R.A.	Wellington v Canterbury	Christchurch	2000/01
127	Nevin C.J.	Jones R.A.			
141	Cumming C.D.	Mohammad Wasim	Otago v Wellington	Wellington	2002/03
147	Gaffaney C.B.	Cumming C.D.			
104 & 118	Richardson M.H.	McIntosh T.G.	Auckland v Northern Districts	Auckland	2002/03
169 & 121*	Raval J.A.	McIntosh T.G.	Auckland v Wellington	Auckland	2009/10
227 & 133	Rutherford H.D.	Wilson B.S.	Otago v Central Districts	Nelson	2016/17

HIGHEST PARTNERSHIPS BY WICKET

1st	432	Papps M.H.W. & Woodcock L.J.	Wellington v Auckland	Wellington	2017/18
2nd	317	Hart R.T. & Briasco P.S.	Central Districts v Canterbury	New Plymouth	1983/84
3rd	467	Jones A.H. & Crowe M.D.	New Zealand v Sri Lanka	Wellington	1990/91
4th	369	Williamson K.S. & Nicholls H.M.	New Zealand v Pakistan	Christchurch	2020/21
5th	359	Shakib Al Hasan & Mushfiqur Rahim	Bangladesh v New Zealand	Wellington	2016/17
6th	379*	Stewart S.L. & van Wyk C.F.K.	Canterbury v Central Districts	New Plymouth	2009/10
7th	265	Powell J.L. & Dorreen N.	Canterbury v Otago	Christchurch	1929/30
8th	433	Trumper V.T. & Sims A.	Sims' Australian XI v Canterbury	Christchurch	1913/14
9th	239	Cave H.B. & Leggat I.B.	Central Districts v Otago	Dunedin	1952/53
10th	184	Blunt R.C. & Hawksworth W.	Otago v Canterbury	Christchurch	1931/32

HIGHEST PARTNERSHIPS BY RUNS

	wkt				
467	3rd	Jones A.H. & Crowe M.D.	New Zealand v Sri Lanka	Wellington	1990/91
445	3rd	Whitelaw P.E. & Carson W.N.	Auckland v Otago	Dunedin	1936/37
433	8th	Trumper V.T. & Sims A.	Sims' Australian XI v Canterbury	Christchurch	1913/14
432	1st	Papps M.H.W. & Woodcock L.J.	Wellington v Auckland	Wellington	2017/18
428	1st	Ingram P.J. & How J.M.	Central Districts v Wellington	Wellington	2009/10
394*	3rd	Kennedy P.G. & Latham R.T.	Canterbury v Northern Districts	Rotorua	1990/91
387	1st	Turner G.M. & Jarvis T.W.	New Zealand v West Indies	Georgetown	1971/72
379*	6th	Stewart S.L. & van Wyk C.F.K.	Canterbury v Central Districts	New Plymouth	2009/10
377	6th	Munro C. & Cachopa Craig	Auckland v Wellington	Auckland	2012/13
373	1st	Sutcliffe B. & Watt L.	Otago v Auckland	Auckland	1950/51

FAMILIES IN FIRST-CLASS CRICKET

Four Generations

Snedden A.N.C.	(A)	Snedden W.N.	(A)	Snedden M.C.	(A)	Snedden M.W.	(W)

Great-grandfather and Great-grandson

Orchard S.A.	(C)	Orchard M.G.	(ND)

Three Generations

Anderson W.M.	(C)	Anderson R.W.	(C, ND, O, CD)	Anderson T.R.	(CD)
*Blair J.R.	(O)	Blair R.A.J.	(O)	Blair W.L. Blair B.R.	(O) (O, ND)
Burton H.G.E.L.	(W)	Burton H.E.L.	(W, A)	Burton J.E.L.	(W)
*Burtt N.V.	(C)	Burtt J.W.	(C, CD)	Burtt L.M.	(C)
Smith F.A.	(C)	Smith F.B.	(C)	Smith G.B.	(C)
*Carson W.	(O)	Carson W.N.	(A)	Carson J.R.	(A, ND)

** J.R. Blair is the uncle of R.A.J. Blair. The Carsons are uncles and nephews. J.W. Burtt is the uncle of L.M. Burtt.*

Grandfather and Grandson

Anderson I.P.	(C)	Anderson F.G.	(C)
Dowker R.T.	(C)	Wheeler B.M.	(CD)
Guillen S.C.	(C)	van Beek L.V.	(C, W)
Milnes L.A.	(O)	Milnes G.S.	(CD)
Pritchard T.L.	(W)	Meiring D.T.	(CD)
Roberts H.	(W)	du Chateau V.H.	(W)
Rapley A.F.	(C)	Sheat F.W.	(C)

Father and Three Sons

Cotterill A.J.	(C)	Cotterill A.K.	(HB)	Cotterill B.W.	(HB)	Cotterill G.R.	(HB)
Hadlee W.A.	(C, O)	Hadlee B.G.	(C)	Hadlee D.R.	(C)	Hadlee R.J.	(C)

Father and Two Sons

Blacklock J.W.	(W)	Blacklock C.P.	(W)	Blacklock J.P.	(W)
Blair R.A.J.	(O)	Blair W.L.	(O)	Blair B.R.	(O, ND)
Crowe D.W.	(W,C)	Crowe M.D.	(A, CD, W)	Crowe J.J.	(A, SA)
Garrard C.W.	(C)	Garrard W.R.	(A)	Garrard D.R.	(A)
Furlong B.D.M.	(CD)	Furlong J.B.M.	(CD)	Furlong C.J.M.	(CD)
Harris P.G.Z.	(C)	Harris B.Z.	(C, O)	Harris C.Z.	(C)
Howell J.H.	(CD)	Howell L.G.	(C, CD, A, ND)	Howell G.A.	(C, W)
McCullum S.J.	(O)	McCullum B.B.	(O, C)	McCullum N.L.	(O)
McVicar A.C.	(Minor Assocs)	McVicar S.A.	(W)	McVicar C.C.	(CD)
Puna N.	(ND)	Puna K.N.	(ND)	Puna A.	(ND)
Reaney P.S.	(HB)	Reaney H.E.I.	(W)	Reaney T.P.L.	(W, CD)

Father and One Son

Airey W.F.	(W)	Airey D.M.L.	(W)
Aldridge C.W.	(C)	Aldridge G.W.	(ND)
Allen R.	(W)	Allen G.S.	(W)
Alpe S.	(A, C, W)	Alpe F.G.	(W)
Andrews S.	(C)	Andrews B.	(C, CD, O)
Astle A.M.	(CD)	Astle T.D.	(C)
Baker J.C.	(O)	Clark J.B.	(O)

Barclay W.S.	(W)	Barclay C.W.	(CD)
Barton P.H.	(ND, O)	Barton H.D.	(A, C)
Beard D.D.	(W, CD, ND)	Beard D.A.	(ND)
Blackmore J.H.	(ND)	Blackmore S.J.	(W)
Boyle J.G.	(C)	Boyle J.C.T.	(C)
Bracewell B.P.	(CD, O, ND)	Bracewell D.A.J.	(CD)
Bracewell M.A.	(O)	Bracewell M.G.	(O, W)
Bradburn W.P.	(ND)	Bradburn G.E.	(ND)
Burgess G.C.	(A)	Burgess M.G.	(A)
Burtt N.V.	(C)	Burtt J.W.	(C, CD)
Cairns B.L.	(CD, O, ND)	Cairns C.L.	(ND, C)
Campbell K.O.	(O)	Campbell P.A.	(O)
Carter R.M.	(C)	Carter L.J.	(C)
Child E.L.	(A, ND)	Child M.J.	(ND)
Clark L.G.	(O)	Clark L.A.	(W, O, A)
Collins W.E.	(W)	Collins D.C.	(W)
Cooper B.G.	(ND)	Cooper H.R.	(ND)
Cuff L.A.	(C, A)	Cuff A.G.	(Tasmania)
Cunis R.S.	(A, ND)	Cunis S.J.	(C)
Dawson G.J.	(O)	Dawson G.J.	(C)
Douglas G.W.	(CD)	Douglas M.W.	(CD, W)
Edgar A.J.	(W)	Edgar B.A.	(W)
Freeman T.A.	(O)	Freeman B.T.	(O)
Fulton F.	(O, HB)	Fulton P.R.	(HB)
Gasson E.A. snr	(C)	Gasson E.A. jnr	(C)
Gearry G.N.	(C)	Gearry R.M.	(C, CD)
Gedye A.E.	(W)	Gedye S.G.	(A)
Gilbertson J.	(S)	Gilbertson A.W.	(O)
Greenfield A.	(N)	Greenfield F.E.	(N)
Hartland I.R.	(C)	Hartland B.R.	(C)
Hastings B.F.	(W, CD, C)	Hastings M.A.	(C)
Hay W.P.C.	(A)	Hay S.C.	(A)
Hill A.J.	(CD)	Hill J.V.	(CD)
Hill J.	(O)	Hill R.J.	(O)
Hoar F.R.	(W)	Hoar N.R.	(W)
Holden W.J.	(O)	Holden A.C.	(O)
Horne P.A.	(A)	Horne B.J.	(A)
Howden C.E.	(O)	Howden C.P.	(O)
Ibadulla K.	(O)	Ibadulla K.B.K.	(O)
Jefferson R.G.	(O, W)	Jefferson M.R.	(W, ND)
Kelly J.W.H.	(W)	Kelly P.J.	(A)
Kerr A.C.	(A)	Kerr A.C.	(A)
Kuggeleijn C.M.	(ND)	Kuggeleijn S.C.	(W, ND)
Lankham G.	(A)	Lankham W.	(A)
Latham R.T.	(C)	Latham T.W.M.	(C)
Lowry T.H.	(HB)	Lowry T.C.	(A, W)
McEwan P.E.	(C)	McEwan M.B.	(C, W, A)
McGirr W.P.	(W)	McGirr H.M.	(W)
McKnight S.G.	(O)	McKnight K.J.	(O)
McKenzie N.M.	(O)	McKenzie M.N.	(C, O)
Mills G.	(A, HB, O)	Mills J.E.	(A)
Monaghan H.W.	(W, C)	Monaghan D.W.	(SI Army)
Morgan H.A.	(W)	Morgan R.G.	(ND, A)
Murdoch D.H.	(O)	Murdoch G.H.	(O)
Newman A.	(W)	Newman P.A.	(CD)
North T.H.	(C)	North R.H.	(WC)

Nuttall A.J.	(C)	Nuttall E.J.	(C)
O'Brien J.J.	(HB)	O'Brien M.A.	(W)
Oakley J.H.	(W)	Oakley D.F.	(W)
Ollivier A.M.	(C)	Ollivier K.M.	(C)
Ongley A.M.	(HB)	Ongley J.A.	(W, CD)
Parker N.M.	(O, C)	Parker M.M.	(O)
Postles A.J.	(A)	Postles B.J.	(A)
Pringle M.R.	(A)	Pringle O.M.R.	(A)
Redmond R.E.	(W, A)	Redmond A.J.	(C, O)
Rees W.L.	(A)	Rees A.W.	(A, HB)
Reese T.W.	(C)	Reese D.W.	(C)
Reid J.R.	(W, O)	Reid R.B.	(W, A)
Roberts A.	(W)	Roberts S.A.	(A)
Roberts H.	(W)	Roberts E.J.	(W)
Rutherford K.R.	(O)	Rutherford H.D.	(O)
Sale E.V.	(A)	Sale V.S.	(A)
Sears M.J.	(W)	Sears B.V.	(W)
Standidge J.A.	(W)	Standidge P.H.	(W)
Stead D.W.	(C)	Stead G.R.	(C)
Stoyanoff P.A.	(U23)	Stoyanoff B.P.	(CD)
Tindill E.W.T.	(W)	Tindill P.	(W)
Tuke C.L.	(HB)	Tuke H.L.	(HB)
Vance R.A.	(W)	Vance R.H.	(W)
Vivian H.G.	(A)	Vivian G.E.	(A)
Wallace W.M.	(A)	Wallace G.M.	(A)
Ward J.T.	(C)	Ward B.J.	(C)
Wilding F.	(C)	Wilding A.F.	(C)
Wright G.T.	(C)	Wright J.G.	(ND, C, A)

Father and Son in Same First-class Match

Reese T.W. & Reese D.W.	Canterbury v Otago	Dunedin	1917/18

Five Brothers

Cotterill A.J. (C) Cotterill C.N. (HB) Cotterill E.J. (C, A) Cotterill H. (C) Cotterill W.J. (C)

Four Brothers

Bayly A.	(T)	Bayly F.	(T)	Bayly G.T.	(T)	Bayly H.	(T)
Bracewell B.P.	(CD, O, ND)	Bracewell D.W.	(CD, C)	Bracewell J.G.	(O, A)	Bracewell M.A.	(O)
Mills E.	(A)	Mills G.	(A, HB, O)	Mills I.	(A)	Mills W.	(T, A)

Three Brothers

Alloo A.P.	(O)	Alloo A.W.	(O)	Alloo H.C.	(O)
Blacklock A.	(W)	Blacklock J.W.	(W)	Blacklock R.V.	(W)
Cachopa B.	(A, C)	Cachopa Carl	(A, CD)	Cachopa Craig	(W, A)
Carlton W.	(A, C)	Carlton A.R.	(Vic)	Carlton J.	(Vic)
Cotterill A.K.	(HB)	Cotterill B.W.	(HB)	Cotterill G.R.	(HB)
Eden J.	(N)	Eden T.G.	(N)	Eden W.	(N)
Fowler G.	(N)	Fowler L.A.	(N)	Fowler S.	(N)
Gore A.H.	(W, HB)	Gore C.S.	(W)	Gore R.	(W)
Hadlee B.G.	(C)	Hadlee D.R.	(C)	Hadlee R.J.	(C)
Harman A.F.G.	(C)	Harman R.D.	(C)	Harman T.D.	(C)
Knapp C.H.	(N)	Knapp K.J.	(N)	Knapp W.H.	(N)
Lusk Hugh B.	(A, HB)	Lusk R.B.	(T)	Lusk W.N.B.	(A)

Mace C.	(O)	Mace H.	(W)	Mace J.	(O)
McCormick A.D.	(O)	McCormick C.E.	(A)	McCormick E.	(A)
Meldrum A.L.	(A)	Meldrum D.	(A)	Meldrum W.	(A)
Newman A.	(W)	Newman J.	(C, W)	Newman S.	(W)
Parker K.J.	(A)	Parker J.M.	(ND)	Parker N.M.	(O, C)
Reese D.	(C)	Reese J.B.	(C)	Reese T.W.	(C)
Ridley A.E.	(C)	Ridley H.C.	(C)	Ridley R.A.	(C)
Salmon I.J.	(W)	Salmon J.A.N.	(W)	Salmon W.J.	(W, HB, T)
Tucker K.H.	(W)	Tucker S.J.	(W)	Tucker W.C.	(T)
Williams A.M.	(HB)	Williams G.C.	(HB)	Williams N.T.	(A)

Two Brothers

Aberhart D.C.	(CD, C)	Aberhart W.M.	(W)
Alabaster G.D.	(O, C, ND)	Alabaster J.C.	(O)
Austin G.G.	(O)	Austin T.T.L.	(O)
Baker E.G.H.	(W)	Baker W.A.	(W)
Bannerman J.W.H.	(S)	Bannerman W.E.	(O)
Barton P.H.	(ND, O)	Barton R.H.	(ND)
Beal C.E.	(O, C)	Beal W.M.	(O)
Beuth D.	(CD)	Beuth A.J.	(ND)
Bigg-Wither A.	(N)	Bigg-Wither J.	(N)
Billcliff I.S.	(O, W, A)	Billcliff M.R.	(O)
Bishop H.A.	(HB, C)	Bishop R.E.	(HB)
Blacklock C.P.	(W)	Blacklock J.P.	(W)
Blair B.R.	(O, ND)	Blair W.L.	(O)
Blakely D.J.	(O)	Blakely J.W.	(O)
Blamires E.O.	(W, O)	Blamires H.L.	(HB)
Boddington E.R.	(N, W)	Boddington H.A.	(N, O)
Boult J.J.	(ND)	Boult T.A.	(ND)
Boyle D.J.	(C)	Boyle J.G.	(W, C)
Broad C.H.	(N)	Broad E.W.	(N)
Broom D.J.	(O)	Broom N.T.	(C, O)
Burtt N.V.	(C)	Burtt T.B.	(C)
Cairns A.E.	(O)	Cairns H.W.	(O)
Cameron D.S.	(O)	Cameron H.R.	(O)
Cederwall B.W.	(W)	Cederwall G.N.	(W)
Chadwick C.S.	(O)	Chadwick L.N.	(O)
Clarke D.B.	(A, ND)	Clarke D.S.	(ND)
Collins J.U.	(N, C)	Collins W.E.	(W)
Coney C.J.	(W)	Coney J.V.	(W)
Cornelius C.J.	(C)	Cornelius W.A.	(C)
Cresswell A.E.	(W, CD)	Cresswell G.F.	(W, CD)
Cross C.S.	(N, W)	Cross W.H.S.	(N)
Crowe J.J.	(A, South Australia)	Crowe M.D.	(A, CD, W, Somerset)
Cummings E.M.	(O)	Cummings G.B.	(O)
Dacre C.C.R.	(A)	Dacre L.M.	(A)
Doull L.J.	(W)	Doull S.B.	(ND)
Dryden C.H.	(W)	Dryden W.E.	(W)
Dufaur E.T.	(A)	Dufaur P.P.R.	(A)
Duffy J.A.	(O)	Duffy R.M.	(O)
Farrant A.J.	(C)	Farrant D.G.	(C)
Fenwick F.F.	(O)	Fenwick H.S.	(C)
Findlay J.L.	(C)	Findlay J.W.	(W)
Fisher A.H.	(O)	Fisher R.L.	(C)
Frankish E.H.	(C)	Frankish F.S.	(C)
Frith C.	(C, O)	Frith W.	(C, O, W)

Fulton F.	(O, HB)	Fulton J.C.	(O)
Fulton D.H.	(C)	Fulton P.G.	(C)
Furlong C.J.M.	(CD)	Furlong J.B.M.	(CD)
Garrard D.R.	(A)	Garrard W.R.	(A)
Gatenby D.J.	(C)	Gatenby P.R.	(Tasmania)
Gilbertson J.	(S)	Gilbertson J.H.	(S)
Godby H.E.	(O)	Godby M.J.	(O, C)
Graham A.C.	(O)	Graham C.G.	(O)
Hamilton A.J.	(S)	Hamilton D.C.	(S)
Hampton B.L.	(CD)	Hampton I.R.	(CD)
Harris B.Z.	(C, O)	Harris C.Z.	(C)
Hart M.N.	(ND)	Hart R.G.	(ND)
Hatch R.K.	(W)	Hatch R.J.	(W)
Hatwell B.J.	(ND)	Hatwell J.G.	(ND)
Hay T.D.B.	(A)	Hay W.P.C.	(A)
Hewat D.F.	(W)	Hewat R.	(O)
Hickson H.C.	(W)	Hickson W.R.S.	(W)
Hindmarsh H.S.W.	(HB)	Hindmarsh J.S.	(HB)
Holdship A.R.	(W)	Holdship W.E.J.	(Middlesex)
Horne M.J.	(A, O)	Horne P.A.	(A)
Howarth G.P.	(A, ND, Surrey)	Howarth H.J.	(A)
Howell L.G.	(C, CD, A, ND)	Howell G.A.	(C, W)
Howden A.M.	(A)	Howden C.E.	(O)
Labatt A.B.M.	(C, A)	Labatt F.H.D.	(C)
Lash E.G.	(T)	Lash F.W.	(W)
Lynch D.J.F.	(A)	Lynch R.F.	(W)
Lynch R.K.	(A)	Lynch S.M.	(A)
McCullum B.B.	(O, C)	McCullum N.L.	(O)
McVicar S.A.	(W)	McVicar C.C.	(CD)
Marshall J.M.	(T)	Marshall P.	(A)
Marshall J.A.H.	(ND)	Marshall H.J.H.	(ND, Glos, W)
Martin J.H.	(HB)	Martin H.	(HB)
Matthias H.R.	(C)	Matthias R.B.	(C)
Morris J.B.	(A)	Morris P.P.W.	(A)
Naughton D.O.	(W)	Naughton M.P.	(W)
Neill R.	(A)	Neill T.	(A)
Nicholson C.R.	(C, O)	Nicholson K.A.	(O)
O'Donnell R.R.	(A)	O'Donnell W.T.	(A)
O'Rourke M.H.	(A)	O'Rourke P.W.	(W)
Ogier H.J.	(W)	Ogier P.H.W.	(C)
Ollivier A.M.	(C)	Ollivier F.M.	(C)
Ormiston I.W.	(W)	Ormiston R.W.	(CD, W)
Papps M.H.W.	(C, W)	Papps T.J.T.	(C)
Parlane M.E.	(ND, W)	Parlane N.R.	(ND, W, A)
Perry A.	(C)	Perry C.T.H.	(C)
Phillips D.N.	(O)	Phillips G.D.	(A)
Powell J.L.	(C)	Powell R.F.J.	(C)
Powys A.L.	(C)	Powys R.A.N.	(C)
Puna A.	(ND)	Puna K.N.	(ND)
Reaney H.E.I.	(W)	Reaney T.P.L.	(W, CD)
Richardson C.A.	(W)	Richardson W.A.	(NSW)
Ritchie A.W.	(A)	Ritchie D.C.	(A)
Robertson G.K.	(CD)	Robertson S.P.	(CD)
Rutherford I.A.	(O, CD)	Rutherford K.R.	(O)
Schofer J.W.J.	(W)	Schofer P.J.	(W)
Scott A.H.	(A)	Scott V.J.	(A)

Shaw G.S.	(A, O)	Shaw L.J.	(A)
Snedden A.N.C.	(A)	Snedden Cyril A.	(A)
Snedden Colin A.	(A)	Snedden W.N.	(A)
Sorenson B.J.	(A)	Sorenson R.G.	(A)
Stevens G.R.	(HB)	Stevens J.A.M.	(HB)
Studholme E.C	(C)	Studholme W.P.	(C)
Toomey C.D.G.	(O)	Toomey F.J.	(O)
Thomson K.	(C)	Thomson W.A.	(C)
Turnbull A.J.	(O)	Turnbull P.J.	(O)
Wallace G.F.	(A)	Wallace W.M.	(A)
Watson E.A.	(O)	Watson L.F.	(O)
Watson G.	(C)	Watson F.E.	(WC)
Watson H.C.	(O)	Watson L.C.	(O)
Webb M.G.	(O, C)	Webb R.J.	(O)
Weir A.F.	(A)	Weir G.L.	(A)
West G.L.	(CD, ND)	West R.M.	(CD, W)
Westbrook K.R.	(Tasmania)	Westbrook R.A.	(O, Tasmania)
White N.M.	(HB)	White P.C.	(HB)
Williams P.F.C.	(Gloucestershire)	Williams J.N.	(HB)
Wilson A.C.	(C)	Wilson W.C.	(C)
Wilkie J.L.	(O)	Wilkie R.A.	(O)
Wyatt I.E.	(A)	Wyatt J.L.	(ND)

Uncle and Nephew

instances not included in previous lists

Bailey J.F.	(ND)	Bailey M.D.	(ND)
Burtt J.W.	(C, CD)	Burtt L.M.	(C)
Carlton W.	(A, C)	Carlton T.A.	(C, O)
Carson W.	(O)	Carson W.N.	(A)
Carson W.N.	(A)	Carson J.R.	(A, ND)
Crawford C.G.	(C)	Playle W.R.	(A)
Cunningham W.H.R.	(C)	Anderson G.F.	(C)
Dacre C.C.R. (A) & Dacre L.M.	(A)	Coleman D.D.	(A)
Fulton J.	(O)	Fulton F. (O, HB) & Fulton J.C.	(O)
Fulton R.W.	(C, ND)	Fulton D.H. & Fulton P.G.	(C)
Griffiths B.G.	(W)	Maguiness S.J.	(W)
Pocock M.G.	(ND)	Pocock B.A.	(A, ND)
Roberts B.L.	(ND)	Cairns C.L.	(ND, C)
Westbrook N.R.	(Tasmania)	Westbrook R.A.	(O, Tasmania)
Wilson R.S.	(O)	Paul J.M.	(O)
Wilson T.J.	(O)	Wilson J.W.	(O)

Cousins

Bateman G.C.	(C)	Bateman S.N.	(C)
Bracewell D.A.J.	(CD)	Bracewell M.G.	(O, W)
Hoskin R.N.	(O)	Lamont M.J.	(O)
Hotter S.J.	(W)	Verry R.A.	(W)
Leggat I.B.	(CD)	Leggat J.G.	(C)
Lusk Harold B.	(A, C, W)	Lusk Hugh B.	(A, HB)
		Lusk R.B.	(T)
		Lusk W.N.B.	(A)
McMillan C.D.	(C)	McMillan J.M.	(O)
Pringle M.R.	(A)	Webb P.N.	(A)
Reid B.A.	(WA)	Reid J.F.	(A)
Studholme E.C.	(C)	Studholme W.P.	(C)
Talbot G.L.	(C)	Talbot R.O.	(C, O)

Vettori D.L.	(ND)	Hill J.V.	(CD)
Williamson K.S.	(ND)	Cleaver D.	(CD)

Miscellaneous

C.R.W. Dickel (O, C) is son of first cousin of T.H.V. Dickel (O).

G.A.W. Blakely (O) is son of first cousin of D.J. and J.W. Blakely (O).

A. Barron (C, W) and J.R. Barron (O) — fathers were first cousins.

D.W. Lamason (CD) is grandson of first cousin of J.R. Lamason (W).

W.H. Cooper (A) is great-uncle of B.G. Cooper (ND).

W.J. Pocock (NSW, C) and W.L. Rees (Vic, A) were related to the Graces and other first-class cricketers as follows:

W.R. Gilbert (Middx, Glos) and G.H.B. Gilbert (Middx, NSW) were half-brothers. They had the same father and their mothers were sisters (Pococks). W.J. Pocock (NSW, C), W.L. Rees (Vic, A) W.G. Rees (NSW) and the Graces all had a (different) parent who was a brother or sister of the two Pocock sisters.

NB: *Only instances where relationships have been verified have been included in these lists.*
There are numerous other possibilities and we would welcome any additional information on this subject.

REDPATH CUP

Presented by Mr David Redpath

Awarded to the New Zealand batsman whose performances in first-class cricket have been, in the opinion of the Board of Control, the most meritorious since the award was last made.

HOLDERS

Season's first-class figures

		Team	In	NO	HS	Runs	Ave
1920/21	Anthony A.	Auckland	5	1	113	251	62.75
1921/22	Hiddleston J.S.	Wellington	8	1	118	396	56.57
1922/23	Blunt R.C.	Canterbury	12	1	174	583	53.00
1923/24	Hiddleston J.S.	Wellington	12	0	163	619	51.58
1924/25	Worker R.V. de R.	Otago	12	2	121*	491	49.10
1925/26	Allcott C.F.W.	Auckland	9 †	2	116	359	51.28
1926/27	Blunt R.C.	Otago	12 §	1	187	758	69.80
1927/28	Dempster C.S.	Wellington	12	1	145	616	56.00
1928/29	Weir G.L.	Auckland	4	2	106*	262	131.00
1929/30	Dempster C.S.	Wellington	10	4	141*	559	93.16
1930/31	Dempster C.S.	Wellington	42 †	6	212	1901	52.80
1931/32	Roberts A.W.	Canterbury	10	1	181	476	52.88
1932/33	Dempster C.S.	Wellington	9	2	83*	336	48.00
1933/34	Vivian H.G.	Auckland	5	0	64	263	52.60
1934/35	Whitelaw P.E.	Auckland	7	0	155	472	67.42
1935/36	Kerr J.L.	Canterbury	13 †	2	146	655	59.54
1936/37	Whitelaw P.E.	Auckland	6	1	195	410	82.00
1937/38	Uttley K.F.M.	Otago	6	0	138	420	70.00
1938/39	Wallace W.M.	Auckland	6	1	105	270	54.00
1939/40	Donnelly M.P.	Canterbury	5	1	104	302	75.50
1940-45	no award						
1945/46	Hadlee W.A.	Otago	7	0	198	449	66.14
1946/47	Sutcliffe B.	Auckland & Otago	8	1	197	722	103.14
1947/48	Sutcliffe B.	Otago	10	1	208*	911	101.22
1948/49	Sutcliffe B.	Auckland	6	0	141	511	85.16
1949/50	Sutcliffe B.	Otago	9	0	355	695	77.55
1950/51	Sutcliffe B.	Otago	12	0	275	798	66.50
1951/52	Scott V.J.	Auckland	10	2	151*	459	57.37
1952/53	Miller L.S.M.	Central Districts	9	3	128*	545	90.83
1953/54	Sutcliffe B.	Otago	34 †	2	196	1691	52.84
1954/55	Reid J.R.	Wellington	15	2	106	505	38.84
1955/56	Reid J.R.	New Zealand	33 †	6	150*	1227	45.44
1956/57	Miller L.S.M.	Wellington	13	3	83	559	55.90
1957/58	Miller L.S.M.	Wellington	14	1	95	549	42.23
1958/59	Pairaudeau B.H.	Northern Districts	11	1	80	456	45.60
1959/60	Reid J.R.	Wellington	16	1	165	724	48.26
1960/61	Harris P.G.Z.	Canterbury	14	2	108	597	49.75
1961/62	Reid J.R.	Wellington	40 †	2	203	2188	57.57
1962/63	Reid J.R.	Wellington	14	1	296	681	52.38
1963/64	Sinclair B.W.	Wellington	15	1	138	641	45.78
1964/65	Pollard V.	Central Districts	43 †	6	85	1081	29.21
1965/66	Sinclair B.W.	Wellington	17	2	114	700	56.66
1966/67	Dowling G.T.	Canterbury	18	2	102*	871	46.66
1967/68	Dowling G.T.	Canterbury	18	1	239	968	56.94
1968/69	Hastings B.F.	Canterbury	15	4	117*	872	79.27
1969/70	Murray B.A.G.	Wellington	51 †	3	157	2079	43.31

		Team	In	NO	HS	Runs	Ave
1970/71	Dowling G.T.	Canterbury	16	1	102	667	44.66
1971/72	Turner G.M.	Otago	27 †	5	259	1708	77.63
1972/73	Congdon B.E.	Otago	38 †	6	126	1728	54.00
1973/74	Turner G.M.	Otago	17 †	2	110*	714	47.60
1974/75	Turner G.M.	Otago	15	1	186*	838	59.85
1975/76	Turner G.M.	Otago	20	4	177*	1244	77.75
1976/77	Burgess M.G.	Auckland	28 †	1	138	1064	39.40
1977/78	Howarth G.P.	Northern Districts	22	1	122	685	32.61
1978/79	Howarth G.P.	Northern Districts	11	1	147*	505	50.50
1979/80	Howarth G.P.	Northern Districts	22	2	151	767	38.35
1980/81	Reid J.F.	Auckland	18	4	173	817	58.35
1981/82	Edgar B.A.	Wellington	19	1	161	934	51.88
1982/83	Edgar B.A.	Wellington	30 †	5	146	1116	44.64
1983/84	Coney J.V.	Wellington	19 †	4	174*	736	49.06
1984/85	Coney J.V.	Wellington	26 †	4	111*	877	39.86
1985/86	Crowe M.D.	Central Districts	31 †	9	242*	1667	75.77
1986/87	Crowe M.D.	Central Districts	22 †	3	175*	1703	89.63
1987/88	Crowe M.D.	Central Districts	16 †	2	144	1064	76.00
1988/89	Jones A.H.	Wellington	25 †	2	181*	1079	46.91
1989/90	Wright J.G.	Auckland	32 †	5	185	1641	60.77
1990/91	Crowe M.D.	Wellington	15 †	3	299	847	70.58
1991/92	Wright J.G.	Auckland	14	0	116	518	37.00
1992/93	Rutherford K.R.	Otago	26 †	3	105	907	39.43
1993/94	Jones A.H.	Wellington	20 †	0	143	934	46.70
1994/95	Parore A.C.	New Zealand	36 †	7	127*	1050	36.20
1995/96	Twose R.G.	New Zealand	10 †	2	119*	452	56.50
1996/97	Fleming S.P.	Canterbury	16 †	1	129	629	41.93
1997/98	Horne M.J.	Otago	22 †	1	241	1114	53.04
1998/99	Horne M.J.	Otago	19	2	132	887	52.17
1999/00	Cairns C.L.	New Zealand	26 †	3	109	903	39.26
2000/01	Richardson M.H.	Otago	45 †	5	306	2672	66.80
2001/02	Astle N.J.	Canterbury	15 †	3	223	899	74.91
2002/03	Richardson M.H.	Auckland	25 †	2	113	885	38.47
2003/04	Styris S.B.	Northern Districts	17 †	1	170	663	41.43
2004/05	Marshall H.J.H.	Northern Districts	16 †	0	160	730	45.62
2005/06	Sinclair M.S.	Central Districts	18 †	2	121	848	53.00
2006/07	Papps M.H.W.	Canterbury	18 †	0	188	1141	63.38
2007/08	Taylor L.R.P.L.	Central Districts	19 †	0	152	717	42.17
2008/09	Ryder J.D.	Wellington	18 †	2	201	777	48.56
2009/10	Taylor L.R.P.L.	Central Districts	17 †	0	138	852	50.12
2010/11	Ingram P.J.	Central Districts	21 †	0	143	969	46.14
2011/12	Guptill M.J.	Auckland	23 †	1	195*	927	42.13
2012/13	Fulton P.G.	Canterbury	23	2	136	1249	59.47
2013/14	Taylor L.R.P.L.	Central Districts	17 †	4	217*	861	66.23
2014/15	Williamson K.S.	Northern Districts	15 †	3	242*	1070	89.16
2015/16	Williamson K.S.	Northern Districts	19 †	2	166	1068	62.82
2016/17	Williamson K.S.	Northern Districts	21 †	3	176	1079	59.94
2017/18	Taylor L.R.P.L.	Central Districts	8	1	107*	375	53.57
2018/19	Williamson K.S.	Northern Districts	13 †	2	200*	885	80.45
2019/20	Latham T.W.M.	Canterbury	20 †	1	224	875	46.05
2020/21	Williamson K.S.	Northern Districts	4	0	251	639	159.75

† including matches for New Zealand teams overseas

§ these figures include Blunt's scores for Otago and New Zealand against the Melbourne Cricket Club

WINSOR CUP

Presented by Sir Arthur Donnelly to perpetuate the memory of Mr W.H. Winsor

Presented to the New Zealand bowler whose performances in first-class cricket have been, in the opinion of the Board of Control, the most meritorious since the award was last made.

HOLDERS

Season's first-class figures

		Team	Matches	O	M	R	W	Ave
1938/39	Cowie J.	Auckland	4	150	20	444	21	21.14
1939/40	Pritchard T.L.	Wellington	3	113.3	9	404	23	17.56
1940-45	no award							
1945/46	Cowie J.	Auckland	5	209	69	433	24	18.04
1946/47	Cowie J.	Auckland	5	257.4	61	578	26	22.23
1947/48	Burtt T.B.	Canterbury	4	256	57	666	26	25.61
1948/49	Cresswell A.E.	Wellington	4	152	27	343	22	15.59
1949/50	Cresswell G.F.	Wellington	4	235	111	304	20	15.20
1950/51	Burtt T.B.	Canterbury	6	363.2	151	673	44	15.29
1951/52	Burtt T.B.	Canterbury	6	317	120	643	37	17.37
1952/53	Rabone G.O.	Auckland	5	174	44	405	23	17.60
1953/54	MacGibbon A.R.	Canterbury†	17	463.7	98	1271	63	20.17
1954/55	Reid J.R.	Wellington	8	279.1	121	496	30	16.53
1955/56	Cave H.B.	Central Districts*	18	673.4	271	1259	50	25.18
1956/57	Cave H.B.	Central Districts	9	358.3	138	685	41	16.70
1957/58	Hayes J.A.	Auckland	6	244.3	49	568	48	11.83
1958/59	Hough K.W.	Auckland	8	411.3	151	701	46	15.23
1959/60	Alabaster J.C.	Otago	9	313	78	824	47	17.53
1960/61	Alabaster J.C.	Otago	10	426.3	125	964	49	19.61
1961/62	Blair R.W.	Wellington	6	252	96	535	44	12,15
1962/63	Blair R.W.	Wellington	7	244.2	77	562	32	17.56
1963/64	Blair R.W.	Wellington	9	408.1	135	856	49	17.46
1964/65	Motz R.C.	Canterbury*	26	890	272	2179	93	23.43
1965/66	Puna N.	Northern Districts	8	338	126	706	38	18.57
1966/67	Pollard V.	Central Districts	11	345.4	141	672	41	16.39
1967/68	Motz R.C.	Canterbury	10	369.2	115	907	47	19.29
1968/69	Motz R.C.	Canterbury	9	265.2	54	880	40	22.00
1969/70	Howarth H.J.	Auckland*	24	991.4	355	2173	100	21.73
1970/71	Collinge R.O.	Wellington	9	230.6	46	677	37	18.29
1971/72	Taylor B.R.	Wellington*	15	560.5	118	1474	69	21.36
1972/73	Collinge R.O.	Wellington*	23	659.2	149	1806	83	21.75
1973/74	Hadlee D.R.	Canterbury*	13	336.3	35	1451	38	38.18
1974/75	Alabaster G.D.	Otago	6	182.2	26	684	34	20.11
1975/76	Collinge R.O.	Northern Districts	9	215.3	39	623	43	14.48
1976/77	Hadlee R.J.	Canterbury	15	418.2	41	1768	49	36.08
1977/78	Hadlee R.J.	Canterbury	10	266.1	56	860	42	20.47
1978/79	Hadlee R.J.	Canterbury	10	299.1	56	909	50	18.18
1979/80	Hadlee R.J.	New Zealand	3	161.3	50	361	19	19.00
1980/81	Hadlee R.J.	New Zealand*	8	349	89	855	37	23.10
1981/82	Hadlee R.J.	Canterbury	10	424.2	135	868	59	14.74
1982/83	Hadlee R.J.	Canterbury*	12	498	147	1132	59	19.18
1983/84	Hadlee R.J.	Canterbury*	10	310.4	111	587	48	12.22
1984/85	Hadlee R.J.	Canterbury*	12	429.5	119	1061	53	20.01
1985/86	Hadlee R.J.	Canterbury*	11	553.1	129	1314	72	18.25
1986/87	Hadlee R.J.	Canterbury*	12	446.1	116	1047	66	15.86
1987/88	Chatfield E.J.	Wellington*	9	355.1	114	672	24	28.00

		Team	Matches	O	M	R	W	Ave
1988/89	Hadlee R.J.	Canterbury*	7	247.5	59	541	34	15.91
1989/90	Hadlee R.J.	New Zealand*	9	349	71	1014	43	23.58
1990/91	Watson W.	New Zealand	8	333.3	92	807	26	31.03
1991/92	Cairns C.L.	Canterbury	8	294	67	872	42	20.76
1992/93	Morrison D.K.	Auckland	8	263.2	66	598	38	15.73
1993/94	Morrison D.K.	Auckland*	9	327.3	59	1021	28	36.46
1994/95	Morrison D.K.	Auckland*	11	368.5	82	1016	40	25.40
1995/96	Cairns C.L.	New Zealand*	8	232.4	62	631	26	24.26
1996/97	Doull S.B.	New Zealand*	8	255.3	67	715	33	21.66
1997/98	Cairns C.L.	Canterbury*	12	399	113	1124	51	22.03
1998/99	Penn A.J.	Central Districts	9	288	76	763	40	19.07
1999/00	Cairns C.L.	New Zealand*	17	508.5	124	1541	67	23.00
2000/01	Tuffey D.R.	Northern Districts*	12	396.5	118	1104	54	20.44
2001/02	Drum C.J.	Auckland	9	317.3	96	827	53	15.60
2002/03	Bond S.E.	Canterbury*	6	183.5	44	600	30	20.00
2003/04	Martin C.S.	Canterbury	12	448	141	1144	53	21.68
2004/05	Vettori D.L.	Northern Districts*	8	395.5	102	1052	40	26.30
2005/06	Martin C.S.	Auckland*	13	386.3	90	1199	50	23.98
2006/07	Martin C.S.	Auckland*	13	452	94	1424	52	27.38
2007/08	Martin C.S.	Auckland*	9	311.2	74	975	38	25.65
2008/09	Vettori D.L.	Northern Districts*	10	457.3	106	1071	40	26.77
2009/10	Vettori D.L.	New Zealand*	8	433.1	112	1176	32	36.75
2010/11	Martin C.S.	Auckland*	15	521.2	131	1536	60	25.60
2011/12	Bracewell D.A.J.	Central Districts*	10	301.3	54	977	41	23.82
2012/13	Southee T.G.	Northern Districts*	8	315	71	928	42	22.09
2013/14	Southee T.G.	Northern Districts*	9	320	60	967	48	20.14
2014/15	Boult T.A.	Northern Districts*	9	327	77	882	35	25.20
2015/16	Boult T.A.	Northern Districts*	10	418	72	1443	43	33.55
2016/17	Wagner N.	Otago*	15	550.2	118	1541	70	22.01
2017/18	Wagner N.	Otago	10	372.1	89	1090	43	25.34
2018/19	Boult T.A.	Northern Districts*	8	283.2	76	844	35	24.11
2019/20	Southee T.G.	Northern Districts*	9	341.5	84	915	41	22.31
2020/21	Jamieson K.A.	Auckland	7	230.1	77	548	47	11.65

† including 16 matches for New Zealand overseas
** includes matches for New Zealand teams overseas*

SUTCLIFFE MEDAL

For outstanding services to cricket.

1997/98	Morrison B.D.
	Curtis W.H.M.
1998/99	Neely D.O.
1999/00	Gallaway I.W.
2000/01	Hadlee W.A.
2001/02	Reid J.R.
2002/03	Cameron F.J.
2003/04	Dowling G.T.
2004/05	Wallace W.M.
2005/06	Sharp P.A.
2006/07	Shrimpton M.J.F.
2007/08	Sir Richard Hadlee
2008/09	Whimp A.D.
2009/10	Horton M.J.
2010/11	Renwick C.
2011/12	Bull C.L.
2012/13	no award
2013/14	Astle A.M.
2014/15	Dykes R.A.
2015/16	Smith R.
2016/17	Sulzberger L.N.
2017/18	Malcon P.J.
2018/19	Chatfield E.J.
2019/20	Smith I.D.S.
2020/21	Crowe J.J.

TOURING TEAMS IN NEW ZEALAND

		FIRST-CLASS MATCHES				ALL MATCHES			
		P	W	L	D	P	W	L	D
1863/64	G. Parr's England Team	—	—	—	—	4	3	—	1
1876/77	J. Lillywhite's England Team	—	—	—	—	8	6	—	2
1877/78	Australia	—	—	—	—	7	5	1	1
1880/81	Australia	—	—	—	—	10	6	1	3
1881/82	A. Shaw's England Team	—	—	—	—	7	5	—	2
1883/84	Tasmania	4	—	3	1	7	2	3	2
1886/87	Australia	—	—	—	—	5	2	—	3
1887/88	C.A. Smith's England Team	—	—	—	—	3	—	—	3
1888/89	English Footballers	—	—	—	—	1	—	—	1
1889/90	New South Wales	5	4	—	1	7	6	—	1
1893/94	New South Wales	7	4	1	2	8	4	1	3
1894/95	Fiji	6	2	2	2	8	4	2	2
1895/96	New South Wales	5	3	1	1	5	3	1	1
1896/97	Australia	—	—	—	—	5	3	—	2
1896/97	Queensland	5	3	1	1	8	4	1	3
1899/00	Melbourne Cricket Club	—	—	—	—	7	6	—	1
1902/03	Lord Hawke's England Team	7	7	—	—	18	18	—	—
1904/05	Australia	4	3	—	1	6	4	—	2
1905/06	Melbourne Cricket Club	—	—	—	—	10	8	—	2
1906/07	MCC	11	6	2	3	16	10	2	4
1909/10	Australia	6	5	—	1	9	7	—	2
1913/14	A. Sims' Australian Team	8	6	—	2	16	8	—	8
1920/21	Australia	9	6	—	3	15	12	—	3
1922/23	MCC	8	6	—	2	14	11	—	3
1923/24	New South Wales	6	5	—	1	12	8	—	4
1924/25	Victoria	6	1	1	4	12	4	1	7
1926/27	Melbourne Cricket Club	—	—	—	—	13	5	—	8
1927/28	Australia	6	4	—	2	13	6	—	7
1929/30	MCC	8	2	—	6	17	9	—	8
1930/31	West Indies	—	—	—	—	1	—	—	1
1931/32	South Africa	3	3	—	—	3	3	—	—
1932/33	MCC	3	—	—	3	3	—	—	3
1935/36	MCC	8	2	1	5	18	5	1	12
1936/37	MCC	3	1	—	2	3	1	—	2
1938/39	Sir Julien Cahn's XI	1	—	—	1	10	2	—	8
1945/46	Australia	5	5	—	—	5	5	—	—
1946/47	MCC	4	2	—	2	4	2	—	2
1947/48	Fiji	5	2	3	—	17	6	3	8
1949/50	Australia B	5	3	—	2	14	9	—	5
1950/51	MCC	4	3	—	1	4	3	—	1
1951/52	West Indies	4	2	—	2	5	3	—	2
1952/53	South Africa	4	1	—	3	5	1	—	4
1953/54	Fiji	4	1	3	—	17	8	6	3
1954/55	MCC	4	4	—	—	4	4	—	—
1955/56	West Indies	8	6	1	1	15	11	1	3
1956/57	Australia B	7	5	—	2	12	7	—	5
1958/59	MCC	5	3	—	2	5	3	—	2
1959/60	Australia B	6	2	—	4	9	4	—	5

		FIRST-CLASS MATCHES				ALL MATCHES			
		P	W	L	D	P	W	L	D
1960/61	MCC	10	4	1	5	21	11	1	9
1961/62	Fiji	—	—	—	—	22	9	9	4
1961/62	R.A. Roberts' Commonwealth XI	2	2	—	—	3	2	—	1
1962/63	MCC	4	4	—	—	4	4	—	—
1963/64	South Africa	4	1	—	3	7	1	—	6
1964/65	Pakistan	10	2	—	8	12	4	—	8
1965/66	MCC	4	—	—	4	4	—	—	4
1966/67	Australia B	9	1	2	6	10	2	2	6
1967/68	Fiji	—	—	—	—	25	12	7	6
1967/68	India	6	4	1	1	6	4	1	1
1968/69	West Indies	6	1	2	3	7	1	2	4
1969/70	Australia B	8	2	—	6	8	2	—	6
1970/71	MCC	2	1	—	1	5	3	1	1
1972/73	Pakistan	8	5	1	2	11	6	3	2
1973/74	Australia	7	2	1	4	11	6	1	4
1974/75	MCC	3	1	—	2	5	1	—	4
1975/76	India	6	3	1	2	9	3	4	2
1976/77	Australia	6	5	—	1	8	5	2	1
1977/78	Fiji	—	—	—	—	15	5	4	6
1977/78	England	8	3	1	4†	9	4	1	4†
1978/79	Pakistan	8	5	—	3	10	6	1	3
1979/80	West Indies	5	—	2	3	8	2	3	3
1979/80	D.H. Robins' XI	2	—	—	2	8	5	1	2
1980/81	India	5	1	1	3	7	1	3	3
1981/82	Australia	5	1	1	3	11	4	4	3
1982/83	England	—	—	—	—	3	—	3	—
1982/83	Sri Lanka	4	—	3	1	9	1	7	1
1983/84	England	7	1	1	5	11	4	2	5
1984/85	Pakistan	5	1	2	2	9	1	5	3
1985/86	Australia	5	1	1	3	11	5	3	3
1986/87	West Indies	5	1	1	3	9	5	1	3
1987/88	England	7	2	1	4	12	5	3	4
1988/89	Pakistan	5	1	—	4	12	2	5	5
1989/90	India	6	1	1	4	10	2	4	4
1989/90	Australia	1	—	1	—	6	5	1	—
1990/91	Sri Lanka	7	1	—	6	10	1	3	6
1990/91	England	—	—	—	—	3	1	2	—
1991/92	England	7	4	—	3	11	8	—	3
1991/92	Zimbabwe	—	—	—	—	3	1	2	—
1991/92	Australia	—	—	—	—	1	1	—	—
1991/92	Sri Lanka	—	—	—	—	1	1	—	—
1992/93	Pakistan	1	1	—	—	4	2	2	—
1992/93	Australia	4	2	1	1	10	5	4	1
1993/94	Pakistan	5	2	1	2	11	6	2	3†
1993/94	India	3	—	—	3	7	2	2	3
1994/95	West Indies	3	1	—	2	8	6	—	2
1994/95	Australia	—	—	—	—	4	3	1	—
1994/95	South Africa	2	2	—	—	6	3	2	1†
1994/95	India	—	—	—	—	4	2	2	—
1994/95	Sri Lanka	4	2	—	2	9	4	2	3
1994/95	Australian Academy	1	1	—	—	5	5	—	—

		FIRST-CLASS MATCHES				ALL MATCHES			
		P	W	L	D	P	W	L	D
1995/96	Pakistan	1	1	—	—	5	3	2	—
1995/96	Zimbabwe	4	1	—	3	8	3	2	3
1996/97	England	6	4	1	1	12	6	3	3†
1996/97	Sri Lanka	2	—	2	—	6	2	3	1
1997/98	Bangladesh	4	—	4	—	7	—	6	1
1997/98	Zimbabwe	4	1	3	—	10	3	7	—
1998/99	Pakistan A	5	—	1	4	10	1	4	5
1998/99	India	4	1	2	1	10	3	5	2
1998/99	South Africa	5	1	—	4	13	5	2	6
1999/00	England A	5	3	—	2	10	7	—	3
1999/00	West Indies	4	—	2	2	10	—	8	2
1999/00	Australia	5	4	—	1	11	8	1	2
2000/01	Zimbabwe	2	—	—	2	6	3	1	2
2000/01	Sri Lanka	—	—	—	—	6	4	2	—
2000/01	Pakistan	5	1	2	2	10	3	5	2
2001/02	Bangladesh	3	—	3	—	4	—	3	1
2001/02	England	5	1	1	3	12	4	5	3
2002/03	India	3	—	2	1	11	2	8	1
2003/04	Pakistan	3	1	—	2	9	3	4	2
2003/04	South Africa	4	1	1	2	11	3	6	2
2003/04	Sri Lanka A	4	—	3	1	6	—	5	1
2004/05	Sri Lanka	3	—	1	2	5	—	2	3
2004/05	FICA World XI	—	—	—	—	3	1	2	—
2004/05	Australia	3	2	—	1	9	8	—	1
2005/06	Australia	—	—	—	—	3	2	1	—
2005/06	Sri Lanka	—	—	—	—	4	1	3	—
2005/06	West Indies	3	—	2	1	9	1	7	1
2006/07	Sri Lanka	2	1	1	—	10	4	4	2
2006/07	Australia	—	—	—	—	3	—	3	—
2007/08	Bangladesh	2	—	2	—	9	1	7	1
2007/08	England	4	2	1	1	14	7	4	3†
2008/09	West Indies	3	—	—	3	10	2	3	5
2008/09	India	3	1	—	2	10	4	3	3
2008/09	England Lions	2	—	—	2	7	—	3	4
2009/10	Pakistan	3	1	1	1	4	1	1	2
2009/10	Bangladesh	1	—	1	—	5	—	5	—
2009/10	Australia	2	2	—	—	9	6	3	—
2010/11	Pakistan	2	1	—	1	13	5	5	3
2011/12	Zimbabwe	1	—	1	—	7	—	6	1
2011/12	South Africa	3	1	—	2	10	7	1	2
2012/13	India A	2	—	—	2	6	1	1	4
2012/13	England	4	—	1	3	13	5	4	4
2013/14	West Indies	3	—	2	1	10	2	6	2
2013/14	India	2	—	1	1	8	—	5	3†
2014/15	Afghanistan	—	—	—	—	4	1	3	—
2014/15	Scotland	—	—	—	—	4	1	3	—
2014/15	Ireland	—	—	—	—	4	—	3	1
2014/15	Sri Lanka	2	—	2	—	12	2	8	2
2014/15	Zimbabwe	—	—	—	—	5	4	—	1
2014/15	South Africa	—	—	—	—	2	1	1	—
2015/16	Sri Lanka A	2	—	1	1	8	2	5	1

		FIRST-CLASS MATCHES				ALL MATCHES			
		P	W	L	D	P	W	L	D
2015/16	Sri Lanka	2	—	2	—	10	1	7	2
2015/16	Pakistan	—	—	—	—	5	1	4	—
2015/16	Australia	2	2	—	—	5	3	2	—
2016/17	Pakistan	3	—	2	1	3	—	2	1
2016/17	Bangladesh	2	—	2	—	9	—	9	—
2016/17	Australia	—	—	—	—	2	—	2	—
2016/17	South Africa	3	1	—	2	9	5	2	2
2017/18	West Indies	2	—	2	—	10	—	8	2
2017/18	Pakistan	—	—	—	—	9	3	6	—
2017/18	Australia	—	—	—	—	1	—	1	—
2017/18	England	2	—	1	1	11	4	4	3
2018/19	Sri Lanka	2	—	1	1	7	—	5	2
2018/19	India	—	—	—	—	8	5	3	—
2018/19	Bangladesh	2	—	2	—	7	—	6	1
2019/20	England	3	—	1	2	11	4	4	3
2019/20	India	2	—	2	—	11	5	5	1
2020/21	West Indies	3	—	2	1	7	—	4	3
2020/21	West Indies A	2	—	2	—	2	—	2	—
2020/21	Pakistan A	1	1	—	—	6	3	3	—
2020/21	Pakistan	2	—	2	—	5	1	4	—
2020/21	Australia	—	—	—	—	5	2	3	—
2020/21	Bangladesh	—	—	—	—	6	—	6	—

† *includes a tie*

NB: From 1900 the basis for inclusion is any of the following:

a) First-class matches were played.
b) The touring side was its country's official team.
c) The touring side played an official New Zealand team.
d) Matches in the 1992 and 2015 World Cups are not included, although preliminary games played by Zimbabwe, Australia and Sri Lanka in 1992 and by Zimbabwe, South Africa and Sri Lanka in 2015 are.

NEW ZEALAND TOURING TEAMS

		FIRST-CLASS MATCHES				ALL MATCHES			
		P	W	L	D	P	W	L	D
1898/99	Australia	2	—	2	—	4	1	2	1
1913/14	Australia	4	1	2	1	9	5	2	2
1925/26	Australia	4	—	1	3	9	3	1	5
1927	Great Britain	26	7	5	14	38	12	5	21
	Ceylon	—	—	—	—	1	—	—	1
1927/28	Australia	1	—	1	—	1	—	1	—
1931	Great Britain	32	6	3	23	36	7	3	26
1937	Great Britain	32	9	9	14	38	14	9	15
	Ceylon	—	—	—	—	1	—	—	1
1937/38	Australia	3	—	3	—	3	—	3	—
1949	Great Britain	32	13	1	18	35	14	1	20
	West Germany	—	—	—	—	1	1	—	—
1953/54	South Africa	16	3	4	9	17	3	4	10
	Australia	3	2	—	1	3	2	—	1
1955/56	Pakistan	6	1	3	2	6	1	3	2
	India	10	2	3	5	10	2	3	5
1958	Great Britain	31	7	6	18 †	35	7	6	22
1961/62	South Africa	18	5	2	11	24	7	2	15
	Australia	3	—	2	1	3	—	2	1
1964/65	India	4	—	1	3	4	—	1	3
	Pakistan	3	—	2	1	3	—	2	1
1965	Great Britain	19	3	6	10	21	4	6	11
	Holland	—	—	—	—	1	—	—	1
	Bermuda	—	—	—	—	2	—	—	2
	USA	—	—	—	—	1	1	—	—
1967/68	Australia	4	—	2	2	7	2	2	3
1969	Great Britain	18	4	3	11	22	5	4	13
1969/70	India	5	1	1	3	5	1	1	3
1969/70	Pakistan	4	1	—	3	4	1	—	3
1969/70	Australia	3	—	—	3	8	3	—	5
1970/71	Australia	1	—	—	1	2	—	1	1
1971/72*	Australia	—	—	—	—	2	1	—	1
1971/72	West Indies	13	1	—	12	16	4	—	12
1972/73	Australia	1	—	—	1	3	2	—	1
1973	Great Britain	19	3	2	14	23	4	3	16
1973/74	Australia	9	2	5	2	13	5	6	2
1974/75	Australia	—	—	—	—	3	3	—	—
1975	England *(Prudential Cup)*	—	—	—	—	4	2	2	—
1976/77	Pakistan	6	1	3	2	7	2	3	2
	India	3	—	2	1	3	—	2	1
1978	Great Britain	16	5	4	7	20	5	8	7
1979	Great Britain *(Prudential Cup)*	—	—	—	—	4	2	2	—
1980/81	Australia	7	1	2	4	29	14	9	6
1982/83	Australia	2	—	—	2 †	4	1	1	2 †
1982/83	Australia	—	—	—	—	18	12	6	—
1983	England	13	7	3	3	21	11	6	4
1983/84	Sri Lanka	5	2	—	3	8	4	1	3
1984/85	Sri Lanka	—	—	—	—	2	1	1	—
	Pakistan	5	—	2	3	9	1	5	3
1984/85	Australia *(WCC)*	—	—	—	—	4	1	2	1
1984/85	West Indies	7	—	2	5	12	—	7	5
1985/86	Australia	6	2	1	3	8	2	1	5

		FIRST-CLASS MATCHES				ALL MATCHES			
		P	W	L	D	P	W	L	D
1985/86	Australia	—	—	—	—	11	3	6	2
1985/86	Sri Lanka	—	—	—	—	2	1	1	—
	Sharjah	—	—	—	—	2	—	2	—
	Hong Kong (China)	—	—	—	—	2	2	—	—
1986	England	15	4	—	11	18	5	1	12
	Holland	—	—	—	—	2	1	1	—
1986/87	Sri Lanka	2	—	—	2	2	—	—	2
1987/88	India *(Reliance World Cup)*	—	—	—	—	6	2	4	—
1987/88	Australia	6	1	2	3	19	8	8	3
1987/88	Sharjah	—	—	—	—	4	2	2	—
1988/89	India	6	1	2	3	10	1	6	3
1988/89	Australia	—	—	—	—	1	—	1	—
1989/90	Australia	3	—	—	3	4	—	1	3
1990	Sharjah	—	—	—	—	3	1	2	—
	England	12	4	2	6	19	8	5	6
1990/91	Pakistan	5	—	3	2	8	—	6	2
1990/91	Australia	—	—	—	—	10	3	7	—
1991/92	Australia	—	—	—	—	6	4	2	—
1992/93	Zimbabwe	3	2	—	1	6	5	—	1
	Sri Lanka	2	—	1	1	7	—	5	2
1993/94	Australia	7	2	3	2	16	5	9	2
1994	Sharjah	—	—	—	—	3	1	2	—
	Great Britain	12	1	3	8	21	8	5	8
1994/95	India	—	—	—	—	4	—	3	1
	South Africa	7	2	3	2	16	3	9	4
1995/96	India	6	—	1	5	11	2	4	5
1995/96	India & Pakistan *(Wills World Cup)*	—	—	—	—	6	3	3	—
1995/96	West Indies	4	1	2	1	13	7	5	1
1996/97	Sharjah	—	—	—	—	5	1	3	1†
1996/97	Pakistan	3	1	1	1	6	2	3	1
1996/97	India *(Independence Cup)*	—	—	—	—	3	1	2	—
1997/98	Kenya	—	—	—	—	3	2	—	1
	Zimbabwe	3	—	—	3	7	2	1	4†
1997/98	Australia	6	—	5	1	21	5	13	3†
1997/98	Sharjah	—	—	—	—	4	1	3	—
1997/98	Sri Lanka	5	1	2	2	11	3	4	4
1998	Malaysia *(Commonwealth Games)*	—	—	—	—	5	4	1	—
1998/99	Bangladesh *(Wills International Cup)*	—	—	—	—	2	1	1	—
1999	England	10	5	2	3	26	14	8	4
1999/00	India	6	—	2	4	11	2	5	4
2000/01	Singapore	—	—	—	—	2	—	2	—
2000/01	Zimbabwe	4	2	—	2	8	4	2	2
2000/01	Kenya	—	—	—	—	3	3	—	—
2000/01	South Africa	6	2	2	2	14	4	7	3
2000/01	Sharjah	—	—	—	—	4	1	3	—
2001/02	Sri Lanka	—	—	—	—	7	3	4	—
2001/02	Australia	5	—	1	4	21	6	8	7
2001/02	Sharjah	—	—	—	—	4	1	3	—
2001/02	Pakistan	1	—	1	—	4	—	4	—
2001/02	West Indies	2	1	—	1	8	3	3	2
2002/03	Australia	—	—	—	—	4	4	—	—
2002/03	Sri Lanka *(ICC Champions Trophy)*	—	—	—	—	4	2	2	—
2002/03	South Africa *(World Cup)*	—	—	—	—	11	7	4	—
2002/03	Sri Lanka	2	—	—	2	9	3	2	4

		FIRST-CLASS MATCHES				ALL MATCHES			
		P	W	L	D	P	W	L	D
2003/04	India	4	—	—	4	10	1	4	5
2003/04	Pakistan	—	—	—	—	5	—	5	—
2004	England	7	1	4	2	16	7	5	4
2004	England *(ICC Champions Trophy)*	—	—	—	—	2	1	1	—
2004/05	Bangladesh	2	2	—	—	6	5	—	1
2004/05	Australia	3	—	3	—	6	2	4	—
2005/06	{ Namibia	—	—	—	—	2	2	—	—
2005/06	{ Zimbabwe	2	2	—	—	8	7	1	—
2005/06	South Africa	—	—	—	—	8	3	4	1
2005/06	South Africa	4	—	2	2	4	—	2	2
2006/07	India *(ICC Champions Trophy)*	—	—	—	—	6	4	2	—
2006/07	Australia	—	—	—	—	8	2	6	—
2006/07	West Indies *(ICC World Cup)*	—	—	—	—	12	8	4	—
2007/08	South Africa *(Twenty20 World Championship)*	—	—	—	—	6	3	3	—
2007/08	{ South Africa	4	1	3	—	8	2	6	—
2007/08	{ Australia	—	—	—	—	5	—	4	1
2008	England	7	1	2	4	17	4	4	6
2008/09	Bangladesh	2	1	—	1	5	3	1	1
2008/09	Australia	3	—	3	—	3	—	3	—
2008/09	Australia	—	—	—	—	7	2	4	1
2009	England *(ICC World Twenty20)*	—	—	—	—	5	2	3	—
2009/10	Sri Lanka	4	—	2	2	9	2	5	2
2009/10	South Africa *(ICC Champions Trophy)*	—	—	—	—	5	3	2	—
2009/10	United Arab Emirates	—	—	—	—	5	2	3	—
2009/10	West Indies *(ICC World Twenty20)*	—	—	—	—	5	3	2	—
2009/10	United States of America	—	—	—	—	2	1	1	—
2010/11	Sri Lanka	—	—	—	—	6	3	2	1
2010/11	Bangladesh	—	—	—	—	4	—	4	—
2010/11	India	3	—	1	2	8	—	6	2
2010/11	India, Sri Lanka, Bangladesh *(ICC World Cup)*	—	—	—	—	10	6	4	—
2011/12	Zimbabwe	1	1	—	—	7	5	1	1
2011/12	Australia	3	1	1	1	3	1	1	1
2012	{ United States of America	—	—	—	—	2	—	2	—
2012	{ West Indies	3	—	2	1	8	1	6	1
2012/13	India	2	—	2	—	4	1	2	1
2012/13	Sri Lanka *(ICC World Twenty20)*	—	—	—	—	5	1	4	—
2012/13	Sri Lanka	2	1	1	—	8	1	4	3
2012/13	South Africa	2	—	2	—	10	4	5	1
2013	England	4	1	2	1	12	5	4	3
2013/14	{ Bangladesh	2	—	—	2	6	1	3	2
2013/14	{ Sri Lanka	—	—	—	—	4	1	1	2
2013/14	Bangladesh *(ICC World Twenty20)*	—	—	—	—	4	2	2	—
2013/14	West Indies	3	2	1	—	7	4	2	1
2014/15	Pakistan *(played in United Arab Emirates)*	3	1	1	1	11	5	4	2
2015	England	3	2	1	—	11	6	5	—
2015/16	{ Zimbabwe	—	—	—	—	4	3	1	—
2015/16	{ South Africa	—	—	—	—	7	4	3	—
2015/16	Australia	4	—	2	2	7	1	2	4
2015/16	India *(ICC World Twenty20)*	—	—	—	—	5	4	1	—
2015/16	{ Zimbabwe	2	2	—	—	3	3	—	—
2015/16	{ South Africa	2	—	1	1	2	—	1	1
2016/17	India	3	—	3	—	9	2	6	1
2016/17	Australia	—	—	—	—	3	—	3	—

		FIRST-CLASS MATCHES				ALL MATCHES			
		P	W	L	D	P	W	L	D
2017	Ireland	—	—	—	—	4	3	1	—
2017	England *(ICC Champions Trophy)*	—	—	—	—	5	1	3	1
2017/18	India	—	—	—	—	8	3	5	—
2018/19	United Arab Emirates	3	2	1	—	10	4	5	1
2019	England *(ICC World Cup)*	—	—	—	—	12	7	5	—
2019/20	Sri Lanka	2	1	1	—	7	4	2	1
2019/20	Australia	3	—	3	—	4	—	3	1
2019/20	Australia	—	—	—	—	1	—	1	—
2021	England	3	2	—	1	3	2	—	1

† *includes a tie*

NB: 1) All tours refer to those undertaken by official New Zealand sides. Unofficial practice matches have not been included in the totals.

2) The first team from New Zealand to tour overseas was Canterbury who visited Victoria and Tasmania in 1878/79. This was the first tour ever undertaken by a domestic association from any country. (None of the games are ranked as first-class.)

3) Where countries are bracketed it indicates this represented a single tour. Where there is more than one entry for the same season but countries are not bracketed, the tours were not connected.

4) The 1974/75, second 1982/83, 1990/91, 1993/94 and 1997/98 tours to Australia included a return trip after the teams had come back to New Zealand. They are all listed as single tours for the purposes of this article.

5) The 1986/87 tour to Sri Lanka was scheduled for 8 matches. The team returned home after 2 matches due to unrest in Sri Lanka.

6) One match played in Australia as part of the Trans-Tasman Twenty20 Tri-Series in 2017/18 is not regarded as a tour.

A total of 131 official New Zealand sides have toured overseas since the first in February, 1899. The teams were as follows:

1) **1898/99 to Australia**
L.T. Cobcroft *(captain)*, F.L. Ashbolt, J.C. Baker, C. Boxshall, A.D. Downes, A.H. Fisher, F.S. Frankish, Hugh B. Lusk, G. Mills, I. Mills, D. Reese, A. Sims, E.F. Upham.

2) **1913/14 to Australia**
D. Reese *(captain)*, J.H. Bennett, C. Boxshall, T.A. Carlton, L.G. Hemus, R.G. Hickmott, W.R. Patrick, C.W. Robinson, D.M. Sandman, A.N.C. Snedden, R.C. Somervell, L.G. Taylor, H.J. Tattersall, B.J. Tuckwell.

3) **1925/26 to Australia**
W.R. Patrick *(captain)*, C.F.W. Allcott, A.W. Alloo, R.C. Blunt, C.G. Crawford, W.H.R. Cunningham, C.C.R. Dacre, H.D. Gillespie, R.W. Hope, K.C. James, T.C. Lowry, D.J. McBeath, C.J. Oliver, R.V. de R. Worker.

4) **1927 to Great Britain, Ceylon and Australia**
T.C. Lowry *(captain)*, C.F.W. Allcott, E.H.L. Bernau, E.D. Blundell*, R.C. Blunt, W.H.R. Cunningham, C.C.R. Dacre, C.S. Dempster, R.H. Fox*, T.D.B. Hay*, M. Henderson, K.C. James, H.M. McGirr, W.E. Merritt, J.E. Mills, C.J. Oliver, M.L. Page.

5) **1931 to Great Britain**
T.C. Lowry *(captain)*, C.F.W. Allcott, R.C. Blunt, I.B. Cromb, C.S. Dempster, K.C. James, J.L. Kerr, A.M. Matheson, W.E. Merritt, J.E. Mills, M.L. Page, R.O. Talbot, H.G. Vivian, G.L. Weir.

6) **1937 to Great Britain, Ceylon and Australia**
M.L. Page *(captain)*, W.N. Carson, J. Cowie, M.P. Donnelly, J.A. Dunning, N. Gallichan, W.A. Hadlee, J.L. Kerr, J.R. Lamason, T.C. Lowry, D.A.R. Moloney, C.K. Parsloe*, A.W. Roberts, E.W.T. Tindill, H.G. Vivian, W.M. Wallace, G.L. Weir.

7) **1949 to Great Britain and West Germany**
W.A. Hadlee *(captain)*, C. Burke, T.B. Burtt, H.B. Cave, J. Cowie, G.F. Cresswell, M.P. Donnelly, J.A. Hayes, F.L.H. Mooney, G.O. Rabone, J.R. Reid, V.J. Scott, F.B. Smith, B. Sutcliffe, W.M. Wallace.

8) **1953/54 to South Africa and Australia**
G.O. Rabone *(captain)*, J.E.F. Beck, W. Bell, R.W. Blair, M.E. Chapple, E.W. Dempster, I.B. Leggat, J.G. Leggat*, A.R. MacGibbon, L.S.M. Miller, F.L.H. Mooney, G.W.F. Overton, M.B. Poore, J.R. Reid, B. Sutcliffe.

9) **1955/1956 to Pakistan and India**
H.B. Cave *(captain)*, J.C. Alabaster, J.W. Guy, N.S. Harford, J.A. Hayes, P.G.Z. Harris, J.G. Leggat, A.R. MacGibbon, S.N. McGregor, T.G. McMahon, A.M. Moir, E.C. Petrie, M.B. Poore, J.R. Reid, B. Sutcliffe.

10) **1958 to Great Britain**
J.R. Reid *(captain)*, J.C. Alabaster, R.W. Blair, H.B. Cave, J.W. D'Arcy, N.S. Harford, J.A. Hayes, A.R. MacGibbon, T. Meale, L.S.M. Miller, A.M. Moir, E.C. Petrie, W.R. Playle, J.T. Sparling, B. Sutcliffe, J.T. Ward.

11) **1961/62 to South Africa and Australia**
J.R. Reid *(captain)*, J.C. Alabaster, G.A. Bartlett, P.T. Barton, F.J. Cameron, M.E. Chapple, A.E. Dick, G.T. Dowling, J.W. Guy, P.G.Z. Harris, S.N. McGregor, R.C. Motz, J.T. Sparling, J.T. Ward, B.W. Yuile.

12) **1964/65 to India, Pakistan, Great Britain, Holland, Bermuda and USA**
J.R. Reid *(captain)*, F.J. Cameron, R.O. Collinge, B.E. Congdon, A.E. Dick*, G.T. Dowling, T.W. Jarvis, R.W. Morgan, R.C. Motz, V. Pollard, B.W. Sinclair, B. Sutcliffe, B.R. Taylor, G.E. Vivian, J.T. Ward, B.W. Yuile.

13) **1967/68 to Australia**
B.W. Sinclair *(captain)*, J.C. Alabaster, M.G. Burgess, R.O. Collinge, B.E. Congdon, R.I. Harford, T.W. Jarvis, R.C. Motz, B.A.G. Murray, V. Pollard, B.R. Taylor, K. Thomson, B.W. Yuile.

14) **1969 to Great Britain, India and Pakistan**
G.T. Dowling *(captain)*, M.G. Burgess, R.O. Collinge, B.E. Congdon, R.S. Cunis, D.R. Hadlee, B.F. Hastings, H.J. Howarth, B.D. Milburn, B.A.G. Murray, V. Pollard, B.R. Taylor, D.G. Trist*, G.M. Turner, K.J. Wadsworth, B.W. Yuile.

15) **1969/70 to Australia**
G.T. Dowling *(captain)*, M.G. Burgess, R.O. Collinge, B.E. Congdon, R.S. Cunis, D.R. Hadlee, B.F. Hastings, H.J. Howarth, R.W. Morgan*, B.W. Sinclair, G.M. Turner, G.E. Vivian, K.J. Wadsworth.

16) **1970/1971 to Australia**
G.T. Dowling *(captain)*, M.G. Burgess, R.O. Collinge, B.E. Congdon, R.S. Cunis, H.J. Howarth, T.W. Jarvis, R.W. Morgan, B.R. Taylor, G.M. Turner, G.E. Vivian, K.J. Wadsworth.

17) **1971/72 to Australia**
R.W. Morgan *(captain)*, R.W. Anderson, B. Andrews, B. Dunning, B.G. Hadlee, R.J. Hadlee, W.A. Greenstreet, G.A. Newdick, R.E. Redmond, M.L. Ryan, M.J.F. Shrimpton, D.G. Trist.

18) **1971/72 to West Indies**
G.T. Dowling *(captain)*, J.C. Alabaster, M.G. Burgess, K.O. Campbell, M.E. Chapple*, R.O. Collinge, B.E. Congdon, R.S. Cunis, B.F. Hastings, H.J. Howarth, T.W. Jarvis, R.W. Morgan*, B.R. Taylor, G.M. Turner, G.E. Vivian, K.J. Wadsworth, M.G. Webb.

19) **1972/73 to Australia**
B.E. Congdon *(captain)*, B. Andrews, R.S. Cunis, B. Dunning, R.J. Hadlee, B.F. Hastings, A.B. Jordan, D.R. O'Sullivan, R.E. Redmond, G.M. Turner, G.E. Vivian, K.J. Wadsworth.

20) **1973 to Great Britain**
B.E. Congdon *(captain)*, R.W. Anderson, M.G. Burgess, R.O. Collinge, E.K. Gillott, D.R. Hadlee, R.J. Hadlee, B.F. Hastings, H.J. Howarth, J.M. Parker, V. Pollard, R.E. Redmond, B.R. Taylor, G.M. Turner, K.J. Wadsworth.

21) **1973/74 to Australia**
B.E. Congdon *(captain)*, G.D. Alabaster, B. Andrews, B.L. Cairns, K.O. Campbell, J.V. Coney*, D.R. Hadlee, R.J. Hadlee, B.F. Hastings, J.F.M. Morrison, D.R. O'Sullivan, J.M. Parker, M.J.F. Shrimpton, G.M. Turner, K.J. Wadsworth.

22) **1974/75 to Australia**
B.E. Congdon *(captain)*, B.L. Cairns, E.J. Chatfield, R.O. Collinge, G.N. Edwards, D.R. Hadlee, B.F. Hastings, G.P. Howarth, H.J. Howarth, J.F.M. Morrison, J.M. Parker, G.M. Turner, K.J. Wadsworth.

23) **1975 to England** *(World Cup)*
G.M. Turner *(captain)*, B.L. Cairns, R.O. Collinge, B.G. Hadlee, D.R. Hadlee, R.J. Hadlee, B.F. Hastings, G.P. Howarth, H.J. Howarth, B.J. McKechnie, J.F.M. Morrison, D.R. O'Sullivan, J.M. Parker, K.J. Wadsworth.

24) **1976/77 to Pakistan and India**
G.M. Turner *(captain)*, R.W. Anderson, M.G. Burgess, B.L. Cairns, R.O. Collinge, R.J. Hadlee, G.P. Howarth, W.K. Lees, J.F.M. Morrison, D.R. O'Sullivan, J.M. Parker, N.M. Parker, P.J. Petherick, A.D.G. Roberts, G.B. Troup.

25) **1978 to Great Britain**
M.G. Burgess *(captain)*, R.W. Anderson, S.L. Boock, B.P. Bracewell, B.L. Cairns, R.O. Collinge*, B.E. Congdon, B.A. Edgar, G.N. Edwards, D.R. Hadlee, R.J. Hadlee, G.P. Howarth, J.M. McIntyre, J.M. Parker, G.B. Thomson, G.B. Troup*, J.G. Wright.

26) **1979 to England** *(World Cup)*
M.G. Burgess *(captain)*, B.L. Cairns, E.J. Chatfield, J.V. Coney, B.A. Edgar, R.J. Hadlee, G.P. Howarth, W.K. Lees, B.J. McKechnie, J.F.M. Morrison, L.W. Stott, G.B. Troup, G.M. Turner, J.G. Wright.

27) **1980/81 to Australia**
G.P. Howarth *(captain)*, S.L. Boock, B.P. Bracewell*, J.G. Bracewell, M.G. Burgess, B.L. Cairns, E.J. Chatfield, J.V. Coney, B.A. Edgar, R.J. Hadlee, W.K. Lees, P.E. McEwan, B.J. McKechnie*, J.M. Parker, I.D.S. Smith, M.C. Snedden, G.B. Troup, J.G. Wright.

28) **1982/83 to Australia**
G.P. Howarth *(captain)*, B.R. Blair, S.M. Carrington, E.J. Chatfield, J.V. Coney, M.D. Crowe, B.A. Edgar, W.K. Lees, J.F.M. Morrison, J.F. Reid, G.K. Robertson, M.C. Snedden, G.B. Troup.

29) **1982/83 to Australia**
G.P. Howarth *(captain)*, B.L. Cairns, E.J. Chatfield, J.V. Coney, J.J. Crowe, M.D. Crowe*, B.A. Edgar, T.J. Franklin*, R.J. Hadlee, W.K. Lees, J.F.M. Morrison, M.C. Snedden, G.B. Troup, G.M. Turner, P.N. Webb, R.J. Webb*, J.G. Wright.

30) **1983 to England**
G.P. Howarth *(captain)*, J.G. Bracewell, B.L. Cairns, E.J. Chatfield, J.V. Coney, J.J. Crowe, M.D. Crowe, B.A. Edgar, T.J. Franklin, E.J. Gray, R.J. Hadlee, W.K. Lees, I.D.S. Smith, M.C. Snedden, S.R. Tracy*, G.M. Turner, J.G. Wright.

31) **1983/84 to Sri Lanka**
G.P. Howarth *(captain)*, S.L. Boock, J.G. Bracewell, B.L. Cairns, E.J. Chatfield, J.V. Coney, J.J. Crowe, M.D. Crowe, B.A. Edgar, R.J. Hadlee, J.F. Reid, I.D.S. Smith, D.A. Stirling, J.G. Wright.

32) **1984/85 to Pakistan and Sri Lanka**
J.V. Coney *(captain)*, S.L. Boock, J.G. Bracewell, B.L. Cairns, E.J. Chatfield, J.J. Crowe, M.D. Crowe, B.A. Edgar, E.J. Gray, P.E. McEwan, J.F. Reid, I.D.S. Smith, M.C. Snedden, D.A. Stirling, J.G. Wright.

33) **1984/85 to Australia** *(World Championship of Cricket)*
G.P. Howarth *(captain)*, B.P. Bracewell, J.G. Bracewell, B.L. Cairns, E.J. Chatfield, J.V. Coney, J.J. Crowe, M.D. Crowe, R.J. Hadlee, P.E. McEwan, J.F. Reid, I.D.S. Smith, M.C. Snedden, J.G. Wright.

34) **1984/85 to West Indies**
G.P. Howarth *(captain)*, S.L. Boock, J.G. Bracewell, B.L. Cairns, E.J. Chatfield, J.V. Coney, J.J. Crowe, M.D. Crowe, R.J. Hadlee, R.T. Hart, K.R. Rutherford, I.D.S. Smith, D.A. Stirling, G.B. Troup, J.G. Wright.

35) **1985/86 to Australia**
J.V. Coney *(captain)*, S.L. Boock, J.G. Bracewell*, V.R. Brown, B.L. Cairns, E.J. Chatfield, J.J. Crowe, M.D. Crowe, B.A. Edgar, T.J. Franklin, R.J. Hadlee, E.B. McSweeney*, J.F. Reid, I.D.S. Smith, M.C. Snedden, J.G. Wright.

36) **1985/86 to Australia**
J.V. Coney *(captain)*, B.R. Blair, S.L. Boock, J.G. Bracewell, E.J. Chatfield, J.J. Crowe, M.D. Crowe, B.A. Edgar, S.R. Gillespie, R.J. Hadlee, E.B. McSweeney, J.F. Reid, M.C. Snedden, J.G. Wright.

37) **1985/86 to Sri Lanka, Sharjah and Hong Kong (China)**
J.G. Wright *(captain)*, T.E. Blain, B.R. Blair, J.G. Bracewell, E.J. Chatfield, J.J. Crowe, M.D. Crowe, E.J. Gray, E.B. McSweeney, G.K. Robertson, K.R. Rutherford, M.C. Snedden, W. Watson.

38) **1986 to England and Holland**
J.V. Coney *(captain)*, B.J. Barrett, T.E. Blain, J.G. Bracewell, E.J. Chatfield, J.J. Crowe, M.D. Crowe, B.A. Edgar, T.J. Franklin, E.J. Gray, R.J. Hadlee, K.R. Rutherford, I.D.S. Smith, D.A. Stirling, W. Watson, J.G. Wright.

39) **1986/87 to Sri Lanka**
J.J. Crowe *(captain)*, J.G. Bracewell, E.J. Chatfield, M.D. Crowe, E.J. Gray, R.J. Hadlee, P.A. Horne, A.H. Jones, E.B. McSweeney, D.K. Morrison, D.N. Patel, K.R. Rutherford, I.D.S. Smith, M.C. Snedden.

40) **1987/88 to India** *(World Cup)*
J.J. Crowe *(captain)*, S.L. Boock, J.G. Bracewell, E.J. Chatfield, M.D. Crowe, P.A. Horne, A.H. Jones, D.K. Morrison, D.N. Patel, K.R. Rutherford, I.D.S. Smith, M.C. Snedden, W. Watson, J.G. Wright.

41) **1987/88 to Australia**
J.J. Crowe *(captain)*, T.E. Blain*, J.G. Bracewell, V.R. Brown*, E.J. Chatfield, M.D. Crowe, S.R. Gillespie*, E.J. Gray, R.J. Hadlee, P.A. Horne, A.H. Jones, D.K. Morrison, D.N. Patel, K.R. Rutherford, I.D.S. Smith, M.C. Snedden, W. Watson, J.G. Wright.

42) **1987/88 to Sharjah**
J.G. Wright *(captain)*, T.E. Blain, E.J. Chatfield, M.J. Greatbatch, R.J. Hadlee, A.H. Jones, C.M. Kuggeleijn, D.K. Morrison, D.N. Patel, K.R. Rutherford, I.D.S. Smith, R.H. Vance, W. Watson.

43) **1988/89 to India**
J.G. Wright *(captain)*, T.E. Blain, J.G. Bracewell, E.J. Chatfield, T.J. Franklin, E.J. Gray, M.J. Greatbatch, R.J. Hadlee, A.H. Jones, C.M. Kuggeleijn, D.K. Morrison, K.R. Rutherford, I.D.S. Smith, M.C. Snedden, R.H. Vance, W. Watson*.

44) **1988/89 to Australia**
J.G. Wright *(captain)*, E.J. Chatfield, J.J. Crowe, M.D. Crowe, M.J. Greatbatch, A.H. Jones, C.M. Kuggeleijn, D.K. Morrison, I.D.S. Smith, M.C. Snedden, R.H. Vance, W. Watson.

45) **1989/90 to Australia**
J.G. Wright *(captain)*, B.P. Bracewell, J.G. Bracewell, C.L. Cairns*, J.J. Crowe, M.D. Crowe, M.J. Greatbatch, A.H. Jones, D.K. Morrison, D.N. Patel*, G.K. Robertson, I.D.S. Smith, M.C. Snedden, R.H. Vance, W. Watson.

46) **1990 to Sharjah and England**
J.G. Wright *(captain)*, J.G. Bracewell, J.J. Crowe, M.D. Crowe, T.J. Franklin, M.J. Greatbatch, Sir R.J. Hadlee, A.H. Jones, J.P. Millmow, D.K. Morrison, A.C. Parore, M.W. Priest, C. Pringle*, K.R. Rutherford, I.D.S. Smith, M.C. Snedden, S.A. Thomson, W. Watson*.

47) **1990/91 to Pakistan**
M.D. Crowe *(captain)*, G.E. Bradburn, T.J. Franklin, M.J. Greatbatch, P.A. Horne, D.K. Morrison, A.C. Parore, D.N. Patel, M.W. Priest, C. Pringle, S.J. Roberts, K.R. Rutherford, I.D.S. Smith, W. Watson, D.J. White.

48) **1990/91 to Australia**
M.D. Crowe *(captain)*, G.E. Bradburn, M.J. Greatbatch, C.Z. Harris, A.H. Jones, G.R. Larsen*, R.T. Latham, D.K. Morrison, R.G. Petrie, C. Pringle, R.B. Reid*, K.R. Rutherford, I.D.S. Smith, W. Watson, J.G. Wright, B.A. Young.

49) **1991/92 to Australia**
M.D. Crowe *(captain)*, G.E. Bradburn, C.L. Cairns, T.J. Franklin, M.J. Greatbatch, C.Z. Harris, A.H. Jones, D.K. Morrison, A.C. Parore, D.N. Patel, C. Pringle, I.D.S. Smith, S.A. Thomson, W. Watson, K.A. Wealleans.

50) **1992/93 to Zimbabwe and Sri Lanka**
M.D. Crowe *(captain)*, G.E. Bradburn*, S.B. Doull, M.J. Greatbatch, C.Z. Harris, B.R. Hartland, M.J. Haslam, A.H. Jones, G.R. Larsen, R.T. Latham, D.J. Nash, M.B. Owens*, A.C. Parore, D.N. Patel, C. Pringle*, K.R. Rutherford, M.L. Su'a, J.T.C. Vaughan*, W. Watson, J.G. Wright*.

51) **1993/94 to Australia**
M.D. Crowe *(captain)*, T.E. Blain, C.L. Cairns, S.B. Doull, R.P. de Groen*, M.J. Greatbatch, C.Z. Harris*, M.J. Haslam, A.H. Jones, G.R. Larsen*, R.T. Latham*, D.K. Morrison, D.N. Patel, B.A. Pocock, C. Pringle*, K.R. Rutherford, M.L. Su'a, S.A. Thomson*, W. Watson, D.J. White*, B.A. Young.

52) **1994 to Sharjah and England**
K.R. Rutherford *(captain)*, M.D. Crowe, H.T. Davis, M.W. Douglas, S.B. Doull, S.P. Fleming, M.J. Greatbatch, C.Z. Harris, M.N. Hart, B.R. Hartland, G.R. Larsen, D.K. Morrison, D.J. Nash, M.B. Owens*, A.C. Parore, B.A. Pocock, C. Pringle, S.J. Roberts*, S.A. Thomson, B.A. Young. (Harris and Douglas were selected only for Sharjah but Douglas re-appeared as an additional player during the England tour. Larsen captained the team in Sharjah as Rutherford was not available for that part of the tour).

53) **1994/95 to India and South Africa**
K.R. Rutherford *(captain)*, M.D. Crowe, R.P. de Groen, S.B. Doull, S.P. Fleming, L.K. Germon, C.Z. Harris, M.N. Hart, B.R. Hartland, D.K. Morrison*, D.J. Murray, D.J. Nash, A.C. Parore, M.W. Priest*, C. Pringle, M.L. Su'a, S.A. Thomson, B.A. Young.

54) **1995/96 to India**
L.K. Germon *(captain)*, N.J. Astle*, C.L. Cairns, M.D. Crowe, S.B. Doull, S.P. Fleming, A.J. Gale, M.J. Greatbatch, M.N. Hart, M.J. Haslam, G.R. Larsen*, D.K. Morrison, D.J. Nash, A.C. Parore, S.A. Thomson, R.G. Twose, B.A. Young.

55) **1995/96 to India and Pakistan** *(World Cup)*
L.K. Germon *(captain)*, N.J. Astle, C.L. Cairns, S.P. Fleming, C.Z. Harris, R.J. Kennedy, G.R. Larsen, D.K. Morrison, D.J. Nash, A.C. Parore, D.N. Patel, C.M. Spearman, S.A. Thomson, R.G. Twose.

56) **1995/96 to West Indies**
L.K. Germon *(captain)*, N.J. Astle, M.D. Bailey*, C.L. Cairns, S.P. Fleming, C.Z. Harris, M.J. Haslam*, R.J. Kennedy, G.R. Larsen, D.K. Morrison, D.J. Nash, A.C. Parore, D.N. Patel, C.M. Spearman, S.A. Thomson, R.G. Twose, J.T.C. Vaughan*.

57) **1996/97 to Sharjah and Pakistan**
L.K. Germon *(captain)*, N.J. Astle, C.L. Cairns, S.B. Doull, S.P. Fleming, M.J. Greatbatch, C.Z. Harris, M.N. Hart*, M.J. Haslam, G.R. Jonas*, R.J. Kennedy*, G.R. Larsen, D.K. Morrison, A.C. Parore, D.N. Patel, C.M. Spearman, J.T.C. Vaughan, P.J. Wiseman*, B.A. Young.

58) **1996/97 to India** *(Independence Cup)*
S.P. Fleming *(captain)*, N.J. Astle, C.L. Cairns, H.T. Davis, C.Z. Harris, M.J. Horne, G.R. Larsen, C.D. McMillan, S.B. O'Connor, A.C. Parore, D.N. Patel, A.J. Penn, D.L. Vettori, B.A. Young.

59) **1997/98 to Kenya and Zimbabwe**
S.P. Fleming *(captain)*, N.J. Astle, C.L. Cairns, H.T. Davis, C.Z. Harris, M.J. Horne, G.R. Larsen, C.D. McMillan, S.B. O'Connor, A.C. Parore, B.A. Pocock, D.G. Sewell, C.M. Spearman, D.L. Vettori, P.J. Wiseman.

60) **1997/98 to Australia**
S.P. Fleming *(captain)*, G.I. Allott, N.J. Astle, C.L. Cairns, H.T. Davis, S.B. Doull, C.J. Drum*, C.Z. Harris*, M.J. Horne, G.R. Larsen*, C.D. McMillan, D.J. Nash*, S.B. O'Connor, A.C. Parore, B.A. Pocock, C.M. Spearman*, R.G. Twose*, D.L. Vettori, B.A. Young.

61) **1997/98 to Sharjah**
S.P. Fleming *(captain)*, N.J. Astle, C.L. Cairns, S.B. Doull, C.Z. Harris, M.J. Horne, L.G. Howell, C.D. McMillan, D.J. Nash, S.B. O'Connor, A.C. Parore, M.W. Priest, P.J. Wiseman.

62) **1997/98 to Sri Lanka**
S.P. Fleming *(captain)*, N.J. Astle, C.L. Cairns, S.B. Doull, C.Z. Harris, M.J. Horne, C.D. McMillan, D.J. Nash, S.B. O'Connor, A.C. Parore, M.W. Priest, C.M. Spearman, A.R. Tait*, D.L. Vettori, P.J. Wiseman, B.A. Young.

63) **1998 to Malaysia** *(Commonwealth Games)*
S.P. Fleming *(captain)*, G.I. Allott, N.J. Astle, M.D. Bailey, M.D. Bell, C.J. Drum, C.Z. Harris, M.J. Horne, C.D. McMillan, S.B. O'Connor, A.C. Parore, A.R. Tait, D.L. Vettori, P.J. Wiseman.

64) **1998/99 to Bangladesh** *(Wills International Cup)*
S.P. Fleming *(captain)*, G.I. Allott, N.J. Astle, M.D. Bailey, M.D. Bell, S.B. Doull, C.Z. Harris, M.J. Horne, C.D. McMillan, S.B. O'Connor, A.C. Parore, A.R. Tait, D.L. Vettori, P.J. Wiseman.

65) **1999 to England**
S.P. Fleming *(captain)*, G.I. Allott, N.J. Astle, M.D. Bell*, C.E. Bulfin, C.L. Cairns, M.G. Croy*, S.B. Doull, C.Z. Harris, M.N. Hart, M.J. Horne, G.R. Larsen, C.D. McMillan, D.J. Nash, S.B. O'Connor*, A.C. Parore, A.J. Penn*, R.G. Twose, D.L. Vettori, B.G.K. Walker*.

66) **1999/00 to India**
S.P. Fleming *(captain)*, N.J. Astle, M.D. Bell, C.L. Cairns, C.J. Drum, C.Z. Harris, M.J. Horne, C.D. McMillan, D.J. Nash, S.B. O'Connor, A.C. Parore, A.J. Penn, C.M. Spearman, G.R. Stead*, S.B. Styris*, A.R. Tait*, R.G. Twose*, D.L. Vettori, P.J. Wiseman.

67) **2000/01 to Singapore, Zimbabwe, Kenya and South Africa**
S.P. Fleming *(captain)*, G.I. Allott, N.J. Astle, C.L. Cairns, C.Z. Harris, M.J. Horne, C.D. McMillan, H.J.H. Marshall, C.S. Martin, D.J. Nash, C.J. Nevin, S.B. O'Connor, A.C. Parore, A.J. Penn, M.H. Richardson, M.S. Sinclair, C.M. Spearman, S.B. Styris, G.P. Sulzberger, D.R. Tuffey, R.G. Twose, D.L. Vettori, B.G.K. Walker, K.P. Walmsley, P.J. Wiseman. (Apart from a number of players being replaced because of injury, this party was reselected and changed several times depending on the nature of the matches being played).

68) **2000/01 to Sharjah**
C.D. McMillan *(captain)*, A.R. Adams, M.D. Bell, G.E. Bradburn, J.E.C. Franklin, C.Z. Harris, K.D. Mills, C.J. Nevin, J.D.P. Oram, M.S. Sinclair, D.R.Tuffey, L. Vincent, B.G.K. Walker.

69) **2001/02 to Sri Lanka**
S.P. Fleming *(captain)*, N.J. Astle, G.E. Bradburn, J.E.C. Franklin, C.Z. Harris, K.D. Mills, C.D. McMillan, D.J. Nash, J.D.P. Oram, A.C. Parore, M.S. Sinclair, D.R.Tuffey, D.L. Vettori, L. Vincent.

70) **2001/02 to Australia**
S.P. Fleming *(captain)*, A.R. Adams, N.J. Astle, M.D. Bell, S.E. Bond*, C.L. Cairns, C.J. Drum*, J.E.C. Franklin, C.Z. Harris, B.B. McCullum, C.D. McMillan, C.S. Martin, D.J. Nash, S.B. O'Çonnor, A.C. Parore, M.H. Richardson, M.S. Sinclair, S.B. Styris, G.P. Sulzberger, D.R. Tuffey, D.L. Vettori, L. Vincent, P.J. Wiseman*.

71) **2001/02 to Sharjah and Pakistan**
S.P. Fleming *(captain)*, A.R. Adams, N.J. Astle, I.G. Butler, J.E.C. Franklin, C.Z. Harris, R.G. Hart, M.J. Horne, C.D. McMillan, C.S. Martin, C.J. Nevin, J.D.P. Oram, M.H. Richardson, M.S. Sinclair, S.B. Styris, D.R. Tuffey, D.L. Vettori, L. Vincent, B.G.K. Walker.

72) **2001/02 to West Indies**
S.P. Fleming *(captain)*, N.J. Astle, S.E. Bond, I.G. Butler, C.Z. Harris, M.N. Hart, R.G. Hart, P.A. Hitchcock, M.J. Horne, C.D. McMillan, C.S. Martin, C.J. Nevin, J.D.P. Oram, M.H. Richardson, S.B. Styris, D.R. Tuffey, D.L. Vettori, L. Vincent.

73) **2002/03 to Australia and Sri Lanka** *(ICC Champions Trophy)*
S.P. Fleming *(captain)*, N.J. Astle, S.E. Bond, I.G. Butler*, C.Z. Harris, M.N. Hart*, P.A. Hitchcock, M.J. Horne*, C.D. McMillan*, K.D. Mills, C.J. Nevin, J.D.P. Oram, M.S. Sinclair, S.B. Styris, G.P. Sulzberger, D.R. Tuffey, D.L. Vettori, L. Vincent, B.G.K. Walker*, J.A.F. Yovich*.

74) **2002/03 to South Africa** *(World Cup)*
S.P. Fleming *(captain)*, A.R. Adams, N.J. Astle, S.E. Bond, C.L. Cairns, C.Z. Harris, B.B. McCullum, C.D. McMillan, K.D. Mills, J.D.P. Oram, M.S. Sinclair, S.B. Styris, D.R. Tuffey, D.L. Vettori, L. Vincent.

75) **2002/03 to Sri Lanka**
S.P. Fleming *(captain)*, A.R. Adams, S.E. Bond, I.G. Butler, C.L. Cairns, C.Z. Harris, R.G. Hart, M.J. Horne, R.A. Jones, B.B. McCullum, K.D. Mills, C.J. Nevin, J.D.P. Oram, M.H. Richardson, M.S. Sinclair, S.B. Styris, D.R. Tuffey, D.L. Vettori, L. Vincent, P.J. Wiseman.

76) **2003/04 to India**
S.P. Fleming *(captain)*, N.J. Astle, I.G. Butler, C.L. Cairns*, C.Z. Harris*, R.G. Hart, P.A. Hitchcock*, R.A. Jones, B.B. McCullum*. C.D. McMillan, M.J. Mason, K.D. Mills*, C.J. Nevin*, J.D.P. Oram, M.H. Richardson, S.B. Styris, D.R. Tuffey, D.L. Vettori, L. Vincent, P.J. Wiseman.

77) **2003/04 to Pakistan**
C.L. Cairns *(captain)*, T.K. Canning, C.D. Cumming, C.Z. Harris, P.A. Hitchcock, R.A. Jones, B.B. McCullum, H.J.H. Marshall, M.J. Mason, J.D.P. Oram, M.S. Sinclair, D.R. Tuffey, D.L. Vettori, M.D.J. Walker, K.P. Walmsley.

78) **2004 to England**
S.P. Fleming *(captain)*, A.R. Adams*, N.J. Astle, S.E. Bond, I.G. Butler*, C.L. Cairns, J.E.C. Franklin*, C.Z. Harris*, G.J. Hopkins*, B.B. McCullum, C.D. McMillan, H.J.H Marshall*, C.S. Martin, K.D. Mills, J.D.P. Oram, M.H.W Papps, M.H. Richardson, S.B. Styris, D.R. Tuffey, D.L. Vettori.

79) **2004 to England** *(Champions Trophy)*
S.P. Fleming *(captain)*, N.J. Astle, I.G. Butler, C.L. Cairns, C.Z. Harris, B.B. McCullum, C.D. McMillan, H.J.H. Marshall, K.D. Mills, J.D.P Oram, M.H.W. Papps, S.B. Styris, D.R. Tuffey, D.L. Vettori.

80) **2004/05 to Bangladesh**
S.P. Fleming *(captain)*, A.R. Adams*, N.J. Astle, I.G. Butler, C.L. Cairns*, J.E.C. Franklin, P.G.Fulton*, C.Z. Harris*, B.B. McCullum, C.D. McMillan*, H.J.H. Marshall, C.S. Martin, K.D. Mills, J.D.P. Oram, M.H. Richardson, M.S. Sinclair, S.B. Styris, D.L. Vettori, P.J. Wiseman.

81) **2004/05 to Australia**
S.P. Fleming *(captain)*, A.R. Adams*, N.J. Astle, I.G. Butler, C.L. Cairns*, T.K. Canning*, J.E.C. Franklin, C.Z. Harris*, G.J.Hopkins*, B.B. McCullum, C.D. McMillan*, H.J.H. Marshall, C.S. Martin, K.D. Mills, J.D.P.Oram, M.H. Richardson, M.S. Sinclair, S.B. Styris, D.L. Vettori, P.J. Wiseman.

82) **2005/06 to Namibia and Zimbabwe**
S.P. Fleming *(captain)*, A.R. Adams*, N.J. Astle, S.E. Bond, C.L. Cairns*, C.D. Cumming, J.E.C. Franklin, B.B. McCullum, C.D. McMillan*, H.J.H. Marshall, J.A.H. Marshall, C.S. Martin, K.D. Mills, J.D.P. Oram, J.S. Patel*, S.B. Styris, D.L. Vettori, L. Vincent, P.J. Wiseman.

83) **2005/06 to South Africa**
S.P. Fleming *(captain)*, A.R. Adams, N.J. Astle, S.E. Bond, J.E.C. Franklin, H.J.H. Marshall, J.A.H. Marshall, B.B. McCullum, C.D. McMillan, K.D. Mills, J.D.P. Oram, J.S. Patel, S.B. Styris, D.L. Vettori, L. Vincent.

84) **2005/06 to South Africa**
S.P. Fleming *(captain)*, N.J. Astle, S.E. Bond, J.E.C. Franklin, P.G. Fulton, J.M. How, B.B. McCullum, H.J.H Marshall, C.S. Martin, M.J. Mason*, K.D. Mills, J.D.P. Oram, M.H.W. Papps, J.S. Patel, S.B. Styris, D.L. Vettori

85) **2006/07 to India** *(ICC Champions Trophy)*
S.P. Fleming *(captain)*, N.J. Astle, S.E. Bond, J.E.C. Franklin, P.G. Fulton, M.R. Gillespie, B.B. McCullum, H.J.H. Marshall, K.D. Mills, J.D.P. Oram, J.S. Patel, S.B. Styris, L.R.P.L. Taylor*, D.L. Vettori, L. Vincent.

86) **2006/07 to Australia**
S.P. Fleming *(captain)*, A.R. Adams, N.J. Astle, S.E. Bond, J.E.C. Franklin, P.G. Fulton, M.R. Gillespie, B.B. McCullum, C.D. McMillan, H.J.H. Marshall, M.J. Mason, K.D. Mills*, J.D.P. Oram*, J.S. Patel, S.B. Styris*, L.R.P.L. Taylor, D.L. Vettori, L. Vincent*.

87) **2006/07 to West Indies** *(World Cup)*
S.P. Fleming *(captain)*, S.E. Bond, J.E.C. Franklin, P.G. Fulton, M.R. Gillespie, B.B. McCullum, C.D. McMillan, H.J.H. Marshall*, C.S. Martin*, M.J. Mason, J.D.P. Oram, J.S. Patel, S.B. Styris, L.R.P.L. Taylor, D.R. Tuffey, D.L. Vettori, L. Vincent.

88) **2007/08 to South Africa** *(Twenty20 World Championship)*
D.L. Vettori *(captain)*, S.E. Bond, P.G. Fulton, M.R. Gillespie, G.J. Hopkins, B.B. McCullum, N.L. McCullum, C.D. McMillan, C.S. Martin, J.D.P. Oram, J.S. Patel, B.E. Scott, S.B. Styris, L.R.P.L. Taylor, L. Vincent.

89) **2007/08 to South Africa and Australia**
D.L. Vettori *(captain)*, S.E. Bond, C.D.Cumming, S.P. Fleming, M.R. Gillespie, G.J. Hopkins*, J.M. How*, B.B. McCullum, C.S. Martin, M.J. Mason, K.D. Mills*, I.E. O'Brien, J.D.P. Oram, M.H.W. Papps, J.S. Patel, M.S. Sinclair*, S.B. Styris, L.R.P.L. Taylor, L. Vincent.

90) **2008 to England**
D.L. Vettori *(captain)*, G.D. Elliott*, D.R. Flynn, P.G. Fulton, M.R. Gillespie*, G.J. Hopkins, J.M. How, B.B. McCullum, J.A.H. Marshall, C.S. Martin, M.J. Mason, K.D. Mills, I.E. O'Brien, J.D.P. Oram, J.S. Patel, A.J. Redmond, T.G. Southee, S.B. Styris*, L.R.P.L. Taylor.

91) **2008/09 to Bangladesh**
D.L. Vettori *(captain)*, G.D. Elliott, D.R. Flynn, M.R. Gillespie, G.J. Hopkins, J.M. How, B.B. McCullum, M.J. Mason, K.D. Mills, I.E. O'Brien*, J.D.P. Oram, J.S. Patel, A.J. Redmond*, J.D. Ryder, T.G. Southee, S.B. Styris, L.R.P.L. Taylor.

92) **2008/09 to Australia**
D.L. Vettori *(captain)*, G.D. Elliott, D.R. Flynn, P.G. Fulton, M.R. Gillespie, G.J. Hopkins, J.M. How, B.B. McCullum, C.S. Martin, K.D. Mills, I.E. O'Brien, J.S. Patel*, A.J. Redmond, J.D. Ryder, T.G. Southee, L.R.P.L. Taylor.

93) **2008/09 to Australia**
D.L. Vettori *(captain)*, T.A. Boult, N.T. Broom, I.G. Butler*, C.D. Cumming, B.J. Diamanti, G.D. Elliott, J.E.C. Franklin*, P.G. Fulton, M.J. Guptill, G.J. Hopkins*, B.B. McCullum, N.L. McCullum*, P.D. McGlashan*, K.D. Mills, I.E. O'Brien, J.S. Patel, T.G. Southee, L.R.P.L. Taylor.

94) **2009 to England** *(ICC World Twenty20)*
D.L. Vettori *(captain)*, N.T. Broom, I.G. Butler, B.J. Diamanti, J.E.C. Franklin, M.J. Guptill, B.B. McCullum, N.L. McCullum, P.D. McGlashan, K.D. Mills, I.E. O'Brien, J.D.P. Oram, A.J. Redmond*, J.D. Ryder, S.B. Styris, L.R.P.L. Taylor.

95) **2009/10 to Sri Lanka**
D.L. Vettori *(captain)*, S.E. Bond, N.T. Broom, I.G. Butler, C.D. Cumming, B.J. Diamanti, G.D. Elliott, D.R. Flynn, M.J. Guptill, G.J. Hopkins, B.B. McCullum, N.L. McCullum, P.D. McGlashan, T.G. McIntosh, C.S. Martin, K.D. Mills, I.E. O'Brien, J.D.P. Oram, J.S. Patel, J.D. Ryder, L.R.P.L. Taylor, D.R. Tuffey.

96) **2009/10 to South Africa** *(ICC Champions Trophy)*
D.L. Vettori *(captain)*, S.E. Bond, N.T. Broom, I.G. Butler, B.J. Diamanti, G.D. Elliott, J.E.C. Franklin*, M.J. Guptill, G.J. Hopkins, B.B. McCullum, K.D. Mills, I.E. O'Brien*, J.D.P. Oram, J.S. Patel, A.J. Redmond*, J.D. Ryder, S.B. Styris*, L.R.P.L. Taylor, D.R. Tuffey.

97) **2009/10 to United Arab Emirates**
D.L. Vettori *(captain)*, S.E. Bond, N.T. Broom, I.G. Butler, J.E.C. Franklin, M.J. Guptill, B.B. McCullum, N.L. McCullum, K.D. Mills, J.D.P. Oram, A.J. Redmond, T.G. Southee, S.B. Styris, L.R.P.L. Taylor, B-J. Watling.

98) **2009/10 to West Indies** *(ICC World Twenty20)*
D.L. Vettori *(captain)*, S.E. Bond, I.G. Butler, M.J. Guptill, G.J. Hopkins, B.B. McCullum, N.L. McCullum, K.D. Mills, R.J. Nicol, J.D.P. Oram, A.J. Redmond, J.D. Ryder, T.G. Southee, S.B. Styris, L.R.P.L. Taylor.

99) **2009/10 to United States of America**
D.L. Vettori *(captain)*, I.G. Butler, M.J. Guptill, G.J. Hopkins, B.B. McCullum, N.L. McCullum, A.J. McKay, K.D. Mills, R.J. Nicol, J.D.P. Oram, A.J. Redmond, T.G. Southee, S.B. Styris, L.R.P.L. Taylor.

100) **2010/11 to Sri Lanka**
L.R.P.L. Taylor *(captain)*, G.D. Elliott, M.J. Guptill, G.J. Hopkins, P.J. Ingram, N.L. McCullum A.J. McKay, K.D. Mills, J.D.P. Oram, J.S. Patel, T.G. Southee, S.B. Styris, D.R. Tuffey, B-J. Watling, K.S. Williamson.

101) **2010/11 to Bangladesh**
D.L. Vettori *(captain)*, H.K. Bennett, G.D. Elliott, B.B. McCullum, N.L. McCullum, A.J. McKay, K.D. Mills, A.J. Redmond, J.D. Ryder, T.G. Southee, S.L. Stewart, L.R.P.L. Taylor, D.R. Tuffey, B-J. Watling, K.S. Williamson.

102) **2010/11 to India**
D.L. Vettori *(captain)*, B.J. Arnel, H.K. Bennett, G.D. Elliott, J.E.C. Franklin*, M.J. Guptill, G.J. Hopkins, J.M. How, B.B. McCullum, N.L. McCullum, T.G. McIntosh, A.J. McKay, C.S. Martin, K.D. Mills, J.S. Patel, J.D. Ryder, T.G. Southee, S.B. Styris, L.R.P.L. Taylor, D.R. Tuffey, B-J. Watling, K.S. Williamson.

103) **2010/11 to India, Sri Lanka and Bangladesh** *(ICC World Cup)*
D.L. Vettori *(captain)*, H.K. Bennett, J.E.C. Franklin, M.J. Guptill, J.M. How, B.B. McCullum, N.L. McCullum, A.J. McKay*, K.D. Mills, J.D.P. Oram, J.D. Ryder, T.G. Southee, S.B. Styris, L.R.P.L. Taylor, D.R. Tuffey*, K.S. Williamson, L.J. Woodcock.

104) **2011/12 to Zimbabwe**
L.R.P.L. Taylor *(captain)*, G.W. Aldridge, D.A.J. Bracewell, D.G. Brownlie, J.E.C. Franklin, M.J. Guptill, B.B. McCullum, N.L. McCullum, A.J. McKay, C.S. Martin, K.D. Mills, R.J. Nicol, J.D.P. Oram, J.S. Patel, J.D. Ryder, D.L. Vettori, B-J. Watling, K.S. Williamson, L.J. Woodcock, R.A. Young.

105) **2011/12 to Australia**
L.R.P.L. Taylor *(captain)*, B.J. Arnel*, T.A. Boult, D.A.J. Bracewell, D.G. Brownlie, M.J. Guptill, B.B. McCullum, C.S. Martin, J.D. Ryder, T.G. Southee, D.L. Vettori, B-J. Watling, K.S. Williamson, R.A. Young.

106) **2012 to United States of America and West Indies**
L.R.P.L. Taylor *(captain)*, T.A. Boult, D.A.J. Bracewell, D.G. Brownlie, A.M. Ellis, D.R. Flynn, M.J. Guptill, R.M. Hira, T.W.M. Latham, B.B. McCullum, N.L. McCullum, C.S. Martin, K.D. Mills, T.S. Nethula, R.J. Nicol, J.D.P. Oram, T.G. Southee, C.F.K. van Wyk, D.L. Vettori, N. Wagner, B-J. Watling, K.S. Williamson.

107) **2012/13 to India**
L.R.P.L. Taylor *(captain)*, T.A. Boult, D.A.J. Bracewell, D.R. Flynn, J.E.C. Franklin, M.J. Guptill, R.M. Hira, B.B. McCullum, N.L. McCullum, C.S. Martin, K.D. Mills, A.F. Milne, T.S. Nethula, R.J. Nicol, J.D.P. Oram, J.S. Patel, T.G. Southee, C.F.K. van Wyk, D.L. Vettori, N. Wagner, B-J. Watling, K.S. Williamson.

108) **2012/13 to Sri Lanka** *(ICC World Twenty20)*
L.R.P.L. Taylor *(captain)*, D.A.J. Bracewell, J.E.C. Franklin, M.J. Guptill, R.M. Hira, B.B. McCullum, N.L. McCullum, K.D. Mills, A.F. Milne, R.J. Nicol, J.D.P. Oram, T.G. Southee, D.L. Vettori, B-J. Watling, K.S. Williamson.

109) **2012/13 to Sri Lanka**
L.R.P.L. Taylor *(captain)*, T.D. Astle, T.A. Boult, D.A.J. Bracewell, A.M. Ellis, D.R. Flynn, J.E.C. Franklin, M.J. Guptill, R.M. Hira, T.W.M. Latham, B.B. McCullum, N.L. McCullum, K.D. Mills, A.F. Milne, R.J. Nicol, J.D.P. Oram, J.S. Patel, T.G. Southee, C.F.K. van Wyk, B-J. Watling, K.S. Williamson.

110) **2012/13 to South Africa**
B.B. McCullum *(captain)*, C.J. Anderson, M.D. Bates, T.A. Boult, D.A.J. Bracewell, D.G. Brownlie, D.C. de Boorder, G.D. Elliott, D.R. Flynn, J.E.C. Franklin, P.G. Fulton, M.J. Guptill, R.M. Hira, M.J. McClenaghan, N.L. McCullum, B.P. Martin, C.S. Martin, K.D. Mills, C. Munro, J.D.S. Neesham, R.J. Nicol, J.S. Patel, N. Wagner, B-J. Watling, K.S. Williamson.

111) **2013 to England**
B.B. McCullum *(captain)*, T.A. Boult, D.A.J. Bracewell, D.G. Brownlie, I.G. Butler, G.D. Elliott, J.E.C. Franklin, P.G. Fulton, M.R. Gillespie, M.J. Guptill, R.M. Hira, T.W.M. Latham, N.L. McCullum, B.P. Martin, K.D. Mills, C. Munro, L. Ronchi, H.D. Rutherford, T.G. Southee, L.R.P.L. Taylor, D.L. Vettori, N. Wagner, B-J. Watling, K.S. Williamson.

112) **2013/14 to Bangladesh and Sri Lanka**
B.B. McCullum *(captain)*, C.J. Anderson, T.A. Boult, D.A.J. Bracewell, N.T. Broom*, D.G. Brownlie, A.P. Devcich, G.D. Elliott, A.M. Ellis*, P.G. Fulton, M.R. Gillespie, T.W.M. Latham, M.J. McClenaghan. N.L. McCullum, B.P. Martin, K.D. Mills, A.F. Milne, C. Munro, J.D.S. Neesham, R.J. Nicol*, L. Ronchi, H.D. Rutherford, I.S. Sodhi, T.G. Southee, L.R.P.L. Taylor, N. Wagner, B-J. Watling, K.S. Williamson.

113) **2013/14 to Bangladesh** *(ICC World Twenty20)*
B.B. McCullum *(captain)*, C.J. Anderson, T.A. Boult, A.P. Devcich, M.J. Guptill, R.M. Hira, M.J. McClenaghan. N.L. McCullum, K.D. Mills, C. Munro, J.D.S. Neesham, L. Ronchi, T.G. Southee, L.R.P.L. Taylor, K.S. Williamson.

114) **2014 to West Indies**
B.B. McCullum *(captain)*, C.J. Anderson, T.A. Boult, M.D. Craig, P.G. Fulton, T.W.M. Latham, J.D.S. Neesham, L. Ronchi, H.D. Rutherford, I.S. Sodhi, T.G. Southee, L.R.P.L. Taylor, N. Wagner, B-J. Watling, K.S. Williamson.

115) **2014/15 to United Arab Emirates**
B.B. McCullum *(captain)*, C.J. Anderson, T.A. Boult, D.A.J. Bracewell, D.G. Brownlie, M.D. Craig, A.P. Devcich, M.P. Guptill, M.J. Henry, T.W.M. Latham, M.J. McClenaghan, N.L. McCullum, K.D. Mills, A.F. Milne, J.D.S. Neesham, L. Ronchi, H.D. Rutherford, I.S. Sodhi, T.G. Southee, L.R.P.L. Taylor, D.L. Vettori, N. Wagner, B-J. Watling, K.S. Williamson.

116) **2015 to England**
B.B. McCullum *(captain)*, C.J. Anderson, T.A. Boult, D.A.J. Bracewell, M.D. Craig, J.A. Duffy*, G.D. Elliott, M.J. Guptill, M.J. Henry, T.W.M. Latham, M.J. McClenaghan, N.L. McCullum, A.W. Mathieson*, C. Munro*, L. Ronchi, H.D. Rutherford, M.J. Santner, T.G. Southee, L.R.P.L. Taylor, N. Wagner, B-J. Watling, B.M. Wheeler*, K.S. Williamson.

117) **2015/16 to Zimbabwe and South Africa**
K.S. Williamson *(captain)*, D.A.J. Bracewell, G.D. Elliott, M.J. Guptill, M.J. Henry, T.W.M. Latham, M.J. McClenaghan, N.L. McCullum, A.F. Milne, C. Munro, J.D.S. Neesham, L. Ronchi, I.S. Sodhi, L.R.P.L. Taylor, B.M. Wheeler, G.H. Worker.

118) **2015/16 to Australia**
B.B. McCullum *(captain)*, T.A. Boult, D.A.J. Bracewell, M.D. Craig, M.J. Guptill, M.J. Henry, T.W.M. Latham, M.J. McClenaghan*, J.D.S. Neesham, L. Ronchi, H.D. Rutherford, M.J. Santner, T.G. Southee, L.R.P.L. Taylor, N.Wagner*, B-J. Watling, K.S. Williamson.

119) **2015/16 to India** *(ICC World Twenty20)*
K.S. Williamson *(captain)*, C.J. Anderson, T.A. Boult, G.D. Elliott, M.J. Guptill, M.J. McClenaghan, N.L. McCullum, A.F. Milne, C. Munro, H.M. Nicholls, L. Ronchi, M.J. Santner, I.S. Sodhi, T.G. Southee, L.R.P.L. Taylor.

120) **2016/17 to Zimbabwe and South Africa**
K.S. Williamson *(captain)*, T.A. Boult, D.A.J. Bracewell, M.D. Craig, M.J. Guptill, M.J. Henry, T.W.M. Latham, H.M. Nicholls, J.A. Raval, L. Ronchi, M.J. Santner, I.S. Sodhi, T.G. Southee, L.R.P.L. Taylor, N. Wagner, B-J. Watling.

121) **2016/17 to India**
K.S. Williamson *(captain)*, C.J. Anderson, T.A. Boult, D.A.J. Bracewell, M.D. Craig, A.P. Devcich, M.J. Guptill, M.J. Henry*, T.W.M. Latham, J.D.S. Neesham, H.M. Nicholls, J.S. Patel*, L. Ronchi, M.J. Santner, I.S. Sodhi, T.G. Southee, L.R.P.L. Taylor, N. Wagner, B-J. Watling.

122) **2016/17 to Australia**
K.S. Williamson *(captain)*, T.D. Astle, T.A. Boult, C. de Grandhomme, L.H. Ferguson, M.J. Guptill, M.J. Henry, T.W.M. Latham, C. Munro, J.D.S. Neesham, H.M. Nicholls, M.J. Santner, T.G. Southee, B-J. Watling.

123) **2017 to Ireland**
T.W.M. Latham *(captain)*, C.J. Anderson*, H.K. Bennett, N.T. Broom, M.J. Henry*, S.C. Kuggeleijn, A.F. Milne*, C. Munro, J.D.S. Neesham, H.M. Nicholls, J.S. Patel, S.H.A. Rance, L. Ronchi, M.J. Santner, I.S. Sodhi, L.R.P.L. Taylor, N. Wagner, G.H. Worker.

124) **2017 to England** *(ICC Champions Trophy)*
K.S. Williamson *(captain)*, C.J. Anderson, T.A. Boult, N.T. Broom, C. de Grandhomme, M.J. Guptill, T.W.M. Latham, M.J. McClenaghan, A.F. Milne, J.D.S. Neesham, J.S. Patel, L. Ronchi, M.J. Santner, T.G. Southee, L.R.P.L. Taylor.

125) **2017/18 to India**
K.S. Williamson *(captain)*, T.D. Astle, T.A. Boult, T.C. Bruce, C. de Grandhomme, M.J. Guptill, M.J. Henry, T.W.M. Latham, A.F. Milne, C. Munro, H.M. Nicholls, G.D. Phillips, M.J. Santner, I.S. Sodhi, T.G. Southee, L.R.P.L. Taylor, G.H. Worker.

126) **2018/19 to United Arab Emirates**
K.S. Williamson *(captain)*, C.J. Anderson, T.A. Blundell, T.A. Boult, M.S. Chapman, C. de Grandhomme, L.H. Ferguson, M.J. Henry, T.W.M. Latham, A.F. Milne, C. Munro, H.M. Nicholls, A.Y. Patel, G.D. Phillips, S.H.A. Rance, J.A. Raval, T.L. Seifert, I.S. Sodhi, W.E.R. Somerville, T.G. Southee, L.R.P.L. Taylor, N. Wagner, B-J. Watling, G.H. Worker.

127) **2019 to England** *(ICC World Cup)*
K.S. Williamson *(captain)*, T.A. Blundell, T.A. Boult, C. de Grandhomme, L.H. Ferguson, M.J. Guptill, M.J. Henry, T.W.M. Latham, C. Munro, J.D.S. Neesham, H.M. Nicholls, M.J. Santner, I.S. Sodhi, T.G. Southee, L.R.P.L. Taylor.

128) **2019/20 to Sri Lanka**
K.S. Williamson *(captain)*, T.D. Astle, T.A. Blundell, T.A. Boult, T.C. Bruce, C. de Grandhomme, L.H. Ferguson, M.J. Guptill, S.C. Kuggeleijn, T.W.M. Latham, D.J. Mitchell, C. Munro, H.M. Nicholls, A.Y. Patel, S.H.A. Rance, J.A. Raval, H.D. Rutherford*, M.J. Santner, T.L. Seifert, I.S.Sodhi, W.E.R. Somerville, T.G. Southee, L.R.P.L. Taylor, N. Wagner, B-J. Watling.

129) **2019/20 to Australia**
K.S. Williamson *(captain)*, T.D. Astle, T.A. Blundell, T.A. Boult, C. de Grandhomme, L.H. Ferguson, M.J. Henry, K.A. Jamieson*, T.W.M. Latham, H.M. Nicholls, G.D. Phillips*, J.A. Raval, M.J. Santner, W.E.R. Somerville*, T.G. Southee, L.R.P.L. Taylor, N. Wagner, B-J. Watling.

130) **2019/20 to Australia**
K.S.Williamson *(captain)*, T.A. Blundell, T.A. Boult, C. de Grandhomme, L.H. Ferguson, M.J. Guptill, M.J. Henry, K.A. Jamieson, T.W.M. Latham, J.D.S. Neesham, H.M. Nicholls, M.J Santner, I.S. Sodhi, T.G. Southee, L.R.P.L. Taylor.

131) **2021 to England**
K.S.Williamson *(captain)*, T.A. Blundell, T.A. Boult, D.A.J. Bracewell, D.P. Conway, C. de Grandhomme, J.A. Duffy, M.J. Henry, K.A. Jamieson, T.W.M. Latham, D.J. Mitchell, H.M. Nicholls, A.Y. Patel, R. Ravindra, M.J. Santner, T.G. Southee, L.R.P.L. Taylor, N. Wagner, B-J. Watling, W.A. Young.

** replacement or temporary addition to the touring party*

NEW ZEALAND TEST RECORDS

REGISTER OF PLAYERS

	Born	Died	Type		Test Career
Adams Andre Ryan	17/7/1975 Auckland		RHB	RFM	2001/02
Alabaster John Chaloner	11/7/1930 Invercargill		RHB	RLB	1955/56-1971/72
Allcott Cyril Francis Walter	7/10/1896 Lower Moutere	19/11/1973 Auckland	LHB	LM	1929/30-1931/32
Allott Geoffrey Ian	24/12/1971 Christchurch		RHB	LFM	1995/96-1999
Anderson Corey James	13/12/1990 Christchurch		LHB	LFM	2013/14-2015/16
Anderson Robert Wickham	2/10/1948 Christchurch		RHB	RLB	1976/77-1978
Anderson William McDougall	8/10/1919 Westport	21/12/1979 Christchurch	LHB	RLBG	1945/46
Andrews Bryan	4/4/1945 Christchurch		RHB	RFM	1973/74
Arnel Brent John	3/1/1979 Hamilton		RHB	RFM	2009/10-2011/12
Astle Nathan John	15/9/1971 Christchurch		RHB	RM	1995/96-2006/07
Astle Todd Duncan	24/9/1986 Palmerston North		RHB	RLB	2012/13-2019/20
Badcock Frederick Theodore	9/8/1897 Abbottabad, India	19/9/1982 Perth	RHB	RM	1929/30-1932/33
Barber Richard Trevor	3/6/1925 Otaki	7/8/2015 Christchurch	RHB	WK	1955/56
Bartlett Gary Alex	3/2/1941 Blenheim		RHB	RF	1961/62-1967/68
Barton Paul Thomas	9/10/1935 Wellington		RHB	SLA	1961/62-1962/63
Beard Donald Derek	14/1/1920 Palmerston North	15/7/1982 Lancaster	RHB	RM	1951/52-1955/56
Beck John Edward Francis	1/8/1934 Wellington	23/4/2000 Waikanae	LHB		1953/54-1955/56
Bell Matthew David	25/2/1977 Dunedin		RHB		1998/99-2007/08
Bell William	5/9/1931 Dunedin	23/7/2002 Auckland	RHB	RLB	1953/54
Bennett Hamish Kyle	22/2/1987 Timaru		LHB	RF	2010/11
Bilby Grahame Paul	7/5/1941 Wellington		RHB		1965/66
Blain Tony Elston	17/2/1962 Nelson		RHB	WK	1986-1993/94
Blair Robert William	23/6/1932 Petone		RHB	RFM	1952/53-1963/64
Blundell Thomas Ackland	1/9/1990 Wellington		RHB	WK	2017/18- 2021
Blunt Roger Charles	3/11/1900 Durham, England	22/6/1966 London	RHB	RLBG	1929/30-1931/32
Bolton Bruce Alfred	31/5/1935 Christchurch		RHB	RLB	1958/59
Bond Shane Edward	7/6/1975 Christchurch		RHB	RF	2001/02-2009/10
Boock Stephen Lewis	20/9/1951 Dunedin		RHB	SLA	1977/78-1988/89
Boult Trent Alexander	22/7/1989 Rotorua		RHB	LFM	2011/12-2021

	Born	Died	Type		Test Career
Bracewell Brendon Paul	14/9/1959 Auckland		RHB	RFM	1978-1984/85
Bracewell Douglas Andrew John	28/9/1990 Tauranga		RHB	RFM	2011/12-2016/17
Bracewell John Garry	15/4/1958 Auckland		RHB	ROB	1980/81-1990
Bradburn Grant Eric	26/5/1966 Hamilton		RHB	ROB	1990/91-2000/01
Bradburn Wynne Pennell	24/11/1938 Thames	25/9/2008 Hamilton	RHB	RSM	1963/64
Broom Neil Trevor	20/11/1983 Christchurch		RHB		2016/17
Brown Vaughan Raymond	3/11/1959 Christchurch		LHB	ROB	1985/86
Brownlie Dean Graham	30/7/1984 Perth, Australia		RHB	RM	2011/12-2013
Burgess Mark Gordon	17/7/1944 Auckland		RHB	ROB	1967/68-1980/81
Burke Cecil	22/3/1914 Auckland	4/8/1997 Auckland	RHB	RLB	1945/46
Burtt Thomas Browning	22/1/1915 Christchurch	24/5/1988 Christchurch	RHB	SLA	1946/47-1952/53
Butler Ian Gareth	24/11/1981 Auckland		RHB	RF	2001/02-2004/05
Butterfield Leonard Arthur	29/8/1913 Christchurch	5/7/1999 Christchurch	RHB	RM	1945/46
Cairns Bernard Lance	10/10/1949 Picton		RHB	RM	1973/74-1985/86
Cairns Christopher Lance	13/6/1970 Picton		RHB	RFM	1989/90-2004
Cameron Francis James	1/6/1932 Dunedin		RHB	RFM	1961/62-1965
Cave Henry Butler	10/10/1922 Wanganui	15/9/1989 Wanganui	RHB	RM	1949-1958
Chapple Murray Ernest	25/7/1930 Christchurch	31/7/1985 Hamilton	RHB	SLA	1952/53-1965/66
Chatfield Ewen John	3/7/1950 Dannevirke		RHB	RM	1974/75-1988/89
Cleverley Donald Charles	23/12/1909 Oamaru	16/2/2004 Southport, Aust.	LHB	RFM	1931/32-1945/46
Collinge Richard Owen	2/4/1946 Wellington		RHB	LFM	1964/65-1978
Colquhoun Ian Alexander	8/6/1924 Wellington	26/2/2005 Paraparaumu Beach	RHB	WK	1954/55
Coney Jeremy Vernon	21/6/1952 Wellington		RHB	RSM	1973/74-1986/87
Congdon Bevan Ernest	11/2/1938 Motueka	10/2/2018 Auckland	RHB	RM	1964/65-1978
Conway Devon Philip	8/7/1991 Johannesburg, South Africa		LHB	WK	2021
Cowie John	30/3/1912 Auckland	3/6/1994 Lower Hutt	RHB	RFM	1937-1949
Craig Mark Donald	23/3/1987 Auckland		LHB	ROB	2014-2016/17
Cresswell George Fenwick	22/3/1915 Wanganui	10/1/1966 Blenheim	LHB	RM	1949-1950/51
Cromb Ian Burns	25/6/1905 Christchurch	6/3/1984 Christchurch	RHB	RM	1931-1931/32
Crowe Jeffrey John	14/9/1958 Auckland		RHB		1982/83-1989/90
Crowe Martin David	22/9/1962 Auckland	3/3/2016 Auckland	RHB	RM	1981/82-1995/96
Cumming Craig Derek	31/8/1975 Timaru		RHB	RM	2004/05-2007/08
Cunis Robert Smith	5/1/1941 Whangarei	9/8/2008 Whangarei	RHB	RFM	1963/64-1971/72

	Born	Died	Type		Test Career
D'Arcy John William	23/4/1936 Christchurch		RHB		1958
de Grandhomme Colin	22/7/1986 Harare, Zimbabwe		RHB	RM	2016/17-2021
de Groen Richard Paul	5/8/1962 Otorohanga		RHB	RM	1993/94-1994/95
Davis Heath Te-Ihi-O-Te-Rangi	30/11/1971 Lower Hutt		RHB	RF	1994-1997/98
Dempster Charles Stewart	15/11/1903 Wellington	12/2/1974 Wellington	RHB		1929/30-1932/33
Dempster Eric William	25/1/1925 Wellington	15/8/2011 Dunedin	LHB	SLA	1952/53-1953/54
Dick Arthur Edward	10/10/1936 Middlemarch		RHB	WK	1961/62-1965
Dickinson George Ritchie	11/3/1903 Dunedin	17/3/1978 Lower Hutt	RHB	RF	1929/30-1931/32
Donnelly Martin Paterson	17/10/1917 Ngaruawahia	22/10/1999 Sydney	LHB	SLA	1937-1949
Doull Simon Blair	6/8/1969 Pukekohe		RHB	RM	1992/93-1999/00
Dowling Graham Thorne	4/3/1937 Christchurch		RHB		1961/62-1971/72
Drum Christopher James	10/7/1974 Auckland		RHB	RFM	2000/01-2001/02
Dunning John Angus	6/2/1903 Omaha	24/6/1971 Adelaide	RHB	RM	1932/33-1937
Edgar Bruce Adrian	23/11/1956 Wellington		LHB	WK	1978-1986
Edwards Graham Neil	27/5/1955 Nelson	6/4/2020 Nelson	RHB	WK	1976/77-1980/81
Elliott Grant David	21/3/1979 Johanesburg, S. Africa		RHB	RM	2007/08-2009/10
Emery Raymond William George	28/3/1915 Auckland	18/12/1982 Auckland	RHB	RM	1951/52
Ferguson Lachlan Hammond	13/9/1991 Auckland		RHB	RF	2019/20
Fisher Frederick Eric	28/7/1924 Johnsonville	19/6/1996 Palmerston North	RHB	LM	1952/53
Fleming Stephen Paul	1/4/1973 Christchurch		LHB		1993/94-2007/08
Flynn Daniel Raymond	16/4/1985 Rotorua		LHB	SLA	2008-2012
Foley Henry	28/1/1906 Wellington	16/10/1948 Brisbane	LHB		1929/30
Franklin James Edward Charles	7/11/1980 Wellington		LHB	LFM	2000/01-2012/13
Franklin Trevor John	18/3/1962 Auckland		RHB	RM	1983-1990/91
Freeman Douglas Linford	8/9/1914 Sydney, Australia	31/5/1994 Sydney	RHB	RLBG	1932/33
Fulton Peter Gordon	1/2/1979 Christchurch		RHB	RM	2005/06-2014
Gallichan Norman	3/6/1906 Palmerston North	25/3/1969 Taupo	RHB	SLA	1937
Gedye Sidney Graham	2/5/1929 Otahuhu	10/8/2014 Auckland	RHB		1963/64-1964/65
Germon Lee Kenneth	4/11/1968 Christchurch		RHB	WK	1995/96-1996/97
Gillespie Mark Raymond	17/10/1979 Wanganui		RHB	RFM	2007/08-2011/12
Gillespie Stuart Ross	2/3/1957 Wanganui		RHB	RFM	1985/86
Gray Evan John	18/11/1954 Wellington		RHB	SLA	1983-1988/89

	Born	Died	Type		Test Career
Greatbatch Mark John	11/12/1963 Auckland		LHB		1987/88-1996/97
Guillen Simpson Clairmonte	24/9/1924 Port of Spain, Trinidad	1/3/2013 Christchurch	RHB	WK	1955/56
Guptill Martin James	30/9/1986 Auckland		RHB	ROB	2008/09-2016/17
Guy John William	29/8/1934 Nelson		LHB		1955/56-1961/62
Hadlee Dayle Robert	6/1/1948 Christchurch		RHB	RM	1969-1977/78
Hadlee Richard John	3/7/1951 Christchurch		LHB	RFM	1972/73-1990
Hadlee Walter Arnold	4/6/1915 Lincoln	29/9/2006 Christchurch	RHB		1937-1950/51
Harford Noel Sherwin	30/8/1930 Winton	30/3/1981 Auckland	RHB	RM	1955/56-1958
Harford Roy Ivan	30/5/1936 London, England		LHB	WK	1967/68
Harris Chris Zinzan	20/11/1969 Christchurch		LHB	RM	1992/93-2001/02
Harris Parke Gerald Zinzan	18/7/1927 Christchurch	1/12/1991 Christchurch	RHB	ROB	1955/56-1964/65
Harris Roger Meredith	27/7/1933 Otahuhu		RHB	RM	1958/59
Hart Matthew Norman	16/5/1972 Hamilton		LHB	SLA	1993/94-1995/96
Hart Robert Garry	2/12/1974 Hamilton		RHB	WK	2001/02-2003/04
Hartland Blair Robert	22/10/1966 Christchurch		RHB		1991/92-1994
Haslam Mark James	26/9/1972 Bury, England		LHB	SLA	1992/93-1995/96
Hastings Brian Frederick	23/3/1940 Wellington		RHB		1968/69-1975/76
Hayes John Arthur	11/1/1927 Auckland	25/12/2007 Auckland	RHB	RF	1950/51-1958
Henderson Matthew	2/8/1895 Auckland	17/6/1970 Wellington	LHB	LFM	1929/30
Henry Matthew James	14/12/1991 Christchurch		RHB	RFM	2015-2021
Hopkins Gareth James	24/11/1976 Lower Hutt		RHB	WK	2008-2010/11
Horne Matthew Jeffery	5/12/1970 Auckland		RHB	RM	1996/97-2002/03
Horne Philip Andrew	21/1/1960 Upper Hutt		LHB		1986/87-1990/91
Hough Kenneth William	24/10/1928 Sydney, Australia	20/9/2009 Gladstone	RHB	RM	1958/59
How Jamie Michael	19/5/1981 New Plymouth		RHB	ROB	2005/06-2008/09
Howarth Geoffrey Philip	29/3/1951 Auckland		RHB	ROB	1974/75-1984/85
Howarth Hedley John	25/12/1943 Auckland	7/11/2008 Auckland	LHB	SLA	1969-1976/77
Ingram Peter John	25/10/1978 Hawera		RHB		2009/10
James Kenneth Cecil	12/3/1904 Wellington	21/8/1976 Palmerston North	RHB	WK	1929/30-1932/33
Jamieson Kyle Alex	30/12/1994 Auckland		RHB	RFM	2019/20-2021
Jarvis Terrence Wayne	29/7/1944 Auckland		RHB		1964/65-1972/73
Jones Andrew Howard	9/5/1959 Wellington		RHB	ROB	1986/87-1994/95

	Born	Died	Type			Test Career
Jones Richard Andrew	22/10/1973 Auckland		RHB			2003/04
Kennedy Robert John	3/6/1972 Dunedin		RHB	RFM		1995/96
Kerr John Lambert	28/12/1910 Dannevirke	27/5/2007 Christchurch	RHB			1931-1937
Kuggeleijn Christopher Mary	10/5/1956 Auckland		RHB	ROB		1988/89
Larsen Gavin Rolf	27/9/1962 Wellington		RHB	RM		1994-1995/96
Latham Rodney Terry	12/6/1961 Christchurch		RHB			1991/92-1992/93
Latham Thomas William Maxwell	2/4/1992 Christchurch		LHB	WK		2013/14-2021
Lees Warren Kenneth	19/3/1952 Dunedin		RHB	WK		1976/77-1983
Leggat Ian Bruce	7/6/1930 Invercargill		RHB	RM		1953/54
Leggat John Gordon	27/5/1926 Wellington	9/3/1973 Christchurch	RHB			1951/52-1955/56
Lissette Allen Fisher	6/11/1919 Morrinsville	24/1/1973 Hamilton	RHB	SLA		1955/56
Loveridge Greg Riaka	15/1/1975 Palmerston North		RHB	RLB		1995/96
Lowry Thomas Coleman	17/2/1898 Fernhill	20/7/1976 Hastings	RHB	ROB	WK	1929/30-1931
McCullum Brendon Barrie	27/9/1981 Dunedin		RHB		WK	2003/04-2015/16
McEwan Paul Ernest	19/12/1953 Christchurch		RHB	RM		1979/80-1984/85
MacGibbon Anthony Roy	28/8/1924 Christchurch	6/4/2010 Christchurch	RHB	RFM		1950/51-1958
McGirr Herbert Mendelson	5/11/1891 Wellington	14/4/1964 Nelson	RHB	RFM		1929/30
McGregor Spencer Noel	18/12/1931 Dunedin	21/11/2007 Christchurch	RHB			1954/55-1964/65
McIntosh Timothy Gavin	4/12/1979 Auckland		LHB			2008/09-2010/11
McKay Andrew John	17/4/1980 Auckland		RHB	LF		2010/11
McLeod Edwin George	14/10/1900 Auckland	14/9/1989 Wellington	LHB	RLB		1929/30
McMahon Trevor George	8/11/1929 Wellington		RHB	WK		1955/56
McMillan Craig Douglas	13/9/1976 Christchurch		RHB	RM		1997/98-2004/05
McRae Donald Alexander Noel	25/12/1912 Christchurch	10/8/1986 Christchurch	LHB	LM		1945/46
Marshall Hamish John Hamilton	15/2/1979 Warkworth		RHB	RM		2000/01-2005/06
Marshall James Andrew Hamilton	15/2/1979 Warkworth		RHB	RM		2004/05-2008
Martin Bruce Philip	25/4/1980 Whangarei		RHB	SLA		2012/13-2013/14
Martin Christopher Stewart	10/12/1974 Christchurch		RHB	RFM		2000/01-2012
Mason Michael James	27/8/1974 Carterton		RHB	RFM		2003/04
Matheson Alexander Malcolm	27/2/1906 Omaha	31/12/1985 Auckland	RHB	RFM		1929/30-1931
Meale Trevor	11/11/1928 Auckland	21/5/2010 Auckland	LHB			1958
Merritt William Edward	18/8/1908 Sumner	9/6/1977 Christchurch	RHB	RLBG		1929/30-1931

	Born	Died	Type		Test Career
Meuli Edgar Milton	20/2/1926 Hawera	15/4/2007 Auckland	RHB	RLB	1952/53
Milburn Barry Douglas	24/11/1943 Dunedin		RHB	WK	1968/69
Miller Lawrence Somerville Martin	31/3/1923 New Plymouth	17/12/1996 Kapiti	LHB	LSM	1952/53-1958
Mills John Ernest	3/9/1905 Dunedin	11/12/1972 Hamilton	LHB		1929/30-1932/33
Mills Kyle David	15/3/1979 Auckland		RHB	RFM	2004-2008/09
Mitchell Daryl Joseph	20/5/1991 Hamilton		RHB	RM	2019/20-2021
Moir Alexander McKenzie	17/7/1919 Dunedin	17/6/2000 Dunedin	RHB	RLB	1950/51-1958/59
Moloney Denis Andrew Robert	11/8/1910 Dunedin	15/7/1942 El Alamein	RHB	RLB	1937
Mooney Francis Leonard Hugh	26/5/1921 Wellington	8/3/2004 Wellington	RHB	WK	1949-1953/54
Morgan Ross Winston	12/2/1941 Auckland		RHB	ROB	1964/65-1971/72
Morrison Bruce Donald	17/12/1933 Lower Hutt		LHB	RM	1962/63
Morrison Daniel Kyle	3/2/1966 Auckland		RHB	RFM	1987/88-1996/97
Morrison John Francis MacLean	27/8/1947 Wellington		RHB	SLA	1973/74-1981/82
Motz Richard Charles	12/1/1940 Christchurch	29/4/2007 Christchurch	RHB	RFM	1961/62-1969
Munro Colin	11/3/1987 Durban, South Africa		LHB	RM	2012/13
Murray Bruce Alexander Grenfell	18/9/1940 Wellington		RHB	RLB	1967/68-1970/71
Murray Darrin James	4/9/1967 Christchurch		RHB		1994/95
Nash Dion Joseph	20/11/1971 Auckland		RHB	RFM	1992/93-2001/02
Neesham James Douglas Sheahan	17/9/1990 Auckland		LHB	RFM	2013/14-2016/17
Newman Jack	3/7/1902 Brightwater	23/9/1996 Nelson	RHB	LM	1931/32-1932/33
Nicholls Henry Michael	15/11/1991 Christchurch		LHB	WK	2015/16-2021
Nicol Robert James	28/5/1983 Auckland		RHB	ROB	2011/12
O'Brien Iain Edward	10/7/1976 Lower Hutt		RHB	RM	2004/05-2009/10
O'Connor Shayne Barry	15/11/1973 Hastings		LHB	LFM	1997/98-2001/02
Oram Jacob David Philip	28/7/1978 Palmerston North		LHB	RM	2002/03-2009/10
O'Sullivan David Robert	16/11/1944 Palmerston North		RHB	SLA	1972/73-1976/77
Overton Guy William Fitzroy	8/6/1919 Dunedin	7/9/1993 Winton	LHB	RFM	1953/54
Owens Michael Barry	11/11/1969 Christchurch		RHB	RFM	1992/93-1994
Page Milford Laurenson	8/5/1902 Lyttelton	13/2/1987 Christchurch	RHB	ROB	1929/30-1937
Papps Michael Hugh William	2/7/1979 Christchurch		RHB		2003/04-2007/08
Parker John Morton	21/2/1951 Dannevirke		RHB	WK	1972/73-1980/81
Parker Norman Murray	28/8/1948 Dannevirke		RHB	RLB	1976/77

	Born	*Died*	*Type*			*Test Career*
Parore Adam Craig	23/1/1971 Auckland		RHB	WK		1990-2001/02
Patel Ajaz Yunus	21/10/1988 Bombay, India		LHB	SLA		2018/19-2021
Patel Dipak Narshibhai	25/10/1958 Nairobi, Kenya		RHB	ROB		1986/87-1996/97
Patel Jeetan Shashi	7/5/1980 Wellington		RHB	ROB		2005/06-2016/17
Petherick Peter James	25/9/1942 Ranfurly	7/6/2015 Perth, Australia	RHB	ROB		1976/77
Petrie Eric Charlton	22/5/1927 Ngaruawahia	14/8/2004 Omokoroa	RHB	WK		1955/56-1965/66
Phillips Glenn Dominic	6/12/1996 East London, South Africa		RHB	ROB	WK	2019/20
Playle William Rodger	1/12/1938 Palmerston North	27/2/2019 Coffs Harbour, Australia	RHB			1958-1962/63
Pocock Blair Andrew	18/6/1971 Papakura		RHB			1993/94-1997/98
Pollard Victor	7/9/1945 Burnley, England		RHB	ROB		1964/65-1973
Poore Matt Beresford	1/6/1930 Christchurch	11/6/2020 Auckland	RHB	ROB		1952/53-1955/56
Priest Mark Wellings	12/8/1961 Greymouth		LHB	SLA		1990-1997/98
Pringle Christopher	26/1/1968 Auckland		RHB	RFM		1990/91-1994/95
Puna Narotam	28/10/1929 Surat, India	7/6/1996 Hamilton	RHB	ROB		1965/66
Rabone Geoffrey Osborne	6/11/1921 Gore	19/1/2006 Auckland	RHB	ROB		1949-1954/55
Raval Jeet Ashok	22/5/1988 Ahmedabad, India		LHB	RLB		2016/17-2019/20
Redmond Aaron James	23/9/1979 Auckland		RHB	RLB		2008-2013/14
Redmond Rodney Ernest	29/12/1944 Whangarei		LHB	SLA		1972/73
Reid John Fulton	3/3/1956 Auckland	28/12/2020 Christchurch	LHB	RLB	WK	1978/79-1985/86
Reid John Richard	3/6/1928 Auckland	19/10/2020 Auckland	RHB	RFM	WK	1949-1965
Richardson Mark Hunter	11/6/1971 Hastings		LHB	SLA		2000/01-2004/05
Roberts Andrew Duncan Glenn	6/5/1947 Te Aroha	26/10/1989 Wellington	RHB	RM		1975/76-1976/77
Roberts Albert William	20/8/1909 Christchurch	13/5/1978 Clyde	RHB	RM		1929/30-1937
Robertson Gary Keith	15/7/1960 New Plymouth		RHB	RFM		1985/86
Ronchi Luke	23/4/1981 Dannevirke		RHB		WK	2015-2016/17
Rowe Charles Gordon	30/6/1915 Glasgow, Scotland	9/6/1995 Palmerston North	RHB			1945/46
Rutherford Hamish Duncan	27/4/1989 Dunedin		LHB			2012/13-2014/15
Rutherford Kenneth Robert	26/10/1965 Dunedin		RHB	RM		1984/85-1994/95
Ryder Jesse Daniel	6/8/1984 Masterton		LHB	RM		2008/09-2011/12
Santner Mitchell Josef	5/2/1992 Hamilton		LHB	SLA		2015/16-2021
Scott Roy Hamilton	6/3/1917 Clyde	5/8/2005 Christchurch	RHB	RM		1946/47
Scott Verdun John	31/7/1916 Devonport	2/8/1980 Devonport	RHB	RM		1945/46-1951/52

	Born	*Died*	*Type*		*Test Career*
Sewell David Graham	20/10/1977 Christchurch		RHB	LFM	1997/98
Shrimpton Michael John Froud	23/6/1940 Feilding	13/6/2015 Hastings	RHB	RLBG	1962/63-1973/74
Sinclair Barry Whitley	23/10/1936 Wellington		RHB		1962/63-1967/68
Sinclair Ian McKay	1/6/1933 Rangiora	25/8/2019 Tauranga	LHB	ROB	1955/56
Sinclair Mathew Stuart	9/11/1975 Katherine, Australia		RHB		1999/00-2009/10
Smith Frank Brunton	13/3/1922 Rangiora	6/7/1997 Christchurch		RHB	1946/47-1951/52
Smith Horace Dennis	8/1/1913 Toowoomba, Australia	25/1/1986 Christchurch	RHB	RFM	1932/33
Smith Ian David Stockley	28/2/1957 Nelson		RHB	WK	1980/81-1991/92
Snedden Colin Alexander	7/1/1918 Auckland	23/4/2011 Auckland	RHB	ROB	1946/47
Snedden Martin Colin	23/11/1958 Auckland		LHB	RFM	1980/81-1990
Sodhi Inderbir Singh	31/10/1992 Ludhiana, India		RHB	RLB	2013/14-2018/19
Somerville William Edgar Richard	9/8/1984 Wellington		RHB	ROB	2018/19-2019/20
Southee Timothy Grant	11/12/1988 Whangarei		RHB	RFM	2007/08-2021
Sparling John Trevor	24/7/1938 Auckland		RHB	ROB	1958-1963/64
Spearman Craig Murray	4/7/1972 Auckland		RHB		1995/96-2000/01
Stead Gary Raymond	9/1/1972 Christchurch		RHB	RLB	1998/99-1999/00
Stirling Derek Alexander	5/10/1961 Upper Hutt		RHB	RFM	1984/85-1986
Styris Scott Bernard	10/7/1975 Brisbane, Australia		RHB	RM	2001/02-2007/08
Su'a Murphy Logo	7/11/1966 Wanganui		LHB	LFM	1991/92-1994/95
Sutcliffe Bert	17/11/1923 Auckland	20/4/2001 Auckland	LHB	SLA	1946/47-1965
Taylor Bruce Richard	12/7/1943 Timaru	6/2/2021 Lower Hutt	LHB	RFM	1964/65-1973
Taylor Donald Dougald	2/3/1923 Auckland	5/12/1980 Auckland	RHB	RLBG	1946/47-1955/56
Taylor Luteru Ross Poutoa Lote	8/3/1984 Lower Hutt		RHB	ROB	2007/08-2021
Thomson Keith	26/2/1941 Methven		RHB		1967/68
Thomson Shane Alexander	27/1/1969 Hamilton		RHB	ROB	1989/90-1995/96
Tindill Eric William Thomas	18/12/1910 Nelson	1/8/2010 Wellington	LHB	WK	1937-1946/47
Troup Gary Bertram	3/10/1952 Taumarunui		RHB	LFM	1976/77-1985/86
Truscott Peter Bennetts	14/8/1941 Pahiatua		RHB		1964/65
Tuffey Daryl Raymond	11/6/1978 Milton		RHB	RFM	1999/00-2009/10
Turner Glenn Maitland	26/5/1947 Dunedin		RHB		1968/69-1982/83
Twose Roger Graham	17/4/1968 Torquay, England		LHB	RM	1995/96-1999
Vance Robert Howard	31/3/1955 Wellington		RHB		1987/88-1989/90

	Born	Died	Type		Test Career
van Wyk Cornelius Francoius Kruger	7/2/1980 Wolmaransstad, South Africa		RHB	WK	2011/12-2012/13
Vaughan Justin Thomas Caldwell	30//8/1967 Hereford, England		LHB	RM	1992/93-1996/97
Vettori Daniel Luca	27/1/1979 Auckland		LHB	SLA	1996/97-2014/15
Vincent Lou	11/11/1978 Warkworth		RHB	WK	2001/02-2007/08
Vivian Graham Ellery	28/2/1946 Auckland		LHB	RLB	1964/65-1971/72
Vivian Henry Gifford	4/11/1912 Auckland	12/8/1983 Auckland	LHB	SLA	1931-1937
Wadsworth Kenneth John	30/11/1946 Nelson	19/8/1976 Nelson	RHB	WK	1969-1975/76
Wagner Neil	13/3/1986 Pretoria, South Africa		LHB	LFM	2012-2021
Walker Brooke Graeme Keith	25/3/1977 Auckland		RHB	RLB	2000/01-2001/02
Wallace Walter Mervyn	19/12/1916 Auckland	21/3/2008 Auckland	RHB		1937-1952/53
Walmsley Kerry Peter	23/8/1973 Dunedin		RHB	RFM	1994/95-2000/01
Ward John Thomas	11/3/1937 Timaru	12/1/2021 Timaru	RHB	WK	1963/64-1967/68
Watling Bradley-John	9/7/1985 Durban, South Africa		RHB	WK	2009/10-2021
Watson William	31/8/1965 Auckland		RHB	RFM	1986-1993/94
Watt Leslie	17/9/1924 Waitati	15/11/1996 Dunedin	RHB		1954/55
Webb Murray George	22/6/1947 Invercargill		RHB	RFM	1970/71-1973/74
Webb Peter Neil	14/7/1957 Auckland		RHB	WK	1979/80
Weir Gordon Lindsay	2/6/1908 Auckland	31/10/2003 Auckland	RHB	RM	1929/30-1937
White David John	26/6/1961 Gisborne		RHB	ROB	1990/91
Whitelaw Paul Erskine	10/2/1910 Auckland	28/8/1988 Auckland	RHB		1932/33
Williamson Kane Stuart	8/8/1990 Tauranga		RHB	ROB	2010/11-2021
Wiseman Paul John	4/5/1970 Auckland		RHB	ROB	1997/98-2004/05
Wright John Geoffrey	5/7/1954 Darfield		LHB	RM	1977/78-1992/93
Young Bryan Andrew	3/11/1964 Whangarei		RHB	WK	1993/94-1998/99
Young Reece Alan	15/9/1979 Auckland		RHB	WK	2010/11-2011/12
Young William Alexander	22/12/1992 New Plymouth		RHB		2020/21-2021
Yuile Bryan William	29/10/1941 Palmerston North		RHB	SLA	1962/63-1969/70

TEST UMPIRES

The following is the complete list of New Zealand test umpires:

Umpire	Tests
Bowden B.F.	84 *
Hill A.L.	40 *
Dunne R.S.	39 *
Gaffaney C.B.	37 *
Aldridge B.L.	26 *
Goodall F.R.	24
Woodward S.J.	24
Cowie D.B.	22 *
Martin W.T.	15
Copps D.E.A.	13
Gardiner W.R.C.	9
Shortt R.W.R.	9
MacKintosh E.C.A.	8
Hastie J.B.R.	7
Cave K.H.	6
Monteith R.L.	6
Quested D.M.	5
Pengelly M.F.	4
Harris J.C.	4
Morris G.C.	4
Cobcroft L.T.	3
McLellan J.M.	3
Pearce T.M.	3
Cowie J.	3
Gwynne W.J.C.	3
Kinsella D.A.	3
McHarg R.L.	3
King C.E.	3
Watkin E.A.	3
Butler W.P.	2
Forrester J.T.	2
Brown J.M.A.	2
Tomkinson S.B.	2
Currie R.G.	2
Clark L.G.	2
Dumbleton D.P.	2
Knights W.R.	2
Brown C.M.	2
Page W.P.	1
Burgess T.W.	1
Torrance R.C.	1
Gourlay H.W.	1
Montgomery O.R.	1
Brook E.G.	1
Vine B.W.	1
Jelley A.E.	1
Tindill E.W.T.	1
Johnston L.C.	1
Burns D.C.	1
Cassie H.B.	1
Bricknell B.A.	1
Higginson I.C.	1

* *includes test matches overseas*

The following overseas umpires have stood in test matches in New Zealand:

Umpire	Tests
Harper D.J. *(Aus)*	13
Tucker R.J. *(Aust)*	11
Reiffel P.R. *(Aus)*	10
Koertzen R.E. *(SA)*	10
Kettleborough R.A. *(Eng)*	9
Llong N.J. *(England)*	8
Davis S.J. *(Aus)*	7
Gould I.J. *(England)*	7
Aleem Dar *(Pak)*	7
Oxenford B.N.J. *(Aust)*	7
de Silva E.A.R. *(SL)*	6
Taufel S.J.A. *(Aus)*	6
Hair D.B. *(Aus)*	5
Doctrove B.R. *(WI)*	5
Bucknor S.A. *(WI)*	4
Asad Rauf *(Pak)*	4
Illingworth R.K. *(Eng)*	4
Dharmasena H.P.D.K. *(SL)*	4
Randell S.G. *(Aus)*	3
Orchard D.L. *(SA)*	3
Tiffin R.B. *(Zim)*	3
Shepherd D.R. *(Eng)*	3
Benson M.R. *(Eng)*	3
Venkataraghavan S. *(Ind)*	3
Gough M.A. *(Eng)*	3
Ramaswamy V.K. *(Ind)*	2
Cooray B.C. *(SL)*	2
Francis K.T. *(SL)*	2
Mahboob Shah *(Pak)*	2
Bird H.D. *(Eng)*	2
Jerling B.G. *(SA)*	2
Parker P.D. *(Aus)*	2
Saheba A.M. *(India)*	2
Ravi S. *(India)*	2
Erasmus M. *(SA)*	2
Palliyaguruge R.S.A. *(SL)*	1
Robinson I.D. *(Zim)*	1
Nicholls E.A. *(WI)*	1
Plews N.T. *(Eng)*	1
Riazuddin *(Pak)*	1
Jayaprakash A.V. *(Ind)*	1
Khizar Hayat *(Pak)*	1
Elliott C.S. *(Eng)*	1
Barker L.H. *(WI)*	1
Lloyds J.W. *(Eng)*	1
Howell I.L *(SA)*	1
Enamul Haq *(Ban)*	1
Martinesz R.E.J. *(SL)*	1
Fry S.D. *(Aus)*	1
Wilson J.S. *(WI)*	1
Wilson P. *(Aus)*	1

The following pairs of umpires have stood together in the most tests:

Umpires	Tests
Goodall F.R. & Woodward S.J.	10
Aldridge B.L. & Dunne R.S.	7
Aldridge B.L. & Woodward S.J.	6
Copps D.E.A. & Gardiner W.R.C.	5
Copps D.E.A. & Martin W.T.	4
MacKintosh E.C.A. & Shortt R.W.R.	4
Harris J.C. & Pearce T.M.	3
MacKintosh E.C.A. & Martin W.T.	3
Cobcroft L.T. & Cave K.H.	3
Dunne R.S. & Woodward S.J.	3

These umpires have stood in every test of a series *(minimum 3 matches):*

Cave K. (4)	v England	1929/30
Martin W.T. (3)	v England	1965/66
MacKintosh E.C.A. (3)	v West Indies	1968/69
Goodall F.R. (3)	v England	1983/84
Woodward S.J. (3)	v England	1983/84
Aldridge B.L. (3)	v Sri Lanka	1990/91
Aldridge B.L. (3)	v England	1991/92
Dunne R.S. (3)	v England	1991/92
Aldridge B.L. (3)	v Australia	1992/93

The following pairs stood in three tests during a series:

Cobcroft L.T. & Cave K.	v England	1929/30 *(4 test series)*
Copps D.E.A. & Martin W.T.	v India	1967/68 *(4 test series)*
Goodall F.R. & Woodward S.J.	v England	1983/84 *(3 test series)*
Aldridge B.L. & Dunne R.S.	v England	1991/92 *(3 test series)*

Woodward S.J. was appointed to all three tests v Pakistan 1988/89 but stood in only two as the first test was abandoned.

TEAM RECORDS

New Zealand's Test Victories

1) **v West Indies** at Auckland 1955/56
NZ 255 & 157-9d WI 145 & 77
NZ won by 190 runs

2) **v South Africa** at Cape Town 1961/62
NZ 385 & 212-9d SA 190 & 335
NZ won by 72 runs

3) **v South Africa** at Port Elizabeth 1961/62
NZ 275 & 228 SA 190 & 273
NZ won by 40 runs

4) **v India** at Christchurch 1967/68
NZ 502 & 88-4 I 288 & 301
NZ won by 6 wickets

5) **v West Indies** at Wellington 1968/69
WI 297 & 148 NZ 282 & 166-4
NZ won by 6 wickets

6) **v India** at Nagpur 1969/70
NZ 319 & 214 I 257 & 109
NZ won by 167 runs

7) **v Pakistan** at Lahore 1969/70
P114 & 208 NZ 241 & 82-5
NZ won by 5 wickets

8) **v Australia** at Christchurch 1973/74
A 223 & 259 NZ 255 & 230-5
NZ won by 5 wickets

9) **v India** at Wellington 1975/76
I 220 & 81 NZ 334
NZ won by an innings and 33 runs

10) **v England** at Wellington 1977/78
NZ 228 & 123 E 215 & 64
NZ won by 72 runs

11) **v West Indies** at Dunedin 1979/80
WI 140 & 212 NZ 249 & 104-9
NZ won by 1 wicket

12) **v India** at Wellington 1980/81
NZ 375 & 100 I 233 & 190
NZ won by 62 runs

13) **v Australia** at Auckland 1981/82
A 210 & 280 NZ 387 & 109-5
NZ won by 5 wickets

14) **v Sri Lanka** at Christchurch 1982/83
NZ 344 SL 144 & 175
NZ won by an innings and 25 runs

15) **v Sri Lanka** at Wellington 1982/83
SL 240 & 93 NZ 201 & 134-4
NZ won by 6 wickets

16) **v England** at Leeds 1983
E 225 & 252 NZ 377 & 103-5
NZ won by 5 wickets

17) **v England** at Christchurch 1983/84
NZ 307 E 82 & 93
NZ won by an innings and 132 runs

18) **v Sri Lanka** at Kandy 1983/84
NZ 276 & 201-8d SL 215 & 97
NZ won by 165 runs

19) **v Sri Lanka** at Colombo 1983/84
SL 225 & 142 NZ 459
NZ won by an innings and 61 runs

20) **v Pakistan** at Auckland 1984/85
P 169 & 183 NZ 451-9d
NZ won by an innings and 99 runs

21) **v Pakistan** at Dunedin 1984/85
P274 & 223 NZ 220 & 278-8
NZ won by 2 wickets

22) **v Australia** at Brisbane 1985/86
A 179 & 333 NZ 553-7d
NZ won by an innings and 41 runs

23) **v Australia** at Perth 1985/86
A 203 & 259 NZ 299 & 164-4
NZ won by 6 wickets

24) **v Australia** at Auckland 1985/86
A 314 & 103 NZ 258 & 160-2
NZ won by 8 wickets

25) **v England** at Nottingham 1986
E 256 & 230 NZ 413 & 77-2
NZ won by 8 wickets

26) **v West Indies** at Christchurch 1986/87
WI 100 & 264 NZ 332-9d & 33-5
NZ won by 5 wickets

27) **v India** at Bombay 1988/89
NZ 236 & 279 I 234 & 145
NZ wonby 136 runs

28) **v India** at Christchurch 1989/90
NZ 459 & 2-0 I 164 & 296
NZ won by 10 wickets

29) **v Australia** at Wellington 1989/90
A 110 & 269 NZ 202 & 181-1
NZ won by 9 wickets

30) **v Zimbabwe** at Harare 1992/93
NZ 335 & 262-5d Z 283-9d & 137
NZ won by 177 runs

31) **v Australia** at Auckland 1992/93
A 139 & 285 NZ 224 & 201-5
NZ won by 5 wickets

32) **v Pakistan** at Christchurch 1993/94
P 344 & 179 NZ 200 & 324-5
NZ won by 5 wickets

33) v **South Africa** at Johannesburg 1994/95
NZ 411 & 194 SA 179 & 289
NZ won by 137 runs

34) v **Pakistan** at Lahore 1996/97
NZ 155 & 311 P 191 & 231
NZ won by 44 runs

35) v **Sri Lanka** at Dunedin 1996/97
NZ 586-7d SL 222 & 328
NZ won by an innings & 36 runs

36) v **Sri Lanka** at Hamilton 1996/97
NZ 222 & 273 SL 170 & 205
NZ won by 120 runs

37) v **Zimbabwe** at Wellington 1997/98
Z 180 & 250 NZ 411 & 20-0
NZ won by 10 wickets

38) v **Zimbabwe** at Auckland 1997/98
Z 170 & 277 NZ 460
NZ won by an innings and 13 runs

39) v **Sri Lanka** at Colombo 1997/98
NZ 305 & 444-6d SL 285 & 297
NZ won by 167 runs

40) v **India** at Wellington 1998/99
I 208 & 356 NZ 352 & 215-6
NZ won by 4 wickets

41) v **England** at Lord's 1999
E 186 & 229 NZ 358 & 60-1
NZ won by 9 wickets

42) v **England** at The Oval 1999
NZ 236 & 162 E 153 & 162
NZ won by 83 runs

43) v **West Indies** at Hamilton 1999/00
WI 365 & 97 NZ 393 & 70-1
NZ won by 9 wickets

44) v **West Indies** at Wellington 1999/00
NZ 518-9d WI 179 & 234
NZ won by an innings and 105 runs

45) v **Zimbabwe** at Bulawayo 2000/01
Z 350 & 119 NZ 338 & 132-3
NZ won by 7 wickets

46) v **Zimbabwe** at Harare 2000/01
NZ 465 & 74-2 Z 166 & 370
NZ won by 8 wickets

47) v **Pakistan** at Hamilton 2000/01
P 104 & 118 NZ 407-4d
NZ won by an innings & 185 runs

48) v **Bangladesh** at Hamilton 2001/02
NZ 365-9d B 205 & 108
NZ won by an innings and 52 runs

49) v **Bangladesh** at Wellington 2001/02
B 132 & 135 NZ 341-6d
NZ won by an innings and 74 runs

50) v **England** at Auckland 2001/02
NZ 202 & 269-9d E 160 & 233
NZ won by 78 runs

51) v **West Indies** at Bridgetown 2001/02
NZ 337 & 243 WI 107 & 269
NZ won by 204 runs

52) v **India** at Wellington 2002/03
I 161 & 121 NZ 247 & 36-0
NZ won by 10 wickets

53) v **India** at Hamilton 2002/03
I 99 & 154 NZ 94 & 160-6
NZ won by 4 wickets

54) v **South Africa** at Auckland 2003/04
SA 296 & 349 NZ 595 & 53-1
NZ won by 9 wickets

55) v **Bangladesh** at Dhaka 2004/05
B 177 & 126 NZ 402
NZ won by an innings and 99 runs

56) v **Bangladesh** at Chittagong 2004/05
NZ 545-6d B 182 & 262
NZ won by an innings and 101 runs

57) v **Sri Lanka** at Wellington 2004/05
SL 211 & 273 NZ 522-9d
NZ won by an innings and 38 runs

58) v **Zimbabwe** at Harare 2005/06
NZ 452-9d Z 59 & 99
NZ won by an innings and 294 runs

59) v **Zimbabwe** at Bulawayo 2005/06
Z 231 & 207 NZ 484
NZ won by an innings and 46 runs

60) v **West Indies** at Auckland 2005/06
NZ 275 & 272 WI 257 & 263
NZ won by 27 runs

61) v **West Indies** at Wellington 2005/06
WI 192 & 215 NZ 372 & 37-0
NZ won by 10 wickets

62) v **Sri Lanka** at Christchurch 2006/07
SL 154 & 179 NZ 206 & 119-5
NZ won by 5 wickets

63) v **Bangladesh** at Dunedin 2007/08
B 137 & 254 NZ 357 & 39-1
NZ won by 9 wickets

64) v **Bangladesh** at Wellington 2007/08
B 143 & 113 NZ 393
NZ won by an innings and 137 runs

65) v **England** at Hamilton 2007/08
NZ 470 & 177-9d E 348 & 110
NZ won by 189 runs

66) v **Bangladesh** at Chittagong 2008/09
B 245 & 242 NZ 171 and 317-7
NZ won by 3 wickets

67) v **Pakistan** at Dunedin 2009/10
NZ 429 & 153 P 332 & 128
NZ won by 32 runs

68) v **Bangladesh** at Hamilton 2009/10
NZ 553-7d & 258-5d B 408 & 282
NZ won by 121 runs

69) v **Zimbabwe** at Bulawayo 2011/12
NZ 426 & 252-8d Z 313 & 331
NZ won by 34 runs

70) v **Australia** at Hobart 2011/12
NZ 150 & 226 A 136 & 233
NZ won by 7 runs

71) v **Zimbabwe** at Napier 2011/12
NZ 495-7d Z 51 & 143
NZ won by an innings and 301 runs

72) v **Sri Lanka** at Colombo 2012/13
NZ 412 & 194-9d SL 244 & 195
NZ won by 167 runs

73) v **West Indies** at Wellington 2013/14
NZ 441 WI 193 & 175
NZ won by an innings and 73 runs

74) v **West Indies** at Hamilton 2013/14
WI 367 & 103 NZ 349 & 124-2
NZ won by 8 wickets

75) v **India** at Auckland 2013/14
NZ 503 & 105 I 202 & 366
NZ won by 40 runs

76) v **West Indies** at Kingston 2014
NZ 508-7d & 156-8d WI 262 & 216
NZ won by 186 runs

77) v **West Indies** at Bridgetown 2013/14
NZ 293 & 331-7d WI 317 & 254
NZ won by 53 runs

78) v **Pakistan** at Sharjah 2014/15
P 351 & 259 NZ 690
NZ won by an innings and 80 runs

79) v **Sri Lanka** at Christchurch 2014/15
NZ 441 & 107-2 SL 138 & 407
NZ won by 8 wickets

80) v **Sri Lanka** at Wellington 2014/15
NZ 221 & 524-5d SL 356 & 196
NZ won by 193 runs

81) v **England** at Leeds 2015
NZ 350 & 454-8d E 350 & 255
NZ won by 199 runs

82) v **Sri Lanka** at Dunedin 2015/16
NZ 431 & 267-3d SL 294 & 282
NZ won by 122 runs

83) v **Sri Lanka** at Hamilton 2015/16
SL 292 & 133 NZ 237 & 189-5
NZ won by 5 wickets

84) v **Zimbabwe** at Bulawayo 2016/17
Z 164 & 295 NZ 576-6d
NZ won by an innings and 117 runs

85) v **Zimbabwe** at Bulawayo 2016/17
NZ 582-4d & 166-2d Z 362 & 132
NZ won by 254 runs

86) v **Pakistan** at Christchurch 2016/17
P 133 & 171 NZ 200 & 108-2
NZ won by 7 wickets

87) v **Pakistan** at Hamilton 2016/17
NZ 271 & 313-5d P 216 & 230
NZ won by 138 runs

88) v **Bangladesh** at Wellington 2016/17
B 595-8d & 160 NZ 539 & 217-3
NZ won by 7 wickets

89) v **Bangladesh** at Christchurch 2016/17
B 289 & 173 NZ 354 & 111-1
NZ won by 9 wickets

90) v **West Indies** at Wellington 2017/18
WI 134 & 319 NZ 520-9d
NZ won by an innings and 67 runs

91) v **West Indies** at Hamilton 2017/18
NZ 373 & 281-8d WI 221 & 293
NZ won by 140 runs

92) v **England** at Auckland 2017/18
E 58 & 320 NZ 427-9d
NZ won by an innings and 49 runs

93) v **Pakistan** at Abu Dhabi 2018/19
NZ 153 & 249 P 227 & 171
NZ won by 4 runs

94) v **Pakistan** at Abu Dhabi 2018/19
NZ 274 & 353-7d P 348 & 156
NZ won by 123 runs

95) v **Sri Lanka** at Christchurch 2018/19
NZ 178 & 585-4d SL 104 & 236
NZ won by 423 runs

96) v **Bangladesh** at Hamilton 2018/19
B 234 & 429 NZ 715-6d
NZ won by an innings & 52 runs

97) v **Bangladesh** at Wellington 2018/19
B 211 & 209 NZ 432-6d
NZ won by an innings & 12 runs

98) v **Sri Lanka** at Colombo 2019/20
SL 244 & 122 NZ 431-6d
NZ won by an innings and 65 runs

99) v **England** at Mt Maunganui 2019/20
E 353 & 197 NZ 615-9d
NZ won by an innings and 65 runs

100) v **India** at Wellington 2019/20
I 165 & 191 NZ 348 & 9-0
NZ won by 10 wickets

101) v **India** at Christchurch 2019/20
I 242 & 124 NZ 235 & 132-3
NZ won by 7 wickets

102) v **West Indies** at Hamilton 2020/21
NZ 519-7d WI 138 & 247
NZ won by an innings and 134 runs

103) v **West Indies** at Wellington 2020/21
NZ 460 WI 131 & 317
NZ won by an innings and 12 runs

104) v **Pakistan** at Mt Maunganui 2020/21
NZ 431 & 180-5d P 239 & 271
NZ won by 101 runs

105) v **Pakistan** at Christchurch 2020/21
P 297 & 186 NZ 659-6d
NZ won by an innings and 176 runs

106) v **England** at Birmingham 2021
E 303 & 122 NZ 388 & 41-2
NZ won by 8 wickets

107) v **India** at Southampton 2021
I 217 & 170 NZ 249 & 140-2
NZ won by 8 wickets

Test Record by Series

Season	Opponent	TOTAL Won	TOTAL Lost	TOTAL Drawn	Cumulative Won	Cumulative Lost	Cumulative Drawn	BY OPPONENT Won	BY OPPONENT Lost	BY OPPONENT Drawn
1929/30	England*	—	1	3	—	1	3	—	1	3
1931	England	—	1	2	—	2	5	—	2	5
1931/32	South Africa*	—	2	—	—	4	5	—	2	—
1932/33	England*	—	—	2	—	4	7	—	2	7
1937	England	—	1	2	—	5	9	—	3	9
1945/46	Australia*	—	1	—	—	6	9	—	1	—
1946/47	England*	—	—	1	—	6	10	—	3	10
1949	England	—	—	4	—	6	14	—	3	14
1950/51	England*	—	1	1	—	7	15	—	4	15
1951/52	West Indies*	—	1	1	—	8	16	—	1	1
1952/53	South Africa*	—	1	1	—	9	17	—	3	1
1953/54	South Africa	—	4	1	—	13	18	—	7	2
1954/55	England*	—	2	—	—	15	18	—	6	15
1955/56	Pakistan	—	2	1	—	17	19	—	2	1
1955/56	India	—	2	3	—	19	22	—	2	3
1955/56	West Indies*	1	3	—	1	22	22	1	4	1
1958	England	—	4	1	1	26	23	—	10	16
1958/59	England*	—	1	1	1	27	24	—	11	17
1961/62	South Africa	2	2	1	3	29	25	2	9	3
1962/63	England*	—	3	—	3	32	25	—	14	17
1963/64	South Africa*	—	—	3	3	32	28	2	9	6
1964/65	Pakistan*	—	—	3	3	32	31	—	2	4
1964/65	India	—	1	3	3	33	34	—	3	6
1964/65	Pakistan	—	2	1	3	35	35	—	4	5
1965	England	—	3	—	3	38	35	—	17	17
1965/66	England*	—	—	3	3	38	38	—	17	20
1967/68	India*	1	3	—	4	41	38	1	6	6
1968/69	West Indies*	1	1	1	5	42	39	2	5	2
1969	England	—	2	1	5	44	40	—	19	21
1969/70	India	1	1	1	6	45	41	2	7	7
1969/70	Pakistan	1	—	2	7	45	43	1	4	7
1970/71	England*	—	1	1	7	46	44	—	20	22
1971/72	West Indies	—	—	5	7	46	49	2	5	7
1972/73	Pakistan*	—	1	2	7	47	51	1	5	9
1973	England	—	2	1	7	49	52	—	22	23
1973/74	Australia	—	2	1	7	51	53	—	3	1
1973/74	Australia*	1	1	1	8	52	54	1	4	2
1974/75	England*	—	1	1	8	53	55	—	23	24
1975/76	India*	1	1	1	9	54	56	3	8	8
1976/77	Pakistan	—	2	1	9	56	57	1	7	10
1976/77	India	—	2	1	9	58	58	3	10	9
1976/77	Australia*	—	1	1	9	59	59	1	5	3
1977/78	England*	1	1	1	10	60	60	1	24	25
1978	England	—	3	—	10	63	60	1	27	25
1978/79	Pakistan*	—	1	2	10	64	62	1	8	12
1979/80	West Indies*	1	—	2	11	64	64	3	5	9
1980/81	Australia	—	2	1	11	66	65	1	7	4
1980/81	India*	1	—	2	12	66	67	4	10	11
1981/82	Australia*	1	1	1	13	67	68	2	8	5
1982/83	Sri Lanka*	2	—	—	15	67	68	2	—	—

Season	Opponent	TOTAL Won	TOTAL Lost	TOTAL Drawn	Cumulative Won	Cumulative Lost	Cumulative Drawn	BY OPPONENT Won	BY OPPONENT Lost	BY OPPONENT Drawn
1983	England	1	3	—	16	70	68	2	30	25
1983/84	England*	1	—	2	17	70	70	3	30	27
1983/84	Sri Lanka	2	—	1	19	70	71	4	—	1
1984/85	Pakistan	—	2	1	19	72	72	1	10	13
1984/85	Pakistan*	2	—	1	21	72	73	3	10	14
1984/85	West Indies	—	2	2	21	74	75	3	7	11
1985/86	Australia	2	1	—	23	75	75	4	9	5
1985/86	Australia*	1	—	2	24	75	77	5	9	7
1986	England	1	—	2	25	75	79	4	30	29
1986/87	West Indies*	1	1	1	26	76	80	4	8	12
1986/87	Sri Lanka	—	—	1	26	76	81	4	—	2
1987/88	Australia	—	1	2	26	77	83	5	10	9
1987/88	England*	—	—	3	26	77	86	4	30	32
1988/89	India	1	2	—	27	79	86	5	12	11
1988/89	Pakistan*	—	—	2	27	79	88	3	10	16
1989/90	Australia	—	—	1	27	79	89	5	10	10
1989/90	India*	1	—	2	28	79	91	6	12	13
1989/90	Australia*	1	—	—	29	79	91	6	10	10
1990	England	—	1	2	29	80	93	4	41	34
1990/91	Pakistan	—	3	—	29	83	93	3	13	16
1990/91	Sri Lanka*	—	—	3	29	83	96	4	—	5
1991/92	England*	—	2	1	29	85	97	4	33	35
1992/93	Zimbabwe	1	—	1	30	85	98	1	—	1
1992/93	Sri Lanka	—	1	1	30	86	99	4	1	6
1992/93	Pakistan*	—	1	—	30	87	99	3	14	16
1992/93	Australia*	1	1	1	31	88	100	7	11	11
1993/94	Australia	—	2	1	31	90	101	7	13	12
1993/94	Pakistan*	1	2	—	32	92	101	4	16	16
1993/94	India*	—	—	1	32	92	102	6	12	14
1994	England	—	1	2	32	93	104	4	34	37
1994/95	South Africa	1	2	—	33	95	104	3	11	6
1994/95	West Indies*	—	1	1	33	96	105	4	9	13
1994/95	South Africa*	—	1	—	33	97	105	3	12	6
1994/95	Sri Lanka*	—	1	1	33	98	106	4	2	7
1995/96	India	—	1	2	33	99	108	6	13	16
1995/96	Pakistan*	—	1	—	33	100	108	4	17	16
1995/96	Zimbabwe*	—	—	2	33	100	110	1	—	3
1995/96	West Indies	—	1	1	33	101	111	4	10	14
1996/97	Pakistan	1	1	—	34	102	111	5	18	16
1996/97	England*	—	2	1	34	104	112	4	36	38
1996/97	Sri Lanka*	2	—	—	36	104	112	6	2	7
1997/98	Zimbabwe	—	—	2	36	104	114	1	—	5
1997/98	Australia	—	2	1	36	106	115	7	15	13
1997/98	Zimbabwe*	2	—	—	38	106	115	3	—	5
1997/98	Sri Lanka	1	2	—	39	108	115	7	4	7
1998/99	India*	1	—	1	40	108	116	7	13	17
1998/99	South Africa*	—	1	2	40	109	118	3	13	8
1999	England	2	1	1	42	110	119	6	37	39
1999/00	India	—	1	2	42	111	121	7	14	19
1999/00	West Indies*	2	—	—	44	111	121	6	10	14
1999/00	Australia*	—	3	—	44	114	121	7	18	13
2000/01	Zimbabwe	2	—	—	46	114	121	5	—	5

		TOTAL			Cumulative			BY OPPONENT		
Season	Opponent	Won	Lost	Drawn	Won	Lost	Drawn	Won	Lost	Drawn
2000/01	South Africa	—	2	1	46	116	122	3	15	9
2000/01	Zimbabwe*	—	—	1	46	116	123	5	—	6
2000/01	Pakistan*	1	1	1	47	117	124	6	19	17
2001/02	Australia	—	—	3	47	117	127	7	18	16
2001/02	Bangladesh*	2	—	—	49	117	127	2	—	—
2001/02	England*	1	1	1	50	118	128	7	38	40
2001/02	Pakistan	—	1	—	50	119	128	6	20	17
2001/02	West Indies	1	—	1	51	119	129	7	10	15
2002/03	India*	2	—	—	53	119	129	9	14	19
2002/03	Sri Lanka	—	—	2	53	119	131	7	4	9
2003/04	India	—	—	2	53	119	133	9	14	21
2003/04	Pakistan*	—	1	1	53	120	134	6	21	18
2003/04	South Africa*	1	1	1	54	121	135	4	16	10
2004	England	—	3	—	54	124	135	7	41	40
2004/05	Bangladesh	2	—	—	56	124	135	4	—	—
2004/05	Australia	—	2	—	56	126	135	7	20	16
2004/05	Australia*	—	2	1	56	128	136	7	22	17
2004/05	Sri Lanka*	1	—	1	57	128	137	8	4	10
2005/06	Zimbabwe	2	—	—	59	128	137	7	—	6
2005/06	West Indies*	2	—	1	61	128	138	9	10	16
2005/06	South Africa	—	2	1	61	130	139	4	18	11
2006/07	Sri Lanka*	1	1	—	62	131	139	9	5	10
2007/08	South Africa	—	2	—	62	133	139	4	20	11
2007/08	Bangladesh*	2	—	—	64	133	139	6	—	—
2007/08	England*	1	2	—	65	135	139	8	43	40
2008	England	—	2	1	65	137	140	8	45	41
2008/09	Bangladesh	1	—	1	66	137	141	7	—	1
2008/09	Australia	—	2	—	66	139	141	7	24	17
2008/09	West Indies*	—	—	2	66	139	143	9	10	18
2008/09	India*	—	1	2	66	140	145	9	15	23
2009/10	Sri Lanka	—	2	—	66	142	145	9	7	10
2009/10	Pakistan†	1	1	1	67	143	146	7	22	19
2009/10	Bangladesh*	1	—	—	68	143	146	8	—	1
2009/10	Australia*	—	2	—	68	145	146	7	26	17
2010/11	India	—	1	2	68	146	148	9	16	25
2010/11	Pakistan*	—	1	1	68	147	149	7	23	20
2011/12	Zimbabwe	1	—	—	69	147	149	8	—	6
2011/12	Australia	1	1	—	70	148	149	8	27	17
2011/12	Zimbabwe*	1	—	—	71	148	149	9	—	6
2011/12	South Africa*	—	1	2	71	149	151	4	21	13
2012	West Indies	—	2	—	71	151	151	9	12	18
2012/13	India	—	2	—	71	153	151	9	18	25
2012/13	Sri Lanka	1	1	—	72	154	151	10	8	10
2012/13	South Africa	—	2	—	72	156	151	4	23	13
2012/13	England*	—	—	3	72	156	154	8	45	44
2013	England	—	2	—	72	158	154	8	47	44
2013/14	Bangladesh	—	—	2	72	158	156	8	—	3
2013/14	West Indies*	2	—	1	74	158	157	11	12	19
2013/14	India*	1	—	1	75	158	158	10	18	26
2014	West Indies	2	1	—	77	159	158	13	13	19
2014/15	Pakistan+	1	1	1	78	160	159	8	24	21
2014/15	Sri Lanka*	2	—	—	80	160	159	12	8	10

Season	Opponent	TOTAL Won	TOTAL Lost	TOTAL Drawn	Cumulative Won	Cumulative Lost	Cumulative Drawn	BY OPPONENT Won	BY OPPONENT Lost	BY OPPONENT Drawn
2015	England	1	1	—	81	161	159	9	48	44
2015/16	Australia	—	2	1	81	163	160	8	29	18
2015/16	Sri Lanka*	2	—	—	83	163	160	14	8	10
2015/16	Australia*	—	2	—	83	165	160	8	31	18
2016/17	Zimbabwe	2	—	—	85	165	160	11	—	6
2016/17	South Africa	—	1	1	85	166	161	4	24	14
2016/17	India	—	3	—	85	169	161	10	21	26
2016/17	Pakistan*	2	—	—	87	169	161	10	24	21
2016/17	Bangladesh*	2	—	—	89	169	161	10	—	3
2016/17	South Africa*	—	1	2	89	170	163	4	25	16
2017/18	West Indies*	2	—	—	91	170	163	15	13	19
2017/18	England*	1	—	1	92	170	164	10	48	45
2018/19	Pakistan+	2	1	—	94	171	164	12	25	21
2018/19	Sri Lanka*	1	—	1	95	171	165	15	8	11
2018/19	Bangladesh*	2	—	—	97	171	165	12	—	3
2019/20	Sri Lanka	1	1	—	98	172	165	16	9	11
2019/20	England*	1	—	1	99	172	166	11	48	46
2019/20	Australia	—	3	—	99	175	166	8	34	18
2019/20	India*	2	—	—	101	175	166	12	21	26
2020/21	West Indies*	2	—	—	103	175	166	17	13	19
2020/21	Pakistan*	2	—	—	105	175	166	14	25	21
2021	England	1	—	1	106	175	167	12	48	47
2021	India	1	—	—	107	175	167	13	21	26

** home series*

† scheduled as a Pakistan home series but was played in New Zealand

+ scheduled as a Pakistan home series but was played in United Arab Emirates

Summary of Results

	Played	Won	Lost	Drawn
v England	107	12	48	47
v Australia	60	8	34	18
v India	60	13	21	26
v Pakistan	60	14	25	21
v West Indies	49	17	13	19
v South Africa	45	4	25	16
v Sri Lanka	36	16	9	11
v Zimbabwe	17	11	—	6
v Bangladesh	15	12	—	3
Total	**449**	**107**	**175**	**167**

Highest Totals

For

715-6d	v Bangladesh	Hamilton	2018/19
690	v Pakistan	Sharjah	2014/15
680-8d	v India	Wellington	2013/14
671-4	v Sri Lanka	Wellington	1990/91
659-6d	v Pakistan	Christchurch	2020/21
630-6d	v India	Mohali	2003/04
624	v Australia	Perth	2015/16
619-9d	v India	Napier	2008/09
615-9d	v England	Mt Maunganui	2019/20

609-9d	v West Indies	Dunedin	2013/14
595	v South Africa	Auckland	2003/04
593-8d	v South Africa	Cape Town	2005/06
586-7d	v Sri Lanka	Dunedin	1996/97
585-4d	v Sri Lanka	Christchurch	2018/19
582-4d	v Zimbabwe	Bulawayo	2016/17
578	v Sri Lanka	Wellington	2018/19
576-6d	v Zimbabwe	Bulawayo	2016/17
563	v Pakistan	Hamilton	2003/04
561	v Sri Lanka	Napier	2004/05
553-7d	v Australia	Brisbane	1985/86
553-7d	v Bangladesh	Hamilton	2009/10
551-9d	v England	Lord's	1973
545-6d	v Bangladesh	Chittagong	2004/05
543-3d	v West Indies	Georgetown	1971/72
539	v Bangladesh	Wellington	2016/17
537	v England	Wellington	1983/84
534-9d	v Australia	Perth	2001/02
524-5d	v Sri Lanka	Wellington	2014/15
523	v England	Lord's	2015
522-9d	v Sri Lanka	Wellington	2004/05
520-9d	v West Indies	Wellington	2017/18
519-7d	v West Indies	Hamilton	2020/21
518-9d	v West Indies	Wellington	1999/00
515-7d	v Sri Lanka	Colombo	2002/03
512-6d	v England	Wellington	1987/88
509	v South Africa	Hamilton	2003/04
508-7d	v West Indies	Kingston	2014
505	v South Africa	Cape Town	1953/54
503	v India	Auckland	2013/14
502	v India	Christchurch	1967/68
Against			
660-5d	by West Indies	Wellington	1994/95
643	by Pakistan	Lahore	2001/02
621-5d	by South Africa	Auckland	1998/99
616-5d	by Pakistan	Auckland	1988/89
607-6d	by Australia	Brisbane	1993/94
595-8d	by Bangladesh	Wellington	2016/17
593-6d	by England	Auckland	1974/75
585	by Australia	Brisbane	2004/05
583-7d	by India	Ahmedabad	1999/00
580-9d	by England	Christchurch	1991/92
575-8d	by Australia	Adelaide	2004/05
571-8d	by Pakistan	Christchurch	2000/01
570-8d	by Australia	Wellington	2004/05
567-8d	by England	Nottingham	1994
566-8d	by India	Nagpur	2010/11
566-3d	by Pakistan	Abu Dhabi	2014/15
565-9d	by Pakistan	Karachi	1976/77
564-8	by West Indies	Bridgetown	1971/72
562-7d	by England	Auckland	1962/63
562	by Australia	Wellington	2015/16
561	by Pakistan	Lahore	1955/56
560-8d	by England	Christchurch	1932/33
559-9d	by Australia	Perth	2015/16

558-8d	by Australia	Hobart	2001/02
557-5d	by India	Indore	2016/17
556	by Australia	Brisbane	2015/16
552	by Australia	Christchurch	1976/77
550	by England	Christchurch	1950/51

Lowest Totals

For

26	v England	Auckland	1954/55
42	v Australia	Wellington	1945/46
45	v South Africa	Cape Town	2012/13
47	v England	Lord's	1958
54	v Australia	Wellington	1945/46
65	v England	Christchurch	1970/71
67	v England	Leeds	1958
67	v England	Lord's	1978
68	v England	Lord's	2013
70	v Pakistan	Dacca	1955/56
73	v Pakistan	Lahore	2001/02
74	v West Indies	Dunedin	1955/56
74	v England	Lord's	1958
76	v Australia	Brisbane	2004/05
79	v South Africa	Johannesburg	1953/54
79	v Pakistan	Rawalpindi	1964/65
85	v England	Manchester	1958
89	v England	Auckland	1962/63
90	v Pakistan	Dubai	2018/19
93	v Pakistan	Hamilton	1992/93
94	v England	Birmingham	1958
94	v West Indies	Bridgetown	1984/85
94	v India	Hamilton	2002/03
97	v England	Nottingham	1973

Against

51	by Zimbabwe	Napier	2011/12
58	by England	Auckland	2017/18
59	by Zimbabwe	Harare	2005/06
64	by England	Wellington	1977/78
77	by West Indies	Auckland	1955/56
81	by India	Wellington	1975/76
82	by England	Christchurch	1983/84
83	by India	Mohali	1999/00
88	by India	Bombay	1964/65
89	by India	Hyderabad	1969/70
93	by Sri Lanka	Wellington	1982/83
93	by England	Christchurch	1983/84
97	by Sri Lanka	Kandy	1983/84
97	by West Indies	Hamilton	1999/00
99	by India	Hamilton	2002/03
99	by Zimbabwe	Harare	2005/06

Longest Innings

Mins	Runs			
904	680-8d	v India	Wellington	2013/14
851	671-4	v Sri Lanka	Wellington	1990/91
845	615-9d	v England	Mt Maunganui	2019/20
815	459	v Sri Lanka	Colombo	1983/84
802	630-6d	v India	Mohali	2003/04
790	406-5	v Sri Lanka	Colombo	1986/87
784	512-6d	v England	Wellington	1987/88
780	543-3d	v West Indies	Georgetown	1971/72

Largest First Innings Leads

*481	v Bangladesh	Hamilton	2018/19
*444	v Zimbabwe	Napier	2011/12
*412	v Zimbabwe	Bulawayo	2016/17
396	v West Indies	Dunedin	2013/14
*393	v Zimbabwe	Harare	2005/06
*386	v West Indies	Wellington	2017/18
*381	v West Indies	Hamilton	2020/21
*374	v Australia	Brisbane	1985/86
*369	v England	Auckland	2017/18
*364	v Sri Lanka	Dunedin	1996/97
*363	v Bangladesh	Chittagong	2004/05
*362	v Pakistan	Christchurch	2020/21

** New Zealand won the match*

Opposition Following-on

South Africa	Cape Town	1953/54
India	Bombay	1964/65
*India	Christchurch	1967/68
*Sri Lanka	Christchurch	1982/83
*England	Christchurch	1983/84
*India	Christchurch	1989/90
*Sri Lanka	Dunedin	1996/97
*West Indies	Wellington	1999/00
*Zimbabwe	Harare	2000/01
*Bangladesh	Hamilton	2001/02
India	Mohali	2003/04
*Bangladesh	Chittagong	2004/05
*Zimbabwe	Harare	2005/06
India	Napier	2008/09
*Zimbabwe	Napier	2011/12
West Indies	Dunedin	2013/14
*West Indies	Wellington	2013/14
*Sri Lanka	Christchurch	2014/15
*West Indies	Hamilton	2020/21
*West Indies	Wellington	2020/21

** New Zealand won the match*

NB: *New Zealand did not enforce the follow-on v South Africa at Cape Town, 1961/62, v West Indies at Bridgetown, 2001/02, v India at Auckland, 2013/14 and v Zimbabwe at Bulawayo, 2016/17 although they could have done so. They eventually won all four games.*

GROUNDS

Results by Grounds

In New Zealand	P	W	L	D
Eden Park, Auckland	50	11	15	24
Lancaster Park, Christchurch	40	8	16	16
Basin Reserve, Wellington	65	21	20	24
Carisbrook, Dunedin	10	3	4	3
McLean Park, Napier	10	1	2	7
Seddon Park, Hamilton	27	13	6	8
University of Otago Oval, Dunedin	8	3	—	5
Hagley Oval, Christchurch	8	6	1	1
Bay Oval, Mt Maunganui	2	2	—	—
Total	**220**	**68**	**64**	**88**

In Australia	P	W	L	D
Melbourne Cricket Ground	4	—	2	2
Sydney Cricket Ground	3	—	2	1
Adelaide Oval	5	—	4	1
WACA Ground, Perth	7	1	2	4
Woolloongabba, Brisbane	10	1	8	1
Bellerive Oval, Hobart	4	1	1	2
Optus Stadium, Perth	1	—	1	—
Total	**34**	**3**	**20**	**11**

In Bangladesh				
National Stadium, Dhaka	1	1	—	—
Chittagong Stadium	3	2	—	1
National Stadium, Mirpur	2	—	—	2
Total	**6**	**3**	**—**	**3**

In England				
Lord's, London	18	1	8	9
The Oval, London	9	1	4	4
Headingley, Leeds	8	2	5	1
Trent Bridge, Nottingham	9	1	6	2
Old Trafford, Manchester	7	—	3	4
Edgbaston, Birmingham	5	1	4	—
Rose Bowl, Southampton	1	1	—	—
Total	**57**	**7**	**30**	**20**

In Pakistan	P	W	L	D
National Stadium, Karachi	6	—	3	3
Bagh-e-Jinnah, Lahore	1	—	1	—
Dacca Stadium, Dacca	2	—	—	2
Niaz Stadium, Hyderabad	2	—	2	—
Rawalpindi Club Ground	1	—	1	—
Lahore (Gaddafi) Stadium	7	2	4	1
Iqbal Stadium, Faisalabad	1	—	1	—
Rawalpindi Cricket Stadium	1	—	1	—
Total	**21**	**2**	**13**	**6**

In India				
Brabourne Stadium, Bombay	3	—	2	1
Wankhede Stadium, Bombay	2	1	1	—
Fateh Maidan, (Lal Bahadur Stadium) Hyderabad	3	—	1	2
Feroz Shah Kotla, Delhi	2	—	1	1
Eden Gardens, Calcutta	3	—	1	2
Corporation Stadium, Madras	2	—	1	1
Chepauk, (Chidambaram Stadium) Madras	2	—	1	1
VCA Ground, Nagpur	2	1	1	—
Green Park, Kanpur	3	—	2	1
Chinnaswamy Stadium, Bangalore	2	—	2	—
Barabati Stadium, Cuttack	1	—	—	1
Punjab C.A. Stadium, Mohali	2	—	—	2
Sardar Patel Stadium, Ahmedabad	3	—	—	3
Rajiv Gandhi International Stadium, Hyderabad	1	—	—	1
Holkar Stadium, Indore	1	—	1	—
Total	**32**	**2**	**14**	**16**

In South Africa	P	W	L	D
Kingsmead, Durban	4	—	3	1
Ellis Park, Johannesburg	2	—	2	—
New Wanderers, Johannesburg	6	1	3	2
Newlands, Cape Town	5	1	2	2
St George's Park, Port Elizabeth	4	1	3	—
Goodyear Park, Bloemfontein	1	—	1	—
SuperSport Park, Centurion	3	—	3	—
Total	**25**	**3**	**17**	**5**

In Sri Lanka				
Asgiriya Stadium, Kandy	2	1	—	1
Sinhalese Sports Club Ground, Colombo	4	—	3	1
Colombo C.C. Ground	2	1	—	1
Tyrone Fernando Stadium, Moratuwa	1	—	—	1
R. Premadasa Stadium, Colombo	1	1	—	—
Galle International Stadium	4	—	4	—
P. Saravanamuttu Stadium Colombo	3	2	—	1
Total	**17**	**5**	**7**	**5**

In West Indies

Queen's Park Oval, Port of Spain	4	—	1	3
Sabina Park, Kingston	4	1	2	1
Kensington Oval, Bridgetown	5	2	2	1
Bourda, Georgetown	2	—	—	2
St Johns Recreation Ground, Antigua	1	—	—	1
Queen's Park, Grenada	1	—	—	1
Sir Vivian Richards Stadium, Antigua	1	—	1	—
Total	**18**	**3**	**6**	**9**

In United Arab Emirates

Sheikh Zayed Stadium, Abu Dhabi	3	2	1	—
Dubai International Cricket Stadium	2	—	1	1
Sharjah Cricket Stadium	1	1	—	—
Total	**6**	**3**	**2**	**1**

In Zimbabwe

Bulawayo Athletic Club	1	—	—	1
Harare Sports Club, Harare	4	3	—	1
Queens Sports Club, Bulawayo	6	5	—	1
Total	**11**	**8**	**—**	**3**

Record Performances in Tests on Each NZ Ground v All Countries

Venue	Highest Total by NZ v NZ	Lowest Total by NZ v NZ	Highest Individual Innings by NZ v NZ	Best Bowling by NZ v NZ
Eden Park, Auckland 50 Tests	595 2003/04 v South Africa 621-5d 1998/99 by South Africa	26 1954/55 v England 58 2017/18 by England	224 McCullum B.B. 2013/14 v India 336* Hammond W.R. 1932/33 for England	7-87 Vettori D.L. 1999/00 v Australia 8-76 Prasanna E.A.S. 1975/76 for India
Lancaster Park, Christchurch 40 Tests	502 1967/68 v India 580-9d 1991/92 by England	65 1970/71 v England 82 1983/84 by England	239 Dowling G.T. 1967/68 v India 258 Nurse S.M. 1968/69 for West Indies	7-116 Hadlee R.J. 1985/86 v Australia 7-47 Tufnell P.C.R. 1991/92 for England
Carisbrook, Dunedin 10 Tests	586-7d 1996/97 v Sri Lanka 507-6d 1972/73 by Pakistan	74 1955/56 v West Indies 140 1979/80 by West Indies	267* Young B.A. 1996/97 v Sri Lanka 201 Mushtaq Mohammad 1972/73 for Pakistan	6-51 Hadlee R.J. 1984/85 v Pakistan 7-52 Intikhab Alam 1972/73 for Pakistan
Basin Reserve, Wellington 65 Tests	680-8d 2013/14 v India 660-5d 1994/95 by West Indies	42 1945/46 v Australia 64 1977/78 by England	302 McCullum B.B. 2013/14 v India 267 de Silva P.A. 1990/91 for Sri Lanka	7-23 Hadlee R.J. 1975/76 v India 7-37 Walsh C.A. 1994/95 for West Indies
McLean Park, Napier 10 Tests	619-9d 2008/09 v India 498 2004/05 by Sri Lanka	109 1994/95 v Sri Lanka 51 2011/12 by Zimbabwe	201 Ryder J.D. 2008/09 v India 197 Gayle C.H. 2008/09 for West Indies	6-26 Martin C.S. 2011/12 v Zimbabwe 7-47 Sidebottom R.J. 2007/08 for England
Seddon Park, Hamilton 27 Tests	715-6d 2018/19 v Bangladesh 520 2008/09 by India	93 1992/93 v Pakistan 97 1999/00 by West Indies	251 Williamson K.S. 2020/21 v West Indies 226 Root J.E. 2019/20 for England	7-27 Cairns C.L. 1999/00 v West Indies 6-49 Sidebottom R.J. 2007/08 for England
University of Otago Oval, Dunedin 8 Tests	609-9d 2013/14 v West Indies 507 2013/14 by West Indies	153 2009/10 v Pakistan 137 2008/09 by Bangladesh	217* Taylor L.R.P.L. 2013/14 v West Indies 218 Bravo D.M. 2013/14 for West Indies	6-56 Vettori D.L. 2008/09 v West Indies 5-94 Maharaj K.A. 2016/17 for South Africa
Hagley Oval, Christchurch 8 Tests	659-6d 2020/21 v Pakistan 505 2015/16 by Australia	200 2016/17 v Pakistan 124 2019/20 by India	238 Williamson K.S. 2020/21 v Pakistan 170 Burns J.A. 2015/16 for Australia	6-30 Boult T.A. 2018/19 v Sri Lanka 6-54 Broad S.C.J. 2017/18 for England
Bay Oval, Mt Maunganui 2 Tests	615-9d 2019/20 v England 353 2019/20 by England	431 2020/21 v Pakistan 197 2019/20 by England	205 Watling B-J. 2019/20 v England 102 Fawad Alam 2020/21 for Pakistan	5-44 Wagner N. 2019/20 v England 3-119 Curran S.M. 2019/20 for England
ALL TESTS IN NZ 220 Tests	715-6d 2018/19 v Bangladesh Hamilton 660-5d 1994/95 by West Indies Wellington	26 1954/55 v England Auckland 51 2011/12 by Zimbabwe Napier	302 McCullum B.B. 2013/14 v India Wellington 336* Hammond W.R. 1932/33 for England Auckland	7-23 Hadlee R.J. 1975/76 v India Wellington 8-76 Prasanna E.A.S. 1975/76 for India Auckland

Record Performances in Tests v All Opponents

Opponent	Highest Total by NZ / v NZ	Lowest Total by NZ / v NZ	Highest Individual Innings by NZ / v NZ	Best Bowling by NZ / v NZ
England	615-9d Mt Maunganui 2019/20 593-6 Auckland 1974/75	26 Auckland 1954/55 58 Auckland 2017/18	222 Astle N.J. Christchurch, 2001/02 336* Hammond W.R. Auckland, 1932/33	7-74 Cairns B.L. Leeds, 1983 7-32 Underwood D.L. Lord's, 1969
Australia	624 Perth 2015/16 607-6d Brisbane 1993/94	42 Wellington 1945/46 103 Auckland 1985/86	290 Taylor L.R.P.L.. Perth, 2015/16 250 Walters K.D. Christchurch, 1977/78	9-52 Hadlee R.J. Brisbane, 1985/86 6-31 Warne S.K. Hobart 1993/94
South Africa	595 Auckland 2003/04 621-5d Auckland 1998/99	45 Cape Town 2012/13 148 Johannesburg 1953/54	262 Fleming S.P. Cape Town, 2005/06 275* Cullinan D.J. Auckland, 1998/99	6-60 Reid J.R. Dunedin, 1963/64 8-53 Lawrence G.B. Johannesburg, 1961/62
West Indies	609-9d Dunedin 2013/14 660-5d Wellington 1994/95	74 Dunedin 1955/56 77 Auckland 1955/56	259 Turner G.M. Georgetown, 1971/72 258 Nurse S.M. Christchurch, 1968/69	7-27 Cairns C.L. Hamilton, 1999/00 7-37 Walsh C.A. Wellington, 1994/95
India	680-8d Wellington 2013/14 583-7d Ahmedabad 1999/00	94 Hamilton 2002/03 81 Wellington 1975/76	302 McCullum B.B. Wellington, 2013/14 231 Mankad M.H. Madras, 1955/56	7-23 Hadlee R.J. Wellington, 1975/76 8-72 Venkataraghavan S. Delhi, 1964/65
Pakistan	690 Sharjah 2014/15 643 Lahore 2001/02	70 Dacca 1955/56 102 Faisalabad 1990/91	238 Williamson K.S. Christchurch, 2020/21 329 Inzamam-ul-Haq Lahore, 2001/02	7-52 Pringle C. Faisalabad 1990/91 8-41 Yasir Shah Dubai, 2018/19
Sri Lanka	671-4 Wellington 1990/91 498 Napier 2004/05	102 Colombo 1992/93 93 Wellington 1982/83	299 Crowe M.D. Wellington, 1990/91 267 de Silva P.A. Wellington, 1990/91	7-130 Vettori D.L. Wellington 2006/07 6-43 Herath H.M.R.K.B. Galle, 2012/13
Zimbabwe	582-4d Bulawayo 2016/17 461 Bulawayo 1997/98	207 Harare 1997/98 51 Napier 2011/12	173* Taylor L.R.P.L. Bulawayo, 2016/17 203* Whittall G.J. Bulawayo, 1997/98	6-26 Martin C.S. Napier, 2011/12 8-109 Strang P.A. Bulawayo, 2000/01
Bangladesh	715-6d Hamilton 2018/19 595-8d Wellington 2016/17	171 Chittagong 2008/09 108 Hamilton 2001/02	202 Fleming S.P. Chittagong, 2004/05 217 Shakib Al Hasan. Wellington, 2016/17	7-53 Cairns C.L. Hamilton, 2001/02 7-36 Shakib Al Hasan Chittagong, 2008/09

INDIVIDUAL RECORDS

BATTING

Test Centuries

(308 instances)

302	McCullum B.B. v India at Wellington	2013/14
299	Crowe M.D. v Sri Lanka at Wellington	1990/91
290	Taylor L.R.P.L. v Australia at Perth	2015/16
274*	Fleming S.P. v Sri Lanka at Colombo	2002/03
267*	Young B.A. v Sri Lanka at Dunedin	1996/97
264*	Latham T.W.M. v Sri Lanka at Wellington	2018/19
262	Fleming S.P. v South Africa at Cape Town	2005/06
259	Turner G.M. v West Indies at Georgetown	1971/72
251	Williamson K.S. v West Indies at Hamilton	2020/21
242*	Williamson K.S. v Sri Lanka at Wellington	2014/15
239	Dowling G.T. v India at Christchurch	1967/68
238	Williamson K.S. v Pakistan at Christchurch	2020/21
230*	Sutcliffe B. v India at New Delhi	1955/56
225	McCullum B.B. v India at Hyderabad	2010/11
224	Vincent L. v Sri Lanka at Wellington	2004/05
224	McCullum B.B. v India at Auckland	2013/14
223*	Turner G.M. v West Indies at Kingston	1971/72
222	Astle N.J. v England at Christchurch	2001/02
217*	Taylor L.R.P.L. v West Indies at Dunedin	2013/14
214	Sinclair M.S. v West Indies at Wellington	1999/00
206	Donnelly M.P. v England at Lord's	1949
205	Watling B-J. v England at Mount Maunganui	2019/20
204*	Sinclair M.S. v Pakistan at Christchurch	2000/01
202	Fleming S.P. v Bangladesh at Chittagong	2004/05
202	McCullum B.B. v Pakistan at Sharjah	2014/15
201	Ryder J.D. v India at Napier	2008/09
200*	Williamson K.S. v Bangladesh at Hamilton	2018/19
200	Taylor L.R.P.L. v Bangladesh at Wellington	2018/19
200	Conway D.P. v England at Lord's	2021
195	McCullum B.B. v Sri Lanka at Christchurch	2014/15
192	Fleming S.P. v Pakistan at Hamilton	2003/04
192	Williamson K.S. v Pakistan at Sharjah	2014/15
189	Guptill M.J. v Bangladesh at Hamilton	2009/10
188	Crowe M.D. v West Indies at Georgetown	1984/85
188	Crowe M.D. v Australia at Brisbane	1985/86
186	Jones A.H. v Sri Lanka at Wellington	1990/91
185	Wright J.G. v India at Christchurch	1989/90
185	McCullum B.B. v Bangladesh at Hamilton	2009/10
182	Jarvis T.W. v West Indies at Georgetown	1971/72
180	Reid J.F. v Sri Lanka at Colombo	1983/84
177	Latham T.W.M. v Bangladesh at Wellington	2016/17
176	Congdon B.E. v England at Nottingham	1973
176	Williamson K.S. v South Africa at Hamilton	2016/17
176	Latham T.W.M. v Sri Lanka at Christchurch	2018/19
175	Congdon B.E. v England at Lord's	1973
174*	Coney J.V. v England at Wellington	1983/84
174*	Fleming S.P. v Sri Lanka at Colombo	1997/98
174	Crowe M.D. v Pakistan at Wellington	1988/89

174	Nicholls H.M. v West Indies at Wellington	2020/21
173*	Taylor L.R.P.L v Zimbabwe at Bulawayo	2016/17
173	Smith I.D.S. v India at Auckland	1989/90
171	Rutherford H.D. v England at Dunedin	2012/13
170*	Jones A.H. v India at Auckland	1989/90
170	Styris S.B. v South Africa at Auckland	2003/04
166*	Congdon B.E. v West Indies at Port of Spain	1971/72
166	Williamson K.S. v Australia at Perth	2015/16
162*	Nicholls H.M. v Sri Lanka at Christchurch	2018/19
161*	Williamson K.S. v West Indies at Bridgetown	2014
161	Edgar B.A. v Australia at Auckland	1981/82
161	Latham T.W.M. v Bangladesh at Hamilton	2018/19
160	Marshall H.J.H. v Sri Lanka at Napier	2004/05
158*	Reid J.F. v Pakistan at Auckland	1984/85
158	Cairns C.L. v South Africa at Auckland	2003/04
157	Horne M.J. v Zimbabwe at Auckland	1997/98
157	Nicholls H.M. v Pakistan at Christchurch	2020/21
156*	Astle N.J. v Australia at Perth	2001/02
156	Guptill M.J. v Sri Lanka at Dunedin	2015/16
154*	Taylor L.R.P.L. v England at Manchester	2008
154	Latham T.W.M. v Sri Lanka at Colombo	2019/20
152	Lees W.K. v Pakistan at Karachi	1976/77
151*	Sutcliffe B. v India at Calcutta	1964/65
151*	Hadlee R.J. v Sri Lanka at Colombo	1986/87
151	Taylor L.R.P.L. v India at Napier	2008/09
150	Jones A.H. v Australia at Adelaide	1987/88
150	Sinclair M.S. v South Africa at Port Elizabeth	2000/01
148	Reid J.F. v Pakistan at Wellington	1984/85
147	Howarth G.P. v West Indies at Christchurch	1979/80
146*	Greatbatch M.J. v Australia at Perth	1989/90
146	Marshall H.J.H. v Australia at Christchurch	2004/05
145*	Nicholls H.M. v England at Auckland	2017/18
145	Richardson M.H. v India at Mohali	2003/04
145	McCullum B.B. v Australia at Christchurch	2015/16
143	Dowling G.T. v India at Dunedin	1967/68
143	Crowe M.D. v England at Wellington	1987/88
143	Jones A.H. v England at Wellington	1991/92
143	Jones A.H. v Australia at Perth	1993/94
143	Richardson M.H. v Bangladesh at Hamilton	2001/02
143	McCullum B.B. v Bangladesh at Dhaka	2004/05
142*	Watling B-J. v Sri Lanka at Wellington	2014/15
142	Reid J.R. v South Africa at Johannesburg	1961/62
142	Crowe M.D. v England at Lord's	1994
142	McMillan C.D. v Sri Lanka at Colombo	1997/98
142	McMillan C.D. v Zimbabwe at Wellington	2000/01
142	Taylor L.R.P.L. v Sri Lanka at Colombo	2012/13
141	Wright J.G. v Australia at Christchurch	1981/82
141	Astle N.J. v Zimbabwe at Wellington	2000/01
140	Crowe M.D. v Zimbabwe at Harare	1992/93
140	Vettori D.L. v Sri Lanka at Colombo	2009/10
140	Williamson K.S. v Australia at Brisbane	2015/16
139	McMillan C.D. v Zimbabwe at Wellington	1997/98
139	Williamson K.S. v Pakistan at Abu Dhabi	2018/19
138	Sinclair B.W. v South Africa at Auckland	1963/64
138	Wright J.G. v West Indies at Wellington	1986/87
138	Taylor L.R.P.L. v Australia at Hamilton	2009/10

137*	Sutcliffe B. v India at Hyderabad	1955/56
137*	Howarth G.P. v India at Wellington	1980/81
137*	Vettori D.L. v Pakistan at Hamilton	2003/04
137*	Neesham J.D.S. v India at Wellington	2013/14
137	Crowe M.D. v Australia at Christchurch	1985/86
137	Crowe M.D. v Australia at Adelaide	1987/88
137	Latham T.W.M. v Pakistan at Dubai	2014/15
136	Dempster C.S. v England at Wellington	1929/30
136	McIntosh T.G. v West Indies at Napier	2008/09
136	Fulton P.G. v England at Auckland	2012/13
136	Latham T.W.M. v Zimbabwe at Bulawayo	2016/17
135	Reid J.R. v South Africa at Cape Town	1953/54
135	Williamson K.S. v Sri Lanka at Colombo	2012/13
134	Vettori D.L. v Pakistan at Napier	2009/10
133	Greatbatch M.J. v Pakistan at Hamilton	1992/93
133	Horne M.J. v Australia at Hobart	1997/98
133	Oram J.D.P. v South Africa at Centurion	2005/06
132	Congdon B.E. v Australia at Wellington	1973/74
132	Williamson K.S. v England at Lord's	2015
132	Raval J.A. v Bangladesh at Hamilton	2018/19
131	Williamson K.S. v India at Ahmedabad	2010/11
131	Taylor L.R.P.L. v West Indies at Hamilton	2013/14
130	Sinclair B.W. v Pakistan at Lahore	1964/65
130	Wright J.G. v England at Auckland	1983/84
130	Fleming S.P. v West Indies at Bridgetown	2001/02
130	Williamson K.S. v South Africa at Dunedin	2016/17
129	Dowling G.T. v India at Bombay	1964/65
129	Edgar B.A. v Pakistan at Christchurch	1978/79
129	Fleming S.P. v England at Auckland	1996/97
129	Taylor L.R.P.L. v West Indies at Wellington	2013/14
129	Williamson K.S. v Pakistan at Mt Maunganui	2020/21
128	Reid J.R. v Pakistan at Karachi	1964/65
128	Crowe J.J. v England at Auckland	1983/84
128	Astle N.J. v Zimbabwe at Bulawayo	2005/06
127	Edgar B.A. v West Indies at Auckland	1979/80
127	Vettori D.L. v Zimbabwe at Harare	2005/06
126*	Oram J.D.P. v Australia at Brisbane	2004/05
126*	Nicholls H.M. v Pakistan at Abu Dhabi	2018/19
126	Congdon B.E. v West Indies at Bridgetown	1971/72
126	Cairns C.L. v India at Hamilton	1998/99
126	Santner M.J. v England at Mount Maunganui	2019/20
125	Astle N.J. v West Indies at Bridgetown	1995/96
124*	Taylor L.R.P.L. v Zimbabwe at Bulawayo	2016/17
124	Taylor B.R. v West Indies at Auckland	1968/69
124	Cairns C.L. v Zimbabwe at Harare	2000/01
124	Watling B-J. v India at Wellington	2013/14
123*	Reid J.F. v India at Christchurch	1980/81
123	Howarth G.P. v England at Lord's	1978
122*	Franklin J.E.C. v South Africa at Cape Town	2005/06
122*	Taylor L.R.P.L. v Zimbabwe at Napier	2011/12
122	Howarth G.P. v England at Auckland	1977/78
122	Jones A.H. v Sri Lanka at Hamilton	1990/91
121	Parker J.M. v England at Auckland	1974/75
121	Blundell T.A. v Australia at Melbourne	2019/20
120*	Crowe J.J. v Sri Lanka at Colombo	1986/87
120*	Thomson S.A. v Pakistan at Christchurch	1993/94

120	Dempster C.S. v England at Lord's	1931
120	Reid J.R. v India at Calcutta	1955/56
120	Young B.A. v Pakistan at Christchurch	1993/94
120	Cairns C.L. v Zimbabwe at Auckland	1995/96
120	Taylor L.R.P.L. v England at Hamilton	2007/08
120	Watling B-J. v England at Leeds	2015
119*	Reid J.R. v India at Delhi	1955/56
119*	Burgess M.G. v Pakistan at Dacca	1969/70
119*	Oram J.D.P. v South Africa at Hamilton	2003/04
119	Wright J.G. v England at The Oval	1986
119	Crowe M.D. v West Indies at Wellington	1986/87
119	Latham R.T. v Zimbabwe at Bulawayo	1992/93
119	Styris S.B. v India at Mohali	2003/04
118	Vettori D.L. v India at Hamilton	2008/09
118	Nicholls H.M. v South Africa at Wellington	2016/17
117*	Hastings B.F. v West Indies at Christchurch	1968/69
117*	Wright J.G. v Australia at Wellington	1989/90
117	Mills J.E. v England at Wellington	1929/30
117	Morrison J.F.M. v Australia at Sydney	1973/74
117	Turner G.M. v India at Christchurch	1975/76
117	Fleming S.P. v England at Nottingham	2004
117	Oram J.D.P. v Bangladesh at Dunedin	2007/08
116	Hadlee W.A. v England at Christchurch	1946/47
116	Sutcliffe B. v England at Christchurch	1950/51
116	Pollard V. v England at Nottingham	1973
116	Wright J.G. v England at Wellington	1991/92
116	Anderson C.J. v Bangladesh at Mirpur	2013/14
115	Crowe M.D. v England at Manchester	1994
115	McCullum B.B. v India at Napier	2008/09
114	Sinclair B.W. v England at Auckland	1965/66
114	Howarth G.P. v Pakistan at Napier	1978/79
114	Astle N.J. v Zimbabwe at Auckland	1997/98
114	Astle N.J. v Sri Lanka at Napier	2004/05
114	Williamson K.S. v Bangladesh at Chittagong	2013/14
113*	Smith I.D.S. v England at Auckland	1983/84
113*	Wright J.G. v India at Napier	1989/90
113	Turner G.M. v India at Kanpur	1976/77
113	Crowe M.D. v India at Auckland	1989/90
113	Taylor L.R.P.L. v India at Bangalore	2012/13
113	McCullum B.B. v West Indies at Dunedin	2013/14
113	Williamson K.S. v India at Auckland	2013/14
113	Williamson K.S. v West Indies at Kingston	2014
113	Williamson K.S. v Zimbabwe at Bulawayo	2016/17
112	Crowe J.J. v West Indies at Kingston	1984/85
112	Spearman C.M. v Zimbabwe at Auckland	1995/96
111*	Coney J.V. v Pakistan at Dunedin	1984/85
111	McGregor S.N. v Pakistan at Lahore	1955/56
111	Burgess M.G. v Pakistan at Lahore	1976/77
111	McCullum B.B. v Zimbabwe at Harare	2005/06
110*	Turner G.M. v Australia at Christchurch	1973/74
110	Turner G.M. v Pakistan at Dacca	1969/70
110	Hastings B.F. v Pakistan at Auckland	1972/73
110	Wright J.G. v India at Auckland	1980/81
110	Bracewell J.G. v England at Nottingham	1986
110	Horne M.J. v Zimbabwe at Bulawayo	2000/01
110	Parore A.C. v Australia at Perth	2001/02

110	Vettori D.L. v Pakistan at Wellington	2010/11
110	Fulton P.G. v England at Auckland	2012/13
109*	Latham T.W.M. v Sri Lanka at Dunedin	2015/16
109	Barton P.T. v South Africa at Port Elizabeth	1961/62
109	Cairns C.L. v Australia at Wellington	1999/00
109	Guptill M.J. v Zimbabwe at Bulawayo	2011/12
109	Brownlie D.G. v South Africa at Cape Town	2012/13
108*	Crowe M.D. v Pakistan at Lahore	1990/91
108*	Williamson K.S. v Sri Lanka at Hamilton	2015/16
108	Parker J.M. v Australia at Sydney	1973/74
108	Reid J.F. v Australia at Brisbane	1985/86
108	Styris S.B. v England at Nottingham	2004
107*	Congdon B.E. v Australia at Christchurch	1976/77
107*	Greatbatch M.J. v England at Auckland	1987/88
107*	Rutherford K.R. v England at Wellington	1987/88
107*	McMillan C.D. v England at Manchester	1999
107*	Blundell T.A. v West Indies at Wellington	2017/18
107*	Taylor L.R.P.L. v West Indies at Hamilton	2017/18
107	Rabone G.O. v South Africa at Durban	1953/54
107	Redmond R.E. v Pakistan at Auckland	1972/73
107	Wright J.G. v Pakistan at Karachi	1984/85
107	Crowe M.D. v Sri Lanka at Colombo	1992/93
107	Styris S.B. v West Indies at St George's	2001/02
107	Bell M.D. v Bangladesh at Dunedin	2007/08
107	Taylor L.R.P.L. v India at Wellington	2008/09
107	Neesham J.D.S. v West Indies at Kingston	2014
107	Watling B-J. v Zimbabwe at Bulawayo	2016/17
107	Nicholls H.M. v Bangladesh at Wellington	2018/19
106	Reid J.F. v Pakistan at Hyderabad	1984/85
106	Crowe M.D. v England at Lord's	1986
106	Richardson M.H. v Pakistan at Hamilton	2000/01
106	McMillan C.D. v Bangladesh at Hamilton	2001/02
106	Vincent L. v India at Mohali	2003/04
105*	Pollard V. v England at Lord's	1973
105*	Watling B-J. v Sri Lanka at Colombo	2019/20
105*	Taylor L.R.P.L. v England at Hamilton	2019/20
105	Taylor B.R. v India at Calcutta	1964/65
105	Hastings B.F. v West Indies at Bridgetown	1971/72
105	Burgess M.G. v England at Lord's	1973
105	Rutherford K.R. v Sri Lanka at Moratuwa	1992/93
105	Bell M.D. v Pakistan at Hamilton	2000/01
105	Fleming S.P. v Australia at Perth	2001/02
105	Latham T.W.M. v Zimbabwe at Bulawayo	2016/17
105	de Grandhomme C. v West Indies at Wellington	2017/18
105	Latham T.W.M. v England at Hamilton	2019/20
104*	Williamson K.S. v Bangladesh at Wellington	2016/17
104*	Williamson K.S. v England at Hamilton	2019/20
104	Page M.L. v England at Lord's	1931
104	Congdon B.E. v England at Christchurch	1965/66
104	Burgess M.G. v England at Auckland	1970/71
104	Parker J.M. v India at Bombay	1976/77
104	Crowe M.D. v West Indies at Auckland	1986/87
104	Vincent L. v Australia at Perth	2001/02
104	McCullum B.B. v Australia at Wellington	2009/10
104	Taylor L.R.P.L. v Pakistan at Dubai	2014/15

103*	Styris S.B. v West Indies at Auckland	2005/06
103	Hadlee R.J. v West Indies at Christchurch	1979/80
103	Wright J.G. v England at Auckland	1987/88
103	Astle N.J. v West Indies at St John's	1995/96
103	Astle N.J. v India at Ahmedabad	2003/04
103	Ryder J.D. v India at Ahmedabad	2010/11
103	Watling B-J. v Bangladesh at Chittagong	2013/14
103	Latham T.W.M. v Pakistan at Abu Dhabi	2014/15
102*	Astle N.J. v England at Auckland	1996/97
102*	Watling B-J. v Zimbabwe at Napier	2011/12
102*	Williamson K.S. v South Africa at Wellington	2011/12
102*	Taylor L.R.P.L. v Pakistan at Hamilton	2016/17
102*	Mitchell D.J. v Pakistan at Christchurch	2020/21
102	Guy J.W. v India at Hyderabad	1955/56
102	Howarth G.P. v England at Auckland	1977/78
102	Rutherford K.R. v Australia at Christchurch	1992/93
102	Ryder J.D. v India at Hamilton	2008/09
102	McIntosh T.G. v India at Hyderabad	2010/11
102	Williamson K.S. v England at Auckland	2017/18
101*	Coney J.V. v Australia at Wellington	1985/86
101	Sutcliffe B. v England at Manchester	1949
101	Harris P.G.Z. v South Africa at Cape Town	1961/62
101	Burgess M.G. v West Indies at Kingston	1971/72
101	Hastings B.F. v Australia at Wellington	1973/74
101	Turner G.M. v Australia at Christchurch	1973/74
101	Franklin T.J. v England at Lord's	1990
101	Wright J.G. v Sri Lanka at Hamilton	1990/91
101	Astle N.J. v England at Manchester	1999
101	Richardson M.H. v England at Lord's	2004
101	Oram J.D.P. v England at Lord's	2008
100*	Jones A.H. v Sri Lanka at Hamilton	1990/91
100*	Parore A.C. v West Indies at Christchurch	1994/95
100*	McMillan C.D. v India at Mohali	2003/04
100	Vivian H.G. v South Africa at Wellington	1931/32
100	Reid J.R. v England at Christchurch	1962/63
100	Crowe M.D. v England at Wellington	1983/84
100	Horne M.J. v England at Lord's	1999

Century on Test Debut

117 & 7	Mills J.E. v England at Wellington	1929/30
105 & 0*	Taylor B.R. v India at Calcutta	1964/65
107 & 56	Redmond R.E. v Pakistan at Auckland	1972/73
11 & 107*	Greatbatch M.J. v England at Auckland	1987/88
214	Sinclair M.S. v West Indies at Wellington	1999/00
104 & 54	Vincent L. v Australia at Perth	2001/02
107 & 69*	Styris S.B. v West Indies at St George's	2001/02
131	Williamson K.S. v India at Ahmedabad	2010/11
171	Rutherford H.D. v England at Dunedin	2012/13
137*	Neesham J.D.S. v India at Wellington	2013/14
107*	Blundell T.A. v West Indies at Wellington	2017/18
200 & 23	Conway D.P. v England at Lord's	2021

Centuries in Both Innings of a Test

101 & 110*	Turner G.M. v Australia at Christchurch	1973/74
122 & 102	Howarth G.P. v England at Auckland	1977/78
122 & 100*	Jones A.H. v Sri Lanka at Hamilton	1990/91
136 & 110	Fulton P.G. v England at Auckland	2012/13

NB: *In the same match that Jones achieved this feat A.P. Gurusinha (119 & 102) also scored a century in each innings. This is only the second occasion that a player from each side has scored centuries in each innings of a test (A.R. Morris and D.C.S. Compton, Australia v England, Adelaide, 1946/47).*

A Century and a Fifty in a Test

136 & 80*	Dempster C.S. v England at Wellington	1929/30
52 & 120	Dempster C.S. v England at Lord's	1931
100 & 73	Vivian H.G. v South Africa at Wellington *(aged 19)*	1931/32
107 & 68	Rabone G.O. v South Africa at Durban	1953/54
60 & 142	Reid J.R. v South Africa at Johannesburg	1961/62
74 & 100	Reid J.R. v England at Christchurch	1962/63
128 & 76	Reid J.R. v Pakistan at Karachi	1964/65
59 & 119*	Burgess M.G. v Pakistan at Dacca	1969/70
166* & 82	Congdon B.E. v West Indies at Port of Spain	1971/72
107 & 56	Redmond R.E. v Pakistan at Auckland	1972/73
75 & 138	Wright J.G. v West Indies at Wellington	1986/87
150 & 64	Jones A.H. v Australia at Adelaide	1987/88
76 & 146*	Greatbatch M.J. v Australia at Perth	1989/90
140 & 61	Crowe M.D. v Zimbabwe at Harare	1992/93
105 & 53	Rutherford K.R. v Sri Lanka at Moratuwa	1992/93
57 & 102	Rutherford K.R. v Australia at Christchurch	1992/93
70 & 115	Crowe M.D. v England at Manchester	1994
57 & 120	Cairns C.L. v Zimbabwe at Auckland	1995/96
54 & 125	Astle N.J. v West Indies at Bridgetown	1995/96
78 & 174*	Fleming S.P. v Sri Lanka at Colombo	1997/98
109 & 69	Cairns C.L. v Australia at Wellington	1999/00
141 & 51*	Astle N.J. v Zimbabwe at Wellington	2000/01
204 & 50*	Sinclair M.S. v Pakistan at Christchurch	2000/01
104 & 54	Vincent L. v Australia at Perth	2001/02
107 & 69*	Styris S.B. v West Indies at St George's	2001/02
274* & 69*	Fleming S.P. v Sri Lanka at Colombo	2002/03
103 & 51	Astle N.J. v India at Ahmedabad	2003/04
93 & 101	Richardson M.H. v England at Lord's	2004
189 & 56*	Guptill M.J. v Bangladesh at Hamilton	2009/10
142 & 74	Taylor L.R.P.L. v Sri Lanka at Colombo	2012/13
114 & 74	Williamson K.S. v Bangladesh at Chittagong	2013/14
69 & 242*	Williamson K.S. v Sri Lanka at Wellington	2014/15
140 & 59	Williamson K.S. v Australia at Brisbane	2015/16
113 & 68*	Williamson K.S. v Zimbabwe at Bulawayo	2016/17
124* & 67*	Taylor L.R.P.L. v Zimbabwe at Bulawayo	2016/17
53 & 104*	Williamson K.S. v Bangladesh at Wellington	2016/17
89 & 139	Williamson K.S. v Pakistan at Abu Dhabi	2018/19
53 & 105*	Taylor L.R.P.L. v England at Hamilton	2019/20

Redmond's feat of scoring a century and a fifty in his only test is unique. Only he and A.G. Ganteaume (112 WI v England, Port of Spain 1947/48) have made a century in their only test.

Centuries in Three Successive Test Innings

Jones A.H. 186, Wellington, 122 and 100* Hamilton v Sri Lanka 1990/91

Centuries in Two Successive Test Innings

Reid J.R. 119*, Delhi and 120, Calcutta v India 1955/56
Burgess M.G. 119*, Dacca v Pakistan 1969/70 and 104, Auckland v England 1970/71
Congdon B.E. 176, Nottingham and 175, Lord's v England 1973
Pollard V. 116, Nottingham and 105*, Lord's v England 1973
Turner G.M. 101 and 110*, Christchurch v Australia 1973/74
Howarth G.P. 122 and 102, Auckland v England 1977/78 – 94 v England, Oval 1978
Crowe M.D. 143, Wellington v England 1987/88 and 174, Wellington v Pakistan 1988/89
Wright J.G. 185, Christchurch and 113* Napier v India 1989/90
Astle N.J. 125, Bridgetown and 103, St Johns v West Indies 1995/96
Fulton P.G. 136 and 110, Auckland v England 2012/13
Taylor L.R.P.L. 129, Wellington and 131, Hamilton v West Indies 2013/14
Neesham J.D.S. 137*, Wellington v West Indies 2013/14 and 107, Kingston v West Indies 2014
Williamson K.S. 242* v Sri Lanka at Wellington 2014/15 and 132 v England at Lords 2015
Latham T.W.M. 105 and 136, Bulawayo v Zimbabwe 2016/17
Taylor L.R.P.L. 173* and 124*, Bulawayo v Zimbabwe 2016/17
Latham T.W.M. 176 v Sri Lanka at Christchurch and 161 v Bangladesh at Hamilton 2018/19
Williamson K.S. 251 v West Indies at Hamilton 2020/21 and 129 v Pakistan at Mt Maunganui 2020/21

M.G. Burgess scored centuries in three successive tests – all played in different countries. He followed the two centuries above with 15 & 101 v West Indies at Kingston, 1971/72.
L.R.P.L. Taylor scored centuries in three successive tests against West Indies in 2013/14 – 217 & 16* at Dunedin, 129 at Wellington and 131 & 2* at Hamilton.*
B.E. Congdon scored centuries in successive tests v West Indies 1971/72 – 166 & 82 at Port of Spain and 126 at Bridgetown.*
G.T. Dowling did likewise with 143 & 10 at Dunedin and 239 & 5 at Christchurch v India 1967/68.
B.B. McCullum scored 224 & 1 at Auckland and 8 & 302 at Wellington in successive tests v India 2013/14
K.S. Williamson scored 140 & 59 at Brisbane and 166 & 32 at Adelaide in successive tests v Australia 2015/16*
In successive tests v Pakistan 1984/85 J.F. Reid scored 106 & 21 at Hyderabad, 97 at Karachi, 148 & 3 at Wellington and 158 at Auckland.*
K.S.Williamson scored centuries in three successive tests. 251 v West Indies at Hamilton, 129 & 21 v Pakistan at Mt Maunganui and 238 v Pakistan at Christchurch in 2020/21

Fifty on Test Debut

3 & 51	Vivian H.G. v England at The Oval *(aged 18)*	1931
52 & 56	Wallace W.M. v England at Lord's	1937
64 & 0	Moloney D.A.R. v England at Lord's	1937
58	Sutcliffe B. v England at Christchurch	1946/47
50 & 25	Reid J.R. v England at Manchester	1949
93 & 64	Harford N.S. v Pakistan at Lahore	1955/56
54 & 23	Barton P.T. v South Africa at Durban	1961/62
74 & 58	Dowling G.T. v South Africa at Johannesburg	1961/62
64 & 1	Yuile B.W. v England at Auckland	1962/63
10 & 52	Gedye S.G. v South Africa at Wellington	1963/64
66 & 5	Morgan R.W. v Pakistan at Auckland	1964/65
17 & 54	Murray B.A.G. v India at Dunedin	1967/68
50 & 39	Burgess M.G. v India at Dunedin	1967/68
69 & 0*	Thomson K. v India at Christchurch	1967/68
6 & 51*	Howarth G.P. v England at Auckland	1974/75
14 & 92	Anderson R.W. v Pakistan at Lahore	1976/77
55 & 19	Wright J.G. v England at Wellington	1977/78
56 & 0*	Harris C.Z. v Sri Lanka at Moratuwa	1992/93
38 & 53	Young B.A. v Australia at Brisbane	1993/94
16 & 92	Fleming S.P. v India at Hamilton	1993/94
54 & 0	McMillan C.D. v Australia at Brisbane	1997/98
59 & 12	Papps M.H.W. v South Africa at Hamilton	2003/04
57 & 19*	McCullum B.B. v South Africa at Hamilton	2003/04
74 & 7	Cumming C.D. v Australia at Christchurch	2004/05

5 & 77*	Southee T.G. v England at Napier	2007/08
18 & 60*	Watling B-J. v Pakstan at Napier	2009/10
63 & 9	Brownlie D.G. v Zimbabwe at Bulawayo	2011/12
88 & 31	Ronchi L. v England at Leeds	2015
8 & 59	Nicholls H.M. v Australia at Wellington	2015/16
55 & 36*	Raval J.A. v Pakistan at Christchurch	2016/17
73	Mitchell D.J. v England at Hamilton	2019/20
51 & 0	Phillips G.D. v Australia at Sydney	2019/20

H.M. McGirr scored 51 in his first (and only) test innings but it was his second test appearance

Two Fifties in a Test

52 & 56	†Wallace W.M. v England at Lord's	1937
58 & 50	Vivian H.G. v England at Old Trafford	1937
96 & 54*	Smith F.B. v England at Headingley	1949
75 & 80	Donnelly M.P. v England at Old Trafford	1949
88 & 54	Sutcliffe B. v England at The Oval	1949
55 & 58	Wallace W.M. v England at The Oval	1949
93 & 64	†Harford N.S. v Pakistan at Lahore	1955/56
74 & 58	†Dowling G.T. v South Africa at Johannesburg	1961/62
55 & 55	Pollard V. v England at Lord's *(aged 19)*	1965
66 & 60	Burgess M.G. v India at Wellington	1967/68
58 & 58	Morrison J.F.M. v England at Auckland	1974/75
54 & 54	Congdon B.E. v India at Auckland	1975/76
55 & 54	Edwards G.N. v England at Auckland	1977/78
62 & 76	Edgar B.A. v England at Nottingham	1983
62 & 60	Howarth G.P. v Sri Lanka at Kandy	1983/84
57 & 84	Crowe M.D. v Pakistan at Dunedin	1984/85
50 & 52	Edgar B.A. v Australia at Sydney	1985/86
56 & 59	Wright J.G. v Australia at Auckland	1985/86
82 & 79	Crowe M.D. v Australia at Melbourne	1987/88
87 & 88	Greatbatch M.J. v Zimbabwe at Bulawayo	1992/93
74 & 89	Rutherford K.R. v Zimbabwe at Harare	1992/93
63 & 59	Rutherford K.R. v India at Hamilton	1993/94
79 & 53	Fleming S.P. v South Africa at Cape Town	1994/95
59 & 51*	Twose R.G. v Pakistan at Christchurch	1995/96
57 & 52	Cairns C.L. v England at Christchurch	1996/97
92 & 84	McMillan C.D. v India at Hamilton	1998/99
93 & 60	Horne M.J. v South Africa at Auckland	1998/99
57 & 99	Fleming S.P. v South Africa at Bloemfontein	2000/01
57 & 71	Vincent L. v England at Wellington	2001/02
95 & 71	Richardson M.H. v West Indies at St George's	2001/02
55 & 55	Richardson M.H. v Sri Lanka at Kandy	2002/03
54 & 83*	McMillan C.D. v India at Ahmedabad	2003/04
53 & 55	Taylor L.R.P.L. v England at Wellington	2007/08
59 & 66	Fleming S.P. v England at Napier	2007/08
55 & 76*	Vettori D.L. v Bangladesh at Chittagong	2008/09
57 & 59*	Ryder J.D. v West Indies at Napier	2008/09
94 & 59	Taylor L.R.P.L. v Pakistan at Dunedin	2009/10
78 & 52	Taylor L.R.P.L. v Pakistan at Wellington	2010/11
76 & 76	Taylor L.R.P.L. v Zimbabwe at Bulawayo	2011/12
97 & 67	Guptill M.J. v West Indies at North Sound	2012
63 & 63	Watling B-J. v South Africa at Port Elizabeth	2012/13
73 & 59	Fulton P.G. v Bangladesh at Chittagong	2013/14
58 & 56	Williamson K.S. v West Indies at Hamilton	2013/14
83 & 73	Latham T.W.M. v West Indies at Kingston	2014

78 & 51	Neesham J.D.M. v West Indies at Bridgetown	2014
61* & 59	Watling B-J. v England at Lord's	2015
88 & 71	Williamson K.S. v Sri Lanka at Dunedin	2015/16
52 & 52	Latham T.W.M. v India at Christchurch	2019/20

† *on debut*

Fifties in Successive Test Innings

The following reached 50 in four successive test innings:

Donnelly M.P. 62, 206, 75 & 80 v England, 1949
Sutcliffe B. 101, 88, 54 v England 1949 and 116 v England 1950/51
Congdon B.E. 166*, 82, 126 and 61* v West Indies 1971/72
54, 54, 58 & 52 v India 1975/76
Coney J.V. 101*, 98, 93 v Australia 1985/86 and 51 v England 1986
Rutherford K.R. 74, 89 v Zimbabwe and 105, 53 v Sri Lanka 1992/93
Ryder J.D. 89, 57, 59* v West Indies and 102 v India 2008/09
Taylor L.R.P.L. 78, 52 v Pakistan 2010/11 and 76, 76 v Zimbabwe 2011/12
Williamson K.S. 97 v Australia 2015/16 and 91, 113 and 68* v Zimbabwe 2016/17

Highest Score in Each Batting Position

Position					
1 or 2	267*	Young B.A.	v Sri Lanka	Dunedin	1996/97
3	274*	Fleming S.P.	v Sri Lanka	Colombo	2002/03
4	299	Crowe M.D.	v Sri Lanka	Wellington	1990/91
5	302	McCullum B.B.	v India	Wellington	2013/14
6	205	Watling B-J.	v England	Mt Maunganui	2019/20
7	185	McCullum B.B.	v Pakistan	Dunedin	2009/10
8	140	Vettori D.L.	v Sri Lanka	Colombo	2009/10
9	173	Smith I.D.S.	v India	Auckland	1989/90
10	83*	Bracewell J.G.	v Australia	Sydney	1985/86
11	68*	Collinge R.O.	v Pakistan	Auckland	1972/73

Century Partnership for The First Wicket

					Final innings total
276	Dempster C.S. Mills J.E.	v England	Wellington	1929/30	440
133	Sutcliffe B. Hadlee W.A.	v England	Christchurch	1946/47	345-9d
112	Sutcliffe B. Scott V.J	v England	Leeds	1949	195-2
121	Sutcliffe B. Scott V.J.	v England	The Oval	1949	345
126	Rabone G.O. Chapple M.E.	v South Africa	Cape Town	1953/54	505
101	McGregor S.N. Leggat J.G.	v India	Delhi	1955/56	112-1
136	Dowling G.T. Jarvis T.W.	v Pakistan	Lahore	1964/65	482-6d
126	Dowling G.T. Murray B.A.G.	v India	Christchurch	1967/68	502
112	Dowling G.T. Turner G.M.	v West Indies	Auckland	1968/69	297-8d
115	Dowling G.T. Turner G.M.	v West Indies	Christchurch	1968/69	367-6
106	Dowling G.T. Murray B.A.G.	v India	Hyderabad	1969/70	181
387	Turner G.M. Jarvis T.W.	v West Indies	Georgetown	1971/72	543-3d
159	Redmond R.E. Turner G.M.	v Pakistan	Auckland	1972/73	402
107	Parker J.M. Turner G.M.	v Australia	Auckland	1973/74	158
100	Wright J.G. Edgar B.A.	v Australia	Sydney	1985/86	193
117	Wright J.G. Franklin T.J.	v England	Auckland	1987/88	350-7d
149	Wright J.G. Franklin T.J.	v India	Napier	1989/90	178-1
185	Wright J.G. Franklin T.J.	v England	Lord's	1990	462-9d
134	Franklin T.J. Wright J.G.	v Sri Lanka	Wellington	1990/91	671-4
161	Franklin T.J. Wright J.G.	v Sri Lanka	Hamilton	1990/91	374-6d
116	Greatbatch M.J. Latham R.T.	v Zimbabwe	Bulawayo	1992/93	325-3d
102	Greatbatch M.J. Latham R.T.	v Zimbabwe	Bulawayo	1992/93	222-5d

Runs	Partners	Opponent	Venue	Season	Total
110	Hartland B.R. Wright J.G.	v Sri Lanka	Moratuwa	1992/93	195-5
110	Greatbatch M.J. Hartland B.R.	v Pakistan	Hamilton	1992/93	264
111	Greatbatch M.J. Wright J.G.	v Australia	Wellington	1992/93	329
214	Spearman C.M. Twose R.G.	v Zimbabwe	Auckland	1995/96	441-5d
107	Young B.A. Horne M.J.	v South Africa	Christchurch	1998/99	127-1
131	Horne M.J. Stead G.R.	v India	Ahmedabad	1999/00	252-2
102	Richardson M.H. Bell M.D.	v Pakistan	Christchurch	2000/01	476
181	Richardson M.H. Bell M.D.	v Pakistan	Hamilton	2000/01	407-4d
104	Richardson M.H. Horne M.J.	v Bangladesh	Wellington	2001/02	341-6d
117	Richardson M.H. Vincent L.	v West Indies	St George's	2001/02	256-5
231	Richardson M.H. Vincent L.	v India	Mohali	2003/04	630-6d
163	Richardson M.H. Fleming S.P.	v England	Nottingham	2004	384
125	McIntosh T.G. McCullum B.B.	v India	Hyderabad	2010/11	448-8d
120	Guptill M.J. McCullum B.B.	v Pakistan	Wellington	2010/11	356
124	McCullum B.B. Guptill M.J.	v Zimbabwe	Napier	2011/12	495-7d
158	Fulton P.G. Rutherford H.D.	v England	Dunedin	2012/13	460-9d
148	Guptill M.J. Latham T.W.M.	v England	Lord's	2015	523
169	Guptill M.J. Latham T.W.M.	v Zimbabwe	Bulawayo	2016/17	582-4d
118	Guptill M.J. Latham T.W.M.	v India	Indore	2016/17	299
121	Raval J.A. Latham T.W.M.	v Sri Lanka	Christchurch	2018/19	585-4d
254	Raval J.A. Latham T.W.M.	v Bangladesh	Hamilton	2018/19	715-6d
103	Latham T.W.M. Blundell T.A.	v India	Christchurch	2019/20	132-3
111	Latham T.W.M. Blundell T.A.	v Pakistan	Mt Maunganui	2020/21	180-5d

Pairs in Test Matches Involving New Zealand

By New Zealand *(64)*

*James K.C. v England at Christchurch	1929/30
*Badcock F.T. v England at Christchurch	1929/30
Cowie J. v England at Manchester	1937
*Rowe C.G. v Australia at Wellington	1945/46
*Butterfield L.A. v Australia at Wellington	1945/46
Miller L.S.M. v South Africa at Johannesburg	1953/54
Poore M.B. v England at Auckland	1954/55
Colquhoun I.A. v England at Auckland	1954/55
Hayes J.A. v England at Auckland	1954/55
Blair R.W. v West Indies at Dunedin	1955/56
Cave H.B. v West Indies at Dunedin	1955/56
MacGibbon A.R. v India at Madras	1955/56
Harford N.S. v England at Leeds	1958
Motz R.C. v South Africa at Cape Town	1961/62
Blair R.W. v England at Christchurch	1962/63
Blair R.W. v South Africa at Auckland	1963/64
Shrimpton M.J.F. v South Africa at Auckland	1963/64
Dick A.E. v Pakistan at Rawalpindi	1964/65
Bartlett G.A. v England at Christchurch	1965/66
Jarvis T.W. v Pakistan at Wellington	1972/73
Lees W.K. v England at Christchurch	1977/78
*Bracewell B.P. v England at The Oval	1978
Cairns B.L. v Australia at Brisbane	1980/81
Edgar B.A. v Australia at Perth	1980/81
Troup G.B. v India at Wellington	1980/81
Coney J.V. v Australia at Christchurch	1981/82
Smith I.D.S. v Australia at Christchurch	1981/82
Bracewell J.G. v Pakistan at Hyderabad	1984/85
*Rutherford K.R. v West Indies at Port of Spain	1984/85
Wright J.G. v England at Lord's	1986
Morrison D.K. v Australia at Melbourne	1987/88
*Kuggeleijn C.M. v India at Bangalore	1988/89
Snedden M.C. v India at Hyderabad	1988/89
Morrison D.K. v Sri Lanka at Hamilton	1990/91
Hartland B.R. v England at Auckland	1991/92
Su'a M.L. v Pakistan at Hamilton	1992/93
Morrison D.K. v Australia at Hobart	1993/94
Doull S.B. v West Indies at Wellington	1994/95
Nash D.J. v Sri Lanka at Napier	1994/95
Harris C.Z. v West Indies at Bridgetown	1995/96
Patel D.N. v England at Auckland	1996/97
Doull S.B. v England at Wellington	1996/97
Fleming S.P. v Australia at Hobart	1997/98
Vettori D.L. v Sri Lanka at Galle	1997/98
Wiseman P.J. v India at Wellington	1998/99
Twose R.G. v England at Edgbaston	1999
Wiseman P.J. v India at Kanpur	1999/00
O'Connor S.B. v Australia at Hamilton	1999/00
*Franklin J.E.C. v Pakistan at Auckland	2000/01
Martin C.S. v Pakistan at Auckland	2000/01
Martin C.S. v Pakistan at Lahore	2001/02
Martin C.S. v Australia at Brisbane	2004/05
Martin C.S. v West Indies at Auckland	2005/06

Martin C.S. v South Africa at Johannesburg	2007/08
*Gillespie M.R. v South Africa at Centurion	2007/08
O'Brien I.E. v South Africa at Centurion	2007/08
O'Brien I.E. v Australia at Adelaide	2008/09
Martin C.S. v Australia at Adelaide	2008/09
McIntosh T.G. v India at Ahmedabad	2010/11
Bracewell D.A.J. v South Africa at Hamilton	2011/12
Martin C.S. v India at Hyderabad	2012/13
van Wyk C.F.K. v Sri Lanka at Colombo	2012/13
Flynn D.R. v South Africa at Port Elizabeth	2012/13
Boult T.A. v Pakistan at Dubai	2018/19

* *on debut*

Against New Zealand *(47)*

Javed Burki for Pakistan at Wellington	1964/65
Jaisimha M.L. for India at Hyderabad	1969/70
Knott A.P.E. for England at Lord's	1973
Stackpole K.R. for Australia at Auckland	1973/74
Chandrasekhar B.S. for India at Wellington	1975/76
Hendrick M. for England at Wellington	1977/78
Kallicharran A.I. for West Indies at Dunedin	1979/80
Wood G.M. for Australia at Perth	1980/81
Holland R.G. for Australia at Brisbane	1985/86
*Patel R.G. for India at Bombay	1988/89
Malcolm D.E. for England at Birmingham	1990
Waqar Younis for Pakistan at Faisalabad	1990/91
Aamer Sohail for Pakistan at Hamilton	1992/93
Langer J.L. for Australia at Auckland	1992/93
Streak H.H. for Zimbabwe at Harare	1997/98
Rennie G.J. for Zimbabwe at Auckland	1997/98
Mbangwa M. for Zimbabwe at Auckland	1997/98
Walsh C.A. for West Indies at Wellington	1999/00
Nkala M.L. for Zimbabwe at Harare	2000/01
Monjurul Islam for Bangladesh at Wellington	2001/02
Dillon M. for West Indies at Bridgetown	2001/02
Laxman V.V.S. for India at Wellington	2002/03
Khan Z. for India at Hamilton	2002/03
Tareq Aziz for Bangladesh at Dhaka	2004/05
Mohammad Ashraful for Bangladesh at Chittagong	2004/05
Mpofu C.B. for Zimbabwe at Harare	2005/06
*Silva L.P.C. for Sri Lanka at Christchurch	2006/07
Malinga S.L. for Sri Lanka at Wellington	2006/07
Muralitharan M. for Sri Lanka at Wellington	2006/07
Aftab Ahmed for Bangladesh at Dunedin	2007/08
Shahadat Hossain for Bangladesh at Dunedin	2007/08
Mohammad Asif for Pakistan at Napier	2009/10
Rubel Hossain for Bangladesh at Hamilton	2009/10
Johnson M.G. for Australia at Hamilton	2009/10
Mpofu C.B. for Zimbabwe at Bulawayo	2011/12
Masakadza H. for Zimbabwe at Napier	2011/12
Vitori B.V. for Zimbabwe at Napier	2011/12
Finn S.T. for England at Auckland	2012/13
Prior M.J. for England at Lord's	2013
Sammy D.J.G. for West Indies at Wellington	2013/14
Gabriel S.T. for West Indies at Wellington	2013/14
Samuels M.N. for West Indies at Kingston	2014

Wahab Riaz for Pakistan at Hamilton	2016/17
Powell K.O.A. for West Indies at Hamilton	2017/18
Perera M.D.K.J. for Sri Lanka at Colombo	2019/20
Chase R.L. for West Indies at Wellington	2020/21
Shan Masood for Pakistan at Christchurch	2020/21
Bumrah J.J. for India at Southampton	2021

** on debut*

BOWLING

Ten Wickets in a Match

(26 instances)

15-123	Hadlee R.J. v Australia at Brisbane	1985/86
12-149	Vettori D.L. v Australia at Auckland	1999/00
12-170	Vettori D.L. v Bangladesh at Chittagong	2004/05
11-58	Hadlee R.J. v India at Wellington	1975/76
11-102	Hadlee R.J. v West Indies at Dunedin	1979/80
11-117	Jamieson K.A. v Pakistan at Christchurch	2020/21
11-152	Pringle C. v Pakistan at Faisalabad	1990/91
11-155	Hadlee R.J. v Australia at Perth	1985/86
11-169	Nash D.J. v England at Lord's	1994
11-180	Martin C.S. v South Africa at Auckland	2003/04
10-80	Boult T.A. v West Indies at Wellington	2013/14
10-88	Hadlee R.J. v India at Bombay	1988/89
10-99	Bond S.E. v Zimbabwe at Bulawayo	2005/06
10-100	Hadlee R.J. v England at Wellington	1977/78
10-100	Cairns C.L. v West Indies at Hamilton	1999/00
10-102	Hadlee R.J. v Sri Lanka at Colombo	1983/84
10-106	Bracewell J.G. v Australia at Auckland	1985/86
10-108	Southee T.G. v England at Lord's	2013
10-124	Chatfield E.J. v West Indies at Port of Spain	1984/85
10-140	Cowie J. v England at Manchester	1937
10-140	Hadlee R.J. v England at Nottingham	1986
10-144	Cairns B.L. v England at Leeds	1983
10-166	Troup G.B. v West Indies at Auckland	1979/80
10-176	Hadlee R.J. v Australia at Melbourne	1987/88
10-183	Vettori D.L. v Sri Lanka at Wellington	2006/07
10-203	Craig M.D. v Pakistan at Sharjah	2014/15

Five Wickets in an Innings

(218 instances)

9-52	Hadlee R.J. v Australia at Brisbane	1985/86
7-23	Hadlee R.J. v India at Wellington	1975/76
7-27	Cairns C.L. v West Indies at Hamilton	1999/00
7-39	Wagner N. v West Indies at Wellington	2017/18
7-52	Pringle C. v Pakistan at Faisalabad	1990/91
7-53	Cairns C.L. v Bangladesh at Hamilton	2001/02
7-64	Southee T.G. v India at Bangalore	2012/13
7-65	Doull S.B. v India at Wellington	1998/99
7-74	Taylor B.R. v West Indies at Bridgetown	1971/72
7-74	Cairns B.L. v England at Leeds	1983
7-87	Boock S.L. v Pakistan at Hyderabad	1984/85
7-87	Vettori D.L. v Australia at Auckland	1999/00
7-89	Morrison D.K. v Australia at Wellington	1992/93

7-94	Craig M.D. v Pakistan at Sharjah	2014/15
7-116	Hadlee R.J. v Australia at Christchurch	1985/86
7-130	Vettori D.L. v Sri Lanka at Wellington	2006/07
7-143	Cairns B.L. v England at Wellington	1983/84
6-26	Hadlee R.J. v England at Wellington	1977/78
6-26	Martin C.S. v Zimbabwe at Napier	2011/12
6-27	Nash D.J. v India at Mohali	1999/00
6-28	Vettori D.L. v Bangladesh at Dhaka	2004/05
6-30	Boult T.A. v Sri Lanka at Christchurch	2018/19
6-32	Bracewell J.G. v Australia at Auckland	1985/86
6-32	Boult T.A. v England at Auckland	2017/18
6-37	Morrison D.K. v Australia at Auckland	1992/93
6-38	Bartlett G.A. v India at Christchurch	1967/68
6-40	Cowie J. v Australia at Wellington	1945/46
6-40	Bracewell D.A.J. v Australia at Hobart	2011/12
6-40	Boult T.A. v West Indies at Wellington	2013/14
6-41	Wagner N. v Zimbabwe at Bulawayo	2016/17
*6-41	de Grandhomme C. v Pakistan at Christchurch	2016/17
6-43	Southee T.G. v England at Lord's	2021
6-46	Butler I.G. v Pakistan at Wellington	2003/04
6-49	Jamieson K.A. v Pakistan at Christchurch	2020/21
6-49	Hadlee R.J. v India at Bombay	1988/89
6-50	Hadlee R.J. v West Indies at Christchurch	1986/87
6-50	Patel D.N. v Zimbabwe at Harare	1992/93
6-50	Southee T.G. v England at Lord's	2013
6-51	Hadlee R.J. v Pakistan at Dunedin	1984/85
6-51	Bracewell J.G. v India at Bombay	1988/89
6-51	Bond S.E. v Zimbabwe at Bulawayo	2005/06
6-52	Cairns C.L. v England at Auckland	1991/92
6-53	Hadlee R.J. v England at The Oval	1983
6-54	Tuffey D.R. v England at Auckland	2001/02
6-54	Martin C.S. v Sri Lanka at Wellington	2004/05
6-56	Vettori D.L. v West Indies at Dunedin	2008/09
6-57	Hadlee R.J. v Australia at Melbourne	1980/81
6-60	Reid J.R. v South Africa at Dunedin	1963/64
6-62	Southee T.G. v England at Christchurch	2017/18
6-63	Motz R.C. v India at Christchurch	1967/68
6-63	Collinge R.O. v India at Christchurch	1975/76
6-64	Vettori D.L. v Sri Lanka at Colombo	1997/98
6-67	Cowie J. v England at Manchester	1937
6-68	Rabone G.O. v South Africa at Cape Town	1953/54
6-68	Hadlee R.J. v West Indies at Dunedin	1979/80
6-68	Boult T.A. v England at Auckland	2012/13
6-68	Southee T.G. v Sri Lanka at Wellington	2018/19
6-69	Motz R.C. v West Indies at Wellington	1968/69
6-69	Morrison D.K. v West Indies at Christchurch	1994/95
6-70	Vettori D.L. v Bangladesh at Chittagong	2004/05
6-71	Hadlee R.J. v Australia at Brisbane	1985/86
6-73	Chatfield E.J. v West Indies at Port of Spain	1984/85
6-75	O'Brien I.E. v West Indies at Napier	2008/09
6-76	Cunis R.S. v England at Auckland	1970/71
6-76	Nash D.J. v England at Lord's	1994
6-76	Martin C.S. v South Africa at Auckland	2003/04
6-77	Cairns C.L. v England at Lord's	1999
6-78	Watson W. v Pakistan at Lahore	1990/91
6-80	Hadlee R.J. v England at Lord's	1986

6-80	Hadlee R.J. v England at Nottingham	1986
6-80	Southee T.G. v Pakistan at Hamilton	2016/17
6-83	Cowie J. v England at Christchurch	1946/47
6-85	Cairns B.L. v West Indies at Christchurch	1979/80
6-85	Bracewell J.G. v Australia at Wellington	1989/90
6-87	Vettori D.L. v Australia at Perth	2001/02
6-90	Hadlee R.J. v Australia at Perth	1985/86
6-95	Troup G.B. v West Indies at Auckland	1979/80
6-100	Hadlee R.J. v Australia at Christchurch	1981/82
6-100	Vettori D.L. v Bangladesh at Chittagong	2004/05
6-105	Hadlee R.J. v West Indies at Auckland	1986/87
6-106	Wagner N. v Australia at Christchurch	2015/16
6-113	Patel D.N. v Zimbabwe at Bulawayo	1992/93
6-113	Gillespie M.R. v South Africa at Wellington	2011/12
6-119	Franklin J.E.C v Australia at Auckland	2004/05
6-127	Vettori D.L. v India at Kanpur	1999/00
*6-155	Moir A.M. v England at Christchurch	1950/51
6-162	Burtt T.B. v England at Manchester	1949
*6-168	Cresswell G.F. v England at The Oval	1949
5-26	Taylor B.R. v India at Bombay	1964/65
5-28	Hadlee R.J. v England at Christchurch	1983/84
5-28	Boock S.L. v Sri Lanka at Kandy	1983/84
5-28	Franklin J.E.C v Bangladesh at Dhaka	2004/05
5-29	Hadlee R.J. v Sri Lanka at Colombo	1983/84
5-31	Cairns C.L. v England at The Oval	1999
5-31	Cairns C.L. v Zimbabwe at Bulawayo	2000/01
5-31	Jamieson K.A. v India at Southampton	2021
5-32	Southee T.G. v West Indies at Wellington	2020/21
5-33	Cairns B.L. v India at Wellington	1980/81
5-34	Cameron F.J. v Pakistan at Auckland	1964/65
5-34	Howarth H.J. v India at Nagpur	1969/70
5-34	Hadlee R.J. v West Indies at Dunedin	1979/80
5-34	Jamieson K.A. v West Indies at Wellington	2020/21
5-37	Martin C.S. v South Africa at Johannesburg	2005/06
5-39	Hadlee R.J. v Australia at Wellington	1989/90
5-41	Taylor B.R. v West Indies at Port of Spain	1971/72
5-41	Morrison D.K. v Pakistan at Hamilton	1992/93
5-44	Cairns C.L. v West Indies at Wellington	1999/00
5-44	Wagner N. v England at Mt Maunganui	2019/20
5-45	Wagner N. v Bangladesh at Wellington	2018/19
5-45	Jamieson K.A. v India at Christchurch	2019/20
5-46	Doull S.B. v Pakistan at Lahore	1996/97
5-47	Hadlee R.J. v India at Christchurch	1980/81
5-47	Wagner N. v Bangladesh at Hamilton	2018/19
5-48	Cameron F.J. v South Africa at Cape Town	1961/62
5-50	Cairns C.L. v Zimbabwe at Harare	1997/98
5-51	O'Connor S.B. v Australia at Hamilton	1999/00
5-53	Hadlee R.J. v England at Birmingham	1990
5-53	Franklin J.E.C. v West Indies at Wellington	2005/06
5-55	Cairns B.L. v India at Madras	1976/77
5-55	Martin C.S. v South Africa at Wellington	2003/04
*5-55	Southee T.G. v England at Napier	2007/08
5-57	Boult T.A. v England at Leeds	2013
5-58	Doull S.B. v Sri Lanka at Dunedin	1996/97
5-59	Vettori D.L. v Bangladesh at Chittagong	2008/09

5-59	Gillespie M.R. v South Africa at Hamilton	2011/12
*5-59	Patel A.Y. v Pakistan at Abu Dhabi	2018/19
5-60	Boult T.A. v Australia at Adelaide	2015/16
5-61	Morrison D.K. v West Indies at St Johns	1995/96
5-61	Southee T.G. v India at Wellington	2019/20
5-62	Moir A.M. v England at Auckland	1954/55
5-62	Hadlee R.J. v Pakistan at Christchurch	1978/79
5-62	Cairns C.L. v Sri Lanka at Colombo	1997/98
5-62	Vettori D.L. v Australia at Auckland	1999/00
5-62	Southee T.G. v Sri Lanka at Colombo	2012/13
5-63	Hadlee R.J. v Australia at Auckland	1981/82
5-63	Chatfield E.J. v Sri Lanka at Colombo	1983/84
5-63	Davis H.T. v Sri Lanka at Hamilton	1996/97
5-63	Martin C.S. v India at Ahmedabad	2010/11
5-64	MacGibbon A.R. v England at Birmingham	1958
5-64	Wagner N. v Bangladesh at Mirpur	2013/14
5-65	Congdon B.E. v India at Auckland	1975/76
5-65	Hadlee R.J. v Australia at Sydney	1985/86
5-65	Hadlee R.J. v Australia at Perth	1985/86
5-65	Hadlee R.J. v India at Bangalore	1988/89
5-65	Martin C.S. v Bangladesh at Wellington	2007/08
5-66	Doull S.B. v Pakistan at Auckland	1993/94
5-66	Vettori D.L. v England at Manchester	2008
5-66	Vettori D.L. v Bangaldesh at Mirpur	2008/09
5-67	Boock S.L. v England at Auckland	1977/78
5-67	Hadlee R.J. v Australia at Melbourne	1987/88
5-68	Snedden M.C. v West Indies at Christchurch	1986/87
5-68	Hadlee R.J. v Australia at Adelaide	1987/88
5-69	Burtt T.B. v West Indies at Christchurch	1951/52
5-69	Morrison D.K. v England at Christchurch	1987/88
5-69	Bond S.E. v West Indies at Auckland	2005/06
5-69	Vettori D.L. v England at Lord's	2008
5-69	Southee T.G. v Australia at Perth	2019/20
5-69	Jamieson K.A. v Pakistan at Christchurch	2020/21
5-71	Martin C.S. v Zimbabwe at Wellington	2000/01
5-73	Hadlee R.J. v Sri Lanka at Colombo	1983/84
5-73	Su'a M.L. v Pakistan at Hamilton	1992/93
5-73	Doull S.B. v South Africa at Durban	1994/95
5-74	Collinge R.O. v England at Leeds	1973
5-75	Bracewell J.G. v India at Auckland	1980/81
5-75	Morrison D.K. v India at Christchurch	1989/90
5-75	Cairns C.L. v Sri Lanka at Auckland	1990/91
5-75	Doull S.B. v England at Wellington	1996/97
5-77	Hart M.N. v South Africa at Johannesburg	1994/95
5-78	Bond S.E. v West Indies at Bridgetown	2001/02
5-79	Cairns C.L. v England at Nottingham	2004
5-80	Howarth H.J. v Pakistan at Karachi	1969/70
5-82	Collinge R.O. v Australia at Auckland	1973/74
*5-82	Wiseman P.J. v Sri Lanka at Colombo	1997/98
5-83	Cameron F.J. v South Africa at Johannesburg	1961/62
5-84	Hadlee R.J. v England at Lord's	1978
5-84	Vettori D.L. v Sri Lanka at Hamilton	1996/97
5-85	Su'a M.L. v Zimbabwe at Harare	1992/93
5-85	Bracewell D.A.J. v Zimbabwe at Bulawayo	2011/12
5-85	Boult T.A. v England at Lord's	2015

*5-86	Taylor B.R. v India at Calcutta	1964/65
5-86	Motz R.C. v India at Dunedin	1967/68
5-86	Wagner N. v Zimbabwe at Bulawayo	2016/17
5-87	Cairns B.L. v Australia at Brisbane	1980/81
5-87	Hadlee R.J. v Australia at Perth	1980/81
5-87	Tuffey D.R. v Pakistan at Hamilton	2003/04
5-89	Patel A.Y. v Sri Lanka at Galle	2019/20
5-90	Wiseman P.J. v Zimabwe at Bulawayo	2000/01
5-93	Hadlee R.J. v England at Lord's	1983
5-93	Patel D.N. v Australia at Auckland	1992/93
5-93	Nash D.J. v England at Lord's	1994
5-94	Southee T.G. v Bangladesh at Christchurch	2016/17
5-95	Chatfield E.J. v England at Leeds	1983
5-97	Burtt T.B. v England at Leeds	1949
5-98	Morrison D.K. v India at Napier	1989/90
5-104	Hadlee R.J. v Pakistan at Auckland	1978/79
5-104	Bond S.E. v West Indies at St George's	2001/02
5-104	Martin C.S. v South Africa at Auckland	2003/04
5-106	Vettori D.L. v Australia at Christchurch	2004/05
5-107	Bond S.E. v Pakistan at Dunedin	2009/10
5-108	Motz R.C. v England at Birmingham	1965
5-109	Hadlee R.J. v Australia at Melbourne	1987/88
5-109	Vettori D.L. v Zimbabwe at Bulawayo	2011/12
5-110	Patel J.S. v West Indies at Napier	2008/09
5-113	Motz R.C. v West Indies at Christchurch	1968/69
5-117	Boock S.L. v Pakistan at Wellington	1984/85
5-121	Hadlee R.J. v Pakistan at Lahore	1976/77
5-123	Boult T.A. v Bangladesh at Hamilton	2018/19
5-124	Wagner N. v England at Hamilton	2019/20
5-127	Cowie J. v England at Leeds	1949
5-135	Vettori D.L. v India at Hyderabad	2010/11
*5-136	Gillespie M.R. v South Africa at Centurion	2007/08
5-137	Cairns C.L. v Pakistan at Rawalpindi	1996/97
5-138	Vettori D.L. v Australia at Hobart	2001/02
5-145	Morrison D.K. v India at Auckland	1989/90
5-146	Cairns C.L. v Australia at Brisbane	2001/02
5-148	O'Sullivan D.R. v Australia at Adelaide	1973/74
5-152	Martin C.S. v Australia at Brisbane	2004/05
5-152	Vettori D.L. v Australia at Adelaide	2004/05
5-153	Morrison D.K. v Sri Lanka at Wellington	1990/91

** on debut*

Hat-tricks

*Petherick P.J. v Pakistan at Lahore	1976/77
Franklin J.E.C. v Bangladesh at Dhaka	2004/05

** on debut*

ALL-ROUND CRICKET

Rabone G.O. 56 and 6-68 & 1-16 v South Africa at Cape Town	1953/54
Taylor B.R. 105 & 0 and 5-86 v India at Calcutta	1964/65
Congdon B.E. 54 & 54 and 5-65 v India at Auckland	1975/76
Hadlee R.J. 54* & 5 and 5-104 & 0-8 v Pakistan at Auckland	1978/79
Hadlee R.J. 51 & 17 and 5-34 & 6-68 v West Indies at Dunedin	1979/80
Hadlee R.J. 84 & 11 and 6-53 & 2-99 v England at The Oval	1983
Cairns B.L. 3 & 64 and 7-143 v England at Wellington	1983/84
Hadlee R.J. 99 and 3-16 & 5-28 v England at Christchurch	1983/84
Hadlee R.J. 54 and 9-52 & 6-71 v Australia at Brisbane	1985/86
Hadlee R.J. 68 and 6-80 & 4-60 v England at Nottingham	1986
Bracewell J.G. 52 & 32 and 2-81 & 6-51 v India at Bombay	1988/89
Patel D.N. 6 & 58* and 2-81 & 6-50 v Zimbabwe at Harare	1992/93
Nash D.J. 56 and 6-76 & 5-93 v England at Lord's	1994
Cairns C.L. 12 & 71* and 5-50 & 0-44 v Zimbabwe at Harare	1997/98
Cairns C.L. 11 & 80 and 5-31 & 1-50 v England at The Oval	1999
Cairns C.L. 72 and 3-73 & 7-27 v West Indies at Hamilton	1999/00
Cairns C.L. 61 & 43 and 5-146 & 1-29 v Australia at Brisbane	2001/02
Vettori D.L. 20 & 59 and 5-152 & 1-35 v Australia at Adelaide	2004/05
Vettori D.L. 0 & 51 and 3-53 & 7-130 v Sri Lanka at Wellington	2006/07
Southee T.G. 5 & 77 and 5-55 & 0-84 v England at Napier	2007/08
Vettori D.L. 55 & 76* and 5-59 & 4-74 v Bangladesh at Chittagong	2008/09
Craig M.D. 65 and 7-94 & 3-109 v Pakistan at Sharjah	2014/15
Southee T.G. 50 & 0* and 6-62 & 1-65 v England at Christchurch	2017/18

* *On debut. Taylor is the only player from any country to score a century and take five wickets in an innings on debut.*

WICKETKEEPING AND FIELDING

MOST DISMISSALS IN AN INNINGS BY A WICKETKEEPER

7*	Smith I.D.S. v Sri Lanka at Hamilton *(all caught)*	1990/91
6	Watling B-J. v India at Auckland *(all caught)*	2013/14
6	Watling B-J. v Sri Lanka at Dunedin *(all caught)*	2015/16
5	Harford R.I. v India at Wellington *(all caught)*	1967/68
5	Wadsworth K.J. v Pakistan at Auckland *(all caught)*	1972/73
5	Lees W.K. v Sri Lanka at Wellington *(all caught)*	1982/83
5	Smith I.D.S. v England at Auckland *(4ct 1st)*	1983/84
5	Smith I.D.S. v Sri Lanka at Auckland *(all caught)*	1990/91
5	Parore A.C. v England at Auckland *(all caught)*	1991/92
5	Parore A.C. v Sri Lanka at Colombo *(4ct 1st)*	1992/93
5	Parore A.C. v Zimbabwe at Harare *(all caught)*	2000/01
5	Parore A.C. v Pakistan at Auckland *(all caught)*	2000/01
5	McCullum B.B. v England at Hamilton *(all caught)*	2007/08
5	McCullum B.B. v West Indies at Napier *(all caught)*	2008/09
5	McCullum B.B. v Pakistan at Napier *(all caught)*	2009/10
5	McCullum B.B. v England at Leeds *(all caught)*	2013
5	Watling B-J. v West Indies at Hamilton *(all caught)*	2013/14
5	Watling B-J. v India at Wellington *(all caught)*	2013/14
5	Watling B-J. v West Indies at Kingston *(all caught)*	2014
5	Watling B-J. v Sri Lanka at Wellington *(4ct 1st)*	2014/15
5	Watling B-J. v Sri Lanka at Wellington *(all caught)*	2018/19
5	Watling B-J. v Sri Lanka at Colombo *(all caught)*	2019/20

* *equals world test record*

MOST DISMISSALS IN A MATCH BY A WICKETKEEPER

9	McCullum B.B. v Pakistan at Napier *(8ct, 1st)*	2009/10
9	Watling B-J. v India at Auckland *(all caught)*	2013/14
9	Watling B-J. v Sri Lanka at Dunedin *(all caught)*	2015/16
8	Lees W.K. v Sri Lanka at Wellington *(all caught)*	1982/83
8	Smith I.D.S. v Sri Lanka at Hamilton *(all caught)*	1990/91
8	Watling B-J. v West Indies at Hamilton *(all caught)*	2013/14
8	Watling B-J. v West Indies at Kingston *(all caught)*	2014
8	Watling B-J. v Pakistan at Mt Maunganui *(all caught)*	2020/21
8	Blundell T.A. v England at Birmingham *(all caught)*	2021
7	Dick A.E. v South Africa at Durban *(6ct 1st)*	1961/62
7	Harford R.I. v India at Wellington *(all caught)*	1967/68
7	Smith I.D.S. v India at Wellington *(all caught)*	1980/81
7	Smith I.D.S. v England at Leeds *(all caught)*	1983
7	Parore A.C. v Pakistan at Auckland *(all caught)*	2000/01
7	Parore A.C. v Pakistan at Hamilton *(all caught)*	2000/01
7	McCullum B.B. v Australia at Brisbane *(all caught)*	2008/09
7	Watling B-J. v Sri Lanka at Wellington *(6ct 1st)*	2014/15
7	Watling B-J. v Australia at Perth *(5ct 2st)*	2015/16
7	Watling B-J. v Bangladesh at Christchurch *(all caught)*	2016/17
7	Watling B-J. v India at Wellington *(all caught)*	2019/20

MOST STUMPINGS IN AN INNINGS

2	Mooney F.L.H. v England at Leeds	1949
2	Milburn B.D. v West Indies at Christchurch	1968/69
2	Lees W.K. v Pakistan at Hyderabad	1976/77
2	Lees W.K. v Pakistan at Karachi	1976/77
2	Lees W.K. v India at Madras	1976/77
2	Watling B-J. v Australia at Perth	2015/16

MOST STUMPINGS IN A MATCH

2	Mooney F.L.H. v England at Leeds	1949
2	Milburn B.D. v West Indies at Christchurch	1968/69
2	Lees W.K. v Pakistan at Hyderabad	1976/77
2	Lees W.K. v Pakistan at Karachi	1976/77
2	Lees W.K. v India at Madras	1976/77
2	Smith I.D.S. v Australia at Sydney	1985/86
2	Parore A.C. v Australia at Auckland	1999/00
2	McCullum B.B. v Zimbabwe at Harare	2005/06
2	McCullum B.B. v Banladesh at Chittagong	2008/09
2	Watling B-J. v Australia at Perth	2015/16

MOST CATCHES IN AN INNINGS BY A FIELDER

5*	Fleming S.P. v Zimbabwe at Harare	1997/98
4	Crowe J.J. v West Indies at Bridgetown	1984/85
4	Crowe M.D. v West Indies at Kingston	1984/85
4	Fleming S.P. v Australia at Brisbane	1997/98
4	Fleming S.P. v Zimbawe at Harare	2005/06
4	Fleming S.P. v West Indies at Wellington	2005/06
4	Brownlie D.G. v Zimbabwe at Napier	2011/12

** equals world test record*

MOST CATCHES IN A MATCH BY A FIELDER

7	Fleming S.P. v Zimbabwe at Harare	1997/98
6	Young B.A. v Pakistan at Auckland	1993/94
6	Fleming S.P. v Australia at Brisbane	1997/98
6	Fleming S.P. v West Indies at Wellington	2005/06
5	Harris C.Z. v Zimbabwe at Bulawayo	1997/98
5	Fleming S.P. v India at Wellington	1998/99
5	Sinclair M.S. v Bangladesh at Chittagong	2004/05
5	Guptill M.J. v Pakistan at Napier	2009/10
5	Brownlie D.G. v Zimbabwe at Napier	2011/12
5	Williamson K.S. v Sri Lanka at Colombo	2011/12
5	Latham T.W.M. v India at Southampton	2021

REPLACEMENT WICKETKEEPERS IN TEST MATCHES

Wicketkeeper	*Replacement*	*Dismissal*			
Mooney F.L.H.	Sutcliffe B.	—	v South Africa	Port Elizabeth	1953/54
Petrie E.C.	Reid J.R.	Richardson P.E. *(st)*	v England	Manchester	1958
Petrie E.C.	Reid J.R.	—	v England	Christchurch	1958/59
Ward J.T.	Morgan R.W.	Jaisimha M.L. *(c)*	v India	Calcutta	1964/65
Ward J.T.	Congdon B.E.	Hanumant Singh *(c)*	v India	Delhi	1964/65
Dick A.E.	Reid J.R.	—	v Pakistan	Lahore	1964/65
Dick A.E.	Congdon B.E. *(sub)*	Pervez Sajjad *(st)*	v Pakistan	Lahore	1964/65
Lees W.K.	Anderson R.W.	—	v Pakistan	Hyderabad	1976/77
Smith I.D.S.	Edgar B.A.	Laird B.M. *(c)*	v Australia	Christchurch	1981/82
Smith I.D.S.	Crowe M.D.	—	v West Indies	Kingston	1984/85
Smith I.D.S.	Horne P.A.	—	v Australia	Melbourne	1987/88
Smith I.D.S.	Blain T.E.	—	v India	Hyderabad	1988/89
Smith I.D.S.	Horne P.A.	—	v Pakistan	Faisalabad	1990/91
Smith I.D.S.	Parore A.C. *(sub)*	Shoaib Mohammad *(c)* Aaqib Javed *(c)*	v Pakistan	Faisalabad	1990/91
McCullum B.B.	Sinclair M.S.	Jayawardene D.P.M.D.	v Sri Lanka	Wellington	2006/07
van Wyk C.F.K.	McCullum B.B.	—	v India	Bangalore	2012/13
Watling B-J.	McCullum B.B.	Swann G.P. *(c)*	v England	Lord's	2013
Watling B-J.	Latham T.W.M.	Root J.E. *(c)* Ali M.M. *(c)* Broad S.J.C. *(c)* Cook A.N. *(c)* Bell I.R. *(c)* Buttler J.C. *(c)*	v England	Lord's	2015
Watling B-J.	Latham T.W.M.	Sikandar Raza *(c)*	v Zimbabwe	Bulawayo	2016/17
Watling B-J.	Ronchi L.	Sharma R.G. *(c)*	v India	Calcutta	2016/17
Watling B-J.	Latham T.W.M.	—	v Pakistan	Abu Dhabi	2018/19
Watling B-J.	Bocock P.D. *(sub)*	—	v Bangladesh	Wellington	2018/19
Watling B-J.	Latham T.W.M.	—	v England	Mt Maunganui	2019/20
Watling B-J.	Blundell T.A. *(sub)*	—	v India	Southampton	2021

RECORD PARTNERSHIPS

NEW ZEALAND v ALL COUNTRIES

For

1st	387	Turner G.M. & Jarvis T.W. v West Indies	Georgetown	1971/72
2nd	297	McCullum B.B. & Williamson K.S. v Pakistan	Sharjah	2014/15
3rd	467	Jones A.H. & Crowe M.D. v Sri Lanka	Wellington	1990/91
4th	369	Williamson K.S. & Nicholls H.M. v Pakistan	Christchurch	2020/21
5th	222	Astle N.J. & McMillan C.D. v Zimbabwe	Wellington	2000/01
6th	365*	Williamson K.S.& Watling B-J. v Sri Lanka	Wellington	2014/15
7th	261	Watling B-J. & Santner M.J. v England	Mt Maunganui	2019/20
8th	256	Fleming S.P. & Franklin J.E.C. v South Africa	Cape Town	2005/06
9th	136	Smith I.D.S. & Snedden M.C. v India	Auckland	1989/90
10th	151	Hastings B.F. & Collinge R.O. v Pakistan	Auckland	1972/73

Against

1st	413	Mankad M.H. & Roy P. for India	Madras	1955/56
2nd	369	Edrich J.H. & Barrington K.F. for England	Leeds	1965
3rd	330	Amla H.M. & Kallis J.H. for South Africa	Johannesburg	2007/08
4th	365	Kohli V. & Rahane A. for India	Indore	2016/17
5th	359	Shakib Al Hasan & Mushfiqur Rahim for Bangladesh	Wellington	2016/17
6th	281	Thorpe G.P. & Flintoff A. for England	Christchurch	2001/02
7th	308	Waqar Hassan & Imtiaz Ahmed for Pakistan	Lahore	1955/56
8th	246	Ames L.E.G. & Allen G.O.B. for England	Lord's	1931
9th	163*	Cowdrey M.C. & Smith A.C. for England	Wellington	1962/63
10th	114	Gillespie J.N. & McGrath G.D. for Australia	Brisbane	2004/05

NEW ZEALAND v ENGLAND

New Zealand

1st	276	Dempster C.S. & Mills J.E.	Wellington	1929/30
2nd	241	Wright J.G. & Jones A.H.	Wellington	1991/92
3rd	213*	Williamson K.S. & Taylor L.R.P.L.	Hamilton	2019/20
4th	174	Conway D.P. & Nicholls H.M.	Lord's	2021
5th	180	Crowe M.D. & Thomson S.A.	Lord's	1994
6th	142	Watling B-J. & de Grandhomme C.	Christchurch	2017/18
7th	261	Watling B-J. & Santner M.J. v England	Mt Maunganui	2019/20
8th	104	Roberts A.W. & Moloney D.A.R.	Lord's	1937
9th	118	Coney J.V. & Cairns B.L.	Wellington	1983/84
10th	118	Astle N.J. & Cairns C.L.	Christchurch	2001/02

England

1st	231	Cook A.N. & Compton N.R.D.	Dunedin	2012/13
2nd	369	Edrich J.H. & Barrington K.F.	Leeds	1965
3rd	245	Hammond W.R. & Hardstaff J.	Lord's	1937
4th	266	Denness M.H. & Fletcher K.W.R.	Auckland	1974/75
5th	242	Hammond W.R. & Ames L.E.G.	Christchurch	1932/33
6th	281	Thorpe G.P. & Flintoff A.	Christchurch	2001/02
7th	193	Root J.E. & Pope O.J.D.	Hamilton	2019/20
8th	246	Ames L.E.G. & Allen G.O.B.	Lord's	1931
9th	163*	Cowdrey M.C. & Smith A.C.	Wellington	1962/63
10th	59	Knott A.P.E. & Gifford N.	Nottingham	1973

NEW ZEALAND v AUSTRALIA

New Zealand

1st	111	Greatbatch M.J. & Wright J.G.	Wellington	1992/93
2nd	132	Horne M.J. & Parore A.C.	Hobart	1997/98
3rd	265	Williamson K.S. & Taylor L.R.P.L.	Perth	2015/16
4th	229	Congdon B.E. & Hastings B.F.	Wellington	1973/74
5th	179	McCullum B.B. & Anderson C.J.	Christchurch	2015/16
6th	158	Brownlie D.G. & Vettori D.L.	Brisbane	2011/12
7th	132*	Coney J.V. & Hadlee R.J.	Wellington	1985/86
8th	253	Astle N.J. & Parore A.C.	Perth	2001/02
9th	73	Howarth H.J. & Hadlee D.R.	Christchurch	1976/77
10th	124	Bracewell J.G. & Boock S.L.	Sydney	1985/86

Australia

1st	237	Burns J.A. & Warner D.A.	Brisbane	2015/16
2nd	302	Warner D.A. & Khawaja U.T.	Perth	2015/16
3rd	289	Burns J.A. & Smith S.P.D.	Christchurch	2015/16
4th	184	Langer J.L. & Lehmann D.S.	Adelaide	2004/05
5th	253	Clarke M.J. & North M.J.	Wellington	2009/10
6th	256	Martyn D.R. & Gilchrist A.C.	Wellington	2004/05
7th	217	Walters K.D. & Gilmour G.J.	Christchurch	1976/77
8th	135	Gilchrist A.C. & Lee B.	Brisbane	2001/02
9th	74	Gilchrist A.C. & Kasprowicz M.S.	Auckland	2004/05
	74	Nevill P.M. & Lyon N.M.	Adelaide	2015/16
10th	114	Gillespie J.N. & McGrath G.D.	Brisbane	2004/05

NEW ZEALAND v SOUTH AFRICA

New Zealand

1st	126	Rabone G.O. & Chapple M.E.	Cape Town	1953/54
2nd	190	Raval J.A. & Williamson K.S.	Hamilton	2016/17
3rd	125	Richardson M.H. & Styris S.B.	Auckland	2003/04
4th	171	Sinclair B.W. & McGregor S.N.	Auckland	1963/64
5th	176	Reid J.R. & Beck J.E.F.	Cape Town	1953/54
6th	116	Nicholls H.M. & Watling B-J.	Wellington	2016/17
7th	225	Cairns C.L. & Oram J.D.P.	Auckland	2003/04
8th	256	Fleming S.P. & Franklin J.E.C.	Cape Town	2005/06
9th	87	Oram J.D.P. & Wiseman P.J.	Hamilton	2003/04
10th	59	Watling B-J. & Boult T.A.	Port Elizabeth	2012/13

South Africa

1st	196	Mitchell B. & Christy J.A.H.	Christchurch	1931/32
2nd	315*	Gibbs H.H. & Kallis J.H.	Christchurch	1998/99
3rd	330	Amla H.M. & Kallis J.H.	Johannesburg	2007/08
4th	171	Smith G.C. & Kirsten G.	Wellington	2003/04
5th	141	Cullinan D.J. & Rhodes J.N.	Auckland	1998/99
6th	131	du Plessis F. & Elgar D.	Port Elizabeth	2012/13
7th	246	McGlew D.J. & Murray A.R.A.	Wellington	1952/53
8th	136	McKenzie N.D. & Boje N.	Port Elizabeth	2000/01
9th	60	Pollock P.M. & Adcock N.A.T.	Port Elizabeth	1961/62
10th	57	Philander V.D. & Morkel M.	Wellington	2016/17

NEW ZEALAND v WEST INDIES

New Zealand

1st	387	Turner G.M. & Jarvis T.W.	Georgetown	1971/72
2nd	210	Howarth G.P. & Crowe J.J.	Kingston	1984/85
3rd	241	Wright J.G. & Crowe M.D.	Wellington	1986/87
4th	195	Taylor L.R.P.L. & McCullum B.B.	Dunedin	2013/14
5th	144	Astle N.J. & Vaughan J.T.C.	Bridgetown	1995/96
6th	220	Turner G.M. & Wadsworth K.J.	Kingston	1971/72
7th	148	de Grandhomme C. & Blundell T.A.	Wellington	2017/18
8th	136	Congdon B.E. & Cunis R.S.	Port of Spain	1971/72
9th	99	Watling B-J. & Craig M.D.	Port of Spain	2014
10th	78*	Blundell T.A. & Boult T.A.	Wellington	2017/18

West Indies

1st	276	Griffith A.F.G. & Campbell S.L.	Hamilton	1999/00
2nd	269	Fredericks R.C. & Rowe L.G.	Kingston	1971/72
3rd	221	Lara B.C. & Adams J.C.	Wellington	1994/95
4th	182	Brathwaite K.C. & Bravo D.M.	Port of Spain	2014
5th	189	Worrell F.M.M. & Walcott C.L.	Auckland	1951/52
6th	254	Sobers G.S. & Davis C.A.	Bridgetown	1971/72
7th	155	Blackwood J. & Joseph A.S.	Hamilton	2020/21
8th	83	Richards I.V.A. & Marshall M.D.	Bridgetown	1984/85
9th	70	Marshall M.D. & Garner J.	Bridgetown	1984/85
10th	82	Benn S.J. & Shillingford S.	Kingston	2014

NEW ZEALAND v INDIA

New Zealand

1st	231	Richardson M.H. & Vincent L.	Mohali	2003/04
2nd	155	Dowling G.T. & Congdon B.E.	Dunedin	1967/68
3rd	222*	Sutcliffe B. & Reid J.R.	New Delhi	1955/56
4th	271	Taylor L.R.P.L. & Ryder J.D.	Napier	2008/09
5th	194	Ryder J.D. & Williamson K.S.	Ahmedabad	2010/11
6th	352	McCullum B.B. & Watling B-J.	Wellington	2013/14
7th	186	Ryder J.D. & Vettori D.L.	Hamilton	2008/09
8th	137	Nash D.J. & Vettori D.L.	Wellington	1998/99
9th	136	Smith I.D.S. & Snedden M.C.	Auckland	1989/90
10th	61	Ward J.T. & Collinge R.O.	Madras	1964/65

India

1st	413	Mankad M.H. & Roy P.	Madras	1955/56
2nd	237	Sehwag V. & Dravid R.S.	Ahmedabad	2010/11
3rd	238	Umrigar P.R. & Manjrekar V.L.	Hyderabad	1955/56
4th	365	Kohli V. & Rahane A.	Indore	2016/17
5th	182	Dravid R.S. & Ganguly S.C.	Ahmedabad	2003/04
6th	193*	Sardesai D.N. & Hanumant Singh	Bombay	1964/65
	193	Dravid R.S. & Dhoni M.S.	Nagpur	2010/11
7th	163	Laxman V.V.S. & Harbhajan Singh	Ahmedabad	2010/11
8th	144	Dravid R.S. & Srinath J.	Hamilton	1998/99
9th	105	Kirmani S.M.H. & Bedi B.S.	Bombay	1976/77
	105	Kirmani S.M.H. & Yadav N.S.	Auckland	1980/81
10th	105	Harbhajan Singh & Sreesanth S.	Hyderabad	2010/11

NEW ZEALAND v PAKISTAN

New Zealand

1st	181	Richardson M.H. & Bell M.D.	Hamilton	2000/01
2nd	297	McCullum B.B. & Williamson K.S.	Sharjah	2014/15
3rd	178	Sinclair B.W. & Reid J.R.	Lahore	1964/65
4th	369	Williamson K.S. & Nicholls H.M.	Christchurch	2020/21
5th	212	Williamson K.S. & Nicholls H.M.	Abu Dhabi	2018/19
6th	176	Vettori D.L. & McCullum B.B.	Napier	2009/10
7th	186	Lees W.K. & Hadlee R.J.	Karachi	1976/77
8th	125	Fleming S.P. & Vettori D.L.	Hamilton	2003/04
9th	99	Vettori D.L. & Tuffey D.R.	Hamilton	2003/04
10th	151	Hastings B.F. & Collinge R.O.	Auckland	1972/73

Pakistan

1st	178	Mohammad Hafeez & Ahmed Shehzad	Abu Dhabi	2014/15
2nd	262	Saeed Anwar & Ijaz Ahmed	Rawalpindi	1996/97
3rd	248	Shoaib Mohammad & Javed Miandad	Auckland	1988/89
4th	350	Mushtaq Mohammad & Asif Iqbal	Dunedin	1972/73
5th	281	Javed Miandad & Asif Iqbal	Lahore	1976/77
6th	217	Hanif Mohammad & Majid Khan	Lahore	1964/65
7th	308	Waqar Hassan & Imtiaz Ahmed	Lahore	1955/56
8th	89	Anil Dalpat & Iqbal Qasim	Karachi	1984/85
9th	78	Inzamam-ul-Haq & Shoaib Akhtar	Lahore	2001/02
	78	Asad Shafiq & Rahat Ali	Sharjah	2014/15
10th	81	Sarfraz Ahmed & Rahat Ali	Dubai	2014/15

NEW ZEALAND v SRI LANKA

New Zealand

1st	161	Franklin T.J. & Wright J.G.	Hamilton	1990/91
2nd	173	Guptill M.J. & Williamson K.S.	Dunedin	2015/16
3rd	467	Jones A.H. & Crowe M.D.	Wellington	1990/91
4th	240	Fleming S.P. & McMillan C.D.	Colombo	1997/98
5th	153	McCullum B.B. & Neesham J.D.S.	Christchurch	2014/15
6th	365*	Williamson K.S. & Watling B-J.	Wellington	2014/15
7th	124	Oram J.D.P. & Vettori D.L.	Colombo	2009/10
8th	98	Vincent L. & Mills K.D.	Wellington	2004/05
9th	69	Vettori D.L. & O'Brien I.E.	Colombo	2009/10
10th	52	Lees W.K. & Chatfield E.J.	Christchurch	1982/83

Sri Lanka

1st	161	Karunaratne F.D.M. & Thirimanne H.D.R.L.	Galle	2019/20
2nd	137	Mahanama R.S. & Gurusinha A.P.	Moratuwa	1992/93
3rd	184	Atapattu M.S. & Jayawardene D.P.M.D.	Napier	2004/05
4th	274*	Mendis B.K.G. & Mathews A.D.	Wellington	2018/19
5th	138	Mathews A.D. & Siriwardana T.A.M.	Hamilton	2015/16
6th	156	Jayawardene D.P.M.D. & Mathews A.D.	Galle	2012/13
7th	137	Kaluwitharana R.S. & Vaas W.P.J.U.C.	Dunedin	1996/97
8th	89	Samaraweera T.T. & Chandana U.D.U.	Wellington	2004/05
9th	67	Sangakkara K.C. & Lakmal R.A.S.	Wellington	2014/15
10th	71	Kaluwitharana R.S. & Muralitharan M.	Colombo	1997/98

NEW ZEALAND v ZIMBABWE

New Zealand

1st	214	Spearman C.M. & Twose R.G.	Auckland	1995/96
2nd	160	Latham T.W.M. & Williamson K.S.	Bulawayo	2016/17
3rd	140*	Williamson K.S. & Taylor L.R.P.L.	Bulawayo	2016/17
4th	243	Horne M.J. & Astle N.J.	Auckland	1997/98
5th	222	Astle N.J. & McMillan C.D.	Wellington	2000/01
6th	253	Taylor L.R.P.L. & Watling B-J	Bulawayo	2016/17
7th	108	McMillan C.D. & Nash D.J.	Wellington	1997/98
8th	144	Cairns C.L. & Nash D.J.	Harare	2000/01
9th	78	Parore A.C. & Vettori D.L.	Bulawayo	2000/01
10th	27	McMillan C.D. & Doull S.B.	Auckland	1997/98

Zimbabwe

1st	156	Rennie G.J. & Flower G.W.	Harare	1997/98
2nd	107	Arnott K.J. & Campbell A.D.R.	Harare	1992/93
3rd	96	Mawoyo T.M.K. & Taylor B.R.M.	Bulawayo	2011/12
4th	130	Rennie G.J. & Flower A.	Wellington	2000/01
5th	131	Flower A. & Whittall G.J.	Harare	2000/01
6th	151	Whittall G.J. & Streak H.H.	Harare	2000/01
7th	118	Cremer A.G. & Williams S.C.	Bulawayo	2016/17
8th	94	Campbell A.D.R. & Streak H.H.	Wellington	1997/98
9th	85	Masvaure P.S. & Tiripano D.T.	Bulawayo	2016/17
10th	40	Whittall G.J. & Matambanadzo E.	Bulawayo	1997/98

NEW ZEALAND v BANGLADESH

New Zealand

1st	254	Raval J.A & Latham T.W.M.	Hamilton	2018/19
2nd	126	Fulton P.G. & Williamson K.S.	Chittagong	2013/14
3rd	204	Fleming S P & Styris S B	Chittagong	2004/05
4th	216	Taylor L.R.P.L. & Nicholls H.M.	Wellington	2018/19
5th	190	Richardson M.H. & McMillan C.D.	Hamilton	2001/02
6th	339	Guptill M.J. & McCullum B.B.	Hamilton	2009/10
7th	110*	Williamson K.S. & de Grandhomme C.	Hamilton	2018/19
8th	57	McCullum B.B. & Franklin J.E.C.	Dhaka	2004/05
	57	Watling B-J. & Bracewell DA.J.	Chittagong	2013/14
9th	93	Anderson C.J. & Sodhi I.S.	Mirpur	2013/14
10th	127	Watling B-J. & Boult T.A.	Chittagong	2013/14

Bangladesh

1st	161	Tamim Iqbal & Zunaed Siddique	Dunedin	2007/08
2nd	67	Tamim Iqbal & Marshall Ayub	Mirpur	2013/14
3rd	157	Tamim Iqbal & Mominul Haque	Mirpur	2013/14
4th	115	Rajin Saleh & Mohammad Ashraful	Dhaka	2004/05
5th	359	Shakib Al Hasan & Mushfiqur Rahim	Wellington	2016/17
6th	79	Shakib Al Hasan & Mushfiqur Rahim	Hamilton	2009/10
7th	145	Shakib Al Hasan & Mahmudullah	Hamilton	2009/10
8th	39	Mushfiqur Rahman & Mohammad Rafique	Chittagong	2004/05
9th	105	Sohag Gazi & Robiul Islam	Chittagong	2013/14
10th	45	Tapash Baisya & Enamul Haque	Chittagong	2004/05

CAREER RECORDS

Averages

	M	I	NO	HS	Runs	Ave	100	50	Ct	St	Wkts	Runs	Ave	Best	5WI	10WM
Adams A.R.	1	2	0	11	18	9.00	—	—	1	—	6	105	17.50	3-44	—	—
Alabaster J.C.	21	34	6	34	272	9.71	—	—	7	—	49	1863	38.02	4-46	—	—
Allcott C.F.W.	6	7	2	33	113	22.60	—	—	3	—	6	541	90.17	2-102	—	—
Allott G.I.	10	15	7	8*	27	3.37	—	—	2	—	19	1111	58.47	4-74	—	—
Anderson C.J.	13	22	1	116	683	32.52	1	4	7	—	16	659	41.18	3-47	—	—
Anderson R.W.	9	18	0	92	423	23.50	—	3	1	—	—	—	—	—	—	—
Anderson W.M.	1	2	0	4	5	2.50	—	—	1	—	—	—	—	—	—	—
Andrews B.	2	3	2	17	22	22.00	—	—	1	—	2	154	77.00	2-40	—	—
Arnel B.J.	6	12	4	8*	45	5.62	—	—	3	—	9	566	62.88	4-95	—	—
Astle N.J.	81	137	10	222	4702	37.02	11	24	70	—	51	2143	42.01	3-27	—	—
Astle T.D.	5	6	1	35	98	19.60	—	—	3	—	7	368	52.57	3-39	—	—
Badcock F.T.	7	9	2	64	137	19.57	—	2	1	—	16	610	38.13	4-80	—	—
Barber R.T.	1	2	0	12	17	8.50	—	—	1	—	—	—	—	—	—	—
Bartlett G.A.	10	18	1	40	263	15.47	—	—	8	—	24	792	33.00	6-38	1	—
Barton P.T.	7	14	0	109	285	20.36	1	1	4	—	—	—	—	—	—	—
Beard D.D.	4	7	2	31	101	20.20	—	—	2	—	9	302	33.56	3-22	—	—
Beck J.E.F.	8	15	0	99	394	26.27	—	3	—	—	—	—	—	—	—	—
Bell M.D.	18	32	2	107	729	24.30	2	3	19	—	—	—	—	—	—	—
Bell W.	2	3	3	21*	21	—	—	—	1	—	2	235	117.50	1-54	—	—
Bennett H.K.	1	1	0	4	4	4.00	—	—	—	—	0	47	—	—	—	—
Bilby G.P.	2	4	0	28	55	13.75	—	—	3	—	—	—	—	—	—	—
***Blain** T.E.	11	20	3	78	456	26.82	—	2	19	2	—	—	—	—	—	—
Blair R.W.	19	34	6	64*	189	6.75	—	1	5	—	43	1515	35.23	4-85	—	—
***Blundell** T.A.	11	17	2	121	572	38.13	2	2	15	—	0	13	—	—	—	—
Blunt R.C.	9	13	1	96	330	27.50	—	1	5	—	12	472	39.33	3-17	—	—
Bolton B.A.	2	3	0	33	59	19.67	—	—	1	—	—	—	—	—	—	—
Bond S.E.	18	20	7	41*	168	12.92	—	—	8	—	87	1922	22.09	6-51	5	1
Boock S.L.	30	41	8	37	207	6.27	—	—	14	—	74	2564	34.64	7-87	4	—
Boult T.A.	73	86	42	52*	687	15.61	—	1	39	—	292	8080	27.67	6-30	8	1
Bracewell B.P.	6	12	2	8	24	2.40	—	—	1	—	14	585	41.78	3-110	—	—
Bracewell D.A.J.	27	45	4	47	568	13.85	—	—	10	—	72	2796	38.83	6-40	2	—
Bracewell J.G.	41	60	11	110	1001	20.42	1	4	31	—	102	3653	35.81	6-32	4	1
Bradburn G.E.	7	10	2	30*	105	13.12	—	—	6	—	6	460	76.66	3-134	—	—
Bradburn W.P.	2	4	0	32	62	15.50	—	—	2	—	—	—	—	—	—	—
Broom N.T.	2	3	0	20	32	10.66	—	—	—	—	—	—	—	—	—	—
Brown V.R.	2	3	1	36*	51	25.50	—	—	3	—	1	176	176.00	1-17	—	—
Brownlie D.G.	14	25	1	109	711	29.62	1	4	17	—	1	52	52.00	1-13	—	—
Burgess M.G.	50	92	6	119*	2684	31.21	5	14	34	—	6	212	35.33	3-23	—	—
Burke C.	1	2	0	3	4	2.00	—	—	—	—	2	30	15.00	2-30	—	—
Burtt T.B.	10	15	3	42	252	21.00	—	—	2	—	33	1170	35.45	6-162	3	—
Butler I.G.	8	10	2	26	76	9.50	—	—	4	—	24	884	36.83	6-46	1	—
Butterfield L.A.	1	2	0	0	0	0.00	—	—	—	—	0	24	—	—	—	—
Cairns B.L.	43	65	8	64	928	16.28	—	2	30	—	130	4279	32.91	7-74	6	1
Cairns C.L.	62	104	5	158	3320	33.53	5	22	14	—	218	6410	29.40	7-27	13	1
Cameron F.J.	19	30	20	27*	116	11.60	—	—	2	—	62	1849	29.82	5-34	3	—
Cave H.B.	19	31	5	22*	229	8.81	—	—	8	—	34	1467	43.15	4-21	—	—
Chapple M.E.	14	27	1	76	497	19.12	—	3	10	—	1	84	84.00	1-24	—	—
Chatfield E.J.	43	54	33	21*	180	8.57	—	—	7	—	123	3958	32.17	6-73	3	1
Cleverley D.C.	2	4	3	10*	19	19.00	—	—	—	—	0	130	—	—	—	—

	M	I	NO	HS	Runs	Ave	100	50	Ct	St	Wkts	Runs	Ave	Best	5WI	10WM
Collinge R.O.	35	50	13	68*	533	14.41	—	2	10	—	116	3393	29.25	6-63	3	—
†**Colquhoun** I.A.	2	4	2	1*	1	0.50	—	—	4	—	—	—	—	—	—	—
Coney J.V.	52	85	14	174*	2668	37.57	3	16	64	—	27	966	35.77	3-28	—	—
***Congdon** B.E.	61	114	7	176	3448	32.22	7	19	44*	—	59	2154	36.51	5-65	1	—
Conway D.P.	3	6	0	200	379	63.16	1	2	—	—	—	—	—	—	—	—
Cowie J.	9	13	4	45	90	10.00	—	—	3	—	45	969	21.53	6-40	4	1
Craig M D.	15	25	9	67	589	36.81	—	3	14	—	50	2326	46.52	7-94	1	1
Cresswell G.F.	3	5	3	12*	14	7.00	—	—	—	—	13	292	22.46	6-168	1	—
Cromb I.B.	5	8	2	51*	123	20.50	—	1	1	—	8	442	55.25	3-113	—	—
Crowe J.J.	39	65	4	128	1601	26.24	3	6	41	—	0	9	—	—	—	—
Crowe M.D.	77	131	11	299	5444	45.36	17	18	71	—	14	676	48.28	2-25	—	—
Cumming C.D.	11	19	2	74	441	25.94	—	1	3	—	—	—	—	—	—	—
Cunis R.S.	20	31	8	51	295	12.83	—	1	1	—	51	1887	37.00	6-76	1	—
D'Arcy J.W.	5	10	0	33	136	13.60	—	—	—	—	—	—	—	—	—	—
de Grandhomme C.	26	39	5	105	1207	35.50	1	8	16	—	47	1555	33.08	6-41	1	—
de Groen R.P.	5	10	4	26	45	7.50	—	—	—	—	11	505	45.90	3-40	—	—
Davis H.T.	5	7	4	8*	20	6.66	—	—	4	—	17	499	29.35	5-63	1	—
Dempster C.S.	10	15	4	136	723	65.73	2	5	2	—	0	10	—	—	—	—
Dempster E.W.	5	8	2	47	106	17.67	—	—	1	—	2	219	109.50	1-24	—	—
†**Dick** A.E.	17	30	4	50*	370	14.73	—	1	47	4	—	—	—	—	—	—
Dickinson G.R.	3	5	0	11	31	6.20	—	—	3	—	8	245	30.63	3-66	—	—
Donnelly M.P.	7	12	1	206	582	52.91	1	4	7	—	0	20	—	—	—	—
Doull S.B.	32	50	11	46	570	14.61	—	—	16	—	98	2872	29.30	7-65	6	—
Dowling G.T.	39	77	3	239	2306	31.16	3	11	23	—	1	19	19.00	1-19	—	—
Drum C.J.	5	5	2	4	10	3.33	—	—	4	—	16	482	30.12	3-36	—	—
Dunning J.A.	4	6	1	19	38	7.60	—	—	2	—	5	493	98.60	2-35	—	—
***Edgar** B.A.	39	68	4	161	1958	30.59	3	12	14*	—	0	3	—	—	—	—
***Edwards** G.N.	8	15	0	55	377	25.13	—	3	7*	—	—	—	—	—	—	—
Elliott G.D.	5	9	1	25	86	10.75	—	—	2	—	4	140	35.00	2-8	—	—
Emery R.W.G.	2	4	0	28	46	11.50	—	—	—	—	2	52	26.00	2-52	—	—
Ferguson L.H.	1	2	2	1*	1	—	—	—	—	—	0	47	—	—	—	—
Fisher F.E.	1	2	0	14	23	11.50	—	—	—	—	1	78	78.00	1-78	—	—
Fleming S.P.	111	189	10	274*	7172	40.06	9	46	172	—	—	—	—	—	—	—
Flynn D.R.	24	45	5	95	1038	25.95	—	6	10	—	0	0	—	—	—	—
Foley H.	1	2	0	2	4	2.00	—	—	—	—	—	—	—	—	—	—
Franklin J.E.C.	31	46	7	122*	808	20.71	1	2	12	—	82	2786	33.97	6-119	3	—
Franklin T.J.	21	37	1	101	828	23.00	1	4	8	—	—	—	—	—	—	—
Freeman D.L.	2	2	0	1	2	1.00	—	—	—	—	1	169	169.00	1-91	—	—
Fulton P.G.	23	39	1	136	967	25.44	2	5	25	—	—	—	—	—	—	—
Gallichan N.	1	2	0	30	32	16.00	—	—	—	—	3	113	37.67	3-99	—	—
Gedye S.G.	4	8	0	55	193	24.13	—	2	—	—	—	—	—	—	—	—
†**Germon** L.K.	12	21	3	55	382	21.22	—	1	27	2	—	—	—	—	—	—
Gillespie M.R.	5	8	1	27	76	10.85	—	—	1	—	22	631	28.68	6-113	3	—
Gillespie S.R.	1	1	0	28	28	28.00	—	—	—	—	1	79	79.00	1-79	—	—
Gray E.J.	10	16	0	50	248	15.50	—	1	6	—	17	886	52.11	3-73	—	—
Greatbatch M.J.	41	71	5	146*	2021	30.62	3	10	27	—	0	0	—	—	—	—
†**Guillen** S.C.	3	6	0	41	98	16.33	—	—	4	1	—	—	—	—	—	—
Guptill M.J.	47	89	1	189	2586	29.38	3	17	50	—	8	298	37.25	3-11	—	—
Guy J.W.	12	23	2	102	440	20.95	1	3	2	—	—	—	—	—	—	—
Hadlee D.R.	26	42	5	56	530	14.32	—	1	8	—	71	2389	33.65	4-30	—	—
Hadlee R.J.	86	134	19	151*	3124	27.16	2	15	39	—	431	9611	22.29	9-52	36	9
Hadlee W.A.	11	19	1	116	543	30.17	1	2	6	—	—	—	—	—	—	—
Harford N.S.	8	15	0	93	229	15.27	—	2	—	—	—	—	—	—	—	—
†**Harford** R.I.	3	5	2	6	7	2.33	—	—	11	—	—	—	—	—	—	—

	M	I	NO	HS	Runs	Ave	100	50	Ct	St	Wkts	Runs	Ave	Best	5WI	10WM
Harris C.Z.	23	42	4	71	777	20.44	—	5	14	—	16	1170	73.12	2-16	—	—
Harris P.G.Z.	9	18	1	101	378	22.24	1	1	6	—	0	14	—	—	—	—
Harris R.M.	2	3	0	13	31	10.33	—	—	—	—	—	—	—	—	—	—
Hart M.N.	14	24	4	45	353	17.65	—	—	9	—	29	1438	49.58	5-77	1	—
†**Hart** R.G.	11	19	3	57*	260	16.25	—	1	29	1	—	—	—	—	—	—
Hartland B.R.	9	18	0	52	303	16.83	—	1	5	—	—	—	—	—	—	—
Haslam M.J.	4	2	1	3	4	4.00	—	—	2	—	2	245	122.50	1-33	—	—
Hastings B.F.	31	56	6	117*	1510	30.20	4	7	23	—	0	9	—	—	—	—
Hayes J.A.	15	22	7	19	73	4.87	—	—	3	—	30	1217	40.57	4-36	—	—
Henderson M.	1	2	1	6	8	8.00	—	—	1	—	2	64	32.00	2-38	—	—
Henry M.J.	14	17	4	66	236	18.15	—	1	6	—	37	1712	46.27	4-93	—	—
†**Hopkins** G.J.	4	7	1	15	71	11.83	—	—	9	—	—	—	—	—	—	—
Horne M.J.	35	65	2	157	1788	28.38	4	5	17	—	0	26	—	—	—	—
Horne P.A.	4	7	0	27	71	10.14	—	—	3	—	—	—	—	—	—	—
Hough K.W.	2	3	2	31*	62	62.00	—	—	1	—	6	175	29.17	3-79	—	—
How J.M.	19	35	1	92	772	22.70	—	4	18	—	0	4	—	—	—	—
Howarth G.P.	47	83	5	147	2531	32.44	6	11	29	—	3	271	90.33	1-13	—	—
Howarth H.J.	30	42	18	61	291	12.13	—	1	33	—	86	3178	36.95	5-34	2	—
Ingram P.J.	2	4	0	42	61	15.25	—	—	—	—	—	—	—	—	—	—
†**James** K.C.	11	13	2	14	52	4.73	—	—	11	5	—	—	—	—	—	—
Jamieson K.A.	8	8	2	51*	256	42.66	—	1	3	—	46	652	14.17	6-48	5	1
Jarvis T.W.	13	22	1	182	625	29.76	1	2	3	—	0	3	—	—	—	—
Jones A.H.	39	74	8	186	2922	44.27	7	11	25	—	1	194	194.00	1-40	—	—
Jones R.A.	1	2	0	16	23	11.50	—	—	—	—	—	—	—	—	—	—
Kennedy R.J.	4	5	1	22	28	7.00	—	—	2	—	6	380	63.33	3-28	—	—
Kerr J.L.	7	12	1	59	212	19.27	—	1	4	—	—	—	—	—	—	—
Kuggeleijn C.M.	2	4	0	7	7	1.75	—	—	1	—	1	67	67.00	1-50	—	—
Larsen G.R.	8	13	4	26*	127	14.11	—	—	5	—	24	689	28.70	3-57	—	—
Latham R.T.	4	7	0	119	219	31.28	1	—	5	—	0	6	—	—	—	—
***Latham** T.W.M.	59	103	5	264*	4056	41.38	11	20	66	—	—	—	—	—	—	—
†**Lees** W.K.	21	37	4	152	778	23.57	1	1	52	7	0	4	—	—	—	—
Leggat I.B.	1	1	0	0	0	0.00	—	—	2	—	0	6	—	—	—	—
Leggat J.G.	9	18	2	61	351	21.94	—	2	—	—	—	—	—	—	—	—
Lissette A.F.	2	4	2	1*	2	1.00	—	—	1	—	3	124	41.33	2-73	—	—
Loveridge G.R.	1	1	1	4*	4	—	—	—	—	—	—	—	—	—	—	—
Lowry T.C.	7	8	0	80	223	27.88	—	2	8	—	0	5	—	—	—	—
***McCullum** B.B.	101	176	9	302	6453	38.64	12	31	198	11	1	88	88.00	1-1	—	—
McEwan P.E.	4	7	1	40*	96	16.00	—	—	5	—	0	13	—	—	—	—
MacGibbon A.R.	26	46	5	66	814	19.85	—	3	13	—	70	2160	30.86	5-64	1	—
McGirr H.M.	2	1	0	51	51	51.00	—	1	—	—	1	115	115.00	1-65	—	—
McGregor S.N.	25	47	2	111	892	19.82	1	3	9	—	—	—	—	—	—	—
McIntosh T.G.	17	33	2	136	854	27.54	2	4	10	—	—	—	—	—	—	—
McKay A.J.	1	2	1	20*	25	25.00	—	—	—	—	1	120	120.00	1-120	—	—
McLeod E.G.	1	2	1	16	18	18.00	—	—	—	—	0	5	—	—	—	—
†**McMahon** T.G.	5	7	4	4*	7	2.33	—	—	7	1	—	—	—	—	—	—
McMillan C.D.	55	91	10	142	3116	38.46	6	19	22	—	28	1257	44.89	3-48	—	—
McRae D.A.N.	1	2	0	8	8	4.00	—	—	—	—	0	44	—	—	—	—
Marshall H.J.H.	13	19	2	160	652	38.35	2	2	1	—	0	4	—	—	—	—
Marshall J.A.H.	7	11	0	52	218	19.81	—	1	5	—	—	—	—	—	—	—
Martin B.P.	5	6	1	41	74	14.80	—	—	—	—	12	646	53.33	4-43	—	—
Martin C.S.	71	104	52	12*	123	2.36	—	—	14	—	233	7878	33.81	6-26	10	1
Mason M.J.	1	2	0	3	3	1.50	—	—	—	—	0	105	—	—	—	—
Matheson A.M.	2	1	0	7	7	7.00	—	—	2	—	2	136	68.00	2-7	—	—
Meale T.	2	4	0	10	21	5.25	—	—	—	—	—	—	—	—	—	—

	M	*I*	*NO*	*HS*	*Runs*	*Ave*	*100*	*50*	*Ct*	*St*	*Wkts*	*Runs*	*Ave*	*Best*	*5WI*	*10WM*
Merritt W.E.	6	8	1	19	73	10.43	—	—	2	—	12	617	51.42	4-104	—	—
Meuli E.M.	1	2	0	23	38	19.00	—	—	—	—	—	—	—	—	—	—
†**Milburn** B.D.	3	3	2	4*	8	8.00	—	—	6	2	—	—	—	—	—	—
Miller L.S.M.	13	25	0	47	346	13.84	—	—	1	—	0	1	—	—	—	—
Mills J.E.	7	10	1	117	241	26.78	1	—	1	—	—	—	—	—	—	—
Mills K.D.	19	30	5	57	289	11.56	—	1	4	—	44	1453	33.02	4-16	—	—
Mitchell D.J.	5	5	1	102*	232	58.00	1	1	4	—	1	133	133.00	1-7	—	—
Moir A.M.	17	30	8	41*	327	14.86	—	—	2	—	28	1418	50.64	6-155	2	—
Moloney D.A.R.	3	6	0	64	156	26.00	—	1	3	—	0	9	—	—	—	—
†**Mooney** F.L.H.	14	22	2	46	343	17.15	—	—	22	8	0	0	—	—	—	—
***Morgan** R.W.	20	34	1	97	734	22.24	—	5	12*	—	5	609	121.80	1-16	—	—
Morrison B.D.	1	2	0	10	10	5.00	—	—	1	—	2	129	64.50	2-129	—	—
Morrison D.K.	48	71	26	42	379	8.42	—	—	14	—	160	5549	34.68	7-89	10	—
Morrison J.F.M.	17	29	0	117	656	22.62	1	3	9	—	2	71	35.50	2-52	—	—
Motz R.C.	32	56	3	60	612	11.55	—	3	9	—	100	3148	31.48	6-63	5	—
Munro C.	1	2	0	15	15	7.50	—	—	—	—	2	40	20.00	2-40	—	—
Murray B.A.G.	13	26	1	90	598	23.92	—	5	21	—	1	0	0.00	1-0	—	—
Murray D.J.	8	16	1	52	303	20.20	—	1	6	—	—	—	—	—	—	—
Nash D.J.	32	45	14	89*	729	23.51	—	4	13	—	93	2649	28.48	6-27	3	1
Neesham J.D.S.	12	22	1	137*	709	33.76	2	4	12	—	14	675	48.21	3-42	—	—
Newman J.	3	4	0	19	33	8.25	—	—	—	—	2	254	127.00	2-76	—	—
Nicholls H.M.	40	59	6	174	2264	42.71	7	11	27	—	—	—	—	—	—	—
Nicol R.J.	2	4	0	19	28	7.00	—	—	2	—	0	13	—	—	—	—
O'Brien I.E.	22	34	5	31	219	7.55	—	—	7	—	73	2429	33.27	6-75	1	—
O'Connor S.B.	19	27	9	20	105	5.83	—	—	6	—	53	1724	32.52	5-51	1	—
O'Sullivan D.R.	11	21	4	23*	158	9.29	—	—	2	—	18	1221	67.83	5-148	1	—
Oram J.D.P.	33	59	10	133	1780	36.32	5	6	15	—	60	1983	33.05	4-41	—	—
Overton G.W.F.	3	6	1	3*	8	1.60	—	—	1	—	9	258	28.67	3-65	—	—
Owens M.B.	8	12	6	8*	16	2.66	—	—	3	—	17	585	34.44	4-99	—	—
Page M.L.	14	20	0	104	492	24.60	1	2	6	—	5	231	46.20	2-21	—	—
Papps M.H.W.	8	16	1	86	246	16.40	—	2	11	—	—	—	—	—	—	—
Parker J.M.	36	63	2	121	1498	24.56	3	5	30	—	1	24	24.00	1-24	—	—
Parker N.M.	3	6	0	40	89	14.83	—	—	2	—	—	—	—	—	—	—
***Parore** A.C.	78	128	19	110	2865	26.28	2	14	197	7	—	—	—	—	—	—
Patel A.Y.	9	11	3	20	73	9.12	—	—	5	—	26	792	30.46	5-59	2	—
Patel D.N.	37	66	8	99	1200	20.68	—	5	15	—	75	3154	42.05	6-50	3	—
Patel J.S.	24	38	8	47	381	12.70	—	—	13	—	65	3078	47.35	5-110	1	—
Petherick P.J.	6	11	4	13	34	4.86	—	—	4	—	16	685	42.81	3-90	—	—
†**Petrie** E.C.	14	25	5	55	258	12.90	—	1	25	—	—	—	—	—	—	—
Phillips G.D.	1	2	0	52	52	26.00	—	1	1	—	—	—	—	—	—	—
Playle W.R.	8	15	0	65	151	10.07	—	1	4	—	—	—	—	—	—	—
Pocock B.A.	15	29	0	85	665	22.93	—	6	5	—	0	20	—	—	—	—
Pollard V.	32	59	7	116	1266	24.35	2	7	19	—	40	1853	46.33	3-3	—	—
Poore M.B.	14	24	1	45	355	15.43	—	—	1	—	9	367	40.78	2-28	—	—
Priest M.W.	3	4	0	26	56	14.00	—	—	—	—	3	158	52.66	2-42	—	—
Pringle C.	14	21	4	30	175	10.29	—	—	3	—	30	1389	46.30	7-52	1	1
Puna N.	3	5	3	18*	31	15.50	—	—	1	—	4	240	60.00	2-40	—	—
Rabone G.O.	12	20	2	107	562	31.22	1	2	5	—	16	635	36.69	6-68	1	—
Raval J.A.	24	39	1	132	1143	30.07	1	7	21	—	1	34	34.00	1-33	—	—
Redmond A.J.	8	16	1	83	325	21.66	—	2	5	—	3	80	26.66	2-47	—	—
Redmond R.E.	1	2	0	107	163	81.50	1	1	—	—	—	—	—	—	—	—
Reid J.F.	19	31	3	180	1296	46.28	6	2	9	—	0	7	—	—	—	—
***Reid** J.R.	58	108	5	142	3428	33.28	6	22	43*	1	85	2835	33.35	6-60	1	—
Richardson M.H.	38	65	3	145	2776	44.77	4	19	26	—	1	21	21.00	1-16	—	—

	M	I	NO	HS	Runs	Ave	100	50	Ct	St	Wkts	Runs	Ave	Best	5WI	10WM
Roberts A.D.G.	7	12	1	84*	254	23.09	—	1	4	—	4	182	45.50	1-12	—	—
Roberts A.W.	5	10	1	66*	248	27.56	—	3	4	—	7	209	29.86	4-101	—	—
Robertson G.K.	1	1	0	12	12	12.00	—	—	—	—	1	91	91.00	1-91	—	—
***Ronchi** L.	4	8	0	88	319	39.87	—	2	5	—	—	—	—	—	—	—
Rowe C.G.	1	2	0	0	0	0.00	—	—	1	—	—	—	—	—	—	—
Rutherford H.D.	14	25	1	171	650	27.08	1	1	10	—	—	—	—	—	—	—
Rutherford K.R.	56	99	8	107*	2465	27.08	3	18	32	—	1	161	161.00	1-38	—	—
Ryder J.D.	18	33	2	201	1269	40.93	3	6	12	—	5	280	56.00	2-7	—	—
Santner M.J.	24	32	1	126	766	24.70	1	2	16	—	41	1871	45.63	3-53	—	—
Scott R.H.	1	1	0	18	18	18.00	—	—	—	—	1	74	74.00	1-74	—	—
Scott V.J.	10	17	1	84	458	28.63	—	3	7	—	0	14	—	—	—	—
Sewell D.G.	1	1	1	1*	1	—	—	—	—	—	0	90	—	—	—	—
Shrimpton M.J.F.	10	19	0	46	265	13.95	—	—	2	—	5	158	31.60	3-35	—	—
Sinclair B.W.	21	40	1	138	1148	29.44	3	3	8	—	2	32	16.00	2-32	—	—
Sinclair I.M.	2	4	1	18*	25	8.33	—	—	1	—	1	120	120.00	1-79	—	—
***Sinclair** M.S.	33	56	5	214	1635	32.05	3	4	31	—	0	14	—	—	—	—
Smith F.B.	4	6	1	96	237	47.40	—	2	1	—	—	—	—	—	—	—
Smith H.D.	1	1	0	4	4	4.00	—	—	—	—	1	113	113.00	1-113	—	—
†**Smith** I.D.S.	63	88	17	173	1815	25.56	2	6	168	8	0	5	—	—	—	—
Snedden C.A.	1	—	—	—	—	—	—	—	—	—	0	46	—	—	—	—
Snedden M.C.	25	30	8	33*	327	14.86	—	—	7	—	58	2199	37.91	5-68	1	—
Sodhi I.S.	17	25	4	63	448	21.33	—	3	11	—	41	1992	48.58	4-60	—	—
Somerville W.E.R.	4	6	2	40*	72	18.00	—	—	—	—	15	487	32.46	4-75	—	—
Southee T.G.	79	111	11	77*	1728	17.28	—	5	60	—	314	8862	28.22	7-64	12	1
Sparling J.T.	11	20	2	50	229	12.72	—	1	3	—	5	327	65.40	1-9	—	—
Spearman C.M.	19	37	2	112	922	26.34	1	3	20	—	—	—	—	—	—	—
Stead G.R.	5	8	0	78	278	34.75	—	2	2	—	0	1	—	—	—	—
Stirling D.A.	6	9	2	26	108	15.42	—	—	1	—	13	601	46.23	4-88	—	—
Styris S.B.	29	48	4	170	1586	36.04	5	6	23	—	20	1015	50.75	3-28	—	—
Su'a M.L.	13	18	5	44	165	12.69	—	—	8	—	36	1377	38.25	5-73	2	—
Sutcliffe B.	42	76	8	230*	2727	40.10	5	15	20	—	4	344	86.00	2-38	—	—
Taylor B.R.	30	50	6	124	898	20.41	2	2	10	—	111	2953	26.60	7-74	4	—
Taylor D.D.	3	5	0	77	159	31.80	—	1	2	—	—	—	—	—	—	—
Taylor L.R.P.L.	108	189	24	290	7564	45.84	19	35	159	—	2	48	24.00	2-4	—	—
Thomson K.	2	4	1	69	94	31.33	—	1	—	—	1	9	9.00	1-9	—	—
Thomson S.A.	19	35	4	120*	958	30.90	1	5	7	—	19	953	50.15	3-63	—	—
†**Tindill** E.W.T.	5	9	1	37*	73	9.13	—	—	6	1	—	—	—	—	—	—
Troup G.B.	15	18	6	13*	55	4.58	—	—	2	—	39	1454	37.28	6-95	1	1
Truscott P.B.	1	2	0	26	29	14.50	—	—	1	—	—	—	—	—	—	—
Tuffey D.R.	26	36	10	80*	427	16.42	—	1	15	—	77	2445	31.75	6-54	2	—
Turner G.M.	41	73	6	259	2991	44.64	7	14	42	—	0	5	—	—	—	—
Twose R.G.	16	27	2	94	628	25.12	—	6	5	—	3	130	43.33	2-36	—	—
Vance R.H.	4	7	0	68	207	29.57	—	1	—	—	—	—	—	—	—	—
†**van Wyk** C.F.K.	9	17	1	71	341	21.31	—	1	23	1	—	—	—	—	—	—
Vaughan J.T.C.	6	12	1	44	201	18.27	—	—	4	—	11	450	40.90	4-27	—	—
Vettori D.L.	113	174	23	140	4531	30.00	6	23	58	—	362	12441	34.36	7-87	20	3
Vincent L.	23	40	1	224	1332	34.15	3	9	19	—	0	2	—	—	—	—
Vivian G.E.	5	6	0	43	110	18.33	—	—	3	—	1	107	107.00	1-14	—	—
Vivian H.G.	7	10	0	100	421	42.10	1	5	4	—	17	633	37.24	4-58	—	—
†**Wadsworth** K.J.	33	51	4	80	1010	21.49	—	5	92	4	—	—	—	—	—	—
Wagner N.	54	69	19	66*	695	13.90	—	1	12	—	229	6046	26.40	7-39	9	—
Walker B.G.K.	5	8	2	27*	118	19.66	—	—	—	—	5	399	79.80	2-92	—	—
Wallace W.M.	13	21	0	66	439	20.90	—	5	5	—	0	5	—	—	—	—

	M	I	NO	HS	Runs	Ave	100	50	Ct	St	Wkts	Runs	Ave	Best	5WI	10WM
Walmsley K.P.	3	5	0	5	13	2.60	—	—	—	—	9	391	43.44	3-70	—	—
†**Ward** J.T.	8	12	6	35*	75	12.50	—	—	16	1	—	—	—	—	—	—
***Watling** B-J.	75	117	16	205	3790	37.52	8	19	267	8	—	—	—	—	—	—
Watson W.	15	18	6	11	60	5.00	—	—	4	—	40	1387	34.67	6-78	1	—
Watt L.	1	2	0	2	2	1.00	—	—	—	—	—	—	—	—	—	—
Webb M.G.	3	2	0	12	12	6.00	—	—	—	—	4	471	117.75	2-114	—	—
Webb P.N.	2	3	0	5	11	3.67	—	—	2	—	—	—	—	—	—	—
Weir G.L.	11	16	2	74*	416	29.71	—	3	3	—	7	209	29.86	3-38	—	—
White D.J.	2	4	0	18	31	7.75	—	—	—	—	0	5	—	—	—	—
Whitelaw P.E.	2	4	2	30	64	32.00	—	—	—	—	—	—	—	—	—	—
Williamson K.S.	85	148	14	251	7230	53.95	24	33	72	—	30	1207	40.23	4-44	—	—
Wiseman P.J.	25	34	8	36	366	14.07	—	—	11	—	61	2903	47.59	5-82	2	—
Wright J.G.	82	148	7	185	5334	37.82	12	23	38	—	0	5	—	—	—	—
Young B.A.	35	68	4	267*	2034	31.78	2	12	54	—	—	—	—	—	—	—
†**Young** R.A.	5	10	3	57	169	24.14	—	1	8	—	—	—	—	—	—	—
Young W.A.	3	4	0	82	138	34.50	—	1	1	—	—	—	—	—	—	—
Yuile B.W.	17	33	6	64	481	17.81	—	1	12	—	34	1213	35.68	4-43	—	—

Note: There have been 81 dismissals made by substitutes: M.J. Greatbatch (5), J.G. Bracewell, J.J. Crowe, T.W. Jarvis (4), C.Z. Harris (3), J.M. How, J.A.H. Marshall, D.R. O'Sullivan, A.C. Parore, K.R. Rutherford, G.E. Vivian, M.J. Guptill, T.G. Southee (2), J.C. Alabaster, R.W. Anderson, T.A. Blundell, S.E. Bond, S.L. Boock, G.E. Bradburn, C. Burke, Carl Cachopa, R.O. Collinge, B.E. Congdon, D.P. Conway, M.D. Crowe, H.T. Davis, C.J. Drum, E.W. Dempster, G.T. Dowling, S.W. Eathorne, B.A. Edgar, G.N. Edwards, S.G. Gedye, M.N. Hart, M.A. Hastings, M.J. Henry, N.K.W. Horsley, I.B. Leggat, T.G. McMahon, P.E. McEwan, M.N. McKenzie, H.J.H. Marshall, M.J. Mason, S.M. Mills, D.J. Mitchell, R.C. Motz, J.D.S. Neesham, S.B. O'Connor, N.M. Parker, J.S. Patel, M.W. Priest, T.D. Ritchie, M.J. Santner, L. Vincent, B.G.K. Walker, W.A. Young, B-J. Watling catches and B.E. Congdon a stumping. The latter is one of only two instances in tests of a substitute making a stumping.

† all test appearances were as wicketkeeper. A.C. Parore had 67 tests as wicketkeeper, B-J. Watling 67, B.B. McCullum 52, T.E. Blain 9, G.N. Edwards 4, T.A. Blundell 4, B.A. Edgar, J.R. Reid and L. Ronchi one each.

** record includes catches taken while keeping wicket as follows: B-J. Watling 257, A.C. Parore 194, B.B. McCullum 168, T.E. Blain 18, T.A. Blundell 12, T.W.M. Latham 7, B.A. Edgar 4, J.R. Reid 2 and B.E. Congdon, R.W. Morgan and M.S. Sinclair one each. Edwards' and Ronchi's catches were all made while keeping wicket.*

Vettori's record includes one match for ICC World XI.

SUMMARY OF TEST CAREER RECORDS

Most Matches

Vettori D.L.	113	Southee T.G.	79	Congdon B.E.	61
Fleming S.P.	111	Parore A.C.	78	Latham T.W.M.	59
Taylor L.R.P.L.	108	Crowe M.D.	77	Reid J.R.	58
McCullum B.B.	101	Watling B-J.	75	Rutherford K.R.	56
Hadlee R.J.	86	Boult T.A.	73	McMillan C.D	55
Williamson K.S.	85	Martin C.S.	71	Wagner N.	54
Wright J.G.	82	Smith I.D.S.	63	Coney J.V.	52
Astle N.J.	81	Cairns C.L.	62	Burgess M.G.	50

Most Runs

Taylor L.R.P.L.	7564	Congdon B.E.	3448	Burgess M.G.	2684
Williamson K.S.	7230	Reid J.R.	3428	Coney J.V.	2668
Fleming S.P.	7172	Cairns C.L.	3320	Guptill M.J.	2586
McCullum B.B.	6453	Hadlee R.J.	3124	Howarth G.P.	2531
Crowe M.D.	5444	McMillan C.D.	3116	Rutherford K.R.	2465
Wright J.G.	5334	Turner G.M.	2991	Dowling G.T.	2306
Astle N.J.	4702	Jones A.H.	2922	Nicholls H.M.	2264
Vettori D.L.	4531	Parore A.C.	2865	Young B.A.	2034
Latham T.W.M.	4056	Richardson M.H.	2776	Greatbatch M.J.	2021
Watling B-J.	3790	Sutcliffe B.	2727		

Most Wickets

Hadlee R.J.	431	Wagner N.	229	Collinge R.O.	116
Vettori D.L.	362	Cairns C.L.	218	Taylor B.R.	111
Southee T.G.	314	Morrison D.K.	160	Bracewell J.G.	102
Boult T.A.	292	Cairns B.L.	130	Motz R.C.	100
Martin C.S.	233	Chatfield E.J.	123		

Most Catches

Fleming S.P.	172	Astle N.J.	70	Southee T.G.	60
Taylor L.R.P.L.	159	Latham T.W.M	65	Vettori D.L.	58
Williamson K.S.	72	Coney J.V.	64	Young B.A.	54
Crowe M.D.	71				

Most Wicketkeeping Dismissals

	Ct	*St*	*Total*
Watling B-J.	257	8	265
Parore A.C.	194	7	201
McCullum B.B.	168	11	179
Smith I.D.S.	168	8	176
Wadsworth K.J.	92	4	96
Lees W.K.	52	7	59
Dick A.E.	47	4	51

Test Captains

		RESULTS				TOSS	
		P	W	L	D	W	L
Fleming S.P.	1996/97 to 2006/07	80	28	27	25	37	43
Williamson K.S.	2016/17 to 2021	37	22	6	9	20	17
Reid J.R.	1955/56 to 1965	34	3	18	13	17	17
Vettori D.L.	2007/08 to 2010/11	32	6	16	10	17	15
McCullum B.B.	2012/13 to 2015/16	31	11	11	9	12	19
Howarth G.P.	1979/80 to 1984/85	30	11	7	12	17	13
Dowling G.T.	1967/68 to 1971/72	19	4	7	8	10	9
Rutherford K.R.	1992/93 to 1994/95	18	2	11	5	12	6
Congdon B.E.	1971/72 to 1974/75	17	1	7	9	4	13
Crowe M.D.	1990/91 to 1993/94	16	2	7	7	8	8
Coney J.V.	1984/85 to 1986/87	15	5	4	6	8	7
Wright J.G.	1987/88 to 1990	14	3	3	8	8	6
Taylor L.R.P.L.	2011/12 to 2016/17	14	4	8	2	8	6
Germon L.K.	1995/96 to 1996/97	12	1	5	6	6	6
Turner G.M.	1975/76 to 1976/77	10	1	6	3	2	8
Burgess M.G.	1977/78 to 1980/81	10	1	6	3	4	6
Cave H.B.	1955/56	9	0	5	4	5	4
Hadlee W.A.	1945/46 to 1950/51	8	0	2	6	4	4
Lowry T.C.	1929/30 to 1931	7	0	2	5	5	2
Page M.L.	1931/32 to 1937	7	0	3	4	4	3
Crowe J.J.	1986/87 to 1987/88	6	0	1	5	3	3
Rabone G.O.	1953/54 to 1954/55	5	0	4	1	2	3
Sutcliffe B.	1951/52 to 1953/54	4	0	3	1	4	0
Sinclair B.W.	1965/66 to 1967/68	3	0	1	2	3	0
Nash D.J.	1998/99	3	0	1	2	3	0
Latham T.W.M.	2019/20 to 2021	3	2	1	0	0	3
Wallace W.M.	1952/53	2	0	1	1	0	2
Chapple M.E.	1965/66	1	0	0	1	0	1
Parker J.M.	1976/77	1	0	0	1	0	1
Smith I.D.S.	1990/91	1	0	0	1	1	0
Totals		**449**	**107**	**175**	**167**	**224**	**225**

Test Debuts

New Zealand has now played 449 test matches. In 266 there have been no new test caps. In the other 183 the records are:

11 players making debut 1929/30 v England at Christchurch (NZ's first test match)
6 players making debut 1937 v England at Lord's (NZ's first test since 1932/33)
6 players making debut 1945/46 v Australia at Wellington
6 players making debut 1946/47 v England at Christchurch (test after one above)
5 players making debut 1961/62 v South Africa at Durban

Of the 12 players who made their debuts in the 1945/46 and 1946/47 tests above, seven did not appear again. In eight successive tests at least one player made his test debut — South Africa 1963/64 (3), Pakistan 1964/65 (3), India 1964/65 (2). In nine successive tests there were no new caps — England 1969 (2), India 1969/70 (3), Pakistan 1969/70 (3), England 1970/71 (1) and South Africa 1998/99 (1), England 1999 (4), India 1999/00 (3), West Indies 1999/00 (1).

Youngest/Oldest Test Players

YOUNGEST PLAYERS			***Bat***	***Bowl***
18 years 10 days	Vettori D.L. v England at Wellington	1996/97	3* & 2*	2-98
18 years 197 days	Freeman D.L. v England at Christchurch	1932/33	1	0-78
18 years 267 days	Vivian H.G. v England at The Oval	1931	3 & 51	2-96
18 years 295 days	Collinge R.O. v Pakistan at Wellington	1964/65	0*	2-51 & 3-43
18 years 316 days	Bracewell B.P. v England at The Oval	1978	0 & 0	2-46 & 1-26
19 years 5 days	Vivian G.E. v India at Calcutta	1964/65	1 & 43	0-37 & 1-14
19 years 102 days	Southee T.G. v England at Napier	2007/08	5 & 77*	5-55 & 0-84
19 years 145 days	Beck J.E.F. v South Africa at Johannesburg	1953/54	16 & 7	
19 years 154 days	Rutherford K.R. v West Indies at Port of Spain	1984/85	0 & 0	
19 years 157 days	Crowe M.D. v Australia at Wellington	1981/82	9	0-14
19 years 163 days	Parore A.C. v England at Birmingham	1990	12* & 20	4ct/1st
19 years 164 days	Cairns C.L. v Australia at Perth	1989/90	1 & 28	0-60
19 years 173 days	Pollard V. v India at Madras	1964/65	3	3-90 & 1-32
19 years 186 days	Playle W.R. v England at Birmingham	1958	4 & 8	
19 years 252 days	Donnelly M.P. v England at Lord's	1937	0 & 21	
19 years 340 days	Sewell D.G. v Zimbabwe at Bulawayo	1997/98	1*	0-81 & 0-9
19 years 344 days	Sparling J.T. v England at Leeds	1958	9* & 18	1-78

OLDEST PLAYERS *(age on last day of final test)*

41 years 247 days	Alabaster J.C. v West Indies at Port of Spain	1971/72	18	0-49 & 1-5
41 years 196 days	Sutcliffe B. v England at Birmingham	1965	4* & 53	
40 years 198 days	Congdon B.E. v England at Lord's	1978	2 & 3	0-12

OLDEST PLAYER ON DEBUT

38 years 101 days	McGirr H.M.† v England at Auckland	1929/30		0-46

† he made 51 in his first test innings in his second test

YOUNGEST CENTURY MAKERS

19 years 121 days†	Vivian H.G. 100 v South Africa at Wellington	1931/32
20 years 91 days	Williamson K.S. 131 v India at Ahmedabad	2010/11

† world record at that time

OLDEST CENTURY MAKERS

41 years 109 days	Sutcliffe B. 151* v India at Calcutta	1964/65
39 years 12 days	Congdon B.E. 107* v Australia at Christchurch	1976/77

YOUNGEST CAPTAINS

23 years 319 days	Fleming S.P. v England at Christchurch	1996/97	62 & 11
25 years 252 days	Parker J.M. v Pakistan at Karachi	1976/77	24 & 16
25 years 355 days	Williamson K.S. v Zimbabwe at Bulawayo	2016	91

OLDEST CAPTAINS *(age on last day of final test)*

37 years 40 days	Reid J.R. v England at Leeds	1965	54 & 5	
37 years 22 days	Congdon B.E. v England at Christchurch	1974/75	38	0-27
36 years 150 days	Burgess M.G. v Australia at Perth	1980/81	43 & 18	
36 years 88 days	Wallace W.M. v South Africa at Auckland	1952/53	23	

LONGEST INTERVAL BETWEEN TEST APPEARANCES

14 years 28 days — Cleverley D.C. — v South Africa at Christchurch 1/3/1932
v Australia at Wellington 29/3/1946

Only A.J. Traicos (22 years 222 days), G. Gunn (17 years 316 days), Younis Ahmed (17 years 111 days) and J.M.M. Commaille (14 years 95 days) have a longer interval between tests but Cleverley is unique in that the above matches were his only two tests.

NEW ZEALAND LIMITED-OVERS RECORDS

This section of the *Almanack* is devoted to limited-overs matches in New Zealand (other than one-day internationals) and has been compiled from the following games:

1. 1099 matches in national competitions (Shell Cup, State Shield, Ford Trophy etc) from 1971/72 to 2020/21.

2. 55 matches between provincial sides and overseas teams from 1970/71 to 2007/08.

1970/71	Wellington v MCC
	Otago v MCC
	Central Districts v MCC
1972/73	Central Districts v Pakistan
1973/74	Wellington v Australia
	Central Districts v Australia
1975/76	Wellington v India
1977/78	Northern Districts v England XI
1978/79	Auckland v Pakistan
	Canterbury v Pakistan
1979/80	Auckland XI v West Indies
	Central Districts v West Indies
1981/82	Northern Districts v Australia
	Central Districts v Australia
1983/84	Otago v England XI
1984/85	Wellington v New South Wales
1985/86	Auckland v Australia
1986/87	Auckland v West Indies
	Central Districts v South Australia *(4 matches)*
1987/88	Wellington v England
	Auckland v Victoria *(2 matches)*
	Wellington v Queensland
	Canterbury v Queensland
	Otago v Queensland
1988/89	Auckland v Pakistan
1991/92	Auckland v England
	Auckland v Australia
	Northern Districts v Zimbabwe *(2 matches)*
1993/94	Canterbury v New South Wales
1994/95	Auckland v West Indies
	Central Districts v India
	Wellington v South Africa
	Canterbury v Sri Lanka
1996/97	Central Districts v Sri Lanka
1997/98	Canterbury v Bangladesh
1998/99	Northern v Pakistan A
2000/01	Wellington v New South Wales
	Canterbury v Zimbabwe
2001/02	Northern Districts v England *(2 matches)*
2003/04	Wellington v Pakistan
	Northern Districts v South Africa
2004/05	Central Districts v Sri Lanka
2007/08	Northern Districts v Bangladesh *(2 matches)*
	Auckland v Bangladesh
	Canterbury v England *(2 matches)*

3. Three matches in the Data General competition in 1986/87.

4. Six matches in the Shell Shield competition in 1997/98.

5. 39 other matches not involving provincial sides.

1972/73	New Zealand Under 23 XI v Pakistan
1976/77	Australia v Invitation XIs *(2 matches)*
1981/82	North Island v South Island
1982/83	Sri Lanka v NZ Minor Associations *(2 matches)*
1992/93	New Zealand President's XI v Australia
1993/94	North Island v South Island
	Sir Ron Brierley XI v Pakistan
1994/95	North Island v South Island
	Sir Ron Brierley XI v West Indies
	New Zealand Academy XI v Sri Lanka
	New Zealand Academy XI v Australian Academy XI
1996/97	New Zealand Academy XI v England
1997/98	New Zealand Academy XI v Zimbabwe
1998/99	New Zealand A v Pakistan A *(3 matches)*
	New Zealand Academy XI v South Africa
1999/00	New Zealand Academy XI v England A *(2 matches)*
	New Zealand A v England A *(3 matches)*
2000/01	North Island Selection XI v Sri Lanka
2003/04	South Island v North Island
	New Zealand A v Sri Lanka A *(2 matches)*
2004/05	New Zealand v FICA World XI *(3 matches)*
	North Island v South Island
2008/09	New Zealand A v England Lions *(2 matches)*
2017/18	New Zealand XI v Pakistan
2018/19	New Zealand A v India A *(3 matches)*
2019/20	New Zealand XI v India A *(2 matches)*
	New Zealand A v India A *(3 matches)*

TEAM RECORDS

Highest Totals

427-8	Wellington v Otago	Wellington	2020/21
417-6	Central Districts v Northern Districts	Hamilton	2012/13
410-5	Canterbury v Otago	Timaru	2009/10
407-4	Otago v Central Districts	Dunedin	2019/20
405	Central Districts v Canterbury	New Plymouth	2014/15
405-6	Central Districts v Canterbury	Timaru	2014/15
405-6	Central Districts v Canterbury	New Plymouth	2015/16
401-8	Central Districts v Northern Districts	New Plymouth	2016/17
401-8	Auckland v Canterbury	Christchurch	2019/20

Lowest Totals

48	Pakistan v Auckland	Auckland	1988/89
58	Central Districts v Wellington	Wellington	2001/02
64	Otago v Wellington	Alexandra	1984/85
64	Otago v Central Districts	Invercargill	2004/05
66	Wellington v Canterbury	Wellington	1996/97
67	Otago v Central Districts	Invercargill	2000/01
67	Central Districts v Canterbury	Christchurch	2002/03
70	Auckland v Northern Districts	Pukekohe	1977/78

Most Extras in an Innings

55	Northern Districts (271-8)	v Wellington (228)	Hamilton	2002/03
51	NZ Academy XI (183)	v England A (184-4)	Lincoln	1999/00
48	Wellington (211-7)	v Otago (208-8)	Wellington	1996/97
45	Wellington (251-8)	v Otago (250-6)	Alexandra	1997/98
45	England A (219-7)	v New Zealand A (216)	Auckland	1999/00

Fewest Extras in an Innings

1	Canterbury (205-6)	v Wellington (203)	Timaru	1986/87
1	New Zealand A (299-9)	v India A (300-5)	Mt Maunganui	2018/19
2	Pakistan (216-4)	v NZ Under 23 XI	Rotorua	1972/73
2	Otago (114)	v Canterbury (113)	Christchurch	1979/80
2	Auckland (163-4)	v Otago (162)	Oamaru	1981/82
2	Auckland (105)	v Otago (214-9)	Dunedin	1993/94
2	Otago (279-5)	v Central Districts (275-7)	Palmerston North	2006/07
2	Wellington (149)	v Auckland (230)	Auckland	2009/10
2	Canterbury (300-5)	v Wellington (299-7)	Christchurch	2009/10
2	Otago (222-7)	v Canterbury (221-9)	Rangiora	2017/18

Tied Match

Wellington v South Africa	Wellington	1994/95
Northern Districts v Auckland	Hamilton	2005/06
Auckland v Canterbury	Auckland	2009/10
Northern Districts v Otago	Whangarei	2010/11
Wellington v Otago *(D/L)*	Wellington	2015/16

Close Finishes

RUNS *(winning team listed first)*

1	Northern Districts v Canterbury	Hamilton	1982/83
1	Northern Districts v Zimbabwe	Pukekohe	1991/92
1	Auckland v Central Districts	Auckland	1994/95
1	Otago v Auckland	Alexandra	1995/96
1	Central Districts v Wellington	Wellington	1996/97
1	Northern Districts v Wellington *(D/L)*	Taupo	2004/05
1	Otago v Northern Districts	Taupo	2005/06
1	Canterbury v Northern Districts	Christchurch	2019/20

ONE WICKET *(winning team listed first)*

Wellington v Auckland	Wellington	1973/74
Otago v Canterbury	Christchurch	1979/80
Central Districts v Australia	New Plymouth	1981/82
Canterbury v Central Districts	Christchurch	1986/87
Otago v Northern Districts	Gisborne	1986/87
Auckland v Northern Districts	Hamilton	1989/90
Otago v Auckland	Auckland	1990/91
Wellington v Otago	Alexandra	1992/93
Central Districts v Wellington	Masterton	1993/94
Wellington v Northern Districts	Wellington	1996/97
Central Districts v Canterbury	Napier	1996/97
Wellington v Northern Districts	Whangarei	1999/00
Auckland v Northern Districts	Auckland	1999/00
Otago v Wellington	Dunedin	2000/01
Central Districts v Wellington	Waikanae	2000/01
Canterbury v Auckland	Auckland	2001/02

Otago v Northern Districts	Invercargill	2003/04
Northern Districts v Wellington	Wellington	2008/09
Wellington v Otago	Invercargill	2008/09
Northern Districts v Central Districts	Palmerston North	2010/11
Auckland v Northern Districts	Auckland	2014/15
Northern Districts v Wellington	Wellington	2019/20
Wellington v Northern Districts	Wellington	2020/21

SCORES LEVEL *(won by team listed first, having lost fewer wickets)*

Otago (223-5) v Wellington (223-9)	Dunedin	1979/80
Canterbury (182-7) v Auckland (182-9)	Christchurch	1983/84
Canterbury (136-9) v Auckland (136)	Ashburton	1985/86
Queensland (174-8) v Wellington (174)	Wellington	1987/88
Wellington (227-8) v Auckland (227)	Wellington	1995/96
Canterbury (238-6) v Auckland (238-7)	Auckland	1995/96

Large Victories

RUNS *(winning team listed first)*

227	Central Districts v Northern Districts	New Plymouth	2016/17
222	Otago v Northern Districts	Alexandra	2014/15
221	Otago v Wellington	Invercargill	2015/16
217	Central Districts v Canterbury	New Plymouth	2014/15
216	Canterbury v Auckland	Rangiora	2020/21
211	Auckland v Central Districts	Auckland	2012/13
210	Otago v Auckland	Dunedin	2019/20
200	Central Districts v Otago	Hastings	1998/99
200	Central Districts v Otago	Invercargill	2004/05

TEN WICKETS *(winning team listed first)*

Northern Districts (71-0) v Auckland (70)	Pukekohe	1977/78
West Indies (132-0) v Central Districts (130)	New Plymouth	1979/80
Canterbury (120-0) v Auckland (119)	Christchurch	1987/88
Auckland (81-0) v Central Districts (78)	New Plymouth	1988/89
Wellington (205-0) v Canterbury (202-7)	Wellington	1994/95
Auckland (164-0) v Central Districts (163)	Auckland	1998/99
Canterbury (97-0) v Central Districts (94)	Christchurch	2013/14

Most Run Outs

INNINGS

5	Wellington v Auckland	Wellington	1974/75
5	Northern Districts v Wellington	Hamilton	1992/93
5	Central Districts v Northern Districts	Hamilton	2000/01
5	Otago v Canterbury	Alexandra	2004/05

MATCH

7	Wellington v Auckland	Wellington	1974/75
7	Auckland v Canterbury	Auckland	1999/00

INDIVIDUAL RECORDS

Highest Scores

222	How J.M.	Central Districts v Northern Districts	Hamilton	2012/13
194	Worker G.H.	Central Districts v Canterbury	Timaru	2014/15
181	Worker G.H.	Central Districts v Northern Districts	New Plymouth	2016/17
178	Nicholls H.M.	Canterbury v Wellington	Wellington	2014/15
177	Pyke J.K.	South Australia v Central Districts	Palmerston North	1986/87
177	How J.M.	Central Districts v Canterbury	New Plymouth	2014/15
174*	Munro C.	Auckland v Canterbury	Auckland	2017/18
171*	Nicol R. J.	Canterbury v Northern Districts	Mt Maunganui	2012/13
170	McCullum B.B.	Otago v Auckland	Auckland	2007/08
167	Munro C.	Auckland v Canterbury	Christchurch	2019/20
164	Broom N.T.	Otago v Canterbury	Timaru	2009/10
162*	Papps M.H.W	Wellington v Otago	Wellington	2012/13
161	Hartland B.R.	Canterbury v Northern Districts	Timaru	1993/94
161	McIntosh T.G.	Auckland v Otago	Auckland	2010/11
159*	Vincent L.	Auckland v Canterbury	Christchurch	2010/11
159	Worker G.H.	Central Districts v Canterbury	New Plymouth	2015/16
157	Chapman M.S.	Auckland v Central Districts	Auckland	2015/16
156	Guptill M.J.	Auckland v Canterbury	Christchurch	2009/10
156	How J.M.	Central Districts v Auckland	Auckland	2013/14
156	Phillips G.D.	Auckland v Otago	Lincoln	2019/20
155	Rutherford H.D.	Otago v Central Districts	Dunedin	2019/20
154	Papps M.H.W	Wellington v Central Districts	Wellington	2012/13
154	Rutherford H.D.	Otago v Canterbury	Dunedin	2018/19
153	Vincent L.	Auckland v Canterbury	Christchurch	2010/11
152*	Marshall J.A.H.	Northern Districts v Canterbury	Christchurch	2006/07
152	Solia S.M.	Auckland v Northern Districts	Auckland	2016/17
151	Munro C.	Auckland v Canterbury	Auckland	2012/13
151	Blundell T.A.	Wellington v Otago	Wellington	2020/21
150	Papps M.H.W.	Canterbury v Central Districts	Rangiora	2009/10

Fastest Centuries

Balls				
50	Fulton P.G.	Canterbury v Wellington	Rangiora	2016/17
50	Allen F.H.	Wellington v Otago	Wellington	2020/21
52	McCullum B.B.	Otago v Auckland	Auckland	2007/08
54	Fleming S.P.	New Zealand v FICA World XI	Christchurch	2004/05
57	Munro C.	Auckland v Canterbury	Christchurch	2019/20
58	Munro C.	Auckland v Otago	Auckland	2019/20
59	Kitchen A.K.	Otago v Northern Districts	Dunedin	2016/17
60	How J.M.	Central Districts v Northern Districts	Hamilton	2012/13
61	How J.M.	Central Districts v Canterbury	New Plymouth	2014/15
63	Latham T.W.M.	Canterbury v Auckland	Rangiora	2020/21
65	de Silva P.A.	Auckland v Canterbury	Auckland	1996/97
65	Munro C.	Auckland v Northern Districts	Lincoln	2018/19
65	Worker G.H.	Central Districts v Otago	New Plymouth	2020/21
67	Cooper H.R.	Northern Districts v Wellington	Hamilton	2020/21
69	Munro C.	Auckland v Otago	Alexandra	2015/16
70	Munro C.	Auckland v Canterbury	Auckland	2012/13

Fastest Fifties

Balls				
16	Bruce T.C.	Central Districts v Canterbury	New Plymouth	2015/16
19	McGlashan P.D.	Northern Districts v Auckland	Hamilton	2007/08
19	Stewart S.L.	Canterbury v Otago	Timaru	2009/10
20	Cairns C.L.	Canterbury v Northern Districts	Timaru	2002/03
20	Napier G.R.	Central Districts v Northern Districts	Palmerston North	2009/10
20	Marshall H.J.H.	Wellington v Canterbury	Rangiora	2016/17
21	Rutherford H.R.	Otago v Central Districts	New Plymouth	2020/21
22	Maynard M.P.	Otago v Auckland	Alexandra	1997/98
22	Napier G.R.	England Lions v New Zealand A	Palmerston North	2008/09
22	Styris S.B.	Auckland v Otago	Oamaru	2009/10
22	Anderson C.J.	Northern Districts v Wellington	Wellington	2011/12
22	Bracewell D.A.J.	Central Districts v Auckland	Auckland	2015/16
23	Greatbatch M.J.	Central Districts v Otago	New Plymouth	1996/97
23	Butler I.G.	Otago v Canterbury	Timaru	2009/10
23	Bracewell D.A.J.	Central Districts v Canterbury	New Plymouth	2014/15
23	How J.M.	Central Districts v Wellington	Nelson	2014/15
23	Noema-Barnett K	Central Districts v Northern Districts	Gisborne	2014/15
23	Colson F.J.	Wellington v Central Districts	Wellington	2019/20
24	Ryder J.D.	Wellington v Otago	Invercargill	2012/13
24	van Beek L.V.	Wellington v Northern Districts	Wellington	2017/18
24	Bruce T.C.	Central Districts v Canterbury	Palmerston North	2019/20
25	Mascarenhas A.D.	Otago v Central Districts	New Plymouth	2008/09

Note: I.D.S. Smith reached fifty from 24 balls for Auckland v Central Districts at Auckland, 1989/90 but the game was abandoned and restarted the following day and none of the performances in the game are included in any records.

Most Wickets in an Innings

7-0-23-7	Watson W.	Auckland v Otago	Auckland	1984/85
8-1-28-7	Penn A.J.	Wellington v Northern Districts	Mt Maunganui	2000/01
10-1-35-7	Rae M.D.	Otago v Auckland	Auckland	2020/21
7.1-0-49-7	Marshall E.J.	Otago v Auckland	Dunedin	1993/94
10-5-12-6	Barrett B.J.	Northern Districts v Otago	Gisborne	1986/87
5.5-0-12-6	Cairns C.L.	New Zealand v FICA World XI	Hamilton	2004/05
10-2-19-6	McCone R.J.	Canterbury v Northern Districts	Christchurch	2013/14
9-2-20-6	Thompson E.P.	Central Districts v Canterbury	New Plymouth	2009/10
9.3-1-25-6	Mason M.J.	Central Districts v Auckland	Auckland	2003/04
9.5-3-26-6	Vaughan J.T.C.	Auckland v Otago	Auckland	1995/96
8-2-27-6	Ferguson L.J.	Auckland v Northern Districts	Auckland	2016/17
10-2-26-6	Su'a M.L.	Auckland v Central Districts	New Plymouth	1995/96
10-1-30-6	Davey S.B.	Canterbury v Wellington	Christchurch	2020/21
7.7-2-31-6	Intikhab Alam	Pakistan v NZ Under 23 XI	Rotorua	1972/73
10-1-35-6	Duffy J.A.	Otago v Canterbury	Christchurch	2018/19
10-1-37-6	Cairns C.L.	Canterbury v Wellington	Christchurch	1996/97
8.3-0-38-6	Gillespie M.R.	Wellington v Northern Districts	Wellington	2012/13
9.3-0-41-6	McClenaghan M.J.	Auckland v Wellington	Auckland	2011/12
9.3-0-43-6	Wisneski W.A.	Canterbury v Auckland	Christchurch	1996/97
10-1-45-6	Bennett H.K.	Canterbury v Auckland	Auckland	2007/08
10-0-45-6	Henry M.J.	Canterbury v Auckland	Auckland	2012/13
10-1-49-6	Penn A.J.	Central Districts v Northern Districts	Napier	1996/97
9.3-0-51-6	Lister B.G.	Auckland v Northern Districts	Whangarei	2019/20

Most Expensive Bowling

10-0-97-5	Ellis A.M.	Canterbury v Central Districts	New Plymouth	2014/15
10-0-97-2	Ellis A.M.	Canterbury v Central Districts	New Plymouth	2015/16
10-0-95-1	Kuggeleijn S.C.	Northern Districts v Otago	Dunedin	2016/17
10-0-93-2	Presland C.M.	Northern Districts v Auckland	Gisborne	1982/83
10-3-92-1	Yasir Arafat	Otago v Auckland	Oamaru	2009/10
10-1-92-0	Arnel B.J.	Northern Districts v Canterbury	Mt Maunganui	2012/13
10-0-90-1	Ellis A.M.	Canterbury v Central Districts	Timaru	2014/15
10-0-90-0	Arnel B.J.	Wellington v Canterbury	Wellington	2014/15
ALSO NOTE *(8-ball overs)*				
1-0-18-0	Payton D.H.	Central Districts v Wellington	Wellington	1973/74
1-0-18-1	Redpath I.R.	Australia v Central Districts	New Plymouth	1973/74
2-0-29-0	Child M.J.	Northern Districts v Central Districts	Palmerston North	1975/76
3-0-37-0	Dunning B.	Northern Districts v Canterbury	Christchurch	1977/78
4-0-42-1	Maingay C.T.	Auckland v Wellington	Wellington	1971/72
5-0-48-0	Coles M.J.	Wellington v Canterbury	Christchurch	1975/76
6-0-56-0	Cater S.B.	Wellington v Auckland	Auckland	1977/78
6-0-56-0	Gilmour G.J.	Australia v Invitation XI	Christchurch	1976/77
7-0-68-1	Aldridge C.W.	Northern Districts v Auckland	Auckland	1978/79
ALSO NOTE *(6-ball overs)*				
1-0-22-0	Pryor C.R.	Auckland v Wellington	Wellington	1998/99
1-0-22-0	Solia S.M.	Auckland v Northern Districts	Lincoln	2018/19
1.5-0-27-0	Houghton M.V.	Wellington v Auckland	Auckland	2007/08
2-0-26-0	Roberts S.J.	Canterbury v Wellington	Ohoka	1990/91
2-0-26-0	Lennox J.R.	Central Districts v Otago	New Plymouth	2020/21
2.1-0-30-0	McConchie C.E.	Canterbury v Central Districts	Rangiora	2016/17
3-0-42-1	McMillan C.D.	Canterbury v Central Districts	Napier	1996/97
3.1-0-57-0	Muralitharan M.	FICA World XI v New Zealand	Christchurch	2004/05
4-0-53-0	Toole R.L.	Central Districts v Otago	New Plymouth	2020/21
5-0-57-0	Nethula T.S.	Auckland v Central Districts	New Plymouth	2017/18
6-0-74-1	Yasir Arafat	Otago v Canterbury	Timaru	2009/10
7-0-75-1	Rae M.D.	Otago v Wellington	Wellington	2020/21
8-0-81-0	Hutchinson D.S.	Wellington v Central Districts	Palmerston North	2015/16

Most Economical Bowling

10-7-5-2	Boock S.L.	Otago v Central Districts	Alexandra	1986/87
10-5-6-2	Larsen G.R.	Wellington v Otago	Alexandra	1992/93
*8-3-7-2	Williams J.C.	Auckland v Northern Districts	Auckland	1971/72
10-6-8-1	Hills P.W.	Otago v Auckland	Oamaru	1981/82
10-6-8-2	Nuttall A.J.	Canterbury v Wellington	Christchurch	1988/89
10-4-8-0	Duff S.W.	Central Districts v Wellington	New Plymouth	1989/90
10-5-8-3	Vaughan J.T.C.	Auckland v Central Districts	Waikanae	1993/94
10-5-8-1	Harris C.Z.	Canterbury v Auckland	Christchurch	1995/96
*7-0-9-0	Dunning B.	Northern Districts v Canterbury	Christchurch	1976/77
10-6-9-1	Boock S.L.	Otago v Canterbury	Christchurch	1979/80
10-4-9-1	de Mel A.L.F.	Sri Lanka v Minor Associations	Wanganui	1982/83
10-5-9-2	Astle N.J.	Canterbury v Northern Districts	Christchurch	1991/92
10-4-9-2	Astle N.J.	Canterbury v Wellington	Christchurch	1993/94
10-3-9-1	de Groen R.P.	Northern Districts v Central Districts	Levin	1995/96
10-6-9-2	McCullum N.J.	Otago v Auckland	Auckland	2000/01
*7-1-10-2	Kirk C.M.	Canterbury v Otago	Christchurch	1973/74
10-5-10-3	McIntyre J.M.	Auckland v Canterbury	Auckland	1980/81
10-4-10-2	Pigott A.C.S.	Wellington v Northern Districts	Tauranga	1983/84

10-6-10-0	Bracewell J.G.	Auckland v Canterbury	Auckland	1986/87
10-7-10-4	Duers K.G.	Zimbabwe v Northern Districts	Cambridge	1991/92
10-3-10-2	Williams B.R.	Wellington v Northern Districts	Gisborne	1993/94
10-3-10-3	Larsen G.R.	Wellington v Canterbury	Rangiora	1994/95

** 8-ball overs*

(Note: C.M. Brown had figures of 10-5-6-2 for Auckland v Otago at Dunedin, 1993/94 but the game was abandoned and none of the performances in the game are included in any records).

Hat-tricks

7-0-23-7	Watson W.	Auckland v Otago	Auckland	1984/85
10-0-48-4	Briasco P.S.	Central Districts v Auckland	Napier	1989/90
10-1-40-3	Walker M.D.J.	Wellington v Otago	Dunedin	2000/01

Wicketkeeping

DISMISSALS

	(ct/st)				
7	(7/0)	Johns L.R.	Wellington v Canterbury	Wellington	2018/19
6	(5/1)	Murray D.A.	West Indies v Central Districts	New Plymouth	1979/80
6	(6/0)	McSweeney E.B.	Wellington v Auckland	Wellington	1982/83
6	(6/0)	McSweeney E.B.	Wellington v Northern Districts	Wellington	1988/89
6	(6/0)	McRae G.P.	Central Districts v Wellington	Masterton	1994/95
6	(6/0)	Hopkins G.J.	Auckland v Central Districts	Auckland	2012/13

THREE STUMPINGS IN AN INNINGS

Milburn B.D.	Otago v Wellington	Alexandra	1982/83
Rixon S.J.	NSW v Wellington	Wellington	1984/85
Dyer G.C.	NSW v Wellington	Wellington	1986/87

Fielding

CATCHES

5	Wilson J.W.	Otago v Auckland	Dunedin	1993/94
4	Redmond R.E.	Auckland v Otago	Auckland	1972/73
4	Sampson H.C.	Otago v Canterbury	Christchurch	1974/75
4	Howarth G.P.	Invitation XI v Australia	Auckland	1976/77
4	Wiltshire J.R.	Auckland v Northern Districts	Auckland	1978/79
4	Dickeson C.W.	Northern Districts v Canterbury	Hamilton	1980/81
4	Cooper B.G.	Northern Districts v Central Districts	Palmerston North	1982/83
4	Hore A.J.	Otago v Canterbury	Christchurch	1998/99
4	Brownlie D.G.	Northern Districts v Central Districts	New Plymouth	2014/15
4	Beghin G.K.	Auckland v Canterbury	Christchurch	2017/18

HISTORY OF THE LIMITED-OVER COMPETITION IN NEW ZEALAND

2020/21 was the 50th season of limited over competition among the six New Zealand first-class sides. In that time there have been several changes both in sponsorship and format.

For the first six seasons a knock-out competition was sponsored by the New Zealand Motor Corporation. Each innings was limited to 40 eight-ball overs during the initial two seasons, reduced to 35 thereafter. In 1977/78 and 1978/79 the sponsors changed and the teams competed for the Gillette Cup. In the first season 30 eight-ball overs were used but the limit reverted to 35 the following year. There was no sponsorship for the competition in 1979/80, known simply as the National Knock-out, where 50 six-ball overs was the limit for each innings.

In 1980/81, the Shell Cup, previously contested for as part of the first-class season, became the limited-over prize and the contest was run on a league basis for the first time with each side playing the other once.

In keeping with the previous limited-over competitions, a final was arranged, this time between the top two teams of the league table, points gained being disregarded at this stage. Fifty six-ball overs was the limit on each innings.

From 1985/86 the competition was held, in its entirety, prior to the Shell Trophy series with no final. From 1989/90 the top four teams in the league table went on to semi-final play-offs, previous points being disregarded. The top two teams gained home ground advantage, the venue for the final being decided in a similar manner.

From 1993/94 to 1998/99 the top two sides played each other, with the winner going into the grand final. The loser then played the winner of the game between third and fourth to find the other finalist. From 1999/00, the leading team after the round robin went straight to the final with the second and third-placed sides meeting in a semi-final to find the other finalist. The finals became a best-of-three series.

From 2001/02 to 2008/09 the competition was known as the State Shield and the format remained unaltered except the final reverted to a single game. In 2009/10 and 2010/11, with no sponsor, the tournament was reduced to eight games per side but the semi-finals were increased to three games with the top four sides taking part. In 2011/12 it became the Ford Trophy, played under the same conditions.

In 2018/19 the competition was played over two full rounds (ten games each) with the top-placed side after the round robin qualifying to host the final and the second and third teams playing in an eliminator to determine the other finalist.

Winners of Limited-over Competitions

NEW ZEALAND MOTOR CORPORATION KNOCK-OUT

1971/72	Canterbury
1972/73	Auckland
1973/74	Wellington
1974/75	Wellington
1975/76	Canterbury
1976/77	Canterbury

GILLETTE CUP

1977/78	Canterbury
1978/79	Auckland

NATIONAL KNOCK-OUT

1979/80	Northern Districts

SHELL CUP

1980/81	Auckland
1981/82	Wellington
1982/83	Auckland
1983/84	Auckland
1984/85	Central Districts
1985/86	Canterbury
1986/87	Auckland
1987/88	Otago
1988/89	Wellington
1989/90	Auckland
1990/91	Wellington
1991/92	Canterbury
1992/93	Canterbury
1993/94	Canterbury
1994/95	Northern Districts
1995/96	Canterbury
1996/97	Canterbury
1997/98	Northern Districts
1998/99	Canterbury
1999/00	Canterbury
2000/01	Central Districts

STATE SHIELD

2001/02	Wellington
2002/03	Northern Districts
2003/04	Central Districts
2004/05	Northern Districts
2005/06	Canterbury
2006/07	Auckland
2007/08	Otago
2008/09	Northern Districts

ONE-DAY COMPETITION

2009/10	Northern Districts
2010/11	Auckland

FORD TROPHY

2011/12	Central Districts
2012/13	Auckland
2013/14	Wellington
2014/15	Central Districts
2015/16	Central Districts
2016/17	Canterbury
2017/18	Auckland
2018/19	Wellington
2019/20	Auckland
2020/21	Canterbury

Table of Results

1971/72 – 2020/21

	P	W	L	T	NR
Auckland	380	184	170	2	24
Canterbury	386	205	154	1	26
Central Districts	364	154	179	–	31
Northern Districts	373	173	184	2	14
Otago	357	137	196	2	22
Wellington	374	191	161	1	21

The Auckland and Central Districts totals include a match won by the toss of a coin against Central Districts and Northern Districts respectively.

INTER-PROVINCIAL RECORDS

	Highest Score	Lowest Score	Highest Individual Score	Best Bowling
Auckland	401-8 v Canterbury 2019/20	70 v ND 1977/78	C. Munro 174* v Canterbury 2017/18	W. Watson 7-0-23-7 v Otago 1984/85
Canterbury	410-5 v Otago 2009/10	75 v Otago 1973/74	H.M. Nicholls 178 v Wellington 2014/15	R.J. McCone 10-2-19-6 v ND 2013/14
Central Districts	417-6 v ND 2012/13	58 v Wellington 2001/02	J.M. How 222 v ND 2012/13	E.P. Thompson 9-2-20-6 v Canterbury 2009/10
Northern Districts	398 v CD 2012/13	76 v CD 1987/88	J.A.H. Marshall 152* v Canterbury 2006/07	B.J. Barrett 10-5-12-6 v Otago 1986/87
Otago	407-4 v CD 2019/20	64 v Wellington 1984/85 v CD 2004/05	B.B. McCullum 170* v Auckland 2007/08	M.D. Rae 10-1-35-7 v Auckland 2020/21
Wellington	427-8 v Otago 2020/21	66 v Canterbury 1996/97	M.H.W. Papps 162* v Otago 2012/13	A.J. Penn 8-1-28-7 v ND 2000/01

	Most Economical Bowling	Most Expensive Bowling	Most Dismissals in an Innings
Auckland	J.T.C. Vaughan 10-5-8-3 v CD 1993/94 J.C. Williams 8-3-7-2 v ND 1971/72*	L.H. Ferguson 10-0-87-0 v CD 2015/16	G.J. Hopkins 6c v CD 2012/13
Canterbury	A.J. Nuttall 10-6-8-2 v Wellington 1988/89 C.Z. Harris 10-5-8-1 v Auckland 1995/96	A.M.Ellis 10-0-97-5 v CD 2014/15 A.M.Ellis 10-0-97-2 v CD 2015/16	L.K. Germon 5c v Otago 1988/89
Central Districts	S.W. Duff 10-4-8-0 v Wellington 1989/90	B.M. Wheeler 8-0-89-1 v ND 2012/13	G.P. McRae 6c v Wellington 1994/95
Northern Districts	R.P. de Groen 10-3-9-1 v CD 1995/96	S.C. Kuggeleijn 10-0-95-1 v Otago 2016/17	M.J.E. Wright 5c v Auckland 1982/83
Otago	S.L. Boock 10-7-5-2 v C.D. 1986/87	Yasir Arafat 10-3-92-1 v Canterbury 2009/10	B.D. Milburn 5c v CD 1982/83 J.W. Wilson 5c v Auckland 1993/94
Wellington	G.R. Larsen 10-5-6-2 v Otago 1992/93	B.J.Arnel 10-0-90-0 v Canterbury 2014/15	L.R. Johns 7c v Canterbury 2018/19

** 8-ball overs*

RECORD PARTNERSHIPS

AUCKLAND

1st	226	Solia S.M. & Briggs C.J.	v Central Districts	Auckland	2020/21
2nd	235	Guptill M.J. & Phillips G.D.	v Otago	Lincoln	2019/20
3rd	242	Jones R.A. & Nicol R.J.	v Northern Districts	Auckland	2007/08
4th	157	Nicol R.J. & Barnes A.C.	v Otago	Auckland	2003/04
5th	† 229	Munro C. & de Grandhomme C.	v Canterbury	Auckland	2012/13
6th	116	Munro C. & Grobbelaar D.J.	v Canterbury	Auckland	2012/13
7th	126	Chapman M.S. & Grobbelaar D.J.	v Central Districts	Auckland	2015/16
8th	121	Canning T.K. & Morgan R.G.	v Otago	Alexandra	2000/01
9th	81	Grobbelaar D.J. & Bates M.D.	v Central Districts	Auckland	2014/15
10th	65*	Bates M.D. & Quinn M.R.	v Canterbury	Timaru	2014/15

CANTERBURY

1st	168	Papps M.H.W. & Astle N.J.	v Wellington	Timaru	2004/05
2nd	† 291	Nicholls H.M. & Broom N.T.	v Wellington	Wellington	2014/15
3rd	174	McMillan C.D. & Latham R.T.	v Central Districts	Christchurch	1994/95
4th	† 221	Howell L.G. & Stead G.R.	v Otago	Oamaru	1997/98
5th	198	Cairns C.L. & Germon L.K.	v Wellington	Christchurch	1992/93
6th	142	Cairns C.L. & Fleming S.P.	v Central Districts	Napier	1993/94
7th	124	Ellis A.M. & Jamieson K.A.	v Central Districts	Palmerston Nth	2017/18
8th	91	Harris C.Z. & Wiseman P.J.	v Central Districts	Christchurch	2003/04
9th	62	van Beek L.V. & Henry M.J.	v Auckland	Auckland	2012/13
10th	57*	Williams W.S.A. & Sheat F.W.	v Auckland	Auckland	2017/18

CENTRAL DISTRICTS

1st	† 321	Raval J.A. & How J.M.	v Northern Districts	Hamilton	2012/13
2nd	224	Worker G.H. & Smith B.S.	v Otago	Nelson	2019/20
3rd	231	Robinson D.S. & Sinclair M.S.	v Canterbury	Rangiora	2011/12
4th	147	Young W.A. & Bruce T.C.	v Northern Districts	New Plymouth	2015/16
5th	211	Young W.A. & Clarkson J.A.	v Auckland	Auckland	2017/18
6th	115	Cleaver D. & Schmulian B.D.	v Northern Districts	Lincoln	2019/20
7th	† 163	Ryder J.D. & Wheeler B.M.	v Canterbury	Christchurch	2015/16
8th	105	Wheeler B.M. & McCone R.J.	v Wellington	Lincoln	2018/19
9th	92	Loveridge G.R. & Penn A.J.	v Canterbury	Napier	1996/97
10th	50	Garner C.D. & Alcock A.J.	v Otago	Oamaru	1993/94

NORTHERN DISTRICTS

1st	181	Flynn D.R. & Devcich A P	v Otago	Mt Maunganui	2012/13
2nd	240	Watling B-J. & Flynn D.R.	v Wellington	Whangarei	2007/08
3rd	210	Flynn D.R. & Marshall J.A.H.	v Canterbury	Christchurch	2007/08
4th	155	Mitchell D.J. & Marshall J.A.H.	v Central Districts	Nelson	2012/13
5th	157	Brownlie D.G. & Mitchell D.J.	v Wellington	Wellington	2017/18
6th	† 196	Williamson K.S. & McGlashan P.D.	v Canterbury	Hamilton	2008/09
7th	119	Devcich A.P. & Hiini B.C.	v Otago	Hamilton	2011/12
8th	93*	Southee T.G. & Aldridge G.W.	v Auckland	Hamilton	2012/13
9th	† 117	Mitchell D.J. & Baker J.D.	v Central Districts	New Plymouth	2015/16
10th	62	Aldridge G.W. & Butler I.G.	v Canterbury	Hamilton	2003/04

OTAGO

1st	189	Rutherford H.D. & Renwick M.	v Central Districts	Dunedin	2019/20
2nd	158	Bracewell M.G. & Broom N.T.	v Auckland	Invercargill	2015/16
3rd	194	McCullum B.B. & Cumming C.D.	v Auckland	Auckland	2007/08
4th	190	Trott I.J.L. & Broom N.T.	v Northern Districts	Hamilton	2005/06
5th	150	McCullum N.L. & Robertson I.A.	v Wellington	Queenstown	2014/15
6th	165*	Broom D.J. & de Boorder D.C.	v Northern Districts	Queenstown	2010/11
7th	116	Todd G.R. & Yasir Arafat	v Auckland	Oamaru	2009/10
8th †	146	Rippon M.J.G. & Viljoen C.	v Wellington	Dunedin	2018/19
9th	59	Wagner N. & Scott B.E.	v Central Districts	Dunedin	2014/15
	59	Wagner N. & Scott B.E.	v Canterbury	Alexandra	2015/16
10th †	67	Smith N.G. & Rae M.D.	v Wellington	Wellington	2020/21

WELLINGTON

1st	222	Fletcher A.T. & Ravindra R.	v Auckland	Lincoln	2019/20
2nd	273	Papps M.H.W. & Murdoch S.J.	v Otago	Wellington	2012/13
3rd †	244*	Fleming S.P. & Twose R.G.	v Otago	Wellington	2000/01
4th	162	Parlane N.R. & Elliott G.D.	v Northern Districts	Wellington	2008/09
5th	137	Blundell T.A. & Neesham J.D.S.	v Canterbury	Wellington	2019/20
6th	122	Franklin J.E.C. & Woodcock L.J.	v Northern Districts	Wellington	2012/13
7th	130*	Bell M.D. & Mather S.R.	v Northern Districts	Mt Maunganui	1997/98
8th	98*	Taylor B.R. & Collinge R.O.	v Central Districts	Lower Hutt	1971/72
9th	98	Doull L.J. & Williams B.R.	v Otago	Alexandra	1993/94
10th	42	Woodcock L.J. & O'Brien I.E.	v Canterbury	Christchurch	2008/09
	42	Gillespie M.R. & McKay A.J.	v Auckland	Wellington	2010/11

† record for all teams

DOMESTIC ONE-DAY CAREER RECORDS

BATTING		M	In	NO	HS	Runs	Ave	100s	50s
Papps M.H.W.	*C, W*	141	140	9	162*	5163	39.41	11	28
Broom N.T.	*C, O*	130	120	13	164	4455	41.63	9	28
Sinclair M.S.	*CD*	143	137	22	123	4398	38.24	3	36
Worker G.H.	*CD, C*	107	106	7	194	4397	44.41	12	26
Parlane M.E.	*ND, W*	153	152	10	132	4225	29.75	5	23
Harris C.Z.	*C*	145	133	45	107	3893	44.23	1	23
Nicol R.J.	*A, C, O*	121	119	10	171*	3864	35.44	5	24
Marshall J.A.H.	*ND*	120	114	10	152*	3755	36.10	5	25
Stewart S.L.	*C*	108	107	9	120	3432	35.02	4	18
Hopkins G.J.	*ND, C, O, A*	156	139	22	142	3401	29.06	4	13
Cumming C.D.	*C , O*	124	117	8	123	3379	31.00	4	19
Nevin C.J.	*W*	136	129	10	149	3339	28.05	5	15
Watling B-J.	*ND*	90	89	11	145*	3288	42.15	7	22
Astle N.J.	*C*	99	90	12	131	3285	42.11	8	16
Fulton P.G.	*C*	113	104	9	116*	3274	34.46	3	25
How J.M.	*CD*	105	103	4	222	3159	31.90	3	20
Bell M.D.	*ND, W*	130	124	10	124	3058	26.82	4	14
Howell L.G.	*C. CD, A, ND*	105	105	14	134*	3022	33.20	5	22

BOWLING		M	O	M	R	W	Ave	R/O	Best
Aldridge G.W.	ND	131	1002.4	66	4844	178	27.21	4.83	5-34
Martin C.S.	C, A	103	854.2	73	4125	150	27.50	4.83	5-21
Harris C.Z.	C	145	1153.4	72	4336	138	31.42	3.76	4-28
Gillespie M.R.	W	81	674.1	42	3491	137	25.48	5.18	6-38
Mason M.J.	CD	96	771.4	85	3305	136	24.30	4.28	6-25
Ellis A.M.	C	109	750.1	44	3903	133	29.34	5.20	5-17
Tait A.R.	ND	90	757.4	75	3138	128	24.51	4.14	4-29
Arnel B.J.	ND, W	92	774	54	3949	128	30.85	5.10	4-26
Hitchcock P.A.	A, W	89	706.5	38	3441	127	27.09	4.87	5-10
Tuffey D.R.	ND, A	100	824.5	63	3750	120	31.25	4.55	4-33
Petrie R.G.	C, W	100	736	58	3146	119	26.43	4.27	5-24
Yovich J.A.F.	ND	111	588.2	26	3172	119	26.65	5.39	4-44
Scott B.E.	O, ND	98	790.4	42	3978	116	34.29	5.03	4-63
McSkimming W.C.	O	89	718.5	61	3413	108	31.60	4.75	5-9
Styris S.B.	ND, A	100	672.3	50	2883	108	26.69	4.29	4-19
Bennett H.K.	C, W	77	557.3	33	2854	108	26.42	5.12	6-45
Priest M.W.	C	89	724.5	69	2668	106	25.16	3.68	5-26
Wagner N.	O, ND	66	549.4	38	3007	106	28.36	5.47	5-34
Adams A.R.	A	66	573.1	42	2473	104	23.77	4.31	5-7
Cairns C.L.	ND, C	91	587.2	39	2412	103	23.41	4.11	6-37
Astle N.J.	C	99	728.2	86	2479	102	24.30	3.40	4-14
Kuggeleijn S.C.	W, ND	66	552.5	32	3132	102	30.70	5.67	5-24
Mills K.D.	A	76	636	64	2693	101	26.66	4.23	4-40
Thompson E.P.	CD	63	518.1	40	2364	100	23.64	4.56	6-20

MOST ECONOMICAL BOWLING *(qualification 100 overs)*

		O	M	R	W	Ave	R/O
Hadlee R.J.	C	174.4	33	440	29	15.17	2.52
Boock S.L.	O	338.2	74	947	47	20.12	2.80
McIntyre J.M.	A	118	25	335	15	22.33	2.84
Webb R.J.	O	117.4	16	344	20	17.20	2.92
Mallender N.A.	O	458.4	83	1356	72	18.83	2.96
Chatfield E.J.	W	305	68	902	50	18.04	2.96

FIELDING		Ct	St	Total
Hopkins G.J.	ND, C, O, A	171	26	197
Nevin C.J.	W	163	13	176
Hart R.G.	ND	117	30	147
de Boorder D.C.	O	116	14	130
McSweeney E.B.	CD, W	97	26	123
Griggs B.B.J.	CD	108	6	114
van Wyk C.F.K.	C, CD	95	12	107
Germon L.K.	C, O	88	18	106
McGlashan P.D.	CD, O, ND	81	15	96
Young R.A.	A, C	78	13	91
Sinclair M.S.	CD	82	1	83
Papps M.H.W.	C, W	78	3	81
Blain T.E.	CD, C	62	15	77
Fletcher C.D.	ND, C	67	9	76
Harris C.Z.	C	74	—	74
Croy M.G.	O	64	9	73
Vincent L.	A	68	3	71

NEW ZEALAND ONE-DAY INTERNATIONAL RECORDS

TEAM RECORDS

Results

1972/73	Pakistan	Christchurch	NZ 187	P 165	*NZ won by 22 runs*
1973	England	Swansea	NZ 158	E 159-3	*England won by 7 wickets*
	England	Manchester	E 167-8		*abandoned*
1973/74	Australia	Dunedin	NZ 194-9	A 195-3	*Australia won by 7 wickets*
	Australia	Christchurch	A 265-5	NZ 234-6	*Australia won by 31 runs*
1974/75	England	Dunedin	E 136	NZ 15-0	*abandoned*
	England	Wellington	NZ 227	E 35-1	*abandoned*
1975	East Africa	Birmingham	NZ 309-5	EA 128-8	*NZ won by 181 runs*
World Cup	England	Nottingham	E 266-6	NZ 186	*England won by 80 runs*
	India	Manchester	I 230-9	NZ 233-6	*NZ won by 4 wickets*
	West Indies	The Oval	NZ 158	WI 159-5	*West Indies won by 5 wickets*
1975/76	India	Christchurch	I 154	NZ 155-1	*NZ won by 9 wickets*
	India	Auckland	NZ 236-8	I 156	*NZ won by 80 runs*
1976/77	Pakistan	Sialkot	NZ 198-8	P 197-9	*NZ won by 1 run*
1978	England	Scarborough	E 206-8	NZ 187-8	*England won by 19 runs*
	England	Manchester	E 278-5	NZ 152	*England won by 126 runs*
1979	Sri Lanka	Nottingham	SL 189	NZ 190-1	*NZ won by 9 wickets*
World Cup	India	Leeds	I 182	NZ 183-2	*NZ won by 8 wickets*
	West Indies	Nottingham	WI 244-7	NZ 212-9	*West Indies won by 32 runs*
	England	Manchester	E 221-8	NZ 212-9	*England won by 9 runs*
1979/80	West Indies	Christchurch	WI 203-7	NZ 207-9	*NZ won by 1 wicket*
1980/81	Australia	Adelaide	A 217-9	NZ 219-7	*NZ won by 3 wickets*
	Australia	Sydney	A 289-3	NZ 195	*Australia won by 94 runs*
	Australia	Melbourne	NZ 156	A 159-6	*Australia won by 4 wickets*
	India	Perth	I 162	NZ 157	*India won by 5 runs*
	India	Brisbane	I 204	NZ 205-7	*NZ won by 3 wickets*
	India	Adelaide	I 230-7	NZ 224	*India won by 6 runs*
	India	Melbourne	I 112-9	NZ 113-0	*NZ won by 10 wickets*
	Australia	Sydney	NZ 220-8	A 219-7	*NZ won by 1 run*
	India	Brisbane	NZ 242-9	I 220	*NZ won by 22 runs*
	Australia	Sydney	A 180	NZ 23-1	*abandoned*
	Australia	Sydney	NZ 233-6	A 155	*NZ won by 78 runs*
	Australia	Melbourne	NZ 126	A 130-3	*Australia won by 7 wickets*
	Australia	Melbourne	A 235-4	NZ 229-8	*Australia won by 6 runs*
	Australia	Sydney	NZ 215-8	A 218-4	*Australia won by 6 wickets*
1980/81	India	Auckland	NZ 218-6	I 140-9	*NZ won by 78 runs*
	India	Hamilton	NZ 210-8	I 153	*NZ won by 57 runs*

1981/82	Australia	Auckland	NZ 240-6	A 194	*NZ won by 46 runs*
	Australia	Dunedin	NZ 159-9	A 160-4	*Australia won by 6 wickets*
	Australia	Wellington	NZ 74	A 75-2	*Australia won by 8 wickets*
1982/83	Australia	Melbourne	NZ 181	A 182-2	*Australia won by 8 wickets*
	England	Melbourne	NZ 239-8	E 237-8	*NZ won by 2 runs*
	England	Brisbane	E 267-6	NZ 213	*England won by 54 runs*
	Australia	Sydney	NZ 226-8	A 179	*NZ won by 47 runs*
	England	Sydney	NZ 199	E 200-2	*England won by 8 wickets*
	Australia	Melbourne	NZ 246-6	A 188	*NZ won by 58 runs*
	England	Adelaide	E 296-5	NZ 297-6	*NZ won by 4 wickets*
	Australia	Adelaide	NZ 200-9	A 153	*NZ won by 47 runs*
	England	Perth	E 88-7	NZ 89-3	*NZ won by 7 wickets*
	Australia	Perth	A 191-9	NZ 164	*Australia won by 27 runs*
	Australia	Sydney	NZ 193-7	A 155-4	*Australia won on faster scoring rate*
	Australia	Melbourne	A 302-8	NZ 153	*Australia won by 149 runs*
1982/83	England	Auckland	E 184	NZ 187-4	*NZ won by 6 wickets*
	England	Wellington	NZ 295-6	E 192	*NZ won by 103 runs*
	England	Christchurch	NZ 211-8	E 127	*NZ won by 84 runs*
	Sri Lanka	Dunedin	NZ 183-8	SL 118-9	*NZ won by 65 runs*
	Australia	Sydney	NZ 138-8	A 124	*NZ won by 14 runs*
	Sri Lanka	Napier	SL 167-8	NZ 168-3	*NZ won by 7 wickets*
	Sri Lanka	Auckland	NZ 304-5	SL 188-6	*NZ won by 116 runs*
1983 *World Cup*	England	The Oval	E 322-6	NZ 216	*England won by 106 runs*
	Pakistan	Birmingham	NZ 238-9	P 186	*NZ won by 52 runs*
	Sri Lanka	Bristol	SL 206	NZ 209-5	*NZ won by 5 wickets*
	England	Birmingham	E 234	NZ 238-8	*NZ won by 2 wickets*
	Sri Lanka	Derby	NZ 181	SL 184-7	*Sri Lanka won by 3 wickets*
	Pakistan	Nottingham	P 261-3	NZ 250	*Pakistan won by 11 runs*
1983/84	England	Christchurch	E 188-9	NZ 134	*England won by 54 runs*
	England	Wellington	NZ 135	E 139-4	*England won by 6 wickets*
	England	Auckland	E 209-9	NZ 210-3	*NZ won by 7 wickets*
1983/84	Sri Lanka	Colombo	NZ 234-6	SL 130	*NZ won by 104 runs*
	Sri Lanka	Moratuwa	SL 157-8	NZ 116	*Sri Lanka won by 41 runs*
	Sri Lanka	Colombo	NZ 201-8	SL 115	*NZ won by 86 runs*
1984/85	Sri Lanka	Colombo	NZ 171-6	SL 174-6	*Sri Lanka won by 4 wickets*
	Sri Lanka	Moratuwa	SL 114-9	NZ 118-3	*NZ won by 7 wickets*
	Pakistan	Peshawar	P 191-5	NZ 145	*Pakistan won by 46 runs*
	Pakistan	Faisalabad	P 157-5	NZ 152-7	*Pakistan won by 5 runs*
	Pakistan	Sialkot	NZ 187-9	P 153-8	*NZ won by 34 runs*
	Pakistan	Multan	NZ 213-8	P 214-9	*Pakistan won by 1 wicket*
1984/85	Pakistan	Napier	NZ 277-6	P 167-9	*NZ won by 110 runs*
	Pakistan	Hamilton	P 221-4	NZ 222-6	*NZ won by 4 wickets*
	Pakistan	Christchurch	NZ 264-8	P 251	*NZ won by 13 runs*
	Pakistan	Auckland	P 189		*abandoned*
1984/85 *World Championship of Cricket*	West Indies	Sydney	NZ 57-2		*abandoned*
	Sri Lanka	Melbourne	NZ 223	SL 172	*NZ won by 51 runs*
	India	Sydney	NZ 206	I 207-3	*India won by 7 wickets*
	West Indies	Sydney	NZ 138-9	WI 139-4	*West Indies won by 6 wickets*

1984/85	West Indies	Antigua	WI 231-8	NZ 208-8	*West Indies won by 23 runs*
	West Indies	Port of Spain	NZ 51-3	WI 55-4	*West Indies won by 6 wickets*
	West Indies	Berbice	WI 259-5	NZ 129	*West Indies won by 130 runs*
	West Indies	Port of Spain	NZ 116	WI 117-0	*West Indies won by 10 wickets*
	West Indies	Bridgetown	WI 265-3	NZ 153-8	*West Indies won by 112 runs*
1985/86	Australia	Melbourne	NZ 161-7		*abandoned*
	India	Brisbane	NZ 259-9	I 263-5	*India won by 5 wickets*
	Australia	Sydney	NZ 152	A 153-6	*Australia won by 4 wickets*
	India	Perth	I 113	NZ 115-7	*NZ won by 3 wickets*
	Australia	Perth	NZ 159-6	A 161-6	*Australia won by 4 wickets*
	India	Melbourne	I 238-8	NZ 239-5	*NZ won by 5 wickets*
	India	Adelaide	NZ 172	I 174-5	*India won by 5 wickets*
	Australia	Adelaide	NZ 276-7	A 70	*NZ won by 206 runs*
	Australia	Sydney	A 239-7	NZ 140	*Australia won by 99 runs*
	India	Launceston	I 202-9	NZ 168-9	*India won by 21 runs (target adjusted)*
1985/86	Australia	Dunedin	NZ 186-6	A 156	*NZ won by 30 runs*
	Australia	Christchurch	NZ 258-7	A 205	*NZ won by 53 runs*
	Australia	Wellington	NZ 229-9	A 232-7	*Australia won by 3 wickets*
	Australia	Auckland	A 231	NZ 187-9	*Australia won by 44 runs*
1985/86	Sri Lanka	Colombo	SL 137-9	NZ 140-4	*NZ won by 6 wickets*
	Pakistan	Colombo	NZ 214-8	P 217-6	*Pakistan won by 4 wickets*
	India	Sharjah	NZ 132-8	I 134-7	*India won by 3 wickets*
	Pakistan	Sharjah	NZ 64	P 66-0	*Pakistan won by 10 wickets*
1986	England	Leeds	NZ 217-8	E 170	*NZ won by 47 runs*
	England	Manchester	NZ 284-5	E 286-4	*England won by 6 wickets*
1986/87	West Indies	Dunedin	WI 237-9	NZ 142	*West Indies won by 95 runs*
	West Indies	Auckland	NZ 213	WI 217-4	*West Indies won by 6 wickets*
	West Indies	Wellington	*abandoned without a ball being bowled*		
	West Indies	Christchurch	NZ 191-9	WI 192-0	*West Indies won by 10 wickets*
1987/88 *World Cup*	Zimbabwe	Hyderabad	NZ 242-7	Z 239	*NZ won by 3 runs*
	India	Bangalore	I 252-7	NZ 236-8	*India won by 16 runs*
	Australia	Indore	A 199-4	NZ 196-9	*Australia won by 3 runs*
	Zimbabwe	Calcutta	Z 227-5	NZ 228-6	*NZ won by 4 wickets*
	Australia	Chandigarh	A 251-8	NZ 234	*Australia won by 17 runs*
	India	Nagpur	NZ 221-9	I 224-1	*India won by 9 wickets*
1987/88	Australia	Perth	NZ 232-9	A 231	*NZ won by 1 run*
	Sri Lanka	Sydney	SL 174	NZ 178-4	*NZ won by 6 wickets*
	Australia	Melbourne	A 216	NZ 210-9	*Australia won by 6 runs*
	Sri Lanka	Adelaide	SL 241	NZ 242-6	*NZ won by 4 wickets*
	Sri Lanka	Hobart	NZ 199-7	SL 200-6	*Sri Lanka won by 4 wickets*
	Sri Lanka	Brisbane	SL 164-8	NZ 167-6	*NZ won by 4 wickets*
	Australia	Brisbane	NZ 176-5	A 177-5	*Australia won by 5 wickets*
	Australia	Sydney	A 221-8	NZ 143	*Australia won by 78 runs*
	Australia	Melbourne	NZ 177	A 180-2	*Australia won by 8 wickets*
	Australia	Sydney	NZ 168-5	A 169-4	*Australia won by 6 wickets*

1987/88	England	Dunedin	NZ 204	E 207-5	*England won by 5 wickets*
	England	Christchurch	NZ 186-8	E 188-4	*England won by 6 wickets*
	England	Napier	E 219	NZ 223-3	*NZ won by 7 wickets*
	England	Auckland	E 208	NZ 211-6	*NZ won by 4 wickets*
1987/88	India	Sharjah	I 267-6	NZ 194-8	*India won by 73 runs*
	Sri Lanka	Sharjah	NZ 258-8	SL 159	*NZ won by 99 runs*
	Sri Lanka	Sharjah	NZ 249-7	SL 206-9	*NZ won by 43 runs*
	India	Sharjah	I 250-7	NZ 198	*India won by 52 runs*
1988/89	India	Visakhapatnam	NZ 196-9	I 197-6	*India won by 4 wickets*
	India	Cuttack	NZ 160-7	I 161-5	*India won by 5 wickets*
	India	Indore	I 222-6	NZ 169-9	*India won by 53 runs*
	India	Baroda	NZ 278-3	I 282-8	*India won by 2 wickets*
	India	Jammu	*abandoned without a ball being bowled*		
1988/89	Pakistan	Dunedin	P 170-9	NZ 174-2	*NZ won by 8 wickets*
	Pakistan	Christchurch	P 170-7	NZ 171-3	*NZ won by 7 wickets*
	Pakistan	Wellington	P 253-6	NZ 254-4	*NZ won by 6 wickets*
	Pakistan	Auckland	NZ 249	P 251-3	*Pakistan won by 7 wickets*
	Pakistan	Hamilton	P 138-9	NZ 139-3	*NZ won by 7 wickets*
1989/90	India	Dunedin	NZ 246-6	I 138	*NZ won by 108 runs*
	Australia	Christchurch	A 244-8	NZ 94	*Australia won by 150 runs*
	India	Wellington	I 221	NZ 220	*India won by 1 run*
	Australia	Auckland	A 239-6	NZ 167-2	*Australia won on faster scoring rate*
	Australia	Auckland	NZ 162	A 164-2	*Australia won by 8 wickets*
1989/90	Australia	Sharjah	A 258-5	NZ 195-7	*Australia won by 63 runs*
	Bangladesh	Sharjah	NZ 338-4	B 177-5	*NZ won by 161 runs*
	Pakistan	Sharjah	NZ 74	P 75-2	*Pakistan won by 8 wickets*
1990	England	Leeds	E 295-6	NZ 298-6	*NZ won by 4 wickets*
	England	The Oval	NZ 212-6	E 213-4	*England won by 6 wickets*
1990/91	Pakistan	Lahore	P 196-8	NZ 177	*Pakistan won by 19 runs*
	Pakistan	Peshawar	NZ 127	P 128-2	*Pakistan won by 8 wickets*
	Pakistan	Sialkot	P 223-2	NZ 118	*Pakistan won by 105 runs*
1990/91	Australia	Sydney	A 236-9	NZ 174-7	*Australia won by 61 runs target reduced*
	England	Adelaide	NZ 199-6	E 192-9	*NZ won by 7 runs*
	Australia	Adelaide	NZ 208-7	A 210-4	*Australia won by 6 wickets*
	England	Perth	NZ 158	E 161-6	*England won by 4 wickets*
	Australia	Melbourne	A 263-7	NZ 224-8	*Australia won by 39 runs*
	England	Sydney	E 194	NZ 161	*England won by 33 runs*
	England	Brisbane	E 203-6	NZ 204-2	*NZ won by 8 wickets*
	Australia	Hobart	NZ 194-6	A 193	*NZ won by 1 run*
	Australia	Sydney	NZ 199-7	A 202-4	*Australia won by 6 wickets*
	Australia	Melbourne	NZ 208-6	A 209-3	*Australia won by 7 wickets*
1990/91	Sri Lanka	Napier	SL 177-8	NZ 178-5	*NZ won by 5 wickets*
	Sri Lanka	Auckland	NZ 242-5	SL 201	*NZ won by 41 runs*
	Sri Lanka	Dunedin	NZ 272-6	SL 165	*NZ won by 107 runs*
	England	Christchurch	E 230-7	NZ 216-8	*England won by 14 runs*
	England	Wellington	NZ 196-8	E 187	*NZ won by 9 runs*
	England	Auckland	NZ 224-7	E 217	*NZ won by 7 runs*

1991/92	England	Auckland	NZ 178-7	E 179-3	*England won by 7 wickets*
	England	Dunedin	NZ 186-7	E 188-7	*England won by 3 wickets*
	England	Christchurch	E 255-7	NZ 184-8	*England won by 71 runs*
1991/92 *World Cup*	Australia	Auckland	NZ 248-6	A 211	*NZ won by 37 runs*
	Sri Lanka	Hamilton	SL 206-9	NZ 210-4	*NZ won by 6 wickets*
	South Africa	Auckland	SA 190-7	NZ 191-3	*NZ won by 7 wickets*
	Zimbabwe	Napier	NZ 163-3	Z 105-7	*NZ won by 49 runs target reduced*
	West Indies	Auckland	WI 203-7	NZ 206-5	*NZ won by 5 wickets*
	India	Dunedin	I 230-6	NZ 231-6	*NZ won by 4 wickets*
	England	Wellington	E 200-8	NZ 201-3	*NZ won by 7 wickets*
	Pakistan	Christchurch	NZ 166	P 167-3	*Pakistan won by 7 wickets*
	Pakistan	Auckland	NZ 262-7	P 264-6	*Pakistan won by 4 wickets*
1992/93	Zimbabwe	Bulawayo	NZ 244-7	Z 222-9	*NZ won by 22 runs*
	Zimbabwe	Harare	Z 271-6	NZ 272-6	*NZ won by 4 wickets*
1992/93	Sri Lanka	Colombo	NZ 166-9	SL 41-2	*abandoned*
	Sri Lanka	Colombo	NZ 190-7	SL 192-2	*SL won by 8 wickets*
	Sri Lanka	Colombo	SL 262-6	NZ 231	*SL won by 31 runs*
1992/93	Pakistan	Wellington	P 158-8	NZ 108	*Pakistan won by 50 runs*
	Pakistan	Napier	P 136-8	NZ 137-4	*NZ won by 6 wickets*
	Pakistan	Auckland	P 139	NZ 140-4	*NZ won by 6 wickets*
1992/93	Australia	Dunedin	A 258-4	NZ 129	*Australia won by 129 runs*
	Australia	Christchurch	NZ 196-8	A 197-9	*Australia won by 1 wicket*
	Australia	Wellington	NZ 214	A 126	*NZ won by 88 runs*
	Australia	Hamilton	A 247-7	NZ 250-7	*NZ won by 3 wickets*
	Australia	Auckland	A 232-8	NZ 229-8	*Australia won by 3 runs*
1993/94	South Africa	Adelaide	*abandoned without a ball being bowled*		
	Australia	Adelaide	NZ 135	A 136-2	*Australia won by 8 wickets*
	Australia	Melbourne	A 202-5	NZ 199-9	*Australia won by 3 runs*
	South Africa	Hobart	SA 147-7	NZ 148-6	*NZ won by 4 wickets*
	South Africa	Brisbane	NZ 256-7	SA 219-8	*NZ won by 9 runs target reduced*
	Australia	Sydney	NZ 198-9	A 185	*NZ won by 13 runs*
	South Africa	Perth	NZ 150	SA 151-5	*SA won by 5 wickets*
	Australia	Melbourne	A 217-3	NZ 166	*Australia won by 51 runs*
1993/94	Pakistan	Dunedin	NZ 122-9	P 123-5	*Pakistan won by 5 wickets*
	Pakistan	Auckland	P 146	NZ 110	*Pakistan won by 36 runs*
	Pakistan	Wellington	P 213-6	NZ 202-8	*Pakistan won by 11 runs*
	Pakistan	Auckland	P 161-9	NZ 161	*Tie*
	Pakistan	Christchurch	P 145-9	NZ 146-3	*NZ won by 7 wickets*
	India	Napier	NZ 240-5	I 212-9	*NZ won by 28 runs*
	India	Auckland	NZ 142	I 143-3	*India won by 7 wickets*
	India	Wellington	I 255-5	NZ 243-9	*India won by 12 runs*
	India	Christchurch	I 222-6	NZ 223-4	*NZ won by 6 wickets*
1993/94	Australia	Sharjah	NZ 207-9	A 208-3	*Australia won by 7 wickets*
	Sri Lanka	Sharjah	NZ 217-8	SL 215-9	*NZ won by 2 runs*
	Pakistan	Sharjah	P 328-2	NZ 266-7	*Pakistan won by 62 runs*
1994	England	Birmingham	E 224-8	NZ 182	*England won by 42 runs*
	England	Lord's	*abandoned without a ball being bowled*		

1994/95	West Indies	Goa	WI 123	NZ 25-1	*abandoned*
	India	Baroda	NZ 269-4	I 271-3	*India won by 7 wickets*
	West Indies	Guwahati	WI 306-6	NZ 171-9	*West Indies won by 135 runs*
	India	Delhi	I 289-3	NZ 182	*India won by 107 runs*
1994/95	South Africa	Cape Town	SA 203-8	NZ 134	*South Africa won by 69 runs*
	Sri Lanka	Bloemfontein	SL 288-4	NZ 66-1	*abandoned*
	South Africa	Verwoerdburg	SA 314-7	NZ 233	*South Africa won by 81 runs*
	Pakistan	Port Elizabeth	NZ 201	P 206-5	*Pakistan won by 5 wickets*
	Sri Lanka	East London	NZ 255-4	SL 257-5	*Sri Lanka won by 5 wickets*
	Pakistan	East London	NZ 172	P 175-5	*Pakistan won by 5 wickets*
1994/95	West Indies	Auckland	NZ 167-6	WI 149-1	*West Indies won by 9 wickets target reduced*
	West Indies	Wellington	WI 246-7	NZ 205	*West Indies won by 41 runs*
	West Indies	Christchurch	NZ 146	WI 149-1	*West Indies won by 9 wickets*
1994/95	India	Napier	I 160	NZ 162-6	*NZ won by 4 wickets*
	Australia	Auckland	A 254-5	NZ 227-9	*Australia won by 27 runs*
	South Africa	Christchurch	NZ 249-7	SA 203	*NZ won by 46 runs*
	Australia	Auckland	NZ 137-9	A 138-4	*Australia won by 6 wickets*
1994/95	Sri Lanka	Christchurch	NZ 271-6	SL 238	*NZ won by 33 runs*
	Sri Lanka	Hamilton	NZ 280-6	SL 117-6	*NZ won by 57 runs target reduced*
	Sri Lanka	Auckland	SL 250-6	NZ 199	*Sri Lanka won by 51 runs*
1995/96	India	Jamshedpur	I 236	NZ 237-2	*NZ won by 8 wickets*
	India	Amritsar	NZ 145	I 146-4	*India won by 6 wickets*
	India	Goa	*abandoned without a ball being bowled*		
	India	Pune	NZ 235-6	I 236-5	*India won by 5 wickets*
	India	Nagpur	NZ 348-8	I 249	*NZ won by 99 runs*
	India	Bombay	NZ 126	I 128-4	*India won by 6 wickets*
1995/96	Pakistan	Dunedin	P 189-9	NZ 169	*Pakistan won by 20 runs*
	Pakistan	Christchurch	P 232-9	NZ 236-9	*NZ won by 1 wicket*
	Pakistan	Wellington	P 261-4	NZ 207	*Pakistan won by 54 runs*
	Pakistan	Auckland	NZ 244-8	P 212	*NZ won by 32 runs*
1995/96	Zimbabwe	Auckland	NZ 278-5	Z 204	*NZ won by 74 runs*
	Zimbabwe	Wellington	Z 181-9	NZ 184-4	*NZ won by 6 wickets*
	Zimbabwe	Napier	Z 267-7	NZ 246	*Zimbabwe won by 21 runs*
1995/96	England	Ahmedabad	NZ 239-6	E 228-9	*NZ won by 11 runs*
World Cup	Holland	Baroda	NZ 307-8	H 188-7	*NZ won by 119 runs*
	South Africa	Faisalabad	NZ 177-9	SA 178-5	*Sth Africa won by 5 wickets*
	UAE	Faisalabad	NZ 276-8	UAE 167-9	*NZ won by 109 runs*
	Pakistan	Lahore	P 281-5	NZ 235	*Pakistan won by 46 runs*
	Australia	Madras	NZ 286-9	A 289-4	*Australia won by 6 wickets*
1995/96	West Indies	Kingston	NZ 243	WI 247-9	*West Indies won by 1 wicket*
	West Indies	Port of Spain	WI 238-7	NZ 239-6	*NZ won by 4 wickets*
	West Indies	Port of Spain	NZ 219-8	WI 225-3	*West Indies won by 7 wickets*
	West Indies	Georgetown	NZ 158	WI 154	*NZ won by 4 runs*
	West Indies	Arnos Vale	NZ 241-8	WI 242-3	*West Indies won by 7 wickets*
1996/97	Sri Lanka	Sharjah	NZ 206-8	SL 177	*NZ won by 29 runs*
	Pakistan	Sharjah	NZ 197	P 198-6	*Pakistan won by 4 wickets*
	Sri Lanka	Sharjah	NZ 169-8	SL 169	*Tie*
	Pakistan	Sharjah	NZ 192	P 196-6	*Pakistan won by 4 wickets*
	Pakistan	Sharjah	P 160	NZ 119	*Pakistan won by 41 runs*

1996/97	Pakistan	Gujranwala	P 228-8	NZ 217	*Pakistan won by 11 runs*
	Pakistan	Sialkot	P 277-9	NZ 231	*Pakistan won by 46 runs*
	Pakistan	Karachi	P 234-4	NZ 235-3	*NZ won by 7 wickets*
1996/97	England	Christchurch	NZ 222-6	E 226-6	*England won by 4 wickets*
	England	Auckland	NZ 253-8	E 134-4	*England won by 6 wickets target reduced*
	England	Napier	NZ 237	E 237-8	*Tie*
	England	Auckland	NZ 153	E 144	*NZ won by 9 runs*
	England	Wellington	NZ 228-8	E 200	*NZ won by 28 runs*
1996/97	Sri Lanka	Auckland	*abandoned without a ball being bowled*		
	Sri Lanka	Christchurch	NZ 201-9	SL 202-4	*Sri Lanka won by 6 wickets*
	Sri Lanka	Wellington	NZ 201	SL 132	*NZ won by 69 runs*
1996/97	Pakistan	Mohali	NZ 285-7	P 263-9	*NZ won by 22 runs*
	India	Bangalore	NZ 220-9	I 221-2	*India won by 8 wickets*
	Sri Lanka	Hyderabad	SL 214	NZ 162	*Sri Lanka won by 52 runs*
1997/98	Zimbabwe	Bulawayo	Z 233-8	NZ 233-9	*Tie*
	Zimbabwe	Harare	NZ 185-7	Z 188-7	*Zimbabwe won by 3 wickets*
	Zimbabwe	Harare	NZ 294-7	Z 211	*NZ won by 83 runs*
1997/98	South Africa	Adelaide	NZ 224-6	SA 177	*NZ won by 47 runs*
	Australia	Adelaide	NZ 260-7	A 263-7	*Australia won by 3 wickets*
	South Africa	Hobart	SA 174-9	NZ 173-7	*South Africa won by 1 run*
	Australia	Melbourne	NZ 141	A 142-4	*Australia won by 6 wickets*
	South Africa	Brisbane	SA 300-6	NZ 298-9	*South Africa won by 2 runs*
	Australia	Sydney	A 250	NZ 119	*Australia won by 131 runs*
	South Africa	Perth	SA 233-7	NZ 166	*South Africa won by 67 runs*
	Australia	Melbourne	A 251-4	NZ 253-6	*NZ won by 4 wickets*
1997/98	Zimbabwe	Hamilton	NZ 248-7	Z 208	*NZ won by 40 runs*
	Zimbabwe	Wellington	Z 138	NZ 139-2	*NZ won by 8 wickets*
	Australia	Christchurch	NZ 212-7	A 215-3	*Australia won by 7 wickets*
	Australia	Wellington	A 297-6	NZ 231	*Australia won by 66 runs*
	Australia	Napier	A 236	NZ 240-3	*NZ won by 7 wickets*
	Australia	Auckland	NZ 223-7	A 193	*NZ won by 30 runs*
	Zimbabwe	Christchurch	Z 228-7	NZ 227-9	*Zimbabwe won by 1 run*
	Zimbabwe	Napier	Z 207-8	NZ 211-1	*NZ won by 9 wickets*
	Zimbabwe	Auckland	NZ 231-9	Z 229-9	*NZ won by 2 runs*
1997/98	India	Sharjah	I 220-9	NZ 205	*India won by 15 runs*
	Australia	Sharjah	NZ 159	A 160-4	*Australia won by 6 wickets*
	India	Sharjah	I 181	NZ 183-6	*NZ won by 4 wickets*
	Australia	Sharjah	NZ 259-5	A 261-5	*Australia won by 5 wickets*
1997/98	Sri Lanka	Colombo	NZ 200-9	SL 201-3	*Sri Lanka won by 7 wickets*
	India	Colombo	NZ 219-8	I 131-3	*abandoned*
	Sri Lanka	Galle	*abandoned without a ball being bowled*		
	India	Galle	*abandoned without a ball being bowled*		
	India	Colombo	NZ 128-5		*abandoned*
	Sri Lanka	Colombo	SL 293-4	NZ 206	*Sri Lanka won by 87 runs*
1998/99	Zimbabwe	Dhaka	Z 258-7	NZ 260-5	*NZ won by 5 wickets*
ICC Knockout	Sri Lanka	Dhaka	NZ 188	SL 191-5	*Sri Lanka won by 5 wickets*

Season	Opponent	Venue	Score	Score	Result
1998/99	India	Taupo	I 257-5	NZ 200-5	*NZ won by 5 wickets (D/L)*
	India	Napier	NZ 213	I 214-8	*India won by 2 wickets*
	India	Wellington	I 208-4	NZ 89-2	*abandoned*
	India	Auckland	NZ 207-7	I 208-5	*India won by 5 wickets*
	India	Christchurch	NZ 300-8	I 230	*NZ won by 70 runs*
1998/99	South Africa	Dunedin	SA 211	NZ 215-7	*NZ won by 3 wickets*
	South Africa	Christchurch	NZ 220-9	SA 224-3	*SA won by 7 wickets*
	South Africa	Auckland	SA 212-7	NZ 215-3	*NZ won by 7 wickets*
	South Africa	Napier	NZ 257-8	SA 10-0	*abandoned*
	South Africa	Napier	NZ 191	SA 194-8	*SA won by 2 wickets*
	South Africa	Auckland	SA 290-5	NZ 147	*SA won by 143 runs*
	South Africa	Wellington	SA 249-4		*abandoned*
1999 *World Cup*	Bangladesh	Chelmsford	B 116	NZ 117-4	*NZ won by 6 wickets*
	Australia	Cardiff	A 213-8	NZ 214-5	*NZ won by 5 wickets*
	West Indies	Southampton	NZ 156	WI 158-3	*WI won by 7 wickets*
	Pakistan	Derby	P 269-8	NZ 207-8	*Pakistan won by 62 runs*
	Scotland	Edinburgh	S 121	NZ 123-4	*NZ won by 6 wickets*
	Zimbabwe	Leeds	Z 175	NZ 70-3	*abandoned*
	South Africa	Birmingham	SA 287-5	NZ 213-8	*SA won by 74 runs*
	India	Nottingham	I 251-6	NZ 253-5	*NZ won by 5 wickets*
	Pakistan	Manchester	NZ 241-7	P 242-1	*Pakistan won by 9 wickets*
1999/00	India	Rajkot	NZ 349-9	I 306	*NZ won by 43 runs*
	India	Hyderabad	I 376-2	NZ 202	*India won by 174 runs*
	India	Gwalior	I 261-5	NZ 247-8	*India won by 14 runs*
	India	Guwahati	NZ 236-9	I 188	*NZ won by 48 runs*
	India	Delhi	NZ 179-9	I 181-3	*India won by 7 wickets*
1999/00	West Indies	Auckland	WI 268-7	NZ 250-7	*NZ won by 3 wickets (D/L)*
	West Indies	Taupo	WI 192	NZ 194-3	*NZ won by 7 wickets*
	West Indies	Napier	WI 159	NZ 160-6	*NZ won by 4 wickets*
	West Indies	Wellington	WI 171-9	NZ 172-2	*NZ won by 8 wickets*
	West Indies	Christchurch	NZ 302-6	WI 282	*NZ won by 20 runs*
1999/00	Australia	Wellington	A 119-1	NZ	*abandoned*
	Australia	Auckland	NZ 122	A 123-5	*Australia won by 5 wickets*
	Australia	Dunedin	A 310-4	NZ 260	*Australia won by 50 runs*
	Australia	Christchurch	A 349-6	NZ 301-9	*Australia won by 48 runs*
	Australia	Napier	NZ 243-9	A 245-5	*Australia won by 5 wickets*
	Australia	Auckland	A 191	NZ 194-3	*NZ won by 7 wickets*
2000/01	Pakistan	Singapore	P 191-6	NZ 179	*Pakistan won by 12 runs*
	South Africa	Singapore	NZ 158	SA 159-2	*SA won by 8 wickets*
2000/01	Zimbabwe	Harare	Z 183-8	NZ 184-3	*NZ won by 7 wickets*
	Zimbabwe	Bulawayo	Z 273-5	NZ 252	*Zimbabwe won by 21 runs*
	Zimbabwe	Bulawayo	NZ 264-8	Z 268-4	*Zimbabwe won by 6 wkts*
2000/01 *ICC Knockout*	Zimbabwe	Nairobi	NZ 265-7	Z 201	*NZ won by 64 runs*
	Pakistan	Nairobi	P 252	NZ 255-6	*NZ won by 4 wickets*
	India	Nairobi	I 264-6	NZ 265-6	*NZ won by 4 wickets*
2000/01	South Africa	Potchefstroom	SA 191-2	NZ	*abandoned*
	South Africa	Benoni	NZ 194-8	SA 197-4	*SA won by 6 wkts*
	South Africa	Centurion	SA 324-4	NZ 189	*SA won by 115 runs (D/L)*
	South Africa	Kimberley	NZ 287-6	SA 289-5	*SA won by 5 wickets*
	South Africa	Durban	NZ 114-5	SA 158-4	*SA won by 6 wickets(D/L)*
	South Africa	Cape Town	NZ 256-9	SA 258-7	*SA won by 3 wickets*

2000/01	Zimbabwe	Taupo	Z 300-7	NZ 210	*Zimbabwe won by 70 runs (D/L)*
	Zimbabwe	Wellington	Z 236-7	NZ 237-2	*NZ won by 8 wickets*
	Zimbabwe	Auckland	NZ 273-9	Z 274-9	*Zimbabwe won by 1 wicket*
2000/01	Sri Lanka	Napier	SL 213-8	NZ 152	*Sri Lanka won by 61 runs*
	Sri Lanka	Wellington	NZ 205-8	SL 209-7	*Sri Lanka won by 3 wickets*
	Sri Lanka	Auckland	NZ 181	SL 182-1	*Sri Lanka won by 9 wickets*
	Sri Lanka	Hamilton	NZ 182-9	SL 155-5	*Sri Lanka won by 3 runs (D/L)*
	Sri Lanka	Christchurch	NZ 282-6	SL 269	*NZ won by 13 runs*
2000/01	Pakistan	Auckland	NZ 149	P 150-4	*Pakistan won by 6 wickets*
	Pakistan	Napier	P 135	NZ 136-4	*NZ won by 6 wickets*
	Pakistan	Wellington	P 243-9	NZ 215	*Pakistan won by 28 runs*
	Pakistan	Christchurch	NZ 284-5	P 146	*NZ won by 138 runs*
	Pakistan	Dunedin	P 285	NZ 290-6	*NZ won by 4 wickets*
2000/01	Sri Lanka	Sharjah	SL 269-9	NZ 163	*Sri Lanka won by 106 runs*
	Pakistan	Sharjah	NZ 266-7	P 270-2	*Pakistan won by 8 wickets*
	Pakistan	Sharjah	NZ 127	P 131-3	*Pakistan won by 7 wickets*
	Sri Lanka	Sharjah	NZ 248-6	SL 169-8	*NZ won by 79 runs*
2001/02	Sri Lanka	Colombo	SL 220	NZ 204-9	*Sri Lanka won by 16 runs*
	India	Colombo	NZ 211-8	I 127	*NZ won by 84 runs*
	Sri Lanka	Colombo	NZ 236-8	SL 240-5	*Sri Lanka won by 5 wickets*
	India	Colombo	NZ 200	I 133	*NZ won by 67 runs*
	Sri Lanka	Colombo	SL 221-6	NZ 115-9	*Sri Lanka won by 106 runs*
	India	Colombo	NZ 264-7	I 267-3	*India won by 7 wickets*
2001/02	Australia	Melbourne	NZ 199-8	A 176	*NZ won by 23 runs*
	South Africa	Hobart	SA 257-7	NZ 231-9	*SA won by 26 runs*
	Australia	Sydney	NZ 235-9	A 212	*NZ won by 23 runs*
	South Africa	Brisbane	SA 241	NZ 244-6	*NZ won by 4 wickets*
	Australia	Adelaide	NZ 242-5	A 165	*NZ won by 77 runs*
	South Africa	Adelaide	SA 253-5	NZ 160	*SA won by 93 runs*
	Australia	Melbourne	NZ 245-8	A 248-8	*Australia won by 2 wickets*
	South Africa	Perth	SA 270-5	NZ 203-8	*SA won by 67 runs*
	South Africa	Melbourne	NZ 190	SA 191-2	*SA won by 8 wickets*
	South Africa	Sydney	NZ 175	SA 173-4	*SA won by 6 wickets (D/L)*
2001/02	England	Christchurch	E 196	NZ 198-6	*NZ won by 4 wickets*
	England	Wellington	NZ 244-8	E 89	*NZ won by 155 runs*
	England	Napier	E 244-5	NZ 201	*England won by 43 runs*
	England	Auckland	E 193-6	NZ 189	*England won by 33 runs (D/L)*
	England	Dunedin	E 218-8	NZ 223-5	*NZ won by 5 wickets*
2001/02	Sri Lanka	Sharjah	NZ 218-8	SL 207	*NZ won by 11 runs*
	Pakistan	Sharjah	P 288-6	NZ 237-8	*Pakistan won by 51 runs*
	Sri Lanka	Sharjah	SL 243-9	NZ 197-9	*Sri Lanka won by 46 runs*
	Pakistan	Sharjah	NZ 213-9	P 217-2	*Pakistan won by 8 wickets*
2001/02	Pakistan	Karachi	P 275-6	NZ 122	*Pakistan won by 153 runs*
	Pakistan	Rawalpindi	NZ 277-5	P 278-7	*Pakistan won by 3 wickets*
	Pakistan	Lahore	P 278-5	NZ 212	*Pakistan won by 66 runs*
2001/02	West Indies	Kingston	NZ 176	WI	*abandoned*
	West Indies	Gros Islet	NZ 248-7	WI 250-4	*West Indies won by 6 wickets*
	West Indies	Gros Islet	NZ 210-7	WI 211-3	*West Indies won by 7 wickets*
	West Indies	Port of Spain	NZ 212-5	WI 202-9	*NZ won by 9 runs (D/L)*
	West Indies	Arnos Vale	NZ 291-8	WI 292-6	*West Indies won by 4 wickets*

2002/03	Australia	Colombo	A 296-7	NZ 132	*Australia won by 164 runs*
Champions Trophy	Bangladesh	Colombo	NZ 244-9	B 77	*NZ won by 167 runs*
2002/03	India	Auckland	I 108	NZ 109-7	*NZ won by 3 wickets*
	India	Napier	NZ 254-9	I 219	*NZ won by 35 runs*
	India	Christchurch	I 108	NZ 109-5	*NZ won by 5 wickets*
	India	Queenstown	I 122	NZ 123-3	*NZ won by 7 wickets*
	India	Wellington	NZ 168	I 169-8	*India won by 2 wickets*
	India	Auckland	NZ 199-9	I 200-9	*India won by 1 wicket*
	India	Hamilton	I 122	NZ 125-4	*NZ won by 6 wickets*
2002/03	Sri Lanka	Bloemfontein	SL 272-7	NZ 225	*Sri Lanka won by 47 runs*
World	West Indies	Port Elizabeth	NZ 241-7	WI 221	*NZ won by 20 runs*
Cup	South Africa	Johannesburg	SL 306-6	NZ 229-1	*NZ won by 9 wickets (D/L)*
	Kenya	Nairobi			*NZ forfeited the match*
	Bangladesh	Kimberley	B 198-7	NZ 199-3	*NZ won by 7 wickets*
	Canada	Benoni	C 196	NZ 197-5	*NZ won by 5 wickets*
	Zimbabwe	Bloemfontein	Z 252-7	NZ 253-4	*NZ won by 6 wickets*
	Australia	Port Elizabeth	A 208-9	NZ 112	*Australia won by 96 runs*
	India	Centurion	NZ 146	I 150-3	*India won by 7 wickets*
2002/03	Pakistan	Dambulla	P 116	NZ 117-3	*NZ won by 7 wickets*
	Sri Lanka	Dambulla	NZ 139	SL 143-5	*Sri Lanka won by 5 wickets*
	Sri Lanka	Dambulla	NZ 156-8	SL 147	*NZ won by 9 runs*
	Pakistan	Dambulla	P 203-9	NZ 181	*Pakistan won by 22 runs*
	Pakistan	Dambulla	P 198	NZ 200-6	*NZ won by 4 wickets*
2003/04	India	Chennai	I 141-3	NZ	*abandoned*
	Australia	Faridabad	NZ 97	A 101-2	*Australia won by 8 wickets*
	Australia	Pune	NZ 258-9	A 259-8	*Australia won by 2 wickets*
	India	Cuttack	I 246-6	NZ 249-6	*NZ won by 4 wickets*
	Australia	Guwahati	A 225-7	NZ 181	*Australia won by 44 runs*
	India	Hyderabad	I 353-5	NZ 208	*India won by 145 runs*
2003/04	Pakistan	Lahore	NZ 291-5	P 292-7	*Pakistan won by 3 wickets*
	Pakistan	Lahore	P 281-6	NZ 157	*Pakistan won by 124 runs*
	Pakistan	Faisalabad	P 314-7	NZ 263-7	*Pakistan won by 51 runs*
	Pakistan	Rawalpindi	NZ 183	P 184-3	*Pakistan won by 7 wickets*
	Pakistan	Rawalpindi	P 277-4	NZ 228-6	*Pakistan won by 49 runs*
2003/04	Pakistan	Auckland	P 229-7	NZ 230-6	*NZ won by 4 wickets*
	Pakistan	Queenstown	NZ 235-8	P 236-4	*Pakistan won by 6 wickets*
	Pakistan	Christchurch	P 255-9	NZ 259-3	*NZ won by 7 wickets*
	Pakistan	Napier	P 126	NZ 127-2	*NZ won by 8 wickets*
	Pakistan	Wellington	NZ 307-8	P 303	*NZ won by 4 runs*
2003/04	South Africa	Auckland	NZ 225-8	SA 226-5	*SA won by 5 wickets*
	South Africa	Christchurch	SA 253-8	NZ 255-5	*NZ won by 5 wickets*
	South Africa	Wellington	NZ 254-5	SA 249-7	*NZ won by 5 runs*
	South Africa	Dunedin	SA 259-7	NZ 264-4	*NZ won by 6 wickets*
	South Africa	Auckland	NZ 193-8	SA 175-5	*NZ won by 2 runs (D/L)*
	South Africa	Napier	SA 186-9	NZ 190-5	*NZ won by 5 wickets*
2004	England	Manchester	*abandoned without a ball being bowled*		
	West Indies	Birmingham	WI 122-4	NZ 97-2	*abandoned*
	England	Chester-le-Street	E 101	NZ 103-3	*NZ won by 7 wickets*
	West Indies	Cardiff	WI 216	NZ 220-5	*NZ won by 5 wickets*
	England	Bristol	E 237-7	NZ 241-4	*NZ won by 6 wickets*
	West Indies	Southampton	*abandoned without a ball being bowled*		
	West Indies	Lord's	NZ 266	WI 159	*NZ won by 107 runs*

2004	USA	The Oval	NZ 347-4	USA 137	*NZ won by 210 runs*
Champions Trophy	Australia	The Oval	NZ 198	A 199-3	*Australia won by 7 wickets*
2004/05	Bangladesh	Chittagong	NZ 224	B 86	*NZ won by 138 runs*
	Bangladesh	Dhaka	B 146	NZ 148-7	*NZ won by 3 wickets*
	Bangladesh	Dhaka	NZ 250-7	B 167-7	*NZ won by 83 runs*
2004/05	Australia	Melbourne	A 246-9	NZ 247-6	*NZ won by 4 wickets*
	Australia	Sydney	A 261-7	NZ 244	*Australia won by 17 runs*
	Australia	Brisbane	*abandoned without a ball being bowled*		
2004/05	Sri Lanka	Auckland	SL 141	NZ 144-3	*NZ won by 7 wickets*
2004/05	Australia	Wellington	A 236-7	NZ 226	*Australia won by 10 runs*
	Australia	Christchurch	A 314-6	NZ 208	*Australia won by 106 runs*
	Australia	Auckland	A 264-5	NZ 178	*Australia won by 86 runs*
	Australia	Wellington	NZ 233	A 236-3	*Australia won by 7 wickets*
	Australia	Napier	A 347-5	NZ 225-8	*Australia won by 122 runs*
2005/06	Zimbabwe	Bulawayo	NZ 397-5	Z 205	*NZ won by 192 runs*
	India	Bulawayo	NZ 215	I 164	*NZ won by 51 runs*
	Zimbabwe	Harare	NZ 238	Z 211	*NZ won by 27 runs*
	India	Harare	NZ 278-9	I 279-4	*India won by 6 wickets*
	India	Harare	I 276	NZ 278-4	*NZ won by 6 wickets*
2005/06	South Africa	Bloemfontein	NZ 249-8	SA 250-8	*SA won by 2 wickets*
	South Africa	Cape Town	SA 201-9	NZ 182	*SA won by 19 runs*
	South Africa	Port Elizabeth	NZ 243-9	SA 245-6	*SA won by 4 wickets*
	South Africa	Durban	SA 79-2	NZ	*abandoned*
	South Africa	Centurion	NZ 215	SA 140-5	*SA won by 5 wickets (D/L)*
2005/06	Australia	Auckland	A 252-8	NZ 105	*Australia won by 147 runs*
	Australia	Wellington	A 322-5	NZ 320	*Australia won by 2 runs*
	Australia	Christchurch	A 331-7	NZ 332-8	*NZ won by 2 wickets*
2005/06	Sri Lanka	Queenstown	SL 164	NZ 166-3	*NZ won by 7 wickets*
	Sri Lanka	Christchurch	SL 255-7	NZ 256-5	*NZ won by 5 wickets*
	Sri Lanka	Wellington	NZ 224-9	SL 203	*NZ won by 21 runs*
	Sri Lanka	Napier	SL 273-6	NZ 253	*Sri Lanka won by 20 runs*
2005/06	West Indies	Wellington	NZ 288-9	WI 207	*NZ won by 81 runs*
	West Indies	Queenstown	WI 200-9	NZ 204-7	*NZ won by 3 wickets*
	West Indies	Christchurch	NZ 276-6	WI 255	*NZ won by 21 runs*
	West Indies	Napier	NZ 324-6	WI 233-8	*NZ won by 91 runs*
	West Indies	Auckland	NZ 233	WI 234-7	*West Indies won by 3 wickets*
2006/07	South Africa	Mumbai	NZ 195	SA 108	*NZ won by 87 runs*
Champions Trophy	Sri Lanka	Mumbai	NZ 165	SL 166-3	*Sri Lanka won by 7 wkts*
	Pakistan	Chandigarh	NZ 274-7	P 223	*NZ won by 51 runs*
	Australia	Chandigarh	A 240-9	NZ 206	*Australia won by 34 runs*
2006/07	Sri Lanka	Napier	NZ 285-8	SL 289-3	*Sri Lanka won by 7 wickets*
	Sri Lanka	Queenstown	SL 224-7	NZ 228-9	*NZ won by 1 wicket*
	Sri Lanka	Christchurch	SL 112	NZ 110-6	*NZ won by 4 wickets (D/L)*
	Sri Lanka	Auckland	SL 262-6	NZ 73	*Sri Lanka won by 189 runs*
	Sri Lanka	Hamilton	*abandoned without a ball being bowled*		
2006/07	Australia	Hobart	A 289-8	NZ 184	*Australia won by 105 runs*
	England	Hobart	NZ 205-9	E 206-7	*England won by 3 wickets*
	Australia	Sydney	NZ 218	A 224-8	*Australia won by 2 wickets*
	England	Adelaide	NZ 210	E 120	*NZ won by 90 runs*
	Australia	Perth	A 343-5	NZ 335-5	*Australia won by 8 runs*

	England	Perth	NZ 318-7	E 260-8	*NZ won by 58 runs*
	Australia	Melbourne	NZ 290-7	A 291-5	*Australia won by 5 wickets*
	England	Brisbane	E 270-7	NZ 256-8	*England won by 14 runs*
2006/07	Australia	Wellington	A 148	NZ 149-0	*NZ won by 10 wickets*
	Australia	Auckland	A 336-4	NZ 340-5	*NZ won by 5 wickets*
	Australia	Hamilton	A 346-5	NZ 350-9	*NZ won by 1 wicket*
2006/07	England	Gros Islet	E 209-7	NZ 210-4	*NZ won by 6 wickets*
World Cup	Kenya	Gros Islet	NZ 331-7	K 183	*NZ won by 148 runs*
	Canada	Gros Islet	NZ 363-5	C 249	*NZ won by 114 runs*
	West Indies	Antigua	WI 177	NZ 179-3	*NZ won by 7 wickets*
	Bangladesh	Antigua	B 174	NZ 178-1	*NZ won by 9 wickets*
	Ireland	Guyana	NZ 263-8	I 134	*NZ won by 129 runs*
	Sri Lanka	Grenada	NZ 219-7	SL 222-4	*Sri Lanka won by 6 wickets*
	South Africa	Grenada	SA 193-7	NZ 196-5	*NZ won by 5 wickets*
	Australia	Grenada	A 348-6	NZ 133	*Australia won by 215 runs*
	Sri Lanka	Kingston	SL 289-5	NZ 208	*Sri Lanka won by 81 runs*
2007/08	South Africa	Durban	NZ 248-6	SA 249-8	*South Africa won by 2 wickets*
	South Africa	Port Elizabeth	SA 209-9	NZ 210-3	*NZ won by 7 wickets*
	South Africa	Cape Town	NZ 238-8	SA 242-5	*South Africa won by 5 wickets*
2007/08	Australia	Adelaide	NZ 254-7	A 255-3	*Australia won by 7 wickets*
	Australia	Sydney	NZ 30-3		*abandoned*
	Australia	Hobart	A 282-6	NZ 168	*Australia won by 114 runs*
2007/08	Bangladesh	Auckland	B 201	NZ 203-4	*NZ won by 6 wickets*
	Bangladesh	Napier	NZ 335-5	B 181-6	*NZ won by 102 runs (D/L)*
	Bangladesh	Queenstown	B 93	NZ 95-0	*NZ won by 10 wickets*
2007/08	England	Wellington	E 130	NZ 131-4	*NZ won by 6 wickets*
	England	Hamilton	E 158	NZ 165-0	*NZ won by 10 wickets (D/L)*
	England	Auckland	NZ 234-9	E 229-4	*England won by 6 wickets (D/L)*
	England	Napier	E 340-6	NZ 340-7	*Tie*
	England	Christchurch	E 242-7	NZ 213-6	*NZ won by 34 runs (D/L)*
2008	England	Chester-le-Street	E 307-5	NZ 193	*England won by 114 runs*
	England	Birmingham	E 162	NZ 127-2	*abandoned*
	England	Bristol	NZ 182	E 160	*NZ won by 22 runs*
	England	The Oval	E 245	NZ 246-9	*NZ won by 1 wicket*
	England	Lord's	NZ 266-5	E 215	*NZ won by 51 runs*
	Ireland	Aberdeen	NZ 402-2	I 112	*NZ won by 290 runs*
	Scotland	Aberdeen	S 101	NZ 102-2	*NZ won by 8 wickets*
2008/09	Bangladesh	Mirpur	NZ 201-9	B 202-3	*Bangladesh won by 7 wickets*
	Bangladesh	Mirpur	NZ 212-9	B 137	*NZ won by 75 runs*
	Bangladesh	Chittagong	NZ 249-7	B 170-8	*NZ won by 79 runs*
2008/09	West Indies	Queenstown	WI 129-5		*abandoned*
	West Indies	Christchurch	NZ 152-8	WI 158-5	*West Indies by 5 wks (D/L)*
	West Indies	Wellington	WI 128	NZ 129-3	*NZ won by 7 wickets*
	West Indies	Auckland	NZ 275-4	WI 64-0	*abandoned*
	West Indies	Napier	WI 293-9	NZ 211-5	*NZ won by 9 runs (D/L)*
2008/09	Australia	Perth	A 181	NZ 182-8	*NZ won by 2 wickets*
	Australia	Melbourne	A 225-5	NZ 226-4	*NZ won by 6 wickets*
	Australia	Sydney	A 301-9	NZ 269	*Australia won by 32 runs*
	Australia	Adelaide	NZ 244-8	A 247-4	*Australia won by 6 wickets*
	Australia	Brisbane	A 168-4	NZ 123-6	*abandoned*

2008/09	India	Napier	I 273-4	NZ 162-9	*India won by 53 runs (D/L)*
	India	Wellington	I 188-4		*abandoned*
	India	Christchurch	I 392-4	NZ 334	*India won by 58 runs*
	India	Hamilton	NZ 270-5	I 201-0	*India won by 84 runs (D/L)*
	India	Auckland	I 149	NZ 151-2	*NZ won by 8 wickets*
2009/10	Sri Lanka	Colombo	SL 216-7	NZ 119	*Sri Lanka won by 97 runs*
	India	Colombo	NZ 155	I 156-4	*India won by 6 wickets*
2009/10	South Africa	Centurion	NZ 214	SA 217-5	*South Africa won by 5 wickets*
Champions Trophy	Sri Lanka	Johannesburg	NZ 315-7	SL 277	*NZ won by 38 runs*
	England	Johannesburg	E 146	NZ 147-6	*NZ won by 4 wickets*
	Pakistan	Johannesburg	P 233-9	NZ 234-5	*NZ won by 5 wickets*
	Australia	Centurion	NZ 200-9	A 206-4	*Australia won by 6 wickets*
2009/10	Pakistan	Abu Dhabi	P 287-9	NZ 149	*Pakistan won by 138 runs*
	Pakistan	Abu Dhabi	NZ 303-8	P 239	*NZ won by 64 runs*
	Pakistan	Abu Dhabi	NZ 211	P 204	*NZ won by 7 runs*
2009/10	Bangladesh	Napier	NZ 336-9	B 190	*NZ won by 146 runs*
	Bangladesh	Dunedin	B 183-8	NZ 185-5	*NZ won by 5 wickets*
	Bangladesh	Christchurch	B 241-9	NZ 244-7	*NZ won by 3 wickets*
2009/10	Australia	Napier	A 275-8	NZ 281-8	*NZ won by 2 wickets*
	Australia	Auckland	A 273-7	NZ 253	*Australia won by 12 runs (D/L)*
	Australia	Hamilton	NZ 245	A 248-4	*Australia won by 6 wickets*
	Australia	Auckland	NZ 238	A 202-4	*Australia won by 6 wickets (D/L)*
	Australia	Wellington	NZ 241-9	A 190	*NZ won by 51 runs*
2010/11	India	Dambulla	NZ 288	I 88	*NZ won by 200 runs*
	Sri Lanka	Dambulla	NZ 192	SL 195-7	*Sri Lanka won by 3 wickets*
	Sri Lanka	Dambulla	SL 203-3		*abandoned*
	India	Dambulla	I 223	NZ 118	*India won by 105 runs*
2010/11	Bangladesh	Mirpur	B 228	NZ 200-8	*Bangladesh won by 9 runs (D/L)*
	Bangladesh	Mirpur	*abandoned without a ball being bowled*		
	Bangladesh	Mirpur	NZ 173	B 177-3	*Bangladesh won by 7 wickets*
	Bangladesh	Mirpur	B 241	NZ 232	*Bangladesh won by 9 runs*
	Bangladesh	Mirpur	B 174	NZ 171	*Bangladesh won by 3 runs*
2010/11	India	Guwahati	I 276	NZ 236	*India won by 40 runs*
	India	Jaipur	NZ 258-8	I 259-2	*India won by 8 wickets*
	India	Vadodara	NZ 224-9	I 229-1	*India won by 9 wickets*
	India	Bangalore	NZ 315-7	I 321-5	*India won by 5 wickets*
	India	Chennai	NZ 103	I 107-2	*India won by 8 wickets*
2010/11	Pakistan	Wellington	P 124	NZ 125-1	*NZ won by 9 wickets*
	Pakistan	Queenstown	P 31-0		*abandoned*
	Pakistan	Christchurch	P 293-7	NZ 250-9	*Pakistan won by 43 runs*
	Pakistan	Napier	NZ 262-7	P 264-8	*Pakistan won by 2 wickets*
	Pakistan	Hamilton	P 268-9	NZ 227	*Pakistan won by 41 runs*
	Pakistan	Auckland	NZ 311-7	P 254	*NZ won by 57 runs*
2010/11	Kenya	Chennai	K 69	NZ 72-0	*NZ won by 10 wickets*
World Cup	Australia	Nagpur	NZ 206	A 207-3	*Australia won by 7 wickets*
	Zimbabwe	Ahmedabad	Z 162	NZ 166-0	*NZ won by 10 wickets*
	Pakistan	Pallekele	NZ 302-7	P 192	*NZ won by 110 runs*
	Canada	Mumbai	NZ 358-6	C 261-9	*NZ won by 97 runs*
	Sri Lanka	Mumbai	SL 265-9	NZ 153	*Sri Lanka won by 112 runs*
	South Africa	Mirpur	NZ 221-8	SA 172	*NZ won by 49 runs*
	Sri Lanka	Colombo	NZ 217	SL 220-5	*Sri Lanka won by 5 wickets*

2011/12	Zimbabwe	Harare	Z 231-6	NZ 232-1	*NZ won by 9 wickets*
	Zimbabwe	Harare	Z 259-8	NZ 261-6	*NZ won by 4 wickets*
	Zimbabwe	Bulawayo	NZ 328-5	Z 329-9	*Zimbabwe won by 1 wicket*
2011/12	Zimbabwe	Dunedin	NZ 248	Z 158	*NZ won by 90 runs*
	Zimbabwe	Whangarei	NZ 372-6	Z 231-8	*NZ won by 141 runs*
	Zimbabwe	Napier	NZ 373-8	Z 171	*NZ won by 202 runs*
2011/12	South Africa	Wellington	NZ 253-9	SA 254-4	*South Africa won by 6 wickets*
	South Africa	Napier	NZ 230	SA 231-4	*South Africa won by 6 wickets*
	South Africa	Auckland	NZ 206	SA 208-5	*South Africa won by 5 wickets*
2012	West Indies	Kingston	NZ 190-9	WI 136-1	*West Indies won by 9 wkts (D/L)*
	West Indies	Kingston	WI 315-5	NZ 260	*West Indies won by 55 runs*
	West Indies	Basseterre	NZ 249-9	WI 161	*New Zealand won by 88 runs*
	West Indies	Basseterre	WI 264	NZ 240	*West Indies won by 24 runs*
	West Indies	Basseterre	WI 241-9	NZ 221	*West Indies won by 20 runs*
2012/13	Sri Lanka	Pallakele	*abandoned without a ball being bowled*		
	Sri Lanka	Pallakele	NZ 250-6	SL 118-3	*Sri Lanka won by 14 runs (D/L)*
	Sri Lanka	Pallakele	NZ 188-6	SL 200-3	*Sri Lanka won by 7 wkts (D/L)*
	Sri Lanka	Hambantota	NZ 131-8	SL 131-3	*Sri Lanka won by 7 wkts (D/L)*
	Sri Lanka	Hambantota	SL 123-8	NZ	*abandoned*
2012/13	South Africa	Paarl	SA 208	NZ 209-9	*NZ won by 1 wicket*
	South Africa	Kimberley	NZ 279-8	SA 252	*NZ won by 27 runs*
	South Africa	Potchefstroom	NZ 260-9	SA 264-9	*South Africa won by 1 wicket*
2012/13	England	Hamilton	E 258	NZ 259-7	*NZ won by 3 wickets*
	England	Napier	NZ 269	E 270-2	*England won by 8 wickets*
	England	Auckland	NZ 185	E 186-5	*England won by 5 wickets*
2013	England	Lord's	E 227-9	NZ 231-5	*NZ won by 5 wickets*
	England	Southampton	NZ 359-3	E 273	*NZ won by 86 runs*
	England	Nottingham	E 287-6	NZ 253	*England won by 34 runs*
2013	Sri Lanka	Cardiff	SL 138	NZ 139-9	*NZ won by 1 wicket*
Champions Trophy	Australia	Birmingham	A 243-8	NZ 51-2	*abandoned*
	England	Cardiff	E 169	NZ 159-8	*England won by 10 runs*
2013/14	Bangladesh	Mirpur	B 265	NZ 162	*Bangladesh won by 43 runs (D/L)*
	Bangladesh	Mirpur	B 247	NZ 207	*Bangladesh won by 40 runs*
	Bangladesh	Fatullah	NZ 307-5	B 309-6	*Bangladesh won by 4 wickets*
2013/14	Sri Lanka	Hambantota	SL 288-9	NZ 13-1	*abandoned*
	Sri Lanka	Hambantota	SL 138-1	NZ 203-6	*NZ won by 4 wickets (D/L)*
	Sri Lanka	Dambulla	SL 211-8	NZ 126-6	*Sri Lanka won by 36 runs (D/L)*
2013/14	West Indies	Auckland	NZ 156	WI 157-8	*West Indies won by 2 wickets*
	West Indies	Napier	*abandoned without a ball being bowled*		
	West Indies	Queenstown	NZ 283-4	WI 124-5	*NZ won by 159 runs*
	West Indies	Nelson	NZ 285-6	WI 134-5	*NZ won by 58 runs (D/L)*
	West Indies	Hamilton	WI 363-4	NZ 160	*West Indies won by 203 runs*
2013/14	India	Napier	NZ 292-7	I 268	*NZ won by 24 runs*
	India	Hamilton	NZ 271-7	I 277-9	*NZ won by 15 runs (D/L)*
	India	Auckland	NZ 314	I 314-9	*Tied*
	India	Hamilton	I 278-5	NZ 280-3	*NZ won by 7 wickets*
	India	Wellington	NZ 303-5	I 216	*NZ won by 87 runs*
2014/15	South Africa	Mt Maunganui	NZ 230	SA 236-4	*South Africa won by 6 wickets*
	South Africa	Mt Maunganui	SA 282-9	NZ 210	*South Africa won by 72 runs*
	South Africa	Hamilton	SA 157-3		*abandoned*

2014/15	Pakistan	Dubai	NZ 246-7	P 250-7	*Pakistan won by 3 wickets*
	Pakistan	Sharjah	P 252	NZ 255-6	*NZ won by 4 wickets*
	Pakistan	Sharjah	P 364-7	NZ 217	*Pakistan won by 147 runs*
	Pakistan	Abu Dhabi	NZ 299-5	P 292-8	*NZ won by 7 runs*
	Pakistan	Abu Dhabi	NZ 275-4	P 207	*NZ won by 68 runs*
2014/15	Sri Lanka	Christchurch	SL 218-9	NZ 219-7	*NZ won by 3 wickets*
	Sri Lanka	Hamilton	NZ 248	SL 252-4	*Sri Lanka won by 6 wickets*
	Sri Lanka	Auckland	NZ 145-3		*abandoned*
	Sri Lanka	Nelson	SL 276	NZ 280-6	*NZ won by 4 wickets*
	Sri Lanka	Dunedin	NZ 360-5	SL 252	*NZ won by 108 runs*
	Sri Lanka	Dunedin	NZ 315-8	SL 195	*NZ won by 120 runs*
	Sri Lanka	Wellington	SL 287-6	NZ 253	*Sri Lanka won by 34 runs*
2014/15	Pakistan	Wellington	P 210	NZ 213-3	*NZ won by 7 wickets*
	Pakistan	Napier	NZ 369-5	P 250	*NZ won by 119 runs*
2014/15	Sri Lanka	Christchurch	NZ 331-6	SL 233	*NZ won by 98 runs*
World Cup	Scotland	Dunedin	S 142	NZ 146-7	*NZ won by 3 wickets*
	England	Wellington	E 123	NZ 125-2	*NZ won by 8 wickets*
	Australia	Auckland	A 151	NZ 152-9	*NZ won by 1 wicket*
	Afghanistan	Napier	A 186	NZ 188-4	*NZ won by 6 wickets*
	Bangladesh	Hamilton	B 288-7	NZ 290-7	*NZ won by 3 wickets*
	West Indies	Wellington	NZ 393-6	WI 250	*NZ won by 143 runs*
	South Africa	Auckland	SA 281-5	NZ 299-6	*NZ won by 4 wickets (D/L)*
	Australia	Melbourne	NZ 183	A 186-3	*Australia won by 7 wickets*
2015	England	Birmingham	E 408-9	NZ 198	*England won by 210 runs*
	England	The Oval	NZ 398-5	E 365-9	*NZ won by 13 runs (D/L)*
	England	Southampton	E 302	NZ 306-7	*NZ won by 3 wickets*
	England	Nottingham	NZ 349-7	E 350-3	*England won by 3 wickets*
	England	Durham	NZ 283-9	E 192-7	*England won by 3 wickets (D/L)*
2015/16	Zimbabwe	Harare	NZ 303-4	Z 304-3	*Zimbabwe won by 7 wickets*
	Zimbabwe	Harare	Z 235-9	NZ 236-0	*NZ won by 10 wickets*
	Zimbabwe	Harare	NZ 273-6	Z 235	*NZ won by 38 runs*
2015/16	South Africa	Centurion	SA 304-7	NZ 284	*South Africa won by 20 runs*
	South Africa	Potchefstroom	SA 204	NZ 207-2	*NZ won by 8 wickets*
	South Africa	Durban	SA 283-7	NZ 221	*South Africa won by 62 runs*
2015/16	Sri Lanka	Christchurch	SL 188	NZ 191-3	*NZ won by 7 wickets*
	Sri Lanka	Christchurch	SL 117	NZ 118-0	*NZ won by 10 wickets*
	Sri Lanka	Nelson	NZ 276-8	SL 277-2	*Sri Lanka won by 8 wickets*
	Sri Lanka	Nelson	NZ 75-3		*abandoned*
	Sri Lanka	Mt Maunganui	NZ 294-5	SL 258	*NZ won by 36 runs*
2015/16	Pakistan	Wellington	NZ 280-8	P 210	*NZ won by 70 runs*
	Pakistan	Napier	*abandoned without a ball being bowled*		
	Pakistan	Auckland	P 290	NZ 265-7	*NZ won by 3 wickets (D/L)*
2015/16	Australia	Auckland	NZ 307-8	A 148	*NZ won by 159 runs*
	Australia	Wellington	NZ 281-9	A 283-6	*Australia won by 4 wickets*
	Australia	Hamilton	NZ 246	A 191	*NZ won by 55 runs*
2016/17	India	Dharamsala	NZ 190	I 194-4	*India won by 6 wickets*
	India	Delhi	NZ 242-9	I 236	*NZ won by 6 runs*
	India	Mohali	NZ 285	I 289-3	*India won by 7 wickets*
	India	Ranchi	NZ 260-7	I 241	*NZ won by 19 runs*
	India	Visakhapatnam	I 269-6	NZ 79	*India won by 190 runs*

2016/17	Australia	Sydney	A 324-8	NZ 256	*Australia won by 68 runs*
	Australia	Canberra	A 378-5	NZ 262	*Australia won by 116 runs*
	Australia	Melbourne	A 264-8	NZ 147	*Australia won by 117 runs*
2016/17	Bangladesh	Christchurch	NZ 341-7	B 264	*NZ won by 77 runs*
	Bangladesh	Nelson	NZ 251	B 184	*NZ won by 67 runs*
	Bangladesh	Nelson	B 236-9	NZ 239-2	*NZ won by 8 wickets*
2016/17	Australia	Auckland	NZ 286-9	A 280	*NZ won by 6 runs*
	Australia	Napier	*abandoned without a ball being bowled*		
	Australia	Hamilton	NZ 281-9	A 257	*NZ won by 24 runs*
2016/17	South Africa	Hamilton	NZ 207-7	SA 210-6	*South Africa won by 4 wickets*
	South Africa	Christchurch	NZ 289-4	SA 283-9	*NZ won by 6 runs*
	South Africa	Wellington	SA 271-8	NZ 112	*South Africa won by 159 runs*
	South Africa	Hamilton	SA 279-8	NZ 280-3	*NZ won by 7 wickets*
	South Africa	Auckland	NZ 149	SA 150-4	*South Africa won by 6 wickets*
2017	Ireland	Dublin	NZ 289-7	I 238	*NZ won by 51 runs*
	Bangladesh	Dublin	B 257-9	NZ 258-6	*NZ won by 4 wickets*
	Ireland	Dublin	NZ 344-6	I 154	*NZ won by 190 runs*
	Bangladesh	Dublin	NZ 270-8	B 271-5	*Bangladesh won by 5 wickets*
2017	Australia	Birmingham	NZ 291	A 53-3	*abandoned*
Champions Trophy	England	Cardiff	E 310	NZ 223	*England won by 87 runs*
	Bangladesh	Cardiff	NZ 265-8	B 268-5	*Bangladesh won by 5 wickets*
2017/18	India	Mumbai	I 280-8	NZ 284-4	*NZ won by 6 wickets*
	India	Pune	NZ 230-9	I 232-4	*India won by 6 wickets*
	India	Kanpur	I 337-6	NZ 331-7	*India won by 6 runs*
2017/18	West Indies	Whangarei	WI 248-9	NZ 249-5	*NZ won by 5 wickets*
	West Indies	Christchurch	NZ 325-6	WI 121	*NZ won by 204 runs*
	West Indies	Christchurch	NZ 131-4	WI 99-9	*NZ won by 66 runs (D/L)*
2017/18	Pakistan	Wellington	NZ 315-7	P 166-6	*NZ won by 61 runs (D/L)*
	Pakistan	Nelson	P 246-9	NZ 151-2	*NZ won by 8 wickets (D/L)*
	Pakistan	Dunedin	NZ 257	P 74	*NZ won by 183 runs*
	Pakistan	Hamilton	P 262-8	NZ 263-5	*NZ won by 5 wickets*
	Pakistan	Wellington	NZ 271-7	P 256	*NZ won by 15 runs*
2017/18	England	Hamilton	E 284-8	NZ 287-7	*NZ won by 3 wickets*
	England	Mt Maunganui	NZ 223	E 225-4	*England won by 6 wickets*
	England	Wellington	E 234	NZ 230-8	*England won by 4 runs*
	England	Dunedin	E 335-9	NZ 339-5	*NZ won by 5 wickets*
	England	Christchurch	NZ 223	E 229-3	*England won by 7 wickets*
2018/19	Pakistan	Abu Dhabi	NZ 266-9	P 219	*NZ won by 47 runs*
	Pakistan	Abu Dhabi	NZ 209-9	P 212-4	*Pakistan won by 6 wickets*
	Pakistan	Dubai	P 279-8	NZ 35-1	*abandoned*
2018/19	Sri Lanka	Mt Maunganui	NZ 371-7	SL 326	*NZ won by 45 runs*
	Sri Lanka	Mt Maunganui	NZ 319-7	SL 298	*NZ won by 21 runs*
	Sri Lanka	Nelson	NZ 364-4	SL 249	*NZ won by 115 runs*
2018/19	India	Napier	NZ 157	I 156-2	*India won by 8 wickets (D/L)*
	India	Mt Maunganui	I 324-4	NZ 234	*India won by 90 runs*
	India	Mt Maunganui	NZ 243	I 245-3	*India won by 7 wickets*
	India	Hamilton	I 92	NZ 93-2	*NZ won by 8 wickets*
	India	Wellington	I 252	NZ 217	*India won by 35 runs*
2018/19	Bangladesh	Napier	B 232	NZ 233-2	*NZ won by 8 wickets*
	Bangladesh	Christchurch	B 226	NZ 229-2	*NZ won by 8 wickets*
	Bangladesh	Dunedin	NZ 330-6	B 242	*NZ won by 88 runs*

2019	Sri Lanka	Cardiff	SL 136	NZ 137-0	*NZ won by 10 wickets*
World Cup	Bangladesh	The Oval	B 244	NZ 248-8	*NZ won by 2 wickets*
	Afghanistan	Taunton	A 172	NZ 173-3	*NZ won by 7 wickets*
	India	Nottingham	*abandoned without a ball being bowled*		
	South Africa	Birmingham	SA 241-6	NZ 245-6	*NZ won by 4 wickets*
	West Indies	Manchester	NZ 291-8	WI 286	*NZ won by 5 runs*
	Pakistan	Birmingham	NZ 237-6	P 241-4	*Pakistan won by 6 wickets*
	Australia	Lord's	A 243-9	NZ 157	*Australia won by 86 runs*
	England	Chester-le-Street	E 305-8	NZ 186	*England won by 119 runs*
	India	Manchester	NZ 239-8	I 221	*NZ won by 18 runs*
	England	Lord's	NZ 241-8	E 241	*England won on countback*
2019/20	India	Hamilton	I 347-4	NZ 348-6	*NZ won by 4 wickets*
	India	Auckland	NZ 273-8	I 251	*NZ won by 22 runs*
	India	Mt Maunganui	I 296-7	NZ 300-5	*NZ won by 5 wickets*
2019/20	Australia	Sydney	A 258-7	NZ 187	*Australia won by 71 runs*
2020/21	Bangladesh	Dunedin	B 131	NZ 132-2	*NZ won by 8 wickets*
	Bangladesh	Christchurch	B 271-6	NZ 275-5	*NZ won by 5 wickets*
	Bangladesh	Wellington	NZ 318-6	B 154	*NZ won by 164 runs*

Summary of Results

	Played	*Won*	*Lost*	*Tie*	*Abandoned*
v Australia	138	39	98	—	7
v India	110	49	55	1	5
v Pakistan	107	48	55	1	3
v Sri Lanka	99	49	41	1	8
v England	91	43	42	2	4
v South Africa	71	25	41	—	5
v West Indies	65	28	30	—	7
v Zimbabwe	38	27	9	1	1
v Bangladesh	38	28	10	—	—
v Ireland	4	4	—	—	—
v Canada	3	3	—	—	—
v Scotland	3	3	—	—	—
v Kenya	2	2	—	—	—
v Afghanistan	2	2	—	—	—
v East Africa	1	1	—	—	—
v Holland	1	1	—	—	—
v UAE	1	1	—	—	—
v USA	1	1	—	—	—
TOTALS	**775**	**354**	**375**	**6**	**40**

In addition, New Zealand forfeited their match against Kenya, at Nairobi, 2002/03

One-day International Captains

		Results					*Toss*	
		P	*W*	*L*	*Tie*	*NR*	*W*	*L*
Fleming S.P.	1996/97 to 2006/07	218	98	106	1	13	106	112
Vettori D.L.	2004/05 to 2010/11	82	41	33	1	7	46	36
Williamson K.S.	2012 to 2019/20	79	42	35	—	2	37	42
McCullum B.B.	2008/09 to 2015/16	62	36	22	1	3	28	34
Howarth G.P.	1979/80 to 1984/85	60	31	26	—	3	23	37
Crowe M.D.	1989/90 to 1992/93	44	21	22	—	1	28	16
Rutherford K.R.	1993/94 to 1994/95	37	10	24	1	2	18	19
Germon L.K.	1995/96 to 1996/97	36	15	19	2	—	17	19
Wright J.G.	1982/83 to 1990	31	16	15	—	—	21	10
Coney J.V.	1984/85 to 1986/87	25	8	16	—	1	13	12
Taylor L.R.P.L	2009/10 to 2012/13	20	6	12	—	2	10	10
Crowe J.J.	1985/86 to 1987/88	16	4	12	—	—	5	11
Latham T.W.M.	2017-2020/21	15	13	1	—	1	7	8
Burgess M.G.	1978 to 1980/81	8	2	6	—	—	6	2
McMillan C.D.	2000/01 to 2001/02	8	2	6	—	—	3	5
Congdon B.E.	1972/73 to 1974/75	7	1	3	—	3	5	2
Turner G.M.	1974/75 to 1976/77	7	5	2	—	—	4	3
Nash D.J.	1998/99	7	3	3	—	1	4	3
Cairns C.L.	2001/02 to 2003/04	7	1	6	—	—	3	4
Mills K.D.	2013/14	4	1	2	—	1	2	2
Larsen G.R.	1993/94	3	1	2	—	—	2	1
Jones A.H.	1992/93	2	—	2	—	—	1	1
Southee T.G.	2017/18	1	—	1	—	—	—	1
TOTAL		**775**	**354**	**375**	**6**	**40**	**387**	**388**

Other One-day Internationals Played in New Zealand

Season	Venue					Result
1989/90	Christchurch	A	187-9	I	169	*Australia won by 18 runs*
	Hamilton	I	211-8	A	212-3	*Australia won by 7 wickets*
1991/92	New Plymouth	Z	312-4	SL	313-7	*Sri Lanka won by 3 wickets*
World Cup	Wellington	SA	195	SL	198-7	*Sri Lanka won by 3 wickets*
	Christchurch	SA	200-8	WI	136	*South Africa won by 64 runs*
	Hamilton	I	203-7	Z	104-1	*India won by 55 runs**
	Wellington	I	197	WI	195-5	*West Indies won by 5 wickets**
1994/95	Wellington	SA	123	A	124-7	*Australia won by 3 wickets*
	Hamilton	SA	223-6	I	209-9	*South Africa won by 14 runs*
	Dunedin	A	250-6	I	252-5	*India won by 5 wickets*
2014/15	Hamilton	SA	339-4	Z	277	*South Africa won by 52 runs*
World Cup	Nelson	WI	304-7	IRE	307-6	*Ireland won by 4 wickets*
	Nelson	UAE	258-7	Z	286-6	*Zimbabwe won by 4 wickets*
	Christchurch	WI	310-6	P	160	*West Indies won by 150 runs*
	Dunedin	AFG	232	SL	236-6	*Sri Lanka won by 4 wickets*
	Christchurch	E	303-8	SCO	184	*England won by 119 runs*
	Dunedin	SCO	210	AFG	211-9	*Afghanistan won by 1 wicket*
	Wellington	E	309-6	SL	312-1	*Sri Lanka won by 9 wickets*
	Napier	P	339-6	UAE	210-8	*Pakistan won by 129 runs*
	Nelson	SCO	318-8	B	322-4	*Bangladesh won by 6 wickets*
	Auckland	P	222	SA	202	*Pakistan won by 29 runs (D/L)*
	Hamilton	IRE	259	I	260-2	*India won by 8 wickets*
	Wellington	SA	341-6	UAE	195	*South Africa won by 146 runs*
	Auckland	Z	287	I	288-4	*India won by 6 wickets*
	Napier	UAE	175	WI	176-4	*West Indies won by 6 wickets*

* *target reduced*

Highest Totals

For

402-2	v Ireland	Aberdeen	2008
398-5	v England	The Oval	2015
397-5	v Zimbabwe	Bulawayo	2005/06
393-6	v West Indies	Wellington	2014/15
373-8	v Zimbabwe	Napier	2011/12
372-6	v Zimbabwe	Whangarei	2011/12
371-7	v Sri Lanka	Mt Maunganui	2018/19
369-5	v Pakistan	Napier	2014/15
364-4	v Sri Lanka	Nelson	2018/19
363-5	v Canada	Gros Islet	2006/07
360-5	v Sri Lanka	Dunedin	2014/15
359-3	v England	Southampton	2013
358-6	v Canada	Mumbai	2010/11
350-9	v Australia	Hamilton	2006/07

Against

408-9	by England	Birmingham	2015
392-4	by India	Christchurch	2008/09
378-5	by Australia	Canberra	2016/17
376-2	by India	Hyderabad	1999/00
365-9	by England	The Oval	2015
364-7	by Pakistan	Sharjah	2014/15
363-4	by West Indies	Hamilton	2013/14

353-5	by India	Hyderabad	2003/04
350-3	by England	Nottingham	2015

Lowest Totals

For

64	v Pakistan	Sharjah	1985/86
73	v Sri Lanka	Auckland	2006/07
74	v Australia	Wellington	1981/82
74	v Pakistan	Sharjah	1989/90
79	v India	Visakhapatnam	2016/17
94	v Australia	Christchurch	1989/90
97	v Australia	Faridabad	2003/04

Against

69	by Kenya	Chennai	2010/11
70	by Australia	Adelaide	1985/86
77	by Bangladesh	Colombo	2002/03
86	by Bangladesh	Chittagong	2004/05
88	by India	Dambulla	2010/11
89	by England	Wellington	2001/02
92	by India	Hamilton	2018/19
93	by Bangladesh	Queenstown	2007/08

Highest Match Aggregates

763	New Zealand v England	The Oval	2015
726	New Zealand v India	Christchurch	2008/09
699	England v New Zealand	Nottingham	2015
697	New Zealand v Sri Lanka	Mt Maunganui	2018/19
696	New Zealand v Australia	Hamilton	2006/07
695	New Zealand v India	Hamilton	2019/20
680	New Zealand v England	Napier	2007/08
678	Australia v New Zealand	Perth	2006/07
676	New Zealand v Australia	Auckland	2006/07
674	New Zealand v England	Dunedin	2017/18
668	India v New Zealand	Kanpur	2017/18
663	New Zealand v Australia	Christchurch	2005/06
657	Zimbabwe v New Zealand	Bulawayo	2011/12
655	India v New Zealand	Rajkot	1999/00
650	New Zealand v Australia	Christchurch	1999/00

Lowest Match Aggregates

130	New Zealand v Pakistan	Sharjah	1985/86
141	New Zealand v Kenya	Chennai	2010/11
149	New Zealand v Australia	Wellington	1981/82
149	New Zealand v Pakistan	Sharjah	1989/90
185	New Zealand v India	Hamilton	2018/19
188	New Zealand v Bangladesh	Queenstown	2007/08
198	New Zealand v Australia	Faridabad	2003/04

INDIVIDUAL RECORDS

Centuries

237*	Guptill M.J.	v West Indies	Wellington	2014/15
189*	Guptill M.J.	v England	Southampton	2013
181*	Taylor L.R.P.L.	v England	Dunedin	2017/18
180*	Guptill M.J.	v South Africa	Hamilton	2016/17
172	Vincent L.	v Zimbabwe	Bulawayo	2005/06
171*	Turner G.M.	v East Africa	Birmingham	1975
170*	Ronchi L.	v Sri Lanka	Dunedin	2014/15
166	McCullum B.B.	v Ireland	Aberdeen	2008
161	Marshall J.A.H.	v Ireland	Aberdeen	2008
148	Williamson K.S.	v West Indies	Manchester	2019
146	Nicol R.J.	v Zimbabwe	Whangarei	2011/12
145*	Astle N.J.	v USA	The Oval	2004
145*	Williamson K.S.	v South Africa	Kimberley	2012/13
141	Styris S.B.	v Sri Lanka	Bloemfontein	2002/03
140	Turner G.M.	v Sri Lanka	Auckland	1982/83
139	How J.M.	v England	Napier	2007/08
138	Guptill M.J.	v Sri Lanka	Mt Maunganui	2018/19
137	Latham T.W.M.	v Bangladesh	Christchurch	2016/17
137	Taylor L.R.P.L.	v Sri Lanka	Nelson	2018/19
134*	Fleming S.P.	v South Africa	Johannesburg	2002/03
131*	Taylor L.R.P.L.	v Pakistan	Pallekele	2010/11
131*	Anderson C.J.	v West Indies	Queenstown	2013/14
131	McCullum B.B.	v Pakistan	Abu Dhabi	2009/10
130	Harris C.Z.	v Australia	Madras	1995/96
128*	Taylor L.R.P.L.	v Sri Lanka	Napier	2006/07
126	Conway D.P.	v Bangladesh	Wellington	2020/21
124*	Nicholls H.M.	v Sri Lanka	Nelson	2018/19
123	Williamson K.S.	v Pakistan	Abu Dhabi	2014/15
122*	Astle N.J.	v England	Dunedin	2001/02
122*	Guptill M.J.	v West Indies	Auckland	2008/09
120	Astle N.J.	v Zimbabwe	Auckland	1995/96
120	Astle N.J.	v India	Rajkot	1999/00
119*	Taylor L.R.P.L.	v England	The Oval	2015
119	Astle N.J.	v Pakistan	Dunedin	2000/01
119	Taylor L.R.P.L.	v Zimbabwe	Bulawayo	2011/12
119	McCullum B.B.	v Zimbabwe	Napier	2011/12
118*	Sinclair M.S.	v Sri Lanka	Sharjah	2000/01
118*	Astle N.J.	v West Indies	Christchurch	2005/06
118	Williamson K.S.	v England	Southampton	2015
118	Williamson K.S.	v India	Delhi	2016/17
118	Guptill M.J.	v Bangladesh	Christchurch	2018/19
117*	Guptill M.J.	v Bangladesh	Napier	2018/19
117	Astle N.J.	v Pakistan	Mohali	1996/97
117	Sinclair M.S.	v Pakistan	Sharjah	2000/01
117	Astle N.J.	v India	Colombo	2001/02
117	Taylor L.R.P.L.	v Australia	Auckland	2006/07
117	McMillan C.D.	v Australia	Hamilton	2006/07
117	McCullum B.B.	v Sri Lanka	Hamilton	2014/15
116*	Fleming S.P.	v Australia	Melbourne	1997/98
116*	Guptill M.J.	v Zimbabwe	Harare	2015/16
115*	Fleming S.P.	v Pakistan	Christchurch	2003/04
115*	Astle N.J.	v India	Harare	2005/06

115	Cairns C.L.	v India	Christchurch	1998/99
115	Elliott G.D.	v Australia	Sydney	2008/09
115	Williamson K.S.	v Pakistan	Wellington	2017/18
114*	Turner G.M.	v India	Manchester	1975
114	Astle N.J.	v India	Nagpur	1995/96
114	Guptill M.J.	v Australia	Sydney	2016/17
113	Taylor L.R.P.L.	v England	Hamilton	2017/18
112*	Taylor L.R.P.L.	v India	Hamilton	2013/14
112*	Taylor L.R.P.L.	v Zimbabwe	Harare	2015/16
112*	Williamson K.S.	v England	Wellington	2017/18
112	Fulton P.G.	v Sri Lanka	Napier	2005/06
112	Williamson K.S.	v Pakistan	Napier	2014/15
111*	Fleming S.P.	v Australia	Napier	1997/98
111*	Styris S.B.	v Sri Lanka	Grenada	2006/07
111	Greatbatch M.J.	v England	The Oval	1990
111	Guptill M.J.	v India	Auckland	2013/14
110*	Latham T.W.M.	v Zimbabwe	Harare	2015/16
110*	Latham T.W.M.	v Bangladesh	Christchurch	2020/21
110	Taylor L.R.P.L.	v West Indies	Basseterre	2012
110	Taylor L.R.P.L.	v England	Southampton	2015
109*	Taylor L.R.P.L.	v India	Hamilton	2019/20
109	Broom N.T.	v Bangladesh	Nelson	2016/17
108*	Nicol R.J.	v Zimbabwe	Harare	2011/12
108	Rutherford K.R.	v India	Baroda	1994/95
108	Parore A.C.	v South Africa	Verwoerdburg	1994/95
108	Astle N.J.	v India	Colombo	2001/02
108	Fleming S.P.	v South Africa	Christchurch	2003/04
108	Williamson K.S.	v Bangladesh	Mirpur	2010/11
107*	Crowe M.D.	v India	Jamshedpur	1995/96
107*	Taylor L.R.P.L.	v Bangladesh	Fatullah	2013/14
107	Ryder J.D.	v Pakistan	Auckland	2010/11
107	Taylor L.R.P.L.	v Australia	Hamilton	2016/17
106*	Fleming S.P.	v West Indies	Port of Spain	1995/96
106*	Williamson K.S.	v South Africa	Birmingham	2019
106	Fleming S.P.	v England	Brisbane	2006/07
105*	Crowe M.D.	v England	Auckland	1983/84
105*	Taylor L.R.P.L.	v Pakistan	Dubai	2014/15
105	McMillan C.D.	v Pakistan	Rawalpindi	2001/02
105	Ryder J.D.	v India	Christchurch	2008/09
105	Guptill M.J.	v Zimbabwe	Harare	2011/12
105	Guptill M.J.	v Bangladesh	Hamilton	2014/15
104*	Astle N.J.	v Zimbabwe	Napier	1997/98
104*	McMillan C.D.	v Pakistan	Christchurch	2000/01
104*	Elliott G.D.	v Sri Lanka	Dunedin	2014/15
104	Wadsworth K.J.	v Australia	Christchurch	1973/74
104	Crowe M.D.	v India	Dunedin	1989/90
104	Astle N.J.	v Australia	Napier	1999/00
104	Ryder J.D.	v West Indies	Queenstown	2013/14
104	Latham T.W.M.	v Ireland	Dublin	2017
103*	Guptill M.J.	v England	Lord's	2013
103*	Guptill M.J.	v South Africa	Potchefstroom	2015/16
103*	Latham T.W.M.	v India	Mumbai	2017/18
103	Cairns C.L.	v India	Pune	1995/96
103	Twose R.G.	v South Africa	Cape Town	2000/01
103	Taylor L.R.P.L.	v Bangladesh	Chittagong	2008/09
103	Williamson K.S.	v Sri Lanka	Nelson	2014/15

102*	Edgar B.A.	v Australia	Melbourne	1980/81
102*	Greatbatch M.J.	v England	Leeds	1990
102*	Rutherford K.R.	v Sri Lanka	East London	1994/95
102*	Cairns C.L.	v India	Nairobi	2000/01
102*	Cairns C.L.	v South Africa	Brisbane	2001/02
102*	Astle N.J.	v Zimbabwe	Bloemfontein	2002/03
102*	Fleming S.P.	v Bangladesh	Antigua	2006/07
102*	Taylor L.R.P.L.	v Sri Lanka	Napier	2014/15
102*	Taylor L.R.P.L.	v South Africa	Christchurch	2016/17
102	Vincent L.	v West Indies	Napier	2005/06
102	Taylor L.R.P.L.	v India	Wellington	2013/14
102	Guptill M.J.	v Sri Lanka	Mt Maunganui	2015/16
101*	Marshall H.J.H.	v Pakistan	Faisalabad	2003/04
101*	Styris S.B.	v Pakistan	Auckland	2003/04
101*	Oram J.D.P.	v Australia	Perth	2006/07
101	Congdon B.E.	v England	Wellington	1974/75
101	Wright J.G.	v England	Napier	1987/88
101	Astle N.J.	v England	Ahmedabad	1995/96
101	Styris S.B.	v Australia	Christchurch	2005/06
101	Vincent L.	v Canada	Gros Islet	2006/07
101	McCullum B.B.	v Canada	Mumbai	2010/11
100*	Crowe M.D.	v Australia	Auckland	1991/92
100*	Astle N.J.	v South Africa	Auckland	1998/99
100*	Williamson K.S.	v Zimbabwe	Bulawayo	2011/12
100*	Mitchell D.J.	v Bangladesh	Wellington	2020/21
100	Taylor L.R.P.L.	v England	Napier	2012/13
100	Williamson K.S.	v Australia	Birmingham	2017
100	Guptill M.J.	v Pakistan	Wellington	2017/18

Successive Centuries

Taylor L.R.P.L. (3) 112* and 102 v India and 105* v Pakistan	2013/14 & 2014/15
Greatbatch M.J. (2) 102* and 111 v England	1990
Taylor L.R.P.L. (2) 119 v Zimbabwe and 110 v West Indies	2011/12
Guptill M.J. (2) 103* and 189* v England	2013
Guptill M.J. (2) 105 v Bangladesh and 237* v West Indies	2014/15
Taylor L.R.P.L. (2) 119* and 110 v England	2015
Guptill M.J. (2) 117* and 118 v Bangladesh	2018/19
Williamson K.S. (2) 106* v South Africa and 148 v West Indies	2019

Most Successive Fifties

Jones A.H. (6)	57 v India and 55*, 62*, 67, 82, 63* v Pakistan	1988/89
Taylor L.R.P.L. (6)	181* v England, 80 and 86 v Pakistan, 54, 90 and 137 v Sri Lanka	2017/18 & 2018/19

Five Wickets in an Innings

9-0-33-7	Southee T.G.	v England	Wellington	2014/15
10-3-34-7	Boult T.A.	v West Indies	Christchurch	2017/18
9-3-19-6	Bond S.E.	v India	Bulawayo	2005/06
10-2-23-6	Bond S.E.	v Australia	Port Elizabeth	2002/03
7-0-25-6	Styris S.B.	v West Indies	Port of Spain	2001/02
10-1-33-6	Boult T.A.	v Australia	Hamilton	2016/17
9.2-1-65-6	Southee T.G.	v Bangladesh	Dunedin	2018/19
6-2-7-5	Vettori D.L.	v Bangladesh	Queenstown	2007/08
7.2-1-17-5	Boult T.A.	v Pakistan	Dunedin	2017/18

10-4-21-5	Boult T.A.	v India	Hamilton	2018/19
10-2-22-5	Hart M.N.	v West Indies	Goa	1994/95
8.4-1-22-5	Adams A.R.	v India	Queenstown	2002/03
7-1-23-5	Collinge R.O.	v India	Christchurch	1975/76
9.3-2-23-5	Bond S.E.	v Australia	Wellington	2006/07
10.1-4-25-5	Hadlee R.J.	v Sri Lanka	Bristol	1983
9.2-2-25-5	Bond S.E.	v Australia	Adelaide	2001/02
10-2-25-5	Mills K.D.	v South Africa	Durban	2007/08
8.3-4-26-5	Hadlee R.J.	v Australia	Sydney	1980/81
10-3-26-5	Oram J.D.P.	v India	Auckland	2002/03
10-3-27-5	Boult T.A.	v Australia	Auckland	2014/15
7.4-1-27-5	Neesham J.D.S.	v Bangladesh	Wellington	2020/21
11-3-28-5	Cairns B.L.	v England	Scarborough	1978
9.2-1-30-5	Vettori D.L.	v West Indies	Lord's	2004
9-1-30-5	Henry M.J.	v Pakistan	Abu Dhabi	2014/15
10-1-31-5	Neesham J.D.S.	v Afghanistan	Taunton	2019
9-1-32-5	Hadlee R.J.	v India	Perth	1980/81
10-2-32-5	Hadlee R.J.	v England	Christchurch	1983/84
10-1-32-5	Latham R.T.	v Australia	Auckland	1992/93
9.3-0-33-5	Southee T.G.	v Pakistan	Wellington	2010/11
10-1-34-5	Chatfield E.J.	v Australia	Adelaide	1980/81
10-0-34-5	Morrison D.K.	v Sri Lanka	Sharjah	1996/97
9.4-1-36-5	Oram J.D.P.	v USA	The Oval	2004
10-0-38-5	Hadlee R.J.	v Pakistan	Dunedin	1988/89
10-0-39-5	O'Connor S.B.	v Zimbabwe	Wellington	1997/98
10-1-40-5	Henry M.J.	v Sri Lanka	Mt Maunganui	2015/16
10-0-42-5	Harris C.Z.	v Pakistan	Sialkot	1996/97
7.4-0-42-5	Cairns C.L.	v Australia	Napier	1997/98
10-1-42-5	Franklin J.E.C.	v England	Chester-le-Street	2004
11-1-45-5	Pringle C.	v England	Birmingham	1994
10-0-45-5	Ferguson L.H.	v Pakistan	Dubai	2018/19
10-0-46-5	Morrison D.K.	v Pakistan	Christchurch	1995/96
9.2-0-46-5	O'Connor S.B.	v Pakistan	Nairobi	2000/01
10-0-50-5	Santner M.J.	v Ireland	Dublin	2017
9.3-0-58-5	McClenaghan M.J.	v West Indies	Auckland	2013/14
10-1-63-5	Anderson C.J.	v India	Auckland	2013/14

Most Economical Bowling

10-4-8-1	Chatfield E.J.	v Sri Lanka	Dunedin	1982/83
12-6-10-0	Hadlee R.J.	v East Africa	Birmingham	1975
10-6-10-0	Cairns B.L.	v Sri Lanka	Dunedin	1982/83
10-2-11-2	Tuffey D.R.	v India	Christchurch	2002/03
10-5-12-2	Larsen G.R.	v South Africa	Hobart	1993/94
10-2-12-1	Harris C.Z.	v Pakistan	Napier	2000/01
10-5-13-0	Chatfield E.J.	v India	Adelaide	1985/86
10-3-14-2	Snedden M.C.	v Pakistan	Hamilton	1988/89
10-5-14-1	Larsen G.R.	v Zimbabwe	Wellington	1995/96
10-4-14-4	Vettori D.L.	v Sri Lanka	Dambulla	2002/03
10-3-14-3	Vettori D.L.	v USA	The Oval	2004
10-2-15-2	Chatfield E.J.	v England	Dunedin	1987/88
10-2-15-1	Watson W.	v England	Christchurch	1990/91
10-3-15-3	Allott G.I.	v Scotland	Edinburgh	1999
10-3-15-1	Harris C.Z.	v West Indies	Wellington	1999/00
10-4-15-2	Bond S.E.	v Bangladesh	Antigua	2006/07

Most Expensive Bowling

12-1-105-2	Snedden M.C.	v England	The Oval	1983
10-0-105-0	Southee T.G.	v India	Christchurch	2008/09
10-0-96-1	Anderson C.J.	v Pakistan	Sharjah	2014/15
10-0-93-2	McClenaghan M.J.	v England	Birmingham	2015
10-0-91-0	Henry M.J.	v Australia	Canberra	2016/17
10-0-87-1	Southee T.G.	v England	Dunedin	2017/18
10-0-87-1	Henry M.J.	v Sri Lanka	Mt Maunganui	2018/19
9-0-86-3	McCullum N.L.	v England	The Oval	2015
9-0-85-0	Drum C.J.	v India	Hyderabad	1999/00
10-1-85-2	Southee T.G.	v India	Hamilton	2019/20
11-0-84-0	Cairns B.L.	v England	Manchester	1978
10-0-83-2	Gillespie M.R.	v Australia	Hamilton	2006/07
9-0-82-0	Bond S.E.	v Sri Lanka	Johannesburg	2009/10
8-1-82-2	Southee T.G.	v West Indies	Wellington	2014/15
10-0-81-0	Boult T.A.	v India	Kanpur	2017/18
10-0-81-2	Ferguson L.H.	v India	Mt Maunganui	2018/19
10-0-80-1	Canning T.K.	v Australia	Napier	2004/05
10-0-80-0	Tuffey D.R.	v Australia	Auckland	2006/07
10-0-80-1	Boult T.A.	v Australia	Canberra	2016/17
10-0-80-1	Boult T.A.	v Pakistan	Dubai	2018/19

Hat-tricks

9-1-35-3	Morrison D.K.	v India	Napier	1993/94
10-0-61-4	Bond S.E.	v Australia	Hobart	2006/07
10-1-54-3	Boult T.A.	v Pakistan	Abu Dhabi	2018/19
10-1-51-4	Boult T.A.	v Australia	Lord's	2019

Most Wicketkeeping Dismissals in an Innings

*5	Parore A.C.	v West Indies	Goa	1994/95
†5	McCullum B.B.	v India	Napier	2002/03
5	McCullum B.B	v India	Christchurch	2002/03
5	McCullum B.B.	v South Africa	Napier	2003/04
5	Hopkins G.J.	v Ireland	Aberdeen	2008
5	McCullum B.B.	v Bangladesh	Napier	2009/10
5	McCullum B.B.	v Pakistan	Wellington	2010/11
*5	Latham T.W.M.	v Australia	Auckland	2016/17
5	Latham T.W.M.	v Afghanistan	Taunton	2019

*† includes one stumping * includes two stumpings*

Most Catches in an Innings by a Fielder

4	Bracewell J.G. *(sub)*	v Australia	Adelaide	1980/81
4	Rutherford K.R.	v India	Napier	1994/95
4	Harris C.Z.	v India	Colombo	2001/02
4	Fleming S.P.	v England	Adelaide	2006/07
4	Taylor L.R.P.L.	v India	Dambulla	2010/11
4	How J.M.	v India	Guwahati	2010/11
4	McCullum N.L.	v England	Cardiff	2013
4	Guptill M.J.	v Pakistan	Auckland	2015/16

WALTER HADLEE TROPHIES

Awarded for the most meritorious batting and bowling performances by a New Zealand player in one-day internationals under the board's jurisdiction and other one-day matches as designated from time to time by the Board of Control *(discontinued after 2009/10 season)*.

BATTING

1988/89	Jones A.H.
1989/90	Crowe M.D.
1990/91	Crowe M.D.
1991/92	Crowe M.D.
1992/93	Crowe M.D.
1993/94	Thomson S.A.
1994/95	Parore A.C.
1995/96	Astle N.J.
1996/97	Fleming S.P.
1997/98	Harris C.Z.
1998/99	Astle N.J.
1999/00	Astle N.J.
2000/01	Twose R.G.
2001/02	Astle N.J.
2002/03	Fleming S.P.
2003/04	Fleming S.P.
2004/05	Marshall H.J.H.
2005/06	Astle N.J.
2006/07	Styris S.B.
2007/08	McCullum B.B.
2008/09	Guptill M.J.
2009/10	McCullum B.B.

BOWLING

1988/89	Snedden M.C.
1989/90	Snedden M.C.
1990/91	Pringle C.
1991/92	Patel D.N.
1992/93	Larsen G.R.
1993/94	Pringle C.
1994/95	Pringle C.
1995/96	Larsen G.R.
1996/97	Harris C.Z.
1997/98	Cairns C.L.
1998/99	Allott G.I.
1999/00	Allott G.I.
2000/01	Tuffey D.R.
2001/02	Bond S.E.
2002/03	Bond S.E.
2003/04	Tuffey D.R.
2004/05	Vettori D.L.
2005/06	Bond S.E.
2006/07	Bond S.E.
2007/08	Mills K.D.
2008/09	Mills K.D.
2009/10	Vettori D.L.

RECORD PARTNERSHIPS

New Zealand v All Countries

For				
1st	274	Marshall J.A.H. & McCullum B.B. v Ireland	Aberdeen	2008
2nd	179	Williamson K.S. & Broom N.T. v Bangladesh	Nelson	2016/17
3rd	206	Williamson K.S. & Taylor L.R.P.L. v England	Southampton	2015
4th	200	Taylor L.R.P.L. & Latham T.W.M. v India	Mumbai	2017/18
5th	195	Taylor L.R.P.L. & Williamson K.S. v Zimbabwe	Bulawayo	2011/12
6th	267*	Elliott G.D. & Ronchi L. v Sri Lanka	Dunedin	2014/15
7th	123	Broom N.T. & Oram J.D.P. v Bangladesh	Napier	2009/10
8th	94	Franklin J.E.C. & McCullum N.L. v India	Vadodara	2010/11
9th	84	Neesham J.D.S. & Henry M.J. v India	Mohali	2016/17
10th	76	Ronchi L. & McClenaghan M.J. v South Africa	Mt Maunganui	2014/15
Against				
1st	201	Tharanga W.U. & Jayasuriya S.T. for Sri Lanka	Napier	2006/07
	201*	Gambhir G. & Sehwag V. for India	Hamilton	2008/09
2nd	331	Tendulkar S.R. & Dravid R.S. for India	Hyderabad	1999/00
3rd	198	Root J.E. & Morgan E.J.G. for England	Nottingham	2015
4th	211	Edwards K.A. & Bravo D.J. for West Indies	Hamilton	2013/14
5th	224	Shakib Al Hasan & Mahmudullah for Bangladesh	Cardiff	2017
6th	136*	Clarke M.J. & Hussey M.E.K. for Australia	Auckland	2004/05
7th	177	Buttler J.C. & Rashid A.U. for England	Birmingham	2015
8th	117	Houghton D.L. & Butchart I.P. for Zimbabwe	Hyderabad	1987/88
9th	118	Yadav Jai P. & Pathan I.K. for India	Bulawayo	2005/06
10th	103	Mohammad Aamer & Saeed Ajmal for Pakistan	Abu Dhabi	2009/10

New Zealand v England

New Zealand				
1st	165*	Ryder J.D. & McCullum B.B.	Hamilton	2007/08
2nd	120	Guptill M.J. & Williamson K.S.	Southampton	2013
3rd	206	Williamson K.S. & Taylor L.R.P.L.	Southampton	2015
4th	187	Taylor L.R.P.L. & Latham T.W.M.	Dunedin	2017/18
5th	138*	Styris S.B. & Oram J.D.P.	Gros Islet	2006/07
6th	122	Rutherford K.R. & Harris C.Z.	Christchurch	1990/91
7th	96	Williamson K.S. & Santner M.J.	Wellington	2017/18
8th	68	Congdon B.E. & Cairns B.L.	Scarborough	1978
9th	69	Santner M.J.& Ferguson L.H.	Mt Maunganui	2017/18
10th	35	McCullum B.B. & Southee T.G.	Auckland	2012/13
England				
1st	193	Gooch G.A. & Athey C.W.J.	Manchester	1986
2nd	190	Bairstow J.M. & Root J.E.	Dunedin	2017/18
3rd	198	Root J.E. & Morgan E.J.G.	Nottingham	2015
4th	136	Pietersen K.P. & Collingwood P.D.	Chester-le-Street	2008
5th	113	Gower D.I. & Randall D.W.	Brisbane	1982/83
6th	80	Bairstow J.M. & Billings S.W.	Chester-le-Street	2015
7th	177	Buttler J.C. & Rashid A.U.	Birmingham	2015
8th	76	Nixon P.A. & Plunkett L.E.	Perth	2006/07
	76	Rashid A.U. & Plunkett L.E.	The Oval	2015
9th	47	Trott I.J.L. & Anderson J.M.	Southampton	2013
10th	29	Sidebottom R.J. & Anderson J.M.	Johannesburg	2009/10

New Zealand v Australia

New Zealand				
1st	149*	Vincent L. & Fleming S.P.	Wellington	2006/07
2nd	151	Vincent L. & Fulton P.G.	Melbourne	2006/07
3rd	125	Williamson K.S. & Neesham J.D.S.	Canberra	2016/17
4th	168	Germon L.K. & Harris C.Z.	Madras	1995/96
5th	148	Twose R.G. & Cairns C.L.	Cardiff	1999
6th	165	McMillan C.D.& McCullum B.B.	Hamilton	2006/07
7th	103	Oram J.D.P. & Vettori D.L.	Mohali	2006/07
8th	72	Harris C.Z. & Vettori D.L.	Melbourne	2001/02
9th	74*	McCullum B.B. & Vettori D.L.	Christchurch	2005/06
10th	50	Mills K.D. & Bond S.E.	Colombo	2002/03
Australia				
1st	189	Waugh M.E. & Gilchrist A.C.	Christchurch	1999/00
2nd	200	Hayden M.L. & Ponting R.T.	Perth	2006/07
3rd	135	Ponting R.T. & Clarke M.J.	Adelaide	2007/08
4th	154	Ponting R.T. & Hodge B.J.	Melbourne	2006/07
5th	220	Symonds A. & Clarke M.J.	Wellington	2005/06
6th	136*	Clarke M.J. & Hussey M.E.K.	Auckland	2004/05
7th	86*	Marsh M.R. & Hastings J.W.	Wellington	2015/16
8th	97	Bevan M.G. & Bichel A.J.	Port Elizabeth	2002/03
9th	46	Marsh R.W. & Lawson G.F.	Adelaide	1980/81
10th	54	Stoinis M.P. & Hazlewood J.R.	Auckland	2016/17

New Zealand v India

New Zealand				
1st	166	Ryder J.D. & McCullum B.B.	Christchurch	2008/09
2nd	153	Guptill M.J. & Williamson K.S.	Auckland	2013/14
3rd	180	Parore A.C. & Rutherford K.R.	Baroda	1994/95
4th	200	Taylor L.R.P.L. & Latham T.W.M.	Mumbai	2017/18
5th	147	Twose R.G. & Cairns C.L.	Pune	1995/96
6th	122	Cairns C.L. & Harris C.Z.	Nairobi	2000/01
7th	79	Burgess M.G. & Cairns B.L.	Adelaide	1980/81
8th	94	Franklin J.E.C. & McCullum N.L.	Vadodara	2010/11
9th	84	Neesham J.D.S. & Henry M.J.	Mohali	2016/17
10th	52*	Vincent L. & Bond S.E.	Auckland	2002/03
India				
1st	201*	Gambhir G. & Sehwag V.	Hamilton	2008/09
2nd	331	Tendulkar S.R. & Dravid R.S.	Hyderabad	1999/00
3rd	158	Sidhu N.S. & Amarnath M.	Sharjah	1987/88
4th	136	Iyer S.S. & Rahul K.L.	Hamilton	2019/20
5th	107	Sehwag V. & Dhoni M.S.	Dambulla	2010/11
	107	Rahul K.L. & Pandey M.K.	Mt Maunganui	2019/20
6th	133*	Pathan Y.K. & Tiwary S.S.	Bangalore	2010/11
7th	116	Dhoni M.S. & Jadeja R.A.	Manchester	2019
8th	82*	Kapil Dev & More K.S.	Bangalore	1987/88
9th	118	Yadav Jai P. & Pathan I.K.	Bulawayo	2005/06
10th	34	Kulkarni D.S. & Yadav U.T.	Ranchi	2016/17

New Zealand v Pakistan

New Zealand

1st	193	Fleming S.P. & Astle N.J.	Dunedin	2000/01
2nd	159	Guptill M.J. & Williamson K.S.	Auckland	2015/16
3rd	135	Astle N.J. & Twose R.G.	Nairobi	2000/01
4th	157	Marshall H.J.H. & McMillan C.D.	Wellington	2003/04
5th	108*	Crowe M.D. & Smith I.D.S.	Wellington	1988/89
6th	132	Neesham J.D.S. & de Grandhomme C.	Birmingham	2019
7th	115	Parore A.C. & Germon L.K.	Sharjah	1996/97
8th	57*	McCullum N.L. & Vettori D.L.	Napier	2010/11
9th	73*	Henry M.J. & McClenaghan M.J.	Wellington	2015/16
10th	33	Germon L.K. & Morrison D.K.	Wellington	1995/96

Pakistan

1st	199	Yasir Hameed & Imran Farhat	Rawalpindi	2003/04
2nd	263	Aamer Sohail & Inzamam-ul-Haq	Sharjah	1993/94
3rd	157*	Saeed Anwar & Inzamam-ul-Haq	Sharjah	2000/01
4th	161	Yousuf Youhana & Younis Khan	Karachi	2001/02
5th	108*	Ijaz Ahmed & Wasim Akram	Karachi	1996/97
6th	105	Haris Sohail & Shadab Khan	Wellington	2017/18
7th	110	Haris Sohail & Shahid Afridi	Dubai	2014/15
8th	70	Shadab Khan & Hasan Ali	Nelson	2017/18
9th	66	Abdul Razzaq & Umar Gul	Pallakele	2010/11
10th	103	Mohammad Aamer & Saeed Ajmal	Abu Dhabi	2009/10

New Zealand v West Indies

New Zealand

1st	136	How J.M. & Astle N.J.	Wellington	2005/06
2nd	156	Vincent L. & Astle N.J.	Napier	2005/06
3rd	170	Astle N.J. & Twose R.G.	Christchurch	1999/00
4th	191	Ryder J.D. & Anderson C.J.	Queenstown	2013/14
5th	99	Astle N.J. & Marshall H.J.H.	Christchurch	2005/06
6th	130	Nicholls H.M. & Astle T.D.	Christchurch	2017/18
7th	111	Parore A.C. & Patel D.N.	Kingston	1995/96
8th	63*	Vettori D.L. & Franklin J.E.C.	Queenstown	2005/06
9th	44*	Harris C.Z. & Vaughan J.T.C.	Arnos Vale	1995/96
10th	48*	Nash D.J. & Pringle C.	Guwahati	1994/95

West Indies

1st	192*	Greenidge C.G. & Haynes D.L.	Christchurch	1986/87
2nd	184	Haynes D.L. & Gomes H.A.	Bridgetown	1984/85
3rd	186	Lara B.C. & Simmons P.V.	Arnos Vale	1995/96
4th	211	Edwards K.A. & Bravo D.J.	Hamilton	2013/14
5th	91	Adams J.C. & Holder R.I.C.	Port of Spain	1995/96
6th	85	Pollard K.A. & Thomas D.C.	Basseterre	2012
7th	98	Sarwan R.R. & Jacobs R.D.	Port Elizabeth	2002/03
8th	48	Perry N.O. & Dillon M.	Napier	1999/00
9th	77	Sarwan R.R. & Bradshaw I.D.R.	Christchurch	2005/06
10th	41	Brathwaite C.R. & Thomas O.R.	Manchester	2019

New Zealand v Sri Lanka

New Zealand

1st	137*	Guptill M.J. & Munro C.	Cardiff	2019
2nd	163	Guptill M.J. & Williamson K.S.	Mt Maunganui	2018/19
3rd	136	Parore A.C. & Rutherford K.R.	East London	1994/95
4th	154	Taylor L.R.P.L. & Nicholls H.M.	Nelson	2018/19
5th	93	Latham T.W.M. & Ronchi L.	Hambantota	2013/14
6th	267*	Elliott G.D. & Ronchi L.	Dunedin	2014/15
7th	85*	Harris C.Z. & Vincent L.	Christchurch	2000/01
8th	64*	Styris S.B. & Franklin J.E.C.	Grenada	2006/07
9th	47*	Cairns B.L. & Boock S.L.	Colombo	1983/84
10th	65	Snedden M.C. & Chatfield E.J.	Derby	1983

Sri Lanka

1st	201	Tharanga W.U. & Jayasuriya S.T.	Napier	2006/07
2nd	170	Jayasuriya S.T. & Tillakaratne H.P.	Bloemfontein	2002/03
3rd	184	Jayasuriya S.T. & Jayawardene D.P.M.D.	Sharjah	2000/01
4th	127*	Dilshan T.M. & Mathews A.D.	Pallekele	2012/13
5th	110	Atapattu M.S. & Arnold R.P.	Colombo	2001/02
6th	127	Samaraweera T.T. & Mathews A.D.	Colombo	2009/10
7th	98	Siriwardana T.A.M. & Kulasekera K.M.D.N.	Christchurch	2015/16
8th	75	Perera N.L.T.C. & Malinga S.L.	Mt Maunganui	2018/19
9th	51	Perera N.L.T.C. & Sandakan P.A.D.L.R	Mt Maunganui	2018/19
10th	44	Perera N.L.T.C. & Pradeep N.	Mt Maunganui	2018/19

New Zealand v Zimbabwe

New Zealand

1st	236*	Guptill M.J. & Latham T.W.M.	Harare	2015/16
2nd	157	Guptill M.J. & McCullum B.B.	Harare	2011/12
3rd	152	Spearman C.M. & Twose R.G.	Harare	2000/01
4th	130	Crowe M.D. & Rutherford K.R.	Harare	1992/93
5th	195	Taylor L.R.P.L. & Williamson K.S.	Bulawayo	2011/12
6th	75	Cairns C.L. & Harris C.Z.	Hamilton	1997/98
7th	57	McCullum N.L. & Ellis A.M.	Dunedin	2011/12
8th	79	Styris S.B. & Vettori D.L.	Harare	2005/06
9th	55	Harris C.Z. & Larsen G.R.	Bulawayo	1997/98
10th	28	Franklin J.E.C. & Martin C.S.	Taupo	2000/01

Zimbabwe

1st	124	Flower A. & Flower G.W.	Harare	1992/93
2nd	120	Masakadza H. & Ervine C.R.	Harare	2015/16
3rd	154	Carlisle S.V. & Flower A.	Taupo	2000/01
4th	123	Rennie G.J. & Campbell A.D.R.	Harare	1997/98
5th	156	Taylor B.R.M. & Mutizwa F.	Harare	2011/12
6th	112	Waller M.N. & Chigumbura E.	Bulawayo	2011/12
7th	68	Taibu T. & Streak H.H.	Bloemfontein	2002/03
8th	117	Houghton D.L. & Butchart I.P.	Hyderabad	1987/88
9th	89	Sikandar Raza & Panyangara T.	Harare	2015/16
10th	23	Strang B.C. & Whittall A.R.	Harare	1997/98

New Zealand v South Africa

New Zealand				
1st	126	Guptill M.J. & Latham T.W.M.	Potchefstroom	2015/16
2nd	154	McCullum B.B. & How J.M.	Port Elizabeth	2007/08
3rd	180	Guptill M.J. & Taylor L.R.P.L.	Hamilton	2016/17
4th	150	Twose R.G. & Cairns C.L.	Cape Town	2000/01
5th	123*	Taylor L.R.P.L. & Neesham J.D.S.	Christchurch	2016/17
6th	124	McMillan C.D. & Harris C.Z.	Adelaide	1997/98
7th	84*	Cairns C.L. & Parore A.C.	Brisbane	2001/02
8th	69	Parore A.C. & Nash D.J.	Brisbane	1997/98
9th	47*	Parore A.C. & Vettori D.L.	Perth	2001/02
	47	Franklin J.E.C. & Mills K.D.	Paarl	2012/13
10th	76	Ronchi L & McClenaghan M.J.	Mt Maunganui	2014/15
South Africa				
1st	176	Kirsten G. & Gibbs H.H.	Birmingham	1999
2nd	185	Amla H.M. & Roussow R.R.	Centurion	2015/16
3rd	139*	Kallis J.H. & Dippenaar H.H.	Melbourne	2001/02
4th	145	Kallis J.H. & Cullinan D.J.	Auckland	1998/99
5th	139*	de Villiers A.B. & Duminy J.P.	Mt Maunganui	2014/15
6th	97*	Rhodes J.N. & Pollock S.M.	Perth	2001/02
7th	84	de Villiers A.B. & Parnell W.D.	Wellington	2016/17
8th	69*	Klusener L. & Abrahams S.	Cape Town	2000/01
9th	61	Pretorious D. & Phehlukwayo A.L.	Christchurch	2016/17
10th	67*	Morkel J.A. & Ntini M.	Napier	2003/04

New Zealand v Bangladesh

New Zealand				
1st	158	Crowe M.D. & Wright J.G.	Sharjah	1989/90
2nd	179	Williamson K.S. & Broom N.T.	Nelson	2016/17
3rd	131	Guptill M.J. & Taylor L.R.P.L.	Hamilton	2014/15
4th	130	Taylor L.R.P.L. & Munro C	Fatullah	2013/14
5th	159	Conway D.P. & Mitchell D.J.	Wellington	2020/21
6th	86	Vettori D.L. & Elliott G.D.	Mirpur	2010/11
7th	123	Broom N.T. & Oram J.D.P.	Napier	2009/10
8th	72	Taylor L.R.P.L. & Mills K.D.	Mirpur	2010/11
9th	37	McCullum N.L. & Mills K.D.	Mirpur	2013/14
10th	45*	Oram J.D.P. & Patel J.S.	Mirpur	2008/09
Bangladesh				
1st	127	Imrul Kayes & Shariar Nafees	Mirpur	2010/11
2nd	136	Tamim Iqbal & Sabbir Rahman	Dublin	2017
3rd	109	Zunaed Siddique & Mohammad Ashraful	Mirpur	2008/09
4th	154	Mushfiqur Rahim & Naeem Islam	Mirpur	2013/14
5th	224	Shakib Al Hasan & Mahmudullah	Cardiff	2017
6th	101	Sabbir Rahman & Mohammad Saifuddin	Dunedin	2018/19
7th	101	Mushfiqur Rahim & Naeem Islam	Dunedin	2009/10
8th	84	Mohammad Mithun & Mohammad Saifuddin	Napier	2018/19
9th	52	Mahmudullah & Rubel Hossain	Wellington	2008/09
10th	34	Mohammad Rafique & Syed Rasel	Antigua	2006/07

CAREER RECORDS

Averages

	M	In	NO	HS	Runs	Ave	100	50	Ct	St	Balls	Runs	Wkts	Ave	5WI	Best	R/100B	B/W
Adams A.R.	42	34	10	45	419	17.45	—	—	8	—	1885	1643	53	31.00	1	5-22	87	35
Aldridge G.W.	2	—	—	—	—	—	—	—	—	—	114	98	1	98.00	—	1-45	86	114
Allott G.I.	31	11	6	7*	17	3.40	—	—	5	—	1528	1207	52	23.21	—	4-35	78	29
Anderson C.J.	49	44	4	131*	1109	27.72	1	4	11	—	1485	1502	60	25.03	1	5-63	101	24
Anderson R.W.	2	2	1	12	16	16.00	—	—	1	—	—	—	—	—	—	—	—	—
Astle N.J.	223	217	14	145*	7090	34.92	16	41	83	—	4850	3809	99	38.47	—	4-43	78	48
Astle T.D.	9	5	2	49	79	26.33	—	—	2	—	270	246	10	24.60	—	3-33	91	27
Bailey M.D.	1	—	—	—	—	—	—	—	—	—	—	—	—	—	—	—	—	—
Bates M.D.	2	1	0	13	13	13.00	—	—	1	—	84	52	2	26.00	—	1-24	61	42
Bell M.D.	7	7	0	66	133	19.00	—	1	1	—	—	—	—	—	—	—	—	—
Bennett H.K.	19	7	5	4*	10	5.00	—	—	3	—	892	820	33	24.84	—	4-16	91	27
Blain T.E.	38	38	11	49*	442	16.37	—	—	37	1	—	—	—	—	—	—	—	—
Blair B.R.	14	14	2	29*	174	12.50	—	—	4	—	30	34	1	34.00	—	1-7	113	30
Blundell T.A.	2	2	0	22	31	15.50	—	—	1	—	—	—	—	—	—	—	—	—
Bond S.E.	82	40	22	31*	292	16.22	—	—	15	—	4295	3070	147	20.88	4	6-19	71	29
Boock S.L.	14	7	4	12	30	10.00	—	—	5	—	700	513	15	34.20	—	3-28	73	46
Boult T.A.	93	40	23	21*	159	9.35	—	—	34	—	5157	4261	169	25.21	5	7-34	82	30
Bracewell B.P.	1	1	1	0*	0	—	—	—	—	—	66	41	1	41.00	—	1-41	62	66
Bracewell D.A.J.	19	12	2	57	158	15.80	—	—	3	—	932	798	23	34.69	—	4-55	85	406
Bracewell J.G.	53	43	12	43	512	16.51	—	—	19	—	2447	1884	33	57.09	—	2-3	76	74
Bradburn G.E.	11	10	3	30	60	8.57	—	—	2	—	385	318	6	53.00	—	2-18	82	64
Broom N.T.	39	39	4	109*	943	26.94	1	5	9	—	—	—	—	—	—	—	—	—
Brown V.R.	3	3	0	32	44	14.66	—	—	2	—	66	75	1	75.00	—	1-24	113	66
Brownlie D.G.	16	15	1	63	361	25.78	—	1	6	—	—	—	—	—	—	—	—	—
Bulfin C.E.	4	2	1	7*	9	9.00	—	—	1	—	102	109	0	—	—	—	106	—
Burgess M.G.	26	20	0	47	336	16.80	—	—	8	—	74	69	1	69.00	—	1-10	93	74
Butler I.G.	26	13	5	25	84	10.50	—	—	8	—	1109	1038	28	37.07	—	4-44	93	39
Cairns B.L.	78	65	6	60	987	16.73	—	2	19	—	4015	2717	89	30.47	1	5-28	67	45
Cairns C.L.	215	193	25	115	4950	29.46	4	26	66	—	8168	6594	201	32.80	1	5-42	80	40
Canning T.K.	4	4	1	23*	52	17.33	—	—	1	—	204	203	5	40.60	—	2-30	100	41
Chapman M.S.	6	6	1	124*	161	32.30	1	—	1	—	—	—	—	—	—	—	—	—
Chatfield E.J.	114	48	37	19*	118	10.72	—	—	19	—	6065	3618	140	25.84	1	5-34	59	43
Collinge R.O.	16	10	4	19	53	8.83	—	—	1	—	915	517	19	27.21	1	5-23	56	48
Coman P.G.	3	3	0	38	62	20.66	—	—	2	—	—	—	—	—	—	—	—	—
Coney J.V.	88	80	19	66*	1874	30.72	—	8	40	—	2931	2039	54	37.75	—	4-46	69	54
Congdon B.E.	12	10	3	101	373	54.71	1	2	1	—	501	322	8	40.25	—	2-17	64	62
Conway D.P.	3	3	0	126	225	75.00	1	1	3	—								
Crowe J.J.	75	71	12	88*	1518	25.72	—	7	28	—	6	1	0	—	—	—	16	—
Crowe M.D.	143	140	18	107*	4704	38.55	4	34	66	—	1296	954	29	32.89	—	2-9	73	44
Cumming C.D.	13	13	1	45*	161	13.41	—	—	6	—	18	17	0	—	—	—	94	—
Davis H.T.	11	6	4	7*	13	6.50	—	—	2	—	432	436	11	39.63	—	4-35	100	39
de Grandhomme C.	42	33	7	74*	722	27.76	—	4	14	—	1458	1180	27	43.70	—	3-26	80	54
de Groen R.P.	12	8	3	7*	12	2.40	—	—	2	—	549	478	8	59.75	—	2-34	87	68
Devcich A.P.	12	11	0	58	195	17.72	—	1	3	—	324	291	4	72.75	—	2-33	89	81
Diamanti B.J.	1	1	1	26*	26	—	—	—	1	—	12	25	0	—	—	—	208	—
Douglas M.W.	6	6	0	30	55	9.16	—	—	2	—	—	—	—	—	—	—	—	—
Doull S.B.	42	27	13	22	172	12.28	—	—	10	—	1745	1459	36	40.52	—	4-25	83	48
Drum C.J.	5	2	2	7*	9	—	—	—	1	—	216	261	4	65.25	—	2-31	120	54
Edgar B.A.	64	64	5	102*	1814	30.74	1	10	12	—	12	5	0	—	—	—	41	—
Edwards G.N.	7	7	0	41	164	23.42	—	—	7	—	6	5	1	5.00	—	1-5	83	6
Elliott G.D.	83	69	11	115	1976	34.06	2	11	17	—	1302	1179	39	30.23	—	4-31	90	33
Ellis A.M.	15	12	1	33	153	13.90	—	—	3	—	480	425	12	35.41	—	2-22	88	40
Ferguson L.H.	37	16	7	19	63	7.00	—	—	10	—	1956	1779	69	25.78	1	5-45	91	28
Fleming S.P.	280	269	21	134*	8037	32.40	8	49	133	—	29	28	1	28.00	—	1-8	96	29
Flynn D.R.	20	17	2	35	228	15.20	—	—	4	—	24	25	0	—	—	—	104	—
Franklin J.E.C.	109	79	27	98*	1265	24.32	—	4	26	—	3836	3334	81	41.16	1	5-42	86	47
Franklin T.J.	3	3	0	21	27	9.00	—	—	—	—	—	—	—	—	—	—	—	—
Fulton P.G.	49	46	5	112	1334	32.53	1	8	17	—	—	—	—	—	—	—	—	—
Germon L.K.	37	31	5	89	519	19.96	—	3	21	9	—	—	—	—	—	—	—	—
Gillespie M.R.	32	14	8	28	93	15.50	—	—	6	—	1521	1369	37	37.00	—	4-58	90	41

	M	*In*	*NO*	*HS*	*Runs*	*Ave*	*100*	*50*	*Ct*	*St*	*Balls*	*Runs*	*Wkts*	*Ave*	*5WI*	*Best*	*R/100B*	*B/W*
Gillespie S.R.	19	11	5	18*	70	11.66	—	—	7	—	963	736	23	32.00	—	4-30	76	41
Gray E.J.	10	7	1	38	98	16.33	—	—	3	—	386	286	8	35.75	—	2-26	74	48
Greatbatch M.J.	84	83	5	111	2206	28.28	2	13	35	—	6	5	0	—	—	—	83	—
Guptill M.J.	186	183	19	237*	6927	42.23	16	37	93	—	109	98	4	24.50	—	2-4	90	27
Hadlee B.G.	2	2	1	19	26	26.00	—	—	—	—	—	—	—	—	—	—	—	—
Hadlee D.R.	12	8	2	20	56	9.33	—	—	3	—	683	410	23	17.82	—	4-34	60	29
Hadlee R.J.	115	98	17	79	1751	21.61	—	4	27	—	6182	3407	158	21.56	5	5-25	55	39
Hamilton L.J.	2	2	2	2*	3	—	—	—	—	—	108	143	1	143.00	—	1-76	132	108
Harris C.Z.	250	213	62	130	4379	29.00	1	16	96		10667	7613	203	37.50	1	5-42	71	53
Hart M.N.	13	8	0	16	61	7.62	—	—	7	—	572	373	13	28.69	1	5-22	65	44
Hart R.G.	2	1	0	0	0	0.00	—	—	1	—	—	—	—	—	—	—	—	—
Hart R.T.	1	1	0	3	3	3.00	—	—	—	—	—	—	—	—	—	—	—	—
Hartland B.R.	16	16	1	68*	311	20.73	—	2	5	—	—	—	—	—	—	—	—	—
Haslam M.J.	1	1	0	9	9	—	—	—	—	—	30	28	1	28.00	—	1-28	93	30
Hastings B.F.	12	10	1	37	176	19.55	—	—	4	—	—	—	—	—	—	—	—	—
Hayes R.L.	1	1	0	13	13	13.00	—	—	—	—	42	31	0	—	—	—	73	—
Henry M.J.	55	21	7	48*	211	15.07	—	—	17	—	2877	2538	98	25.89	2	5-30	88	29
Hitchcock P.A.	14	7	3	11*	41	10.25	—	—	4	—	558	468	12	39.00	—	3-30	83	46
Hopkins G.J.	25	17	1	45	236	14.75	—	—	27	1	—	—	—	—	—	—	—	—
Horne M.J.	50	48	0	74	980	20.41	—	5	12	—	—	—	—	—	—	—	—	—
Horne P.A.	4	4	0	18	50	12.50	—	—	—	—	—	—	—	—	—	—	—	—
How J.M.	41	37	1	139	1046	29.05	1	7	19	—	—	—	—	—	—	—	—	—
Howarth G.P.	71	66	5	76	1384	22.72	—	6	16	—	90	68	3	22.67	—	1-4	75	30
Howarth H.J.	10	6	3	11	21	7.00	—	—	3	—	556	304	14	27.71	—	3-24	54	39
Howell L.G.	12	12	0	68	287	23.92	—	4	2	—	—	—	—	—	—	—	—	—
Ingram P.J.	8	7	0	69	193	27.57	—	1	3	—	—	—	—	—	—	—	—	—
Jamieson K.A.	5	1	1	25*	25	—	—	—	2	—	276	186	5	37.20	—	2-42	67	55
Jones A.H.	87	87	9	93	2784	35.69	—	25	23	—	306	216	4	54.00	—	2-42	70	76
Jones R.A.	5	5	0	63	168	33.60	—	1	—	—	—	—	—	—	—	—	—	—
Kennedy R.J.	7	4	3	8*	17	17.00	—	—	1	—	312	283	5	56.60	—	2-36	90	62
Kuggeleijn C.M.	16	11	2	40	142	15.77	—	—	9	—	817	604	12	50.33	—	2-31	74	68
Kuggeleijn S.C.	2	1	1	11	11	11.00	—	—	—	—	84	58	5	11.60	—	3-41	69	16
Larsen G.R.	121	70	27	37	629	14.62	—	—	23	—	6368	4000	113	35.39	—	4-24	62	56
Latham R.T.	33	33	4	60	583	20.10	—	1	11	—	450	386	11	35.09	1	5-32	85	40
Latham T.W.M.	102	94	11	137	2824	34.02	5	16	85	8	—	—	—	—	—	—	—	—
Lees W.K.	31	24	5	26	215	11.31	—	—	28	2	—	—	—	—	—	—	—	—
McClenaghan M.J.	48	14	10	34*	108	27.00	—	—	4	—	2336	2313	82	28.20	1	5-58	99	28
McCullum B.B.	260	228	28	166	6083	30.41	5	32	262	15	—	—	—	—	—	—	—	—
McCullum N.L.	84	62	11	65	1070	20.98	—	4	41	—	3536	2956	63	46.92	—	3-24	83	56
McEwan P.E.	17	15	0	41	204	13.60	—	—	1	—	420	353	6	58.83	—	2-29	84	70
McGlashan P.D.	4	2	1	56*	63	63.00	—	1	8	—	—	—	—	—	—	—	—	—
McKay A.J.	19	10	7	4*	12	4.00	—	—	3	—	926	800	27	29.62	—	4-53	86	34
McKechnie B.J.	14	8	4	27	54	13.50	—	—	2	—	818	495	19	26.05	—	3-23	60	43
McMillan C.D.	197	183	16	117	4707	28.18	3	28	44	—	1879	1717	49	35.04	—	3-20	91	38
McSweeney E.B.	16	14	5	18*	73	8.11	—	—	14	3	—	—	—	—	—	—	—	—
Marshall H.J.H.	66	62	9	101*	1454	27.43	1	12	18	—	—	—	—	—	—	—	—	—
Marshall J.A.H.	10	10	0	161	250	25.00	1	1	—	—	—	—	—	—	—	—	—	—
Martin C.S.	20	7	2	3	8	1.60	—	—	7	—	948	804	18	44.66	—	3-62	84	52
Mason M.J.	26	7	4	13*	24	8.00	—	—	4	—	1179	1024	31	33.03	—	4-24	86	38
Mathieson A.W.	1	—	—	—	—	—	—	—	—	—	24	40	1	40.00	—	1-40	166	24
Millmow J.P.	5	1	1	0*	0	—	—	—	1	—	270	232	4	58.00	—	2-22	85	67
Mills K.D.	170	101	34	54	1047	15.62	—	2	42	—	8230	6485	240	27.02	1	5-25	79	34
Milne A.F.	40	17	7	36	168	16.80	—	—	21	—	1801	1581	41	38.56	—	3-49	87	43
Mitchell D.J.	3	2	2	100*	112	—	1	—	—	—	30	33	0	—	—	—	110	-
Morrison D.K.	96	43	24	20*	171	9.00	—	—	19	—	4586	3470	126	27.53	2	5-34	75	36
Morrison J.F.M.	19	16	3	55	301	23.15	—	1	6	—	283	199	8	24.87	—	3-24	70	35
Munro C.	57	53	2	87	1271	24.92	—	8	22	—	552	481	7	68.71	—	2-10	87	78
Murray D.J.	1	1	0	3	3	3.00	—	—	—	—	—	—	—	—	—	—	—	—
Nash D.J.	81	53	13	42	624	15.60	—	—	25	—	3416	2622	64	40.96	—	4-38	76	53
Neesham J.D.S.	66	56	10	97	1320	28.69	—	6	24	—	2115	2139	68	31.45	2	5-27	101	31
Nethula T.S.	5	3	1	9*	12	6.00	—	—	2	—	264	249	5	49.80	—	2-41	94	52
Nevin C.J.	37	36	0	74	732	20.33	—	4	16	3	—	—	—	—	—	—	—	—
Nicholls H.M.	52	50	11	124*	1409	36.12	1	11	21	—	—	—	—	—	—	—	—	—
Nicol R.J.	22	21	2	146	586	30.84	2	2	11	—	339	329	10	32.90	—	4-19	97	33
O'Brien I.E.	10	2	2	3*	3	—	—	—	1	—	453	488	14	34.85	—	3-68	107	32

	M	In	NO	HS	Runs	Ave	100	50	Ct	St	Balls	Runs	Wkts	Ave	5WI	Best	R/100B	B/W
O'Connor S.B.	38	13	6	8	24	3.42	—	—	11	—	1487	1397	46	30.36	2	5-39	93	32
O'Sullivan D.R.	3	2	1	1*	2	2.00	—	—	—	—	168	123	2	61.50	—	1-38	73	84
Oram J.D.P.	160	116	15	101*	2434	24.09	1	13	51	—	6911	5047	173	29.17	1	5-26	73	39
Owens M.B.	1	1	0	0	0	0.00	—	—	—	—	48	37	0	—	—	—	77	—
Papps M.H.W.	6	6	2	92*	207	51.75	—	2	1	—	—	—	—	—	—	—	—	—
Parker J.M.	25	21	0	66	280	13.33	—	1	11	1	16	10	1	10.00	—	1-10	62	16
Parker N.M.	1	1	0	0	0	0.00	—	—	1	—	—	—	—	—	—	—	—	—
Parore A.C.	179	161	32	108	3314	25.68	1	14	116	25	—	—	—	—	—	—	—	—
Patel D.N.	75	63	10	71	623	11.75	—	1	23	—	3251	2260	45	50.22	—	3-22	69	72
Patel J.S.	43	15	8	34	95	13.57	—	—	13	—	2014	1691	49	34.51	—	3-11	84	41
Penn A.J.	5	3	1	15	23	11.50	—	—	1	—	159	201	1	201.00	—	1-50	126	159
Petrie R.G.	12	8	3	21	65	13.00	—	—	2	—	660	449	12	37.41	—	2-25	68	55
Pollard V.	3	2	0	55	67	33.50	—	1	1	—	—	—	—	—	—	—	—	—
Priest M.W.	18	14	4	24	103	10.30	—	—	2	—	752	590	8	73.75	—	2-27	78	94
Pringle C.	64	41	19	34*	193	8.77	—	—	7	—	3314	2459	103	23.87	1	5-45	74	32
Rance S.H.A.	2	—	—	—	—	—	—	—	3	—	105	110	1	110.00	—	1-44	105	105
Redmond A.J.	6	6	0	52	152	25.33	—	1	3	—	—	—	—	—	—	—	—	—
Redmond R.E.	2	1	0	3	3	3.00	—	—	—	—	—	—	—	—	—	—	—	—
Reid J.F.	25	24	1	88	633	27.16	—	4	5	—	—	—	—	—	—	—	—	—
Reid R.B.	9	9	0	64	248	27.55	—	2	3	—	7	13	1	13.00	—	1-13	185	7
Richardson M.H.	4	4	0	26	42	10.50	—	—	1	—	—	—	—	—	—	—	—	—
Roberts A.D.G.	1	1	0	16	16	16.00	—	—	1	—	56	30	1	30.00	—	1-30	53	56
Roberts S.J.	2	1	1	1*	1	—	—	—	—	—	42	47	0	—	—	—	111	—
Robertson G.K.	10	6	0	17	49	8.16	—	—	2	—	498	321	6	53.50	—	2-29	64	83
Ronchi L.	85	68	9	170*	1397	23.67	1	4	105	12	—	—	—	—	—	—	—	—
Rutherford H.D.	4	4	0	11	15	3.75	—	—	2	—	—	—	—	—	—	—	—	—
Rutherford K.R.	121	115	9	108	3143	29.65	2	18	41	—	389	323	10	32.30	—	2-39	83	38
Ryder J.D.	48	42	1	107	1362	33.21	3	6	15	—	407	412	12	34.33	—	3-29	101	33
Santner M.J.	75	57	23	67	927	27.26	—	2	30	—	3385	2742	75	36.56	1	5-50	81	45
Seifert T.L.	3	2	0	22	33	16.50	—	—	7	1	—	—	—	—	—	—	—	—
Sinclair M.S.	54	50	4	118*	1304	28.34	2	8	17	—	—	—	—	—	—	—	—	—
Smith I.D.S.	98	77	16	62*	1055	17.29	—	3	81	5	—	—	—	—	—	—	—	—
Snedden M.C.	93	54	19	64	535	15.28	—	1	19	—	4525	3237	114	28.39	—	4-34	71	39
Sodhi I.S.	33	14	3	24	81	7.36	—	—	8	—	1620	1508	43	35.06	—	4-58	93	37
Southee T.G.	143	86	32	55	679	12.57	—	1	39	—	7195	6558	190	34.51	3	7-33	91	37
Spearman C.M.	51	50	0	86	936	18.72	—	5	15	—	3	6	0	—	—	—	—	—
Stewart S.L.	4	4	0	14	26	6.50	—	—	—	—	—	—	—	—	—	—	—	—
Stirling D.A.	6	5	2	13*	21	7.00	—	—	3	—	246	207	6	34.33	—	2-29	84	41
Stott L.W.	1	—	—	—	—	—	—	—	1	—	72	48	3	16.00	—	3-48	66	24
Styris S.B.	188	161	23	141	4483	32.48	4	28	73	—	6114	4839	137	35.32	1	6-25	79	44
Su'a M.L.	12	7	2	12*	24	4.80	—	—	1	—	463	367	9	40.77	—	4-59	79	51
Sulzberger G.P.	3	2	1	6*	9	9.00	—	—	—	—	132	102	3	34.00	—	1-28	77	44
Tait A.R.	5	5	2	13*	35	11.66	—	—	—	—	120	88	3	29.33	—	2-37	73	40
Taylor B.R.	2	1	0	22	22	22.00	—	—	1	—	114	62	4	15.50	—	3-25	54	28
Taylor L.R.P.L.	233	217	39	181*	8581	48.20	21	51	139	—	42	35	0	—	—	—	83	—
Thompson E.P.	1	—	—	—	—	—	—	—	—	—	24	42	0	—	—	—	175	—
Thomson S.A.	56	52	10	83	964	22.95	—	5	18	—	2121	1602	42	38.14	—	3-14	75	50
Troup G.B.	22	12	8	39	101	25.25	—	—	2	—	1180	791	32	23.97	—	4-19	67	36
Tuffey D.R.	94	52	21	36	295	9.51	—	—	20	—	4333	3534	110	32.12	—	4-24	83	39
Turner G.M.	41	40	6	171*	1598	47.00	3	9	13	—	6	0	0	—	—	—	—	—
Twose R.G.	87	81	11	103	2717	38.81	1	20	37	—	272	237	4	59.25	—	2-31	87	68
Vance R.H.	8	8	0	96	248	31.00	—	1	4	—	—	—	—	—	—	—	—	—
Vaughan J.T.C.	18	16	7	33	162	18.00	—	—	4	—	696	524	15	34.93	—	4-33	75	46
Vettori D.L.	295	187	57	83	2253	17.33	—	4	88	—	14060	9674	305	31.71	2	5-7	69	46
Vincent L.	102	99	10	172	2414	27.12	3	11	41	—	20	25	1	25.00	—	1-0	125	20
Vivian G.E.	1	1	0	14	14	14.00	—	—	—	—	—	—	—	—	—	—	—	—
Wadsworth K.J.	14	11	1	104	302	30.20	1	—	15	3	—	—	—	—	—	—	—	—
Walker B.G.K.	11	7	4	16*	47	15.66	—	—	5	—	438	417	8	52.12	—	2-43	95	54
Walker M.D.J.	3	1	0	10	10	10.00	—	—	2	—	132	119	4	29.75	—	4-49	90	33
Walmsley K.P.	2	—	—	—	—	—	—	—	—	—	120	117	2	58.60	—	1-53	97	60
Watling B-J.	28	25	2	96*	573	24.91	—	5	20	—	—	—	—	—	—	—	—	—
Watson W.	61	24	13	21	86	7.81	—	—	9	—	3251	2247	74	30.36	—	4-27	69	43
Webb P.N.	5	5	1	10*	38	9.50	—	—	3	—	—	—	—	—	—	—	—	—
Webb R.J.	3	1	1	6*	6	—	—	—	—	—	161	105	4	26.25	—	2-28	65	40
Wheeler B.M.	6	4	4	39*	58	—	—	—	1	—	309	315	8	39.37	—	3-63	101	38

	M	In	NO	HS	Runs	Ave	100	50	Ct	St	Balls	Runs	Wkts	Ave	5WI	Best	R/100B	B/W
White D.J.	3	3	0	15	37	12.33	—	—	1	—	—	—	—	—	—	—	—	—
Williamson K.S.	151	144	14	148	6173	47.48	13	39	60	—	1467	1310	37	35.40	—	4-22	89	39
Wilson J.W.	6	6	1	44*	103	20.60	—	—	4	—	242	260	4	65.00	—	2-21	107	61
Wiseman P.J.	15	7	5	16	45	22.50	—	—	2	—	450	368	12	30.66	—	4-45	81	37
Wisneski W.A.	3	2	1	6	10	10.00	—	—	1	—	114	123	0	—	—	—	107	—
Woodcock L.J.	4	2	1	11	14	14.00	—	—	—	—	164	155	3	51.66	—	2-58	94	54
Worker G.H.	10	10	2	58	272	34.00	—	3	5	—	6	5	0	—	—	—	83	—
Wright J.G.	149	148	1	101	3891	26.46	1	24	51	—	24	8	0	—	—	—	33	—
Young B.A.	74	73	5	74	1668	24.52	—	9	28	—	—	—	—	—	—	—	—	—
Young W.A.	2	2	1	11*	12	12.00	—	—	1	—								

Cairns' record includes one match for ICC World XI
Chapman's record includes two matches for Hong Kong (China)
Fleming's record includes one match for ICC World XI
Ronchi's record includes four matches for Australia
Vettori's record includes four matches for ICC World XI

SUMMARY OF ONE-DAY INTERNATIONAL CAREER RECORDS

Most Matches

Vettori D.L.	295	Styris S.B.	188	Southee T.G.	143
Fleming S.P.	280	Guptill M.J.	186	Rutherford K.R.	121
McCullum B.B.	260	Parore A.C.	179	Larsen G.R.	121
Harris C.Z.	250	Mills K.D.	170	Hadlee R.J.	115
Taylor L.R.P.L.	233	Oram J.D.P.	160	Chatfield E.J.	114
Astle N.J.	223	Williamson K.S.	151	Franklin J.E.C.	109
Cairns C.L.	215	Wright J.G.	149	Vincent L.	102
McMillan C.D.	197	Crowe M.D.	143	Latham T.W.M.	102

Most Runs

		Ave			*Ave*
Taylor L.R.P.L.	8581	48.20	Wright J.G.	3891	26.46
Fleming S.P.	8037	32.40	Parore A.C.	3314	25.68
Astle N.J.	7090	34.92	Rutherford K.R.	3143	29.65
Guptill M.J.	6927	42.23	Latham T.W.M.	2824	34.02
Williamson K.S.	6173	47.48	Jones A.H.	2784	35.69
McCullum B.B.	6083	30.41	Twose R.G.	2717	38.81
Cairns C.L.	4950	29.46	Oram J.D.P.	2434	24.09
McMillan C.D.	4707	28.18	Vincent L.	2414	27.12
Crowe M.D.	4704	38.55	Vettori D.L.	2253	17.33
Styris S.B.	4483	32.48	Greatbatch M.J.	2206	28.28
Harris C.Z.	4379	29.00			

Most Wickets

		Ave			*Ave*
Vettori D.L.	305	31.71	Bond S.E.	147	20.88
Mills K.D.	240	27.02	Chatfield E.J.	140	25.84
Harris C.Z.	203	37.50	Styris S.B.	137	35.32
Cairns C.L.	201	32.80	Morrison D.K.	126	27.53
Southee T.G.	190	34.51	Snedden M.C.	114	28.39
Oram J.D.P.	173	29.17	Larsen G.R.	113	35.39
Boult T.A.	169	25.21	Tuffey D.R.	110	32.12
Hadlee R.J.	158	21.56	Pringle C.	103	23.87

Most Economical Bowling

(qualification 600 balls)

	Balls bowled	***Runs conceded***	***Runs conceded per 100 balls***		***Balls bowled***	***Runs conceded***	***Runs conceded per 100 balls***
Hadlee R.J.	6182	3407	55.11	Larsen G.R.	6368	4000	62.81
Collinge R.O.	915	517	56.50	Troup G.B.	1180	791	67.03
Chatfield E.J.	6065	3618	59.65	Cairns B.L.	4015	2717	67.67
Hadlee D.R.	683	410	60.02	Petrie R.G.	660	449	68.03
McKechnie B.J.	818	495	60.51	Vettori D.L.	14,060	9674	68.80

Best Strike Rates

(qualification 600 balls)

	Balls bowled	Wickets	Balls per wicket
Anderson C.J.	1485	60	24.75
Bennett H.K.	892	33	27.03
Ferguson L.H.	1956	69	28.35
McClenaghan M.J.	2336	82	28.49
Bond S.E.	4295	147	29.22
Henry M.J.	2877	98	29.36
Allott G.I.	1528	52	29.38
Hadlee D.R.	683	23	29.70
Boult T.A.	5157	169	30.51
Neesham J.D.S.	2115	68	31.10

Register of New Zealand One-day Cricketers Who Have Not Played Test Cricket

	Born	Type	
Aldridge	15/11/1977	RHB	RFM
Graeme William	Christchurch		
Bailey	26/11/1970	RHB	RM
Mark David	Hamilton		
Bates	11/10/1983	RHB	LFM
Michael David	Auckland		
Blair	27/12/1957	LHB	RM
Bruce Robert	Dunedin		
Bulfin	19/8/1973	RHB	RFM
Carl Edwin	Blenheim		
Canning	7/4/1977	RHB	RFM
Tamahau Karangatukituki	Adelaide, Australia		
Chapman	27/6/1994	LHB	SLA
Mark Sinclair	Hong Kong (China)		
Coman	13/4/1943	RHB	
Peter George	Christchurch		
Devcich	28/9/1985	LHB	SLA
Anton Paul	Hamilton		
Diamanti	30/4/1981	RHB	RM
Brendon John	Blenheim		
Douglas	20/10/1968	LHB	
Mark William	Nelson		
Ellis	24/3/1982	RHB	RM
Andrew Malcolm	Christchurch		
Hadlee	14/12/1941	RHB	
Barry George	Christchurch		
Hamilton	5/4/1973	RHB	LFM
Lance John	Papakura		
Hart	7/11/1961	RHB	
Ronald Terence	Lower Hutt		
Hayes	9/5/1971	RHB	RFM
Roydon Leslie	Paeroa		
Hitchcock	23/1/1975	RHB	RM
Paul Anthony	Whangarei		
Howell	8/7/1972	RHB	
Llorne Gregory	Napier		
Kuggeleijn	3/1/1992	RHB	RFM
Scott Christopher	Hamilton		
McClenaghan	11/6/1986	LHB	LFM
Mitchell John	Hastings		
McCullum	1/9/1980	RHB	ROB
Nathan Leslie	Dunedin		
McGlashan	22/6/1979	RHB	WK
Peter Donald	Napier		

McKechnie Brian John	6/11/1953 Gore	RHB	RM
McSweeney Ervin Bruce	8/3/1957 Wellington	RHB	WK
Mathieson Andrew William	10/10/1989 Hamilton	RHB	RFM
Millmow Jonathan Paul	22/9/1967 Wellington	RHB	RFM
Milne Adam Fraser	13/4/1992 Palmerston North	RHB	RF
Nethula Tarun Sai	8/5/1983 Kurnool, India	RHB	RLB
Nevin Christopher John	3/8/1975 Dunedin	RHB	WK
Penn Andrew Jonathan	27/7/1974 Wanganui	RHB	RFM
Petrie Richard George	23/8/1967 Christchurch	RHB	RFM
Rance Seth Hayden Arnold	23/8/1987 Wellington	RHB	RM
Reid Richard Bruce	3/12/1958 Lower Hutt	RHB	
Roberts Stuart James	22/3/1965 Christchurch	RHB	RFM
Seifert Tim Louis	14/12/1994 Wanganui	RHB	WK
Stewart Shanan Luke	21/6/1982 Christchurch	RHB	RM
Stott Leslie Warren	8/12/1946 Rochdale, England	RHB	RM
Sulzberger Glen Paul	14/3/1973 Kaponga	LHB	ROB
Tait Alex Ross	13/6/1972 Paparoa	RHB	RM
Thompson Ewen Paul	17/12/1979 Warkworth	LHB	LFM
Walker Matthew David John	17/1/1977 Opunake	RHB	RM
Webb Richard John	15/9/1952 Invercargill	RHB	RFM
Wheeler Ben Matthew	10/11/1991 Blenheim	RHB	LM
Wilson Jeffrey William	24/10/1973 Invercargill	RHB	RFM
Wisneski Warren Anthony	19/2/1969 New Plymouth	RHB	RM
Woodcock Luke James	19/3/1982 Wellington	LHB	SLA
Worker George Herrick	23/8/1989 Palmerston North	LHB	SLA

NEW ZEALAND TWENTY20 RECORDS

This section of the *Almanack* is devoted to Twenty20 matches in New Zealand (other than Twenty20 internationals) and has been compiled from the following games:

1. 420 matches in national competitions from 2005/06 to 2020/21.

2. 7 matches involving other teams.

2008/09	New Zealand A v England Lions
2011/12	Canterbury v South Africa
2012/13	New Zealand XI v England *(3 matches)*
2014/15	Island of Origin
2015/16	Island of Origin

Winners of Twenty20 Competitions

STATE TWENTY20

2005/06	Canterbury
2006/07	Auckland
2007/08	Central Districts
2008/09	Otago

HRV CUP

2009/10	Central Districts
2010/11	Auckland
2011/12	Auckland
2012/13	Otago
2013/14	Northern Districts

GEORGIE PIE SUPER SMASH

2014/15	Wellington
2015/16	Auckland

McDONALD'S SUPER SMASH

2016/17	Wellington

BURGER KING SUPER SMASH

2017/18	Northern Districts
2018/19	Central Districts

DREAM11 SUPER SMASH

2019/20	Wellington
2020/21	Wellington

TEAM RECORDS

Highest Totals

249-3	Otago v Central Districts	New Plymouth	2016/17
248-4	Central Districts v Otago	New Plymouth	2016/17
230-5	Northern Districts v Central Districts	Napier	2018/19
230-2	Wellington v Auckland	Auckland	2020/21
229-3	Auckland v Wellington	Auckland	2009/10

Lowest Totals

72	Wellington v Northern Districts	Hamilton	2015/16
74	Auckland v Northern Districts	Auckland	2010/11
77	Northern Districts v Otago	Dunedin	2015/16
80	Northern Districts v Central Districts	Hamilton	2018/19
80	Otago v Auckland	Auckland	2020/21

INDIVIDUAL RECORDS

Centuries

120*	M.J. Guptill	Auckland v Canterbury	Rangiora	2011/12
116*	G.D. Phillips	Auckland v Central Districts	Auckland	2016/17
116	D.P.M.D. Jayawardene	Central Districts v Otago	New Plymouth	2016/17
111*	L.R.P.L. Taylor	Central Districts v Northern Districts	Hamilton	2007/08
110	T.W.M. Latham	Canterbury v Central Districts	Napier	2018/19
108*	B.B. McCullum	Otago v Auckland	Dunedin	2009/10
107	T.L. Seifert	Northern Districts v Auckland	Mt Maunganui	2017/18
106*	G.D. Phillips	Auckland v Otago	Auckland	2019/20
106	H.D. Rutherford	Otago v Central Districts	New Plymouth	2016/17
106	G.H. Worker	Central Districts v Otago	Dunedin	2020/21
105*	L. Vincent	Auckland v Wellington	Auckland	2009/10
105*	D.P. Conway	Wellington v Otago	Dunedin	2018/19
103*	B.B. McCullum	Otago v Northern Districts	Hamilton	2011/12
102	J.M. How	Central Districts v Wellington	New Plymouth	2011/12
102	L. Ronchi	Wellington v Auckland	Auckland	2017/18
102	A.P. Devcich	Northern Districts v Central Districts	New Plymouth	2020/21
101*	B.R.M. Taylor	Wellington v Otago	Queenstown	2011/12
101*	R.J. Nicol	Canterbury v Auckland	Auckland	2011/12
101*	D.P. Conway	Wellington v Otago	Dunedin	2019/20
101	C.B. Gaffaney	Otago v Central Districts	Dunedin	2005/06
101	M.S. Chapman	Auckland v Canterbury	Christchurch	2017/18
101	W.A. Young	Central Districts v Canterbury	Auckland	2020/21
100*	A.J. Redmond	Otago v Central Districts	Dunedin	2008/09
100*	Azhar Mahmood	Auckland v Canterbury	Auckland	2011/12
100	C.Z. Harris	Canterbury v Auckland	Christchurch	2006/07
100*	H.J.H. Marshall	Wellington v Otago	Alexandra	2016/17

Fastest Century

Balls				
40	T.L. Seifert	Northern Districts v Auckland	Mt Maunganui	2017/18

Fastest Fifty

Balls				
14	K. Noema-Barnett	Central Districts v Otago	Invercargill	2010/11

Most Wickets in an Innings

4-0-7-6	K.A. Jamieson	Canterbury v Auckland	Auckland	2018/19
3.1-0-23-6	T.S. Nethula	Northern Districts v Central Districts	Napier	2018/19
4-0-28-6	I.G. Butler	Otago v Auckland	Dunedin	2009/10
4-1-28-6	B. Laughlin	Northern Districts v Wellington	Wellington	2013/14
2.2-1-9-5	A.M. Ellis	Canterbury v Northern Districts	Hamilton	2015/16
4-1-10-5	G.H. Worker	Central Districts v Otago	New Plymouth	2015/16
2-0-12-5	W.S.A. Williams	Canterbury v Wellington	Wellington	2019/20
4-0-14-5	J.D.P. Oram	Central Districts v Otago	New Plymouth	2009/10
4-0-14-5	A.M. Ellis	Canterbury v Wellington	Hamilton	2014/15
3.4-0-14-5	N.G. Smith	Otago v Northern Districts	Hamilton	2019/20
4-0-16-5	A.M. Ellis	Canterbury v Otago	Alexandra	2017/18
4-1-18-5	J.A.Duffy	Otago v Canterbury	Christchurch	2015/16
4-1-19-5	B.M. Tickner	Central Districts v Auckland	New Plymouth	2016/17

4-0-20-5	A.R. Adams	Auckland v Central Districts	Auckland	2010/11
4-0-22-5	R.J. Nicol	Canterbury v Northern Districts	Christchurch	2009/10
4-0-23-5	B.W. Hilfenhaus	Canterbury v Otago	Christchurch	2016/17
4-0-32-5	E.P. Thompson	Central Districts v Otago	Napier	2006/07
4-0-39-5	J.A. Duffy	Otago v Canterbury	Christchurch	2017/18
4-0-45-5	O.R. Newton	Wellington v Central Districts	New Plymouth	2019/20

Most Economical Bowling

4-0-7-6	K.A. Jamieson	Canterbury v Auckland	Auckland	2018/19
4-0-8-2	J.M. McMillan	Otago v Auckland	Alexandra	2013/14
4-0-9-2	M.P.F. Davidson	Canterbury v Northern Districts	Christchurch	2008/09
4-0-9-1	B.J. Arnel	Northern Districts v Canterbury	Christchurch	2009/10
4-0-9-0	B.E. Scott	Northern Districts v Auckland	Mt Maunganui	2010/11
4-0-9-0	M.J. Santner	Northern Districts v Otago	Wellington	2014/15
4-0-9-0	M.J. Santner	Northern Districts v Wellington	Hamilton	2014/15

Most Expensive Bowling

4-0-70-0	A.W. Mathieson	Central Districts v Auckland	Auckland	2015/16
4-0-69-0	D.S. Hutchinson	Wellington v Otago	Dunedin	2013/14
4-0-68-1	N. Wagner	Otago v Central Districts	Invercargill	2017/18
4-0-65-0	R.J. McCone	Central Districts v Auckland	Auckland	2016/17
4-0-63-0	D.K. Ferns	Auckland v Central Districts	New Plymouth	2020/21
4-0-61-3	M.D. Bates	Auckland v Central Districts	New Plymouth	2009/10
4-0-61-0	A.P. Devcich	Northern Districts v Canterbury	Christchurch	2019/10
4-0-60-0	L.M. Burtt	Canterbury v Otago	Dunedin	2008/09
4-0-60-0	T.G. Southee	Northern Districts v Auckland	Mt Maunganui	2017/18
4-0-60-3	L.V. van Beek	Wellington v Central Districts	New Plymouth	2017/18
4-0-60-0	S.C. Kuggeleijn	Northern Districts v Central Districts	Napier	2019/20

Hat-tricks

4-0-18-4	T.L. Tsotsobe	South Africa v Canterbury	Christchurch	2011/12
4-1-22-3	S.J.C. Broad	England v New Zealand XI	Whangarei	2012/13
2.3-0-10-4	M.D. Bates	Auckland v Northern Districts	Hamilton	2014/15
2-0-12-5	W.S.A.Williams	Canterbury v Wellington	Wellington	2019/20

Wicketkeeping

DISMISSALS

	(ct/st)				
5	(4/1)	D.C. de Boorder	Otago v Canterbury	Christchurch	2009/10
5	(4/1)	C.D. Fletcher	Canterbury v Northern Districts	Hamilton	2015/16

Fielding

CATCHES

5	P.G. Fulton	Canterbury v Northern Districts	Hamilton	2015/16

RECORD PARTNERSHIPS

1st	201	P.J. Ingram & J.M. How	CD v Wellington	New Plymouth	2011/12
2nd	188*	N.T. Broom & B.B. McCullum	Otago v ND	Hamilton	2011/12
3rd	124	D.P.M.D. Jayawardene & T.C. Bruce	CD v Otago	New Plymouth	2016/17
4th	143	W.A. Young & D. Cleaver	CD v Auckland	Auckland	2018/19
5th	132	D.J. Mitchell & C.D Fletcher	Canterbury v CD	Auckland	2020/21
6th	112*	A.M. Ellis & B.J. Diamanti	Canterbury v CD	Nelson	2012/13
7th	80	D.J. Mitchell & I.S. Sodhi	ND v Wellington	Hamilton	2017/18
8th	68*	M.D. Bell & L.J. Woodcock	Wellington v Auckland	Auckland	2008/09
9th	47*	T.G. Southee & B.E. Scott	ND v Otago	Invercargill	2009/10
10th	40	C.E. McConchie & E.J. Nuttall	Canterbury v Wellington	Wellington	2018/19

DOMESTIC TWENTY20 CAREER RECORDS

BATTING		*M*	*In*	*NO*	*HS*	*Runs*	*Ave*	*100s*	*50s*
N.T. Broom	*O, C*	114	112	11	96*	2839	28.10	–	18
G.H. Worker	*CD, C*	112	107	8	106	2798	28.26	1	14
R.J. Nicol	*A, C, O*	98	88	11	101*	2336	30.33	1	16
A.P. Devcich	*ND*	102	93	8	102	2189	25.75	1	14
H.D. Rutherford	*O*	90	88	3	106	2109	24.81	1	9
A.K. Kitchen	*A, O*	117	106	9	66	2034	20.96	–	6
M.J. Guptill	*A*	62	58	10	120*	1964	40.91	1	13
D.G. Brownlie	*C, ND*	89	85	4	99	1922	23.72	–	7
D.J. Mitchell	*ND, C*	86	75	21	88*	1919	35.53	–	8
M.H.W. Papps	*C, W*	84	81	6	80*	1735	23.13	–	9

BOWLING		*M*	*O*	*M*	*R*	*W*	*Ave*	*R/O*	*Best*
A.M. Ellis	*C*	116	335.3	5	2794	125	22.35	8.33	5-9
R.M. Hira	*A, C, ND*	103	338.2	1	2451	109	22.48	7.24	4-13
L.J. Woodcock	*W*	107	282	1	2159	92	23.46	7.66	3-20
B.J. Arnel	*ND, W*	92	329.2	3	2649	85	31.16	8.04	4-22
J.A. Duffy	*O*	74	251.3	3	2190	83	26.38	8.71	5-18
J.S. Patel	*W*	87	294.4	3	2071	80	25.88	7.03	4-11
S.C. Kuggeleijn	*W, ND*	81	274	3	2392	80	29.90	8.73	4-18
B.M. Tickner	*CD*	48	173	2	1471	79	18.62	8.50	5-19
T.S. Nethula	*CD, A, ND*	70	245.4	2	1867	76	24.56	7.60	6-23
S.H.A. Rance	*CD*	63	211.2	0	1643	76	21.61	7.77	4-13

NEW ZEALAND TWENTY20 INTERNATIONAL RECORDS

TEAM RECORDS

Results

2004/05	Australia	Auckland	A 214-5	NZ 170	*Australia won by 44 runs*
2005/06	South Africa	Johannesburg	SA 133	NZ 134-5	*NZ won by 5 wickets*
2005/06	West Indies	Auckland	WI 126-7	NZ 126-8	*NZ won bowl-out*
2006/07	Sri Lanka	Wellington	NZ 162-8	SL 62-1	*Sri Lanka won by 18 runs (D/L)*
	Sri Lanka	Auckland	SL 115	NZ 116-5	*NZ won by 5 wickets*
2007/08	Kenya	Durban	K 73	NZ 74-1	*NZ won by 9 wickets*
World Twenty20	Sri Lanka	Johannesburg	NZ 164-7	SL 168-3	*Sri Lanka won by 7 wickets*
	India	Johannesburg	NZ 190	I 180-9	*NZ won by 10 runs*
	England	Durban	NZ 164-9	E 159-8	*NZ won by 5 runs*
	South Africa	Durban	NZ 153-8	SA 158-4	*South Africa won by 6 wickets*
	Pakistan	Cape Town	NZ 143-8	P 147-4	*Pakistan won by 6 wickets*
	South Africa	Johannesburg	NZ 129-7	SA131-7	*South Africa won by 3 wickets*
2007/08	Australia	Perth	A 186-6	NZ 132	*Australia won by 54 runs*
2007/08	England	Auckland	E 184-8	NZ 152	*England won by 32 runs*
	England	Christchurch	E 193-8	NZ 143-8	*England won by 50 runs*
2008	England	Manchester	NZ 123-9	E 127-1	*England won by 9 wickets*
2008/09	West Indies	Auckland	NZ 155-7	WI 155-8	*West Indies won eliminator*
	West Indies	Hamilton	NZ 191-9	WI 155-7	*NZ won by 36 runs*
	Australia	Sydney	A 150-7	NZ 149-5	*Australia won by 1 run*
	India	Christchurch	I 162-8	NZ 166-3	*NZ won by 7 wickets*
	India	Wellington	I 149-6	NZ 150-5	*NZ won by 5 wickets*
2009	Scotland	The Oval	S 89-4	NZ 90-3	*NZ won by 7 wickets*
World Twenty20	South Africa	Lord's	SA 128-7	NZ 127-5	*South Africa won by 1 run*
	Ireland	Nottingham	NZ 198-5	I 115	*NZ won by 83 runs*
	Pakistan	The Oval	NZ 99	P 100-4	*Pakistan won by 6 wickets*
	Sri Lanka	Nottingham	SL 158-5	NZ 110	*Sri Lanka won by 48 runs*
2009/10	Sri Lanka	Colombo	NZ 141-8	SL 138-9	*NZ won by 3 runs*
	Sri Lanka	Colombo	NZ 170-4	SL 148-8	*NZ won by 22 runs*
2009/10	Pakistan	Dubai	P 161-8	NZ 112	*Pakistan won by 49 runs*
	Pakistan	Dubai	P 153-5	NZ 146-5	*Pakistan won by 7 runs*
2009/10	Bangladesh	Hamilton	B 78	NZ 79-0	*NZ won by 10 wickets*
2009/10	Australia	Wellington	NZ 118	A 119-4	*Australia won by 6 wickets*
	Australia	Christchurch	NZ 214-6	A 214-4	*NZ won eliminator*
2009/10	Sri Lanka	Providence	SL 135-6	NZ 139-8	*NZ won by 2 wickets*
World Twenty20	Zimbabwe	Providence	Z 84	NZ 36-1	*NZ won by 7 runs (D/L)*
	South Africa	Bridgetown	SA 170-4	NZ 157-7	*South Africa won by 13 runs*
	Pakistan	Bridgetown	NZ 133-7	P 132-7	*NZ won by 1 run*
	England	Gros Islet	NZ 149-6	E 153-7	*England won by 3 wickets*
2009/10	Sri Lanka	Lauderhill	NZ 120-7	SL 92	*NZ won by 28 runs*
	Sri Lanka	Lauderhill	NZ 81	SL 82-3	*Sri Lanka won by 7 wickets*

2010/11	Pakistan	Auckland	P 143-9	NZ 146-5	*NZ won by 5 wickets*
	Pakistan	Hamilton	NZ 185-7	P 146-9	*NZ won by 39 runs*
	Pakistan	Christchurch	P 183-6	NZ 80	*Pakistan won by 103 runs*
2011/12	Zimbabwe	Harare	Z 123-8	NZ 127-0	*NZ won by 10 wickets*
	Zimbabwe	Harare	NZ 187-3	Z 154	*NZ won by 33 runs*
2011/12	Zimbabwe	Auckland	Z 159-8	NZ 160-3	*NZ won by 7 wickets*
	Zimbabwe	Hamilton	Z 200-2	NZ 202-5	*NZ won by 5 wickets*
2011/12	South Africa	Wellington	SA 147-6	NZ 148-4	*NZ won by 6 wickets*
	South Africa	Hamilton	NZ 173-4	SA 174-2	*South Africa won by 8 wickets*
	South Africa	Auckland	SA 165-7	NZ 162-7	*South Africa won by 3 runs*
2012	West Indies	Lauderhill	WI 177-5	NZ 116	*West Indies won by 61 runs*
	West Indies	Lauderhill	WI 209-2	NZ153	*West Indies won by 56 runs*
2012/13	India	Visakhapatnam	*abandoned without a ball being bowled*		
	India	Chennai	NZ 167-5	I 166-4	*NZ won by 1 run*
2012/13	Bangladesh	Pallekele	NZ 191-3	B 132-8	*NZ won by 59 runs*
World Twenty20	Pakistan	Pallekele	P 177-6	NZ 164-9	*Pakistan won by 13 runs*
	Sri Lanka	Pallekele	NZ 174-7	SL 174-6	*Sri Lanka won eliminator*
	England	Pallekele	NZ 148-6	E 149-4	*England won by 6 wickets*
	West Indies	Pallekele	WI 139	NZ 139-7	*W.Indies won eliminator*
	Sri Lanka	Pallekele	NZ 74-7	SL 6-0	*abandoned*
2012/13	South Africa	Durban	NZ 86	SA 87-2	*South Africa won by 8 wickets*
	South Africa	East London	SA 165-5	NZ 169-2	*NZ won by 8 wickets*
	South Africa	Port Elizabeth	SA 179-6	NZ 146-9	*South Africa won by 33 runs*
2012/13	England	Auckland	E 214-7	NZ 174-9	*England won by 40 runs*
	England	Hamilton	NZ 192-6	E 137	*NZ won by 55 runs*
	England	Wellington	NZ 139-8	E 143-0	*England won by 10 wickets*
2013	England	The Oval	NZ 201-4	E 196-5	*NZ won by 5 runs*
	England	The Oval	E 2-1	NZ	*abandoned*
2013/14	Bangladesh	Mirpur	NZ 204-5	B 189-9	*NZ won by 15 runs*
2013/14	Sri Lanka	Pallekele	*abandoned without a ball being bowled*		
	Sri Lanka	Pallekele	NZ 142-7	SL 143-2	*Sri Lanka won by 8 wickets*
2013/14	West Indies	Auckland	NZ 189-5	WI 108-8	*NZ won by 81 runs*
	West Indies	Wellington	WI 159-5	NZ 163-6	*NZ won by 4 wickets*
2013/14	England	Chittagong	E 172-6	NZ 52-1	*NZ won by 9 runs (D/L)*
World Twenty20	South Africa	Chittagong	SA 170-6	NZ 168-8	*South Africa won by 2 runs*
	Sri Lanka	Chittagong	SL 119	NZ 60	*Sri Lanka won by 59 runs*
	Netherlands	Chittagong	N 151-4	NZ 152-4	*NZ won by 6 wickets*
2014	West Indies	Rousseau	WI 132-8	NZ 117-4	*NZ won by 12 runs (D/L)*
	West Indies	Rousseau	WI 165-6	NZ 126	*West Indies won by 39 runs*
2014/15	Pakistan	Dubai	NZ 135-7	P 140-3	*Pakistan won by 7 wickets*
	Pakistan	Dubai	NZ 144-8	P 127	*NZ won by 17 runs*
2015	England	Manchester	E 191-7	NZ 135	*England won by 56 runs*
2015/16	Zimbabwe	Harare	NZ 198-5	Z 118-8	*NZ won by 80 runs*
2015/16	South Africa	Durban	NZ 151-8	SA 152-4	*South Africa won by 6 wickets*
	South Africia	Centurion	NZ 177-7	SA 145-8	*NZ won by 32 runs*
2015/16	Sri Lanka	Mt Maunganui	NZ 182-4	SL 179-9	*NZ won by 3 runs*
	Sri Lanka	Auckland	SL 142-8	NZ 147-1	*NZ won by 9 wickets*

2015/16	Pakistan	Auckland	P 171-8	NZ 155	*Pakistan won by 16 runs*
	Pakistan	Hamilton	P 168-7	NZ 171-0	*NZ won by 10 wickets*
	Pakistan	Wellington	NZ 196-5	P 101	*NZ won by 95 runs*
2015/16	India	Nagpur	NZ 126-7	I 79	*NZ won by 47 runs*
World Twenty20	Australia	Dharamsala	NZ 142-8	A 134-9	*NZ won by 8 runs*
	Pakistan	Mohali	NZ 180-5	P 158-5	*NZ won by 22 runs*
	Bangladesh	Kolkata	NZ 145-8	B 70	*NZ won by 75 runs*
	England	Delhi	NZ 153-8	E 159-3	*England won by 7 wickets*
2016/17	Bangladesh	Napier	B 141-8	NZ 143-4	*NZ won by 6 wickets*
	Bangladesh	Mt Maunganui	NZ 195-7	B 148	*NZ won by 47 run*
	Bangladesh	Mt Maunganui	NZ 194-4	B 167-6	*NZ won by 27 runs*
2016/17	South Africa	Auckland	SA 185-6	NZ 107	*SA won by 78 runs*
2017/18	India	Delhi	I 202-3	NZ 149-8	*India won by 53 runs*
	India	Rajkot	NZ 196-2	I 156-7	*NZ won by 40 runs*
	India	Thiruvinanthapuram	I 67-5	NZ 61-6	*India won by 6 runs*
2017/18	West Indies	Nelson	NZ 187-7	WI 140	*NZ won by 47 runs*
	West Indies	Mt Maunganui	NZ 102-4	WI	*abandoned*
	West Indies	Mt Maunganui	NZ 243-5	WI 124	*NZ won by 119 runs*
2017/18	Pakistan	Wellington	P 105	NZ 106-3	*NZ won by 7 wickets*
	Pakistan	Auckland	P 201-4	NZ 153	*Pakistan won by 48 runs*
	Pakistan	Mt Maunganui	P 181-6	NZ 163-6	*Pakistan won by 18 runs*
2017/18	Australia	Sydney	NZ 117-9	A 96-3	*Australia won by 7 wickets (D/L)*
	England	Wellington	NZ 196-5	E 184-9	*NZ won by 12 runs*
Tri-Series	Australia	Auckland	NZ 243-6	A 245-5	*Australia won by 5 wickets*
	England	Hamilton	E 194-7	NZ 192-4	*England won by 2 runs*
	Australia	Auckland	NZ 150-9	A 121-3	*Australia won by 19 runs (D/L)*
2018/19	Pakistan	Abu Dhabi	P 148-6	NZ 146-6	*Pakistan won by 2 runs*
	Pakistan	Dubai	NZ 153-7	P 154-4	*Pakistan won by 6 wickets*
	Pakistan	Dubai	P 166-3	NZ 119	*Pakistan won by 47 runs*
2018/19	Sri Lanka	Auckland	NZ 179-7	SL 144	*NZ won by 35 runs*
2018/19	India	Wellington	NZ 219-6	I 139	*NZ won by 80 runs*
	India	Auckland	NZ 158-8	I 162-3	*India won by 7 wickets*
	India	Hamilton	NZ 212-4	I 208-6	*NZ won by 4 runs*
2019/20	Sri Lanka	Pallekele	SL 174-4	NZ 175-5	*NZ won by 5 wickets*
	Sri Lanka	Pallekele	SL 161-9	NZ 165-6	*NZ won by 4 wickets*
	Sri Lanka	Pallekele	SL 125-8	NZ 88	*SL won by 37 runs*
2019/20	England	Christchurch	NZ 153-5	E 154-3	*England won by 7 wickets*
	England	Wellington	NZ 176-8	E 155	*NZ won by 21 runs*
	England	Nelson	NZ 180-7	E 166-7	*NZ won by 14 runs*
	England	Napier	E 241-3	NZ 165	*England won by 76 runs*
	England	Auckland	NZ 146-5	E 146-7	*England won eliminator*
2019/20	India	Auckland	NZ 203-5	I 204-4	*India won by 6 wickets*
	India	Auckland	NZ 132-5	I 135-3	*India won by 7 wickets*
	India	Hamilton	I 179-5	NZ 179-6	*India won eliminator*
	India	Wellington	I 165-8	NZ 165-7	*India won eliminator*
	India	Mt Maunganui	I 163-3	NZ 156-9	*India won by 7 runs*
2020/21	West Indies	Auckland	WI 180-7	NZ 179-5	*NZ won by 5 wickets (D/L)*
	West Indies	Mt Maunganui	NZ 238-3	WI 166-9	*NZ won by 72 runs*
	West Indies	Mt Maunganui	WI 25-1		*abandoned*

2020/21	Pakistan	Auckland	P 153-9	NZ 156-5	*NZ won by 5 wickets*
	Pakistan	Hamilton	P 163-6	NZ 164-1	*NZ won by 9 wickets*
	Pakistan	Napier	NZ 173-7	P 177-6	*Pakistan won by 4 wickets*
2020/21	Australia	Christchurch	NZ 184-5	A 131	*NZ won by 53 runs*
	Australia	Dunedin	NZ 219-7	A 215-8	*NZ won by 4 runs*
	Australia	Wellington	A 208-4	NZ 144	*Australia won by 64 runs*
	Australia	Wellington	A 156-6	NZ 106	*Australia won by 50 runs*
	Australia	Wellington	A 142-8	NZ 143-3	*NZ won by 7 wickets*
2020/21	Bangladesh	Hamilton	NZ 210-3	B 144-8	*NZ won by 66 runs*
	Bangladesh	Napier	NZ 173-5	B 142-7	*NZ won by 28 runs (D/L)*
	Bangladesh	Auckland	NZ 141-4	B 76	*NZ won by 65 runs*

Summary of Results

	Played	Won	Lost	NR
v Pakistan	24	10	14	–
v England	21	7	13	1
v Sri Lanka	19	10	8	1
v India	16	8	8	–
v West Indies	16	9	5	2
v South Africa	15	4	11	–
v Australia	14	5	9	–
v Bangladesh	10	10	–	–
v Zimbabwe	6	6	–	–
v Kenya	1	1	–	–
v Ireland	1	1	–	–
v Scotland	1	1	–	–
v Netherlands	1	1	–	–
Total	**145**	**73**	**68**	**4**

Highest Totals

243-5	v West Indies	Mt Maunganui	2017/18
243-6	v Australia	Auckland	2017/18
238-3	v West Indies	Mt Maunganui	2020/21
219-6	v India	Auckland	2018/19
219-7	v Australia	Dunedin	2020/21
214-6	v Australia	Christchurch	2009/10
212-4	v India	Hamilton	2018/19
210-3	v Bangladesh	Hamilton	2020/21
204-5	v Bangladesh	Mirpur	2013/14
203-5	v India	Auckland	2019/20
202-5	v Zimbabwe	Hamilton	2011/12
201-4	v England	The Oval	2013

Twenty20 International Captains

		Results				Toss	
		P	W	L	NR	W	L
Williamson K.S.	2012 to 2020/21	49	23	25	1	21	28
Vettori D.L.	2007/08 to 2009/10	28	14	14	–	16	12
McCullum B.B.	2007/08 to 2015	28	13	14	1	16	12
Taylor L.R.P.L	2010/11 to 2012/13	13	6	6	1	6	7
Southee T.G.	2017/18 to 2020/21	18	12	6	–	7	11
Fleming S.P.	2004/05 to 2006/07	5	3	2	–	4	1
Mills K.D.	2013/14	2	1	1	–	1	1
Santner M.J.	2020/21	2	1	–	1	1	1
TOTAL		**145**	**73**	**68**	**4**	**72**	**73**

INDIVIDUAL RECORDS

Centuries

123	McCullum B.B.	v Bangladesh	Pallekele	2012/13
116*	McCullum B.B.	v Australia	Christchurch	2009/10
109*	Munro C.	v India	Rajkot	2017/18
108	Phillips G.D.	v West Indies	Mt Maunganui	2020/21
105	Guptill M.J.	v Australia	Auckland	2017/18
104	Munro C.	v West Indies	Mt Maunganui	2017/18
101*	Guptill M.J.	v South Africa	East London	2012/13
101	Munro C.	v Bangladesh	Mt Maunganui	2016/17

Five Wickets in an Innings

4-1-18-5	Southee T.G.	v Pakistan	Auckland	2010/11
4-0-21-5	Ferguson L.H.	v West Indies	Auckland	2020/21

Hat-tricks

4-0-33-3	Oram J.D.P.	v Sri Lanka	Colombo	2009/10
4-1-18-5	Southee T.G.	v Pakistan	Auckland	2010/11

Most Economical Bowling

4-1-6-3	Vettori D.L.	v Bangladesh	Hamilton	2009/10
4-0-8-2	Boult T.A.	v South Africa	Auckland	2016/17
4-0-9-2	Butler I.G.	v England	Hamilton	2012/13
4-0-10-2	Milne A.F.	v Zimbabwe	Harare	2015/16

Most Expensive Bowling

3.1-0-64-0	Wheeler B.M.	v Australia	Auckland	2017/18
4-0-60-0	Neesham J.D.S.	v Australia	Wellington	2020/21
4-0-58-0	Rance S.H.A.	v Sri Lanka	Pallekele	2019/20
3.5-0-56-1	de Grandhomme C.	v Australia	Auckland	2017/18
4-0-54-3	Bennett H.K.	v India	Hamilton	2019/20

Most Wicketkeeping Dismissals in an Innings

†4	Phillips G.D.	v West Indies	Nelson	2017/18

† *includes one stumping*

Most Catches in an Innings by a Fielder

4	Anderson C.J.	v South Africa	Port Elizabeth	2012/13
4	de Grandhomme C.	v England	Wellington	2019/20

RECORD PARTNERSHIPS

New Zealand v All Countries

For

1st	171*	Guptill M.J. & Williamson K.S. v Pakistan	Hamilton	2015/16
2nd	131	Guptill M.J. & Williamson K.S. v Australia	Dunedin	2020/21
3rd	184	Conway D.P. & Phillips G.D. v West Indies	Mt Maunganui	2020/21
4th	124	Williamson K.S.& Anderson C.J. v Bangladesh	Mt Maunganui	2016/17
5th	81*	Williamson K.S. & de Grandhomme C. v Bangladesh	Napier	2016/17
6th	85*	McCullum B.B. & Ronchi L. v West Indies	Auckland	2013/14
7th	54	Santner M.J. & Wheeler B.M. v Pakistan	Auckland	2017/18
8th	40	Styris S.B. & Wilson J.W. v Australia	Auckland	2004/05
9th	38*	Santner M.J. & Sodhi I.S. v India	Delhi	2017/18
	38	Taylor L.R.P.L. & Sodhi I.S. v Australia	Auckland	2017/18
10th	36	Southee T.G. & Rance S.H.A. v Sri Lanka	Pallekele	2019/20

Against

1st	158	Sharma R.G. & Dhawan S. for India	Delhi	2017/18
2nd	99	Rahul K.L. & Kohli V. for India	Auckland	2019/20
3rd	182	Malan D.J. & Morgan E.J.G. for England	Napier	2019/20
4th	82	Clarke M.J. & White C.L. for Australia	Christchurch	2009/10
5th	102	Collingwood P.D. & Shah O.A. for England	Christchurch	2007/08
6th	84	Allen F.A. & Pollard K.A. for West Indies	Auckland	2020/21
7th	92	Stoinis M.P.& Sams D.R. for Australia	Dunedin	2020/21
8th	61	Harbhajan Singh & Raina S.K. for India	Christchurch	2008/09
9th	44	Fernando C.R.D. & Malinga S.L. for Sri Lanka	Auckland	2006/07
10th	31*	Shoaib Akhtar & Wahab Riaz for Pakistan	Auckland	2010/11

CAREER RECORDS

	M	*In*	*NO*	*HS*	*Runs*	*Ave*	*100s*	*50s*	*Ct*	*St*	*O*	*M*	*R*	*W*	*Ave*	*R/O*	*Best*
A.R.Adams	4	2	1	7	13	13.00	-	-	1	-	12.5	0	105	3	35.00	8.18	2-20
G.W.Aldridge	1	-	-	-	-	-	-	-	1	-	4	0	45	1	45.00	11.25	1-45
F.H.Allen	3	3	0	71	88	29.33	-	1	-	-							
C.J.Anderson	31	24	4	94*	485	24.25	-	2	19	-	60	0	495	14	35.35	8.25	2-17
N.J.Astle	4	4	1	40*	74	24.66	-	-	3	-	6.5	0	50	4	12.50	7.32	3-20
T.D.Astle	4	2	0	3	4	2.00	-	-	3	-	10	0	82	7	11.71	8.20	4-13
M.D.Bates	3	-	-	-	-	-	-	-	-	-	11	0	107	4	26.75	9.73	3-31
H.K.Bennett	9	1	1	1*	1	-	-	-	-	-	28.5	0	282	9	31.33	9.78	3-54
T.A.Blundell	3	2	1	14	17	17.00	-	-	1	-							
S.E.Bond	20	8	3	8*	21	4.20	-	-	4	-	77.3	2	543	25	21.72	7.01	3-18
T.A.Boult	34	10	5	8	28	5.60	-	-	13	-	125.5	1	1074	46	23.34	8.53	4-34
D.A.J.Bracewell	18	10	5	44	121	24.20	-	-	7	-	47.4	0	457	20	21.85	9.59	3-25
N.T.Broom	11	7	1	36	73	12.16	-	-	4	-							
D.G.Brownlie	5	5	0	5	6	1.20	-	-	3	-							
T.C.Bruce	17	17	2	59*	279	18.60	-	2	15	-							
I.G.Butler	19	6	5	2*	5	5.00	-	-	3	-	59.4	1	481	23	20.91	8.06	3-19
C.L.Cairns	2	2	0	2	3	1.50	-	-	1	-	8	0	52	1	52.00	6.50	1-28
M.S.Chapman *	30	28	4	63*	535	22.29	-	1	10	-	13	0	95	4	23.75	7.30	1-9
D.P.Conway	14	11	3	99*	473	59.12	-	4	7	1							
C.de Grandhomme	36	34	7	59	487	18.03	-	3	18	-	49.5	0	445	11	40.45	8.93	2-22
A.P.Devcich	4	4	0	59	111	27.75	-	1	2	-	12	0	80	2	40.00	6.67	2-16
B.J.Diamanti	1	-	-	-	-	-	-	-	-	-	2	0	19	0	-	9.50	-
J.A.Duffy	1	-	-	-	-	-	-	-	-	-	4	0	33	4	8.25	8.25	4-33
G.D.Elliott	16	14	4	27	157	15.70	-	-	4	-	30	0	218	14	15.57	7.27	4-22
A.M.Ellis	5	5	2	16	25	8.33	-	-	-	-	10	0	105	2	52.50	10.50	2-40
L.H.Ferguson	13	1	0	1	1	1.00	-	-	4	-	46	0	316	24	13.16	6.86	5-21
S.P.Fleming	5	5	0	38	110	22.00	-	-	2	-							
D.R.Flynn	5	5	0	23	59	11.80	-	-	2	-	1	0	7	0	-	7.00	-

	M	In	NO	HS	Runs	Ave	100s	50s	Ct	St	O	M	R	W	Ave	R/O	Best
J.E.C.Franklin	38	31	8	60	463	20.13	-	2	13	-	54.3	0	417	20	20.85	7.65	4-15
P.G.Fulton	12	12	1	25	127	11.54	-	-	4	-							
M.R.Gillespie	11	6	4	7	21	10.50	-	-	1	-	35	3	255	10	25.50	7.29	4-7
M.J.Guptill	102	98	7	105	2939	32.29	2	17	58	-	1	0	11	0	-	11.00	-
M.J.Henry	6	2	1	10	10	10.00	-	-	1	-	22	1	191	7	27.28	8.68	3-44
R.M.Hira	15	3	1	20*	37	18.50	-	-	2	-	42.2	1	337	10	33.70	7.96	2-42
P.A.Hitchcock	1	1	0	13	13	13.00	-	-	-	-	3	0	43	2	21.50	14.33	2-43
G.J.Hopkins	10	8	0	36	86	10.75	-	-	4	2							
J.M.How	5	5	0	31	56	11.20	-	-	1	-							
P.J.Ingram	3	3	1	20*	22	11.00	-	-	1	-							
K.A.Jamieson	8	4	2	30	41	20.50	-	-	3	-	28.4	0	281	4	70.25	9.80	2-15
A.K.Kitchen	5	4	1	16	38	12.66	-	-	3	-	6	0	46	2	23.00	7.67	1-3
S.C.Kuggeleijn	16	8	4	35*	79	19.75	-	-	5	-	47.5	0	430	13	33.38	9.07	3-21
T.W.M.Latham	13	10	0	39	163	16.30	-	-	6	-							
H.J.H.Marshall	3	3	0	8	12	4.00	-	-	1	-							
J.A.H.Marshall	3	2	0	13	14	7.00	-	-	-	-							
C.S.Martin	6	1	1	5*	5	-	-	-	1	-	23	1	193	7	27.57	8.39	2-14
M.J.Mason	3	1	0	2	2	2.00	-	-	-	-	9	0	65	2	32.50	7.22	1-18
M.J.McClenaghan	28	7	4	6*	14	4.66	-	-	7	-	98.2	2	758	30	25.26	7.71	3-17
B.B.McCullum	71	70	10	123	2140	35.66	2	13	36	8							
N.L.McCullum	63	41	15	36*	299	11.50	-	-	25	-	187.1	0	1278	58	22.03	6.83	4-16
P.D.McGlashan	11	9	1	26	61	7.62	-	-	9	-							
A.J.McKay	2	1	0	0	0	0.00	-	-	-	-	5.4	0	31	2	15.50	5.48	2-20
C.D.McMillan	8	7	1	57	187	31.16	-	1	3	-							
K.D.Mills	42	19	7	33*	137	11.41	-	-	8	-	149.3	1	1228	43	28.55	8.21	3-26
A.F.Milne	23	8	8	10*	21	-	-	-	6	-	77.5	1	599	28	21.39	7.69	4-37
D.J.Mitchell	15	13	4	34*	148	16.44	-	-	8	-	11.1	0	110	5	22.00	9.85	2-27
C.Munro	65	62	7	109*	1724	31.34	3	11	17	-	19.4	0	186	4	46.50	9.46	1-12
J.D.S.Neesham	29	22	7	48*	324	21.60	-	-	11	-	52.1	0	493	18	27.38	9.45	3-16
H.M.Nicholls	5	4	0	7	19	4.75	-	-	6	-							
R.J.Nicol	21	19	0	58	327	17.21	-	2	5	-	20.3	0	167	5	33.40	8.15	2-20
I.E.O'Brien	4	-	-	-	-	-	-	-	-	-	13	0	116	6	19.33	8.92	2-30
J.D.P.Oram	36	30	7	66*	474	20.60	-	2	12	-	91	0	793	19	41.73	8.71	3-33
A.Y.Patel	2	-	-	-	-	-	-	-	-	-	6	0	45	1	45.00	7.50	1-27
J.S.Patel	11	4	1	5	9	3.00	-	-	4	-	33.1	1	269	16	16.81	8.11	3-20
G.D.Phillips	25	22	4	108	506	28.11	1	2	17	2	7.3	0	57	2	28.50	7.60	1-11
S.H.A.Rance	8	3	0	8	10	3.33	-	-	-	-	27	0	245	10	24.50	9.07	3-26
A.J.Redmond	7	6	0	63	126	21.00	-	1	3	-	2.5	0	24	2	12.00	8.47	2-24
L.Ronchi †	32	25	6	51*	359	18.89	-	1	24	5							
H.D.Rutherford	8	7	0	62	151	21.57	-	1	1	-							
J.D.Ryder	22	21	1	62	457	22.85	-	3	7	-	10	0	68	2	34.00	6.80	1-2
M.J.Santner	52	37	15	37	335	15.22	-	-	24	-	174.2	1	1287	60	21.45	7.38	4-11
T.L.Seifert	35	32	4	84*	695	24.82	-	5	20	6							
M.S.Sinclair	2	2	0	0	0	0.00	-	-	-	-							
I.S.Sodhi	57	10	4	16*	76	12.66	-	-	16	-	196.3	0	1586	73	21.72	8.07	4-28
T.G.Southee	83	35	13	39	249	11.31	-	-	43	-	297	2	2492	99	25.17	8.39	5-18
S.B.Styris	31	29	2	66	578	21.40	-	1	8	-	51.3	0	349	18	19.38	6.78	3-5
L.R.P.L.Taylor	102	94	21	63	1909	26.15	-	7	46	-							
E.P.Thompson	1	1	1	1*	1	-	-	-	-	-	3	1	18	1	18.00	6.00	1-18
B.M.Tickner	6	1	1	5	5	5.00	-	-	-	-	22	0	212	5	42.40	9.63	2-25
D.R.Tuffey	3	2	1	5*	5	5.00	-	-	-	-	10	0	93	3	31.00	9.30	2-16
D.L.Vettori	34	22	6	38	205	12.81	-	-	9	-	131.1	1	748	38	19.68	5.70	4-20
L.Vincent	9	9	0	42	174	19.33	-	-	1	-							
B-J.Watling	5	4	0	22	38	19.00	-	-	1	-							
B.M.Wheeler	6	4	2	30	37	18.50	-	-	1	-	21.2	0	216	7	30.85	10.13	2-16
K.S.Williamson	67	65	8	95	1805	31.66	-	13	32	-	19.4	0	164	6	27.33	8.34	2-16
J.W.Wilson	1	1	0	18	18	18.00	-	-	-	-	4	0	43	0	-	10.75	-
L.J.Woodcock	3	-	-	-	-	-	-	-	1	-	10	0	70	1	70.00	7.00	1-30
G.H.Worker	2	2	0	62	90	45.00	-	1	1	-	2	0	19	1	19.00	9.50	1-19
W.A.Young	3	2	0	53	67	33.50	-	1	1	-							

** includes 19 games for Hong Kong (China)   † includes three games for Australia*

SUMMARY OF TWENTY20 INTERNATIONAL CAREER RECORDS

Most Matches

Taylor L.R.P.L.	102	McCullum B.B.	71	McCullum N.L.	63
Guptill M.J.	102	Williamson K.S.	67	Sodhi I.S.	57
Southee T.G.	83	Munro C.	65	Santner M.J.	52

Most Runs

Guptill M.J.	2939
McCullum B.B.	2140
Taylor L.R.P.L.	1909
Williamson K.S.	1805
Munro C.	1724

Most Wickets

Southee T.G.	99
Sodhi I.S.	73
Santner M.J.	60
McCullum N.L.	58
Boult T.A.	46
Mills K.D.	43

Register of New Zealand Twenty20 Cricketers Who Have Not Played Test Cricket or One-day Internationals

	Born	*Type*	
Allen	22/4/1999	RHB	
Finnley Hugh	Auckland		
Bruce	2/8/1991	RHB	ROB
Thomas Charles	Te Kuiti		
Duffy	2/8/1994	RHB	RFM
Jacob Andrew	Lumsden		
Hira	23/1/1987	LHB	SLA
Roneel Magan	Auckland		
Tickner	13/10/1993	RHB	RFM
Blair Marshall	Napier		